Jeff Herman's
GUIDE TO
BOOK
PUBLISHERS,
EDITORS,
& LITERARY
AGENTS
2013

Who they are!
What they want!
How to
win them
over!

23RD EDITION

JEFF HERMAN

 sourcebooks

Copyright © 2013 by Jeff Herman
Cover and internal design © 2013 by Sourcebooks, Inc.

Sourcebooks and the colophon are registered trademarks of Sourcebooks, Inc.

Published by Sourcebooks, Inc.
PO Box 4410, Naperville, Illinois 60567-4410
(630) 961-3900
Fax: (630) 961-2168
www.sourcebooks.com

Library of Congress Cataloging-in-Publication Data is on file with the publisher.

Printed and bound in the United States of America.
DR 10 9 8 7 6 5 4 3 2 1

DEDICATION

You can't be lost if searching. Truth is a writer's deliverance, and freedom the reward. When a writer leaps, the universe applauds.

PUBLISHERS, EDITORS, AND LITERARY AGENTS

ADVICE FOR WRITERS

THE INDEPENDENT EDITORS

RESOURCES FOR WRITERS

INTRODUCTION

This book emerged more than twenty editions ago as a way to bring crucial information and improved opportunities to the majority of writers, who were being disrespected at publishers' gates.

In those days, publishing was noticeably infected by a measure of inbred elitism that favored the few who resembled what already prevailed, and too many good books were arbitrarily dismissed due to a gentrified monopoly of access. This book was my way to bring forth the names of the people who publish books, and infuse them with the blood and bones that afflict all mortals. If publishing was a riddle, I wanted writers to have a reasonable shot at solving it and bringing down the walls. A true meritocracy requires egalitarian access.

During these two-plus decades, what had once been a land with many thriving privately owned firms morphed into a few international multimedia conglomerates for which book publishing is an asterisk on management's to-do list. Independent publishers, like the one that publishes the book you now hold, went from being the norm to becoming the exception.

What has also changed is the ability of a writer to be a bona fide publisher of one, without needing to embrace and become embedded within the old structures. Over this still young decade, the struggle isn't simply about getting access to publishers, but is also about redefining what a publisher is and if it will remain relevant. After all, today you and I could sell our books to each other in a matter of easy clicks without a publisher or retailer. On the other hand, the established publishers are also like trusted book clubs that cull the unregulated weeds on the reader's behalf, and reliably nominate what's worthy to read. Many writers will always aspire to receive the valuable validation and credibility that only certain kingdoms can award in any given environment.

Though things have changed and are changing, this book remains as useful and helpful as ever.

Jeff Herman
413-298-0077
www.jeffherman.com | www.waenetwork.com | e-mail: jeff@jeffherman.com

OPPORTUNITY AT A GLANCE

It's all about fit. Just because you've written the perfect book doesn't mean every publisher will want to buy it. McGraw-Hill develops nonfiction—they're not interested in a romance, even a super-steamy one. Likewise, Simon Spotlight, a children's imprint, doesn't want to read your memoir. However, there are dozens (perhaps hundreds) of publishers who might be interested in your book, and we've made it easier to find them.

At the top of every listing, there are images noting the publisher's priority genres. These are the categories of books that they have specifically mentioned as having an interest in acquiring or have demonstrated great success in promoting. As you skim through the front half of the book, you'll get a rough idea of whom you or your agent should approach (especially for a niche like poetry, science fiction, or craft). Then go back and be sure to read the full listings for details about submission guidelines and to learn more about the individual publishers.

 Adult Fiction   Memoir/Biography

 Romance   Cooking

 Fantasy/Science Fiction   Crafts

 Poetry   Mind/Body/Spirit

 Books for Children/Teens   Religion

 Adult Nonfiction

SECTION ONE

PUBLISHING
CONGLOMERATES

THE MULTINATIONAL CONGLOMERATED PUBLISHING ENTITIES

JEFF HERMAN

A long time ago (30+ years), the US book publishing business consisted of hundreds of mom-and-pop companies. Each was generally named for the individual(s) who founded the firm, and the respective catalogues reflected their own special tastes and sensibilities. Separately, none of these entities or individuals had the power to dictate the contemporary status or future direction of publishing. They were a thriving community of several hundred distinct pieces. Collectively, they comprised our nation's entire book publishing structure.

The revolution came and happened quickly. Some of us complained, but it didn't make any difference. It was a funny revolution in that it reversed the usual dynamic. Unlike the breaking away of exploited tribes from masters of conquest, which is revolution in its most romantic form, we watched as faceless and formless conquerors wrapped themselves around most of our precious tribes and soundlessly absorbed them into a small number of obese oceans. Perhaps those who might have cared the most saw gold before they saw the cost. Can we blame them? Should we even judge the result? Perhaps it is wiser to simply adjust.

The largest multinational publishing properties have been consolidated into their own section. It seemed right to do so, since consolidation has been their most striking feature. These companies possess the brand names of the firms they have acquired over the past three decades. While some of the firms may be led by high-profile individuals or greatly influenced by multigenerational families that control large blocks of non-traded stock, it is also safe to say that these firms are greater than any one person or any unified collection of people. At the end of the day, it is the various pension funds, institutional investment firms, and sovereign trust funds that must be satisfied.

There are two other key features of multinational publishers: (1) Most of them are controlled by foreign interests; (2) The book publishing programs are an extremely small part of a much larger agenda, which includes movies, magazines, broadcast and cable channels, newspapers, music, and the Internet.

Do not let my irreverent or ominous tone chase you away. At all of these firms you will find hardworking, dedicated editors who want nothing more than the ability to publish good books. And they manage to achieve that. So join with them and adjust to the system as it is. The best thing you can do is get your book published.

This section is followed by a large number of independent and small houses, each of which is capable of doing as much as, or more than, the big houses. The independent houses are not vestiges from a dead past. To the contrary, they keep the current publishing climate vibrant, and help create the future with their entrepreneurial and innovative ways. Don't ever think twice about joining them.

I have asserted my discretionary powers to place a few houses in the Independent Section that could also fit into the Conglomerates Section. Obviously, not all corporations are the same. Some are the equivalent of Jupiter, while others are more like Mercury (I'm actually referring to size, not "personalities"). When the book division is not a mere asterisk within its corporate envelope, but is instead a crucial piece, you will find it with the independents.

BERTELSMANN AG

A global media firm based in Germany, Bertelsmann AG comprises publishing, music, and broadcasting operations in nearly 60 countries; these include Random House, the world's largest English-language general trade book publisher. Bertelsmann is a privately held company, owned by the Mohn family and their foundation.

Recent Bertelsmann acquisitions—including BBC Books, Multnomah, and Triumph Books—helped Bertelsmann in 2006 achieve their "most successful year in history" with record sales of 19.3 billion euros. CEO Thomas Rabe said they plan to start shopping for more corporate acquisitions, fueling even more growth and opportunity within this media leviathan.

RANDOM HOUSE, INC.

CROWN PUBLISHING GROUP
KNOPF DOUBLEDAY PUBLISHING GROUP
RANDOM HOUSE CHILDREN'S BOOKS
RANDOM HOUSE PUBLISHING GROUP
1745 Broadway, New York, NY 10019
212-782-9000
www.randomhouse.com | Twitter: @randomhouse

Founded in 1925 and acquired by Bertelsmann in 1998, Random House has grown into an intricate web of divisions, publishing groups, and imprints. The years 2008 and 2009 witnessed a massive reorganization and the consolidation of Random House's many components. Divisions such as Bantam Dell, WaterBrook Multnomah, Doubleday, and Knopf were either combined or had their imprints shifted around, leading to the creation of the Knopf Doubleday Publishing Group and the expansion of the Crown Publishing Group and Random House divisions.

The span of this house's titles runs both wide and deep, including a broad array of categories in fiction and nonfiction. Random House publishes in hardcover, trade paperback, mass-market paperback, audio, electronic, and digital, for adults, young adults, and children.

The company was founded when Bennett Cerf and Donald Klopfer purchased The Modern Library, an imprint that reprinted classic works of literature, from publisher Horace Liveright. Two years later, in 1927, the publisher decided to broaden its publishing activities, and the Random House colophon made its debut.

In recent years, Random House revenues have continued to grow, despite a sluggish international marketplace. Partly responsible is the explosive rise of the e-book; in 2010, 20 percent of Random House's US revenue came from digital sales. Random House steadily produces a stellar number of *New York Times* best sellers—37 at number one in 2006 alone. The international nature of the company tends to attract a global audience, with operations in Asia, South Africa, South America, and the United Kingdom, to name a few. In 2007, Random House launched Insight, a US book and audio search and browse service that operates as a widget inside Web browsers. Be sure to explore the Random House website; it's chock full of information, including blogs, podcasts, and newsletters.

In what continues as an endless stream of global consolidation, Random House and Penguin are in the process of merging their US operations.

Random House editors prefer to accept manuscripts submitted by literary agents. They do not accept unsolicited submissions, proposals, manuscripts, or submission queries via e-mail at this time.

CROWN PUBLISHING GROUP

BROADWAY BOOKS
CLARKSON POTTER
CROWN
CROWN ARCHETYPE
CROWN BUSINESS
CROWN FORUM
HARMONY BOOKS
HOGARTH
IMAGE BOOKS
TEN SPEED PRESS
THREE RIVERS PRESS
WATERBROOK MULTNOMAH
WATSON-GUPTILL

The Crown Publishing Group originated in 1933 and is known today for the broad scope of its publishing program and its singular market responsiveness, qualities that are reflected in its savvy selection of authors and books and in its aggressive efforts to market them.

Acquired by Random House in 1988, Crown incorporates a number of Random House imprints and acquisitions that together make up the Crown Publishing Group. In 2008, Random House restructured its organization to incorporate Broadway and WaterBrook Multnomah, once individual imprints, into the Crown Group. Random House has also purchased and incorporated the previously independent Ten Speed Press and Watson-Guptill under the Crown umbrella. New imprints include Crown Archetype, launched in 2010, Hogarth, in 2012, and Image Books, which incorporated elements of the retired Doubleday Religion line.

BROADWAY BOOKS

Broadway generates a variety of nonfiction, including memoir, health and fitness, inspiration and spirituality, history, current affairs and politics, marriage and relationships, animals, travel and adventure narrative, pop culture, humor, and personal finance. The house also provides selective commercial/literary frontlist fiction, primarily by established or highly promotable authors. Broadway's emporium strategy involves publishing unique, marketable books of the highest editorial quality by authors who are authorities in their field and who use their credibility and expertise to promote their work.

Broadway has established many long-running best sellers, including *Saving Graces: Finding Solace* and *Strength from Friends and Strangers* by Elizabeth Edwards; Frances Mayes's *Bella Tuscany* and *Under the Tuscan Sun*; Bill Bryson's *In a Sunburned Country*, *A Walk in the Woods*, and *I'm a Stranger Here Myself*; Bob Costas's *Fair Ball*; and Bill O'Reilly's *Who's Looking Out for You?*

In addition to narrative nonfiction, Broadway publishes a highly successful range of self-help, mind/body/spirit, business, and cooking books.

Recent Broadway titles include *Muzzled: The Assault on Honest Debate* by Juan Williams; *The Fatal Gift of Beauty* by Nina Burleigh; *The Gospel According to the Fix*, by Chris Cillizza; *How to Eat a Small Country* by Amy Finley; and *Amazing Grace* by Jonathan Kozol.

Broadway does not accept unsolicited manuscripts; only agented works are considered.

Charles Conrad, Editorial Director—New nonfiction projects; popular culture, social history, humor, biography, and literary nonfiction; contemporary literary and quality fiction.

CLARKSON POTTER
POTTER CRAFT
POTTER STYLE

Clarkson Potter is a leader in beautifully illustrated nonfiction books on cooking, parenting, pets, crafts and hobbies, decorating, self-help, and other lifestyle topics. Clarkson Potter authors include Ina Garten, Martha Stewart, Giada De Laurentiis, Bobby Flay, Rachael Ray, Colin Cowie, and Celerie Kemble.

In 2006, Clarkson Potter hired a new editorial director, Doris Cooper, who came on board to explore new options in lifestyle publishing.

Recent titles include *Foraged Flavor* by Tama Matsuoka Wong; *Uncorked* by Marco Pasanella; *Easy Sexy Raw* by Carol Alt; *HERS* by Jacqueline deMontravel; and *The Perfectly Imperfect Home* by Deborah Needleman.

Direct query and SASE to:

Pam Kraus, Editor-in-Chief

Doris Cooper, Editor-in-Chief—Lifestyle, cooking, decorating.

Emily Takoudes, Senior Editor—Cooking, nonfiction narrative.

Rica Allannic, Senior Editor—Cooking.

Ashley Phillips, Editor—Cooking and food.

Angelin Borsics, Editor—Decorating, cooking, lifestyle.

POTTER CRAFT

Launched in 2006, Potter Craft publishes books in the areas of crocheting, jewelry making, knitting, paper crafts, sewing, embroidery, and general crafts. Some recent titles include *Handmade to Sell* by Kelly Rand; *The Sketchbook Challenge* by Sue Bleiweiss; *I Spy DIY Style* by Jenni Radosevich; *Noni Flowers* by Nora Bellows; and *Sew What You Love* by Tanya Whelan.

Betty Wong—Crafts, hobbies.

POTTER STYLE

Potter Style publishes high-end gift books; stationery; recipe, trivia, and how-to decks; guided journals; and other paper-based novelty products. It has recently published authors such as Cesar Millan, Jillian Michaels, Rachael Ray, Max Brooks, and Amy Krouse Rosenthal. Some titles include *Mrs. Lilien's Cocktail Swatchbook* by Kelley Lilien; *Paris Versus New York Postcard Box* by Vahram Muratyan; *Life Is Wine Journal* by Graham Harding; and *Sibley Backyard Birding Flashcards* by David Allen Sibley.

See editors as per above.

CROWN

The Crown Group's eponymous imprint's nonfiction encompasses popular titles in health and wellness, biography and memoir, history, politics, current events and parenting, as well as popular and historical fiction. Fiction titles focus on literary and popular works in hardcover.

Bestselling authors include President Barack Obama, Suzanne Somers, Tim Ferriss, Patrick J. Buchanan, Edward Klein, Jillian Michaels, Dr. Nancy L. Snyderman, Benjamin Wallace, and Ruth Rendell.

Recent Crown titles include *Eat the City* by Robin Shulman; *Octopus* by Guy Lawson; *Heartbroken* by Lisa Unger; *Twilight of the Elites* by Christopher Hayes; and *Road to Valor* by Aili McConnon.

Direct queries and SASEs to:

Rick Horgan, Executive Editor—Nonfiction, business narratives, pop culture, sports narratives.

Sean Desmond, Senior Editor—Politics, social narratives, current affairs, conservative points of view.

Charles Conrad, Editor—Music, pop culture, contemporary/social narratives.

Vanessa Mobley, Editor—Popular science, psychology, philosophy, history, current affairs, social narratives.

Molly Stern, Editor—Fiction with contemporary themes, historical/current narratives.

Zack Wagman, Editor—Current affairs, fiction mysteries/thrillers/crime.

Roger Scholl, Editor—Business narratives.

Amanda Cook, Editor—Social trends, cutting-edge psychological and scientific narratives.

CROWN ARCHETYPE

Crown Archetype was launched in 2010 with Tina Constable as Vice President and Publisher. The imprint publishes authors in health and wellness, personal finance/career, celebrity, and pop culture.

It has so far published such authors as Mindy Kaling, Jillian Michaels, Deepak Chopra, Suzanne Somers, Dr. Pierre Dukan, and Tim Ferriss.

Titles include *My Roadmap* by Sam Bracken; *Not Taco Bell Material* by Adam Carolla; *Finding Ultra* by Rich Roll; *Dream New Dreams* by Jai Pausch; and *Bombshell* by Suzanne Somers.

Mauro Dipreta, Editor—Sports narratives.

Sydny Miner, Editor—Parenting, relationships.

Talia Krohn, Editor—Business, diet.

CROWN BUSINESS

Crown Business is one of the leading publishers of business books, producing titles by authors such as Phil Town, Larry Bossidy, Ram Charan, Jean Chatzky, Rosabeth Moss Kanter, Steve Forbes, Keith McFarland, and Suze Orman. Crown Business looks to publish books in management and leadership, business narrative, career advice, and personal finance.

Recent titles include *Key Moments* by Liz Mohn; *Everything Is Obvious* by Duncan J. Watts; *Management in Ten Words* by Terry Leahy; *Dark Pools* by Scott Patterson; and *The Unfair Trade* by Michael J. Casey.

Direct queries and SASEs to:

Talia Krohn, Editor

Roger Scholl, Editor

CROWN FORUM

Serving a conservative readership, Crown Forum includes several bestselling titles from Ann Coulter, Michael Medved, Bill Getz, Newt Gingrich, Joe Scarborough, and Steven F. Hayward.

Recent titles include *The New Leviathan* by David Horowitz and Jacob Laksin; *Coming Apart* by Charles Murray; *American Individualism* by Margaret Hoover; *The Next Wave* by Catherine Herridge; and *Demonic* by Ann Coulter.

Sean Desmond, Editor

HARMONY BOOKS

Though Crown seems to be winding it down, Harmony Books has been a market leader in the area of mind, body, and spirit, as well as biography/memoir, science, and general narrative nonfiction. Its critically acclaimed and bestselling authors include Buzz Aldrin, Tony Curtis, Pattie Boyd, Deepak Chopra, Judith Orloff, MD, Daniel G. Amen, MD, Cesar Millan, David E. Sanger, Byron Katie, Yongey Mingyur Rinpoche, and Shawn Levy.

Recent titles include *Running with the Mind of Meditation* by Sakyong Mipham Rinpoche; *Open Heart, Open Mind* by Tsoknyi Rinpoche; *Ten Poems to Say Goodbye* by Roger Housden; *Four Elements* by John O'Donohue; and *War of the Worldviews* by Deepak Chopra and Leonard Mlodinow.

HOGARTH

Hogarth Press was originally founded in 1917 by Virginia and Leonard Woolf. In order to print cutting-edge books that commercial publishers had rejected—and as a diversion from their own writing—the two bought a hand-operated letterpress, turning their London residence into a publishing house. The Woolfs published volumes by such writers as T. S. Eliot, E. M. Forester, Roger Fry, and Katherine Mansfield, until Chatto & Windus acquired the press in 1946.

In 2012, Random House relaunched Hogarth, envisioning the press as a close collaboration between Crown Publishing, in the United States, and Chatto & Windus, in the United Kingdom. The press publishes between eight and ten fiction titles a year, described by publisher Molly Stern as "worldly, provocative, well-written works for a broad and lasting readership."

Titles include *I Am Forbidden* by Anouk Markovits; *The Kissing List* by Stephanie Reents; *The Dead Do Not Improve* by Jay Caspian Kang; and *The Watch* by Joydeep Roy-Bhattacharya.

Please refer to the editors listed for Crown as per above.

IMAGE BOOKS

A publisher of Catholic resources for over 50 years, Image Books recently incorporated Doubleday Religion as part of a reorganization of Random House's religious program in 2011. The press publishes a mix of contemporary and classic authors such as Blessed Mother Teresa, George Weigel, Scott Hahn, Cardinal Francis George, Thomas Merton, Carl Anderson, and Pope Benedict XVI.

Recent titles include *Following the Path* by Sister Joan Chittister; *Why Catholicism Matters* by Dr. William Donohue; *The Way to Love* by Anthony De Mello; and *Doing Well and Doing Good* by Richard J. Neuhaus.

Gary Jansen, Editor

TEN SPEED PRESS
 CELESTIAL ARTS
  CROSSING PRESS

6001 Shellmound Street, Emeryville, CA 94608
510-559-1600
www.tenspeed.com | Twitter: @tenspeedpress

Founder Philip Wood began the Ten Speed Press in 1971 with *Anybody's Bike Book*, still in print with more than a million copies sold. Ten Speed went on to build its reputation with titles including *What Color Is Your Parachute?*, *Moosewood Cookbook*, *White Trash Cooking*, *Why Cats Paint*, and *Flattened Fauna*. Ten Speed Press publishes 150 books per year under its three imprints: Ten Speed Press, Celestial Arts, and Crossing Press. Tricycle Press, Ten Speed's former children's imprint, was closed in 2010.

Random House recently acquired Ten Speed Press and incorporated it into the Crown Publishing Group; the editorial offices, however, will stay in Berkeley, California. Jenny Frost, former president and publisher of Crown, said, "They have a lot of eclectic and quirky books, and I think maybe the soil in Berkeley helps grow that. I wouldn't want to take that away."

Julie Bennett, editorial director at Ten Speed, says that the press is in the process of expanding its list in the area of "quirky" or "alternative" crafts. "We're hoping it's where the cookbook world was ten to 15 years ago," she said. Other Ten Speed categories include how-to, cooking, business/career, relationships, gardening, gift, humor, and pop culture.

Recent titles from Ten Speed include *Wired for Story* by Lisa Cron; *Heart and Hands* by Elizabeth Davis; *People's Pops* by Nathalie Jordi; *The Detox Diet* by Elson M. Haas; and *The Damn Good Resume Guide* by Yana Parker.

For all Ten Speed imprints, direct queries, proposals, and SASEs to the attention of "Acquisition Editors" for the specific imprint. No unsolicited e-mail submissions.

Aaron Wehner, Editorial Director—Cooking.
Julie Bennett, Editor—Cooking, lifestyle, how-to, careers, health, humor.
Jenny Wapner, Editor—Cooking.
Melissa Moore, Editor—Cooking.
Sarah Golski, Editor—Parenting, health/diet, cooking.

CELESTIAL ARTS

Celestial Arts was founded by poster printer Hal Kramer in San Francisco in 1963. During the Human Potential Movement of the seventies, Celestial Arts blossomed into a book publisher and made a name for itself with best sellers like *Loving Someone Gay* and Virginia Satir's inspirational poem-book *Self-Esteem*.

The imprint was acquired by Ten Speed Press in 1983 and continues to publish a diverse list of alternative medicine, health, nutrition, parenting, inspiration, self-help, and spirituality titles.

Recent titles include *Dogs Can Sign, Too: A Breakthrough Method for Teaching Your Dog to Communicate* by Sean Senechal; *Mother Rising* by Yana Cortlund; *Maui Onion Cookbook* by Barbara Santos; *More Lesbian Sex: Finding and Pleasing Her Sweet Spot* by Jude Schell; and *Words That Heal the Blues* by Douglas Bloch.

CROSSING PRESS

Crossing Press (originally called New Books) began as a small poetry publisher founded by poet John Gill in the village of Trumansburg, New York, just outside of Ithaca, in 1963. He changed the press's name to the Crossing Press in 1969 (after consulting the *I Ching*, as legend has it) and began branching out into literature, feminist and political works, and cookbooks. Early landmarks include *The Male Muse* (1974), a pioneering collection of gay poetry, and unique cookbooks like *Moog's Musical Eatery* (1978). In 1986, the company relocated to northern California and, in 2002, it was acquired by Ten Speed Press.

The Crossing Press publishes a wide range of hardcover and trade paperback editions of books, videos, and audios on natural healing, spirituality, alternative healing practices, and, occasionally, cooking. Dedicated to social and spiritual change, Crossing Press focuses on metaphysics, alternative therapies, mysticism, feminism, herbal medicine, and chakra and color healing.

Recent titles include *Floral Acupuncture* by Warren Bellows; *In God's Garden* by Mahassen Ahmad; *Finding Soul on the Path of Orisa* by Tobe Melora Correal; *Gemstones A to Z* by Diane Stein; and *A Woman's I Ching* by Diane Stein.

THREE RIVERS PRESS

Three Rivers Press publishes original paperbacks and paperback reprints of books issued initially in hardcover by the other Crown imprints. The press is named for the Harlem, East, and Hudson rivers.

Titles representative of the list include *Stop Saying You're Fine* by Mel Robbins; *Apron Anxiety* by Alyssa Shelasky; *My Lucky Life In and Out of Show Business* by Dick Van Dyke; *The Legal Writer* by Steven D. Stark; and *Growing Up Psychic* by Chip Coffey.

Amanda Patten, Editor—Nonfiction, self-help, humor.

WATERBROOK MULTNOMAH

12265 Oracle Boulevard, Suite 200, Colorado Springs, CO 80921
719-590-4999 | fax: 719-590-8977
www.randomhouse.com/waterbrook | e-mail: info@waterbrookmultnomah.com
Twitter: @waterbrookpress

The WaterBrook Multnomah Publishing Group was formed in 2006 when Random House purchased Multnomah from founder Don Jacobson and integrated it with WaterBrook Press. WaterBrook Press and Multnomah operated as distinct imprints before they were restructured into the Crown Publishing Group in 2009 as a single imprint: WaterBrook Multnomah.

WaterBrook Multnomah is committed to creating products that both intensify and satisfy the elemental thirst for a deeper relationship with God. Their publishing list includes books for Christian living and spiritual growth, Bible studies, tips on parenting, inspiring works of fiction for adults and youth, engaging books for children, series for men, and titles on marriage, love, finances, and prophecy.

Recent titles include *The Shape of Mercy* by Susan Meissner; *The Girl's Still Got It* by Liz Curtis Higgs; *The Orphan King* by Sigmund Brouwer; *Breaking Free from Fear* by Kay Arthur; and *Your Life Without Limits* by Nick Vujicic.

WaterBrook Multnomah accepts unsolicited manuscripts only from literary agents. Direct queries and SASEs to:

Shannon Marchese, Editor—Religion, science fiction, fantasy, romance.

Laura Barker, Editor—Popular psychology, self-help, inspiration, spirituality.

WATSON-GUPTILL
AMPHOTO BOOKS
BACK STAGE BOOKS

www.watsonguptill.com | e-mail: info@watsonguptill.com

Watson-Guptill's name is synonymous with design and art instruction. One of America's foremost publishers of lavishly illustrated art and art instruction titles and reference books on performing and visual arts, Watson-Guptill was founded in 1937.

The house publishes under three imprints: Watson-Guptill, Amphoto Books, and Back Stage Books. The Watson-Guptill imprint focuses on technique books for drawing and painting in all media, sculpture, cartooning, animation, crafts, and graphic design. They also publish illustrated young-adult and tween nonfiction in the crafts category. Amphoto Books covers all aspects of photography technique, and Back Stage concentrates on reference titles for theater.

Recent titles from Watson-Guptill include *Draw 50 Athletes* by Lee J. Ames; *Printmaking Revolution* by Dwight Pogue; *Digital Painting for the Complete Beginner* by Carlyn Beccia; and *Calligraphy Bible* by Maryanne Grebenstein.

E-mail submissions and phone calls will not be accepted. Send a proposal and cover letter in writing via regular mail. Address queries and SASEs to the Editors.

Victoria Craven, Editorial Director

AMPHOTO BOOKS

A leading publisher of photography, Amphoto Books is at the forefront in publishing for professionals and amateurs on such vital topics as digital, lighting, nature, glamour, wedding, and the business of photography.

Some recent titles include *The Luminous Portrait* by Elizabeth Messina; *Beyond Snapshots* by Rachel Devine; *The Complete Guide to Nature Photography* by Sean Arbabi; *Going Pro* by Scott Bourne; and *Boudoir Photography* by Critsey Rowe.

BACK STAGE BOOKS

Synonymous with the performing arts, Back Stage Books publishes titles for professionals, students, and enthusiasts on acting, theater, and dance as well as the history and business of theater and its leading performers.

Some titles include *Voice for Hire* by Randy Thomas; *Acting—Make It Your Business* by Paul Russell; *Let's Put on a Musical* by Peter Filichia; *Broadway Babylon* by Boze Hadleigh; and *Acting for Young Actors* by Mary Lou Belli.

KNOPF DOUBLEDAY PUBLISHING GROUP

ALFRED A. KNOPF
ANCHOR BOOKS
DOUBLEDAY
EVERYMAN'S LIBRARY
FLYING DOLPHIN PRESS
NAN A. TALESE
PANTHEON BOOKS
SCHOCKEN BOOKS
VINTAGE

In 2009, Random House created the Knopf Doubleday Publishing Group, reorganizing and combining the previously separate divisions and many imprints of Knopf (pronounced with a hard *k*) and Doubleday Broadway.

ALFRED A. KNOPF

Alfred A. Knopf founded his eponymous press in 1915, publishing European authors neglected in America such as Kafka, Freud, D. H. Lawrence, and Sartre. He had a colorful and outspoken personality, and was dedicated to the quality of his press's output. Knopf merged with Random House in 1960.

Knopf's publishes fiction, select poetry, and nonfiction; its current nonfiction categories include biography, history, nature, travel, and cooking. The house also publishes nature guides and travel guides including National Audubon Society Field Guides, Sibley Field Guides, Knopf Map Guides, and Knopf City Guides.

Recent Knopf titles include *The Impeachment of Abraham Lincoln* by Stephen L. Carter; *The Red Chamber* by Pauline A. Chen; *The Crowded Grave* by Martin Walker; *A Night in Brooklyn* by D. Nurkse; and *Talulla Rising* by Glen Duncan.

Send query letters and SASEs to:
Ann Close, Senior Editor—Literary fiction, social and cultural history, narratives.
Jonathan Segal, Vice President and Senior Editor—Twentieth-century history, contemporary events, biography, health.
Jordan Pavlin, Editor—Fiction.
Andrew Miller, Editor—Nonfiction, history, current affairs.
Dan Frank, Senior Editor—American history
Sonny Mehta, Editor—Fiction, memoirs.
Gary Fisketjon, Editor—Fiction.
Jennifer Jackson, Editor—Fiction.

ANCHOR BOOKS

Anchor Books is the oldest trade paperback publisher in America. It was founded in 1953 by Jason Epstein with the goal of making inexpensive editions of modern classics widely available to college students and the adult reading public. Today, Anchor's list includes award-winning history, science, women's studies, sociology, and quality fiction.

Authors published by Anchor Books include Susan Sontag, Natalie Angier, Thomas Cahill, Ian McEwan, Anne Lamott, and Margaret Atwood.

New titles include *Sex on the Moon* by Ben Mezrich; *The Devil All the Time* by Donald Ray Pollock; *Zone One* by Colson Whitehead; and *The Things We Cherished* by Pam Jenoff.

DOUBLEDAY

Frank Nelson Doubleday, along with magazine publisher Samuel McClure, founded the Doubleday & McClure Company in 1897. Rudyard Kipling became one of their first bestselling authors with his book *The Day's Work*. Perhaps best known for its strong list in commercial fiction, literary fiction, and nonfiction, Doubleday continues to be a dominating force.

Bestselling and prize-winning authors include Anne Applebaum, Pat Barker, Dan Brown, Bill Bryson, William D. Cohan, Barbara Delinsky, Sebastian Faulks, George Friedman, David Grann, John Grisham, Mark Haddon, Jon Krakauer, Jonathan Lethem, Jeff Lindsay, Christopher Reich, Rick Reilly, Edward Rutherfurd, Hampton Sides, Jeffrey Toobin, and Colson Whitehead.

Doubleday nonfiction categories include biography and autobiography, art and photography, current affairs, political science, public affairs, philosophy, ethics, family, marriage, sports and recreation, health, history, home and garden, and self-help.

Recent titles include *The Malice of Fortune* by Michael Ennis; *Birdseye* by Mark Kurlansky; *Some Kind of Fairy Tale* by Graham Joyce; *The Third Gate* by Lincoln Child; and *The Good Father* by Noah Hawley.

Direct query letters and SASEs to:

Bill Thomas, Senior Vice President, Editor-in-Chief, Publisher—Memoir, current affairs, fiction.

Jason Kaufman, Vice President and Executive Editor—Thrillers, action adventure, true crime, narrative nonfiction, science, sports stories, current affairs.

Kristine Puopolo, Senior Editor—Literary nonfiction, current affairs, biography, current affairs.

Gerry Howard, Editor-at-Large—Fiction, memoir, nonfiction narrative, current affairs, cultural issues.

EVERYMAN'S LIBRARY

Everyman's Library was founded in 1906 by London Publisher Joseph Malaby Dent, who sought to put out literature that would appeal to "every kind of reader: the worker, the student, the cultured man, the child, the man and the woman." These beautiful editions feature original introductions, up-to-date bibliographies, and complete chronologies of the authors' lives and works. The series has grown to hundreds of volumes and includes sets such as *100 Essentials, Children's Classics, Contemporary Classics,* and *The Great Poets.*

Titles include *Art and Artists* by Emily Fragos; *Stories of Motherhood* by Diana Secker Tesdell; *Agnes Grey, The Tenant of Wildfell Hall* by Anne Bronte; *Villanelles* by Annie Finch and Marie-Elizabeth Mali; and *The Siege of Krishnapur,Troubles* by J.G. Farrell.

FLYING DOLPHIN PRESS

Flying Dolphin Press focuses on popular culture and fiction titles. Great emphasis is placed on the quality of the writing as well as finding subject matter that examines people and ideas central to contemporary culture. A new imprint, it will release six new titles per year to start.

Recent titles include *We'll Be Here For the Rest of Our Lives* by Paul Shaffer and David Ritz; *Mr. Fooster Traveling on a Whim* by Tom Corwin and Craig Frazier; *Chasing Windmills* by Catherine Ryan Hyde; and *BORAT: Touristic Guidings to Minor Nation of US and A. and Touristic Guidings to Glorious Nation of Kazakhstan* by Borat Sagdiyev.

NAN A. TALESE

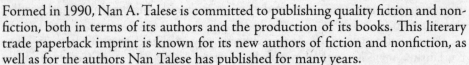

Formed in 1990, Nan A. Talese is committed to publishing quality fiction and nonfiction, both in terms of its authors and the production of its books. This literary trade paperback imprint is known for its new authors of fiction and nonfiction, as well as for the authors Nan Talese has published for many years.

Among its writers are Peter Ackroyd, Margaret Atwood, Pinckney Benedict,

Thomas Cahill, Kevin Canty, Lorene Cary, Pat Conroy, Jennifer Egan, Mia Farrow, Antonia Fraser, David Grand, Nicola Griffith, Aleksandar Hemon, Thomas Keneally, Alex Kotlowitz, Robert MacNeil, Ian McEwan, Gita Mehta, George Plimpton, Edvard Radzinsky, Mark Richard, Nicholas Shakespeare, Barry Unsworth, and Gus Van Sant. Nan A. Talese is also well known as the publisher of the controversial memoir *A Million Little Pieces* by James Frey.

Recent titles include *The Investigation* by Philippe Claudel; *Snow-Storm in August* by Jefferson Morley; *The Paris Directive* by Gerald Jay; *Marilyn & Me* by Lawrence Schiller; and *A Song in the Night* by Bob Massie.

This imprint does not accept unagented or unsolicited submissions.

Nan Talese, Senior Vice President, Publisher, and Editorial Director—Fiction, biography, nonfiction.

Ronit Feldman, Editor

PANTHEON BOOKS

Pantheon handles nonfiction books in categories such as current events, international affairs, contemporary culture, literary criticism and the arts, popular business, psychology, travel, nature, science, and history. The house has a strong list in contemporary fiction, poetry, and drama. Pantheon also offers the Fairytale and Folktale Library.

Pantheon was founded in 1942 by Helen and Kurt Wolff, refugees from Nazi Germany. The Wolffs published translated literature by authors such as Hermann Broch, Giuseppe di Lampedusa, Boris Pasternak, Karl Jung, and Gunter Grass. The press was purchased by Random House in 1961, and it continues to publish works by such authors as Julia Glass, James Gleick, Ha Jin, Anne Morrow Lindbergh, Alexander McCall Smith, Marjane Satrapi, Art Spiegelman, and Studs Terkel.

Representative titles include *Corduroy Mansions* by Alexander McCall Smith; *The Newhate* by Arthur Godwag; *Offspeed* by Terry McDermott; *Borrow: A Brief History of Debt in Modern America* by Louis Hyman; *The Flame Alphabet* by Ben Marcus; *The Pirates of Puntland* by Jay Bahadur; and *Bad Dog: A Love Story* by Martin Kihn.

Recent titles include *Sorry Please Thank You* by Charles Yu; *A Conspiracy of Friends* by Alexander McCall Smith; *The World Without You* by Joshua Henkin; and *China Airborne* by James Fallows.

Direct query letters and SASEs to:

Tim O'Connell, Editor—Fiction and nonfiction.

SCHOCKEN BOOKS

Schocken publishes books of Jewish interest in the following areas: history, biography, memoir, current affairs, spirituality, religion, philosophy, politics, sociology, and fiction.

Founded in Berlin in 1931 by Salman Schocken, a department store magnate, bibliophile, and ardent Zionist, Schocken Verlag was closed down by the Nazis in

1938. Salman Schocken founded Schocken Books in the United States in 1942. The company became a division of Random House in 1987.

Recently published books include *Blooms of Darkness* by Aharon Appelfeld; *When General Grant Expelled the Jews* by Jonathan D. Sarna; *Unterzakhn* by Leela Corman; *Tzili* by Aharon Appelfeld; and *Simon Wiesenthal* by Tom Segev.

Direct queries with SASEs to:

Altie Karper, Editorial Director

VINTAGE BOOKS

Vintage Books is a trade paperback arm of the Knopf Publishing Group.

The Vintage Books publishing list includes a wide range, from world literature to contemporary fiction and distinguished nonfiction, featuring such writers as William Faulkner, Vladimir Nabokov, Albert Camus, Ralph Ellison, Dashiell Hammett, William Styron, A. S. Byatt, Philip Roth, Richard Ford, Cormac McCarthy, Alice Munro, David Guterson, and Arthur Golden. Vintage Crime/Black Lizard titles focus on crime and suspense.

Representative titles include *Maine* by J. Courtney Sullivan; *Fifty Shades Trilogy* by E. L. James; *The Sense of an Ending* by Julian Barnes; *Blue Nights* by Joan Didion; and *The Cat's Table* by Michael Ondaatje.

Send query letters and SASEs to:

Tim O'Connell, Editor

RANDOM HOUSE CHILDREN'S BOOKS

ALFRED A. KNOPF BOOKS FOR YOUNG READERS
BLUEFIRE
DELACORTE BOOKS FOR YOUNG READERS
DRAGONFLY
EMBER
GOLDEN BOOKS
LAUREL-LEAF
ROBIN COREY BOOKS
SCHWARTZ & WADE BOOKS
WENDY LAMB BOOKS
YEARLING BOOKS

Random House Children's Books publishes Dr. Seuss and other well-known licenses, such as Arthur, the Berenstain Bears, Sesame Workshop, and Thomas the Tank Engine. In 2012, the press announced that it had become the primary publisher of Nickelodeon properties. The house also publishes many of children's favorite authors, including Judy Blume, Robert Cormier, Madeleine L'Engle, Leo

Lionni, Mary Pope Osborne, Gary Paulsen, Tamora Pierce, Philip Pullman, Faith Ringgold, and Jerry Spinelli. Random House imprints have published such books as Clare Vanderpool's *Moon Over Manifest* and Rebecca Stead's *When You Reach Me*, winners, respectively, of the 2010 and 2011 John Newbery Medals.

Random House Children's Books publishes popular fiction including *Anne of Green Gables*, *Where the Red Fern Grows*, and *The Phantom Tollbooth*. The Random House list also features Caldecott Honor- and Medal-winning books, including *A Ball for Daisy* by Chris Raschka in 2012, *Tar Beach*, *Time Flies*, *Song and Dance Man*, and the late Leo Lionni's *Frederick*, *Swimmy and Alexander and the Wind-Up Mouse*.

Recent releases from Random House Books for Young Readers include *Magic Tree House #48: A Perfect Time for Pandas* by Mary Pope Osborne; *Princess and the Popstar* by Irene Trimble; *Risky Rails!* by Rev. W. Awdry; *Trick-or-Treat!/Aye-Aye!* by Tish Rabe; and *Beka Cooper: The Hunt Records* by Tamora Pierce.

All submissions to the Random House Books for Young Readers imprint should come via a literary agent.

Suzy Capozzi, Editor—Young adult.
Alice Jonaitis, Editor—Picture books.
Heidi Kilgras, Editor—Illustrated/picture books.
Schuyler Hooke, Editor—Middle grade, young adult.
Shana Corey, Editor—Middle grade.
Jennifer Arena, Editor—Picture books, middle grade.
Chelsea Eberly, Editor—Middle grade, young adult.
Annie Eaton, Editor—Young adult.

ALFRED A. KNOPF BOOKS FOR YOUNG READERS

Alfred A. Knopf Books for Young Readers (BFYR) publishes quality books for children of all ages, toddlers to young adults. The imprint publishes between 60 and 70 new hardcover books each year, ranging from board books to picture books to novels to nonfiction.

Known for both the caliber of its authors and artists and the high quality of its book design and production, Alfred A. Knopf BFYR publishes books intended to entertain, inspire, and endure. The imprint is deeply committed to its authors and illustrators, and believes that by working closely with them, they can create books that children, and adults who read to children, will love for years to come.

Authors and illustrators published by Alfred A. Knopf BFYR include Marc Brown, Robert Cormier, Leo and Diane Dillon, Carl Hiaasen, Leo Lionni, Christopher Paolini, Philip Pullman, Eric Rohmann, Judy Sierra, and Jerry Spinelli.

Some recent titles from Alfred A. Knopf BFYR include *Day by Day* by Susan Gal; *Fury's Fire* by Lisa Papademetriou; *Sammy Keyes and the Power of Justice Jack* by Wendelin Van Draanen; *Hide & Seek* by Il Sung Na; and *I, Galileo* by Bonnie Christensen.

Katherine Harrison, Editor—Picture books, middle-grade, young adult.

BLUEFIRE

Established in 2011, Bluefire is an imprint that specializes in high-fantasy novels for young adult and middle-grade readers. The books feature classic tales of witches, dragons, wizards, and knights. Authors on the list include Tamora Pierce, Isobelle Carmody, Esther Friesner, Eoin McNamee, Henry Neff, N. D. Wilson, and Janni Lee Simne.

Titles include *Blood Magic* (The Blood Journals) by Tessa Gratton; *Faerie Winter: Book 2* by Janni Lee Simner; *The Floating Islands* by Rachel Neumeier; *The Hunt of the Unicorn* by Chris Humphreys; and *Tortall and Other Lands: A Collection of Tales* by Tamora Pierce.

DELACORTE PRESS BOOKS FOR YOUNG READERS

Delacorte Press Books for Young Readers publishes literary and commercial novels for middle-grade and young-adult readers, as well as nonfiction that crosses both educational and general interest categories. Among the many bestselling authors published by Delacorte Press Books for Young Readers are David Almond, Ann Brashares, Libba Bray, Caroline Cooney, Robert Cormier, Lurlene McDaniel, Phyllis Reynolds Naylor, Joan Lowery Nixon, Louis Sachar, Zilpha Keatley Snyder, and R. L. Stine.

The press accepts unsolicited manuscripts only through their contests, The Delacorte Press Contest for a First Young-Adult Novel and the Delacorte Dell Yearling Contest for a First Middle-Grade Novel. You may request the rules and guidelines at the Random House address, at: Contests, or view them online.

Some recent Delacorte BFYR titles are *Diva* by Jillian Larkin; *Don't You Wish* by Roxanne St. Clair; *Poison Tree* by Amelia Atwater-Rhodes; *The Scorpions of Zahir* by Christine Brodien-Jones; and *Diary of a Parent Trainer* by Jenny Smith.

Beverly Horowitz, Vice President and Publisher—Middle grade, young adult.
Francoise Bui, Executive Editor—Young adult, fantasy.
Wendy Loggia, Publishing Director—Young adult, middle-grade children's literature, graphic novels.
Krista Marino, Senior Editor—Young adult.
Michelle Poploff, Editor—Young adult, middle grade.
Krista Vitola, Editor—Middle grade, young adult.

DRAGONFLY

Dragonfly introduces children to talented and award-winning artists and writers through affordable paperback picture books. These inspiring and imaginative full-color books range from first concept books to read-together stories to books for newly independent readers. Through the variety of writing and illustration styles, children reap the rich rewards that Dragonfly's paperback picture books offer. Authors and illustrators include Leo and Diane Dillon, Jarrett J. Krosoczka,

Grace Lin, Leo Lionni, Anita Lobel, Jack Prelutsky, Raffi, Faith Ringgold, Lizzy Rockwell, Eric Rohmann, Judy Sierra, Peter Spier, Meilo So, Nancy Van Laan, and more.

Some Dragonfly books are *Canoe Days* by Gary and Ruth Paulsen; *Confessions of a Former Bully* by Trudy Ludwig; *Rosi's Time: Rosi's Doors* by Edward Eaton; *Lala Mankowicz: Dances with Dogs…Runs from Spiders!* by Basia Kent Belroy; and *Joe & The Lightning Bug Adventure* by Brenda Nelson.

EMBER

A new imprint, Ember was established in 2011. Ember is mostly intended to issue reprints, but it will also publish original paperback titles as well.

Recent tiles from Ember include *Reaching Through Time: Three Novellas* by Lurlene McDaniel; *The Summer I Learned to Fly* by Dana Reinhardt; *Wildcat Fireflies: A Meridian Novel* by Amber Kizer; *You Don't Know About Me* by Brian Meehl; and *All Just Glass* by Amelia Atwater-Rhodes.

GOLDEN BOOKS

In August 2001, Random House acquired all the book-publishing properties of Golden Books Family Entertainment, which produces storybooks, coloring and activity books, puzzle books, educational workbooks, reference books, novelty books, and chapter books. The Golden Books publishing program features Blue's Clues, Rugrats, Bob the Builder, and Barbie; and the *Little Golden Books* series publishes classic favorites such as *Pat the Bunny* and *The Poky Little Puppy*.

Recent Golden Books are *Where Do Giggles Come From?* by Diane E. Muldrow; *The Big Ballet Show* (Dora the Explorer) by Inc. Loter; *The Big Boat Race!* by Kellee Riley; *Blue Mountain Mystery* (Thomas & Friends) by Rev. W. Awdry and Tommy Stubbs; and *The Cow Went Over the Mountain* by Jeanette Krinsley

Diane Muldrow, Editor

LAUREL-LEAF

Laurel-Leaf is a paperback imprint that publishes quality literature for teens. Laurel-Leaf offers reprints of contemporary and classic fiction, mystery, fantasy, romance, suspense, and nonfiction appropriate for ages 12 and up.

The press is the paperback home of such bestselling and beloved authors as Judy Blume, Caroline B. Cooney, Robert Cormier, Lois Duncan, S. E. Hinton, Lois Lowry, Scott O'Dell, Gary Paulsen, Philip Pullman, and Jerry Spinelli.

Recent titles include *Living Up The Street* by Gary Soto; *Swallowing Stones* by Joyce Mcdonald; *For Better, For Worse, Forever* by Lurlene Mcdaniel; *Orphea Proud* by Sharon Dennis Wyeth; and *The Unlikely Romance of Kate Bjorkman* by Louise Plummer.

ROBIN COREY BOOKS

In Fall 2007, Robin Corey Books launched its inaugural list of board books and interactive books for ages four to eight. Noted authors, illustrators, and paper engineers include Sandra Boynton, David A. Carter, Elise Primavera, Chuck Murphy, Charise Mericle Harper, John Stadler, and Hiroe Nakata.

Some of their titles include *My Dad Is the Best Playground* by Luciana Navarro Powell; *The House at the End of Ladybug Lane* by Elise Primavera; *Peas on Earth* by Todd H. Doodler; and *The Lorax Pop-up* by Dr. Seuss and David A. Carter.

Robin Corey, Vice President and Publisher

SCHWARTZ & WADE BOOKS

Established in March 2005, Schwartz & Wade Books is codirected by Anne Schwartz and Lee Wade, who take a unique approach to the creative process and believe that the best books for children grow from a seamless collaboration between editorial and design. The imprint launched its first list in spring 2006 with four picture books and continues to publish approximately 20 hardcover books a year. Authors and illustrators include Tad Hills, Deborah Hopkinson, James E. Ransome, Ronnie Shotter, Giselle Potter, and Valorie Fisher.

Recent titles include *The Honeybee Man* by Lela Nargi; *Rocket Writes a Story* by Tad Hills; *The Little Woods* by McCormick Templeman; *On the Day I Died: Stories from the Grave* by Candace Fleming; and *The Fantastic 5 & 10 Cent Store* by J. Patrick Lewis.

Anne Schwartz, Editorial Director—Young adult, picture books.

WENDY LAMB BOOKS

Wendy Lamb Books, established in 2002, focuses on innovative middle-grade and young-adult fiction by award-winning writers such as Christopher Paul Curtis, Peter Dickinson, Patricia Reilly Giff, Gary Paulsen, and Graham Salisbury. The imprint also seeks new talent and publishes many first novels.

Recent titles include *Crush: The Theory, Practice and Destructive Properties of Love* by Gary Paulsen; *Jersey Angel* by Beth Ann Bauman; *Bears Beware (Afterschool)* by Patricia Reilly Giff; and *Calvin Coconut: Man Trip* by Graham Salisbury.

Wendy Lamb, Publisher—Young adult.

YEARLING BOOKS

Yearling Books celebrates over 40 years of providing parents, teachers, and children ages eight to twelve with distinguished paperback books in an affordable digest format. The Yearling imprint features a wide variety of books: beloved classics, Newbery-award winners, first-rate contemporary and historical fiction, fantasy, mystery, and adventure.

The Yearling brand is recognized by generations of readers as representing quality. Yearling is the middle-reader paperback home of such beloved authors as Judy Blume, Christopher Paul Curtis, Patricia Reilly Giff, Norton Juster, Madeleine L'Engle, Lois Lowry, Gary Paulsen, Philip Pullman, and Louis Sachar, and classic characters such as Encyclopedia Brown, Harriet the Spy, Nate the Great, and Sammy Keyes.

Recent titles include *Eight Keys* by Suzanne M. LaFleur; *R My Name Is Rachel* by Patricia Reilly Giff; *The Fabled Fifth Graders of Aesop Elementary School* by Candace Fleming; *Far-Flung Adventures: Hugo Pepper* by Paul Stewart; and *Noah Barleywater Runs Away* by John Boyne.

THE RANDOM HOUSE PUBLISHING GROUP

BALLANTINE BANTAM DELL
BALLANTINE BOOKS
BANTAM DELL
DEL REY
THE DIAL PRESS
ESPN BOOKS
THE MODERN LIBRARY
ONE WORLD
PRESIDIO
RANDOM HOUSE
RANDOM HOUSE TRADE PAPERBACKS
SPECTRA
SPIEGEL & GRAU
VILLARD BOOKS

The Random House Publishing Group (RHPG) was formed in 2003, uniting the two divisions formerly known as the Random House Trade Group and the Ballantine Books Group. Publishing in all formats—hardcover, trade paperback, and mass-market. In 2010, Random House created the Ballantine Bantam Dell unit, grouping several of their publishers into the same division.

Gina Centrello, President and Publisher
Kate Medina, Executive Vice President, Associate Publisher, and Executive Editorial Director
Susan Kamil, Senior Vice President and Editor-in-Chief
Jennifer Hershey, Senior Vice President, Editorial Director

BALLANTINE BANTAM DELL

Ballantine Bantam Dell was created in 2010, as Random House merged their Ballantine and Bantam Dell divisions with other RHPG imprints such as Del Rey, Delacorte,

ESPN Books, One World, Presidio, Spectra, and Villard Books. The decision was made to "better define our priorities," according to a Random House spokesperson.

BALLANTINE BOOKS

Ballantine Books publishes commercial fiction and general nonfiction, including health, diet, psychology, history, and biography. The mass-market list includes such bestselling authors as John Case, Robert Crais, Fannie Flagg, Sue Grafton, Kristin Hannah, John Irving, Jonathan Kellerman, Richard North Patterson, Anne Perry, Anne Rice, Edward Rutherfurd, and Anne Tyler.

Recent titles include *Maximum Brainwidth* by Collins Hemingway; *Recipe for Style: A Cookbook for Your Closet* by Jessica Schroeder; *I Do…Now What?: Stories and Advice from America's Favorite Couple* by Giuliana Rancic and Bill Rancic; *The Last Great Game* by Gene Wojciechowski; *Friendship Bread* by Darien Gee; *How to Build a Fire* by Erin Bried; and *Homesick and Happy* by Michael Thompson.

Marnie Cochran, Executive Editor—Nonfiction lifestyle, parenting, advice, diet, memoir.

Susanna Porter, Executive Editor—Fiction, mysteries, nonfiction, current affairs, business.

Kate Collins, Senior Editor—Women's fiction, romance, suspense.

Ryan Doherty, Associate Editor—Cooking, sports, food, business.

Pamela Cannon, Editor—Cooking, lifestyle.

Shauna Summers, Editor—Women's fiction/romance.

Jennifer Hershey, Editor—Fiction, mysteries.

Jennifer Smith, Editor—Fiction, advice, relationships.

BANTAM DELL

Established in 1945, Bantam was one of the most successful publishers of adult fiction and nonfiction, and Dell was one of the biggest publishers of paperbacks for more than seven decades. As a part of massive Random House reorganizations, both houses were merged to become Bantam Dell and incorporated into the Random House Publishing Group in 2009. Their fiction list includes commercial novels, mysteries, thrillers, suspense, science fiction and fantasy, romance, women's fiction, and select literary works, and their diverse nonfiction lists cover genres from memoir to current events to history.

Bantam has published such bestselling authors as Dean Koontz, Lisa Gardner, George R. R. Martin, Louis L'Amour, Daniel Goleman, John Glenn, and Dr. Christiane Northrup. Dell has been home to writers such as John Grisham, Danielle Steel, Thomas Harris, Lee Child, and Diana Gabaldon.

Titles include *The Scottish Prisoner* by Diana Gabaldon; *The Stranger You Seek* by Amanda Kyle Williams; *The Odd Thomas* series by Dean Koontz; *The Last Kind Words* by Tom Piccirilli; and *Explosive Eighteen* by Janet Evanovich.

Kate Miciak, Editorial Director—Mysteries, thrillers, other fiction, narrative nonfiction.

Shauna Summers, Senior Editor—Women's fiction, romance, erotica, paranormal.

DEL REY

In 1977, Del Rey was founded as an imprint of Ballantine Books. The press publishes manga, science fiction, fantasy, speculative fiction, and alternate history in hardcover, trade paperback, and mass-market paperback formats. Its founders were the late Judy-Lynn and Lester del Rey, legendary publishers who catapulted science-fiction/fantasy titles onto the national best-sellers lists for the first time. Del Rey is also home to LucasBooks, publishing Star Wars novelizations, spin-off novels, and nonfiction books.

Del Rey's list includes such illustrious authors as Terry Brooks, Arthur C. Clarke, Isaac Asimov, Stephen Donaldson, Anne McCaffrey, David Eddings, Larry Niven, Alan Dean Foster, Katherine Kurtz, Jack L. Chalker, and Barbara Hambly.

Recent titles include *Embassytown* by China Mieville; *Dearly, Departed* by Lia Habel; *The Cold Commands* by Richard K. Morgan; and *The High Druid of Shannara* Trilogy by Terry Brooks.

Betsy Mitchell, Editor-in-Chief—Paranormal fiction, horror, science fiction, fantasy.
Tricia Narwani, Editor
David Pomerico, Editor

THE DIAL PRESS

The Dial Press was originally founded in 1924 by Lincoln MacVeagh, in collaboration with Scofield Thayer, owner of literary magazine *The Dial*. The press grew to publish such authors as James Baldwin, Thomas Berger, Vance Bourjaily, Elizabeth Bowen, James M. Cain, Richard Condon, e. e. cummings, Salvador Dali, Andre Dubus, Shelby Foote, Ford Madox Ford, James Jones, D. H. Lawrence, Robert Ludlum, Norman Mailer, Larry McMurtry, Howard Sackler, Wallace Stegner, Glenway Wescott, and Frank Yerby.

After shutting down for a period, the press was resurrected by Dell Publishing in 1995. It publishes literary fiction and nonfiction, including works by Sophie Kinsella, Allegra Goodman, Justin Cronin, Marie Arana, Patrick Ryan, Elizabeth McCracken, Ian Caldwell, Dustin Thomason, and Sting.

Recent titles include *Tell the Wolves I'm Home* by Carol Rifka Brunt; *A Partial History of Lost Causes* by Jennifer DuBois; *The Cookbook Collector* by Allegra Goodman; *Vaclav & Lena* by Haley Tanner; and *The Imperfectionists* by Tom Rachman.

Direct queries and SASEs to:
Susan Kamil, Vice President and Editorial Director
Noah Eaker, Editor—Fiction.

ESPN BOOKS

ESPN Books began in 2008 when Ballantine and ESPN announced a publishing alliance and a plan to release 10 to 12 books a year.

Recent titles include *The Book of Basketball* by Bill Simmons; *Rules of the Red Rubber Ball* by Kevin Carroll; *Mike and Mike's Rules for Sports and Life* by Mike Greenberg and Mike Golic; and *How Lucky You Can Be* by Buster Olney.

Steve Wulf, Editor—Sports.

THE MODERN LIBRARY

The Modern Library, one of the most beloved lines of American classics, was founded in 1917, established itself as a leading publisher in the 1920s, and continues to thrive to this day. In 1999 it generated spirited debate with its published lists of the 100 Best Novels and the 100 Best Nonfiction Books published in English in the twentieth century. The year 2000 saw the introduction of *Modern Library Chronicles*, short histories by the world's great historians, including *Islam* by Karen Armstrong and *The Age of Shakespeare* by Frank Kermode. That same year the Modern Library introduced its first line of paperback classics, a list that has grown to more than 300 titles. The Modern Library Editorial Board is made up of leading writers and intellectuals, including Maya Angelou, Charles Frazier, Joyce Carol Oates, Salman Rushdie, Oliver Sacks, and Gore Vidal, who continue to provide editorial counsel to the Modern Library and its editors.

Recent titles include *The Korean War* by Bruce Cumings; *The Only Game in Town* by David Remnick; *3 Days Before the Shooting* by Ralph Ellison; *Dusk and Other Stories* by James Salter; and *The Feminist Promise* by Christine Stansell.

ONE WORLD

In 1991, Ballantine launched One World and became the first mainstream publisher to create an imprint devoted to multicultural titles. Its list encompasses subjects of African American, Asian, Latin, and Native American interest across all categories and formats. Its bestselling backlist titles include *The Autobiography of Malcolm X as Told to Alex Haley* by Anita J. Aboulafia and *Dreaming in Cuban* by Cristina Garcia.

Current and forthcoming authors include the bestselling novelist Pearl Cleage, the film historian Donald Bogle, and one of the rising stars of "street lit," Nikki Turner.

Recent titles include *Money Never Sleeps* by Tu-Shonda Whitaker; *Ice: A Memoir of Gangster Life* and *Redemption-from South Central to Hollywood* by Ice-T; *Heartbreak of a Hustler's Wife* by Nikki Turner; *The Strawberry Letter* by Shirley Strawberry; and *Natural Born Hustler* by Nikki Turner.

PRESIDIO PRESS

The military history publisher Presidio Press was acquired by Ballantine in 2002. Presidio Press publishes about 25 new titles per year, under the supervision of Ron Doering. Formats include mass-market, paperback, and hardcover.

Most recent titles include *Charlie Rangers* by Don Ericson; *Death Valley: The Summer Offensive, I Corps, August 1969* by Keith Nolan; *Eyes Behind the Lines: L Company Rangers in Vietnam, 1969* by Gary Linderer; and *War in the Pacific: From Pearl Harbor to Tokyo Bay* by Harry Gailey.

RANDOM HOUSE

The flagship imprint of the Random House Publishing group, Random House publishes distinguished trade fiction and nonfiction covering a broad scope of literary and commercial appeal. The press was founded in 1927, when Modern Library publishers Bennett Cerf and Donald Klopfer started publishing books on the side, "at random." The famous Random House logo, drawn by Rockwell Kent, appeared on the first two books published by the press, illustrated editions of *Candide* and *Moby Dick*.

The press made literary history by publishing James Joyce's *Ulysses* and went on to publish some of the greatest writers of the twentieth century, including William Faulkner, Isak Dinesen, Edgar Snow, Andre Malraux, Robert Graves, Gertrude Stein, W.H. Auden, John O'Hara, Truman Capote, Ralph Ellison, Irwin Shaw, Sinclair Lewis, Robert Penn Warren, Eudora Welty, and James Michener.

Since 1995, it has published four of the bestselling books of all time: *My American Journey* by Colin Powell; *Midnight in the Garden of Good and Evil* by John Berendt; *The Greatest Generation* by Tom Brokaw; and *Seabiscuit* by Laura Hillenbrand.

This group has also become a showcase for fiction and nonfiction authors publishing for the first time. Particularly notable titles include *The Dante Club* by Matthew Pearl; *Reading Lolita in Tehran* by Azar Nafisi; *Shadow Divers* by Rob Kuraon; and *The God of Small Things* by Arundhati Roy.

Recent titles include *The Tools* by Phil Stutz and Barry Michels; *True Believers* by Kurt Andersen; *The Unlikely Pilgrimage of Harold Fry* by Rachel Joyce; *A Daughter's Tale* by Mary Soames; and *Thomas Becket* by John Guy.

Direct queries and SASEs to:

Will Murphy, Editor—Foreign affairs, military history and affairs, cultural issues.

David Ebershoff, Editor-at-Large—Fiction, health, history.

Andy Ward, Editor—Current affairs, humor, science, fiction.

Susan Kamil, Editor—Fiction, personal narratives.

Jonathan Jao, Editor—Narratives, memoirs, history.

RANDOM HOUSE TRADE PAPERBACKS

First launched in 2001, Random House Trade Paperbacks is the paperback imprint of Random House, with an emphasis on serious nonfiction and literary fiction.

The nonfiction list includes the best seller *Reading Lolita in Tehran* by Azar Nafisi; *The Crisis of Islam* by Bernard Lewis; *Paris 1919* by Margaret McMillan; and *Mountains Beyond Mountains* by Tracy Kidder. E. L. Doctorow, Sarah Dunant, David Mitchell, Matthew Pearl, and Arthur Phillips are among its many award-winning fiction writers.

Random House Trade Paperbacks also has a line of mysteries and thrillers called Mortalis, comprising both originals and reprints. Recent Mortalis titles include *Red Square* by Martin Cruz Smith; *From Doon with Death: The First Inspector Wexford Novel* by Ruth Rendell; and *The Last Nightingale: A Novel of Suspense* by Anthony Flacco.

Other recent titles include *The End of Country: Dispatches from the Frack Zone* by Seamus McGraw; *Northwest Corner: A Novel* by John Burnham Schwartz; *The Homecoming of Samuel Lake: A Novel* by Jenny Wingfield; *The Girl in the Blue Beret: A Novel* by Bobbie Ann Mason; and *At Random: The Reminiscences of Bennett Cerf* by Bennett Cerf and Christopher Cerf.

SPECTRA

Celebrating its twenty-fifth anniversary, Spectra has been publishing the finest science-fiction, fantasy, horror, and speculative novels from recognizable authors including Isaac Asimov, Ray Bradbury, Arthur C. Clarke, George R. R. Martin, Kim Stanley Robinson, and M. John Harrison.

Recent titles include *The Wanderers* by Paula Brandon; *Steelhands* by Jaida Jones; *Conquerors' Heritage* by Timothy Zah; *Casket of Souls* by Lynn Flewelling; and *The Master of Heathcrest Hall* by Galen Beckett.

SPIEGEL & GRAU

Julie Grau and Celina Spiegel, former editors at Riverhead Books, founded their eponymous press as an imprint of Doubleday in 2005. Spiegel & Grau publishes books that help us make sense of our lives in a world besieged by conflict, rapid change, ideology, and constant pressures. It aims to create a list of books that share the potential to unite people in a common experience, whether it be through fiction, memoir, narrative journalism, or works on current issues.

Some Spiegel & Grau books include *The Devil in Silver* by Victor LaValle; *Pym* by Mat Johnson; *Coal to Diamonds* by Beth Ditto and Michelle Tea; *Meat Eater* by Steven Rinella; and *Lay the Favorite* by Beth Raymer.

Julie Grau, Senior Vice President and Publisher—Memoirs, advice, self-help, fiction.
Celina Spiegel, Senior Vice President and Publisher—Fiction, nonfiction.
Hana Landes, Editor—Cooking.

VILLARD BOOKS

Villard Books was founded in 1983 and named after the Stanford White brownstone mansion on Madison Avenue that was the home of Random House for 20 years. It publishes a general nonfiction and fiction list that has positioned itself on the leading edge of popular culture. Among the bestselling authors it has published are Jon Krakauer, Eve Ensler, former Governor Jesse Ventura, and the "Travel Detective," Peter Greenberg. Villard is also known for its titles in the areas of humor, personal narrative, and new-voice fiction, including the books of Laurie Notaro and Jon Katz.

Recent titles include *When All Hell Breaks Loose: A Novel* by Camika Spencer; *Hers: Through Women's Eyes* by Nancy Newhouse; *Opium Fiend: A 21st Century Slave to a 19th Century Addiction* by Steven Martin; *Microwave Cooking for Your Baby & Child* by Eileen Behan; and *Anonymous Rex: A Detective Story* by Eric Garcia.

CBS CORPORATION

The CBS Corporation was formed in 2005, when Viacom, Inc., split into two publicly traded companies: Viacom and CBS Corporation. Based in New York, CBS Corporation holds assets in television, radio, digital media, outdoor advertising, and publishing, including Simon & Schuster.

SIMON & SCHUSTER

SIMON & SCHUSTER ADULT PUBLISHING GROUP
SIMON & SCHUSTER CHILDREN'S PUBLISHING
1230 Avenue of the Americas, New York, NY 10020
212-698-7000
www.simonandschuster.com | Twitter: @simonschuster

Simon & Schuster was founded in 1924 by Richard L. Simon and M. Lincoln Schuster. Their initial project was a crossword puzzle book, the first ever produced, and it was a runaway best seller. From that, the company has grown to become a global, multifaceted publishing house releasing more than 1,800 titles annually. Simon & Schuster titles have won 54 Pulitzer Prizes and numerous National Book Awards, Caldecott Medals, and Newbery Medals.

Simon & Schuster today is wholly focused on consumer publishing. Its divisions—the Simon & Schuster Adult Publishing Group, Simon & Schuster Children's Publishing, Simon & Schuster Audio, Simon & Schuster UK, Simon & Schuster Canada, and Simon & Schuster Australia—are home to many distinguished imprints and recognizable brand names, including Simon & Schuster, Scribner, Pocket Books, The Free Press, Atria, Touchstone, Atheneum, Margaret K. McElderry, Aladdin Paperbacks, Little Simon, and Simon Spotlight.

Simon & Schuster does not accept unsolicited manuscripts and recommends working with an agent.

SIMON & SCHUSTER ADULT PUBLISHING GROUP

ATRIA BOOKS
THE FREE PRESS
GALLERY BOOKS
SCRIBNER
SIMON & SCHUSTER
TOUCHSTONE
1230 Avenue of the Americas, New York, NY 10020
212-698-7000

The Simon & Schuster Adult Publishing Group includes a number of publishing units that offer books in several formats. Each unit has its own publisher, editorial group, and publicity department. Common sales and business departments support all the units.

ATRIA BOOKS
BEYOND WORDS
CASH MONEY CONTENT
EMILY BESTLER BOOKS
STREBOR BOOKS
WASHINGTON SQUARE PRESS

The Atria imprint, launched in 2002, publishes a mix of fiction and nonfiction—especially biography and celebrity memoirs. It is the hardcover imprint for Pocket Books, a commercial publishing house pledged to bring the world a wealth of timely, important, and entertaining publications. Atria Books is the home of several best-selling authors including Jennifer Weiner, Jodi Picoult, Judith McNaught, Vince Flynn, and Jude Deveraux.

In recent years, Atria has placed an emphasis on publishing for diverse audiences and has launched a Hispanic/Latino line, acquired Strebor Books, and entered copublishing deals with Beyond Words and Cash Money Records. Atria releases trade paperbacks under the Washington Square Press imprint. The Emily Bestler Books imprint, launched in 2011, publishes popular fiction and nonfiction. In 2010, the imprint announced the launch of Atria Unbound, which develops cutting-edge content from e-books to iPhone applications.

Recent Atria titles include *Let It Go* by T.D. Jakes; *Kill Shot* by Vince Flynn; *Lone Wolf* by Jodi Picoult; *Temptation* by Douglas Kennedy; and *These Girls* by Sarah Pekkanen.

Direct query letters and SASEs to:

Judith Curr, Publisher, founder of the Atria program.

Peter Borland, Editorial Director—High-end fiction and nonfiction.

Greer Hendricks, Vice President and Senior Editor—Literary and commercial fiction, narrative nonfiction, memoir, lifestyle, parenting, health and beauty.

Malaika Adero, Vice President and Senior Editor—Literary fiction, narrative nonfiction, health and fitness, spirituality, memoir, biography, African American interests, art and culture, urban fiction.

Johanna V. Castillo, Vice President and Senior Editor—Hispanic-Latino and Spanish language publishing program, spirituality, inspirational self-help.

Amy Tannenbaum, Editor—Fiction, popular culture, self-help.

Sarah Branham, Senior Editor—Fiction, cooking, diet, mysteries.

Sarah Durand, Senior Editor—Health, celebrity memoirs, fiction suspense/thrillers, self-help.

Sarah Cantin, Associate Editor—Commercial fiction, travel stories, health and fitness, cooking.

Todd Hunter, Assistant Editor—African-American subjects, current affairs, mysteries/thrillers.

BEYOND WORDS

Beyond Words, founded in 1983 as a publisher of coffee-table books, currently releases around 15 new titles a year in the Mind/Body/Spirit category, and is best known for the blockbuster New Age self-help book *The Secret*. They entered into a copublishing agreement with Atria Books in 2006. See the listing for Beyond Words in the Independent Publishers section for more information.

Cynthia Black, Editor

CASH MONEY CONTENT

In collaboration with Atria, hip-hop entrepreneurs Bryan "Birdman" Williams and Ronald "Slim" Williams started Cash Money Content in 2011, publishing books in such categories as urban fiction, money, motivation, health and success, and memoir. The inaugural list included *Raw Law: An Urban Guide to Criminal Justice* by Muhammad Ibn Bashir, the *NYT*-bestselling *Justify My Thug* by Wahida Clark, and the classic *Pimp* by Iceberg Slim.

Recent titles include *An XL Life: Staying Big at Half the Size* by Big Boy; *Get It Girls* by Treasure Blue; *Payback Ain't Enough* by Wahida Clark; *Murderville 2: The Epidemic* by Ashley & JaQuavis; and *Animal* by K'wan.

EMILY BESTLER BOOKS

Emily Bestler Books began in 2011, "with one guiding principle in mind: to find the very best reads available and to put them into the hands of as many readers as we can." Run by Atria Books' former executive editorial director, the imprint publishes fiction and nonfiction, thrillers, cookbooks, memoirs, international crime fiction, and literary novels.

Recent titles include *Black List* by Brad Thor; *Advent* by James Treadwell; *Blessed Are the Dead* by Malla Nunn; *Between the Lines* by Jodi Picoult and Samantha van Leer; and *The Playdate* by Louise Millar.

Emily Bestler, Editor-in-Chief
Kate Cetrullo, Assistant Editor

STREBOR BOOKS

Strebor Books was originally founded in 1999 by the author Zane to publish her first three books. The imprint's editors now focus on popular fiction and nonfiction by African American writers and are on the lookout for the next big thing. It releases 48 new titles per year in hardcover and paperback.

Recent titles from Strebor include *A Cold Piece of Work* by Curtis Bunn; *The Last Prejudice: A Novel* by David Rivera Jr.; *Brick* by Allison Hobbs; *Serial Typical* by Michelle Janine Robinson; and *Antebellum* by R. K Thomas.

Zane, Publisher
Charmaine Parker, Director

WASHINGTON SQUARE PRESS

Atria imprint Washington Square Press publishes literary fiction and topical non-fiction in trade paperback format.

Recent titles from Washington Square Press include *Ten Girls to Watch* by Charity Shumway; *Gone* by Cathi Hanauer; *It's Classified* by Nicolle Wallace; *The Winters in Bloom* by Lisa Tucker; and *The English Monster: or, The Melancholy Transactions of William Ablass* by Lloyd Shepherd.

THE FREE PRESS

For more than 65 years, The Free Press has published cutting-edge nonfiction works in social thought, politics, current affairs, history, science, psychology, religion and spirituality, music, and a broad business list. It also produces college textbooks. Around 80 titles a year are produced in hardcover format, and the press has produced more than 120 *NYT* best sellers in the past ten years alone.

What follows are a few award-winning titles from The Free Press: *The Denial of Death* by Ernest Becker; *Waiting for Snow in Havana* by Carlos Eire; *The Memory Palace* by Mira Bartók; *The White Tiger* by Aravind Adiga; and *The Madonnas of Echo Park* by Brando Skyhorse.

Recent releases include *Wunderkind* by Nikolai Grozni; *Learning to Breathe* by Priscilla Warner; *Obama on the Couch* by Justin A. Frank, MD; *Sybil Exposed* by Debbie Nathan; and *Who's Afraid of Post-Blackness* by Touré.

Direct query letters and SASEs to:

Martha K. Levin, Publisher
Suzanne Donohue, Vice President and Associate Publisher—Celebrity authors.
Dominick Anfuso, Editor-in-Chief—General nonfiction, history, politics, military, health.
Emily Loose, Senior Editor—Nonfiction, current affairs, popular science, social science, history.
Leslie Meredith, Senior Editor—Animals, spirituality, health, pop science, general nonfiction, philosophy, spirituality, self-help.
Leah Miller, Editor—Social history, food, travel, pop science.
Millicent Bennett, Senior Editor—Fiction, social/cultural history, pop psych, womens issues, parenting.

Alessandra Bastagli, Senior Editor—History, current affairs, politics, military, music.

Webster Younce, Senior Editor—History, current affairs, religion, politics, social science, music.

Sabari Bose Kamat, Associate Editor—Cultural history, psychology, food, travel, international fiction.

Donna Loffredo, Associate Editor—Pop history, philosophy, psychology, health, food.

Sydney Tanigawa, Associate Editor—Science, history, pop culture, crime, fiction.

Chloe Perkins, Editorial Assistant—History, current events.

GALLERY BOOKS
POCKET BOOKS
THRESHOLD

Gallery Books is designed to showcase established voices and to introduce emerging new ones both in fiction and nonfiction, and across a variety of genres. With a focus on women's fiction, pop culture, lifestyle, and memoir, Gallery publishes *New York Times* bestselling authors from Tori Spelling to Tim Gunn.

Recent titles include *11/22/63: A Novel* by Stephen King; *The Sinatra Club* by Sal Polisi; *Anne of Hollywood* by Carol Wolper; *The Gap Year* by Sarah Bird; and *City of the Dead* by Daniel Blake.

Gallery Submissions:

Mitchell Ivers, Vice President and Senior Editor—Commercial fiction, true crime, politics, popular history.

Abby Zidle, Senior Editor—Romance, women's fiction, thrillers, pop culture.

Jeremy Ruby-Strauss, Editor—Narratives by pop stars, diet/fitness, TV/Internet tie-ins.

Kathy Sagan, Senior Editor—Historical fiction, women's fiction, suspense/thrillers, politics.

Karen Kostlnyik, Executive Editor—Commercial fiction, narrative nonfiction and memoirs.

Lauren McKenna, Executive Editor—Commercial women's fiction, historical and contemporary romance, pop culture.

Micki Nuding, Senior Editor—Women's fiction, romance, historical fiction, health (unrelated to diets).

Ed Schlesinger, Senior Editor—Dark/horror/thrillers fiction, media tie-ins.

Adam Wilson, Editor—Paranormal/suspense/urban fiction, popular nonfiction.

Emilia Pisani, Assistant Editor—Women's fiction, historical fiction, popular culture.

Kate Dresser, Assistant Editor—Erotica/romance, historical fiction, popular culture.

Julia Fincher, Editorial Assistant—Urban fiction/fantasy, popular culture.

THRESHOLD

Threshold publishes titles for a conservative audience. Recent best sellers include *Liberty and Tyranny* by Mark Levin, *An Inconvenient Book* by Glenn Beck, and *The Obama Nation* by Jerome R. Corsi, PhD.

Threshold counts the following among their authors: Glenn Beck, Karl Rove, Jerome R. Corsi, Mark R. Levin, David Kupelian, Lynne Cheney, Arthur B. Laffer, Mary Cheney, Jerry Doyle, Reid Buckley, Brian Jennings, George Melloan, Burton W. Folsom, and Stephen Moore.

Threshold Submissions:

Louise Burke, Editor—Conservative public affairs narratives.

Mitchell Ivers, Senior Editor

Kathy Sagan, Senior Editor

Abby Zidle, Senior Editor

Ed Schlesinger, Senior Editor

SCRIBNER

Scribner was founded in 1846 by Charles Scribner and Isaac Baker, and initially focused on religious books. As Charles Scribner's Sons, and under legendary editors such as Maxwell Perkins and John Hall Wheelock, the house published many of the giants of nineteenth- and twentieth-century American literature, including Henry James, Edith Wharton, Ring Lardner, Ernest Hemingway, F. Scott Fitzgerald, Thomas Wolfe, and Marjorie Kinnan Rawlings. Many of these authors and their classic works remain in print today as a mainstay of the Scribner list.

Today, Scribner produces fiction and nonfiction titles in hardcover format. Categories include general fiction, history, military, social science, popular culture, and self-help. Scribner authors include Annie Proulx, whose novel *The Shipping News* (1993) won both the Pulitzer Prize and the National Book Award; Frank McCourt, whose memoir *Angela's Ashes* (1996) became a mainstay of the *New York Times* best-seller list, was awarded the Pulitzer Prize and the National Book Critics Circle Award, and was followed by the bestselling *'Tis and Teacher Man*; and Don DeLillo's *Underworld* (1997). Scribner is also the home of bestselling authors Stephen King, Kathy Reichs, and Linda Fairstein.

Recent releases include *Alys, Always* by Harriet Lane; *Suzy's Case* by Andy Siegel; *Buddhaland Brooklyn* by Richard C. Morais; *Stolen Chalice* by Kitty Pilgrim; and *Equal of the Sun* by Anita Amirrezvani.

Send query letters with SASEs to:

Colin Harrison, Senior Editor—True crime, narrative nonfiction, thrillers, current affairs, sports, crime, science, politics.

Brant Rumble, Senior Editor—Pop culture, music, sports.

Alexis Gargagliano, Editor—Fiction, narratives.

Whitney Frick, Editor—Women's fiction, health, psychology, food writing, cookbooks.

Paul Whitlatch, Editor—Thrillers, politics, technology, popular science.

Kelsey Smith, Assistant Editor—Literary fiction and narrative nonfiction.

Shannon Welch, Senior Editor—Health and Wellness, lifestyle, psychology, spirituality, fitness and diet.

John Glynn, Editorial Assistant—Sports, pop culture, health and wellness.

SIMON & SCHUSTER

Simon & Schuster was founded in April 1924 when Richard L. Simon and M. Lincoln Schuster pooled their resources and published *The Cross Word Puzzle Book*, capitalizing on the crossword craze of the time and packaged with a pencil to aid readers in solving the puzzles. In its early years, S&S achieved commercial success from such groundbreaking mega-sellers as Will and Ariel Duran's *The Story of Philosophy* and Dale Carnegie's *How to Win Friends and Influence People*.

Over the years, the name Simon & Schuster has also grown to signify the much larger publishing enterprise of Simon & Schuster, Inc., but the Simon & Schuster trade imprint has remained a cornerstone to the business and one of the most venerated brand names in the world of publishing. It is widely known as a powerhouse publisher of general fiction and nonfiction for readers of all tastes.

Titles representative of this list include *Gold* by Chris Cleave; *In the Shadow of the Banyan* by Vaddey Ratner; *Paterno* by Joe Posnanski; *XO: A Kathryn Dance Novel* by Jeffery Deaver; and *The Kings of Cool: A Prequel to Savages* by Don Winslow.

Send query letters and SASEs to:

Robert Bender, Vice President, Senior Editor—Business, biography, sports, American history, film and music.

Priscilla Painton, Senior Editor—History, politics, religion, science.

Alice Mayhew, Editorial Director—History, politics, social issues.

Marysue Rucci, Editor-in-Chief—Fiction.

Jofie Ferrari-Adler, Senior Editor—Politics, current affairs, recent history, military history, sports.

Anjali Singh, Senior Editor—Fiction and nonfiction.

Sarah Knight, Senior Editor—Pop culture, humor, self-help, travel and food writing, thrillers/suspense.

Ben Loehnen, Senior Editor—Science, business, psychology, nature.

Trish Todd, Executive Editor—Popular fiction, practical nonfiction.

Thomas LeBien, Senior Editor—Sports, business, science.

Karen Marcus, Senior Editor—Suspense fiction, science, health.

Micheal Szczerban, Associate Editor—Commercial fiction, science, technology, food, adventure, "fringe" subjects.

Johanna Li, Associate Editor—Literary fiction, cultural history, sociology.

Michele Bove, Assistant Editor—History, politics, current events, sports, pop culture.

Molly Lindley, Assistant Editor—Fiction and nonfiction that explains the human condition.

Nick Greene, Assistant Editor—Politics, the arts, new voices in fiction.

Sammy Perlmutter, Assistant Editor—Business, baseball, cooking, fine arts.

Emily Graff, Editorial Assistant—Commercial and literary fiction.

TOUCHSTONE
HOWARD BOOKS

Touchstone Fireside was created at Simon & Schuster in 1970 to publish books in trade paperback, although the changing marketplace resulted in the addition of hardcover books in 2003. In 2010, the Fireside name was dropped, and the imprint was renamed as, simply, Touchstone.

Touchstone publishes fiction and serious nonfiction books in all categories of history, politics, military, political science, biography, and autobiography. It publishes almost exclusively original trade paperbacks and hardcovers as well as reprints from other houses in the industry.

Titles representative of Touchstone's list include *Farewell, My Queen: A Novel* by Chantal Thomas; *A Once Crowded Sky* by Tom King and Tom Fowler; *Discretion* by Allison Leotta; *Darkness All Around: A Novel* by Doug Magee; *Madame Serpent* by Jean Plaidy; and *It Calls You Back: An Odyssey through Love, Addiction, Revolutions, and Healing* by Luis J. Rodriguez.

Direct query letters and SASEs to:

Michelle Howry, Senior Editor—Nonfiction, including health, relationships, self-help, food, memoir, investing; especially practical nonfiction and compelling narrative nonfiction.

HOWARD BOOKS

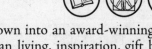

Howard Books was founded in 1969 and has grown into an award-winning publisher of more than 45 titles per year in Christian living, inspiration, gift books, fiction, devotionals, and youth books. Howard Publishing was acquired by Simon & Schuster in 2006 and renamed Howard Books.

Not affiliated with any religious group or denomination, Howard Books maintains a distinctly objective editorial independence, which allows for a broad base of authors and subject matter. Its titles promote biblical principles for godly living as expressed by qualified writers whose lives and messages reflect the heart of Christ. Howard authors include Point of Grace, Andy Stanley, Sandi Patty, Big Idea's VeggieTales, Ed Young, David and Claudia Arp, Tony Campolo, Dr. Ken Canfield, Calvin Miller, and Bill Bright.

Recent titles include *Far from Here* by Nicole Baart; *Man on the Run: Helping*

PUBLISHING CONGLOMERATES

Hyper-Hobbied Men Recognize the Best Things in Life by Zeke Pipher; *An Uncommon Grace* by Serena B. Miller; and *Wish You Were Here* by Beth K. Vogt.

Howard Books is open to unsolicited queries; do not send manuscripts until invited to do so.

Philis Boultinghouse, Senior Editor—Christian inspiration.

Beth Adams, Senior Editor—Inspiration fiction.

Jessica Wong, Associate Editor—Inspirational fiction and nonfiction.

Amanda Demastus, Associate Editor—Christian-themed fiction and nonfiction.

SIMON & SCHUSTER CHILDREN'S PUBLISHING

ALADDIN PAPERBACKS
ATHENEUM BOOKS FOR YOUNG READERS
BEACH LANE BOOKS
LITTLE SIMON
MARGARET K. MCELDERRY BOOKS
PAULA WISEMAN BOOKS
SIMON & SCHUSTER BOOKS FOR YOUNG READERS
SIMON PULSE
SIMON SPOTLIGHT
1230 Avenue of the Americas, New York, NY 10020
212-698-7000

Simon & Schuster Children's Publishing is one of the world's leading children's book publishers. While maintaining an extensive award-winning backlist, the division continues to publish acclaimed and best-selling books in a variety of formats for children ages preschool through teen, including such high-profile characters as Eloise, Raggedy Ann & Andy, Olivia, Henry & Mudge, The Hardy Boys, Nancy Drew, Buffy the Vampire Slayer, and Shiloh.

ALADDIN PAPERBACKS

Aladdin Paperbacks publishes juvenile fiction and nonfiction early readers, chapter books, and middle-grade books, for ages four to twelve. The imprint includes a line for beginning readers; Ready-to-Read books (including the *Henry & Mudge* series by Cynthia Rylant and Suçie Stevenson); and the Ready-for-Chapters line for newly independent readers (including The Bears on Hemlock Mountain by Alice Dalgliesh and *The Unicorn's Secret* series by Kathleen Duey).

The backbone of the Aladdin list is reprints from the hardcover imprints, including some of the most enduring children's books of the modern era, such as classic picture books like *Chicka Chicka Boom Boom* by Bill Martin, Jr., John Archambault, and Lois Ehlert, and *Strega Nona* by Tomie DePaola; honored fiction like *From the Mixed-Up Files of Mrs. Basil E. Frankweiler* by E. L. Konigsburg; *Hatchet* by Gary Paulsen; *Frindle* by Andrew Clements; the Shiloh trilogy by Phyllis Reynolds Naylor; and the Bunnicula books by James Howe. Aladdin's strong reprint list also is supplemented by a limited number of original series and single titles.

Some new and notable titles include the #1 *New York Times* best seller *Beyonders: A World Without Heroes* by Brandon Mull, the upcoming *The Unwanteds* by *New York Times* bestselling author Lisa McMann, *The Rock and the River* by Kekla Magoon (winner of the 2010 Coretta Scott King - John Steptoe Award for New Talent), *Milo: Sticky Notes & Brain Freeze* by Alan Silberberg (winner of the 2011 SCBWI Sid Fleishman Award for Humor), and the *New York Times* best-selling *Dork Diaries* series.

Send query letters with SASEs to:

Bethany Buck, Publisher—Teen fiction with realistic-edgy themes.

Fiona Simpson, Editorial Director—Middle grade through tweens with strong girl characters.

Liesa Abrams, Executive Editor—Fantasy/action adventure.

Karen Nagel, Senior Editor—Illustrated early to middle-grade fiction and non-fiction, mysteries, fantasies, humorous, coming of age, unique characters.

Annie Berger, Editorial Assistant—Fantasy, paranormal, dystopia.

Alyson Heller, Assistant Editor—Picture books through middle grade.

ATHENEUM BOOKS FOR YOUNG READERS

Atheneum Books for Young Readers is a hardcover imprint with a focus on literary fiction and fine picture books for children and young adults. The imprint, founded in 1961 by legendary editor Jean Karl (1928–2000), has garnered over two dozen Newbery and Caldecott Medals and Honors, as well as Coretta Scott King medals, National Book Award nominations, PEN USA Literary Awards, and *New York Times* best sellers, and its books have been named to countless state reading lists.

Some award-winning books are *The View from Saturday* by E. L. Konigsburg; *Alexander and the Terrible, Horrible, No Good, Very Bad Day* by Judith Viorst and Ray Cruz; *Shiloh* by Phyllis Reynolds Naylor; the Bunnicula books by James Howe; Doreen Cronin and Betsy Lewin's *Duck* series; and Sharon Draper's *Ziggy and the Black Dinosaurs* series.

Atheneum has also published novelty books, the first being the *New York Times* #1 best seller *Pirates* by John Matthews.

Recent titles include *Dessert First* by Hallie Durand; *Where Things Come Back* by John Corey Whaley; *No Room for Dessert* by Hallie Durand; and *It Was September When We Ran Away the First Time* by D. James Smith.

Caitlyn Dlouhy, Editorial Director—Picture books, middle grade, teen fiction.

Namrata Tripathi, Executive Editor—Picture books, biographies, young adult.

Emma Ledbetter, Editorial Assistant—Picture books, chapter books, young middle-grade novels, with some humor, heart, and silliness.

Dani Young, Editorial Assistant—Young-adult and middle-grade fiction, fantasy, historical, dystopian.

Ruta Rimas, Associate Editor—Picture books, middle-grade novels, teen novels.

Ariel Colletti, Assistant Editor—Adventurous middle-grade novels and contemporary young adult.

BEACH LANE BOOKS

Beach Lane Books was founded in 2008 in San Diego. The imprint publishes books for all ages and across all genres, with a primary focus on highly visual picture books for young children. Their overarching goal is to publish books that are truly for children, books that connect with readers on a deep level and that become beloved childhood treasures people will return to throughout their lives.

Recent titles include *1-2-3 Peas* by Keith Bake; *ABC ZooBorns!* by Andrew Bleiman; *Brownie & Pearl Get Dolled Up* by Cynthia Rylant; *Boo to You!* by Lois Ehlert; and *Shiver Me Timbers!* by Douglas Floria.

Andrea Welch, Senior Editor—Picture books through teen novels.

LITTLE SIMON
LITTLE SIMON INSPIRATIONS

Little Simon specializes in the most innovative novelty books for children, including pop-ups, lift-the-flap books, board books, sticker books, interactive e-books, and other specialty formats.

Recent titles include *The Happy Little Yellow Box: A Pop-Up Book of Opposites* by David A. Carter; *Bathtime for Twins* by Ellen Weiss; *Captain Awesome Takes a Dive* by Stan Kirby; and *Zoo Babies from Around the World* by Andrew Bleiman.

Direct query letters and SASEs to:

Sonoli Fry, Editorial Director

LITTLE SIMON INSPIRATIONS

Little Simon Inspirations publishes faith-based books that celebrate a child's relationship with God and reaffirm a belief in faith-based family values. This exciting line of children's books goes beyond Bible stories and presents an appreciation for God and God's gifts through a mix of charming, relevant picture and novelty books from inspiring role models who present positive messages to children.

Some recent titles include *The Cat in the Rhinestone Suit* by John Carter Cash; *Daddy Loves His Little Girl* by John Carter Cash; and *You Can Be a Friend* by Tony Dungy.

MARGARET K. MCELDERRY BOOKS

Founded by legendary editor Margaret K. McElderry in 1972, the imprint publishes in hardcover with an emphasis on picture books, poetry, and middle-grade and teen fiction. Recent lists include the first-ever authorized sequel to J. M. Barrie's *Peter Pan*, Geraldine McCaughrean's *Peter Pan in Scarlet*; *Ironside* by Holly Black; and *Skin* by Adrienne Maria Vrettos.

Other recent titles include *Artist Ted* by Andrea Beaty; *The Brixen Witch* by Stacy DeKeyser; *A String in the Harp* by Nancy Bond; *Big Brothers Don't Take Naps* by Louise Borden; *The Demon's Surrender* by Sarah Rees Brennan.

Send query letters with SASEs to:

Karen Wojtyla, Editorial Director—Literary fiction in all genres for all ages.

Emily Fabre, Assistant Editor—Literary fiction, fantasy, humor, illustrated.

PAULA WISEMAN BOOKS

Paula Wiseman, formerly an editorial director at Harcourt, launched her eponymous children's imprint at Simon & Schuster in 2003. Their first book was *Clorinda* by Robert Kinerk and illustrated by Steven Kellogg, and they have since gone on to publish 20 to 30 titles a year and over 50 award-winning and best-selling books. The imprint focuses on stories and art that are wholly childlike, centered in emotion, innovative, and timeless for children of all ages.

Some Paula Wiseman titles include *Wild Card* by Tiki Barber & Ronde Barber; *Fake Friend!* by Marissa Moss; *Cleopatra Confesses* by Carolyn Meyer; *Secret Ingredient* by Laura Schaefer; and *Libby of High Hopes* by Elise Primavera.

Paula Wiseman, Vice President and Publisher

Alexandra Penfold, Editor

SIMON & SCHUSTER BOOKS FOR YOUNG READERS

Simon & Schuster Books for Young Readers, the flagship imprint of the S&S Children's Division, publishes fiction and nonfiction titles for children of all ages, from preschool through teens, in hardcover format. Titles in this house span the spectrum from social situations and self-esteem, to animals and pets, action and adventure, holidays and festivals, science fiction, fantasy, and African American and other ethnic stories.

This list includes the classic Eloise books by Kay Thompson and Hilary Knight; *Sylvester and the Magic Pebble* by William Steig; *Frindle* by Andrew Clements; *Chicka Chicka Boom Boom* by Bill Martin, Jr., John Archambault, and Lois Ehlert; and *Click, Clack Moo: Cows That Type* by Doreen Cronin and Betsy Lewin. SSBFYR includes among its authors and illustrators Loren Long, John Lithgow, Derek Anderson, Kate Brian, and Rachel Cohn.

Recent titles include *Don't Cramp My Style* by Lisa Rowe Fraustino; *Sarah's Ground* by Ann Rinaldi; *Whale* by Cynthia Rylant; *Mouse's First Day of School* by Lauren Thompson; and *Talent Show* by Dan Gutman.

PUBLISHING CONGLOMERATES

Zareen Jaffery, Executive Editor—Young-adult and middle-grade fiction.

Alexandra Cooper, Senior Editor—Picture books, middle-grade and young-adult fiction.

Kristin Ostby, Editor—Middle-grade fiction and picture books, engaging books for boys.

Navah Wolfe, Assistant Editor—Middle-grade and teen novels, commercial picture books.

Julia Maguire, Assistant Editor—Short picture books, young-adult fiction with realistic plots.

SIMON PULSE

Simon Pulse is a hardcover and paperback imprint for late tweens to older teens with a focus on contemporary commercial fiction. Pulse publishes and markets directly to its readership, and addresses topical, edgy, and trend-driven subjects that are prevalent in the teen world today.

Included in Pulse are series like R. L. Stine's *Fear Street*; Cathy Hopkin's *Mates, Dates*; Scott Westerfeld's *Specials*; and *The Au Pairs* by Melissa de la Cruz; contemporary classics like *Go Ask Alice*; National Book Award winners *The House of the Scorpion* by Nancy Farmer and *True Believer* by Virginia Euwer Wolff; and literary titles such as the *Dark Is Rising* sequence by Susan Cooper and the *Tillerman Cycle* series by Cynthia Voigt.

Recent titles include *Forbidden Secrets* by R.L. Stine; *Used to Be* by Eileen Cook; *Nocturne* by Christine Johnson; *Michael Vey: The Prisoner of Cell 25* by Richard Paul Evans; and *Never Enough* by Denise Jaden.

Direct query letters and SASEs to:

Jennifer Klonsky, Editorial Director—Voice-driven fiction, paranormal romance.

Anica Rissi, Executive Editor—Intense or doomed romance, dark humor.

Annette Pollert, Associate Editor—Dark edgy novels, mysteries/thrillers/suspense.

Michael Strother, Editorial Assistant—Magic, romance, mystery.

Nicole Ellul, Editorial Assistant—Romance, historical fiction, contemporary.

SIMON SPOTLIGHT

Simon Spotlight publishes hardcover and mass-market paperback fiction books tied to media properties, such as *The Busy World of Richard Scarry*. Launched in the fall of 1997, this imprint is one of the top-ranked imprints in the children's book industry—releasing titles for preschool through middle-grade children.

Some titles indicative of Simon Spotlight's list include *We Love a Luau* (The Backyardigans) by Jodie Shepherd, illustrated by Carlo Lo Raso; *The Deathless* (Buffy the Vampire Slayer) by Keith R. A. DeCandido; and *High Spirits* (Charmed) by Scott Ciencin.

Recent Spotlight titles include *Time for T-ball* by Alyson Heller; *Annie and*

Snowball and the Cozy Nest by Cynthia Rylant; *Eloise's Mother's Day Surprise* by Hilary Knight; *Presidents' Day* by Margaret McNamara; and *Pinky and Rex and the Just-Right Pet* by James Howe.

Direct query letters and SASE:

Alyson Grubard, Director

HACHETTE LIVRE

Hachette Livre, France's largest publishing company, is a wholly owned subsidiary of Lagardère, a French company that is active on the worldwide stage in the areas of aerospace, defense, and media.

HACHETTE BOOK GROUP USA

CENTER STREET
FAITHWORDS
GRAND CENTRAL PUBLISHING
LITTLE, BROWN AND COMPANY
LITTLE, BROWN BOOKS FOR YOUNG READERS
237 Park Avenue, New York, NY 10017
212-364-1200
www.hachettebookgroup.com | Twitter: @hachettebooks

In 2006, Hachette Livre acquired Time Warner Book Group from Time Warner, and renamed it Hachette Book Group USA. The terms of the sale stipulated that Warner Books must shed its name, and the publisher lost little time in rechristening as Grand Central Publishing. In April 2007, Hachette Book Group moved to new offices on Park Avenue, just north of Grand Central Terminal.

Hachette Book Group USA (HBG) is comprised of the following groups: Grand Central Publishing; Little, Brown and Company; Little, Brown Books for Young Readers; FaithWords; Center Street, Orbit, and Yen Press.

Publishers in the Hachette Book Group USA do not consider unsolicited manuscript submissions or unsolicited queries. The publisher recommends working with a literary agent.

CENTER STREET

Two Creekside Crossing, Ten Cadillac Drive, Suite 220, Brentwood, TN 37027
615-221-0996
e-mail: centerstreetpub@hbgusa.com | Twitter: @centerstreet

Center Street is a general market imprint based near Nashville that was launched in 2005 to publish wholesome entertainment, helpful encouragement, and books of traditional values that appeal to readers in America's heartland. Unlike FaithWords, which publishes specifically for the Christian market, Center Street books are intended for a broad audience.

Recent titles include *Deep in the Wave* by Bear Woznick; *Unsaid* by Neil

Abramson; *Shadowbosses* by Mallory Factor; *Work Happy* by Jill Geisler; and *The Brief Against Obama* by Hugh Hewitt.

Rolf Zettersten, Publisher

Kate Hartson, Editor—Gift books, fitness, current affairs.

FAITHWORDS

JERICHO BOOKS

Two Creekside Crossing, Ten Cadillac Drive, Suite 220, Brentwood, TN 37027
615-221-0996 | fax: 615-221-0962
Twitter: @faithwords

From its headquarters in Tennessee, FaithWords is an imprint that deals with Christian faith, inspiration, spirituality, and religion, with fiction and nonfiction titles. The imprint publishes books for the broad Christian market reflecting a range of denominations and perspectives. Formerly known as Warner Faith, FaithWords titles include Christian chick lit by Lisa Samson and inspirational fiction by T. D. Jakes, as well as traditional nonfiction religious titles. FaithWords is the publisher of the bestselling books *Your Best Life Now* by Joel Osteen and *The Confident Woman: Start Today Living Boldly & Without Fear* by Joyce Meyer.

Recent titles include *The Other Side of Suffering* by John Ramsey; *Indivisible* by James Robison; *Every Day a Friday* by Joel Osteen; *I Never Thought I'd See the Day!* by Dr. David Jeremiah; and *Living Beyond Your Feelings* by Joyce Meyer.

Rolf Zettersten, Publisher

Christina Boys, Editor—Women's fiction, inspirational fiction.

JERICHO BOOKS

Jericho Books, which launched in September of 2012, seeks to publish books that express fresh perspectives on today's culture and growing changes in the Church. The press explores religious, social, and political issues as they relate to faith. At launch, Jericho is home to authors Brian McLaren, Shane Hipps, Jay Bakker, Lillian Daniel, and Becca Stevens.

Wendy Grisham, Editor

GRAND CENTRAL PUBLISHING

5-SPOT
BUSINESS PLUS
FOREVER
FOREVER YOURS
GRAND CENTRAL LIFE AND STYLE
TWELVE
VISION

237 Park Avenue, New York, NY 10017
212-364-1200
www.hachettebookgroupusa.com | Twitter: @grandcentralpub

As Warner Books, Grand Central Publishing was esteemed for publishing mass-market commercial fiction from authors like Nicholas Sparks and James Patterson. Known as Grand Central Publishing since April 2007, it still publishes a lot of commercial fiction, but has also started imprints that move in other directions and expects to become equally well known for those.

As for the name, Grand Central Publishing, publisher Jamie Raab dissects it this way: Grand because they are big and impressive, Central because they embrace a larger audience of readers, and Publishing because emerging forms of publishing go beyond books and paper.

Grand Central produces hardcover, mass-market, and trade paperback originals, as well as reprints. Nonfiction categories include biography, business, cooking, current affairs, history, house and home, humor, popular culture, psychology, self-help, sports, games books, and general reference; fiction titles include commercial novels and works in the categories of mystery and suspense, fantasy and science fiction, action thrillers, horror, and contemporary and historical romance. The Grand Central imprints are 5-Spot, Business Plus, Forever, Forever Yours, Grand Central Life & Style, Twelve, and Vision. Altogether, Grand Central publishes about 300 books per year.

Recent titles include *I Am A Pole (And So Can You!)* by Stephen Colbert; *The Defining Decade* by Meg Jay; *No One Ever Told Us That* by John D. Spooner; *After Camelot* by J. Randy Taraborrelli; and *A Natural Woman* by Carole King.

Jamie Raab, Senior Vice President and Publisher, oversees the publication of all Grand Central titles. She has a particular fondness for fiction, narrative nonfiction, and current affairs, and the authors she has edited include Nicholas Delbanco, Nelson DeMille, Henry Louis Gates, Jr., Jane Goodall, Olivia Goldsmith, Billie Letts, Brad Meltzer, Michael Moore, Rosie O'Donnell, Nicholas Sparks, Jon Stewart, and Lalita Tademy.

Beth de Guzman, Editorial Director of Mass Market, has spent 20 years in publishing and has held positions at Berkley Books, Silhouette Books, and Bantam Books. She has edited over 30 *New York Times* best sellers. At Grand Central, she oversees the mass-market program and acquires commercial fiction and nonfiction.

Amy Pierpont, Senior Editor—Women's fiction.
Ben Greenberg, Editor—Pop culture, humor, memoir, quirky fiction, politics.
Emily Griffin, Associate Editor—Pop culture, advice, new fiction.
Alex Logan, Editor—Romance, women's fiction.
Deb Futter, Editor—Historical biography, narratives, fiction.
Selina McLemore, Editor—Women's fiction, paranormal romance.
Diana Baroni, Editor—Diet, cooking, fitness, healthful living.
Rick Wolff, Editor—Sports narratives/history, business narratives, and how-to.
Latoya Smith, Editor—Women's fiction, paranormal romance.
Michele Bidelspach, Editor—Women's fiction/romance.
Amanda Englander, Editor—Food/cooking, popular culture narratives and issues.
Lauren Plude, Editor—Women's fiction/romance.
Mitch Hoffman, Editor—Mysteries, thrillers, criminals, current affairs, politics.
Meredith Haggerty, Editor—Humorous subjects.

5-SPOT

5-Spot is a list of books for women who want entertainment but refuse to leave their brains at the door. The imprint releases about 15 new fiction and nonfiction titles per year. Recent acquisitions have been primarily in the women's fiction and romance categories.

Recent titles include *Henny on the Couch* by Rebecca Land Soodak; *Leaving Sophie Dean* by Alexandra Whitaker; *I Couldn't Love You More* by Jillian Medoff; and *The Ice Cream Girls* by Dorothy Koomson.

Sara Weiss, Editor

BUSINESS PLUS

Business Plus represents the international outgrowth of Warner Business Books, which was founded in 2000 and has enjoyed great success. The imprint has had nearly 50 books crack the best-sellers lists of the *New York Times*, *Wall Street Journal*, *Publishers Weekly*, and *Business Week*. With sister imprints in Europe and Asia, their books aim to give voice to innovative leaders and thinkers in the business world.

Business Plus authors include Hank Paulson, the former US Treasury Secretary; Jack Welch, former CEO of General Electric; Coach Mike Krzyzewski, the Hall of Fame basketball coach from Duke University; Tony Hsieh, the CEO of Zappos; and Captain D. Michael Abrashoff of the US Navy.

Recent titles include *No One Ever Told Us That* by John D. Spooner; *Worth It …Not Worth It?* by Jack Otter; *You, Inc.* by Harry Beckwith; *18 Minutes* by Peter Bregman; and *Inside Apple* by Adam Lashinsky.

Rick Wolff, Publisher and Editor-in-Chief
John Brodie, Editor

FOREVER

Forever publishes a wide variety of historical and contemporary romance, including paranormal and romantic suspense, in mass-market format. Authors on their list include Larissa Ione, Elizabeth Hoyt, and Sandra Hill.

Recent titles include *Immortal Rider* by Larissa Ione; *Head Over Heels* by Hope Ramsay; *The Sinner* by Margaret Mallory; *Deliciously Sinful* by Lilli Feisty; and *Scandalous Desires* by Elizabeth Hoyt.

FOREVER YOURS

Launched in February 2012, Forever Yours is a digital-only imprint that publishes a mix of new and classic romance. Digital short stories, novellas, and full-length novels are available in historical, paranormal, contemporary, and romantic suspense genres.

Recent titles include *Ember* by Kristen Callihan; *Once Upon a Wicked Night* by Jennifer Haymore; *It Begins with a Kiss* by Eileen Dreyer; *The Darkest Day* by Britt Bury; and *Into the Rift: A Prequel to Secret of the Wolf* by Cynthia Garner.

Same editors as per Grand Central above.

GRAND CENTRAL LIFE AND STYLE

In September 2010, Grand Central Life & Style was launched, absorbing GCP's Springboard Press and Wellness Central imprints. The press publishes practical nonfiction in such categories as beauty, fashion, cooking, diet, fitness, inspiration, self-help, and relationships.

Recent titles include *The Physique 57® Solution* by Tanya Becker; *What Your Doctor May Not Tell You about Heart Disease* by Mark Houston, MD; *The Wholesome Baby Food Guide* by Maggie Meade; *10 Pounds in 10 Days* by Jackie Warner; and *Giant George* by Dave Nasser.

Karen Murgolo, Editor

TWELVE

Because Twelve publishes only 12 new books a year, this imprint looks for books that matter, books that enliven the national conversation, books that will sell at least 50,000 copies. The editors at Twelve look for meaningful stories, true and fictional, and singular books that will entertain and illuminate.

Each book receives the marketing focus of the entire imprint for the month of its release, and is promoted well into its paperback life. This imprint is known to put great marketing and editorial muscle behind each and every title.

Recent titles include *The Defining Decade* by Meg Jay, PhD; *The Missionary Position* by Christopher Hitchens; *No One Left to Lie To* by Christopher Hitchens;

The Trial of Henry Kissinger by Christopher Hitchens; and *They Eat Puppies, Don't They?* by Christopher Buckley.
Cary Goldstein, Editor

VISION

Vision is Grand Central Publishing's mass-market imprint for the best in blockbuster fiction. Recent titles include *Lethal Rider* by Larissa Ione; *The Bourne Dominion* by Eric Van Lustbader; *Tick Tock* by James Patterson; *The Choke Artist* by David Yoo; and *The Drop* by Michael Connelly.

LITTLE, BROWN AND COMPANY

BACK BAY BOOKS
MULHOLLAND BOOKS
ORBIT
REAGAN ARTHUR BOOKS
YEN PRESS
237 Park Avenue, New York, NY 10017
212-364-1100
Twitter: @littlebrown

Founded in 1837, Little, Brown originated as an independent house with a Boston home base, but joined Warner Books in Manhattan in 2002. A former Little, Brown imprint, Bulfinch Press, was dissolved by parent HBG late in 2006. However, the imprimatur "a Bulfinch Press book" is added to traditional art books (photography, art, and museum-related titles) published as Little, Brown titles.

Little, Brown and Company is home to noted debut novelists like Eduardo Santiago and masters of the trade like Herman Wouk. The house publishes David Sedaris's essays and Holly Hobbie's pigs, Walter Mosley's mysteries, and James Patterson's thrillers.

Recent titles from Little, Brown include *NYPD Red* by James Patterson and Marshall Karp; *The Cypress House* by Michael Koryta; *Love Is the Cure: On Life, Loss, and the End of AIDS* by Elton John; *Tigers in Red Weather: A Novel* by Liza Klaussmann; and *The Violinist's Thumb* by Sam Kean.

Michael Pietsch, Senior Vice President and Publisher, has worked with the novelists Martin Amis, Peter Blauner, Michael Connelly, Martha Cooley, Tony Earley, Janet Fitch, Mark Leyrier, Rick Moody, Walter Mosley, James Patterson, George Pelecanos, Alice Sebold, Anita Shreve, Nick Tosches, David Foster Wallace, and Stephen Wright; the nonfiction writers John Feinstein, Peter Guralnick, and David Sedaris; and the cartoonist R. Crumb. Prior to joining Little, Brown in 1991, Michael worked at Harmony Books and before that at Scribner, where he edited a posthumous memoir by Ernest Hemingway, *The Dangerous Summer*. He acquires a range of top selling fiction and nonfiction titles.

Geoff Shandler, Editor, primarily acquires histories, biographies, and journalism. Among the many authors he has worked with are James Bradley, John le Carré, Robert Dallek, Tom Shales, Ann Blackman, Robert Wright, William Least Heat-Moon, Gary Giddins, James Miller, Doug Stanton, Elaine Shannon, Elizabeth Royte, Eileen Welsome, and Luis Urrea. His numerous best sellers and award winners include *An Unfinished Life, Flyboys, Blind Man's Bluff, Black Mass, Paris in the Fifties*, and *In Retrospect*.

Tracy Behar, Editor-in-Chief, joined Little, Brown in 2004 after serving as Editorial Director at Atria and Washington Square Press. At Little, Brown she has edited authors Arianna Huffington and Dr. Mark Liponis from Canyon Ranch. Her editing interests include life-improvement categories such as psychology, parenting, health, creativity, empowerment, science and psychology.

Pat Strachan, Senior Editor, joined Little, Brown in September 2002. She is acquiring literary fiction and general nonfiction. Most recently at Houghton Mifflin, she began her career at Farrar, Straus & Giroux, where she worked as an editor for 17 years. She was then a fiction editor at *The New Yorker*, returning to book publishing in 1991. She received the PEN/Roger Klein Award for Editing. Among the prose writers she has edited are Elizabeth Benedict, Harold Bloom, Ian Frazier, James Kelman, Jamaica Kincaid, Wendy Lesser, Rosemary Mahoney, John McPhee, David Nasaw, Edna O'Brien, Peter Orner, Padgett Powell, Marilynne Robinson, Jim Shepard, Tatyana Tolstaya, and Tom Wolfe. Her Little, Brown books include fiction by Christina Adam, Kathryn Davis, Michelle de Kretser, Lucia Nevai, and Michael Redhill.

Judy Clain, Senior Editor, joined Little Brown in 1998. She began her career as a film agent and was a Sony executive on *Deep End of the Ocean* and *Donnie Brasco*. She has edited novelists including Jody Shields (*The Fig Eater*), Simon Mawer (*The Fall*), Elisabeth Robinson (*The True and Outstanding Adventures of the Hunt Sisters*), and Robb Forman Dew (*The Evidence Against Her*). She has also edited narrative nonfiction by Kien Nguyen (*The Unwanted*) and Daphne de Marneffe (*Maternal Desire*), among others. Acquires a wide range of fiction.

John Parsley, Senior Editor, joined Little, Brown in 2007. His acquisitions focus on serious and narrative nonfiction, including popular and natural science, history, ideas books, music, sports, food, business, humor. He was previously at Thomas Dunne/St. Martin's.

Michael Sand, Editor—Cooking, illustrated nonfiction.

Asya Muchnick, Editor—Fiction.

BACK BAY BOOKS

Little, Brown created the trade paperback imprint Back Bay Books in 1993. The press focuses on long-term publication of the company's best fiction and nonfiction. Back Bay has produced new editions of William Least Heat-Moon's *Blue Highways*,

Tracy Kidder's *The Soul of a New Machine*, Evelyn Waugh's *A Handful of Dust*, and C.S. Forester's Hornblower novels. The imprint also has put out paperback editions of new works by David Sedaris, Anita Shreve, Janet Fitch, and Malcolm Gladwell.

Titles include *The Sun's Heartbeat* by Bob Berman; *Give Us a Kiss: A Novel* by Daniel Woodrell; *The End of Everything: A Novel* by Megan E. Abbott; *The Cut* by George Pelecanos; and *Inside SEAL Team Six: My Life and Missions with America's Elite Warriors* by Don Mann.

Same editors as per Little, Brown above.

MULHOLLAND BOOKS

Mulholland Books, established in April 2011, publishes books of mystery and suspense in such genres as crime novels, thrillers, police procedurals, spy stories, and supernatural suspense. Their slogan: "You never know what's coming around the curve."

Titles include *Fifteen Digits* by Nick Santora; *Slip and Fall* by Nick Santora; *Guilt by Degrees* by Marcia Clark; *Alpha* by Greg Rucka; and *The Wreckage* by Michael Robotham.

Joshua Kendall, Editorial Director
John Schoenfelder, Senior Editor

ORBIT

237 Park Avenue, 16th Floor, New York, NY 10017
212-364-1100
e-mail: orbit@hbgusa.com | Twitter: @orbitbooks

Since 2007, Orbit, the science fiction and fantasy imprint at Hachette Book Group, publishes across the spectrum of science fiction and fantasy—from action-packed urban fantasy to widescreen space opera, from sweeping epic adventures to near-future thrillers. It publishes approximately 40 titles each year from both established and debut authors.

Some Orbit titles are *San Diego 2014: The Last Stand of the California Browncoats* by Mira Grant; *Chimera (The Subterrene War)* by T.C. McCarthy; *Best Served Cold* by Joe Abercrombie; *Sharps* by K. J. Parker; and *Bitter Seeds* by Ian Tregillis.

Tim Holman, Vice President, Publisher—Across the spectrum of fantasy, science fiction.
Devi Pillai, Senior Editor—Science fiction, paranormal, fantasy.

REAGAN ARTHUR BOOKS

Reagan Arthur Books is the imprint of Reagan Arthur, a Little, Brown editor who is noted for signing Tina Fey for a $6 million deal in 2008. The first list was published in Fall 2009, and the press produces 15 to 20 books a year. Acquisitions include

Dare Me: A Novel by Megan E. Abbott; *Summerland* by Elin Hilderbrand; *This Bright River: A Novel* by Patrick Somerville; *Flashback* by Dan Simmons; and *The Taint of Midas* by Anne Zouroudi.

Reagan Arthur, Vice President, Editorial Director—Fiction, nonfiction.
Laura Tisdel, Editor

YEN PRESS

237 Park Avenue, New York, NY 10017
212-364-1100
www.yenpress.com | Twitter: @yenpress

Founded in 2006 by Kurt Hassler and Rich Johnson, Yen Press is a North American publisher of manga and graphic novels for all ages. Bestselling titles include illustrated adaptations of *Maximum Ride* by James Patterson and *Twilight* by Stephanie Meyers.

Some recent titles include *Alice in the Country of Hearts* by QuinRose, art by Soumei Hoshino; *Olympos* by Aki; *Witch & Wizard* by James Patterson, art by Svetlana Chmakova; *Spice and Wolf* by Isuna Hasekura; and *Kobato* by Clamp.

LITTLE, BROWN BOOKS FOR YOUNG READERS

LB KIDS
POPPY
237 Park Avenue, New York, NY 10017
212-364-1100
www.hachettebookgroup.com/kids | Twitter: @lbkids

Little, Brown's children's books division produces picture books, board books, pop-up and lift-the-flap editions, chapter books, manga, and general fiction and nonfiction titles for middle-grade and young-adult readers. This division also issues resource guides and reference titles in careers, social issues, and intellectual topics for higher grade levels and the college-bound. The house offers volumes in Spanish language and in dual Spanish/English editions and is on the lookout for multicultural titles.

Representative Little, Brown Books for Young Readers titles include the bestselling *Twilight* series by Stephanie Meyers, Caldecott winner *Saint George and the Dragon*, illustrated by Trina Schart Hyman; Newbery winner *Maniac Magee* by Jerry Spinelli; *Toot & Puddle* by Holly Hobbie; *Daisy and the Egg* by Jane Simmons; *Kevin and His Dad* by Irene Smalls; *47* by Walter Mosley; *Maximum Ride: The Angel Experiment* by James Patterson.

Recent releases include *The Land of Stories: The Wishing Spell* by Chris Colfer; *Lost Girls* by Ann Kelley; *Nanny Piggins and The Wicked Plan* by R. A. Spratt; *Perfect Escape* by Jennifer Brown; and *A Gift of Magic* by Lois Duncan.

Megan Tingley—Publisher, Picture books through young adult.

Andrea Spooner, Editorial Director—Young adult, picture books, science fiction, middle grade.

Alvina Ling, Editor—Young adult, children's fantasy, picture books.

Liza Baker, Editor—Picture book, children's fiction, young adult.

Julie Scheina, Editor—Young adult, middle grade, picture/illustrated books.

Connie Hsu, Editor—Illustrated biographies, picture books, middle grade, young adult.

Kate Sullivan, Editor—Young adult, paranormal.

LB KIDS

LB Kids publishes novelty and licensed books and focuses primarily on interactive formats, licensed properties, media tie-ins, and baby and toddler focused projects. The press has published award-winning novelty books based on the toy and game brands ALEX and Cranium, as well as authors and artists including Sandra Magsamen, Rachel Hale, and Ed Emberley.

Titles include *The Muppets: Kermit's Costume Caper* by Martha T. Ottersley; *ParaNorman: Attack of the Pilgrim Zombies!* by Annie Auerbach; The First Adventures of Spider by Joyce Cooper Arkhurst; Transformers Prime: Attack of the Scraplets! by Ryder Windham; and Kaleidoscope by Salina Yoon.

Same editors as per Little, Brown Books for Young Readers above.

POPPY

Poppy publishes paperback original series for teen girls. The press has launched several bestselling series, including the national bestselling series *Gossip Girl* and *The It Girl* by Cecily von Ziegesar, *The Clique* by Lisi Harrison, and *The A-List* by Zoey Dean.

Titles include *Falling for Hamlet* by Michelle Ray; *The White Glove War* (The Magnolia League) by Katie Crouch; *Messy* by Heather Cocks; *A Midsummer's Nightmare* by Kody Keplinger; and *Snow White & the Huntsman* by Evan Daugherty.

Cindy Eagan, Editor

VERLAGSGRUPPE GEORG VON HOLTZBRINCK

Verlagsgruppe Georg von Holtzbrinck is Germany's second-largest publisher; holdings include Macmillan in the United Kingdom and Die Zeit in Germany. The American division is based in New York City.

MACMILLAN

FARRAR, STRAUS & GIROUX
HENRY HOLT AND COMPANY
MACMILLAN CHILDREN'S BOOK PUBLISHING GROUP
PALGRAVE MACMILLAN
PICADOR USA
ST. MARTIN'S PRESS
TOR/FORGE
175 Fifth Avenue, New York, NY 10010
212-674-5151
us.macmillan.com | Twitter: @panmacmillan

Macmillan (formerly Holtzbrinck Publishers) is a group of publishing companies, including renowned houses like Farrar, Straus & Giroux; St. Martin's; and Henry Holt; the companies include trade and educational imprints, and the *Scientific American* magazine.

Former Scholastic publisher Jean Feiwel joined Macmillan in 2006 to start a broadly defined children's effort and to guide strategy within the group. As well as creating new children's imprints, like Feiwel & Friends and Square Fish, she is publishing into paperback and other formats.

Most of you will recognize the name Macmillan, because it's one of publishing's most respected brand names. However, for many years it has been a brand without a product. Over the past 20 years both the brand and its catalogue have been traded several times, until finally it was detached from its catalogue to become a name without a body. Somehow Holtzbrinck acquired the rights to the name, even if they didn't actually mean to. And it turned out to be very convenient, because they needed a palatable flagship title for their conglomerated divisions. "Holtzbrinck Gruppe" somehow didn't sound American, which it isn't, but reviving the Macmillan name was a brilliant solution.

FARRAR, STRAUS & GIROUX

FABER, INC.
HILL AND WANG
SARAH CRICHTON BOOKS
18 West 18th Street, New York, NY 10011
212-741-6900
www.fsgbooks.com | e-mail: fsg.editorial@fsgbooks.com | blog: www.fsgpoetry
.com | Twitter: @fsgbooks

Farrar, Straus & Giroux (FSG) was founded in New York City in 1946 by Roger Straus and John Farrar; Robert Giroux joined the company in 1955. The firm is widely acclaimed for its international list of literary fiction, nonfiction, poetry, and children's books. FSG is also known for building authors over time through strong editorial relationships. This was the way Roger Straus built the company, and it continues so under current publisher Jonathan Galassi.

FSG authors have won extraordinary acclaim over the years, including numerous National Book Awards, Pulitzer Prizes, and 22 Nobel Prizes in literature. Nobel Prize winners include Knut Hamsun, Hermann Hesse, T. S. Eliot, Par Lagerkvist, Francois Mauriac, Juan Ramon Jimenez, Salvatore Quasimodo, Nelly Sachs, Czeslaw Milosz, Elias Canetti, William Golding, Wole Soyinka, Joseph Brodsky, Camilo Jose Cela, Nadine Gordimer, Derek Walcott, Seamus Heaney, and Mario Vargas Llosa.

Today's Farrar, Straus & Giroux list includes some of the most renowned names in poetry and fiction, including Elizabeth Bishop, Marilynne Robinson, Ted Hughes, Phillip Larkin, Michael Cunningham, Jonathan Franzen, Alice McDermott, Scott Turow, and Tom Wolfe. FSG is also the distributer for Graywolf Press and Drawn and Quarterly.

History, art history, natural history, current affairs, and science round out the list in nonfiction, represented by Thomas Friedman, Philip Gourevitch, Roy Jenkins, Gina Kolata, Ben Macintyre, Louis Menaud, Giles Milton, and John McPhee.

Recent titles include *All We Know: Three Lives* by Lisa Cohen; *Holding On to Zoe* by George Ella Lyon; *Moonbird: A Year on the Wind with the Great Survivor B95* by Phillip Hoose; *52 Reasons to Hate My Father* by Jessica Brod; and *A Pimp's Notes: A Novel* by Giorgio Faletti and Anthony Shugaar.

FSG does accept unsolicited and unagented manuscripts. All editorial inquiries should be e-mailed to the editorial department at fsg.editorial@fsgbooks.com. FSG does not accept manuscript submissions via e-mail. Queries may be sent via mail with SASEs to:

Jonathan Galassi, Publisher—Fiction, nonfiction, art history, business, poetry, biographies.

Eric Chinski, Editor-in-Chief—Science, history, business, general nonfiction, philosophy, historical memoir.

Courtney Hodell, Executive Editor—Fiction, biography.

Amanda Mood, Editor—Science, philosophy, psychology, sociology.
Sean McDonald, Editor—Fiction, culture, music.
Mark Krotov, Editor—Fiction.

FABER, INC.

Faber specializes in books on the arts and entertainment, pop culture, cultural criticism, and the media, with a special emphasis on music. Among its authors are Courtney Love and Billy Corgan, as well as Pulitzer Prize–winning playwrights David Auburn, Margaret Edson, and Doug Wright; Pulitzer finalist Richard Greenberg; British dramatists Tom Stoppard and David Hare; and filmmaker and playwright Neil LaBute.

Faber also publishes books designed to reach a younger readership, one it feels loves and understands itself through popular culture.

Recent titles include *81 Austerities* by Sam Riviere; *You, Me and Thing 1: The Curse of the Jelly Babies* by Karen McCombie; *Collected Poems of Samuel Beckett* by Samuel Beckett; *The Beautiful Indifference* by Sarah Hall; and *The World's Two Smallest Humans* by Julia Copus.

All editorial inquiries should be e-mailed to the editorial department at fsg.editorial@fsgbooks.com. FSG does not accept manuscript submissions via e-mail. Queries may be sent via mail with SASEs to:

Mitzi Angel, Publisher—International studies, psychology, international fiction.

HILL AND WANG

Hill and Wang focuses on books of academic interest for both the trade and college markets, in both hard- and softcover. The list is strong in American history, world history, politics, and graphic nonfiction. Among its authors are Roland Barthes, Michael Burleigh, William Cronon, Langston Hughes, Robert Wiebe, and Elie Wiesel.

Recent titles include *Not the Israel My Parents Promised Me* by Harvey Pekar; *In the Long Run: A Father, a Son, and Unintentional Lessons in Happiness* by Jim Axelrod; *Clarence Darrow: American Iconoclast* by Andrew Edmund Kersten; *Bottled Lightning: Superbatteries, Electric Cars, and the New Lithium Economy* by Seth Fletcher; and *Trinity: A Graphic History of the First Atomic Bomb* by Jonathan Fetter-Vorm.

SARAH CRICHTON BOOKS

Launched in 2006, Sarah Crichton Books publishes books with a slightly commercial bent; their first title was *The God Factor* by Cathleen Falsani. Recent titles include *The Nightmare: A Novel* by Lars Kepler; *Alphabetter Juice: or, The Joy of Text* by Roy Blount Jr.; *Exit Interview* by David Westin; *When Women Were Birds: Fifty-four Variations on Voice* by Terry Tempest Williams; and *No Biking in the House Without a Helmet* by Melissa Fay Greene.

Sarah Crichton, Publisher

HENRY HOLT AND COMPANY

METROPOLITAN BOOKS
TIMES BOOKS
175 Fifth Avenue, New York, NY 10010
646-307-5095
www.henryholt.com | Twitter: @henryholt

Founded in 1866 by Henry Holt and Frederick Leypoldt, Henry Holt is one of the oldest publishers in the United States. Henry Holt is known for publishing high-quality books, including those by authors such as Erich Fromm, Robert Frost, Hermann Hesse, Norman Mailer, Robert Louis Stevenson, Ivan Turgenev, and H. G. Wells. Today the company continues to build upon its illustrious history by publishing bestselling, award-winning books in the areas of literary fiction, mysteries and thrillers, history, biography, politics, current events, science, psychology, and books for children and young adults.

Recent titles include *Bring Up The Bodies* by Hilary Mantel; *Vengeance: A Novel* by Benjamin Black; *Winter Journal* by Paul Auster; *Me, Who Dove into the Heart of the World: A Novel* by Sabina Berman; and *The Graves Are Walking: The Great Famine and the Saga of the Irish People* by John Kelly.

Henry Holt and its adult imprints do not accept or read any unsolicited manuscripts or queries.

Jack MacRae, Editor—Fiction.
Gillian Blake, Editor—Nonfiction, science, narratives, history, biographies.
Aaron Schlecter, Editor—Fiction.
Sarah Bowlin, Editor—Fiction.
Barbara Jones, Editor—Fiction, memoirs, narratives.

METROPOLITAN BOOKS

Metropolitan Books, established in 1995, publishes American and international fiction and nonfiction. With a mission to introduce unconventional, uncompromising, and sometimes controversial voices, Metropolitan publishes titles in categories ranging from world history to American politics, foreign fiction to graphic novels, and social science to current affairs.

Authors published by Metropolitan Books include Ann Crittenden, Mike Davis, Barbara Ehrenreich, Susan Faludi, Orlando Figes, Michael Frayn, Eduardo Galeano, Atul Gawande, Todd Gitlin, Arlie Russell Hochschild, Michael Ignatieff, Orville Schell, and Tom Segev.

Titles representative of Metropolitan's nonfiction list include *Failed States: The Abuse of Power and the Assault on Democracy* by Noam Chomsky; *What's the Matter with Kansas? How Conservatives Won the Heart of America* by Thomas Frank; *Dancing in the Streets: A History of Collective Joy* by Barbara Ehrenreich; and *Complications: A Surgeon's Notes on an Imperfect Science* by Atul Gawande.

Titles indicative of Metropolitan fiction include *All for Love: A Novel* by Dan Jacobeon; *The Nubian Prince* by Juan Bonilla, translated by Esther Allen; *The Beholder* by Thomas Farber; and *Spies* by Michael Frayn.

Recent titles include *Journalism* by Joe Sacco; *The Outsourced Self: Intimate Life in Market Times* by Arlie Russell Hochschild; *Just Send Me Word: A True Story of Love and Survival in the Gulag* by Orlando Figes; *The Conflict: How Modern Motherhood Undermines the Status of Women* by Elisabeth Badinter; and *Skios: A Novel* by Michael Frayn.

Henry Holt and its adult imprints do not accept or read any unsolicited manuscripts or queries.

Sara Bershtel, Associate Publisher—Nonfiction, nonfiction narrative, history, current events, general fiction.

TIMES BOOKS

Times Books, launched in 2001, is the result of a copublishing agreement between Holt and the *New York Times*; its nonfiction list focuses on politics, current events, international relations, history, science, business, and American society and culture. About half of the imprint's books are written by *New York Times* reporters and the rest are written by other American intellectuals, journalists, and public figures.

Titles representative of this list include *John F. Kennedy* by Alan Brinkley; *First Cameraman* by Arun Chaudhary; *The Crisis Of Zionism* by Peter Beinart; *Straphanger: Saving Our Cities and Ourselves from the Automobile* by Taras Grescoe; and *Reckless Endangerment* by Gretchen Morgenson and Joshua Rosner.

Recent releases include *Boiling Mad* by Kate Zernike; *The Teacher* by Seth Davis; and *Invisible Men* by Michael Addis.

Direct queries and SASEs to:

Paul Golob, Editorial Director—Nonfiction, sports, politics, current events.

Serena Jones, Editor—International politics, investigative journalism.

MACMILLAN CHILDREN'S BOOK PUBLISHING GROUP

FARRAR, STRAUS & GIROUX BOOKS FOR YOUNG READERS
FEIWEL & FRIENDS
HENRY HOLT AND COMPANY BOOKS FOR YOUNG READERS
FIRST SECOND
KINGFISHER
PRIDDY BOOKS
ROARING BROOK PRESS
SQUARE FISH
STARSCAPE
TOR TEEN

175 Fifth Avenue, New York, NY 10010
212-982-3900

The Macmillan Children's Book Publishing Group was created in late 2008 with the consolidation of Macmillan's far-flung children's imprints. Jean Feiwel, senior vice president and codirector of the new division, saw the move as harnessing separate assets to work in tandem and compared the new infrastructure to a "Star Wars federation" of imprints. Each editorial team will be able to pursue its own agenda while drawing upon the shared resources of other departments. As of 2010, the imprints of Macmillan Children's Book Publishing Group do not accept unsolicited manuscripts; they recommend finding representation through a literary agent.

Jean Feiwel, Senior Vice President, Codirector

FARRAR, STRAUS & GIROUX BOOKS FOR YOUNG READERS

www.fsgkidsbooks.com | e-mail: childrens.editorial@fsgbooks.com

The FSG juvenile program publishes fiction and nonfiction books for toddlers to young adults. This list includes many Caldecott, Newbery, and National Book Award winners. Award-winning authors include Jack Gantos, Madeleine L'Engle, Louis Sachar, Uri Shulevitz, Peter Sis, David Small, William Steig, and Sarah Stewart. Newer FSG authors include Kate Banks, Claudia Mills, Jack Gantos, Suzanne Fisher Staples, and Tim Wynne-Jones.

Recent titles include *Dot* by Patricia Intriago; *Desert Elephant* by Helen Cowcher; *All These Things I've Done* by Gabrielle Zevin; *Dead End in Norvelt* by Jack Gantos; and *With a Name Like Love* by Tess Hilmo.

Janine O'Malley, Editor—Children's picture books, young adult.

Wesley Adams, Editor—Young adult.

Joy Peskin, Editor—Young adult.

FEIWEL & FRIENDS

646-307-5151

Feiwel & Friends is a new imprint developed by former Scholastic publisher Jean Feiwel, who joined Macmillan in 2006. They publish innovative children's fiction and nonfiction literature including hardcover, paperback series, and individual titles. The list is eclectic and combines quality and commercial appeal for readers ages zero to sixteen. The imprint is dedicated to "book by book" publishing, bringing the work of distinctive and outstanding authors, illustrators, and ideas to the marketplace. Feiwel & Friends is defined and guided by their principle: Our Books Are Friends for Life.

Titles from Feiwel & Friends include *Monument 14* by Emmy Laybourne; *Of Poseidon* by Anna Banks; *In the Ocean* by Salina Yoon; *Justin Case: Shells, Smells, and the Horrible Flip-Flops of Doom* by Rachel Vail; and *The Raft* by S. A. Bodeen.

Direct queries and SASEs to:

Jean Feiwel, Publisher

HENRY HOLT AND COMPANY BOOKS FOR YOUNG READERS

www.henryholtchildrensbooks.com

Henry Holt and Company Books for Young Readers publishes a wide range of children's books, from picture books for preschoolers to fiction for young adults. Their titles cover a wide variety of genres, featuring imaginative authors and illustrators who inspire young readers.

Their list includes classic picture books like *Panda Bear, Panda Bear, What Do You See?* by Bill Martin, Jr., illustrated by Eric Carle; *Tikki Tikki Tembo* by Arlene Mosel, illustrated by Blair Lent; *The Book of Three* (The Chronicles of Prydain) by Lloyd Alexander; *Whirligig* by Paul Fleischman; *My First Chinese New Year* by Karen Katz; *Frog in Love* by Max Velthuijs; *My Thirteenth Season* by Kristi Robert; and *Beach Patrol* by John O'Brien, illustrated by Max Bilkins.

Recent titles include *Shadow and Bone: The Grisha Trilogy* by Leigh Bardugo; *Because of Shoe and Other Dog Stories* by Ann M. Martin; *Amazing ABC* by Sean Kenney; *Guy-Write: What Every Guy Writer Needs to Know* by Ralph Fletcher; and *Knuckle and Potty Destroy Happy World* by James Proimos.

Noa Wheeler, Editor—Young adult, children's picture book, middle grade.

FIRST SECOND

In 2006, Roaring Brook launched First Second, an imprint devoted to graphic novels. First Second editors seek to acquire titles that attract a diverse audience of readers by working on many different levels. Their publication of Gene Luen Yang's *American Born Chinese* was both the first graphic novel to win the American Library Association's Michael L. Printz Award and the first graphic novel to be a National Book Award finalist.

First Second titles include *Bloody Chester* by J. T. Petty and Hilary Florido; *Marathon* by Boaz Yakin and Joe Infurnari; *The Moon Moth* by Jack Vance and Humayoun Ibrahim; *Baby's in Black* by Arne Bellstorf; and *Mastering Comics: Drawing Words & Writing Pictures Continued* by Jessica Abel.

Mark Siegel, Editorial Director

KINGFISHER

Kingfisher publishes illustrated information books for pre-schoolers and older students. The press puts out books on subjects on subjects as diverse as natural history, science, geography, history, art and philosophy. Their *Basher Science* series has sold over 1.5 million copies.

Recent titles include *Human Body Factory: The Nuts and Bolts of Your Insides* by Dan Green; *Popposites* by Mike Haines and Julia Frohlich; *Discover Science: Desert* by Nicola Davies; *Legendary Journeys: Space* by Dr. Mike Goldsmith; and *Basher Basics: Dinosaurs* by Simon Basher.

PRIDDY BOOKS

Priddy Books publishes photographic children's books specially designed to encourage their development and awareness of the world around them. Their range is aimed at three key age groups: Happy Baby zero to two years, Preschool two to five years and Smart Kids for children ages five and over. They produce books for a worldwide market, with translations into 30 different languages.

Recent titles include *Funny Faces Halloween Jack*; *Rainbow Friends*; *Fuzzy Bee 123*; *Baby Touch and Feel Meow! Meow!*; and *Funny Faces Haunted House* by Roger Priddy.

ROARING BROOK PRESS
212-674-5151

Roaring Brook Press published its debut list of children's books in Spring 2002, and less than a year later one of its picture books, Eric Rohmann's *My Friend Rabbit*, won the Caldecott Medal. Another Roaring Brook picture book, Mordicai Gerstein's *The Man Who Walked Between the Towers*, won the Caldecott Medal in January 2004. This was the first time in 30 years that the Caldecott had been awarded to the same publisher two years in a row (in 1976 and 1977, Dial Press won for *Why Mosquitoes Buzz in People's Ears* by Verna Aardema, illustrated by Leo and Diane Dillon, and *Ashanti to Zulu* by Margaret Musgrove, again illustrated by Leo and Diane Dillon).

Macmillan acquired the Connecticut-based publisher in 2004. Roaring Brook publishes 40 books per year, half picture books and half novels for middle-grade and young-adult readers, and is in the midst of a growth pattern.

Roaring Brook Press is an author-centered publisher with a small but eclectic list. They are seeking long-term relationships with their authors; they don't do series; they don't do merchandise. What they do is edgy teen fiction, middle-grade fiction with humor, and high-quality picture books with an individual approach to art and format.

Recent Roaring Brook titles include *Clover Twig and the Perilous Path* by Kaye Umansky; *The Girl Is Trouble* by Kathryn Miller Haines; *A Home for Bird* by Philip C. Stead; *It's a Dog's Life: How Man's Best Friend Sees, Hears, and Smells the World* by Susan E. Goodman; and *My Snake Blake* by Randy Siegel.

Direct queries and SASEs to:

Simon Boughton, Publisher—Middle-grade children's literature, picture books.
Katherine Jacobs, Editor—Picture books, middle grade, young adult.

SQUARE FISH

Square Fish is a paperback imprint that reprints hardcover children's books from all of the Macmillan publishers. The imprint launched in summer 2007 with Madeleine L'Engle's Time Quintet, which includes the classic *A Wrinkle in Time*. They do not accept submissions.

More recent titles from Square Fish include *Clover Twig and the Magical Cottage* by Kaye Umansky; *Enclave* by Ann Aguirre; *School! Adventures at the Harvey N. Trouble Elementary School* by Kate McMullan; *Molly the Pony* by Pam Kaster; and *Fractions = Trouble!* by Claudia Mills.

Jean Feiwel, Editor
Rose Hilliard, Editor

STARSCAPE

Starscape publishes science fiction and fantasy for middle-grade readers ages ten and up, in hardcover and paperback. All titles are age- and theme-appropriate. Some titles include *Invasion of the Appleheads: Deadtime Stories* by Annette Cascone; *Down the Mysterly River* by Bill Willingham and Mark Buckingham; *House of the Star* by Caitlin Brennan; *Beware the Ninja Weenies: And Other Warped and Creepy Tales* by David Lubar; and *City of Ice* (City Trilogy) by Laurence Yep.

Susan Chang, Editor

TOR TEEN

Tor Teen publishes science fiction and fantasy for young-adult readers ages thirteen and up, in hardcover and paperback. All titles are age- and theme-appropriate. Some titles are *Earthseed* (Seed Trilogy) by Pamela Sargent; *Anna Dressed in Blood* by Kendare Blake; *Last Rite* (Personal Demons Novels) by Lisa Desrochers; *Dark Companion* by Marta Acosta; and *The Galahad Legacy* by Dom Testa.

PALGRAVE MACMILLAN

175 Fifth Avenue, New York, NY 10010
212-982-3900
www.palgrave-usa.com | Twitter: @palgraveusa

Formerly the Scholarly and Reference division of St. Martin's Press, Palgrave Macmillan is a global cross-market publisher specializing in quality nonfiction and cutting-edge academic books. It publishes general-interest books as well as textbooks, journals, monographs, professional, and reference works in subjects ranging from political science, economics, and history, to literature, linguistics, and business.

Recent titles include *Nonbeliever Nation: The Rise of Secular Americans* by David Niose; *Survival Investing* by John R. Talbott; *Prize Fight: The Race and the Rivalry to be the First in Science* by Morton Meyers; *Masters of the Planet: The Search for Our Human Origins* by Ian Tattersall; and *Stealing Rembrandts* by Anthony M. Amore and Tom Mashberg.

Direct query letters and SASEs to:

Luba Ostashevsky, Editor—Latin American studies, African studies, psychology, science, parenting.
Emily Carleton, Editor—Economics, politics, political history, international affairs.
Karen Wolny, Editorial Director—Business, economics, social history.
Laurie Harting, Editor—Economics, business, management, leadership.

PICADOR USA

175 Fifth Avenue, 19th Floor, New York, NY 10010
212-674-5151 | fax: 212-253-9627
www.picadorusa.com | Twitter: @picadorusa

Picador USA was founded by St. Martin's Press and is now the reprint house for Farrar, Straus & Giroux; Henry Holt; and other Macmillan publishers. With an international list of world-class authors, Picador has rapidly established itself as one of the country's literary trade paperback imprints.

Representative titles include *Winter under Water* by James Hopkin; *Bridget Jones's Diary* by Helen Fielding; *The Ice Soldier* by Paul Watkins; *Physical: An American Checkup* by James McManus; and *A Taxonomy of Barnacles: A Novel* by Galt Niederhoffer.

Recent titles include *East of the West: A Country in Stories* by Miroslav Penkov; *The Devil She Knows: A Novel* by Bill Loehfelm; *None to Accompany Me: A Novel* by Nadine Gordimer; *The Age of Deception: Nuclear Diplomacy in Treacherous Times* by Mohamed ElBaradei; and *The Summer Without Men: A Novel* by Siri Hustvedt.

ST. MARTIN'S PRESS

GRIFFIN
MINOTAUR
THOMAS DUNNE BOOKS
TRUMAN TALLEY BOOKS

175 Fifth Avenue, New York, NY 10010
212-674-5151
www.stmartins.com | Twitter: @stmartinspress

Founded in 1952 by Macmillan Publishers of England, St. Martin's Press is now one of the largest publishers in America. Together, their imprints produce over 700 books a year, and their editors are as equally committed to establishing new and innovative authors, as to maintaining a strong backlist of titles. Publishing in hardcover, trade paperback, and mass-market formats enables St. Martin's Press to offer a diverse assortment of titles with wide-ranging appeal. St. Martin's is looking for new authors to discover, to build, and to support.

The house is particularly strong in a number of specialty areas, some with associated lines and imprints (including popular culture, international arts and letters, relationships, multicultural topics, science, business, and professional topics). St. Martin's publishes across the spectrum of trade nonfiction and hosts a wide range of popular and literary fiction.

Representative titles include *Twelve Sharp* by Janet Evanovich; *Running with Scissors: A Memoir* by Augusten Burroughs; *Big Papi: The Story of How My Baseball Dreams Came True* by David Ortiz and Tony Massoroti; *Brendan Wolf* by Brian Malloy; *How Not to Be Afraid of Your Own Life: Opening Your Heart to Confidence, Intimacy, and Joy* by Susan Piver; *10 Things Your Minister Wants to Tell You (But Can't Because He Needs the Job)* by Oliver Thomas; *Cat O'Nine Tales* by Jeffrey Archer; *Friends in High Places* by Marne Davis Kellogg; and *Vicente Minnelli: Hollywood's Dark Dreamer* by Emanuel Levy.

Recent titles include *Shine Shine Shine* by Lydia Netzer; *Nixon's Darkest Secrets: The Inside Story of America's Most Troubled President* by Don Fulsom; *A Place in the Country* by Elizabeth Adler; and *Spark: A Sky Chasers Novel* by Amy Kathleen Ryan.

Queries and SASEs may be directed to:

George Witte, Editor-in-Chief—Quality literary and commercial fiction, current affairs and issues, and narrative nonfiction. "During my twenty-two years here, I've taken particular pleasure in the number of first books we've published—many of those authors are now writing their fifth, tenth, fifteenth, or even twentieth book for us. Discovery, energy, and commitment to authors are the driving forces of our house."

David Rogers, Editor—Fiction.

Charles Spicer, Executive Editor—Commercial fiction: crime, suspense, mysteries, and historical fiction; nonfiction: true crime, biography and history. "I also oversee the True Crime Library Imprint, which has long been the most successful publisher of nonfiction crime, with many *New York Times* best sellers and Edgar winners to its credit."

Elizabeth Beier, Executive Editor—"I couldn't be more enthusiastic about the kinds of books I work on—they span a generous variety of categories, from issues-oriented books to pop culture, cookbooks to fiction, celebrity memoir to biography. Especially exciting is to work with first-time authors—I love introducing a writer to the process, trying to smooth the bumps along the way, and watching them take leaps as we pull the book together."

Hope Dellon, Executive Editor—Mysteries, serious contemporary and historical novels. "In nonfiction, my interests include biography, social history, and psychological memoirs. As the wife of a psychiatrist and mother of two daughters, I also find myself drawn to books on parenting, education, women's issues, and medicine."

Jennifer Enderlin, Associate Publisher—Fiction, thriller, cooking, women's fiction, romance, pop psychology, self-help, memoirs, humor.

Jennifer Weis, Executive Editor—Commercial fiction: women's, thrillers, romance; young adult; nonfiction: people books, narrative nonfiction, cookbooks, self-help, health and parenting, humor and popular culture. "The common theme of the novels I acquire is that they tell a story. From the most boldly commercial, to the quieter, what we call literary commercial crossover titles, they must make me keep turning the pages—usually, far into the night!" She is also looking, from a content/book perspective, to tie in with opportunities in areas of new media, branding, and Hollywood.

Keith Kahla, Executive Editor—Thrillers, crime fiction, historical, literary fiction, Asian fiction (domestic and translated), new age works, divination systems, biography, and history. "What draws me to a particular book is the quality of the writing, and a distinct, compelling authorial voice. Editorially, I believe it isn't the topic, story, or 'hook' that is the determining factor for interesting and successful books—it's the execution of the work by a uniquely talented author."

B. J. Berti, Senior Editor—She started at St. Martin's in 2005 with a mandate to reinvigorate the line of craft, style, and home books and develop a range of new titles in this area. In addition to practical nonfiction titles like *Easy Knitted Socks*, she is also interested in considering books that are not specifically craft but have a strong practical "how-to" component, like *The Art of Friendship*. She writes, "An attractively designed book with unique projects of information and something new to teach is what appeals to me most."

Alyse Diamond, Editor—Health, self-help, beauty, fashion, psychology, parenting, business, cooking, lifestyle.

Marc Resnick, Executive Editor—Outdoor adventure, sports, military, popular culture, memoirs, thrillers, commercial fiction. "I have been working at St. Martin's Press since 1996—my first job in publishing."

Michael Flamini, Executive Editor—History, politics, current affairs, memoirs, and cookbooks. He says, "It's an eclectic list, but why be boring? Life's too short and I hope my publishing reflects that philosophy."

Monique Patterson, Executive Editor—All areas of commercial fiction.

Nichole Argyres, Senior Editor—"The search for a good story drives me both as a reader and as an editor. I love discovering stories with strong voices, beautiful language, and mysterious secrets. In nonfiction, I acquire idea books, memoirs, and platform-driven nonfiction of all kinds. I have a special interest in women's issues, current events, mental health, and medicine, as well as popular science and anything Greek."

Rose Hilliard, Editor—Women's fiction and romance. "I'm on the lookout for exciting new romance authors in every subgenre, from romantic suspense to romantic comedy." She looks for stories with a great hook, an appealing voice, and winning characters that have her rooting for them from page one—and bonus points for a story that makes her laugh aloud or tear up. She is also considering branching out in the direction of pop-culture books.

Michael Homler, Editor—Biographies, history, pop science, crime fiction, sophisticated thrillers, and literary novels. "I'm really fascinated by material that breaks convention. At the same time, I look for solid voice-driven writing—something that makes the book and the author stand out from the pack. A sense of humor doesn't hurt either. In addition, I'm looking for more sports books, with a particular interest in baseball, which I can never get enough of."

Daniela Rapp, Editor—Humor, pets, biography, food/travel/wine, pop science, mysteries, thrillers, historical fiction, literary fiction. "I am actively looking for young Native American writers, as well as fiction in translation (I read German, French, and Italian), and am intrigued by literary references and anything to do with sword fights."

Hilary Teeman, Editor—Social and cultural history, narrative nonfiction, popular sociology, playful self-help, memoirs, up-market women's fiction, romantic suspense, chick lit, literate commercial fiction, thrillers, and edgy young adult novels. "I'm particularly interested in anything geared toward the twenty-to-thirty-something market."

Yaniv Soha, Associate Editor—Nonfiction, pop culture, health, humor, narrative reporting.

Kathryn Huck, Executive Editor—Wide range of self-help/how-to, health, lifestyle, politics.

Vicki Lame, Associate Editor—Literary fiction, women's fiction, and young adult.

Matt Martz, Associate Editor—Crime fiction, journalistic narratives, American history, social and economic trends/theories.

Dori Weintraub, Editor-at-Large—Fiction, biographies, general nonfiction.

Dan Weiss, Publisher-at-Large—Fiction and nonfiction for readers between the ages of 20 and 35.

Sara Goodman, Associate Editor—"Gritty" and paranormal young-adult novels.

GRIFFIN

The Griffin list features a wide range of contemporary paperbacks and includes hundreds of bestselling works of fiction—from commercial, literary, and graphic novels to titles of African American and young-adult interest. Their varied nonfiction publishing program includes such categories as biography, memoir, pop-culture, politics, business, self-help, humor, reference, gay, health and fitness, home and travel, crafts, hobbies, nature, medicine, crossword puzzles, and sudoku.

Recent releases include *Adele: The Biography* by Marc Shapiro; *Deep Future: The Next 100,000 Years of Life on Earth* by Curt Stager; *The Boy in the Moon: A Father's Journey to Understand His Extraordinary Son* by Ian Brown; *21st Century Dead: A Zombie Anthology* by Christopher Golden; and *The Complete Guide to Machine Quilting* by Joanie Zeier Poole.

MINOTAUR
www.minotaurbooks.com

Minotaur publishes mystery and all its sub-genres, but doesn't kill itself with gravity. A comic crime novel is not an oxymoron at this imprint. The position at Minotaur is that a good mystery is any good novel that has a crime as the foundation of the story. St. Martin's Press began releasing mystery novels in the 1950s—publishing classics like *Enter a Murderer* by Ngaio Marsh—and created Minotaur in 1999 to recognize the importance of the genre to the list.

Andy Martin, formerly of Crown and Sterling, became Minotaur's publisher in 2006; he has said that the fun in his job is discovering, launching, and marketing major new talent, like John Hart, Marcus Sakey, Chelsea Cain, and Louise Penny. Minotaur publishes about 135 books per year.

Recent Minotaur titles include *Gone Missing: A Thriller* by Kate Burkholder; *Leader of the Pack* by David Rosenfelt; *The Seven Wonders: A Novel of the Ancient World* by Steven Saylor; and *The Trust* by Norb Vonnegut.

Direct queries with SASEs to:

Andrew Martin, Publisher—Mysteries and crime fiction; everything from cozies and international thrillers to police procedurals and amateur sleuths.

Ms. Kelley Ragland, Executive Editor—Mystery, suspense fiction, crime. "My taste in crime runs the gamut from cozy to hardboiled but is becoming increasingly dark and more serious."

THOMAS DUNNE BOOKS
www.thomasdunnebooks.com

The Thomas Dunne imprint produces roughly 200 titles per year—about 50/50 fiction/nonfiction—and covers a wide array of interests that include commercial fiction, literary fiction, thrillers, biography, politics, sports, popular science, and more.

Thomas Dunne editors have a wide range of tastes, backgrounds, even ages—from mid-twenties to late eighties. They believe that almost any book of commercial or literary merit will find a good home in their house.

Recent releases include *Ruler of the World* by Alex Rutherford; *Some Like It Hawk* by Donna Andrews; *Bushville Wins!* by John Klima; *Ripper* by David L. Golemon; and *Marilyn Monroe: The Final Years* by Keith Badman.

Queries and SASEs should be directed to:

Thomas L. Dunne, Vice President, Executive Editor, Publisher—Eclectic interests, commercial women's fiction, mysteries, military histories, biographies, divination systems, politics, philosophy, humor, literary fiction, and current events; he says that many of the biggest authors he has personally edited have been British—Rosamunde Pilcher, Frederick Forsyth, Wilbur Smith, Michael Palin—but also he has edited first books by Americans Dan Brown and Madeleine Wickham (aka Sophie Kinsella). In nonfiction, he has a particular interest in politics, history, biography, and current events.

Peter Wolverton, Executive Editor and Associate Publisher—Fiction: commercial and popular literature, genre mysteries; and a wide range of nonfiction consistent with the Thomas Dunne list; he says, "During my seventeen years in the business, I've published a wide variety of titles, but inevitably I find myself drawn to sports books (of all kinds), explosive thrillers and mysteries, outdoor literature (a particular passion—I'm always looking for the next Stegner or Mosher), the early years of NASA and the Apollo missions, and I occasionally journey into every genre."

Rob Kirkpatrick, Senior Editor—Pop culture, sports, politics, current events; "I'm on the lookout for strong, platform-friendly nonfiction titles in sports, pop culture, history, and politics, as well as (on a very, very select basis) fiction."

Marcia Markland, Senior Editor—Fiction and nonfiction; "As a former editor of The Mystery Guild, my taste naturally leans toward suspense fiction. My favorite category right now is what I think of as the semi-literary thriller. I also like police procedurals and legal thrillers. International suspense writing fascinates me. I devour disaster novels of any stripe, so if any given topic will make me lose sleep, that's the project for me." In nonfiction, she likes issue books, nature, and animals. She likes reading manuscripts that are a bit offbeat, and is most likely to request a manuscript that reflects a passionate belief on the part of the author, regardless of subject matter.

Karyn Marcus, Editor—Nonfiction with a focus on science, music, food, and humor. "I'm looking to acquire fiction projects which combine quality prose with clever plotting, particularly those with strong female protagonists. I'm also interested in writers working on a series of thrillers or historicals who are prolific enough to do a book a year. In nonfiction, my interests range from layman's science, psychology, and sociology to memoir and contemporary biography. Books about dogs, and animals in general, always make the top of my list."

Kathleen Gilligan, Editor—Women's fiction, romance, mysteries, food, cooking.

Peter Joseph, Editor—History, science, biography/autobiography, narrative nonfiction, travel, humor, pop-culture, film, music, social history, mysteries, thrillers, historical, and literary fiction. He also manages the Tony Hillerman Prize for first mysteries set in the Southwest.

Toni Plummer, Editor—Fiction and nonfiction, including sassy relationship advice, humor, and mysteries. "My nonfiction interests include memoir, narrative, advice/relationships, and social issues. My taste in mysteries runs the gamut, from gritty police procedurals to eloquent historicals to hilarious cozies."

Brendan Deneen, Editor—Fiction, paranormal fiction, horror, thriller, science fiction, fantasy.

TRUMAN TALLEY BOOKS

The Truman Talley imprint was run by Truman "Mac" Talley, who had been one of New York's most respected editors over the past 40 years. He retired in 2008. The list focuses on law, business, and leadership.

Recent titles include *Managing in the Next Society* by Peter F. Drucker; *Accomplice to Evil: Iran and the War Against the West* by Michael A. Ledeen; *Getting Everything You Can Out of All You've Got* by Jay Abraham; *The Iranian Time Bomb: The Mullah Zealots' Quest for Destruction* by Michael A. Ledeen; and *FutureWealth: Investing In The Second Great Wave Of Technology* by Francis McInerney and Sean White.

TOR/FORGE

TOR
FORGE
175 Fifth Avenue, New York, NY 10010
212-388-0100
www.tor-forge.com | Twitter: @torbooks

TOR

Tor was created in 1981 at Tom Doherty and Associates, an independent publishing company known for its science fiction and fantasy list, including the bestselling *Sword of Truth* series by Terry Goodkind.

Today, Tor publishes science fiction and fantasy in both paperback and hardcover formats. Forge Books, an imprint of Tor, publishes nonfiction, thrillers, suspense, mysteries, historicals, and Westerns, targeted to the mainstream audience.

Recent Tor titles include *The Girl Who Heard Dragons* by Anne McCaffrey; *The Inconstant Moon* by Alaya Johnson; *Loco* by Rudy Rucker and Bruce Sterling; and *Cat in a Vegas Gold Vendetta* by Carole Nelson Douglas.

Direct query letters and SASEs to:

Bob Gleason, Editor—Fiction, thriller, mystery and crime fiction, fantasy.

David Hartwell, Editor—Science fiction, fantasy, general fiction.

Melissa Singer, Editor—Science fiction, fantasy.

Paul Stevens, Editor—Science fiction, fantasy, thrillers.

Jim Frenkel, Editor—Science fiction.

FORGE

The Forge imprint publishes a wide range of fiction, including a strong line of historical novels and thrillers, plus mysteries, women's fiction, and a variety of nonfiction titles. Forge has also become a leading modern publisher of American Westerns.

Recent Forge titles include *Angel* by Nicole "Coco" Marrow and Laura Hayden;

Kings of Vice by Ice-T and Mal Radcliff; *Hell on Earth: The Wildfire Pandemic* by David L. Porter; *A City of Broken Glass* (Hannah Vogel) by Rebecca Cantrell; and *Castro's Daughter* (Kirk Mcgarvey) by David Hagberg.

Bob Gleason, Editor—Thrillers and aliens.

Kristin Sevick, Editor—Fiction.

Claire Eddy, Editor—Historical fiction.

NEWS CORPORATION

News Corporation is a worldwide media and entertainment corporation with subsidiaries that include HarperCollins, one of the world's largest English-language publishers. News Corp. founder Rupert Murdoch turned his family's business into a multinational media corporation, which now has 51,000 employees and annual revenues in excess of $33 billion.

News Corp.'s $61 billion in assets include Fox Broadcasting, Twentieth Century Fox, Blue Sky Studios, the *New York Post*, many radio stations, newspapers, magazines, and the National Rugby League.

HARPERCOLLINS PUBLISHERS
HARPERCOLLINS GENERAL BOOKS GROUP
HARPERCOLLINS CHILDREN'S BOOKS GROUP
HARPERCOLLINS CHRISTIAN PUBLISHING
HARPERONE

HarperCollins publishes a diverse list of commercial, trade, professional, academic, and mass-market books in hardcover, paperback, and multimedia editions—fiction, nonfiction, poetry, history, reference, business, children's books, cookbooks, romance, mystery, art, and style. If the subject exists, there's likely a HarperCollins title representing it, or will be very soon.

The company was formed by the merger of two esteemed publishers: Harper and Row, and William Collins and Sons. Harper and Row (founded in 1817) was an early publisher of Mark Twain, the Brontë sisters, and Charles Dickens. In the United Kingdom, William Collins and Sons, founded in 1819, published H. G. Wells, C. S. Lewis, and Agatha Christie. HarperCollins formed when News Corp. acquired both of these publishers in 1987 and 1990. The publisher has continued to expand with subsequent acquisitions including Avon Books and William Morrow.

Recent changes at HarperCollins include the 2012 acquisition of Thomas Nelson, one of the largest publishers of religious books. Thomas Nelson will be integrated with the Zondervan imprint into a new division, the HarperCollins Christian Publishing unit; however, the two imprints will maintain distinct identities.

Recent HarperCollins best sellers include *American Sniper* by Chris Kyle; *The Pioneer Woman Cooks: Food from My Frontier* by Ree Drummond; *It Worked for Me* by Colin Powell; and *Portrait of a Spy* by Daniel Silva.

HarperCollins has publishing groups in the United States, Canada, the United Kingdom, Australia/New Zealand, and India. The company has revenues that top $1 billion annually, serves an enormous audience, and provides a home for hundreds of authors—from debut novelists like Bryan Charles (*Grab On to Me Tightly as if I Knew the Way*) to former Secretary of State Madeleine Albright (*The Mighty and the Almighty*).

For submissions to all imprints, please note that HarperCollins Publishers prefers material submitted by literary agents and previously published authors.

HARPERCOLLINS GENERAL BOOKS GROUP

AMISTAD PRESS
AVON
AVON IMPULSE
AVON INSPIRE
AVON RED
BROADSIDE BOOKS
ECCO
HARPER
HARPER DESIGN
HARPER PERENNIAL
IT BOOKS
NEWMARKET PRESS
WILLIAM MORROW

10 East 53rd Street, New York, NY 10022-5299
212-207-7000
www.harpercollins.com | Twitter: @harpercollins

HarperCollins is a publisher with strengths in a broad range of literary and commercial fiction, business books, cookbooks, mystery, romance, reference, religious, and spiritual books. The company has revenues that top $1 billion annually.

In 2009, the Collins imprint was closed and integrated its operations with the rest of the company. The Collins general nonfiction list is now published under Harper; Collins Design and Collins Business are now published as Harper Design and Harper Business. Collins trade paperbacks have been folded into Harper Perennial and Harper paperbacks.

HarperCollins has three blogs, which will be useful to check for insider tips and information. One of the blogs, called Publishing Insider, is from marketing guru Carl Lennertz and is at publishinginsider.typepad.com. The Harper Perennial blog, named after their oval-shaped logo, is The Olive Reader, at www.olivereader.com. The HarperCollins poetry blog, called Cruelest Month, is at cruelestmonth.typepad.com. Many of the imprints also have Twitter accounts and Facebook pages.

AMISTAD PRESS

In operation for almost 40 years, Amistad Press is the oldest New York press dedicated to producing books for the African American market. Amistad Press publishes works by and about people of African descent on subjects and themes that have significant influence on the intellectual, cultural, and historical perspectives of a world audience.

Recent titles include *A Cupboard Full of Coats* by Yvvette Edwards; *Escaping the Delta: Robert Johnson and the Invention of the Blues* by Elijah Wald; *All the Right Stuff* by Walter Dean Myers; *By Love Possessed: Stories* by Lorna Goodison; *American Tapestry: The Ancestors of Michelle Obama* by Rachel L. Swarns; and *Lone Bean* by Chudney Ross.

AVON

Founded in 1941, Avon Books is the second-oldest paperback publishing house in the US Acquired by HarperCollins in 1999, Avon publishes titles for adults and young readers. It is recognized for pioneering the historical romance category and continues to produce commercial literature for the broadest possible audience in mass-market paperback format. In trade paperback, Avon Trade focuses on contemporary romance and other chick-lit titles. An imprint called Avon Red publishes steamy erotic romance. Avon Inspire publishes Christian fiction for women, and is run from HarperOne in San Francisco. A new imprint launched in 2011, Avon Impulse, is dedicated to publishing digital titles.

Recent Avon titles include *Night of Fire* by Nico Rosso; *Dark Desire* by Christine Freeman; *The Love Potion* by Sandra Hill; *Lessons from a Scandalous Bride: Forgotten Princesses* by Sophie Jordan; and *The Cowboy and the Princess* by Lori Wilde.

Avon Books is actively seeking imaginative stories that can establish new voices in historical and contemporary romance, romantic suspense, and African American romance. Detailed manuscript and submission guidelines are available online or by written request with SASE.

Send a brief query with no more than a two-page description of the book. Avon editors prefer e-mail queries with the word "Query" in the subject line. You will receive a response one way or another within approximately six to eight weeks. The e-mail address is: avonromance@harpercollins.com. To query by mail, be sure to include an SASE.

Lucia Macro, Editor—Women's fiction, romance.

Erika Tsang, Executive Editor—Romance, self-help for women.

Esi Sogah, Editor—Romance, paranormal, women's fiction.

Tessa Woodward, Editor—Women's fiction, mysteries, romance.

May Chen, Editor—Romance.

BROADSIDE BOOKS

Launched in 2010, Broadside Books specializes in conservative nonfiction writing. Broadside publishes works covering the full range of serious right-of-center thought and opinion—in hardcover, paperback, and e-book formats. The imprint prides itself on discovering new writers and younger talent as it seeks to create a forum for cutting-edge conservative ideas. Broadside authors seek to redefine and reinvigorate the conservative tradition.

Recent titles include *Bumper Sticker Liberalism* by Mark Goldblatt; *What the (Bleep) Just Happened?* by Monica Crowley; *Spoiled Rotten* by Jay Cost; *Ron Paul's rEVOLution* by Brian Doherty; and *Still the Best Hope* by Dennis Prager.

Adam Bellow, Editor

ECCO

Ecco publishes approximately 60 titles per year by such critically acclaimed authors as John Ashbery, Paul Bowles, Italo Calvino, Gerald Early, Louise Glück, Robert Hass, Zbigniew Herbert, Erica Jong, Cormac McCarthy, Czeslaw Milosz, Joyce Carol Oates, Josef Skvorecky, Mark Strand, and Tobias Wolff. The imprint has also created a number of literary series that enjoy a special celebrity in the world of book publishing.

Recent titles include *You & Me* by Padgett Powell; *Higgs Discovery: The Power of Empty Space* by Lisa Randall; *5 Stories and a Piece of You & Me* by Padgett Powell; *Lost Memory of Skin* by Russell Banks; and *Up Jumps the Devil* by Michael Poore.

Query letters and SASEs should be directed to:

Daniel Halpern, Editor-in-Chief—Fiction, memoirs, food cooking, biography.

Lee Boudreaux, Editorial Director—Fiction, horror.

Hilary Redmon, Editor—Science, history, current affairs, animals.

Libby Edelson, Editor—Fiction, cooking, musician biographies.

Bill Strachan, Editor-at-Large—Narrative histories.

HARPER

Harper produces adult hardcover books, trade paperbacks, and mass-market paperback editions that cover the breadth of trade publishing categories, including feature biographies (celebrities, sports, and historical), business, mysteries and thrillers, popular culture, humor, inspiration, and how-to (including cookbooks and health), in addition to works in most reference categories. The editors strive to find books that come from the heart of our literary, popular, and intellectual culture.

Best-selling authors include Milan Kundera, Michael Chabon, Barbara Kingsolver, Michael Crichton, Dr. Laura Schlessinger, Emeril Lagasse, Tony Hillerman, Barbara Taylor Bradford, Louise Erdrich, Anne Rivers Siddons, and Ursula K. Le Guin.

Recent fiction books include *Carnival of Souls Sneak Peek* by Melissa Marr; *Stanley in Space* by Jeff Brown; *Beautiful Days: A Bright Young Things Novel* by Anna Godbersen; *No Escape* by Michelle Gagnon; and *Endlessly Unabridged* by Kiersten White.

Direct queries and SASEs to:

Claire Wachtel, Executive Editor—Mysteries, contemporary narratives, biographies.

Terry Karten, Editor—Fiction, biography, memoirs.
Gail Winston, Editor—Psychology, health, parenting.
Jennifer Barth, Editor—Biography, current affairs, fiction.
Johnathan Burnham, Editor—Fiction, memoirs, current affairs.
Iris Tupholme, Editor—Fiction.
Karen Rinaldi, Editor—Health.
Michael Signorelli, Editor—Fiction, memoirs, narratives.
Barry Harbaugh, Editor—Fiction, current affairs.

HARPER BUSINESS

Harper Business titles formerly were published under the Collins Business name. Following the dissolution of Collins, Harper Business has incorporated Collins Business. Some titles include *Guerrilla P.R. 2.0* by Michael Levine; *The Great Reset* by Richard Florida; *Multipliers* by Liz Wiseman; *Brainsteering: The Breakthrough Approach to Developing More and Better Ideas of Any Kind* by Kevin and Shawn Coyne; *Talespin* by Larry Kramer; and *Beta* by Jeff Jarvis.

    Hollis Heimbouch, Vice President and Publisher

HARPER PERENNIAL
HARPER PERENNIAL MODERN CLASSICS

Home of such esteemed and award-winning authors as Barbara Kingsolver, Ann Patchett, Howard Zinn, and Harper Lee, Harper Perennial has been publishing fiction, nonfiction, and the classics for nearly 50 years. Perennial's broad range varies from Matt Groening's *The Simpsons* to Thomas Moore's *Care of the Soul*. A trade paperback format imprint, Harper Perennial publishes fiction and nonfiction originals and reprints.

    Titles representative of Perennial's list include *Border to Border* by Kevin Moffett; *The Party* by Richard McGregor; *Redeemers* by Enrique Krauze; *How to Be a Woman* by Caitlin Moran; and *The Thread* by Victoria Hislop.

    All division editors are eligible to acquire original titles for the paperback program.

HARPER PERENNIAL MODERN CLASSICS

The Harper Perennial Modern Classics imprint is home to many great writers and their most significant works. Featuring classic books from writers as diverse as Richard Wright, Harper Lee, Thomas Pynchon, Aldous Huxley, Sylvia Plath, and Thornton Wilder, Harper Perennial Modern Classics is the foundation stone for Harper Perennial itself. The Harper Perennial Modern Classics line is being expanded to include more contemporary classics.

    Recent titles include *Maggie-Now: A Novel* by Betty Smith; *The Illustrated Man* by Ray Bradbury; *Zelda: A Biography* by Nancy Milford; *The Sheltering Sky* by Paul Bowles; and *The Betsy-Tacy Treasury: The First Four Betsy-Tacy Books* by Maud Hart Lovelace.

IT BOOKS

It Books, founded in March 2009, focuses on pop culture, sports, style, and entertainment. HarperEntertainment's pending titles have been merged into the imprint. Some upcoming titles include *Not Young, Still Restless* by Jeanne Cooper; *Power Chord* by Thomas Scott McKenzie; *Radioactive Man* by Matt Groening; *The Burning House* by Foster Huntington; and *Wayne of Gotham* by Tracy Hickman.

Denise Oswald, Editor—Music, pop culture, celebrity narratives, memoirs and biographies.

Carrie Thorton, Editor—Music, celebrity narratives, memoirs, biographies.

Jennifer Schuster, Editor—Pop culture themes with photos and art.

NEWMARKET PRESS

Publisher Esther Margolis first launched Newmarket Press in 1981; the press ran independently until its acquisition by HarperCollins in 2011. Newmarket focuses on the areas of film, theater, and performing arts—publishing illustrated book counterparts for movies such as *The Matrix*, *Saving Private Ryan*, and *Moulin Rouge*.

Recent titles include *Titanic and the Making of James Cameron* by Paula Parisi; *Hugo: The Shooting Script* (Newmarket Shooting Script) by John Logan; and *Anonymous and the Shakespeare Authorship Question: The Theories, the Contenders, and the Evidence* by Paul Sugarman et al.

Esther Margolis, Publisher

WILLIAM MORROW

William Morrow, acquired in 1999 by HarperCollins Publishing, is one of the nation's leading publishers of general trade books, including bestselling fiction, non-fiction, and cookbooks.

William Morrow has an 80-year legacy of bringing fiction and nonfiction to the broadest possible audience, including works from bestselling authors Bruce Feiler, Neil Gaiman, Dennis Lehane, Neal Stephenson, John Grogan, Elmore Leonard, Ray Bradbury, Steven Levitt and Stephen J. Dubner, Susan Elizabeth Phillips, Christopher Moore, Sena Jeter Naslund, James Rollins, and Cokie Roberts.

Recent titles include *Under the Olive Tree* by Courtney Miller Santo; *Judgment Call* by J. A. Jance; *Hints of Heloise: Three Stories* by Laura Lippman; *Have Mother, Will Travel* by Claire Fontaine and Mia Fontaine; and *The Great Escape* by Susan Elizabeth Phillips.

Direct query letters and SASEs to:

(As is common practice, Harper, Morrow, and their respective divisions liberally share editors.)

Jennifer Brehl, Senior Vice President—High level fiction, celebrity books.

Henry Ferris, Executive Editor—Nonfiction narrative, history, fiction.

David Highfill, Executive Editor—Fiction, thriller, suspense, nonfiction narratives.

Cassie Jones, Executive Editor—Diet, cooking, health.
Katherine Nintzel, Editor—Fiction.
Peter Hubbard, Editor—General nonfiction, science, politics, current affairs, history, military, celebrity narratives.
Carrie Feron, Editor—Women's fiction, romance, crime fiction.
Matt Harper, Editor—Music, sports, celebrity biographies and narratives.
Rachel Kahan, Editor—Fiction.
Lisa Sharkey, Editor—Music/sports/celebrity biographies and memoirs.
Adam Korn, Editor—Music/celebrity memoirs.
Lynn Grady, Editor—Music/celebrity memoirs.
Emily Krump, Editor—Fiction.

HARPERCOLLINS CHILDREN'S BOOKS GROUP

BALZER AND BRAY
GREENWILLOW BOOKS
HARPERCOLLINS CHILDREN'S BOOKS
HARPERFESTIVAL
HARPERTEEN
HARPERTROPHY
HARPERVOYAGER
KATHERINE TEGEN BOOKS
WALDEN POND PRESS
1350 Avenue of the Americas, New York, NY 10019
212-261-6500
www.harpercollinschildrens.com
www.harperteen.com

The broad range of imprints within HarperCollins Children's Group reflects the strength of the house as it both embraces new markets and values traditional literature for children. This group is impressively successful and has been cited as being responsible for much of the publishing house's recent growth.

BALZER AND BRAY

Balzer and Bray is the eponymous imprint of Donna Bray and Alessandra Balzer, who were formerly editorial director and executive editor respectively at Hyperion. The imprint debuted in 2009 and publishes across the spectrum of children's literature, from picture books to young adult.

Some upcoming titles include *My Brave Year of Firsts* by Jamie Lee Curtis; *Chloe* by Peter McCarty; *Never Fall Down* by Patricia McCormick; *Ungifted* by Gordon Korman; and *Jake and Lily* by Jerry Spinelli.

Donna Bray, Copublisher—Middle-grade children's literature, young adult, children's picture books.

Alessandra Balzer, Copublisher—Middle-grade children's literature, young adult.

Kristin Daly Rens, Editor—Young adult.

GREENWILLOW BOOKS

Greenwillow, founded in 1974, publishes books in hardcover and library bindings for children of all ages. They strive for books filled with emotion, honesty, and depth, books that have something to say to children and an artful way of saying it.

Recent titles that are representative of the Greenwillow list include *It's Time for Preschool!* by Esme Raji Codell; *Blackwatch (The Secrets of Wintercraft)* by Jenna Burtenshaw; *Frank and Tank: Lost at Sea* by Sharon Phillips Denslow; *Amelia Bedelia, Cub Reporter* by Herman Parish; and *The Shadow Cats: A Girl of Fire and Thorns Story* by Rae Carson.

Virginia Duncan, Vice-President, Publisher—Young adult, picture books.

Martha Mihalick, Editor—Young adult.

HARPERCOLLINS CHILDREN'S BOOKS

HarperCollins Children's Books is known worldwide for its tradition of publishing quality books in hardcover, library binding, and paperback for children, from toddlers through teens. This imprint also releases several successful series, such as *I Can Read*, *Math Start*, and *Let's Read and Find Out*, plus seemingly nonstop titles from authors Meg Cabot and Lemony Snicket.

Titles representative of this list are *A Hat Full of Sky* by Terry Pratchett; *Two Times the Fun* by Beverly Cleary, illustrated by Carol Thompson; *Ten Go Tango* by Arthur Dorros; *I'm Not Going to Chase the Cat Today!* by Jessica Harper; *The Princess Diaries* by Meg Cabot; *Arabat: Days of Magic, Nights of War* by Clive Barker; and *A Series of Unfortunate Events* by Lemony Snicket.

Recent releases include *Arise* by Tara Hudson; *Big Nate Fun Blaster* by Lincoln Peirce; *A Midsummer Tights Dream* by Louise Rennison; *The Ingo Chronicles: Ingo* by Helen Dunmore; and *Harry the Poisonous Centipede's Big Adventure* by Lynne Reid Banks.

Send query letters and SASEs to:

Maria Modugno, Editorial Director—Picture books.

Anne Hoppe, Executive Editor—Young adult and middle grade.

Barbara Lalicki, Editor—Middle grade and young adult.

Phoebe Yeh, Editor—Middle grade, young adult, picture books.

Rosemary Brosnan, Editor—Young adult, middle grade.

Andrew Harwell, Editor—Young adult, middle grade.

HARPERFESTIVAL

HarperFestival is home to books, novelties, and merchandise for the very young: children up to six years of age. Classic board books, such as *Goodnight Moon* and *Runaway Bunny*, established the list over ten years ago. Today, Harper Festival produces a wide range of novelty and holiday titles as well as character-based programs such as Biscuit, Little Critter, and the Berenstain Bears.

Recent books include *Mia: Time to Trick or Treat!* by Robin Farley; *Pinkalicious: Purpledoodles* by Victoria Kann; *The Berenstain Bears' Dinosaur Dig* by Jan and Mike Berenstain; *Batman Classic: Batman and the Toxic Terror* by Jodi Huelin; and *Little Critter: Just Big Enough* by Mercer Mayer.

HARPERTEEN

HarperTeen produces original titles and previously published books in both hardcover and paperback formats, as well as original titles for young adults. In addition to typical teen fare, HarperTeen regularly publishes fiction that deals with difficult personal and social issues like the death of a parent or senseless violence. The imprint has published such authors as Meg Cabot, Walter Dean Myers, Louise Rennison, Chris Crutcher, and Joyce Carol Oates.

Recent titles include *Endlessly (Paranormalcy)* by Kiersten White; *Drain You* by M. Beth Bloom; *The Lying Game #2: Never Have I Ever* by Sara Shepard; *Cruise Control* by Terry Trueman; and *Alex Van Helsing: The Triumph of Death* by Jason Henderson.

Sarah Landis, Editor—Young adult.
Kari Southerland, Editor—Young adult.

HARPERTROPHY

HarperTrophy is a leading paperback imprint for children, producing original fiction and nonfiction, as well as paperback reprints of previously published titles. From picture books by Maurice Sendak to novels by Laura Ingalls Wilder, E. B. White, Katherine Paterson, and Beverly Cleary, Trophy continues its tradition of offering a broad list of the old and the new.

Recent titles include *Mittens at School* by Lola M. Schaefer; *Monster School: First Day Frights* by Dave Keane; *A Birthday for Frances* by Russell Hoban; *Fairest* by Gail Carson Levine; and *Gilbert and the Lost Tooth* by Diane deGroat.

HARPERVOYAGER

Previously known as Eos—the press was rebranded in 2010—HarperVoyager offers exciting and innovative titles for the young-adult science fiction and fantasy reader. The books are intended to be engaging enough to appeal to adults and include *Fire-us* trilogy by Jennifer Armstrong and Nancy Butche; *The Books of Magic*

PUBLISHING CONGLOMERATES

by Hillari Bell; and *Sacred Sacrament* by Sherryl Jordan, author of several critically acclaimed and award-winning books including *The Raging Quiet*, a School Library Journal Best Book and ALA Best Book for Young Adults.

Recent HarperVoyager books include *Aloha from Hell* by Richard Kadrey; *The Steel Queen* by Karen L. Azinger; *Jack Cloudie* by Stephen Hunt; *Kill the Dead* by Richard Kadrey; and *Insatiable* by Meg Cabot.

Direct query letters and SASEs to:

Diana Gill, Executive Editor—Thriller, science fiction, fantasy.

KATHERINE TEGEN BOOKS

This imprint is looking for books made from stories that entertain, inform, and capture the excitement and emotions of children's lives. Katherine Tegen is a publisher who believes that "narratives created through memorable characters and original voices are the most powerful way to connect the reader with the experience of growing up in our world." The editors buy fantasy, middle-grade, and young-adult fiction, as well as picture books.

Recent titles include *Destiny* by Gillian Shields; *Walls Within Walls* by Maureen Sherry; *Fins Are Forever* by Tera Lynn Childs; *The Lost Code: Book One of the Atlanteans* by Kevin Emerson; and *The Magnificent 12: The Trap* by Michael Grant.

Direct queries and SASEs to:

Katherine Tegen, Publisher

WALDEN POND PRESS

A collaboration between HarperCollins and Walden Media, Walden Pond Press launched in 2010. The imprint aims to publish the next generation of middle-grade classics—seeking fast-paced, funny, engaging, compulsively readable stories.

Titles include *Guys Read: The Sports Pages* by Dan Gutman et al.; *The Mask of Destiny (Archer Legacy)* by Richard Newsome; *The Fourth Stall Part II* by Chris Rylander; *Juniper Berry* by M. P. Kozlowsky; and *The Hero's Guide to Saving Your Kingdom* by Christopher Healy.

HARPERCOLLINS CHRISTIAN PUBLISHING

THOMAS NELSON
ZONDERVAN
ZONDERKIDZ

HarperCollins Christian Publishing is a new unit, launched in 2012, consolidating Zondervan with the newly acquired Thomas Nelson publishing group. The two publishers are far more than just imprints: Thomas Nelson, founded in 1798, was the largest independent Christian publisher in the world, and Zondervan is the world's largest publisher of Bibles. The acquisition prompted the Department of Justice to launch a year-long review, which declared the merger to be legal in August 2012. Things are still in flux, so be on the watch for changes in this massive new publishing entity.

ZONDERVAN

5300 Patterson Avenue SE, Grand Rapids, MI 49530
616-698-6900 | fax: 616-698-3454
www.zondervan.com | e-mail: submissions@zondervan.com

Zondervan Publishing House (founded in 1931) became a division of HarperCollins in 1988. Zondervan publishes both fiction and nonfiction Christian-oriented books and has frequently held multiple top-ten positions on the Christian Booksellers best-seller lists.

Zondervan is publisher of the 20-million-copy best seller *The Purpose-Driven Life: What on Earth Am I Here For?* by Rick Warren, as well as other notable titles like *The Myth of a Christian Nation: How the Quest for Political Power Is Destroying the Church* by Gregory A. Boyd; *Boundaries* by Dr. Henry Cloud and Dr. John Townsend; and *The Case for Christ: A Journalist's Personal Investigation of Evidence for Jesus* by Lee Strobel.

Zondervan also publishes faith-based fiction for adults and children including *Faithgirlz* series for nine- to twelve-year-olds and the *Kanner Lake* series for adults.

Although Zondervan specializes in publishing Bibles and books, the house also produces a wide variety of resources, including audio books, e-books, videos, and inspirational gifts. The company sells its products through its different brands: Zondervan, Zonderkidz, Zondervan Academic, and Editorial Vida.

As the world's largest Bible publisher, Zondervan holds exclusive publishing rights to the New International Version of the Bible—the most popular translation of the Bible—and has distributed more than 150 million copies worldwide. Zondervan publishes approximately 50 Bible products, 150 books, 80 gifts, and 50 new media products each year.

Recent titles include *Who Is This Man?: The Unpredictable Impact of the Inescapable Jesus* by John Ortberg; *Christian Apologetics: An Anthology of Primary Sources* by Chad V. Meister; *Game Plan for Life* by Joe Gibbs; *Four Views on the Apostle Paul (Counterpoints: Bible and Theology)* by Michael F. Bird, et al.; and *The Dark Side of the Supernatural* by Bill Myers and David Wimbish.

Currently Zondervan is only seeking manuscripts in academic, reference, and ministry resources categories. Zonderkidz is not currently accepting unsolicited manuscripts.

Direct queries and SASEs to:

Sue Brower, Editor—Inspiration fiction, Christian romance.

Jacque Alberta, Editor—Young adult, middle grade.

Carolyn McCready, Editor—Inspirational fiction and nonfiction, lifestyles, cooking.

ZONDERKIDZ

Zonderkidz was formed in 1998 to represent the children's and juvenile division at Zondervan. Zonderkidz is now the leading publisher of children's Bibles, children's Christian books, and other related products.

Titles include *Speed to Glory: The Cullen Jones Story* by Natalie Davis Mille; *K Is for Kite: God's Springtime Alphabet* by Kathy-jo Wargin; *Aldo's Fantastical Movie Palace* by Jonathan Friesen; *NIV Teen Study Bible* by Lawrence O. Richards and Sue W. Richards; and *Voices of Christmas* by Nikki Grimes.

HARPER ONE

353 Sacramento Street, Suite 500, San Francisco, CA 94111
415-477-4400

In 2007, HarperSanFrancisco changed its name to HarperOne to completely dispel the idea that it is a regional publisher. This imprint publishes books important and subtle, large and small, titles that explore the full range of spiritual and religious literature. It releases about 85 titles annually, with a backlist of some 800 titles.

HarperOne strives to be the preeminent publisher of the most important books across the spectrum of religion, spirituality, and personal growth, with authors who are the world's leading voices of wisdom, learning, faith, change, hope, and healing.

By respecting all spiritual traditions, the editors strive to offer their readers paths leading to personal growth and well-being. In addition to traditional religious titles, HarperOne publishes inspirational fiction—including their classic titles *The Alchemist* by Paulo Coehlo; *The Heart of Christianity: Rediscovering a Life of Faith* by Marcus J. Borg; *God's Politics: Why the Right Gets It Wrong and the Left Doesn't Get It* by Jim Wallis; *The Essential Rumi* by Coleman Banks; *The Right Questions: Ten Essential Questions to Guide You to an Extraordinary Life* by Debbie Ford; and *The World's Religions* by Huston Smith.

Recent titles representative of this list include *Awakening the Heroes Within: Twelve Archetypes to Help Us Find Ourselves and Transform Our World* by Carol S. Pearson; *Fierce Medicine: Breakthrough Practices to Heal the Body and Ignite the Spirit* by Ana T. Forrest; and *Drops Like Stars: A Few Thoughts on Creativity and Suffering* by Rob Bell.

Query letters and SASEs should be directed to:

Gideon Weil, Executive Editor—Religion, spirituality, psychology, health.

Nancy Hancock, Editor—Fitness, diet, health.

Mark Tauber, Editor—Spiritual memoirs, health.

PEARSON

Pearson is an international media company based in the United Kingdom with businesses in education, business information, and consumer publishing. Pearson's 37,000 employees are in more than 70 countries, connecting a family of businesses that draws on common assets and shares a common purpose: to help customers live and learn. In addition to the Penguin Group, Pearson divisions include Pearson Education and the Financial Times Group.

The Penguin Group, with primary operations in the United Kingdom, Australia, the United States, and Canada, and smaller operations in South Africa and India, is led by CEO and Chairman John Makinson. The Penguin Group is the world's second-largest English-language trade book publisher.

PENGUIN GROUP (USA), INC.
PENGUIN PUTNAM ADULT DIVISION
PENGUIN PUTNAM YOUNG READERS DIVISION

Penguin Group (USA), Inc., is the US affiliate of the Penguin Group. Formed in 1996 as a result of the merger between Penguin Books USA and the Putnam Berkley Group, Penguin Group (USA), under the stewardship of CEO David Shanks, is a leading US adult and children's trade book publisher.

Penguin Group (USA) publishes under a wide range of prominent imprints and trademarks, among them Berkley Books, Dutton, Grosset & Dunlap, New American Library, Penguin, Philomel, G. P. Putnam's Sons, and Riverhead Books. The Penguin Group's roster of bestselling authors includes, among hundreds of others, Dorothy Allison, Nevada Barr, Saul Bellow, A. Scott Berg, Maeve Binchy, Harold Bloom, Sylvia Browne, Tom Clancy, Robin Cook, Patricia Cornwell, Catherine Coulter, Clive Cussler, Eric Jerome Dickey, Richard Paul Evans, Helen Fielding, Ken Follett, Sue Grafton, W. E. B. Griffin, Nick Hornby, Spencer Johnson, Jan Karon, Anne Lamott, James McBride, Terry McMillan, Arthur Miller, Jacqueline Mitchard, Toni Morrison, Kathleen Norris, Joyce Carol Oates, Robert B. Parker, Nora Roberts, John Sandford, Carol Shields, John Steinbeck, Amy Tan, Kurt Vonnegut, and the Dalai Lama.

In what continues as an endless stream of global consolidation, Penguin and Random House are in the process of merging their US operations.

PENGUIN PUTNAM ADULT DIVISION

ALPHA BOOKS
AMY EINHORN BOOKS
AVERY BOOKS
BERKLEY BOOKS
BLUE RIDER PRESS
CURRENT
DUTTON
GOTHAM BOOKS
HUDSON STREET PRESS
NEW AMERICAN LIBRARY/NAL
PAMELA DORMAN BOOKS
PENGUIN PRESS
PERIGEE BOOKS
PLUME
PORTFOLIO
G. P. PUTNAM'S SONS
RIVERHEAD BOOKS
SENTINEL
TARCHER
THE VIKING PRESS

375 Hudson Street, New York, NY 10014
212-366-2000 | fax: 212-366-2666
www.us.penguingroup.com | Twitter: @penguinusa | blog: thepenguinblog
.typepad.com

The Adult Division of Penguin Putnam has been a strong performer for many years. As Penguin USA President Susan Petersen Kennedy said, "It's very nice when both the economic side and the artistic side coincide."

The company has continued to perform well in a tough marketplace, with a very strong first half in 2011 which included bestselling titles such as Tom Clancy's *Against All Enemies*, *The Battle Hymn of the Tiger Mother* by Amy Chua and the hardcover, paperback, and e-book phenomenon *The Help*, which sold well over 2 million copies in the first six months of the year.

Authors should definitely check out the Penguin blog, where editors post the latest news from the company: new acquisitions, sneak previews from works in progress, industry gossip, and advice on how to get published. Although it comes from the UK editorial office, the blog offers insight into the day-to-day running of the company and how books are made.

Penguin Putnam houses www.PenguinClassics.com, an online community devoted to classic titles. In addition, Penguin Putnam resumed its *Pelican Shakespeare* series, which has remained one of the bestselling series of Shakespeare's plays since the line was introduced in the mid-1960s.

ALPHA BOOKS

800 E. 96th Street, Indianapolis, IN 46240
375 Hudson Street, New York, NY 10014
212-366-2000
www.idiotsguides.com | e-mail: submissions@idiotsguides.com

With the slogan "knowledge for life," Alpha Books publishes original nonfiction and how-to titles for adults who seek to learn new skills or otherwise enrich their lives. Alpha publishes the very popular series, *The Complete Idiot's Guides*.

With over 35 million copies sold, in 26 languages, *The Complete Idiot's Guides* is one of the world's most easily recognizable title series. Despite the dizzying success of the series, ideas and manuscripts are continually welcomed. Best-selling topics include personal finance, business, health/fitness, foreign language, New Age, and relationships.

A random selection of recent titles is *The Complete Idiot's Guide to Genealogy* by Fasg Rose; *The Complete Idiot's Guide to Using Your Computer—For Seniors* by Paul McFedries; *The Complete Idiot's Guide to Quick Total Body Workouts* by Tom Seabourne; and *The Complete Idiot's Guide to Google +* by Michael Miller.

Send electronic submissions with proposals as an e-mail attachment. Submit to the attention of the Editorial Coordinator in the Indianapolis office or at share @idiotsguides.com. Detailed submission guidelines are available on the website.

Mike Sanders, Editorial Director (IN office)
Tom Stevens, Acquisitions Editor (IN office)
Brook Fahrling, Editor (IN Office)

AMY EINHORN BOOKS

Amy Einhorn Books was founded in 2007 by Amy Einhorn and launched in February of 2009. The first title published in the imprint was the number-one *New York Times* best seller *The Help* by Kathryn Stockett, which sold more than 10 million copies in the United States and was made into an Academy Award–nominated movie. The imprint publishes fiction, narrative nonfiction, and commercial nonfiction. The overarching tenet of Amy Einhorn Books is intelligent writing with a strong narrative, always with great storytelling at its core. It seeks the perfect blend of literary and commercial.

Some new titles include *The Hypnotist's Love Story* by Liane Moriarty; *Faith Bass Darling's Last Garage Sale* by Lynda Rutledge; *The Gods of Gotham* by Lyndsay Faye; *Next Stop: A Memoir* by Glen Finland; and *Let's Pretend This Never Happened: (A Mostly True Memoir)* by Jenny Lawson.

Amy Einhorn, Vice President and Publisher—Memoir, fiction.

AVERY BOOKS

Avery's publishing program is dedicated primarily to complementary medicine, nutrition, and healthful cooking. It was established in 1976 as a college textbook publisher specializing in niche areas. Through a series of alliances, most notably with Hippocrates Health Institute, Avery began a program of health books by such authors as Ann Wigmore and Michio Kushi, whose work on macrobiotics helped propel the Avery list in the health food and alternative markets. The firm was acquired by the Penguin Group in 1999 and currently publishes 30 new titles per year. Avery's scope of titles has broadened to include psychology, inspirational memoir, and sociology.

In addition to producing original titles in hardcover and paperback formats, Avery has a backlist of several hundred titles in trade and mass-market formats that include works by pioneers in alternative healing, scientists, and health care professionals involved in cutting-edge research.

Titles representative of the Avery list are *Oh, Baby!: Pregnancy Tales and Advice from One Hot Mama to Another* by Tia Mowry; *Healthy Tipping Point: A Powerful Program for a Stronger, Happier You* by Caitlin Boyle; *The New Rules of Lifting For Life* by Lou Schuler and Alwyn Cosgrove; and *I Talk, You Walk* by Thomas P. Casselman.

Direct your query letter and SASE to:

Megan Newman, Vice President, Editorial Director—High-profile memoir, health, diet.

Lucia Watson, Editor—Cooking, relationships, parenting, health, psychology, lifestyle.

Rachel Holtzman, Editor—Narrative and prescriptive nonfiction, science, personal finance, self-help.

BERKLEY BOOKS
ACE BOOKS
BERKLEY PRIME CRIME
DAW
JOVE BOOKS

Berkley Books was founded in 1955 by a group of independent investors. The quiet but profitable company ran for ten years, and in 1965 was bought by G. P. Putnam's Sons, which in turn was bought by MCA ten years later. In 1982, Putnam bought Grosset & Dunlap and Playboy Press, and the Ace and Playboy lists were added to Berkley. The Playboy list was eventually absorbed into Berkley, while the Jove and Ace Lists have continued as distinct imprints.

Under the leadership of President and Publisher Leslie Gelbman, Berkley publishes more than 500 titles per year under their imprints, in mass-market paperback, trade paperback, hardcover, and multimedia formats.

Recent titles include *All the Truth* by Laura Brodie; *The Secret Crown* by Chris Kuzneski; *Haven* by Kay Hooper; *Gabriel's Inferno* by Sylvain Reynard; and *Dark Hunger* by Christine Feehan.

Direct query letters and SASEs to:

Natalee Rosenstein, Vice President, Senior Executive Editor—General fiction, mystery, thrillers, history, politics, military.

Cindy Hwang, Senior Editor—Women's fiction, romance.

Denise Silvestro, Executive Editor—Relationships, sex, spirituality.

Kate Seaver, Senior Editor—Fiction including paranormal romance, erotica, Berkley Heat.

Jackie Cantor, Editor—Women's fiction, romance, mysteries.

Leis Pederson, Editor—Women's fiction, romance.

Andie Avila, Editor—Popular/quirky reference, lifestyle, self-help.

Emily Rapoport, Assistant Editor—Fiction.

Wendy McCurdy, Editor—Women's fiction, romance.

Shannon Jamieson Vazquez, Editor—Mystery, true crime nonfiction.

Faith Black, Editor—Mystery, crime fiction.

Ginjer Buchanan, Editor—Science fiction, fantasy, horror, mystery and crime fiction.

Michelle Vega, Editor—Mysteries, crime fiction.

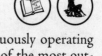

ACE BOOKS

Ace Books, founded in 1953 by A. A. Wyn, is the oldest continuously operating science-fiction publisher in the United States. Ace released some of the most outstanding science-fiction writers of the 1950s and 1960s, including Frank Herbert, William Gibson, Samuel R. Delany, Philip K. Dick, Ursula K. Le Guin, and Robert Silverberg.

Ace produces original titles in hardcover and mass-market paperback, as well as reprints previously published in hardcover and trade paperback fiction.

Recent titles include *Bared Blade* by Kelly McCullough; *The Apocalypse Codex* by Charles Stross; *Mad Men Yourself—A Gentleman's Guide to Personal Development* by Izzy Traub; *Prince of Thorns (The Broken Empire)* by Mark Lawrence; and *Gunmetal Magic: A Novel in the World of Kate Daniels* by Ilona Andrews.

Direct query letters and SASEs to:

Ginjer Buchanan, Editor-in-Chief—Science fiction, fantasy.

Anne Sowards, Editor—Science fiction and fantasy, young adult, paranormal fiction.

Jessica Wade, Editor—Science fiction, fantasy, mystery, crime.

Kat Sherbo, Editor—Science fiction, fantasy, thriller.

BERKLEY PRIME CRIME

Berkley Prime Crime publishes mystery and crime fiction. Some recent titles include *Naughty In Nice* by Rhys Bowen; *Peril in Paperback* by Kate Carlisle; *A Witch Before Dying* by Heather Blake; *When the Cookie Crumbles* by Virginia Lowell; and *Death of a Schoolgirl* by Joanna Campbell Slan.

Michelle Vega, Editor—Mystery and crime fiction.

Kate Seaver, Editor—Mysteries, paranormal.

PUBLISHING CONGLOMERATES

Faith Black, Editor—Mystery/crime fiction.
Sandy Harding, Editor—Mystery/crime fiction.

DAW

Founded in 1971 by veteran paperback editor Donald A. Wollheim, along with his wife, Elsie B. Wollheim, DAW Books was the first publishing company ever devoted exclusively to science fiction and fantasy. The press has debuted such authors as Tad Williams, C. J. Cherryh, Mercedes Lackey, Melanie Rawn, C.S. Friedman, Jennifer Roberson, and Tanith Lee.

Recent titles include *Libriomancer* by Jim C. Hine; *The Grass King's Concubine* by Kari Sperring; *Shadowlands* by Violette Malan; *Love on the Run* by Katharine Kerr; and *The Diviner* by Melanie Rawn.

Sheila Gilbert, Editor
Betsy Wollheim, Editor

JOVE BOOKS

Jove is the mass-market paperback imprint of the Berkley group. It originated as Pyramid Books, which was founded in 1949 by Alfred R. Plaine and Matthew Huttner, and was sold to the Walter Reade Organization in the late 1960s. In the early 1970s, Pyramid published the first four titles in John Jakes's popular Kent Family Chronicles. Harcourt Brace Jovanovich was looking for a paperback division, and in 1975, Pyramid was bought by HBJ and its name changed to Jove.

The Jove imprint has published such authors as Nora Roberts, Catherine Coulter, Steve Martini, Jayne Ann Krentz, Dick Francis, and W. E. B. Griffin.

Recent titles include *The Gunsmith #368: The University Showdown* by J. R. Roberts; *Samurai Game* by Christine Feehan; *Happy Ever After* by Nora Roberts; *Charmed By His Love* by Janet Chapman; and *Split Second (An FBI Thriller)* by Catherine Coulter.

BLUE RIDER PRESS

Blue Rider Press debuted in 2011 and publishes a mix of suspense fiction, popular biography, literary novels, humor, music, and contemporary politics. The imprint is named for Der Blaue Reiter an iconoclastic twentieth-century movement in music and painting that was determined to promote individual expression and break free of any conventional artistic restraints.

Recent titles include *The Empty Glass* by J.I. Baker; *The Watchers* by Jon Steele; *Swimming Studies* by Leanne Shapton; *It's the Middle Class, Stupid!* by James Carville and Stan Greenberg; and *Dial M for Murdoch: News Corporation and the Corruption of Britain* by Tom Watson and Martin Hickman.

Sarah Hochman, Editor—Memoirs.

David Rosenthal, Editor—Fiction, memoirs, current issues.
Vanessa Kehren, Editor—Memoirs, fiction.

CURRENT

Launched in 2010, Current publishes sciences books for a general audience. The imprint publishes five to eight titles a year that explore the newest and most powerful ideas in a wide range of scientific fields, from genetics to quantum physics to neuroscience.

Recent titles include *Biopunk: Solving Biotech's Biggest Problems in Kitchens and Garages* by Marcus Wohlsen; *The Man Who Lied to His Laptop: What We Can Learn About Ourselves from Our Machines* by Clifford Nass and Corina Yen; and *The Youth Pill: Scientists at the Brink of an Anti-Aging Revolution* by David Stipp.

Brooke Carey, Editor

DUTTON

Dutton dates back to 1852, when Edward Payson Dutton founded a bookselling firm, E. P. Dutton, in Boston. Dutton currently publishes about 40 hardcover titles per year, fiction and nonfiction; about one in four will hit the *New York Times* bestseller list each year.

Dutton authors include Ken Follett, Eckhart Tolle, Harlan Coben, Al Franken, Raymond Khoury, Eric Jerome Dickey, John Hodgman, John Lescroart, John Jakes, and Jenny McCarthy.

Recent titles include *Thirteen* by Kelley Armstrong; *Kill Decision* by Daniel Suarez; *Amelia Anne is Dead and Gone* by Kat Rosenfield; *Skin: A Mike Hammer Story* by Max Allan Collins; and *Murder in Mumbai: A Dutton Guilt Edged Mystery* by K. D. Calamur.

Direct query letters and SASEs to:

Brian Tart, President and Publisher—Fiction, thrillers, business stories, memoirs.
Stephen Morrow, Executive Editor—Entertaining books on serious subjects, popular science, economics, psychology, investigative journalism.
Ben Sevier, Editor-in-Chief—Fiction, mystery, crime fiction
Denise Roy, Senior Editor—Contemporary and historical fiction.
Jessica Horvath, Associate Editor—Fiction.
Jill Schwartzman, Executive Editor—Pop culture, humor, memoir, music.

GOTHAM BOOKS

Launched in 2001, The Gotham Books imprint strives for both commercial and literary success in its titles. This nonfiction imprint publishes 35 books per year. Its emphasis is on self-help, spirituality, business, sports, travel writing, biography, food, current affairs, health, humor, and narrative nonfiction. Its colophon, designed by Eric Baker of Eric Baker Designs, evokes a mythic skyscraper made of open books.

Representative titles include *Eats, Shoots & Leaves: The Zero Tolerance Approach to Punctuation* by Lynne Truss; *The Man Who Heard Voices: Or, How M. Night Shyamalan Risked His Career on a Fairy Tale* by Michael Bamberger; *Me and a Guy Named Elvis* by Jerry Schilling with Chuck Crisafulli; and *Curb Your Enthusiasm: The Book* by Deirdre Dolan.

Recent releases include *A Golden Voice: How Faith, Hard Work, and Humility Brought Me from the Streets to Salvation* by Ted Williams; *Thoughts without Cigarettes: A Memoir* by Oscar Hijuelos; *The Rules of the Tunnel: My Brief Period of Madness* by Ned Zema; *Nerd Do Well: A Small Boy's Journey to Becoming a Big Kid* by Simon Pegg; and *Big Day Coming: Yo La Tengo and the Rise of Indie Rock* by Jesse Jarnow.

Direct query letters and SASEs to:

Lauren Marino, Executive Editor—Celebrity memoirs, humorous narratives, business, pop culture, food, travel, style.

Patrick Mulligan, Editor—Narrative nonfiction, history, sports, music, pop culture, humor.

Bill Shinker, Publisher—Memoir, sports, general nonfiction, business, careers, self-help, golf.

HUDSON STREET PRESS

Hudson Street Press's list was launched in the winter of 2005. Hudson Street focuses on narrative and practical nonfiction: memoirs, biography, sex, self-help, relationships, money, women's issues, health/diet, science, and popular history.

Hudson Street Press looks for books exploring issues that keep people up at night and for voice-driven narratives with emotional resonance. Its mission is to publish authors who bring a new perspective or a unique voice to the traditionally successful nonfiction categories. It publishes approximately 30 books per year.

Recent titles include *Words Can Change Your Brain: 12 Conversation Strategies to Build Trust, Resolve Conflict, and Increase Intimacy* by Andrew Newberg; *Man of War* by Charlie Schroeder; *Emotional Chaos to Clarity* by Phillip Moffitt; and *The First 20 Minutes* by Gretchen Reynolds.

Caroline Sutton, Editor-in-Chief—Science nonfiction, health, parenting, religion and spirituality, business and investing, relationship advice.

NEW AMERICAN LIBRARY/NAL
OBSIDIAN MYSTERIES
ONYX
ROC
SIGNET

Kurt Enoch and Victor Weybright, two former Penguin editors, started the New American Library—popularly known as NAL—in 1948. With Signet and

Mentor as their leading imprints, NAL published titles such as William Faulkner's *Sanctuary*, D. H. Lawrence's *Lady Chatterley's Lover*, John Steinbeck's *Tortilla Flat*, James Jones's *From Here to Eternity*, and, later, the popular fiction of Ian Fleming and Mickey Spillane.

NAL publishes a diverse and exciting range of paperback books, including *New York Times* best sellers by Maeve Binchy, Stuart Woods, John Lescroart, Ken Follett, Sylvia Browne, Catherine Coulter, Greg Iles, and John Jakes. Under the Signet, Onyx, and Roc imprints, NAL publishes both fiction and nonfiction, with trade paperback and hardcover programs in addition to their core mass-market format. Its editors are looking for strong, innovative authors who offer distinctive voices and original ideas.

Recent titles include *The Elusive Mr. McCoy* by Brenda L. Baker; *Lethal Outlook: A Psychic Eye Mystery* by Victoria Laurie; *Kindred Spirits* by Sarah Strohmeyer; *In a Witch's Wardrobe: A Witchcraft Mystery* by Juliet Blackwell; and *How to Dine on Killer Wine: A Party-Planning Mystery* by Penny Warner.

For all of NAL, direct queries and SASEs to:

Claire Zion, Editorial Director—Fiction, women's fiction, paranormal, romance.

Ellen Edwards, Executive Editor—Fiction, romance, mystery, crime.

Tracy Bernstein, Executive Editor—Mystery, romance, self-help, lifestyle.

Mark Chait, Senior Editor—History, politics, humor, health, sports, true crime, public affairs.

Kerry Donovan, Associate Editor—Romance/women's fiction.

Brent Howard, Associate Editor—History.

Danielle Perez, Editor—Women's fiction.

Jhanteigh Kupihea, Editor—Romance/women's fiction.

Jessica Wade, Editor—Science fiction, paranormal fiction.

OBSIDIAN MYSTERIES

Obsidian Mysteries publishes mystery novels of all kinds. Some titles include *Death on a Platter* by Elaine Viets; *To Catch a Leaf* by Kate Collins; *Ink Flamingos* by Karen E. Olson; *The Fine Art of Murder* by Jessica Fletcher; and *A Parfait Murder* by Wendy Lyn Watson.

ONYX

Onyx produces mass-market and trade paperbacks, both reprints and originals. Titles representative of the list include *Lover Revealed: A Novel of the Black Dagger Brotherhood* by J. R. Ward; *Dead Past: A Diane Fallon Forensic Investigation* by Beverly Connor; *A Garden of Vipers* by Jack Kerley; *Unwound* by Jonathan Baine; and *Nothing but Trouble* by Michael McGarrity.

Recent titles include *Final Sins* by Michael Prescott; *The Duchess Diaries* by Jillian Hunter; *Nightborn: Lords of the Darkyn* by Lynn Viehl; *Silent Mercy* by Linda A. Fairstein; and *A Duke's Temptation* by Jillian Hunter.

ROC

Roc publishes science fiction and fantasy, reprints and originals, in hardcover, trade paperback, and mass-market formats.

Recent releases include *Downpour: A Greywalker Novel* by Kat Richardson; *Tin Swift: The Age of Steam* by Devon Monk; *Iron Gray Sea: Destroyermen* by Taylor Anderson; *Grave Memory: An Alex Craft Novel* by Kalayna Price; and *Dragon Rule: Book Five of the Age of Fire* by E.E. Knight.

Anne Sowards, Editor
Ginjer Buchanan, Editor

SIGNET

This imprint produces mass-market paperback reprints, as well as some original titles in mass-market paperback format.

Recent Signet titles include *Getting to Happy* by Terry McMillan; *Blood Before Sunrise: A Shaede Assassin Novel* by Amanda Bonilla; *How to Dine on Killer Wine: A Party-Planning Mystery* by Penny Warner; *The Bells of El Diablo* by Frank Leslie; and *Heart of Gold* by J. R. Ward.

Jesse Feldman, Editor

PAMELA DORMAN BOOKS

An editor at Viking for more than 20 years, Pamela Dorman has a reputation for spotting debut novels that sell millions of copies. Some of her titles include *Bridget Jones's Diary*, *The Secret Life of Bees*, *The Memory Keeper's Daughter*, and *The Deep End of the Ocean*. She has returned to Penguin in 2010 after a brief hiatus at Hyperion to head her own imprint.

Some upcoming titles include *Little Night: A Novel* by Luanne Rice; *The Dark Rose: A Novel* by Erin Kelly; *A Surrey State of Affairs: A Novel* by Ceri Radford; *Alice Bliss: A Novel* by Laura Harrington; and *The Last Letter from Your Lover: A Novel* by Jojo Moyes.

Pamela Dorman, Director

PENGUIN PRESS

Founded in 2003 and dedicated to publishing literary nonfiction and select fiction, this is an imprint that embraces new writers. Penguin Press publishes 40 titles a year, including those by authors Alan Greenspan, Al Gore, Thomas Pynchon, Ruth Reichl, and Nicholas Wade. In 2005, the Penguin Press introduced *The Penguin History of American Life*, a series of 50 books that range across all of American history.

Recent titles that are indicative of this list include *Can We Have Our Balls Back, Please?* by Julian Norridge; *The Twilight War: The Secret History of America's Thirty-Year Conflict with Iran* by David Crist; *Scotland's Empire* by T. M. Devine; *Where the*

Heart Beats: John Cage, Zen Buddhism, and the Inner Life of Artists by Kay Larson; and *The Odyssey of KP2: An Orphan Seal, a Marine Biologist, and the Fight to Save a Species* by Terrie M. Williams.

Direct query letters and SASEs to:

Ann Godoff, President, Publisher—Public affairs, history, politics, fiction.

Laura Stickney, Editor—Narrative nonfiction, politics, economics, science.

Colin Dickerman, Editor—Science, popular reference, fiction.

Andrea Walker, Editor—Fiction, memoir.

Scott Moyers, Editor—Sports, current affairs.

PERIGEE BOOKS

Perigee Books, originally created as the trade paperback imprint for G. P. Putnam's Sons, has expanded into hardcover as well as original paperback publishing. This imprint features an eclectic range of nonfiction titles including careers, decorating, cookbooks, parenting, health, fitness, relationships, self-help, humor, puzzles, and memoirs. This house also publishes the *52 Brilliant Ideas* how-to series with recent titles: *Discover Your Roots, Raising Pre-Teens, Land Your Dream Job, Defeat Depression*, and *Boost Your Heart Health*.

Other recent titles include *Our Valued Customers: Conversations from the Comic Book Store* by Tim Chamberlain; *Remembering Ritalin: A Doctor and Generation Rx Reflect on Life and Psychiatric Drugs* by Lawrence H. Diller; *F My Life World Tour: Life's Crappiest Moments from Around the Globe* by Maxime Valette and Guillaume Passaglia; and *Suffering Succotash* by Stephanie V.W. Lucianovic.

Direct query letters and SASEs to:

John Duff, Publisher—Self-help/how-to, health, popular psychology.

Marian Lizzi, Editor-in-Chief—Prescriptive nonfiction, health/fitness, parenting, relationships and communication, science.

Meg Leder, Editor—Pop culture, lifestyle, communications, fashion.

Jeanette Shaw, Editor—Cooking, lifestyle.

PLUME

Plume, founded in 1970 as the trade paperback imprint of New American Library, is now recognized as one of the preeminent trade paperback imprints.

Throughout its history, Plume has been dedicated to giving an opportunity to voices previously neglected by mainstream publishing. The pioneering program in multicultural literature, which began with Toni Morrison and Jamaica Kincaid, has expanded to include groundbreaking works by Latino, African American, and Asian American authors. Plume was also a pioneer in gay publishing, with such classics as Edmund White's *A Boy's Own Story* and Andrew Holleran's *Dancer from the Dance*, which built the foundation for an exceptional gay and lesbian publishing program.

Recent Plume titles include *Rush: Why We Thrive in the Rat Race* by Todd G.

Buchholz; *The Dyslexic Advantage: Unlocking the Hidden Potential of the Dyslexic Brain* by Brock L. Eide; *Rav Hisda's Daughter, Book I: Apprentice: A Novel of Love, the Talmud, and Sorcery* by Maggie Anton; *The Keeper of Lost Causes: A Department Q Novel* by Jussi Adler-Olsen; and *I'm Losing You: A Novel* by Bruce Wagner.

Direct query letters and SASEs to:

Becky Cole, Senior Editor—Health, mystery and crime fiction, pop culture, memoir, self-help.

Denise Roy, Editor—Fiction.

Kate Napolitano, Editor—Humor.

PORTFOLIO

Portfolio is an imprint that publishes business and career books exclusively. It publishes books in the fields of management, leadership, marketing, business narrative, investing, personal finance, economics, and career advice. The press produces 45 hardcover and 20 paperback titles a year.

Recent titles include *The Pumpkin Plan: A Simple Strategy to Grow a Remarkable Business in Any Field* by Mike Michalowicz; *Trust Me, I'm Lying: Confessions of a Media Manipulator* by Ryan Holiday; *Bought and Paid For: The Hidden Relationship Between Wall Street and Washington* by Charles Gasparino; *Malled: My Unintentional Career in Retail* by Caitlin Kelly; and *Eat People: And Other Unapologetic Rules for Game-Changing Entrepreneurs* by Andy Kessler.

Direct queries and SASEs to:

Adrian Zackheim, President and Publisher

Maria Gagliano, Editor

Joel Rickett, Editor

Emily Angell, Editor

Niki Papadopoulos, Editor

G. P. PUTNAM'S SONS

For over two decades, G. P. Putnam's Sons has led the publishing industry with more hardcover fiction and nonfiction *New York Times* best sellers than any other imprint in the publishing industry. The company began in 1838 when 24-year-old George Putnam joined with John Wiley in the firm Wiley & Putnam. Ten years later, when the two men parted ways, George went into business under his own name, where he published such luminaries as William Cullen Bryant, Thomas Carlyle, Samuel Taylor Coleridge, James Fenimore Cooper, Nathaniel Hawthorne, Washington Irving, and Edgar Allan Poe.

The press is also known for the taboo-breaking publications of 1955's *Deer Park* by Norman Mailer and Vladmir Nabokov's *Lolita* in 1958.

Recent titles include *Cold Fury* by T.M. Goeglein; *Mysteries According to Humphrey* by Betty G. Birney; *Juliet in August* by Dianne Warren; *Halfway to Perfect: A Dyamonde Daniel Book* by Nikki Grimes; and *The Renegades* by Tom Young.

Direct query letters with SASEs to:

Neil Nyren, Editor-in-Chief—Serious and commercial fiction and nonfiction.
Christine Pepe, Senior Editor—Fiction.
Ivan Held, President—Fiction.

RIVERHEAD BOOKS

Founded in 1994 by Susan Petersen Kennedy, Riverhead Books is now well established as a publisher of bestselling literary fiction and quality nonfiction.

Recent titles include *India Becoming: A Portrait of Life in Modern India* by Akash Kapur; *Beijing Welcomes You: Unveiling the Capital City of the Future* by Tom Scocca; *Jack 1939* by Francine Mathews; and *The Man Without a Face: The Unlikely Rise of Vladimir Putin* by Masha Gessen.

Direct query letters and SASEs to:

Jake Morrissey, Executive Editor—Narrative nonfiction, science, history, historical fiction, thrillers.
Sarah McGrath, Senior Editor—Fiction, food.
Megan Lynch, Senior Editor—Fiction, memoirs.
Laura Perciasepe, Associate Editor—Fiction.
Sara Stein, Editor—Memoir, fiction.

SENTINEL

Sentinel is a politically conservative imprint of Penguin, established in 2003. It has a mandate to publish right-of-center books on politics, history, public policy, culture, and religion. The imprint publishes ten to fifteen new titles per year, in both hardcover and paperback. The name Sentinel symbolizes a tough-minded defense of America's fundamental values and national interests.

Recent titles include *Keeping the Republic: Saving America by Trusting Americans* by Mitchell Elias Daniels; *The Tyranny of Cliches: How Liberals Cheat in the War of Ideas* by Jonah Goldberg; *Known and Unknown: A Memoir* by Donald Rumsfeld; *An American Son: A Memoir* by Senator Marco Rubio; and *Can't Is Not an Option: My American Story* by Nikki Haley.

Direct queries and SASEs to:

Adrian Zackheim, President and Publisher

TARCHER

Jeremy P. Tarcher was founded 35 years ago in Los Angeles, California, and was purchased by Putnam in 1991. The press publishes some 60 titles annually in both hardcover and paperback, covering a broad spectrum of topics that range from current affairs, social commentary, literary nonfiction, and creativity to spirituality/religion, health, psychology, parenting, business, and other topics. It has had numerous national best sellers including *Drawing on the Right Side of the Brain* and *Seven Years in Tibet*. Recent best sellers include *Quarterlife Crisis*; *Trust Us, We're Experts*; and *The Hard Questions*. Tarcher also produces paperback reprints of previously published titles.

Recent titles include *2012: The Return of Quetzalcoatl* by Daniel Pinchbeck; *Self-Healing with Reiki: How to Create Wholeness, Harmony & Balance for Body, Mind & Spirit* by Penelope Quest; *50 Ways to Play: BDSM for Nice People* by Don Macleod; and *The Not-So-Nude Ride of Lady Godiva: & Other Morsels of Misinformation from the History Books* by David Haviland.

Direct query letters and SASEs to:

Joel Fotinos, Publisher

Sara Carder, Editor—Practical nonfiction, narrative nonfiction, lifestyles, health, self-help.

THE VIKING PRESS

In 1925, Harold K. Guinzburg and George S. Oppenheimer founded The Viking Press in order "To publish a strictly limited list of good nonfiction, such as biography, history and works on contemporary affairs, and distinguished fiction with some claim to permanent importance rather than ephemeral popular interest."

The press has published many groundbreaking and influential authors, such as Mohandas Gandhi, Bertrand Russell, James Joyce, John Steinbeck, Arthur Miller, Jack Kerouac, William S. Burroughs, Hannah Arendt, Thomas Pynchon, Stephen King, Phillip Roth, Bruce Chatwin, Don DeLillo, Jorge Luis Borge, and J. M. Coetzee.

Recent titles include *Shadow of Night: A Novel* by Deborah Harkness; *Rabid: A Cultural History of the World's Most Diabolical Virus* by Bill Wasik; *Broken Harbor: A Novel* by Tana French; *Guide to the Beasts of East Africa* by Nicholas Drayson; and *A Year Up* by Gerald Chertavian.

PENGUIN PUTNAM YOUNG READERS DIVISION

DIAL BOOKS FOR YOUNG READERS
DUTTON CHILDREN'S BOOKS
FIREBIRD
FREDERICK WARNE
GROSSET & DUNLAP
PHILOMEL BOOKS
PUFFIN BOOKS
G. P. PUTNAM'S SONS CHILDREN'S BOOKS
RAZORBILL
VIKING CHILDREN'S BOOKS

345 Hudson Street, New York, NY 10014
212-414-3600

Penguin Putnam Books for Young Readers produces titles for children of all ages. This house offers an array of distinctive divisions, imprints, and affiliates of Penguin Putnam's component houses, including Dial Books for Young Readers, Dutton, Firebird, Grosset & Dunlap, Philomel, Puffin Books, G. P. Putnam's Children's Books, Razorbill, and Viking Children's Books. Together, these imprints produce a broad range of titles serving every market in children's book publishing.

DIAL BOOKS FOR YOUNG READERS

Dial Books for Young Readers is a hardcover trade children's book division publishing around 50 titles per year for children from preschool age through young adult, fiction and nonfiction titles. This Penguin Group (USA), Inc., imprint traces its roots to 1880 and the founding of *The Dial*, a monthly literary magazine that published such literary giants as e. e. cummings, T. S. Eliot, D. H. Lawrence, and Gertrude Stein.

Since the children's list was launched in 1961, Dial has been known for books of high literary merit and fine design for readers of all ages. It has pioneered books for the young, including the first quality board books published in the United States. Dial introduced its *Easy-to-Read* series in 1979 to publish full-color early readers with popular children's book authors and artists, including James Marshall, creator of the *Fox* series.

Recent titles include *This Monster Needs a Haircut* by Bethany Barton; *Olympig!* by Victoria Jamieson; *The Girl With Borrowed Wings* by Rinsai Rossetti; *Monkey See, Look at Me!* by Lorena Siminovich; and *What To Do If An Elephant Stands On Your Foot* by Michelle Robinson.

Dial Books for Young Readers accepts unsolicited manuscripts of entire picture books or the first ten pages of longer works, with cover letters. Do not include SASEs, as they will only contact within four months those authors they want to publish. All other submissions will be recycled without comment. Send submissions through the mail only to:

Lauri Hornik, Vice President and Publisher—Young adult, children's picture books, middle grade.

Kathy Dawson, Associate Editorial Director—Young adult, fantasy.

Kate Harrison, Senior Editor—Middle grade, young adult, graphic novels, picture books.

Nancy Conescu, Editor—Middle grade, picture books.

Jessica Garrison, Editor—Young adult.

Liz Waniewski, Editor—Picture books, middle grade.

Heather Alexander, Editor—Middle grade, young adult.

Jennifer Bailey Hunt, Editor—Young adult.

DUTTON CHILDREN'S BOOKS

Dutton Children's Books is one of the oldest continually operating children's publishers in the United States. Edward Payson Dutton opened the doors of his Boston bookshop in 1852 and shortly thereafter began to release "fresh and entertaining" books for young readers.

More than 150 years later, Dutton's tagline, "Every book a promise," reflects the imprint's mission to create high-quality books that will transport young readers. Today, the Dutton list looks very different, but its commitment to excellence, freshness, and entertainment has not changed.

The recent list includes *Amelia Anne is Dead and Gone* by Kat Rosenfield; *Little Monsters: The Creatures that Live on Us and in Us* by Albert Marrin; *The Fault in Our Stars* by John Green; *The Disenchantments* by Nina LaCour; and *The Best Night of Your (Pathetic) Life* by Tara Altebrando.

Direct query letters and SASEs to:

Julie Strauss-Gabel, Associate Publisher—Middle-grade children's literature, young adult.

FIREBIRD

Firebird is a paperback science-fiction and fantasy imprint specifically designed to appeal to both teenagers and adults. Launched in January 2002, Firebird books are all reprints, drawn from a variety of sources: the children's imprints at PPI; adult genre imprints (Ace and Roc); outside hardcover houses; and the authors themselves. All have covers by adult genre artists and feature a short essay or autobiography written by their authors. The imprint publishes between 12 and 18 books each year. More information is available at the website: www.firebirdbooks.com.

Some recent titles include *Land of Myth (The Dragon Wars Saga)* by Becka Sutton; *The Sable Quean (Redwall)* by Brian Jacques; *Singing the Dogstar Blues* by Alison Goodman; *Dogsbody* by Diana Wynne Jones and Neil Gaiman; and *Fire: Tales of Elemental Spirits (Firebird Fantasy)* by Robin McKinley and Peter Dickinson.

Sharyn November, Editorial Director

FREDERICK WARNE

In 1865, Frederick Warne, a bookseller turned publisher, started producing a well-regarded list of illustrated children's books. The press was the original publisher of *The Tale of Peter Rabbit*, leading to a highly successful partnership and the first merchandising program based around a children's book. The press was bought by Penguin in 1983 and started acquiring other classic children's book properties, such as Cicely Mary Barker's *Flower Fairies* and *Spot* by Eric Hill.

Recent titles include *The Pied Piper of Hamelin* by Robert Browning and Kate Greenaway; *The Story of the Three Little Pigs* by L. Leslie Brooke; *Spot Loves Sport* by Eric Hill; and *Beatrix Potter: The Complete Tales* by Beatrix Potter.

GROSSET & DUNLAP

Grosset & Dunlap produces about 135 mass-market children's books each year in hardcover, paperback, library binding, and other formats. Since the 1940s, in addition to the original *Nancy Drew* and *Hardy Boys* series, Grosset has published the Illustrated Junior Library. This collection of hardcover editions of *Little Women*, *Tom Sawyer*, and other classics is a mainstay of practically every bookstore selling children's books.

Other series include *Smart About Art* (all about art for kids five to nine); *Katie Kazoo*; *Strawberry Shortcake*; *Spot*; *Miss Spider*; *The Wiggles*; *The Weebles*; and *Who Was…?* (a biography series for kids eight to eleven).

Recent titles include *Rocking Out!* by AJ Stern; *Katie Kazoo, Switcheroo* by Nancy Krulik; *The Ship of Lost Souls* by Rachelle Delaney; *Kindergarten, Here I Come!* by D.J. Steinberg; and *Meet Cherry Jam! (Strawberry Shortcake)* by Amy Ackelsberg.

Direct query letters and SASEs to:

Jordan Hamessley, Editor—Middle grade.

Sarah Fabiny, Editor—Middle grade.

PHILOMEL BOOKS

Philomel Books was created in the early 1980s from World Publishing Books for Young People, by Editor and Publisher Ann Beneduce. Ms. Beneduce was a pioneer as far as books that would sell to both trade and institutional markets, so for the new list she chose the name Philomel, a term for an English nightingale that means literally "love of learning." The name implied that these books would be distinguished, beautiful in concept and form, fine enough to be sought as gifts, and original and handsome enough to be bought by libraries and schools.

Some recent titles from Philomel include *Stronger: A Super Human Clash* by Michael Carroll; *You Are My Wonders* by Maryann Cusimano Love; *The World's Greatest Lion* by Ralph Helfer and Ted Lewin; *Small Damages* by Beth Kephart; and Andrew Henry's *Meadow* by Doris Burn.

Michael Green, President and Publisher—Children's picture books, middle grade.

Jill Santopolo, Editor—Young adult, middle grade.

Tamra Tuller, Editor—Young adult.

PUFFIN BOOKS

Puffin Books was founded on a strong literary tradition and a commitment to publishing a successful mix of classic children's fiction and brand-new literature for children. Over the years, Puffin has transformed from a small, yet distinguished, paperback house into one of the largest and most diverse children's publishers in the business, publishing over 225 titles a year—everything from picture books to groundbreaking middle-grade and teen fiction. In addition to publishing new editions of quality literary fiction, Puffin has started several original series with broad commercial appeal.

Puffin produces titles for young readers in every age group: lift-the-flaps and picture books for young children, Puffin Easy-to-Reads for first-time readers, Puffin Chapters and historical and contemporary fiction for middle-graders, and critically acclaimed novels for teens under the Speak imprint. The house has a backlist packed with award-winning children's literature, including Robert McCloskey's Caldecott Medal winner *Make Way for Ducklings*; Ludwig Bemelmans's Caldecott Honor book *Madeline*; and Don Freeman's classic *Corduroy*.

Classic Puffin picture book titles include *The Gingerbread Boy* by Ludwig Bemelmans, illustrated by Jan Brett; *The Very Hungry Caterpillar* by Eric Carle; *Strega Nona* by Tomie dePaola; *The Snowy Day* by Ezra Jack Keats; and *Max and Ruby* by Rosemary Wells. Middle-graders and teen readers titles include *Time Cat and The Chronicles of Prydain* by Lloyd Alexander; *Charlie and the Chocolate Factory* by Roald Dahl; *Amber Brown* by Paula Danziger; *The Outsiders* by S. E. Hinton; *Pippi Longstocking* by Astrid Lindgren; *Roll of Thunder, Hear My Cry* by Mildred D. Taylor; and *Miracle's Boys* by Jacqueline Woodson.

Recent titles include *Henry and the Bully* by Nancy L. Carlson; *King Jack and the Dragon* by Peter Bently; *The Clueless Girl's Guide to Being a Genius* by Janice Repka; *War and Watermelon* by Richard Wallace; and *Four Mice Deep in the Jungle* by Geronimo Stilton.

Titles from Speak include *Wicked Jealous: A Love Story* by Robin Palmer; *The Summer My Life Began* by Shannon Greenland; *Imaginary Girls* by Nova Ren Suma; *Where She Went* by Gayle Forman; and *Chime* by Franny Billingsley.

Direct query letters and manuscripts with SASEs to:

Jennifer Bonnell, Editor—Young adult, middle grade.

G. P. PUTNAM'S SONS CHILDREN'S BOOKS

Putnam Children's publishes about 60 trade hardcover books for children per year. It publishes popular novels and picture books for toddlers to middle-readers, ages nine to twelve.

G. P. Putnam's Sons is the home of celebrated picture book creators Tomie dePaola, Jan Brett, Eric Hill, Rachael Isadora, Maira Kalman, Keiko Kasza, and Peggy Rathmann. Award-winning authors for older readers include Joan Bauer, Paula Danziger, Jean Fritz, Vicki Grove, Suzy Kline, Robin McKinley, Jacqueline Woodson, and Laurence Yep.

Recent titles include *Dog Gone* by Leeza Hernandez; *Mysteries According to Humphrey* by Betty G. Birney; *Halfway to Perfect: A Dyamonde Daniel Book* by Nikki Grimes; *Cold Fury* by T.M. Goeglein; and *The Perfect Present* by Fiona Roberton.

Direct queries and SASEs to:

Stacey Barney, Director—Young adult, middle grade.

Jennifer Besser, Editor—Young adult, middle grade.
Susan Kochan, Editor—Picture books.

RAZORBILL

Razorbill, which launched in Fall 2004, is dedicated to publishing teen and tween books for "kids who love to read, hate to read, want to read, need to read." A typical Razorbill book is contemporary commercial fiction, with a high-concept plot hook and a fresh, eye-catching package—a book that a young reader will pick up on his or her own.

The imprint publishes about 40 new titles a year, both stand-alone titles and limited series (three to six books). Formats range from paperback to hardcover, with an emphasis on alternative formats and trim sizes. Hardcovers and trade paperbacks appear in mass-market formats 12 to 18 months after initial publication. In November 2011, Razorbill also published its first picture book, an adaptation of the Internet sensation "Marcel the Shell," *Marcel the Shell with Shoes On: Things About Me* by Jenny Slate and Dean Fleischer-Camp.

Recent titles include *Zoe Letting Go* by Nora Price; *The Probability of Miracles* by Wendy Wunder; *All You Desire (Eternal Ones)* by Kirsten Miller; *The Golden Lily: A Bloodlines Novel* by Richelle Mead; and *Ripple* by Mandy Hubbard.

Ben Schrank, President and Publisher—Young adult, middle grade.
Laura Arnold, Editor—Middle grade.
Caroline Donofrio, Editor—Young adult.

VIKING CHILDREN'S BOOKS

Viking Children's Books, founded in 1933, publishes approximately 60 titles per year, ranging from books for very young children, such as board and lift-the-flap books, to sophisticated fiction and nonfiction for teens. The current Viking list is known for classic characters such as Madeline, Corduroy, Pippi Longstocking, Roald Dahl's Matilda, Rosemary Wells's Max and Ruby, The Stinky Cheese Man, Cam Jansen, and Froggy.

Among the groundbreaking titles published by Viking are *The Outsiders* (1969), still the bestselling young-adult book ever published; *The Snowy Day* (1963), which brought multicultural books mainstream recognition; and *The Stinky Cheese Man* (1992), widely hailed for its innovative design.

Recent titles include *Horrible Harry and the Scarlet Scissors* by Suzy Kline; *The Unfortunate Son* by Constance Leeds; *Tokyo Heist* by Diana Renn; *My Life in Black and White* by Natasha Friend; and *Keeping The Castle* by Patrice Kindl.

Direct query letters and SASEs to:
Regina Hayes, Publisher
Tracy Gates, Editor— Picture Books.
Kendra Levin, Editor—Young adult, middle grade.
Leila Sales, Editor—Picture books, young adult.
Sharyn November, Editor—Young adult, middle grade.

SECTION TWO

INDEPENDENT US PRESSES

INDEPENDENT US PRESSES

JEFF HERMAN

I get to see things a bit differently as an agent than I would as a writer. As discussed elsewhere, publishing houses have more or less fallen into two huge categories: the "globalized" conglomerates and everyone else. The former can be counted on your fingers, yet they constitute most of all trade book revenues. The latter are countless in number and always expanding like an unseen universe.

Some of these players—the "micro-presses" not included here—have revenues that could be rivaled by a nine-year-old's lemonade stand, whereas others are eight-figure operations.

Together, the "independents" are the other half of the game. As a unified force, they are smaller than they were a decade ago, and are likely to keep getting smaller. But as their market share shrinks, their indispensability only grows.

The choice of the word "independent" reflects the best word I could come up with, but it's not a perfect description. There are many shades of gray, as in all things. Here you will find a few imprints of major houses that I felt operate in a particularly independent fashion. There are also cases where an independent house is distributed by one of the large mega-publishers, and it is listed here rather than with its large umbrella house.

In the end, it's quality that counts, not quantity. And the long-term consequences of the growing consolidation in the industry are not clear yet. Dominance leads to comfort, which leads to inertia. When the asteroids return, it's the ponderous dominators who will be the first to fall.

But it wasn't me who predicted that the meek will inherit the Earth.

***

So welcome to the world of the independent publisher. Rest assured, we have been very careful not to include any vanity publishers or "fly-by-nights" who will take your money and promise the world without any intention of delivering. The publishing houses we have included are established and reputable.

Independent publishers tend to be more open to direct queries and proposals from authors, rather than requiring that work be submitted through agents.

For some, an independent press might be a stepping stone to a mega-press. For others, the right independent house is exactly the place to be and stay. Large house refugees sometimes choose to go with the independents due to the enhanced flexibility and author involvement that's offered. Often, a smaller press can provide more editorial attention, more authorial involvement throughout the process, and a more focused, long-term involvement with specialized audiences of readers and their communities.

It all depends—on you, on your work, and on the methods of the publisher involved. So study each listing that seems of possible interest and look closely at their books.

In all cases, be sure to scrutinize their guidelines and prepare your material carefully. You want to put your best foot forward, and a clear query, followed by a well-written, well-organized proposal, is just as important for a small house as for a large one.

ABBEVILLE PUBLISHING GROUP

ABBEVILLE PRESS
ABBEVILLE FAMILY
ARTABRAS
137 Varick Street, 5th Floor, New York, NY 10013
212-366-5585 | fax: 212-366-6966
www.abbeville.com | e-mail: abbeville@abbeville.com

Since 1977, Abbeville has published a wide variety of distinctive art, photographic, and illustrated books. With an active backlist of over 700 titles, Abbeville Publishing Group releases approximately 40 new titles annually in subjects ranging from the arts, gardening, fashion, and food and wine to travel and history. Titles are published in hardcover and trade paperback editions, with close attention given to production standards. Abbeville also produces printed gift items.

ABBEVILLE PRESS

The Abbeville Press imprint publishes fine art and illustrated books for an international readership. Their Tiny Folio and miniSeries lines include palm-sized volumes popular in the gift shop sections of museums and bookstores.

Recent titles from Abbeville Press include *Fine Bonsai* by Dr. Jonathan M. Singer and William N. Valavanis; *The Grand Medieval Bestiary: The Animal in Illuminated Manuscripts* by Christian Heck; and *Rémy Cordonnier: Greek and Roman Mosaics* by Umberto Pappalardo and Rosario Ciardello.

ABBEVILLE FAMILY

Abbeville Family is an imprint for high-quality illustrated books that appeal to the youth market, especially designed to teach children about ways of seeing the world by interacting with art. Titles from Abbeville Family include *T. Rex and the Great Extinction* by Matteo Bacchin and Marco Signore; *Sometimes It's Grandmas and Grandpas: Not Mommies and Daddies* by Gayle Byrne and Mary Haverfield; *123 Caterpillar* by Calino; *Animal Fables* by Aesop Charles Perrault, Marie-France Floury, and Jacob and Wilhelm Grimm; *Giant vs. Giant: Argentinosaurus* by Matteo Bacchin and Marco Signore.

ARTABRAS

The Artabras imprint makes select Abbeville titles available at bargain prices. Some titles include *Ansel Adams: The National Park Service Photographs* by Ansel Adams and Alice Gray; *The Art of Florence* by Glenn M. Andrews et al; and *Hot Rods and Cool Customs* by Pat Ganahl.

Abbeville Press is not currently accepting unsolicited book proposals. Should they decide to expand their list in the future, they'll post a notice on their website. Abbeville Kids is accepting submissions in parenting subjects and illustrated books for all ages of children.

They claim not to be even considering new submissions for several years. If true, it would mean that recent titles were acquired long ago or initiated in-house.

ABC-CLIO

PO Box 1911, Santa Barbara, CA 93116-1911
805-968-1911 | 800-368-6868 | fax: 866-270-3856
www.abc-clio.com

GREENWOOD PUBLISHING GROUP
88 Post Road West, Box 5007, Westport, CT 06881-5007
203-226-3571 | fax: 203-222-1502
e-mail: editorial@greenwood.com

HEINEMANN USA
361 Hanover Street, Portsmouth, NH 03801
603-431-7894
www.heinemann.com | e-mail: proposals@heinemann.com

Established in 1953, ABC-CLIO is a family-owned business specializing in history reference. It annually publishes approximately 80 encyclopedias, guides, and handbooks for teachers, students, and scholars. Its best-known reference works are the annotated *Historical Abstracts* and *America: History and Life*, both accessible online, which together represent the largest bibliographic history database in the world. Since 1961, ABC-CLIO has won over 80 best-reference awards from the American Library Association and *Library Journal*. They also have a large e-book program, with all reference book titles published in both print and electronic formats.

The company's corporate headquarters are in Santa Barbara, California, with offices in Denver, Colorado, and Oxford, England. ABC-CLIO was founded by Eric Boehm and is headed today by Ron Boehm.

ABC-CLIO recently became the publisher for Greenwood Books and all associated imprints.

ABC-CLIO's publishing focus is on American and world history, politics, law, government, geography, popular and traditional culture, current issues, and history of religion, science, technology, and medicine. They generally accept single-volume titles of approximately 80,000 to 150,000 words.

Query letters or proposals with CVs and SASEs should be addressed to the attention of the Editorial Director, Books. Or, **Brian Romer**, Editor.

GREENWOOD PUBLISHING GROUP
GREENWOOD PRESS
PRAEGER PUBLISHERS
LIBRARIES UNLIMITED

The Greenwood Publishing Group is one of the world's leading publishers of reference titles, academic and general interest books, texts, books for librarians and other professionals, and electronic resources. With over 18,000 titles in print, GPG publishes some 1,000 books each year, many of which are recognized with annual awards from *Choice*, *Library Journal*, the American Library Association, and other scholarly and professional organizations.

For submissions to Praeger and Greenwood, please classify your project as either reference (Greenwood Press) or non-reference (Praeger), and send your proposal to the appropriate editor. If you cannot identify the appropriate editor, or if you are writing on an interdisciplinary topic such as women's studies, send an e-mail outlining your proposal to editorial@greenwood.com or send via mail to the Acquisitions Department. Send proposals or queries via e-mail or regular mail with SASEs.

GREENWOOD PRESS

GPG imprint Greenwood Press publishes reference books in all subject areas taught in middle schools, high schools, and colleges, as well as on topics of general interest. Their many award-winning titles in the social sciences and humanities range from in-depth multivolume encyclopedias to more concise handbooks, guides, and even biographies.

Recent titles from Greenwood include *Documenting Steppe Empires and Silk Roads: Historical Sources on the World of Genghis Khan* by George Lane; *America's Service Meltdown: Restoring Service Excellence in the Age of the Customer* by Raul Pupo; *Boy Culture* by Shirley Steinberg et al; *Contesting History: The Bush Counterinsurgency Legacy in Iraq* by Matthew Flynn; and *The Cultural Context of Medieval Music* by Nancy Van Deusen.

Jeff Olsen—Business and economics; jeff.olsen@greenwood.com

Kristi Ward—Contemporary music, popular culture and media, sports; kristi.ward@greenwood.com

Sandy Towers—Current events, media literacy; sandy.towers@greenwood.com

Wendi Schnaufer—Food, social issues, world cultures, multicultural/African American/Latino American/Asian American/Native American issues; wendi.schnaufer@greenwood.com

Debby Adams—Health and medicine, high school reference, young-adult literature, arts; debra.adams@greenwood.com

Kevin Downing—Health and medicine; kevin.downing@greenwood.com

George Butler—Literature/college reference; gbutler@greenwood.com

PRAEGER PUBLISHERS

GPG Imprint Praeger Publishers has a distinguished history (since 1949) of producing scholarly and professional books in the social sciences and humanities, with special strengths in modern history, military studies, psychology, business, current events and social issues, international affairs, politics, visual and performing arts, and literature. Praeger books serve the needs of scholars and general readers alike by providing the best of contemporary scholarship to the widest possible audience.

Recent titles from Praeger include *Diversity in Mind and in Action* by Jean Lau Chin; *Religious Myths and Visions of America* by Christopher Buck; *Women in India* by Sita Raman; *Light, Bright, and Damned Near White* by Stephanie Bird; and *Gender and Violence in the Middle East* by David Ghanim.

Suzanne Staszak-Silva—Crime, literature, religion; sstaszak@greenwood.com
Daniel Harmon—Contemporary music, popular culture and media, sports, arts; daniel.harmon@greenwood.com
Robert Hutchinson—Interdisciplinary; robert.hutchinson@greenwood.com
Debora Carvalko—Psychology, social work; dcarvalk@greenwood.com
Adam Kane—Military history; adam.kane@greenwood.com

LIBRARIES UNLIMITED

Libraries Unlimited serves the needs of the library profession through quality publications for library and information science students and faculty, practicing librarians, media specialists, and teachers. Titles include *100+ Literacy Lifesavers: A Survival Guide for Librarians and Teachers K–12* by Pamela S. Bacon and Tammy K. Bacon; *American Reference Books Annual: 2009* by Shannon Graff Hysell; and *Best Books for High School Readers, Grades 9–12* by Catherine Barr and John T. Gillespie.

For Libraries Unlimited submissions, please query one of the following editors below via e-mail prior to sending a proposal.

Barbara Ittner—Public library and high school reference books; barbara.ittner@lu.com
Sharon Coatney—School library books; sharon.coatney@lu.com
Sue Easun—Textbooks and reference books; sue.easun@lu.com

HEINEMANN USA

Heinemann USA is a national leader in the publishing of professional books for teachers of language arts K–12, and has growing lists in math, science, social studies, and art education. In 1987, Boynton/Cook, the leading publisher of professional books for English teachers at the middle and high school levels and for college English teachers, joined Heinemann. The company also has an active presence in several niche markets, most notably in theater and arts, and Third World writing, with literature lists in the Caribbean, Asia, the Middle East, and Africa.

Recent Heinemann titles include *Classroom Reading Assessments* by Frank

Serafini; *Code-Switching Lessons* by Rebecca Wheeler and Rachel Swords; *What's the Big Idea?* by Jim Burke; *Reading Ladders* by Teri Lesesne; and *The Drama of AIDS* by Michael Kearns.

To submit to Heinemann, e-mail proposals@heinemann.com or send your proposal or query via regular mail with SASE to the Acquisitions Editor.

ABINGDON PRESS

DIMENSIONS FOR LIVING
KINGSWOOD BOOKS
201 Eighth Avenue South, PO Box 801, Nashville, TN 37202-0801
615-749-6000
www.abingdonpress.com

Abingdon Press is one of the oldest houses in religious publishing. It has been in existence since 1789 and began as an imprint of the United Methodist Publishing House. Its efforts expanded in the 1920s with books in many different subject areas such as academics, inspirational, and materials for church communities. In the early 1920s, Abingdon began publishing a wide array of academic, professional, inspirational, and life-affirming religious literature with the goal of enriching church communities across the globe.

Abingdon is open to a wide range of subject matter, which provides opportunity for writers who do not fit within the more narrow guidelines of other houses. Abingdon looks to include popular material, as long as it has contemporary spiritual and ethical themes that influence the lives of its readership. For example, in *50 Ways to Pray: Practices from Many Traditions and Times*, Teresa A. Blythe considers a wide variety of prayer types, gleaned from centuries-old practices of Christian spiritual leaders, including the Christian mystics.

Abingdon publishes hardback and paperback editions, covering religious specialty, religious trade, and popular markets. They also publish professional reference and resources for the clergy, as well as academic and scholarly works in the fields of religious and biblical history and theory. One new example of an adult Bible study book is *Hurry Less, Worry Less at Christmastime* by Judy Christie. This book helps busy people learn to celebrate more joyfully, peacefully, and deeply during the "holiday season" between Thanksgiving and New Year's Day.

Abingdon also issues several series of books for children and resources for Sunday school and general Christian education.

Recent Abingdon titles include *Changing Forward: Experiencing God's Unlimited Power* by Bishop Paul Morton; *Make It Count: 180 Devotions for the School Year* by Sue Christian; *Forgiveness: Finding Peace Through Letting Go* by Adam Hamilton; *American Dream 2.0: A Christian Way Out of the Great Recession* by Thomas Frank; *A Shared Christian Life* by Dr. Ben Witherington, III; *A New History of*

Christianity by Hans J. Hillerbrand; *Healing Waters Participant Book: A Bible Study on Forgiveness, Grace and Second Chances* by Melody Carlson; *Embraced by God Bible Study Participant Book: Seven Promises for Every Woman* by Babbie Mason.

Dimensions for Living books help Christian apply their faith to daily life. Recognizing that living faithfully in today's world isn't easy, Dimensions for Living offers daily meditations, inspiration, practical suggestions, faith-filled advice, and other helps for Christian living.

Kingswood Books is an academic imprint devoted the scholarly works in all periods and areas of Methodist and Wesleyan studies. This imprint honors John Wesley's lifelong commitment to an informed and reflective Christian life.

DIMENSIONS FOR LIVING

Dimensions for Living is an imprint of Abingdon devoted to general-interest religious trade books on practical Christian living. It publishes inspiration, devotion, self-help, home and family, as well as gift volumes. The editorial approach is to combine contemporary themes with mainstream Christian theology: "Quality books that celebrate life and affirm the Christian faith." Dimensions for Living is currently no longer producing new titles.

Dimensions for Living titles include *Lessons I Learned from My Grandchildren* by Delia Halverson; *Healing Where It Hurts* by James W. Moore; *Goodbye, Murphy's Law: Whatever Can Go Wrong, God Can Make Right* by Judy Pace Christie; *My Tummy Talked in Church Today* by Christy Colby Heno; and *The Wide Open Spaces of God: A Journey with God through the Landscapes of Life* by Beth Booram.

KINGSWOOD BOOKS

Kingswood Books is an Abingdon imprint that publishes scholarly works in all areas of Methodist and Wesleyan studies. The imprint honors John Wesley's lifelong commitment to the Christian lifestyle. This commitment, which found expression in his extensive writing and publishing, took form in his establishment of the Kingswood School, near Bristol, England.

Recent Kingswood titles include *Doctrine in Experience: A Methodist Theology of Church and Ministry* by Russell E. Richey; *The Manuscript Journal of the Rev. Charles Wesley, M.A.*, Volume 1 by S. T. Kimbrough, Jr. and Kenneth G. C. Newport; and *Early Methodist Spirituality* by Paul W. Chilcote.

In addition to distributing its own books, Abingdon Press handles the lists of several other smaller religious publishers. No multiple submissions. Query letters and SASEs should be directed to:

Pamela Clements, Associate Publisher

Lil Cpan, Senior Editor

John Kutsho, Editor—Academic and professional books.

HARRY N. ABRAMS, INC.

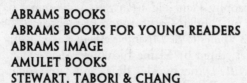

ABRAMS BOOKS
ABRAMS BOOKS FOR YOUNG READERS
ABRAMS IMAGE
AMULET BOOKS
STEWART, TABORI & CHANG
115 West 18th Street, 6th Floor, New York, NY 10011
212-206-7715 | fax: 212-519-1210
www.hnabooks.com

Harry N. Abrams, Inc. (HNA), is a prominent publisher of high-quality art and illustrated books. This house publishes and distributes approximately 250 titles annually and currently has more than 2,000 titles in print. HNA encompasses Abrams Books; Stewart, Tabori & Chang; Abrams Books for Young Readers; Amulet Books for middle grade and young adult; and Abrams Image.

ABRAMS BOOKS

Abrams is a specialist house and acquires nonfiction projects on a selective basis, giving particular weight to the national or international renown and credentials of artists, photographers, and writers. Their illustrated volumes (mainly in hardcover, with some trade paperback editions and series, as well as works in electronic formats) focus primarily on the fields of fine art; architecture; design; anthropology; archaeology; ethnology and culture; gardening and the home; crafts, especially knitting; literary and art criticism; world history; travel; the natural sciences; and the creative use of technology and new media.

Abrams Books titles include *Brother Jimmy's BBQ* by Josh Lebowitz and Eva Pesantez; *P.S. I Still Hate It Here: More Kids' Letters from Camp* by Diane Falanga; *Custom Knits Accessories: Unleash Your Inner Designer...and More* by Wendy Bernard.

Deborah Aaronson, Editorial Director

ABRAMS BOOKS FOR YOUNG READERS

Authors of middle-grade and young-adult fiction should not overlook Abrams Books for Young Readers. Abrams Books for Young Readers include *Library Mouse: A Friend's Tale* by Daniel Kirk; *All in a Day* by Cynthia Rylant; *Beyond* by Michael Benson; *My First Nursery Book* by Franciszka Themerson; *Good Night, Baby Ruby* by Rohan Henry.

Susan Van Metre, Senior Editor

ABRAMS IMAGE

The Abrams Image imprint focuses on edgy pop culture books, but also had a best seller with the 2007 book about philosophy, *Plato and a Platypus Walk into a Bar: Understanding Philosophy through Jokes* by Thomas Cathcart and Daniel Klein.

Abrams Image titles include *11,002 Things to Be Miserable About* by Lia Romeo and Nick Romeo; *Poem in Your Pocket* edited by Elaine Bleakney; *Spott's Canine Miscellany* by Mike Darton; *Itty Bitty Kitty Ditties* by Alex Boies and Tim Hodapp; *Sh*tty Mom: The Parenting Guide for the Rest of Us* by Laurie Kilmartin, Karen Moline, Alicia Ybarbo, and Mary Ann Zoellner.

AMULET BOOKS

Amulet has a bestselling series, *The Sisters Grimm* by Michael Buckley, and publishes books for teens and young readers. Some other titles are *Diary of a Wimpy Kid* by Jeff Kinney; *My Life in Pink & Green* by Lisa Greenwald; and *Escape the Mask* by David Ward.

Susan Van Metre, Senior Editor
Tamar Brazis, Editorial Director
Howard Reeves, Editor-at-Large

STEWART, TABORI & CHANG

Stewart, Tabori & Chang editor Melanie Falick is one of the most respected publishing professionals focusing on crafts, especially knitting. This imprint also releases bestselling lifestyle, environmental, and food titles.

Stewart, Tabori & Chang titles include *1,000 Ways to Be a Slightly Better Woman* by Pamela Redmond Satran; *1,001 Reasons to Love Dogs* by Christine Miele and Mary Tiegreen; and *100 Years of Oz* by Willard Carroll and John Fricke.

Leanna Allday, Senior Editor
Abrams distributes its own books in the United States and Canada.

Query letters and SASEs should be directed to the Editorial Department of the specific imprint to which you are submitting. If you are a nonfiction author, proposals may be sent directly to Abrams Books for Young Readers, Amulet Books, and Abrams Books only. Due to heavy volume, Stewart, Tabori & Chang cannot accept unsolicited book proposals at this time, and Abrams Books for Young Readers and Amulet Books cannot accept unsolicited works of fiction (picture books, novels, or related formats).

ACADEMY CHICAGO PUBLISHERS

363 West Erie Street, 7E, Chicago, IL 60654
312-751-7300 | 800-248-READ | fax: 312-751-7306
www.academychicago.com | e-mail: info@academychicago.com

A small press with a noteworthy list, Academy Chicago publishes general nonfiction, art, history, and cultural studies, as well as fiction (including mysteries). The house also offers a line of classic reprints. Academy Chicago makes notable contributions to American letters.

Nonfiction from Academy Chicago includes popular works with an emphasis on contemporary culture, current events, and historical interpretation. The house does not publish science fiction, thrillers, cookbooks, self-help, books dealing with the supernatural, horror, books of photography, children's books, or books with explicit, gratuitous sex and violence.

Recent Academy Chicago titles include *Resisting Elegy: On Grief and Recovery* by Joel Peckham; *Roll On* by Fred Afflerbach; *From Animal House to Our House: A Love Story* by Ron Tanner; *Country, Life, Death, and Politics at Chicago's Public Hospital* by David A. Ansell, MD, MPH.

Academy Chicago handles its own distribution. All submissions must be by regular mail, not by e-mail or fax. Send the first three to four chapters, synopsis, cover letter, and SASE to the Editorial Department.

Anita Miller, Editorial Director

ADAMS MEDIA

Owned by F+W Publications
   POLKA DOT PRESS
   PROVENANCE PRESS
57 Littlefield Street, Avon, MA 02322
508-427-7100 | fax: 800-872-5628
www.adamsmedia.com

This midsize trade house has long been known for specific, high-quality content and impressive design. Primary areas of interest covered are business, leadership, parenting, pets, personal finance, motivational guidance, travel, weddings, and writing. Adams publishes both single-title breakouts and signature series, and releases under two imprints: Polka Dot Press and Provenance Press.

With their motto, "Value looks good," Adams Media particularly innovates in the fields of business, self-help, and New Age how-to books. Since being acquired by F + W Publications in 2003, Adams has been extending its reach and now has a list with over 300 books in 25 categories.

National best sellers in the single-title category include *A Beginner's Guide to Day Trading Online* by Toni Turner; *Why Men Love Bitches* by Sherry Argov; *Please Stop Laughing at Me* by Jodee Blanco; *The Verbally Abusive Relationship* by Patricia Evans; and the teen hit *Mean Chicks, Cliques and Dirty Tricks* by Erika V. Shearin Karres. Career and business best sellers like Martin Yate's *Knock 'Em Dead* and Stephan Schiffman's *Closing Techniques* are also popular.

Perhaps the best known of Adams Media's output is the *Everything* series. This is the ubiquitous user-friendly how-to series with titles like *The Everything Father's First Year Book* and *The Everything Dog Book*. The Streetwise line is dedicated specifically to the small businessperson. The *Cup of Comfort* and *Small Miracles* series are meant to inspire readers with anthologies of true stories. Many of these anthologies have regular calls for submissions on the Adams Media website.

Recent Adams Media titles include *Math for Grownups: Relearn the Arithmetic You Forgot from School* by Laura Laing; *Meditation for Multitaskers with CD: Your Guide to Finding Peace Between the Pings* by David Dillard-Wright, PhD; *The Misanthrope's Guide to Life (Go Away!)* by Meghan Rowland and Chris Turner-Neal.

Peter Archer, Associate Editor—Business, personal finance, reference.
Andrea Hankanson, Editor
Erik Herman, Editor
Brendan O'Neill, Editor

POLKA DOT PRESS

The Polka Dot Press imprint specializes in nonfiction for female readers ages 18 to 35. Polka Dot Press aims to bring the witty energy of chick lit to the self-help shelf. Titles include *The 10 Women You'll Be Before You're 35* by Alison James; *28 Days* by Gabrielle Lichterman; *Tales from the Scale* by Erin J. Shea; and The Dating Cure by Rhonda Findling.

Chelsea King, Associate Editor

PROVENANCE PRESS

The Provenance Press imprint adds to the New Age shelf with "sophisticated books for the intermediate practitioner." Titles include *Power Spellcraft for Life* by Arin Murphy-Hiscock; *The Way of the Hedge Witch: Rituals and Spells for Hearth and Home* by Arin-Murphy-Hiscock; and *The Healing Power of Faery: Working with Elementals and Nature Spirits to Soothe the Body and Soul* by Edain McCoy.

Adams does its own distribution in the United States, also operating through wholesalers and jobbers. In the United Kingdom and elsewhere, Adams distributes via overseas distributors.

Adams Media welcomes book proposal submissions, including those from first-time authors. Mail your proposals with SASEs to "Book Proposals."

Karen Cooper, Publisher
Andrea Norville, Assistant Editor

A. K. PETERS, LTD.

5 Commonwealth Rd., Suite 2C, Natick, MA 01760
508-651-0887 | fax: 508-651-0889
www.akpeters.com | e-mail: editorial@akpeters.com

A. K. Peters, founded in 1992 by Alice and Klaus Peters, is a leading independent scientific technical publisher that specializes in computer science, mathematics, computer graphics, game development, history of science, and physics. The list ranges from textbooks to advanced professional publications, specialist trade titles, and scholarly monographs. A. K. Peters publishes around 20 new titles annually, and has over 200 titles in print. The guiding principle behind the company is its philosophy of working in service to the scientific community.

Recent titles from A. K. Peters include *Discrete Mathematics with Ducks* by Sarah-Marie Belcastro; *The Complete Guide to Blender Graphics: Computer Modeling and Animation* by John M. Blain; *Buttonless: Incredible iPhone and iPad Games and the Stories Behind Them* by Ryan Rigney; *Divided Spheres: Geodesics and the Orderly Subdivision of the Sphere* by Edward S. Popko; *Ancient Loons: Stories Pingree Told Me* by Philip J. Davis.

Send queries and SASEs to:
Alice Peters, Publisher
Klaus Peters, Publisher

ALLWORTH PRESS

10 East 23rd Street, Suite 510, New York, NY 10010
212-777-8395 | fax: 212-777-8261
www.allworth.com

Allworth specializes in practical business and self-help books for creative professionals—artists, designers, photographers, writers, filmmakers, and performers, as well as books about business, law, and personal finance for the general public. Founded in 1989 by author, attorney, and artists' rights advocate Tad Crawford, the press first published a revised edition of Crawford's *Legal Guide for the Visual Artist*. Later titles offered helpful advice to both artists and the general public on marketing, promotion, pricing, copyright, contracts, safety on the job, personal finance, and more. Today, Allworth Press publishes 40 titles annually and has a full-time staff of ten. The press has also published books of contemporary and classic critical writings on the visual arts.

Recent noteworthy titles from Allworth include *Interior Design Clients: The Designer's Guide to Building and Keeping a Great Clientele* by Thomas L. Williams; *Interior Design Practice* edited by Cindy Coleman; *The Art of Motion Picture Editing:*

An Essential Guide to Methods, Principles, Processes, and Terminology by Vincent LoBrutto; *The Business of Writing: Professional Advice on Proposals, Publishers, Contracts, and More for the Aspiring Writer* by Jennifer Lyons.

Allworth Press enjoys excellent relationships with a number of publishing partners, including the School of Visual Arts, the American Institute of Graphic Arts, the American Society of Media Photographers, the Authors Guild, *Communication Arts* magazine, the Direct Marketing Institute, and the Graphic Artists Guild.

With over 250 titles in print, Allworth Press continues to publish practical guidance for creative people. Suggestions and insights are welcomed as an aid in determining the best projects and authors for the future.

Query letters and SASEs should be directed to:

Tad Crawford, Publisher

Robert A. Porter, Associate Publisher

ALPHA BOOKS [SEE PEARSON/PENGUIN GROUP]

AMACOM (AMERICAN MANAGEMENT ASSOCIATION)

1601 Broadway, New York, NY 10019-7420
212-586-8100 | fax: 212-903-8168
www.amanet.org

AMACOM is the book publishing division of the American Management Association. AMACOM's titles focus on business and professional leadership issues. They explore the changing workplace, the old and new concerns of managers of all kinds, and the means of improving team performance.

AMACOM trade nonfiction lines include works that cover the fields of accounting and finance, customer service, human resources, international business, manufacturing, organization development, strategy, information and communication technology, personal finance, marketing, advertising and public relations, personal development, small business, supervision, sales, management, and training. AMACOM Books is now publishing books in health, parenting, emerging sciences, current events, and public policy.

AMACOM seeks world-class educators, successful executives, business owners, trainers, consultants, and journalists—all eager to share their insights and techniques with a broad audience. The primary audience is managers in large and small companies looking to improve their effectiveness, make their organizations more competitive, keep up with current trends and thinking, energize their staff, and inspire employees at all levels. AMACOM readers are definitely not mass-market consumers. They want specialized materials and information on business issues that concern them most. AMACOM book buyers want more than a quick fix. They crave in-depth ideas and practical approaches they can try out on the job. They like to be on the leading edge and get a jump on the competition. They do not want secondhand information. They want to go straight to the source.

Noteworthy titles from AMACOM's list include *Transnational Leadership Development* by Beth Fisher-Yoshida and Kathy D. Geller; *A Class with Drucker* by William A. Cohen; *Freeing Tibet* by John Roberts II and Elizabeth Roberts; *Want It, See It, Get It!* by Gini Graham Scott; *The ROI of Human Capital* by Jac Fitzenz; *Identifying and Managing Project Risk* by Rom Kendrick; and *Managing Your Government Career* by Stewart Liff.

AMACOM distributes its own products through multiple marketing channels, including retail trade, direct marketing, special sales, and international sales (through McGraw-Hill).

Proposals and SASEs should be directed to the appropriate editor:

Ellen Kadin, Executive Editor—Marketing, career, communication skills, parenting, biography/memoirs, current events, pop psychology; ekadin@amanet.org

Bob Nirkind, Senior Editor—Real estate, sales, customer service, parenting, biography/memoirs, current events; rnirkind@amanet.org

Christina M. Parisi, Executive Editor—Management, human resources, leadership, parenting, biography/memoirs, current events; cparisi@amanet.org

AMAZON PUBLISHING

276 Fifth Avenue, Suite 1007, New York, NY 10001
Media Hotline: 206-266-7180
www.amazon.com

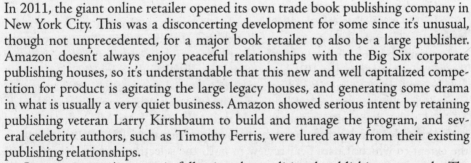

In 2011, the giant online retailer opened its own trade book publishing company in New York City. This was a disconcerting development for some since it's unusual, though not unprecedented, for a major book retailer to also be a large publisher. Amazon doesn't always enjoy peaceful relationships with the Big Six corporate publishing houses, so it's understandable that this new and well capitalized competition for product is agitating the large legacy houses, and generating some drama in what is usually a very quiet business. Amazon showed serious intent by retaining publishing veteran Larry Kirshbaum to build and manage the program, and several celebrity authors, such as Timothy Ferris, were lured away from their existing publishing relationships.

In most ways, Amazon is following the traditional publishing protocols. The major exception is that in many cases, it is releasing major front list books in digital formats only. This is something that few other publishers are inclined to do, especially if it means losing lucrative hardcover profit margins.

Amazon has established the following imprints dedicated to specific genres.

Montlake Romance, which is of course romance.

Thomas and Mercer will focus on mysteries and thrillers.

47North will provide urban fantasies, supernatural horror, and alternate histories.

AmazonEncore will focus on previously published books that may find a second life.

The Domino Project will publish small books by prominent individuals and thought leaders.

Current acquisition editors are:

Larry Kirshbaum, Publisher

Julia Cheiffetz, Editorial Director

Maria Gomez, Editor

Carly Hoffman, Assistant Editor

Carmen Johnson, Associate Editor

David Moldower, Senior Editor

Ed Park, Senior Editor

Katie Salisbury, Associate Editor

AMERICAN PSYCHIATRIC PUBLISHING, INC.

1000 Wilson Boulevard, Suite 1825, Arlington, VA 22209-3901
703-907-7322, 800-368-5777 | fax: 703-907-1091
www.appi.org | e-mail: appi@psych.org

American Psychiatric Publishing, Inc. (APPI), is one of the most respected publishers of books, journals, and multimedia on psychiatry, mental health, and behavioral science. The house releases professional, reference, and trade books, as well as college textbooks. APPI publishes a midsize booklist in hardcover and trade paper and also produces a number of professional journals. Selected reference works are issued in electronic formats.

APPI is a wholly owned subsidiary of the American Psychiatric Association. Its purpose is twofold: to serve as the distributor of publications of the Association and to publish books independent of the policies and procedures of the American Psychiatric Association. APPI has grown since its founding in 1981 into a full-service publishing house, including a staff of editorial, production, marketing, and business experts devoted to publishing for the field of psychiatry and mental health.

Under the direction of Robert E. Hales, MD, and John McDuffie, editorial acquisition and development have the highest priority at APPI. APPI is unique in the extent to which it uses peer review in both the selection and final approval of publishing projects. Proposals are reviewed and developed at the earliest stages by an Editorial Board that brings psychiatric expertise from a diverse spectrum of the field. Full manuscripts are then peer-reviewed in their entirety, with final acceptance of the manuscript dependent on appropriate response to the peer reviews. Each year more than 200 projects are reviewed by as many as 750 specialist reviewers, and fewer than 30 are accepted in the typical year.

Although by far the major portion of the American Psychiatric list is geared toward the professional and academic markets, the house catalogs a small number of books in the areas of patient information and books for the general public, among which are selected titles marketed through trade channels.

Recent noteworthy titles from APPI include *Clinical Manual of Neuropsychiatry* by Stuart C. Yudofsky, MD, and Robert E. Hales, MD, MBA; *Health Care Reform, A Primer for Psychiatrists* by American Psychiatric Association; *Clinical Manual for Treatment of Schizophrenia* by John Lauriello, MD, and Stefano Pallanti, MD; *The American Board of Psychiatry and Neurology: Looking Back and Moving Ahead* by Michael J. Aminoff, MD, DSc, FRCP, and Larry R. Faulkner, MD; *Psychiatry Review and Canadian Certification Exam Preparation Guide* by James A. Bourgeois, OD, MD, FRCPC, Usha Parthasarathi, MBBS, FRCPC, and Ana Hategan, MD, FRCPC.

American Psychiatric Publishing is also the publisher of the profession's acknowledged clinical guidebook, *Diagnostic and Statistical Manual of Mental Disorders* (4th Edition, Text Revision), also known as *DSM-IVTR*.

American Psychiatric Publishing distributes through several regional distribution services.

To receive full consideration, prospective authors must submit a completed Author Questionnaire, found on the APPI website. Query letters and SASEs should be directed to:

John McDuffie, Editorial Director
Samantha Luck, Editorial Support Services Manager, ngray@psych.org

---

AMERICAN PSYCHOLOGICAL ASSOCIATION, INC.

MAGINATION PRESS
750 First Street, NE, Washington, DC 20002-4242
800-374-2721 | 202-336-5500 | fax: 202-336-5502
www.apa.org | e-mail: books@apa.org

Based in Washington, DC, and founded in 1892, the American Psychological Association (APA) is a scientific and professional organization that represents psychology in the United States. With 150,000 members, APA is the largest association of psychologists worldwide. In their publications, the APA aims to promote psychological knowledge and the usefulness of psychologists through high standards of ethics, conduct, education, and achievement. They hope to advance scientific interests and inquiry, and the application of research findings to the promotion of health, education, and the public welfare.

Virtually all aspects of psychology are examined in APA publications: methodology, history, student aids, teaching, health, business strategies, violence, personality, and clinical issues. APA produces books, journals, publishing resources, continuing-education/home-study programs, CDs, videotapes, and databases. *Life Tools* is a special series of APA books written to help the general public find the best advice that psychology can offer.

Recent entries in the APA list include *Graduate Study in Psychology*, 2013 Edition by American Psychological Association; *Humanity's Dark Side: Evil, Destructive Experience, and Psychotherapy* by Arthur C. Bohart, PhD, Barbara S. Held, PhD, Edward Mendelowitz, PhD, and Kirk J. Schneider, PhD; *Preventive Stress Management in Organizations*, Second Edition by James Campbell Quick, PhD, Thomas A. Wright, PhD, Joyce A. Adkins, PhD, Debra L. Nelson, PhD, and Jonathan D. Quick, MD, MPH, FACPM; *Transforming Negative Reactions to Clients: From Frustration to Compassion* by Abraham W. Wolf, PhD, Marvin R. Goldfried, PhD, and J. Christopher Muran, PhD.

MAGINATION PRESS

Magination Press is an APA children's imprint that publishes innovative books to help children ages four to eighteen deal with the challenges and problems they face growing up. Topics include everyday situations such as starting school and the growing family, as well as more serious psychological, clinical, or medical problems, such as divorce, depression, anxiety, asthma, attention disorders, bullying, death, and more. Formats include picture books, illustrated readers, interactive books, and nonfiction.

Examples of recent Magination titles are *Max Archer, Kid Detective: The Case of the Recurring Stomachaches* by Howard J. Bennett, MD; *Harry Goes to the Hospital: A Story for Children About What It's Like to Be in the Hospital* by Howard J. Bennett, MD

Query letters and SASEs should be directed to:

Edward Porter, Editorial Assistant (APA Books)
Julia Frank-McNeil, Director (APA Books)
Shenny Wu, Editorial Assistant (Magination Press)
Becky Shaw, Editor (Magination Press)

AMERICAN SOCIETY FOR TRAINING AND DEVELOPMENT (ASTD) BOOKS

1640 King Street, PO Box 1443, Alexandria, VA 22313-2043
703-683-8100 | fax: 703-683-8103
www.astd.org | e-mail: customercare@astd.org

ASTD Books is a business-information specialist providing guides on workplace learning and performance, HR development, management, career building, consulting, teamwork, IT issues, and creative problem solving. In addition to books, ASTD offers training kits, diagnostic tools, presentation materials, games and simulations, videos, audiocassettes, and computer software.

Founded in 1944, ASTD Books is the publishing wing of the American Society for Training and Development, a nonprofit membership organization. ASTD aims to address the most current workplace topics, innovative techniques, and experienced authors in the field. Books listed in the ASTD catalog are reviewed and selected by a distinguished and professional peer group.

Recent titles from ASTD include *Real World Training Design* by Jenn Labin; *The Self-Aware Leader* by Daniel Gallagher and Joseph Costal; *The ASTD Management Development Handbook* by Lisa Hanenberg; *Informal Learning Basics* by Saul Carliner.

ASTD Books distributes its own list via a catalog, easy ordering, and an online store. Some ASTD books are available through other publishing houses. ASTD also distributes and copublishes books from a variety of other business-oriented publishers, including McGraw-Hill, Jossey-Bass, Berrett-Koehler, and others. ASTD also distributes through Amazon.com.

If you are writing a book targeted to trainers that you think ASTD might like to publish, please contact ASTD at 703-683-9205. Guidelines for submitting a book proposal are available upon request. Query letters and SASEs should be directed to:

Justin Brusino, Project Manager, jbrusino@astd.org

AMG PUBLISHERS

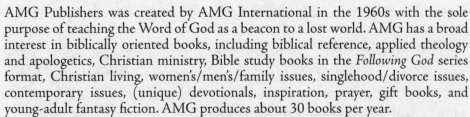

GOD AND COUNTRY PRESS
LIVING INK BOOKS
6915 Shallowford Road, Chattanooga, TN 37421
800-266-4977 | 423-894-6060 | fax: 800-265-6690 | 423-894-9511
www.amgpublishers.com | e-mail: info@amgpublishers.com

AMG Publishers was created by AMG International in the 1960s with the sole purpose of teaching the Word of God as a beacon to a lost world. AMG has a broad interest in biblically oriented books, including biblical reference, applied theology and apologetics, Christian ministry, Bible study books in the *Following God* series format, Christian living, women's/men's/family issues, singlehood/divorce issues, contemporary issues, (unique) devotionals, inspiration, prayer, gift books, and young-adult fantasy fiction. AMG produces about 30 books per year.

AMG Publishers' focus is on books that help the reader get into the Bible, facilitate interaction with Scripture, encourage and facilitate a reader's personal growth in areas such as personal devotion and skillful use of the Bible, and encourage studying, understanding, and applying Scripture.

Recent examples include *The Key of Living Fire* by Scott Appleton; *Stories of Faith and Courage from the Homefront* by Jocelyn Green and Karen Whiting; *Quest for Celestia: A Reimagining of the Pilgrim's Process* by Steven James; *What Does Every*

Bible Chapter Say…The Ultimate Bible Outline/Theme Book by John Hunt; *The Believer's Payday* by Paul N. Benware.

GOD AND COUNTRY PRESS

God and Country Press is a new imprint that publishes books dealing with themes of Christianity and war, patriotism, history, faith, and politics. Some titles from God and Country Press include *The Faith of America's First Ladies* by Jane Hampton Cook; *The Faith of America's Presidents* by Daniel Mount; *The Pledge: One Nation Under God* by William J. Murray; *Stories of Faith and Courage from World War II* by Larkin Spivey; and *Stories of Faith and Courage from the War in Iraq & Afghanistan* by Jane Hampton Cook.

LIVING INK BOOKS

Living Ink Books is an imprint of AMG Publishers that focuses on subjects like Christian living, fiction, inspiration and devotion, and specialty gift book products. This imprint also publishes several series, including *Matterhorn the Brave, Oracles of Fire, Angel Light, Dragons in Our Midst, Made Simple,* and *Twenty-third Psalm.*

Living Ink titles include *The Bones of Makaidos* by Bryan Davis; *The Ark, the Reed, and the Fire Cloud* by Jenny Cote; *Last of the Nephilim* by Bryan Davis; *The Believer's Guide to Legal Issues* by Stephan Bloom; *Not My Child: Contemporary Paganism and the New Spirituality* by Linda Harvey; *Angela's Answer* by Pat Matuszak; and *Prayer: The Timeless Secret of High-Impact Leaders* by Dave Earley.

Query by e-mail or regular mail with SASE to:

Rick Steele, Editor, Acquisitions—Bible study, Christian living.

AMULET BOOKS [SEE HARRY N. ABRAMS, INC.]

ANDREWS MCMEEL PUBLISHING

ACCORD

1130 Walnut Street, Kansas City, MO 64106
800-851-8923 | fax: 816-932-6684
www.andrewsmcmeel.com

Andrews McMeel Publishing (AMP), a division of Andrews McMeel Universal, is a leading publisher of general nonfiction trade books, gift and humor books, and calendars, publishing as many as 300 new works annually. Its titles—such as *The Complete Far Side* by Gary Larson and *The Blue Day Book* by Bradley Trevor—have enjoyed long stays on the *New York Times* best-seller lists. In recent years, Andrews McMeel Publishing has expanded its scope and now offers books on a wide range of subjects (popular culture and lifestyles, popular psychology, self-help, and women's issues) appealing to readers of all ages and interests.

Recent titles are *Feed Your Best Friend Better: Easy Nutritious Meals and Treats for Dogs* by Rick Woodford; *Tomatoland: How Modern Industrial Agriculture Destroyed Our Most Alluring Fruit* by Barry Estabrook; *Curses and Blessings for All Occasions* by Bradley Trevor Greive.

ACCORD

AMP publishes children's books under the Accord imprint. Titles include *Bee & Me* by Elle J. McGuinness and Heather Brown; *Silly Dogs* by Gandee Vasan; *Here's Looking at You: In Your Dreams* by Leslie Jomath and Jana Christy; *Eyeball Animation Drawing Book: African Safari Edition* by Jeff Cole; *Happy Birthday Mouse* by Katie Stone.

AMP is also the country's premier calendar publisher, annually publishing calendars based on many top-selling properties such as The Far Side, Dilbert, Disney, Mary Engelbreit, and Jeopardy! Gift books, such as those from the *Tiny Tomes* series, are also a specialty of this house.

Agents, please query. No unsolicited manuscripts are accepted. Query letters should be addressed: Attn. Book Submissions.

JuJu Johnson, Acquisitions—All categories.

Kirsty Melville, Publisher—Cooking.

Dorothy O'Brien, Vice President and Managing Director—Humor, general nonfiction.

Patty Rice, Senior Editor, Book Division/Editorial Director, Gift Books—General nonfiction, gift books.

Jean Lucas, Senior Editor—General nonfiction, illustrated books, humor, New Age.

Lane Butler, Editor—Humor.

THE APEX PRESS

THE BOOTSTRAP PRESS
4501 Forbes Blvd, Suite 200, Lanham, MD 20706
800-462-6420 | fax: 800-388-4450
rowman.com/page/apex

Introduced in 1990, the Apex Press is an imprint of the nonprofit research, education, and publishing group the Council on International and Public Affairs (CIPA). Apex publishes books to build a better world: hardcover and paperback titles offering critical analyses of and new approaches to economic, social, and political issues in the United States, other industrialized nations, and the Third World. Subjects include corporate accountability, grassroots and worker organization, and intercultural understanding. The primary focus is on justice, human rights, and the impact of technology on contemporary society.

The Council on International and Public Affairs was founded in 1954 and is a nonprofit research, education, and publishing group. The Council seeks to further the study and public understanding of problems and affairs of the peoples of the United States and other nations of the world through conferences, research, seminars and workshops, publications, and other means.

The Apex Press is the official publisher of books for POCLAD (the Program on Corporations, Law, and Democracy). POCLAD is a group dedicated to instigating conversations and actions to contest the authority of corporations to define culture, control governments, and plunder the earth.

Titles from Apex Press include *Gaveling Down the Rabble: How "Free Trade" Is Stealing Our Democracy* by Jane Anne Morris; *Through Japanese Eyes*, 4th Edition by Richard H. Minear; *The Rule of Property* by Karen Coulter; *Through Indian Eyes*, 5th Edition by Donald J. Johnson and Jean E. Johnson; and *Through Chinese Eyes: Tradition, Revolution, and Transformation*, 3rd Edition by Edward Vernoff and Peter J. Seybolt.

The Apex Press handles its own distribution. The house catalog includes books and additional resources (including videos) from a number of publishers worldwide.

THE BOOTSTRAP PRESS

The Bootstrap Press (inaugurated in 1988) is an imprint of the Intermediate Technology Development Group of North America (ITDG/North America) in cooperation with the Council on International and Public Affairs. Bootstrap's publishing interest focuses on social economics and community economic change; the house covers small-scale and intermediate-scale or appropriate technology in both industrialized and emerging countries, with an aim to promote more just and sustainable societies. Its books explore business and industry theory and how-to, gardening and agriculture, building and construction, and communications.

Representative titles from Bootstrap include *Chicken Little, Tomato Sauce, and Agriculture: Who Will Produce Tomorrow's Food?* by Joan Dye Gussow; *A World That Works: Building Blocks for a Just and Sustainable Society* edited by Trent Schroyer; and *Greening Cities: Building Just and Sustainable Communities* by Joan Roelofs.

Bootstrap publications are distributed with those of sibling operation the Apex Press.

For both Apex and Bootstrap, e-mail queries are preferred: cipa@cipa-apex.org. Letters and SASEs should be directed to:

Ward Morehouse, Publisher

JASON ARONSON, INC., PUBLISHERS [SEE ROWMAN & LITTLEFIELD PUBLISHING GROUP]

AUGSBURG FORTRESS BOOKS

FORTRESS PRESS
100 South Fifth Street, Suite 600, Minneapolis, MN 55402-1222
Mailing address:
PO Box 1209, Minneapolis, MN 55440-1209
612-330-3300 | 800-426-0115 | fax: 612-330-3455
www.augsburgfortress.org | e-mail: booksub@augsburgfortress.org

Augsburg Fortress, the publishing house of the Evangelical Lutheran Church in America, publishes titles in popular and professional religious categories. The publishing house produces about 100 books each year. The Augsburg Fortress list accents works of interest to general readers, in addition to books that appeal primarily to a mainstream religious readership and a solid selection of works geared to professional clergy and practitioners of pastoral counseling.

Categories include theology and pastoral care, biblical and historical academic studies, the life and tradition of Martin Luther, self-improvement and recovery, and books for younger readers from nursery to young adults.

Recent titles include *American Civil Religion* by Gary Laderman; *The Theology of Martin Luther: A Critical Assessment* by Hans-Martin Barth; *2 Chronicles: Hermeneia* by Ralph W. Klein; *1 Enoch: The Hermeneia Translation* by George W.E. Nickelsburg and James C. VanderKam; *Jewish Interpretation of the Bible: Ancient and Contemporary* by Karin Hedner Zetterholm; *Religions of the World: An Introduction to Culture and Meaning* Lawrence E. Sullivan.

Authors should note: Augsburg Fortress prefers to receive a proposal rather than a completed manuscript.

FORTRESS PRESS

The Fortress Press is the academic book imprint of Augsburg Fortress. Fortress Press focuses on the ever-changing religious worldview of the contemporary world. The Fortress list is keyed to issues of topical interest, tackled with vision and precision; these works address political and cultural issues and are often on the cusp of current religious debate, and the press is noted for significant publishing in the areas of Jewish-Christian studies, African American religion, religion and science, and feminist theology. The Fortress market orientation tilts toward both the general trade and the religious trade.

Titles from Fortress Press include *Christians and War: A History of Practices and Teachings* by A. James Reimer; *Green Christianity: Five Ways to a Sustainable Future* by Mark I. Wallace; *New Proclamation: Year C, 2010, Easter to Christ the King* by David B. Lott; *The Bible: An Introduction* by Jerry L. Sumney; and *The Priestly Vision of Genesis I* by Mark S. Smith.

Query letters and SASEs should be directed to Book Submissions via regular mail or e-mail: booksub@augsburgfortress.org.

Beth Lewis, President and CEO

AVALON BOOKS (ACQUIRED BY AMAZON PUBLISHING)

1202 Lexington Avenue Suite 283, New York, NY 10028
212-598-0222 | fax: 212-979-1862
www.avalonbooks.com | e-mail: editorial@avalonbooks.com

Established as an imprint of Thomas Bouregy & Company, Inc., in 1950, the aim of Avalon Books (not to be confused with the Avalon Publishing Group) is to provide readers with quality fiction in a variety of genres. The emphasis has always been on good and wholesome entertainment primarily for distribution to library and institutional markets on a subscriber basis. The specialties are mystery, mainstream romance, historical romance, and traditional genre Westerns. Avalon also produces a line of literary classics in reprint (on the Airmont Classics imprint).

The house emphasis on new original novels caters to the tastes and preferences of the all-important library readership. Stories should consist of those likely to be of high interest to the patrons of this wholesome core market. The house publishes 60 books per year.

Recent titles from Avalon Books include *Sunny Day for Sam* by Jennifer Shirk; *A Grand Deception* by Shirley Marks; *Whispers of the Stone* by Loretta Jackson and Vickie Britton; *The Gingerbread House* by Nell Carson; *Deadly Policy: A Silver Sleuth Mystery* by Mitzi Kelly; *In Shining Whatever* by Carolyn Brown.

Submission guidelines for Avalon are not clear due to recent acquisition by Amazon.

B&H PUBLISHING GROUP

127 9th Avenue, North, MSN 114, Nashville, TN 37234-0115
1-800-448-8032 | fax: 1-615-251-3914
www.bhpublishinggroup.com

B&H is the trade publishing division of LifeWay Christian resources, owned by the Southern Baptist Convention. Formerly Broadman & Holman, this house began as a producer of Bibles, textbooks, and reference books. It is now a major publisher of Christian living, fiction, children's books, and history for the Christian market. The B&H Español imprint focuses on Spanish-language titles.

B&H best sellers include *Praying God's World* by Beth Moore, and *Experiencing God* by Dr. Henry Blackaby, as well as Oliver North's novels and Chuck Norris's autobiography.

In 2004, the company's Holman Bible division introduced the new Holman Christian Standard Bible (HCSB) translation. It is also the largest publisher of Spanish-language Bibles in the United States.

Recent titles include *A Duke's Promise* by Jamie Carie; *Courageous Teens* by Michael Catt and Amy Parker; *Mended* by Angie Smith; *October Baby* by Eric Wilson and Theresa Preston.

Submit query with SASE to:

David Shepherd, Publisher

Thomas Walters, Senior Acquisitions Editor

BAEN BOOKS

PO Box 1188, Wake Forest, NC 27588
www.baen.com | e-mail: info@baen.com

Baen publishes science-fiction and fantasy writing. The house's new releases are generally published in mass-market paperback format with targeted lead titles produced in trade paper and hardcover editions. Baen is also a prominent publisher of fiction series, collections, and anthologies geared to various subgenre traditions in science fiction and fantasy.

Founded in 1984, Baen concentrates its concise list on its proven categories of publishing strength. Baen's roster of writers includes John Ringo, Harry Turtledove, Martin Scott, Mercedes Lackey, Murray Leinster, Andre Norton, Lois McMaster Bujold, and Eric Flint.

Writers are encouraged to familiarize themselves with the house output. For science fiction, solid plot-work with scientific and philosophical undercurrents is a must. For fantasy, magical systems must be coherent and integral to the plot. For any Baen title, style need never call attention to itself.

Recent titles from the Baen catalog are *War Maid's Choice* by David Weber; *Elfhome* by Wen Spencer; *Assignment in Eternity* by Robert A. Heinlein; *Rogue* by Michael Z. Williamson.

Electronic submissions are strongly preferred. Due to spam, submissions are no longer accepted by e-mail. Send manuscripts using the submission form at ftp.baen .com/Slush/submit.aspx. Only Rich Text Format (.rtf) files are accepted. Further details are available on the website. No multiple submissions. Query letters and SASEs may be directed to:

"The Editors"

BAKER PUBLISHING GROUP

BAKER ACADEMIC
BAKER BOOKS
BETHANY HOUSE
BRAZOS PRESS
CHOSEN BOOKS
FLEMING H. REVELL
6030 East Fulton Road, Ada, MI 49301
Mailing address:
PO Box 6287, Grand Rapids, MI 49516-6287
616-676-9185 | fax: 616-676-9573
www.bakerpublishinggroup.com

Baker Publishing Group is a major player in the Christian book market. Their mission is to publish writings that promote historic Christianity, ironically express the concerns of evangelism, and reflect the diversity of this movement. At the 2006 Christianity Today Book Awards, Baker Publishing Group won six, more than any other single publisher. Taking top honors in the Christian Living category was Ron Sider's *The Scandal of the Evangelical Conscience* (Baker Books). *Dictionary for the Interpretation of the Bible* by Kevin Vanhoozer (Baker Academic) took the top award in the Biblical Studies category. Awards of Merit went to *Real Sex: The Naked Truth about Chastity* (Brazos Press); *Startling Joy* (fiction, Fleming H. Revell); *The Changing Face of World Missions* (Baker Academic); and *Is the Reformation Over?* (Baker Academic).

BAKER ACADEMIC

As a Christian academic publisher, Baker Academic seeks thoughtful and scholarly works that enhance the pursuit of knowledge within the context of the Christian faith. Baker Academic publishes textbooks, reference books, and scholarly works.

The main areas of specialty are biblical studies, theology (biblical, systematic, and historical), and church history. They also publish works in the areas of Christian education, Christian mission, and integrative works in a variety of liberal arts disciplines (e.g., literature, communication, ethics, psychology).

Recent Baker Academic titles include *The Early Church on Killing* by Ronald J. Sider; *Turning Points: Decisive Moments in the History of Christianity*, 3rd Edition by Mark A. Noll.

Baker Academic welcomes submissions from authors with academic credentials. Send a proposal by post or e-mail (submissions@bakeracademic.com).

BAKER BOOKS

The primary focus of the Baker trade division is the church. It publishes for pastors and church leaders, concentrating on topics such as preaching, worship, pastoral ministries, counseling, and leadership. Topics include the intersection of Christianity and culture, discipleship, spirituality, encouragement, relationships, marriage, and parenting. In addition, Baker trade publishes books that enable parents to pass their faith to their children.

Highlighting the Baker program: *Christless Christianity: The Alternative Gospel of the American Church* by Michael Horton; *A Great and Terrible Love: A Spiritual Journey into the Attributes of God* by Mark Galli; *The Great Emergence* by Phyllis Tickle; *Heaven's Calling: A Memoir of One Soul's Steep Ascent* by Leanne Payne; and *Holy Questions: Encountering Jesus' Provocative Questions* by Winn Collier.

Baker Books accepts manuscripts only through literary agents. All unsolicited manuscripts received will be returned to the sender without review.

BETHANY HOUSE

fax: 952-996-1304
www.bethanyhouse.com

Recognized as a pioneer and leader in Christian fiction, Bethany House publishes nearly 120 titles annually in subjects including historical and contemporary fiction, Christian living, family, health, devotionals, children's books, classics, and theology. Bethany House titles are often found on the Christian best-seller lists.

Recent titles include *Almost Amish* by Kathryn Cushman; *Arena* (Repackaged Edition) by Karen Hancock; *The Art of Mentoring: Embracing the Great Generational Transition* by Darlene Zschech; *The Deposit Slip* by Christopher J.H. Wright.

Bethany House only accepts one-page facsimile proposals directed to adult nonfiction, adult fiction, or young adult/children's editors. Detailed tips for writing a successful query are on the Bethany House website; in general, familiarize yourself with the Bethany House list and read their books, tell the editor why you chose to query them, and deliver a fantastic one-paragraph description of your manuscript.

BRAZOS PRESS

PO Box 4287, Wheaton, IL 60189
www.brazospress.com | e-mail: rclapp@brazospress.com

Brazos Press is a publisher of theology and theologically based cultural criticism, grounded in and growing out of the Great Tradition common to Roman Catholic, Eastern Orthodox, Anabaptist, Protestant, and Protestant evangelical Christianity.

Recent titles include *Speaking of Dying: Recovering the Church's Voice in the Face of Death* by Fred Craddock, Dale Goldsmith, and Joy V. Goldsmith; *God and Charles Dickens: Recovering the Christian Voice of a Classic Author* by Gary L. Colledge; *Luke* by David Lyle Jeffrey.

Send a short proposal, CV, and one or two sample chapters via e-mail with attachment or by regular mail to:

Rodney Clapp, Editorial Director

CHOSEN BOOKS

Chosen is the division of Bethany that explores the ministry of the Holy Spirit in areas like intercessory prayer, spiritual warfare, evangelism, prophecy, healing, and general charismatic interest. Several hundred titles over more than 30 years, from Charles Colson's *Born Again* to Cindy Jacobs's *Possessing the Gates of the Enemy*, reflect the publishing mandate of Chosen Books to publish well-crafted books that recognize the gifts and ministry of the Holy Spirit and help readers live more empowered and effective lives for Jesus Christ.

Recent titles include *Help for the Fractured Soul: Experiencing Healing and Deliverance from Deep Trauma* by Candyce Roberts; *Word Spirit Power: What Happens When You Seek All God Has to Offer* by R.T. Kendall, Charles Carrin, and Jack Taylor; *Visions of the Coming Days: What to Look For and How to Prepare* by R. Loren Sandford; *God is Faithful: A Daily Invitation into the Father Heart of God* by David Wilkerson.

Chosen Books accepts manuscripts only through literary agents. All unsolicited manuscripts received will be returned to the sender without review.

FLEMING H. REVELL

Revell looks for practical books that help bring the Christian faith to everyday life. The list includes fiction, Christian living, self-help, marriage, family, and youth books.

Recent titles include *Waiting for Sunrise: A Cedar Key Novel* by Eva Marie Everson; *Praying God's Words for Your Husband* by Kathi Lipp; *A Forbidden Love* by Kathleen Morgan; *Mom Connection: Creating Vibrant Relationships in the Midst of Motherhood* by Tracey Bianchi; *The Pursuit of Lucy Banning* by Olivia Newport.

Revell accepts manuscripts only through literary agents. All unsolicited manuscripts received will be returned to the sender without review.

BARRICADE BOOKS, INC.

185 Bridge Plaza North, Suite 308-A, Fort Lee, NJ 07024

201-944-7600 | fax: 201-917-4951

www.barricadebooks.com | e-mail: customerservice@barricadebooks.com

Barricade publishes nonfiction and welcomes provocative material; its mission is to publish books that preserve, protect, and extend the First Amendment. House interests include arts and entertainment, pop culture, cultural studies, biography, history, politics and current events, true crime, Jewish interest, New Age, psychology, health and sexuality, and how-to/self-help.

Barricade Books was founded in 1991 by veteran publisher Lyle Stuart, who had previously founded Lyle Stuart, Inc. (Lyle Stuart, Inc., was sold and eventually became the Carol Publishing Group before Carol closed its doors in late 1999.) Barricade was launched in order to continue the tradition begun in 1956, when Lyle Stuart left his career as a newspaper reporter to become a publisher. That tradition is to specialize in books other publishers might hesitate to publish because the books are too controversial.

Titles from Barricade include *Terrorist Cop* by Mordecai Dzikansky and Robert Slater; *Jailing the Johnston Gang* by Bruce Mowday; *Gaming the Game* by Sean Patrick Griffin; *The Mafia and the Machine* by Frank Hayde; and *Battle of the Two Talmuds* by Leon Charney and Saul Mayzlish.

Complete proposals (including author bio, marketing plan, comparative titles, and sample chapters) and SASEs should be directed to:

Carole Stuart, Publisher
Allan Wilson, Senior Editor

BARRON'S/BARRON'S EDUCATIONAL SERIES, INC.

250 Wireless Boulevard, Hauppauge, NY 11788
800-645-3476 | fax: 631-434-3723
www.barronseduc.com | e-mail: barrons@barronseduc.com

Founded in 1941, Barron's Educational Series, Inc., rapidly became a leading publisher of test preparation manuals and school directories. Among the most widely recognized of Barron's many titles in these areas are its SAT I and ACT test prep books, Regents Exams books, and Profiles of American Colleges. In recent years, Barron's has expanded into many other publishing fields, introducing extensive lines of children's books, foreign language learning books and DVDs, pet care manuals, New Age books, cookbooks, business and financial advice books, parenting advice books, and art instruction books, as well as learning materials on digital formats. On average, Barron's publishes up to 300 new titles a year and maintains an extensive backlist of well over 2,000 titles. The focus remains educational.

The house offers a number of practical business series, retirement and parenting keys, programs on skills development in foreign languages (as well as in English), healthy cooking, arts and crafts techniques, biographies of well-known artists, and home and garden titles. Books on pets and pet care include numerous titles keyed to particular breeds and species of birds, fish, dogs, and cats.

Children's and young-adult books and books of family interest include series on pets, nature and the environment, dinosaurs, sports, fantasy, adventure, and humor. Many of these are picture storybooks, illustrated works, and popular reference titles of general interest.

Barron's offers an extensive general-interest series lineup for students and educators: the *Masters of Music* series, the *Megascope* series, the *Bravo* series, the *History* series, the *Natural World* series, and the *Literature Made Easy* series.

Recent titles from Barron's are *The Spirit of the Dog* by Tamsin Pickeral; *The Steampunk Gazette* by Major Tinker; *100 Gardens You Must See Before You Die*, 2nd Edition by Rae Spencer-Jones; *How to Make Your Own Brewskis: The Go-to Guide for Craft Brew Enthusiasts* by Jordan St. John and Mark Murphy; *Is that You, Wolf? Check Inside the Secret Pockets if You Dare!* by Steve Cox.

Barron's handles its own distribution. Send query letters with SASEs to the Acquisitions Manager.

BASIC BOOKS [SEE PERSEUS BOOKS GROUP]

BASKERVILLE PUBLISHERS

7105 Golf Club Drive, Suite 1102, #112, Fort Worth, TX 76179
817-923-1064 | 866-526-2312 | fax: 817-886-8713
www.baskervillepublishers.com | e-mail: authors@baskervillepublishers.com

Baskerville Publishers is a publisher of literary fiction and nonfiction, particularly books of interest to lovers of serious music and opera.

Recent Baskerville titles include *Samuel Ramey: American Bass* by Jane Scovell; *Mario Lanzo: An American Tragedy* (2nd Edition) by Armando Cesari; *Ris Stevens: A Life in Music* by John Pennino; *George London: Of Gods and Demons* by Nora London.

Send queries and SASEs to:
F. Ann Whitaker, Controller

BEACON PRESS

25 Beacon Street, Boston, MA 02108
617-742-2110 | fax: 617-723-3097
www.beacon.org

Beacon Press celebrated its 150th anniversary in 2004. The Press has been a light of independent American publishing since 1854, when the house was established by the Unitarian Universalist Church. This is an independent publisher of serious nonfiction and fiction. The output is meant to change the way readers think about fundamental issues; they promote such values as freedom of speech and thought, diversity, religious pluralism, anti-racism, and respect for diversity in all areas of life.

Beacon has published many groundbreaking classics, including James Baldwin's *Notes of a Native Son*; Herbert Marcuse's *One-Dimensional Man*; Jean Baker Miller's *Toward a New Psychology of Women*; and Mary Daly's *Gyn/Ecology*. In 1971, Beacon printed the *Senator Gravel Edition of The Pentagon Papers* in five volumes. This groundbreaking achievement marked the first time those papers had appeared in book form. Beacon is also the publisher of Marian Wright Edelman's bestselling book, *The Measure of Our Success: A Letter to My Children and Yours*, and Cornel West's acclaimed *Race Matters*.

Beacon's current publishing program emphasizes African American studies, anthropology, essays, gay/lesbian/gender studies, education, children and family issues, nature and the environment, religion, science and society, and women's studies. Beacon's continuing commitment to diversity is reflected in its *Bluestreak* books, which feature innovative literary writing by women. The series includes many acclaimed books, including the best sellers *Kindred* by Octavia Butler; *The Healing* by Gayl Jones; and *A Thousand Pieces of Gold* by Ruthann Lum McCunn.

Recent publications include *The Land Grabbers: The New Fight Over Who Owns the Earth* by Fred Pearce; *Ethical Chic: The Inside Story of the Companies We Think We Love* by Fran Hawthorne; *Mr. Hornaday's War: How a Peculiar Victorian Zookeeper Waged a Lonely Crusade for Wildlife That Changed the World* by Stefan Bechtel; *Outlaw Marriages: The Hidden Histories of Fifteen Extraordinary Same-Sex Couples* by Rodger Streitmatter.

Beacon is an associate member of the Association of American University Presses and a department of the Unitarian Universalist Association.

Beacon Press is distributed to the trade by Houghton Mifflin.

Query letters, proposals, CVs, and SASEs should be sent by regular mail to the Editorial Department.

Helen Atwan, Editorial Director—Narratives, memoirs, public health, legal issues.

Alexis Rizzuto, Editor—Environmental issues, education issues.

Joanna Green, Associate Editor—Social justice, economics, activism.

Amy Caldwell, Executive Editor—Religion in society, science and society, women's social issues.

BEAR & COMPANY [SEE INNER TRADITIONS/ BEAR & COMPANY]

BENBELLA BOOKS

6440 N. Central Expressway, Suite 617, Dallas, TX 75206
214-750-3600
www.benbellabooks.com | e-mail: feedback@benbellabooks.com

BenBella is an independent publishing house based in Dallas, Texas. Founded by Glenn Yeffeth in 2001, BenBella specializes in nonfiction books on popular culture, health, and nutrition, along with books on science, politics, psychology, and other topics.

BenBella publishes the acclaimed *Smart Pop* series, a series of anthologies on the best of pop culture. The *Smart Pop* series is where the world's smartest philosophers, scientists, psychologists, and religious scholars write—in clear English—about pop culture, and take television and movies seriously—but not too seriously.

Recent titles from BenBella Books include *Rock Your Business* by David Fishof; *Singularity Rising: Surviving and Thriving in a Smarter, Richer, and More Dangerous World* by James D. Miller; *Made With Love: The Meals On Wheels Family Cookbook* by Enid Borden; *Get A Grip: Your Journey to Get Real, Get Simple, and Get Results* by Gino Wickman and Mike Paton.

BenBella is looking for nonfiction only. E-mail queries are accepted. Address queries and SASEs to Editorial Submissions.

Glenn Yeffeth, Publisher, glenn@benbellabooks.com

BERRETT-KOEHLER PUBLISHERS

235 Montgomery Street, Suite 650, San Francisco, CA 94104-2916
415-288-0260 | fax: 415-362-2512
www.bkconnection.com | e-mail: bkpub@bkpub.com

Founded in 1992, Berrett-Koehler Publishers is committed to supporting the movement toward a more enlightened work world. The house specializes in nonfiction titles that help integrate our values with our work and work lives in the hope of creating more humane and effective organizations. More specifically, the books focus on business, management, leadership, career development, entrepreneurship, human resources, and global sustainability.

The work world is going through tumultuous changes, from the decline of job security to the rise of new structures for organizing people and work. BK believes that change is needed at all levels—individual, organizational, community, and global. Their titles address each of these levels, whether applying new scientific models to leadership, reclaiming spiritual values in the workplace, or using humor to cast light on the business world.

Just as BK publications are redefining the boundaries of business literature, the house is also "opening up new space" in the design and operation of its own business. Partnering with authors, suppliers, subcontractors, employees, customers, and societal and environmental communities, BK makes all involved in the creation of their books "stakeholders." They are striving to create a more equitable, open, and participative environment than is typically the case in the increasingly "lean and mean" world of corporate publishing.

Berrett-Koehler's current affairs line is called BK Currents. These titles explore the critical intersections between business and society with an eye on social and economic justice. The *BK Life* series helps people to create positive change, *BK Business* delivers pioneering socially responsible and effective approaches to managing organizations, and *Fast Fundamentals* provides practical expertise in article-length format for busy professionals.

Recent titles include *What To Do When There's Too Much Money* by Laura Stack; *Leaders Make the Future: Future Leadership Skills Indicator*, 2nd Edition by Bob Johansen; *The Shareholder Value Myth* by Lynn Stout; *99 to 1: How Wealth Inequality is Wrecking the World and What We Can Do About It* by Chuck Collins; *Source: The Inner Path of Knowledge Creation* by Joseph Jaworski.

Berrett-Koehler tends its own multichanneled distribution, through bookstores, direct-mail brochures, catalogs, a toll-free telephone-order number, book clubs, association book services, e-books, and special sales to business, government, and nonprofit organizations. The house is distributed to the trade via Publishers Group West.

Query letters and SASEs should be directed to:

Jeevan Sivasubramaniam, Executive Managing Editor
Steven Piersanti, President and Publisher
Neal Maillet, Editorial Director

BETHANY HOUSE [SEE BAKER PUBLISHING GROUP]

BEYOND WORDS

20827 N.W. Cornell Road, Suite 500, Hillsboro, OR 97124-9808
503-531-8700 | fax: 503-531-8773
www.beyondword.com | e-mail: info@beyondword.com

Beyond Words is a publishing company for artists, authors, and readers who share a love of words and images that inspire, delight, and educate. Founded in 1984 by Cynthia Black and Richard Cohen, Beyond Words is a boutique publisher that has published over 250 titles and has nearly 10 million books in print. In 2006, Beyond Words formed a copublishing deal with Simon & Schuster's Atria imprint; while

Beyond Words continues to publish around 15 titles per year, Atria handles the marketing, publication design, and production for all Beyond Words titles.

Subjects include mind, body, and spirit, global native wisdom, spiritual lifestyles, spiritual parenting, holistic health, and science and spirituality. Beyond Words is the publisher of our own Deborah Herman's Spiritual Writing from Inspiration to Publication.

Other recent titles include *Conscious Money* by Patricia Aburdene; *The Game of Life and How to Play It* by Rev. Ruth L. Miller, PhD; *So, You Want to Be a Comic Book Artist (revised)* by Phillip Amara; *Girls Who Rocked The World (revised)* by Michelle Roehm McCann and Ameile Welden; *Macho!* by Victor Villasenor; *Leveraging The Universe* by Mike Dooley; *Why Worry?* by Kathryn Tristan.

Beyond Words looks for authors who have passion for their books and want to work in a collaborative way. Most of their titles are by first-time authors. The editors seek to discover new authors and develop bestselling book projects.

Beyond Words no longer publishes children's, cooking, or photography books. Due to the high volume of submissions, they are unable to accept unsolicited manuscripts; however, they are accepting submissions from literary agents or trusted advisers.

Cynthia Black, President, Editor-in-Chief

BLOOMBERG PRESS (ACQUIRED BY JOHN WILEY & SONS IN 2010)

BLOOMSBURY USA

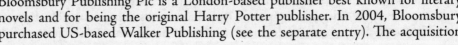

BLOOMSBURY USA
BLOOMSBURY PRESS
BLOOMSBURY CHILDREN'S BOOKS USA
175 Fifth Avenue, 8th Floor, New York, NY 10010
212-674-5151 | fax: 212-780-0115
www.bloomsburyusa.com | e-mail: info@bloomsburyusa.com
WALKER PUBLISHING COMPANY
WALKER BOOKS FOR YOUNG READERS
646-307-5151 | fax: 212-727-0984
www.walker.co.uk

Bloomsbury USA, launched in 1998 by Bloomsbury Publishing Plc, is an independent publisher of high-quality fiction and nonfiction for adults and children. Bloomsbury Publishing Plc is a London-based publisher best known for literary novels and for being the original Harry Potter publisher. In 2004, Bloomsbury purchased US-based Walker Publishing (see the separate entry). The acquisition and integration of Walker enabled Bloomsbury to broaden its presence in the US market, especially in adult narrative nonfiction and children's nonfiction. In 2008, Bloomsbury debuted a new imprint, Bloomsbury Press, devoted to serious nonfiction and headed by Peter Ginna, former editorial director of Oxford University Press.

Bloomsbury USA adult titles include works in fiction, arts, memoir, science, travel, history, biography, food, humor, sports, gardening, relationships and self-help, crime, women's studies, reference, and current affairs.

Recent releases include *Hidden Harmonies* by Robert Kaplan and Ellen Kaplan; *El Narco: Inside Mexico's Criminal Insurgency* by Ioan Grillo; *Volcke: The Triumph of Persistence* by William L. Silber; *What's the Economy for, Anyway?* by John De Graaf, and David K. Batker; *America Aflame: How The Civil War Created A Nation* by David Goldfield.

BLOOMSBURY PRESS

Titles from Bloomsbury Press include *A Difficult Woman: The Life and Times of Lillian Hellman* by Alice Kessler-Harris; *The Great Disruption: Why the Climate Crisis Will Bring On The End of...* by Paul Gilding; *The Dreyfus Affair: The Scandal That Tore France in Two* by Piers Paul Read; *Whatever It Is, I Don't Like It: The Best of Howard Jacobson* by Howard Jacobson.

BLOOMSBURY CHILDREN'S BOOKS USA

Bloomsbury Children's Books welcomes picture-book manuscripts and queries for longer works, whether fiction or nonfiction. They publish picture books, chapter books, easy readers, middle-grade and young adult novels, fantasy, and some nonfiction. With queries, please include a synopsis of the book and the first ten pages or first chapter to the Children's Book Acquisitions Department. Please do not send originals or only copies, because Bloomsbury Children's Books no longer responds to unsolicited submissions, and will only contact authors if they are interested in acquiring the work.

Recent children's titles from Bloomsbury USA include *How They Croaked: The Awful Ends of the Awfully Famous* by Georgia Bragg; *The Lion's Share* by Matthew McElligott; *Even Monsters Need Haircuts* by Mathew McElligott; *The Joshua Files: Zero Moment* by M.G. Harris; *The Death Catchers* by Jennifer Anne Kogler.

Bloomsbury USA does not accept unsolicited submissions, and does not assume responsibility for unsolicited manuscripts they receive. They consider manuscripts represented by established literary agents.

Because of new postal weight regulations, Bloomsbury cannot return any manuscripts, art, or other materials. Please include only recyclable materials with your submission, and send an SASE for their response only.

Anton Mueller, Executive Editor
Melanie Cecka, Executive Editor, Bloomsbury Children's USA

Peter Ginna, Editorial Director, Bloomsbury Press
Benjamin Adams, Senior Editor
Nancy Miller, Editor
Rachel Manheimer, Editor
Peter Beatty, Editor

WALKER PUBLISHING COMPANY

Walker Publishing Company became an imprint of Bloomsbury USA when it was acquired by Bloomsbury in 2004. During the course of its 47-year history as an independent, Walker has published best sellers in its adult and children's lists; recently they have published Dava Sobel's best sellers, *Longitude* and *Galileo's Daughter*; Mark Kurlansky's *Cod and Salt*; Ross King's *Michelangelo and the Pope's Ceiling*; and Judith Finchler's children's classic, *Testing Miss Malarkey*, illustrated by Kevin O'Malley.

Walker currently publishes three lists a year, each consisting of around ten picture books and four to five middle-grade and/or young-adult works, for a total of 40–45 titles annually.

Walker has been credited in *Business Week* as "a pioneer of a now-ubiquitous book genre—stories about forgotten people or offbeat things that changed the world." Sometimes called microhistories, these books are biographies of inanimate objects—like salt or longitude. Walker publisher George Gibson said recently that he looks to acquire manuscripts with great storytelling and fine writing. He publishes books for "thoughtful folks."

The prolific Isaac Asimov published more books with Walker than with any other publisher, and now David Bodanis ($E=mc2$); Simon Singh (*Fermat's Enigma*); Chet Raymo (*Climbing Brandon* and *An Intimate Look at the Night Sky*); and, most recently, Harvard astronomer Owen Gingerich (*The Book Nobody Read*) have published with Walker.

While mystery/thriller publishing is somewhat less the focus of the house, it has published John le Carré. Please note that Walker does not publish adult fiction outside of the mystery category. The house no longer publishes Westerns, thrillers, or Regency romance novels.

Recent Walker titles include *The Accidental Feminist: How Elizabeth Taylor Raised Our Consciousness...* by M.G. Lord; *The Sugar Barons: Family, Corruption, Empire, and War in the West Indies* by Matthew Parker.

WALKER BOOKS FOR YOUNG READERS

Beth Walker started the children's division, which has now been a central part of the company for some 40 years, featuring authors such as Barbara Cooney, Tomie de Paola, Michael McCurdy, and Pat and Fred McKissack, whose *Long Hard Journey* won the Coretta Scott King Award.

Walker Young Readers is actively seeking middle-grade and young adult novels and well-paced picture book manuscripts for the preschool and early elementary age levels. They do not publish folk tales, fairy tales, textbooks, myths, legends, series, novelties, science fiction, fantasy, or horror.

Walker Young Readers titles include *Bedtime for Mommy* by Amy Krouse; *The Wide-Awake Princess* by E.D. Baker; *Little Blog on the Prairie* by Cathleen Davitt Bell; *My Circus* by Xavier Deneux; *Poop Happened!* by Sarah Albee; and *Rules of Attraction* by Simone Elkeles.

Submit your manuscript—or the first 75 pages of it—with SASE for a response only to (they recycle all submissions and return only their response):

George Gibson, Publisher, Walker
Caroline Abbey, Walker Children's
Michelle Nagler, Editor, Children's
Melanie Cecka, Editor, Children's

BLUEBRIDGE BOOKS

240 West 35th Street, Suite 500, New York, NY 10001
212-244-4166 | fax: 212-279-0927
www.bluebridgebooks.com | e-mail: janguerth@bluebridgebooks.com

BlueBridge is an independent publisher of international nonfiction based in New York City. Publisher and founder Jan-Erik Guerth started BlueBridge after four years directing the Hidden Spring imprint of Paulist Press. Guerth left Hidden Spring in 2003 and spent a year preparing for the launch of BlueBridge, which he founded with his own money and investments from friends and family. BlueBridge is currently publishing six to eight books a year.

Recent titles from BlueBridge include *Queen Elizabeth in the Garden* by Trea Martyn; *Island: How Islands Transform the World* by J. Edward Chamberlin; *The Monastery of the Heart: An Invitation to a Meaningful Life* by Joan Chittister; *A Private History of Happiness: 99 Moments of Joy from Around the World* by George Meyerson.

BlueBridge is distributed by IPG. Send queries and SASEs to:

Jan-Erik Guerth, Publisher

BOYDS MILLS PRESS

CALKINS CREEK BOOKS
FRONT STREET
LEMINSCAAT
WORDSONG
A Subsidiary of Highlights for Children

815 Church Street, Honesdale, PA 18431
570-253-1164 | 800-490-5111
www.boydsmillspress.com | e-mail: contact@boydsmillspress.com

Boyds Mills Press, the trade division of Highlights for Children, Inc., was launched in 1990. Publishing books was a logical step for Highlights, which has a long tradition of helping children develop a love of reading. Boyds Mills produces books for children, picture books, novels, nonfiction, and poetry—nonsensical verse, as well as more serious fare. The press promotes a solid seasonal list of new titles and hosts a hefty backlist of titles that challenge, inspire, and entertain.

Boyds Mills Press reaches children primarily through bookstores, libraries, and schools. The list runs about 50 books per year. Poetry is published under the Wordsong imprint, the only imprint of its kind devoted exclusively to poetry for children.

Respect for children is among the highest priorities when Boyds Mills Press acquires a manuscript. They aim to publish good stories with lasting value, avoid the trendy, and never publish a book simply to fill a market need. Whether pure entertainment or more challenging subject matter, the story always comes first.

Recent Boyds Mills titles include *A Beach Tail* by Karen Lynn Williams; *Planet Hunter* by Vicki Wittenstein; *My School in the Rain Forest* by Margriet Ruurs; and *Mama, Will It Snow Tonight?* by Nancy White Carlstrom.

CALKINS CREEK BOOKS

The Calkins Creek Books imprint introduces children to the people, places, and events that shaped American history. Through picture books, chapter books, and novels for ages eight and up, combining original and extensive research with creative energetic writing, Calkins authors transport their readers back in time to recognizable places with living and breathing people. Recent books from Calkins Creek include *Hope and Tears* by Gwenyth Swain and *Write On, Mercy!* by Gretchen Woelfle.

FRONT STREET

Front Street publishes young-adult fiction that deals with children in crisis or children at risk, and offers hope and comfort no matter how difficult the subject matter. Their picture books emphasize art and design. Titles from Front Street include *The Dog in the Wood* by Minoka Scröder; *Planet Pregnancy* by Linda High; and *Wild Things* by Clay Carmichael.

LEMINSCAAT

Leminscaat is a highly esteemed publishing house located in Rotterdam, The Netherlands. Their list represents the broad traditions of European picture books and incorporates the best contemporary art, design, and story. Some titles from

Leminscaat include *Cold Skin* by Steven Herrick; *Loserville* by Peter Johnson; and *Markus and the Girls* by Klaus Hagerup.

WORDSONG

Wordsong is the only imprint in children's publishing in America that is dedicated to poetry. Their books range from the silly to the serious and are infused with the wordplay and imagery that let readers view the world in new and thoughtful ways. Latest from Wordsong include *Bug Off! Creepy Crawly Poems* by Jane Yolen; *Cowboys* by Dan Burr; *Pirates* by David L. Harrison; *Running With Trains* by Michael J. Rosen; *Thunderboom!* by Rob Shepperson.

Boyds Mills Press handles its own distribution.

This publisher is actively seeking picture books, middle-grade and young-adult novels, and nonfiction and poetry for all ages. For all imprints, send manuscripts, query letters, and SASEs to the Manuscript Coordinator.

Larry Rosler, Editorial Director (Boyds Mills)

Carolyn P. Yoder, Editor (Calkins Creek)

Andy Boyles, Editor—Science and natural history.

Joan Hyman, Editor—Wordsong.

GEORGE BRAZILLER, INC.

277 Broadway, Suite 708, New York, NY 10007
212-889-0909 | fax: 212-689-5405
www.georgebraziller.com | e-mail: info@georgebraziller.com

Founded in 1955 and celebrating more than half a century in business, George Braziller, Inc., is a small, independent publishing house based in New York City. The house publishes international literature and beautiful books on art and design, architecture, and art movements and history. The house also publishes selected literary titles, as well as philosophy, science, history, criticism, and biographical works. Much of Braziller's fiction and poetry is foreign literature in translation, although the publisher does publish original literary novels (such as works by Janet Frame) and works in the English language that have received initial publication elsewhere. The house aims to be consistently discovering new writers and exploring new areas in the world of art.

Braziller also has a strong interest in literary criticism and writing relating to the arts, in addition to a small selection of contemporary and modern poetry. *Essential Readings in Black Literature* is a Braziller series that features world-class writers from around the globe. Other Braziller series include *Library of Far Eastern Art* and *New Directions in Architecture*.

Braziller recently introduced a young-adult series with titles including *Figs and Fate: Stories about Growing Up in the Arab World Today* by Elsa Marston; and *Changing, Changing* by Aracelis Girmay.

Other recent titles include *Selected Early Poems* by Charles Simic; *Farewell, My Queen* by Chantal Thomas; *The Donner Party (Revised)* by George Keithley.

Braziller titles are distributed by W. W. Norton & Co.

Submissions with manuscript (nothing in excess of 50 pages) and CV should be directed to:

George Braziller, Publisher

BRAZOS PRESS [SEE BAKER PUBLISHING GROUP]

BURNS & OATES [SEE CONTINUUM INTERNATIONAL PUBLISHING GROUP]

CANONGATE BOOKS [SEE GROVE/ATLANTIC, INC.]

CAREER PRESS

NEW PAGE BOOKS
220 West Parkway, Unit 12, Pompton Plains, NJ 07444
201-848-0310 | 800-227-3371
www.careerpress.com | www.newpagebooks.com

With their motto, "Enriching Your Life One Book at a Time," Career Press publishes general nonfiction that addresses real, practical needs. Their useful, accessible how-to books reach a broad market of average Americans—people grappling with issues relating to job-hunting, career management, education, money management, and personal goals.

Career Press was launched in 1985 with a commitment to publish quality books on careers, business, reference, motivation, sales, personal finance, real estate, and more. Career Press publishes quality books on topics most needed in the marketplace, written by established, credentialed, media-savvy professionals, and then promotes and publicizes them full force. They are seeking books in the categories of business, career, job search, college preparation, small business, entrepreneurship, motivation, sales, negotiation, study aids, and reference. This list is not comprehensive, and other categories are published based on the project's tone, approach, and sales potential.

Recent titles from Career Press include *The Hands-Off Manager* by Steve Chandler and Duane Black; *Homework Helpers: Physics* by Greg Curran; *The Synthesis Effect: Your Direct Path to Personal Power and Transformation* by John McGrail, PhD; *The Zen Leader* by Ginny Whitelow.

NEW PAGE BOOKS

In 2000 Career Press created a new imprint, New Page Books, to expand the category list to include New Age, supernatural/paranormal, ancient mysteries, Wicca, mythology, alternative health, nutrition/wellness, pop history, and weddings.

Recent titles from New Page include *The Last Secrets of Maya Technology* by James A. O'Kon, P.E.; *A New Way to Be Human* by Robert V. Taylor; *The Book of Transformation* by Lisa Barretta; *A.D. After Disclosure: When The Government Finally Reveals the Truth About Alien Contact* by Richard M. Dolan, and Bryce Zabel

Career Press/New Page Books distributes its own list.

Query letters, proposals, and SASEs should be directed to the Acquisitions Department.

Michael Pye, Acquisitions Editor, mpye@careerpress.com
Adam Schwartz, Acquisitions Editor, aschwartz@careerpress.com
Gina Hoogerhyde, Editorial Director, ghoogerhyde@careerpress.com

CEDAR FORT, INC.

BONNEVILLE BOOKS
CFI BOOKS
COUNCIL PRESS
SWEETWATER BOOKS
2373 West 700 South, Springville, UT 84663
801-489-4084 | 800-SKYBOOK | fax: 801-489-1097 | 800-388-3727
www.cedarfort.com | e-mail: submissions@cedarfort.com
HORIZON PUBLISHERS
191 N. 560 East, Bountiful, UT 84010-3628
801-295-9451 | 866-818-6277 | fax: 801-298-1305
http://www.ldshorizonpublishers.com | e-mail: LDSHorizonPublishers@gmail.com

Cedar Fort was founded in May 1896 and initially produced Latter-Day Saints (LDS) books for other publishers as an LDS book printer broker. Founder Lyle Mortimer began distributing LDS books and other items until, in September 1987, the company released its first publication, *Beyond the Veil* by Lee Nelson, which became an immediate best seller.

BONNEVILLE BOOKS

Bonneville Books mainly publishes LDS fiction. Titles from Bonneville Books include *My Loving Vigil Keeping* by Carla Kelly; *The Gift of Angels* by Rachel Ann Nunes; *The Misadventures of Phillip Isaac Penn: PIP Goes to Camp* by Donna L. Peterson; *The Epic Tales of a Misfit Hero* by Matt Peterson.

CFI BOOKS

CFI searches for life-enriching, edifying, and enhancing LDS books geared to the LDS market in any form. In recent years the company has published several highly acclaimed novels and continues to branch out into the world beyond the LDS books market, in the traditional manner, on the Internet, and in alternative markets.

CFI Books publishes LDS doctrinal books, scriptural commentaries, self-help, cookbooks, and some fiction. Recent titles from CFI Books include *The Doctrine and Covenants Made Easier, Part 1: Section 1 through Section 42* by David J. Ridges; *Family Treasures: 15 Lessons, Tips, and Tricks for Discovering your Family History* by Barry J. Ewell; *101 Gourmet Ice Cream Creations for Every Craving* by Wendy Paul; *A Sisterhood of Strength: True Stories of Miraculous Service* by Diony George.

COUNCIL PRESS

Council Press mostly publishes historical fiction and nonfiction. Titles include *Storm Testament III* by Lee Nelson; *The White Bedouin* by George Potter; *The Bearded White God of Ancient America: The Legend of Quetzalcoatl* by Donald Hemingway and W. David Hemmingway; and *Jumping Off Places* by Laura Stratton Friel.

SWEETWATER BOOKS

Sweetwater Books produces books intended primarily for the national market. Titles include *Chester the Chimpanzee* by Les and Genny Nuckolls; *Tombs of Terror, Volume 2: The Lost Curse* by T. Lynn Adams; *Flin's Destiny Series, Book 2: Garden of the Lost Souls* by Erik Olsen; *Silver Falls Series, Volume 3: Rising Winds of Silver Falls* by Rebecca Woods.

E-mail submissions are accepted, but hard copies are preferred. Send a query letter and SASE to an Acquisitions Editor.

Jennifer Fielding, Acquisitions Editor, submissions@cedarfort.com

Jeffrey Marsh, Acquisitions Editor

HORIZON PUBLISHERS

Horizon Publishers is a family-run corporation that publishes wholesome, informative books and DVDs for a variety of marketplaces. In 2004, Horizon was acquired by Cedar Fort, Inc. (CFI), a leading publisher of LDS (Latter-Day Saints) fiction and nonfiction titles since its founding in 1986; CFI now publishes 100 titles per year, roughly 25 percent of the Utah book market. In a unique arrangement, CFI is slowly acquiring Horizon's assets; Horizon continues its editorial operations while CFI picks up production and distribution.

Established in 1971, Horizon Publishers has various product lines in which it has "distinctive competencies"—publishing areas in which it is noted for having a strong offering of products of noteworthy quality. In the general trade market, these areas include such topics as outdoor life, camping, Dutch-oven and outdoor cooking, cookbooks, outdoor survival skills, food storage, gardening, emergency preparedness, life after death and near-death experiences, marriage and family life, and counted cross-stitch designs.

Many of Horizon Publishers' books are written for readers in the general religious marketplace. Numerous books the firm produces are for the general Christian marketplace, including those on marriage, family life, raising and teaching children, Bible studies, and comparative religions.

Recent titles include *Unearthed* by Lara Stauffer

Horizon Publishers is distributed by Cedar Fort.

The editorial board of Horizon Publishers seeks products that will lift, inspire, inform, and entertain their readers. Horizon publishes 20 to 30 new titles per year, selecting its new releases from the 2,000-plus queries and manuscripts it receives annually. E-mail queries are not accepted. Direct queries, proposals, and SASEs to the Editorial Board.

Duane S. Crowther, Founder and CEO

CELESTIAL ARTS [SEE TEN SPEED PRESS]

CHELSEA GREEN PUBLISHING COMPANY

PO Box 428, 85 North Main Street, Suite 120, White River Junction, VT 05001
802-295-6300 | fax: 802-295-6444
www.chelseagreen.com | e-mail: info@chelseagreen.com

Chelsea Green publishes trade nonfiction on sustainable living, organic gardening and food, renewable energy and green building, nature and the environment, and books on political and social issues. Founded in 1984, Chelsea Green Publishing is an independent and individualistic firm; the house continues to grow its list with about 15 new releases each year (in hardcover and trade paper formats) and a hardy backlist with well over 400 titles in print. Chelsea Green sees publishing as a tool for effecting cultural change. Their purpose is "to stop the destruction of the natural world by challenging the beliefs and practices that are enabling this destruction and by providing inspirational and practical alternatives that promote sustainable living."

Some areas of particular interest for Chelsea Green include organic gardening and market farming, local agricultural movements and healthy food supplies, environmentally friendly building techniques, renewable energy sources and energy conservation, simpler lifestyles, economic systems that account for environmental and social needs, political activism that promotes sustainable economies, philosophical writing that promotes sustainable living, and natural science with a cross-disciplinary and ecological perspective.

Recent Chelsea Green titles *Altered Genes, Twisted Truth: How the Venture to Genetically Engineer Our Food Has Subverted Science, Corrupted Government, and Systematically Deceived the Public* by Steven M. Druker; *The Organic Seed Grower: A Farmer's Guide to Vegetable Seed Production* by John Navazio; *Farms with a Future: Creating and Growing a Sustainable Farm Business* by Rebecca Thistlethwaite; *Desert or Paradise: Renaturing Endangered Landscapes, Integrating Diversified Aquaculture, and Creating Biotopes in Urban Spaces* by Sepp Holzer.

Chelsea Green handles its own distribution and distributes for a number of other small, innovative independent presses such as Green Books, Ltd.; Otto Graphics; Ecological Design Press; Harmonious Press; and Seed Savers Exchange.

An electronic query may be addressed to submissions@chelseagreen.com. Proposals with SASEs should be directed via regular mail to:

Margo Baldwin, President and Publisher, mbaldwin@chelseagreen.com
Joni Praded, Editor-in-Chief, jpraded@chelseagreen.com
Susan Warner, Senior Editor, swarner@chelseagreen.com

CHOSEN BOOKS [SEE BAKER PUBLISHING GROUP]

CHRONICLE BOOKS

680 Second Street, San Francisco, CA 94107
415-537-4200 | 800-722-6657 | fax: 415-537-4460
www.chroniclebooks.com | e-mail: frontdesk@chroniclebooks.com

Chronicle Books was founded in 1967 and over the years has developed a reputation for award-winning, innovative books. The company continues to challenge conventional publishing wisdom, setting trends in both subject and format. Chronicle titles include cookbooks, fine art, design, photography, architecture titles, nature books, poetry and literary fiction, travel guides, and gift items. Chronicle publishes about 175 books per year.

Titles of note include Martha Zamora's *Frida Kahlo: The Brush of Anguish* (1990), and Nick Bantock's *Griffin & Sabine* (1991). Originally slated for an edition of 10,000, this interactive book became the most talked-about title of the year and a *New York Times* best seller for 50 weeks. The two subsequent volumes in the trilogy,

Sabine's Notebook and The Golden Mean, were also Times best sellers. A more recent monster hit was the Worst-Case Scenario franchise.

The company brought the same innovative philosophy to cookbooks with its four-color release of Sushi (1981), which sold 90,000 copies and is still in print. Chronicle Books also publishes James McNair's eye-catching cookbooks, all perennial best sellers having sold over 1 million copies.

The Children's list was launched in 1988 and has published the bestselling Mama, Do You Love Me? (over 1 million copies in hardcover); Ten Little Rabbits (450,000 copies); and N.C. Wyeth's Pilgrims (100,000 copies). The list has grown to include not only traditional picture books but also affordable paperbacks, board books, plush toys, and novelty merchandise.

In 1992, Chronicle Books launched its gift division to develop ancillary products such as the Griffin & Sabine address book and writing box, the bestselling 52 Deck series, and a motorcycle journal and address book based on the Harley-Davidson image archives.

Recent Chronicle titles are The Fresh & Green Table: Delicious Ideas for Bringing Vegetables Into Every Meal by Susie Middleton; Fun Without Dick and Jane: Your Guide to a Delightfully Empty Nest by Christie Mellor; Instant Love: How to Make Magic and Memories with Polaroids by Jenifer Altman, Susannah Conway, and Amanda Gilligan; Rad Rides: The Best BMX Bikes of All Time by Gavin Lucas.

Recent Chronicle Children's books include Chloe, Instead by Micah Player; Project Jackalope by Emily Ecton; The Art of Brave by Jenny Lerew; Wookiee Pies, Clone Scones, and Other Galactic Goodies by Robin Davis and Lara Starr.

For adult titles, query letters, proposals, and SASEs should be directed via regular mail only to the Adult Trade Editorial Staff. Chronicle Books is no longer accepting fiction.

With children's titles, projects for older children should be submitted by a query letter, synopsis, and three sample chapters, with SASE. Projects for younger children may be sent in their entirety. Send via regular mail to the Children's Division.

Sarah Malarkey, Publishing Director
Bill LeBlond, Editorial Director—Cookbooks.
Kelli Chipponeri, Executive Editor
Dean Burrell, Editorial Director
Emily Haines, Editor
Lorena Jones, Editor—Children's.
Naomi Kirsten, Editor
Jennifer Kong, Editor
Laura Lee Mattingly, Editor
Amy Treadwell, Editor—Food.

CITADEL [SEE KENSINGTON PUBLISHING]

CITY LIGHTS PUBLISHERS

261 Columbus Avenue, San Francisco, CA 94133
415-362-8193 | fax: 415-362-4921
www.citylights.com | e-mail: staff@citylights.com

City Lights publishes literary essays and criticism, biography, philosophy, literary fiction (including first novels), poetry, books on political and social issues, and ecumenical volumes featuring both words and visual images.

City Lights Booksellers and Publishers is a renowned American institution. Founded in 1953 by Beat poet Lawrence Ferlinghetti, its San Francisco bookstore is a North Beach landmark and, above all else, a resolute cultural tradition.

City Lights initially featured the *Pocket Poets* series, which introduced such writers as Gregory Corso, Allen Ginsberg, Jack Kerouac, and other Beats to a wider audience. Since then, as successive literary generations have commenced and terminated, City Lights continues to flourish. Today, it has nearly 200 titles in print and puts out a dozen new titles each year.

Recent City Lights titles *The Wondrous Mushroom: Mycolatry in Mesoamerica* by R. Gordon Wasson; *National Insecurity: The Cost of American Militarism* by Melvin A. Goodman; *Robert Duncan in San Francisco*, Expanded Edition by Michael Rumaker; *A Long Day's Evening* by Bilge Karasu; *Winged Shoes and a Shield: Collected Stories* by Don Bajema.

City Lights is distributed by Consortium Book Sales and Distribution and has its own in-house mail-order fulfillment department.

City Lights no longer accepts unsolicited submissions.

Elaine Katzenberger, Acquisitions Editor—Latin American literature, women's studies, fiction.

Nancy J. Peters, Publisher

Robert Sharrard, Acquisitions Editor—Poetry, literature.

CLARION BOOKS [SEE HOUGHTON MIFFLIN]

CLEIS PRESS

2246 Sixth Street, Berkeley, CA 94710
510-845-8000 | 800-780-2279 | fax: (510) 845-8001
www.cleispress.com | e-mail: cleis@cleispress.com

Founded in 1980, Cleis Press publishes 34 new books a year on sexual politics and self-help, lesbian and gay studies and culture, sex guides, feminism, fiction, erotica, humor, and translations of world-class literature. Cleis titles cross markets from niches of gender and sexuality to reach the widest possible audiences.

Projects from Cleis Press garner numerous awards and reviews—and include many bestselling books. The house is committed to publishing the most original, creative, and provocative works by women and men in the United States and Canada.

Recent titles from the Cleis list include *Happily Even After: A Guide to Getting Through (and Beyond) the Grief of Widowhood* by Carole Brody Fleet; *The Elements of Expression: Putting Thoughts into Words* by Arthur Plotnik; *Use Your Words: A Writing Guide for Mothers* by Kate Hopper; *She Shifters* by Delilah Devlin.

Cleis Press is represented to the book trade by Publishers Group West.

Please do not send submissions via USPS or any other delivery service. E-mail queries only are accepted. Book proposals and sample chapters with SASEs should be directed to:

Frédérique Delacoste, Publisher and Acquisitions Editor, fdelacoste @cleispress.com

Felice Newman, Publisher, fnewman@cleispress.com

Brenda Knight, Associate Publisher, bknight@cleispress.com

CLEVELAND STATE UNIVERSITY POETRY CENTER

2121 Euclid Avenue, RT 1841, Cleveland, OH 44115-2214
216-687-2000 | 888-278-6473 | fax: 216-687-6943
www.csuohio.edu/poetrycenter | e-mail: poetrycenter@csuohio.edu

The Cleveland State University Poetry Center was founded in 1962 to offer encouragement to poets and writers and to further the public's knowledge of and appreciation for contemporary poetry. The Series Editor and Director is Michael Dumanis. The Poetry Center Manager is Rita Grabowski.

The Poetry Center began publishing in 1971 and since that time has developed a list of over 150 nationally distributed titles. The press publishes poets of local, regional, and international reach, generally under the aegis of one or another of the center's ongoing series. Under its flying-unicorn logo, CSU Poetry Center most often publishes trade paper editions, but has also offered some titles in hardbound editions. Its publications include the national CSU Poetry Series, the Cleveland Poets Series for Ohio writers, as well as other titles of interest, including the *Imagination* series. CSU Poetry Center presents a variety of styles and viewpoints—some with evident sociopolitical bent, others with broadly inspirational themes, and others notable for their strong individualistic inflections.

The current editorial board consists of Kazim Ali, Mary Bettinger, Michael Dumanis, and Sarah Gridley. The Cleveland State University Poetry Center Prize of $1,000 is awarded for the best book-length manuscript in two categories submitted annually from November 1 through April 15. There is a $25.00 reader's fee. The "Open" Competition is limited to poets who have published at least one book-length collection of their poems. The "First Book" Competition is for poets who have not previously published a full-length collection. Send a business-sized, self-addressed, stamped envelope for complete contest guidelines, or check the "Contest Guidelines" link on their website.

Some titles from the Cleveland State University Poetry Center are *You Don't Know What You Don't Know* by John Bradley; *Clamor* by Elyse Fenton; *Brazil* by Jesse Lee Kercheval; *Snaketown* by Kathleen Wakefield; *I Live in a Hut* by S.E. Smith; *Uncanny Valley* by Jon Woodward.

Poetry Center books are distributed through Partners Book Distributing, Ingram, and Spring Church Book Company.

The Poetry Center only accepts manuscripts submitted between November 1 and February 1 ($25 entry fee; full manuscripts only). For complete guidelines on the Center's annual competitions, visit the website or send request plus SASE to:

Michael Dumanis, Director
Rita Grabowski, Manager

COFFEE HOUSE PRESS

79 Thirteenth Avenue NE, Suite 110, Minneapolis, MN 55413
612-338-0125 | fax: 612-338-4004
www.coffeehousepress.org

Coffee House Press was founded in 1984, and took its name from the long tradition of coffee houses as places for the free exchange of ideas, where each individual had equal time for expression, regardless of station or background. The press is an award-winning, nonprofit literary publisher dedicated to innovation in the craft of writing and preservation of the tradition of book arts. Coffee House produces books that present the dreams and ambitions of people who have been underrepresented in published literature, books that shape our national consciousness while strengthening a larger sense of community. The house produces contemporary poetry, short fiction, and novels. Contemporary writing that is challenging, thought-provoking, daring, vibrant, funny, or lyrical is the key.

Coffee House Press aims to enrich our literary heritage, and to contribute to the cultural life of our community. Coffee House Press publishes books that advance the craft of writing; the house colophon is a steaming book that lets the reader know (as the Coffee House motto runs) "where good books are brewing."

Recent titles from Coffee House include *Hold It 'Til It Hurts* by T. Geronimo Johnson; *Kind One* by Laird Hunt; *Read This! Handpicked Favorites from America's Indie Bookstores* by Ann Patchett.

Coffee House Press oversees its own marketing and sales network with the assistance of regional representatives; trade distribution is handled by Consortium.

Coffee House Press accepts manuscripts on an ongoing basis. For fiction, query letters with 20- to 30-page samples and SASEs should be directed to:

Allan Kornblum, Senior Editor and Founder

CONARI PRESS [SEE RED WHEEL/WEISER]

CONTINUUM INTERNATIONAL PUBLISHING GROUP

BURNS & OATES
T&T CLARK, USA
THOEMMES PRESS
A Division of Bloomsbury USA
80 Maiden Lane, Suite 704, New York, NY 10038
212-953-5858 | fax: 212-953-5944
www.continuumbooks.com | e-mail: info@continuumbooks.com

Continuum is the trade and academic imprint of the Continuum International Publishing Group, a growing family of religious, trade, and academic publishers headquartered in London, with offices in New York, Harrisburg, Denver, Bristol, and Poole. It is now a division of Bloomsbury USA. Continuum publishes high-quality nonfiction in the humanities, including theology and religious studies, spirituality, philosophy, education, linguistics, literature, performing arts, the social sciences, women's studies, and popular culture. With a wide range of books from its popular music series, 33⅓, to works by the great Jewish theologian Abraham Joshua Heschel, Jonathan Sacks, Chief Rabbi of Britain and the Commonwealth, and philosopher Roger Scruton, Continuum's books are read by academics, educators, librarians, students, and the intellectually curious around the world. Its output consists of trade books, texts, scholarly monographs, and reference works. Continuum offers about 500 new publications a year, as well as nearly 6,000 established backlist titles.

From the Continuum list are *Brian Eno's Another Green World* by Geeta Dayal; *A Cultural Dictionary of Punk* by Nicholas Rombes; *Bedside, Bathtub & Armchair Companion to Dickens* by Brian Murray; *Wesley: A Guide for the Perplexed* by Jason E. Vickers; *The Power of Comics* by Randy Duncan; *Sin Bravely* by Mark Ellingsen; *Between Heaven and Charing Cross* by Martin Warner; and *The Secret Temple* by Peter Levenda.

BURNS & OATES

Burns & Oates is the premier Roman Catholic publishing imprint in Great Britain, and a leading imprint throughout the English-speaking world. Authors include Timothy Radcliffe OP, Joseph Ratzinger (now Pope Benedict XVI), Cardinal Daneels, Eamon Duffy, Cardinal Walter Kasper, and Anselm Grün. Burns & Oates titles include *St. John of the Cross* by Peter Tyler; *Excellent Mrs. Fry* by Anne Isba; *Islam Today* by Ron Geaves; and *Tudor Queens of England* by David Loades.

T&T CLARK, USA

T&T Clark's tradition of publishing works by world-class scholars in both Europe and North America stretches back to 1821, when it was founded in Edinburgh by Thomas Clark (he was joined in 1846 by his nephew, also named Thomas). T&T Clark became part of Continuum in 2000. In 2003, the three religious academic imprints of Sheffield Academic Press, Trinity Press International, and T&T Clark were united under one imprint.

The list includes past and present biblical scholars such as James D. G. Dunn, Richard Hays, Martin Hengel, and Gerd Theissen, and theologians such as Karl Barth, Wolfhart Pannenberg, Karl Rahner, and T. F. Torrance. Recent T&T Clark titles include *Psalmody and Poetry in Old Testament Ethics* by Dirk J. Human; *Outside of Eden: Cain in the Ancient Versions of Genesis 4.1-16* by M. W. Scarlata; *Edward Schillebeeckx and Contemporary Theology* by Lieven Boeve, Frederiek Depoortere, and Stephan van Erp; *Democracy in the Christian Church: An Historical, Theological and Political Case* by Luca Badini Confalonieri.

THOEMMES PRESS

Thoemmes Press began in 1989 as an adjunct to Thoemmes Antiquarian Books. Subsequently, Thoemmes Press became independent. The press rapidly established an international reputation for scholarly reference publishing. In particular, it published primary source material (often in facsimile form, but sometimes re-set) and Biographical Dictionaries in Philosophy and allied areas of intellectual history. Thoemmes Press titles include *The Bibliography of Modern British Philosophy* by John G. Slater; *The Biographical Dictionary of British Economists* by Donald Rutherford; *British Education: Or, The Source of the Disorders of Great Britain* by Thomas Sheridan; *The Dictionary of Seventeenth-Century French Philosophers* by Luc Foisneau.

Continuum is distributed through Books International. Continuum also distributes the publishing programs of Chiron Publications, Daimon Publications, Spring Publications, and Paragon House.

Query letters via e-mail are preferred, or send via regular mail with SASEs, to the appropriate editor:

David Barker, PhD, Editorial Director (Continuum)—Film, music, popular culture, politics; david@continuumbooks.com

Marie-Claire Antoine, Acquisitions Editor—Politics and international relations; mantoine@continuumbooks.com
Angela Kao, Editor—History

COPPER CANYON PRESS

PO Box 271, Building 313, Fort Worden State Park,
Port Townsend, WA 98368
360-385-4925 | 877-501-1393 | fax: 360-385-4985
www.coppercanyonpress.org | e-mail: poetry@coppercanyonpress.org

Copper Canyon Press was founded in 1972 in the belief that good poetry is essential to the individual spirit and a necessary element in a thriving culture. The press publishes poetry exclusively and has established an international reputation for its commitment to its authors, editorial acumen, and dedication to expanding the audience of poetry. The Copper Canyon mission is to publish poetry distinguished in both content and design, within the context of belief that the publisher's art—like the poet's—is sacramental. The press publishes in hardcover and paperback.

Copper Canyon Press publishes new collections of poetry by both revered and emerging American poets, anthologies, prose books about poetry, translations of classical and contemporary work from many of the world's cultures, and re-issues of out-of-print poetry classics. Within its ambitious vision, there are limitations; Copper Canyon generally does not sign many new writers. The house assigns its resources to furthering its established roster. The publisher's success in its aim is proven through abundant and continuing recognition of its authors via honors, awards, grants, and fellowships.

Copper Canyon has published more than 300 books and CDs, including works by Nobel Laureates Pablo Neruda, Odysseas Elytis, Octavio Paz, Vincente Aleixandre, and Czeslaw Milosz; Pulitzer Prize winners Carolyn Kizer, Maxine Kumin, and W.S. Merwin; and National Book Award winners Hayden Carruth and Lucille Clifton.

Recent titles from Copper Canyon are *After the Point of No Return* by David Wagoner; *Collected Body* by Valzhyna Mort; *The Crossed-Out Swastika* by Cyrus Cassells; *Fall Higher* by Dean Young.

Copper Canyon distributes to the trade via Consortium.

Copper Canyon Press has suspended its annual Hayden Carruth Award while exploring other options for considering the work of new and emerging poets. For now, unsolicited manuscripts will not be accepted; however, queries will be read from poets who have previously published a book.

All queries must include an SASE, a one-page cover letter, and a biographical vitae. Query letters and SASEs should be directed to:

Tonaya Thompson, Managing Editor, Tonaya@coppercanyonpress.org

COUNCIL OAKS BOOKS

WILDCAT CANYON PRESS

2015 E. 15th Street, Suite B, Tulsa, OK 74104
918-743-BOOK | 800-247-8850 | fax: 918-743-4288
www.counciloakbooks.com

Council Oaks Books, founded in 1984, is a publisher of nonfiction books based in personal, intimate history (memoirs, letters, diaries); nature, animals, and wildlife; Native American history and spiritual teachings; African American history and contemporary experience; small illustrated inspirational gift books; and unique vintage photo books and Americana. Best sellers include *The Four Agreements* by Don Miguel Ruiz and *Wise Talk, Wild Women* by Gwen Mazer.

Council Oaks titles include *The Second Life of John Wilkes Booth* by Barnaby Conrad; *The Microbe Factor* by Hiromi Shinya; *The Art of Navigation* by Felix Wolf; *Enzyme Factor* by Hiromi Shinya; *Sound* by Joseph Rael; and *Tibet: 100,000 Prayers of Compassion* by Ken Ballard.

WILDCAT CANYON PRESS

Wildcat Canyon Press publishes books about relationships, women's issues, and home and family, with a focus on personal growth. The editors at this imprint strive to create books that inspire reflection and improve the quality of life. Council Oaks and Wildcat Canyon Press categories include body/mind/spirit, cookbooks, environment/natural world, history, multicultural, and women's studies/feminist.

Wildcat Canyon titles include *Teen Girlfriends* by Julia DeVillers; *Celebrating the Good Times, Getting Through the Hard Times* by Julia DeVillers; *Urban Etiquette* by Charles Purdy; *40 over 40* by Brenda Kinsel; *Hip Girls' Handbook for the Working World* by Jennifer Musselman and Patty Fletcher; and *Taming Your Inner Brat: A Guide for Transforming Self-Defeating Behavior* by Pauline Wallin.

At present, Council Oaks Books is not accepting proposals. Query and SASEs to:
Sally Dennison, PhD, Editor

THE COUNTRYMAN PRESS [SEE W. W. NORTON & COMPANY]

COUNTRYSPORT PRESS [SEE DOWN EAST BOOKS]

CROSSING PRESS [SEE TEN SPEED PRESS]

CROSSROAD PUBLISHING COMPANY

HERDER & HERDER

831 Chestnut Ridge Road, Chestnut Ridge, NY 10977
845-517-0180
www.crossroadpublishing.com | e-mail: ask@crossroadpublishing.com

Crossroad Publishing Company (founded in 1980) publishes general interest and scholarly titles in religion, Catholicism, spirituality, and personal improvement. Its books include spirituality, religion, mind/body/spirit, and counseling for general and popular religious markets.

Crossroad and sibling imprint Herder & Herder is a US-based wing of the international firm Verlag Herder (founded in 1798). The programs of Crossroad and Herder & Herder offer books by some of the most distinguished authors in the United States and abroad in the fields of theology, spirituality, religious education, women's studies, world religions, psychology, and counseling. Crossroad looks for authors who can form long-term and personal publishing relationships.

Titles from Crossroad include *The Enemies of Excellence: 7 Reasons Why We Sabotage Success* by Greg Salciccioli; *Seven from Heaven: How Your Family Can Find Healing, Strength and Protection in the Sacraments* by Elizabeth Ficocelli; *Take Heart: Catholic Writers on Hope in Our Time* by Ben Birnbaum; *Seeking with All My Heart: Encountering God's Presence Today* by Paula D'Arcy; *Path of Wisdom, Path of Peace: A Personal Conversation* by His Holiness the Dalai Lama.

HERDER & HERDER

Herder & Herder publishes books in theology, Christian mysticism, religious studies, and religious education for professionals and active members of Catholic and mainstream Protestant churches. Titles from Herder & Herder include *A Chronicle of the Great Catholic Leader's Quest for Reconciliation and Peace* by Eugene J. Fisher, PhD, Rabbi Leon Klenicki, and Pope John Paul II; *Sharing Ideas and Faith in a Rapidly Changing Culture* by Matthias Scharer and Bernd Jochen Hilberath; *The Complete Mystical Works of Meister Eckhart* by Meister Eckhart and Bernard McGinn.

E-mail submissions are preferred and should be sent to info@crossroadpublishing .com with the word "submission" in the subject line. Query letters and SASE should be directed to:

John Jones, Editorial Director

CROSSWAY BOOKS

1300 Crescent Street, Wheaton, IL 60187-5883
630-682-4300 | fax: 630-682-4785
www.gnpcb.org

Crossway Books (founded in 1938) is a division of Good News Publishers. Crossway produces a small list of books with an evangelical Christian perspective aimed at both the religious and general audience, including issue-oriented nonfiction, evangelical works, inspiration, and fiction.

Crossway Books is interested in acquiring nonfiction areas of books on the deeper Christian life, issue-oriented books, and a select number of academic and professional volumes. It feels called to publish fiction works that fall into these categories: historical, youth/juvenile, adventure, action, intrigue, thriller, and contemporary and Christian realism.

From the Crossway list: *Evangelicalism: What Is It and Is It Worth Keeping?* by D. A. Carson; *The Gospel and the Mind: Recovering and Shaping the Intellectual Life* by Bradley G. Green; *God's Glory in Salvation Through Judgment* by James Hamilton; *Apologetics for the Twenty-First Century* by Louis Markos; and *Redeeming Singleness: How the Storyline of Scripture Affirms the Single Life* by Barry Danylak.

Sample children's books: *The Toddler's 1-2-3 Bible Storybook* by Carolyn Larsen, illustrated by Caron Turk; *Keeping Holiday* by Starr Meade; *ESV Illustrated Family Bible: 270 Selections from the Holy Bible* by Zbigniew Freus; *Kindness Counts* by Debbie Anderson; *Tell Me about Heaven* by Randy Alcorn, illustrated by Ron DiCianni; and *The Big Picture Story Bible* by David Helm, illustrated by Gail Schoonmaker.

Recent Crossway Books titles include *Kingdom through Covenant: A Biblical-Theological Understanding of the Covenants* by Peter J. Gentry and Stephen J. Wellum; *Remember Me* by Penelope Wilcock; *Pursuing Peace: A Christian Guide to Handling Our Conflicts* by Robert D. Jones; *Political Thought: A Student's Guide* by Hunter Baker.

No unsolicited manuscripts will be accepted. Send query letters and SASEs to:
Jill Carter, Editorial Administrator

DA CAPO PRESS [SEE PERSEUS BOOKS GROUP]

DALKEY ARCHIVE PRESS

University of Illinois, 1805 S. Wright Street, MC-011, Champaign, IL 61820
217-244-5700 | fax: 217-244-9142
www.dalkeyarchive.com | e-mail: contact@dalkeyarchive.com

The aim of Dalkey Archive, a division of the Center for Book Culture, is to bring under one roof the best of modern and contemporary literature and to create a space where this literature is protected from the whims of the marketplace. At the heart of the house's mission is a dedication to breakthrough artistic expression in fiction and an educational, interpretive function that goes beyond what most publishers are doing.

Unlike many small presses, and certainly unlike commercial presses, Dalkey has always been rooted in critical inquiry, most evident in the *Review of Contemporary Fiction*, the periodical from which the book publisher is an offshoot and more recently in the new periodical, *CONTEXT*. When the press first started operations in 1984, the *Review* was providing criticism on overlooked writers, and the press was in many cases publishing those same writers, or writers who belonged to a similar subversive aesthetic tradition. Since its founding, the press has published over 250 works of world literature and criticism. Dalkey Archive Press is currently seeking book-length scholarly works.

Recent Dalkey Archive Press titles include *Reticence* by Jean- Philippe Toussaint; *Transparency* by Marek Bienczyk; *Istanbul Was a Fairy Tale* by Mario Levi; *Replacement* by Tor Ulven; *Flowers of Grass* by Takehiko Fukunaga.

Dalkey Archive handles its own distribution.

Dalkey prefers submissions sent by e-mail, directed to submissions@dalkeyarchive .com. Query letters and SASEs should be directed to the "Acquisitions Editor."

John O'Brien, Director
Jeremy Davies, Editor
Aaron Kerner, Assistant Editor

IVAN R. DEE, PUBLISHER [SEE ROWMAN & LITTLEFIELD PUBLISHING GROUP]

DEVORSS & COMPANY

PO Box 1389, Camarillo, CA 93011-1389
805-322-9010 | 800-843-5743 | fax: 805-322-9011
www.devorss.com | e-mail: service@devorss.com

Devorss & Company has been publishing metaphysical and spiritual books since 1929. The house was founded in Los Angeles by Douglas Kimball DeVorss, who set up as a publisher of what today would be called body/mind/spirit books. At that time, the term was New Thought, and Los Angeles was already home to many centers, institutes, and churches that taught a new, "metaphysical" brand of philosophy and spirituality.

Some Devorss titles include *The Magic Story: Updated and Revised* by Frederic

Van Rensselaer Dey; *The Neville Reader: A Collection of Spiritual Writings and Thoughts on Your Inner Power to Create an Abundant Life* by Neville Goddard; *Your Weight or Your Life? Balancing the Scale for a Healthy Life from Within* by Barbara McCalmon; *Fitzpatrick Lane: A Book of Prayers* by Dianne Edleman; and *Communing with Music: Practicing the Art of Conscious Listening* by Matthew Cantello.

Submit queries, proposals, and SASEs via regular mail to Editorial Submissions. Queries only may be sent to editorial@devorss.com.

Gary Peattie, Submissions Editor

DIMENSIONS FOR LIVING [SEE ABINGDON PRESS]

DISNEY PRESS [SEE HYPERION]

DORCHESTER PUBLISHING

Last reports are that the firm has been closed and liquidated. It's possible that the name and backlist catalogue will be acquired and reactivited in the near future.

DOWN EAST BOOKS

PO Box 679, Camden, ME 04843
680 Commercial Street (US Route 1), Rockport, ME 04856
207-594-9544 | fax: 207-594-0147
www.downeastbooks.com | e-mail: info@downeastbooks.com

Down East Enterprise began at a kitchen table in 1954 with the creation of *Down East* magazine. In 1967, *Leroy the Lobster* was published and Down East Books was born. Today, Down East Books is the largest book publisher in the state of Maine and has published over 750 books. With the Countrysport Press imprint, Down East has a backlist of many hundreds of titles that grows by dozens of new books every year.

Although Down East Books is the largest book publisher in Maine, it is still a relatively small, regional publisher specializing in books with a strong Maine or New England theme. Current subject areas include general interest nonfiction, art and photography, regional attractions and travel guides, biography and memoir, gardening, cooking, crafts, history, nature and ecology, nautical books, and fiction. A fully developed regional connection is critical in Down East fiction titles, too.

Down East also publishes children's books, and here also the regional subject and setting are highly desirable. Note that the New England setting must be integral to the work; a story that with little or no change could be set in another region would not meet their requirements.

Recent Down East titles include *Maine Home Cooking* by Sandra Oliver; *Fairy House Handbook* by Liza Walsh; *Cartoons from Maine* by Jeff Pert; *Moxie: Maine in a Bottle* by Jim Baumer.

Mark your package "Book Proposal" and direct queries and SASEs to:

John Viehman, Publisher, jviehman@downeast.com

Paul Doiron, Editor-in-Chief, editorial@downeast.com

WILLIAM B. EERDMANS PUBLISHING COMPANY

EERDMANS BOOKS FOR YOUNG READERS

2140 Oak Industrial Dr. NE, Grand Rapids, MI 49505
616-459-4591 | 800-253-7521 | fax: 616-459-6540
www.eerdmans.com | e-mail: info@eerdmans.com

William B. Eerdmans Publishing Company (founded in 1911) is one of the largest independent nondenominational Christian religious publishers in the United States. Founded in 1911 and still independently owned, Eerdmans Publishing Company has long been known for publishing a wide range of religious books, from academic works in theology, biblical studies, religious history, and reference to popular titles in spirituality, social and cultural criticism, and literature.

Eerdmans publishes titles of general interest; religious, academic, and theological works; books for young readers; regional histories; and American religious history. The house offers a Christian handle on such areas as anthropology, biblical studies, and religious approaches to biography, African American studies, church administration, music, philosophy, psychology, science, social issues, current and historical theology, and women's interests.

New on the Eerdmans list: *After Vatican II* by James L. Heft and John W. O'Malley; *Called to Lead* by Anthony B. Robinson and Robert W. Wall; *Princeton Seminary in American Religion and Culture* by James H. Moorhead; *The Spiritual in the Secular* by Patrick Harries and David Maxwell; *Thomas and the Gospels* by Mark Goodacre.

EERDMANS BOOKS FOR YOUNG READERS

Eerdmans Books for Young Readers, founded in 1995 as an imprint of William B. Eerdmans Publishing Company, seeks to publish beautifully written and illustrated books that nurture children's faith in God and help young people to explore and understand the wonder, joy, and challenges of life.

Eerdmans Books for Young Readers publishes picture books and middle-reader and young-adult fiction and nonfiction. They seek manuscripts that are honest, wise, and hopeful, but also publish stories that simply delight the editors with their story line, characters, or good humor. Stories that celebrate diversity, stories of historical significance, and stories that relate to current issues are of special interest to them at this time. The house considers manuscripts that address spiritual themes in authentic and imaginative ways without being didactic. They currently publish 12 to 18 books a year.

Some recent titles include *Jonah's Whale* by Giuliano Ferri and Eileen Spinelli; *I Lay My Stitches Down* by Cynthia Grady and Michele Wood; *Garmann's Secret* by Stian Hole; *John Jensen Feels Different* by Henrik Hovland and Torill Kove.

Eerdmans Books for Young Readers will only consider exclusive submissions that are clearly marked as such on the outside of the envelope. They do not accept simultaneous submissions and those sent will be discarded. Query letters with proposal or sample chapters and SASEs should be directed to:

Jon Pott, Editor-in-Chief (Eerdmans)

ENTREPRENEUR PRESS

2445 McCabe Way, Suite 400, Irvine, CA 92614
949-261-2325 | 800-864-6864 | fax: 949-261-7729
www.entrepreneurpress.com | e-mail: press@entrepreneur.com

Entrepreneur Press, a division of Entrepreneur Media, Inc. (publishers of *Entrepreneur* magazine), publishes trade books offering practical advice and inspirational success stories for business owners and aspiring entrepreneurs. The goal of the house is to provide essential business information to help plan, run, and grow small businesses. Areas of expertise include instructional business books, and motivational, management, marketing, new economy, e-commerce, and personal finance titles that appeal to a broad spectrum of the business book-buying audience.

Titles include *Flashpoint* by J. K. Harris; *101 Ways to Green Your Business* by Rich Mintzer; *The Social Wave* by Starr Hall; *Maverick Startup* by Yanik Silver; *Start Your Own Restaurant and More* by Jacquelyn Lynn; *What Your CPA Isn't Telling You* by Mark J. Kohler.

Entrepreneur Press books are distributed to the trade by McGraw Hill.

Query letters and SASEs should be directed to:

Ryan Shea, Publisher

ESPN BOOKS [SEE HYPERION]

M. EVANS AND COMPANY [SEE ROWMAN & LITTLEFIELD PUBLISHING GROUP]

FACTS ON FILE

CHECKMARK BOOKS

132 West 31st Street, 17th Floor, New York, NY 10001
212-967-8800 | 800-322-8755 | fax: 212-967-9196 | 800-678-3633
www.factsonfile.com | e-mail: editorial@factsonfile.com

Facts On File (founded in 1940) is a dynamic popular-reference publisher. The house has many award-winning titles to its credit, and many Facts On File publications feature an innovative production approach. The publisher is extremely well tuned to specific category markets, which it targets with marked commercial consistency.

Facts On File is one of the nation's top providers of resources for teaching and learning. They produce high-quality reproducible handouts, online databases, CD-ROMs, and print reference and information titles in a broad popular range, including literature, science, geography, nature, technology, world history, American history, business, popular culture, fashion, design, sports, health, current affairs and politics, and the environment. Facts On File is also the first place that many teachers, students, librarians, and parents turn for general reference works. They offer a broad selection of historical and cultural atlases, dictionaries, and encyclopedias geared toward professional as well as popular interests, and are one of the pioneers of the electronic multimedia-publishing frontier.

Facts On File has made a renewed commitment to its goal of becoming the premier print and electronic reference publisher in the industry. It is striving to be the beacon and a guide for librarians, teachers, students, parents, and researchers to look to for award-winning materials, cutting-edge trends, and innovative products. This is the publisher to seek when the requirements are nebulous and the transitions are turbulent.

Recent Facts On File books include *American Wars* by Ballard C. Campbell, PhD; *Brain and Mind* by Michael Kerchner and Bernard C. Beins, PhD; *The Environment Since 1945* by Marcos Luna, PhD; *History of Western Philosophy* by David Boersema and Kari Middleton.

CHECKMARK BOOKS

The year 1998 brought the launch of the trade imprint Checkmark Books. It was created to provide booksellers and consumers with quality resources focused on topics such as business, careers, fitness, health and nutrition, history, nature, parenting, pop culture, and self-help.

Examples of Checkmark Books are *Field Guide to Finding a New Career in Internet and Media* by Amanda Kirk; *The New Complete Book of Food* by Carol Ann Rinzler et al; *The Student-Athlete's College Recruitment Guide* by Ashley Benjamin et al; *Tae Kwon Do: My Life and Philosophy* by Yeon Hwan Park; and *Virtual Apprentice! Fashion Designer* by Don Rauf and Monique Vescia.

Facts On File utilizes individualized marketing and distribution programs that are particularly strong in the areas of corporate, institutional, and library sales.

Query letters, proposals, and SASEs should be directed to:

Laurie Likoff, Editorial Director

Frank Darmstadt, Editor—Science and math.

FAIRVIEW PRESS (ACQUIRED BY ROWMAN & LITTLEFIELD)

2450 Riverside Avenue, Minneapolis, MN 55454
612-672- 4180 | 800-544-8207 | fax: 612-672-4980
www.fairviewpress.org | e-mail: press@fairview.org

Fairview Press publishes books dedicated to the physical, emotional, and spiritual health of children, adults, and seniors—specializing in books on aging and elder care, grief and bereavement, health and wellness, inspiration, and parenting and child care.

The house is a division of Fairview Health Services, a regional health care provider affiliated with the University of Minnesota. This affiliation, combined with its award-winning books, has caused industry experts to name Fairview Press as one of the "Top 50 Independent Publishers" in the United States. Fairview authors have been featured on CNN, CBS, NBC's *Today* show, National Public Radio, and in hundreds of other local, national, and international media outlets.

At this time, Fairview is particularly interested in acquiring manuscripts that deal with the following topics: pregnancy and childbirth, health issues for young adults, complementary/holistic/integrative medicine, diet and exercise, and inspiration and mindfulness. They are de-emphasizing their previous focus on end-of-life issues, but will consider proposals on any topic pertaining to physical, emotional, or spiritual wellness.

Recent Fairview Press titles include *Daily Comforts for Caregivers* by Pat Samples; *Help Me Say Goodbye* by Janis Silverman; *Out of the Ashes* by Peter and Peggy Holmes; *Raising Strong Daughters* by Jeanette Gadeberg; and *Remembering with Love* by Elizabeth Levang, PhD, and Sherokee Isle.

Fairview Press operates through a variety of sales venues; the press is distributed to the trade through National Book Network.

Query letters, proposals, and SASEs should be addressed to:

Steve Deger, Acquisitions Manager

FALCON GUIDES [SEE THE GLOBE PEQUOT PRESS]

FANTAGRAPHICS BOOKS

7563 Lake City Way NE, Seattle, WA 98115
206-524-1967 | 800-657-1100 | fax: 206-524-2104
www.fantagraphics.com | e-mail: fbicomix@fantagraphics.com | blog: www
.fantagraphics.com/blog

Fantagraphics publishes comics and comic art. The house features a list of mainstream, classic, and underground offerings and also purveys a strong line of erotic comics and comics-related books. Fantagraphics Books (inaugurated in 1976) produces trade paperbacks, hardbound editions, and quality fine-art album editions of graphic productions, in addition to comic books, comics-related magazines, and a line of gift items dedicated to this most accessible literary form.

Comics creators cataloged by Fantagraphics include Peter Bagge, Vaughn Bode, Daniel Clowes, Guido Crepax, Robert Crumb, Dame Darcy, Kim Deitch, Julie Doucet, Jules Feiffer, Frank Frazetta, Drew Friedman, Rick Geary, Los Bros. Hernandez, Peter Kuper, Terry LeBan, Douglas Michael, Joe Sacco, Gilbert Shelton, Art Spiegelman, Ralph Steadman, Basil Wolverton, and Wallace Wood.

Recent Fantagraphics titles include *Buz Sawyer Volume 2: Sultry's Tiger* by Roy Crane; *Jack Jackson's American History: Los Tejanos & Lost Cause* by Jack Jackson; *Observed While Falling: Bill Burroughs, Ah Pook, and Me* by Malcolm McNeill; *The Crumb Compendium* by Carl Richter; *The Hypo: The Melancholic Young Lincoln* by Noah Van Sciver.

Take note of the originality and diversity of the themes and approaches to drawing in such Fantagraphics titles as *Love & Rockets* (stories of life in Latin America and Chicano LA, which draw on influences as diverse as Luis Buñuel, Frida Kahlo, and Hank Ketcham); *Palestine* (journalistic autobiography in the Middle East); *Eightball* (surrealism mixed with kitsch culture in stories alternately humorous and painfully personal); and *Naughty Bits* (feminist humor and short stories which both attack and commiserate). Prior to submitting, try to develop your own, equally individual voice; originality, aesthetic maturity, and graphic storytelling skill are the signs by which Fantagraphics judges whether or not your submission is ripe for publication. Query letters should be accompanied by short, carefully selected samples and an SASE.

FELDHEIM PUBLISHERS

208 Airport Executive Park, Nanuet, NY 10954
845-356-2282 | 800-237-7149 | fax: 845-425-1908
www.feldheim.com

Feldheim Publishers (founded in 1954) is among the leading houses in areas of Jewish thought, translations from Hebrew of classical works, dictionaries and general reference works, textbooks, and guides for Sabbaths and festivals, as well as literature for readers ages three and up. The Feldheim publishing program is expanding, and the house releases an increasing number of titles each season. Feldheim retains a comprehensive backlist.

Recent titles include *Talmudic Wisdom for Today* by Rabbi Dov Beirish Ganz; *Tangled Ties* by Shoshana Schwartz; *Collected Writings of Rabbi Samson Raphael Hirsch*, Volume 9, *Timeless Hashkafah* and *Index Volume* by Rabbi Samson Raphael Hirsch; *Briefcases and Baby Bottles, The Working Mother's Guide to Nurturing a Jewish Home* by Tzivia Reiter; *The Elephant in the Room, Torah, Wisdom and Inspiration for Life* by Rabbi Ron Yitzchok Eisenman.

Feldheim handles its own distribution and offers the books of additional publishers such as American Yisroel Chai Press and Targum Press.

Query letters and SASEs should be directed to:

Yitzchak Feldheim, President

FLUX [SEE LLEWELLYN WORLDWIDE]

FORTRESS PRESS [SEE AUGSBURG FORTRESS BOOKS]

FREE SPIRIT PUBLISHING

217 Fifth Avenue North, Suite 200, Minneapolis, MN 55401-1299
612-338-2068 | 800-735-7323 | fax: 612-337-5050
www.freespirit.com | e-mail: help4kids@freespirit.com

For over 25 years, Free Spirit's mission has been to provide children and teens—and the adults who care for and about them—the tools they need to succeed in life and to make a positive difference in the world.

Based in Minneapolis, Minnesota, Free Spirit Publishing is known for its unique understanding of what kids want (and need) to know to navigate life successfully.

The house built its reputation as the leading publisher of self-help books for teens and kids. Their books and other learning materials are practical, positive, pro-kid, and solution focused. Free Spirit is not afraid to tackle tough topics such as teen depression, kids and anxiety, grief and loss, juvenile justice, and conflict resolution. Free Spirit also offers sound advice with a sense of humor on relevant issues including stress management, character building, puberty, school success, self-esteem, and more. The house aims to meet all kids—toddlers, teens, and in-betweens—where they are (not where we wish they were), and support them to develop their talents, build resiliency, and foster a positive outlook on life so they can reach their goals.

Founded by Judy Galbraith, a former classroom teacher and education specialist, Free Spirit pushes boundaries on behalf of young people. For example, they pioneered use of the term "learning differences" to replace "learning disabilities" because they know that kids with LD are eager and able to learn—just in a different way. Free Spirit is also a recognized leader in meeting the needs of another special population—gifted and talented youth. Judy Galbraith's groundbreaking *The Gifted Kids' Survival Guides*, first published in 1984, have remained perennial best sellers (300,000 copies in print) through several updates and revisions. One of Free Spirit's newest ventures is in expanding early childhood offerings, with titles such as *Hands Are Not for Hitting* (100,000 copies in print).

Recent titles include *Zach Apologizes* by William "Bill" Mulcahy; *What Kids Need to Succeed* by Peter L. Benson, PhD, Judy Galbraith, MA, and Pamela Espeland; *ADHD in HD* by Jonathan Chesner; *The Survival Guide for Kids with Autism Spectrum Disorders* by Elizabeth Verdick and Elizabeth Reeve, MD; *Bookmarked* by Ann Camacho.

Free Spirit's distribution is through the trade market, as well as direct to schools and other youth-serving venues.

Query letters and SASEs should be directed to:

Heidi Stier, Acquisitions Editor

Judy Galbraith, Founder and President

FULCRUM PUBLISHING

4690 Table Mountain Drive, Suite 100, Golden, CO 80403
303-277-1623 | 800-992-2908 | fax: 303-279-7111
www.fulcrum-books.com | e-mail: info@fulcrum-books.com
 SPECK PRESS
PO Box 102004, Denver, CO 80222
303-277-1623 | 800-992-2908 | fax: 800-726-7112
www.speckpress.com | e-mail: books@speckpress.com

Fulcrum is a trade publisher focusing on books that inspire readers to live life to the fullest and learn something new each day. In fiction and nonfiction, subjects include lifestyle, health and wellness, Western culture, outdoor and travel, Native American, memoirs and literature, gardening, environment and nature, and children's titles.

Fulcrum has published books from prominent politicians (Gov. Richard Lamm, Sen. Gary Hart, Sen. Eugene McCarthy), leading Native Americans (Wilma Mankiller, Vine Deloria, Jr., Joseph Bruchac), master gardeners (Lauren Springer, Tom Peace, Richard Hartlage), and important organizations in the environmental community (Campaign for America's Wilderness, World Wilderness Congress, Defenders of Wildlife).

Recent Fulcrum releases are *Rebuilding Justice: Civil Courts in Jeopardy and Why You Should Care* by Rebecca Love Kourlis and Dirk Olin; *Rural Wit and Wisdom: Time-Honored Values from the Heartland* by Jerry Apps; *Planes, Trains, and Auto-Rickshaws: A Journey through Modern India* by Laura Pedersen; *Let Them Paddle: Coming of Age on the Water* by Alan Kesselheim; *Durango: A Novel* by Gary Hart.

SPECK PRESS

Speck Press is an imprint that explores cultures and subcultures through nonfiction and crime fiction books—revealing scenes that are typically invisible to the casual observer. They currently publish around ten new titles a year, in the areas of subculture, music, environment issues, art, politics, travel, and gift books. Some titles from Speck include *The Tattoed Lady: A History* by Amelia Klem Osterud; *The Birth (And Death) of the Cool* by Ted Gioia; *Road Show: Art Cars and the Museum of the Streets* by Eric Dregni and Ruthann Godollei; and *DeKok and the Dead Harlequin* by A. C. Baantjer.

Fulcrum handles its own distribution. Query letters and SASEs should be directed to:

Bob Baron, President and Publisher (Fulcrum)
Derek Lawrence, Publisher (Speck Press)
Susan Hill-Newton, Editor (Speck Press)

GENEVA PRESS [SEE PRESBYTERIAN PUBLISHING CORPORATION]

THE GLOBE PEQUOT PRESS

FALCON GUIDES
FOOTPRINT BOOKS
INSIDERS' GUIDES
KNACK BOOKS
LYONS PRESS
SKIRT! BOOKS

246 Goose Lane, PO Box 480, Guilford, CT 06437
203-458-4500 | 800-820-2329 | fax: 800-508-8938
www.globepequot.com | e-mail: info@globepequot.com

The Pequot Press, whose name was adapted from a local Indian tribe, was founded in 1947 as an adjunct to the Stonington Printing Company in Stonington, Connecticut. The Boston Globe Newspaper Company purchased the press in February 1981, formalizing an association that had begun in 1978. Today, more than 60 years after the publication of its first monograph, The Globe Pequot Press has established an international reputation for publication of regional guides to a myriad of travel destinations in this country and around the world and is among the top three sources for travel books in the United States. Globe Pequot is owned by Georgia-based Morris Communications, a privately held media company with diversified holdings that include newspaper and magazine publishing, outdoor advertising, radio broadcasting, book publishing, and distribution.

Globe Pequot publishes approximately 600 new books each year. In addition to publishing its own imprint, it offers marketing and fulfillment services to client publishers whose combined annual output currently exceeds 200 new titles. Its 75,000-square-foot warehouse holds well over 1 million units representing approximately 4,000 titles in print, comprising books on domestic and international travel, outdoor recreation, sports, how-to, history, fiction, health and fitness, cooking, and nature.

The Globe Pequot line primarily publishes travel guides, with some select nature titles, cookbooks, and home-based business books. Insiders' Guides are travel and relocation guides written by local authors. Falcon Guides specialize in outdoor recreation, both how-to and where-to, with hiking, biking, climbing, and other specialized lines, including regional history. Footprint Guides publishes guides for experienced independent travelers looking to get off the beaten track. The Lyons Press is primarily a publisher of practical and literary books, as well as being the most distinguished publisher of fishing books in the world (see below for Lyons Press).

In the travel arena, Globe Pequot is well regarded for several bestselling series and also distributes for a number of travel-specialist houses. Among Globe Pequot lines: *Quick Escapes* for weekend and day trips keyed to metropolitan areas or regions; *Romantic Days and Nights*; *Recommended Bed & Breakfasts*; *Fun with the Family Guides*; *Cadogan Guides* to destinations worldwide for the discriminating traveler; and the popular *Off-the-Beaten-Path* series. Globe Pequot also updates a variety of annuals, among them *Europe by Eurorail*. Globe Pequot's regionally keyed books also cover such interest areas as biking, hiking, mountaineering, skiing, and family activities in the wilderness and on the beach.

Globe Pequot titles include *Growing Up Mary* by Melissa Sue Anderson; *The Long Walk* by Peter Wier; *Forbidden Creatures* by Peter Laufer; and *The Dangerous World of Butterflies* by Peter Laufer.

FALCON GUIDES

Falcon Guides aspires to be the leading publisher of information for nonconsumptive, human-powered outdoor recreation, conservation, and natural history. Their guides compel readers to move: to strap on their boots, to mount a bike, to climb a mountain, to slip into a kayak, to commandeer a yak!—in short, to ignite the passion for hands-on discovery. Their guidebooks are designed to be highly visual and easily referenced for maximum ease-of-use.

Some titles from Falcon Guides include *The Scout's Backpacking Guide* by Tim and Christine Conners; *The Best Climbs: Grand Teton National Park* by Richard Rossiter; *Best Climbs: Cascade Volcanoes* by Jeff Smoot.

FOOTPRINT BOOKS

The passion for travel and discovery at Footprint has been reflected in guidebooks dating back to the first edition of *The South American Handbook* in 1924: the longest established travel guide in the English-language market. Each book is written by authors with firsthand knowledge of the areas they write about, written for independent travelers looking to get off the beaten track and escape the tourist crowds.

Recent titles include *Morocco Handbook* by Julius Honnor; *Kenya Handbook* by Lizzie Williams; *Andalucia Handbook* by Andy Symington.

INSIDERS' GUIDES

The *Insiders' Guide* series began with one local guidebook to North Carolina's Outer Banks. Today the series has grown to encompass more than 60 cities and regional destinations in the United States and Bermuda. Written by local authors with years of experience writing about their communities, the Insiders' Guides provide newcomers, visitors, and business travelers with a native's perspective of the area. Each guide details hotels, restaurants, annual events, attractions, nightlife, parks and recreation, real estate, and more.

Recent titles from Insiders' Guides include *Insiders' Guide® to New York City* by Shandana Durrani, Susan Finch, John Newton, Sandra Ramani, and William Travis; *Insiders' Guide® to Florida Keys & Key West*, 16th Edition by Juliet Grey; *Insiders' Guide® to North Carolina's Outer Banks*, 31st Edition; *Insiders' Guide® to Glacier National Park*, 6th Edition by Michael McCoy.

KNACK BOOKS

Knack is the how-to and reference imprint of Globe Pequot. It includes stand-alone lead titles featuring authors with visibility on television, radio, education, or the Internet. Some titles from Knack include *Sign Language: A Step-by-Step Guide to Signing* by Suzie Chafin; *Baby's First Year: A Complete Illustrated Guide to Your Child's First Twelve Months* by Robin McClure and Vince Iannelli; *Bartending Basics: More*

than 400 Classic and Contemporary Cocktails for Any Occasion by Cheryl Charming; and *Canoeing for Everyone: A Step-by-Step Guide to Selecting the Gear, Learning the Strokes, and Planning Your Trip* by Daniel A. Gray.

LYONS PRESS

Now an imprint of Globe Pequot, Lyons Press was founded by Nick Lyons in 1984 and has established an international reputation for publishing outstanding titles in its core categories of fishing, hunting, horses, sports, pets, history, adventure, the outdoors, self-reliant living, and reference.

Recent Lyons purchases include a book of ghostly cat tales, the story of a puppy befriending US soldiers in Iraq, a history of the US Space Program, and an exploration of the world of modern-day shipping, indicating an expansion from their core editorial direction.

Titles include *Dead Pet: Send Your Best Little Buddy Off in Style* by Andrew Kirk and Jane Mosely; *Fishing Florida: An Angler's Guide to More than 600 Prime Fishing Spots* by Kris Thoemke; *Newshounds: The Wackiest Dog Stories from Around the World* by Ryan O'Meara; *Ron Paul Speaks* by Philip Haddad and Roger Marsh.

Direct proposals with SASEs to the Submissions Editor.

Lara Asher, Editor
Janice Goldklang, Executive Director
James Jayo, Editor

DAVID R. GODINE, PUBLISHER

BLACK SPARROW BOOKS

Fifteen Court Square, Suite 320, Boston, MA 02108-4715
617-451-9600 | fax: 617-350-0250
www.godine.com | e-mail: info@godine.com

David R. Godine, Publisher, founded in 1970, is a small publishing house located in Boston, producing between 20 and 30 titles per year and maintaining an active reprint program. The company is independent, and its list tends to reflect the individual tastes and interests of its president and founder, David Godine.

At Godine, quality has remained foremost. All of their hardcover and softcover books are printed on acid-free paper. Many hardcovers are still bound in full cloth. The list is deliberately eclectic and features works that many other publishers can't or won't support, books that won't necessarily become best sellers but that still deserve publication. In a world of spinoffs and commercial products, Godine's list stands apart by offering original fiction and nonfiction of the highest rank, rediscovered masterworks, translations of outstanding world literature, poetry, art, photography, and beautifully designed books for children.

Recently, Godine launched two new series: Imago Mundi, a line of original books devoted to photography and the graphic arts; and Verba Mundi, featuring the most notable contemporary world literature in translation. Volumes in the Imago Mundi series, which has received praise from reviewers and booksellers alike, include *Jean Cocteau: The Mirror and the Mask* by Julie Saul and *Small Rooms & Hidden Places* by Ronald W. Wohlauer. Verba Mundi has so far published works by world-renowned authors Georges Perec, José Donoso, Isaac Babel, and Anna Seghers, and has introduced new voices such as Sylvie Germain (whose *Book of Nights* was named a Notable Book of the Year by the *New York Times*) and the acclaimed Swedish novelist Goran Tunstrom, author of *The Christmas Oratorio*.

Recent titles from Godine include *Fauna and Family: More Durrell Family Adventures on Corfu* by Gerald Durrell; *Faith, Hope & Charity: Social Reform and Photography, 1885–1910* by Suzanne Greenberg and Barbara Norfleet; *The African* by J. M. G. Le Clézio; *Printer's Devil: The Life and Work of Frederic Warde* by Simon Loxley.

BLACK SPARROW BOOKS

On July 1, 2002, John Martin, the founder and for 36 years the publisher of Black Sparrow Press, closed down his shop in Santa Rosa, California. After finding new homes for four of his authors—Charles Bukowski, Paul Bowles, John Fante, and Wyndham Lewis—he entrusted the rest of his backlist to a fellow publisher, David R. Godine. The agreement was simple: Godine would keep Black Sparrow's offerings available to the trade, keep the bestselling titles in print, and keep the house's spirit alive through judicious acquisitions. In short, Black Sparrow Press would be reborn—as Black Sparrow Books at David R. Godine, Publisher.

Recent titles from Black Sparrow Books include *Taking What I Like: Stories* by Linda Bamber; *Door to the River* by Aram Saroyan; *By the Waters of Manhattan* by Charles Reznikoff; *Jazz and Twelve O'Clock Tales* by Wanda Coleman; *Holocaust* by Charles Reznikoff; and *Metropolitan Tang* by Linda Bamber.

David R. Godine, Publisher and Black Sparrow Books do not accept unagented unsolicited manuscripts. Authors are advised to have their agents establish contact if they would like their manuscripts to be considered. Do not telephone the office or submit anything via e-mail. Query letters and SASEs should be directed to:

David R. Godine, Publisher

GOSPEL LIGHT PUBLICATIONS

REGAL BOOKS
1957 Eastmen Avenue, Ventura, CA 93003
800-446-7735
www.gospellight.com

Founded in 1933 by Dr. Henrietta Mears, Gospel Light is committed to providing effective resources for evangelism, discipleship, and Christian education through Sunday school and Vacation Bible school curricula, videos, and children's music.

Gospel Light highlights include *Clergy Tax* by J. David Epstein; *A New Kind of Conservative* by Joel Hunter; *Fusion* by Nelson Searcy with Jennifer Henson; *I Want to Believe* by Mel Lawrenz; *Raising Fit Kids in a Fat World* by Judy Halliday, RN, and Joanie Jack, MD; *The Relief of Imperfection* by Joan C. Webb; *Yes, Lord* by Harold Bredesen with Pat King; and *The Big Book of Create-Your-Own Bible Lessons* by Sharon Short.

REGAL BOOKS

The Regal Book Division (founded in 1965) specializes in needs-oriented books and building efforts aimed at church leadership and families. Recent Regal titles include *Arise* by Clayton and Ellen Kershaw, with Ann Higginbottom; *7 Love Letters From Jesus* by Rebecca Hayford Bauer; *A Passion for Prayer* by Vonette Bright; *Armor of God: The Uncommon Junior High Group Study* by Kara Powell.

Queries, proposals, and SASEs should be directed to Acquisitions Editor.

GRAYWOLF PRESS

250 Third Avenue North, Suite 600, Minneapolis, MN 55401
651-641-0077 | fax: 651-641-0036
www.graywolfpress.org

Since 1974, Graywolf has been an important outlet for American poetry and helped keep fine literature off the extinction list. Their list also includes novels, short stories, memoirs, and essays, and features such writers as Elizabeth Alexander, Charles Baxter, Sven Birkerts, Linda Gregg, Eamon Grennan, Tony Hoagland, Jane Kenyon, William Kittredge, Carl Phillips, William Stafford, David Treuer, and Brenda Ueland. A commitment to quality, and a willingness to embrace or invent new models, has kept Graywolf at the forefront of the small press movement. Today, Graywolf is considered one of the nation's leading nonprofit literary publishers. The house publishes about 27 new books per year.

Representative of the Graywolf list are *Rainy Lake* by Mary Rockcastle; *I Am Not Sidney Poitier* by Percival Everett; *How to Escape from a Leper Colony* by Tiphanie Yanique; *The Best Short Stories of William Kittredge* by William Kittredge; and *The Art of Description*.

Graywolf Press accepts submissions in the months of January, May, and September. Submissions received outside of these months will not be considered. Send one hard copy of the finished, book-length manuscript with cover letter to:

Jeff Shotts, Senior Editor
Steve Woodward, Editorial Assistant

GREENWOOD PUBLISHING GROUP [SEE ABC-CLIO]

GROVE/ATLANTIC, INC.

GROVE PRESS
ATLANTIC MONTHLY PRESS
841 Broadway, 4th Floor, New York, NY 10003
212-614-7850 | fax: 212-614-7886
www.groveatlantic.com | e-mail: info@groveatlantic.com

Grove/Atlantic publishes trade nonfiction and fiction; these works often display a contemporary cultural bent or an issue-oriented edge. Grove Press and Atlantic Monthly Press, two formerly independent houses, were united under the Grove/Atlantic corporate crest in 1993. Grove/Atlantic operates from the former Grove headquarters on Broadway (with Atlantic having relocated from its previous digs at nearby Union Square West). The publisher operates essentially as one house, while maintaining the distinction of two major imprints.

GROVE PRESS

Grove Press was founded in 1951 by literary trailblazer Barney Rosset, who established a tradition of enterprising lists that featured some of the finest and most fearless writing from around the globe. This literary institution was purchased by Ann Getty in 1985, in league with the UK-based publisher Weidenfeld & Nicholson; the publisher operated briefly under the sobriquet Grove Weidenfeld. With the early retreat of the Weidenfeld interests, the fate of Grove was a popular topic of publishing tattle rumored to be perpetually on the block, both prior and subsequent to the house's merger with *Atlantic Monthly*.

ATLANTIC MONTHLY PRESS

Atlantic Monthly Press was founded in 1917 as an imprint of Little, Brown. During the next 16 years, the press's books won more than 16 Pulitzer Prizes and National Book Awards. Among the press's bestselling award-winning titles published during those years were *Mutiny on the Bounty*, *Goodbye Mr. Chips*, *Drums Along the Mohawk*, *Ship of Fools*, *Fire in the Lake*, *The Soul of the New Machine*, and *Blue Highways*. In 1985, the press was spun off from the magazine and became independent.

In February 1993, Grove Press and Atlantic Monthly Press merged to form Grove/Atlantic, Inc. Publishing under these two imprints, Grove/Atlantic, Inc., continues to publish books that have been in the forefront of the American literary and publishing scene for more than 75 years. Imprints Canongate Books and

Atlantic Books are based in the United Kingdom and may be reached via e-mail at enquiries@groveatlantic.co.uk.

Recent Grove/Atlantic titles include *The Vanishing Point* by Val McDermid; *Seven Days* by Deon Meyer; *The Greatcoat: A Ghost Story* by Helen Dunmore; *The Jewels of Paradise* by Donna Leon; *The Finish: The Killing of Osama bin Laden* by Mark Bowden

Grove/Atlantic books are distributed by Perseus.

Grove/Atlantic accepts unsolicited manuscripts only from literary agents. Direct queries and SASEs to:

Morgan Entrekin, Publisher
Elisabeth Schmitz, Executive Editor
Corinna Barsan, Editor
Judy Hottenson, Associate Publisher
Amy Hudley, Senior Editor

HAL LEONARD CORPORATION

PO Box 13819, Milwaukee, WI 53213
AMADEUS PRESS
APPLAUSE THEATRE & CINEMA BOOKS
LIMELIGHT EDITIONS
www.halleonard.com
BACKBEAT BOOKS
www.backbeatbooks.com

The Hal Leonard Corporation has its roots in brothers Harold "Hal" Edstrom and Everett "Leonard" Edstrom's traveling band. The print publishing company was founded in 1947 when the band broke up and the brothers began to arrange "popular" music for school bands. Since then it has continued to grow, becoming a world presence in music publishing. It has recently acquired several independent publishers of trade music and entertainment books, such as Applause Theatre and Cinema Books, Amadeus Press, Limelight Editions, and Backbeat Books.

AMADEUS PRESS

Amadeus Press was founded by Richard Abel in 1987 as an imprint of Timber Press. A music lover, Abel recognized a gap between popular music titles of somewhat dubious quality issued by large commercial houses and the narrowly specialized scholarly publications of the university presses. Amadeus Press was started with the mission of publishing books that would appeal to a wide audience of discerning music lovers yet maintain their scholarly integrity.

In 1990, the press received major attention with the publication of *Enrico Caruso: My Father and My Family* by Andrew Farkas and Enrico Caruso, Jr. The company found new acclaim in the early 2000s with its book/CD series called *Unlocking the Masters*, which brings both experienced and new listeners to the world of classical music and opera. In 2006, the imprint was sold to the Hal Leonard Corporation. The mission of Amadeus is focused mainly on creating books that bring new listeners into the exciting world of classical music and opera.

Amadeus Press Books include *Schubert's Instrumental Music: A Listener's Guide* by John Bell Young; *Playing the Beethoven Piano Sonatas* by Robert Taub; *Worlds of Johann Sebastian Bach* by Raymond Erickson; *Zubin Mehta: The Score of My Life* by Zubin Mehta; and *Elisabeth Schwarzkopf: From Flower Maiden to Marschallin* by Kirsten Liese.

APPLAUSE THEATRE & CINEMA BOOKS

Now in its third decade, Applause is well established as one of the country's most important publishers of theater and cinema books. The house is now owned and operated by Hal Leonard Corporation, the world's largest music print publisher.

The catalog covers everything from books on acting to biographies of theater luminaries, reference books on music and film, screenplays, play scripts, anthologies, and many other topics all for seasoned pros, rookies, and aficionados of the entertainment arts. The Applause program covers hardback and paperback editions, among them a number of generously illustrated works.

Applause issues stage plays and screenplays (many in translation and many in professional working-script format) that run the gamut from the classical repertory to contemporary works in drama, comedy, and musicals. Applause also offers audio works and a video library. The publisher's backlist is comprehensive. Special-production volumes encompass works that detail the background and history behind the creation of works for stage and screen, in addition to containing complete scripts.

Recent titles of interest are *The Miles Davis Reader* edited by Frank Alkyer; *I Hate New Music: The Classic Rock Manifesto* by Dave Thompson; *In the Studio with Michael Jackson* by Bruce Swedien; *Broadway: The American Musical* by Laurence Maslon and Michael Kantor; *Neil Young FAQ* by Glen Boyd; *Music, Artistry and Education: A Journey Towards Musical Growth and Enlightenment* by Milton Allen.

LIMELIGHT EDITIONS

Limelight Editions is one of the world's leading small presses of books on the performing arts, theater, cinema, music, and dance. It has recently become a part of the Hal Leonard Performing Arts Publishing Group. Titles from Limelight include *Warren Oates: A Wild Life* by Susan A. Compo; *Collaboration in Theatre: A Practical Guide for Designers and Directors* by Kirk Bomer; and *Fifty Classic American Films* by John White.

BACKBEAT BOOKS

Backbeat Books specializes in music books in rock, jazz, blues, country, classical, and everything in between. Titles shed light on music and its makers. Since 1991, Backbeat Books (originally Miller Freeman Books) has published books for readers who are passionate about music, whether as performers or fans.

Recent titles include *Family Tradition: Three Generations of Hank Williams* by Susan Masino; *Reaching Out with No Hands: Reconsidering Yoko Ono* by Lisa Carver; *Jimi Hendrix* by Keith Shadwick; *Revolver: How the Beatles Re-Imagined Rock 'n' Roll* by Robert Rodriguez; *Exit Music: The Radiohead Story* by Mac Randall.

Editorial submissions for all imprints should be directed to:

John Cerullo, jcerullo@halleonard.com
Hal Leonard Publishing Group
33 Plymouth Street, #302
Montclair, NJ 07042

HAMPTON ROADS

665 Third Street, #400, San Francisco, CA 94107
www.hrpub.com

Hampton Roads was recently acquired by Red Wheel Weiser and is being integrated into their synergistic program. Hampton Roads is a nonfiction publisher that describes its titles as messages for the evolving human spirit. The catalog consists of spiritual self-help from the mystical to the practical; subjects include body/mind/spirit, astrology and divination, dreams and dreaming, past lives, reincarnation, the animal world, psychics, remote viewing, business and leadership, visionary fiction, natural solutions for health problems, self-care health advice, the political dimensions of medicine, new science, studies in consciousness, out-of-body experiences, near-death experiences, exploring the afterlife, earth energies, crop circles, and shamanism. Hampton Roads publishes bestselling authors such as Richard Bach, Neal Donald Walsch, and Mary Summer Rain. The Young Spirit line focuses on New Age titles for children.

Recent titles include *The Easy Vegan: Over 440 Delicious Recipes and Menus For Every Day of the Year* by Janet Hudson; *Jesus, Buddha, Krishna, and Lao Tzu: The Parallel Sayings* by Richard Hooper; *How To Say Yes When Your Body Says No: Discover the Silver Lining in Life's Toughest Health Challenges* by Dr. Lee Jampolsky; *End Your Story, Begin Your Life: Wake Up, Let Go, Live Free* by Jim Dreaver; *365 Dalai Lama: Daily Advice From the Heart* by Tenzin Gyatso, His Holiness the XIV Dalai Lama.

Mail submissions to:

Chris Nelson, Acquisitions Manager

INDEPENDENT US PRESSES

HARCOURT [SEE HOUGHTON MIFFLIN HARCOURT]

HARLEQUIN ENTERPRISES, LTD.

HARLEQUIN BOOKS
HARLEQUIN NONFICTION
HQN BOOKS
KIMANI PRESS
LUNA BOOKS
SILHOUETTE BOOKS
STEEPLE HILL BOOKS
233 Broadway, Suite 1001, New York, NY 10279
212-553-4200
www.harlequin.com

Harlequin Enterprises, Ltd., is the world's leading publisher of romance and women's fiction. The Toronto-based company publishes some 115 titles a month in 25 languages in 95 international markets on six continents. Harlequin is unique in the publishing industry, developing more new authors than any other publisher, and currently publishes over 1,300 authors from around the world. Harlequin is a division of the Torstar Corporation, a Toronto-based media company that also owns over 100 newspapers, a TV station, and various online ventures.

The Harlequin Enterprises home base in Ontario, Canada, issues the greater portion of Harlequin Books series (please see listing for Harlequin Books in the directory of Canadian Presses), while the New York office issues several Harlequin series, as well as the HQN, LUNA, Kimani, Red Dress Ink, Silhouette, and Steeple Hill lists. The editorial acquisitions departments for Mills & Boon, Harlequin Romance, and Harlequin Presents are located at the operation's UK offices (listed with Canada).

Each of the various lines within the Harlequin series of romance novels stakes out particular market-niche segments of reader interest within the overall categories of romance and women's fiction. The best way to learn which imprint is appropriate for your manuscript is to read books already in print. There are many different Harlequin lines, and each has its own submission and editorial guidelines. These guidelines are explored in great detail on the Harlequin website or may be requested via regular mail (with SASE) from the editors.

HARLEQUIN BOOKS

Harlequin Books in New York is home to Harlequin Intrigue. The Harlequin NEXT line has been cancelled.

Harlequin Intrigue features taut, edge-of-the-seat contemporary romantic suspense tales of intrigue and desire. Kidnappings, stalkings, and women in jeopardy coupled with bestselling romantic themes are examples of storylines the editors love most. Whether a murder mystery, a psychological suspense story, or a thriller, the love story must be inextricably bound to the mystery, where all loose ends are tied up neatly and shared dangers lead right to shared passions. As long as they're in jeopardy and falling in love, the heroes and heroines may traverse a landscape as wide as the world itself.

Recent Harlequin Intrigue titles are *Copy That* by HelenKay Dimon; *Gage* by Delores Fossen; *Her Cowboy Avenger* by Kerry Connor; *Mommy Midwife* by Cassie Miles.

Harlequin invites submissions from both published and unpublished writers. They prefer a query with synopsis and one to three chapters. Make sure your query is clear as to which line it is intended for. See writing guidelines on website.

Margaret Marbury, Director of Harlequin Single Titles

HARLEQUIN NONFICTION

Harlequin Nonfiction is a new division that publishes across a diverse list of categories, such as companion pieces, original memoirs, health, fitness, self-help, relationships, and more. Some recent titles include *Eat Your Way to Sexy* by Elizabeth Somer; *The 7-Minute Back Pain Solution* by Dr. Gerard Girasole; *The Beauty Aisle Insider* by Perry Romanowski; *Making Piece* by Beth M. Howard.

Sarah Pelz, Editor

HQN BOOKS

HQN Books publishes mainstream romance fiction for readers around the world. Because HQN Books is a mainstream imprint, there are no tip sheets, although manuscripts are expected to range between 100,000 and 150,000 words. Recent titles include *Always the Best Man* by Fiona Harper; *How the Playboy Got Serious* by Shirley Jump; *Nanny for the Millionaire's Twins* by Susan Meier; *The Navy SEAL's Bride* by Soraya Lane.

Direct your query letter to:
Tara Parson, HQN Books

KIMANI PRESS

Kimani Press, a new division of Harlequin, is home to four of the industry's leading imprints targeting the African American reader including Arabesque, Sepia, TRU, and Kimani Romance, which is the industry's only African American series romance program. As with the other Harlequin divisions, Kimani has different lines, each with its own guidelines available online or by querying the editors via regular mail.

Arabesque offers uplifting, contemporary love stories featuring realistic African American characters that resolve relationship conflicts through the perspective of strong moral beliefs. Arabesque titles may include several points of view, and offer classic contemporary settings.

Arabesque Romances offer contemporary, sophisticated, and entertaining love stories featuring realistic African American characters that resolve natural relationship conflicts such as issues of trust, compatibility, and outlook on life, with satisfying endings. Arabesque Romances may reflect several points of view and can include a wide variety of story subgenres including classic romance, contemporary romance, romantic comedy, and romantic suspense or romantic thriller.

Arabesque titles include *Love Takes Time* by Adrianne Byrd; *Surrender* by Branda Jackson; *Seduced by Moonlight* by Janice Sims; and *First Crush* by Marcia King-Gamble.

Kimani TRU is a new fiction imprint targeted to a younger audience of African American readers. This imprint is aimed at illustrating real-life situations young African American readers encounter without being preachy or naïve. The stories will reflect current trends in pop culture as well as story lines taken straight from the headlines. Kimani TRU titles include *Chasing Romeo* by A. J. Byrd; *Lesson Learned* by Earl Sewell; and *Fast Forward* by Celeste O. Norfleet.

Kimani Romance offers sexy, dramatic, sophisticated, and entertaining love stories featuring realistic African American characters that work through compelling emotional conflicts on their way to committed and satisfying relationships. Told primarily from the heroine's point of view, Kimani Romances will keep it real with true-to-life African American characters that turn up the heat and sizzle with passion.

Recent titles are *Sing to My Heart* by Various Authors.

The Sepia imprint publishes mainstream fiction titles that predominantly feature African American characters. Sepia releases a broad range of books that entertain, inform, and enrich the lives of readers. Sepia editors will review both contemporary and historical novels with subgenre plots, such as suspense-driven thrillers, paranormal and mystery, and novels that focus on social and relationship issues, as well as those that offer a realistic display of urban life. Sepia titles include *Counterfeit Wives* by Philip Thomas Duck; *Love, Lies, and Scandal* by Earl Sewell; and *Pleasure Seekers* by Rochelle Alers.

For all Kimani imprints and lines, send a detailed synopsis and three sample chapters (published authors) or a detailed synopsis and a complete manuscript (unpublished authors).

Glenda Howard, Editor (Kimani)

LUNA BOOKS

LUNA titles deliver a compelling, female-focused fantasy with vivid characters, rich worlds, strong, sympathetic women, and romantic subplots. LUNA Books editors want emotionally complex, sweeping stories that highlight the inner female power. Whether the heroine is on a quest to save the world—or someone or something important to her—discover her past or develop her own abilities, these stories are involving, gripping, and sweep the reader away into a detailed, convincing world.

They also contain romantic subplots that enhance the main story but don't become the focus of the novel.

Titles include *Beauty and the Werewolf* by Mercedes Lackey; *Raven Calls* by C.E. Murphy; *Horizon* by Sophie Littlefield.

Query with synopsis and one to three chapters:

Tara Parson, LUNA

SILHOUETTE BOOKS

Silhouette Books are intense thrillers, mysteries, and even werewolf stories—but always also romances. Each imprint has its own guidelines for length, plot, and characters. We recommend writing to the appropriate editor for guidelines or reading them online prior to writing your manuscript.

Silhouette Desire books are filled to the brim with strong, intense storylines. These sensual love stories immediately involve the reader in the romantic conflict and the quest for a happily-ever-after resolution. The novels should be fast-paced reads, and present the hero and heroine's conflict by the end of chapter one in order for the reader to understand what obstacles will impact the characters for the remainder of the novel. Recent titles include *A Scandal So Sweet* by Ann Major; *Gilded Secrets* by Maureen Child; *Strictly Temporary* by Robyn Grady; *The Cinderella Act* by Jennifer Lewis.

Silhouette Romantic Suspense books offer an escape read where true-to-life heroines find themselves in the throes of extraordinary circumstances, and in the arms of powerful heroes. These books combine all the elements of category novels with the excitement of romantic suspense, creating big, sweeping romances amid dangerous and suspenseful settings. Recent titles include *Secret Assignment* by Paula Graves and *Kansas City Cowboy* by Julie Miller.

Launched at the end of 2006, Silhouette Nocturne is looking for stories that deliver a dark, very sexy read that will entertain readers and take them from everyday life to an atmospheric, complex, paranormal world filled with characters struggling with life-and-death issues. These stories will be fast-paced, action-packed, and mission-oriented, with a strong level of sensuality. The hero is a key figure—powerful, mysterious, and totally attractive to the heroine. In fact, both main characters are very powerful, and their conflict is based on this element. The author must be able to set up a unique existence for the characters, with its own set of rules and mythologies; these are stories of vampires, shape-shifters, werewolves, psychic powers, etc., set in contemporary times. Recent titles include *The Covert Wolf* by Bonnie Vanak; *Sentinels: Tiger Bound* by Doranna Durgin; *Dragon's Curse* by Denise Lynn.

Silhouette Special Edition books are sophisticated, substantial stories packed with emotion. Special Edition demands writers to probe characters deeply, to explore issues that heighten the drama of living and loving, and to create compelling romantic plots. Whether the sensuality is sizzling or subtle, whether the plot is wildly innovative or satisfyingly traditional, the novel's emotional vividness, its depth and dimension, should clearly label it a very special contemporary romance. Subplots are welcome, but must further or parallel the developing romantic relationship in a meaningful way. Recent titles *The Last Single Maverick* by Christine Rimmer; *Puppy Love in Thunder Canyon* by Christyne Butler; *The Doctor and the Single Mom* by Teresa Southwick; *The Princess and the Outlaw* by Leanne Banks.

Krista Stroever, Senior Editor (Silhouette Suspense)
Stacy Boyd, Senior Editor (Silhouette Desire)
Patience Bloom, Associate Senior Editor (Silhouette Romantic Suspense)
Gail Chasan, Senior Editor (Silhouette Special Edition)

STEEPLE HILL BOOKS

Steeple Hill's inspiring fiction features wholesome Christian entertainment that will help women to better guide themselves, their families, and other women in their communities toward purposeful, faith-driven lives. All Steeple Hill editors are looking for authors writing from a Christian worldview and conveying their personal faith and ministry values in entertaining fiction that will touch the hearts of believers and seekers everywhere.

This Harlequin imprint comprises the following lines: Love Inspired, Love Inspired Historical, Love Inspired Suspense, and Steeple Hill Women's Fiction. Steeple Hill Café is for the hip, modern woman of faith.

The Love Inspired line is a series of contemporary, inspirational romances that feature Christian characters facing the many challenges of life and love in today's world. Recent titles include *The Carpenter's Wife* and *Heart of Stone* by Lenora Worth and *A Time to Forgive* and *Promise Forever* by Marta Perry.

Love Inspired Historical is a series of historical romances launched in October 2007 featuring Christian characters facing the many challenges of life and love in a variety of historical time periods. Recent titles include *His Unsuitable Viscountess* by Michelle Stlyes; *Betrothed to the Barbarian* by Carol Townend; *Lady with the Devil's Scar* by Sophia James; *A Not So Respectable Gentleman?* by Diane Gaston.

Steeple Hill Love Inspired Suspense is a series of edge-of-your-seat, contemporary romantic suspense tales of intrigue and romance featuring Christian characters facing challenges to their faith and to their lives. Titles include *End Game* by Roxanne Rustand and *Risky Reunion* by Lenora Worth.

The Steeple Hill Women's Fiction program is dedicated to publishing inspirational Christian women's fiction that depicts the struggles the characters encounter as they learn important lessons about trust and the power of faith. Recent titles include *Journey* by Angela Hunt and *Mother and Daughters: An Anthology* by Linda Bedford.

As with many programs developed for the Christian market, the Steeple Hill books have very specific guidelines, which may be requested from the editors or read online at Harlequin.com.

To submit your work, send a detailed synopsis, three sample chapters, and SASE to:

Joan Marlow Golan, Executive Editor (Steeple Hill Café and Steeple Hill Women's Fiction)

Krista Stroever, Associate Senior Editor (Steeple Hill Love Inspired and Love Inspired Suspense)

Melissa Endlich, Editor (Love Inspired Historical)

THE HARVARD COMMON PRESS

535 Albany Street, Boston, MA 02118
617-423-5803 | fax: 617-695-9794
www.harvardcommonpress.com | e-mail: editorial@harvardcommonpress.com

Founded in 1976, the Harvard Common Press publishes a wide variety of award-winning books on cooking, parenting, childbirth, and home gardening. The house is devoted to the home and home living.

Best sellers from Harvard Common include *The Nursing Mother's Companion* by Kathleen Huggins; *Vegan Planet: 400 Irresistible Recipes with Fantastic Flavors from Home and Around the World* by Robin Robertson; and *Not Your Mother's Slow Cooker Cookbook* by Beth Hensperger and Julie Kaufmann.

Titles include *The Best Quick Breads: 150 Recipes for Muffins, Scones, Shortcakes, Gingerbreads, Cornbreads, Coffeecakes, and More* by Beth Hensperger; *The Dad's Playbook to Labor and Birth: A Practical and Strategic Guide for Preparing for the Big Day* by Theresa and Brad Halvorsen; *The Southwestern Grill: 200 Terrific Recipes for Big and Bold Backyard Barbecue* by Michael McLaughlin; *25 Essentials: Techniques for Gas Grilling* by A. Cort Sinnes.

E-mail queries are accepted; please no full manuscripts. Query letters and SASEs should be directed to the Editorial Department:

Jane Dornbusch, Managing Editor

HARVEST HOUSE PUBLISHERS

990 Owen Loop North, Eugene, OR 97402
541-343-0123 | fax: 541-342-6410
www.harvesthousepublishers.com

Harvest House is one of the largest American publishers of Christian literature with more than 160 new books per year and a backlist of more than 700 titles. The house was founded in 1974 by Bob Hawkins, Sr., and has been run for the past 15 years by current president Bob Hawkins, Jr. Harvest House publishes in three main subject areas: self-help (relationships, family, money, Christian living), Bible help (Bibles, Bible studies, topical studies), and full-color gift books featuring name-brand artists. Recent releases include fiction and nonfiction for children and adults. Subjects include humor, Christian history, media, technology, politics, parenting, youth, relationships, family, Christian living, contemporary values, cults and the occult, personal awareness, inspiration, and spiritual growth.

Harvest House best sellers include *Cassidy and Sabrina* by Lori Wick; *My Beautiful Broken Shell* by Carol Hamblet Adams and D. Morgan; *Grandma, Do You Remember When?* by Jim Daly; *The Power of a Praying Wife* by Stormie Omartian; and *30 Days to Taming Your Tongue* by Deborah Smith Pegues.

Recent titles include *101 Questions to Ask Before You Get Remarried* by H. Norman Wright; *21 Ways to Connect with Your Kids* by Kathi Lipp; *7 Seconds to Success* by Gary Coffey; *The Amish Family Cookbook* by Jerry S. Eicher.

Harvest House is currently not accepting any unsolicited manuscripts or queries, even from agents.

Nick Harrison, Senior Editor
Steve Miller, Senior Editor

HAY HOUSE

NEW BEGINNINGS PRESS
PRINCESS BOOKS
SMILEY BOOKS
PO Box 5100, Carlsbad, CA 92018-5100
1-800-654-5126
www.hayhouse.com | e-mail: editorial@hayhouse.com

Hay House was founded in 1984 by Louise L. Hay to self-publish her first two books, *Heal Your Body* and *You Can Heal Your Life*, both of which became best sellers and established Ms. Hay as a leader in the New Age movement.

Now full-scale, Hay House publishes nonfiction only in the areas of self-help, New Age, sociology, philosophy, psychology, health, business, finance, men's/women's issues, inspirational memoirs, and celebrity biographies. Subjects include social issues, current events, ecology, business, food and nutrition, education, the environment, alternative health/medicine, money and finance, nature, recreation, religion, men's and women's issues, spiritual growth, and fitness. All titles have a positive self-help slant to them.

Hay House currently publishes approximately 300 books and 350 audio programs by more than 130 authors, and employs a full-time staff of 100-plus. They average 50 new titles per year. Imprints include Princess Books (titles from author John Edward of Crossing Over fame), Smiley Books (titles from Hay House author Tavis Smiley), and New Beginnings Press (financial titles).

Best-selling titles from Hay House are *Flower Therapy: Welcome the Angels of*

Nature into Your Life by Doreen Virtue, Robert Reeves; *Meals That Heal Inflammation* by Julie Daniluk; *Back To Sanity: Healing the Madness of Our Minds* by Steve Taylor; *Out of the Darkness* by Steve Taylor.

Hay House titles include *Mystery of the White Lions* by Linda Tucker; *The Three Sisters of the Tao* by Terah Kathryn Collins; and *Women's Bodies, Women's Wisdom* by Dr. Christiane Northrup.

NEW BEGINNINGS PRESS

Recent titles from New Beginnings Press include *How You Can Sell Anyone Anything* by Ben Stein and Barron Thomas; *How to Ruin the United States of America* and *Yes, You Can Get a Financial Life! Your Lifetime Guide to Financial Planning* by Ben Stein and Phil DeMuth.

PRINCESS BOOKS

Princess Books titles include *Final Beginnings: The Tunnel* by John Edward and Natasha Stoynoff; *Practical Praying* by John Edward; and *Cracking the Coconut Code* by Mary Jo McCabe.

SMILEY BOOKS

Smiley Books' latest releases are *Hope on a Tightrope: Words and Wisdom* by Dr. Cornel West; *Brainwashed: Erasing the Myth of Black Inferiority* by Tom Burrell; *America I Am: Legends, Rare Moments and Inspiring Words* by Cheryll Y. and Tavis Smiley; and *The Covenant in Action* by Tavis Smiley.

Hay House only accepts submissions from agents. See the website for details or submit hard-copy proposals by mail only to Editorial Department Submissions.

Reid Tracy, President
Patty Gift, Acquisitions Editor

HAZELDEN PUBLISHING AND EDUCATIONAL SERVICES

15251 Pleasant Valley Road, PO Box 176, RD15, Center City, MN 55012-0176
800-257-7810 | 651-213-4200 | fax: 651-213-4590
www.hazelden.org/bookplace | e-mail: customersupport@hazelden.org

Hazelden Publishing and Educational Services (established 1954) specializes in trade books that address issues relevant to alcoholism, drug addiction, and closely related psychology issues. Related topics include eating disorders, family and relationship issues, spirituality, codependency, compulsive gambling, sex addiction, depression, grief, treatment, and recovery. On the non-trade side of the publishing operation, the house publishes curricula, videos, pamphlets, and other publications for treatment programs, hospitals, schools, churches, correctional facilities, government and military agencies, as well as mental health and counseling agencies. Hazelden Publishing and Educational Services is a division of the Hazelden Foundation, which also operates a network of addiction recovery centers. The publisher has a concentration in materials related to the Twelve-Step approach.

Hazelden publishes information that helps build recovery in the lives of individuals, families, and communities affected by alcoholism, drug dependency, and related diseases. Hazelden publications and services are intended to meet a full range of issues for alcoholics, drug addicts, families, counselors, educators, doctors, and other professionals. Hazelden publications support Twelve-Step philosophy and a holistic approach that addresses the needs of the mind, body, and spirit.

Hazelden editors look for innovative materials that address issues relevant to substance abuse, prevention, treatment, and recovery. Topics include alcoholism, nicotine, and drug addictions; family and relationship issues; spirituality; eating disorders, gambling, and other addictive and compulsive behaviors; mental health; and historical information on the Twelve Steps.

Recent titles include *A Gentle Path through the Twelve Steps, Updated and Expanded* by Patrick Carnes, PhD; *Earnie Larsen: His Last Steps* by Earnie Larsen; *Miles To Go Before I Sleep* by Jackie Nink Pflug; *Living the Twelve Traditions in Today's World: Principles Before Personalities* by Mel B.

Physical submissions are strongly preferred. Submit proposals with sample chapters and SASEs to:

Karen Chernyaev, Senior Editor

HEALTH COMMUNICATIONS, INC.

HCI TEENS
3201 Southwest 15th Street, Deerfield Beach, FL 33442
954-360-0909 | 800-441-5569 | fax: 954-360-0034
www.hcibooks.com

Health Communications, Inc. (HCI), has been publishing books that change lives since 1977. HCI: The Life Issues Publisher has the goal of creating personal abundance for readers and customers, one book at a time.

In 1994, HCI published the first *Chicken Soup for the Soul* book, which not only became a best seller, but also continues to be an international publishing phenomenon. Books in the series have sold nearly 100 million copies.

Originally operating as a publisher of informational pamphlets for the recovery community, HCI moved into mainstream publishing in the 1980s with its first *New York Times* best seller, the 1983 *Adult Children of Alcoholics* by Dr. Janet Woititz, a veritable "bible" of the ACOA movement. This first best seller was followed by *Bradshaw On: The Family* and *Healing the Shame That Binds You*, both by John Bradshaw.

Aware of the significant shifts in the recovery movement, HCI actively expanded its book list to include a broader selection of titles. Now regarded as The Life Issues Publisher, HCI continues a tradition of providing readers with inspiring and motivating personal growth and self-help books.

Publisher of quality books on life issues, HCI's broad base of over 900 titles encompasses self-help, spirituality, addictions and recovery, psychology, parenting, relationships, religion, inspiration, health and wellness, and more.

Recent HCI titles include *Eating Free: The Carb-Friendly Way to Lose Inches...* by Manuel Villacorta, MS, RD, CSSD; *Growing Happy Kids* by Maureen Healy; *Understanding Codependency, Updated and Expanded* by Sharon Wegscheider-Cruse and Joseph Cruse; *Learning to Love Yourself, Revised & Updated* by Sharon Wegscheider-Cruse.

HCI TEENS

HCI Teens delivers the facts and fiction teens are asking for. HCI's commitment to teens is firm, up front, and to the point: Give teens what they want and what they need, and most important, give teens a variety of quality content from which they can learn, grow, and enjoy all life has to offer, now and in the future. The backbone for the imprint includes the bestselling titles from *Chicken Soup for the Teenage Soul* series, the *Taste Berries for Teens* series by Bettie and Jennifer Youngs, and the *Teen Love* series by Kimberly Kirberger.

HCI TEENS titles include *Feed Your Head: Some Excellent Stuff on Being Yourself* by Earl Hipp and L. K. Hanson; *Our Best Days* by Sally Coleman and Nancy Hull-Mast; *Mentors, Masters, and Mrs. MacGregor: Stories of Teachers Making a Difference* by Jane Bluestein; *Help for the Hard Times* by Earl Hipp; and *A Child Called It: One Child's Courage to Survive* by Dave Pelzer.

Health Communications distributes its own list. In addition, HCI is the exclusive trade distributor for Hazelden Publishing.

Due to new postal regulations, HCI can no longer use an SASE to return parcels weighing 16 ounces or more. Therefore, they no longer return any submissions weighing 16 ounces or more, even if an SASE is included. See their website for more detailed submission guidelines. Query letters, proposals, and SASEs should be directed to the editorial staff.

Allison Janse, Editor

HEBREW PUBLISHING COMPANY

PO Box 222, Spencertown, NY 12165
518-392-3322 | fax: 518-392-4280

Hebrew Publishing Company (established in 1901) offers a wide range of titles in such categories as reference materials and dictionaries; religions, law, and thought; Rabbinic literature; literature, history, and biography; children's books; Hebrew-language texts and Hebrew culture; Yiddish; the Bible in English and in Hebrew/English; prayers and liturgy, including daily (Hebrew only and Hebrew/English), Sabbath, high holidays, festivals, memorials, and Purim; Hanukkah; educational materials; sermons and aids of the rabbi; and calendars. The house publishes a limited number of new titles and maintains an established backlist.

On the HPC list: *Yom Kippur* by Philip Birnbaum; *Judaism as a Civilization* by Mordecai Kaplan; *Acharon Hamohikanim (The Last of the Mohicans)* by James Fenimore Cooper; *Business Ethics in Jewish Law* by Leo Jung; *Encyclopedia of Jewish Concepts* by Philip Birnbaum; and *Jewish Tales and Legends* by Menachem Glen.

Hebrew Publishing Company oversees its own distribution, utilizing the services of independent fulfillment and distribution firms.

Query letters and SASEs should be directed to:

Charles Lieber, President

HEBREW UNION COLLEGE PRESS

A Division of the Hebrew Union College-Jewish Institute of Religion
3101 Clifton Avenue, Cincinnati, OH 45220-2488
513-221-1875, extension 3292 | fax: 513-221-0321
www.huc.edu/newspubs/press | e-mail: hucpress@huc.edu

As part of the Hebrew Union College-Jewish Institute of Religion, the Hebrew Union College Press (founded 1921) publishes scholarly Judaica for an international academic readership.

Always concerned with quality of scholarship rather than sales potential, the Hebrew Union College Press has from its inception devoted its resources and efforts to the publication of works of the highest caliber for its niche audience. HUCP has copublishing projects with other institutions, including Harvard University Press, KTAV Publishing House, University of Alabama Press, Yale University Press, Klau Library, Skirball Museum, and Kunstresim.

Titles include *A Window on Their World: The Court Diaries of Rabbi Hayyim Gindersheim Frankfurt am Main, 1773-1794* by Edward Fram; *Remnant Stones: The Jewish Cemeteries of Suriname, Essays* by Aviva Ben-Ur, and Rachel Frankel;

The Greening of American Orthodox Judaism: Yavneh in the 1960's by Benny Kraut; *Yannai on Genesis: An Invitation to Piyyut* by Laura S. Lieber; *Let Me Continue to Speak the Truth: Bertha Pappenheim as Actor and Activist* by Elizabeth Loentz.

Hebrew Union College Press is distributed by Wayne State University Press.

HUCP welcomes the submission of scholarly manuscripts in all areas of Judaica. Address all editorial inquiries to:

Michael A. Meyer, Chair, Publications Committee
Barbara Selya, Managing Editor

HEINEMANN USA [SEE ABC-CLIO]

HERDER & HERDER [SEE CROSSROAD PUBLISHING COMPANY]

HIPPOCRENE BOOKS

171 Madison Avenue, New York, NY 10016
212-685-4373 | fax: 212-779-9338
www.hippocrenebooks.com | e-mail: info@hippocrenebooks.com

Over more than 35 years, Hippocrene Books has become one of America's foremost publishers of foreign-language reference books and ethnic cookbooks. As a small publishing house in a marketplace dominated by conglomerates, Hippocrene has succeeded by continually reinventing its list while maintaining a strong international and ethnic orientation. In addition to cookbooks and foreign-language reference books, Hippocrene publishes on the subjects of history, Judaica, leisure, love poetry, militaria, Polish interest, proverbs, travel, and weddings.

George Blagowidow founded the company in 1970. The name Hippocrene comes from Greek mythology and refers to the sacred fountain of the Muses that was the source of their inspiration. Hippocrene's international focus derives from Blagowidow's passion for travel and his personal history.

Currently, Hippocrene features over 64 cuisines in its cookbook program. In addition to its conventional history list, the company launched a series of Illustrated Histories in 1998. Each book features the political and cultural history of a region, accompanied by black-and-white pictures. Leading titles include *Spain: An Illustrated History* and *The Celtic World: An Illustrated History*. New publishing areas also comprise international editions of poetry, short stories, proverbs, and folk tales. *Classic French Love Poems*, edited by Lisa Neal, and *Pakistani Folk*

Tales: Toontoony Pie and Other Stories by Ashraf Siddiqui and Marilyn Lerch are representative titles.

Recent titles include *India: A Culinary Journey* by Prem Kishore; *The Iraqi Family Cookbook* by Kay Karim; *Cantonese-English/English-Cantonese Dictionary & Phrasebook* by Editors of Hippocrene Books; *Introduction to Russian-English Translation* by Natalia Strelkova.

Query letters and SASEs should be directed to the editorial staff.

Anne McBride, Editor-in-Chief

HOUGHTON MIFFLIN HARCOURT

HOUGHTON MIFFLIN HARCOURT
HOUGHTON MIFFLIN HARCOURT CHILDREN'S BOOK GROUP
HOUGHTON MIFFLIN HARCOURT SCHOOL PUBLISHERS
HOLT MCDOUGAL
Boston office:
222 Berkeley Street, Boston, MA 02116-3764
617-351-5000
New York office:
215 Park Avenue South, New York, NY 10003
212-420-5800
www.hmhco.com

Boston-based Houghton Mifflin Harcourt is one of the leading educational publishers in the United States, publishing textbooks, instructional technology, assessments, and other educational materials for teachers and students of every age. The company also publishes an extensive line of reference works and award-winning trade fiction and nonfiction for adults and young readers.

In December 2006, Houghton Mifflin was acquired by HM Rivergroup, an Irish holding company led by Riverdeep Chief Executive Barry O'Callaghan; the combined group was renamed Houghton Mifflin Riverdeep Group. In 2007, Houghton Mifflin Company acquired Harcourt Education, Harcourt Trade, and Greenwood-Heinemann divisions of Reed Elsevier, and became the largest educational publisher in the world. Houghton Mifflin and Harcourt combined forces to become the Houghton Mifflin Harcourt Trade and Reference Publishing Group. The children's divisions followed suit, leading to the creation of Houghton Mifflin Harcourt Children's.

With its origins dating back to 1832, Houghton Mifflin Harcourt combines its tradition of excellence with a commitment to innovation in order to satisfy the lifelong need to learn and be entertained.

HOUGHTON MIFFLIN HARCOURT

Houghton Mifflin Harcourt launched its first combined trade list in Winter 2009. Under the Houghton Mifflin Harcourt imprint, the adult group will publish approximately 80 new hardcover books each year, and under the Mariner Books imprint (incorporating the Harvest backlist), approximately 90 trade paperbacks, including paperback originals and books acquired from other publishers. The reference division continues to publish the American Heritage dictionaries and other authoritative and popular books about language, for adults and children. In addition, Houghton Mifflin Harcourt distributes books for Beacon Press, The Old Farmer's Almanac, Larousse, and Chambers.

The Houghton Mifflin nonfiction roster has included fine writers in such categories as history, natural history, biography and memoir, science, and economics, including such preeminent figures as Winston Churchill, Arthur M. Schlesinger, Jr., and John Kenneth Galbraith. They also have a proud tradition of publishing works of social criticism that have spoken with great power through the generations, including Rachel Carson's *Silent Spring*, James Agee and Walker Evans's *Let Us Now Praise Famous Men*, the works of Jane Goodall and, recently, the bestselling *Constantine's Sword* by James Carroll and *Fast Food Nation* by Eric Schlosser.

On the literary side, Houghton Mifflin launched the careers of such writers as Willa Cather, A. B. Guthrie, Jr., Robert Penn Warren, Ann Petry, Elizabeth Bishop, Philip Roth, Willie Morris, and Robert Stone. Their fiction list today also includes such distinguished names as Tim O'Brien, John Edgar Wideman, and Edna O'Brien.

Houghton Mifflin's commitment to poetry has spanned well over 100 years. The current roster of poets includes Donald Hall, a poet laureate; Natasha Trethewey, the 2007 winner of the Pulitzer Prize in Poetry; and Galway Kinnell, Grace Schulman, Alan Shapiro, Michael Collier, and Glyn Maxwell, among others.

Harcourt Trade Publishers was established when Alfred Harcourt and Donald Brace left Henry Holt and Company in 1919 to form a new publishing enterprise. Early Harcourt lists featured Sinclair Lewis, Carl Sandburg, and John Maynard Keynes, joined over the decades by Virginia Woolf, George Orwell, C. S. Lewis, Antoine de Saint-Exupéry, Thomas Merton, Robert Lowell, T. S. Eliot, and Robert Penn Warren. In 1961, Helen and Kurt Wolff, cofounders of Pantheon Books, became Harcourt's copublishers and brought with them their eponymous list, which included the luminaries Günter Grass, Hannah Arendt, and Konrad Lorenz. A mainstay of literature in translation, Harcourt has published celebrated international authors such as Italo Calvino, Umberto Eco, and Amos Oz, as well as the Nobel Prize winners Octavio Paz, José Saramago, and A. B. Yehoshua.

The adult trade group does not accept unsolicited manuscript submissions for fiction, nonfiction, or poetry, except through a literary agent. Send lexical submissions to the Dictionary Department at the Boston address.

Andrea Schulz, Vice President, Editor-in-Chief (Boston)—Fiction, popular science.
Susan Canavan, Executive Editor (Boston)—Nonfiction, current affairs, narratives.
Bruce Nichols, Editor—Thrillers, politics, current affairs.
Deanne Urmy, Editor—Fiction, current affairs, philosophy.
Jenna Johnson, Editor—Fiction.
Nicola Angeloro, Editor
Ken Carpenter, Editor—Paperback originals.
Steve Danzis, Editor
Lisa White, Editor—Guidebooks, natural history, illustrated and reference field guides.

HOUGHTON MIFFLIN HARCOURT CHILDREN'S BOOK GROUP CLARION BOOKS

Houghton Mifflin Harcourt Children's Book Group encompasses three award-winning imprints as well as the Graphia and Sandpaper paperback lines. Houghton Mifflin introduced its list of books for young readers in 1937. Houghton Mifflin Books for Children publishes luminaries such as H. A. and Margret Rey, Virginia Lee Burton, Bill Peet, Holling C. Holling, Scott O'Dell, and James Marshall; its contemporary authors and illustrators include Steve Jenkins, D. B. Johnson, Toni Morrison, Marilyn Nelson, Eric Schlosser, Brian Lies, Chris Van Allsburg, Allen Say, Lois Lowry, and David Macaulay. Houghton Mifflin is also home to some of the best-loved children's book characters: Curious George, Lyle the Crocodile, George and Martha, Martha of Martha Speaks, and Tacky the Penguin.

Harcourt Children's Books, known for classics such as *The Little Red Lighthouse and the Great Gray Bridge* and *The Little Prince*, features notable authors and illustrators such as Avi, Janell Cannon, Margaret Chodos-Irvine, Lois Ehlert, Mem Fox, Han Nolan, Gennifer Choldenko, David Shannon, Janet Stevens, Susan Stevens Crummel, and Helen Oxenbury.

Houghton Mifflin Harcourt Children's Books does not respond to any unsolicited submission unless they are interested in publishing it. Please do not include an SASE. Submissions will be recycled, and you will not hear from them regarding the status of your submission unless they are interested, in which case you can expect to hear back within 12 weeks. Send to Submissions at the Boston address.

Mary Ann Wilcox, Vice President, Franchise Director
Julia Richardson, Editorial Director
Kate O'Sullivan, Editor
Betsy Groban, Editor

CLARION BOOKS

Clarion Books began publishing children's fiction and picture books in 1965 with a list of six titles. In 1979, it was bought by and became an imprint of Houghton Mifflin. The list has expanded to nearly 60 titles a year and includes nonfiction as well as fiction and picture books. In 1987, Clarion received its first Newbery Honor Medal, for *On My Honor* by Marion Dane Bauer, and in 1988, it had its first Newbery Medal winner, *Lincoln: A Photobiography* by Russell Freedman. Since then Clarion books have received children's book honors and awards nearly every year. Clarion's award-winning titles include *The Three Pigs* (2002 Caldecott Medal), *Tuesday* (Caldecott Medal), and *Sector 7* (Caldecott Honor), all written and illustrated by David Wiesner; *A Single Shard* (2002 Newbery Medal) by Linda Sue Park; *The Midwife's Apprentice* (Newbery Medal) and *Catherine Called Birdy* (Newbery Honor), both by Karen Cushman; *Sir Walter Raleigh and The Quest for El Dorado* (the inaugural Sibert Medal) by Marc Aronson; and *My Rows and Piles of Coins* (Coretta Scott King Honor for illustration) by Tololwa M. Mollel, illustrated by E. B. Lewis.

Recent titles include *Change Up: Baseball Poems* by Gene Fehler and Donald Wu; *How to Scratch a Wombat: Where to Find It…What to Feed It…Why It Sleeps All Day* by Jackie French and Bruce Whatley; and *Rabbit's Good News* by Ruth Bornstein.

In the picture books area, the editors are looking for active picture-book stories with a beginning, middle, and end—stories that deal fully and honestly with children's emotions. You do not need to provide illustrations or find an illustrator; if your manuscript is accepted, the publisher will handle this. No query letter is necessary for picture book manuscripts and/or dummies.

In the nonfiction area, the editors are interested in hearing about social studies, science, concept, wordplay, holiday, history, and biography ideas for all age levels. Send a query letter or proposal with a sample chapter(s) on all nonfiction projects.

In the fiction area, the editors are seeking lively stories for ages eight to twelve and ages ten to fourteen. They are also looking for transitional chapter books (12 to 20 manuscript pages) for ages six to nine and for short novels of 40 to 80 manuscript pages suitable for ages seven to ten. Clarion is highly selective in the areas of historical fiction, fantasy, and science fiction. A novel must be superlatively written in order to find a place on the list. The editors prefer to see complete manuscripts.

Address all submissions with SASEs to the attention of the Editorial Department in New York.

Dinah Stevenson, Publisher
Ann Rider, Editor
Erica Zappy, Editor
Margaret Raymo, Editor

HOUGHTON MIFFLIN HARCOURT SCHOOL PUBLISHERS

Houghton Mifflin Harcourt School Publishers publishes resources for teachers, students, and parents for pre-K through grade eight. The School Division's renowned author teams rely on extensive market and independent research to inform the pedagogical structure of each program. Ancillary products such as workbooks, teacher guides, audiovisual guides, and computer software provide additional support for students and teachers at each grade level. The school division is headquartered in Boston.

Authors may learn more at www.hmhschool.com.

HOLT MCDOUGAL

Holt McDougal was formed with the combination of the Holt, Rinehart, and Winston division and McDougal Littell. Holt McDougal publishes an extensive offering of print and technology materials for language arts, mathematics, social studies, world languages, and science for grades six to twelve.

More information is available at www.holtmcdougal.hmhco.com.

HUMAN KINETICS

1607 N. Market St., Champaign, Illinois 61820
PO Box 5076, Champaign, IL 61825-5076
800-747-4457 | fax: 217-351-1549
www.humankinetics.com | e-mail: webmaster@hkusa.com

Human Kinetics aims to convert all information about physical activity into knowledge—information that people can use to make a positive difference in their lives. In today's world, survival of the fittest means survival of the best informed. Building that knowledge is the role of Human Kinetics (HK).

Human Kinetics published its first book in 1974. Today, HK produces textbooks and their ancillaries, consumer books, software, videos, audiocassettes, journals, and distance education courses. The world headquarters are located in Champaign, Illinois, with offices in the United Kingdom, Canada, Australia, and New Zealand to bolster their international efforts. Their annual sales, including international operations, surpass $37 million.

A privately held company, Human Kinetics publishes more than 100 books and 20 journals annually. They have expanded operations to that of an "information packager," utilizing whatever media source can best deliver the information to the consumer. Their objective is to make a positive difference in the quality of life of all people by promoting physical activity, and by seeking out the foremost experts in a particular field and assisting them in delivering the most current information in the best format.

HK's two academic book divisions—the Scientific, Technical, and Medical (STM) Division; and the Health, Physical Education, Recreation, and Dance (HPERD) Division—publish textbooks and reference books for students, scholars, and professionals in the company's fields of interest.

HK's Trade Book Division (formerly called Leisure Press) publishes expertly written books for the general public and for such groups as coaches, athletes, and fitness enthusiasts.

Recent titles include *Principles of Sustainable Living* by Richard R. Jurin, PhD; *Teaching Lifetime Outdoor Pursuits* by Jeff Steffen, PhD, and Jim Stiehl, PhD; *Recreation, Event, and Tourism Businesses* by Robert E. Pifster and Patrick T. Tierney, PhD; *Inclusive Recreation by Human Kinetics: Managing Sport Facilities* by Gil Fried, JD.

Query letters, proposals, and SASEs should be directed to the Editorial Department of the division to which you are submitting. Detailed guidelines are available on the website.

Rainer Martens, President and Publisher
Julie Marx Goodreau, Director, Trade Division

HYPERION

HYPERION BOOKS FOR CHILDREN
114 Fifth Avenue, New York, NY 10011
212-456-0100
www.hyperionbooks.com
www.hyperionbooksforchildren.com

Hyperion, which was founded by The Walt Disney Company in 1991, publishes general-interest fiction, literary works, and nonfiction in the areas of popular culture, health and wellness, business, current topical interest, popular psychology, self-help, and humor. The house publishes books in hardcover, trade paperback, and mass-market paperback formats. Hyperion also operates a very strong children's program. Imprint ESPN focuses on sports titles.

Recent adult titles from Hyperion include *The Pleasures of Men* by Kate Williams; *Bright Lights, No City* by Max Alexander; *Sly Fox* by Jeanine Pirro; *Serpent's Kiss* by Melissa de la Cruz; *The Innocents* by Francesca Segal.

Laurie Chittenden, Editor
Leslie Wells, Executive Editor—Cooking, fiction, nonfiction.
Elisabeth Dyssegaard, Editor—Business, sport stories, fiction.
Matt Inman, Editor—Fiction, nonfiction, humor.
Colin Fox, Editor—Nonfiction.

HYPERION BOOKS FOR CHILDREN

Hyperion Books for Children published its first book in August 1991: *See Squares*, a paperback counting book by Joy N. Hulme, illustrated by Carol Schwartz. Since then, Hyperion Books for Children and its imprints have published books by Julie Andrews, Rosemary Wells, Louise Erdrich, William Nicholson, Michael Dorris,

INDEPENDENT US PRESSES

Jules Feiffer, Toni Morrison, Jon Agee, Paul Zindel, and William Wegman, among others. Hyperion Books for Children's imprints include Jump at the Sun, the first children's book imprint to celebrate black culture for all children, and Volo, a paperback original series.

Hyperion Books For Children titles include *The Enemy* by Charlie Higson; *The Kane Chronicles Book One: The Red Pyramid* by Rick Riordan; *For the Love of Soccer* by Pelé; *A Field Guide for Heartbreakers* by Kristen Tracy; and *Passing Strange: A Generation Dead Novel* by Daniel Waters.

Christian Trimmer, Editor—Young Adult.

Tamson Weston, Editor—Children's, illustrated.

IDEALS BOOKS

CANDYCANE PRESS
SMART KIDS PUBLISHING
WILLIAMSON BOOKS

2630 Elm Hill Pike, Suite 100, Nashville, TN 37214
800-586-2572
www.idealsbooks.com | e-mail: atyourservice@guideposts.org

Ideals Books has been publishing book and magazine products since 1944. Ideals is owned by Guideposts in Carmel, New York. Ideals Books publishes over 70 new products annually for the adult and children's markets.

CANDYCANE PRESS

Candycane Press publishes children's books and board books. Some of their titles include *Sweetpea Beauty and the Princess Party!* by Laura Neutzling; *The Story of Joshua* by Patricia A. Pingry; *He's Got the Whole World in His Hands* by Traditional; *Humphrey's First Palm Sunday* by Carol Heyer.

SMART KIDS PUBLISHING

Smart Kids Publishing publishes illustrated books and photo books for children. Some of their titles include *Busy Busy Butterfly* by Molly Carroll and Damon Taylor; *Down in the Deep, Deep Ocean!* by Joann Cleland; *It's Potty Time: Boys* by Chris Sharp and Garry Currant; and *Ladybug, Ladybug, What Are You Doing* by Jo Cleland.

WILLIAMSON BOOKS

Williamson publishes nonfiction books that encourage children to succeed by helping them to discover their creative capacity. *Kids Can!*, *Little Hands*, *Kaleidoscope*

Kids, *Quick Starts for Kids*, and *Good Times* books encourage curiosity and exploration with irresistible graphics and open-ended instruction. The house publishes hands-on learning books in science and nature, arts and crafts, math and history, cooking, social studies, and more, featuring new *Kaleidoscope Kids* and *Kids Can!* titles. Its publishing program is committed to maintaining excellent quality while providing good value for parents, teachers, and children.

Titles from Williamson include *Crafts Across America* by Cindy A. Littlefield; *The Little Hands Art Book* by Judy Press; *China: Kaleidoscope Kids* by Debbi Michiko Florence and Jim Caputo; *Leap into Space* by Nancy Castaldo and Patrick McRae; and *Super Science Concoctions: 50 Mysterious Mixtures for Fabulous Fun* by Jill Frankel Hauser and Michael Kline.

Ideals Publications does not accept submissions by e-mail or fax. Send an SASE to "Guidelines" to receive writers' guidelines. Please address queries and SASEs to "The Editors."

INDUSTRIAL PRESS

989 Avenue of the Americas, 19th Floor, New York, NY 10018
212-889-6330 | 888-528-7852 | fax: 212-545-8327
www.industrialpress.com | e-mail: info@industrialpress.com

Founded in 1883, Industrial Press is the leading technical and reference publisher for engineering, technology, manufacturing, and education.

The house's flagship title, *Machinery's Handbook*, now in its 90th year, remains unchallenged as "The Bible" in its field, the most popular engineering title of all time. The new 28th edition remains true to the *Handbook*'s original design as an extraordinary, comprehensive yet practical and easy-to-use reference for mechanical and manufacturing engineers, designers, draftsmen, toolmakers, and machinists.

Recent titles include *Machine Designer's Reference* by J. Mars, P.E.; *The Art of Gear Fabrication* by Prem H. Daryani; *Roll Form Tool Design Fundamentals* by William Alvarez; *Welding Essentials: Questions and Answers*, 2nd Edition by William Galvery and Frank Marlow; *Art and Science of Steel Estimating* by Kerri Olsen.

Industrial Press handles its own distribution.

Industrial Press is expanding its list of professional and educational titles in addition to starting a new program in electronic publishing. Additional information is available in the Authors section of the website. E-mail proposals are accepted at info@industrialpress.com. Contact with proposals or queries:

John F. Carleo, Editorial Director, jcarleo@industrialpress.com

INNER TRADITIONS/BEAR & COMPANY

BEAR & COMPANY
BEAR CUB BOOKS
BINDU BOOKS
DESTINY BOOKS
HEALING ARTS PRESS
INNER TRADITIONS
PARK STREET PRESS

PO Box 388, One Park Street, Rochester, VT 05767-0388
802-767-3174 | 800-246-8648 | fax: 802-767-3726
www.innertraditions.com | e-mail: submissions@innertraditions.com

Inner Traditions/Bear & Company is one of the largest publishers of books on spiritual and healing traditions of the world. Their titles focus on ancient mysteries, alternative health, indigenous cultures, religion, sexuality, tarot, and divination. With over 1,000 books in print, Inner Traditions has eleven imprints: Inner Traditions, Bear & Co., Bear Cub Books, Bindu Books, Destiny Books, Destiny Recordings, Destiny Audio Editions, Inner Traditions en Español, Healing Arts Press, Park Street Press, and Inner Traditions India.

BEAR & COMPANY

Bear & Company's focus is on ancient wisdom, new science, visionary fiction, Western thought, indigenous traditions, Maya studies, extraterrestrial consciousness, and complementary medicine. Titles from Bear & Company include *Krishna in the Sky with Diamonds* by Scott Teitsworth; *The Earth Chronicles Handbook: A Comprehensive Guide to the Seven Books of the Earth Chronicles* by Zecharia Sitchin; *Breathing through the Whole Body: The Buddha's Instructions on Integrating Mind, Body, and Breath* by Will Johnson.

BEAR CUB BOOKS

Bear Cub Books are books for kids that feed the growing mind, body, and spirit. Titles include *The Magical Adventures of Krishna: How a Mischief Maker Saved the World* by Vatsala Sperling and Pieter Welteverde; *Ganga: The River that Flows from Heaven to Earth* by Vatsala Sperling, Harish Johari, and Pierter Weltevrede; and *Karna: The Greatest Archer in the World* by Vatsala Sperling and Sandeep Johari.

BINDU BOOKS

Bindu Books publishes books on spirituality and self-transformation for young adults and teens. Some titles are *Spiritual Journaling: Writing Your Way to Independence*

by Julie Tallard Johnson; *Awakening to Animal Voices: A Teen Guide to Telepathic Communication with All Life* by Dawn Baumann Brunke; and *Teen Psychic: Exploring Your Intuitive Spiritual Powers* by Julie Tallard Johnson.

DESTINY BOOKS

Destiny Books publishes New Age and metaphysical titles with special emphasis on self-transformation, the occult, and psychological well-being. Some titles include *The Alchemy of Sexual Energy: Connecting to the Universe from Within* by Mantak Chia; *The Way of Tarot: The Spiritual Teacher in the Cards* by Alejandro Jodorowsky and Marianne Costa; *Kalaripayat: The Martial Arts Tradition of India* by Patrick Denaud and Marie-Claire Restoux; and *Living in the Tao: The Effortless Path to Self-Discovery* by Mantak Chia and William U. Wei.

HEALING ARTS PRESS

Healing Arts Press produces works on alternative medicine and holistic health that combine contemporary thought and innovative research with the accumulated knowledge of the world's great healing traditions. Some titles include *The Acid–Alkaline Diet for Optimum Health: Restore Your Health by Creating pH Balance in Your Diet* by Christopher Vasey, ND; *Managing Multiple Sclerosis Naturally: A Self-help Guide to Living with MS* by Judy Graham; *The Subtle Energy Body: The Complete Guide* by Maureen Lockhart, PhD; *The Natural Testosterone Plan For Sexual Health and Energy* by Stephen Harrod Buhner.

INNER TRADITIONS

Inner Traditions publishes works representing the spiritual, cultural, and mythic traditions of the world, focusing on inner wisdom and perennial philosophies. Some titles include *The Elixir of Immortality: A Modern-Day Alchemist's Discovery of the Philosopher's Stone* by Robert E. Cox; *How the World Is Made: The Story of Creation According to Sacred Geometry* by John Mitchell and Allan Brown; and *The Way of Beauty: Five Meditations for Spiritual Transformation* by François Cheng.

PARK STREET PRESS

Park Street Press puts its focus on travel books, psychology, consumer and environmental issues, archaeology, women's and men's studies, and fine art. Some titles include *Morphic Resonance: The Nature of Formative Causation* by Rupert Sheldrake and *The Spiritual Anatomy of Emotion: How Feelings Link the Brain, the Body, and the Sixth Sense* by Michael A. Jawer et al.

Query via e-mail or regular mail with SASE. Send cover letter with manuscript or proposal by regular mail with SASE to the acquisitions editor:

Jon Graham, Acquisitions Editor
Jeanie Levitan, Vice President of Editorial

INSIDERS' GUIDES [SEE THE GLOBE PEQUOT PRESS]

INTERVARSITY PRESS

A Division of InterVarsity Christian Fellowship/USA
 FORMATIO
Letters: PO Box 1400, Downers Grove, IL 60515
Packages: 430 Plaza Dr., Westmont, IL 60559
630-734-4000 | fax: 630-734-4200
www.ivpress.com | e-mail: submissions@ivpress.com

InterVarsity Press is the publishing arm of InterVarsity Christian Fellowship campus ministry and has been publishing Christian books for more than 50 years. Their program is comprised of three imprints: IVP Books (general interest), IVP Academic (research and classroom use), and IVP Connect (study guides for churches and small groups). A new imprint, Formatio, was launched in 2006.

As an extension of InterVarsity Christian Fellowship, InterVarsity Press serves those in the university, the church, and the world by publishing resources that equip and encourage people to follow Jesus as Savior and Lord in all of Life.

Recent titles include *Consequential Leadership* by Mac Pier; *Ashamed No More* by Thomas C. Ryan; *Christian Confidence* by Chris Sinkinson; *The Bible Questions: Shedding Light on the World's Most Important Book* by Hal Seed.

FORMATIO

Andy Le Peau, IVP's editorial director, appealed to tradition to describe their new Formatio imprint: "People are looking for a spirituality that is rooted in the history of the church and in Scripture." Formatio books follow the rich tradition of the church in the journey of spiritual formation. These books are not merely about being informed, but about being transformed by Christ and conformed to his image.

Some new titles from Formatio include *Green Leaves for Later Years* by Emile Griffin; *Discovering Lectio Divina* by James C. Wilhoit and Evan B. Howard; *Reborn on the Fourth of July* by Logan Mehl-Laituri; *Go and Do: Becoming a Missional Christian* by Don Everts.

Current interests are listed on the website. IVP is particularly interested in authors with diverse backgrounds and experiences, especially non-Anglos, women, and "knowledgeable and experienced people more than writers." If you are associated with a college or seminary and have an academic manuscript, you may submit it to the attention of the Academic Editor. If you are a pastor or a previously published author, you may submit it to the attention of the General Books Editor. Their preference is to receive a chapter-by-chapter summary, two complete sample chapters, and your résumé.

Address queries with SASEs to:
Dave Zimmerman, Assistant Editor

ISLAND PRESS

1718 Connecticut Avenue, NW, Suite 300, Washington, DC 20009
202-232-7933 | fax: 202-234-1328
www.islandpress.org | e-mail: info@islandpress.org

Island Press was established in 1984 to meet the need for reliable, peer-reviewed information to help solve environmental problems. The house identifies innovative thinkers and emerging trends in the environmental field. They work with world-renowned experts and aspiring authors to develop cross-disciplinary solutions to environmental challenges, making sure this information is communicated effectively to the widest possible audience.

Island Press publishes approximately 40 new titles per year on such topics as conservation biology, marine science, land conservation, green building, sustainable agriculture, climate change, and ecological restoration. In addition, Island Press is engaged in several collaborative partnerships designed to help facilitate the stimulation of new ideas, new information products, and targeted outreach to specific audiences. Their Communication Partnership for Science and the Sea (COMPASS) is one such example.

Recent titles include *State of the World 2012* by The Worldwatch Institute; *Evolution in a Toxic World* by Emily Monosson; *Fundamentals of Sustainable Dwellings* by Avi Friedman; *City Rules* by Emily Talen; *The Restoring Ecological Health to Your Land Workbook* by Steven I. Apfelbaum and Alan Haney.

Query letters and SASEs should be directed to the Editorial Department.
Todd Baldwin, Vice President and Associate Publisher
Barbara Dean, Executive Editor
Heather Boyer, Senior Editor
Erin Johnson, Assistant Editor
Courtney Lix, Editorial Assistant

JEWISH LIGHTS PUBLISHING

Sunset Farm Offices, Route 4, PO Box 237, Woodstock, VT 05091
802-457-4000 | fax: 802-457-4004
www.jewishlights.com | e-mail: editorial@jewishlights.com

Jewish Lights publishes books that reflect the Jewish wisdom tradition for people of all faiths and backgrounds. Stuart Matlins, founder and publisher of Jewish Lights Publishing, was presented with the 2006 American Jewish Distinguished Service Award for engaging people of all faiths and backgrounds to help them learn about who Jewish people are, where they come from, and what the future can be made to hold.

Jewish Lights' authors draw on the Jewish wisdom tradition to deal with the quest for the self and for finding meaning in life. Jewish Lights books are nonfiction almost exclusively, covering topics including religion, Jewish life cycle, theology, philosophy, history, and spirituality. They also publish two books for children annually.

Recent titles include *The Mitzvah Project Book: Making Mitzvah Part of Your Bar/Bat Mitzvah…and Your Life* by Liz Suneby and Diane Heiman; *Our Religious Brains: What Cognitive Science Reveals about Belief…* by Rabbi Ralph D. Mecklenburger; *Masking and Unmasking Ourselves: Interpreting Biblical Texts on Clothing & Identity* by Dr. Norman J. Cohen; *All Politics Is Religious: Speaking Faith to the Media, Policy Makers and Community* by Rabbi Dennis S. Ross.

Direct proposals and SASEs via regular mail to the Submissions Editor. No digital or e-mail submissions. Jewish Lights does not publish biography, haggadot, or poetry.

Stuart Matlins, Publisher

THE JEWISH PUBLICATION SOCIETY

2100 Arch Street, 2nd Floor, Philadelphia, PA 19103
215-832-0600 | 800-234-3151 | fax: 215-568-2017
www.jewishpub.org | e-mail: jewishbook@jewishpub.org

The Jewish Publication Society (JPS) specializes in books of Jewish interest, especially traditional religious works (including the Torah), folktales, and commentaries and resources for Jewish life. JPS is over a century old, and is a nonprofit publisher.

The JPS collection *Legends of the Jews* first appeared in 1909. Lately, JPS has undertaken documenting Jewish tales and legends from the around the world in a series of six massive volumes. The first, *Folktales of the Jews: Tales from the Sephardic Dispersion*, released late in 2006, also contains a detailed commentary by University of Pennsylvania folklorist Dan Ben-Amos.

Recent titles include *36 Letters* by Joan Sohn; *The Book of Ruth: The JPS Audio*

Version by The Jewish Publication Society; *The Five Megilloth and Jonah* by H. L. Ginsberg and Ismar David; *Folktales of the Jews*, Volume 2 by Dan Ben-Amos; *I Will Wake the Dawn: Illuminated Psalms* by Debra Band.

For children's titles, JPS is most interested in manuscripts for short-story and folktale collections and for young-adult novels—all with strong Jewish themes—and for new titles in their Kids' Catalog series. They generally do not acquire stories on immigrant themes, picture books, catalogs, or the Holocaust. For adult titles, they are not seeking fiction, poetry, memoirs, spirituality, inspiration, monographs, or books about the Holocaust. Please see the website for further details.

Direct queries with résumés and SASEs to Rabbi Barry Schwartz.

JOSSEY-BASS [SEE JOHN WILEY & SONS]

JUDSON PRESS

A Division of the American Baptist Churches, USA
PO Box 851, Valley Forge, PA 19482-0851
via UPS/FedEx: 558 N Gulph Rd., King of Prussia, PA 19406
800-458-3766 | fax: 610-768-2107
www.judsonpress.com | e-mail: acquisitions@judsonpress.com

Judson Press is the publishing arm of the American Baptist Churches, USA, a Protestant denomination that includes 1.5 million members. Judson Press is a religious book publisher specializing in books on African American and multicultural issues, practical resources for churches, Baptist history, self-help, and inspirational titles for adults and children. It puts out 12 to 14 books a year, with more than 300 titles in print, ranging from the classic best seller for pastors, *The Star Book for Ministers*, to the latest inspirational volume, *Before the Thunder Rolls: Devotions for NASCAR Fans*.

Judson Press's primary niches are the following: Baptist history and identity; pastoral and sermon helps; small-group studies; discipleship; Christian education (not curriculum); seasonal program resources; African American resources; sermons; inspiration; and self-help.

Titles include *Missional Preaching: Engage, Embrace, Transform* by Al Tizon; *The Star Book for Stewardship* by Clifford A. Jones, Sr.; *Money on Purpose: Finding a Faith-Filled Balance* by Shayna Lear; *Worship on the Way: Exploring Asian North American Christian Experience* by Russell Yee; *Autism & Alleluias* by Kathleen Deyer Bolduc.

Query with SASE to:
Laura Alden, Publisher
Rebecca Irwin-Diehl, Editor
Marcia Jessen, Curriculum/Production Editor

KAPLAN PUBLISHING

New York Offices:
1440 Broadway, New York, NY 10018
212-453-5140
Chicago Offices:
30 South Wacker Drive, Ste. 2500, Chicago, IL 60606
www.kaplanpublishing.com | e-mail: KaplanEditorial@kaplan.com

Kaplan Publishing is one of the nation's leading education, career, and business publishers, with offices in New York and Chicago. Kaplan produces more than 150 books a year on test preparation, admissions, academic and professional development, general business, management, sales, marketing, real estate, finance, and investing. Imprints include Dearborn Home Inspection Education, Dearborn Real Estate Education, Kaplan AEC Education, Kaplan Business, Kaplan CPA Education, Kaplan Financial, Kaplan Education. The press is in the process of reorganizing the Chicago-based Dearborn imprints.

Kaplan titles are *Kaplan Catholic High School Entrance Exams*; *Kaplan PSAT/NMSQT 2011 Premier*; *Kaplan ACT 2011*; *Kaplan LSAT 180*; and *Kaplan PSAT/NMSQT 2012 Premier*.

There are two divisions of Kaplan: test-prep and trade. Currently, acquisitions for both divisions are being handled out of the New York office. Query letters, proposals, and SASEs should be directed to:

Jennifer Farthing, Editorial Director (NY), jennifer.farthing@kaplan.com

KAR-BEN PUBLISHING [SEE LERNER PUBLISHING GROUP]

KENSINGTON PUBLISHING

APHRODISIA
BRAVA
CITADEL
DAFINA
KENSINGTON BOOKS
PINNACLE BOOKS
ZEBRA BOOKS
850 Third Avenue, New York, NY 10022
877-422-3665
www.kensingtonbooks.com

Kensington Publishing (founded 1974) is an independent US publisher of hardcover, trade, and mass-market paperback books. From the time their first book became a best seller (*Appointment in Dallas* by Hugh McDonald), Kensington has been known as a David-vs.-Goliath publisher of titles in the full spectrum of categories, from fiction and romance to health and nonfiction. Kensington now accounts for about seven percent of all mass-market paperback sales in the United States. Through the Kensington, Zebra, Pinnacle, and Citadel press imprints, the company releases close to 600 new books per year and has a backlist of more than 3,000 titles.

Kensington continues to be a full-range publisher large enough to command respect in the market, yet small enough to maintain author, reader, and retailer loyalty. The company is able to respond quickly to trends, put books into the hands of readers faster than larger publishers can, and support them with targeted promotional and marketing programs to generate reader excitement.

APHRODISIA

Aphrodisia, launched in January 2006, is Kensington's popular line of erotica. New titles include *Blood Fire* by Sharon Page; *Canyon Shadows* by Vonna Harper; *Darkest Desire* by Tawny Taylor; *Dream Unchained* by Kate Douglas; *Island of Desire* by Lorie O'Clare.

BRAVA

Brava publishes three erotic romances in trade paperback each month. Some Brava releases include *Angels in Chains* by Cynthia Eden; *Angel Betrayed* by Cynthia Eden; *Babycakes* by Donna Kauffman; *Blaze* by Joan Swan; *Body Heat* by Susan Fox.

CITADEL

Citadel is Kensington's nonfiction imprint. They publish works of history, biography, military history, self-help, and humor. Citadel is also home to their line of poker titles, Lyle Stuart Books. Some titles are *Choosing Faith Against the Odds* by Evona Frink; *Everybody Must Get Stoned* by R. U. Sirius; *Jungle Breezes: From Amish Farm Boy to Jungle Doctor* by Dara Stoltzfus; *Pregnant Pause* by Carrie Friedman; and *French Women Don't Sleep Alone* by Jamie Cat Callan.

DAFINA

Dafina brings the very best in African American fiction, nonfiction, and young-adult titles. Some examples include *A Gangster and a Gentleman* by Kiki Swinson, and De'Nesha Diamond; *A Natural Woman* by Lori Johnson; *A Price to Pay: A View Park Novel* by Angela Winters; *Crime Partners: A Kenyatta Novel* by Donald Goines; *It Is What It Is: A So For Real Novel* by Nikki Carter; *Sex in the Sanctuary* by Lutishia Lovely.

KENSINGTON BOOKS

Kensington Books is the imprint for the hardcover and trade paperback line. The line is currently made up of five to eight titles each month. The typical genres are alternative health, mysteries (Partners In Crime), romance, erotica, and self-help. Kensington Mass Market features paperback titles with an emphasis on mysteries and fiction. Traditionally these titles are first published in hardcover. Alternative health titles also are published in this format for sale in the mass retailers.

Recent Kensington titles include *Rooster* by Brett Cogburn; *Between Boyfriends* by Michael Salvatore; *Blood Orange* by Drusilla Campbell; and *Blood, Guts, and Whiskey* edited by Todd Robinson.

PINNACLE BOOKS

Pinnacle is the imprint that features bestselling commercial fiction, including thrillers and true crime. Some titles are *A Knife in the Heart* by Michael Benson; *And Then She Killed Him* by Robert Scott; *A Cold Place in Hell* by William Blinn; *Cruel Death* by M. William Phelps; *No Mercy* by John Gilstrap; *Revenge of the Dog Team* by William W. Johnstone and J.A. Johnstone; *The Bike Path Killer* by Michael Beebe and Maki Becker; and *Killing Red* by Henry Perez.

ZEBRA BOOKS

Zebra, the company's flagship imprint, is primarily made up of a large number of historical romance titles, but the list also generally includes one or two lead contemporary romances, Westerns, horror, and humor. Some Zebra titles are *At Her Service* by Susan Johnson; *A Woman Made for Pleasure* by Michele Sinclair; *A Perfect Knight for Love* by Jackie Ivie; *I'm Watching You* by Mary Burton; *Navajo Night* by Carol Ann Didier; *Never Love a Lawman* by Jo Goodman; *Pleasure: The Shadowdwellers* by Jacquelyn Frank; *Seduced by a Stranger* by Eve Silver.

Kensington is open to submissions. Submit completed work or synopsis with the first three chapters to whichever editor you feel is the best person to review your work. No e-mail submissions, only regular mail with SASE.

John Scognamiglio, Editor-in-Chief (Kensington)—All areas of fiction, some nonfiction.

Michaela Hamilton, Editor-in-Chief (Citadel)—All areas of nonfiction, including true crime, some fiction.

Alicia Condon, Editorial Director (Brava)—Paranormal, and fantasy.

Audrey LaFehr, Editorial Director—Romance.

Selena James, Executive Editor (Dafina)—Urban and multicultural fiction.

Gary Goldstein, Senior Editor—True crime, humor, popular culture, judaica, general nonfiction.

Megan Records, Associate Editor—Urban fantasy, young adult, select women's fiction, and romance for Zebra and Brava; mrecords@kensingtonbooks.com

KIMANI PRESS [SEE HARLEQUIN ENTERPRISES, LTD.]

KINGFISHER [SEE MACMILLAN CHILDREN'S BOOK PUBLISHING GROUP]

KINGSWOOD BOOKS [SEE ABINGDON PRESS]

KLUTZ [SEE SCHOLASTIC, INC.]

H. J. KRAMER [SEE NEW WORLD LIBRARY]

KRAUSE PUBLICATIONS

700 East State Street, Iola, WI 54990-0001
800-258-0929 | 715-445-2214 | fax: 715-445-4087
http://www.krausebooks.com

Krause Publications, a division of F+W Publications, is the world's largest publisher of leisure-time periodicals and books on collectibles, arts and crafts, hunting, and fishing. A special-interest publisher targeting hobbyists and enthusiasts, Krause imprints cover writing; crafts; scrapbooking; graphic design; fine art; comics, fantasy art and manga; antiques and collectibles; coins; and the outdoors. The book division publishes over 125 titles annually and currently has 750 titles available.

Recent titles include *Haunted Objects: Stories of Ghosts on Your Shelf* by Christopher Balzano and Tim Weisberg; *Legendary Whitetails III* by Duncan Dobie; *Knitting Know-How: The Indispensable Step-by-Step Reference* by Dorothy T. Ratigan; *The Unofficial Batman Trivia Challenge: Test Your Knowledge and Prove You're a Real Fan!* by Alan Kistler; *Canadian Coin Digest* by George Cuhaj and Thomas Michael.

Query letters and SASEs should be directed to the Editorial Department.
Dianne Wheeler, Publishing Director, Antiques and Collectibles Division
Candy Wiza, Editor, Green and Simple Living

LARK BOOKS

67 Broadway, Asheville, NC 28801
828-253-0467 | fax: 828-253-7952
www.larkbooks.com | e-mail: info@larkbooks.com

Lark Books published their first book 20 years ago, and since then their list has grown to more than 300 books, with 60 to 70 new titles now appearing every year. President and Publisher Carol Taylor calls Lark Books "a destination for do-it-yourselfers looking for information, inspiration, source materials, and a lively exchange of ideas." The Lark Books list is composed primarily of reference and how-to books with step-by-step instructions of practical subjects including ceramics, crafts, pets, and other lifestyle topics. Lark Books has published how-to books teaching basketry, weaving, woodworking, ceramics, knitting, jewelry, paper, needlework, sewing, and general crafts from wreath making to rug hooking. They do not publish fiction, and only rarely publish non-illustrated books. The children's list focuses on nonfiction, including crafts and hobbies, games, science experiments, sports, and illustrated board books. Lark Books also publishes a variety of camera manuals and how-to reference books on photography and digital imaging techniques.

Recent titles from Lark Books include *Making Fabric Jewelry* by Marthe Le Van; *The Collage Workbook* by Randel Plowman; *We Make Dolls!* by Jenny Doh; *A Bounty of Beads & Wire Necklaces* by Nathalie Marnu; *Making Great Gingerbread Houses* by Aaron Morgan, and Paige Gilchrist.

Send queries to the attention of the category editor; e.g., material on a ceramics books should be addressed to the Ceramics Editor, a craft book proposal should be addressed to the Craft Acquisitions Editor, and so on. All children's book submissions should be sent to the attention of the Children's Acquisitions Editor.

LATIN AMERICAN LITERARY REVIEW PRESS

PO Box 17660, Pittsburgh, PA 15235
412-824-7903 | fax: 412-351-0770
www.lalrp.org | e-mail: editor@lalrp.org

Latin American Literary Review Press was established in 1980 with the principal objective of familiarizing readers outside the field with Latin American literature. LALRP's emphasis has been on publishing translations of creative writing (Discovery series) and literary criticism (Exploration series). These initial titles were followed by bilingual Spanish/English editions of poetry, books of Spanish music, and young-adult titles. Currently, LALRP publishes fewer than five new books per year.

The house has always aimed for excellence in publishing, and has relied on a prestigious body of academic editors and distinguished and accomplished translators. The press receives financial support from the National Endowment for the Arts, the Pennsylvania Council on the Arts, and from various other institutions and private foundations.

Titles include *Legends of Guatemala* by Miguel Ángel Asturias; *Friends of Mine* by Ángela Pradelli; *Welcome to Miami, Dr. Leal* by René Vázquez Díaz; *My Heart Flooded With Water: Translations from the Poetry of Alfonsina Storni* by Alfonsina Storni; *And What Have You Done?* by José Castro Urioste.

Query letters and SASEs should be directed to the editorial staff.

Yvette Miller, President

LEARNINGEXPRESS, LLC

Two Rector Street, 26th Floor, New York, NY 10006
212-995-2566 | 800-295-9556 Ext. 2 | fax: 212-995-5512
www.learningexpressllc.com | e-mail: customerservice@learningexpressllc.com

LearningExpress is a leading publisher of print and online study guides, test preparation, career guidance, and practical skills materials. www.LearnATest .com/Library, its online interactive resource, offers practice tests and exercises for academic and career exams. Founded in 1995 in affiliation with Random House, LearningExpress emerged as an industry leader in customized test-preparation publishing and as an expert source for information on targeted careers, vocational professions, and academic exams. In August 1999, Allen & Company, Inc., and a select group of private investors purchased a significant equity interest in the company.

LearningExpress offers more than 300 online, interactive practice exams and course series, as well as over 200 titles in print and more than 150 e-books. All LearningExpress materials are developed by leading educators and industry experts. LearningExpress was named the finalist for two 2008 Codie Awards.

Titles include *California Highway Patrol Exam; EMT-Basic Exam for Firefighters; Health Occupations Entrance Exams; Algebra Success in 20 Minutes a Day; Grammar Success in 20 Minutes a Day;* and *Reasoning Skills Success in 20 Minutes a Day.*

Query letters and SASEs should be directed to the editorial staff.

Karen Wolny, Editorial Director

LERNER PUBLISHING GROUP

CAROLRHODA BOOKS
EDICIONES LERNER
GRAPHIC UNIVERSE
KAR-BEN PUBLISHING
LERNER CLASSROOM
LERNER PUBLICATIONS
TWENTY-FIRST CENTURY BOOKS

241 1st Avenue N., Minneapolis, MN 55401
800-328-4929 | fax: 800-332-1132
www.lernerbooks.com | e-mail: info@lernerbooks.com
Kar-Ben editorial offices:
800-328-4929 x229 | fax: 612-332-7615
www.karben.com | e-mail: editorial@karben.com

Founded in 1959, Lerner Publishing Group is a large independent children's book publisher. With more than 3,500 titles in print, Lerner Publishing Group creates high-quality children's books for schools, libraries, and bookstores on a variety of subjects including biographies, social studies, science, language-arts curriculum, geography, sports, vehicles, picture books, activity books, multicultural issues, and fiction.

Lerner is proud to have published the 2006 Robert F. Silbert Informational Book Medal winner *Secrets of a Civil War Submarine: Solving the Mysteries of the H. L. Hunley* by Sally M. Walker. This important award, established by the Association for Library Service to Children, honors the most distinguished informational book published in English during the preceding year.

Lerner Publishing Group publishes distinctive books for children of all ages including picture books, fiction, and nonfiction. Imprints include Twenty-First Century Books, Carolrhoda Books, Millbrook Press, First Avenue Editions, Ediciones Lerner, Lerner Classroom, Graphic Universe, and Kar-Ben Publishing.

CAROLRHODA BOOKS

Carolrhoda Books publishes grades K through 12 picture books, intermediate and young-adult fiction, and nonfiction titles that inspire readers' imaginations. Some titles from Carolrhoda include *A Secret Keeps* by Marsha Wilson Chall; *The White Zone* by Carolyn Marsden; *Zip It!* by Jane Lindaman; *Beep and Bah* by James Burks.

EDICIONES LERNER

Ediciones Lerner publishes grades K through four Spanish translations of curriculum-related and fiction titles. Each title has a corresponding English edition for dual-language teaching strategies. Some titles include *Adivina que esta creciendo dentro de este huevo* by Mia Posada; *Adonde van las personas cuando mueren* by Mindy Avra Portnoy and Shelly O. Haas; and *A clases otra vez, Mallory* by Laurie Friedman and Tamara Schmitz.

GRAPHIC UNIVERSE

Graphic Universe publishes grades four through eight nonfiction and fiction topics boosted to extreme interest through supreme graphic-novel artwork created by experienced artists of the genre. Some titles include *#3 The Hunt for Hidden Treasure* by Lynda Beauregard; *#20 Peril at Summerland Park* by Paul D. Storrie; *#12 Sherlock Holmes and the Adventure of the Cardboard Box* by Sir Author Conan Doyle; *#3 Night of the Living Dogs* by Trina Robbins; *#1 Freedom!* by Frank Le Gall.

KAR-BEN PUBLISHING

Kar-Ben Publishing offers an expansive Jewish library for children, families, and teachers. The Kar-Ben list encompasses presentations keyed to high holidays, the Sabbath, culture and tradition, and general interest concepts. Kar-Ben was founded in 1975 by two friends to publish the children's Passover Haggadah they had created. *My Very Own Haggadah*, now in its 30th anniversary printing, went on to sell over 2 million copies. Kar-Ben continues to publish 10 to 12 new titles each year.

In 2001, Kar-Ben was purchased by Lerner Publishing Group in Minneapolis, although editorial operations have remained in Maryland. Under Lerner's leadership, Kar-Ben Publishing now publishes over a dozen new titles of Jewish content each year, developing a growing Jewish library for children and branching out from pre-school and young children's works into pre-teen and young-adult fiction and nonfiction. Kar-Ben has created many award-winning children's titles on such subjects as Jewish holidays, crafts, folktales, and contemporary stories.

Kar-Ben considers fiction and nonfiction for preschool through high school, including holiday books, life-cycle stories, Bible tales, folktales, board books, and activity books. In particular, they look for stories that reflect the ethnic and cultural diversity of today's Jewish family. They do not publish games, textbooks, or books in Hebrew.

Recent titles include *The Apple Tree's Discovery* by Peninnah Schram and Rachayl Eckstein Davis; *Sadie and the Big Mountain* by Jamie Korngold; *Barnyard Purim* by Kelly Terwilliger; *Dinosaur Goes to Israel* by Diane Levin Rauchwerger; *Hannah's Way* by Linda Glaser.

LERNER CLASSROOM

Lerner Classroom provides books and teaching guides for grades K through eight in the areas of reading, math, social studies, science, biographies, and high-interest topics. They also offer fiction books, picture books, early readers, and chapter books. Some titles include *When Did Columbus Arrive in the Americas?* by Kathy Allen;

Addition by Kristen Sterling; *Clinic* by Sheila Anderson; *Cone* by Jennifer Boothroyd; and *Count Your Way through Afghanistan* by Jim Haskins and Kathleen Benson.

LERNER PUBLICATIONS

Lerner Publications provides educational, photo-driven titles that support key curriculum topics and engage young minds for grades K though five. Some Lerner titles are *Appaloosas are My Favorite* by Elaine Landau; *The President, Vice President, and Cabinet* by Elaine Landau; *Who Were the Accused Witches of Salem* by Laura Hamilton Waxman; *Can You Tell a Seal from a Sea Lion?* by Buffy Silverman; *Checks and Balances* by Kathiann M. Kowalski; *Barack Obama: President for a New Era* by Marlene Targ Brill.

TWENTY-FIRST CENTURY BOOKS

Twenty-First Century Books publishes curriculum-oriented and high-interest titles that make challenging subjects easy to digest for middle and high school students, grades six through twelve. Some titles are *Persian Gulf and Iraqi Wars* by Lawrence J. Zwier and Matthew S. Weltig; *Peru in Pictures* by Herón Márquez; *Photosynthesis* by Alvin Silverstein, Virginia Silverstein, and Laura Silverstein Nunn; *Plate Tectonics* by Rebecca L. Johnson; *Anxiety Disorders* by Cherry Pedrick, R.N., and Bruce M. Hyman, Ph. D.

Lerner Publishing Group no longer accepts unsolicited submissions as of 2007.

Joanna Sussman, Director

LIBRARIES UNLIMITED [SEE GREENWOOD PUBLISHING GROUP]

LIFT EVERY VOICE [SEE MOODY PUBLISHERS]

LIGUORI PUBLICATIONS

One Liguori Drive, Liguori, MO 63057-9999
800-325-9521 | fax: 636-464-8449
www.liguori.org

Located near St. Louis, Liguori Publications is a midsize Catholic publishing house that produces books, pamphlets, educational materials, *Liguorian* magazine, and software. The purpose of Liguori Publications is to effectively communicate the word of God in the Catholic tradition by growing and expanding their outreach to Catholics of all ages through print and electronic media. They provide English- and Spanish-language (Libros Liguori) products. Imprint Liguori Triumph Books emphasizes an ecumenical perspective in the religious trade market.

Titles include *110 Fun Facts About God's Creation: Is It Animal, Vegetable, or Mineral?* by Bernadette McCarver Snyder; *40 Simple Ways to Keep Lent Meaningful* by Victor Parachin; *7 Steps to Peace with St. Alphonsus Liguori* by Paul Coury CSsR; *A Christian Response to World Hunger* by Stephen Rehrauer CSsR; and *Advent and Christmas Wisdom from St. Thomas Aquinas* by Father Andrew Carl Wisdom OP; *10 Things Pope Benedict Wants You To Know* by John L. Allen, Jr.; *9 Ways To Nurture Your Marriage* by William E. Rabior and Susan C. Rabior.

Submit proposals with SASEs to the Editorial Department or via e-mail to manuscript_submission@liguori.org.

LLEWELLYN WORLDWIDE

FLUX
MIDNIGHT INK
2143 Wooddale Drive, Woodbury, MN 55125
651-291-1970 | 877-639-9753 | fax: 651-291-1908
www.llewellyn.com

Llewellyn Worldwide is one of the oldest and largest independent New Age publishers in the United States, with over a century of leadership in the industry on such subjects as self-help, metaphysical studies, mysticism, alternative health, divination, astrology, tarot, the paranormal, witchcraft, paganism, Wicca, magick, goddess lore, and garden witchery. They are seeking new authors.

In the past few years, Llewellyn has expanded into fiction for adults and young adults. Midnight Ink, a new imprint of Llewellyn, offers paperback mystery novels. Llewellyn's new imprint of young-adult fiction, Flux, debuted in 2006. Llewellyn Español, their Spanish-language imprint, boasts over 50 titles.

The Llewellyn emphasis is on the practical: how it works, how it is done, and self-help material. The book should appeal to readers with basic skills and knowledge, and the information presented should be well within the reach of the average reader.

Recent publications from Llewellyn include *Burn* by Heath Gibson; *Don't Give Up Until You Do: From Mindfulness to Realization on the Buddhist Path* by Fred H. Meyer; *Everything You Want to Know About Magick, But Were Afraid to Ask* by Shawn Martin Scanlon; *Haunted Files from the Edge* by Philip J. Imbrogno; *Innocent Darkness: The Aether Chronicles #1* by Suzanne Lazear.

Llewellyn accepts submissions directly from authors (including first-time authors) and from literary agents. Submit proposals or complete manuscripts through regular mail only with an SASE to:

Elysia Gallo, Editor, elysiag@llewellyn.com

Amy Glazer, Editor

Angela Wix, Editor

FLUX

Flux is an imprint dedicated to fiction for teens, where young adult is a point of view, not a reading level. Their fiction avoids condescension and simplification, instead exploring the comedy, tragedy, ecstasy, pain, and discovery that are a part of every teen's life. Some releases from Flux include *Shadows of the Redwood* by Gillian Summers; *The Sorcerer of Sainte Felice* by Ann Finnin; *A Blue So Dark* by Holly Schindler; *Gigged* by Heath Gibson; and *Choppy Socky Blues* by Ed Briant.

Brian Farrey, Editor (Flux), brianf@fluxnow.com

MIDNIGHT INK

Midnight Ink is committed to publishing suspenseful tales of all types: hard-boiled thrillers, cozies, historical mysteries, amateur sleuth novels, and more. Some releases include *Black Moonlight: The Marjorie McClelland Mysteries #4* by Amy Patricia Meade; *Dead Sleeping Shaman: An Emily Kincaid Mystery #3* by Elizabeth Kane Buzzell; *Photo, Snap, Shot: A Kiki Lowenstein Scrap-N-Craft Mystery #3* by Joanna Campbell Slan; *The Tavernier Stones* by Stephen Parrish; *A House to Die For: A Darby Farr Mystery #1* by Vicki Doudera; and *Diamonds for the Dead* by Alan Orioff.

Terri Bischoff, Editor (Midnight Ink), terrib@midnightinkbooks.com

LONELY PLANET PUBLICATIONS

50 Linden Street, Oakland, CA 94607
800-275-8555 | 510-250-6400 | fax: 510-893-8572
www.lonelyplanet.com | e-mail: info@lonelyplanet.com | blog: www.lonelyplanet
.com/tonywheeler

Lonely Planet began in the early 1970s after founders Tony and Maureen Wheeler completed an overland journey from London through Asia and on to Australia. That trip resulted in the first Lonely Planet guidebook—*Across Asia on the Cheap*—and laid the foundations of the world's leading independent travel publisher. Tony and Maureen are still the proud owners, still on the road, and still finding the time to continually push the boundaries of travel publishing.

Lonely Planet's head office is in Australia; the crew in Oakland publishes books for the Americas.

Lonely Planet creates and delivers the world's most compelling and comprehensive travel content, giving travelers trustworthy information, engaging opinions, powerful images, and informed perspectives on destinations around the globe. They have over 600 guidebooks and products in print. The house's titles cover every corner of the planet with guidebooks published in languages including French, Italian, Spanish, Korean, and Japanese.

Recent titles include *Tokyo City Guide*, 9th Edition by Timothy N. Hornyak and Rebecca Milner; *Banff, Jasper & Glacier National Park Guide* by Oliver Berry and Brendan Sainsbury; *Portuguese Phrasebook* by Robert Landon and Anabela de Azevedo Teixeira Sobrinho; *Boston City Guide*, 5th Edition by Mara Vorhees; *Discover Australia Travel Guide* by Lindsay Brown et al; *Beijing Encounter Guide* by David Eimer; *Berlin Encounter Guide* by Andrea Schulte-Peevers; and *Bolivia Travel Guide* by Anja Mutic et al.

They have a pool of 200 authors from over 20 countries. No matter how obscure the query or specialized the topic, Lonely Planet can usually find an in-house expert. In the United States, Lonely Planet distributes its own publications. See their website for detailed submission guidelines and tips.

Query letters and SASEs should be directed to:

Tony Wheeler, Co-owner
Maureen Wheeler, Co-owner

LOTUS PRESS

PO Box 325, Twin Lakes, WI 53181
Shipping address:
1100 Lotus Drive, Building 3, Silver Lake, WI 53170
262-889-8561 | fax: 262 889 8591
www.lotuspress.com | e-mail: lotuspress@lotuspress.com

Lotus Press is one of the leading publishers in its field of alternative health and wellness. Of particular interest is the Lotus Press list of titles in the field of Ayurveda, which are considered to be the standard works in the field and have been reprinted in many different languages worldwide. Lotus Press titles appear in more than 23 languages thanks to an active foreign rights translation program.

Lotus Press was founded in 1981 by Santosh and Karuna Krinsky. Since that time, the house has grown its list of publications to more than 300 titles, and is currently publishing about 20 to 25 new titles per year.

In addition to Ayurveda, Lotus Press has actively sought out titles on traditional healing modalities as well as energetic healing. This includes herbalism, Native American health, Chinese traditional herbal medicine, aromatherapy, Reiki, and much more.

On the Lotus Press list: *Inner Tantric Yoga: Working with the Universal Shakti: Secrets of Mantras, Deities, and Meditation* by David Frawley; *The Way of Ayurvedic*

Herbs: A Contemporary Introduction and Useful Manual for the World's Oldest Healing System by Karta Purkh Khalsa; *Troubled Tongues* by Crystal Williams; and *Ayurvedic Yoga Therapy* by Mukunda Stiles.

Direct query letters, proposals, and SASEs to:

Cathy Hoselton, Assistant to the President

LUNA BOOKS [SEE HARLEQUIN ENTERPRISES, LTD.]

LYONS PRESS [SEE THE GLOBE PEQUOT PRESS]

MACADAM/CAGE PUBLISHING

155 Sansome Street, Suite 550, San Francisco, CA 94104
415-986-7502 | fax: 415-968-7414
www.macadamcage.com

MacAdam/Cage has been experiencing serious business problems and may have suspended making new acquisitions. You should contact them directly to determine their status.

MacAdam/Cage Publishing was founded as an independent trade publisher in 1998 by David Poindexter with the aim of publishing books of quality fiction and nonfiction. Publishers of *The Time Traveler's Wife* by Audrey Niffenegger, a debut novel that became a publishing phenomenon in Fall 2003, this house is committed to bringing new and talented voices to the literary marketplace.

In 1999 MacAdam/Cage Publishing acquired the independent press MacMurray & Beck, well known in the industry for launching authors such as Patricia Henley (*Hummingbird House*), William Gay (*The Long Home*), and Susan Vreeland (*Girl in Hyacinth Blue*), and heavily supported by the bookselling trade, with many BookSense 76 picks as well as appearances in chain-store fiction programs that highlight new authors. MacAdam/Cage Publishing represents independent publishing at its best.

Recent titles include *All For Now* by Joseph Di Prisco; *The Return of Edgar Cayce* by C. Terry Cline, Jr.; *A Silence of Mockingbirds: The Memoir of a Murder* by Karen Spears Zacharias; *The Investigation of Ariel Warning* by Robert Kalich; *The Weight of Memory* by Jennifer Paddock.

MacAdam/Cage will not accept submissions in these categories: romance, science fiction, fantasy, supernatural, self-help, poetry, thrillers, religion, spirituality, children's, young adult, cookbooks, parenting, family, military science, or medical. They also do not accept one-page proposals, complete manuscripts, submissions on disk, or e-mail submissions. Send a cover letter, brief synopsis, author biography, 30-page sample, and SASE to Manuscript Submissions.

Pat Walsh, Editor-in-Chief
David Poindexter, Publisher

MAGINATION PRESS [SEE AMERICAN PSYCHOLOGICAL ASSOCIATION, INC.]

MANIC D PRESS

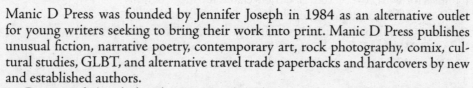

PO Box 410804, San Francisco, CA 94141
415-648-8288
www.manicdpress.com | e-mail: info@manicdpress.com

Manic D Press was founded by Jennifer Joseph in 1984 as an alternative outlet for young writers seeking to bring their work into print. Manic D Press publishes unusual fiction, narrative poetry, contemporary art, rock photography, comix, cultural studies, GLBT, and alternative travel trade paperbacks and hardcovers by new and established authors.

Recent titles include *The Steampunk Coloring and Activity Book: Containing Illustrations, Recipes, Formulas & Other Activities to Entertain…* by Phoebe Longhi; *Fears of Your Life* by Michael Bernard Loggins; *98 Wounds* by Justin Chin; *Gutted* by Justin Chin; *15 Ways to Stay Alive* by Daphne Gottlieb.

Before submitting your work to Manic D, the publisher requests that you read at least one book they have already published to familiarize yourself with their line. In your cover letter, tell them which book you have read and what you thought about it. Be specific.

E-mail submissions are preferred. Send submissions to subs@manicdpress.com. Manuscripts are read twice a year, during the months of January and July only. Send five to ten poems, three to five short stories, or a synopsis and first chapter of a novel with your cover letter and SASE to the attention of the editors.

Jennifer Joseph, Publisher

MCFARLAND & COMPANY

960 NC Highway 88 West, Jefferson, NC 28640
Mailing address:
Box 611, Jefferson, NC 28640
336-246-4460 | fax: 336-246-5018
www.mcfarlandpub.com | e-mail: info@mcfarlandpub.com

McFarland & Company, Inc., Publishers, founded in 1979, is located in Jefferson, North Carolina, a small town nestled in the northwestern corner of the state. The company is now one of the leading publishers of scholarly and reference books in the United States, with 4,000 titles published to date, including nearly 2,400 in print. McFarland publishes 325 new titles each year for a worldwide market; many of them have received awards as outstanding reference or academic titles. McFarland is recognized for its serious works in a variety of fields, including performing arts (especially film), sport and leisure (especially baseball and chess), military history, popular culture, and automotive history, among other topics.

Recent titles include *The IRA on Film and Television: A History* by Mark Connelly; *The Titanic on Film: Myth versus Truth* by Linda Maria Koldau; *Jewish Major Leaguers in Their Own Words: Oral Histories of 23 Players* by Peter Ephross, with Martin Abramowitz; *Arthurian Figures of History and Legend: A Biographical Dictionary* by Frank D. Reno; *The Silverplate Bombers: A History and Registry of the Enola Gay and Other B-29s Configured to Carry Atomic Bombs* by Richard H. Campbell.

Authors may contact the house with a query letter, a full proposal, or a finished manuscript with cover letter. See the website for more details.

Queries may be directed to:

Gary Mitchem, Acquisitions Editor, gmitchem@mcfarlandpub.com
Steve Wilson, Editor Director, swilson@mcfarlandpub.com
David Alff, Editor, dalff@mcfarlandpub.com

THE MCGRAW-HILL COMPANIES, INC.

MCGRAW-HILL BUSINESS
MCGRAW-HILL/OSBORNE MEDIA
1221 Avenue of the Americas, New York, NY 10020
212-512-2000
www.mcgraw-hill.com
160 Spear Street, Suite 700, San Francisco, CA 94105
www.osborne.com

The myriad McGraw-Hill book publishing divisions and imprints may be explored in depth at www.mhprofessional.com and www.mcgraw-hill.com.

MCGRAW-HILL BUSINESS (FINANCE AND MANAGEMENT)

McGraw-Hill Business subjects include accounting, marketing and sales, careers, communication, e-business, economics, finance and investing, general business, human resources and training, international business, management and leadership, personal finance, quality, real estate, and small business and entrepreneurship.

Mary Glenn, Editorial Director—Business management and finance.

Donya Dickerson, Senior Editor—Marketing, sales.
Jennifer Askenazy, Senior Editor—Finance and investing.
Stephanie Frerich, Editor—General business, finance, investing.

MCGRAW-HILL/OSBORNE MEDIA

McGraw-Hill/Osborne Media, a unit of McGraw-Hill Education, is a leading publisher of self-paced computer training materials, including user and reference guides, bestselling series on computer certification, titles on business and technology, and high-level but practical titles on networking, programming, and Web development tools. McGraw-Hill/Osborne Media is the official press of Oracle, Corel, and Intuit. From its home base across the east bay from San Francisco, McGraw-Hill/Osborne Media is seeking proposals from computer-savvy authors.

Titles include *How to Do Everything: Adobe Illustrator CS4* by Sue Jenkins; *Software and Systems Requirements Engineering: In Practice* by Brian Berenbach et al; *Databases: A Beginner's Guide* by Andy Oppel; and *Microsoft Visual Studio 2008 Programming* by Jamie Plenderleith and Steve Bunn.

Direct proposals with SASEs to Manuscript Proposal. See the website for detailed proposal tips and guidelines.

Steve Chapman, Publisher
Roger Stewart, Editorial Director, Consumer Computing, roger_stewart @mcgraw-hill.com
Wendy Rinaldi, Editorial Director, Intelligence, wendy_rinaldi@mcgraw-hill.com
Timothy Green, Senior Acquisitions Editor, Certification & Career, timothy _green@mcgraw-hill.com
Margaret Morin, Acquisitions Editor, Programming, margaret_morin @mcgraw-hill.com

MCSWEENEY'S

McSweeney's West:
849 Valencia Street, San Francisco, CA 94110
McSweeney's East:
826 NYC, 372 Fifth Ave., Brooklyn, NY 11215
www.mcsweeneys.net | e-mail: booksubmissions@mcsweeneys.net

Founded by author Dave Eggers, McSweeney's is a small, independent press based in San Francisco that is committed to helping find new voices—Neal Pollack, Amy Fusselman, and Paul Collins—to publishing works of gifted but under-appreciated writers, such as Lydia Davis and Stephen Dixon—and to always push the literary form forward. One also finds here bestselling authors like Dave Eggers and Nick Hornby.

McSweeney's has a very active website and an amazing quarterly; it is a place to find and share interesting, quirky, and/or brilliant fiction, essays, memoirs, children's titles, and humor.

Recent titles include *The Power of the Story: The Voice of Witness Teacher's Guide to Oral History* by Cliff Mayotte; *A Million Heavens* by John Brandon; *A Hologram for the King* by Dave Eggers; *EMMAUS* translated by Ann Goldstein.

Send complete manuscript or sample chapters via e-mail or regular mail.

Barb Bersche, Publisher

MEADOWBROOK PRESS

6110 Blue Circle Drive Suite 237, Minnetonka, MN 55343
800-338-2232 | fax: 952-930-1940
www.meadowbrookpress.com | e-mail: editorial@meadowbrookpress.com

Meadowbrook Press (founded 1975) specializes in books about parenting, pregnancy, baby care, child care, humorous poetry for children, party planning, and children's activities. Meadowbrook is also the country's number one publisher of baby-name books, with eight baby-naming books in print and total sales of over 6 million copies.

Recent titles include *Baby & Child Emergency First Aid* by Mitchell J. Einzig, MD, and Paula Kelly, MD; *100,000+ Baby Names* by Bruce Lansky; *What I Did on My Summer Vacation: Kids' Favorite Funny Summer Vacation Poems* by Bruce Lansky; *Toddler's Busy Book* by Trish Kuffner; *First-Year Baby Care* by Paula Kelly, MD.

The Meadowbrook editorial staff develops and writes books as well as acquires and edits titles written by outside authors. The house is not currently accepting unsolicited manuscripts or queries for the following genres: adult fiction, adult poetry, humor, and children's fiction. Also, they do not currently publish picture books for children, travel titles, scholarly, or literary works.

See the website for submission guidelines and send all appropriate queries and SASEs to Submissions Editor.

Bruce Lansky, Publisher

MESORAH PUBLICATIONS

4401 Second Avenue, Brooklyn, NY 11232
718-921-9000 | 800-637-6724 | fax: 718-680-1875
www.artscroll.com | e-mail: info@artscroll.com

Mesorah Publications produces books of contemporary Jewish interest written by authors with sophisticated firsthand knowledge of Orthodox religious practices, history, and culture. It is also noted for its works in traditional Judaica, Bible study, Talmud, liturgical materials, Jewish history, and juvenile literature. Founded in 1976, Mesorah Publications remains true to tradition in all of its publications, as expressed in the motto: Mesorah Publications…helping to preserve the heritage, one book at a time.

Recent titles include *Tragedy and Rebirth: Transmitting the History and Messages of Churban Europa to a New Generation* by Rabbi Joseph Elias and Rabbi Yaakov Astor; *A Daily Dose of Torah Series 3/11: Weeks of Mattos through Va'eschanan* by Rabbi Yosaif Asher Weiss; *Lift Me Higher* by Estie Florans; *Rebbetzin Kanievsk: A Legendary Mother to All* by Naftali Weinberger, Naomi Weinberger, and Nina Indig.

Address queries and SASEs to Acquisitions Editor.

MIDNIGHT INK [SEE LLEWELLYN WORLDWIDE]

MILKWEED EDITIONS

1011 Washington Avenue South, Suite 300, Minneapolis, MN 55415-1246
612-332-3192 | 800-520-6455 | fax: 612-215-2550
www.milkweed.org | e-mail: editor@milkweed.org

Milkweed Editions is a nonprofit literary press, publishing 15 to 20 books a year. Founded in 1979, the house publishes literary fiction, nonfiction about the natural world, poetry, and novels for young readers. They have published over 200 titles. The editors at Milkweed Editions believe that literature is a transformative art, and that each book bears a responsibility to convey the essential experiences of the human heart and spirit.

Although a small press, Milkweed also offers prizes for adult fiction and children's literature in their prestigious literary awards. Guidelines for the prizes are available online or by request through regular mail. The World As Home is a Milkweed website that fosters ecological literacy and renewal by linking literary writing about the natural world to specific ecoregions and to organizations active in preserving natural landscapes or focused on the art of writing.

Milkweed authors include Ken Kalfus, Susan Straight, Marilyn Chin, Larry Watson, Bill Holm, Paul Gruchow, Janisse Ray, Pattiann Rogers, and many others, including emerging and mid-career authors.

Titles include *The Wet Collection* by Joni Tevis; *The Fact of the Matter: Poems* by Sally Keith; *I Will Not Leave You Comfortless* by Jeremy Jackson; *Silhouette of a Sparrow* by Molly Beth Griffin; *The Fall of Alice K.* by Jim Heynen.

Milkweed does not accept submissions on disk or via e-mail. Send the complete manuscript or a proposal with sample chapters, outline, and cover letter. Direct submissions to the Fiction Reader (or Nonfiction, Poetry, or Children's, as appropriate); include an SASE.

Daniel Slager, Publisher and CEO
Patrick Thomas, Editor and Program Manager
Allison Wigen, Associate Editor

MOODY PUBLISHERS

LIFT EVERY VOICE

A Division of the Moody Bible Institute
820 North LaSalle Boulevard, Chicago, IL 60610-3284
312-329-2101 | fax: 312-329-4157
www.moodypublishers.org | e-mail: acquisitions@moody.edu

Moody Publishers was founded in 1894 by D. L. Moody eight years after he had founded the Moody Bible Institute, which continues to be a well-known evangelical institution. The house publishes fiction, nonfiction, and children's titles for the Christian markets.

The Moody Publishers' mission is to educate and edify the Christian and to evangelize the non-Christian by ethically publishing conservative, evangelical Christian literature and other media for all ages around the world; and to help provide resources for Moody Bible Institute in its training of future Christian leaders.

Moody titles include *The Global Orphan Crisis: Be the Solution, Change Your World* by Diane Lynn Elliot; *Buyer Beware* by Janet Parshall; *On the Shoulders of Hobbits* by Louis Markos; *Unseduced and Unshaken* by Rosalie A de Rosset; *The White Umbrella* by Mary Frances Bowley.

LIFT EVERY VOICE

Moody Publishers partners with the Institute for Black Family Development in the creation of a joint imprint, Lift Every Voice. The vision for this endeavor is to see African American Christians encouraged in their faith in Jesus Christ through quality books written by African Americans. While Moody Publishers had already published several African American authors, such as Tony Evans, Clarence Schuler, Lois Evans, and Crawford Loritts, Lift Every Voice products will be targeted almost exclusively to African Americans.

Lift Every Voice titles include *Seven Reasons Why God Created Marriage* by James Ford; *Our Voices: Issues Facing Black Women in America* by Amanda Johnson; *The Last Woman Standing* by Tia McCollors; *Learning to Love* by Stephanie Perry Moore; *Coming Across Jordan* by Mabel Elizabeth Singletary; and *Out of the Box: Building Robots, Transforming Lives* by Andrew Williams and Edward Gilbreath.

Moody Publishers currently is not reviewing manuscripts, except from literary agents.

Paul Santhouse, Director of Acquisitions

THE MOUNTAINEERS BOOKS

SKIPSTONE
A Division of The Mountaineers Club
1001 SW Klickitat Way, Suite 201, Seattle, WA 98134
206-223-6303 | fax: 206-223-6306
www.mountaineersbooks.org | e-mail: mbooks@mountaineersbooks.org

The Mountaineers Books specializes in outdoor titles by experts. Born from the hand-scribbled trail maps and wilderness passion of its members, Washington's nearly 100-year-old Mountaineers Club established the nonprofit Mountaineers Books in 1960 to express and share its love of the natural outdoors. The house produces guidebooks, instructional texts, historical works, adventure narratives, natural history guides, and works on environmental conservation.

Today, with more than 500 titles in print, The Mountaineers Books is a leading publisher of quality outdoor books, including many award winners. For those hiking with the family, cycling over a country road, clinging to a big wall, or dreaming of a trek in Nepal, The Mountaineers Books has the guidance for creating the next journey in confidence and safety. The house focuses on non-competitive, non-motorized, self-propelled sports such as mountain climbing, hiking, walking, skiing, snowshoeing, and adventure travel. They also publish works on environmental and conservation subjects, narratives of mountain-eering expeditions and adventure travel, outdoor guidebooks to specific areas, mountaineering history, safety/first aid, and books on skills and techniques for the above sports. The house does not publish fiction, general tourist guides, or guides dealing with hunting, fishing, snowmobiling, RV travel, horseback riding, or team sports.

Mountaineers Press titles include *Kayaking Puget Sound*, 3rd Edition by Rob Casey; *Best Hikes With Kids Colorado* by Maureen Keilty; *75 Classic Rides Washington: The Best Road Biking Routes* by Mike McQuaide; *The Don't Drown Out There Deck* by Adventure Medical Kits.

SKIPSTONE

The Skipstone imprint, launched in 2007, publishes nonfiction books on eco-conscious lifestyle topics, including sustainable home care, food/cooking, pet care, gardening, crafts, humor, and entertaining with a green focus.

Skipstone titles include *The Bar Mitzvah and the Beast: One Family's Cross-Country*

Ride of Passage by Bike by Matt Biers-Ariel; *Backcountry Better Crafting with Style: 50 Nature-Inspired Projects* by Jennifer Worick and Kate Quinby; *Barking Buddha: Simple Soul Stretches for Yogi and Dogi* by Brenda Bryan and Bev Sparks; *The Zen of Mountains & Climbing: Wit, Wisdom, and Inspiration* by Katherine Wroth; and *The Salvage Studio: Sustainable Home Comforts to Organize, Entertain, and Inspire* by Amy Duncan et al.

If you plan to submit an adventure narrative, please request information about the Barbara Savage Miles From Nowhere Memorial Award.

Submit query letters, manuscripts, and/or proposals by regular mail only to Acquisitions.

Kate Rogers, Editor-in-Chief

MUSEUM OF NEW MEXICO PRESS

725 Camino Lejo, Santa Fe, NM 87505
Mailing address:
PO Box 2087, Santa Fe, NM 87504
505-476-1155 | fax: 505-476-1156
www.mnmpress.org

Founded in 1951, the Museum of New Mexico Press is an award-winning publisher of finely designed and crafted books that reflect the collections of the Museum of New Mexico and explore the culture of the Southwest. Specializations include fine art and folk art, photography, Native Americana, the Hispanic Southwest, nature and gardening, and architecture and style.

Recent titles include *New Mexico Art Throughout Time: Prehistory to the Present* by Joseph Traugott; *Tasting New Mexico* by Cheryl Alters Jamison and Bill Jamison; *Living Landscapes: A Roadside View* by William W. Dunmire; *Bhutan: Between Heaven and Earth* by Mary Peck.

The house requests that authors submit book proposals rather than full manuscripts for review. For proposal guidelines, see the website. Send proposals with cover letters, CVs, and SASEs to:

Mary Wachs, Editorial Director, mary.wachs@state.nm.us

NATARAJ PUBLISHING [SEE NEW WORLD LIBRARY]

NATION BOOKS [SEE PERSEUS]

NATIONAL GEOGRAPHIC SOCIETY

National Geographic Books (General Audience):
PO Box 10543, Des Moines, IA 50340
888-647-6733 | 515-362-3345
National Geographic Children's Books
PO Box 4002864, Des Moines, IA 50340
877-873-6846
www.nationalgeographic.com | e-mail: askngs@nationalgeographic.com

Founded in 1888, the National Geographic Society is one of the world's largest nonprofit scientific and educational organizations. Their mission is to increase and diffuse geographic knowledge while promoting the conservation of the world's cultural, historical, and natural resources. National Geographic has funded over 7,000 scientific research projects, supports an education program combating geography illiteracy, and reflects the world through magazines, television programs, books, videos, maps, interactive media, and merchandise.

The Press publishes quality, illustrated nonfiction books, including reference books, photography books, and travel guides. Subjects of focus are adventure and exploration, animals and nature, culture and history, geography and reference, photography, science and space, and educational materials for kids.

Recent titles include *In the Footsteps of Jesus* by Jean-Pierre Isbouts; *Eyewitness to World War II* by Neil Kagan and Stephen G. Hyslop; *Tales of the Weird: Unbelievable True Stories* by David Braun; *Life is Your Best Medicine* by Tieraona Low Dog, MD; *Bird Watcher's Bible* by Jonathan Alderfer.

Query letters and SASEs should be directed to the editorial staff of the Book Division.

Stephen Mico, Senior Vice President, Publisher—Children's and educational titles.
Virginia Koeth, Editor—Children's books.
Lisa Thomas, Senior Editor

NAVAL INSTITUTE PRESS

An imprint of the United States Naval Institute
291 Wood Road, Annapolis, MD 21402
410-224-3378 | fax: 410-269-7940
www.usni.org/store/books

Naval Institute Press, situated on the grounds of the US Naval Academy, is the book-publishing imprint of the US Naval Institute (USNI), a private, independent, nonprofit professional society for members of the military services and civilians who share an interest in naval and maritime affairs. USNI was established in 1873 at the

Naval Academy in Annapolis; the press inaugurated its publishing program in 1898 with a series of basic guides to US naval practice.

Naval Institute Press (NIP) features trade books, in addition to the house's targeted professional and reference titles. Areas of NIP interest include how-to books on boating, navigation, battle histories, and biographies, as well as occasional selected titles in fiction (typically with a nautical adventure orientation). Specific categories encompass such fields as seamanship, naval history and literature, the Age of Sail, aviation, aircraft, World War II naval history, ships and aircraft, current naval affairs, naval science, and general naval resources and guidebooks.

The Press produces more than 70 titles each year. With its long-established tradition of publishing excellence in the fields of naval, military, and maritime history, the NIP provides the serious reader with an invaluable resource. Categories include history and reference.

Recent titles include *The Wreck of Isabella* by David Miller; *Beneath the Waves: The Life and Navy of Capt. Edward L. Beach, Jr.* by Edward Finch; *Shepherds of the Sea: Destroyer Escorts in World War II* by Robert F. Cross; *Guiding Lights: United States Naval Academy Monuments and Memorials* by Nancy Prothro Arbuthnot; and *A Tactical Ethic: Moral Conduct in the Insurgent Battlespace* by Dick Couch.

Submit a proposal or the entire manuscript (paper copy) via regular mail. Send all queries and SASEs to the Acquisitions Editors.

Thomas Cutler, Director of Professional Publishing, tcutler@usni.org
Susan Todd Brook, Acquisitions Editor, sbrook@usni.org
Adam Kane, Acquisitions Editor, akane@usni.org

THOMAS NELSON PUBLISHERS

501 Nelson Place, PO Box 141000, Nashville, TN 37214-1000
800-251-4000
www.thomasnelson.com

Thomas Nelson Publishers is the world's largest Christian publishing company and the ninth-largest publishing company of any kind. Recently purchased by Harper Collins, Thomas Nelson continues with Michael Hyatt as president of this religious publishing company. The company was founded in 1798 by Scotsman Thomas Nelson, who sought to make Christian works and classic literature affordable for the common folk. Today, categories include spiritual growth and Christian thought, fiction, people and culture, Bibles, practical living, children's, gift books, general interest and lifestyle, business, small group curriculum, biblical reference, and Spanish.

Thomas Nelson formerly worked with 18 imprints, but has reorganized itself in a move called the One Company initiative. Thomas Nelson has eliminated all of its imprints and has reorganized its publishing functions around units keyed to BISAC category codes.

Some recent titles from Thomas Nelson include *Love Lifted Me* by Sara Evans; *The Trouble with Cowboys* by Denise Hunter; *Totally Awesome, Super-Cool Bible Stories as Drawn by Nerdy Ned* by Thomas Nelson; *Darkness Rising* by Lis Wiehl; *His Love Endures Forever* by Beth Wiseman.

Brian Hampton, Publisher
Daisy Sutton, Editor, Fiction
Bryan Norman, Editor, Nonfiction

NEW HORIZON PRESS

SMALL HORIZONS

PO Box 669, Far Hills, NJ 07931
908-604-6311 | 800-533-7978 | fax: 908-604-6330
www.newhorizonpressbooks.com | e-mail: nhp@newhorizonpressbooks.com

New Horizon Press (established 1982) publishes 12 to 14 books a year examining the everyday hero among us and social concerns. The company focuses on true crime, battles for justice, current events with a journalistic stance, as well as psychological and social problems, women's and men's issues, and parenting advice written by experts with credentials in their fields. The house develops three primary lines of titles: hardcover, trade paper, and children's books.

Titles include *Don't Say I Do!: Why Women Should Stay Single* by Orna Gadish, MSc; *Coming Around: Parenting Lesbian, Gay, Bisexual and Transgender Kids* by Anne Dohrenwend, PhD, ABPP; *The Spin Doctor: Hero or Cold-Blooded Killer* by Kirk Mitchell; *New Answers to the Mommy Track: Shattering Old Myths & Cracking Glass Ceilings* by Trudi Ferguson, PhD, and Joan S. Dunphy, PhD.

SMALL HORIZONS

Introduced in 1992, Small Horizons teaches crisis, coping, tolerance, and service skills to children. Expanding the scope and success of New Horizon Press's books are targeted promotions and publicity via local and national print, TV shows, and strong subsidiary rights.

Small Horizons titles include *Pretty Plus: How to Look Sexy, Sensational and Successful, No Matter What You Weigh* by Babe Hope; *Troubled Childhood, Triumphant Life: Healing from the Battle Scars of Youth* by James P. Krehbiel; *The Digital Pandemic: Reestablishing Face-to-Face Contact in the Electronic Age* by Mark Hicks, PhD; *Betrayal, Murder and Greed: The True Story of a Bounty Hunter and a Bail Bond Agent* by Pam Phree and Mike "Darkside" Beakley; and *Sun Struck: 16 Infamous Murders in the Sunshine State* by Robert A. Waters and John T. Waters, Jr.

See the website for submission guidelines. Query letters and SASEs should be directed to Ms. P. Patty. To send an e-mail inquiry, put "Attn: Ms. P. Patty" in the subject line and send to nhp@newhorizonpressbooks.com.

NEW LEAF PUBLISHING GROUP

BALFOUR BOOKS
MASTER BOOKS
3142 Highway 103 North, Green Forest, AR 72638
Mailing address:
PO Box 726, Green Forest, AR 72638
800-999-3777 | fax: 870-438-5120
www.newleafpublishinggroup.com | e-mail: nlp@newleafpress.com

New Leaf Publishing (established 1975) is a non-denominational Christian publishing house located in Arkansas. Subjects covered include Christian living, prophecy and eschatology, theology, applied Christianity, Bible study, family/home/marriage, friendship, love, education, evangelism, devotional works, and humor.

In 1996, New Leaf Press bought Master Books, the only publishing house in the world that publishes creation-based material exclusively, including evolution-free homeschool products. In 2003, a third imprint, Balfour Books, was launched to publish books on the importance of Israel and the Middle East, as well their relevance to America.

Recent titles include *Great for God: Missionaries Who Changed the World* by David Shibley; *Life in the Fairway* by Chad Bonham; *When You Ask Why* by Daniel E. Johnson.

BALFOUR BOOKS

Balfour Books publishes books that highlight Israel's global relevance and celebrate its unique position in world history. It also publishes a small range of other non-fiction titles. Some titles include *Smart Dating: How to Find Your Man* by Mary Balfour and Nick Roberts; *Nations United: How the United Nations Undermines Israel and the West* by Alex Grobman; *The Case for Democracy: The Power of Freedom to Overcome Tyranny and Terror* by Natan Sharansky and Ron Dermer; and *God's Covenant with Israel* by Binyamin Elon.

MASTER BOOKS

Master Books publishes creation-based materials for all ages that defend the Bible from the very first verse. Recent titles from Master Books include *American History: Observations & Assessments from Early Settlement to Today* by James P. Stobaugh;

Answers Book for Teens, Volume 2 by Ken Ham, Bodie Hodge, and Dr. Tommy Mitchell; *D is for Dinosaur* by Ken Ham and Mally Ham; *Demolishing Supposed Bible Contradictions*, Volume 2 by Tim Chaffey, Ken Ham, and Bodie Hodge; *Evolution Impossible* by John Ashton.

See the website or write the house to request a proposal guideline document. E-mail submissions should be directed to Craig Froman, craig@newleafpress.com. Send proposal with SASE to:

Craig Froman, Assistant Editor, Acquisitions
Tim Dudley, President and Publisher
Laura Welsh, Senior Editor

NEWMARKET PRESS

A Division of Newmarket Publishing and Communications Company
18 East 48th Street, New York, NY 10017
212-832-3575 | fax: 212-832-3629
www.newmarketpress.com | e-mail: mailbox@newmarketpress.com

Newmarket Publishing and Communications Company, and its publishing arm Newmarket Press, were founded in 1981 by President and Publisher Esther Margolis. Now in its twenty-seventh year with more than 300 books published, Newmarket Press is one of the few mainstream trade publishing houses in New York City under independent, entrepreneurial ownership. With W. W. Norton contracted as its distributor, Newmarket now publishes about 20 to 30 mainly nonfiction books a year, primarily in the areas of child care and parenting, film and performing arts, psychology, health and nutrition, biography, history, business and personal finance, and popular self-help and reference.

In addition, Newmarket has created a successful niche in publishing books in film, theater, and performing arts, and is especially noted for the illustrated movie books published on such films as *The Matrix; Dreamgirls; Planet of the Apes; Moulin Rouge; Crouching Tiger, Hidden Dragon; Magnolia; Cradle Will Rock; Sense and Sensibility; Saving Private Ryan;* and more.

Recent titles include *The Words of Extraordinary Women* edited by Carolyn Warner; *Everything Is Possible: Life and Business Lessons from a Self-Made Billionaire and the Founder of Slim-Fast* by S. Daniel Abraham; *The Last Station: The Shooting Script* by Michael Hoffman; *A Glorious Way to Die: The Kamikaze Mission of the Battleship Yamato* by Russell Spurr; and *A Special Mother: Getting Through the Early Days of a Child's Diagnosis of Learning Disabilities and Related Disorders* by Anne Ford.

See the website for submissions suggestions. No e-mail queries are accepted. Queries, proposals, and SASEs may be directed to the Editorial Department.

Keith Hollaman, Executive Editor, Acquisitions
Esther Margolis, President and Publisher

NEW PAGE BOOKS [SEE CAREER PRESS]

NEW WORLD LIBRARY

H. J. KRAMER
NATARAJ PUBLISHING
STARSEED PRESS
14 Pamaron Way, Novato, CA 94949
415-884-2100 | 800-972-6657 | fax: 415-884-2199
www.newworldlibrary.com

New World Library has been an independent publisher of mind/body/spirit and related titles for over 30 years, located just north of San Francisco. Some of their best sellers include *The Power of Now* by Eckhart Tolle; *The Seven Spiritual Laws of Success* by Deepak Chopra; and *Creative Visualization* by Shakti Gawain. New World Library publishes about 35 to 40 new titles annually, with a backlist of 250 books.

New World seeks manuscripts in the following subject areas: spirituality, personal growth, women's interest, religion, sustainable business, the human-animal relationship, Native American interest, and the environment. Their works appeal to a large, general audience.

Recent titles include *Aromatherapy for the Healthy Child* by Valerie Ann Worwood; *Beginning Mindfulness* by Andrew Weiss; *Body Health* by Francesca McCartney, PhD; *Diet for a New America* by John Robbins.

H. J. KRAMER

In 2000, New World Library entered into a joint venture with H. J. Kramer, the publisher of such authors as Dan Millman, Sanaya Roman, and John Robbins. New World Library assumed responsibility for many functional areas of H. J. Kramer, including sales, marketing, subsidiary rights, fulfillment, production, and accounting. H. J. Kramer has continued to focus on author relationships and acquiring and developing new books, particularly new children's titles from Holly Bea.

NATARAJ PUBLISHING

The Nataraj imprint primarily publishes titles by New World founder Shakti Gawain. Some of his titles include *Creative Visualization: Use the Power of Your Imagination to Create What You Want in Your Life* and *Developing Intuition: Practical Guidance for Daily Life*.

STARSEED PRESS

Starseed Press focuses on titles for younger readers (ages four to eight). Some Starseed titles include *The Fires of Shalsha* by John Michael Greer and Deva Berg; *The 8 Master Keys to Healing What Hurts* by Rue Anne Hass and Angela Treat Lyon; and *A Voyage to the Moon* by Guy Swanson.

E-mail submissions are preferred and can be sent to submit@newworldlibrary .com. Direct physical submissions with SASEs to Submissions Editor.

Jonathan Wichmann, Acquisitions Editor
Georgia Hughes, Editorial Director
Munro Magruder, Associate Publisher
Jason Gardner, Senior Editor

NOLO

950 Parker Street, Berkeley, CA 94710-2524
800-728-3555 | fax: 800-645-0895
www.nolo.com | e-mail: cs@nolo.com

Nolo is one of the nation's leading providers of do-it-yourself legal solutions for consumers and small businesses. The house goal is to help people handle their own everyday legal matters—or learn enough about them to make working with a lawyer a more satisfying experience. According to Nolo, "Americans who are armed with solid legal knowledge are confident, active participants in their legal system—and slowly but inevitably, their participation makes that system more open and democratic. Nolo is proud to be part of that process."

Since 1971, Nolo has offered affordable, plain-English books, forms, and software on a wide range of legal issues, including wills, estate planning, retirement, elder care, personal finance, taxes, housing, real estate, divorce, and child custody. They also offer materials on human resources, employment, intellectual property, and starting and running a small business.

With a staff of lawyer-editors, the house pays attention not only to changes in the law, but to feedback from customers, lawyers, judges, and court staffers. Nolo publishes legal self-help books and software for consumers, small businesses, and nonprofit organizations. They specialize in helping people handle their own legal tasks—for example, write a will, file a small claims court lawsuit, start a small business or nonprofit, or apply for a patent. Nolo does not publish fiction, first-person accounts, biographies, or any other material that strays too far from its step-by-step approach to helping individuals, businesses, and nonprofits solve specific legal problems.

Titles include *101 Law Forms for Personal Use* by Ralph Warner, Attorney, and Robin Leonard, JD; *Nolo's Essential Guide to Child Custody & Support* by Emily Doskow, Attorney; *Tax Savvy for Small Business* by Frederick W. Daily, JD; *Quick &*

Legal Will Book by Denis Clifford, Attorney; *Legal Guide for Starting & Running a Small Business* by Fred S. Steingold, Attorney.

Queries and SASEs should be directed to the Acquisitions Editors.

Mary Randolf, Editor-in-Chief

W. W. NORTON & COMPANY

THE COUNTRYMAN PRESS
NORTON PROFESSIONAL BOOKS
500 Fifth Avenue, New York, NY 10110
212-354-5500 | fax: 212-869-0856
www.wwnorton.com | e-mail: manuscripts@wwnorton.com
The Countryman Press:
43 Lincoln Corners Way/PO Box 748, Woodstock, VT 05091
802-457-4826 | fax: 802-457-1678
www.countrymanpress.com | e-mail: countrymanpress@wwnorton.com

Publishers of adult trade fiction, nonfiction, professional psychology, and architecture books, W. W. Norton & Company is the oldest and largest publishing house owned wholly by its employees. Norton strives to carry out the imperative of its founder to publish books not for a single season, but for the years—in fiction, nonfiction, poetry, college textbooks, cookbooks, art books, and professional books. W. W. Norton & Company now publishes about 400 books annually in hardcover and paperback.

The roots of the company date back to 1923, when William Warder Norton and his wife, Mary D. Herter Norton, began publishing lectures delivered at the People's Institute, the adult education division of New York City's Cooper Union. The Nortons soon expanded their program beyond the Institute, acquiring manuscripts by celebrated academics from America and abroad.

In 1996, Norton acquired the distinguished Vermont firm The Countryman Press and added well-respected nature, history, and outdoor recreation titles to the Norton list. In 2003, Berkshire House Press joined Norton, becoming part of the Vermont operation.

For years, Norton has been known for its distinguished publishing programs in both the trade and the college textbook areas. Early in its history, Norton entered the fields of philosophy, music, and psychology, publishing acclaimed works by Bertrand Russell, Paul Henry Lang, and Sigmund Freud (as his principal American publisher).

In the past few decades, the firm has published bestselling books by such authors as economists Paul Krugman and Joseph Stiglitz; paleontologist Stephen Jay Gould; physicist Richard Feynman; and historians Peter Gay, Jonathan Spence, Christopher Lasch, and George F. Kennan. Norton has also developed a more eclectic list, with prominent titles including *Helter Skelter* by Vincent Bugliosi and Curt Gentry; Jared Diamond's Pulitzer Prize–winning best seller *Guns, Germs, and Steel*; Judy Rogers's *The Zuni Café Cookbook*; Patrick O'Brian's critically acclaimed naval adventures; the works of National Book Award-winning fiction author Andrea Barrett; *Liar's Poker* and *Moneyball* by Michael Lewis; Fareed Zakaria's *The Future of Freedom*; and Sebastian Junger's *The Perfect Storm*.

Recent titles include *Breakout Nations: In Pursuit of the Next Economic Miracles* by Ruchir Sharma; *The Social Conquest of Earth* by Edward O. Wilson; *This Will Be Difficult to Explain: And Other Stories* by Johanna Skibsrud; *Gardening Vertically: 24 Ideas for Creating Your Own Green Walls* by Noémie Vialard and Patrick Blanc; *Siblings Without Rivalry: How to Help Your Children Live Together So You Can Live Too* by Adele Faber and Elaine Mazlish.

THE COUNTRYMAN PRESS

As Vermont's oldest name in publishing, The Countryman Press maintains a tradition of producing books of substance and quality. The company began in Taftsville, Vermont, in 1973, in Peter and Jane Jennison's farmhouse kitchen. In 1996 the press became a division of W. W. Norton & Company, Inc. Countryman retains its own identity, however, with editorial and production offices in Woodstock, Vermont.

Countryman publishes about 50 books per year with more than 250 books in print. Subjects include travel, food, gardening, country living, nature, New England history, and crafts. The Explorer's Guide travel series has sold over half a million copies.

The Backcountry Guides imprint features where-to books on outdoor sports activities, including fishing, cycling, walking, and paddling. The bestselling 50 Hikes series has sold more than 1 million copies.

Some titles from The Countryman Press include *Lobster Shacks: A Road-Trip Guide to New England's Best Lobster Joints* by Mike Urban; *Stand Up and Garden* by Mary Moss-Sprague; *Oregon Coast Memories* by Rod Barbee; *Washington, D.C. Memories* by David Muse; *Maine Coast Memories* by David Middleton.

NORTON PROFESSIONAL BOOKS

In 1985, Norton expanded its publishing program with Norton Professional Books, specializing in books on psychotherapy and, more recently, neuroscience. The Professional Books program has also moved into the fields of architecture and design.

Recent titles from Norton Professional Books includes *Michael Taylor: Interior Design* by Steven M. Salny; *Historic Preservation*, Second Edition by Norman Tyler et al; *The Healthy Aging Brain: Sustaining Attachment, Attaining Wisdom* by Louis Cozolino; and *How to Use Herbs, Nutrients, and Yoga in Mental Health Care* by Richard P. Brown, MD, et al.

W. W. Norton does consider books from the following categories: juvenile or young adult, religious, occult or paranormal, genre fiction such as formula romances, science fiction or Westerns, arts and crafts, and inspirational poetry.

Due to the workload of the editorial staff, Norton is no longer able to accept unsolicited submissions except from literary agents.

Alane Mason, Senior Editor—Cultural and intellectual history, literary fiction.

Amy Cherry, Senior Editor—African American issues, contemporary biographies, social issues.

Jill Bialosky, Vice President—Literary fiction and nonfiction, biographies.

Robert Weil, Executive Editor—Translations, intellectual history, social sciences, German and Jewish subjects.

Drake McFeely, President—Science, social sciences.

Maria Guarnaschelli, Senior Editor—Science, food, fiction.

Kermit Hummel, Editorial Director (The Countryman Press)

O'REILLY MEDIA

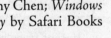

Editorial office:
10 Fawcett Street, Cambridge, MA 01238
Headquarters:
1005 Gravenstein Highway North, Sebastapol, CA 95472
707-827-7000 | 800-998-9938 | fax: 707-829-0104
www.oreilly.com

O'Reilly Media is a premier information source for leading-edge computer technologies. Smart books written for smart people—with animals sketched on the front covers—O'Reilly titles are not for dummies. Some of their subjects include business and culture, databases, digital audio and video, digital photography, hardware, home and office, networking, system administration, operating systems, programming, science, math, security, software engineering, and the Web.

This house is vastly interested in the newest technologies, and thus it's best to check the Author section of their website for the evolving list of what they're looking for right now; you'll find it here: www.oreilly.com/oreilly/author/intro.csp.

Recent titles from O'Reilly include *PostgreSQL: Up and Running* by Regina Obe and Leo Hsu; *Team Geek* by Brian W. Fitzpatrick and Ben Collins-Sussman; *Visual Models for Software Requirements* by Joy Beatty and Anthony Chen; *Windows PowerShell for Developers* by Douglas Finke; *Coding Bibliography* by Safari Books Online Content Team.

Send your proposal via e-mail to proposals@oreilly.com with a descriptive subject line. Physical proposals should be sent to the Cambridge editorial office.

Mike Hendrickson, Associate Publisher

Simon St. Laurent, Senior Editor—Systems, programming.

Brian Sawyer, Editor—Hacks.

OSBORNE MEDIA [SEE MCGRAW-HILL]

THE OVERLOOK PRESS

ARDIS PUBLISHING
THE ROOKERY PRESS
141 Wooster Street, 4B, New York, NY 10012
212-673-2210 | fax: 212-673-2296
www.overlookpress.com | blog: theoverlookpress.blogspot.com
  DUCKWORTH
90-93 Cowcross Street, London, EC1M 6BF
+44 (0) 207-490-7300 | fax: +44 (0) 207-490-0080
www.ducknet.co.uk | e-mail: info@duckworth-publishers.co.uk

The Overlook Press (founded 1971) is an independent, general-interest publisher. The publishing program consists of some 100 new books per year, evenly divided between hardcovers and trade paperbacks. The list is eclectic, but areas of strength include interesting fiction, history, biography, drama, and design.

The house was launched by owner Peter Mayer as a home for distinguished books that had been "overlooked" by larger houses. The publishing formula proved reliable, and now Overlook has nearly 1,000 titles in print. Their fiction includes novels by solidly commercial authors including espionage novelist Robert Littell (*The Company*, 90,000 sold) and international phenomenon Penny Vincenzi, whose Edwardian era family saga *No Angel* is widely acclaimed as stunning entertainment. More success came in April 2004 with *Dragon's Eye* by Andy Oakes, a thriller set in modern Shanghai. In a more literary vein, there is *Hash* by top Swedish novelist Torgny Lindgren, and Michele Slung's anthology of garden writing, *The Garden of Reading*.

History is the mainstay of the house's nonfiction list, and notable books include Paul Cartledge's *The Spartans*, basis of a PBS documentary on this civilization, and Adrienne Mayor's *Greek Fire, Poison Arrows and Scorpion Bombs: Biochemical Warfare in the Ancient World*.

Recent titles from Overlook include *2017* by Olga Slavnikova; *Any Day Now* by Terry Bisson; *The Balloonist* by MacDonald Harris; *Beast Friends Forever* by Robert Forbes and Ronald Searle; *Before Galileo* by John Freely; *AD 381* by Charles Freeman; *Anything Goes* by Lucy Moore; *An Appeal to Reason* by Nigel Lawson; and *Barmy in Wonderland* by P. G. Wodehouse.

ARDIS PUBLISHING

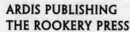

In 2002 Overlook acquired Ardis, the premier publisher of Russian literature in English. They have given that program new presence with handsome new paperback editions of titles long unavailable. Some books include *Selected Poems* by Anna Akhmatova; *A Captive Spirit* by Marina Tsvetaeva; *Envy* by Yury Olesha; *Poor Folk* by Fyodor Dostoevsky; and *Eugene Onegin* by Alexander Pushkin.

THE ROOKERY PRESS

The Rookery Press is a new imprint launched in 2006. Rookery focuses on serious nonfiction and some literary fiction, reprints, a drama list, plus illustrated books on fashion, interiors, design, art, theater, and film. Rookery plans to release 20 titles annually.

Some titles from The Rookery Press include *Ma Gastronomie* by Fernand Point and Thomas Keller; *Paradise with Serpents* by Richard Carver; *The Truth about Sascha Knisch* by Aris Fioretos; *Ten Bad Dates with De Niro: A Book of Alternative Movie Lists* by Richard T. Kelly and Andrew Rae; *Young Pushkin: A Novel* by Yury Tynyanov and Anna Rush; and *St. Trinians: The Entire Appalling Business* by Ronald Searle.

Overlook Press titles are distributed to the trade by Penguin Putnam.

The house currently only accepts submissions from literary agents.

Peter Mayer, President and Publisher

Aaron Schlechter, Editor

Juliet Grames, Editor

DUCKWORTH

Recently Overlook acquired the 106-year-old UK publisher Duckworth. Duckworth publishes literary and commercial fiction and nonfiction, including history, biography, and memoir. Their academic list features important new scholarly monographs in archaeology, classics, ancient history, and ancient philosophy.

Some titles from Duckworth include *Identity Wars* by Cole Stryker; *The Essential Churchill* by Lord Blake; *The Creation of the American Soul: Roger Williams and the Birth of Liberty* by John M. Barry; *Cuba: Contemporary Art* by Andreas Winkler and Sebastiaan Berger; *Beastly Romances* by Robert Forbes and Ronald Searle.

PALADIN PRESS

Gunbarrel Tech Center
7077 Winchester Circle, Boulder, CO 80301
303-443-7250 | fax: 303-442-8741
www.paladin-press.com | e-mail: editorial@paladin-press.com

Controversial even before a 1999 multimillion dollar settlement related to the use of a murder how-to manual *Hit Man*—no longer available—Paladin Press publishes books and DVDs on personal and financial freedom, survival and preparedness, firearms and shooting, martial arts and self-defense, military and police tactics, knives and knife fighting, and more.

The company came into existence in September 1970 when Peder Lund joined Robert K. Brown as a partner in a book publishing venture previously known as Panther Publications. As former military men and adventurers, Lund and Brown were convinced there was a market for books on specialized military and action/adventure topics. Both men also firmly believed that the First Amendment guaranteed Americans the right to read about whatever subjects they desired, and this became the cornerstone of Paladin's publishing philosophy.

Recent titles include *Bob Kasper—The Lost Tapes: Combative Knive Skills* by Bob Kasper; *The Fighting Kukri* by Dwight C. McLemore; *Tactical Ruger: Building Your Own Marksman, Sniper Simulator, and Competition Models* by J.M. Ramos.

E-mail queries are not accepted. Submit a proposal and SASE to the Editorial Department.

Donna Duvall, Editor Director
Cathy Wirtes, Senior Editor

PATHFINDER PRESS

4794 Clark Howell Highway, Suite B-5, College Park, GA 30349
Mailing address:
PO Box 162767, Atlanta, GA 30321-2767
404-669-0600 | fax: 707-667-1141
www.pathfinderpress.com | e-mail: pathfinder@pathfinderpress.com

Since 1940, Pathfinder Press has published books, booklets, pamphlets, posters, and postcards focusing on issues affecting working people worldwide. The house produces titles in English, Spanish, French, Swedish, Farsi, Greek, Icelandic, and Russian. Pathfinder also distributes the journal *New International*.

Subjects include black and African studies; women's rights; the Cuban revolution in world politics; revolutionaries and working-class fighters; fascism, big business, and the labor movement; Russia, Eastern Europe, and the Balkans; scientific views of politics and economics; trade unions: past, present, and future; US history and politics; Latin America and the Caribbean; the Middle East and China; and art, culture, and politics. Pathfinder is usually associated with schools of thought such as populism, internationalism, utopianism, socialism, and communism.

The Pathfinder mural that once adorned the company's original editorial digs in Manhattan's Far West Village featured a depiction of a gargantuan printing press in action, as well as portraits of revolutionary leaders whose writings and speeches were published by Pathfinder; this community cultural icon represented the work of more than 80 artists from 20 countries.

Pathfinder titles include *Women in Cuba: The Making of a Revolution Within the*

Revolution by Vilma Espín, Asela de los Santos, and Yolanda Ferrer; *Malcolm X: Black Liberation and the Road to Workers' Power* by Jack Barnes; *The Inevitable Battle: From the Bay of Pigs to Playa Giron* by Juan Carlos Rodriguez; *Our History Is Still Being Written: The Story of Three Chinese-Cuban Generals in the Cuban Revolution* by Armando Choy et al; and *Capitalism's Long Hot Winter Has Begun* by Jack Barnes.

Direct queries and SASEs to:
Mary-Alice Waters, President
Elizabeth Stone, Managing Editor

PAULIST PRESS

997 Macarthur Boulevard, Mahwah, NJ 07430-9990
201-825-7300 | 800-218-1903 | fax: 800-836-3161
www.paulistpress.com | e-mail: info@paulistpress.com

Founded in 1866 by the Paulist Fathers as the Catholic Publication Society, Paulist Press publishes hardcover and trade originals for general readers, and distinguished scholarly books, in the areas of religion, spirituality, and theology. Paulist Press publishes ecumenical theology, Roman Catholic studies and books on scripture, liturgy, spirituality, church history, and philosophy, as well as works on faith and culture. Their list is oriented toward adult-level nonfiction, although they do offer a growing selection of children's stories and activity books. Children's categories include picture books, prayer books, chapter books, young-adult biographies, Catholic guidebooks, and gift books.

Titles from Paulist Press include *Courageous Hope: The Call of Leadership* by Leonard Doohan; *Understanding the Historical Books of the Old Testament* by Vincent P. Branick; *Seventeenth-Century Lutheran Meditations and Hymns* by Eric Lund; *Living as an American Catholic in the 21st Century: A Short, Self-Guided Retreat* by Richard Gribble, CSC; *My Playtime Angel* by Cat Darens.

Query letters and SASEs should be directed to:
Rev. Lawrence Boadt, CSP, Publisher and President
Susan O'Keefe, Children's Book Editor
Donna Crilly, Managing Editor, dcrilly@paulistpress.com

PEACHPIT PRESS

ADOBE PRESS
APPLE CERTIFIED
LYNDA.COM
NEW RIDERS
NEW RIDERS GAMES

1249 Eighth Street, Berkeley, CA 94710
510-524-2178
www.peachpit.com | e-mail: proposals@peachpit.com

Peachpit Press has been publishing top-notch books on the latest in graphic design, desktop publishing, multimedia, Web publishing, and general computing since 1986. Their titles feature step-by-step explanations, timesaving techniques, savvy insider tips, and expert advice for computer users of all sorts. Peachpit is a part of Pearson Education, the world's largest integrated educational publisher.

Imprints include Peachpit Press, New Riders Press, New Riders Games, Adobe Press, Apple Certified, Lynda.com, and other imprints and series for creative computer users.

Recent titles from Peachpit include *Adobe Flash Professional CS5 Classroom in a Book* by Adobe Creative Team; *InterACT with Web Standards: A Holistic Approach to Web Design* by Erin Anderson et al; *Adobe Flash Catalyst CS5 Classroom in a Book* by Adobe Creative Team; *Nikon D3000: From Snapshots to Great Shots* by Jeff Revell; and *Adobe Flex 4: Training from the Source*, Volume 1 by Michael Labriola et al.

ADOBE PRESS

Adobe Press is the official source of training materials for Adobe software and inspiration for digital communicators. Titles from Adobe Press include *Adobe Flash Professional CS5 Classroom in a Book* by Adobe Creative Team; *Adobe Flash Catalyst CS5 Classroom in a Book* by Adobe Creative Team; and *Adobe Flex 4: Training from the Source*, Volume 1 by Michael Labriola et al.

APPLE CERTIFIED

Books from Apple Certified come with Apple's seal of approval and contain complete courses designed to help users master Mac apps. New titles include *Apple Pro Training Series: Final Cut Pro for Avid Editors*, 4th Edition by Diana Weynand; *Apple Training Series: iLife '11* by Dion Scoppettuolo and Mary Plummer; *Aperture 3 Video Training* by Damian Allen; *Motion 4 Quick-Reference Guide* by Jem Schofield and Brendan Boykin.

LYNDA.COM

Lynda.com is an award-winning education provider of Hands-On Training instructional books, video training on CD and DVD, self-paced online learning, and events for creative designers, developers, instructors, students, hobbyists, and anyone who wants to learn. Titles from Lynda include *Photoshop CS4 Extended for 3D* by Chad Perkins; *Photoshop CS4 Portrait Retouching Essential Training* by Chris Orwig; *Illustrator CS4 One-on-One: Fundamentals* by Deke McClelland; and *Flash CS4 Professional: Object Oriented Programming* by Todd Perkins.

INDEPENDENT US PRESSES

NEW RIDERS

New Riders produces beautiful instruction books that provide a forum for the leading voices in creative and information technologies. New Riders includes the Voices That Matter series and the AIGA Design Press. New titles include *Functional Art* by Alberto Cairo; *Photoshop Masking & Compositing*, 2nd Edition. by Katrin Eismann, Sean Duggan, and James Porto; *Web Designer's Guide to WordPress: Plan, Theme, Build, Launch* by Jesse Friedman; *Implementing Responsive Design: Building sites for an anywhere, everywhere web* by Tim Kadlec; *Adobe Photoshop CS6 Book for Digital Photographers* by Scott Kelby.

NEW RIDERS GAMES

New Riders Games (NRG) takes game books where they've never gone before. As the game resource, NRG touches every category: programming, design, art, and celebrity savvy. Titles include *Creating Games in C++: A Step-by-Step Guide* by David Conger and Ron Little; *Level Design for Games: Creating Compelling Game Experiences* by Phil Co; *3ds max 7 Fundamentals* by Ted Boardman; *Game Character Development with Maya* by Anthony Ward; and *Audio for Games: Planning, Process, and Production* by Alexander Brandon.

Peachpit is always looking for new authors and innovative book ideas. Mail your completed proposal to Book Proposals or e-mail it to proposals@peachpit.com.

Marjorie Baer, Executive Editor
Keasley Jones, Associate Publisher

PEACHTREE PUBLISHERS

1700 Chattahoochee Avenue, Atlanta, GA 30318
404-876-8761 | 800-241-0113 | fax: 404-875-2578 | 800-875-8909
www.peachtree-online.com | e-mail: hello@peachtree-online.com

Peachtree is an award-winning trade publisher featuring children's picture books and chapter books for the very young child through young adult. Other categories include health and parenting, and the best of the South, including fiction, high quality gift, and regional guides. They publish about 20 books per year.

Recent titles include *The Theory of Everything* by J.J. Johnson; *Privateer's Apprentice* by Susan Verrico; *The Universe of Fair* by Leslie Bulion; *Zayde Comes to Live* by Sheri Sinykin; *The Return of Library Dragon* by Carmen Agra Deedy.

Direct submissions and SASEs to Helen Harris.

Helen Harris, Acquisitions Editor
Margaret Quinlin, Publisher
Kathy Landwehr, Associate Publisher

PELICAN PUBLISHING COMPANY

1000 Burmaster Street, Gretna, LA 70053-2246
504-368-1175 | 800-843-1724 | fax: 504-368-1195
www.pelicanpub.com | e-mail: editorial@pelicanpub.com

Called "innovative" by the *New York Times*, Pelican Publishing is the largest independent trade book publisher in the South. Once the publisher of William Faulkner, Pelican is now owned by the Calhouns, a family of self-professed bibliophiles. Significantly, the house managed to make a commendable comeback from the floods of 2005.

The house publishes an average of 70 titles a year and has over 1,500 currently in print. Specialties are art/architecture books, cooking/cookbooks, motivational, travel guides, history (especially Louisiana/regional), nonfiction, children's books (illustrated and otherwise), social commentary, folklore, and textbooks. For fiction, only historical works are considered for publication.

Recent titles include *The Art of Brazilian Cooking* by Sandra Cuza; *Beware, Beware of the Big Bad Bear!* by Dianne de Las Castas; *Clash at Kennesaw: June and July 1864* by Russell J. Blount, Jr.; *The Great Elephant Escape* by Una Belle Townsend; *Mr. Dickey's Barbecue Cookbook* by Roland Dickey.

The editors seek writers on the cutting edge of ideas.

To submit, send a query letter with SASE to the editors. Short children's manuscripts may be sent in their entirety at the initial contact. Direct queries and SASEs to:

Nina Kooij, Editor-in-Chief

PERMANENT PRESS

SECOND CHANCE PRESS
4170 Noyac Road, Sag Harbor, NY 11963
631-725-1101 | fax: 631-725-8215
www.thepermanentpress.com | e-mail: info@thepermanentpress.com

The Permanent Press (founded 1978 by Martin and Judith Shepard) committed itself to publishing works of social and literary merit and has, over the years, gained a reputation as one of the finest small independent presses in America. The Permanent Press is a publisher of literary fiction—and occasionally nonfiction. They publish books that are artfully written, about 12 per year.

Recent titles include *A Cup Full of Midnight* by Jaden Terrell; *Back in the Game* by Charles Holdefer; *Death in a Wine Dark Sea* by Lisa King; *Oregon Hill* by Howard Owen.

SECOND CHANCE PRESS

The imprint Second Chance Press reprints books of merit that had been out of print for at least 20 years. The Second Chance mission is to find literary fiction gems worth republishing; they have published Berry Fleming, Halldor Laxness, Richard Lortz, William Herrick, and Joseph Stanley Pennell.

E-mail queries are not accepted. Send the first 20 pages or so with query letter and SASE. Direct physical submissions to Judith Shepard.

Judith Shepard, Publisher, Acquisitions
Martin Shepard, Publisher

PERSEA BOOKS

277 Broadway, Suite 708, New York, NY 10007
212-260-9256 | fax: 212- 267-3165
www.perseabooks.com | e-mail: info@perseabooks.com

Founded in 1975 by Karen and Michael Braziller, Persea is a small literary press of books for adults and young adults. Their titles cover a wide range of themes, styles, and genres. They have published poetry, fiction, essays, memoir, biography, titles of Jewish and Middle Eastern interest, women's studies, American Indian folklore, and revived classics, as well as a notable selection of works in translation.

They have been expanding their young-adult list with intelligent books by authors such as Anne Mazer, Gary Soto, and Marie Raphael. These works complement their acclaimed series of literary anthologies for youths, which include *America Street: A Multicultural Anthology of Stories*; *Imagining America: Stories from the Promised Land*; *A Walk in My World: International Short Stories About Youth*; *Starting With "I": Personal Essays by Teenagers*; and many more.

Recent Persea titles include *Apocalyptic Swing* by Gabrielle Calvocoressi; *Having Been an Accomplice* by Laura Cronk; *Unexpected Elegies* by Thomas Hardy; *Sightseer* by Cynthia Marie Hoffman; *The Girl in the Mirror: A Novel in Poems and Journal Entries* by Meg Kearney.

Direct queries and SASEs to the attention of the Fiction Editor (or nonfiction or poetry, as appropriate).

Michael Braziller, Publisher
Karen Braziller, Editorial Director

PERSEUS BOOKS GROUP

BASIC BOOKS
250 West 57th Street, 15th Floor, New York, NY 10107
212-340-8100
www.basicbooks.com | e-mail: perseus.promos@perseusbooks.com

SEAL PRESS
1700 4th Street, Berkeley, CA 94710
510-528-1444
www.sealpress.com

DA CAPO LIFELONG BOOKS
DA CAPO PRESS
44 Farnsworth Street, 3rd Floor, Boston, MA 02210
617-252-5200
www.dacapopress.com

NATION BOOKS
PUBLICAFFAIRS
116 East 16th Street, 8th Floor, New York, NY 10003
212-397-6666 | fax: 212-397-4277
www.nationbooks.com
www.publicaffairsbooks.com | e-mail: publicaffairs@perseusbooks.com

RUNNING PRESS
2300 Chestnut Street, Suite 200, Philadelphia, PA 19103
215-567-5080
www.runningpress.com | e-mail: perseus.promos@perseusbooks .com

The Perseus Books Group was founded with the belief that insightful books of quality are both necessary and desirable, that an innovative model is possible, that authors, readers, booksellers—and books—matter. That innovative model includes Perseus' mission to empower independent publishers to reach their potential whether those publishers are owned by Perseus Books, joint venture partnerships, or clients for whom they provide services. Perseus very recently acquired both distributor Consortium and publisher Avalon Publishing Group, and in doing so has greatly expanded its depth and breadth in the publishing world.

In the process of combining Avalon Publishing Group with Perseus operations, several imprints were closed or sold; these include Counterpoint, Shoemaker & Hoard, Thunder's Mouth Press, and Carroll & Graf.

Each of the remaining Perseus and former Avalon imprints is editorially independent and individually focused, with offices from California to Massachusetts. As a whole, Perseus' publishing spans the breakthroughs in science to the great public issues, from military history to modern maternity, from African American scholars to novelists just breaking out, from choosing a great wine or a great president, from gift giving to required reading.

INDEPENDENT US PRESSES

BASIC BOOKS

Since its founding in 1952, Basic Books has helped shape public debate by publishing award-winning books in psychology, science, politics, sociology, current affairs, and history. Basic seeks to publish serious nonfiction by leading intellectuals, scholars, and journalists; to create books that change the way people think.

Recent titles include *Divided We Stand: A Biography of the World Trade Center* by Eric Darton; *America and the Pill: A History of Promise, Peril, and Liberation* by Elaine Tyler May; *Rothstein: The Life, Times, and Murder of the Criminal Genius Who Fixed the 1919 World Series* by David Pietrusza; *The Assassin's Accomplice: Mary Surratt and the Plot to Kill Abraham Lincoln* by Kate Clifford Larson.

Basic does not accept unsolicited proposals or manuscripts.

T. J. Kelleher, Editor—Psychology, science.

Lara Heimert, Executive Editor—Religion, history.

Tim Bartlett, Editor

SEAL PRESS

Seal Press was founded in 1976 to provide a forum for women writers and feminist issues. Since then, Seal has published groundbreaking books that represent the diverse voices and interests of women—their lives, literature, and concerns. Seal's list includes books on women's health, parenting, outdoor adventure and travel, popular culture, gender and women's studies, and current affairs.

Seal publishes books by and for women, with an emphasis on original, lively, radical, empowering, and culturally diverse nonfiction that addresses contemporary issues from a women's perspective.

Recent Seal titles include *Essential Car Care for Women* by Jamie Little and Danielle McCormick; *Something Spectacular: The True Story of One Rockette's Battle with Bulimia* by Greta Gleissner; *A Little F'd Up: Why Feminism Is Not a Dirty Word* by Julie Zeilinger; *Stop Signs: Recognizing, Avoiding, and Escaping Abusive Relationships* by Lynn Fairweather; *Lessons from the Monk I Married* by Katherine Jenkins.

Seal Press is not acquiring fiction at this time. Send proposal with SASE to the Acquisitions Editor.

Krista Lyons-Gould, Publisher

Brooke Warner, Acquisitions Editor

Laura Mazer, Executive Editor—Women's nonfiction.

DA CAPO PRESS

Da Capo is an Italian musical term meaning "from the beginning," and Da Capo Press was once known primarily as a publisher of music and culture titles. Da Capo is an imprint of Perseus, where a reorganization in 2004 expanded Da Capo when it absorbed the Perseus health, parenting, and reference/how-to program. This means titles such as *Third Coast: OutKast, Timbaland and the Rise of Dirty South Hip Hop* by Roni Sarig and *Muscle Your Way Through Menopause* by Judith Sherman-Wolin all find a home at Da Capo.

With editorial offices in both New York and Massachusetts, Da Capo Press publishes hardcover and paperback editions in American and world history, biography, music, film, art, photography, sports, humor, and popular culture.

A Da Capo imprint launched in 2004, Lifelong Books, consolidated Da Capo titles on pregnancy, parenting, health, fitness, and relationships. New titles from Lifelong include the Staying Sane series edited by Pam Brodowsky and Evelyn Fazio; Mari Winsor's Pilates best sellers; and Dr. Mike Riera's *Field Guide to the American Teenager*. The Marlowe & Company brand from Da Capo also focuses on health and wellness titles.

Most recent Da Capo titles include *When I Left Home: My Story* by Buddy Guy; *I Got a Name: The Jim Croce Story* by Ingrid Croce and Jimmy Rock; *Grilling Vegan Style: 125 Fired-Up Recipes to Turn Every Bite into a Backyard BBQ* by John Schlimm; *Ballet Beautiful* by Mary Bowers; *Fire and Rain: The Beatles, Simon and Garfunkel, James Taylor, CSNY, and the Lost Story of 1970* by David Browne.

Da Capo Press does not accept unsolicited manuscripts or proposals.

Ben Schafer, Editor (NY)—Pop culture, music.

Robert Pigeon, Senior Editor (Philadelphia)—History, science, current affairs.

Renee Sedliar, Senior Editor (Emeryville)—Health, fitness.

Jonanthan Crowe, Editor (NY)—Narratives, general nonfiction.

NATION BOOKS

Nation Books, a copublishing venture with The Nation Institute, publishes works from a progressive perspective. Nation Books is dedicated to continuing the long tradition of progressive, critical thought in America, publishing new nonfiction works on politics, current events, human rights, feminism, race, gay and lesbian issues, history, art and culture, popular science, and the environment.

Recent titles include *Days of Destruction, Days of Revolt* by Chris Hedges and Joe Sacco; *Desert Reckoning* by Deanne Stillman; *100 Greatest Americans of the 20th Century: A Social Justice Hall of Fame* by Peter Dreier; *Rebuild the Dream* by Van Jones; *La Roja: How Soccer Conquered Spain and How Spanish Soccer Conquered the World* by Jimmy Burns.

No unsolicited manuscripts or proposals. Direct queries with SASEs to:

Carl Bromley, Editorial Director

PUBLICAFFAIRS

PublicAffairs is one of the nation's primary providers of good books about things that matter. The house specializes in current events, recent history, and other pressing issues affecting contemporary society. PublicAffairs publishes original nonfiction works by field experts from journalists to politicians, from political dissidents to leaders in the arts. PublicAffairs specializes in journalism, history, biography, and memoir.

Recent titles include *Who Gets What: Fair Compensation after Tragedy and Financial Upheaval* by Kenneth R. Feinberg; *The Betrayal of the American Dream* by Donald L. Barlett and James B. Steele; *Ascent of the A-Word Assholism: The First Sixty Years* by Geoffrey Nunberg.

No e-mail submissions. Direct proposals and SASEs to PublicAffairs Submissions.

John Mahaney, Editor

Clive Priddle, Executive Editor

Brandon Proia, Editor

Lisa Kaufman, Editor

RUNNING PRESS

One of the country's largest independent trade publishers, Running Press Publishers has been providing consumers with an innovative list of quality books and book-related kits since 1972.

Running Press creates more than 200 new titles a year under four imprints: Running Press, Running Press Miniature Editions, Running Press Kids, and Courage Books. Titles cover a broad range of categories, including general nonfiction, science, history, children's fiction and nonfiction, food and wine, pop culture, lifestyle, photo-essay, and illustrated gift books.

Recent titles include *Cornered: 14 Stories of Bullying and Defiance* by Rhoda Belleza; *Downside of Being Charlie* by Jenny Torres Sanche; *Cowgirl Chef: Texas Cooking with a French Accent* by Ellise Pierce; *Food in Jars: Preserving in Small Batches Year-Round* by Marisa McClellan; *Gardener and the Grill: The Bounty of the Garden Meets the Sizzle of the Grill* by Judith Fertig and Karen Adler.

For children's titles, to submit a proposal for interactive nonfiction, basic concepts books (such as letters, numbers, opposites, or shapes), or beginning reading projects, send a query letter accompanied by a brief outline or table of contents. When submitting a picture-book proposal, send the entire manuscript. Note that at this time Running Press Kids is not publishing novels or any fiction longer than picture-book length.

For their general-interest lists (Running Press and Courage Books), they specialize in publishing illustrated nonfiction. They very rarely publish any new fiction or poetry and are not seeking submissions in those categories at this time. They also do not accept proposals for Miniature Editions of any kind. To submit a proposal for an appropriate work of nonfiction, please send a query letter accompanied by a brief outline or table of contents.

Direct all Running Press submissions to the Philadelphia office, to the attention of the Submissions Editor at Running Press Kids, or the Assistant of the Editorial Director at Running Press Book Publishers for adult titles.

Jennifer Kasius, Senior Editor—Cooking, self-help.
Greg Jones, Editorial Director—Pop culture, humor.
Geoffrey Stone, Editor—Humor, pop culture, cooking.
Jordana Tusman, Editor—Humor, lifestyle.
Kristen Green Wiewora, Editor—Cooking.
Lisa Cheng, Editor—Children's books.

PETERSON'S

A Division of the Thomson Corporation
Princeton Pike Corporate Center
2000 Lenox Drive, PO Box 67005, Lawrenceville, NJ 08648
609-896-1800
www.petersons.com

Peterson's is one of the nation's most comprehensive education resources. Since 1966, Peterson's has helped to connect individuals, educational institutions, and corporations through critically acclaimed books. The house reaches an estimated 105 million consumers annually with information about colleges and universities, career schools, graduate programs, distance learning, executive training, private secondary schools, summer opportunities, study abroad, financial aid, test preparation, and career exploration.

Peterson's is part of the Thomson Corporation, a global leader in providing integrated information solutions to business and professional customers.

Titles from Peterson's include *Master the GRE 2010* by Mark Allen Stewart; *Nursing Programs 2010*; *The Russia Balance Sheet* by Anders Aslund and Andrew Kuchins; *Global Warming and the World Trading System* by Steve Charnovitz et al; and *US Pension Reform: Lessons from Other Countries* by Martin Neil Baily and Jacob Kirkegaard.

Query letters and SASEs should be directed to the Editorial Department.
Therese D'Angelis, Senior Editor

THE PILGRIM PRESS

UNITED CHURCH PRESS
700 Prospect Avenue, East Cleveland, OH 44115-1100
216-736-3764 | fax: 216-736- 2207
www.pilgrimpress.com | e-mail: pilgrim@ucc.org

The Pilgrim Press (founded in 1645 and established in the United States in 1895) is the book publishing banner of the publishing wing of the United Church of Christ.

The house has a tradition of publishing books and other resources that challenge, encourage, and inspire, and are crafted in accordance with fine standards of content, design, and production.

Comprised of two imprints—Pilgrim Press and United Church—Pilgrim's trade motto is: Books at the Nexus of Religion and Culture. The Pilgrim Press is a Christian-related imprint that focuses on three areas: theological ethics (including science, technology, and medicine); human identity, relationships, and sexuality (including feminist and gay/lesbian issues); and activist spirituality (having a social dimension).

Titles indicative of the Pilgrim list include *Equipping the Saint: Best Practices in Contextual Theological Education* edited by David Jenkins and P. Alice Rogers; *Forgiving Yourself: Why You Must, How You Can* by Robert and Jeanette Lauer; *Our Money, Our Values: Building a Just and Sustainable World* by Holley Hewitt Ulbrich and Catherine Mobley; and *Water Bugs and Dragonflies: Explaining Death to Young Children* by Doris Stickney.

UNITED CHURCH PRESS

United Church Press is a Pilgrim imprint geared primarily toward readers of inspirational materials. They publish 50 to 60 new titles each year. Titles from United Church include *Catholics in the United Church of Christ* by J. Mary Luti and Andrew B. Warner; *Affirming Faith: A Confirmand's Journal* by Thomas E. Dipko; and *Theology and Identity: Traditions, Movements, and Polity in the United Church of Christ* by Daniel L. Johnson and Charles E. Hambrick-Stowe.

The Pilgrim Press oversees its own distribution.

See the website for an e-mail submission form. As well, queries may be sent via regular mail with SASE to:

Kim Sadler, Editorial Director

PINNACLE BOOKS [SEE KENSINGTON PUBLISHING]

PLATINUM PRESS [SEE ADAMS MEDIA]

POLKA DOT PRESS [SEE ADAMS MEDIA]

POMEGRANATE COMMUNICATIONS, INC.

775A Southpoint Boulevard, Petaluma, CA 94954-1495
Mailing address:
PO Box 808022, Petaluma, CA 94975-8022
707-782-9000 | 800-227-1428 | fax: 707-782-9810
www.pomegranatecommunications.com | e-mail: info@pomegranate.com

Pomegranate publishes an attractive array of lavish graphic titles and specialty items around subjects such as fine art, architecture, travel, ethnic culture, and crafts. Pomegranate is also among the premier publishers of calendars, posters and poster art, note cards, games, puzzles, specialty sets, and popular topical card decks. The house is located in Northern California.

Pomegranate has its roots in San Francisco's 1960s psychedelic art explosion, when founder Thomas F. Burke distributed posters from the Avalon Ballroom and the Fillmore Auditorium. He worked with seminal poster companies such as East Totem West—two of whose iconic posters, White Rabbit and Cheshire Cat, are still in Pomegranate's line.

Recent titles include *Frank Lloyd Wright's Buffalo Ventures* by Jack Quinan; *Angels and Tomboys: Girlhood in Nineteenth-Century American Art* by Holly Pyne Connor; *American Moderns, 1910-1960: From O'Keeffe to Rockwell* by Karen A. Sherry; *The Osbick Bird* by Edward Gorey; *Thoughtful Alphabets: The Just Dessert & The Deadly Blotter* by Edward Gorey.

E-mail queries are not accepted. Query letters and SASEs should be directed to the Submissions Editor.

Thomas F. Burke, President
Zoe Katherine (Katie) Burke, Publisher

POTOMAC BOOKS, INC.

22841 Quicksilver Drive, Dulles, VA 20166
703-661-1548 | fax: 703-661-1547
www.potomacbooksinc.com | e-mail: pbimail@presswarehouse.com

Founded in 1983 as part of Brassey's Ltd., a distinguished British publishing house dating back to the nineteenth century, Potomac Books was acquired by American book distributor Books International in 1999. With strong roots in military history, Potomac Books has expanded its editorial focus to include general history, world and national affairs, foreign policy, defense and national security, intelligence, memoirs, biographies, and sports. The house publishes 85 new titles per year.

Recent titles include *Long Journey with Mr. Jefferson: The Life of Dumas Malone* by William G. Hyland, Jr.; *Joel Barlow: American Diplomat and Nation Builder* by

Peter P. Hill; *No Stone Unturned: A Father's Memoir of His Son's Encounter with Traumatic Brain Injury* by Joel Goldstein; *Two Pioneers: How Hank Greenberg and Jackie Robinson Transformed Baseball and America* by Robert C. Cottrell.

E-mail submissions can be sent to either Elizabeth Demers or Hilary Claggett. See website for further details. Query letters and proposals with SASEs may be directed to the Editorial Department.

Elizabeth Demers, Editor—History: military and naval, diplomatic, political, and other; current events; international relations; intelligence; security studies; terrorism; and military life; Elizabeth.Demers@booksintl.com

Hilary Claggett, Editor—Politics, public policy, current events, environment energy, media, democracy, and social movements; Hilary.Claggett @booksintl.com

PRAEGER PUBLISHERS [SEE GREENWOOD PUBLISHING GROUP]

PRESBYTERIAN PUBLISHING CORPORATION

GENEVA PRESS
WESTMINSTER JOHN KNOX PRESS
100 Witherspoon Street, Room 2047, Louisville, KY 40202-1396
502-569-5052 | 800-227-2872 | fax: 502-569-5113 | 800-541-5113
www.ppcbooks.com | e-mail: customer_service@presbypub.com

The Presbyterian Publishing Corporation (PPC) is the denominational publisher for the Presbyterian Church (USA), but the materials it issues under its Westminster John Knox Press imprint cover the spectrum of modern religious thought and represent the work of scholarly and popular authors of many different religious affiliations. PPC's Geneva Press imprint is for a specifically Presbyterian audience. The house publishes 95 new books each year and manages a backlist of over 1,600 titles.

For 160 years, PPC and its predecessors have served clergy, scholars, students, and lay people. Most of its publications are used in the spiritual formation of clergy and laity, the training of seminarians, the dissemination of religious scholars' work, and the preparation for ministry of lay church leaders. One of PPC's principal aims is to help readers of its publications achieve biblical and theological literacy. It is a nonprofit corporation, sustained by its sales.

Geneva Press titles include *A Children's Guide to Worship* by Ruth Boling et al; *Making Worship Real* by Aimee Wallis Buchanan et al; *Following Jesus* by Sonja Stewart; and *Come Worship Me* by Ruth Boling and Tracy Carrier.

WESTMINSTER JOHN KNOX PRESS

Westminster John Knox Press (WJK) represents the publications unit of the Presbyterian Church (USA). The house unites the former independents Westminster Press and John Knox Press, which were originally founded as one entity in 1838, then separated into distinct enterprises, and again merged as WJK following the reunion of the Northern and Southern Presbyterian Churches in 1983.

WJK publishes general-interest religious trade books, as well as academic and professional works in biblical studies, theology, philosophy, ethics, history, archaeology, personal growth, and pastoral counseling. Among its series are *Literary Currents in Biblical Interpretation, Family Living in Pastoral Perspective, Gender and the Biblical Tradition*, and the *Presbyterian Presence: The Twentieth-Century Experience*. It has also gained popularity for its unofficial series of "Gospel According to…" books that explore religion and pop culture.

WJK's recent titles include *A Thicker Jesus: Incarnational Discipleship in a Secular Age* by Glen H. Stassen; *An Introduction to Biblical Aramaic* by Andreas Schuele; *Calvin's Theology and Its Reception* by I. John Hesselink and J. Todd Billings; *Don't Stop Believin': Pop Culture and Religion from Ben-Hur to Zombies* by Craig Detweiler, Robert K. Johnston, and Barry Taylor; *God: The Sources of Christian Theology* by Lois Malcolm.

WJK distributes its list through Spring Arbor. The house also represents titles from other publishers, including Orbis Books, Pilgrim Press, Saint Andrew Press of Scotland, and Presbyterian Publishing Corporation.

E-mail queries are fine. Query letters and SASEs should be directed to:

Jana Riess, Acquisitions Editor, jreiss@wjkbooks.com
Don McKim, Theology and Reference Editor, dmckim@wjkbooks.com
Jon Berquist, Editor, jberquist@wjkbooks.com
David Maxwell, Executive Editor (Geneva Press), dmaxwell@wjkbooks.com
David Dobson, Executive Director of Publishing and Editorial

PROFESSIONAL PUBLICATIONS

1250 Fifth Avenue, Belmont, CA 94002
650-593-9119 | 800-426-1178 | fax: 650-592-4519
www.ppi2pass.com | e-mail: acquisitions@ppi2pass.com

Professional Publications (PP), located in Belmont, California, was established as an independent publisher of professional licensing exam review materials in 1975. The house maintains a reputation as a leader in engineering, architecture, and interior design exam review. More than 800,000 exam candidates have used these publications. The mission is simple: to help readers pass their exams.

PP is currently looking for Civil and Structural PEs with code, timber, and bridges expertise.

PP titles include *Civil Engineering Reference Manual for the PE Exam (CERM13)*, 13th Edition by Michael R. Lindeburg, PE; *Nuclear Engineering Solved Problems (NESP2)*, 2nd Edition by John A. Camara, PE; *ARE Schematic Design Passing Zone*; *ARE Site Planning & Design Passing Zone*.

Queries may be directed to acquisitions@ppi2pass.com or to the Acquisitions Editor at the mailing address above.

PROMETHEUS BOOKS

HUMANITY BOOKS
PYR

59 John Glenn Drive, Amherst, NY 14228-2197
716-691-0133 | 800-421-0351 | fax: 716-691-0137
www.prometheusbooks.com | e-mail: editorial@prometheusbooks.com
www.pyrsf.com | Pyr blog: pyrsf.blogspot.com

One of the leading publishers in philosophy, popular science, and critical thinking, Prometheus Books has more than 1,500 books in print and produces an average of 100 new titles each year. Founded in 1969, this house took its name from the courageous Greek god who gave fire to humans, lighting the way to reason, intelligence, and independence, among other things. The house is located near Buffalo, New York.

Among the categories of books published are popular science, science and the paranormal, contemporary issues, social science and current events, children's fiction and nonfiction, history, religion and politics, philosophy, humanism, Islamic studies, Jewish studies, biblical criticism, psychology, women's issues, health, self-help, sexuality, reference, and more. Prometheus also maintains a strong backlist that includes hundreds of established classics in literature, philosophy, and the sciences.

Recent titles from Prometheus include *The Secrets of Triangles: A Mathematical Journey* by Alfred S. Posamentier and Ingmar Lehmann; *The Stardust Revolution: The New Story of Our Origin in the Stars* by Jacob Berkowitz; *That's Not What They Meant! Reclaiming the Founding Fathers from America's Right Wing* by Michael Austin; *Radical Distortion: How Emotions Warp What We Hear* by John W. Reich.

HUMANITY BOOKS

Humanity Books publishes academic works across the humanities. Recent Humanity Books titles include *Citizens of the World: Cosmopolitan Ideals for the 21st Century* edited by Hugh Silverman et al; *Beyond God: Evolution and the Future of Religion* by Kenneth Kardong; *Democracy's Debt: The Historical Tensions Between Political and Economic Liberty* by M. Lane Bruner; and *Culture and Conflict in the Middle East* by Philip Carl Salzman.

PYR

Pyr (the Greek word for fire) publishes science fiction and speculative fiction. Recent titles from Pyr include *The Devoured Earth: Books of the Cataclysm: Four* by Sean Williams; *The Dusk Watchman: Book Five of the Twilight Reign* by Tom Lloyd; *A Guile of Dragons: A Tournament of Shadows Book One* by James Enge; *Reaper* by K. D. McEntire.

Query via regular mail or e-mail (do not send attachments with e-mails).

Steven L. Mitchell, Editor-in-Chief, editorial@prometheusbooks.com

---

QUARRY BOOKS [SEE QUAYSIDE PUBLISHING GROUP]

QUAYSIDE PUBLISHING GROUP

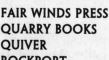

FAIR WINDS PRESS
QUARRY BOOKS
QUIVER
ROCKPORT
33 Commercial Street, Gloucester, MA 01930
978-282-3550
www.quaysidepublishinggroup.com
CREATIVE PUBLISHING INTERNATIONAL
MOTORBOOKS
MVP BOOKS
VOYAGEUR PRESS
400 First Avenue North, Suite 300, Minneapolis, MN 55401
612-344-8100 | 800-328-0590 | fax: 612-344-8691

The Quayside Publishing Group was formed in 2004 upon Rockport Publishers' acquisition of Creative Publishing International. In 2007, Quayside acquired the MBI Publishing Company and its three imprints: Motorbooks, Voyageur Press, and Zenith Press. In 2009, it launched sports and fitness imprint MVP Books.

In 2001, Rockport Publishers launched Fair Winds Press to focus on a wide range of mind, body, and spirit topics that excite readers and help them answer life's fundamental questions. The Quarry Books imprint, launched in 2003, provides practical general reference in categories such as crafts, home style, pet care, and personal improvement. Quiver, launched in 2006, offers titles about sex.

FAIR WINDS PRESS

Fair Winds offers nonfiction books in a range of practical categories, including cooking, health, household hints, fitness, and self-improvement. Fair Winds books are distinguished by their unique approaches to popular subjects, innovative packaging, and dynamic authors.

Recent Fair Winds titles include *365 Winter Warmer Slow Cooker Recipes* by Carol Hildebr, Robert Hildebr, and Suzanne Bonet; *Beat Sugar Addiction Now! for Kids* by Jacob Teitelbaum and Deborah Kennedy; *Fast and Simple Gluten-Free* by Gretchen Brown; *World's Best Cocktails* by Tom Sandham; *Face to Face* by Scott Barnes.

QUARRY BOOKS

Quarry Books provides practical reference in categories such as artisan crafts, home style, pet care, and hobbies. Their books are defined by their full-color photography and illustration and their informative text.

Recent Quarry titles include *The Sweet Book of Candy Making* by Elizabeth LaBau; *Playing with Paper* by Helen Hiebert; *I Just Love Making Things* by Lilla Rogers; *Drawing Comics Lab* by Robyn Chapman; *How to Make Stuffed Animals* by Sian Keegan.

QUIVER

Quiver books are for couples who want to take their sex lives to the next level. Their books feature sex positions, techniques, erotic stories, color photography, kama sutra, and tantra. Their books celebrate erotic pleasure and intimacy through beautiful, sophisticated photography and inspiring text.

Recent Quiver titles include *Hot Sex Tips, Tricks, and Licks* by Jessica O'Reilly; *Sex Games You'll Never Forget* by Beverly Cummings; *365 Sex Moves* by Randi Foxx; *Acrobatic Sex Positions* by Emily Dubberley; *Getting the Sex You Want* by Tammy Nelson.

ROCKPORT

Rockport Publishers creates beautiful illustrated source books for professional designers and artisans of all types. Their books present the best design work from around the world, showing how work gets done, and the inspiration behind the art. Rockport's editors are constantly looking for the newest and most noteworthy trends in the design industry as well as keeping abreast of the best work being done in the traditional areas of commercial design and art.

Recent Rockport titles include *Design/Type: A Seductive Collection of Alluring Type Designs* by Paul Burgess and Tony Seddon; *Writing and Research for Graphic Designers* by Steven Heller; *The Best of Brochure Design 11* by Kiki Eldridge; *Interactive Design* by Andy Pratt and Jason Nunes.

CREATIVE PUBLISHING INTERNATIONAL

Founded in 1969, Creative Publishing International is a worldwide publisher of how-to books. They offer books on home improvement, home decorating, sewing, crafting, hunting, fishing, and photography. Over the past 15 years CPI has developed high-quality photography step-by-step books with nationally recognized brands like Black and Decker and Singer.

Some titles include *Black & Decker Codes for Homeowners* by Bruce Barker; *Building with Secondhand Stuff* by Chris Peterson; *Black & Decker: The Complete Guide to Room Additions* by Chris Peterson; *Upgrade Your House* by Philip Schmidt; *Black & Decker Here's How…Trimwork* by Editors of CPI.

MOTORBOOKS

Motorbooks began in the garage of founder Thomas Warth in 1965, when the automobile aficionado was unable to find quality car, motorcycle, and racing books. It continued to grow and was acquired by the Quayside Publishing Group in 2007.

Some titles include *Dream Garages* by Kris Palmer; *How to Ride Off-Road Motorcycles* by Gary LaPlante; *The Harley in the Barn* by Tom Cotter; *How to Restore and Customize Automotive Interiors* by Dennis W. Parks; *The Chevrolet Small-Block Bible* by Thomas J. Madigan.

MVP BOOKS

Established in 2009, MVP Books is an expansion of the sports category begun under Voyageur Press. Built on a decade of sports publishing experience, their versatile list of books is highlighted by four-color photography and informative, entertaining text, providing high-quality publishing for the sports and fitness enthusiast.

Some recent releases by MVP Books include *The Big Book of Whitetail* by Gary Clancy; *The Ultimate Super Bowl Book* by Bob McGinn; *The Ultimate Book of March Madness* by Tom Hager; *New York Knicks* by Alan Hahn; *New York Giants* by Lew Freedman.

VOYAGEUR PRESS

Since 1972, Voyageur Press has published books and calendars on subjects like nature, science, regional interest, travel, American heritage, country life, crafts, sports, wild animals, pets, and more.

Some titles from Voyageur Press include *Swedish Handknits: A Collection of Heirloom Designs* by Janine Kosel; *Barnyard Confidential: An A to Z Reader of Life Lessons, Tall Tales, and Country Wisdom* by Melinda Keefe; *The Art of Punk* by Russ Bestley and Alex Ogg; *Planet Ink* by Dale Rio; *Neil Young: Long May You Run* by Daniel Durchholz and Gary Graff.

Please see their website for all submission guidelines.

QUIRK BOOKS

215 Church Street, Philadelphia, PA 19106
215-627-3581 | fax: 215-627-5220
www.quirkbooks.com | e-mail: general@quirkbooks.com

Founded by the folks who authored the Worst-Case Scenario franchise, Quirk Books editors seek to be publishers of high-quality irreverence. The mission of this house is to originate, develop, and publish nontraditional and innovative nonfiction books that are objects of desire editorially, graphically, and physically. Quirk also functions as a book packager, developing and selling recent titles to St. Martin's and Potter, among others.

Quirk's recent titles include *Stuff Every American Should Know* by Denise Kiernan and Joseph D'Agnese; *The Cookie Dough Lover's Cookbook* by Lindsay Landis; *Pregnancy Countdown Book: Nine Months of Practical Tips, Useful Advice, and Uncensored Truths* by Kara Nakisbendi, MD, and Susan Magee; *How to Con Your Kid* by David Borgenicht and James Grace; *Marshmallow Madness!* by Shauna Sever.

Direct brief queries to Editorial Submissions via fax, e-mail (submissions @quirkbooks.com), or regular mail with SASE.

Jason Rekulak, Editorial, Submissions, and Design, jason@quirkbooks.com
Margaret McGuire, Editor
Stephen H. Segal, Editor

RED WHEEL/WEISER

CONARI PRESS
WEISER BOOKS
665 Third Street, #400, San Francisco, CA 94107
www.redwheelweiser.com

Red Wheel/Weiser, LLC, is the publisher of Weiser and Conari Press. The house primarily publishes in the category of body/mind/spirit, about 60 books per year among the three imprints.

In 2006, the entire Red Wheel/Weiser Conari editorial department relocated from Boston to San Francisco. At the same time, Red Wheel/Weiser Conari consolidated its Maine operations department and the Boston sales and marketing department moved to a new office in Newburyport, Massachusetts.

CONARI PRESS

Conari Press, founded in 1989 in Berkeley, California, was acquired by Red Wheel/ Weiser in 2002. Conari topics include spirituality, personal growth, parenting, and social issues. Some titles include *No Happy Cows: Dispatches from the Frontlines of the Food Revolution* by John Robbins; *The Yoga Back Book: The Natural Solution to Freedom from Pain* by Stella Weller; *The Insulin Resistance Factor* by Antony J. Haynes; *Stop Eating Your Heart Out: The 21-Day Program to Free Yourself From Emotional Eating* by Meryl Hershey Beck, MA, MEd, LPCC; *Getting Unstuck* by Karen Casey.

WEISER BOOKS

Weiser Books has a long history as one of America's preeminent publishers of esoteric and occult teachings from traditions around the world and throughout time. Areas of Weiser publishing interest include self-transformation, alternative healing methods, meditation, metaphysics, consciousness, magic, astrology, tarot, astral projection, Kabbalah, earth religions, Eastern philosophy and religions, Buddhism, t'ai chi, healing, and Tibetan studies. The publisher specializes in books relating to all facets of the secret and hidden teachings worldwide.

Recent titles from Weiser include *Dowsing Beyond Duality: Access Your Power to Create Positive Change* by David Ian Cowan and Erina Cowan; *The Book of Enoch the Prophet* by Robert Henry Charles; *Live Your Divinity: Inspiration for New Consciousness* by Adamus Saint-Germain; *Quantum Affirmations* by Monte Farber; *Mystery Teachings From the Living Earth: An Introduction to Spiritual Ecology* by John Michael Greer.

Submissions are accepted via regular mail only. For both imprints, query letters, proposals, or manuscripts with SASEs should be directed to:

Caroline Pincus, Editor
Jan Johnson, Publisher
Pat Bryce, Editor

REGNERY

A Division of Eagle Publishing
One Massachusetts Avenue, NW, Washington, DC 20001
202-216-0600 | 888-219-4747 | fax: 202-216-0612
www.regnery.com | e-mail: submissions@regnery.com

Founded in 1947, Regnery has become the country's most popular publisher of books for conservatives. Regnery publishes books in the fields of current affairs, politics, history, culture, and biography.

In 1993 Regnery became part of the newly founded Eagle Publishing, which also includes *Human Events*, the national conservative weekly; the Conservative Book Club; and the Evans & Novak Political Report.

Recent titles include *The Great Destroyer* by David Limbaugh; *Defending the Free*

Market by Robert A. Sirico; *The Amateur* by Edward Klein; *Marked for Death* by Geert Wilders; *Fast and Furious* by Katie Pavlich.

Regnery only accepts manuscripts and proposals submitted by agents.

Marjory Ross, Publisher

FLEMING H. REVELL [SEE BAKER PUBLISHING GROUP]

RIZZOLI, USA

UNIVERSE INTERNATIONAL PUBLICATIONS

A Division of RCS Media Group, Italy

300 Park Avenue South, 3rd Floor, New York, NY 10010

212-387-3400 | fax: 212-387-3535

www.rizzoliusa.com | e-mail: submissions@rizzoliusa.com

Rizzoli began its New York operations in 1974 as an integral part of its parent company, the Italian communications giant, RCS Media Group. The house is a leader in illustrated books in the fields of art, architecture, interior design, photography, haute couture, and gastronomy. In 1990, Rizzoli added the Universe imprint, marking Rizzoli's entrée into the pop-culture worlds of humor, fashion, beauty, sports, performing arts, and gay and alternative lifestyles. It also contributed a successful calendar program and published economical versions of Rizzoli books.

Under the direction of Senior Editor Robb Pearlman, who joined the company in 2006, the company plans to expand its children's book and calendar lines.

Recent Rizzoli titles include *101 Classic Cookbooks* by The Fales Library; *1001 Dream Cars You Must Drive Before You Die* by Simon Heptinstall; *12 Days of Christmas in New York* by Michael Storrings; *A Third Decade of Guess Images* by Paul Marciano; *African Art* by Ezio Bassani.

Rizzoli titles are distributed through St. Martin's Press.

Rizzoli does accept unsolicited proposals. E-mail proposals can be sent to submissions@rizzoliusa.com. All queries with SASEs should be directed to Editorial Submissions.

Charles Miers, Publisher

Robb Pearlman, Senior Editor—Children's books, calendars, licensing.

RODALE, INC.

33 East Minor Street, Emmaus, PA 18098-0099

610-967-5171 | fax: 610-967-8963

New York address:
733 Third Avenue, 15th Floor, New York, NY 10017-3204
212-697-2040 | fax: 212-682-2237
www.rodale.com | e-mail: reader_service@rodale.com

Rodale publishes acclaimed nonfiction books on health, fitness, cooking, gardening, spirituality, self-help, nature, and more. Recent *New York Times* best sellers include Al Gore's *An Inconvenient Truth*; *The Abs Diet for Women* by David Zinczenko; *LL Cool J's Platinum Workout* by LL Cool J; *The South Beach Heart Program* by Arthur Agaston; and *Joy Bauer's Food Cures* by Joy Bauer.

Rodale Books has also been developing titles in new genres including memoirs, biographies, narrative nonfiction, self-help, science and nature, psychology, current events, and personal finance.

Recent titles include *The Belly Melt Diet™: The 6-Week Plan to Harness Your Body's Natural Rhythms to Lose Weight for Good!* by The Editors of Prevention; *The Organic Food Handbook* by Ken Roseboro; *Winter Gardening in the Maritime Northwest: Cool Season Crops for the Year-Round Gardener* by Binda Colebrook; *Onward: How Starbucks Fought for Its Life without Losing Its Soul* by Howard Schultz and Joanne Gordon; *Get It, Understand It: Get Ahead Companion Workbook* by James Taylor.

Please send proposals and SASEs to the editors via regular mail (NY) or e-mail at bookproposals@rodale.com.

Ursula Cary, Editor
Alex Postman, Editor
Mark Weinstein, Executive Editor

ROUTLEDGE

An Imprint of Taylor and Francis Books
711 3rd Avenue, 8th Floor, New York, NY 10017, USA
212-216-7800 | fax: 212-563-2269
www.routledge-ny.com

Routledge produces adult nonfiction for the trade and academic markets. The house produces titles in the humanities and social sciences with more specific focus on current events, communications, media, cultural studies, education, self-improvement, world political studies, philosophy, economics, feminist theory, gender studies, history, and literary criticism. Routledge is an imprint of the Taylor and Francis Group.

Recent titles include *Critical Realism* by Roy Bhaskar; *Debates in Modern Philosophy* by Stewart Duncan and Antonia LoLordo; *Bible and Cinema: Fifty Key Films* by Adele Reinhartz; *The Buddhist World* by John Powers; *Authoring the Past: Writing and Rethinking History* by Alun Munslow.

See the website for submission guidelines. Send your proposal with SASE via regular mail to the Editorial Department; your proposal will be forwarded to the appropriate editor.

Michael Kerns—Politics.
Catherine Bernard—Education.
Matthew Byrnie—Media studies, communications, literature, cultural studies.
Kimberly Guinta—History.
Constance Ditzel—Music.

ROWMAN & LITTLEFIELD PUBLISHING GROUP

ALTAMIRA
HAMILTON BOOKS
JASON ARONSON, INC., PUBLISHERS
LEXINGTON BOOKS
SCARECROW PRESS
SHEED & WARD
UNIVERSITY PRESS OF AMERICA
4501 Forbes Boulevard, Suite 200, Lanham, MD 20706
301-459-3366 | fax: 301-429-5748
www.rowmanlittlefield.com
www.hamiltonbooks.com
www.lexingtonbooks.com
www.univpress.com
New York office:
200 Park Avenue South, Suite 1109, New York, NY 10003
212-529-3888 | fax: 212-529-4223
   M. EVANS
   TAYLOR TRADE
5360 Manhattan Circle, #100, Boulder, CO 80303
www.rlpgtrade.com | e-mail: tradeeditorial@rowman.com
   IVAN R. DEE, PUBLISHER
   NEW AMSTERDAM BOOKS
   J. S. SANDERS
1332 North Halsted Street, Chicago, IL, 60622-2694
312-787-6262 | fax: 312-787-6269
www.ivanrdee.com | e-mail: elephant@ivanrdee.com

The Rowman & Littlefield Publishing Group (RLPG) is one of the largest and fastest-growing independent publishers and distributors in North America. The company publishes more than 20 imprints in virtually all fields in the humanities and social sciences for the academic and trade markets. Rowman & Littlefield also owns National Book Network, which is North America's second-largest distributor of independent trade book publishers. NBN recently created two new divisions: Biblio Distribution for small trade publishers and FaithWorks for CBA publishers.

RLPG built its list quickly by acquiring small companies and niche publishers, especially over the past five years. These have been either merged into existing imprints or have continued to exist as stand-alone RLPG imprints.

Rowman & Littlefield is an independent press devoted to publishing scholarly books in the best tradition of university presses; innovative, thought-provoking texts for college courses; and crossover trade books intended to convey scholarly trends to an educated readership.

Recent titles include *Anthropology and Contemporary Human Problems*, 6th Edition by John H. Badley; *Introducing Medical Anthropology*, 2nd Edition by Merrill Singer and Hans Baer; *Hopelessly Divided: The New Crisis in American Politics and What it Means for 2012 and Beyond* by Douglas E. Schoen.

An academic or scholarly author would do well to explore online the various RLPG imprints, or to query this publisher for guidelines. To submit to Rowman & Littlefield, direct your query to the appropriate editor:

Jonathan Sisk, Senior Editor (MD)—American government, philosophy, political theory, public policy; jsisk@rowmanlittlefield.com

Jack Meinhardt, Acquisitions Editor (MD)—Anthropology, archaeology, Smithsonian Institution Scholarly Press; jmeinhardt@rowman.com

Sarah Stanton, Associate Editor (MD)—Sociology, religion, Cowley Publications; sstanton@rowman.com

Suzanne Staszak-Silva, Senior Editor (MD)—Crime/criminal justice, health, psychology; sstaszak-silva@rowman.com

Patti Belcher, Acquisitions Editor for Education, ACE and AERA

ALTAMIRA

AltaMira Press exists to disseminate high-quality information to those who research, study, practice, and read the humanities and social sciences, with a particular focus on helping in the professional development of those who work in the cultural life of a community—the museum, historical society, arts center, and church. They are a preeminent publisher in the field of archaeology, and also publish in anthropology, Asian American studies, Native American studies, and comparative religion. AltaMira welcomes submissions from prospective authors.

Some titles include *Three World Cuisines: Italian, Mexican, and Chinese* by Ken Albala and *Appetites and Aspirations in Vietnam: Food and Drink in the Long Nineteenth Century* by Erica J. Peters.

HAMILTON BOOKS

Hamilton Books was launched as a new imprint of the Rowman and Littlefield Publishing Group in 2003. Potential authors include corporate leaders, politicians, scholars, war veterans, and family historians. Their publishing program is based on an alternative model, where the author is offered a contract that specifies a quantity for pre-publication purchase by the author to share a portion of up-front production expenses. Hamilton covers the costs of all copies beyond the initial order, no matter what the quantity.

Some titles include *Lurps: A Ranger's Diary of Tet, Khe Sanh, A Shau, and Quang Tri*, Revised Edition by Robert C. Ankony; *Objectivism in One Lesson: An Introduction to the Philosophy of Ayn Rand* by Andrew Bernstein; and *What's The Beef? Sixty Years of Hard-Won Lessons for Today's Leaders in Labor, Management, and Government* by Wayne L. Horvitz.

JASON ARONSON, INC., PUBLISHERS

Jason Aronson is the publisher of highly regarded psychotherapy and Judaica books. Dedicated to publishing professional, scholarly works, their list of Judaica authors spans the entire spectrum of approaches to Jewish tradition: Orthodox, Hasidic, Reconstructionist, Reform, Conservative, Renewal, unaffiliated, and secular. Topics include anti-Semitism, Baal Shem Tov, classics in translation, family, folklore and storytelling, Gematria, Hasidism, history, holidays, Holocaust, Israel, Jewish law, Kabbalah, Maimonides, marriage, meditation, prayer, Talmud, theology, Torah, travel, women's studies, and more.

In the subject of psychotherapy, Jason Aronson, Inc., offers more titles from a broader range of psychotherapists than any other publisher. Topics include child therapy, family therapy, eating disorders, substance abuse, short-term therapy, bereavement, stress, trauma, object relations therapy, personality disorder, depression, couples therapy, sexual abuse, play therapy, psychoanalysis, psychology, transference, and more.

Some titles include *Working With Trauma: Lessons from Bion and Lacan* by Marilyn Charles; *Stress Response Syndromes: PTSD, Grief…*, 5th Edition by Mardi J. Horowitz; *Outsmarting the Riptide of Sometic Violence* by Pat Pernicano; *The Impact of Complex Trauma on Development* by Cheryl Arnold and Ralph Fisch; *Dynamic Psychotherapy with Adult Survivors: Living Past Neglect* by Lori Bennett.

Send proposal with CV and SASE to:

Arthur T. Pomponio, Editorial Director for Jason Aronson (NY), apomponio @rowman.com

Mary Catherine La Mar, Acquisitions Editor for Jason Aronson (NY), mlamae@rowman.com

LEXINGTON BOOKS

Lexington Books is Rowman & Littlefield's division for publishing specialized new work by established and emerging scholars. Lexington publishes high-quality scholarly work that may not have a wide audience but makes a substantial contribution to scholarship in particular and related fields.

Lexington welcomes proposals in the fields of Africana studies, American history, American studies, anthropology, archaeology, Asian studies, cultural studies, geography, history, international relations, literary criticism, Middle East studies, philosophy, political science, political theory, public policy, religion, and sociology.

Some titles include *A Delaware Album, 1900-1930* by George Miller; *Taking Socialism Seriously* by Richard Schmitt and Anatole Anton; *Philosophy in Children's Literature* by Peter R. Costello; *The Commercial Church: Black Churches and the New Religious Marketplace in America* by Mary Hinton; *Waiving Our Rights: The Personal Data Collection and Its Threat to Privacy and Civil Liberties* by Orlan Lee.

SCARECROW PRESS

Scarecrow Press was purchased by R&L in 1995 and is known for its scholarly bibliographies, historical dictionaries, library science, and reference working in the humanities, particularly music and film. It is broadening its to include textbooks in library and information science, new series that address the technological frontiers of the profession, handbooks for librarians serving children, and a greater scope of materials in music.

Some titles include *Leaving Home: A Hollywood Blacklisted Writer's Years Abroad* by Anne Edwards; *Out of the Canon: Expanding the Canon of Classic Film Noir* by Gene D. Phillips; *Building Blocks for Planning Functional Library Space*, 3rd Edition by The American Library Association; *Preserving Local Writers, Geneology, Photographs, Newspapers, and Related Materials* by Carol Smallwood and Elaine S. Williams; *Encyclopedia of National Anthems*, 2nd Edition (2 Volumes) by Xing Hang.

SHEED & WARD

Founded in 1926 by Australian lawyer Francis Joseph Sheed and his British wife Maisie Ward, Sheed & Ward is one of the most eminent Catholic publishing houses in the world today. Some of their titles include *The Gospel of Cesar Chavez: My Faith in Action* by Mario T. Garcia; *Before I Go: Letters to Our Children about What Really Matters* by Peter Kreeft; and *The Genius of Pope John Paul II: The Great Pope's Moral Wisdom* by Richard A. Spinello.

UNIVERSITY PRESS OF AMERICA

The University Press of America is an academic publisher committed to the belief that the most important question relevant to the publication decision is: Does this work provide a significant contribution to scholarship?

The UPA publishes works across disciplines as various as African American studies, African studies, American history, American literature, anthropology, art history, Asian studies, biblical studies, Catholicism, classics, communications, criminology, Eastern European studies, economics, education, ethics, GLBT studies, gender studies, geography, history, international studies, Jewish studies, language studies, Latin American studies, legal studies, literary studies, marketing, minority studies, organization, peace and conflict studies, philosophy, political science, psychology, public health, religious studies, sociology, US public policy, and world history.

Some titles include *Pearl of Great Price: A Literary Translation of the Middle English Pearl* by David Gould; *Wild Socialism: Workers Councils in Revolutionary Berlin, 1918-21* by Martin Comack; *C.D. Jackson: Cold War Propagandist for Democracy and Globalism* by John Allen Stern; *The Poverty of Nations* by Robert J. Tata.

Prospective authors can visit their website to view the proposal questionnaire.

M. EVANS

Recently acquired by Rowman & Littlefield, M. Evans and Company, Inc., has been publishing thought-provoking titles with a clear, constantly honed commercial focus in its favored market niches for over 40 years. M. Evans has become an imprint of Taylor Trade, with editorial operations in Colorado, as well.

The M. Evans front list features high-profile offerings in topical issues, investigative stories in politics, business, and entertainment, and popular biography. The core Evans program accents popular nonfiction books, primarily self-help related, in the areas of health and fitness, human relationships, business and finance, and lifestyle and cuisine.

Recent M. Evans titles include *The Essential Guide to Hysterectomy*, 2nd Edition by Lauren F. Streicher, MD; *Muhammad Ali's Greatest Fight: Cassius Clay vs. the United States of America* by Howard Bingham and Max Wallace; *Sex So Great She Can't Get Enough* by Barbara Keesling.

Query letters and SASEs should be directed to the Editorial Department; e-mail generates the quickest response. If querying by e-mail, note "Book Proposal" in the subject line.

Rick Rinehart, Editorial Director, rrinehart@rowman.com
Dulcie Wilcox, Acquisitions Editor, dwilcox@rowman.com

TAYLOR TRADE

The Taylor Trade Publishing program consists of an award-winning list of books on gardening, health, history, family issues, sports, entertainment, nature, field guides, house and home, cooking, Texana/Western history, and children's titles. Taylor Trade operates out of Boulder, Colorado.

Recent Taylor titles include *Mill Reef Style* by Elizabeth Ballantine and Stephen S. Lash; *Houses of Mexico* by Verna Cook Shipway and Warren Shipway; *Adobe, Homes and Interiors...* by Sandra Seth and Laurel Seth; *Spanish Colonial or Adobe Architecture of California 1800-1850* by Donald R. Hannaford and Revel Edwards; *Early Reagan* by Anne Edwards.

IVAN R. DEE, PUBLISHER

Ivan R. Dee publishes serious nonfiction trade books in history, politics, biography, literature, philosophy, and theater. Similar to Basic Books and the Free Press in their heyday, Ivan R. Dee produces books that are provocative, controversial, and aimed at the intelligent layperson. They are routinely reviewed in the *New York Times*, the *Washington Post*, the *New York Review of Books*, and other influential publications. Ivan R. Dee paperbacks are also used extensively in college courses as supplementary reading.

Founded in 1988 by Ivan Dee, the house was acquired in 1998 by the Rowman & Littlefield Publishing Group. Ivan Dee continues as publisher in the company's Chicago headquarters.

Some titles include *The Founders' Second Amendment: Origins of the Right to Bear Arms* by Stephen P. Halbrook; *Rethinking Kennedy: An Interpretive Biography* by Michael O'Brien; *Pay to Play: How Rod Blagojevich Turned Political Corruption into a National Sideshow* by Elizabeth Brackett; and *No Sense of Decency: The Army-McCarthy Hearings* by Robert Shogan.

NEW AMSTERDAM BOOKS

New Amsterdam Books, an imprint of Ivan R. Dee, Publisher, publishes distinguished books for the serious general reader. Highlights include art and art history, fiction in translation, theater, Scottish studies, Victorian studies, religion, and history. New Amsterdam Books is not currently accepting submissions.

Some titles are *Broken April* by Ismail Kadare; *Understanding Design* by Kees Dorst; and *The Immortal Dinner: A Famous Evening of Genius and Laughter in Literature* by Penelope Hughes-Hallett.

J. S. SANDERS

J. S. Sanders & Company, an imprint of Ivan R. Dee, Publisher, was founded by John Sanders of Nashville, Tennessee, to publish and republish general trade books on Southern culture, history, and literature, including the Southern Classics series, which "restores to our awareness some of the South's most important writers of the nineteenth and twentieth centuries" (Hudson Review). Many classic novels about the South, as well as histories and biographies of the region and its leaders, are still in print today thanks to J. S. Sanders. J. S. Sanders is not currently accepting submissions.

Some titles include *Nashville 1864* by Madison Jones; *The War the Women Lived* by Walter Sullivan; *Bedford Forrest and His Critter Company* by Andrew Nelson Lyte; and *John Brown: The Making of a Martyr* by Robert Penn Warren.

J. S. SANDERS [SEE ROWMAN & LITTLEFIELD]

SASQUATCH BOOKS

1904 Third Ave., Suite 710, Seattle, WA 98101
206-467-4300 | 800-775-0817 | fax: 206-467-4301
www.sasquatchbooks.com

Sasquatch Books is one of the nation's premier regional presses, with titles for and about the Pacific Northwest, Alaska, and California. Founded in 1986, Sasquatch's publishing program celebrates regionally written works. Their top-selling Best Places travel guides serve the most popular destinations and locations of the West. Sasquatch also publishes widely in the subjects of food, wine, gardening, nature, photography, children's books, and regional history. With more than 200 books on the West, this house offers an exploration of the lifestyle, landscape, and worldview of its region.

Some titles include *The Creaky Knees Guide Oregon* by Seabury Blair, Jr.; *Larry Gets Lost in San Francisco* by John Skewes; *Swirl, Sip & Savor: Northwest Wine and Small Plate Pairings* by Carol Frieberg; *Pugetopolis: A Mossback Takes on Growth Addicts, Weather Wimps, and the Myth of Seattle Nice* by Knute Berger; and *The Collector: David Douglas and the Natural History of the Northwest* by Jack Nisbet.

E-mail queries are not accepted at this time. Submit a query, proposal, or complete manuscript to the Acquisitions Department.

Gary Luke, President and Publisher
Terence Maikels, Acquisitions Editor

SCHOLASTIC, INC.

ARTHUR A. LEVINE BOOKS
THE BLUE SKY PRESS
CARTWHEEL BOOKS
557 Broadway, New York, NY 10012
212-343-6100
www.scholastic.com
CHICKEN SOCKS
KLUTZ
KLUTZ LATINO
450 Lambert Avenue, Palo Alto, CA 94306
650-857-0888 | 800-737-4123
www.klutz.com | e-mail: thefolks@klutz.com

Scholastic is a global children's publishing and media company and is the United States' largest publisher and distributor of children's books. Recognizing that literacy is the cornerstone of a child's intellectual, personal, and cultural growth, Scholastic creates quality products and services that educate, entertain, and motivate children, and are designed to help enlarge their understanding of the world around them.

Scholastic publishes over 750 new books each year. The list includes *Harry Potter, Captain Underpants, Clifford the Big Red Dog, I Spy,* and *The Magic Schoolbus.* Best-selling titles include *How Do Dinosaurs Say Goodnight?, No, David!, Inkheart, Charlie Bone, Chasing Vermeer,* and *The Day My Butt Went Psycho.*

Scholastic imprints include Scholastic Press, Arthur A. Levine Books, Cartwheel Books, and The Blue Sky Press. Scholastic acquired Klutz (see below) five years ago.

Scholastic Library Publishing is a leading provider of print and online reference products for school and public libraries, with a broad array of products through its well-known Grolier, Children's Press, Franklin Watts, and Grolier Online imprints.

Recent titles include *Captain Underpants and the Terrifying Return of Tippy Tinkletrousers* by Dav Pilkey; *The Raven Boys* by Maggie Stiefvater; *Diary of a Wimpy Kid 7: The Third Wheel* by Jeff Kinney; *Fancy Nancy's Fabulously Fancy Treasury* by Jane O'Connor; *I Am Number Four: The Lost Files, The Legacies* by Pittacus Lore.

ARTHUR A. LEVINE BOOKS

Arthur A. Levine Books was founded at Scholastic, Inc., in 1996, publishing their first book, *When She Was Good* by Norma Fox Mazer, in the fall of 1997. Since then, they publish a small high-quality list of hardcover literary fiction, picture books, and nonfiction for children and teenagers.

Some of their titles include *Absolutely Maybe* by Lisa Yee; *Marcelo in the Real World* by Francisco X. Stork; and *Tales from Outer Suburbia* by Shaun Tan.

THE BLUE SKY PRESS

The Blue Sky Press publishes picture books and chapter books for grade schoolers. Some titles from The Blue Sky Press include *Our Abe Lincoln* by Jim Aylesworth; *Living Sunlight: How Plants Bring the Earth to Life* by Molly Bang and Penny Chisholm; *Dumb Bunnies' Easter* by Dav Piley; and *Book of Love for Mothers and Sons* by Rob D. Walker.

CARTWHEEL BOOKS

Cartwheel Books publishes picture books for toddlers. Some titles from Cartwheel Books include *Bedtime Kiss for Little Fish* by Lorie Ann Grover; *Don't Lose Your Shoes!* by Elizabeth Mills; *Lily's Twinkly Bedtime* by Katie Peters; and *What Do You See?* by Reyna Lindert.

Scholastic considers submissions from agents or previously published authors. Arthur A. Levine considers queries from everyone. Submissions and SASEs should be directed to David Saylor.

Arthur A. Levine, Vice President and Editorial Director (Arthur A. Levine Books)
David Levitan, Editor

Abby McAden, Editor
Nick Eliopulos, Editor
Brenda Murray, Editor

KLUTZ

Based in Palo Alto, California, Klutz is the creator of kids' activity products including books, kits, toys, and other kids' stuff that stimulate their growth through creativity. Klutz products combine clear instructions with everything you need to give kids a hands-on learning experience that ranges from the artistic to the scientific, and beyond. Founded in 1977 by three Stanford students, Klutz was purchased by Scholastic in 2002, but maintains editorial offices in California's Silicon Valley. Klutz makes cool stuff; their credo is: create wonderful things, be good, have fun.

Imprints include Klutz Latino (Spanish language) and Chicken Socks (for readers ages four to eight).

Recent titles include *The Super Scissors Book* by the Editors of Klutz; *Castle Fold Out* by the Editors of Klutz; *Boom Splat Kablooey* by the Editors of Klutz; *Klutz Build-a-Book: My Really Good Friends* by the Editors of Klutz.

Query with SASE to:
John Cassidy, Founder and Chief Creative Officer

SEAL PRESS [SEE PERSEUS BOOKS GROUP]

SELF-COUNSEL PRESS

4152 Meridian Street Suite 105-471, Bellingham, WA 98226
360-676-4530 | 800-663-3007 | fax: 360-676-4549
www.self-counsel.com | e-mail: orderdesk@self-counsel.com
Vancouver editorial office:
1481 Charlotte Road, North Vancouver, BC V7J 1H1, Canada
604-986-3366 | 800-663-3007 | fax: 604-986-3947

A pioneer in the self-help law titles in North America, Self-Counsel Press published its first divorce guide in 1971. Self-Counsel produces business how-to, legal reference, self-help, and practical psychology books. Topical areas include entrepreneurship, the legal system, business training, the family, and human resources development and management. The house also produces titles geared to lifestyles and business and legal issues in Florida, Oregon, and Washington.

The house tries to anticipate a need for basic, understandable information and fill that need by publishing an informative, clearly written, and reasonably priced how-to book for the layperson. They publish as many as 30 new titles each year, as well as revising more than 50 of their backlist titles to ensure that their books are always up to date regarding changes in legislation or current procedures and practices. All legal titles are authored by lawyers.

Some titles include *A Canadian's Best Tax Haven: The US* by Robert Keats; *Estate Planning for the Blended Family* by L. Paul Hood, Jr., and Emily Bouchard; *Start & Run a Pet Business* by Heather Mueller; *Writing Screenplays* by Jessie Coleman and Paul Peditto; *Your First Home: A Buyer's Kit* by Kimberley Marr.

E-mail queries can be sent to orders@self-counsel.com. Direct physical proposals and SASEs to the Acquisitions Editor in either Canada or the United States, depending on the market for which you are writing.

Diana Douglas, President, ddouglas@self-counsel.com

SEVEN STORIES

SIETE CUENTOS
140 Watts Street, New York, NY 10013
212-226-8760 | fax: 212-226-1411
www.sevenstories.com | e-mail: info@sevenstories.com

Seven Stories Press is an independent book publisher based in New York City, with distribution throughout the United States, Canada, England, Australia, and New Zealand. Under the direction of publisher Dan Simon, perhaps no other small independent house in America has consistently attracted so many important voices away from the corporate publishing sector.

Authors include Nelson Algren, Kate Braverman, Octavia Butler, Harriet Scott Chessman, Assia Djebar, Ariel Dorfman, Martin Duberman, Alan Dugan, Annie Ernaux, Barry Gifford, Stanley Moss, Peter Plate, Charley Rosen, Ted Solotaroff, Lee Stringer, Alice Walker, Martin Winckler, and Kurt Vonnegut, together with political titles by voices of conscience, including Daw Aung San Suu Kyi, Tom Athanasiou, the Boston Women's Health Book Collective, the Center for Constitutional Rights, Fairness & Accuracy in Reporting, Noam Chomsky, Angela Davis, Shere Hite, Robert McChesney, Phil Jackson, Ralph Nader, Gary Null, Benjamin Pogrund, Project Censored, Luis J. Rodriguez, Barbara Seaman, Vandana Shiva, Leora Tanenbaum, Koigi wa Wamwere, Gary Webb, and Howard Zinn.

On several notable occasions, Seven Stories has stepped in to publish—on First Amendment grounds—important books that were being refused the right to publish for political reasons, including Pulitzer Prize-winning journalist Gary Webb's *Dark Alliance*, about the CIA-Contra-crack cocaine connection; Carol Felsenthal's biography of the Newhouse family, *Citizen Newhouse*; and distinguished journalist and death row inmate Mumia Abu-Jamal's censored essays in *All Things Censored*.

Recent Seven Stories titles include *Billionaires & Ballot Bandits: Election Games 2012* by Greg Palast; *Live Through This: On Creativity and Self Destruction*, 2nd Edition by Sabrina Chap; *Ma, He Sold Me for a Few Cigarettes: A Memoir of Dublin in the 1950s* by Martha Long; *The Rich Don't Always Win: The Forgotten Triumph over Plutocracy that Created the American Middle Class* by Sam Pizzigati; *Meme Wars: The Creative Destruction of Neoclassical Economics* by Kalle Lasn.

SIETE CUENTOS

Siete Cuentos, Seven Stories' Spanish-language imprint, launched in 2000 and now edited by Sara Villa, represents a major ongoing effort on the part of Seven Stories to introduce important English-language texts to Spanish-language readers on the one hand—for example the Spanish-language editions of *Our Bodies, Ourselves, Nuestros cuerpos, nuestras vidas*, a project of the Boston Women's Health Book Collective and Howard Zinn's *A People's History of the United States, La otra historia de los Estados Unidos*—and on the other hand to provide Spanish-language readers in the United States with the best in fiction and literature written in Spanish. The literary side of Siete Cuentos has published new and classic texts by Ariel Dorfman, including *Death and the Maiden, La muerte y la doncella* and *Heading South, Looking North, Rumbo al sur, deseando el norte*, and new fiction by Ángela Vallvey and Sonia Rivera-Valdés.

Titles from Siete Cuentos include *11 de Septiembre* by Noam Chomsky; *A la caza del ultimo hombre salvaje* by Angela Vallvey; *La muerte y la doncella* by Ariel Dorfman; and *Nuestros cuerpos, nuestras vidas* by the Boston Women's Health Book Collective.

Seven Stories is accepting submissions of query letters with one or two sample chapters only. Direct your submission to Acquisitions.

Dan Simon, Publisher

SHAMBHALA

NEW SEEDS
TRUMPETER BOOKS
WEATHERHILL BOOKS
PO Box 308, Boston, MA 02115
617-424-0030 | fax: 617-236-1563
www.shambhala.com | e-mail: editors@shambhala.com

With classic titles like *Meditation in Action* by Chögyam Trungpa, *Writing Down the Bones* by Natalie Goldberg, and *The Tao of Physics* by Fritjof Capra, Shambhala is a foremost representative of the wave of publishers specializing in the arena of contemporary globalized spiritual and cultural interest. Since Shambhala's inception (the house was founded in 1969), the field has blossomed into a still-burgeoning readership, as underscored by the many smaller independent presses and large corporate houses that tend this market. Yet Shambhala quietly continues to publish "what's real and not the glitz."

Shambhala publishes hardcover and paperback titles on creativity, philosophy, psychology, medical arts and healing, mythology, folklore, religion, art, literature, cooking, martial arts, and cultural studies. Shambhala generally issues a modest list of new titles each year and tends a flourishing backlist; the house periodically updates some of its perennial sellers in revised editions.

Shambhala produces a number of distinct lines, including gift editions and special-interest imprints. Shambhala Dragon Editions accents the sacred teachings of Asian masters. Shambhala Centaur Editions offers classics of world literature in small-sized gift editions. The New Science Library concentrates on titles relating to science, technology, and the environment. Shambhala copublishes C. G. Jung Foundation Books with the C. G. Jung Foundation for Analytical Psychology. Shambhala Redstone Editions are fine-boxed sets composed of books, postcards, games, art objects, and foldouts. Shambhala Lion Editions are spoken-word DVD presentations. New Seeds publishes such Christian mystics as Thomas Merton; Trumpeter Books publishes humanistic titles with mainstream marketability. Integral Books, an imprint with author Ken Wilber as editorial director, was launched in 2007. Shambhala purchased Weatherhill in 2004, giving it the classic *Zen Mind, Beginner's Mind* by Japanese Zen master Shunryu Suzuki.

Recent titles from Shambhala include *The Heart Is Noble: Changing the World from the Inside Out* by Ogyen Trinley Dorje the Karmapa; *Twenty Poems to Bless Your Marriage And One to Save It* by Roger Housden; *The Book of Five Rings: A Graphic Novel* by Miyamoto Musashi and Sean Michael Wilson; *Hunger Mountain: A Field Guide to Mind and Landscape* by David Hinton; *Restoring Your Life Energy: Simple Chi Gung Practices to Reduce Stress and Enhance Well-Being* by Waysun Liao.

NEW SEEDS

New Seeds is a new imprint dedicated to publishing books that present the wisdom of the Christian faith for everyone—with a special emphasis on prayer and contemplation. Some new titles include *Where God Happens: Discovering Christ in One Another* by Rowan Williams; *The Practice of the Presence of God* by Brother Lawrence; and *No Man Is an Island* by Thomas Merton.

TRUMPETER BOOKS

Trumpeter Books is a new imprint from Shambhala covering a broad range of topics and genres—including psychology, health, literature, and personal growth—all aimed at nourishing and celebrating our positive human potential. Some titles include *The Autism Mom's Survival Guide* (for dads, too!) by Susan Senator; *Beyond the Abbey Gates* by Catherine MacCoun; *Black Elk in Paris* by Kate Horsley; *Climbing Jacob's Ladder: One Man's Journey to Rediscover a Jewish Spiritual Tradition* by Alan Morinis; and *The Creative Family: How to Encourage Imagination and Nurture Family Connections* by Amanda Blake Soule.

WEATHERHILL BOOKS

Weatherhill specializes in books on art, martial arts, and Eastern culture. Shambhala purchased Weatherhill and its backlist of 150 titles in 2004. Some Weatherhill titles are *77 Dances: Japanese Calligraphy by Poets, Monks, and Scholars 1568–1868* by Stephen Addiss; *The Art of Ancient India* by John Huntington et al; and *The Art of Ground Fighting: Principles and Techniques* by Marc Tedeschi.

Shambhala distributes to the trade via Random House and also services individual and special orders through its own house fulfillment department.

Proposals and SASEs should be directed to the Editorial Assistant, James Rudnickas. E-mail submissions can go to customerservice@shambhala.com.

Sara Bercholtz, Vice President
Emily Bower, Editor, Trumpeter Books
Beth Frankl, Editor
Julie Saidenberg, Editor
Nikko Odiseos, Editor
Rochelle Bourgault, Editor

M. E. SHARPE

EAST GATE BOOKS
SHARPE REFERENCE
80 Business Park Drive, Armonk, NY 10504
914-273-1800 | 800-541-6563 | fax: 914-273-2106

Founded in 1958, M. E. Sharpe is a privately held publisher of books and journals in the social sciences and humanities, including economics, political science, management, public administration, and history. It also publishes both original works and translations in Asian and East European studies. Several Nobel Prize winners, including Ōe Kenzaburo and Wasily Leontief, are among the M. E. Sharpe authors.

The East Gate imprint publishes in Asian studies. M. E. Sharpe also publishes single- and multivolume reference works designed to meet the needs of students and researchers from high school through college under the Sharpe Reference imprint.

Recent titles include *The Foreign Policy of Russia: Changing Systems, Enduring Interests* by Robert Donaldson and Joseph Nogee; *Handbook of Urban Services: A Basic Guide for Local Governments* by Charles K. Coe; *Dagestan: Russian Hegemony and Islamic Resistance in the North Caucasus* by Robert Ware and Enver Kisriev; and *Entrepreneurial Financial Management: An Applied Approach* by Jeffery Cornwall et al.

EAST GATE BOOKS

The East Gate Books imprint is dedicated to the publication of works that lead to a greater understanding of Asia and its peoples. It represents the best in Asian Studies publishing by scholars, students, and general interest audiences. Recent titles include *Christianity in China: A Scholars' Guide to Resources in the Libraries* by Xiaoxin Wu; *End of the Maoist Era: Chinese Politics During the Twilight of Cultural Revolution 1972–1976* by Frederick Teiwes and Warren Sun; and *Modern East Asia: An Introductory History* by John H. Miller.

SHARPE REFERENCE

Sharpe Reference was created to meet the needs of students and researchers in the high school, public, and college library. Their books provide easy access to a broad array of curriculum-related information in the social sciences and humanities; music, art, history, politics, and civil rights are among the fields covered.

Some titles include *Global Social Issues: An Encyclopedia* by Christopher G. Bates, and James Ciment; *Native Peoples of the World: An Encyclopedia of Groups, Cultures, and Contemporary Issues* by Steven Danver; *World Food: An Encyclopedia of History, Culture, and Social Influence from Hunter-Gatherers to the Age of Globalization* by Mary Ellen Snodgrass

All queries with SASEs may be directed to Patricia Kolb. Please, no e-mail queries.

Patricia Kolb, Editorial Director—All areas, all disciplines; pkolb@mesharpe.com

Harry Briggs, Executive Editor—Management, marketing, public administration; hbriggs@mesharpe.com

George Lobell, Executive Editor—Economics and Finance; globell @mesharpe.com.

SIERRA CLUB BOOKS

85 Second Street, 2nd Floor, San Francisco, CA 94105
415-977-5500 | fax: 415-977-5799
www.sierraclub.org/books | e-mail: books.publishing@sierraclub.org

The Sierra Club, founded in 1892 by John Muir, has for more than a century stood in the forefront of the study and protection of the earth's scenic, environmental, and ecological resources; Sierra Club Books is part of the nonprofit effort the club carries on as a public trust.

INDEPENDENT US PRESSES

Sierra Club publishes works in the categories of nature, technology, outdoor activities, mountaineering, health, gardening, natural history, travel, and environmental issues. Sierra Club series include the Adventure Travel Guides, Sierra Club Tote books, Naturalist's Guides, Natural Traveler, the John Muir Library, and Guides to the Natural Areas of the United States. Sierra Club Books has a strong division that publishes works dedicated to children and young adults.

The books represent the following areas: the finest in outdoor photographic artistry; thought-provoking discussions of ecological issues; literary masterworks by naturalist authors; and authoritative handbooks to the best recreational activities the natural world offers. Today, the need to protect and expand John Muir's legacy is greater than ever—to help stop the relentless abuse of irreplaceable wilderness land, save endangered species, and protect the global environment.

Recent titles include *Edible Landscaping* by Rosalind Creasy; *Coming Clean: Breaking America's Addiction to Oil and Coal* by Michael Brune; *Hey Mr. Green: Sierra Magazine's Answer Guy Tackles Your Toughest Green Living Questions* by Bob Schildgen; *Shooting in the Wild: An Insider's Account of Making Movies in the Animal Kingdom* by Chris Palmer.

Sierra Club Books are distributed by the University of California Press.

E-mail submissions will not be accepted. Sierra Club Books for Children is not currently accepting any unsolicited manuscripts. Direct queries and SASEs to the Editorial Department.

Helen Sweetland, Publisher

Ellen Landau, Acting Editorial Director

SIETE CUENTOS [SEE SEVEN STORIES]

SIGNATURE BOOKS

564 West 400 North Street, Salt Lake City, UT 84116-3411
801-531-1483 | fax: 801-531-1488
www.signaturebooks.com | e-mail: people@signaturebooks.com

Signature Books was founded in 1980 to promote the study of Mormonism and related issues pertaining to the Rocky Mountain area. The Signature list emphasizes contemporary literature, as well as scholarly works relevant to the Intermountain West. Signature Books publishes subjects that range from outlaw biographies and Mormonism to speculative theology, from demographics to humor. In addition, Signature publishes novels and collections of poetry of local interest. They publish 12 new titles per year.

Recent titles include *The Backslider* by Levi S. Peterson; *The Amazing Colossal Apostle* by Robert M. Price; *Her Side of It* by Marilyn Bushman-Carlton; *The*

Midwife: A Biography of Laurine Ekstrom Kingston by Victoria D. Burgess; *The Nauvoo City* and *High Council Minutes* by John S. Dinger.

Signature Publications oversees distribution of its titles via in-house ordering services and a national network of wholesalers. Their acquisitions editors prefer submissions from authors who have been previously published in peer-reviewed forums. Query letters and SASEs should be directed to the Acquisitions Editor.

Ron Priddis, Managing Director
Jani Fleet, Editor

SILHOUETTE BOOKS [SEE HARLEQUIN ENTERPRISES, LTD.]

SKYHORSE PUBLISHING

307 West 36th Street, 11th Floor, New York, NY 10018
212-643-6816 | fax: 212- 643-6819
www.skyhorsepublishing.com

Skyhorse Publishing was launched in 2006 by publishing veteran Tony Lyons. The company has more than 100 titles in print, including a current best seller by Jesse Ventura. The firm's nonfiction list includes sports, narratives, memoirs, history, military, business, and perhaps anything else that appears to be unique or simply commercial.

Recent titles include *Burqalicious: The Dubai Diaries* by Becky Wicks; *Cutting-Edge Therapies for Autism* (Updated Edition) by Tony Lyons, Ken Siri; *Fuhrer* by Konrad Heiden; *The Sex Habits of Americans* by Amy Winter; *Short Course in Beer* by Lynn Hoffman.

Mark Weinstein, Acquisition Editor
Ann Treistman, Acquisition Editor
Julie Matysik, Acquisition Editor

GIBBS SMITH, PUBLISHER

PO Box 667, Layton, UT 84041
801-544-9800 | fax: 801-544-5582
www.gibbs-smith.com

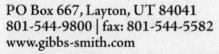

Founded in 1969, Gibbs Smith, Publisher, specializes in beautifully illustrated lifestyle books, with topics including design and architecture, cooking, business, holiday, sports, and children's books. From their farm in Utah, the editors produce books with a mission to enrich and inspire humankind the world over.

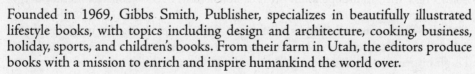

Recent titles include *Trailerama* by Phil Noyes; *Wedding Inspiration* by Kimberly Schlegel Whitman; *Tropical Flowers* by Eileen W. Johnson; *The Night Before Christmas in Paris* by Betty Lou Philips and Roblyn Herndon; *Italian Slanguage* by Mike Ellis.

Gibbs Smith no longer accepts physical manuscripts. E-mail duribe @gibbs-smith.com for manuscript submission guidelines.

Suzanne Taylor, Vice President and Editorial Director
Linda Nimori, Editor
Melissa Barlow, Editor
Jennifer Grillone, Senior Editor

SMITHSONIAN BOOKS

PO Box 37012, Washington, DC 20013
www.smithsonianbooks.com

Smithsonian Books, in collaboration with the Smithsonian Institution, publishes a select list of narrative nonfiction and illustrated books. Their publishing program includes categories where the Smithsonian's authority is unparalleled, such as history, science, technology, art, museums, collections, and artifacts. Among the distinguished list of Smithsonian Books authors are Mark Stein and Joy Hakim. Smithsonian Books is distributed by Random House Publisher Services.

Some recent titles include *5,000 Years of Textiles* by Jennifer Harris; *A Guide to Smithsonian Architecture* by Heather Ewing and Amy Ballard; *A Guide to Smithsonian Gardens* by Carole Ottesen; *A Legal Primer on Managing Museum Collections* by Marie C. Malaro and Ildiko DeAngelis; *A Revolution in Wood* by Nicholas Bell.

Christina Wiginton, Editor

SOHO PRESS, INC.

SOHO CONSTABLE
SOHO CRIME
853 Broadway, New York, NY 10003
212-260-1900 | fax: 212-260-1902
www.sohopress.com | e-mail: soho@sohopress.com

Soho Press, Inc., an independent press established in 1986, publishes literary fiction and nonfiction.

Soho Press primarily publishes fiction, with the occasional autobiography or cultural historical account. They are eager to find work from new writers and place a high priority on publishing quality unsolicited materials.

Recent titles include *Leviathan* by James Lilliefors; *The Ionia Sanction* by Gary Corby; *Death Comes to Vicenza* by David Dickenson; *Murder Below Montparnasse* by Cara Black; *The Woman Who Wouldn't Die* by Colin Cotterill.

SOHO CONSTABLE

Soho Constable is a new imprint launched in 2008. The press will be releasing mysteries published across the pond by British house Constable & Robinson. The books are both historical and modern-day mysteries set mostly in England and Scotland. Some recent titles include *The Fourth Crow* by Pat McIntosh and *The Silence* by Alison Bruce.

SOHO CRIME

The Soho Crime imprint focuses on procedurals set in exotic locales. Some recent titles include *The Fear Artist* by Timothy Hallinan; *Port Villa Blues* by Garry Disher; *Not My Blood* by Barbara Cleverly; *Death's Door* by James R. Benn.

No submissions via e-mail. The editors prefer a query letter with three chapters of a completed work (preferably the first three chapters), with a brief outline and CV. Direct submissions with SASEs to:

Katie Herman, Editor

SOURCEBOOKS, INC.

CUMBERLAND HOUSE
DAYS OF OUR LIVES PUBLICATIONS
LANDMARK
MEDIAFUSION
SPHINX PUBLISHING
1935 Brookdale Road, Suite 139, Naperville, IL 60563
630-961-3900 | 800-43-BRIGHT | fax: 630-961-2168
www.sourcebooks.com | e-mail: info@sourcebooks.com
CASABLANCA
18 Cherry Street, Suite 1W, Milford, CT 06460
203-876-9790
FIRE
JABBERWOCKY
232 Madison Ave., Suite 1100, New York, NY 10018
212-414-1701

Chicago's leading independent book publisher, Sourcebooks is exceptionally strong in reference, romance, parenting, self-help, children's, and fiction titles. Under the

MediaFusion imprint, Sourcebooks also publishes mixed media titles including *Poetry Speaks to Children* and the Sourcebooks Shakespeare series. The house was founded in 1987 by Dominique Raccah, and it has been one of the fastest-growing companies in America, with many best sellers.

Sourcebooks is the publisher of *Jeff Herman's Guide to Book Publishers, Editors, and Literary Agents.*

In 2007, Sourcebooks launched the Jabberwocky imprint for children's and young-adult titles, including *The Fairy Chronicles* by J. H. Sweet and *New York Times* best seller *I Love You More* by Laura Duksta, illustrated by Karen Keesler. In the Landmark fiction imprint, the house has done very well with books that continue famous stories from Jane Austen, including *Mr. Darcy's Diary* and *More Letters from Pemberley: Mrs. Darcy's Story Unfolds* by Jane Dawkins.

Other Sourcebooks imprints include Casablanca, with romance genre fiction and nonfiction titles, and Sphinx Publishing, which focuses on self-help law titles. In 2008, Sourcebooks acquired Cumberland House, publishers of Gregory Lang's *Why a Daughter Needs a Dad* and other various titles.

Recent Sourcebooks titles include *That Book about Harvard* by Eric Kester; *Fiske Guide to Colleges 2013* by Edward Fiske; *Pride and Pyramids: Mr. Darcy in Egypt* by Amanda Grange and Jacqueline Webb; *Gruber's Complete ACT Guide 2013* by Gary Gruber.

Sourcebooks is actively seeking romance fiction, and authors of romance may submit a Word document including their first four chapters via e-mail to deb.werksman@sourcebooks.com. For all genres other than romance, the house is only accepting fiction from agents. Nonfiction authors should direct book proposals by mail to Editorial Submissions. Sourcebooks is no longer accepting print submissions. Please see the Sourcebooks website for additional information and submissions guidelines.

Agents may direct submissions to:

Shana Drehs, Editorial Manager, Landmark (IL)—Adult trade, gift books, parenting, relationships, inspiration, sex, historical and women's fiction, pop culture, women's commercial fiction; shana.drehs@sourcebooks.com

Deborah Werksman, Editorial Manager (CT)—Romance (all genres) and women's fiction; deb.werksman@sourcebooks.com

Leah Hultenschmidt, Senior Editor (NY)—Young-adult fiction; leah.hultenschmidt@sourcebooks.com

Steve Geck, Editorial Manager (NY)—Toddler through age 14, picture books; steve.geck@sourcebooks.com

Suzanna Bainbridge, Editorial Manager (IL)—Education, college guides; suzanna.bainbridge@sourcebooks.com

Todd Stocke, Vice President and Editorial Director (IL)—Mixed media projects that combine print and digital aspects; todd.stocke@sourcebooks.com

Stephanie Bowen, Editor (IL)—Adult trade, humor, memoir; stephanie.bowen@sourcebooks.com

Aubrey Poole, Associate Editor, (NY)—Children's ages seven and up; aubrey
.poole@sourcebooks.com

SPRINGER

233 Spring Street, New York, NY 10013
212-460-1500 | 800-SPRINGER | fax: 212-460-1575
www.springer.com | e-mail: service-ny@springer.com

Springer is one of the world's most renowned scientific publishing companies. Its publications cover subjects ranging from the natural sciences, mathematics, engineering, and computer science to medicine and psychology. In the fields of economics and law, Springer offers an increasing number of books in management science. Since the 2004 merger with Dutch scientific house Kluwer Academic Publishing, the range of products has increased; it now includes publications on the arts and social science.

Springer's authors are highly qualified experts. More than 150 Nobel Prize winners, plus scientists, doctors, and engineers such as Robert Koch, Fredinand Sauerbruch, Albert Einstein, Werner von Siemens, and Otto Hahn have published their works at Springer.

Recent titles include *The Chemical Cosmos* by Steve Miller; *A Handbook of Transcription Factors* edited by Timothy R. Hughes; *Analytical Techniques in Biochemistry and Molecular Biology* by Rajan Katoch; *Earth and Life* edited by John A. Talent.

Submit proposals and SASEs to:

William Curtis, Editorial Director—Life sciences and medicine; william
.curtis@springer.com

Hans Koelsch, Directorial Editor—Mathematics, physics, engineering; hans
.koelsch@springer.com

John Kimmel, Executive Editor—Statistics, computer science; john.kimmel
@springer.com

SQUARE ONE PUBLISHERS

115 Herricks Road, Garden City Park, NY 11040
516-535-2010 | 877-900-BOOK | fax: 516-535-2014
www.squareonepublishers.com

Square One publishing sees itself as recapturing the spirit of the 1920s, '30s, and '40s: the Golden Age of independent publishing. They feel that advances in print technology have given birth to a revival of the original sense of entrepreneurial spirit and excitement that characterized the early pioneers. Supporting this conviction, *Publishers Weekly* has named Square One Publishers one of the fastest-growing indie publishers in the United States for the third year in a row. Square One is interested in manuscripts on alternative health, collectibles, cooking, gambling, health, how-to, parenting, personal finance, postcards, self-help, and writing.

Recent titles from Square One include *The Big Beautiful Brown Rice Cookbook* by Wendy Esko; *Blue Sky, White Clouds* by Eliezer Sobel; *The Book of Macrobiotics* by Michio Kushi and Alex Jack; *Buddha Speaks* by Rashmi Khilnani; *Coming Full Circle: Ancient Teachings for a Modern World* by Lynn V. Andrews.

Address queries and SASEs to the Acquisitions Editor.

ST. ANTHONY MESSENGER PRESS

Franciscan Communications
28 West Liberty Street, Cincinnati, OH 45202
513-241-5615 | 800-488-0488 | fax: 513-241-0399
www.sampbooks.org | e-mail: samadmin@americancatholic.org

St. Anthony Messenger Press (founded in 1970) and Franciscan Communications publishes Catholic religious works and resources for parishes, schools, and individuals. The house also owns the video/print imprints Ikonographics and Fischer Productions.

Areas of St. Anthony Messenger's publishing interest include Franciscan topics, Catholic identity, family life, morality and ethics, parish ministry, pastoral ministry, prayer helps, sacraments, saints and Christian heroes, Scripture, seasonal favorites, small-group resources, spirituality for every day, children's books, and youth ministry. The house produces books (hardcover and paperback, many in economically priced editions), magazines, DVDs and CDs, as well as educational programs and an award-winning website.

Recent titles include *Fools, Liars, Cheaters, and Other Bible Heroes* by Barbara Hosbach; *Catholic Update Guide to Vocations* by Mary Carol Kendzia; *Firmly on the Rock: 120 Reflections on Faith* by Debra Herbeck; *Francis: The Journey and the Dream* by Murray Bodo; *Catholic and Confident: Simple Steps to Share Your Faith* by Henry Libersat.

St. Anthony Messenger Press also offers music CDs, computer software, and DVDs.

St. Anthony Messenger Press distributes books through Ingram, Spring Arbor, Riverside Distributors, Appalachian, Inc., Baker & Taylor, and ABS/Guardian.

Query letters and SASEs should be directed to:
Lisa Biedenbach, Editorial Director, Books—LisaB@AmericanCatholic.org

STEEPLE HILL BOOKS [SEE HARLEQUIN ENTERPRISES, LTD.]

STERLING PUBLISHING CO., INC.

A division of Barnes and Noble
387 Park Avenue South, 10th Floor, New York, NY 10016-8810
212-532-7160
www.sterlingpublishing.com | e-mail: specialsales@sterlingpublishing.com

Sterling Publishing (founded 1949 and acquired by Barnes and Noble in 2003) is one of the world's leading publishers of nonfiction titles, with more than 5,000 books in print. Among its bestselling titles are *The Big Book of Knitting*, *The Good Housekeeping Cookbook*, and *Windows on the World Complete Wine Course*. Subject categories in which the company excels include puzzles and games, crafts, gardening, woodworking, health, and children's books.

With an unusual title and packaging, *Yoga for Wimps* became a best seller in 2001 and marked the launch of an ongoing series that includes *Orchids for Wimps* and *Meditation for Wimps*. Another success is the novelty-packaged *Sit and Solve* series. Many of Sterling's children's books, such as *Sometimes I Like to Curl Up in a Ball* and *I Know a Rhino*, are critically acclaimed best sellers.

Recent titles include *Horten's Incredible Illusions* by Lissa Evans; *The New York Times Book of Wine* by Howard G. Goldberg; *Every Seventh Wave* by Daniel Glattauer; *At Home with Town and Country* by Sarah Medford; *Playboy's Greatest Covers* by Damon Brown.

To submit to Sterling, send a proposal with CV and SASE via regular mail. Submissions should be sent to the attention of the category editor, e.g., the material on a woodworking book should be addressed to the Woodworking Editor; a craft book proposal should be addressed to the Craft Editor; and so on. All children's book submissions should be sent to the attention of the Children's Book Editor.

Michael Fragnito, Vice President, Editorial Director
Barbara Berger, Executive Editor

STEWART, TABORI & CHANG [SEE HARRY N. ABRAMS, INC.]

SYBEX, INC. [SEE JOHN WILEY & SONS]

 (right margin, vertical text) INDEPENDENT US PRESSES

THAMES & HUDSON, INC.

500 Fifth Avenue, New York, NY 10110
212-354-3763 | fax: 212-398-1252
www.thamesandhudsonusa.com | e-mail: BookInfo@thames.wwnorton.com

Thames & Hudson is one of the world's most eminent publishers of illustrated books. The house releases high-quality, well-printed books on art, architecture, design, photography, decorative arts, archaeology, history, religion, and spirituality, as well as a number of titles for children.

Recent titles include *Joan Miro: The Ladder of Escape* by Matthew Gale and Marko Daniel; *The Art of Not Making* by Michael Petry; *Heirloom Fruits and Vegetables* by Toby Musgrave; *The Most Beautiful Villages of Provence* by Michael Jacobs and Hugh Palmer; *Head to Toe: My Body and How it Works* by Okido.

Thames & Hudson is distributed in the United States by W. W. Norton & Company, Inc., and in Canada by Penguin.

Authors send queries with SASE to Submissions or e-mail BookInfo@thames .wwnorton.com.

Peter Warner, President
Susan Dwyer, Vice President

THEATRE COMMUNICATIONS GROUP

520 Eighth Avenue, 24th Floor, New York, NY 10018-4156
212-609-5900 | fax: 212-609-5901
www.tcg.org | e-mail: tcg@tcg.org

The mission of the Theatre Communications Group (TCG) is to strengthen, nurture, and promote the not-for-profit professional American theater by celebrating differences in aesthetics, culture, organizational structure, and geography. The house produces *American Theatre* magazine and the ArtSEARCH employment bulletin. They also publish plays, translations, and theater reference books. TCG awards grants to individuals and institutions; interested authors should peruse the house website for a myriad of opportunities to connect to the professional theater world.

Recent titles include *Boleros of the Disenchanted and Other Plays* by Jose Rivera; *Chekhov's Three Sisters and Woolf's Orlando* by Sasha Ruhl; *The Color of Desire/ Hurricane* by Nilo Cruz; *But the Giraffe and Brundibar* by Tony Kushner; *Chinglish* by David Henry Hwang.

Direct queries with SASEs to either Kathy Sova or Molly Metzler. E-mail submissions can be sent to tcg@tcg.org.

Terence Nemeth, Publisher

Kathy Sova, Editorial Director
Molly Metzler, Associate Editor
Alexander Barreto, Associate Editor

TIN HOUSE BOOKS

2601 N.W. Thurman Street, Portland, OR 97210
503-473-8663
www.tinhouse.com/books | e-mail: tinhousebooks@tinhouse.com

After three years working with Bloomsbury USA on a joint publishing venture known as Tin House Books/Bloomsbury, Tin House Books is now an independent company with offices in Portland, Oregon. Tin House continues to publish new literary voices as well as reprints of contemporary and classic works of fiction and nonfiction. The mission of Tin House Books remains constant: to publish compelling and authentic narratives of our time. Tin House salutes the artistic edge but remains rooted in the tenets of the classic storytelling tradition.

Tin House Books' first focus is the launch of the New Voice Series: story cycles, collections, novels, and memoirs by first-time authors. The house also publishes the *Tin House* literary journal.

Recent titles include *Misfit* by Adam Braver; *Beside the Sea* by Veronique Olmi; *Writer's Notebook II: Craft Essays* from Tin House; *Me and Mr. Booker* by Cory Taylor.

Tin House Books no longer reads unsolicited submissions by authors without representation, but this may change. Check the Tin House Books website for more information.

Meg Storey, Associate Editor
Tony Perez, Associate Editor

TRAFALGAR SQUARE BOOKS

PO Box 257, 388 Howe Hill Road, North Pomfret, VT 05053
802-457-1911 | 800-423-4525
www.horseandriderbooks.com | e-mail: info@horseandriderbooks.com

Trafalgar Square published its first horse book, *Centered Riding* by Sally Swift, in 1985 and the book remains one of the bestselling horse books of all time. This book was the spark that led Ted and Caroline Robbins, Trafalgar Square's owners, to start up a horse book publishing business. Previously, Trafalgar Square was a book distribution outlet for British publishers. Since its beginnings in 1985, Trafalgar Square has published over 85 horse books, and has a growing list of titles on dressage, jumping, training, western riding, horse care, driving, and more. Trafalgar Square has also ventured into video, DVD, and audio publishing.

Trafalgar Square has published such authors as Jane Savoi, Linda Tellington-Jones, William Steinkraus, Mary Wanless, Clinton Anderson, Charles de Kunffy, Sylvia Loch, Richard Shrake, Betsy Steiner, Kyra Kyrklund, Alois Podhajsky, Paul Belasik, Jessica Jahiel, and more.

Recent titles from Trafalgar Square include *Balancing Act* by Dr. Gerd Heuschmann; *Creative Dressage Schooling* by Julia Kohl; *Crown Prince* by Linda Snow McLoon; *Know You, Know Your Horse* by Eunice Rush and Marry Morrow; *Modern Eventing with Phillip Dutton* by Phillip Dutton and Amber Heintzberger.

Send queries and SASEs by e-mail to info@horseandriderbooks.com.

TUTTLE PUBLISHING

A Member of the Periplus Publishing Group
364 Innovation Drive, North Clarendon, VT 05759
802-773-8930 | 800-526-2778 | fax: 802-773-6993 | 800-329-8885
www.tuttlepublishing.com | e-mail: info@tuttlepublishing.com

Tuttle Publishing was founded by Charles Tuttle in Tokyo in 1948. The publisher's mission was to publish "books to span the East and West." In the early 1950s the company began publishing a large number of titles on Japanese language, arts, and culture. In 1983, Charles Tuttle was awarded the Order of the Sacred Treasure by the Emperor of Japan for his services to Japanese-American understanding. Tuttle is now the US arm of the Periplus Publishing Group, the world's leading publisher of books on Asia.

Eric Oey, a cousin of Charles E. Tuttle, founded Periplus Editions in 1988 in Berkeley, California, and merged the two companies in 1996. With offices in Vermont, Singapore, Tokyo, Hong Kong, and Jakarta, Tuttle Publishing has become the largest English-language book publishing and distribution company in Asia.

Recent titles include *Japanese Hiragana & Katakana Flash Cards Kit* by Glen McCabe; *Ninja Attack!: True Tales of Assassins, Samurai, and Outlaws* by Hiroko Yoda and Matt Alt; *Origami Studio Kit: 30 Step-by-Step Lessons with an Origami Master* by Michael G. LaFosse and Richard L. Alexander; *Phantoms of Asia* by Mami Kataoka and Allison Harding; *Little Vietnam…80 Exciting Vietnamese Dishes to Prepare at Home* by Nhut Huynh and Jeremy McNamara.

No e-mail submissions, please. To submit, send a complete book proposal and SASE to Editorial Acquisitions.

William Notte, Associate Editor, Acquisitions

TYNDALE HOUSE PUBLISHERS

351 Executive Drive, Carol Stream, IL 60188
800-323-9400 | fax: 800-684-0247
www.tyndale.com | e-mail: customer@tyndale.com

Tyndale House Publishers (founded in 1962) offers a comprehensive program in Christian living: devotional, inspirational, and general nonfiction, from a nondenominational evangelical perspective. Tyndale's publishing interest also encompasses religious fiction and children's books. The house publishes the bestselling Living Bible and the Left Behind series. Tyndale produces hardcover, trade paperback, and mass-market paperback originals, as well as reprints.

Tyndale children's books target all ages from birth through high school. Most are on topics of specific interest to children in Christian families (e.g., the Bible or prayer). The others are on themes that interest all children (e.g., friends or fears), but these themes are presented from a clearly Christian perspective.

Tyndale fiction includes mainstream novels, as well as a number of inspirational romance series, including works set in Revolutionary War and Civil War milieus. The house is interested in evangelical Christian-theme romance in other historical periods (including Regency), as well as those with a humorous twist.

Recent Tyndale titles include *The Last Temple* by Hank Hanegraaff and Sigmund Brouwer; *You're Stronger Than You Think* by Les Parrott; *The End* by Mark Hitchcock; *Abducted* by Janice Cantore; *Life Application Study Bible NLT, TuTone* by Tyndale.

Tyndale House oversees its own distribution. Tyndale also distributes books from Focus on the Family.

Tyndale is not accepting manuscript proposals from anyone except literary agents or writers whose work has already been published.

Jonathan Farrar, Acquisitions Director
Carol Traver, Acquisitions Editor

UPPER ROOM PUBLISHING

DISCIPLESHIP RESOURCES
Delivery address:
1908 Grand Avenue, Nashville, TN 37212
Mailing address:
PO Box 840, Nashville, TN 37202-0840
615-340-7200
www.upperroom.org

A program of the General Board of Discipleship, Upper Room is an ecumenical nonprofit religious publisher focused on books that help readers discover, develop, and enrich a life of devotion and attention to God. Books published by Upper Room present to individuals and groups the possibility and promise of an intimate, life-giving relationship with God. These books further assist readers along their spiritual path by offering guidance toward a disciplined life that includes prayer and action. The Upper Room publishes between 25 and 30 books each year.

Recent titles from Upper Room Books include *10 Life-Charged Words: Real Faith for Men* by Derek Maul; *My Story, My Song* by Lucimarian Roberts; *That We May Perfectly Love Thee* by Robert Benson; *"Pray for Me": The Power in Praying for Others* by Kenneth H. Carter, Jr.; *The Leadership Lab* by Hank Hilliard.

DISCIPLESHIP RESOURCES

Discipleship Resources is now an imprint of Upper Room Publishing. Areas of publishing interest encompass United Methodist history, doctrine, and theology, as well as Bible study, Christian education, ethnic church concerns, evangelism, ministry of the laity, stewardship, United Methodist men, and worship.

The mission of Discipleship Resources is "to provide quality resources that respond to the needs of United Methodist leaders and congregation members, as they seek to become and encourage others to become disciples of Jesus Christ."

Recent titles from Discipleship Resources include *Does Your Church Have a Prayer? In Mission Toward the Promised Land* by Marc Brown et al; *What Kind of Man Is Joseph, and What Kind of Man Are You?* by Eugene Blair; *A Blueprint for Discipleship: Wesley's General Rules as a Guide for Christian Living* by Kevin Watson; and *Not Just a One-Night Stand: Ministry with the Homeless* by John Flowers and Karen Vannoy.

Query letters with one sample chapter and SASEs should be directed to the Editor; e-mail submissions may be sent to kduncan@gbod.org.

URJ PRESS

633 Third Avenue, New York, NY 10017
888-489-8242 | 212-650-4120 | fax: 212-650-4119
www.urjpress.com | e-mail: press@urj.org

Formerly UAHC Press, URJ Press publishes in the areas of religion (Jewish), Reform Judaism, textbooks, audiovisual materials, social action, biography, and life cycles and holidays. In its trade categories, URJ Press accents juvenile fiction and adult nonfiction books, as well as titles in basic Judaism and inspirational works. The house catalogs books, CDs, DVDs, and multimedia products, suitable for use in both the classroom and the home.

URJ Press provides the highest quality in religious educational materials and has done so for well over 100 years. The publishers are committed to providing their readers with the foremost in materials and service, to be a continuing resource for books, publications, CDs, DVDs, and multimedia.

Indicative of URJ Press interests are *Anthology of Jewish Art Song, Volume III: A Sametenem Ponim* by Richard Hereld; *Did Moses Really Have Horns? And Other Myths About Jews and Judaism* by Rifat Sonsino; *Entrée to Judaism: A Culinary Exploration of the Jewish Diaspora* by Tina Wasserman; and *Galilee Diary: Reflections on Daily Life in Israel* by Marc Rosenstein.

Some recent titles include *Seekers of Meaning: Baby Boomers, Judaism, and the Pursuit of Healthy Aging* by Rabbi Richard F. Address; *Noah's Swim-a-Thon* by Ann Koffsky; *Finding Words* by Merle Feld; *Jewish Living: A Guide to Contemporary Reform Practice* (Revised Edition) by Mark Washofsky; *Love Tales from the Talmud* by Edwin Goldberg.

Query letters, proposals, and SASEs should be directed to:

Michael H. Goldberg, Editor-in-Chief

VEDANTA PRESS

Vedanta Society of Southern California
1946 Vedanta Place, Hollywood, CA 90068
800-816-2242 | 323-960-1736
www.vedanta.com | e-mail: info@vedanta.com

Vedanta's publishing interests include meditation, religions and philosophies, and women's studies. In addition to its list of titles imported from the East (primarily from Indian publishers), Vedanta's program embraces works of Western origin. The publisher catalogs titles from other publishers and also sells CDs and DVDs.

The house publishes books on the philosophy of Vedanta, with an aim to engage a wide variety of temperaments, using a broad spectrum of methods, in order to attain the realization of each individual personality's divinity within. Vedanta Press (founded in 1947) is a subsidiary of the Vedanta Society of Southern California.

Recent titles include *Inner Peace in a Busy World* by Cliff Johnson; *Reminiscences of Swami Brahmananda: The Mind-born Son of Sri Ramakrishna* by Brahmachari Akshayachaitanya; *Swami Vivekananda on Himself* by Swami Vivekananda; *You Will Be a Paramahamsa: Reminiscenses of Sw. Kalyananda* by Swami Sarvagatananda; *Self Mastery* by Swami Paramananda.

Vedanta publishes many classic Vedic works in a variety of editions and translations. Among them is *Bhagavad Gita: The Song of God* (translated by Swami Prabhavananda and Christopher Isherwood; introduction by Aldous Huxley).

Vedanta Press handles its own distribution, with many titles available from Baker & Taylor, DeVross and Company, and New Leaf Distributors.

Vedanta's books originate in-house, though the publisher is open to considering additional projects that may fall within its program. Vedanta does not wish to receive unsolicited manuscripts.

Query letters and SASEs should be directed to:

Bob Adjemian, General Manager

VERSO

20 Jay Street, 10th Floor, Brooklyn, NY 11201-8346
718-246-8160 | fax: 781-246-8165
www.versobooks.com | e-mail: versony@versobooks.com

With global sales approaching $3 million per year and over 350 titles in print, Verso can justifiably claim to be the largest radical publisher in the English-language world. The house publishes critical nonfiction in social science, humanities, history, and current affairs, such as Tariq Ali's *The Clash of Fundamentalism* and Laura Flanders' *Bushwomen: How They Won the White House for Their Man*, and trade titles such as Karen Finley's *George and Martha*.

Verso (meaning, in printers' parlance, "the left-hand page") was founded in 1970 by the London-based *New Left Review*, a journal of left-wing theory with a world-wide readership of 40,000. The company remains independent to this day. The company's head office is located in London, where a staff of 12 produces a program of 60 new titles each year.

Originally trading as New Left Books, the company developed an early reputation as a translator of classic works of European literature and politics by authors such as Jean-Paul Sartre, Walter Benjamin, Louis Althusser, Theodor Adorno, Herbert Marcuse, Ernest Mandel, and Max Weber. More recent translations include the work of Giovanni Arrighi, Norberto Bobbio, Guy Debord, Giles Deleuze, Che Guevara, Carlo Ginzburg, André Gorz, Jürgen Habermas, Gabriel García Marquez, and Paul Virilio.

Commissioning intelligent, critical works located at the intersection of the academic and trade markets, Verso has many key authors in English in the social sciences and humanities, with particular strength in politics, cultural studies, history, philosophy, sociology, and literary criticism. Such writers include Tariq Ali, Benedict Anderson, Perry Anderson, Michèle Barrett, Robin Blackburn, Terry Eagleton, Paul Gilroy, Stuart Hall, Eric Hobsbawm, Victor Kiernan, Steven Lukes, E. P. Thompson, and Raymond Williams.

From early on in its life, the company retained US rights and has added to its imports a range of distinguished North America-based writers. Editors located on both East and West coasts have signed authors including Noam Chomsky, Alexander Cockburn, Marc Cooper, Mike Davis, Juan Gonzalez, Christopher Hitchens, Frederic Jameson, Andrew Kopkind, Lewis Lapham, Manning Marable, David Roediger, Andrew Ross, Edward Said, and Michele Wallace.

North America today comprises 65 percent of the company's worldwide sales. In the spring of 1995 Verso opened an office in New York. Primarily handling marketing and publicity work, the American office now has a staff of four.

Verso stands today as a publisher combining editorial intelligence, elegant production, and marketing flair. Having quadrupled in size over the past decade, the company will continue its progress towards the mainstream of the industry without compromising its radical commitment.

Recent titles include *The Faith of the Faithless: Experiments in Political Theology* by Simon Critchley; *Britain's Empire* by Richard Gott; *The Metamorphoses of Kinship* by Maurice Godelier; *I'm With the Bears: Short Stories from a Damaged Planet* by Mark Martin; *Occupy! Scenes From Occupied America* by Sarah Leonard, Sarah Resnick, and Astra Taylor.

E-mail queries are preferred; send them to verso@versobooks.com. Send proposals (lengths of ten pages or fewer) and SASEs to the Editorial Department.

VISIBLE INK PRESS

43311 Joy Road, #414, Canton, MI 48187-2075
734-667-3211 | fax: 734-667-4311
www.visibleink.com

A Detroit phenomenon since 1990 and a continuing surprise to everyone involved, Visible Ink Press publishes mega-works of popular reference that inform and entertain in the areas of culture, science, history, religion, and government. All of their titles could be classified as popular reference.

Recent titles include *African American Almanac: 400 Years of Triumph, Courage and Excellence* by Lean'tin Bracks, PhD; *Conspiracies and Secret Societies: The Complete Dossier* (2nd Edition) by Brad Steiger and Sherry Hansen Steiger; *The Handy Math Answer Book* (2nd Edition) by Patricia Barnes-Svarney and Thomas E. Svarney; *The Handy Religion Answer Book* (2nd Edition) by John Renard, PhD.

Visible Ink is not currently accepting unsolicited manuscripts, but the editors encourage authors to check the website, as this policy may soon change. Direct queries and SASEs to:

Roger Janecke, President
Megan Hiller, Editorial Director

WALKER PUBLISHING COMPANY [SEE BLOOMSBURY USA]

WATERBROOK MULTNOMAH [SEE RANDOM HOUSE]

WEISER BOOKS [SEE RED WHEEL/WEISER]

JOHN WILEY & SONS

JOSSEY-BASS
SYBEX
989 Market Street, San Francisco, CA 94103-1741
415-433-1740 | fax: 415-433-0499
www.josseybass.com
www.sybex.com | e-mail: sybexproposals@wiley.com
WILEY-BLACKWELL
Commerce Place, 350 Main Street, Malden, MA 02148
781-388-8200 | fax: 781-388-8210
www.blackwellpublishing.com
WILEY HIGHER EDUCATION
WILEY PROFESSIONAL/TRADE
111 River Street, Hoboken, NJ 07030-5774
201-748-6000 | fax: 201-748-6088
www.wiley.com | e-mail: info@wiley.com
Indianapolis:
10475 Crosspoint Boulevard, Indianapolis, IN 46256
317-572-3000
www.dummies.com

Wiley was founded in 1807, during the Jefferson presidency. In the early years, Wiley was best known for the works of Washington Irving, Edgar Allan Poe, Herman Melville, and other nineteenth-century American literary giants. By the turn of the century, Wiley was established as a leading publisher of scientific and technical information. The company went public in 1962 and was listed on the NYSE in 1995.

In 2007, Wiley acquired academic and professional publisher Blackwell Publishing for over $1 billion. Blackwell was merged into Wiley's global scientific, technical, and medical business. Also in 2007, its bicentennial year, Wiley announced record revenue.

Wiley is a global publisher of print and electronic products, specializing in scientific, technical, and medical books and journals under the Wiley-Blackwell Division; professional and consumer books under the Wiley Professional and Trade Division; and textbooks and other educational materials for undergraduate and graduate students as well as lifelong learners under the Wiley Higher Education Division. Wiley publishes in a variety of formats.

Wiley's proposal submission guidelines are rather specific. Please see the page

"Submission Guidelines" on the website. It is Wiley's policy not to accept unsolicited proposals for books in the *For Dummies* series. For everything else, send a proposal with SASE to the attention of the appropriate division (Professional and Trade Division or Scientific, Technical, and Medical Division).

JOSSEY-BASS

Jossey-Bass publishes books, periodicals, and other media to inform and inspire those interested in developing themselves, their organizations, and their communities. Jossey-Bass publications feature the work of some of the world's best-known authors in leadership, business, education, religion and spirituality, parenting, nonprofit, public health and health administration, conflict resolution, and relationships. Publishing nearly 250 new titles each year, Jossey-Bass was acquired by Wiley in 1999, but maintains largely independent operations in San Francisco.

As of press time, Jossey-Bass was in the process of reassessing its non-business publishing program and new acquisitions for those titles were placed "on hold". In religion and spirituality, Jossey-Bass publishes a broad range of trade books that support readers in their spiritual journeys, including some that combine general spirituality and self-improvement. Most of their books have been drawn from Christian and Jewish traditions, but they are looking to expand in a thoughtful way into other traditions. They are also looking for books on the intersection of faith/spirituality, culture, and history.

Recent titles include *Managing Nonprofit Organizations* by Mary Tschirhart and Wolfgang Bielefeld; *First-Generation College Students...* by Lee Ward, Michael J. Siegel, and Zebulun Davenport; *Protect Your Child from Bullying* by Allan L. Beane; *Environmental Policy and Public Health: Air Pollution, Global Climate Change, and Wilderness* by William N. Rom.

Submit proposals, queries, and SASEs to the Editorial Assistant for the relevant series (Business, Education, Health, Higher Education, Nonprofit and Social Leadership, General Interest, Psychology, or Religion).

Cedric Crocker, Vice President and Publisher

Susan Williams, Executive Editor—Business, leadership, management; swilliams@wiley.com

Karen Murphy, Senior Editor—Nonprofits; kmurphy@wiley.com

Genovesa Llosa, Editor—Leadership, careers; gllosa@wiley.com

Sheryl Fullerton, Editor—Spirituality, religion.

Kate Bradford, Editor—Education, K through 12 text and teaching guides.

SYBEX

Sybex pioneered computer book publishing in 1976 and has as its mission to bring practical skills to computer users through comprehensive, high-quality education and reference materials. Their series range from the reputable Mastering best sellers, used by millions to gain in-depth understanding of the latest computer topics, to certification Study Guides that help students prepare for challenging exams, to Maya Press books that service the needs of highly specialized 3D imaging and design markets. Sybex was acquired by John Wiley & Sons in 2005 and publishes about 100 new books per year.

Recent titles include *ZBrush Professional Tips and Techniques* by Paul Gaboury; *Microsoft Private Cloud Computing* by Aidan Finn, Hans Vredevoort, Patrick Lownds, and Damian Flynn; *VCP5 VMware Certified Professional on vSphere 5 Study Guide: Exam VCP-510* by Brian Atkinson; *Website Optimization: An Hour a Day* by Rich Page; *AutoCAD 2013 and AutoCAD LT 2013: No Experience Required* by Donnie Gladfelter.

Direct queries and proposals to sybexproposals@wiley.com and include the word Proposal at the beginning of the subject line.

WILEY-BLACKWELL

Wiley-Blackwell was formed in February 2007 as a result of the merger between Blackwell Publishing Ltd. and John Wiley & Sons, Inc.'s Scientific, Technical, and Medical business. Wiley-Blackwell is organized into five broad divisions: Life Science, Physical Sciences, Professional, Medical, Social Sciences, and Humanities. Blackwell-Wiley is run by Senior Vice President for Scientific, Technical, and Medical Publishing, Eric Swanson. By June 2008, Wiley-Blackwell integrated the two businesses by combining many infrastructure and distribution processes as well as launching a single Web platform.

Recent titles from Wiley-Blackwell include *Designing and Implementing Global Selection Systems* by Ann Marie Ryan; *The Epigenics of Autoimmune Diseases* by Moncef Zouali; *Essential Mathematics and Statistics for Science* by Graham Currell; *The European Reformations* by Carter Lindberg; and *Planets and Planetary Systems* by Stephen Eales.

Recent titles from Wiley-Blackwell Professional include *Carbon Capture and Sequestration: Integrating Technology, Monitoring, Regulation* by Elizabeth Wilson and David Gerard; *Physics at a Glance* by Tim Mills; *Structure and Reactivity in Organic Chemistry* by Mark Moloney; *Trans Fatty Acids* by Alberst Dijkstra, Richard J. Hamilton, and Wolf Hamm.

If you have an idea for a new book, journal, or electronic product that falls into the chemistry, life sciences, medicine, mathematical and physical sciences, humanities, or social sciences, and would like to be contacted by an editor, please send your proposal to John Wiley & Sons, Wiley Blackwell Division.

Janyne M. Fargnoli, Executive Editor, Art History, Cultural Studies
Elizabeth Swayze, Senior Editor, Media Studies
Peter Coveney, Executive Editor, American History
Jeffrey T. Dean, Executive Editor, Philosophy

WILEY HIGHER EDUCATION

Wiley Higher Education publishes textbooks and other educational materials in English, German, and Chinese (and translated into many other languages) in a variety of formats, both print and online, in the United States, Canada, Europe, Asia, and Australia. Their products are used globally by undergraduate and graduate students, educators, and lifelong learners. Wiley's higher education programs are targeted toward two- and four-year colleges and universities, for-profit career colleges, and advanced placement classes. They are a leader in courses in the sciences, engineering, computer science, mathematics, business and accounting, statistics, geography, hospitality, and the culinary arts, with a growing presence in education, psychology, and modern languages.

WILEY PROFESSIONAL/TRADE

The Professional and Trade Division produces nonfiction books and electronic products for the professional, business, and general interest consumer markets. Its primary fields of interest are accounting, architecture, engineering, business, finance and investment, children, computers, society (including current affairs, health, parenting, self-help, reference, history, biography, science, and nature), hospitality, law, psychology, and real estate. Also included are the following Wiley brands: Bible, CliffsNotes, Cracking the Code, Dummies, Howell, Novell Press, Secrets, 3D Visual, Webster's New World Dictionary, and Weekend Crash Course. Wiley content travels well. Approximately 40 percent of the company's revenue is generated outside the United States.

The company provides "must-have" content to targeted communities of interest. Wiley's deep reservoir of quality content, constantly replenished, offers a tremendous source of competitive advantage. Technology is making this content more accessible to customers worldwide and is adding value for them by delivering it in interactive and/or fully searchable formats. Approximately 25 percent of global revenue is currently Web-enabled. A couple of years ago Wiley purchased Bloomberg Press and it's large catalogue of notable investment and finance titles.

With about 3,500 employees worldwide, Wiley has operations in the United States, Europe (England, Germany, and Russia), Canada, Asia, and Australia. The Company has US publishing, marketing, and distribution centers in New Jersey, California, Virginia, Illinois, Indiana, and Ohio. Wiley's worldwide headquarters are located in Hoboken, New Jersey, just across the river from Manhattan.

Recent titles from the Wiley Professional/Trade division include J.K. Lasser's *Your Income Tax*, Professional Edition 2013 by J.K. Lasser Institute; J.K. Lasser's *Small Business Taxes 2012: Your Complete Guide to a Better Bottom Line* by Barbara Weltman; *The Unofficial Guide to Walt Disney World with Kids 2013* by Bob Sehlinger, Liliane J. Opsomer, and Len Testa.

David Pugh, Senior Editor (NJ)—Finance, investing, e-commerce, corporate tie-ins.

Stephen Power, Senior Editor (NJ)—Popular science, current events, biography.

Debra Englander, Executive Editor (NJ)—Investing, finance, money.
Richard Narramore, Senior Editor (NJ)—General business.
Timothy Burgard, Editor (NJ)—Finance, technology.
Laura Walsh, Editor (NJ)—Investing.
Eric Nelson, Editor (NJ)—Current affairs, history.
Lauren Murphy, Editor (NJ)—Careers, management.

WESTMINSTER JOHN KNOX PRESS [SEE PRESBYTERIAN PUBLISHING CORPORATION]

WILLOW CREEK PRESS, INC.

PO Box 147, Minocqua, WI 54548
715-358-7010 | 800-850-9453 | fax: 715-358-2807
www.willowcreekpress.com | e-mail: info@willowcreekpress.com

Willow Creek Press is a publisher whose primary commitment is to publish books specializing in nature, outdoor and sporting topics, gardening, wildlife and animal books, and cookbooks. They also publish nature, wildlife, fishing, and sporting calendars.

Its location in the Wisconsin Northwoods helps keep Willow Creek Press off the publishing world's radar. But, a few years ago, the house did get noticed with the release of *Just Labs*, a unique and colorful tribute to Labrador retrievers. The book quickly became a best seller (with over 250,000 copies in print). Now an entire line of popular Willow Creek Press titles evokes the myriad joys of dog and cat ownership. Today they are known for these high-quality, light-hearted books and feature over 40 such titles in a continually expanding line.

Recent titles include *Underwater Dogs 2013 Calendar*; *A Gardener's Guide to Frost* by Philip Harnden; *What Pets Teach Us*; *It's a Small Town If…* by Sam Breck; *Remote Locations* by Chris Dorsey

Please provide SASE with all correspondence if you want your materials returned. Address all inquiries or proposals to:
Donnie Rubo, Acquisitions, Donnie@willowcreekpress.com

WISDOM PUBLICATIONS

199 Elm Street, Somerville, MA 02144
617-776-7416 | fax: 617-776-7841
www.wisdompubs.org | e-mail: editors@wisdompubs.org

Wisdom Publications, a not-for-profit publisher, is dedicated to making available authentic Buddhist works for the benefit of all. The house publishes translations of the sutras and tantras, commentaries and teachings of past and contemporary Buddhist masters, and original works by the world's leading Buddhist scholars. Wisdom Publications was named one of the top ten fastest-growing small publishers in the country (the company has been in the United States since 1989) by Publishers Weekly in 1996.

Wisdom titles are published in appreciation of Buddhism as a living philosophy and with the commitment to preserve and transmit important works from all the major Buddhist traditions. Wisdom products are distributed worldwide and have been translated into a dozen foreign languages.

Wisdom publishes the celebrated *Tibetan Art Calendar*, containing 13 full-color reproductions of the world's finest Indo-Tibetan thangka paintings, accompanied by detailed iconographical descriptions.

Wisdom Publications has made a commitment to producing books with environmental mindfulness.

Recent Wisdom titles include *The Mindful Writer: Noble Truths of the Writing Life* by Dinty W. Moore; *Making Zen Your Own: Giving Life to Twelve Key Golden Age Ancestors* by Janet Jiryu Abels; *Enlightenment to Go: Shantideva and the Power of Compassion to Transform Your Life* by David Michie; *Tibetan Calligraphy: How to Write the Alphabet and More* by Sanje Elliott; *Essential Mind Training* by Geshe Thupten Jinpa.

Wisdom Publications is distributed to the trade in the United States and Canada by National Book Network (NBN). Query letters and SASEs should be directed to Acquisitions Editor via regular mail or e-mail. Complete proposal specifications are available on the website.

Tim McNeill, Publisher

INDEPENDENT US PRESSES

WORKMAN PUBLISHING GROUP

ALGONQUIN BOOKS OF CHAPEL HILL
SHANNON RAVENEL BOOKS

PO Box 2225, Chapel Hill, NC 27515
919-967-0108 | fax: 919-933-0272
www.algonquin.com | e-mail: inquiry@algonquin.com

ARTISAN BOOKS
WORKMAN PUBLISHING COMPANY

225 Varick St., New York, NY 10014-4381
212-254-5900 | fax: 212-677-6692
www.workman.com
www.artisanbooks.com | e-mail: artisaninfo@workman.com

BLACK DOG AND LEVENTHAL

151 West 19th Street, New York, NY 10011
212-647-9336 | fax: 212-871-9530
www.blackdogandleventhal.com | e-mail: information@blackdogandleventhal.com

STOREY PUBLISHING

210 MASS MoCA Way, North Adams, MA 01247
413-346-2100 | fax: 413-346-2199
storey.workman.com

TIMBER PRESS

113 SW 2nd Avenue, Suite 450, Portland, OR 97204
503-227-2878 | fax: 503-227-3070
timberpress.workman.com | e-mail: info@timberpress.com

Workman Publishing Company, a medium-sized independent publisher, is the creator of calendars; cookbooks; parenting/pregnancy guides; fun, educational children's titles; gardening; humor; self-help; and business books. They also include several imprints, including Algonquin Books of Chapel Hill, Artisan, HighBridge Audio, Storey Publishing, and Timber Press, as well as acting as distributor for Black Dog and Leventhal, Greenwich Workshop Press, and Fearless Critic Media.

ALGONQUIN BOOKS OF CHAPEL HILL

Algonquin Books was founded in 1982 with the mission statement, "Though we hope and expect that our books will gain their share of book club adoptions, mass paperback sales, and movie and television adaptations, it is their quality that will be our foremost consideration, for we believe that it is still possible to publish worthy fiction and nonfiction that will also be financially profitable for author, publisher, and bookseller."

This division of Workman Publishing Company maintains a literary orientation in commercial fiction and nonfiction. The house list represents the American tradition, ranging from the homespun to the progressive. Algonquin Books of Chapel Hill presents its titles in hardcover and trade paper editions with a look and feel befitting the publisher's emphasis on both the classical and contemporary—books designed to be comfortably handled when read. The Algonquin editorial organization operates from both the Chapel Hill and New York Workman offices. They publish 20 to 25 new books per year, of fiction, nonfiction, cookbooks, and lifestyle books.

Recent Algonquin titles include *The Art Forger* by B.A. Shapiro; *The Beach at Galle Road* by Joanna Luloff; *Life Among Giants* by Bill Roorbach; *Hikikomori and the Rental* by Jeff Backhaus; *The Revised Fundamentals of Caregiving* by Jonathan Evinson.

Amy Gash, Editor—Fiction and nonfiction.

Andra Miller, Editor—Fiction and nonfiction.

Kathy Pories, Editor—Fiction.

SHANNON RAVENEL BOOKS

Algonquin founder Shannon Ravenel's imprint at Algonquin publishes both nonfiction and fiction with titles such as *Brave Enemies: A Novel of the American Revolution* by Robert Morgan; *The Ghost at the Table: A Novel* by Suzanne Berne; *On Agate Hill: A Novel* by Lee Smith; and *Saving the World* by Julia Alvarez.

Shannon Ravenel, Director

ARTISAN BOOKS

Artisan Books, another division of Workman, is known for excellence of content, quality of illustration, and innovative printing. Their authors seek to contribute to the cultural life of a diverse and visually sophisticated readership. Recent titles include *How to Build an A* by Sara Midda; *Tavern on the Green* by Kay LeRoy and Jennifer Oz LeRoy; *Frank Stitt's Bottega Favorita: A Southern Chef's Love Affair with Italian Food* by Frank Stitt; *Under Pressure: Cooking Sous Vide* by Thomas Keller; and *Medal of Honor: Portraits of Valor Beyond the Call of Duty* by Nick Del Calzo and Peter Collier.

Judy Pray, Editor—Cooking, decorating.

WORKMAN PUBLISHING COMPANY

Books, calendars, trends. Workman is a publisher that's always around big ideas. B. Kliban's *Cat*, *1,000 Places to See Before You Die*, *The Silver Palate Cookbook*, *Bad Cat*, the original Page-A-Day Calendars, the What to Expect books, BRAIN QUEST—landmark best sellers such as these reflect a knack for publishing books and calendars that lead.

Workman's first book, 1968's *Yoga 28-Day Exercise Plan*, is currently in its twenty-eighth printing. Their books are known for having an appealing trade-paperback format with high standards of design and production. Authors who are authorities, who tour extensively and are spokespeople for their subjects, work with

Workman. Workman also sometimes goes with unexpected formats such as the packaging of books with objects. And above all, the house prides itself on value through conscientious, aggressive pricing.

Once a book is published, Workman stays after it through promotion and publicity. Take, for example, the case of *The Official Preppy Handbook*, and how an idiosyncratic best seller was transformed into a phenomenon, complete with posters and stationery—even pins and nightshirts. Or *What to Expect When You're Expecting*, which started with a modest 6,700-copy advance in 1984 and has grown into America's pregnancy bible, currently with 10 million copies in print.

Perhaps more telling is the fact that over two-thirds of all the books the house has published in the last 28 years are still in print, with a fair share of titles that have over 1 million copies in print, including BRAIN QUEST, *The Silver Palate Cookbook*, *The New Basics Cookbook*, *All I Need to Know I Learned from My Cat*, *The Magic Locket*, and *The Bones Book & Skeleton*.

Some recent titles from Workman include *I Will Teach You to Be Rich* by Ramit Sethi; *Sell Your Business for the Max!* by Steve Kaplan; *Good Egg* by Barney Saltzberg; and *How to Make Someone Fall in Love with You in 90 Minutes or Less* by Nicholas Boothman.

Peter Workman, Publisher
Bob Miller, Editor-in-Chief
Suzanne Rafer, Executive Editor
Janet Harris, Editor—Non-book products (calendars).
Raquel Jaramillo, Director of Children's Publishing
Mary Ellen O'Neill, Editor
Bruce Tracy, Editor

BLACK DOG AND LEVENTHAL

Black Dog and Leventhal seeks to publish strikingly original books of light reference, humor, cooking, sports, music, film, mysteries, entertainment, history, biography, and more. Many are unusual in format and rich with color and imagery. Titles include *The Manhattan Project: The Birth of the Atomic Bomb in the Words of Its Creators, Eyewitnesses, and Historians* by Cynthia Kelly; *Blue Ribbon Recipes* by Barbara Greenman; *The Cube: The Ultimate Guide to the World's Best-Selling Puzzle: Secrets, Stories, Solutions* by Jerry Slocum et al; *Splitters, Squeezes, and Steals: The Inside Story of Baseball's Greatest Techniques, Strategies, and Plays* by Derek Gentile; and *Hopes and Dreams: The Story of Barack Obama: The Inaugural Edition* by Steve Dougherty.

Beck Koh, Editor

STOREY PUBLISHING

Storey Publishing began on July 1, 1983, with about 65 books and 100 bulletins on topics as varied as building your own log cabin, tanning leather yourself, and canning your garden's bumper crop of fruits and vegetables. Since then, Storey has maintained its independent streak while keeping a backlist of more than 450 titles. Storey wants books that offer fresh ideas, lend encouragement, and help the reader succeed at something specific.

Recent titles from Storey Press include *Sew What! Bags: 18 Pattern-Free Projects You Can Customize to Fit Your Needs* by Lexi Barnes; *The Gardener's A–Z Guide to Growing Organic Food* by Tanya Denckla; *Growing Chinese Vegetables in Your Own Backyard* by Geri Harrington; *Happy Baby, Happy You: Quick Tips for Nurturing, Pampering, and Bonding with Your Baby* by Karyn Siegel-Maier; *The Cattle Health Handbook* by Heather Smith Thomas; and *The Ever-Blooming Flower Garden: A Blueprint for Continuous Bloom* by Lee Schneller.

Deborah Balmuth, Editorial Director—Building and mind/body/spirit.
Deborah Burns, Acquiring Editor—Horses, animals, nature.
Gwen Steege, Acquiring Editor—Crafts.
Margaret Sutherland, Acquiring Editor—Cooking, wine, and beer.
Carleen Madigan, Editor—Gardening.

TIMBER PRESS

Timber Press, located in Portland, Oregon, has over 400 titles in print and is considered the preeminent publisher of horticulture books. Timber Press began in 1980, publishing J. D. Vertee's *Japanese Maples*, which is still in print. Besides horticulture, Timber Press also seeks to publish books about landscape design, food-related topics, fruit-growing titles, natural history, and the Pacific Northwest.

Timber Press titles include *Huntleyas and Related Orchids* by Patricia A. Harding; *The Pruning of Trees, Shrubs, and Conifers* by George Brown and Tony Kirkham; *The Oregon Companion: A Historical Gazetteer of the Useful, the Curious, and the Arcane* by Richard H. Engeman; *Green Flowers: Unexpected Beauty for the Garden, Container, or Vase* by Alison Hoblyn; *Perennial Companions: 100 Dazzling Plants for Every Season* by Tom Fischer and Richard Bloom; and *The Art of Botanical Drawing* by Agathe Ravet-Haevermans.

To submit your manuscript, send a 20-page sample of your work, a cover letter, a self-addressed envelope, and a check to cover return postage to the attention of the Editorial Department.

Tom Fischer, Editor-in-Chief

WRITER'S DIGEST

4700 E. Galbraith Road, Cincinnati, OH 45236
513-531-2690
www.writersdigest.com | e-mail: writersdig@fwpubs.com

Writer's Digest is the world's leading magazine for writers, founded in 1920. Today this house provides a variety of books, magazines, special interest publications, educational courses, conferences, websites, and more.

Publications include: *Writer's Yearbook*, published annually; *Scriptwriting Secrets*, *Getting Started in Writing*; *Start Writing Now*; and a variety of other special interest publications for writers.

All are part of F&W Publications, a leading publisher of books and magazines for creative people. F&W Publications is headquartered in Cincinnati, Ohio, with additional offices in New York, Denver, and Devon, England.

Recent titles include *7 Things I've Learned So Far* by Leah Bobet; *How to Blog a Book: Write, Publish, and Promote Your Work One Post at a Time* by Nina Amir; *Sell Your Book Like Wildfire* by Rob Eagar; *Writing 21st Century Fiction* by Donald Maass; *Where Do You Get Your Ideas? A Writer's Guide to Transforming Notions Into Narratives* by Fred White.

Send a query and SASE to:

Phil Sexton, Editorial Director

ZEBRA BOOKS [SEE KENSINGTON PUBLISHING]

SECTION THREE

UNIVERSITY PRESSES

THE UNIVERSITY AS PUBLISHER

FROM ACADEMIC PRESS TO COMMERCIAL PRESENCE

WILLIAM HAMILTON
Director, University of Hawai'i Press
2840 Kolowalu Street, Honolulu, HI 96822

You nod as you glance at the ads in the book reviews, you are aware of the spots you heard or saw on radio and late-night television, and you recognize the authors from television interviews and radio call-in shows. So you know that today's university presses publish much more than scholarly monographs and academic tomes.

Although the monograph is—and will always be—the bread and butter of the university press, several factors over the past quarter-century have compelled university presses to look beyond their primary publishing mission of disseminating scholarship. The reductions in financial support from parent institutions, library-budget cutbacks by federal and local governments, and the increasing scarcity of grants to underwrite the costs of publishing monographs have put these presses under severe financial pressure. The watchword for university presses, even in the 1970s, was survival.

While university presses were fighting for their lives, their commercial counterparts also experienced difficult changes. The commercial sector responded by selling off unprofitable and incompatible lists or merging with other publishers; many houses were bought out by larger concerns. Publishers began to concentrate their editorial and marketing resources on a few new titles that would generate larger revenues. Books that commercial publishers now categorized as financial risks, the university presses saw as means of entry into new markets and opportunities to revive sagging publishing programs.

Take a look through one of the really good bookstores in your area. You'll find university press imprints on regional cookbooks, popular fiction, serious nonfiction, calendars, literature in translation, reference works, finely produced art books, and a considerable number of upper-division textbooks. Books and other items normally associated with commercial publishers are now a regular and important part of university press publishing.

UNIVERSITY PRESSES

There are approximately 100 university presses in North America, including US branches of the venerable Oxford University Press and Cambridge University Press. Of the largest American university presses—California, Chicago, Columbia, Harvard, MIT, Princeton, Texas, and Yale—each publishes well over 100 books per year. Many of these titles are trade books that are sold in retail outlets throughout the world.

The medium-sized university presses—approximately 20 fit this category—publish between 50 and 100 books a year. Presses such as Washington, Indiana, Cornell, North Carolina, Johns Hopkins, and Stanford are well established as publishers of important works worthy of broad circulation.

All but the smallest university presses have developed extensive channels of distribution, which ensure that their books will be widely available in bookstores and wherever serious books are sold. Small university presses usually retain larger university presses or commissioned sales firms to represent them.

UNIVERSITY PRESS TRADE PUBLISHING

The two most common trade areas in which university presses publish are (1) regional titles and (2) nonfiction titles that reflect the research interests of their parent universities.

For example, University of Hawai'i Press publishes approximately 30 new books a year with Asian or Pacific Rim themes. Typically, eight to ten of these books are trade titles. Recent titles have included Japanese literature in translation, a lavishly illustrated book on Thai textiles, books on forms of Chinese architecture, and a historical guide to ancient Burmese temples. This is a typical university press trade list—a diverse, intellectually stimulating selection of books that will be read by a variety of well-informed, responsive general readers.

For projects with special trade potential, some of the major university presses enter into copublishing arrangements with commercial publishers—notably in the fields of art books and serious nonfiction with a current-issues slant—and there seems to be more of these high-profile projects lately.

Certain of the larger and medium-sized university presses have in the past few years hired editors with experience in commercial publishing to add extra dimensions and impact to the portion of their program with a trade orientation.

It's too early to know whether these observations represent trends. Even if so, the repercussions remain to be seen. Obviously, with the publishing community as a whole going through a period of change, it pays to stay tuned to events.

UNIVERSITY PRESS AUTHORS

Where do university press authors come from? The majority of them are involved in one way or another with a university, research center, or public agency, or are experts in a particular academic field. Very few would list their primary occupation as author. Most of the books they write are the result of years of research or reflect years of experience in their fields.

The university press is not overly concerned about the number of academic degrees following its trade book authors' names. What matters is the author's thoroughness in addressing the topic, regardless of his or her residence, age, or amount of formal education. A rigorous evaluation of content and style determines whether the manuscript meets the university press's standards.

THE UNIVERSITY PRESS ACQUISITION PROCESS

Several of the other essays in this volume provide specific strategies for you to follow to ensure that your book idea receives consideration from your publisher of choice—but let me interject a cautionary note: The major commercial publishers are extremely difficult to approach unless you have an agent, and obtaining an agent can be more difficult than finding a publisher!

The commercial publishers are so overwhelmed by unsolicited manuscripts that you would be among the fortunate few if your proposal or manuscript even received a thorough reading. Your unagented proposal or manuscript will most likely be read by an editorial assistant, returned unread, or thrown on the slush pile unread and unreturned.

An alternative to the commercial publisher is the university press. Not only will the university press respond, but the response will also generally come from the decision maker—the acquisitions editor.

Before approaching any publisher, however, you must perform a personal assessment of your expectations for your book. If you are writing because you want your book to be on the best-seller list, go to a medium to large commercial press. If you are writing to make a financial killing, go to a large commercial publisher. If you are writing in the hope that your book will be a literary success, contribute to knowledge, be widely distributed, provide a modest royalty, and be in print for several years, you should consider a university press.

SHOULD A UNIVERSITY PRESS BE YOUR FIRST CHOICE?

That depends on the subject matter. It is very difficult to sell a commercial publisher on what appears on the surface to be a book with a limited market. For example, Tom Clancy was unable to sell *The Hunt for Red October* to a commercial publisher because the content was considered too technical for the average reader of action-adventure books. Clancy sent the manuscript to a university press that specialized in military-related topics. Naval Institute Press had the foresight to see the literary and commercial value of Clancy's work. As they say, the rest is history. Tom Clancy created the present-day technothriller genre and has accumulated royalties well into the millions of dollars. Once Clancy became a known commodity, the commercial publishers began courting him. All of his subsequent books have been published by commercial houses.

How do you find the university press that is suitable for you? You must research the university press industry. Start by finding out something about university presses. In addition to the listings in the directory of publishers and editors appearing in this book, most university presses are listed in *Literary Market Place*.

A far better and more complete source is *The Association of American University Presses Directory*. The AAUP directory offers a detailed description of each AAUP member press, with a summary of its publishing program. The directory lists the names and responsibilities of each press's key staff, including the acquisitions editors. Each press states its editorial program—what it will consider for publication. A section on submitting manuscripts provides a detailed description of what the university press expects a proposal to contain. Another useful feature is the comprehensive subject grid, which identifies more than 125 subject areas and lists the university presses that publish in each of them.

An updated edition of *The Association of American University Presses Directory* is published every fall and is available for a nominal charge from the AAUP central offices in New York City or through its distributor, University of Chicago Press.

Most university presses are also regional publishers. They publish titles that reflect local interests and tastes and are intended for sale primarily in the university press's local region. For example, University of Hawai'i Press has more than 250 titles on Hawai'i. The books—both trade and scholarly—cover practically every topic one can think of. Books on native birds, trees, marine life, local history, native culture, and an endless variety of other topics can be found in local stores, including chain bookstores.

This regional pattern is repeated by university presses throughout the country. University of Washington Press publishes several titles each year on the Pacific Northwest and Alaska. Rutgers University Press publishes regional fiction. University of New Mexico Press publishes books on art and photography, most dealing with the desert Southwest. Louisiana State University Press publishes Southern history and literature. Nebraska publishes on the American West.

Almost all university presses publish important regional nonfiction. If your book naturally fits a particular region, you should do everything possible to get a university press located in that region to evaluate your manuscript.

Do not mistake the regional nature of the university press for an inability to sell books nationally—or globally. As mentioned earlier, most university presses have established channels of distribution and use the same resources that commercial publishers use for book distribution. The major difference is that the primary retail outlets for university press books tend to be bookstores associated with universities, smaller academic bookstores, specialized literary bookstores, and independent bookstores that carry a large number of titles.

Matching books to buyers is not as difficult as you might think. Most patrons of university press bookstores know these stores are likely to carry the books they want.

Traditionally, very few university press titles are sold through major chain bookstores outside their local region. Even so, this truism is subject to change. Some of the biggest bookstore chains are experimenting with university press sections in their large superstores.

WHAT TO EXPECT AT A UNIVERSITY PRESS

You should expect a personal reply from the acquisitions editor. If the acquisitions editor expresses interest, you can expect the evaluation process to take as long as six to eight months. For reasons known only to editorial staffs—commercial, as well as those of university presses—manuscripts sit and sit and sit. Then they go out for review, come back, and go out for review again!

Once a favorable evaluation is received, the editor must submit the book to the press's editorial board. It is not until the editorial board approves the manuscript for publication that a university press is authorized to publish the book under its imprint.

A word about editorial boards: The imprint of a university press is typically controlled by an editorial board appointed from the faculty. Each project presented to the editorial board is accompanied by a set of peer reviews, the acquisitions editor's summary of the reviews, and the author's replies to the reviews. The project is discussed with the press's management and voted upon.

Decisions from the editorial board range from approval, through conditional approval, to flat rejection. Most university presses present to the editorial board only those projects they feel stand a strong chance of acceptance—approximately 10 to 15 percent of the projects submitted annually. So if you have been told that your book is being submitted to the editorial board, there's a good chance that the book will be accepted.

Once a book has been accepted by the editorial board, the acquisitions editor is authorized to offer the author a publishing contract. The publishing contract of a university press is quite similar to a commercial publisher's contract. The majority of the paragraphs read the same. The difference is most apparent in two areas—submission of the manuscript and financial terms.

University presses view publishing schedules as very flexible. If the author needs an extra six to twelve months to polish the manuscript, the market is not going to be affected too much. If the author needs additional time to proofread the galleys or page proofs, the press is willing to go along. Why? Because a university press is publishing for the long term. The book is going to be in print for several years. It is not unusual for a first printing of a university press title to be available for ten or more years. Under normal circumstances the topic will be timeless, enduring, and therefore of lasting interest.

University presses go to great lengths to ensure that a book is as close to error-free as possible. The academic and stylistic integrity of the work is foremost in the editor's mind. Not only the content, but the notes, references, bibliography, and index should be flawless—and all charts, graphs, maps, and other illustrations perfectly keyed.

It does not matter whether the book is a limited-market monograph or serious nonfiction for a popular trade. The university press devotes the same amount of care to the editorial and production processes to ensure that the book is as accurate and complete as possible. Which leads us to the second difference—the financial terms.

Commercial publishers follow the maxim that time is money. The goal of the organization is to maximize shareholder wealth. Often the decision to publish a book is based solely on financial considerations. If a book must be available for a specific season in order to meet its financial goals, pressure may be applied to editorial by marketing, and editorial in turn puts pressure on the author to meet the agreed-upon schedule. This pressure may result in mistakes, typos, and inaccuracies—but will also assure timely publication and provide the publisher with the opportunity to earn its expected profit. At the commercial publishing house, senior management is measured by its ability to meet annual financial goals.

University presses are not-for-profit organizations. Their basic mission is to publish books of high merit that contribute to universal knowledge. Financial considerations are secondary to what the author has to say. A thoroughly researched, meticulously documented, and clearly written book is more important than meeting a specific publication date. The university press market will accept the book when it appears.

Do not get the impression that university presses are entirely insensitive to schedules or market conditions. University presses are aware that certain books—primarily textbooks and topical trade titles—must be published at specific times of the year if sales are to be maximized. But less than 20 percent of any year's list would fall into such a category.

UNIVERSITY PRESSES AND AUTHOR REMUNERATION

What about advances? Royalties? Surely, university presses offer these amenities—which is not to suggest they must be commensurate with the rates paid by commercial houses.

No and yes. No royalties are paid on a predetermined number of copies of scholarly monographs—usually 1,000 to 2,000.

A royalty is usually paid on textbooks and trade books. The royalty will be based on the title's sales revenue (net sales) and will usually be a sliding-scale royalty, ranging from as low as 5 percent to as high as 15 percent.

As with commercial publishers, royalties are entirely negotiable. Do not be afraid or embarrassed to discuss them with your publisher. Just remember that university presses rarely have surplus funds to apply to generous advances or high royalty rates. However, the larger the university press, the more likely you are to get an advance for a trade book.

Never expect an advance for a monograph or supplemental textbook.

WHEN CONSIDERING A UNIVERSITY PRESS

When you're deciding where to submit your manuscript, keep the following in mind. University presses produce approximately 10 percent of the books published in the United States each year. University presses win approximately 20 percent of the annual major book awards. Yet university presses generate just 2 percent of the annual sales revenue.

So if you want to write a book that is taken seriously and will be carefully reviewed and edited; if you want to be treated as an important part of the publishing process and want your book to have a good chance to win an award; and if you are not too concerned about the financial rewards—then a university press may very well be the publisher for you.

CAMBRIDGE UNIVERSITY PRESS

32 Avenue of the Americas, New York, NY 10013-2473
212-337-5000 | fax: 212-691-3239
www.cambridge.org/us | e-mail: newyork@cambridge.org
Twitter: @CambridgeUP_NY

Dating back to 1534, Cambridge University Press is the world's oldest printing and publishing house, and is dedicated to the advancement and dissemination of knowledge. Internationally, Cambridge publishes over 4,000 titles and 300 journals every year.

The Manhattan office acquires and publishes books in many areas of the humanities and social sciences, with particular focus on subjects including law, history, political science, and economics; it is also active across a broad spectrum of science and medicine publishing. It administers some of the prestigious journals issued by the press, and it also publishes an extremely successful list of books aimed at those learning American English as a foreign or second language.

The press is now in a real sense a "world publisher." English is the dominant world language of scholarship and science, and the press seeks to attract the best authors and publish the best work in the English language worldwide; it currently has over 45,000 authors in over 100 countries. The press publishes and distributes the whole of this varied output through its own network around the world: There are branches in North America, Australia, Africa, Brazil, and Spain, all representing the whole list, supported by sales offices in every major center; there are editorial offices in New York, Melbourne, Cape Town, Madrid, Singapore, and Tokyo, each contributing its own related publishing programs; and the press's websites are visited by over 2.5 million people worldwide.

Recent Cambridge University titles include *King Henry V* by Andrew Gurr; *Justice Denied* by Marci Hamilton; *International Negotiations* by Mark Powell; *MRS Communications* by Peter Green; and *Checkpoint Mathematics* by Greg Byrd et al.

Submit queries (with SASEs if by regular mail) to the appropriate editor:

Adina Berk—Psychology, education; aberk@cambridge.org

Robert Dreesen—Political Science, sociology, political philosophy and theory; rdreesen@cambridge.org

Ray Ryan—Literature; rryan@cambridge.org

Vince Higgs—Astronomy and physics; vhiggs@cambridge.org

Matt Lloyd—Earth and environmental science; mlloyd@cambridge.org

Ada Brunstein—Computer science; abrunstein@cambridge.org

Ben Harris—Latin, Greek; bharris@cambridge.org

Daniele Gibney—Sciences, ICT; dgibney@cambridge.org

Sheryl Borg—Grammar; sborg@cambridge.org

Jeff Krum—Adult courses; jkrum@cambridge.org

Beatrice Rehl—Philosophy, classical art and archaeology; brehl@cambridge.org

Eric Crahan—History and political science; ecrahan@cambridge.org

Scott Parris—Economics and finance; sparris@cambridge.org

John Berger—Law; jberger@cambridge.org

Marigold Acland—The Middle East, Asia, Islamic studies; macland@cambridge.org
Lewis Bateman—Political science, history; lbateman@cambridge.org
Lauren Cowles—Academic computer science, statistics; lcowles@cambridge.org
Peter Gordon—Mechanical, chemical, and aerospace engineering; pgordon @cambridge.org
Richard Westood—Education: literacy/English, mathematics/numeracy, cross-curricular studies; rwestwood@cambridge.org
Claudia Bickford-Smith—International, IB and other; cbickford-smith @cambridge.org
Debbie Goldblatt—English for language teaching: adult courses; dgoldblatt @cambridge.org
Bruce Myint—English for language teaching: adult education; bamyint @cambridge.org
Kathleen Corley—English for language teaching: applied linguistics and professional books for teachers; kcorley@cambridge.org
Bernard Seal—English for academic purposes and pre-academic ESL reading and writing; bseal@cambridge.org
Lesley Koustaff—Primary and secondary courses; lkoustaff@cambridge.org
Paul Heacock—Reference and vocabulary; pheacock@cambridge.org
Karen Brock—Short courses and general EFL listening, speaking, reading, and writing; kbrock@cambridge.org

---

COLUMBIA UNIVERSITY PRESS

61 W. 62nd Street, New York, NY 10023
212-459-0600 | fax: 212-459-3678
cup.columbia.edu | Twitter: @ColumbiaUP

Columbia University Press was founded in 1893 as a nonprofit corporation, separate from Columbia University although bearing its name and associated closely with it. The purpose of the press expressed in the Certificate of Incorporation was to "promote the study of economic, historical, literary, scientific and other subjects; and to promote and encourage the publication of literary works embodying original research in such subjects."

In its first quarter century, the list focused on politics with books by two US presidents, Woodrow Wilson and William Howard Taft. In 1927, the press began publishing major multivolume works. By 1931 the press had grown to such an extent that it published an annual list of 83 new titles—more than any other American university press and 25th among all US publishers.

With the publication of *The Columbia Encyclopedia* in 1935, the press began to develop a list of general reference works in print (several are now in electronic form) that has set it apart from all other American university presses. King's Crown Press was established in 1940 as an imprint for Columbia dissertations: publication was a requirement for a Columbia PhD until the 1950s. In addition, Columbia University's professional program in social work stimulated a strong list of books in that field.

In the 1960s the press became the first—and it is still the only—American university press to publish music. The imprints Columbia University Music Press (for BMI composers) and King's Crown Music Press (for ASCAP composers) were created to publish new music written by Americans. In 2007 the Press launched Columbia Business School Publishing, an imprint that publishes practical works of importance by academic and financial professionals.

Columbia now publishes around 160 titles a year in the areas of Asian studies, literature, biology, business, culinary history, current affairs, economics, environmental sciences, film and media studies, finance, history, international affairs, literary studies, Middle Eastern studies, New York City history, philosophy, neuroscience, paleontology, political theory, religion, and social work.

Recent titles include *Moving Data: The iPhone and the Future of Media* by Pelle Snickars; *The Economists' Voice 2.0* by Aaron S. Edlin and Joseph Stiglitz; *Taking It Big* by Stanley Aaronowitz; and *River Republic: The Fall and Rise of America's Rivers* by Daniel McCool.

Columbia University Press accepts proposals by e-mail or regular mail. However, do not send large files by e-mail. Direct proposals (with SASEs if by regular mail) to the appropriate editor:

Jennifer Crewe, Associate Director and Editorial Director—Asian humanities, film, food history, New York City; jc373@columbia.edu

Patrick Fitzgerald, Publisher for the Life Sciences—Conservation biology, environmental sciences, ecology, neuroscience, paleobiology, public health, biomedical sciences; pf2134@columbia.edu

Philip Leventhal, Editor—Literary studies, cultural studies, journalism, media; pl2164@columbia.edu

Wendy Lochner, Publisher for philosophy and religion—Animal studies, religion, philosophy; wl2003@columbia.edu

Jennifer Perillo, Senior Executive Editor—Criminology, gerontology, psychology, social work; jp3187@columbia.edu

Anne Routon, Editor—Asian history, international relations, Middle East studies; akr36@columbia.edu

Myles Thompson, Publisher, Finance and Economics—Finance, economics; mt2312@columbia.edu

---

CORNELL UNIVERSITY PRESS

Sage House, 512 East State Street, Ithaca, NY 14850
607-277-2338 | fax: 607-277-2374
www.cornellpress.cornell.edu

Cornell University Press was established in 1869, giving it the distinction of being the first university press to be established in the United States, although it was inactive for several decades between 1890 and 1930. The house offers 150 new titles a year in many disciplines, including anthropology, Asian studies, biological sciences, classics, cultural studies, history, industrial relations, literary criticism and theory, medieval studies, philosophy, politics and international relations, psychology and psychiatry, veterinary subjects, and women's studies. Submissions are not invited in poetry or fiction. Its many books in the life sciences and natural history are published under the Comstock Publishing Associates imprint, and a list of books in industrial and labor relations is offered under the ILR Press imprint.

Recent titles include *Memory, Metaphor, and Aby Warburg's Atlas of Images* by Christopher D. Johnson; *How Do We Help? The Free Market in Development Aid* by Patrick Develtere; *Warlords: Strong-arm Brokers in Weak States* by Kimberly Marten; *Air Plants: Epiphytes and Aerial Gardens* by David H. Benzing; *Earth: A Tenant's Manual* by Frank H. T. Rhodes

The house distributes its own titles. Queries and SASEs may be directed to:

Peter J. Potter, Editor-in-Chief—Literature, medieval studies, classics, and ancient history; pjp33@cornell.edu

John G. Ackerman, Director—European history, intellectual history, Russian/East European studies, music; jga4@cornell.edu

Frances Benson, Editorial Director—Business, labor, workplace issues, health care; fgb2@cornell.edu

Roger Haydon, Executive Editor—Political science, international relations, Asian studies, philosophy; rmh11@cornell.edu

Michael J. McGandy, Acquisitions Editor—American history, American politics, law, New York State, regional books; mjm475@cornell.edu

Heidi Steinmetz Lovette, Science Acquisitions Editor, Comstock Publishing Associates—Biology and natural history, ornithology, herpetology, ichthyology, mammology, entomology, botany, plant sciences; hsl22@cornell.edu

Katherine Liu, Acquisitions Assistant

Sarah Grossman, Acquisitions Assistant

DUKE UNIVERSITY PRESS

905 West Main Street, Suite 18B, Durham, NC 27701
919-687-3600 | fax: 919-688-4574
www.dukeupress.edu | e-mail: dukepress@duke.edu

Duke University Press publishes approximately 120 books annually and more than 30 journals. This places the press's books publishing program among the 20 largest at American university presses, and the journals publishing program among the five largest. The relative magnitude of the journals program within the press is unique

UNIVERSITY PRESSES

among American university presses: There is no other publisher of more than 15 journals that also publishes fewer than 175 books per year.

The press publishes primarily in the humanities and social sciences and issues a few publications for primarily professional audiences (e.g., in law or medicine). It is best known for its publications in the broad and interdisciplinary area of theory and history of cultural production, and it is known in general as a publisher willing to take chances with nontraditional and interdisciplinary publications, both books and journals.

Like many other university presses, in addition to scholarly titles, Duke looks for books with crossover appeal for general audiences. For example, *In Search of First Contact* by Annette Kolodny; *Go-Go Live* by Natalie Hopkinson; *Food, Farms, and Solidarity* by Chaia Heller.

Duke University Press requests that you submit a printed copy of your proposal by mail. If you'd like to inquire about potential interest in your project, you may submit a short query by e-mail. Do not submit full proposals electronically unless specifically asked to do so. Direct queries and submissions to:

Ken Wissoker, Editorial Director—Anthropology; cultural studies; postcolonial theory; lesbian and gay studies; construction of race, gender, and national identity; social studies of science; new media; literary criticism; film and television; popular music; visual studies; kwiss@duke.edu

Valerie Millholland, Senior Editor—Latin American history and politics, European history and politics, American history, women's history, environmental studies, labor history, political science; vmill@duke.edu

Miriam Angress, Associate Editor—Religion, women's studies, world history, humanities, cultural studies; mangress@dukeupress.edu

Courtney Berger, Assistant Editor—Political theory, social theory, film and television, geography, gender studies, American studies, Asian American studies, cultural studies of food; cberger@dukeupress.edu

---

THE FEMINIST PRESS AT THE CITY UNIVERSITY OF NEW YORK

365 Fifth Avenue, Suite 5406, New York, NY 10016
212-817-7915 | fax: 212-817-1593
www.feministpress.org

The mission of the Feminist Press is to publish and promote the most potent voices of women from all eras and all regions of the globe. Now in its thirty-ninth year, the press has brought more than 300 critically acclaimed works by and about women into print, enriching the literary canon, expanding the historical record, and influencing public discourse about issues fundamental to women.

In addition to publishing new works, this renowned house recovers precious out-of-print and never-in-print documents, establishing the history of women around the globe. The press develops core curriculum materials for all classroom levels, providing young women with strong role models. In recognition of its special role in bringing awareness to international women's issues, the Feminist Press was granted NGO status with the Economic and Social Council of the United Nations in 2000.

The Feminist Press is interested in acquiring primary texts that will have broad, long-term sales in bookstores, as well as the possibility of consistent adoption for college classrooms or use in secondary school classrooms. Through publications and projects, The Feminist Press attempts to contribute to the rediscovery of the history of women in the United States and internationally, and to the emergence of a more humane society.

Please note that this house does not publish original fiction, original poetry, drama, doctoral dissertations, or original literary criticism. For the time being, the house has also ceased publishing books for children.

Recent titles from the Feminist Press include: *I Still Believe Anita Hill* by Amy Richards and Cynthia Greenberg; *Spit and Passion* by Cristy C. Road; *A Question of Choice: Roe v. Wade 40th Anniversary* by Sarah Weddington; *The Feminist Porn Book: The Politics of Producing Pleasure* by Tristan Taormino, Constance Penley, Celine Parrenas Shimizu, and Mireille Miller-Young.

To submit, send an e-mail of no more than 200 words describing your book project with the word "submission" in the subject line. Your e-mail should very briefly explain the type of book you are proposing and who you are. Do not send a proposal unless the editors request it, as they will discard all submission materials that arrive without an invitation. Send e-mail query to: editor@feministpress.org.

FORDHAM UNIVERSITY PRESS

2546 Belmont Avenue, University Box L, Bronx, NY 10458
718-817-4795 | fax: 718-817-4785
www.fordhampress.com

Fordham University Press was established in 1907 not only to represent and uphold the values and traditions of the University itself, but also to further those values and traditions through the dissemination of scholarly research and ideas.

The press publishes primarily in the humanities and the social sciences, with an emphasis on the fields of philosophy, theology, history, classics, communications, economics, sociology, business, political science, and law, as well as literature and the fine arts. Additionally, the press publishes books focusing on the metropolitan New York region and books of interest to the general public.

Recent titles include *Neighbors and Missionaries: A History of the Sisters of Our Lady of Christian Doctrine* by Margaret M. McGuinness; *Raised by the Church* by

Edward Rohs and Judith Estrine; *New Bedford's Civil War* by Earl F. Mulderink, III; *From Slave Ship to Harvard: Yarrow Mamout and the History of an African American Family* by James H. Johnston; *Hidden: Reflections on Gay Life, AIDS, and Spiritual Desire* by Richard Giannone.

Submissions are not accepted via e-mail. Direct proposals and SASEs to:

Helen Tartar, Editorial Director—Philosophy, religion, theology, literary studies, anthropology, law, or any other fields in the humanities or social sciences; tartar@fordham.edu

---

GEORGETOWN UNIVERSITY PRESS

3240 Prospect Street, NW, Washington, DC 20007
202-687-5889 | fax: 202-687-6340
press.georgetown.edu | e-mail: **gupress@georgetown.edu**

Georgetown University Press supports the academic mission of Georgetown University by publishing scholarly books and journals for a diverse, worldwide readership. These publications, written by an international group of authors representing a broad range of intellectual perspectives, reflect the academic and institutional strengths of the university. They publish peer-reviewed works in five subjects: bioethics; international affairs and human rights; languages and linguistics; political science, public policy, and public management; and religion and ethics.

The beginnings of Georgetown University Press can be traced to 1964; it currently publishes approximately 40 new books a year, as well as two journals, with an active list of close to 500 titles. These publications primarily serve the scholarly community, and many also reach into the general reading public. Many help to unite people speaking different languages, literally and figuratively, and all attempt to illuminate, clarify, and respond to the world's most difficult questions.

Recent titles include *Ethics Beyond War's End* by Eric Patterson; *Federal Management Reform in a World of Contradictions* by Beryl A. Radin; *Afghan Endgames* by Hy Rothstein and John Arquilla; *Between Terror and Tolerance* by Timothy D. Sisk; *Christianity in Evolution* by Jack Mahoney.

Georgetown University Press does not publish poetry, fiction, memoirs, children's books, Festschriften, symposium proceedings, or unrevised dissertations. Send cover letter, prospectus, and SASE via regular mail:

Richard Brown, PhD, Director—Bioethics, international affairs and human rights, religion and politics, and religion and ethics; reb7@georgetown.edu

Hope J. Smith LeGro—Languages, linguistics, and Director, Georgetown Languages; hjs6@georgetown.edu

Donald Jacobs, Acquisitions Editor—International affairs, human rights, public policy, public management; dpj5@georgetown.edu

HARVARD BUSINESS SCHOOL PRESS

60 Harvard Way, Boston, MA 02163
617-783-7400 | fax: 617-783-7555
New York office:
75 Rockefeller Plaza, 15th Floor, New York, NY 10019-6926
www.hbsp.harvard.edu | e-mail: asandoval@hbsp.harvard.edu

Harvard Business School Press seeks to influence real-world change by maximizing the reach and impact of its essential offering—ideas. The editors accept proposals for books that take a harder, broader look at the questions that business people face every day. The press is a business unit of Harvard Business School Publishing (HBSP).

HBSP was founded in 1994 as a not-for-profit, wholly-owned subsidiary of Harvard University. Its mission is to improve the practice of management in a changing world. HBSP does this by serving as a bridge between academia and enterprises around the globe through its publications and reach into three markets: academic, enterprise, and individual managers.

HBSP has about 250 employees, primarily based in Boston, with an office in New York City. Its business units are *Harvard Business Review* magazine and article reprints, Harvard Business School Press, Harvard Business School Publishing Newsletters, Harvard Business School Publishing Conferences, Harvard Business School Publishing Higher Education, and Harvard Business School Publishing eLearning.

Recent titles include *Cost and Effect: Using Integrated Cost Systems to Drive Profitability and Performance* by Robert S. Kaplan and Robin Cooper; *The Balanced Scorecard: Translating Strategy into Action* by Robert S. Kaplan and David P. Norton; *If We Can Put a Man on the Moon…: Getting Big Things Done in Government* by William D. Eggers and John O'Leary; *Managerial Economics: Concepts and Principles* by Donald N. Stengel; *Billions of Entrepreneurs: How China and India Are Reshaping Their Futures and Yours* by Tarun Khanna; *The Entrepreneurial Mindset: Strategies for Continuously Creating Opportunity in an Age of Uncertainty* by Rita Gunther McGrath and Ian MacMillan.

Harvard Business School Press distributes through Perseus.

Send proposals and SASEs via regular mail or e-mail to Courtney E. Schinke, Editorial Coordinator (Boston); cschinke@hbsp.harvard.edu.

Jacqueline Murphy, Senior Editor (Boston)

Jeff Kehoe, Senior Editor (Boston)

Melinda Adams Merino, Editor (Boston)

Kirsten D. Sandberg, Executive Editor (NY)

UNIVERSITY PRESSES

HARVARD UNIVERSITY PRESS

BELKNAP PRESS
79 Garden Street, Cambridge, MA 02138
617-495-2600 | fax: 617-495-5898
www.hup.harvard.edu | e-mail: contact_HUP@harvard.edu | blog: harvardpress
.typepad.com

Publisher of enduring tomes such as Lovejoy's *Great Chain of Being*; Giedion's *Space, Time, and Architecture*; Langer's *Philosophy in a New Key*; and Kelly's *Eleanor of Aquitaine and the Four Kings*; Harvard University Press (HUP) holds an exalted position within the university press world. Still, its editors look to attract an audience of general readers as well as scholars, and the press welcomes considered nonfiction proposals.

HUP publishes scholarly books and thoughtful books for the educated general reader in history, philosophy, American literature, law, economics, public policy, natural science, history of science, psychology, and education, and reference books in all the above fields. The Belknap Press imprint, established in 1949, strives to publish books of long-lasting importance, superior scholarship and production, chosen whether or not they might be profitable, thanks to the bequest of Waldron Phoenix Belknap, Jr.

Recent HUP titles include *Dreaming and Historical Consciousness in Island Greece* by Charles Stewart; *Financing Health in Latin America, Volume 1: Household Spending and Impoverishment* by Felicia Maria Knaul, Rebeca Wong, and Héctor Arreola-Ornelas; *How To Be Gay* by David M. Halperin; *The Money Doctors from Japan* by Michael Schiltz; *What the Best College Students Do* by Ken Bain.

All HUP books are published in English, with translation rights bought by publishers in other countries. The house does not publish original fiction, original poetry, religious inspiration or revelation, cookbooks, guidebooks, children's books, art and photography books, Festschriften, conference volumes, unrevised dissertations, or autobiographies.

The HUP website offers photographs of the editors that you may or may not wish to peruse prior to submitting, as well as detailed submission guidelines that you will not want to miss. No electronic submissions. Submit proposals and SASEs to:

Susan Wallace Boehmer, Editor-in-Chief
Michael Fisher, Editor-in-Chief—Evolutionary theory, evolutionary developmental biology, biological and evolutionary anthropology, neuroscience, systems biology and bioinformatives, human genetics, science and society, animal cognition and behavior, history of technology; also books for general readers in physics, astronomy, earth science, chemistry, engineering, and mathematics.
Joyce Seltzer, Senior Executive Editor for History and Contemporary Affairs— Serious and scholarly nonfiction that appeals to a general intellectual audience

as well as to students and scholars in a variety of disciplines, especially history across a broad spectrum, American studies, contemporary politics, social problems, and biography.

Lindsay Waters, Executive Editor for the Humanities—Philosophy, literary studies, cultural studies, film, Asian cultural studies, pop culture, conflicting relations among the races in the United States and around the world.

Michael Aronson, Senior Editor for Social Sciences—Economics, business, law, political science, sociology, especially the problems of capitalism such as distribution and inequality.

Elizabeth Knoll, Senior Editor for Behavioral Sciences and Law—Education, psychology, law, especially political and social aspects of education, universities, and developmental psychology.

Shamila Sen, Editor for the Humanities—World religions, classics, ancient history, religion.

Kathleen McDermott, Editor for History and Social Sciences—American history, Atlantic history, European history from late medieval to modern, Russian and Central European history, Asian history, international relations, global history, military history, US Western history, Native American history, legal history.

John Kulka, Executive Editor-at-Large—American, English, and world literature; modernism; history of criticism; theory; the American publishing industry; political journalism; globalization; democracy; and human dignity.

HOWARD UNIVERSITY PRESS

2225 Georgia Avenue, NW, Suite 718, Washington, DC 20059
202-238-2570 | fax: 202-588-9849
www.hupress.howard.edu | e-mail: **howardupress@howard.edu**

Howard University Press is dedicated to publishing noteworthy new scholarship that addresses the contributions, conditions, and concerns of African Americans, other people of African descent, and people of color around the globe.

Recent titles include *No Boundaries: A Cancer Surgeon's Odyssey* by LaSalle D. Leffall, Jr., MD; *Horace T. Ward: Desegregation of the University of Georgia, Civil Rights Advocacy, and Jurisprudence* by Maurice C. Daniels; *And Then We Heard the Thunder* by John Oliver Killens; *First Freed: Washington D.C. in the Emancipation Era* edited by Elizabeth Clark-Lewis; *One-Third of a Nation: African American Perspectives* edited by Lorenzo Morris and Ura Jean Oyemade Bailey; *The American Paradox: Politics and Justice* by Patrick J. Gallo; *The Black Seminole Legacy and North American Politics, 1693–1845* by Bruce Edward Tyman; *Genocide in Rwanda: A Collective Memory* edited by John A. Berry and Carol Pott Berry; and *Manichean Psychology: Racism and the Minds of People of African Descent* by Camera Jules P. Harrell.

Please submit proposals, résumés, and SASEs by regular mail to the attention of the Editorial Department.

D. Kamali Anderson, Director; danderson@howard.edu

INDIANA UNIVERSITY PRESS

QUARRY BOOKS

601 N. Morton Street, Bloomington, IN 47404
812-855-8817 | 800-842-6796 | fax: 812-855-8507
www.iupress.indiana.edu | e-mail: iupress@indiana.edu

Currently the second-largest public university press, Indiana University Press (IU Press) wants to publish books that will matter 20 or even 100 years from now—books that make a difference today and will live on into the future through their reverberations in the minds of teachers and writers. IU Press also publishes books with Midwest regional interest through its Quarry Books imprint.

As an academic press, its mandate is to serve the world of scholarship and culture as a professional, not-for-profit publisher. Founded in 1950, IU Press is recognized internationally as a leading academic publisher specializing in the humanities and social sciences. It produces more than 140 new books annually, in addition to 30 journals, and maintains a backlist of some 2,000 titles. The press emphasizes scholarship but also publishes text, trade, and reference titles. Its program is financed primarily by income from sales, supplemented, to a minor extent, by gifts and grants from a variety of outside sources.

IU Press books have won many awards for scholarly merit and design, including two National Book Awards, three Herskovits Awards in African studies, and several National Jewish Book Awards. Numerous IU Press titles are selected every year by Choice as outstanding academic books.

Major subject areas include African, African American, Asian, cultural, Jewish and Holocaust, Middle East, Russian and East European, and gender studies; anthropology, film, history, bioethics, music, paleontology, philanthropy, philosophy, and religion.

Recent titles include *Earth before the Dinosaurs* by Sébastien Steyer; *Before the Chinrest: A Violinist's Guide to the Mysteries of Pre-Chinrest Technique and Style* by Stanley Ritchie; *Buenas Noches, American Culture: Latina/o Aesthetics of Night* by María DeGuzmán; *Claiming Society for God: Religious Movements and Social Welfare* by Nancy J. Davis and Robert V. Robinson; *Confessions of a Guilty Freelancer* by William O'Rourke; *Jewish Masculinities: German Jews, Gender, and History* by Benjamin Maria Baader, Sharon Gillerman, and Paul Lerner.

Quarry Books focuses on everything about Indiana and the Midwest, exploring subjects such as photography, history, gardening, cooking, sports, leisure, people, and places. Some books from Quarry include *An American Hometown: Terre Haute,*

Indiana 1927 by Tom Roznowski; *An Amish Patchwork: Indiana's Old Orders in the Modern World* by Thomas J. Meyers and Steven M. Nolt; *The Artists of Brown County* by Lyn Letsinger-Miller; and *Bean Blossom Dreams: A City Family's Search for a Simple Country Life* by Sallyann J. Murphy.

Please submit your inquiry to one editor only. Preliminary inquiries without attachments may be posted by e-mail, but it is recommended that submissions be sent by mail. Direct submissions to:

Janet Rabinowitch, Director—Russian and East European studies, art, Jewish and Holocaust studies, international studies; jrabinow@indiana.edu

Robert Sloan, Editorial Director—US history, African-American studies, bioethics, philanthropy, military history, paleontology, natural history; rjsloan @indiana.edu

Dee Mortensen, Senior Sponsoring Editor—African studies, religion, philosophy; mortense@indiana.edu

Rebecca Tolen, Sponsoring Editor—Anthropology, Asian studies, political science/international relations, folklore; retolen@indiana.edu

Linda Oblack, Assistant Sponsoring Editor—Regional trade, regional natural history, railroads past and present; loblack@indiana.edu

JOHNS HOPKINS UNIVERSITY PRESS

2715 North Charles Street, Baltimore, MD 21218-4363
410-516-6900 | fax: 410-516-6968
www.press.jhu.edu

Daniel Coit Gilman, the first president of the Johns Hopkins University, inaugurated the press in 1878. For Gilman, publishing, along with teaching and research, was a primary obligation of a great university. Since that time, the Johns Hopkins University Press has carried the name and mission of the university to every corner of the world. The press has published more than 6,000 titles, of which almost half remain in print today.

The press began as the University's Publication Agency, publishing the *American Journal of Mathematics* in its first year and the *American Chemical Journal* in its second. The agency published its first book, *Sidney Lanier: A Memorial Tribute*, in 1881 to honor the poet who was one of the university's first writers in residence. In 1891, the Publication Agency became the Johns Hopkins Press; since 1972, it has been known as the Johns Hopkins University Press (JHU Press). Today JHU Press is one of the world's largest university presses, publishing 60 scholarly periodicals and more than 200 new books each year.

Recent JHU Press titles include *In Full Glory Reflected* by Ralph E. Eshelman and Burton K. Kummerow; *Plants of the Chesapeake Bay* by Lytton John Musselman and David A. Knepper; *Success on the Tenure Track* by Cathy Ann Trower; *Cultivating*

Inquiry-Driven Learners by Clifton Conrad and Laura Dunek; *Mathematical Expeditions* by Frank J. Swetz.

Direct queries with SASEs to the appropriate acquiring editor:

Gregory M. Britton, Editorial Director; gb@press.jhu.edu

Jacqueline C. Wehmueller, Executive Editor—Consumer health, history of medicine, education; jcw@press.jhu.edu

Robert J. Brugger, Senior Acquisitions Editor—American history, history of science and technology, regional books; rjb@press.jhu.edu

Vincent J. Burke, Senior Acquisitions Editor—Biology and life sciences; vjb @press.jhu.edu

Suzanne Flinchbaugh, Associate Editor—Political science, health policy, and Copublishing Liaison; skf@press.jhu.edu

Greg Nicholl, Assistant Editor—American studies, regional books, and anabaptist and pietist studies; gan@press.jhu.edu

---

KENT STATE UNIVERSITY PRESS

1118 University Library, 1125 Risman Drive, PO Box 5190, Kent, OH 44242-0001
330-672-7913 | fax: 330-672-3104
upress.kent.edu | e-mail: ksupress@kent.edu

The Kent State University Press began in 1965 under the direction of Howard Allen and published in the university faculty strengths in literary criticism. In 1972, Paul Rohmann became the press's second director and expanded the press's publishing program to include regional studies and ethnomusicology. In 1985, historian John Hubbell assumed the directorship, and for 15 years he saw the staff and publishing program grow to include widely regarded lists in Civil War history and Ohio history. Today, under director Will Underwood, the press publishes 30 to 35 titles a year and reaches a large and appreciative audience.

The Kent State University Press is especially interested in acquiring scholarly works in history, including military, Civil War, US diplomatic, American cultural, women's, and art history; literary studies; titles of regional interest for Ohio; scholarly biographies; archaeological research; the arts; and general nonfiction.

Recent titles include *NATO after Sixty Years* by James Sperling and S. Victor Papacosma; *White Coats* by Jacqueline Marino and Tim Harrison; *Connie Mack: Grand Old Man of Baseball* by Frederick Lieb; *Pacific Time on Target: Memoirs of a Marine Artillery Officer, 1943-1945* by Christopher Donner and Jack H. McCall; *Rust Belt Resistance* by Perry Bush; *You Stink!* by Eric J. Wittenberg and Michael Aubrecht.

Direct query letters with SASEs to:

Joyce Harrison, Acquiring Editor

Will Underwood, Director
Mary D. Young, Managing Editor

LOUISIANA STATE UNIVERSITY PRESS

PO Box 25053, Baton Rouge, LA 70894-5053
800-848-6224 | fax: 225-576-6461
lsupress.org

Founded in 1935, the Louisiana State University Press (LSU Press) is a nonprofit book publisher dedicated to the publication of scholarly, general-interest, and regional books. As an integral part of LSU, the press shares the university's goal of the dissemination of knowledge and culture. LSU Press is one of the oldest and largest university presses in the South and the only university press to have won Pulitzer Prizes in both fiction and poetry.

The press is perhaps most widely recognized as the original publisher of John Kennedy Toole's Pulitzer Prize-winning novel *A Confederacy of Dunces*. The winner of the 2006 Pulitzer Prize for poetry, *Late Wife* by Claudia Emerson, was also published by the press. Through the years, its books have earned many prestigious honors, including a total of three Pulitzer Prizes, the National Book Award, the National Book Critics Circle Award, the Booker Prize, the American Book Award, the *Los Angeles Times* Book Prize, the Bancroft Prize, the Lincoln Prize, the Lamont Poetry Selection by the Academy of American Poets, and numerous others.

LSU Press publishes approximately 80 new books each year, as well as a backlist of some 1,000 titles. Their primary areas of focus include Southern history, biography, and literature; the Civil War and World War II; poetry; political philosophy and political communications; music studies, particularly jazz; geography and environmental studies; and illustrated books about the Gulf South region. In the mid-1990s, the press launched the acclaimed paperback fiction reprint series Voices of the South, and in 2005, after a hiatus of about a decade, it resumed publishing original fiction under the new series Yellow Shoe Fiction, edited by Michael Griffith.

This is a press that cares whether people outside a narrow theory specialty will understand a text. "We want work that is as accessible as possible," said executive editor John Easterly.

Recent titles include *The Angelic Mother and the Predatory Seductress: Poor White Women in Southern Literature of the Great Depression* by Ashley Craig Lancaster; *The Battlefield and Beyond: Essays on the American Civil War* by Clayton E. Jewett; *Best of LSU Fiction* by Judy Kahn and Nolde Alexius; *Democracy's Lawyer: Felix Grundy of the Old Southwest* by J. Roderick Heller III; *A Cold War Turning Point: Nixon and China, 1969-1972* by Chris Tudda.

Proposals for everything except fiction should include a cover letter, table of contents, sample chapters, information about competitive titles, and a résumé or

UNIVERSITY PRESSES

curriculum vitae. Fiction proposals should include a cover letter, a one-page summary of the work, a brief sample from the work, and a résumé. The press is not currently accepting poetry manuscripts. Submit to the appropriate acquisitions editor by regular mail:

John Easterly, Executive Editor—Poetry, fiction, literary studies, regional interest.
Rand Dotson, Senior Editor—Slavery, Civil War, Reconstruction, nineteenth- and twentieth-century South, Louisiana roots music.
Margaret Hart, Trade Editor—General interest.
Alisa Plant, Editor—European/Atlantic world history and media studies.

MASSACHUSETTS INSTITUTE OF TECHNOLOGY/ THE MIT PRESS

55 Hayward Street, Cambridge, MA 02142-1493
617-253-5646 | fax: 617-258-6779
mitpress.mit.edu | blog: mitpress.typepad.com

The MIT Press is the only university press in the United States whose list is based in science and technology. This does not mean that science and engineering are all it publishes; rather, it is committed to the edges and frontiers of the world—to exploring new fields and new modes of inquiry.

The press publishes about 200 new books a year and is a major publishing presence in fields as diverse as architecture, social theory, economics, cognitive science, and computational science. The MIT Press has a long-term commitment to both design excellence and the efficient and creative use of new technologies. Its goal is to create books that are challenging, creative, attractive, and yet affordable to individual readers.

The MIT Press history starts in 1926, when the physicist Max Born visited MIT to deliver a set of lectures on Problems of Atomic Dynamics. The institute published the lectures under its own imprint, and that book is numbered one in the archives of The MIT Press. In 1932, James R. Killian, Jr.—editor of MIT's alumni magazine, future scientific advisor to President Kennedy, and tenth president of MIT—engineered the creation of an institute-sponsored imprint called Technology Press, which published eight titles over the next five years. In 1937, John Wiley & Sons took on editorial and marketing functions for the young imprint, which during the next 25 years published 125 titles. In 1962, MIT amicably severed the Wiley connection and upgraded its imprint to an independent publishing house, naming it The MIT Press.

The creative burst and explosive growth of the 1960s slackened with the library cutbacks of the early 1970s, and by the end of that decade the press knew that it had to rethink what it was doing. It developed a strategy of focusing the list on a few key areas and publishing in depth in those areas. The initial core consisted of architecture, computer science and artificial intelligence, economics, and the emerging interdiscipline of cognitive science. The plan worked wonderfully, and by the mid-1980s, the press was again thriving. As the list developed, occasional offshoots sprouted (neuroscience, for example, was spun off from cognitive science in 1987), while a few smaller areas in which it continued to publish—technology studies, aesthetic theory, design, and social theory—have remained viable and interesting components of what has become a unique mix. Its latest addition was an environmental science list, started in the early 1990s.

Recent titles include *The Small Worlds of Corporate Governance* by Bruce Kogut; *Boosting: Foundations and Algorithms* by Robert E. Schapire and Yoav Freund; *The Environment: Philosophy, Science, and Ethics* by William P. Kabasenche, Michael O'Rourke, and Matthew H. Slater; *Internet Success: A Study of Open Source Software Commons* by Charles M. Schweik and Robert C. English; *The New Handbook of Multisensory Processing* by Barry E. Stein; *Burdens of Proof: Cryptographic Culture and Evidence Law in the Age of Electronic Documents* by Jean-François Blanchette; *The Cognitive Science of Science: Explanation, Discovery, and Conceptual Change* by Paul Thagard.

The MIT Press accepts proposals via e-mail or regular mail with SASE. Submit your proposal to the appropriate editor:

Gita Manaktala, Editorial Director; manak@mit.edu

Phillip Laughlin, Senior Acquisitions Editor—Cognitive science, philosophy; laughlin@mit.edu

John S. Covell, Senior Acquisitions Editor—Economics, finance, business; jcovell @mit.edu

Jane Macdonald, Acquisitions Editor—Economics, finance, business; janem @mit.edu

Clay Morgan, Senior Acquisitions Editor—Environmental and political science, bioethics; claym@mit.edu

Robert Prior, Executive Editor—Life sciences, neuroscience, biology; prior @mit.edu

Doug Sery, Senior Acquisitions Editor—Design, new media, game studies; dsery@mit.edu

Marguerite Avery, Acquisitions Editor—Science, technology and society, information science; mavery@mit.edu

---

NEW YORK UNIVERSITY PRESS

838 Broadway, 3rd Floor, New York, NY 10003-4812
212-998-2575 | fax: 212-995-3833
www.nyupress.org | e-mail: information@nyupress.org

The NYU Press believes in the idea that academic research and opinion can and should have a prominent place at the table of public debate. At a time of continued upheaval in publishing, some presses, NYU Press among them, detect profound opportunities in this unstable landscape. Rather than bemoaning a lost age, when libraries more or less financed university press operations, these presses are emphasizing their strengths. Convinced that intellectual heft and a user-friendly efficiency need not be mutually exclusive, the staff at NYU Press has sought, in recent years, to redefine what it means to be a university press.

Most importantly, they do not believe that the sole purpose of a university press is to publish works of objective social science, though to be sure this remains an important role of the house mandate. Rather, NYU Press also eagerly embraces the role of a gadfly. It oftentimes publishes books on the same issue from different poles of the political spectrum in the same catalog, to generate dialogue, engender debate, and resist pat categorization of the publishing program. Rather than praise diversity as an abstract goal, it embraces ideological diversity as a crucial, defining ingredient for a healthy program. It does so with a list of around 100 new books a year and a backlist of over 1,500 titles.

On a logistical level, NYU Press believes that, in the world of nonfiction publishing, the scales have far too long been tipped in favor of the publishers. The house therefore rejects exclusive review, encouraging authors to submit their manuscripts widely, should they wish to do so, to ensure their decision, if they publish with this house, is an educated one, not the result of artificial restrictions. NYU Press believes that any long-term relationship between an author and publisher must be predicated on mutual respect. Thus, it places enormous emphasis on a close working relationship with authors. Further, it provides high-quality production and decades of craft experience. Importantly, it can provide all these advantages alongside one crucial guarantee: No one will ever take this house over.

NYU Press is interested in titles that explore issues of race and ethnicity. They are also highly interested in media studies and American studies.

Recent titles include *American Arabesque: Arabs and Islam in the Nineteenth Century Imaginary* by Jacob Rama Berman; *Astrology and Cosmology in the World's Religions* by Nicholas Campion; *At Liberty to Die: The Battle for Death with Dignity in America* by Howard Ball; *Killing McVeigh: The Death Penalty and the Myth of Closure* by Jody Lyneé Madeira; *Not Guilty: Are the Acquitted Innocent?* by Daniel Givelber and Amy Farrell.

No submissions through e-mail. Query letters and SASEs should be directed to:

Eric Zinner, Editor-in-Chief—Literary criticism and cultural studies, media studies, American history; eric.zinner@nyu.edu

Ilene Kalish, Executive Editor—Sociology, criminology, politics; ilene.kalish @nyu.edu

Jennifer Hammer, Editor—Religion, psychology, anthropology; jennifer .hammer@nyu.edu

Deborah Gershenowitz, Senior Editor—American history to 1900, American military history, law; deborah.gershenowitz@nyu.edu

NORTHWESTERN UNIVERSITY PRESS

629 Noyes Street, Evanston, IL 60208-4210
847-491-2046 | fax: 847-491-8150
nupress.northwestern.edu | e-mail: nupress@northwestern.edu

From its inception, Northwestern University Press has striven to be at the forefront in publishing not only scholarly works in different disciplines, but also quality works of fiction, nonfiction, and literary criticism.

Founded in 1893, the press dedicated its early years to the publication of legal periodicals and scholarly books dealing with the law. In 1957, the press was established as a separate university publishing company and began expanding its offerings with new series in various fields, including African studies, phenomenology and existential philosophy, literature, and literary criticism.

In the late 1960s, the press published Viola Spolin's landmark volume, *Improvisation for the Theater: A Handbook of Teaching and Directing Techniques.* This "bible" of improvisational theater has sold more than 100,000 copies since its publication and, with several other Spolin titles, forms a cornerstone of the press's publishing program. The press continues its commitment to theater and performance studies, most recently with the publication of Mary Zimmerman's *Metamorphoses,* the script of her Broadway show that was nominated for the 2002 Tony award for Best Play and Best Scenic Design, and won the 2002 Tony award for Best Director.

Since 1992, Northwestern University Press has doubled its publishing output. In addition to the works of contemporary European writers, the press has also begun to reissue lost or previously untranslated works of important European authors, including Nobel Prize winners Heinrich Böll and Grazia Deledda. Scholarly series include Rethinking Theory, Studies in Russian Literature and Theory, Writings from an Unbound Europe, Avant-Garde and Modernism Studies, and Studies in Phenomenology and Existential Philosophy. In 1992, the press joined forces with *TriQuarterly* magazine—Northwestern University's innovative literary journal aimed at a sophisticated and diverse readership—to establish the TriQuarterly Books imprint, which is devoted primarily to contemporary American fiction and poetry. In addition, the press has a second trade imprint, Hydra Books, which features contemporary fiction, poetry, and nonfiction in translation. In 1997, *TriQuarterly* magazine itself became a publication of the press. In 2002, the press began publishing Chicago regional titles, such as *A Court That Shaped America: Chicago's Federal Court from Abe Lincoln to Abbie Hoffman* by Richard Cahan.

Recent titles include *See You in the Dark: Poems* by Lynne Sharon Schwartz; *Sweet Spot: Poems* by J. T. Barbarese; *Head Off & Split: Poems* by Nikky Finney; *Fowling Piece: Poems* by Heidy Steidlmayer.

To submit fiction, poetry, or general nonfiction, please send the complete manuscript or several sample chapters along with biographical information on the author,

UNIVERSITY PRESSES

including a list of previously published books. Because of the high volume of submissions, allow at least 16 weeks for the review of your manuscript.

To submit a scholarly manuscript, please send a proposal, cover letter, and CV. Allow approximately 12 weeks for the review of your manuscript.

Please do not call. Send queries and SASEs to: Acquisitions Department.

Henry L. Carrigan Jr., Senior Editor; h-carrigan@northwestern.edu

Mike Levine, Acquisitions Editor; mike-levine@northwestern.edu

Anne Gendler, Managing Editor; a-gendler@northwestern.edu

Heather Antti, Senior Project Editor; h-antti@northwestern.edu

---

OHIO STATE UNIVERSITY PRESS

180 Pressey Hall, 1070 Carmack Road, Columbus, OH 43210-1002
614-292-6930 | fax: 614-292-2065
www.ohiostatepress.org | e-mail: info@osupress.org

The Ohio State University Press was established in 1957 and currently publishes 30 new books a year. Areas of specialization include literary studies, including narrative theory; history, including business history, medieval history, and history of crime; political science, including legislative studies; and Victorian studies, urban studies, and women's health. They also publish annual winners of short fiction and poetry prizes, the details of which are available at www.ohiostatepress.org.

Recent titles include *German Writing, American Reading: Women and the Import of Fiction, 1866–1917* by Lynne Tatlock; *London, Radical Culture, and the Making of the Dickensian Aesthetic* by Sambudha Sen; *Writing AIDS: (Re)Conceptualizing the Individual and Social Body in Spanish American Literature* by Jodie Parys; *Green Speculations: Science Fiction and Transformative Environmentalism* by Eric C. Otto; *Fear, Loathing, and Victorian Xenophobia* by Marlene Tromp, Maria K. Bachman, and Heidi Kaufman.

Ohio State University Press oversees its own sales and distribution.

Scholars proposing manuscripts for publication should submit whatever materials they feel are necessary for the acquisitions department at Ohio State University Press to make informed decisions about the project. Query letters and SASEs should be directed to:

Sandy Crooms, Senior Editor—Literary studies, Victorian studies, narrative, American studies, women's studies, women and health; sandy.crooms @osupress.org

Malcolm Litchfield, Acquisitions Editor—Medieval studies, literary theory other than narrative; ml@osupress.org

Eugene O'Connor, PhD, Acquisitions Editor—Classics; eugene@osupress.org

OXFORD UNIVERSITY PRESS

198 Madison Avenue, New York, NY 10016
212-726-6000
www.oup.com/us | blog: blog.oup.com

Oxford University Press, Inc. (OUP USA), is by far the largest American university press and perhaps the most diverse publisher of its type. It publishes works that further Oxford University's objective of excellence in research, scholarship, and education.

The press had its origins in the information technology revolution of the late fifteenth century, which began with the invention of printing from movable type. The first book was printed in Oxford in 1478. In 1586, the university itself obtained a decree confirming its privilege to print books. This was further enhanced in the Great Charter secured by Archbishop Laud from King Charles I, which entitled the university to print "all manner of books." The university first appointed delegates to oversee this privilege in 1633. Minutes recording their deliberations date back to 1668, and OUP as it exists today began to develop in a recognizable way from that time.

OUP's international expansion began with the opening of a US office in 1896. The office was established initially simply to sell bibles published in Oxford, but by the 1920s, the office began to produce books on its own. The first nonfiction work published by OUP USA, *The Life of Sir William Osler*, won the Pulitzer Prize in 1926. Six more Pulitzers, several National Book Awards, and over a dozen Bancroft Prizes in American history have followed since.

Oxford's New York office is editorially independent of the British home office and handles distribution of its own list, as well as titles originating from Oxford's branches worldwide. OUP USA publishes at a variety of levels, for a wide range of audiences in almost every academic discipline. The main criteria in evaluating new titles are quality and contribution to the furtherance of scholarship and education. OUP USA produces approximately 500 titles each year, of which 250 are scholarly research monographs, and imports close to 800 such works from its UK and branch offices. OUP USA has 3,300 scholarly books in print and stocks another 8,700 imports from other OUP offices around the world. All publications are first vetted by OUP's delegates, who are leading scholars at Oxford University and other top US institutions.

OUP editor Shannon McMahan said recently that the press is especially interested in acquiring titles that explore "material based studies," and such topics as print culture, environmentalism, and literature and the law.

Recent titles include *The American Dream: A Short History of an Idea that Shaped a Nation* by Jim Cullen; *Sharp's Dictionary of Power and Struggle: Language of Civil Resistance in Conflicts* by Gene Sharp; *Showdown in the Sonoran Desert: Religion, Law, and the Immigration Controversy* by Ananda Rose; *Elusive Victories: The American Presidency at War* by Andrew J. Polsky; *Cracking the Egyptian Code: The Revolutionary Life of Jean-Francois Champollion* by Andrew Robinson.

OUP USA welcomes submissions. Potential authors should include a cover letter, a copy of their CV, a prospectus, and sample chapters from the work (if available). In general, all material should be unbound and double-spaced on single-sided paper. Material may be sent in care of the appropriate editor:

Niko Pfund, Academic Publisher

Stefan Vranka, Editor—Classical studies; stefan.vranka@oup.com

James Cook, Editor—Criminology; james.cook@oup.com

David McBride, Editor—Current affairs, political science, law (trade), sociology (trade); david.mcbride@oup.com

Sarah Harrington, Editor—Developmental psychology; sarah.harrington @oup.com

Joan Bossert, Associate Publisher—Neuroscience, consumer health, psychological and behavioral sciences; joan.bossert@oup.com

Catharine Carlin, Associate Publisher—Cognitive neuroscience, ophthalmology, cognitive psychology; catharine.carlin@oup.com

Susan Ferber, Editor—American and world history, art history, academic art and architecture; susan.ferber@oup.com

Larry Selby, Editor—Law (practitioner); larry.selby@oup.com

Chris Collins, Editor—Law (academic); chris.collins@oup.com

Tisse Takagi, Editor—Life sciences; tisse.takagi@oup.com

Jeremy Lewis, Editor—Chemistry; jeremy.lewis@oup.com

Peter Ohlin, Editor—Bioethics, linguistics, philosophy; peter.ohlin@oup.com

Phyllis Cohen, Editor—Mathematics and statistics; phyllis.cohen@oup.com

Cynthia Read, Senior Editor—Religion (trade); cynthia.read@oup.com

Donald Kraus, Executive Editor—Bibles; donald.kraus@oup.com

Andrea Seils, Editor—Anesthesiology; andrea.seils@oup.com

Shannon McLachlan, Editor—American studies, classical studies, English language and literature, literary studies, film; shannon.mclachlan@oup.com

Terry Vaughn, Editor—Business management, economics, finance and financial economics; terry.vaughn@oup.com

Mariclaire Cloutier, Editor—Forensic psychology, clinical psychology; mariclaire.cloutier@oup.com

Craig Panner, Editor—Neurology; craig.panner@oup.com

Shelley Reinhardt, Editor—Neuropsychology; shelley.reinhardt@oup.com

Lori Handelman, Editor—Social psychology; lori.handelman@oup.com

Maura Roessner, Editor—Social work; maura.roessner@oup.com

Theo Calderera, Editor—Religion (academic); theo.calderera@oup.com

William Lamsback, Editor—Medicine, neurology, public health; william .lamsback@oup.com

Suzanne Ryan, Editor—Music (books); suzanne.ryan@oup.com

Todd Waldman, Editor—Music (sheet music); todd.waldman@oup.com

Sonke Adlung, Editor—Physics; sonke.adlung@oup.com

PENN STATE UNIVERSITY PRESS

820 North University Drive, University Support Building 1, Suite C, University Park, PA 16802-1003
814-865-1327 | fax: 814-863-1408
www.psupress.org | e-mail: info@psupress.org

The Penn State University Press is dedicated to serving the university community, the citizens of Pennsylvania, and the worldwide network of scholars by publishing books and journals of the highest quality. In fulfilling its role as part of the University's division of research and graduate education, the press promotes the advance of scholarship by disseminating knowledge—new information, interpretations, methods of analysis—and strives to reflect academic strengths of the university. As an integral part of the university community, the press collaborates with alumni, friends, faculty, and staff in producing books about aspects of university life and history. As the publishing arm of a land-grant and state-supported institution, the press recognizes its special responsibility to develop books about Pennsylvania, both scholarly and popular, that enhance interest in the region and spread awareness of the state's history, culture, and environment.

The origins of the press go back to 1945, when a committee at the university was appointed "to study the advisability and practicability of establishing a Pennsylvania State College Press." No immediate action was taken, but in 1953, as a first experiment in university press publishing, the Department of Public Information (then directed by Louis H. Bell) issued a book entitled *Penn State Yankee: The Autobiography of Fred Lewis Pattee*, which Mr. Bell himself edited and designed. The experiment evidently proved successful enough to persuade the trustees board in 1956 to establish the Pennsylvania State University Press "on an experimental basis."

The press's strengths include core areas such as art history and literary criticism as well as fields such as philosophy, religion, history (mainly US and European), and some of the social sciences (especially political science and sociology).

Recent titles include *Princeton: America's Campus* by W. Barksdale Maynard; *The Breathless Zoo: Taxidermy and the Cultures of Longing* by Rachel Poliquin; *Second Atlas of Breeding Birds in Pennsylvania* by Andrew M. Wilson, Daniel W. Brauning, and Robert S. Mulvihill; *The Evolving Citizen: American Youth and the Changing Norms of Democratic Engagement* by Jay P. Childers; *Philadelphia on Stone: Commercial Lithography in Philadelphia, 1828-1878* by Erika Piola.

If you have questions about submissions, Penn State Press invites you to call or e-mail with "Manuscript Submissions" in the subject line. Direct queries and SASEs to:

Patrick H. Alexander, Editor-in-Chief—American studies, European history and culture, history, medieval and early modern studies, philosophy, regional studies, religion, religious studies, romance studies, and Slavic studies; pha3@psu.edu

UNIVERSITY PRESSES

Eleanor Goodman, PhD, Executive Editor for the Arts & Humanities—Art and art history, architectural history, European history and culture (Spanish, French), literature, medieval and early modern studies, visual culture; ehg11@psu.edu

PRINCETON UNIVERSITY PRESS

41 William Street, Princeton, NJ 08540-5237
609-258-4900 | fax: 609-258-6305
press.princeton.edu
UK office:
3 Market Place, Woodstock, Oxfordshire OX20 1SY, UK
011-44-1993-814500

Princeton University Press, which celebrated its 100th anniversary in 2005, is one of the country's largest and oldest university presses. The press publishes some 200 new books in hardcover each year and another 90 paperback reprints. With a goal to disseminate scholarship both within academia and to society at large, the press produces publications that range across more than 40 disciplines, from art history to ornithology and political science to philosophy.

The press is an independent publisher with close connections, both formal and informal, to Princeton University. Its five-member editorial board, which makes controlling decisions about which books will bear the press's imprint, is appointed from the faculty by the president of the university, and nine of the fifteen members of the press's board must have a Princeton University connection.

Recent titles include *The Best of All Possible Worlds: A Story of Philosophers, God, and Evil in the Age of Reason* by Steven Nadler; *The Church in the Shadow of the Mosque: Christians and Muslims in the World of Islam* by Sidney H. Griffith; *Democracy and Knowledge: Innovation and Learning in Classical Athens* by Josiah Ober; *God and Race in American Politics: A Short History* by Mark A. Noll; *Greece: A Jewish History* by K. E. Fleming; and *Luxury Fever: Money and Happiness in an Era of Excess* by Robert H. Frank.

The Bollingen Series, established in 1941, is sponsored by the Bollingen Foundation and has been published by Princeton since 1967. Bollingen titles are works of original scholarship, translations, or new editions of classics. An ongoing Bollingen project is Mythos: The Princeton/Bollingen series in world mythology. Titles representative of the list include *The Collected Works of Samuel Taylor Coleridge, Volume 15: Opus Maximum* edited by Thomas McFarland; *The I Ching or Book of Changes* edited by Hellmut Wilhelm and translated by Cary F. Baynes; and *Essays on a Science of Mythology: The Myth of the Divine Child and the Mysteries of Eleusis* by C. G. Jung and C. Kerényi.

Books from the Princeton Science Library include *Why Adjudicate?* by Christina L. Davis; *Sin* by Paula Fredriksen; *Why Cats Land on Their Feet* by Mark Levi;

Pursuits of Wisdom by John M. Cooper; *The Spirit of Compromise* by Amy Gutmann and Dennis Thompson.

Princeton University Press handles distribution through the offices of California/Princeton Fulfillment Services, as well as regional sales representation worldwide.

Princeton University Press does not accept unsolicited proposals or manuscripts via e-mail. Queries or brief proposals, along with a copy of your CV and SASEs, should be mailed via regular mail addressed to the Editorial Administrator.

Peter Dougherty, Director

Brigitta van Rheinberg, Editor-in-Chief—History (American, European, Middle Eastern, Jewish, Asian, medieval, ancient, and world).

Fred Appel, Associate Editor—Music, anthropology, literature.

Seth Ditchik, Senior Editor—Economics, finance, behavioral and cognitive sciences.

Ingrid Gnerlich, Senior Editor—Physical sciences, earth sciences.

Alison Kalett, Editor—Biology, earth sciences.

Vickie Kearn, Executive Editor—Mathematics.

Robert Kirk, Executive Editor—Natural history, biology, ornithology, field guides.

Chuck Myers, Executive Editor—Political science, law.

Anna Savarese, Senior Editor—Reference.

Eric Schwartz, Editor—Sociology, cognitive sciences.

Robert Tempio, Editor—Philosophy, classics, ancient world.

RUTGERS UNIVERSITY PRESS

RIVERGATE BOOKS
100 Joyce Kilmer Avenue, Piscataway, NJ 08854-8099
848-445-7762 | fax: 732-445-7039
rutgerspress.rutgers.edu

Since its founding in 1936 as a nonprofit publisher, Rutgers University Press has been dedicated to the advancement and dissemination of knowledge to scholars, students, and the general reading public. An integral part of one of the leading public research and teaching universities in the United States, the press reflects and is essential to the university's missions of research, instruction, and service. To carry out these goals, the house publishes books in print and electronic format in a broad array of disciplines across the humanities, social sciences, and sciences. Fulfilling a mandate to serve the people of New Jersey, it also publishes books of scholarly and popular interest on the state and surrounding region.

Working with authors throughout the world, the house seeks books that meet high editorial standards, facilitate the exchange of ideas, enhance teaching, and make scholarship accessible to a wide range of readers. The press's overriding ambition is nothing less than to help make the world better, one book at a time, through a publication program of superior scholarship and popular appeal. The press celebrates and affirms its role as a major cultural institution that contributes significantly to the ideas that shape the critical issues of our time.

The press's strengths include history, sociology, anthropology, religion, media, film studies, women's studies, African American studies, Asian American studies, public health, history of medicine, evolutionary biology, the environment, and books about the Mid-Atlantic region.

Recent titles published by Rutgers University Press include *Arabs of the Jewish Faith: The Civilizing Mission in Colonial Algeria* by Joshua Schreier; *Loyal Subjects: Bonds of Nation, Race, and Allegiance in Nineteenth-Century America* by Elizabeth Duquette; *Sex and the University: Celebrity, Controversy, and a Student Journalism Revolution* by Daniel Reimold; *New Urban Development: Looking Back to See Forward* by Claude Gruen.

Rutgers is proud to announce Rivergate Books, an imprint devoted to New Jersey and surrounding states. New titles from Rivergate include *Knickerbocker: The Myth Behind New York* by Elizabeth L. Bradley; *No Minor Accomplishment: The Revival of New Jersey Professional Baseball* by Bob Golon; *How Newark Became Newark: The Rise, Fall, and Rebirth of an American City* by Brad R. Tuttle; *Local Heroes: The Asbury Park Music Scene* by Anders Martensson; and *The George Washington Bridge: Poetry in Steel* by Michael Aaron Rockland.

Rutgers University Press handles its own distribution.

Query letters and SASEs should be directed to:

Leslie Mitchner, Associate Director and Editor-in-Chief—Humanities, literature, film, communications; lmitch@rutgers.edu

Peter Mickulas, Editor; mickulas@rutgers.edu

Katie Keeran, Editorial Assistant; ckeeran@rutgers.edu

Lisa Boyajian, Editorial Assistant; lboyajian@rutgerspress.rutgers.edu

STANFORD UNIVERSITY PRESS

1450 Page Mill Road, Palo Alto, CA 94304-1124
650-723-9434 | fax: 650-725-3457
www.sup.org | e-mail: info@www.sup.org

Stanford University Press maintains specific publishing strategies that mirror not only Stanford's commitment to the unfettered creation and communication of new knowledge, but also its commitment to offering an undergraduate education that is unrivaled among research universities, and its commitment to training tomorrow's leaders in a range of graduate professional disciplines.

It does this by making available a range of highly specialized and peer-reviewed research that otherwise might not be published; making major foreign-language works available in translation here, and making books available in foreign-language editions abroad; keeping books in print and debate alive, often for decades;

publishing the work of new scholars, thereby adding their voices and views to ongoing debates—and often precipitating new ones; publishing textbooks for upper-level undergraduate courses and graduate courses; publishing reference works for professional practitioners; and making all works for which the house has electronic rights available through the main electronic aggregators, including ebrary, netLibrary, Questia, Google, and Books 24x7.

In pursuit of these strategies, the press publishes about 130 books per year. About two-thirds of these books are scholarly monographs and textbooks in the humanities and the social sciences, with strong concentrations in history, literature, philosophy, and Asian studies, and growing lists in politics, sociology, anthropology, and religion. The remaining one-third are textbooks, professional reference works, and monographs in law, business, economics, public policy, and education. Tenure monographs account for about 20 percent of the press's scholarly output, and translations account for about 12 percent.

In keeping with the high intellectual quality of the works the house publishes, the press ensures that every title it releases benefits from exacting professional standards for editing, design, and manufacturing. It also ensures that each book is carefully positioned in the market channel most appropriate for reaching its primary audience—that is, libraries, bookstores, online vendors, electronic collections, and searchable databases.

Working hard to maintain this commitment to intellectual quality and high production values is a creative, energetic, and enthusiastic staff who work closely together to make the whole process from manuscript creation to publication both seamless for the author and timely for the buyer. Their efforts are augmented by a global sales, marketing, and distribution network that gives access to wholesale and retail buyers in all the key markets of the Americas, Europe, Asia, and Australia.

Recent titles include *Global Futures in East Asia: Youth, Nation, and the New Economy in Uncertain Times* by Ann Anagnost, Andrea Arai, and Hai Ren; *Private Management and Public Policy: The Principle of Public Responsibility* by Lee E. Preston and James E. Post; *The Global Organ Shortage: Economic Causes, Human Consequences, Policy Responses* by T. Randolph Beard, David L. Kaserman, and Rigmar Osterkamp; *A Goy Who Speaks Yiddish: Christians and the Jewish Language in Early Modern Germany* by Aya Elyada; *The Secrets of Law* by Austin Sarat, Lawrence Douglas, and Martha Merrill Umphrey.

Stanford University Press books are distributed by Cambridge University Press Distribution Center.

Initial inquiries about publication should be made directly to the appropriate sponsoring editor at the press. Do not send complete manuscripts until invited to do so by the editor. Query letters and SASEs should be directed to:

Geoffrey Burn, Director and Acquisitions Editor—Business strategy and security studies; grhburn@stanford.edu

Norris Pope, Director of Scholarly Publishing—History, Latin American studies, Jewish studies; npope@stanford.edu

Kate Wahl, Executive Editor—Sociology, law, Middle East studies; kwahl @stanford.edu

Margo Beth Crouppen, Acquisitions Editor—Economics and organizational studies; mbcrouppen@stanford.edu

Stacy Wagner, Acquisitions Editor—Asian studies, Asian American studies, political science; swagner@stanford.edu

Emily-Jane Cohen, Acquisitions Editor—Literature, philosophy, religion; beatrice@stanford.edu

STATE UNIVERSITY OF NEW YORK PRESS

EXCELSIOR EDITIONS

22 Corporate Woods Boulevard, 3rd Floor, Albany, NY 12210- 2504
866-430-7869 | fax: 518-472-5038
www.sunypress.edu | e-mail: info@sunypress.edu

State University of New York Press (SUNY Press) publishes scholarly and trade books in support of the university's commitments to teaching, research, and public service. With an editorial board made up of SUNY faculty from throughout the state, SUNY Press has a large catalog, featuring authors from around the world.

From a modest beginning in 1966, SUNY Press has become one of the largest public university presses in the United States, with an annual output of some 170 books and a backlist of more than 4,000 titles. The press publishes chiefly in the humanities and social sciences, and has attained national recognition in the areas of education, philosophy, religion, Jewish studies, Asian studies, political science, and sociology, with increasing growth in the areas of literature, film studies, communication, women's studies, and environmental studies.

Recent titles include *In the Hamptons Too: Further Encounters with Farmers, Fisherman, Artists, Billionaires, and Celebrities* by Dan Rattinere; *Blows to the Head: How Boxing Changed My Mind* by Binnie Klein; *Truckin' with Sam: A Father and Son, The Mick and the Dyl, Rockin' and Rollin', on the Road* by Lee Gutkind; *The Italian Actress: A Novel* by Frank Lentricchia; and *The Smoking Horse: A Memoir in Pieces* by Stephen Spotte.

Excelsior Editions showcases the history of New York and surrounding states while at the same time making available noteworthy and essential popular books, both classic and contemporary. Some titles from Excelsior Editions include *The Revelation of the Breath: A Tribute to Its Wisdom, Power, and Beauty* by Sharon G. Mijares; *Frank: The Story of Frances Folsom Cleveland, America's Youngest First Lady* by Annette Dunlap; *Once an Engineer: A Song of the Salt City* by Joe Amato; *Letters to a Best Friend* by Richard Seltzer; and *The Firekeeper: A Narrative of the New York Frontier* by Robert Moss.

SUNY Press accepts simultaneous submissions of proposals; however, at the manuscript review stage they prefer an exclusive review. To submit, send a proposal with SASE to:

James Peltz, Codirector, Excelsior Editions
Nancy Ellegate, Senior Acquisitions Editor—Religious studies, Asian studies.
Dr. Michael Rinella, Senior Acquisitions Editor—Political science, African American studies.
Andrew Kenyon, Acquisitions Editor—Philosophy.

SYRACUSE UNIVERSITY PRESS

621 Skytop Road, Suite 110, Syracuse, NY 13244-5290
315-443-5534 | fax: 315-443-5545
www.syracuseuniversitypress.syr.edu | e-mail: supress@syr.edu

Syracuse University Press was founded in 1943 by Chancellor William Pearson Tolley, with the intent to enhance the school's academic standing. With more than 1,200 titles in print today, the press consistently earns international critical acclaim and attracts award-winning authors of note.

Each year Syracuse University Press publishes new books in specialized areas including New York State, Middle East studies, Judaica, geography, Irish studies, Native American studies, religion, television, and popular culture.

Recent titles include *Radical Chapters: Pacifist Bookseller Roy Kepler and the Paperback Revolution* by Michael Doyle; *The Arab and the Brit: The Last of the Welcome Immigrants* by Bill Rezak; *The American Dream: A Cultural History* by Lawrence R. Samuel; *The Time Remaining* by Samuel Hazo; *Tree of Pearls: Queen of Egypt* by Jurji Zaydan.

Syracuse University Press distributes its list via its own in-house offices and utilizes a variety of distribution services worldwide.

Please send a proposal, abstract, and CV with SASE to:
Suzanne Guiod, Editor-in-Chief; seguiod@syr.edu
Jennika Baines, Acquisitions Editor; jsbaines@syr.edu
Deanna McCay, Acquisitions Editor; dhmccay@syr.edu
Kelly Balenske, Editorial Assistant; klbalens@syr.edu

UNIVERSITY PRESSES

TEXAS A&M UNIVERSITY PRESS CONSORTIUM

John H. Lindsey Building, Lewis Street, 4354 TAMU,
College Station, TX, 77843-4354
979-845-1436 | fax: 949-847-8752
www.tamu.edu/upress | e-mail: dlv@tampress.tamu.edu

TEXAS STATE HISTORICAL ASSOCIATION PRESS
1155 Union Circle #311580, Denton, TX 76203-5017
940-369-5200 | fax: 940-369-5248
www.tshaonline.org

TEXAS CHRISTIAN UNIVERSITY PRESS
3000 Sandage, Fort Worth, TX 76109
817-257-7822 | fax: 817-257-5075
www.prs.tcu.edu

UNIVESITY OF NORTH TEXAS PRESS
1155 Union Circle, #311336, Denton, TX 76203-5017
940-565-2142 | fax: 940-565-4590
www.unt.edu/untpress

STATE HOUSE PRESS/MCWHINEY FOUNDATION PRESS
PO Box 818, Buffalo Gap, TX 79508
325-572-3974 | fax: 325-572-3991

TEXAS REVIEW PRESS
PO Box 2146, SHSU Div. of English and Foreign Languages, Evans Bldg.,
Rm. #152, Huntsville, TX 77341-2146
936-294-1992 | fax: 936-294-3070
www.shsu.edu/~www_trp

Founded in 1974, Texas A&M University Press is the principal publishing arm of one of this nation's leading research institutions. The press's primary mission is to select, produce, market, and disseminate scholarly publications of outstanding quality and originality and thereby help the university achieve its paramount purposes of teaching, research, public service, and dissemination of the results of scholarly inquiry. In conjunction with the long-term development of its editorial program, the press draws on and supports the intellectual activities of the university and reflects the standards and stature of scholarship that are fostered by this institution.

The press falls under the administrative aegis of the provost, the chief academic officer of the University, and is an integral part of its parent institution. The press imprint is controlled by an advisory committee composed of senior members of the university's faculty, who are chosen for their own scholarly acumen and publishing experience. Manuscripts, whether by outside authors or by members of the Texas A&M faculty (currently around 15 percent of the total author list), must have been reviewed favorably by both the press's director and editorial staff and at least two experts in that field before being submitted to the faculty advisory committee for approval. Of the hundreds of manuscripts and proposals that come to the press each year, most do not survive this rigorous selection process.

The press's editorial interests span a range of significant fields, including agriculture, anthropology, nautical archaeology, architecture, borderland studies, Eastern Europe, economics, military history, natural history, presidential studies, veterinary medicine, and works on the history and culture of Texas and the surrounding region. Many of these fields of interest reflect outstanding departmental and programmatic strengths at Texas A&M University. Overall, the press seeks to maintain high standards in traditional areas of academic inquiry while also exploring innovative fields of research and new forms of scholarly communication.

The press currently publishes more than 70 new titles a year in these fields. Of the total of nearly 930 books published by the press in its 34-year history, the great majority remain in print or are available in on-demand and electronic editions.

Recent titles include *Waiting* by Linda Moore-Lanning; *Lovin' that Lone Star Flag* by E. Joe Deering; *Spanish Water, Anglo Water: Early Development in San Antonio* by Charles R. Porter Jr.; *To the Line of Fire!: Mexican Texans and World War I* by Jose A. Ramirez; *War and the Environment: Military Destruction in the Modern Age* edited by Charles E. Closmann; and *13 Days to Glory: The Siege of the Alamo* by Lon Tinkle.

The Texas State Historical Association was the first member of the Texas A&M University Press Consortium. Founded in 1897, the TSHA Press specializes in books of Texas History and Texana, both new titles and reprints of classics. Some new titles include *Road, River, and Ol' Boy Politics: A Texas County's Path from Farm to Supersuburb* by Linda Scarbrough; *Giant under the Hill: A History of the Spindletop Oil Discovery at Beaumont, Texas, in 1901* by Jo Ann Stiles et al; *General Vicente Filisola's Analysis of Jose Urrea's Military Diary* by Gregg J. Dimmick; and *Biracial Unions on Galveston's Waterfront, 1865–1925* by Clifford Farrington.

Texas Christian University Press is among the smallest university publishers in the nation, having decided that it was more important to do a few books well than to increase the list. TCU Press focuses on the history and literature of the American Southwest. Some recent titles include *Walk across Texas* by Jon McConal; *Purple Hearts* by C. W. Smith; and *Manhunters* by Elmer Kelton.

State House Press and the McWhiney Foundation Press are located in Buffalo Gap, Texas. They see their missions as making history approachable, accessible, and interesting with special emphasis on Texas, West Texas, the Civil War, military, and southern history. New titles include *The Illustrated Alamo 1836: A Photographic Journey* by Mark Lemon; *The States Were Big and Bright, Volume 1: The United States Army Air Forces and Texas During World War II* by Thomas E. Alexander; and *Texian Macabre: A Melancholy Tale of a Hanging in Early Houston* by Stephen L. Hardin.

Texas Review Press was established in 1979, but published only chapbooks and an occasional anthology until 1992, when it introduced the Southern and Southwestern Writers Breakthrough Series. It now publishes six to eight books a year and has over 40 titles in print in fiction, poetry, and prose nonfiction. Some

UNIVERSITY PRESSES

books include *Living Witness: Historic Trees of Texas* by Ralph Yznaga; *River of Contrasts: The Texas Colorado* by Margie Crisp

Query letters and SASEs for TAMU Press should be directed to:

Diana L. Vance, Editorial Assistant, Acquisitions (TAMU Press); dvance@tamu.edu

Mary Lenn Dixon, Editor-in-Chief (TAMU Press); mary-dixon@tamu.edu

Shannon Davies, Senior Editor, Natural Sciences (TAMU Press); sdavies@tamu.edu

Thom Lemmons, Managing Editor (TAMU Press); thom.lemmons@tamu.edu

UNIVERSITY OF ALABAMA PRESS

USPS Address: Box 870380, Tuscaloosa, AL 35487-0380
Physical/Shipping Address: 200 Hackberry Lane, 2nd Floor McMillan Bldg., Tuscaloosa, AL 35401
205-348-5180 | fax: 205-348-9201
www.uapress.ua.edu

As the university's primary scholarly publishing arm, the University of Alabama Press seeks to be an agent in the advancement of learning and the dissemination of scholarship. The press applies the highest standards to all phases of publishing, including acquisitions, editorial, production, and marketing. An editorial board comprising representatives from all doctoral degree-granting state universities within Alabama oversees the publishing program. Projects are selected that support, extend, and preserve academic research. The press also publishes books that foster an understanding of history of cultures of this state and region.

The University of Alabama Press publishes in the following areas: American history; Southern history and culture; American religious history; Latin American history; American archaeology; Southeastern archaeology; Caribbean archaeology; historical archaeology; ethnohistory; anthropology; American literature and criticism; rhetoric and communication; creative nonfiction; linguistics, especially dialectology; African American studies; Native American studies; Judaic studies; public administration; theater; natural history and environmental studies; American social and cultural history; sports history; military history; regional studies of Alabama and the southern United States, including trade titles. Submissions are not invited in poetry, fiction, or drama.

Special series from Alabama include Classics in Southeastern Archaeology; Contemporary American Indian Studies; Deep South Books; Alabama: The Forge of History; Judaic Studies; Library of Alabama Classics; Modern and Contemporary Poetics; The Modern South; Religion and American Culture; Rhetoric, Culture, and Social Critique; and Studies in American Literary Realism and Naturalism.

Recent Alabama titles include *Desert Rose: The Life and Legacy of Coretta Scott*

King by Edythe Scott Bagley; *Darkroom, A Memoir in Black and White* by Lila Quintero Weaver; *Old Havana/La Habana Vieja: Spirit of the Living City/Elespiritu de la ciudad viva* by Chip Cooper and Nestor Marti; *Circling Faith: Southern Women on Spirituality* by Wendy Reed and Jennifer Horne.

Submit your proposal with cover letter and CV by regular mail to the appropriate acquisitions editor (for questions, feel free to contact the appropriate editor by e-mail):

Daniel Waterman, Acquisitions Editor for Humanities—American literature and criticism, rhetoric and communication, creative nonfiction, linguistics, African American studies, public administration, theater, natural history and environmental studies; waterman@uapress.ua.edu

Elizabeth Motherwell, Acquisitions Editor for Natural History and the Environment—Natural history and environmental trade titles; emother@uapress.ua.edu

Claire Lewis Evans, Associate Editor for Digital and Electronic Publishing—Digital projects; cevans@uapress.ua.edu

UNIVERSITY OF ARIZONA PRESS

Main Library Building, 5th Floor, 1510 E. University Blvd., PO Box 210055, Tuscon, AZ 85721-0055
520-621-1441 | fax: 520-621-8899
www.uapress.arizona.edu | e-mail: uapress@uapress.arizona.edu

The University of Arizona Press (UA Press), founded in 1959 as a department of the University of Arizona, is a nonprofit publisher of scholarly and regional books. As a delegate of the University of Arizona to the larger world, the press publishes the work of scholars wherever they may be, concentrating on scholarship that reflects the special strengths of the University of Arizona, Arizona State University, and Northern Arizona University.

The University of Arizona Press publishes about 55 books annually and has some 783 books in print. These include scholarly titles in American Indian studies, anthropology, archaeology, environmental studies, geography, Chicano studies, history, Latin American studies, and the space sciences.

The UA Press also publishes general interest books on Arizona and the Southwest borderlands. In addition, the press publishes books of personal essays, such as Nancy Mairs's Plaintext and two series in literature: Sun Tracks: An American Indian Literary Series and Camino del Sol: A Chicana/o Literary Series.

Recent titles include *With Blood in Their Eyes* by Thomas Cobb.

University of Arizona Press handles its own distribution and also distributes titles originating from the publishing programs of such enterprises and institutions as Oregon State University Press, the Arizona State Museum, and archaeological and environmental consulting firms.

Query letters and SASEs should be directed to:

Allyson Carter, Editor-in-Chief, Social Sciences and Sciences—Anthropology, archaeology, ecology, geography, natural history, environmental science, astronomy and space sciences, and related regional titles; acarter@uapress@arizona.edu
Kristen Buckles, Acquiring Editor; kbuckles@uapress.arizona.edu
Scott De Herrera, Editorial Assistant; scott@uapress.arizona.edu

UNIVERSITY OF ARKANSAS PRESS

McIlroy House, 105 N. McIlroy Ave, Fayetteville, AR 72701
479-575-3246 | 800-626-0090 | fax: 479-575-6044
www.uapress.com | e-mail: uapress@uark.edu

The University of Arkansas Press was founded in 1980 as the book publishing division of the University of Arkansas. A member of the Association of American University Presses, it publishes approximately 20 titles a year in the following subjects: history, Southern history, African American history, Civil War studies, poetics and literary criticism, Middle East studies, Arkansas and regional studies, music, and cultural studies. About a third of its titles fall under the general heading of Arkansas and Regional Studies. The press also publishes books of poetry and the winners of the Arabic Translation Award.

The press is charged by the university's trustees with the publication of books in service to the academic community and for the enrichment of the broader culture, especially works of value that are likely to be turned aside by commercial houses. This press, like all university presses, has as its central and continuing mission the dissemination of the fruits of research and creative activity.

Recent titles include *And The New…: An Inside Look at Another Year in Boxing* by Thomas Hauser; *In Broken Latin: Poems* by Annette Spaulding-Convy; *Beware of Limbo Dancers: A Correspondent's Adventures with the New York Times* by Roy Reed; *The Empty Loom: Poems* by Robert Gibb.

Query letters and SASEs should be directed to:

Lawrence J. Malley, Director and Acquisitions Editor—US history, African American history, civil rights studies, Middle East studies, sport history; lmalley @uark.edu

UNIVERSITY OF CALIFORNIA PRESS

2120 Berkeley Way, Berkeley, CA 94720-1012
510-642-4247 | fax: 510-643-7127
www.ucpress.edu | e-mail: askucp@ucpress.edu

Founded in 1893, University of California Press (UC Press) is one of the nation's largest and most adventurous scholarly publishers. Each year it publishes approximately 200 new books and 50 multi-issue journals in the humanities, social sciences, and natural sciences, and keeps about 4,000 book titles in print.

The nonprofit publishing arm of the University of California system, UC Press attracts manuscripts from the world's foremost scholars, writers, artists, and public intellectuals. About one-fourth of its authors are affiliated with the University of California.

UC Press publishes in the areas of art, music, cinema and media studies, classics, literature, anthropology, sociology, archaeology, history, religious studies, Asian studies, biological sciences, food studies, natural history, and public health.

Recent titles include *Changing Planet, Changing Health: How the Climate Crisis Threatens Our Health and What We Can Do about It* by Paul R. Epstein and Jeffrey Sachs; *Why Geology Matters: Decoding the Past, Anticipating the Future* by Doug Macdougall; *The Banjo Clock* by Karen Garthe; *Negro Building: Black Americans in the World of Fairs and Museums* by Mabel O. Wilson.

University of California Press distributes its own list.

Query letters and SASEs should be directed to:

Charles R. Crumly, Editor—Organismal biology, ecology, evolution, environment.

Blake Edgar, Editor—Enology, biology, archaeology, viticulture.

Kari Dahlgren, Art History Editor—Art history, museum copublications.

Stephanie Fay, Editor—Art history, classical studies.

Mary Francis, Editor—Music, cinema.

Niels Hooper, Editor—History (except Asia), American studies.

Hannah Love, Associate Editor for Health—Health.

Reed Malcolm, Editor—Religion (sociology/history/anthropology), politics, Asian studies.

Maura Roessner, Senior Editor for social sciences—Criminology, sociology, law and society, criminal justice.

Naomi Schneider, Executive Editor—Sociology, politics, anthropology, Latin American studies.

UNIVERSITY OF CHICAGO PRESS

1427 East 60th Street, Chicago, IL 60637
773-702-7700 | fax: 773-702-9756
www.press.uchicago.edu | blog: pressblog.uchicago.edu

Since its founding in 1891 as one of the three original divisions of the University of Chicago, the press has embraced as its mission the obligation to disseminate scholarship of the highest standard and to publish serious works that promote education, foster public understanding, and enrich cultural life. Through its books and journals programs, it seeks not only to advance scholarly conversation within and

across traditional disciplines but, in keeping with the University of Chicago's experimental tradition, to help define new areas of knowledge and intellectual endeavor.

In addition to publishing the results of research for communities of scholars, the press presents innovative scholarship in ways that inform and engage general readers. The editors develop reference works and educational texts that draw upon and support the emphases of the university's scholarly programs and that extend the intellectual reach of the press. The house publishes significant nonscholarly work by writers, artists, and intellectuals from within and beyond the academy; translations of important foreign-language texts, both historical and contemporary; and books that contribute to the public's understanding of Chicago and its region. In all of this, the press is guided by the judgment of individual editors who work to build a broad but coherent publishing program engaged with authors and readers worldwide.

Recent titles include *Troy, Unincorporated* by Francesca Abbate; *Snapshots from Deep Time: The 52- Million-Year-Old Communities of the Fossil Butte Member, Locked in Stone* by Lance Grande; *Parker* by Richard Stark; *The Birth of the Republic, 1763-89*, Fourth Edition by Edmund S. Morgan.

University of Chicago Press distributes its own list.

Query letters and SASEs should be directed to:

Paul Schellinger, Editorial Director, Reference—Dictionaries, encyclopedias, guides, atlases, and other general reference; pschellinger@press.uchicago.edu

Alan G. Thomas, Editorial Director, Humanities and Sciences—Literary criticism and theory, religious studies; athomas@press.uchicago.edu

John Tryneski, Editorial Director, Social Sciences and Paperback Publishing—Political science, law and society; jtryneski@press.uchicago.edu

Susan Bielstein, Executive Editor—Art, architecture, ancient archeology, classics, film studies; sbielstein@press.uchicago.edu

T. David Brent, Executive Editor—Anthropology, paleoanthropology, philosophy, psychology; dbrent@press.uchicago.edu

Karen Merikangas Darling, Editor—Science studies (history, philosophy, social studies of science, medicine, technology); kdarling@press.uchicago.edu

Robert P. Devens, Editor—American history, Chicago, other regional publishing; rdevens@press.uchicago.edu

Elizabeth Branch Dyson, Associate Editor—Ethnomusicology, interdisciplinary philosophy, education; ebranchdyson@press.uchicago.edu

Kathleen K. Hansell, Editor—Music; khansell@press.uchicago.edu

Christie Henry, Executive Editor—Biological science, behavior, conservation, ecology, environment, evolution, natural history, paleobiology, geography, earth sciences; chenry@press.uchicago.edu

Margaret Hivnor, Paperback Editor; mhivnor@press.uchicago.edu

Jennifer S. Howard, Associate Editor—Physical sciences (astrophysics, general physics, mathematics); jhoward@press.uchicago.edu

Douglas Mitchell, Executive Editor—Sociology, history, sexuality studies, rhetoric; dmitchell@press.uchicago.edu

David Morrow, Senior Editor—Reference works, including regional reference;
dmorrow@press.uchicago.edu

Randolph Petilos, Assistant Editor—Medieval studies, poetry in translation;
rpetilos@press.uchicago.edu

UNIVERSITY OF GEORGIA PRESS

330 Research Drive, Athens, GA 30602-4901
706-369-6130 | fax: 706-369-6131
www.ugapress.org | e-mail: books@ugapress.uga.edu

The University of Georgia Press is the oldest and largest publishing house in the state and one of the largest publishing houses in the South. The press publishes 70 to 80 titles each year, in a range of academic disciplines as well as books of interest to the general reader, and has nearly 1,000 titles in print.

Since its founding in 1938, the University of Georgia Press has as its primary mission to support and enhance the university's place as a major research institution by publishing outstanding works of scholarship and literature by scholars and writers throughout the world as well as the university's own faculty.

As the publishing program of the press has evolved, this mission has taken on three distinct dimensions:

Works of scholarship. The press is committed to publishing important new scholarship in the following subject areas: American and Southern history and literature, African American studies, civil rights history, legal history, Civil War studies, Native American studies, folklore and material culture, women's studies, and environmental studies.

Regional books. The press has a long history of publishing books about the state and region for general readers. Their regional publishing program includes architectural guides, state histories, field guides to the region's flora and fauna, biographies, editions of diaries and letters, outdoor guides, and the work of some of the state's most accomplished artists, photographers, poets, and fiction writers.

Creative and literary works. This area of the list includes books published in conjunction with the Flannery O'Connor Award for Short Fiction, the Associated Writing Programs Award for Creative Nonfiction, and the Cave Canem Poetry Prize. Please write to the press for entry requirements and submission guidelines for these awards.

Recent titles include *Margaret Fuller, Wandering Pilgrim* by Meg McGavran Murray; *Creolization and Contraband: Curaçao in the Early Modern Atlantic World* by Linda M. Rupert; *Unfinished Business: Why International Negotiations Fail* by Guy Olivier Faure; *This Compost: Ecological Imperatives in American Poetry* by Jed Rasula; *My Paddle to the Sea: Eleven Days on the River of the Carolinas* by John Lane.

The University of Georgia Press oversees its own distribution.

UNIVERSITY PRESSES

Query letters and SASEs should be directed to:

Nancy Grayson, Associate Director and Editor-in-Chief—American and Southern history, American literature, Southern studies, African American studies, legal history, women's studies, international affairs; ngrayson@ugapress.uga.edu

Regan Huff, Acquisitions Editor; rhuff@ugapress.uga.edu

Beth Snead, Assistant Acquisitions Editor; bsnead@ugapress.uga.edu

---

UNIVERSITY OF HAWAI'I PRESS

2840 Kolowalu Street, Honolulu, HI 96822-1888
1-808-956-8255 | fax: 808-988-6052
www.uhpress.hawaii.edu | e-mail: uhpbooks@hawaii.edu

Areas of University of Hawai'i Press (UHP) publishing interest include cultural history, economics, social history, travel, arts and crafts, costumes, marine biology, natural history, botany, ecology, religion, law, political science, anthropology, and general reference; particular UHP emphasis is on regional topics relating to Hawai'i, and scholarly and academic books on East Asia, South and Southeast Asia, and Hawai'i and the Pacific.

University of Hawai'i Press (started in 1947) publishes books for the general trade, as well as titles keyed to the academic market. UHP also issues a series of special-interest journals. The house maintains an established backlist.

Recent titles include *Remembering the Kanji 2: A Systematic Guide to Reading the Japanese Characters*, 4th Edition by James W. Heisig; *Passionate Friendship: The Aesthetics of Girl's Culture in Japan* by Deborah Shamoon; *If It Swings, It's Music: The Autobiography of Hawaii's Gabe Baltazar Jr.* by Gabe Baltazar Jr. and Theo Garneau; *Divorce with Decency: The Complete How-To Handbook and Survivor's Guide to the Legal, Emotional, Economic, and Social Issues*, Fourth Edition by Bradley A. Coates; *Plaited Arts from the Borneo Rainforest* by Bernard Sellato.

The University of Hawai'i Press handles its own distribution via a network that includes in-house fulfillment services, as well as independent sales representatives.

Query letters and SASEs should be directed to:

Patricia Crosby, Executive Editor—East Asian studies (all disciplines except literature), anthropology, Buddhist studies; pcrosby@hawaii.edu

Masako Ikeda, Acquisitions Editor—Hawai'ian and Pacific studies (all disciplines), Asian American studies (all disciplines), general-interest books on Hawai'i and the Pacific; masakoi@hawaii.edu

Pamela Kelley, Acquisitions Editor—Southeast Asian studies (all disciplines), East Asian literature; pkelley@hawaii.edu

Nadine Little, Acquisitions Editor—general interest, Hawaiiana, natural history, natural science; nlittle@hawaii.edu

Cheri Dunn, Managing Editor; cheri@hawaii.edu
Ann Ludeman, Managing Editor; aludeman@hawaii.edu

UNIVERSITY OF ILLINOIS PRESS

1325 South Oak Street, Champaign, IL 61820-6903
217-333-0950 | fax: 217-244-8082
www.press.uillinois.edu | e-mail: uipress@uillinois.edu

The University of Illinois Press was established in 1918 as a not-for-profit scholarly publisher at the university. It became one of the founding members of the Association of American University Presses in 1937 and now ranks as one of the country's larger and most distinguished university presses. The house publishes works of high quality for scholars, students, and the citizens of the state and beyond. Its local staff of 46 brings out about 120 books each year, as well as 26 journals.

The University of Illinois Press publishes scholarly books and serious nonfiction, with special interests in Abraham Lincoln studies; African American studies; American history; anthropology; Appalachian studies; archaeology; architecture; Asian American studies; communications; folklore; food studies; immigration and ethnic history; Judaic studies; labor history; literature; military history; Mormon history; music; Native American studies; philosophy; poetry; political science; religious studies; sociology; southern history; sport history; translations; transnational cultural studies; western history; and women's studies. Note that this press does not publish original fiction, and only considers poetry submissions in February.

Recent titles include *Farmers' Markets of the Heartland* by Janine MacLachlan; *Then Sings My Soul: The Culture of Southern Gospel Music* by Douglas Harrison; *The Organs of J. S. Bach: A Handbook* by Christoph Wolff and Markus Zepf; *A People's History of Baseball* by Mitchell Nathanson; *The Poco Field: An American Story of Place* by Talmage A. Stanley; *Illinois in the War of 1812* by Gillum Ferguson.

The University of Illinois Press distributes its own list, as well as books from other university publishers, including Vanderbilt University Press.

Proposals and SASEs should be directed to the appropriate editor:

Willis G. Regier, Director—Lincoln studies, Nietzsche studies, classics, translations, sports history, military history, ancient religion, literature; wregier @uillinois.edu

Laurie Matheson, Senior Acquisitions Editor—American history, Appalachian studies, labor history, music, sociology; lmatheso@uillinois.edu

David Nasset, Assistant Acquisition Editor; dnasset@uillinois.edu

Vijay Shah, Assistant Acquisition Editor; vshah@uillinois.edu

Dawn M. Durante, Assistant Acquisitions Editor; durante9@uillinois.edu

UNIVERSITY OF IOWA PRESS

119 West Park Road, 100 Kuhl House, Iowa City, IA 52242-1000
319-335-2000 | fax: 319-335-2055
www.uiowapress.org | e-mail: uipress@uiowa.edu

Established in 1938, the University of Iowa Press operated for many years as an irregular imprint of the university. In 1969, John Simmons was named the first director of the press, and the imprint was officially organized under a board of faculty advisors. Since 1985, the press has published 30 to 35 new titles a year. As always, it seeks good manuscripts from campus authors, but its efforts have expanded significantly, and press authors and customers now come from countries around the world. As Daniel Coit Gilman, founder of the first university press at Johns Hopkins University, said, it is a university's task to "advance knowledge, and to diffuse it not merely among those who can attend the daily lectures—but far and wide." The University of Iowa Press considers this to be its main trust.

As one of the few book publishers in the state of Iowa, the press considers it a mission to publish excellent books on Iowa and the Midwest. But since the press's role is much broader than that of a regional press, the bulk of its list appeals to a wider audience. The University of Iowa Press books receive national attention in a great variety of scholarly journals, newspapers, magazines, and other major book-reviewing media.

The University of Iowa Press seeks proposals to add to its list in the following areas: literary studies, including Whitman studies and poetics; letters and diaries; American studies, literary nonfiction and thematic edited anthologies, particularly poetry anthologies; the craft of writing; literature and medicine; theater studies; archaeology; the natural history of the Upper Midwest; and regional history and culture. Single-author short fiction and poetry are published through series only.

Moreover, the press is actively looking for literary works dealing with the intersection of the humanities and medicine, works of narrative medicine, fiction, poetry, and memoir by health care professionals and patients, and conceptual works that illuminate health and illness from the perspective of the humanities. They have recently published titles on Midwestern archeology and the Andean region.

Recent titles include *Always Put in a Recipe and Other Tips for Living from Iowa's Best-Known Homemaker* by Evelyn Birkby; *American Literature and Culture in an Age of Cold War* by Steven Belletto and Daniel Grausam; *Jefferson in His Own Time* by Kevin J. Hayes; *The Jewish Kulturbund Theatre Company in Nazi Berlin* by Rebecca Rovit; *The Iowa Lakeside Laboratory* by Michael J. Lannoo.

University of Iowa Press books are distributed by the University of Chicago Distribution Center.

Query letters and SASEs should be directed to:
Holly Carver, Director and Editor; holly-carver@uiowa.edu

Catherine Cocks, Acquisitions Editor; cath-campbell@uiowa.edu
Elisabeth Chretien, Acquisitions Editor; elisabeth-chretien@uiowa.edu
Faye Schillig, Assistant to the Director; faye-schillig@uiowa.edu

---

UNIVERSITY OF MASSACHUSETTS PRESS

East Experiment Station, 671 North Pleasant Street, Amherst, MA 01003
413-545-2217 | fax: 413-545-1226
www.umass.edu/umpress | e-mail: info@umpress.umass.edu

Founded in 1963, the University of Massachusetts Press (UMass Press) is the book publishing arm of the University of Massachusetts. Its mission is to publish first-rate books, edit them carefully, design them well, and market them vigorously. In so doing, it supports and enhances the university's role as a major research institution.

The editors at UMass Press think of book publishing as a collaborative venture—a partnership between author and press staff—and they work hard to see that their authors are happy with every phase of the process.

Since its inception, the press has sold more than 2 million volumes. Today, it has over 900 titles in print. Seven employees, along with student assistants and outside sales representatives, produce and distribute some 30 to 40 new titles annually.

The press imprint is overseen by a faculty committee, whose members represent a broad spectrum of university departments. In addition to publishing works of scholarship, the press produces books of more general interest for a wider readership. With the annual Juniper Prizes, the press also publishes fiction and poetry. For the rules of the contests, please refer to the website or request guidelines via regular mail.

Recent titles include *Agent Orange: History, Science, and the Politics of Uncertainty* by Edwin A. Martini; *To Fight Aloud Is Very Brave: American Poetry and the Civil War* by Faith Barrett; *The Mistakes of Yesterday, the Hopes of Tomorrow: The Story of the Prisonaires* by John Dougan; *Tragic No More: Mixed Race Women and the Nexus of Sex and Celebrity* by Caroline A. Streeter; *Creating a World on Paper: Harry Fenn's Career in Art* by Sue Rainey.

The University of Massachusetts Press publishes scholarly books and serious nonfiction. Please note that it considers fiction and poetry only through its annual Juniper Prize contests. Also, it does not normally publish Festschriften, conference proceedings, or unrevised doctoral dissertations.

Submit proposals with SASEs or e-mail queries to:
Clark Dougan, Acquisitions Editor; cdougan@umpress.umass.edu
Brian Halley, Acquisitions Editor; brian.halley@umb.edu

UNIVERSITY OF MICHIGAN PRESS

839 Greene Street, Ann Arbor, MI 48104-3209
734-764-4388 | fax: 734-615-1540
www.press.umich.edu

University of Michigan Press publishes trade nonfiction and works of scholarly and academic interest. Topic areas and categories include African American studies, anthropology, archaeology, Asian studies, classical studies, literary criticism and theory, economics, education, German studies, history, linguistics, law, literary biography, literature, Michigan and the Great Lakes region, music, physical sciences, philosophy and religion, poetry, political science, psychology, sociology, theater and drama, women's studies, disability studies, and gay and lesbian studies.

Recent titles *American Legal English*, 2nd Edition by Debra S. Lee, Charles Hall, and Susan Barone; *Antiquarianism and Intellectual Life in Europe and China, 1500–1800* by Peter N. Miller and Francois Louis; *Architecture and Modern Literature* by David Spur; *The Art of Cooking Moewla* by Ruth Mossok Johnston.

Query letters and SASEs should be directed to:

Tom Dwyer, Editor-in-Chief—Communications studies, new media, literary studies, cultural studies; thdwyer@umich.edu

Ellen Bauerle, Manager, Acquisitions Department—Classics, archaeology, German studies, music, fiction, early modern history; bauerle@umich.edu

LeAnn Fields, Senior Executive Editor—Class studies, disability studies, theater, performance studies; lfields@umich.edu

Christopher J. Hebert, Editor at Large—Popular music, jazz; hebertc@umich.edu

Melody Herr, Acquiring Editor—Politics, law, American history; mrherr@umich.edu

Kelly Sippell, Executive Editor—ESL, applied linguistics; ksippell@umich.edu

UNIVERSITY OF MINNESOTA PRESS

111 Third Avenue South, Suite 290, Minneapolis, MN 55401
612-627-1970 | fax: 612-627-1980
www.upress.umn.edu | e-mail: ump@umn.edu

The University of Minnesota Press (founded in 1925) is a not-for-profit publisher of academic books for scholars and selected general-interest titles. Areas of emphasis include American studies, anthropology, art and aesthetics, cultural theory, film and media studies, gay and lesbian studies, geography, literary theory, political and social theory, race and ethnic studies, sociology, and urban studies. The Press is among the most active publishers of translations of significant works of European and

Latin American thought and scholarship. The Press also maintains a long-standing commitment to publish books that focus on Minnesota and the Upper Midwest, including regional nonfiction, history, and natural science. It does not publish original fiction or poetry.

Recent titles include *The Mestizo State: Reading Race in Modern Mexico* by Joshua Lund; *Once Were Pacific: Maori Connections to Oceania* by Alice Te Punga Somerville; *Native Orchids of Minnesota* by Welby R. Smith; *A Black Communist in the Freedom Struggle: The Life of Harry Haywood* by Gwendolyn Midlo Hall; *Opacity and the Closet Queer Tactics in Foucault, Barthes, and Warhol* by Nicholas de Villiers.

University of Minnesota Press order fulfillment is handled by the Chicago Distribution Center and in the UK and Europe through Plymbridge Distributors, Ltd.

Proposals in areas not listed below should be addressed to the Executive Editor. Query letters, proposals, and SASEs should be directed to:

Richard Morrison, Executive Editor—American studies, art and visual culture, literary and cultural studies; morri094@umn.edu

Todd Orjala, Senior Editor for Regional Studies and Contemporary Affairs—Regional history and culture, regional natural history; t-orja@umn.edu

Pieter Martin, Editor—Architecture, legal studies, politics and international studies, Scandinavian studies, urban studies; marti190@umn.edu

Jason Weidemann, Editor—Anthropology, Asian culture, cinema and media studies, geography, native studies, sociology; weide007@umn.edu

UNIVERSITY OF MISSOURI PRESS

2910 LeMone Boulevard, Columbia, MO 65201
573-882-7641 | fax: 573-884-4498
www.umsystem.edu/upress | e-mail: upress@umsystem.edu

The University of Missouri Press was founded in 1958 by William Peden, writer and dedicated member of Missouri's English Department faculty. The press has now grown to publish more than 70 titles per year in the areas of American and world history, including intellectual history and biography; African American studies; women's studies; American, British, and Latin American literary criticism; journalism; political science, particularly philosophy and ethics; regional studies of the American heartland; short fiction; and creative nonfiction.

The University of Missouri Press's chief areas of publishing emphasis are American history, political philosophy, journalism, and literary criticism with a primary focus on American and British literature. However, it is glad to receive inquiries from almost any area of work in the humanities. It does publish creative nonfiction and an occasional short-story collection, but no poetry or original novels.

Recent titles include *American Girls, Beer, and Glenn Miller: GI Morale in World War II* by James J. Cooke; *Broken Butterfly: My Daughter's Struggle with Brain Injury* by Karin Finell; *Strong Advocate: The Life of a Trial Lawyer* by Thomas Strong; *The Brothers Robidoux and the Opening of the American West* by Robert J. Willoughby.

Query letters and SASEs should be directed to Mr. Clair Willcox.

Clair Willcox, Editor-in-Chief; willcoxc@umsystem.edu

John Brenner, Acquisitions Editor; brennerj@umsystem.edu

Sara Davis, Managing Editor; davissd@umsystem.edu

UNIVERSITY OF NEBRASKA PRESS

1111 Lincoln Mall, Lincoln, NE 68588-0630
402-472-3581 | fax: 402-472-6214
www.nebraskapress.unl.edu | e-mail: pressmail@unl.edu

As a publisher of scholarly and popular books for more than 60 years, the University of Nebraska Press is a distinctive member of the University of Nebraska–Lincoln (UNL) community. Through the work of its staff and resulting publications, the press fulfills the three primary missions of its host university: research, teaching, and service. Reporting to the vice chancellor for research and in cooperation with a faculty advisory board, the press actively encourages, develops, publishes, and disseminates first-rate, creative literary work, memoirs, and the results of national and international scholarly research in several fields. The press facilitates teaching through its publications and develops projects particularly suited for undergraduate and graduate university classrooms. The press serves the university community directly by publishing the work of many UNL faculty authors, maintaining long-term publishing associations with prominent university organizations, sponsoring campus-wide events, hosting publishing workshops, and enhancing the international visibility of the university through its publicity efforts and reviews of its books. The press's sustained commitment to publications on the peoples, culture, and heritage of Nebraska reflects decades of service to its home state.

Recent University of Nebraska Press titles include *Island of Bones: Essays* by Joy Castro; *Called to Justice: The Life of a Federal Trial Judge* by Warren K. Urbom; *Backstage: Stories from My Life in Public Television* by Ron Hull; *Embracing Fry Bread: Confessions of a Wannabe* by Roger Welsch; *Singer's Typewriter and Mine: Reflections on Jewish Culture* by Ilan Stavans; *From Gods to God: How the Bible Debunked, Suppressed, or Changed Ancient Myths and Legends* by Avigdor Shinan and Yair Zakovitch.

Bison Books is the quality trade paperback imprint of the University of Nebraska Press. Launched in 1960, priced inexpensively, and sold in drugstores and highway tourist gift shops as well as bookstores, the Bison Books line appeared as an affordable means of publishing "original works and reissues of books of permanent value in all fields of knowledge." The idea of the Bison Books imprint was a particularly bold and far-sighted move for a smallish university press in 1960—publishing scholarship in paperback, rather than the more "dignified" cloth, was a rather radical notion, as was selling books in drugstores and gift shops. Today Bison Books publishes in a wide variety of subject areas, including Western Americana; Native American history and culture; military history; sports; Bison Frontiers of Imagination, a science fiction line; classic Nebraska authors, including Willa Cather, Mari Sandoz, John G. Neihardt, Wright Morris, Weldon Kees, and Loren Eiseley; and philosophy and religion.

Recent titles from Bison Books include *Ed Barrow: The Bulldog Who Built the Yankees' First Dynasty* by Daniel R. Levitt and *The Recipe Reader: Narratives, Contexts, Traditions* edited by Janet Floyd and Laurel Forster.

Queries and SASEs should be directed to:

Matt Bokovoy, Acquiring Editor—Native studies; mbokovoy2@unl.edu
Kristen Elias Rowley, Humanities Editor; keliasrowley2@unl.edu
Rob Taylor, Acquiring Editor—Sports; rtaylor6@unl.edu
Tom Swanson, Manager (Bison Books); tswanson3@unl.edu
Alicia Christensen, Bison Books Editor; achristensen6@unl.edu
Bridget Barry, History Editor; bbarry2@unl.edu
Wes Piper, Editorial Assistant; wpiper2@unl.edu

UNIVERSITY OF NEW MEXICO PRESS

MSC05 3185, 1 University of New Mexico, Albuquerque, NM 87131-0001
505-277-2346 | fax: 505-272-7778
www.unmpress.com | e-mail: unmpress@unm.edu

University of New Mexico Press (UNM Press) is a publisher of general, scholarly, and regional trade books in hardcover and paperback editions. Among areas of strong interest are anthropology, archaeology, cultures of the American West, folkways, Latin American studies, literature, art and architecture, photography, crafts, biography, women's studies, travel, and the outdoors. UNM Press offers a robust list of books in subject areas pertinent to the American Southwest, including native Anasazi, Navajo, Hopi, Zuni, and Apache cultures; Nuevomexicano (New Mexican) culture; the pre-Columbian Americas; and Latin American affairs. UNM Press also publishes works of regional fiction and belles lettres, both contemporary and classical.

Recent titles include *Fractal Architecture: Organic Design Philosophy in Theory and Practice* by James Harris; *The Future of Indian and Federal Reserved Water Rights: The Winters Centennial* by Barbara Cosens and Judith V. Royster; *The Mermaid and the Lobster Diver: Gender, Sexuality, and Money on the Miskito Coast* by Laura Hobson Herlihy; *Up the Winds and Over the Tetons: Journal Entries and Images from the 1860 Raynolds Expedition* by Marlene Deahl Merrill and Daniel D. Merrill.

Query letters and SASEs should be directed to:

W. Clark Whitehorn, Editor-in-Chief; wcwhiteh@unm.edu
Elise M. McHugh, Production Editor
Elizabeth Albright, Professional Intern

UNIVERSITY OF NORTH CAROLINA PRESS

116 South Boundary Street, Chapel Hill, NC 27514-3808
919-966-3561 | fax: 919-966-3829
www.uncpress.unc.edu | e-mail: uncpress@unc.edu

For more than 80 years, the University of North Carolina Press (UNC Press) has earned national and international recognition for quality books and the thoughtful way they are published. A fundamental commitment to publishing excellence defines UNC Press, made possible by the generous support of individual and institutional donors who created its endowment.

Reflecting the mission of its parent institution, the 16-campus UNC system, the press exists both to advance scholarship by supporting teaching and research and to serve the people of the state and beyond. Since 1922, the first university press in the South and one of the first in the nation, UNC Press has published outstanding work in pursuit of its dual aims.

UNC Press books explore important questions, spark lively debates, generate ideas, and move fields of inquiry forward. They illuminate the life of the mind. With more than 4,000 titles published and almost 1,500 titles still in print, UNC Press produces books that endure.

When the press was founded in 1922, university presses published work strictly for scholars and by scholars, primarily those from the home faculty. Today, press authors come from all across the nation and around the world. UNC Press's readers come from inside and outside academia, as the press reaches a crossover audience of general readers with titles like *Pets in America: A History* by Kathleen C. Grier and *Gardening with Heirloom Seeds* by Lynn Coulter.

Areas of interest include American studies, African American studies, American history, literature, anthropology, business/economic history, Civil War history, classics, ancient history, European history, folklore, gender studies, Latin American and Caribbean studies, legal history, media studies, Native American studies, North Caroliniana, political science, public policy, regional books, religious studies, rural studies, social medicine, southern studies, and urban studies.

Other recent titles include *Two Captains from Carolina: Moses Grandy, John Newland Maffitt, and the Coming of the Civil War* by Bland Simpson; *The Fire of Freedom: Abraham Galloway and the Slaves' Civil War* by David S. Cecelski; *The Color of Christ: The Son of God and the Saga of Race in America* by Edward J. Blum and Paul Harvey; *Fred Thompson's Southern Sides: 250 Dishes That Really Make the Plate* by Fred Thompson; *Buttermilk: A Savor the South™ Cookbook* by Debbie Moose.

University of North Carolina Press handles its own distribution with the assistance of regional sales representatives.

Query letters and SASEs should be directed to:

David Perry, Assistant Director and Editor-in-Chief—History, regional trade, Civil War; david_perry@unc.edu

Charles Grench, Assistant Director and Senior Editor—American history, European history, law and legal studies, classics and ancient history, business and economic history, political science, social science; charles_grench@unc.edu

Elaine Maisner, Senior Editor—Religious studies, Latin American studies, Caribbean studies, regional trade; elaine_maisner@unc.edu

Joseph Parsons, Senior Editor—Social science, humanities.

Zachary Read, Assistant Editor

Sara Cohen, Editorial Assistant

UNIVERSITY OF OKLAHOMA PRESS

1005 Asp Avenue, Norman, OK 73019-6051
405-325- 2000
www.oupress.com | e-mail: **acquisitions@ou.edu**

During its more than 75 years of continuous operation, the University of Oklahoma Press (OU Press) has gained international recognition as an outstanding publisher of scholarly literature. It was the first university press established in the Southwest, and the fourth in the western half of the country.

The press began as the idea of William Bennett Bizzell, fifth president of the University of Oklahoma and a wide-ranging humanist and book collector. Over the years, the press has grown from a staff of one—the first director, Joseph A. Brandt—to an active and capable team of some 50 members.

Building on the foundation laid by their four previous directors, OU Press continues its dedication to the publication of outstanding scholarly works. Under the guidance of the present director, John Drayton, the major goal of the press is to strengthen its position as a preeminent publisher of books about the American West and American Indians, while expanding its program in other scholarly disciplines, including classical studies, military history, political science, and natural science.

Recent titles include *WinterSun: Poems* by Shi Zhi; *Zebulon Pike, Thomas Jefferson, and the Opening of the American West* by Matthew L. Harris and Jay H. Buckley; *The North American Journals of Prince Maximilian of Wied, Volume 3: September 1833–August 1834* by Prince Maximilian Alexander Philipp; *Gunfight at the Eco-Corral: Western Cinema and the Environment* by Robin L. Murray and Joseph K. Heumann; *Into the Breach at Pusan: The 1st Provisional Marine Brigade in the Korean War* by Kenneth W. Estes.

For additional information, e-mail acquisitions@ou.edu. Query letters with SASEs should be directed to:

Charles E. Rankin, Associate Director, Editor-in-Chief—American West, military history; cerankin@ou.edu

Alessandra Tamulevich, Editor—American Indian, Mesoamerican, and Latin American studies; jacobi@ou.edu

John Drayton, Senior Associate Director and Publisher—Classical studies; jdrayton@ou.edu

Connie Arnold, Administrative Assistant; carnold@ou.edu

Jay Dew, Editor—Twentieth-century American West, Texas history, politics and political history, environmental history; jaydew@ou.edu

UNIVERSITY OF SOUTH CAROLINA PRESS

1600 Hampton Street, 5th Floor, Columbia, SC 29208
803-777-5245 | fax: 803-777-0160
www.sc.edu/uscpress

The University of South Carolina Press shares the central mission of its university: to advance knowledge and enrich the state's cultural heritage. Established in 1944, it is one of the oldest publishing houses in the South and among the largest in the Southeast. With more than 1,500 published books to its credit, 800 in print, and 50 new books published each year, the press is important in enhancing the scholarly reputation and worldwide visibility of the University of South Carolina.

The University of South Carolina Press publishes works of original scholarship in the fields of history (American, African American, Southern, Civil War, culinary, maritime, and women's), regional studies, literature, religious studies, rhetoric, and social work.

Recent titles include *The Aftermath of Slavery: A Study of the Condition and Environment of the American Negro* by William A. Sinclair; *Blood and Bone: Truth and Reconciliation in a Southern Town* by Jack Shuler; *A Book of Exquisite Disasters* by Charlene Spearen; *British Abolitionism and the Question of Moral Progress in History* by Donald A. Yerxa; *Challengers to Duopoly: Why Third Parties Matter in American Two-Party Politics* by J. David Gillespie.

Queries with SASEs should be directed to:

Linda Haines Fogle, Assistant Director for Operations—Trade titles, literature, religious studies, rhetoric, social work, general inquiries; lfogle@gwm.sc.ude

Alexander Moore, Acquisitions Editor—History, regional studies; alexm@gwm.sc.edu

Jim Denton, Acquisitions Editor—Literature, religious studies, rhetoric, social work; dentoja@mailbox.sc.edu

UNIVERSITY OF TENNESSEE PRESS

110 Conference Center, 600 Henley Street, Knoxville, TN 37996-4108
865-974-3321 | fax: 865-974-3724
www.utpress.org

The University of Tennessee Press is dedicated to playing a significant role in the intellectual life of the University of Tennessee system, the academic community in general, and the citizens of the state of Tennessee by publishing high-quality works of original scholarship in selected fields as well as highly accurate and informative regional studies and literary fiction. By utilizing current technology to provide the best possible vehicles for the publication of scholarly and regional works, the press preserves and disseminates information for scholars, students, and general readers.

The University of Tennessee Press was established as a scholarly publisher in 1940 by the university trustees. Its mandate was threefold: to stimulate scholarly research in many fields; to channel such studies to a large readership; and to extend the university's regional leadership by publishing worthy projects about the South, including those by non-university authors.

Recent titles include *Into the Classroom: A Practical Guide for Starting Student Teaching* by Rosalyn McKeown; *Tennessee Tragedies: Natural, Technological, and Societal Disasters in the Volunteer State* by Allen R. Coggins; *David Schenck and the Contours of Confederate Identity* by Rodney Steward; *The Spirit of the Appalachian Trail: Community, Environment, and Belief* by Susan Power Bratton; *Presbyterians in North Carolina: Race, Politics, and Religious Identity in Historical Perspective* by Walter H. Conser Jr., and Robert J. Cain.

Query letters and SASEs should be directed to:
Scot Danforth, Acquisitions Director—American Civil War, American religion, special projects; danforth@utk.edu
Carrie Webb, Acquisitions Editor—African American studies, American history, Appalachian studies, folklore, literary criticism, material culture, nature and environment, sport and popular culture, Tennessee studies; cwebb@utk.edu
Thomas Wells, Editorial Assistant—Archaeology, Native American studies; twells@utk.edu

UNIVERSITY OF TEXAS PRESS

PO Box 7819, Austin, TX 78713-7819
512-471-7233 | fax: 512-232-7178
www.utexas.edu/utpress | e-mail: utpress@uts.cc.utexas.edu

By launching a scholarly press in 1950, the University of Texas made several important statements: Books matter; books educate; and publishing good books

UNIVERSITY PRESSES

is a public responsibility and a valuable component of the state's system of higher education.

As part of its mission to serve the people of Texas, the press also produces books of general interest for a wider audience, covering, in particular, the history, culture, arts, and natural history of the state. To these, the press has recently added accounts of the contributions of African and Native Americans, Latinos, and women. Major areas of concentration are anthropology, Old and New World archaeology, architecture, art history, botany, classics and the Ancient World, conservation and the environment, Egyptology, film and media studies, geography, landscape, Latin American and Latino studies, literary modernism, Mexican American studies, marine science, Middle Eastern studies, ornithology, pre-Columbian studies, Texas and Western studies, and women's studies.

The University of Texas Press has published more than 2,000 books over five decades. Currently a staff of 50, under the direction of Joanna Hitchcock, brings out some 90 books and 11 journals annually.

Recent titles include *A Thousand Deer: Four Generations of Hunting and the Hill Country* by Rick Bass; *Speech Presentation in Homeric Epic* by Deborah Beck; *Tricholomas of North America: A Mushroom Field Guide* by Alan E. Bessette, Arleen R. Bessette, William C. Roody, and Steven A. Trudell; *Tomorrow We're All Going to the Harvest: Temporary Foreign Worker Programs and Neoliberal Political Economy* by Leigh Binford; *Las Sombras/The Shadows* by Kate Breakey; *A Future for Amazonia: Randy Borman and Cofán Environmental Politics* by Michael Cepek; *Contentious: Immigration, Affirmative Action, Racial Profiling, and the Death Penalty* by Anthony Cortese.

University of Texas Press handles its own distribution.

Query letters and SASEs should be directed to:

Theresa May, Editor-in-Chief—Latin American studies, Latino/a studies, Native American studies, anthropology, New World archaeology, photography.

William Bishel, Sponsoring Editor—Texana, ornithology, botany, natural history, environmental studies.

Jim Burr, Sponsoring Editor—Classics and ancient world, film and media studies, Middle East studies, Jewish studies, Old World archaeology, architecture, applied languages.

Allison Faust, Sponsoring Editor—Music, geography, art, Texas art, culture; allison@utpress.ppb.utexas.edu

Casey Kittrell, Assistant Editor—Fiction in translation; casey@utpress.ppb .utexas.edu

---

UNIVERSITY OF VIRGINIA PRESS

Box 400318, Charlottesville, VA 22904
434-924-3468
www.upress.virginia.edu | e-mail: upressva@virginia.edu

The University of Virginia Press (UVaP) was founded in 1963 to advance the intellectual interests not only of the University of Virginia, but also of institutions of higher learning throughout the state. UVaP currently publishes 50 to 60 new titles annually.

The UVaP editorial program focuses primarily on the humanities and social sciences with special concentrations in American history, African American studies, Southern studies, literature, ecocriticism, and regional books. While it continuously pursues new titles, UVaP also maintains a backlist of over 1,000 titles in print.

Active series include the Papers of George Washington; the Papers of James Madison; the Victorian Literature and Culture Series; CARAF Books (translations of Francophone literature); New World Studies; the Carter G. Woodson Institute Series in Black Studies; Under the Sign of Nature: Explorations in Ecocriticism; The American South Series; A Nation Divided: New Studies in the Civil War; Constitutionalism and Democracy; Race, Ethnicity, and Politics; Reconsiderations in Southern African History; Studies in Early Modern German History; Studies in Religion and Culture; Southern Texts Society; and the Virginia Bookshelf series of regional reprints.

Other recent titles include *Whispers of Rebellion: Narrating Gabriel's Conspiracy* by Michael L. Nicholls; *Sustainable, Affordable, Prefab: The ecoMOD Project* by John D. Quale; *William Wordsworth and the Ecology of Authorship: The Roots of Environmentalism in Nineteenth-Century Culture* by Scott Hess; *Fatalism in American Film Noir, Some Cinematic Philosophy* by Robert B. Pippin; *Consuming Visions: Cinema, Writing, and Modernity in Rio de Janeiro* by Maite Conde; *"Those Who Labor for My Happiness": Slavery at Thomas Jefferson's Monticello* by Lucia Stanton.

The Electronic Imprint of the UVaP publishes digital scholarship in the humanities and social sciences issued under the Rotunda imprint (www.upress.virginia .edu/rotunda). Rotunda was created for the publication of original digital scholarship along with newly digitized critical and documentary editions in the humanities and social sciences. For further information, contact Rotunda via e-mail at rotunda-upress @virginia.edu.

Submit UVaP queries and SASEs to:
Cathie Brettschneider, Humanities Editor; cib8b@virginia.edu
Richard K. Holway, History and Social Sciences Editor; rkh2a@virginia.edu
Boyd Zenner, Architecture and Environmental Editor; bz2v@virginia.edu

---

UNIVERSITY OF WASHINGTON PRESS

PO Box 50096, Seattle, WA 98145-5096
206-543-4050 | fax: 206-543-3932
www.washington.edu/uwpress | e-mail: uwpress@u.washington.edu

The University of Washington Press (UW Press) publishes titles that cover a wide variety of academic fields, with especially distinguished lists in Asian studies,

Middle Eastern studies, environmental history, biography, anthropology, Western history, natural history, marine studies, architectural history, and art. The Press has published approximately 3,800 books, of which about 1,400 are still in print. UW Press publishes about 60 new titles a year.

The press is recognized as the world's foremost publisher on the art and culture of the Northwest Coast Indians and Alaskan Eskimos, and as the leader in the publication of materials dealing with the Asian American experience. Such series as A History of East Central Europe, Studies in Modernity and National Identity, American Ethnic and Cultural Studies, Asian Law Series, Korean Studies of the Henry M. Jackson School of International Studies, Studies on Ethnic Groups in China, Literary Conjugations, In Vivo, and the Pacific Northwest Poetry Series, have brought distinction to the press and the university.

The imprint of the University of Washington Press is under the control of a faculty committee appointed by the university's president. The approval of the University Press Committee is required before any book may be published. The press's editors work closely with the faculty committee to select those books that will carry the University of Washington imprint. About one-third of the books published by the press originate within the University of Washington. Of the manuscripts and proposals that are submitted annually from all over the world, less than 5 percent are accepted for publication.

Recent titles include *Contagion: Health, Fear, Sovereignty* by Bruce Magnusson and Zahi Zalloua; *Disappearing Traces: Holocaust Testimonials, Ethics, and Aesthetics* by Dorota Glowacka; *The Promise of Wilderness: American Environmental Politics since 1964* by James Morton Turner; *Where the Salmon Run: The Life and Legacy of Billy Frank Jr.* by Trova Heffernan.

Query letters and SASEs should be directed to:

Lorri Hagman, Executive Editor—Asian studies, cultural and environmental anthropology; lhagman@u.washingon.edu

Marianne Keddington-Lang, Acquisitions Editor—Western history, environmental studies, Native American studies; mkedlang@u.washington.edu

Tim Zimmermann, Assistant Editor; tjz@uw.edu

UNIVERSITY OF WISCONSIN PRESS

1930 Monroe Street, 3rd Floor, Madison, WI 53711-2059
608-263-1110 | fax: 608-263-1120
uwpress.wisc.edu | e-mail: uwiscpress@uwpress.wisc.edu

Located in Madison, Wisconsin, the University of Wisconsin Press was founded in 1936, and publishes both books and journals. Since its first book appeared in 1937, the press has published and distributed more than 3,000 titles. It has more than 1,400 titles currently in print, including books of general interest (biography, fiction, natural history, poetry, photography, fishing, food, travel, etc.), scholarly books (American studies, anthropology, art, classics, environmental studies, ethnic studies, film, gay and lesbian studies, history, Jewish studies, literary criticism, Slavic studies, etc.), and regional books about Wisconsin and the Upper Midwest. They publish and distribute new books each year in these fields.

Among their book series are the Brittingham Prize in Poetry, the Felix Pollak Prize in Poetry, Wisconsin Studies in Autobiography, Wisconsin Studies in Classics, Living Out: Gay and Lesbian Autobiography, Studies in Dance History, the George L. Mosse Series in Modern European Cultural and Intellectual History, the History of American Thought and Culture, and Publications of the Wisconsin Center for Pushkin Studies.

The press is a division of the Graduate School of the University of Wisconsin–Madison. Residing within the university's graduate school, UW Press draws on and supports the intellectual activities of the graduate school and its faculty and enhances the university's overall missions of research and instruction. Although it publishes many books and journals produced by faculty from the University of Wisconsin campuses, it also publishes books and journals from scholars around the United States and the world. The house has authors residing in many different countries, from Australia to Zimbabwe. It has copublished English-language books with publishers in England, Ireland, Turkey, Italy, and Japan. University of Wisconsin Press books have been translated into dozens of foreign languages.

Recent titles include *Letters Home to Sarah: The Civil War Letters of Guy C. Taylor, Thirty-Sixth Wisconsin Volunteers* by Guy C. Taylor; *Endless Empire: Spain's Retreat, Europe's Eclipse, America's Decline* by Alfred McCoy, Josep M. Fradera, and Stephan Jacobson; *Against the Tide: Immigrants, Day-Laborers, and Community in Jupiter, Florida* by Sandra Lazo de la Vega and Timothy J. Steigenga; *A Horse Named Sorrow* by Trebor Healey; *Paternity Test* by Michael Lowenthal.

Query letters and SASEs should be directed to:

Raphael Kadushin, Senior Acquisitions Editor—Autobiography/memoir, biography, classical studies, dance, performance, film, food, gender studies, GLBT studies, Jewish studies, Latino/a memoirs, travel; kadushin@wisc.edu

Gwen Walker, PhD, Acquisitions Editor—African studies, anthropology, environmental studies, Irish studies, Latin American studies, Slavic studies, Southeast Asian studies, US history; gcwalker@wisc.edu

UNIVERSITY PRESS OF COLORADO

5589 Arapahoe Avenue, Suite 206C, Boulder, CO 80303
720-406-8849 | fax: 720-406-3443
www.upcolorado.com

Founded in 1965, the University Press of Colorado is a nonprofit cooperative publishing enterprise supported, in part, by Adams State College, Colorado State

University, Fort Lewis College, Mesa State College, Metropolitan State College of Denver, University of Colorado, University of Northern Colorado, and Western State College of Colorado. The press publishes 30 to 35 new titles each year, with the goal of facilitating communication among scholars and providing the peoples of the state and region with a fair assessment of their histories, cultures, and resources. The press has extended the reach and reputation of supporting institutions and has made scholarship of the highest level in many diverse fields widely available.

The University Press of Colorado is currently accepting manuscript proposals in anthropology, archaeology, environmental studies, history, law, Native American studies, and the natural sciences, as well as projects about the state of Colorado and the Rocky Mountain region. It is also accepting submissions for the following series: Atomic History & Culture, Mesoamerican Worlds, Mining the American West, Timberline Books, and The Women's West (nonfiction only). The University Press of Colorado is not currently accepting proposals in fiction or poetry.

Recent titles include *Agency in Ancient Writing* by Joshua Englehardt; *An American Provence* by Thomas P. Huber; *Ancient Households of the Americas: Conceptualizing What Households Do* by John G. Douglass, and Nancy Gonlin; *The Anthropological Study of Class and Consciousness* by E. Paul Durrenberger; *The Anthropology of Labor Unions* by E. Paul Durrenberger and Karaleah S. Reichart.

Scholars proposing manuscripts for publication should submit a prospectus to the acquisitions department before submitting a complete manuscript. Submissions are accepted via mail and e-mail. No phone calls. Address manuscript submission inquiries to:

Darrin Pratt, Director and Acquiring Editor; darrin@upcolorado.com

---

UNIVERSITY PRESS OF FLORIDA

15 NW 15th Street, Gainesville, FL 32611
352-392-1351 | 800-226-3822 | fax: 352-392-0590
www.upf.com | e-mail: press@upf.com

The University Press of Florida (UPF), the scholarly publishing arm of the State University System, representing all ten universities, is charged by the Board of Regents with publishing books of intellectual distinction and significance, books that will contribute to improving the quality of higher education in the state, and books of general and regional interest and usefulness to the people of Florida, reflecting its rich historical, cultural, and intellectual heritage and resources. The press may publish original works by State University System faculty members, meritorious works originating elsewhere, important out-of-print books, and other projects related to its backlist that will contribute to a coherent and effective publishing program—one that will supplement and extend programs of instruction and research offered by the universities.

UPF has published over 2,500 volumes since its inception and currently releases nearly 100 new titles each year.

Subjects include African studies, anthropology and archaeology, art, dance, music, law, literature, Middle Eastern studies, natural history, Russian studies, history, Florida, Latin American studies, political science, science and technology, and sociology.

Recent titles *Field to Feast: Recipes Celebrating Florida Farmers, Chefs, and Artisans* by Pam Bramdon, Katie Farmand, and Heather McPherson; *Redheads Die Quickly and Other Stories* by Gil Brewer; *Homegrown in Florida* by William McKeen; *Calling Me Home: Gram Parsons and the Roots of Country Rock* by Bob Kealing; *Forever Young: A Life of Adventure in Air and Space* by John W. Young.

To submit a manuscript, send a one-page letter of inquiry to Editor-in-Chief John Byram, to determine the University Press of Florida's interest in your project. Please include your full postal address.

Amy Gorelick, Assistant Director and Assistant Editor-in-Chief
Shannon McCarthy, Acquisitions Assistant

UNIVERSITY PRESS OF KANSAS

2502 Westbrooke Circle, Lawrence, KS 66045-4444
785-864-4155 | fax 785-864-4586
www.kansaspress.ku.edu | e-mail upress@ku.edu

The University Press of Kansas publishes scholarly books that advance knowledge and regional books that contribute to the understanding of Kansas, the Great Plains, and the Midwest. Founded in 1946, it represents the six state universities: Emporia State University, Fort Hays State University, Kansas State University, Pittsburg State University, the University of Kansas, and Wichita State University.

Profiled by *The Chronicle of Higher Education* (3 July 1998) as "a distinctive model of success in turbulent times," the press focuses generally on history, political science, and philosophy. More specifically, it concentrates on presidential studies, military studies, American history (especially political, cultural, intellectual, and western), US government and public policy, legal studies, and social and political philosophy.

Recent titles include *Leak: How Mark Felt Became Deep Throat* by Max Holland; *Scarlet Fields: The Combat Memoir of a World War I Medal of Honor Hero* by John Lewis Barkley; *The CIA's Greatest Covert Operation: Inside the Daring Mission to Recover a Nuclear-Armed Soviet Sub* by David H. Sharp; *Beyond Rosie the Riveter: Women of World War II in American Popular Graphic Art* by Donna B. Knaff; *George Henry Thomas: As True as Steel* by Brian Steel Wills.

Direct queries, proposals, and SASEs to:
Fred M. Woodward, Director—American government and public policy,

presidential studies, American political thought, urban politics, Kansas and regional studies; fwoodward@ku.edu

Michael Briggs, Editor-in-Chief—Military history and intelligence studies, law and legal history, political science; mbrigss@ku.edu

UNIVERSITY PRESS OF MISSISSIPPI

3825 Ridgewood Road, Jackson, MS 39211-6492
601-432-6205 | 800-737-7788 | fax: 601-432-6217
www.upress.state.ms.us | e-mail: press@ihl.state.ms.us

The University Press of Mississippi (UPM) was founded in 1970 and is supported by Mississippi's eight state universities. UPM publishes scholarly books and books that interpret the South and its culture to the nation and the world. From its offices in Jackson, the University Press of Mississippi acquires, edits, distributes, and promotes more than 60 new books every year. Over the years, the press has published more than 900 titles and distributed more than 2.5 million copies worldwide, each with the Mississippi imprint. Out of the approximately 600 submissions it receives, the UPM publishes an average of 60 manuscripts a year.

The University Press of Mississippi is a nonprofit publisher that serves an academic and general audience. The editorial program focuses on the following areas: scholarly and trade titles in African American studies; American studies, literature, history, and culture; art and architecture; biography and memoir; ethnic studies; film studies; folklore and folk art; health; memoir and biography; military history; music; natural sciences; performance; photography; popular culture; reference; Southern studies; sports; women's studies; other liberal arts. Special series include American Made Music, Chancellor Porter L. Fortune Symposium in Southern History, Conversations with Comic Artists, Conversations with Filmmakers, Faulkner and Yoknapatawpha, Hollywood Legends, Literary Conversations, Margaret Walker Alexander Series in African American Studies, Southern Icons, Studies in Popular Culture, Understanding Health and Sickness, Willie Morris Books in Memoir and Biography, and Writers and Their Works.

Recent titles include *Abraham Polonsky: Interviews* by Andrew Dickos; *Aerosol Kingdom: Subway Painters of New York City* by Ivor L. Miller; *The Artistry of Afro-Cuban Bata Drumming: Aesthetics, Transmission, Bonding, and Creativity* by Kenneth Schweitzer; *Campus Traditions: Folklore from the Old-Time College to the Modern Mega-University* by Simon J. Bronner; *Civil Rights in the White Literary Imagination: Innocence by Association* by Jonathan W. Gray.

Submit proposal, CV, and SASE to the appropriate editor:

Leila W. Salisbury, Director—American studies, film studies, popular culture; lsalisbury@ihl.state.ms.us

Craig Gill, Assistant Director and Editor-in-Chief—Art, architecture, folklore and folk art, history, music, natural sciences, photography, Southern studies; cgill@ihl.state.ms.us

Anne Stascavage, Managing Editor—Performance studies; astascavage @ihl.state.ms.us

Walter Biggins, Acquiring Editor—American literature, comics studies, American studies, Caribbean studies; wbiggins@ihl.state.ms.us

Valerie Jones, Editorial Assistant; vjones@mississippi.edu

Katie Keene, Editorial Assistant; kkeene@mississippi.edu

UNIVERSITY PRESS OF NEW ENGLAND

1 Court Street, Suite 250, Lebanon, NH 03766
603-448-1533 | fax: 603-448-7006
www.upne.com

University Press of New England (UPNE) is an award-winning university press supported by a consortium of schools—Brandeis University, Dartmouth College, the University of New Hampshire, Northeastern University, Tufts University, and University of Vermont—and based at Dartmouth College since 1970. UPNE has earned a reputation for excellence in scholarly, instructional, reference, literary and artistic, and general-interest books. Many of these are published cooperatively with one of the member institutions and carry a joint imprint. Others are published under the University Press of New England imprint.

The publishing program reflects strengths in the humanities; liberal arts; fine, decorative, and performing arts; literature; New England culture; and interdisciplinary studies. The press publishes and distributes more than 80 titles annually, with sales of more than $2.5 million. A professional staff of 24 maintains high standards in editorial, design and production, marketing, order fulfillment, and business operations.

University Press of New England publishes books for scholars, teachers, students, and the general public. The press concentrates in American studies; literature; history; cultural studies; art, architecture, and material culture; ethnic studies (including African American, Jewish, Native American, and Shaker studies); international studies; nature and the environment; and New England history and culture. The Hardscrabble Books imprint publishes fiction of New England.

Recent titles include *A Murder in Wellesley: The Inside Story of an Ivy-League Doctor's Double Life, His Slain Wife, and the Trial That Gripped the Nation* by Tom Farmer and Marty Foley; *Killer Show, The Station Nightclub Fire: America's Deadliest Rock Concert* by John Barylick; *Edward Hopper in Vermont* by Bonnie Tocher Clause; *Picasso and the Chess Player: Pablo Picasso, Marcel Duchamp, and the Battle for the Soul of Modern Art* by Larry Witham; *A Newer World: Politics, Money, Technology, and What's Really Being Done to Solve the Climate Crisis* by William F. Hewitt.

UNIVERSITY PRESSES

It is best to contact this press early in one's development process, even at the proposal stage. Send a proposal with SASE to:

Michael P. Burton, Director—Art, photography, decorative arts, material culture, historic preservation, distribution titles; michael.p.burton@dartmouth.edu

Phyllis Deutsch, Editor-in-Chief—Jewish studies, nature and environment, environment and health, sustainability studies, nineteenth-century studies, American studies, criminology with a gendered component; phyllis.d.deutsch @dartmouth.edu

Stephen Hull, Acquisitions Editor—New England regional, African American studies, New England sports, sports and society, music and technology, international studies with a civil society component; stephen.p.hull@dartmouth.edu

Richard Pult, Acquisitions Editor—New England regional/Boston, New England sports, marine biology/ecology, criminology, music/opera, Native American studies, American studies, visual culture, institutional histories; richard .pult@dartmouth.edu

Lori Miller, Editorial Assistant—New England regional, African American studies, women's studies, American studies, ethnic studies, Arctic studies, Canadian-American border studies, political science, historic preservation, material culture, decorative arts; lori.miller@dartmouth.edu

UTAH STATE UNIVERSITY PRESS

7800 Old Main Hill, Logan, UT 84322
435-797-1362 | fax: 435-797-0313
www.usu.edu/usupress

Utah State University Press is a refereed scholarly publisher and division of Utah State University. Established in 1972, the press's mandate is to acquire and publish books of superior quality that win the esteem of readers and that appropriately represent the university to the community of scholars. Vital also to its mission is publication for a broader community, including students, who use the books in their studies, and general readers, who find in them enjoyment as well as enlightenment.

Utah State University Press is an established publisher in the fields of composition studies, creative writing, folklore, Native American studies, nature and environment, and Western history, including Mormon history and Western women's history. They also sponsor the annual May Swenson Poetry Award.

Recent titles include *Presumed Incompetent: The Intersections of Race and Class for Women in Academia* by Gabriella Gutiérrez y Muhs, Yolanda Flores Niemann, Carmen G. González, and Angela P. Harris; *Wildflowers of the Mountain West* by Richard M. Anderson, JayDee Gunnell, and Jerry L. Goodspeed; *Folk Culture in the Digital Age: New Perspectives on Folklore and the Internet* by Trevor J. Blank; *National Healing: Race, State and the Teaching of Composition* by Claude Hurlbert;

Warrior Ways: Explorations in Modern Military Folklore edited by Eric A. Eliason and Tad Tuleja.

Direct proposals with SASEs to:

Michael Spooner, Director; michael.spooner@usu.edu
Kelly Neumann, Editorial Assistant

VANDERBILT UNIVERSITY PRESS

Box 1813 Station B, Nashville, TN 37235-1813
615-322-3585 | fax: 615-343-8823
www.vanderbiltuniversitypress.com | e-mail: vupress@vanderbilt.edu

Established in 1940, Vanderbilt University Press is the principal publishing arm of one of the nation's leading research universities. The press's primary mission is to select, produce, market, and disseminate scholarly publications of outstanding quality and originality. In conjunction with the long-term development of its editorial program, the press draws on and supports the intellectual activities of the university and its faculty. Although its main emphasis falls in the area of scholarly publishing, the press also publishes books of substance and significance that are of interest to the general public, including regional books. In this regard, the press also supports Vanderbilt's service and outreach to the larger local and national community.

The editorial interests of Vanderbilt University Press include most areas of the humanities and social sciences, as well as health care and education. The press seeks intellectually provocative and socially significant works in these areas, as well as works that are interdisciplinary or that blend scholarly and practical concerns. In addition, the press maintains an active copublishing program with Nashville-based Country Music Foundation Press. At present, Vanderbilt publishes some 20 new titles each year. Of the total of some 300 works published by the press in its five-decade history, more than 125 remain in print.

Recent titles include *Lone Wolf: Terror and the Rise of Leaderless Resistance* by George Michael; *Dignity and Health* by Nora Jacobson; *Making Myself at Home in a Nursing Home* by Sandra J. Gaffney; *Seeking a New Majority: The Republican Party and American Politics, 1960–1980* by Robert Mason and Iwan Morgan; *Creation Story: Gee's Bend Quilts and the Art of Thornton Dial* by Mark W. Scala; *Divided Conversations: Identities, Leadership, and Change in Public Higher Education* by Kristin G. Esterberg and John Wooding.

Direct query letters and SASEs to:

Michael Ames, Director; vupress@vanderbilt.edu
Eli Bortz, Acquisitions Editor; eli.bortz@vanderbilt.edu
Joell Smith-Borne, Managing Editor; joell.smith-borne@vanderbilt.edu

WAYNE STATE UNIVERSITY PRESS

The Leonard N. Simons Building, 4809 Woodward Avenue,
Detroit, MI 48201-1309
313-577-6120 | fax: 313-577-6131
wsupress.wayne.edu

Wayne State University Press is a distinctive urban publisher committed to support-ing its parent institution's core research, teaching, and service mission by generating high-quality scholarly and general interest works of global importance. Through its publishing program, the press disseminates research, advances education, and serves the local community, while expanding the international reputation of the press and the university.

Wayne State University Press is an established midsize university press that publishes approximately 40 new books and six journals per year. Subject areas fea-tured in the current publishing program include Africana studies, Armenian studies, children's studies, classical studies, fairy-tale and folklore studies, film and television studies, German studies, Great Lakes and Michigan, humor studies, Jewish studies, labor and urban studies, literature, and speech and language pathology.

Recent titles include *Inventing the Modern Yiddish Stage: Essays in Drama, Performance, and Show Business* by Joel Berkowitz and Barbara Henry; *The Amphibians and Reptiles of Michigan: A Quaternary and Recent Faunal Adventure* by J. Alan Holman; *Geology and Landscape of Michigan's Pictured Rocks National Lakeshore and Vicinity* by William L. Blewett; *Before the Crash: Early Video Game History* by Mark J. P. Wolf; *Bearing Witness to African American Literature: Validating and Valorizing Its Authority, Authenticity, and Agency* by Bernard W. Bell.

To submit, send a letter of inquiry or proposal with SASE to:

Kathryn Wildfong, Acquisitions Manager—Africana studies, Jewish studies, Great Lakes and Michigan; k.wildfong@wayne.edu

Annie Martin, Acquisitions Editor—Film and TV studies, fairy-tale studies, children's studies, Made in Michigan Writers Series, speech and language pathology; annie.martin@wayne.edu

Kristina Stonehill, Assistant Editor

WESLEYAN UNIVERSITY PRESS

215 Long Lane, Middletown, CT 06459
860-685-7711 | fax: 860-685-7712
www.wesleyan.edu/wespress

The mission of Wesleyan University Press is to develop and maintain a sound and vigorous publishing program that serves the academic ends and intellectual life of the university. In addition, the press formulated three broad goals meant to ensure that the press would fulfill its mission: "To acquire and publish scholarly and broadly intellectual works that make significant contributions to knowledge in traditional fields of inquiry or expression, and to new and cross-disciplinary fields of inquiry or expression; to enhance the intellectual life of the Wesleyan community through the involvement of faculty and students in the publishing programs and activities of the press; and to project the name and image of the university and to enhance its reputation as an academic institution of the highest quality."

Publishing in its current form since 1959, Wesleyan University Press has lived through many transitions while continuing to thrive. It has published an internationally renowned poetry series since its inception, releasing more than 250 titles and collecting four Pulitzer Prizes, a Bollingen, and two National Book Awards in that one series alone.

Recent titles include *Carved in Stone: The Artistry of Early New England Gravestones* by Thomas E. Gilson; *Ella Grasso: Connecticut's Pioneering Governor* by Jon E. Purmont; *Garnet Poems: An Anthology of Connecticut Poetry Since 1776* by Dennis Barone; *Collected Poems* by Joseph Caravolo; *Musicking Bodies: Gesture and Voice in Hinduistani Music* by Matthew Rahim; *Music, Politics, and Violence* by Susan Fast and Kip Pegley.

The Wesleyan Poetry Program accepts manuscripts by invitation only until further notice. Its publications in nonfiction concentrate in the areas of dance, music/culture, film/TV and media studies, and science-fiction studies. It will accept proposals for books in these areas only. The equivalent of a cover letter may be submitted by e-mail/ attachment, but do not submit full proposals electronically unless asked to do so.

Direct queries with CVs and SASEs to:

Suzanna Tamminen, Director and Editor-in-Chief—Dance; stamminen @wesleyan.edu

Parker Smathers, Editor—Music/culture, film/TV and media studies, science-fiction studies, Connecticut history; psmathers@wesleyan.edu

YALE UNIVERSITY PRESS

302 Temple Street, New Haven, CT 06511
PO Box 209040, New Haven, CT 06520-9040
203-432-0960 | fax: 203-432-0948
www.yale.edu/yup | e-mail: yupmkt@yalevm.cis.yale.edu
London office:
47 Bedford Square, London WC1B 3DP UK
www.yalebooks.co.uk | blog: yalepress.wordpress.com

By publishing serious works that contribute to a global understanding of human affairs, Yale University Press aids in the discovery and dissemination of light and

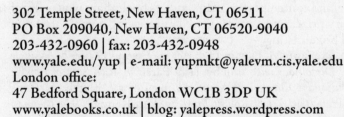

truth, lux et veritas, which is a central purpose of Yale University. The press's publications are books and other materials that further scholarly investigation, advance interdisciplinary inquiry, stimulate public debate, educate both within and outside the classroom, and enhance cultural life. Through the distribution of works that combine excellence in scholarship with skillful editing, design, production, and marketing, the press demonstrates its commitment to increasing the range and vigor of intellectual pursuits within the university and elsewhere. With an innovative and entrepreneurial spirit, Yale University Press continually extends its horizons to embody university press publishing at its best.

One hundred years and over 7,000 titles ago, Yale University Press was founded by a young graduate and his wife. In its first few years, the press was owned entirely by the founders and guided by a committee of the Yale Corporation; whimsy played a part in the publishing of dozens of books of poetry, many from the literary renaissance then at Yale—MacLeish, Farrar, Luce, and the Benéts, for example—and soon the Yale Shakespeare and the Yale Series of Younger Poets, which are going strong today. Then there were the many books for children, another surprise from a university press. These were in addition to such works of solid scholarship as *Farrand's 1911 Records of the 1787 Constitutional Convention*, also still in print, and the *Chronicles of America*, the *Yale Review* from time to time, and the many long Yale series of studies in history, literature, economics, and language. Beyond their content, these books were distinguished by their looks, for Carl Purington Rollins designed them over three decades, gathering praise all the while. Among the press's series then and now are the many shelves of volumes of the papers of Walpole and Franklin and Edwards, and today's new and ambitious series on the Culture and Civilization of China and the Annals of Communism. The *Yale Pelican History of Art* recently joined a long list of art books that was already perhaps the best in the world.

The London office of the Yale Press was first established in 1961 as a marketing base, and in 1973 commenced publishing its own list. It now has a unique position as the only American university press with a full-scale publishing operation and publishing program in Europe. Working closely with the Paul Mellon Centre for Studies in British Art, it swiftly built a preeminent reputation for its art history and architecture titles. Its range now extends to trade history and biography, politics, music, religion, literature, and contemporary affairs, and its books have won many of the leading British literary prizes and awards, as well as receiving notable attention in reviews, journals, and broadcasting.

Recent titles include *Exorcism: A Play in One Act* by Eugine O'Neill; *A Single Roll of the Dice: Obama's Diplomacy with Iran* by Trita Parsi; *"A Rich Spot of Earth": Thomas Jefferson's Revolutionary Garden at Monticello* by Peter J. Hatch; *In God's Shadow* by Michael Walzer; *The Art of Robert Frost* by Tim Kendall; *The Woman Reader* by Belinda Jack.

Query letters, proposals, and SASEs should be directed to:
New Haven Office:

Jean E. Thomson Black, Executive Editor—Life sciences, physical sciences, environmental sciences, medicine.

Jennifer Banks, Editor—Literature in translation, religion.

Jonathan Brent, Editor-at-Large—Literature, literary studies, theater, Slavic studies.

Laura Davulis, Assistant Editor, Coordinator of Editorial Internships—History, current events.

Patricia Fidler, Publisher—Art and architecture.

William Frucht, Executive Editor—Political science, international relations.

Michelle Komie, Senior Editor—Art and architecture.

Sarah Miller, Assistant Editor

Michael O'Malley, PhD, Executive Editor—Business, economics, law.

Mary Jane Peluso, Publisher—Foreign languages and ESL.

Christopher Rogers, Executive Editor—History, current events.

Tim Shea, Development Editor—Foreign languages and ESL.

Vadim Staklo, Associate Editor—Reference.

Alison MacKeen, Editor—Media and technology, literary studies, education.

Ileene Smith, Editor-at-Large—Trade list.

Lindsay Toland, Publishing Coordinator—Art and architecture.

London Office:

Robert Baldock, Managing Director, London, and Editorial Director (Humanities)—History, biography, politics, music, history of religion, contemporary affairs.

Gillian Malpass, Publisher (Art and Architecture)—History of art, history of architecture, history of fashion.

Heather McCallum, Publisher, (Trade Books)—History, politics, current affairs, international affairs, biography, history of science.

Sally Salvesen, Publisher (Pevsner Architectural Guides)—Politics, economics, current affairs.

SECTION FOUR

CANADIAN BOOK PUBLISHERS

CANADIAN BOOK PUBLISHING
AND THE CANADIAN MARKET

GREG IOANNOU
President
Colborne Communications, Toronto
416-214-0183
www.colcomm.ca | e-mail: greg@colcomm.ca

Colborne Communications provides a full range of services to the book publishing industry, taking books from initial conception through writing, editing, design, layout, and print production.

There's good and bad news about the Canadian publishing industry for writers. First, the bad: Breaking in isn't easy. The good news: Most Canadian publishers are interested in new writers. They have to be, because small- to mid-sized Canadian houses operate mainly on government grant money. In order to get that grant money, houses must publish Canadian authors. They also can't afford bidding wars. Instead, they often find new authors, develop them, and hope that they stay—or that their fame will add value to the house's backlist.

The key to getting published is to make sure that you're sending the right manuscript to the right publisher, using an appropriate style for submissions. Publishers are less frustrated by poor writing than they are by poorly executed submissions.

If you've written a nonfiction book about rural Nova Scotia, don't send your manuscript to a children's publisher in Vancouver. Research the publishers first instead of spamming busy editors with manuscripts that don't fit their house's list.

The Internet is a fantastic tool for writers. It's easier to research potential publishers online than it is to sit at the library and search through *Quill & Quire's Canadian Publishers Directory*—though that is still a valuable resource.

Do an online search for Canadian publishers. A few places to start are the Association of Canadian Publishers—who provide a search form by genre and province—and the Canadian Publishers' Council. The Canadian Children's Book Centre is particularly focused and has an annual publication that lists publishers who accept unsolicited manuscripts and artwork. If you see a publisher whose mandate seems to match your book idea, visit their website and locate their submission requirements, or contact a Canadian agent.

Rather than sending your manuscript everywhere, write custom proposals that show the publisher that you know what they publish, you've read their submission guidelines thoroughly, and your manuscript adheres to those requirements. It is okay to show enthusiasm for the press, or to suggest where you think your manuscript fits on their list. But don't act as though the publisher would be lucky to get your book. Do not threaten publishers with deadlines; you may bully yourself into an automatic rejection. Take the time to write a brief but informative proposal, including a chapter-by-chapter outline if appropriate, and send a sample of your work. Include the approximate word count, genre, and reading level in the cover letter. Consider contacting the Canadian Authors Association or The Writers' Union of Canada for more information on writing for the Canadian market.

If you're a foreign writer hoping to be published in Canada, offer some form of subject-matter expertise. It's like immigrating to another country: You need to have a skill that a Canadian doesn't have.

American writers should remember that Canada is not part of the United States; Canadian publishers cannot use US stamps to return manuscripts. Use International Reply Coupons (available at any post office) instead.

ANNICK PRESS LIMITED

15 Patricia Avenue, Toronto, ON M2M 1H9, Canada
416-221-4802 | fax: 416-221-8400
www.annickpress.com

Annick Press publishes children's literature, specifically picture books, nonfiction, and juvenile and young-adult novels. The company has won many prestigious design and publishing awards. Annick Press was the first children's publisher to receive the Canadian Booksellers Association's Publisher of the Year award. Annick publishes books for children ages six months to 12 years and for young adults, approximately 30 titles annually. A select number of books are published in French and Spanish editions.

While continuing to publish picture books, Annick has added contemporary fiction and nonfiction to its list. It seeks titles that speak to issues young people deal with every day, such as bullying, teen sexuality, advertising, and alienation. It also publishes books on science, fantasy, pop culture, and world conflict.

Recent titles include *Erebos* by Ursula Poznanski; *The Research Virtuoso* by the Toronto Public Library; *Seeing Red* by Tanya Lloyd Kyi; *50 Climate Questions* by Peter Christie; *The World in Your Lunch Box* by Claire Eamer; *Latin Americans Thought of It* by Eva Salinas; and *Birthday Suit* by Olive Senior.

Annick Press is committed to publishing only Canadian authors. Further, it is not currently accepting manuscripts for picture books. However, it is interested in receiving manuscripts featuring teen fiction, middle-reader (ages eight to eleven) fiction, and middle-reader and teen nonfiction. Address all submissions to The Editors, so that they may properly register your manuscript. Do not send manuscripts by e-mail or fax.

Rick Wilks, Director
Colleen MacMillan, Associate Publisher

ANVIL PRESS

278 East First Avenue, Vancouver, BC V5T 1A6, Canada
604-876-8710 | fax: 604-879-2667
www.anvilpress.com

Anvil Press is a literary publisher interested in contemporary, progressive literature in all genres. It was created in 1988 to publish *subTERRAIN* magazine, which explores alternative literature and art; three years later, the press moved into publishing books as well. The Anvil Press mission is to discover, nurture, and promote new and established Canadian literary talent. It publishes eight to ten titles per year and sponsors the International 3-Day Novel Writing Contest, which involves writing an entire novel over the Labour Day Weekend and is explained in detail at www.3daynovel.com. It is not interested in publishing genre novels (science fiction, horror, romance, etc).

Recent Anvil titles include *Five Little Bitches* by Teresa McWhirter; *Valery the Great* by Elaine McCluskey; *A Dark Boat* by Patrick Friesen; *You Exist. Details Follow.* by Stuart Ross; *Mutant Sex Party & Other Plays* by Ed Macdonald; *Mayan Horror* by Bob Robertson; and *A Credit to Your Race* by Truman Green.

Direct query letters and SASEs to:

Brian Kaufman, Publisher

Jenn Farrell, Assistant Editor

ARSENAL PULP PRESS

#101–211 East Georgia Street, Vancouver, BC V6A 1Z6, Canada
604-687-4233 | fax: 604-687-4283
www.arsenalpulp.com | Twitter: @Arsenalpulp

Arsenal Pulp Press is a publisher of over 200 provocative and stimulating books in print that challenge the status quo in the following genres: cultural studies, political/sociological studies, regional studies and guides (particularly for British Columbia), cookbooks, gay and lesbian literature, visual art, multicultural literature, literary fiction, youth culture, and health. It has been a four-time nominee for Small Press Publisher of the Year, given by the Canadian Booksellers Association (2004, 2008, 2010, 2012). No genre fiction, such as science fiction, thrillers, or romance. It has had particular success with cookbooks and publishes around 14 to 20 new titles a year.

Recent Arsenal titles include *The Anti-Capitalist Resistance Comic Book* by Gord Hill; *Class Warfare* by D.M. Fraser; *The Dirt Chronicles* by Kristyn Dunnion; *The Mere Future* by Sarah Schulman; *Persistence* edited by Ivan E. Coyote; *Talk – Action = 0* by Joe Keithley; and *Zero Patience* by Susan Knabe and Wendy Gay Pearson.

Submissions should include a marketing analysis, synopsis, and a 50-page sample. Direct your query and SASE to the Editorial Board.

Brian Lam, Publisher; blam@arsenalpulp.com

Robert Ballantyne, Associate Publisher

Susan Safyan, Associate Editor

BEACH HOLME PUBLISHING

409 Granville Street, Suite 1010, Vancouver, BC V6C 1T2, Canada
604-733-4868 | fax: 604-733-4860

Beach Holme Publishing specializes in Canadian literary fiction, plays, poetry, literary nonfiction, and young-adult fiction. It brings indigenous creative writing to a wider Canadian audience and has published award-winning authors including Evelyn Lau, Joe Rosenblatt, and Dorothy Park.

Beach Holme's line of young-adult fiction is geared to children ages 8 to 13, and often features historical Canadian settings and situations.

Recent titles include *White Jade Tiger* by Julie Lawson; *False Shuffles* by Jane Urquhart; *Last Days in Africaville* by Dorothy Perk; *Little Emperors: A Year with the Future of China* by JoAnn Dionne; *Natural Disasters* by Andrea MacPherson; and *Hesitation before Birth* by Bert Almon.

Direct queries and SASEs to:

Michael Carroll, Publisher; bhp@beachholme.bc.ca

BRICK BOOKS

431 Boler Road, Box 20081, London, ON N6K 4G6, Canada
519-657-8579
www.brickbooks.ca | e-mail: brick.books@sympatico.ca | Twitter: @BrickBooks

Brick Books is a small literary press based in London, Ontario, which seeks to foster interesting, ambitious, and compelling work by Canadian poets. It is the only press in Canada that specializes in publishing poetry books. Brick Books was nominated for the prestigious Canadian Booksellers Association Libris Award for Best Small Press Publisher of the Year 2006. It publishes seven new books and an average of nine reprints every year.

Recent titles include *Omens in the Year of the Ox* by Steven Price; *Monkey Ranch* by Julie Bruck; *Between Dusk and Night* by Emily McGiffin; *I see my love more clearly from a distance* by Nora Gould; *Everything, now* by Jessica Moore; and *The Rapids* by Susan Gillis.

Brick Books can publish only authors who are Canadian citizens or landed immigrants. To submit, you may send the fully completed manuscript or a sample of eight to ten poems. Please note that they will only accept submissions between January 1 and April 30. Submissions received outside of the reading period will be returned. E-mail submissions are not accepted. Please address submissions to Brick Books and allow three to four months for a response.

Don McKay, Copublisher
Stan Dragland, Copublisher
John Barton
Barry Dempster
John Donlan
Alayna Munce
Elizabeth Philips
Sue Sinclair
Jan Zwicky

CORMORANT BOOKS

390 Steelcase Road East, Markham, ON L3R 1G2, Canada
905-475-5571
www.cormorantbooks.com | Twitter: @cormorantbooks

Established by Jan and Gary Geddes in 1986, Cormorant Books seeks to publish the best new work in the area of literary fiction and creative nonfiction for the adult market. This award-winning house publishes a select list of literary fiction, trade nonfiction, and works of fiction in translation.

Recent titles from Cormorant include *The Whirling Girl* by Barbara Lambert; *The City's Gates* by Peter Dubé; *The Family Took Shape* by Shashi Bhat; *My Life Among the Apes* by Cary Fagan; *Whiskey Creek* by Dave Hugelschaffer; *It's All About Kindness* edited by Margaret McBurney; and *Pinboy* by George Bowering.

Cormorant Books is not currently accepting unsolicited manuscripts, and unsolicited manuscripts will be recycled. Check their website to see if this policy has changed.

Query letters and SASEs should be directed to:

Marc Côté, Publisher
Barry Jowett, Associate Publisher; b.jowett@cormorantbooks.com
Robyn Sarah, Poetry Editor; r.sarah@cormorantbooks.com
Bryan J. Ibeas, Acquisitions and Marketing; b.ibeas@cormorantbooks.com

COTEAU BOOKS

2517 Victoria Avenue, Regina, SK S4P 0T2, Canada
306-777-0170 | fax: 306-522-5152
www.coteaubooks.com | e-mail: coteau@coteaubooks.com | Twitter: @CoteauBooks

Based in Regina, Coteau publishes novels, juvenile fiction, regional and creative nonfiction, drama, and authors from all parts of Canada. The press seeks to give literary voice to its community, and places a special emphasis on Saskatchewan and prairie writers. It also has an active program of presenting and developing new writers. Coteau releases more than a dozen new titles each year. It publishes novels for young readers aged 9 to 12, ages 13 to 15, and 16 and up. It does not publish kids' picture books.

Recent Coteau titles include *The Anatomy of Edouard Beaupre* by Sarah York; *A Book of Great Worth* by Dave Margoshes; *Day of the Cyclone* by Penny Draper; *Drummer Girl* by Karen Bass; *Full Steam to Canada* by Anne Patton; *Gardening, Naturally* by Sara Williams; and *Outcasts of River Falls* by Jacqueline Guest.

Coteau publishes only authors who are Canadian citizens. Fiction submissions are only accepted between January 1 and April 30; children's literature submissions between May 1 and August 31; and poetry between September 1 and December

31. Nonfiction submissions are accepted at any time. No simultaneous submissions, and only hard-copy submissions are considered. You may send the full manuscript or a sample (3 to 4 stories or chapters; 20 to 25 poems) accompanied by an SASE of appropriate size to:

Nik Burton, Managing Editor; coteau@coteaubooks.com

D&M PUBLISHERS, INC.

GREYSTONE BOOKS
NEW CATALYST BOOKS
NEW SOCIETY PUBLISHERS
Suite 201, 2323 Quebec Street, Vancouver, BC V5T 4S7, Canada
604-254-7191 | 1-800-667-6902 | fax: 604-254-9099
Toronto office:
Suite 405, 130 Spadina Avenue, Toronto, ON M5V 2R4, Canada
416-537-2501 | fax: 416-537-4647
www.dmpibooks.com | e-mail: dm@dmpibooks.com
New Society Publishers:
PO Box 189, Gabirola Island, BC, V0R 1X0, Canada
250-247-9737 | fax: 250-247-7471
www.newsociety.com | e-mail: info@newsociety.com | Twitter: @NewSocietyPub

D&M Publishers, Inc., recently changed its name from Douglas & McIntyre Publishing Group after the acquisition of New Society Publishers. D&M is an independent publishing house with three unique imprints: Douglas & McIntyre, Greystone Books, and New Society Publishers. The group publishes popular Canadian trade books for a global market, with many international successes, particularly in the areas of natural science and the environment.

Douglas & McIntyre publishes a broad general program of adult fiction and nonfiction, with an emphasis on art and architecture, First Nations issues, Pacific Northwest history, cookbooks, and current events. It publishes around 35 nonfiction books a year while maintaining a distinguished literary fiction list.

Greystone Books titles focus on natural history and science, the environment, popular culture, sports, and outdoor recreation. It publishes around 30 new books a year.

New Society Publishers is an activist press focused on social justice and ecological issues. Its mission is to publish books that contribute in fundamental ways to building an ecologically sustainable and just society. It publishes books on food, gardening, health and wellness, energy, sustainable living, urban issues, green building, education, and parenting. All its books are printed on 100 percent post-consumer recycled paper with vegetable-based inks.

Recent titles from Douglas & McIntyre include *Traffic* by Grant Arnold and

Karen Henry; *Canada at War* by Paul Keery and Michael Wyatt; *East Meets West* by Stephanie Yuen; and *Discovering Totem Poles* by Aldona Jonaitis.

Some titles indicative of the Greystone list include *Everything Under the Sun* by David Suzuki; *The Power of More* by Marnie McBean; *Everyone's Birthday* by Marc Kielburger; and *The Bear's Embrace* by Patricia and Martha Van Tighem.

Recent titles from New Society Publishers include *Making Home* by Sharon Astyk; *High Steaks* by Eleanor Boyle; *Life Rules* by Ellen LaConte; *The Intelligent Gardener* by Steve Solomon; and *Beautiful Corn* by Anthony Boutard.

Query letters and SASEs should be directed to the Editorial Panel. Electronic submissions to New Society Publishers should be sent to editor@newsociety.com.

Scott McIntyre, Publisher (D&M)

Chris Labonté, Editor (D&M)—Fiction.

Rob Sanders, Publisher (Greystone Books)

Judith Plant, Publisher (New Society Publishers)

Chris Plant, Acquisitions Editor, Editorial Director (New Society Publishers)

DRAWN AND QUARTERLY

PO Box 48056, Montréal, QC H2V 4S8, Canada
514-279-2221
www.drawnandquarterly.com | Twitter: @DandQ

Drawn and Quarterly is an award-winning publisher of graphic novels, comic books, and comic book series with over 20 new titles per year. The publisher acquires new comic books, art books, and graphic novels by renowned cartoonists and newcomers from around the globe.

Drawn and Quarterly welcomes submissions for consideration in a number of its publishing venues, including a new talent forum (Drawn and Quarterly Showcase), a regular anthology (Drawn and Quarterly), and a seasonal selection of general graphic novels, comic books, and comic book series.

Recent titles include *Birdseye Bristoe* by Dan Zettwoch; *Gloriana* by Kevin Huizenga; *Anna & Froga: Want a Gumball?* by Anouk Ricard; *The Making Of* by Brecht Evens; *Back Alleys and Urban Landscapes* by Michael Cho; and *Ed the Happy Clown* by Chester Brown.

Drawn and Quarterly prefers to receive electronic submissions. E-mail website URLs or JPEG samples of your work to chris@drawnandquarterly.com.

If you are unable to submit via e-mail, mail black-and-white photocopies of your work, no more than eight pages. Do not include an SASE, as Drawn and Quarterly will not return work and will contact you only if they're interested in publishing your art.

Chris Oliveros, Publisher; chris@drawnandquarterly.com

Peggy Burns, Associate Publisher; peggy@drawnandquarterly.com

THE DUNDURN GROUP

NATURAL HERITAGE BOOKS
3 Church Street, Suite 500-3, Toronto, ON M5E 1M2, Canada
416-214-5544 | fax: 416-214-5556
www.dundurn.com | e-mail: info@dundurn.com | Twitter: @dundurnpress

The Dundurn Group began as Dundurn Press Limited, established in 1972 to bring Canadian history and biography to a general readership. Politics, history, and biography were the original mandate, which quickly expanded to include literary and art criticism, and large illustrated art books.

In the 1990s, Dundurn acquired three other Canadian publishing houses: Hounslow Press, Simon & Pierre, and Boardwalk Books. These companies further broadened Dundurn's editorial mandate to include popular nonfiction, literary fiction, young-adult books, and mysteries. It publishes about 75 to 80 new titles a year and is now one of the largest publishers of adult and children's fiction and nonfiction in Canada.

In 2007, Dundurn acquired the assets of Natural Heritage Books, which concentrates on publishing titles that focus on Canadian heritage, natural history, and biography. Natural Heritage releases seven to twelve new books a year.

Dundurn acquired Napoleon and Co. in 2011 and uses this imprint to publish fiction and young adult books.

Recent titles include *The Blue Guitar* by Ann Ireland; *Dazed but Not Confused* by Kevin Callan; *The Emerald Key* by Christopher Dinsdale; *Hope and Heartbreak in Toronto* by Peter Robinson; *The Slaidburn Angel* by M. Sheelagh Whittaker; *Transmigration* by Nicholas Maes; and *Toronto Sketches 11* by Mike Filey.

To submit, please send the complete proposal or manuscript or three sample chapters to the attention of the Acquisitions Editor. Fiction submissions will be reviewed twice annually, in the spring and in the fall. E-mail submissions are not considered. While authors outside Canada are considered, be sure to include an international reply coupon with the SASE.

Kirk Howard, President and Publisher
Michael R. Carroll, Editorial Director
Shannon Whibbs, Senior Editor
Allison Hirst, Assistant Editor

ECW PRESS

2120 Queen Street East, Suite 200, Toronto, ON M4E 1E2, Canada
416-694-3348 | fax: 416-698-9906
www.ecwpress.com | e-mail: info@ecwpress.com | Twitter: @ecwpress

ECW Press (Entertainment, Culture, Writing) publishes nonfiction and fiction for the adult market. ECW has published close to 1,000 books that have been distributed throughout the English-speaking world and translated into dozens of languages. Its list includes poetry and fiction, pop culture and political analysis, sports books, biography, and travel guides. ECW releases around 50 new titles per year.

Recent titles include *The King of New Orleans* by Greg Klein; *Physical Chess* by Billy Robinson; *Shooters* by Jonathan Snowden; *Fifty Sides of the Beach Boys* by Mark Dillon; *Mickey Cohen: The Life and Times of L.A.'s Notorious Mobster* by Tere Tereba; and *The Complete Lockpick Pornography* by Joey Comeau.

ECW publishes only Canadian-authored poetry and fiction. For nonfiction (literary and commercial), they consider proposals from anywhere. Instead of an SASE, you may include an e-mail address in your cover letter for a reply to your query. Please send a proposal and SASE to the appropriate editor:

Jack David, Copublisher—Business, sports, mystery fiction, true crime, biographies; jack@ecwpress.com

Jennifer Hale, Senior Editor—Pop culture, music, celebrity biographies, television, film, fiction, creative nonfiction; jen@ecwpress.com

Michael Holmes, Senior Editor—Literary fiction, poetry, wrestling; michael@ecwpress.com

Crissy Boylan, Managing Editor; crissy@ecwpress.com

Jennifer Knoch, Editor; jenk@ecwpress.com

FIREFLY BOOKS LTD.

66 Leek Crescent, Richmond Hill, ON L4B 1H1, Canada
416-499-8412 | fax: 416-499-8313
www.fireflybooks.com | e-mail: service@fireflybooks.com | Twitter: @FireflyMike

Firefly Books, established in 1977, is a North American publisher and distributor of nonfiction and children's books. Firefly's admirable goal is to bring readers beautifully produced books written by experts at reasonable prices.

Firefly Books has particular strengths in cookbooks, gardening, astronomy, health, natural history, pictorial books, reference books (especially for children), and sports.

Recent titles include *Great White Shark* by Alexandrine Civard-Racinais; *Owls of the World* by Heimo Mikkola; *The Brain Book* by Ken Ashwell; *Night Sky Atlas* by Robin Scagell; *200 Tips for Kitchen and Bathrooms* by Xavier Torras Isla; *Kids' Party Cakes* by Anneka Manning; *Stanley Cup* by Eric Zweig; and *The Munschworks* by Robert Munsch.

Firefly Books does not accept unsolicited manuscripts. However, it does accept proposals for illustrated nonfiction. Firefly does not publish children's books or accept e-mail submissions. Direct queries and SASEs to:

Lionel Koffler, President and Publisher
Michael Warrick, Associate Publisher

FITZHENRY & WHITESIDE LTD.

195 Allstate Parkway, Markham, ON L3R 4T8, Canada
905-477-9700 | 800-387-9776 | fax: 800-260-9777
www.fitzhenry.ca
FIFTH HOUSE PUBLISHERS
1511-1800 4 Street SW, Calgary, AB T2S 2S5, Canada
403-571-5230

Fitzhenry & Whiteside Ltd. specializes in trade nonfiction and children's books. The firm also offers a textbook list and a small list of literary fiction. It publishes or reprints 60 to 80 titles per year. The house specializes in history, natural sciences, forestry, ecology, biography, psychology, reference, Canadiana, antiques, art, photography, children's and young-adult fiction and nonfiction.

Fitzhenry & Whiteside nonfiction titles range throughout Canadian history, biography, Native studies, nature, and antiques and collectibles. The children's book list includes early readers, picture books, and middle-grade and young-adult novels. Markets include trade, school, library, professional and reference, college, mail order, and specialty.

In 1998 Fitzhenry & Whiteside purchased the Calgary-based publisher Fifth House Publishers. It selects books that contribute to the understanding of western Canadian history, culture, and environment, publishing around 15 titles a year.

Recent Fitzhenry & Whiteside titles include *Beginner's Guide to Minerals and Rocks* by Joel Grice; *Five Days of the Ghost* by William Bell; *Hockey Talk* by John Goldner; *Sila's Revenge* by Jamie Bastedo; and *The Nine Lives of Travis Keating* by Jill MacLean.

Titles from Fifth House include *A Bend in the Willows* by Paul Dolphin; *Against the Flow: Rafferty-Alameda and the Politics of the Environment* by George N. Hood; and *Mustang Wranglers* by Curly R. V. Guenter.

Query letters and SASEs should be directed to:

Sharon Fitzhenry, President
Gail Winskill, Publisher—Children's books.
Stephanie Stewart, Publisher; stewart@fifthhousepublishers.ca

GASPEREAU PRESS

47 Church Avenue, Kentville, NS B4N 2M7, Canada
1-902-678-6002 | 877-230-8232 | fax: 902-678-7845
www.gaspereau.com | e-mail: info@gaspereau.com

Gaspereau Press is a Nova Scotia-owned and operated trade publisher specializing in short-run editions of both literary and regional interest for the Canadian market. Its list includes poetry, local history books, literary essays, novels, and short-story collections. Gaspereau was nominated for the prestigious Canadian Booksellers Association's Libris Award for Best Small Press Publisher of the Year 2006.

Gaspereau is one of a handful of Canadian trade publishers that prints and binds books in-house. With only 16 paces between the editor's desk and the printing press, Gaspereau Press practices a form of "craft" publishing that is influenced more by William Morris and the private press movement of the nineteenth century than by the contemporary publishing culture.

Recent titles include *A Short History of Forgetting* by Paul Tyler; *I Do Not Think That I Could Love a Human Being* by Johanna Skibsrud; *The Annotated Bee and Me* by Tim Bowling; *The Geography of Arrival: A Memoir* by George Sipos; and *Through Darkling Air: The Poetry of Richard Outram* by Peter Sanger.

When submitting, please include a cover letter, a list of previous publications, and an SASE. E-mail submissions are not considered. It typically takes four to eight months to hear back from this publisher.

Gary Dunfield, Publisher
Andrew Steeves, Publisher

GOOSE LANE EDITIONS

500 Beaverbrook Court, Suite 330, Fredericton, NB E3B 5X4, Canada
506-450-4251 | 888-926-8377 | fax: 506-459-4991
www.gooselane.com | e-mail: info@gooselane.com

Canada's oldest independent publisher, Goose Lane Editions is a small publishing house that specializes in literary fiction, poetry, and a select list of nonfiction titles including history, biography, Canadiana, and fine art books. It does not publish commercial fiction, genre fiction, or confessional works of any kind. Nor does it publish for the children's market.

Recent titles include *Night Street* by Kristel Thornell; *A Neighborly War* by Robert Dallison; *The Rest is Silence* by Scott Fotheringham; *Master & Madman* by Peter Thomas; *Fair Trade* by Éric St-Pierre; *YOU comma Idiot* by Doug Harris; and *IAIN BAXTER&: Works 1958–2011* by David Moos.

Goose Lane considers submissions from outside Canada only rarely, and only when both the author and the material have significant Canadian connections and the material is of extraordinarily high interest and literary merit. Writers should submit a synopsis, outline, and sample (30 to 50 pages) with an SASE if in Canada; international authors should include SASEs and international reply coupons with submissions. No electronic submissions.

Please query by mail or phone before submitting; direct queries and SASEs to:

Susanne Alexander, Publisher; s.alexander@gooselane.com

Angela Williams, Publishing Assistant; awilliams@gooselane.com

James Duplacey, Managing Editor; jduplacey@gooselane.com

Ross Leckie, Editor—Poetry; rleckie@gooselane.com

Bethany Gibson, Editor—Fiction; bgibson@gooselane.com

Colleen Kitts-Gougen, Editor—Nonfiction Acquisitions; ckitts@gooselane.com

GREAT PLAINS PUBLICATIONS

ENFIELD & WIZENTY
GREAT PLAINS TEEN FICTION
955 Arthur Street, Suite 345, Winnipeg, MB R3G 0P9, Canada
204-475-6799 | fax: 204-475-0138
www.greatplains.mb.ca | e-mail: info@greatplains.mb.ca

Great Plains Publications is an award-winning, prairie-based, general trade publisher specializing in regional history and biography. It has recently established two new imprints, Enfield & Wizenty and Great Plains Teen Fiction.

Great Plains Publications' mandate is to publish books that are written by Canadian prairie authors. It also publishes books by Canadian authors not living on the prairies, but of specific interest to people living in this region (content, setting). Great Plains Teen Fiction and Enfield & Wizenty publish fiction from across the country.

Recent titles from Great Plains Publications include *Ain't Got No Cigarettes* by Lyle E. Style; *Noah's Last Canoe* by Doug Evans; *To the Grave* by Mike McIntyre; *A Dog's Breakfast* by Jess Young; *Horses Don't Lie* by Chris Irwin; and *The Lake* by Jake MacDonald.

Recent titles from Great Plains Teen Fiction include *The Break* by Nelsa Roberto; *The Green-Eyed Queen of Suicide City* by Kevin Marc Fournier; *How to Tend a Grave* by Jocelyn Shipley; *Cape Town* by Brenda Hammond; and *Chance to Dance for You* by Dail Sidonie Sobat.

Recent titles from Enfield & Wizenty include *The Moon of Letting Go* by Richard Van Camp; *Blue Becomes You* by Bettina von Kampen; *Rats of Las Vegas* by Lisa Pasold; *Man and Other Natural Disasters* by Nerys Parry.

Currently, Great Plains is not accepting proposals or manuscripts for poetry or children's picture books, how-to books, cookbooks, or self-help books. Address queries with sample chapters and SASEs to the attention of the Fiction

Editor, Nonfiction Editor, or young-adult Editor, depending on the genre of your work.

Gregg Shilliday, Publisher
Ingeborg Boyens, Executive Editor (Great Plains Publications)
Maurice Mierau, Associate Editor (Enfield & Wizenty)
Anita Daher, Associate Editor (Great Plains Teen Fiction)

HARLEQUIN ENTERPRISES LIMITED

HARLEQUIN BOOKS (CANADA)
MILLS & BOON/HARLEQUIN ENTERPRISES LTD.
WORLDWIDE LIBRARY
225 Duncan Mill Road, Don Mills, ON M3B 3K9, Canada
888-432-4879
www.harlequin.com
www.millsandboon.co.uk

Harlequin Enterprises Limited is the world's leading publisher of romance fiction and women's fiction. The Toronto-based company publishes over 110 titles a month in 29 languages in 111 international markets on six continents. These books are written by more than 1,200 authors. With 390 best-seller placements in 2010—and 95 percent of sales outside Canada—it is both the country's most successful publisher and one of its most international businesses.

The Harlequin Enterprises home base in Ontario, Canada, issues the greater portion of the Harlequin Books series, while the New York office issues several Harlequin series, as well as the HQN, Kimani, Red Dress, Steeple Hill, and Silhouette lists (please see listing for Harlequin Books in the directory of Independent United States Presses). The editorial acquisitions departments for Mills & Boon, Harlequin Romance, and Harlequin Presents are located at the operation's United Kingdom offices (listed below). Harlequin Enterprises Limited in Canada also publishes the Worldwide Library, which features titles in the mystery, suspense, and thriller genres.

Each of the various lines within the Harlequin series of romance novels published in Canada, like their American counterparts, stakes out particular market-niche segments of reader interest within the overall categories of romance fiction and women's fiction. Each line has its own submission and editorial guidelines. These guidelines are explored in great detail on the Harlequin website.

HARLEQUIN BOOKS (CANADA)

Harlequin Books (Canada) is home to Harlequin Everlasting, American Romance, Blaze, Superromance, MIRA, and Spice. The best way to learn which imprint is appropriate for your manuscript is to read books already in print. Harlequin offers detailed tip sheets on its website, www.harlequin.com, or by written request. Following are general guidelines to the imprints handled in Canada:

Harlequin Everlasting, brand-new in 2007, is a contemporary romance series. The novels in this series follow the life and relationship/s of one couple. These emotionally intense stories span considerably more time than the typical series romance—years or even an entire lifetime—and at 75,000 words, the books are longer than usual as well. Recent titles include *Pictures of Us* by Amy Garvey; *Meant for Each Other* by Lee Duran; *A Christmas Wedding* by Tracy Wolff; and *Always a Mother* by Linda Warren.

American Romance features fast-paced, heartwarming stories about the pursuit of love, marriage, and family in America today. They're set in small towns and big cities, on ranches and in the wilderness, from Texas to Alaska—everywhere people live and love. For this series, Harlequin is looking for energetic writing and well-constructed plots based on contemporary characters. Titles indicative of the list include *His Baby Surprise* by Lisa Childs; *A Mother's Wedding Day* by Rebecca Winters and Dominique Burton; and *An Unexpected Father* by Lisa Ruff.

The Harlequin Blaze series features sensuous, highly romantic, innovative stories that are sexy in premise and execution. The tone of the books can run from fun and flirtatious to dark and sensual. Writers can push the boundaries in terms of characterization, plot, and sexual explicitness. Recent titles include *Just Fooling Around* by Julie Kenner and Kathleen O'Reilly; *The Drifter* by Kate Hoffmann; and *While She Was Sleeping…* by Lisabel Sharpe.

The aim of a Harlequin Superromance novel is to produce a contemporary, involving read with a mainstream tone in its situations and characters, using romance as the major theme. To achieve this, emphasis should be placed on individual writing styles and unique and topical ideas. Titles include *Her Best Friend* by Sarah Mayberry; *Trusting the Bodyguard* by Kimberly Can Meter; and *Always a Temp* by Jeannie Watt.

MIRA Books is dedicated to mainstream single-title women's fiction in hardcover and paperback editions. Of interest to a primarily women's readership, MIRA titles span all genres, including thrillers, historical romances, relationship novels, and suspense. Recent titles include *The Memorist* by M. J. Rose; *Home in Carolina* by Sherryl Woods; and *Out of Mind* by Stella Cameron.

New in 2006, Spice is Harlequin's single-title imprint for erotic fiction for the modern woman who also wants a great read. Titles include *Rampant* by Saskia Walker; *Naughty Bits* by Lacy Danes et al; *Addicted* by Charlotte Featherstone; *Stranger* by Megan Hart; *The Duchess, the Maid, the Groom & Their Lover* by Victoria Janssen; *Enchanted Again* by Nancy Madore; *The Diary of Cozette* by Amanda McIntrye; and *Obsession* by Kayla Perrin.

Harlequin will send prospective authors full editorial guidelines with suggested heroine and hero profiles, as well as information pertaining to manuscript length, setting, and sexual approach and content. This information is available upon written request from the publisher and online at eHarlequin.com.

Harlequin invites submissions from both published and unpublished writers. It prefers a query with synopsis and one to three chapters. Make sure your query is clear as to which line it is intended for: Harlequin Everlasting, American Romance, Blaze, Harlequin Superromance, MIRA, or Spice. Direct your submission to:

Valerie Grey, Executive Editor (MIRA Books, Spice)

Wanda Ottewell, Senior Editor (Harlequin Superromance)

Paula Eykelhof, Executive Editor—Single titles.

Kathleen Scheibling, Senior Editor (American Romance)

Susan Swinwood, Editor (MIRA Books)

Brenda Chin, Senior Editor (Blaze)

Victoria Curran, Editor (Superromance)

Kathyrn Lye, Editor (Blaze, RDI)

Johanna Raisanen, Associate Editor (American Romance)

MILLS & BOON/HARLEQUIN ENTERPRISES LTD.

HARLEQUIN PRESENTS
HARLEQUIN ROMANCE
Eton House, 18–24 Paradise Road, Richmond, Surrey TW9 1SR, UK

Acquisitions for Mills & Boon, Harlequin Romance, and Harlequin Presents are through the UK offices. You may query the offices to request a set of editorial guidelines supplied to prospective authors or read them online at www.harlequin.com.

A new line, Mills & Boon Modern books explore cosmopolitan, city romances between upscale men and women. Young characters in affluent urban settings—either North American or international—meet; flirt; share experiences; have great, passionate sex; and fall in love, finally making a commitment that will bind them together, forever. Titles include *Greek Tycoon, Wayward Wife* by Sabrina Philips; *The Italian's Passionate Revenge* by Lucy Gordon; *The Greek Tycoon's Baby Bargain* by Sharon Kendrick; *Di Cesare's Pregnant Mistress* by Chantelle Shaw; *The Billionaire's Virgin Mistress* by Sandra Field; *At the Sicilian Count's Command* by Carole Mortimer; and *Blackmailed for Her Baby* by Elizabeth Power.

The Mills & Boon Medical Romance line involves intense emotional romances and medical drama set in a modern medical community. Recent titles include *Her Long-Lost Husband* by Josie Metcalfe; *English Doctor, Italian Bride* by Carol Marinelli; *The Heart Surgeon's Baby Surprise* by Meredith Webber; *A Wife for the Baby Doctor* by Josie Metcalfe; and *Surgeon Boss, Surprise Dad* by Janice Lynn.

Mills & Boon Historical Romance novels cover a wide range of British and European historical civilizations up to and including the Second World War. Titles include *Untamed Rogue, Scandalous Mistress* by Bronwyn Scott; *Kidnapped: His Innocent Mistress* by Nicola Cornick; *His Cavalry Lady* by Joanna Maitland; *Questions of Honor* by Kate Welsh; and *Conquering Knight, Captive Lady* by Anne O'Brien.

Harlequin Romance is the original line of romance fiction, the series that started it all—more than 35 years ago. These are warm, contemporary novels, filled with compassion and sensitivity, written by world-famous authors and by newcomers. Titles include *Brady: The Rebel Rancher* by Patricia Thayer; *Italian Groom, Princess Bride* by Rebecca Winters; *Falling for Her Convenient Husband* by Jessica Steele; and *Cinderella's Wedding Wish* by Jessica Hart.

Harlequin Presents is overall the bestselling Harlequin line, published in 16 different languages and sold in almost every country of the world. This line features heartwarming romance novels about spirited, independent women and strong, wealthy men. Although grounded in reality and reflective of contemporary, relevant trends, these fast-paced stories are essentially escapist romantic fantasies that take the reader on an emotional roller-coaster ride. Written in the third person, they can be from the male or female point of view, or seen through the eyes of both protagonists. Titles include *The Italian's Ruthless Marriage Command* by Helen Bianchin; *The Spaniard's Virgin Housekeeper* by Diana Hamilton; *The Greek's Million-Dollar Baby Bargain* by Julia James; and *At the Argentinean Billionaire's Bidding* by India Grey.

Please submit the first three chapters along with a one- to two-page synopsis of your novel, with appropriate SASE to:

Tessa Shapcott, Senior Editor (Harlequin Presents, Mills & Boon Modern Romance, Modern Xtra Sensual)

Bryony Green, Senior Editor (Harlequin Romance, Mills & Boon Tender Romance)

Linda Fildew, Senior Editor—Historical romance.

Sheila Hodgson, Senior Editor—Medical.

WORLDWIDE LIBRARY

WORLDWIDE MYSTERY
GOLD EAGLE BOOKS

The Worldwide Library division of Harlequin Enterprises hosts two major imprints, Worldwide Mystery and Gold Eagle Books. Worldwide Library emphasizes genre fiction in the categories of mystery and suspense, action-adventure, futuristic fiction, war drama, and post-Holocaust thrillers. The house gives its titles (primarily mass-market paperbacks) solid marketing and promotional support.

The Worldwide Mystery imprint specializes in mainstream commercial mystery and detective fiction in reprint. This imprint has not been issuing previously unpublished, original fiction; however, Worldwide is not to be overlooked as a resource regarding potential reprint-rights sales in this field. The house generally keeps lines of popular writers' ongoing series in print for a number of seasons, sometimes indefinitely. Titles at Worldwide include *Of All Sad Words* by Bill Crider; *Flawed* by Jo Bannister; and *Murder at Wrightsville Beach* by Ellen Elizabeth Hunter.

Gold Eagle Books is known for a fast-and-furious slate of men's action and adventure series with paramilitary and future-world themes. Series include Deathlands, the Destroyer, the Executioner, and Stony Man. Gold Eagle also publishes Super

Books keyed to the various series—longer novels with more fully developed plots. Prospective authors should be familiar with the guidelines and regular characters associated with each series.

Query letters and SASEs should be directed to:

Feroze Mohammed, Senior Editor
Nicole Brebner, Editor

HOUSE OF ANANSI PRESS

ANANSI INTERNATIONAL
GROUNDWOOD BOOKS
LIBRO TIGRILLO
SPIDERLINE
110 Spadina Avenue, Suite 801, Toronto, ON M5V 2K4, Canada
416-363-4343 | fax: 416-363-1017
www.houseofanansi.com

House of Anansi Press specializes in finding and developing Canada's new writers of literary fiction, poetry, and nonfiction, and in maintaining a culturally significant backlist that has accumulated since the house was founded in 1967. Anansi publishes five new fiction titles, eight new nonfiction titles, and four new poetry titles per year.

Anansi started as a small press with a mandate to publish only Canadian writers, and quickly gained attention for publishing significant authors such as Margaret Atwood, Matt Cohen, Michael Ondaatje, and Erin Mouré, as well as George Grant and Northrop Frye. French-Canadian works in translation have also been an important part of the list, and prominent Anansi authors in translation include Roch Carrier, Anne Hébert, Lise Bissonnette, and Marie-Claire Blais.

Today, Anansi publishes Canadian and international writers of literary fiction, poetry, and serious nonfiction. It does not publish genre fiction (mysteries, thrillers, science fiction, or romance novels), nor does it publish self-help nonfiction.

The company launched Spiderline, an imprint dedicated to the crime fiction genre, in 2010. The same year, the imprint Anansi International was started to reflect the company's commitment to publishing voices from around the world.

New titles include *A Few Bites* by Cybele Young; *A Troublsome Boy* by Paul Vasey; *Ablutions* by Patrick DeWitt; *After a Funeral* by Diana Athill; *All Made Up* by Janice Galloway; and *Ancient Thunder* by Leo Yerxa.

GROUNDWOOD BOOKS

Groundwood Books, an independent imprint of House of Anansi Press, is based in Toronto and publishes children's books for all ages, including fiction, picture books, and nonfiction.

Its primary focus has been on works by Canadians, though it sometimes also buys manuscripts from authors in other countries. Many of its books tell the stories of people whose voices are not always heard. Books by the First Peoples of this hemisphere have always been a special interest, as well as French-Canadian works in translation. Since 1998, Groundwood has been publishing works by people of Latin American origin living in the Americas, both in English and in Spanish, under its Libro Tigrillo imprint.

Recent Groundwood titles include *A daisy is a daisy is a daisy* by Linda Wolfsgruber; *Banjo of Destiny* by Cary Fagan; *Benedict* by Teresa Duran; *City Numbers* by Joanne Schwartz; *Eddie Longpants* by Mireille Levert; and *Gangs* by Richard Swift.

In lieu of sending complete unsolicited manuscripts, House of Anansi prefers to receive proposals in hard copy along with a detailed literary curriculum vitae and a 10- to 15-page sample from the manuscript. These materials should be sent to Manuscript Submissions.

Groundwood Books is always looking for new authors of novel-length fiction for children in all age areas, but does not accept unsolicited manuscripts for picture books. They like character-driven literary fiction and note that they do not publish high-interest/low-vocabulary fiction or stories with anthropomorphic animals or elves/fairies as their main characters.

Sarah MacLachlan, President (Anansi); sarah@anansi.ca
Janie Yoon, Managing Editor (Anansi); janie@anansi.ca
Patsy Aldana, Vice President and Publisher (Groundwood)
Nan Froman, Managing Editor (Groundwood)

INSOMNIAC PRESS

520 Princess Avenue, London, ON N6B 2B8, Canada
416-504-6270 | fax: 416-504-9313
www.insomniacpress.com | Twitter: @InsomniacPress

Insomniac Press is a midsize independent press that publishes nonfiction, fiction, and poetry for the adult markets. Insomniac always strives to publish the most exciting new writers it can find. Celebrated authors like Natalee Caple, Lynn Crosbie, Stephen Finucan, and A. F. Moritz either got their start at Insomniac, or have published important books with the house.

While it publishes a broad range of titles, Insomniac has also developed special niche areas, including black studies books, gay and lesbian books, celebrity musician-authored books (including titles by Matthew Good, Jann Arden, and Terri Clark), and gay mysteries. Insomniac is actively seeking commercial and creative nonfiction on a wide range of subjects, including business, personal finance, gay and lesbian studies, and black Canadian studies.

Recent titles include *Bad Mommy* by Willow Yamauchi; *Breaking Out II* by Kevin Alderson; *Doom* by Natalie Zina Walschots; *Dos Equis* by Anthony Bidulka;

Entry Level by Julie McIsaac; *Oranges and Lemons* by Liz Bugg; *Tapas on the Ramblas* by Anthony Bidulka; and *The Hard Return* by Marcus McCann.

The house does not publish science fiction, cookbooks, romance, or children's books. The poetry list is also full for the foreseeable future. Insomniac does accept unsolicited manuscripts, but suggests that you query first with a short letter or e-mail describing the project. E-mail mike@insomniacpress.com.

Queries and SASEs can be directed to:

Mike O'Connor, Publisher; mike@insomniacpress.com

Dan Varrette, Managing Editor; dan@insomniacpress.com

JAMES LORIMER & COMPANY LIMITED

317 Adelaide Street West, Suite 1002, Toronto, ON M5V 1P9, Canada
416-362-4762 | fax: 416-362-3939
www.lorimer.ca | Twitter: @LorimerBooks

James Lorimer is a publisher of nonfiction, children's, young-adult novels, and illustrated guidebooks. It publishes Canadian authors for a Canadian audience and is currently seeking manuscripts in the following genres: cultural or social history, natural history, cookbooks with a Canadian or regional focus, education, public issues, travel and recreation, and biography. It is especially interested in projects for the southwestern Ontario marketplace.

Recent titles include *Isaac Brock* by Cheryl MacDonald; *Our Lives: Canada after 1945* by Alvin Finkel; *Casa Loma* by Bill Freeman; *Voyage of the Iceberg* by Richard Brown; *The Canadian Labour Movement* by Craig Heron; *Hey Malarek!* by Victor Malarek; and *To Wawa with Love* by Tom Douglas.

Do not send entire manuscripts, just a proposal. E-mail queries are not acceptable. Queries and SASEs should be mailed to the attention of the Acquisition Editor.

James Lorimer, Publisher; jlorimer@lorimer.ca

Diane Young, Editorial Director; diane.young@lorimer.ca

Carrie Gleason, Children's Book Editor; childrenseditor@lorimer.ca

LOBSTER PRESS LTD.

1620 Sherbrooke Street West, Suites C & D, Montréal, QC H3H 1C9, Canada
514-904-1100 | fax: 514-904-1101
www.lobsterpress.com

Lobster Press publishes fiction and nonfiction books for children, tweens, teens, and their families. Lobster Press is seeking fresh, edgy fiction for young adults, high-interest fiction for reluctant readers, and nonfiction for preteens and teens. It particularly seeks titles that appeal to boys. Lobster Press also publishes a bestselling series of family guidebooks, *The Lobster Kids' Guides to Cities in the USA and Canada*.

Recent titles include *The Divided Realms, Book 2: The Darkening* by Maggie L. Wood; *Grim Hill, Book 5: Forest of Secrets* by Linda DeMeulemeester; *Loon Island* by Donna Gamache; and *The Archaeolojesters, Book 3: Trouble at Impact Lake* by Andreas Oertel.

Lobster Press is actively seeking new picture book submissions by Canadian citizens and permanent residents. Manuscripts should be under 600 words. Submit via e-mail only to lobsterpresssubmissions@gmail.com

Alison Fripp, President and Publisher; fripp@lobsterpress.com

Cameron McKeich, Acting Managing Editor; editorial@lobsterpress.com

OWLKIDS BOOKS

10 Lower Spadina Avenue, Suite 400, Toronto, ON M5V 2Z2, Canada
416-340-2700 | fax: 416-340-9767
www.owlkids.com | e-mail: owlkids@owlkids.com

Based in Toronto, Owlkids Books has been publishing children's books for more than 30 years. It specializes in science and nature titles, but also looks for nonfiction in a wide range of subjects, including Canadian culture, sports, crafts, activities, history, humor, and picture books.

Recent titles from Owlkids Books include *Magic up Your Sleeve: Amazing Illusions, Tricks, and Science Facts You'll Never Believe* by Helaine Becker; *SOS! Titanic!: Canadian Flyer Adventures #14* by Frieda Wishinsky; and *Wow Canada!: Exploring this Land from Coast to Coast to Coast* by Vivien Bowers.

Owlkids Books publishes Canadian authors almost exclusively. It especially welcomes submissions for children's books targeted to ages three to twelve. Please send to the attention of the Submissions Editor.

Sheba Meland, Publisher

MCCLELLAND & STEWART

DOUGLAS GIBSON BOOKS
TUNDRA BOOKS

75 Sherbourne Street, 5th Floor, Toronto, ON M5A 2P9, Canada
416-598-1114 | fax: 416-598-7764
www.mcclelland.com | e-mail: mail@mcclelland.com | Twitter: @McClelland Books
www.tundrabooks.com | Twitter: @TundraBooks

Celebrating its 106th anniversary this year, McClelland & Stewart (M&S) is something of a Canadian institution and was an early publisher of Lucy Maud

Montgomery's *Anne of Green Gables* and Winston Churchill's *History of the English Speaking Peoples*. Today, it publishes a wide range of poetry, fiction, and nonfiction.

M&S authors include Margaret Atwood, Sandra Birdsell, Mavis Gallant, Jack Hodgins, Alistair MacLeod, Rohinton Mistry, Alice Munro, Michael Ondaatje, and Jane Urquhart, but it also publishes debut authors such as Madeleine Thien.

In 2012, Random House of Canada, a long-time part owner, bought McClelland & Stewart, but so far no major staffing changes have occurred.

Recent titles include *A Most Beautiful Deception* by Michael Ennis; *A Room Full of Bones* by Elly Griffiths; *Unworthy Creature* by Aruna Papp; *The Stranger Passage* by Steve Lillebuen; *Above All Things* by Tanis Rideout; and *Religion for Atheists* by Alain de Botton.

DOUGLAS GIBSON BOOKS

Douglas Gibson was the first editorial imprint in Canada when it was established in 1986. The list is kept small at five to ten titles a year, and represents Gibson's eclectic tastes in politics, history, biography, high adventure, and fine fiction.

Recent titles from Douglas Gibson include *Dear Life* by Alice Munro; *Up and Down* by Terry Fallis; *The Truth About Canada* by Mel Hurtig; *Here Be Dragons: Telling Tales of People, Passion, and Power* by Peter C. Newman; *Still at the Cottage* by Charles Gordon; and *On Six Continents* by James K. Bartleman.

TUNDRA BOOKS

In 1995, M&S bought Tundra, a children's book publisher known for combining art and story in innovative ways. Tundra's newest venture is the re-introduction of a storybook format that was popular before World War II, combining the beauty of picture books with more complex and longer stories.

Recent titles from Tundra include *The French Fry King* by Rogé; *The Rumor* by Anushka Ravishankar; *Spot the Difference* by Tak Bui; *Wanda and the Wild Hair* by Barbara Azore; and *Wanda's Freckles* by Barbara Azore.

Please do not send manuscript submissions by e-mail. Tundra does not accept unsolicited manuscripts for picture books. Direct queries and SASEs to:

Douglas Pepper, President and Publisher (McClelland & Stewart)
Ellen Seligman, Vice President and Publisher (McClelland & Stewart)
Susan Renouf, COO (McClelland & Stewart)—Nonfiction.
Kathy Lowinger, Publisher (Tundra Books)
Douglas Gibson, Publisher (Douglas Gibson Books)

MCGILL-QUEEN'S UNIVERSITY PRESS

Montréal office:
McGill University, 1010 Sherbrooke West, Suite 1720, Montréal, QC H3A 2R7, Canada
514-398-3750 | fax: 514-398-4333
Kingston office:
Queen's University, Kingston, ON K7L 3N6, Canada
613-533-2155 | fax: 613-533-6822
www.mqup.mcgill.ca | e-mail: mqup@mcgill.ca | Twitter: @scholarmqup

McGill-Queen's University Press (MQUP) publishes original scholarly books and well-researched general-interest books in all areas of the social sciences and humanities. While its emphasis is on providing an outlet for Canadian authors and scholarship, some of its authors are from outside Canada. More than half of its sales are international.

A joint venture of McGill University in Montréal, Quebec, and Queen's University in Kingston, Ontario, MQUP is both a specialist in the Canadian perspective and a publisher of international themes. A Canadian press with a global reach, the house aims to advance scholarship and contribute to culture by selling books.

Recent titles include *Picturing the Land* by Marylin J. McKay; *A Bridge of Ships* by James Pritchard; *Failure's Opposite* by Norman Ravvin and Sherry Simon; *Barbaric Civilization* by Christopher Powell; *Contemporary Majority Nationalism* by Alain Gagnon, et al.; and *Imposing Their Will* by Jack Lipinsky.

Extensive submitting details are on their website. In general, they welcome proposals quite early in the development process. Query letters and SASEs should be directed to:

Donald H. Akenson, Senior Editor (Kingston); mqup@queensu.ca
Joan Harcourt, Editor (Kingston); bjh@queensu.ca
Jeffrey Brison, Deputy Senior Editor (Kingston); brison.mqup@queensu.ca
Philip J. Cercone, Executive Director and Senior Editor (Montréal); philip.cercone@mcgill.ca
John Zucchi, Senior Editor (Montréal); editorial1.mqup@mcgill.ca
Kyla Madden, Editor (Montréal); kyla.madden@mcgill.ca
Mark Abley, Editor (Montréal); mark.abley@mcgill.ca
Jonathon Crago, Editor (Montréal); jonathan.crago@mcgill.ca

CANADIAN BOOK PUBLISHERS

MCGRAW-HILL RYERSON LTD.

300 Water Street, Whitby, ON L1N 9B6, Canada
905-430-5000 | 1-800-565-5758
www.mcgrawhill.ca | Twitter: @McGrawHillCDN

One of the 111 McGraw-Hill Companies around the globe, McGraw-Hill Ryerson is staffed and managed by Canadians but reports to its parent company in New York. Though primarily an educational division, McGraw-Hill Ryerson also has a thriving trade arm.

McGraw-Hill Ryerson's trade division publishes and distributes reference books on a wide array of subjects, including business, computing, engineering, science, reference, travel, and self-study foreign language programs. Other areas include outdoor recreation, child care, parenting, health, fine arts, music, sports, fitness, cooking, and crafts.

Recent titles include *A Book About My Mother* by Toby Talbot; *Canadian Income Taxation* by William. Buckwold; *Investments*, 7th Edition by Zvi Bodie; *Advertising & Promotion* by George Belch; and *Business Statistics* by Bruce Bowerman.

Query letters and SASEs should be directed to:
Claudio Pascucci, President of Professional Division
Lynda Walthert, Assistant to the President of Professional Division

THE MERCURY PRESS

PO Box 672, Station P, Toronto, ON M5S 2Y4, Canada
416-531-4338 | fax: 416-531-0765
www.themercurypress.ca | e-mail: contact@themercurypress.ca

The Mercury Press, shortlisted for 1997 Publisher of the Year by the Canadian Booksellers Association, specializes in cutting-edge fiction and poetry, as well as nonfiction and murder mysteries. All titles are Canadian-authored.

The Mercury Press also publishes *Word: Canada's Magazine for Readers + Writers*. *Word* features literary event listings, columns, and reviews, and is a good starting place for learning about this publisher.

Recent Mercury Press titles include *The Battle of the Five Spot* by David Lee; *Herbie Nichols: A Jazzist's Life* by Mark Miller; *The Port's Seasonal Rental* by Gerry Shikatani; *Way Down That Lonesome Road* by Mark Miller; *Looking for Livingstone* by M. Nourbese Philip; and *A Few Sharp Sticks* by Brian Dedora.

Mercury Press is not currently considering unsolicited manuscripts. Check on their websites to see if this policy changes.

NOVALIS

10 Lower Spadina Ave, Suite 400, Toronto, ON M5V 2Z2, Canada
416-363-3303 | 877-702-7773 | fax: 416-363-9409 | 877-702-7775
613-236-1393 | fax: 613-782-3004
www.novalis.ca | e-mail: comments@novalis.ca

Novalis is a religious publishing house in the Catholic tradition and is a part of Saint Paul University. Novalis publishes and distributes periodicals, books, brochures, and audio-visual resources touching on all aspects of spiritual life, especially from the Christian and Jewish traditions. While the greater part of its production is for the general public, Novalis also publishes more specialized works in the area of theology and religious studies. It is the largest bilingual religious publisher in Canada.

Subjects include personal growth, self-help, spirituality and prayer, children's books, gardening, meditation, Church history, and Celtic spirituality, among others. Novalis has equally strong publishing programs in both of Canada's official languages.

Recent titles include *Stepping into Mystery* by Monty Williams, SJ; *On Earth as It Is in Heaven* by Josephine Lombardi; *Living with the Liturgical Year* by Josephine Lombardi; and *All is Grace* by Jim Forest.

Direct queries and SASEs to:

Joseph Sinasac, Publishing Director; joseph.sinasac@novalis.ca
Grace Deutsch, Editorial Director; grace.deutsch@novalis.ca
Anne-Loiuse Mahoney, Managing Editor; anne-louise.mahoney@novalis.ca

OOLICHAN BOOKS

PO Box 2278, Fernie, BC V0B 1M0, Canada
250-423-6113 | fax: 866-299-0026
www.oolichan.com | e-mail: oolichanbooks@telus.net | Twitter: @OolichanBooks

Oolichan Books is a literary press, publishing poetry, fiction, and creative nonfiction titles including literary criticism, memoirs, and books on regional history, First Nations, and policy issues. Their name is taken from the small fish, once plentiful in West Coast waters and a staple in the diet of First Nations people to whom it was sacred. The oolichan, often referred to as the candlefish, is believed to possess healing powers and guarantee longevity.

Oolichan publishes around ten titles a year, including two or three poetry books, and two or more each of fiction, nonfiction, and children's/young adult.

Recent Oolichan titles include *Grows That Way* by Susan Ketchen; *Sneaker Wave* by Jeff Beamish; *The Village of Many Hats* by Caroline Woodward; *YVR* by W. H. New; *What Echo Heard* by Gordon Sombrowski; and *Day and Night* by Dorothy Livesay.

Oolichan Books publishes only Canadian authors. Please send up to ten poems or three chapters of a manuscript, along with a cover letter and CV. Note that they will not read a submission that arrives without a proper SASE for its return. E-mail submissions are not accepted. You may direct submissions to:

Randal Macnair, Publisher
Christa Moffat, Assistant to the Publisher
Ron Smith, Editor
Pat Smith, Consulting Editor

ORCA BOOK PUBLISHERS

PO Box 5626, Station B, Victoria, BC V8R 6S4, Canada
800-210-5277 | fax: 877-408-1551
www.orcabook.com | e-mail: orca@orcabook.com | Twitter: @orcabook

Orca Book Publishers focuses on children's books: picture books, and juvenile and young-adult fiction. Its limited adult list focuses on general trade nonfiction, including travel and recreational guides, regional history, and biography. With over 500 titles in print and 65 new titles a year, it releases books in its Orca Soundings, Orca Currents, Orca Sports, Orca Echoes, and Orca Young Readers lines.

Orca is presently seeking manuscripts written by Canadian authors in the following genres: children's picture books, early chapter books, juvenile fiction, young-adult fiction, and graphic novels. It is not seeking seasonal stories, board books, or "I Can Read" books.

Recent titles include *A Winter Kill* by Vicki Delany; *Accro d'la planche* by Lesley Choyce; *Assault on Juno* by Mark Zuehlke; and *Best Girl* by Sylvia Warsh.

The Orca Soundings line features short, high-interest novels with contemporary themes written expressly for teens reading below grade level. New releases include *Breaking Point* by Lesley Choyce; *Cuts Like a Knife* by Darlene Ryan; and *One Way* by Norah McClintock.

The Orca Currents line seeks short, high-interest novels with contemporary themes written expressly for middle-school students reading below grade level. Titles include *Agent Angus* by K. L. Denman; *Hold the Pickles* by Vicki Grant; and *Maxed Out* by Daphne Greer.

Their Orca Sports line features sports action combined with mystery/suspense. For ages ten and up, Orca Sports seeks strong plots, credible characters, simple language, and high-interest chapters. Some Orca Sports books include *Dawn Patrol* by Jeff Ross and *Haze* by Erin Thomas.

The Orca Echoes line features early chapter books for readers ages seven to nine at a Grade 2 reading level with engaging characters, easy-to-follow plots with exciting stories, and generous illustrations. Some titles include *Flood Warning* by Jacqueline Pearce; *Justine McKeen, Walk the Talk* by Sigmund Brouwer; and *The Wrong Bus* by Lois Peterson.

The Orca Young Readers line has historical and contemporary stories for ages eight to eleven, with age-appropriate plots and storylines. Orca Young Readers has had many best sellers and award-winning titles. Some recent titles include *Addy's Race* by Debby Waldman; *I Owe You One* by Natalie Hyde; and *The Paper House* by Lois Peterson.

While picture books submissions may be sent in their entirety, all other authors should query with sample chapters prior to sending the complete manuscript. Please send to the appropriate editor, or check the website for further information.

Andrew Woolridge, Publisher; andrew@orcabook.com
Bob Tyrrell, Editorial Director
Christi Howes, Editor (Orca Echoes)—Children's and picture books.
Sarah Harvey, Editor—Young readers, juvenile novels, teen fiction.
Melanie Jeffs, Editor (Orca Currents)

PENGUIN GROUP (CANADA)

HAMISH HAMILTON CANADA
PUFFIN CANADA
VIKING CANADA
90 Eglinton Avenue East, Suite 700, Toronto, ON M4P 2Y3, Canada
416-925-2249 | fax: 416-925-0068
www.penguin.ca | e-mail: info@ca.penguingroup.com | Twitter: @PenguinCanada
www.hamishhamilton.ca
www.puffinbooks.ca | e-mail: info@penguin.ca | Twitter: @PuffinCanada

Penguin Group (Canada)—once called Penguin Books—was founded in 1974. Initially a distribution arm for Penguin International, Penguin Books began publishing indigenous Canadian work in 1982 with such notable titles as Peter C. Newman's landmark history of the Hudson's Bay Company, *Company of Adventurers*, and fiction by Robertson Davies, Timothy Findley, Alice Munro, and Mordecai Richler. It also publishes books under three imprints, Hamish Hamilton Canada, Puffin Canada, and Viking Canada.

Penguin Group (Canada) is determined to publish books that speak to the broadest reading public and address leading issues of social importance. Penguin's books cover subjects as diverse as Canadian nationalism, homelessness and mental illness, and health care and education.

Recent titles include *Imagine* by Jonah Lehrer; *Truth Be Told* by Larry King; *All Men Are Liars* by Alberto Manguel; *The Penguin Book of Crime Stories* by Peter Robinson; *The Witch of Babylon* by D. J. McIntosh; and *The Storm* by Clive Cussler and Graham Brown.

Hamish Hamilton Canada is the Canadian counterpart of one of Britain's most distinguished literary lists. Hamish Hamilton has provided a home for an exciting and eclectic group of authors united by the distinctiveness and excellence of their writing. Hamish Hamilton Canada maintains a deep commitment to literary value, embracing both young and old, the experimental and the new, and continues to be selective with a list of five to ten titles a year.

Recent titles include *Bobcat and Other Stories* by Rebecca Lee; *Y* by Marjorie Celona; *Once You Break a Knuckle* by D. W. Wilson; and *The Third Reich* by Roberto Bolaño.

Puffin Canada publishes juvenile fiction and nonfiction in hardcover and paperback. Titles from Puffin Canada include *Hey! Who Stole the Toilet?* by Nancy Krulik; *Skippy Jon Jones Class Action* by Judy Schnachner; and *Spot's Little Learning Library* by Eric Hill.

Viking Canada, Penguin Canada's counterpart to the Viking Press, publishes both adult and juvenile material. Titles include *A Thousand Farewells: A Reporter's Journey from Refugee Camp to the Arab Spring* by Nahlah Ayed; *River of Smoke* by Amitav Ghosh; and *Nice Recovery* by Susan Juby.

Penguin Group (Canada) no longer accepts unsolicited manuscripts, and will not enter into correspondence about unpublished work, except with literary agents.

Mike Bryan, President
Nicole Winstanley, Publisher
Diane Turbide, Editorial Director

PLAYWRIGHTS CANADA PRESS

269 Richmond Street West, Suite 202, Toronto, Ontario, Canada, M5V 1X1
416-703-0013 | fax: 416-408-3402
www.playwrightscanada.com | e-mail: submissions@playwrightscanada.com |
Twitter: @PlayCanPress

Playwrights Canada Press publishes Canadian plays, theater criticism, history, biographies, and memoirs, and is the largest exclusive publisher of Canadian drama. It publishes roughly 30 books of plays, theater history, and criticism every year. This publisher exists to raise the profile of Canadian playwrights and Canadian theater and theater practitioners. French plays by Canadian authors are published in translation, and the Press's mandate includes printing plays for young audiences.

Recent titles include *The Mommiad* by Sky Gilbert; *Penny Plain* by Ronnie Burkett; *Mrs. Dexter and Her Daily* by Joanna Glass; *Brothel #9* by Anusree Roy; and *The Romeo Initiative* by Trina Davies.

Single new plays must have had at least one professional production in the last ten years. Production information should be submitted along with the manuscript. Query letters and SASEs should be directed to:

Annie Gibson, Publisher; annie@playwrightscanada.com
Blake Sproule, Editorial and Production Manager; blake@playwrightscanada.com

THE PORCUPINE'S QUILL

PO Box 160, 68 Main Street, Erin, ON N0B 1T0, Canada
519-833-9158 | fax: 519-833-9845
porcupinesquill.ca | e-mail: pql@sentex.net

Since 1974, The Porcupine's Quill has been publishing literary titles, especially novels, short stories, and poetry. The Porcupine's Quill is a small publisher with a tradition of publishing first books of poetry; it is proud that many of its writers have graduated to large trade houses to publish best sellers. Today it publishes some 12 books per year.

Recent titles include *A Calendar of Days* by The Wood Engravers; *The Essential Tom Marshall* by David Helwig and Michael Ondaatje; *Down in the Bottom of the Bottom of the Box* by JonArno Lawson; and *High-Water Mark* by Nicole Dixon.

The Porcupine's Quill does not accept unsolicited work. Instead, they seek out writers whose work has appeared in literary magazines such as *The New Quarterly*. Direct your query and SASE to:

Tim Inkster, Publisher
Doris Cowan, Fiction Editor; dorrida@gmail.com
George A. Walker, Graphic Novels Editor; george.walker@sympatico.ca
Carmine Starnino, Nonfiction Editor; cstarnino@yahoo.com
Wayne Clifford, Poetry Editor; wwcliff@nb.sympatico.ca

RANDOM HOUSE CANADA

ANCHOR CANADA
BOND STREET BOOKS
DOUBLEDAY CANADA
KNOPF CANADA
RANDOM HOUSE CANADA
SEAL BOOKS
VINTAGE CANADA

One Toronto Street, Suite 300, Toronto, ON M5C 2V6, Canada
416-364-4449 | fax: 416-364-6863
www.randomhouse.ca | Twitter: @RandomHouseCA

Random House Canada was established in 1944 and in 1986 established its own indigenous Canadian publishing program. Doubleday Canada marked its 75th anniversary in 2012. Following the international merger of Random House and Bantam Doubleday in 1998, the two companies officially became one in Canada in 1999, representing sister companies' titles in this country and maintaining thriving Canadian publishing programs.

The Random House Canada imprint features a diverse list of literary and commercial fiction, Canadian and international cookbooks, and bold nonfiction. Some titles include *One Good Hustle* by Billie Livingston; *Thirteen* by Kelley Armstrong; *The Lost Souls of Angelkov* by Linda Holeman; and *The Tools* by Phil Stutz and Barry Michels.

Anchor Canada is a publisher of quality trade paperback books, fiction and nonfiction. Launched in 2001, it began by publishing affordable editions of Doubleday Canada's hardcover titles and other titles published elsewhere. In 2002, Anchor Canada published its first Anchor Trade Paperback Original, and it continues to produce original fiction and nonfiction works. Some titles include *The Great Depression: 1929–1939* by Pierre Berton; *Willful Blindness: Why We Ignore the Obvious at Our Peril* by Margaret Heffernan; *Now You See Her* by Joy Fielding; and *The Balfour Declaration* by Jonathan Schneer.

The Bond Street Books imprint was launched in 2005, taking its name from the small historic street from which Doubleday Canada began publishing. It is dedicated to publishing fiction and nonfiction titles from around the world. Bond Street Books are supported by an encompassing, dynamic marketing campaign to ensure they reach a wide readership in Canada. Some titles include *The Pigeon Pie Mystery* by Julia Stuart; *The Unlikely Pilgrimage of Harold Fry* by Rachel Joyce; *Tigers in Red Weather* by Liza Klaussmann; *The Age of Miracles* by Karen Thompson Walker; and *Fooling Houdini* by Alex Stone.

Doubleday Canada has been one of Canada's most prominent publishers for over 50 years and is committed to producing fine fiction from both established and new voices, and developing challenging and entertaining nonfiction. It also maintains a young-adult publishing program. Some titles include *The Green Red Green* by Red Green; *The Twelve* by Justin Cronin; *The Wisdom of Psychopaths* by Kevin Dutton; *Wild Girls* by Mary Stewart Atwell; and *A Dangerous Inheritance* by Alison Weir.

Knopf Canada was launched in 1991, when Sonny Mehta, president of Alfred A. Knopf, approached prominent editor Louise Denny to create and run a Canadian arm of Knopf in the offices of Random House Canada. It is interested in thoughtful nonfiction and fiction with literary merit and strong commercial potential. Some titles include *A Conspiracy of Friends* by Alexander McCall Smith; *Days of Destruction, Days of Revolt* by Chris Hedges; *The Watch* by Joydeep Roy-Bhattacharya; and *Home* by Toni Morrison.

Seal Books is a mass-market publishing house, publishing original books and specializing in reprints of major hardcover fiction titles, such as books by Margaret Atwood and Lucy Maud Montgomery. Some of their titles include *The Law of Nines* by Terry Goodkind; *The Birth House* by Ami McKay; *Never Look Away* by Linwood Barclay; and *An Echo in the Bone* by Diana Gabaldon.

Vintage Canada publishes quality trade paperback editions, selecting its books primarily from titles originally published by Knopf Canada and Random House Canada.

Random House Canada does not accept unsolicited manuscripts. Query letters and SASEs should be directed to:

Louise Dennys, Publisher, Executive Vice President

Anne Collins, Publisher, Vice President (Random House Canada)

Marion Garner, Publisher (Vintage Canada)
Nita Pronovost, Senior Editor (Anchor, Doubleday, Bond Street)
Diane Martin, Acquisitions Editor (Knopf, Seal, Vintage Canada)

RED DEER PRESS

ROBERT J. SAWYER BOOKS
195 Allstate Parkway, Markham, ON L3R 4T8 Canada
1-800-387-9776
www.reddeerpress.com | Twitter: @RedDeerPress

Red Deer Press is an award-winning publisher of literary fiction, nonfiction, children's illustrated books, juvenile fiction, teen fiction, drama, and poetry. Red Deer Press's mandate is to publish books by, about, or of interest to Canadians, with special emphasis on the Prairie West. Red Deer Press publishes 18 to 20 new books per year, all written or illustrated by Canadians. Approximately 20 percent of their program is comprised of first-time authors and illustrators.

Recent titles indicative of the list include *Rainbow Crow* by David Bouchard; *Night Madness* by Richard Pyves; *The Imposter* by Gary Blackwood; *Before We Go* by Amy Bright; and *The White Bicycle* by Beverly Brenna.

In 2004, Red Deer Press launched the Robert J. Sawyer Books imprint, a line of literate, philosophically rich science-fiction titles personally selected by "the dean of Canadian Science Fiction." The books in this imprint appeal to both science-fiction fans and general readers who enjoy a mingling of the intimately human with the grandly cosmic.

Some titles from this imprint include *Distant Early Warnings* edited by Robert J. Sawyer; *The Savage Humanists* edited by Fiona Kelleghan; *Valley of Day-Glo* by Nick DiChario; and *The Commons* by Matthew Hughes.

Send queries and SASEs to:
Richard Dionne, Publisher; dionne@reddeerpress.com
Peter Carver, Children's Editor
Robert J. Sawyer, Publisher (Robert J. Sawyer Books); sawyer@sfwriter.com

RONSDALE PRESS

3350 West 21st Avenue, Vancouver, BC V6S 1G7, Canada
604-738-4688 | 855-738-4688 | fax: 604-731-4548
www.ronsdalepress.com | e-mail: ronsdale@shaw.ca | Twitter: @ronsdalepress

A literary publishing house, Ronsdale Press is dedicated to publishing books from across Canada and books that give Canadians new insights into themselves and their country. Ronsdale publishes fiction, poetry, regional history, biography and autobiography, plays, books of ideas about Canada, and children's books. The press looks for thoughtful works that reveal the author has read deeply in contemporary and earlier literature and is working to create a text with innovative combinations of form and content that can bring genuinely new insights. Ronsdale accepts submissions only from Canadian authors.

Recent titles include *Father Augustin Brabant: Saviour or Scourge?* by Jim McDowell; *A Covenant in Wonder with the World* by J. Edward Chamberlin; *Vladmir Krajina* by Jan Drabek; *The Flicker Tree: Oknangan Poems* by Nancy Holmes.

Authors are welcome to send finished manuscripts or queries with samples, along with SASEs.

Ronald B. Hatch, General Acquisitions Editor
Veronica Hatch, Children's Acquisition Editor

SECOND STORY PRESS

20 Maud Street, Suite 401, Toronto, ON M5V 2M5, Canada
416-537-7850 | fax: 416-537-0588
www.secondstorypress.ca | e-mail: info@secondstorypress.ca
Twitter: @_secondstory

The Second Story Press list spans adult fiction and nonfiction; children's fiction, nonfiction, and picture books; and young-adult fiction and nonfiction. As a feminist press, it looks for manuscripts dealing with the many diverse and varied aspects of the lives of girls and women. Some of its special interest areas include Judaica, ability issues, coping with cancer, and queer rights. They publish about 16 new books per year, primarily from Canadian authors.

Recent titles include *Yesterday's Dead* by Pat Bourke; *Rachel's Secret* by Shelly Sanders; *Bernadette to the Rescue* by Susan Glickman; *Support the Girls* by West Parry Sound Health Centre; and *Writing the Revolution* by Michele Landsberg.

Second Story accepts unsolicited manuscripts with SASEs. E-mail manuscripts are not considered. Direct submissions to:

Margie Wolfe, Publisher
Carolyn Jackson, Managing Editor

TALON BOOKS LTD.

PO Box 2076, Vancouver BC, Canada, V6B 3S3
604-444-4889 | 1-888-445-4176 | fax: 604-444-4119
www.talonbooks.com | e-mail: info@talonbooks.com | Twitter: @Talonbooks

Talon Books was founded as a poetry magazine at Magee High School in Vancouver in 1963. Since then it has grown into one of Canada's largest independent presses. It publishes drama, fiction, and nonfiction of the political, social, critical, and ethnographic variety.

Recent titles include *Against the Wind* by Madeleine Gagnon; *Billy Bishop Goes to War* by John Gray; *Bolsheviki* by David Fennario; *Chinese Blue* by Weyman Chan; *Cold Comfort* by Gil McElroy; and *Crossing the Continent* by Michel Tremblay.

Submissions of drama, fiction, criticism, history, and cultural studies are welcomed. Poetry, self-help, how-to, children's books, and genre books are not considered. E-mail submissions are not accepted. Send submission and SASE to:

Kevin Williams, President; kevin@talonbooks.com

Greg Gibson, Managing Editor; production@talonbooks.com

TRANSIT PUBLISHING

1996 Saint-Joseph Boulevard East, Montréal, QC H2H 1E3, Canada
514-273-0123 | fax: 1-866-258-7772
www.transitpublishing.com | e-mail: direction@transitmedias.com

Transit Publishing, founded in March 2009, primarily publishes celebrity-oriented investigative journalism. Transit is expanding into differing genres of fiction, including mystery, as well as health and lifestyle books.

Recent titles include *The Great Heist* by Kenneth Del Vecchio; *Blood for Blood* by Gipsy Paladini; *Escort Girl* by Melodie Nelson; *The First Person* by Pierre Turgeon; and *Mickey Rourke: Wrestling with Demons* by Sandro Monetti.

Send submission and SASE to:

Pierre Turgeon, President and Publisher; direction@transitmedias.com

UNIVERSITY OF ALBERTA PRESS

Ring House 2, University of Alberta, Edmonton, AB T6G 2E1, Canada
780-492-3662 | fax: 780-492-0719
www.uap.ualberta.ca

A scholarly house, the University of Alberta Press publishes in the areas of biography, history, language, literature, natural history, regional interest, travel narratives, and reference books. The press seeks to contribute to the intellectual and cultural life of Alberta and Canada by publishing well-edited, research-based knowledge and creative thought that has undergone rigorous peer review, is of real value to natural constituencies, adheres to quality publication standards, and is supported by diligent marketing efforts.

The University of Alberta Press is looking for original works of significant

CANADIAN BOOK PUBLISHERS

scholarship that are written for a reasonably wide readership. Canadian works that are analytical in nature are especially welcome, as are works by scholars who wish to interpret Canada, both past and present.

Recent titles include *Countering Displacements* by Daniel Coleman et al.; *Cross-Media Ownership and Democratic Practice in Canada* by Walter Soderlund et al.; *Civilizing the Wilderness* by A. A. den Otter; and *Anti-Saints* by Sheila Delany.

Submit queries and SASEs to:

Linda Cameron, Director; linda.cameron@ualberta.ca

Peter Midgley, Senior Acquisitions Editor; petem@ualberta.ca

Fred Bohm, Acquiring Editor; frederic@ualberta.ca

Mary Lou Roy, Production Editor; marylou.roy@ualberta.ca

UNIVERSITY OF BRITISH COLUMBIA PRESS

2029 West Mall, Vancouver, BC V6T 1Z2, Canada
604-822-5959 | 877-377-9378 | fax: 604-822-6083
www.ubcpress.ubc.ca | e-mail: frontdesk@ubcpress.ca | Twitter: @UBCPress

University of British Columbia Press (UBC Press) is the publishing branch of the University of British Columbia. Established in 1971, it is among the largest university presses in Canada. It publishes 70 new books annually and has an active backlist of more than 800 titles.

UBC Press is widely acknowledged as one of the foremost publishers of political science, Native studies, and forestry books. Other areas of particular strength are Asian studies, Canadian history, environmental studies, planning, and urban studies. The Press publishes several series: Legal Dimensions, Law and Society, Canada and International Relations, Studies in Canadian Military History, Sexuality Studies, Sustainability and the Environment, Urbanization in Asia, First Nations Languages, Contemporary Chinese Studies, Pioneers of British Columbia, Pacific Rim Archaeology, and the Brenda and David McLean Canadian Studies series.

Recent titles include *Contesting White Supremacy* by Timothy Stanley; *Indigenous Women and Feminism* by Cheryl Suzack et al.; *Oral History on Trial* by Bruce Miller; *Retail Nation* by Donica Belisle; and *Wet Prairie* by Shannon Bower.

Query letters and SASEs should be directed to:

Peter Milroy, Director—Special projects, international rights; milroy@ubcpress.ca

Melissa Pitts, Director; pitts@ubcpress.ca

Emily Andrew, Senior Editor—Asian studies, political science and political philosophy, military history, transnational and multicultural studies, communications; andrew@ubcpress.ca

Randy Schmidt, Senior Editor—Forestry, environmental studies, urban studies and planning, sustainable development, geography, law and society; schmidt@ubcpress.ca

Darcy Cullen, Acquisitions Editor—Canadian history, regional, native studies, sexuality studies, northern and Arctic studies, health studies, education; cullen @ubcpress.ca

UNIVERSITY OF MANITOBA PRESS

301 St. John's College, University of Manitoba, Winnipeg, MB R3T 2M5, Canada
204-474-9495 | fax: 204-474-7566
www.umanitoba.ca/uofmpress | e-mail: uofmpress@umanitoba.ca

Founded in 1967, the University of Manitoba Press publishes innovative and exceptional books of scholarship and serious Canadian nonfiction. Its list includes books on Native studies, Canadian history, women's studies, Icelandic studies, aboriginal languages, film studies, biography, geography, nature, and Canadian literature and culture. It publishes five to eight books a year, meaning each book receives the concentrated focus and attention that are often not possible in a larger press.

Recent titles include *Louis Riel and the Creation of Modern Canada* by Jennifer Reid; *Psychedelic Psychiatry* by Erika Dyck; and *Settlement, Subsistence, and Change Among the Labrador Inuit* by David C. Natcher et al.

Queries and SASEs may be submitted to:

David Carr, Director and Editor; carr@cc.umanitoba.ca
Jean Wilson, Senior Acquisitions Editor; jeanwilson@shaw.ca
Glenn Bergen, Managing Editor

UNIVERSITY OF OTTAWA PRESS/ LES PRESSES DE L'UNIVERSITÉ D'OTTAWA

542 King Edward, Ottawa, ON K1N 6N5, Canada
613-562-5246 | fax: 613-562-5247
www.press.uottawa.ca | e-mail: puo-uop@uottawa.ca | Twitter: @uOttawaPress

As Canada's only officially bilingual press, the University of Ottawa Press (UOP) is both uniquely Canadian and unique in Canada. Since 1936, UOP has supported cultural development through the publication of books in both French and English aimed at a general public interested in serious nonfiction.

UOP's editorial team works closely with its authors. Writers are supported in the preparation of their manuscript through peer reviews that help tighten the focus of the work before its final submission. By the time a manuscript is submitted to the Editorial Board to decide if it will be published, it has received a good deal of editorial development and revision.

CANADIAN BOOK PUBLISHERS

Recent titles include *The Pillow Book in Translation* by Valerie Henitiuk; *Tours et detours* by Catherine Khordoc; *Francophonies d'Amérique 31*; *Questions ultimes* by Thomas De Konick; and *Charcot in Morocco* by Jean-Martin Charcot.

Please direct query and SASE to:

Lara Mainville, Director; lara.mainville@uottawa.ca

Marie Clausén, Production Manager; msec@uottawa.ca

Sylvie Dugas, Production Manager; sylvie.dugas@uottawa.ca

Jessica Pearce, Editorial Assistant

UNIVERSITY OF TORONTO PRESS

10 Saint Mary Street, Suite 700, Toronto, ON M4Y 2W8, Canada
416-978-2239 | fax: 416-978-4738
www.utpress.utoronto.ca | Twitter: @utpress

University of Toronto Press is Canada's oldest and largest scholarly publisher, and is among the top 15 university presses in North America in size. It is always on the lookout for strong, innovative, and interesting works of scholarship.

Established in 1901, University of Toronto Press publishes scholarly, reference, and general-interest books on Canadian history and literature, medieval studies, and social sciences among other subjects, as well as scholarly journals. Approximately 200 new titles are released each year, and a backlist of more than 3,500 titles is maintained in print.

The house publishes in a range of fields, including history and politics; women's studies; health, family, and society; law and crime; economics; workplace communication; theory/culture; language, literature, semiotics, and drama; medieval studies; Renaissance studies; Erasmus; Italian-language studies; East European studies; classics; and nature. The list includes topical titles in Canadian studies, Native studies, sociology, anthropology, urban studies, modern languages, and music. A complete list of subjects, as well as details on creating and submitting a manuscript, is available on the University of Toronto Press website.

Recent titles include *Staying Human During Residency Training* by Alla D. Peterkin, MD; *A History of Science in Society: From Philosophy to Utility* by Andrew Ede; *Indigenous Peoples of North America* by Robert J. Muckle; and *Intrapreneurship: Managing Ideas Within Your Organization* by Kevin C. Desouza.

Query letters and SASEs should be directed to:

John Yates, President, Publisher, and CEO; jtyates@utpress.utoronto.ca

Virgil Duff, Executive Editor—Social sciences, scholarly medical books, law and criminology, women's studies.

Len Husband, Editor—Canadian history, natural science, philosophy.

Richard Ratzlaff, Editor—Book history, English literature, modern languages, Victorian studies.

Siobhan McMenemy, Editor—Cultural studies, digital futures, film studies.

Suzanne Rancourt, Editor—Humanities, rights and translations, classics, medieval and renaissance studies, music, religion and theology.

Ron Schoeffel, Editor—Erasmus studies, Italian studies, literary criticism, religion and theology.

VÉHICULE PRESS

SIGNAL EDITIONS
ESPLANADE BOOKS

PO Box 125, Place du Parc Station, Montréal, QC H2X 4A3, Canada
514-844-6073 | fax: 514-844-7543
www.vehiculepress.com | e-mail: vp@vehiculepress.com | Twitter: @VehiculePress

For more than 35 years, Véhicule Press has been publishing prize-winning poetry, fiction, social history, Quebec studies, Jewish studies, jazz history, and restaurant guides.

Signal Editions is the poetry imprint of Véhicule Press. Since 1981, 72 poetry titles have been published, one-third of those by first-time authors. Esplanade Books is the fiction imprint of Véhicule Press. Esplanade publishes novels, novellas, and short-story collections—books that fall between the cracks, works of unusual structure and form, and short sharp monologues.

Recent Véhicule Press titles include *Sumptuary Laws* by Nyla Matuk; *The Body on Mount Royal* by David Montrose; *Canada's Forgotten Slaves* by Marcel Trudel; *A Message for the Emperor* by Mark Frutkin; and *The Golden Book of Bovinities* by Robert Moore.

For poetry and nonfiction submissions, please query first. For fiction submissions, please include a 25- to 30-page excerpt. Véhicule mostly publishes Canadian authors.

Simon Dardick, Publisher
Nancy Marrelli, Publisher
Andrew Steinmetz, Editor (Esplanade Books)
Carmine Starnino, Editor (Signal Editions)

WHITECAP BOOKS

WALRUS BOOKS

351 Lynn Avenue, North Vancouver, BC V7J 2C4, Canada
604-980-9852 | fax: 604-980-8197
www.whitecap.ca | Twitter: whitecapbooks

Whitecap Books is one of Canada's largest independent publishers. In addition to the cookbooks, gift books, and coffee-table books that it is primarily known for,

Whitecap publishes gardening and crafts, photo-scenic, history, arts and entertainment, children's fiction and nonfiction, travel, sports, and transportation books. Walrus Books is its imprint for children's books, publishing series fiction for teenagers and science nonfiction.

With a head office in Vancouver, British Columbia, and warehouse operations in Markham, Ontario, the house generates sales across Canada, from coast to coast. In addition to traditional bookstores, Whitecap books can be found in many retail outlets, ranging from museums and clothing stores to gardening centers and cookware suppliers; thus special sales manuscripts might be successfully placed here.

Recent titles include *Canada's Favourite Recipes* by Rose Murray and Elizabeth Baird; *Everyone Can Cook Everything* by Eric Akis; *Okanagan Wine Tour Guide* by John Schreiner; and *Choose It or Lose It* by Rose Reisman.

Whitecap is delighted to receive submissions of queries with proposals and sample chapters. Be sure to include SASEs (and international reply coupons) and direct to Rights and Acquisitions.

Robert McCullough, Publisher
Taryn Boyd, Managing Editor
Grace Yaginuma, Editor

SECTION FIVE

LITERARY AGENTS

WHAT MAKES THIS AGENT DIRECTORY SPECIAL?

JEFF HERMAN

There are many books and websites that include lists of literary agents, but this directory is truly extraordinary because we go way beyond providing names, addresses, and basic statistics. We have offered the agents included here the chance to "talk" about themselves, both professionally and personally, and to share their insights about all aspects of the publishing business. You will not only know who represents what and how to solicit them, but you will also get a sense about many of them as human beings and as potential business partners.

I am frequently asked why certain agents are not listed. I wish to be clear that literally dozens of excellent agents are not listed here, though I would like them to be. Each year I invite the 200-plus members of the Association of Author Representatives (AAR), as well as many excellent nonmember agents, to be in this book. However, just because an agent is not here does not mean that that agent is not qualified to be included. The truth is that many agents are already saturated with as many clients as they can or want to handle. They are not eager to invite unsolicited submissions from the general public because their existing rosters and a few trusted referrals are more than they want to handle. Most agencies are small "mom and pop" businesses that are not inclined to take on a lot of staff and overhead. Their business model is to maximize revenues by limiting expenses and administrative tasks. Yet many qualified agents happily accept my invitation to be listed because they want to hear from as many fresh prospects as possible. If an agent does not explicitly confirm that he or she wants to be in this book, that agent is not included here.

Each year many "false agents" endeavor to be included, and we do our best to keep them out. A false agent is anyone who masquerades as an agent for the sole purpose of stealing money from writers through various acts of clever deception. Letting such people into this book would be tantamount to inviting Colonel Sanders into a hen house. With regret, I must concede instances in the past where I have been deceived by some of these individuals. The consequences for these errors were predictable: I received numerous complaints from writers who came close to getting snagged by these hoodlums. Fortunately, most of the writers smelled the odor before it was too late; however, sometimes I would hear from writers who didn't know what hit them until they were already pinched for a few bucks.

The bottom line is that my staff and I exercise due diligence about who gets listed. Nevertheless, some charlatans may manage to slip through our filters. Like hybrid software viruses, some of these serial grifters have the chutzpah to simply change their names and addresses as soon as word gets out about their scams. I am largely dependent upon you, the writers, to immediately let me know about any wrongful experiences you might have with any of the agencies in this book. That is how I can keep them out of future editions and help sound the alarm elsewhere, as can you. Please see the essay section for more information about this issue. Of course, do not shoot venom only because someone has rejected or disrespected you.

I am not trying to spread fear and paranoia. These unfortunate situations are very much the exception, not the rule. Any agent who has a bona fide list of sales to recognized publishers is legitimate.

THE AARON PRIEST AGENCY

708 3rd Avenue, 23rd Floor, New York, NY 10017
212-818-0344 | fax: 212-573-9417
www.aaronpriest.com

Agent's name: Aaron Priest
Born: Providence, Rhode Island
Education: Graduated from Columbia College in 1959
Career history: Aaron Priest handles about 75 percent fiction and 25 percent nonfiction. Having worked for several years as a sales rep for Doubleday, he started the agency in 1974. Aaron Priest was a founding member of the Independent Literary Agents Association (ILAA), which is now the Association of Author's Representatives. Aaron is a member of the Board of Trustees for the Jewish Theological Seminary and is also on the board of the Schechter Institute of Jewish Studies in Jerusalem.

What's the best way for writers to solicit your interest: E-mail a query to one of our agents using the e-mail address listed below. Please do not submit to more than one agent at this agency. (We urge you to check our website and consider each agent's emphasis before submitting.) Your query letter should be about one page long and describe your work as well as your background. You may also paste the first chapter of your work in the body of the e-mail. Do not send attachments. We will respond within three weeks, but only if interested.

What are some representative titles that you have sold: *Divine Justice* by David Baldacci, *The White Mary* by Kira Salak, *Long Lost* by Harlan Coben, *An Accidental Light* by Elizabeth Diamond, *Trust No One* by Gregg Hurwitz, *Power Down* by Ben Coes

Agent's name: Lisa Erbach Vance
Born: Born and raised outside of Chicago
Education: BA in English literature from Northwestern University
Career history: Lisa Erbach Vance has been with the Aaron Priest Literary Agency since 1993. Her clients include Harlan Coben, Gregg Hurwitz, Gayle Lynds, Matt Beynon Rees, Kathleen Sharp, Aaron Elkins, Sindiwe Magona, Amanda Stevens, and Ann Howard Creel. Her publishing career began at Random House, Inc., where she was selected as one of the first participants in their new management trainee program, after which she became an associate in the foreign rights department at Crown Publishers, before moving to Aaron Priest.

Categories/Subjects that you are most enthusiastic about agenting: Contemporary fiction, especially women's fiction, with a well-defined narrative voice. Observant, thoughtful fiction about families and friends, with fresh perspectives on modern relationships. Thrillers/suspense with propulsive plots enhanced with well-developed characters. Psychological suspense. Contemporary gothic fiction. Unique ghost stories. International fiction (not translation) that takes the reader deep into another culture. Narrative nonfiction, current or historical topics. No poetry, no screenplays, and no sci-fi. In every category, Lisa is looking for original premises, characters she'll be passionate about, and stories she can't put down.

Do you charge reading or management fees: No

Agent's name: Nicole Kenealy
Categories/Subjects that you are most enthusiastic about agenting: Young-adult fiction, nonfiction (narrative, how-to, political, and pop culture), literary and commercial fiction (specifically dealing with social and cultural issues). No poetry, no screenplays, and no sci-fi.

Do you charge reading or management fees: No

Agent's name: Lucy Childs
Career history: Lucy's been at the agency since 1995, having switched from professional actress to literary agent. Her clients include Frances Sherwood, Elizabeth Diamond, and Peter Charles Melman.
Categories/Subjects that you are most enthusiastic about agenting: Literary and commercial fiction, memoir, edgy women's fiction. Not interested in seeing horror, fantasy, sci-fi, self-help, or poetry.

Do you charge reading or management fees: No

ALLEN O'SHEA LITERARY AGENCY

615 Westover Road, Stamford, CT 06902
203-359-9965 | fax: 203-357-9909
www.allenoshea.com
www.publishersmarketplace.com/members/AllenOShea

Agent's name: Marilyn Allen
E-mail: marilyn@allenoshea.com
Education: Trained as an English teacher
Career history: I worked for many years on the publishing side in senior sales and marketing positions for Warner, Penguin, Simon & Schuster, and HarperCollins.
Hobbies/Personal interests: Travel, reading, tennis
Categories/Subjects that you are most enthusiastic about agenting: Nonfiction: Health, parenting, business, cooking, lifestyle, history; Narrative nonfiction
Categories/Subjects writers shouldn't bother pitching to you: Poetry, children's, fiction, memoirs
If you were not an agent, what might you be doing instead: Running marketing department for a publisher or teaching literature
What's the best way for fiction writers to solicit your interest: Not my area of interest

What's the best way for nonfiction writers to solicit your interest: E-mail me.

Do you charge reading or management fees: Never

What are the most common mistakes writers make when pitching to you: Failure to research competition and no marketing plans

Describe the client from hell, even if you don't have any: A client who has unreasonable expectations about the industry; expects things like a quick sale to a publisher, a large advance, extensive marketing, and book reviews

What's your definition of a great client: A great client is a writer who creates a smart proposal, understands his audience and the marketplace, and works collaboratively with me. Love writers who are experts in their field and have cutting-edge research.

How and why did you become an agent: I became an agent because I like to work with writers. I started my agency after a long publishing career.

What can a writer do to increase the odds of you becoming his or her agent: Send me a good proposal with a fresh new idea. I love submissions that are complete and well thought out. Remember, this is a business, so act professionally.

How would you describe what you do as an agent to someone (or something) from another planet: I help writers shape their book projects, find them a publishing home, and do everything in between.

How do you feel about editors and publishers: Really love working with most of them

How do you feel about writers: Really love working with most of them

What do you see in the near future for book publishing: Fewer books being published and e-book sales increasing

What are your favorite books, movies, and TV shows, and why: I have so many favorite books. I just finished *The Story of Edgar Sawtelle* by David Wroblewski and loved it. I look forward to vacation so that I can select books I want to read for pleasure. I enjoy the History Channel and Travel Channel.

In your opinion, what do editors think of you: They trust me and like to work with me. I have a marketing background, and they often look to me for ideas. I solve problems for them.

On a personal level, what do you think people like and dislike about you: They think I'm fun and collegial.

What are some representative titles that you have sold: Many books sold. Please check our web page.

ANDREA BROWN LITERARY AGENCY

650-853-1976

www.andreabrownlit.com

How to contact: Andrea Brown Literary Agency accepts e-mail queries only. Please visit the agency website for submission guidelines.

Agent's name: Jennifer Jaeger

E-mail: Jennifer@andreabrownlit.com

Born: Los Angeles, California

Education: BA in English from UC Davis; minor in social and ethnic relations with a focus on multicultural literature. Spent one year at the University of East Anglia in England. Studied education at Dominican University.

Career history: I worked in journalism and education before becoming a literary agent.

Hobbies/Personal interests: Reading (of course), cooking, martial arts, stock market, travel, spa days, theater, early US history

Categories/Subjects that you are most enthusiastic about agenting: Picture books through young adult, with a special interest in middle grade. I like humorous, literary, multicultural, edgy, and offbeat material. I enjoy some paranormal, fantasy, and historical manuscripts. Though I do not represent adult fiction, I am interested in cross-over fiction.

Categories/Subjects writers shouldn't bother pitching to you: Please, no adult works

If you were not an agent, what might you be doing instead: I would be teaching, learning languages in foreign countries, or working the counter at a bakery.

What's the best way for fiction writers to solicit your interest: Please e-mail your query along with the first 10 pages of your manuscript in the body of an e-mail. For picture books, include the entire manuscript. No attachments, please.

Do you charge reading or management fees: No

What are the most common mistakes writers make when pitching to you: No personalized greeting, no knowledge about my interests or the Andrea Brown Literary Agency, and unprofessional and unpolished query letters.

Describe the client from hell, even if you don't have any: Such a client would be inflexible, greedy, and unnecessarily dramatic.

What's your definition of a great client: Great clients know their market and the business, they work tirelessly on their craft, and they're open to revising and are willing to promote their work. They're also very patient.

How and why did you become an agent: Agenting is the perfect combination of my skills and interests: writing and editing, communication, and business. It is thrilling to know that I play a role in helping great and important books get published.

How do you feel about writers: I think authors are brave souls and the true celebrities.

What are your favorite books, movies, and TV shows, and why: Books: *Even Cowgirls Get the Blues*; *Catherine Called Birdy*; *The Schwa Was Here*; *A Passage to India*; and books by Jonathan Safran Foer and Toni Morrison. TV shows: *The Office*. Movies: *Dirty Dancing, Rushmore, Sweet Home Alabama,* and *Little Miss Sunshine*.

What are some representative titles that you have sold: (Please note that titles are subject to change.) *The Down-to-Earth Guide to Global Warming* (Orchard/Scholastic); *Las mantas de milagros* (Holt); *Farwalker* (Bloomsbury); *Before You*

Were Here and *The Cazuela That the Farm Maiden Stirred* (Viking and Charlesbridge, respectively); *Paris Pan Takes the Dare* (Puffin and Putnam/Penguin)

Agent name: Andrea Brown

E-mail: andrea@andreabrownlit.com

What are some representative titles that you have sold: *Unwind* by Neal Shusterman (Simon & Schuster); *Circle Unbroken* by Margot Theis Raven (Farrar, Straus & Giroux)

How do you feel about writers: I got into publishing because I loved books, but I realized after becoming an agent that I really loved writers even more than books. I am still, after 26 years as an agent, in awe of writers who can finish a book and keep a reader hooked.

How would you describe what you do as an agent to someone (or something) from another planet: I tell everyone who will listen that I have the best career: I get to work with intelligent, creative, wonderful people every day (that includes all my associates at the agency, not just our fabulous clients).

You're welcome to share your thoughts and sentiments about the business of writing and publishing: It is a wonderful time for children's book authors—the best in the 30 years I [have been] in the business. It is also imperative that writers think about their audience more than ever. They must write the best book possible and also make certain that it is commercial. Ask, "Would you pay $25 for this book?"

Will our business exist as we know it in 10 years or so: I think book publishing will always exist, but I think big changes are on the horizon, and the authors that can adapt will continue to be published. I don't think it will exist as it is.

Agent's name: Caryn Wiseman

Education: MBA, Anderson School, UCLA; BS, University of Virginia

Career history: I have been an agent since 1983 and have sold almost 175 books and counting. I represent *New York Times* best sellers, such as *Origami Yoda* author Tom Angleberger and *The Jellybeans* author Nate Evans, as well as debut authors and authors at every stage between.

Categories/Subjects that you are most enthusiastic about agenting: I handle children's books only: young-adult and middle-grade fiction and nonfiction, chapter books, and picture books. My particular interests include humorous middle-grade fiction for girls and for boys; young adult that falls at the intersection of commercial and literary; and non-institutional biography and other unique nonfiction for children and teens. I would love to see more contemporary multicultural middle grade or young adult—books that deeply explore another culture, as well as books in which the ethnicity of the character is not the issue; contemporary middle-grade or young-adult fiction with a touch of magical realism; page-turning thrillers; unique twists on paranormal and dystopian themes; and realistic fiction with an environmental theme. I am always open to terrific children's work that doesn't fit these categories, however. For fiction, a fresh, unique voice is paramount. A literary bent to a well-crafted commercial story in which ordinary characters find themselves in extraordinary situations would capture my attention. I do not represent adult projects. Please do not query me regarding adult work.

Categories/Subjects writers shouldn't bother pitching to you: Any adult projects

What are some representative titles that you have sold: *NY Times* best seller Tom Angleberger's *Darth Paper Strikes Back*, *The Strange Case of Origami Yoda*, and *Horton Halfpott* (Abrams/Amulet); *Time between Us* (fka MOBIUS) by Tamara Ireland Stone (Disney/Hyperion); *Flutter* by Gina Linko (Random House); *Me, Frida* by Amy Novesky (Abrams); *Ballpark Mysteries* series by David Kelly (Random House); and *A Year of Goodbyes* by Debbie Levy (Disney/Hyperion)

Agent name: Laura Rennert

E-mail: laura@andreabrownlit.com

Education: PhD in English Literature, University of Virginia; BA, magna cum laude, Cornell University

Career history: Literary agent, 10 years. Professor, eight years of teaching English literature at Santa Clara University, the University of Virginia; and visiting professor at Osaka University of Foreign Studies in Japan

Hobbies/Personal interests: Travel, movies, theater, good food and wine, and reading and writing, of course

Categories/Subjects that you are most enthusiastic about agenting: Ambitious voice-driven fiction, whether children's books or adult; literary mysteries and thrillers, compelling story-based narrative nonfiction; literary-commercial middle-grade and young-adult fiction; cross-over fiction; fiction. Regardless of genre, I look for works that are emotionally powerful and resonant.

Categories/Subjects writers shouldn't bother pitching to you: Westerns, adult fantasy, adult science fiction, prescriptive nonfiction, screenplays, New Age fiction, and nonfiction

What's the best way for fiction writers to solicit your interest: Follow the guidelines on our website and choose one agent to e-query. Target the agent for whom you feel your work is the best fit and take the time to do a little research. A strong query that demonstrates you've done your homework makes a good first impression. When someone tells me why they're approaching me particularly and demonstrates some knowledge of the market, I look closely at their work. Professionalism, passion, and confidence (not hubris) are attractive. A strong voice is one of my main criteria in work I choose to take on, and I'm already on the lookout for it as I read query letters.

What's the best way for nonfiction writers to solicit your interest: I'm looking for a strong proposal and sample chapters—and pretty much look for the same criteria I mention above for fiction.

If you were not an agent, what might you be doing instead: If I weren't agenting, I'd probably be an editor, a professor of English literature, or a writer…pretty predictable, I'm afraid, although I do also have a secret fascination with dinosaurs—so maybe also paleontologist.

Do you charge reading or management fees: No

What categories do you represent, by percentages: Children's books: 70 percent; adult fiction and nonfiction: 30 percent

Describe the client from hell, even if you don't have any: The client from hell wants constant updates, hand-holding, and attention all the time.

What are your favorite books, movies, and TV shows, and why: Some of my favorite books are Jonathan Lethem's *Motherless Brooklyn*, A. S. Byatt's *Possession*, Barry Eisler's *The Last Assassin*, J. K. Rowling's *Harry Potter* novels, Terry Pratchett's *Wee Free Men* trilogy, all of Jane Austen's novels, and Madeleine L'Engle's *A Wrinkle in Time*. Although they are very different, what all of these works have in common is a marvelous, individualistic voice; characters that get under your skin; emotional power and resonance; masterful storytelling; a unique perspective; and vivid, evocative, visceral writing.

What are some representative titles that you have sold: *The Five Ancestors* series (Random House); *Becoming Chloe* (Knopf); *Storky: How I Won the Girl and Lost My Nickname* (Putnam); *Monsoon Summer* (Random House); *The Squishiness of Things* (Knopf); *The Strongbow Saga: Viking Warrior Book 1* (HarperCollins); *First Daughter: Extreme American Make-Over* (Dutton); *Revolution Is Not a Dinner Party* (Holt); *Evolution, Me, and Other Freaks of Nature* (Knopf); *Glass* (Margaret McElderry/Simon & Schuster); *Love in the Present Tense* (Doubleday); *Thirteen Reasons Why* (Razorbill/Penguin Group); *The Day I Killed James* (Knopf); *Chasing Windmills* (Doubleday); and *Madapple* (Knopf)

ANDREA HURST LITERARY MANAGEMENT

5050 Laguna Blvd., Ste. 112-330, Elk Grove, CA 95758
www.andreahurst.com

Agent's name: Judy Mikalonis
E-mail: judy@andreahurst.com

Categories/Subjects that you are most enthusiastic about agenting: Christian nonfiction, Christian fiction, adult nonfiction, young-adult fiction

Categories/Subjects writers shouldn't bother pitching to you: No science fiction, no historical fiction, no supernatural thrillers

What's the best way for fiction writers to solicit your interest: Write amazingly well and tell a transformative story

What's the best way for nonfiction writers to solicit your interest: Write a damn good proposal and have an amazing platform

Do you charge reading or management fees: No

What are the most common mistakes writers make when pitching to you: Not being prepared to sell their story. No immediate relevance to the reader apparent in their pitch. Can't tell me what their protagonist wants (fiction).

What can a writer do to increase the odds of you becoming his or her agent: Write really well. Write a good proposal. Follow directions and e-mail queries only. Do not mail a query.

Agent's name: Andrea Hurst
E-mail: andrea@andreahurst.com
Born: Los Angeles, California
Education: Bachelor's degree in expressive arts
Career history: As president of Andrea Hurst Literary Management, Andrea works with both major and regional publishing houses, and her client list includes emerging new voices and *New York Times* best-selling authors such as Dr. Bernie Siegel. With over 20 years in the publishing industry, Andrea is a published author (*Lazy Dog's Guide to Enlightenment*), skilled acquisition and development editor, speaker, and literary judge. Her areas of expertise include sales, promotion, and production in the publishing and entertainment fields. She is an instructor for the Northwest Institute of Literary Arts MFA program and teaches webinars for *Writers Digest*.

Hobbies/Personal interests: Animal welfare, reading fine novels, writing fiction, gourmet natural food

Categories/Subjects that you are most enthusiastic about agenting: Prescriptive and narrative nonfiction: Parenting, relationships, women's issues, personal growth, health and wellness, science, business, true crime, animals, pop culture, humor, cookbooks, gift books, spirituality, metaphysical, psychology, and self-help, memoirs. Fiction: Adult commercial fiction, women's fiction, thrillers, romance.

Categories/Subjects writers shouldn't bother pitching to you: Science fiction/fantasy, Western, horror

If you were not an agent, what might you be doing instead: I would be a best-selling fiction author.

What's the best way for fiction writers to solicit your interest: Take the time to learn the craft of writing and have your work professionally edited before sending it out. Be sure your query letter is compelling and shows off your writing style.

What's the best way for nonfiction writers to solicit your interest: Write a knockout book proposal with a long and detailed marketing section. Send a query letter first by e-mail.

Do you charge reading or management fees: No

What are the most common mistakes writers make when pitching to you: Not researching to find the appropriate agency match for their work. It is very easy to locate an agent's website and figure out what they are looking for, how they want it submitted, and what their name is! Not following directions and not having a strong query letter.

Describe the client from hell, even if you don't have any: A writer who is not familiar with the publishing business and has unrealistic expectations can turn quickly into a client from hell. Particularly someone who is not willing to edit their work, can't make deadlines, and has an attitude that everyone else should accommodate [them].

What's your definition of a great client: Luckily, I have many of those. A great client follows directions willingly, meets and exceeds deadlines and expectations, and has a can-do attitude. We have a mutual trust, and they let me do my job.

What can a writer do to increase the odds of you becoming his or her agent: Write exceptionally well and have a unique, well-researched idea that is pitched through a complete book proposal for nonfiction or a synopsis and sample chapters for fiction. Have a strong platform that you are building on a daily basis and be committed to a long-term writing career. Be willing to work hard to promote your writing and continue to improve your craft through classes, critique groups, conferences, etc.

How and why did you become an agent: The publishing business has been in my blood from a very early age. As a writer myself, I understand the business from both sides. My first book published was *Everybody's Natural Foods Cookbook* through New World Library. Marc Allen, the publisher, taught me the business from the ground up. After that, I was hooked. I worked as a freelance editor, ghostwriter, and instructor for many years, including a position as an acquisition and development editor for a children's publisher in Seattle. My extensive list of editorial contacts, coupled with my strong marketing background acquired through working at Columbia Records, led me on a natural course to becoming an agent.

How would you describe what you do as an agent to someone (or something) from another planet: Just about everything from editing to selling and from networking to acting as a coach and mentor. The job is never done.

How do you feel about editors and publishers: They are the gatekeepers that provide the opportunity for wonderful books to reach the world.

How do you feel about writers: I am always looking for the exceptional ones who have a great story to tell or wonderful information to share. Every query I receive is another opportunity to discover a great writer.

In your opinion, what do editors think of you: That I am professional, accessible, genuine, and represent talented and reliable clients

What are some representative titles that you have sold: *No Buddy Left Behind, A Book of Miracles, How to Sell Your Crafts Online, Culinary Birds, Biba's Spaghetti Sauces, The Santa Barbara Table, Going Organic Can Kill You, A Course in Happiness* by Dr. Mardi Horowitz (Tarcher/Penguin); *True Self, True Wealth* by Peter Cole (Daisy Reese); *Beyond Words* (Atria); *Best Recipes from Italy's Food Festivals* by James Fraioli/Leonardo Curti Gibbs (Smith Publishers)

ANDY ROSS LITERARY AGENCY

767 Santa Ray Avenue, Oakland, CA 94610
510-238-8965
andyrossagency@hotmail.com

> **Agent's name:** Andy Ross
> **Born:** Dallas, Texas, 1946

Education: BA, political science, Brandeis University, MA, European history, University of Oregon

Career history: I was the owner of Cody's Books in Berkeley, California, for 30 years from 1977–2007. Cody's was one of America's great independent book stores. It was three blocks from the University of California. We were well known for our breadth of stock, particularly of intellectual subjects. Over the years, we had the world's greatest writers speaking at the store. It was a wonderful experience. I left Cody's in 2007. Sadly, Cody's closed its doors for the last time in 2008, the victim of history and changing buying habits. I opened my agency in 2008. Buying books for Cody's for so many years, getting pitched about 50,000 titles, talking to real book buyers, and doing returns of the books that didn't sell gave me a different perspective than many other agents.

Hobbies/Personal interests: Reading (of course). Photography. Fooling around with my kids.

Categories/Subjects that you are most enthusiastic about agenting: Politics, history, current events, narrative nonfiction, science, journalism, literary and mainstream fiction, young-adult fiction

Categories/Subjects writers shouldn't bother pitching to you: Poetry, genre fiction

If you were not an agent, what might you be doing instead: I would be wishing I was agenting. I love it.

What's the best way for fiction writers to solicit your interest: I am just looking for subjects that are of interest to me and writers who speak with some authority on what they write about. I don't believe in clever pitches.

Do you charge fees separate from your commission or offer nonagenting fee-based services: No

What are some representative titles that you have sold: *The American Doomsday Machine* by Daniel Ellsberg (Bloomsbury Press), *The Dog Who Never Stopped Loving* by Jeffrey Masson (HarperCollins), *The Jewish Gospels* by Dr. Daniel Boyarin (New Press), *God and His Demons* by Michael Parenti (Prometheus Books)

How and why did you become an agent: I became an agent after I left Cody's. After 30 years in the retail book business, I was concerned that my future might lie in bagging groceries at Safeway. But I woke up one night and realized that I wanted to work with authors at the other end of the book food chain. It was the right decision. Fortunately most people in the book business knew about Cody's, and they were very welcoming and encouraging.

How do you feel about writers: I love working with my writers and feel triumphant when I can get a book I believe in published.

How would you describe what you do as an agent to someone (or something) from another planet: I would be delighted to represent a spaceman or a person from an alternative universe, as long as they had an impressive "platform."

What are your favorite books, movies, and TV shows, and why: My favorite book was *War and Peace* because I like historical epics, and I didn't want it to end, and it didn't. My favorite movie is *The Seventh Seal* because it, too, is an epic. I also like *Casablanca* because everyone likes *Casablanca*. The movie I have seen the most is *High School Musical* because I have a little kid. I don't watch television.

Describe the client from hell, even if you don't have any: He expects me to get him a $200,000 advance for his book on *The Idea of Nature in Kant's Metaphysical Writings*. When I submit it to publishers, it turns out that it has already gone around New York. He thinks his book is perfect as is and won't listen to his agent and his publisher. He thinks he will be on *Oprah*. He won't. He thinks it will make a good movie. It won't.

Describe the publisher and/or editor from hell: Since business has been so bad in publishing, most publishers and editors are in hell, not from hell. They are, as a group, pretty good.

What do you like best about your clients and the editors and publishers you work with: Some of my clients are trying to change the world through their writing. Some are just trying to have fun. I admire how much spirit they put into their work and the risks they take. I believe that writing is an act of courage, and I admire this in all writers. I feel as if the editors and publishers are all in this together with me. The publishers I have enjoyed working with are committed book lovers.

Will our business exist as we know it in 10 years or so: Nothing stays the same in this world. I suspect that books will become digital eventually. The future of bookstores, particular independent stores, is in doubt. This is not what I would hope, but it is what I would expect. But people still read, and a digital book is still a book. The Internet has, sadly, created a society with attention deficit disorder. Books require patience and commitment. Texting and twittering [are] very bad news for those who believe in a literate society.

THE ANGELA RINALDI LITERARY AGENCY

PO Box 7877, Beverly Hills, CA 90212-7877
310-842-7665 | fax: 310-837-3143
www.rinaldiliterary.com

Agent's name: Angela Rinaldi
E-mail: amr@RinaldiLiterary.com
Career history: Executive editor, NAL/Signet; senior editor, Pocket Books; executive editor, Bantam Books; manager of book publishing for the *Los Angeles Times*. Taught publishing programs at UCLA. Member of the Literature Panel for the California Arts Council, AAR, and PEN.
Categories/Subjects that you are most enthusiastic about agenting: Fiction: Mainstream and literary fiction, upmarket contemporary women's fiction, suspense, mysteries, thrillers, historical fiction. Nonfiction: Narrative nonfiction like *Blink* or *Freakonomics*—books that present a quirky aspect of the usual, memoirs, women's issues/studies, current issues, cultural and social history, biography, psychology,

popular reference, prescriptive and proactive self-help, health books that address specific issues, business, career, personal finance. Books written by journalists, academics, doctors and therapists, motivational, children's, and young adult.

Categories/Subjects writers shouldn't bother pitching to you: Humor, techno thrillers, KGB/CIA espionage, drug thrillers, category romances, science fiction, fantasy, horror, Westerns, cookbooks, poetry, film scripts, magazine articles, religion, gift, how-to, Christian, religious, celebrity bios, or tell-alls.

If you were not an agent, what might you be doing instead: Editorial consultant/ freelance editor

What's the best way for fiction writers to solicit your interest: Brief synopsis and the first three chapters. Do not send the entire ms, unless requested. Do not query by phone or fax. E-mail inquiries: please be brief, no attachments. Please tell me if I have your work exclusively or if it is a multiple submission. Include SASE. No metered mail or certified mail. UPS and FedEx will not deliver to a post office box. Please allow four weeks for response.

What's the best way for nonfiction writers to solicit your interest: Queries with detailed covering letter or proposal. Do not query by phone or fax. E-mail inquiries; please be brief, no attachments. Please tell me if I have your work exclusively or if it is a multiple submission. Include SASE. No metered mail or certified mail. UPS and FedEx will not deliver to a post office box. Please allow four weeks for response.

Do you charge reading or management fees: No

What are the most common mistakes writers make when pitching to you: Not knowing the genre they are writing in. Not researching the marketplace for similar titles. Pitching a novel that isn't finished and asking the agent to read incrementally. Pitching an undeveloped proposal. Pitching ideas that have been done many times over. Pitching more than one book at a time. Pitching novels and nonfiction at the same time. Not knowing the type of book I represent. Pitching to more than one agent and not letting each agent know. Mentioning that their previous agent died or is sick.

What can a writer do to increase the odds of you becoming his or her agent: Having a strong platform and knowing what that means. Being an expert in their field. Having stories published in journals. Big ideas, original ideas, or noticing trends. Having ideas that explain the way we live. Having a "brand." Being able to get endorsements. Lovely writing. Good storytelling. Distinct voice. Writing a novel that combines literary writing with a commercial hook.

What are some representative titles that you have sold: *Who Moved My Cheese?* by Dr. Spencer Johnson; *Zen Golf: Mastering the Mental Game* by Dr. Joseph Parent (Doubleday); *Zen Putting: Mastering the Mental Game on the Greens* by Dr. Joseph Parent (Gotham Books); *Calling in "The One"* by Katherine Woodward Thomas (Three Rivers); *Welcome to the Real World* by Stacy Kravetz (Norton); *My First Crush* by Linda Kaplan (The Lyons Press); *Bone Lake* by Drusilla Campbell (Bookspan); *Blood Orange* by Drusilla Campbell (Kensington); *Rescue Me* by Megan Clark (Kensington); *The Starlite Drive-In* by Marjorie Reynolds (Morrow); *Blind Spot, Quiet Time* by Stephanie Kane (Bantam); *TWINS! Pregnancy, Birth, and the*

First Year of Life by Dr. Connie Agnew, Dr. Alan H. Klein, and Jill Alison Ganon (HarperCollins); *The Thyroid Solution* by Dr. Ridha Arem (Ballantine); *Before Your Pregnancy* by Amy Ogle, MS, RD and Dr. Lisa Mazzullo

---

ANN RITTENBERG LITERARY AGENCY, INC.

15 Maiden Lane, Suite 206, New York, NY 10038
212-684-6936 | fax: 212-684-6929
www.rittlit.com

Agent's name: Ann Rittenberg
Born: Brooklyn, New York
Hobbies/Personal interests: Reading, fashion, outdoors, travel, technology
Education: BA comparative literature, Eckerd College 1979
Career history: After graduating and working briefly at the *St. Petersburg Times*, I moved to New York and joined Atheneum Publishers as an editorial assistant. Worked my way up to editor, and then joined the Julian Bach Agency as an agent. Opened my own agency in 1992.

Categories/Subjects that you are most enthusiastic about agenting: Upmarket suspense, thrillers, mysteries, and women's fiction (i.e., those with very strong writing, characterizations, and plot); literary fiction; cultural and social history

Categories/Subjects writers shouldn't bother pitching to you: Poetry, sci-fi, genre fiction, how-to, gift books

If you were not an agent, what might you be doing instead: Traveling; studying French; getting a graduate degree in literature; volunteering for nonpolitical causes such as literacy, women's health and safety, teaching life skills to teenagers, and preserving urban green spaces

What's the best way for fiction writers to solicit your interest: Write me a brief, cogent letter.

Do you charge fees separate from your commission or offer nonagenting fee-based services: NO!

What are some representative titles that you have sold: *Where on Earth*, Doug Magee (Simon & Schuster, 2010); *The Poacher's Son*, Paul Doiron (St. Martin's Press); *Mystic River*, Dennis Lehane (William Morrow & Co.); *House and Home*, Kathy McCleary (Hyperion); *Afterimage*, Kathleen George (St. Martin's Press); *The Cure for Grief*, Nellie Herrmann (Scribner)

How and why did you become an agent: I became an agent not only because I wanted to discover wonderful new writers and see them get published, but also because I wanted to advocate for writers. Having worked in a publishing house, I saw how hard it was for every writer on a publisher's list to get equal attention, and I thought that if I worked on the side of the author, I'd be able to help them get the attention they deserved.

How do you feel about writers: I think they're crucially important members of our society. We need storytellers to make sense of a chaotic world.

How would you describe what you do as an agent to someone (or something) from another planet: I tell them I help writers find publishers. If they need a more detailed explanation, I tell them to read the book I cowrote with my client Laura Whitcomb, *Your First Novel*. It explains the entire publishing process in a way that has helped many people.

What are your favorite books, movies, and TV shows, and why: *Great Expectations*, because it's heavenly on every page; *Gone with the Wind*, because Scarlett helped me get where I am; *All about Eve*, because I love Bette Davis and because it depicts an industry's behind-the-scenes in a fresh and compelling manner; the short stories of Katherine Mansfield, because they are simply the best; *Lost*, because it's like a novel on TV.

Describe the client from hell, even if you don't have any: Only gets in touch to complain

Describe the publisher and/or editor from hell: Never returns calls, hates to work collaboratively, withholds information

What do you like best about your clients and the editors and publishers you work with: They're smart and creative, and they surprise me constantly with their wonderful ideas and passion.

You're welcome to share your thoughts and sentiments about the business of writing and publishing: I did this extensively in the book I cowrote with Laura Whitcomb, *Your First Novel*.

Will our business exist as we know it in 10 years or so: It will exist, and it will be recognizable, but I hope it will have embraced all sorts of new technologies while retaining printed books.

ARTISTS AND ARTISANS, INC./ MOVABLE TYPE MANAGEMENT

244 Madison Avenue, Suite 334, New York, NY 10016
212-924-9619 | fax: 212-931-8377
www.mtmgmt.net
www.artistsandartisans.com

Agent name: Jamie Brenner
E-mail: Jamie@artistsandartisans.com
Born: Philadelphia, Pennsylvania, 1974
Education: The George Washington University, BA English
Career history: Started in publishing as a publicity assistant at HarperCollins. I worked on books by supertalented writers like Barbara Kingsolver, Louise Erdrich, and Erica Jong. Then a former colleague lured me over to Barnes & Noble—the company was just launching their online store to compete with Amazon. I worked

there as an editor/buyer for a few years. During this time, a film industry connection got me a freelance job reading manuscripts for Miramax films, and I eventually became a book scout for a film production company. In 2007 I started at Artists and Artisans as a literary agent.

Hobbies/Personal interests: I'm very into pop culture, music, film. I'm fascinated by ballet. I'm interested in politics though I try not to be because there's so much disappointment.

Categories/Subjects that you are most enthusiastic about agenting: Women's fiction, especially novels straddling the line between commercial and literary fiction. I like horror novels that have a strong psychological element. I am always looking for memoirs. I like political thrillers and literary mysteries.

Categories/Subjects writers shouldn't bother pitching to you: Children's books, fantasy, science fiction, sports, spirituality.

If you were not an agent, what might you be doing instead: I don't know—but it would be something with books.

What's the best way for fiction writers to solicit your interest: A simple e-mail query that gives me a clear pitch for the book and an idea who the writer is.

Do you charge fees separate from your commission or offer nonagenting fee-based services: I never charge separate fees, nor do I offer fee-based services.

What are some representative titles that you have sold: *Insatiable, A Memoir* by Erica Rivera (Berkeley); *Liver Let Die* by Annelise Ryan (Kensington)

How and why did you become an agent: When I was scouting books for a film company, I routinely met with agents to hear about the books they had coming down the pike. One of these was my current colleague, Adam Chromy. It was his idea that I try agenting. Needless to say, he was very persuasive. And it was one of the best decisions I ever made.

How do you feel about writers: Writers are the people who helped shaped me. It is their words, stories, pain, insight, that have influenced the way I see the world and even brought the world to me when I was just a suburban girl. To me, they are the most important artists.

How would you describe what you do as an agent to someone (or something) from another planet: I never talk to entities from other planets about my job. Like Europeans, they think we discuss work too much.

What are your favorite books, movies, and TV shows, and why: Favorite books—I could go on forever. I've read almost every Nelson DeMille book. I loved Cathi Hanauer's *Sweet Ruin*. I'm a big fan of Dani Shapiro's *Black and White* and *Slow Motion*. For family sagas, I love Susan Howatch's *The Wheel of Fortune*. Favorite in horror is Bentley Little's *The Mailman*. I have to stop now! Favorite films: *25th Hour, Pulp Fiction, Roger Dodger, A Walk on the Moon, About Last Night, High Art*.

Describe the client from hell, even if you don't have any: One who doesn't take the time to understand that this is a business

Describe the publisher and/or editor from hell: One who could just as easily be buying/selling widgets

What do you like best about your clients and the editors and publishers you work with: At the end of the day, we share a passion.

Agent's name: Adam Chomry

Education: New York University Stern School of Business, BS, 1992

Career history: After a brief stint at a renowned literary agency, Adam Chomry went out on his own to represent a novel written by a close friend. The gamble paid off, and the book was sold on a preemptive offer. Since that auspicious start in 2002, Adam's fresh, rule-breaking approach has led to dozens of book deals at major publishing houses, a national and *New York Times* best seller, and a number of film deals for his clients' projects.

Categories/Subjects that you are most enthusiastic about agenting: I am still signing authors of fiction and narrative nonfiction as long as the writing is exceptional and the authors have something truly unique to say. I am also interested in practical nonfiction from authors with strong platforms and/or a point of view that challenges the status quo.

Categories/Subjects writers shouldn't bother pitching to you: Screenplays, photo or children's books

What's the best way for writers to solicit your interest: Read and follow the submission guidelines on my website—www.artistsandartisans.com.

What are the most common mistakes writers make when pitching to you: Pitching half-baked ideas or projects is a turnoff.

Do you charge reading or management fees: No

What categories do you represent, by percentages: I spend half my time on fiction and [half on] nonfiction, but because fiction is a tougher sell we end up with a list comprised of slightly more nonfiction.

Describe the client from hell, even if you don't have any: I do not have any (at least not for long).

How would you describe the perfect client: They understand that being a professional author is 50 percent writing and 50 percent marketing, and they energetically and enthusiastically pursue both.

What can a writer do to increase the odds of you becoming his or her agent: The author should do everything possible to make sure their book is of the highest quality AND make sure they understand the book's market and how to reach it. If they make this clear in a query, then it is hard to pass up.

How would you describe what you do as an agent to someone (or something) from another planet: I wouldn't waste time telling someone from another planet what I do; I would be trying to sign them for their memoir.

What do you think the future holds for writers, publishers, and agents: I like to remind my authors about the railroad companies of the last century and how they went out of business because they thought of themselves as "railroad companies" and not "transportation companies." So we don't just focus on authors' books; we focus on the value of their stories and messages as intellectual property and plan ahead for delivering that IP through books, websites, TV, film, or anything else that comes along.

On a personal level, what do you think people like and dislike about you: I think I get both reactions because I am a straight shooter.

What are some representative titles that you have sold: *The Hookup Handbook* (Simon Spotlight; film setup at Weinstein Bros.); *Pomegranate Soup* (Random House, international best seller); *Jewtopia* (Warner, based on the hit off-Broadway play); *World Made by Hand* and the sequel to the best seller *The Long Emergency* (Grove/Atlantic). Additional titles on my website.

ASHLEY GRAYSON LITERARY AGENCY

1342 W. 18th Street, San Pedro, CA 90732
310-514-0267 | 310-548-4672 | fax: 310-831-0036
www.graysonagency.com/blog

Agent's name: Lois Winston

Education: BFA graphic design/illustration, Tyler School of Art/Temple University

Career history: Art director, designer, and editor in consumer crafts industry; published author of two novels; contributor to three fiction and one nonfiction anthologies; author of numerous magazine articles; agent since 2005

Hobbies/Personal interests: Broadway theater, reading, travel, wandering around art museums

Categories/Subjects that you are most enthusiastic about agenting: We love to agent books that make us want to run out and tell the world about the book and the author. We love novels that are exceedingly well written, with characters we want to spend time with; clever, high-concept ideas often with a good dose of humor; wonderful, fresh stories that draw us in, keep us turning the pages, and are just so darn fun to read. In nonfiction, we look for books that are fresh, commercial, high concept and promotable, from an author with a national platform. We're especially looking for narrative-driven nonfiction books about health and science topics and cultural history. In children's books, we seek authors and books with unique voice and the right sensibilities for the market, whether quirky and fun or more serious. We are extremely selective about children's nonfiction. I look for women's fiction, romance (all subgenres except inspiration romance), romantic suspense, thrillers, and traditional mysteries. Humor is always a plus, but not slapstick.

Categories/Subjects writers shouldn't bother pitching to you: The agency does not represent screenplays, poetry, short stories, novellas, most novelty books, textbooks, or most memoirs, especially stories of abuse or addiction recovery. In fiction, dark fiction is fine; gore solely for the sake of shocking the reader is not for us. I'm not partial to dark paranormals (light and/or humorous paranormals are okay), and I prefer historical novels over historical romances.

If you were not an agent, what might you be doing instead: Working on my own novels

What's the best way for fiction writers to solicit your interest: Send us something smart, fresh, captivatingly written, and beautifully crafted. Write a book that is truly new and fills a need, not just a version of something that's currently popular. My interests are very specific, so research them carefully before sending your work to me. List publications you've published in and organizations you belong to that demonstrate your interest in the field. For fiction: We are still accepting clients who are previously published by a known publisher. The agency is temporarily closed to queries from writers who are not published at book length, with the following exceptions: (1) Authors recommended by a client, published author, or editor who has read the work in question; (2) Authors we have met at conferences and from whom we have requested submissions; (3) Authors who have been published in quality small presses or magazines. We have had excellent success selling first-time novelists, but at this time we must concentrate on the needs of professional authors who need our intellectual property management and financial skills. If you meet these criteria, please query us, listing publishing credits with titles, publishers, and dates published. Query by e-mail only. Include the first three pages of the manuscript in the body of your e-mail; do not send attachments unless requested. For nonfiction: Query with proposal. Note: We cannot review self-published works to evaluate moving them to mainstream publishers. Please send query letter by e-mail, including brief bio or CV, and the Market and Competition sections of your proposal.

Do you charge fees separate from your commission or offer nonagenting fee-based services: We do not offer nonagenting fee-based services. We do charge for some extraordinary expenses such as bank wires, overnight mail delivery, or posting books to foreign lands.

What are some representative titles that you have sold: *Tales of the Madman Underground* by John Barnes (Viking Children's Books); *Move Your Stuff, Change Your Life* by Karen Rauch Carter (Simon & Schuster); *The Middle of Somewhere* by J. B. Cheaney (Knopf Books for Young Readers); *Moongobble and Me* (series) by Bruce Coville (Simon & Schuster Children's Books); *Ball Don't Lie* by Matt de la Peña (Delacorte); *Be Bless'd* by Denise Dumars (New Page); *Grease Monkey* by Tim Eldred (Tor); *Bride of the Fat White Vampire* by Andrew Fox (Ballantine); *Child of a Dead God* by Barb and J. C. Hendee (ROC/Penguin); *Mars Crossing* by Geoffrey A. Landis (Tor); *Tiny Little Troubles* by Marc Lecard (St. Martin's); *Sleeping Freshmen Never Lie* by David Lubar (Dutton); *Théâtre Illuminata: Eyes Like Stars* by Lisa Mantchev (Feiwel and Friends); *The Healing Power of Faery* by Edain McCoy (Provenance/Adams Media); *Sex Starved and Sex Drive* by Jill Myles (Pocket Books); *But I Don't Feel Too Old to Be a Mommy* by Doreen Nagle (Health Communications); *Phoenix Unrisen* by Kathleen Nance (Dorchester); *Alosha* by Christopher Pike (Tor/Forge); *Cave Paintings to Picasso* by Henry Sayre (Chronicle Books); *Wiley and Grampa's Creature Features* (series) by Kirk Scroggs (Little Brown

Books for Young Readers); *Cat Yoga* by Rick Tillotson (Clarkson Potter); *The Boy with the Lampshade on His Head* by Bruce Wetter (Atheneum); *Raven* by Allison van Diepen (Simon Pulse); *Kitty and the Silver Bullet* by Carrie Vaughn (Warner); *I Wish I Never Met You* by Denise Wheatley (Simon & Schuster/Touchstone); *Love, Lies, and a Double Shot of Deception* by Lois Winston (Dorchester).

How and why did you become an agent: Ashley thought I'd be an asset to the agency, and I've worked my way up to agenting.

What are your favorite books, movies, and TV shows, and why: My clients' books. TV: *House, Lost, Bones, The Shield, Burn Notice, Law & Order.* Movies: *Chicago, Casablanca, Singing in the Rain, Same Time Next Year, Shakespeare in Love.*

How would you describe what you do as an agent to someone (or something) from another planet: Many people think we get paid to read for a living, but that's only the beginning of what we do. We use our judgment to select and market wonderful manuscripts to the most appropriate editors at the most appropriate houses; we read contracts with a thoroughgoing understanding of terms and negotiate the best terms we can in every deal; read royalty statements with an eagle eye; work with publishers and authors to promote the books; sell subrights, including negotiating contracts for foreign editions, film, and TV; and are the authors' advocates in all publishing matters.

Describe the client from hell, even if you don't have any: An author who believes every word he/she has written is etched in platinum and refuses to even consider revising.

Describe the client, publisher, and/or editor from hell: We love our clients—they always have great ideas simmering for the next book or two; their works are continually fresh and exciting; they continue to charm and delight us with their innovative and creative ideas and work and are genuinely enthusiastic about the business; and they understand publishing is a business. They are relentlessly surprising and never bewildering—their work is stunning. We love editors for their enthusiasm for books and authors. We look forward to continuing to work with editors and publishers to find ways to publish and sell creative works as technology, industry business models, and even the form of the book, change.

Will our business exist as we know it in 10 years or so: No, it will not. Readers have changed in their style of reading and reasons to read, as well as what, where, and how they read. The new Generation Y population neither lives, thinks, nor reads like the Boomers and Gen X readers. New best sellers must address these changes and authors must adapt to sell big now and continue to win loyal readers in the next 15 years. Publishers, distributors, and retailers have demonstrated repeatedly that they do not want to continue performing the activities associated with their traditional businesses and desire to move to a model in which no book is manufactured or stocked until the customer buys it. This works well for downloadable games and software, and it is inevitable that books will be next. As an agency, we are prepared to operate in such a future and to protect and grow our clients' intellectual property investments. We are paying attention but are not worried.

Agent's name: Carolyn Grayson

Education: BA, English, Wellesley College; MBA, UCLA

Career history: Market research analyst, marketing consultant, agent since 1994

Hobbies/Personal interests: Reading, gardening, roses, beach, investing, wine, cooking

Categories/Subjects that you are most enthusiastic about agenting: We love to agent books that make us want to run out and tell the world about the book and the author. We love novels that are exceedingly well written, with characters we want to spend time with; clever, high-concept ideas often with a good dose of humor; wonderful, fresh stories that draw us in, keep us turning the pages, and are just so darn fun to read. In nonfiction, we look for books that are fresh, commercial, high concept and promotable, from an author with a national platform. We're especially looking for narrative-driven nonfiction books about health and science topics and cultural history. In children's books, we seek authors and books with unique voice and the right sensibilities for the market, whether quirky and fun or more serious. We are extremely selective about children's nonfiction. I particularly look for women's fiction (including romance and multicultural), historical fiction, mysteries, suspense, women-oriented fantasy, horror, and children's books, from chapter books to young adult. Nonfiction: contemporary self-help, business, pop culture, science, true crime, and a very few gift or highly illustrated books, narrative nonfiction.

Categories/Subjects writers shouldn't bother pitching to you: The agency does not represent screenplays, poetry, short stories, novellas, most novelty books, textbooks, or most memoirs, especially stories of abuse or addiction recovery. In fiction, dark fiction is fine; gore solely for the sake of shocking the reader is not for us. I'm not inclined to read and represent women's fiction in which the life of the heroine is full of depression and angst; I do like a happy ending.

How and why did you become an agent: I love to read, including contracts, and I love to help authors move up in their careers.

What are your favorite books, movies, and TV shows, and why: My favorite books are my clients', of course. I like movies with clever screenwriting: many of the Coen brothers' movies, especially *Barton Fink* and *The Man Who Wasn't There*. TV Shows: *Law & Order*; *CSI: Las Vegas*; *Mystery!*

What's the best way for fiction writers to solicit your interest: Send us something smart, fresh, captivatingly written, and beautifully crafted. For fiction: We are still accepting clients who are previously published by a known publisher. The agency is temporarily closed to queries from writers who are not published at book length, with the following exceptions: (1) Authors recommended by a client, a published author, or an editor who has read the work in question; (2) Authors we have met at conferences and from whom we have requested submissions; (3) Authors who have been published in quality small presses or magazines. We have had excellent success selling first-time novelists, but at this time we must concentrate on the needs of professional authors who need our intellectual property management skills and financial skills. If you meet these criteria, please query us, listing publishing credits with titles, publishers, and dates published. Query by e-mail only. Include the first three pages of the manuscript in the body of your e-mail; do not send attachments unless requested. For nonfiction: Query with proposal. Note: We cannot review self-published works to evaluate moving them to mainstream publishers. Please send query letter by e-mail, including brief bio or CV, and the Market and Competition sections of your proposal.

Do you charge fees separate from your commission or offer nonagenting fee-based services: We do not offer nonagenting fee-based services. We do charge for some extraordinary expenses such as bank wires, overnight mail delivery, or posting books to foreign lands.

Agent's name: Denise Dumars

Education: BA in English/creative writing, Cal State Univ. Long Beach; MA in English/creative writing, Cal State Univ. Dominguez Hills

Career history: Library professional, college English instructor, journalist, literary agent, published author of three books, five chapbooks, and numerous articles, reviews, poems, and short stories

Hobbies/Personal interests: Travel, horror films, metaphysics, attending poetry readings, experimental theater, and punk rock concerts

Categories/Subjects that you are most enthusiastic about agenting: We love to agent books that make us want to run out and tell the world about the book and the author. We love novels that are exceedingly well written, with characters we want to spend time with; clever, high-concept ideas often with a good dose of humor; wonderful, fresh stories that draw us in, keep us turning the pages, and are just so darn fun to read. In nonfiction, we look for books that are fresh, commercial, high concept and promotable, from an author with a national platform. We're especially looking for narrative-driven nonfiction books about health and science topics and cultural history. In children's books, we seek authors and books with a unique voice and the right sensibilities for the market, whether quirky and fun or more serious. We are extremely selective about children's nonfiction. I particularly am interested in horror and dark fantasy fiction, offbeat literary and women's fiction, ethnic fiction; and nonfiction that is related to pop-culture topics, especially Goth and noir; and metaphysical writings, especially those related to Wicca, paganism, magick, goddess religion, and general New Age topics—as long as it is positive in tone.

Categories/Subjects writers shouldn't bother pitching to you: The agency does not represent screenplays, poetry, short stories, novellas, most novelty books, textbooks, or most memoirs, especially stories of abuse or addiction recovery. In fiction, dark fiction is fine; gore solely for the sake of shocking the reader is not for us.

If you were not an agent, what might you be doing instead: Writing, teaching, and traveling, which I pretty much do already

What's the best way for fiction writers to solicit your interest: Send us something smart, fresh, captivatingly written, and beautifully crafted. Write a book that is truly new and fills a need, not just a version of something that's currently popular.

My interests are very specific, so research them carefully before sending your work to me. List publications you've published in and organizations you belong to that demonstrate your interest in the field. For fiction: We are still accepting clients who are previously published by a known publisher. The agency is temporarily closed to queries from writers who are not published at book length, with the following exceptions: (1) Authors recommended by a client, published author, or editor who has read the work in question; (2) Authors we have met at conferences and from whom we have requested submissions; (3) Authors who have been published in quality small presses or magazines. We have had excellent success selling first-time novelists, but at this time we must concentrate on the needs of professional authors who need our intellectual property management skills and financial skills. If you meet these criteria, please query us, listing publishing credits with titles, publishers, and dates published. I prefer queries sent by ordinary post; include first three pages and SASE. Do not send queries by overnight service and never, ever by certified mail. Do not query more than one agent in our agency, whether by e-mail or post; we will make sure that your query reaches the right person. For nonfiction: Query with proposal. Note: We cannot review self-published works to evaluate moving them to mainstream publishers. Please send query letter by e-mail, including brief bio or CV, and the Market and Competition sections of your proposal.

Do you charge fees separate from your commission or offer nonagenting fee-based services: We do not offer nonagenting fee-based services. We do charge for some extraordinary expenses such as bank wires, overnight mail delivery, or posting books to foreign lands.

How and why did you become an agent: Because I was tired of seeing people signing book contracts without understanding them. I wanted to help authors, especially those I knew in the genre fiction and New Age arenas. On suggestion from Dan Hooker, Ashley Grayson took me on as a manuscript evaluator, reading the slush pile, and gradually I worked my way up to agent.

What are your favorite books, movies, and TV shows, and why: Favorite TV shows: currently, *Lost* and *Heroes*. Movies: My all-time favorite movies are *Repo Man*, *Casablanca*, and *Interview with the Vampire*. I also enjoyed *Pan's Labyrinth*.

Describe the client from hell, even if you don't have any: A person who is unprofessional—doesn't return calls or make deadlines. Someone who is not interested in being a professional writer but instead sees writing only as advancing an agenda or as a charity project; clients who listen to gossip and believe it instead of believing their agent. Not that I've ever heard of such a writer, of course.

Will our business exist as we know it in 10 years or so: Niche marketing, which is what I see already on MySpace and similar areas. When my students started wearing T-shirts of death metal bands from Outer Mongolia that I had never heard of, and they in turn had never heard of the MTV and VH1 rock bands I listen to, I realized that there had been a quantum shift in how people relate to entertainment in general. Maybe it will signal a return to the independent bookstore that caters to a particular clientele. We can only hope.

Agent's name: Ashley Grayson

Education: BS in physics

Career history: Computer sales, management consultant, founded Ashley Grayson Literary Agency in 1976

Hobbies/Personal interests: Languages, opera, gardening

Categories/Subjects that you are most enthusiastic about agenting: We love to agent books that make us want to run out and tell the world about the book and the author. We love novels that are exceedingly well written, with characters we want to spend time with; clever, high-concept ideas often with a good dose of humor; wonderful, fresh stories that draw us in, keep us turning the pages, and are just so darn fun to read. In nonfiction, we look for books that are fresh, commercial, high concept and promotable, from an author with a national platform. We're especially looking for narrative-driven nonfiction books about health and science topics and cultural history. In children's books, we seek authors and books with unique voice and the right sensibilities for the market, whether quirky and fun or more serious. We are extremely selective about children's nonfiction. I especially like strong, well-written literary and commercial fiction, historical fiction, dark fantasy, mysteries, thrillers, young adult, humorous or edgy children's fiction.

Categories/Subjects writers shouldn't bother pitching to you: The agency does not represent screenplays, poetry, short stories, novellas, most novelty books, textbooks, or most memoirs, especially stories of abuse or addiction recovery. In fiction, dark fiction is fine; gore solely for the sake of shocking the reader is not for us.

How and why did you become an agent: I love to read books and sell new ideas. The real reason I became an agent is that Judy-Lynn Del Rey (the late founder of the Del Rey imprint at Random House) told me in 1976 that I should. She had great insight—I'm still having a great time.

Describe the client from hell, even if you don't have any: Of course, we don't represent any writers from hell, but such a person is more interested in the celebrity of being an author than in actually writing books. Anyone who doesn't work on the next book until the present one sells. Any clients who want to second-guess their agent.

What's the best way for fiction writers to solicit your interest: Send us something smart, fresh, captivatingly written, and beautifully crafted. For fiction: We are still accepting clients who are previously published by a known publisher. The agency is temporarily closed to queries from writers who are not published at book length, with the following exceptions: (1) Authors recommended by a client, published author, or editor who has read the work in question; (2) Authors we have met at conferences and from whom we have requested submissions; (3) Authors who have been published in quality small presses or magazines. We have had excellent success selling first-time novelists, but at this time we must concentrate on the needs of professional authors who need our intellectual property management skills and financial skills. If you meet these criteria, please query us, listing publishing credits with titles, publishers, and dates published. Query by e-mail only. Include the first three pages of the manuscript in the body of your e-mail; do not send attachments unless requested.

For nonfiction: Query with proposal. Note: We cannot review self-published works to evaluate moving them to mainstream publishers. Please send query letter by e-mail, including brief bio or CV, and the Market and Competition sections of your proposal.

Do you charge fees separate from your commission or offer nonagenting fee-based services: We do not offer nonagenting fee-based services. We do charge for some extraordinary expenses such as bank wires, overnight mail delivery, or posting books to foreign lands.

THE AUGUST AGENCY

www.augustagency.com

Agent's name: Cricket Freeman

Career history: Cricket Freeman, cofounder and agent: After years as a business owner engaged in sales and marketing, Cricket redirected her creativity toward the writing business, freelancing for magazines (more adventure than money) and business clients (more money than adventure). For a time she even slaved daily as the editor-in-chief of a national full-color glossy. In 1991, Cricket intertwined her art education, business experience, and writing skills and established Possibilities Press to support small book publishers with writing, editing, design, and production services. Ever the entrepreneur, a decade later she shifted her focus exclusively to literary representation and founded the Christina Pechstein Agency. In 2004 she saw another fine opportunity to expand her business and her horizons and joined forces with Jeffery McGraw to launch the August Agency, where she operates from its headquarters in Florida.

Our company mind-set: Of any national literature, "the Augustan age" is considered the period of its highest state of excellence and refinement. The expression originated with the reign of Emperor Augustus, who fostered the golden age of Roman literature. Since then, the name has been ascribed to subsequent eras of great prosperity in artistic writing. The August Agency is founded on many of the same principles Augustus set in place to facilitate a stimulating venue where distinguished writers could flourish. More than just another literary and media management company in the business of selling creative projects, we approach the industry with a fresh point of view and innovative strategies that set us apart from other agencies. We firmly believe an agent is, among other things, an author's ultimate advocate, anchor, arbitrator, and advisor. At the August Agency, we not only embrace our authors' works but also the writers themselves and their careers.

What writers can expect from the August Agency: With our rich background of experience, we have developed a unique approach to the publishing industry that seems to work well for us and our authors. Our fundamental belief is that we are all in this together. Neither of us is the employer, nor the employee, and we don't treat each other that way. Instead, we prefer to think of both parties as business partners in a mutually thrilling venture. The August Agency is a nurturing place where we all learn from each other, sell a lot of books, and have fun along the way. Our primary commitment as agents is taking care of our authors, helping to get their proposals in the best shape possible, and effectively marketing their work to publishing houses and beyond. We encourage our authors to follow our lead: Be a team player, meet deadlines, honor contracts, and, no matter how anxious they are about their work, try to have reasonable expectations. While we cannot promise publication for every writer's project, we can guarantee that their work will be put in front of the right people at the right time with the right degree of passion and enthusiasm behind it.

Categories/Subjects that you are most enthusiastic about agenting: The August Agency accepts electronic queries exclusively. We actively pursue a diverse array of writers to represent, with an emphasis in the following areas: Media/current events (seasoned journalists receive special favor here); popular culture, arts, and entertainment; political science; self-help, health, and spirituality; lifestyle, family, and home (including cookbooks, diet, and fitness); science; social sciences; criminology and investigation; history; economics; business and technology; biographies and memoirs; creative narrative nonfiction. In particular, we favor persuasive and prescriptive works, each with a full-bodied narrative command and an undeniable contemporary relevance.

Categories/Subjects writers shouldn't bother pitching to you: At this time, we are not accepting submissions in the following areas: self-published works; screenplays; children's books; cozy mysteries; genre romance; horror; poetry; science fiction; fantasy; short story collections; Westerns; projects by blowhards, bigots, braggarts, bitches, and bastards!

What's the best way for fiction writers to solicit your interest: To submit, please visit www.augustagency.com for complete details of and any updates to our submission guidelines, which currently include sending an e-mail to submissions@augustagency.com containing the following: (1) The word *query* in the subject line; (2) A detailed summary of your book (one to two paragraphs only); (3) A chapter outline (for nonfiction only); (4) A brief paragraph explaining who you are and why you have chosen to write this particular book; (5) MOST IMPORTANT: The first 1,000 words or first chapter (note: this must be pasted within the body of your e-mail; all e-mails with unsolicited attachments or lack of this writing sample within the body of the e-mail may be deleted without being read); (6) The total page or word count of your completed manuscript; (7) Your full contact information (including telephone and e-mail address). If you want to be an ordinary writer, write an ordinary book. But if you want to be an extraordinary author, be prepared to go the extra mile. Our staff is made up of highly selective, seasoned publishing professionals who will give serious consideration to original, creative, and quality manuscripts from extraordinary authors. Due to the volume of submissions we receive, we are unable to respond to all incoming e-mail. However, please note that every query is read and thoroughly reviewed by our staff. If we are interested in your project, you should receive a response to your e-mail within two to three weeks. At that time you will receive further instructions on how to submit a full-length copy of your proposal. We appreciate the opportunity to review your work and look forward to hearing from you.

Do you charge fees separate from your commission or offer nonagenting fee-based services: We do not charge a reading fee. The August Agency retains a commission of 15 percent of all domestic sales and 20 percent of all foreign, film, dramatic, merchandising, and other sales.

Agent's name: Jeffery McGraw. Jeffery directs the New York operations of The August Agency, LLC. He brings to the company a wide range of experience in publishing and television, with a concentrated background in editorial, legal, publicity, and content sales. He has worked for magazine and book publishers, large and small, including *Soap Opera Weekly* as contributing reporter, HarperCollins as editor, Harry N. Abrams as publicity manager, and Leisure Publishing as magazine columnist. Throughout his career he has had the privilege to work with many different types of books—from exquisite art and illustrated coffee table tomes to *New York Times* best-selling fiction and nonfiction—and an equally diverse roster of remarkable authors and artists—among them Nancy Bartholomew, Elizabeth Berg, Cathy East Dubowski, Patricia Gaffney, Olivia Goldsmith, Andy Goldsworthy, Al Hirschfeld, Mary-Kate and Ashley Olsen, Bill O'Reilly, Joanne Pence, Betty Rollin, Ben Schonzeit, and Hunt Slonem.

Categories/Subjects that you are most enthusiastic about agenting: The August Agency accepts electronic queries exclusively. We actively pursue a diverse array of writers to represent, with an emphasis in the following areas: Media/current events (seasoned journalists receive special favor here); popular culture, arts, and entertainment; political science; self-help, health, and spirituality; lifestyle, family, and home (including cookbooks, diet, and fitness); science; social sciences; criminology and investigation; history; economics; business and technology; biographies and memoirs; creative narrative nonfiction. In particular, we favor persuasive and prescriptive works, each with a full-bodied narrative command and an undeniable contemporary relevance.

Categories/Subjects writers shouldn't bother pitching to you: At this time, we are not accepting submissions in the following areas: Self-published works; screenplays; children's books; cozy mysteries; genre romance; horror; poetry; science fiction; fantasy; short story collections; Westerns; projects by blowhards, bigots, braggarts, bitches, and bastards!

What's the best way for fiction writers to solicit your interest: To submit, please visit www.augustagency.com for complete details of and any updates to our submission guidelines, which currently include sending an e-mail to submissions@ augustagency.com containing the following: (1) The word *query* in the subject line; (2) A detailed summary of your book (one to two paragraphs only); (3) A chapter outline (for nonfiction only); (4) A brief paragraph explaining who you are and why you have chosen to write this particular book; (5) MOST IMPORTANT: The first 1,000 words or first chapter (note: this must be pasted within the body of your e-mail; all e-mails with unsolicited attachments or lack of this writing sample within the body of the e-mail may be deleted without being read); (6) The total page or word count of your completed manuscript; (7) Your full contact information (including telephone and e-mail address). If you want to be an ordinary writer, write an ordinary book. But if you want to be an extraordinary author, be prepared to go the extra mile. Our staff is made up of highly selective, seasoned publishing professionals who will give serious consideration to original, creative, and quality manuscripts from extraordinary authors. Due to the volume of submissions we receive, we are unable to respond to all incoming e-mail. However, please note that every query is read and thoroughly reviewed by our staff. If we are interested in your project, you should receive a response to your e-mail within two to three weeks. At that time you will receive further instructions on how to submit a full-length copy of your proposal. We appreciate the opportunity to review your work and look forward to hearing from you.

Do you charge fees separate from your commission or offer nonagenting fee-based services: We do not charge a reading fee. The August Agency retains a commission of 15 percent of all domestic sales and 20 percent of all foreign, film, dramatic, merchandising, and other sales.

BARER LITERARY, LLC

270 Lafayette Street, Suite 1504, New York, NY 10023
212-691-3513 | fax: 212-691-3540
www.barerliterary.com

> **Agent's name:** Julie Barer
> **E-mail:** submissions@barerliterary.com
> **Born:** New York, New York
> **Education:** Vassar College
> **Career history:** After working for six years at the prestigious New York literary agency Sanford J. Greenburger Associates, I left to start my own agency, Barer Literary, in December 2004. I represent a wide range of fiction writers who publish across the literary spectrum, and I am especially attracted to voice-driven projects that feel original and fresh. My list is extremely selective, and I am interested in developing long-term relationships with my clients. I attended the Jerusalem Book Fair as an Agent Fellow in 2003, and I am a member of the Association of Author Representatives. Before becoming an agent, I worked at Shakespeare & Co. Booksellers in New York City.
>
> **Categories/Subjects that you are most enthusiastic about agenting:** Literary fiction, historical fiction, women's fiction, international fiction and nonfiction, narrative nonfiction, history, biography, memoir, travel

Categories/Subjects writers shouldn't bother pitching to you: Barer Literary does NOT handle the following: health and fitness; business, investing, or finance; sports; mind, body, and spirit; reference; thrillers or suspense; military; romance; children's books, picture books, or young-adult books; screenplays.

If you were not an agent, what might you be doing instead: As old-fashioned as it sounds, if I weren't an agent, I'd love to own a bookstore.

What's the best way for fiction writers to solicit your interest: Do your research and make sure that our agency represents the kind of book you've written. Then send a well-written and professional query letter with a self-addressed stamped envelope.

Do you charge fees separate from your commission or offer nonagenting fee-based services: No

What are some representative titles that you have sold: *Then We Came to the End* by Joshua Ferris (Little, Brown & Co.); *Still Life with Husband* by Lauren Fox (Alfred A. Knopf); *What You Have Left* by Will Allison (Free Press); *Finding Nouf* by Zoe Ferraris (Houghton Mifflin); *People I Wanted to Be: Stories* by Gina Ochsner (Houghton Mifflin)

How and why did you become an agent: I became an agent first and foremost because I love to read, and I love the moment of discovering a wonderful novel or story that no one else has read yet and being the person who helps bring that book out into the world. I also love being able to work closely with writers and help shape their work, as well as their careers. Being an agent allows me to be involved with so many aspects of a book's life—from editing and placing a book with the right publisher to helping conceptualize cover art and promotion and beyond.

BLEECKER STREET ASSOCIATES, INC.

217 Thompson St., #519, New York, NY 10012
212-677-4492 | fax: 212-388-0001

Agent's name: Agnes Birnbaum
E-mail: Bleeckerst@hotmail.com
Born: Budapest, Hungary
Career history: 16 years as editor before starting agency in 1984; senior editor at Pocket, NAL; editor-in-chief of Award Books, later a division of Berkley

Categories/Subjects that you are most enthusiastic about agenting: History, biography, science, investigative reporting, true crime, health, psychology, true adventure, women's issues, also mystery/suspense, women's fiction

Categories/Subjects writers shouldn't bother pitching to you: Poetry, science fiction, Western, children's, film/TV scripts, plays, professional/academic books

What's the best way for writers to solicit your interest: Short letter with SASE; no fax or e-mail

Do you charge reading or management fees: No

What categories do you represent, by percentages: Fiction: 10 percent, Nonfiction: 90 percent

How and why did you become an agent: Love to read

What can a writer do to increase the odds of you becoming his or her agent: Send a great short letter about the book and themselves. We don't respond without an SASE.

How do you feel about editors and publishers: I like them; having been an editor, I can understand their problems.

What are your favorite books, movies, and TV shows, and why: The movie *The Big Lebowski*—wonderfully funny

What are some representative titles that you have sold: *The Indifferent Stars Above* by Daniel James Brown (Morrow); *Surviving the College Search* (St. Martin's); *Inside the Nazi War Machine* (NAL); *Fossil Hunter* (Palgrave Macmillan); *Everyday Ethics* (Viking); *Ophelia Speaks* (HarperCollins); *How the South Could Have Won the Civil War* (Crown); *Sex, Lies, and Handwriting* (Simon & Schuster); *Puppy Miracles* (Adams); *Big, Beautiful, and Pregnant* (Marlowe & Co.); *Buddha Baby* (Avon); *Phantom Warrior* (Berkley); *The Flag, the Poet, and the Song* (Dutton)

THE BLUMER LITERARY AGENCY, INC.

809 W. 181st Street, Suite 201, New York, NY 10033
212-947-3040 | fax: 212-947-0460

Agent's name: Olivia B. Blumer

E-mail: blumerliterary@earthlink.net

Born: Long Island, New York

Education: BA, English from Goucher College

Career history: Worked for three publishers (Doubleday, Atheneum, and Warner Books) before becoming an agent 15 years ago

Hobbies/Personal interests: Gardening, food and cooking, travel, tennis, reading (believe it or not)

Categories/Subjects that you are most enthusiastic about agenting: Memoirs with a larger purpose, expository books on social and cultural phenomena, books that spark interest in both ordinary and extraordinary things, groundbreaking guides/how-to books, novels that explore the unexplored (in literature and in life)

Categories/Subjects writers shouldn't bother pitching to you: Victim lit, PhD theses turned "intellectual" exposés, opportunistic books with no larger picture, science fiction, category romance

If you were not an agent, what might you be doing instead: Animal rescue

What's the best way for writers to solicit your interest: A well-crafted, short, unambiguous letter with neither hype nor typos. Just the facts, please.

Do you charge reading or management fees: No

What categories do you represent, by percentages: Nonfiction: 60 percent, fiction: 40 percent

What are the most common mistakes writers make when pitching to you: Too much author bio and not enough information about the actual book (or vice versa); self-congratulatory author bio—don't tell me that all your friends love your book; nonstandardized, small (less than 12-point) type that is not double-spaced drives us crazy!

Describe the client from hell, even if you don't have any: Those deaf to suggestions and those eager to please; whiners

How would you describe the perfect client: Thick-skinned, talented, patient, hardworking, long-term vs. short-term thinker who is not looking to get rich quick, attentive to suggestions, and thorough in their execution

How and why did you become an agent: A chance to invest in my own taste

What can a writer do to increase the odds of you becoming his or her agent: Don't nag; let your writing speak for itself.

How would you describe what you do as an agent to someone (or something) from another planet: Matchmaker, manager of expectations, career counselor

How do you feel about editors and publishers: Majority are overworked and risk averse.

On a personal level, what do you think people like and dislike about you: Dislike: Direct, impatient; Like: Passionate, organized, eclectic taste, lots of varied experience in the book biz from retail to rights to publicity to editorial

---

BOOKS & SUCH LITERARY AGENCY

52 Mission Circle, Suite 122, PMB 170, Santa Rosa, CA 94509
www.booksandsuch.biz

Agents' names: Wendy Lawton, Rachel Zurakowski, Etta Wilson, Janet Kobobel Grant

E-mail: representation@booksandsuch.biz

Categories/Subjects that you are most enthusiastic about agenting: Adult fiction and nonfiction, teen, middle readers

Categories/Subjects writers shouldn't bother pitching to you: Fantasy, sci-fi, paranormal, gift books, poetry, plays

If you were not an agent, what might you be doing instead: Edit fiction

What's the best way for fiction writers to solicit your interest: Have a short, snappy hook that piques my interest. A great title also helps.

What's the best way for nonfiction writers to solicit your interest: Focus the idea on a specific but significantly populated group of potential readers and a unique approach to a perennially popular topic.

Do you charge reading or management fees: No

What are the most common mistakes writers make when pitching to you: Not being able to talk about an idea succinctly. I don't want to hear an entire plotline nor an entire history of why someone wrote a manuscript.

Describe the client from hell, even if you don't have any: E-mails several times a day; suffers from huge insecurity, and needs to be assured several times a week that, yes, publishing is insane but he/she is not; unrealistic expectations in terms of the financial reward of writing; unwilling to take criticism of work; doesn't meet deadlines; isn't willing to do the hard work of actually writing a great book—and a great proposal.

What's your definition of a great client: An innate sense of where the market is and how to write accordingly; capable of putting together a dazzling title and concept; works hard at improving the craft; has strong ideas on how to publicize him/herself as well as his/her writing; has the smarts to know when we need to talk and when we don't; relates well with everyone.

What can a writer do to increase the odds of you becoming his or her agent: Study our website to learn what type of writing really interests us and query us in the way we ask to be queried. An author who thinks his/her work is worthy of making an exception to the query process is just asking to be turned down.

How and why did you become an agent: As an editor, I found what I loved most about the publishing process was discovering authors and introducing them to the reading world. Eventually it occurred to me that agents do that a much higher percentage of the time than editors.

In your opinion, what do editors think of you: I've often been told that I'm tough but fair and that I have good instincts about what each publishing house is looking for.

What are some representative titles that your agency has sold: *Hideaway* series by Robin Jones Gunn (Simon & Schuster); *One Simple Act* by Debbie Macomber (Simon & Schuster); *A Woman Named Sage* by DiAnn Mills (Zondervan); *Breach of Trust* by DiAnn Mills (Tyndale); *Smotherly Love* by Debi Stack (Thomas Nelson); *Unleashing the Courageous Faith* by Paul Coughlin (Bethany House); *Murder by Family* by Kent Whitaker (Simon & Schuster); *Getting Old Ain't for Wimps* by Karen O'Connor (Harvest House); *Having a Mary Heart in a Martha World* by Joanna Weaver (WaterBrook); *Summer of Light* by Dale Cramer (Bethany House)

BRADFORD LITERARY AGENCY

5694 Mission Center Road, #347, San Diego, CA 92108
619-521-1201
www.bradfordlit.com

Agent's name: Laura Bradford
E-mail: laura@bradfordlit.com
Born: February 6, San Leandro, California
Education: BA in English Literature, University of California at San Diego

Career history: I came to agenting pretty much straight out of college. I started with my first agency as an intern less than six months after I graduated.

Categories/Subjects that you are most enthusiastic about agenting: Commercial fiction, specifically genre fiction. I love romance (all subgenres), mystery, thrillers, women's fiction, urban fantasy, and young adult. I do some select nonfiction as well.

Categories/Subjects writers shouldn't bother pitching to you: Westerns, horror, epic fantasy, Christian fiction/nonfiction, poetry, screenplays, New Age, picture books/early reader/middle grade

If you were not an agent, what might you be doing instead: I went to college as a premed major. The original plan was to go into oncology. I switched to English in my second year, and I haven't looked back since.

Do you charge fees separate from your commission or offer nonagenting fee-based services: No

What are some representative titles that you have sold: Lauren Dane, *Bound by Magic* (Berkley Sensation); Ann Aguirre, *Enclave* (Feiwel and Friends); Juliana Stone, *Wicked Road to Hell* (Avon); Katie Lane, *Catch Me a Cowboy* (Grand Central); Elisabeth Naughton, *Tempted* (Dorchester); Beth Kery, *Claiming Colleen* (Harlequin Special Edition); Ava Gray, *Skin Dive* (Berkley Sensation); Megan Hart, *All Fall Down* (Mira); Stacey Kade, *Queen of the Dead* (Hyperion); Anya Bast, *Midnight Enchantment* (Berkley Sensation); Maggie Robinson, *Mistress by Marriage* (Kensington Brava); Ellen Connor, *Daybreak* (Berkley/Ace); Emma Lang, *Circle Eight: Matthew* (Kensington Brava); Jenn Bennett, *Summoning the Night* (Pocket); Karina Cooper, *All Things Wicked* (Avon); Jennifer Echols, *The One That I Want* (Simon Pulse); Soraya Lane, *Rodeo Daddy* (Harlequin Romance); Suzanne Lazear, *Innocent Darkness* (Flux)

How and why did you become an agent: Once upon a time, I thought I might like to be a novelist, and I joined Romance Writers of America so I could learn what was what. At my first meeting, the speaker was a literary agent, which was something I had never heard of before. I was instantly fascinated. I researched what the job was and how to go about getting started. It seemed like the perfect job for someone who loved books and business, and it would allow me to be around my favorite people: authors. Despite the fact that one of the agents I called about an internship told me that agenting was the worst job on earth and that I shouldn't pursue it, I persevered. Within a couple of months, I had landed an internship with Manus and Associates (500 miles away from where I was living). I quit my job and moved. I worked as a bookstore manager to support myself while I was an unpaid intern. I lived in a relative's house for free until I finally got officially hired at the agency as an assistant. A few years later, after becoming an agent, I struck out on my own so I could focus on genre fiction.

How do you feel about writers: They are crazy and I love them. Just kidding (about the crazy part).

How do you really feel about editors: I think that they are in this business, like

I am, because they love it. I have a lot of respect for that kind of passion in the work-place. If they didn't care about this business…well, there are easier jobs out there.

What are your favorite books, movies, and TV shows, and why: I don't watch a ton of TV, and my movie tastes are all over the map (but nothing too scary, too gory, or too highfalutin, aka artsy). As for books, it is much easier to name my favorite authors: Anne Stuart, Linda Howard, Lisa Kleypas, Jennifer Cruisie, Julie Garwood, Susan Elizabeth Phillips, Janet Evanovich, Kathy Reichs.

Describe the client from hell, even if you don't have any: I think writers come in infinite variety, and I am pleased to work with a lot of different "types." As for some characteristics I don't particularly love…it is hard to work with someone with unrealistic expectations, someone who isn't a team player (and publishing IS a team sport), someone who does not respect his or her deadlines. My least favorite characteristic of all? Someone who doesn't comport themselves professionally in public. That includes online dealings.

What's the best way for writers to solicit your interest: A simple, professional query letter is very important—one that is specific, articulate, and concise. I don't need an author to be zany to grab my attention…Just cut right to the heart of what your manuscript is about and give me a strong hook. Don't be vague. As far as sub-missions go, I only take queries via e-mail. Please e-mail a query letter along with the first chapter of your manuscript and a synopsis. Please be sure to include the genre and word count in your cover letter.

Are you optimistic, pessimistic, neutral, or catatonic about the book biz in the future: I am optimistic as a general rule, and I definitely feel optimistic about the future of publishing. Judging by the pace of my own sales this year, things seem to be moving in a delightfully positive direction.

Explain what you like and dislike about your job: I love that my days are totally varied. I love the fellowship of being around creative, talented people. I love the sat-isfaction of being part of something special when I see my authors' books on the bookshelves. As far as what I dislike…I don't think anyone really likes to be a part of disappointing people, and agents hand out A LOT of rejection. I REALLY don't like whenever I get a nastygram from an author who is angry about me passing on their work. It is surprisingly common and it is unnecessary, unprofessional, and unpleasant.

CARDENAS LITERARY SERVICES

10608 Brookline Pl NW, Albuquerque, NM 87114
www.cardenasliteraryservices.com

Agent's name: Melissa Cardenas
E-mail: cardenasliterary@gmail.com
Categories/Subjects that you are most enthusiastic about agenting: Mystery, thriller/horror, crime/true crime, paranormal, suspense, historical fiction, and nonfiction

What's the best way for writers to solicit your interest: Submissions may be made through e-mail or traditional mail service. If mail is sent through snail mail, it must be sent certified or return receipt requested. To submit a manuscript for acceptance, send only the first three (3) chapters along with a query letter and author bio.

Born: May 10, 1980, in Austin, TX

Education: Associates degree in business management

Career history: My journey as an editor began during my senior year in high school. I was approached by a number of classmates to help with editing their senior thesis papers. Soon thereafter, several others asked for my assistance with their college admittance letters. I realized that with my love for reading and my gift of editing written works, I could make a living being an editor. It took some time to become established, however, and I had to prove myself with freelancing and odd editorial jobs. I have literally edited hundreds of resumes. When the opportunity to afford college presented itself, I jumped at the chance. I had my choice to gain a degree in literature but decided, instead, to pursue a degree in business. My goal was to run my own agency. Now, 15 years have passed since my first thesis paper, and I own Cardenas Literary Services. And my love of reading is still just as strong as ever.

Hobbies/Personal interests: I love anything and everything about the paranormal. While I have yet to venture into true ghost hunting, I plan on embarking on that adventure in the near future. I also enjoy photography, although not portrait photography. I am a bit of a thrill seeker as well. The idea of jumping out of a perfectly good airplane is exciting. Anything that gets my adrenaline pumping, please, sign me up!

Categories/Subjects writers shouldn't bother pitching to you: Self-help, academia, technology, cookbooks, astrology, occult

If you were not an agent, what might you be doing instead: If I weren't doing this, I would probably work in some boring computer job. The only other thing I do besides read is mess with computers. I suppose if I had to do something else, it ought to be something I know something about.

Do you charge fees separate from your commission or offer nonagenting fee-based services: My services as an agent are strictly commission based. The editing side of my business is another deal altogether.

What are some representative titles that you have sold: None. After 15 years in editing, I have decided to expand my business into the agenting field. I do, however, have several authors ready to be published.

How and why did you become an agent: I became an agent simply by deciding to take the step forward. My decision in doing so was based solely on the desire to help authors have a chance to see their dream of becoming a published author a reality.

How do you feel about writers: Writers are who keep me busy. They are unique in their writing, just as unique as the characters they invent.

How do you feel about editors and publishers: Being an editor myself, I understand how crucial editing is in the literary process. Editing runs a fine line between too much and not enough. A good editor knows how to walk the line with confidence. Publishers are the proverbial stairways to the fountains of gold. An author must climb that stairway, but it is steep ascension. I respect the job of the publishers to find the best sellers among the thousands of submissions received.

How would you describe what you do as an agent to someone (or something) from another planet: My job is pretty simple. I read…a lot. As an editor, I read slowly, nitpicking every detail until I am pleased with the result. As an agent, I spend a great deal of time researching publishers to find the right one for my clients and being the liaison between them.

What are your favorite books, movies, and TV shows, and why: My favorite books, or, more specifically, genres, are suspense, crime fiction, and paranormal. I love the works of Dean Koontz and Patricia Cornwell. Reading has always been a passion for me. As for movies, that list could go on forever. The term *movie guru* does not even begin to cover it, but if I were to chose a favorite, *Ever After* with Drew Barrymore and Anjelica Huston. My guilty pleasure movie, however, is *Independence Day*. Please do not try to understand; I have no idea either. As for television, I watch only one show, *Ghost Hunters*. Since the induction of reality television infiltrating every station, I have lost my desire to watch almost everything. While *Ghost Hunters* is considered a reality show, it covers one of my favorite things: the paranormal.

Describe the client from hell, even if you don't have any: In my eyes, the "writer from hell" is a writer who refuses to accept constructive criticism. When a person is not open to new ideas, it becomes frustrating, and, to make matters worse, it is hard to explain to your client why their book will never sell when they refuse to consider something different.

Describe yourself: Why does this question always make me feel like I'm speed dating? Well, I am total romantic. I love romantic comedies and Disney movies. I have an adventurous spirit. I love to read. I am a fantastic cook. My biggest pet peeve is reality TV and people who emulate anything resembling what they have learned from these intelligence-sucking shows. I am blunt and have even been accused of completely lacking the skill of "sugar coating." It has been my experience that people want to know the truth, even when they don't want to know. What it comes down to is I am funny, I love to laugh, I love to enjoy life, and I love to love.

Describe the publisher and/or editor from hell: An editor is supposed to help polish a manuscript to its full potential to become a prospective best seller. A publisher is supposed to pick out the best seller. The one thing that gets me going is when either one of these is not consistent. When an editor begins to slack in their work because they accepted a manuscript they probably should have left alone, or a publisher fluctuates too much in what they do accept, it makes my work harder.

What's the best way for writers to solicit your interest: I want every writer to come dressed in cowboy outfits and sing their first chapter in true honky-tonk style. I am kidding entirely. Please do not do that. I will sic my ankle-biting dachshund on you. I prefer receiving pitches in a standard, laid-back manner. I do not want bells and whistles. I like things simple. Give me the first three chapters, an author bio (or writer resume), and a hook. That is all I need. I give every manuscript I receive a chance. If you have already self-published, please do not send me the book. Send me the regular print form.

Will e-readers significantly change the business: Absolutely, but I feel it will be for the better. With the rise of technology, young readers have begun to slowly slip away. Now with e-readers, people have the ability to combine technology with the written word. Granted, it is hard to curl up with a flat screen, but that is why we have pillows.

Are you optimistic, pessimistic, neutral, or catatonic about the book biz in the future: I am fully optimistic. Technology is booming, authors are becoming more and more imaginative, and readers are pouring out from everywhere.

Explain what you like and dislike about your job: I absolutely love my job. I enjoy reading immensely. I love helping people realize a dream to become a published author. The one thing I do not like about my job is having to turn manuscripts down.

Describe a book you might like writing: My favorite genre of writing is true crime, especially murder mysteries. I love the research and the real passion behind the stories as told by each person affected. Mark Twain said it best: Truth is stranger than fiction, but it is because fiction is obliged to stick to possibilities; truth isn't. It never ceases to amaze me what one human can do to another. One day, I hope to find that event, that one person who has a true story to be told.

CASTIGLIA LITERARY AGENCY

1155 Camino del Mar, Del Mar, CA 92014
www.castigliaagency.com

Agent's name: Julia Castiglia

Categories/Subjects writers shouldn't bother pitching to you: Horror, fantasy, poetry

If you were not an agent, what might you be doing instead: Making movies, gardening, reading, traveling, cooking, and lying on the beach

What's the best way for fiction writers to solicit your interest: Query letter, two pages of sample writing plus a synopsis, publishing credits

What's the best way for nonfiction writers to solicit your interest: Query letter listing credentials, education, and experience plus any marketing ability, connections, etc.

Do you charge reading or management fees: No

What are the most common mistakes writers make when pitching to you: Unprofessional presentation, spelling errors, lack of knowledge about the publishing industry; lack of information about themselves; calling instead of writing; lack of brevity; submitting more than one project at a time to more than one agent in our office

Describe the client from hell, even if you don't have any: Not listening to our advice, not trusting our judgment; telling us what to do and how to do it

What's your definition of a great client: Appreciative, loyal, trusting, trustworthy, knowing that we care deeply about their work; sense of humor, sends chocolates

What can a writer do to increase the odds of you becoming his or her agent: Write a query that will knock our socks off; be referred by editors, clients, other professionals, or simply be a brilliant writer.

How and why did you become an agent: It was my destiny.

How would you describe what you do as an agent to someone (or something) from another planet: We sell manuscripts from writers unknown and known to publishers who magically turn them into books.

How do you feel about editors and publishers: Thank God for all of them.

How do you feel about writers: It depends if they can write.

What do you see in the near future for book publishing: I don't want to think about it.

What are your favorite books, movies, and TV shows, and why: *Child 44*, *The Perfect Storm*, *Atonement*, *The Glass Castle*, *The Nature of Air and Water*, *Motherless Brooklyn*, *The Devil in the White City*. TV shows: *House*, *24*, design and architecture shows, chopping block movies, *Slumdog Millionaire*, *Empire of the Sun*, *La Strada*, *Notes on a Scandal*, *The Reader*

In your opinion, what do editors think of you: They respect and like us. We are consummate professionals, aggressive when we need to be but always polite and pleasant. They recognize integrity, and they are aware of our good reputation.

On a personal level, what do you think people like and dislike about you: Everyone loves us; why wouldn't they? Our friends think we have a very glamorous job. We don't tell them the truth.

What are some representative titles that your agency has sold: *The Islanders* (HarperCollins) by Sandra Rodriguez Barron; *Freefall* by Reese Hirsch (Berkley); *America Libre* by Raul Ramos y Sanchez (Grand Central); *Why Did He Cheat on Me?* by Rona Subotnik (Adams Media); *The Leisure Seeker* by Michael Zadoorian (Morrow/Harper); *Waiting for the Apocalypse* by Veronica Chater (Norton); *From Splendor to Revolution* by Julia Gelardi (St. Martin's); *Beautiful: The Life of Hedy Lamarr* by Stephen Shearer (St. Martin's); *Forever L.A.* by Doug Keister (Gibbs Smith); *Barry Dixon Interiors* by Brian Coleman (Gibbs Smith); *Wesley the Owl* by Stacey O'Brien (Free Press/Simon & Schuster)

Agent's name: Deborah Ritchken
How and why did you become an agent: The Devil made me do it.

Agent's name: Winifred Golden
How and why did you become an agent: I thought it was the CIA.

THE CHARLOTTE GUSAY LITERARY AGENCY

10532 Blythe Avenue, Los Angeles, CA 90064
310-559-0831 | fax: 310-559-2639
www.gusay.com

Agent's name: Charlotte Gusay
E-mail: gusay1@ca.rr.com
Education: BA in English literature/theater; General Secondary Life Teaching Credential
Career history: Taught in secondary schools for several years. Interest in film-making developed. Founded (with partners) a documentary film company in the early 1970s. Soon became interested in the fledgling audio-publishing business. Became the managing editor for the Center for Cassette Studies/Scanfax, producing audio programs, interviews, and documentaries. In 1976 founded George Sand, Books, in West Hollywood, one of the most prestigious and popular bookshops in Los Angeles. It specialized in fiction and poetry, sponsored readings, and events. Patronized by the Hollywood community's glitterati and literati, George Sand, Books, was the place to go when looking for the "best" literature and quality books. It was here that the marketing of books was preeminent. It closed in 1987. Two years later the Charlotte Gusay Literary Agency was opened.
Hobbies/Personal interests: Gardens and gardening, architecture, magazines (a magazine junkie), good fiction (especially juicy novels), reading, anything French, anything Greek
Categories/Subjects that you are most enthusiastic about agenting: I enjoy both fiction and nonfiction. Prefer commercial, mainstream but quality material. Especially like books that can be marketed as film material. Also, like material that is innovative, unusual, eclectic, nonsexist. Will consider literary fiction with cross-over potential. TCGLA is a signatory to the Writers' Guild and so represents screenplays and screenwriters selectively. I enjoy unusual children's books and illustrators but have begun to limit children's projects to young-adult novels, especially if they have film possibilities.
Categories/Subjects writers shouldn't bother pitching to you: Prefer not [to] consider science fiction or horror, poetry or short stories (with few exceptions), or the romance genres per se.
If you were not an agent, what might you be doing instead: I would travel to Istanbul and become a foreign agent. I would reread all of Marcel Proust. I would reread Jane Austen. Work on my French. Study Greek (actually I do now). Play the piano. Tap dance.
What's the best way for writers to solicit your interest: First: Send one-page query letter with SASE. Then: After we've read your query and if we request your material (book, proposal, whatever it is), note the following guidelines: For fiction: Send approximately the first 50 pages and a synopsis, along with your credentials

(i.e., list of previous publications, and/or list of magazine articles, and/or any pertinent information, education, and background). For nonfiction: Send a proposal consisting of an overview, chapter outline, author biography, sample chapters, marketing and audience research, and survey of the competition. Important note: Material will not be returned without an SASE. Second important note: Seduce me with humor and intelligence. Always be polite and professional.

Do you charge reading or management fees: No reading fee. No editorial fees. When a client is signed, the client and I share out-of-pocket expenses 50/50. In certain cases, I charge a nominal processing fee, especially when considering unsolicited submissions decided upon as and when queries arrive in my office. (Note: Charlotte—ever the teacher—sponsors a mentoring internship program for young college graduates interested in entering and training in the publishing/book business. Any such processing fees help fund this program.)

What categories do you represent, by percentages: Nonfiction, 40 percent; fiction, 15 percent; children's, 10 percent; books to film/screenplays, 35 percent

What are the most common mistakes writers make when pitching to you: Clients must understand the role of agents and that agents represent only the material they feel they can best handle or—more importantly—material they are completely enthusiastic about and feel they can sell. Potential clients must understand that any given agent may or may not be an editor, a sounding board, a proposal writer, or a guidance counselor. Because of the enormous amount of submissions, queries, and proposals, we most often have only time to say yes or no to your project. Above all, when clients don't understand why in the world we can't respond to a multiple submission with regard to their "900-page novel" within a few days, all we can do is shake our heads and wonder if that potential client realizes we are human.

Describe the client from hell, even if you don't have any: The client from hell is the one who does not understand the hard work we do for our clients. Or the one who refuses to build a career in a cumulative manner but rather goes from one agent to the next and so on. Or clients who circulate their manuscripts without cooperating with their agents. Or those who think it all happens by magic. Or those who have not done their homework and who do not understand the nuts and bolts of the business.

How would you describe the perfect client: The perfect client is the one who cooperates; the one who appreciates how hard we work for our clients; the one who submits everything on time, in lean, edited, proofed, professional copies of manuscripts and professionally prepared proposals; clients who understand the crucial necessity of promoting their own books until the last one in the publisher's warehouse is gone; those who work hard on their book selling in tandem with the agent. The author/agent relationship, like a marriage, is a cooperative affair built on mutual trust, and it is cumulative. The dream client will happily do absolutely whatever is necessary to reach the goal.

How and why did you become an agent: With a great entrepreneurial spirit, cold calls, seat-of-the-pants daring, 12 years in the retail book business (as founder and owner of a prestigious book shop in Los Angeles called George Sand, Books), and 25 years of business experience, including producing films and editing spoken-word audio programs. Agenting is the most challenging and rewarding experience I've ever had.

What can a writer do to increase the odds of you becoming his or her agent: A writer must be professional. Be courteous. Be patient. Understand that we are human. Pay careful attention to the kinds of projects we represent. Query us only if your project fits with our agency profile. Know what we are overworked, always swamped with hundreds of queries. Know that we love and understand writers.

How would you describe what you do as an agent to someone (or something) from another planet: My job is essentially that of a bookseller. I sell books. To publishers, producers, and ultimately to the retail book trade. Sometimes, I develop a book idea. Sometimes, I develop someone's story, help the writer get a proposal written. I've even written proposals myself because I believed strongly in the book, or the person's story, or the salability of an idea. For fiction writers with potential, I sometimes make cursory suggestions. However, I must be clear—I am not an editor. Most often I help writers find a professional editor to work on their novel before it is submitted to a publishing house. That is key. The manuscript must be pristine. I repeat: A manuscript must be complete, polished, and professional.

How do you feel about editors and publishers: Publishers continue to be in great flux and continue to have a difficult time these days. The "conglomeratizing" and "electrifying" aspects of the publishing business are taking over the publishing/book businesses. It's going to be very interesting to see where especially the electronics of the book business ends up. However, still and all, publishers are still and always looking for the next great writer, the next great book, and a way to make both successful. (That means making money.) Editors are still overworked and underpaid. Therefore, if you wish to have the best chance of having your work accepted, you must do their work for them and don't complain. That is the reality of the editor's milieu. Editors are usually very smart. Most always, if they're any good, they are temperamental, and they know their particular publisher's market. If interested, they know how to make your work fit into their list. Do what your editor (and agent) tells you. No argument. The publishing business continues to be overpublished. I read somewhere that 240,000 books were published within the last year. Be reminded that only 1 percent of manuscripts submitted to publishing houses were actually accepted for publication (according to Dee Power, coauthor with Brian Hill, in their book *The Making of a Best Seller*).

What do you think the future holds for writers, publishers, and agents: As long as there is intelligent life on Earth, there will be writers who must express themselves in whatever way or medium they will. As to whether that work will be published—in book form by a major, established publisher paying actual money for it—is doubtful. I repeat my note above, only 1 percent of manuscripts submitted to publishing houses will actually be accepted for publication. If you have an agent who is enthusiastic about your work or your book, you will certainly increase your odds of being in that percentage. Remember that most major publishing houses will accept manuscripts only from agents.

What are your favorite books, movies, and TV shows, and why: Recent films and not-so-recent films I liked: *Shakespeare in Love, Slam, Chasing Amy,* Bas Luhrman's *Romeo and Juliet,* the Marx Brothers films. A few of my all-time favorite films are *Runaway Train, The English Patient, Dr. Zhivago, Cabaret, Rebel Without a Cause, Woman in the Dunes.* A few favorite television shows: Any *Masterpiece Theatre; American Idol, Entourage, Weeds.* And many, many books—a few all-time favorites: Austen's *Pride and Prejudice;* Hemingway's *The Sun Also Rises; The English Patient, Dr. Zhivago, Housekeeping,* and many more. The one thing these have in common for me: They held my attention and I was moved in some important way, and the writing is superb.

On a personal level, what do you think people like and dislike about you: People like my intelligence and enthusiasm. In my agent mode, people don't like my selectivity or they don't understand it. If I reject a project, often the writer feels bleak and…well…rejected. Hopefully, writers will come to understand that I accept projects very selectively. That is important for writers to understand.

What are some representative titles that you have sold: *Wild West 2.0: Reputation and Privacy on the Digital Frontier—The Battle to Take Back Your Good Name and Regain Your Privacy* (AMACOM Books); *Mother Ash* (Red Hen Press) and *American Fugue* (Etruscan Press), both by National Endowment of the Arts International Award Recipient Alexis Stamatis (from Greece); *Honesty Sells: How to Make More Money and Increase Business Profits* (John Wiley & Sons, Inc., Publishers); *Forty-One Seconds: From Terror to Freedom* (Presidio Press/Ballantine); *Richard Landry Estates* (Oro Editions); *Beachglass* (St. Martin's Press); *The Dead Emcee Scrolls: The Lost Teachings of Hip Hop* (MTV/Simon & Schuster); *Said the Shotgun to the Head* (MTV/Simon & Schuster); *Meeting Across the River: Stories Inspired by the Haunting Bruce Springsteen Song,* story contributed by Randy Michael Signor (Bloomsbury Publishing); *Other Sorrows, Other Joys: The Marriage of Catherine Sophia Boucher and William Blake: A Novel* (St. Martin's Press); *Imperial Mongolian Cooking: Recipes from the Kingdoms of Genghis Khan* by Marc Cramer (Hippocrene Publishers); *Somebody's Child: Stories from the Private Files of an Adoption Attorney* by Randi Barrow (Perigee/Penguin Putnam, Inc.); *Retro Chic: A Guide to Fabulous Vintage and Designer Resale Shopping in North America and Online* by Diana Eden and Gloria Lintermans (Really Great Books); *The Spoken Word Revolution,* an essay, poem, and an audio contribution by Saul Williams (Sourcebooks); *Rio L.A.: Tales from the Los Angeles River* by Patt Morrison, with photographs by Mark Lamonica (Angel City Press). Films: *What Angels Know: The Story of Elizabeth Barrett and Robert Browning* (screenplay optioned by producer Marta Anderson); *Somebody's Child: Stories from the Private Files of an Adoption Attorney* by Randi Barrow (Perigee/Penguin Putnam, Inc.), optioned by Green/Epstein/Bacino Productions for a television series; *A Place Called Waco: A Survivor's Story* by David Thibodeau and Leon Whiteson (PublicAffairs/Perseus Book Group), optioned to Showtime for a television movie; *Love, Groucho: Letters from Groucho Marx to His Daughter Miriam*, edited by Miriam Marx Allen (Faber & Faber, Straus & Giroux US, and Faber & Faber UK), sold to CBS. At this writing, we have just signed the film rights to popular Irish novelist Maeve Binchy's novel *Light a Penny Candle* (Viking/NAL/Signet). We have many books in submission and development at this writing and at any given time.

CREATIVE CONVERGENCE

11040 Santa Monica Blvd., Suite 200, Los Angeles, CA 90025
310-954-8480 | fax: 310-954-8481
www.creativecvg.com

Agent's name: Philippa Burgess
Born: October 1974 in Trenton, NJ
Education: Grew up in Upper Montclair, NJ, and New York City; graduated from USC: studied international relations and cinema-television
Career history: Started at ICM and went on to found boutique literary management company that evolved into Creative Convergence
Categories/Subjects that you are most enthusiastic about agenting: We represent and corepresent published literary properties to bring to film and television, as well as work with branded clients to develop literary properties that are part of a larger media brand.
If you were not an agent, what might you be doing instead: We love entertainment, media, and entrepreneurship. When we are not representing clients or packaging projects, we are writing, teaching, and speaking to writers and content creators.
Do you charge reading or management fees: Our literary management department represents screenwriters and directors on commission only. Our production department is paid fee for services and is paid by the studio. Our entertainment consulting services provide brand development and brand management for business endeavors that can be a combination of fees, commissions, or profit participation, depending on the nature of the services rendered, that often include PR, media, and business development. We also offer a brand development course entitled "Your Signature Story: From Content Creator to Media Brand" for a nominal fee.
What are the most common mistakes writers make when pitching to you: Lack clarity about what the author brings to the story from their own experience, what they bring to the table in terms of knowledge about the industry, who their audience is and how this story is relevant to them, what type of platform they are building to reach, and remaining engaged with their audience.
Describe the client from hell, even if you don't have any: A general lack of respect for our time and the realities of the business is a turnoff. Not to mention a

gross sense of entitlement that [is] often tied to a lack of ability or interest in doing their work to deliver a quality product.

What's your definition of a great client: Someone who takes responsibility for doing their work well and who continues to grow in their craft, relationships, and understanding of the business. We want a client to see our relationship as a team effort.

What can a writer do to increase the odds of you becoming his or her agent: Give us something amazing. Get it to us through a referral. Otherwise keep growing and learning, and it will come back around if it really is the right match.

How and why did you become an agent: Started at ICM and really liked it but saw there was a knowledge gap, so I moved into management. The business kept changing, and I found that the knowledge gap was widening and a lot more people needed the information and coaching, specifically media brands. We retained our literary management while expanding into film and television production and entertainment consulting.

How would you describe what you do as an agent to someone (or something) from another planet: We take books and package them for film and television. Specifically in television, we are looking for properties that we can package for network and cable series. We also look to work with content creators that are media brands that we can work to move their content across media platforms.

How do you feel about editors and publishers: We can only manage so many relationships, so we don't actually deal very often with editors and publishers. Rather we work through literary agents when it comes to the publishing side of things. Being an entertainment company in Los Angeles, we work closely with the equivalent in film and television.

How do you feel about writers: We love the smart ones! No really, we are passionate about writers and content creators. Beyond representing clients, packaging literary properties, or managing media brands, we look to be a resource to writers and are frequently found at writers conferences or teaching classes about the business.

What do you see in the near future for book publishing: Film, television, media, and publishing all need each other more than ever before. There is going to be a lot more cooperation between these different arenas of entertainment and media. However, the author needs to recognize that these professionals don't all speak the same language and thus needs to take a greater responsibility for moving their message across media platforms (and in doing so well, will stand to gain a lot more attention and regard from all parties).

In your opinion, what do editors think of you: We'd like to think that industry professionals see us as professional, resourceful, and forthright.

On a personal level, what do you think people like and dislike about you: We'd like to think that people see us as professional, resourceful, and forthright.

What are some representative titles that you have sold: *52 Fights* by Jennifer Jeanne Patterson (Penguin/Putnam), sold and produced as a TV pilot for ABC/Touchstone; *Men's Guide to the Women's Bathroom* (HarperCollins), sold as a TV pilot to CBS/Paramount (slated for production); *Thieves of Baghdad* (Bloomsbury), sold as a feature film to Warner Brothers with our client Jonathan Hunt coproducing; *They Come Back*, an original script written by Gary Boulton-Brown sold and produced for Lifetime; *Queensize*, an original script written by Rod Johnson sold to Lifetime (slated for production)

THE CROCE AGENCY

www.thecroceagency.com

Agent's name: Nicholas Croce
E-mail: submissions@thecroceagency.com
Born: Secaucus, NJ, January 9
Education: BA, major in English, minor in Journalism, University of New Mexico, certification in book publishing, New York University
Career history: I began my career in college as a fiction editor at the literary journals *Conceptions Southwest* and *Blue Mesa Review*. After college I started as an editorial assistant at John Wiley & Sons. I later moved on to Rosen Publishing, where I was an editor and then managing editor. I later started a small press, which was eventually named by *Writers Digest* as one of the top 50 publishers for first-time authors because of our commitment to strong relationships with writers. I closed the press in 2007 to start the Croce Agency.
Hobbies/Personal interests: I love writing fiction. I'm also a lifelong acoustic guitar player and am now starting to get into classical guitar. Aside from that I love cooking. Recipes and novels have a lot in common.
Categories/Subjects that you are most enthusiastic about agenting: I exclusively represent fiction and lean toward more commercial genres including historical, women's, romance, mystery, thriller, suspense, sci-fi, Western, and, more selectively, literary fiction. I'm pretty open to taking a look at all fiction, though, with unique voice and plotting.
Categories/Subjects writers shouldn't bother pitching to you: Poetry, short stories, nonfiction, screenplays
If you were not an agent, what might you be doing instead: A writer
Do you charge fees separate from your commission or offer nonagenting fee-based services: No, I don't charge any fees. I don't get paid until I sell a client's project.
What are some representative titles that you have sold: My most representative sales of what I'm looking for moving forward are *The Stolen Crown* by Susan Higginbotham (Sourcebooks), *The Queen of Last Hopes* by Susan Higginbotham (Sourcebooks), *The Boleyn Wife* by Brandy Purdy (Kensington), *Mary and Elizabeth: A Novel of the Daughters of Henry VIII* by Brandy Purdy (Kensington), and *Mr. Darcy's Little Sister* by C. Allyn Pierson (Sourcebooks).
How and why did you become an agent: I've had a pretty comprehensive career in book publishing, having been a writer, editor, manager, and publisher. It's good

for agents to have expertise in each of these areas, so it seemed like a natural next step for me.

How do you feel about writers: Though you can't paint all writers with the same brush, I have enormous respect for them on the whole. The job is most often thankless but simultaneously one of the most rewarding.

How do you feel about editors and publishers: Editors and publishers on the whole genuinely care about their books, and I respect them immensely for the amount of effort and insight they offer.

How would you describe what you do as an agent to someone (or something) from another planet: Basically a literary agent introduces the right writers to the right editors. We're literary matchmakers. Further, we help authors make wise career decisions. Most authors are so excited about just signing the first contract that they don't think long term.

What are your favorite books, movies, and TV shows, and why: I love challenging fiction, novels that leave you thinking. One of the best books I've read recently is *Netherland* by Joseph O'Neill. It's pretty much a modern-day *Great Gatsby* in post–9/11 New York, but aside from the plot or setting or themes, O'Neill's voice and his characters' nuances left me thinking about the book long after I put it down. As for TV, I don't think there'll ever be a show as wonderfully written as *Northern Exposure*. It's sad that a show like that would never make it to air today. One of my favorite movies of all time is *Lonestar*. It's one of the most perfectly plotted mystery movies.

Describe the client from hell, even if you don't have any: I wouldn't say there's a writer from hell, but there are certainly ones don't understand that publishing is a business, which can make them difficult to work with. I've turned down writers whose books I loved but whose attitudes I felt were unproductive. They might have had unreasonable expectations or weren't willing to take advice.

Describe yourself: I work hard at being professional, organized, and dependable. This is a small industry where everyone pretty much knows everyone, and professionalism is recognized, not just among agents but also authors.

Describe the publisher and/or editor from hell: Just like with writers, I wouldn't say there's a publisher or an editor from hell. Ones who aren't professional, though, tend to fall to the bottom of my list.

Describe hell: Hell is a place without books!

What's the best way for writers to solicit your interest: I only accept submissions by e-mail at submissions@thecroceagency.com. Brevity is key and is the mark of a good writer. I just ask for a one-sentence "hook," a one-paragraph synopsis, and one sample chapter all in the body of the e-mail. If I like what I see, I then ask the author to send me the full manuscript for a two-week exclusive read.

Will e-readers significantly change the business: I think e-readers will certainly offer growth opportunities. In the end though it's the content that matters more than the platform. There will always be a demand for good writing. Nonetheless, as an agent I'm always looking out for new technologies that can offer opportunities for my authors.

Are you optimistic, pessimistic, neutral, or catatonic about the book biz in the future: I'm definitely optimistic. Books have been around in one form or another for millennia. The business isn't leaving us any time soon.

Explain what you like and dislike about your job: What I love most about my job is taking a good manuscript and making it great, either by developing the characters, giving it a more marketable angle, adding themes or more dimension, etc. What I like least is when an editor doesn't share my enthusiasm for a book. However, this usually forces me to revisit the manuscript and make it better.

Describe a book you might like writing: Though I prefer reading character-driven fiction, I'd love to write a plot-driven page-turner, either mystery or suspense. I think it'd be fun.

Do you think some/most of these questions are stupid: I loved these questions! They really help you get to know the agent on a more casual level.

CS INTERNATIONAL LITERARY AGENCY

43 West 39th St., New York, NY 10018
212-921-1610
www.csliterary.com

Agent's name: Cynthia Neeseman
E-mail: csliterary@aol.com
Education: Columbia University
Categories/Subjects that you are most enthusiastic about agenting: Fiction, nonfiction, screenplays
Categories/Subjects writers shouldn't bother pitching to you: Pornography
If you were not an agent, what might you be doing instead: Real estate and writing
What's the best way for fiction writers to solicit your interest: Send short query letters that grab one's attention. Include telephone numbers, if available, as well as e-mail and snail-mail addresses. I like to talk to potential clients over the phone as a fast and efficient way to determine whether we will connect and be able to work together.
What's the best way for nonfiction writers to solicit your interest: See above.
Do you charge reading or management fees: I charge reading fees if I believe a writer might need revision and/or I have doubts about marketability of subject matter and/or interest in submitted subject. I expect a writer to pay for expenses as they occur. My fees are very fair and moderate. I analyze manuscripts and screenplays in addition to agenting, because many writers benefit from revision. I like to help writers produce material that will sell, and therefore I discuss all aspects of their efforts, including marketability, up front. It saves time and effort. I also read partial manuscripts. Sometimes a smaller first submission can be beneficial.
What are the most common mistakes writers make when pitching to you: They have not mastered the art of being succinct but pithy. In short, they ramble.

How and why did you become an agent: I have always been interested in writing and obtaining interesting information. I was a foreign correspondent and worked for a literary agent.

How do you feel about writers: Writers are wonderful.

What do you see in the near future for book publishing: More and more self-publishing. Marketing is often the secret to becoming a successful writer.

CURTIS BROWN, LTD.

10 Astor Place, New York, NY 10003
212-473-5400
www.curtisbrown.com

Agent's name: Ginger Knowlton

Born: Before the 1960s in Princeton, New Jersey

Education: Questionable, Navy brat–quality

Career history: I worked in a factory assembling display cases in Mystic, Connecticut, for a time. Gained numerous pounds one summer working in a bakery in Mendocino, California. I've taught preschool and I directed an infant and toddler child-care center. That means I organized a lot of fundraisers. I started working at Curtis Brown in 1986.

Categories/Subjects that you are most enthusiastic about agenting: Middle-grade and teenage novels

Categories/Subjects writers shouldn't bother pitching to you: I prefer to remain open to all ideas.

What's the best way for writers to solicit your interest: A simple, straightforward letter with a return envelope works well.

If you were not an agent, what might you be doing instead: I love my job, but if I had the luxury of not having to work, I would play tennis even more than I already do; I would tend my gardens more fastidiously; and I would spend more time playing with others.

What categories do you represent, by percentages: Nonfiction, 5 percent; fiction, 5 percent; children's, 90 percent

What are the most common mistakes writers make when pitching to you: Expecting an answer within a week, but mostly poor-quality writing.

Describe the client from hell, even if you don't have any: Happy to report that I still don't have firsthand experience with a "client from hell," so once again I will refrain from describing one (for fear of a self-fulfilling prophecy).

How would you describe the perfect client: Professional authors who respect my job as I respect theirs, who will maintain an open dialogue so we may learn from each other and continue to grow, who are optimistic and enthusiastic, and who continue to write books worthy of publication

How and why did you become an agent: I asked Dad for money for graduate school. He offered me a job at Curtis Brown instead.

Do you have any particular opinions or impressions of editors or publishers in general: I have a lot of respect for editors, and I think they have an incredibly difficult job. As in all professions, some are more gifted than others.

Agent's name: Elizabeth Harding

Education: BA in English, University of Michigan (Ann Arbor)

Categories/Subjects that you are most enthusiastic about agenting: Children's literature

What's the best way for writers to solicit your interest: Query letter or sample chapters

What categories do you represent, by percentages: Children's: 100 percent

Agent's name: Laura Blake Peterson

Education: BA, Vassar College

Career history: 1986–present, Curtis Brown, Ltd.

Hobbies/Personal interests: Gardening, pets, regional equestrian competitions

Areas most interested in agenting: Exceptional fiction, narrative nonfiction, young-adult fiction, anything outstanding

Categories/Subjects writers shouldn't bother pitching to you: Fantasy, science fiction, poetry

If you were not an agent, what might you be doing instead: Teaching, gardening, who knows?

What's the best way for writers to solicit your interest: The best way is through a referral from either a client of mine or an editor with whom I work.

What categories do you represent, by percentages: Fiction: 40 percent; nonfiction: 40 percent; children's: 20 percent

What are the most common mistakes writers make when pitching to you: Calling, rather than sending a query letter

Describe the client from hell, even if you don't have any: Authors who call incessantly, preventing me from accomplishing anything on their behalf

How would you describe the perfect client: A talented writer who knows the idiosyncrasies of the publishing business yet nonetheless remains determined to be a part of it; a writer with the skills and patience to participate in an often frustrating and quirky industry

How and why did you become an agent: I love language. I can't imagine a better job than helping to bring a skilled writer to the attention of the book-buying public.

What can a writer do to increase the odds of you becoming his or her agent: Do their homework. Find out what I (or whomever they're contacting) like to read and represent, what books I've sold in the past, etc. Read this survey!

D4EO LITERARY AGENCY

7 Indian Valley Road, Weston, CT 06883
203-544-7180 | fax: 203-544-7160
www.d4eoliteraryagency.com

Agent's name: Robert Diforio

E-mail: d4eo@optonline.net

Born: March 19, 1940; Mamaroneck, New York

Education: Williams College 1964, advanced management program (AMP) at Harvard Business School 1978

Career history: Kable News Company 1964–1972: book and magazine sales rep 1964–1966, manager, paperback books division 1966–1969, Vice President book sales 1969–1972; New American Library 1972–1989, Vice President general sales manager 1972–1974, senior Vice President marketing director 1975–1978, executive Vice President 1979, president, publisher 1980, chairman and CEO 1981–1989; founded D4EO Literary Agency 1989

Hobbies/Personal interests: Golf

Categories/Subjects that you are most enthusiastic about agenting: Commercial fiction and nonfiction

Categories/Subjects writers shouldn't bother pitching to you: Anything I don't like.

If you were not an agent, what might you be doing instead: Publisher

What's the best way for writers to solicit your interest: Recommendation from a publisher or client

Do you charge reading or management fees: No

How and why did you become an agent: As a publisher I loved launching new writers, now I do it as an agent.

What can a writer do to increase the odds of you becoming his or her agent: Send me a MS that I absolutely love.

How would you describe what you do as an agent to someone (or something) from another planet: I find the right editor/publisher for my client's work.

What are some representative titles that you have sold: *To Sin with a Scoundrel, To Surrender to a Rogue* (Mira); *The Hunt Chronicles* trilogy (Tor and Droemer Knaur); *Game Over* trilogy (Tor); *Libertine's Kiss* (Harlequin); *Boca Knights and Boca Mournings* (Tor); *Reindeer Christmas* and *The Very Best Pumpkin* (Paula Wiseman/ S&S); *Betrayed, Captured, Escape, Malice, Counterplay, Hoax, Fury* (all of the Butch Karp legal thrillers by Robert Tanenbaum; Vanguard/Atria Books/Pocket Books); *Havoc, Deep Fire Rising, River of Ruin, Medusa Stone, Pandora's Curse, Charon's Landing, Vulcan's Forge* (Dutton/NAL); *Felony Murder, Shoot the Moon, Flat Lake in Winter, Irreparable Damage, Fog* (St. Martin's Press); *My Name Is Jillian Gray* (Albin Michel); *The Mermaid's Song* (Delacort); *The 10th Case, Bronx Justice,* and *Depraved Indifference* (Mira); *Anxiety Free* and *Here Comes the Sun* (Hay House); *Putting My*

Way [Jack Nicklaus, Ken Bowden] (John Wiley & Sons); *Debates on Science*, seven-book series (Facts on File); *The Words You Should Know to Sound Smart* (Adams Media); *Don't Be That Boss* (John Wiley); *Age of Fire* (St. Martin's); Michael Phelps biography (St. Martin's); *S.K.I.R.T.S. in the Boardroom* (John Wiley); *Undress for Success* (John Wiley); *Murder for Hire* (St. Martin's); *The CIG to Biology* (Alpha); *Roux Memories Cookbook* and *Knack Chinese Cooking* (Globe Pequot); *Everything Soup, Stew, and Chili* (Adams Media); *Knack Drums* (Globe Pequot); *Starting a Web-Based Business* (Adams Media); *The Wealthy Freelancer* (Adams Media); *Bear Trap* (foreign sales China, Taiwan, Korea, and Poland); *Hyper-Performance* (Jossey Bass); *New Résumé, New Career* (Alpha Books); *The Little Book of Bullet-Proof Investing* (John Wiley); *Betrayal* (Union Square Press); *Reel Terror* (St. Martin's Press); *Teeing Off* (Triumph Books); *Everything I Needed to Know I Learned at McDonald's* (McGraw-Hill); *Accidental Landlord* and *Accidental Tycoon* (Alpha Books); *The Faraway Fairies* (Hatchette Australia); *Reindeer Christmas* (Paula Wiseman/Simon & Schuster); *The History of Medicine* and *Controversies in Science* and *Ocean Sciences*, multibook series (Facts on File); *Crazy Love, Cruising* (Pocket Books); *Expired, Criss Cross, Out "A" Order* (Kensington); *The Tiger's Mistress, Kiss of Spice* (Pocket Books); *Hellions* (Warner); *Take Me Out of the Bathtub, I'm Still Here in the Bathtub* (Margaret McElderry); *McKeag's Mountain, Wolf Mountain, Stranahan, Gavagan, O'Rourke's Revenge* (Kensington); *House of Pain, Behold a Pale Horse* (Tor); *The Last Pope* (Sourcebooks); *Via Magna*—Spain, *DiFel*—Portugal, *Eddie's World, Jimmy Bench Press, Charlie Opera, Cheapskates* (Carroll & Graf and UK and Russia sales); *Shakedown* (Pegasus); *Rift Zone* (Tor); *4th & Fixed* (Sourcebooks); *Dangerous Deceptions* (NAL); *Red Meat Cures Cancer* (Vintage); *Heretic: The Templar Chronicles* (Pocket Books); *Droemer-Knaur*—Germany, *Alfaret*—Russia, *Pleasure Control* trilogy (Avon Red); *Allure Author's Anthology* (Avon Red); *Sexy Beast, Hell Kat, Inferno* (Aphrodisia); *Wild, Wild Women of the West* (Aphrodisia); *Vampire Erotica 1* and *Vampire Erotica 2* (Avon Red); *Solomon's Code, The Voynich Code* (sales in Russia, Bulgaria, Brazil); *The Worry Cure* (Harmony Books); *Application Suicide* (Gotham).

Agent's name: Mandy Hubbard
E-mail: mandy@d4eo.com
Personal website: www.mandyhubbard.com
Born: Enumclaw, Washington
Education: Associate of arts degree, Green River Community College
Career history: Mandy Hubbard began her career in publishing on the other side of the desk, as an author. Her titles include *Prada and Prejudice* (Razorbill/Penguin, 2009); *Driven* (Harlequin, 2010); *You Wish* (Razorbill/Penguin, 2010); *But I Love Him* (Flux, 2011); *Ripple* (Razorbill/Penguin, 2011); *In Too Deep* (Flux, 2012), and *Dangerous Boy* (Razorbill/Penguin 2012). She interned with The Bent Agency before joining D4EO Literary, where she is now building a list of middle-grade and young-adult fiction.
Hobbies/Personal interests: Hiking, reading, horseback riding, ATVs, camping

The Categories/Subjects that you are most enthusiastic about agenting: Middle-grade and young-adult fiction

Categories/Subjects writers shouldn't bother pitching to you: Nonfiction, books for the adult market, poetry, screenplays, picture books

If you were not an agent, what might you be doing instead: I am currently—and always will be—an author.

Do you charge fees separate from your commission or offer nonagenting fee-based services: No

What are some representative titles that you have sold: *Virtuosity* (and untitled book 2) by Jessica Martinez, Simon Pulse; *Linked* (and sequel) by Imogen Howson, Simon & Schuster Books for Young Readers; *The Patron Saint of Beans* by Emily Murdoch, St Martin's

How and why did you become an agent: As an author, I've had many, many writers come to me for advice. This industry is crazy and maddening and so dang hard to break into. I really love trying to play tour guide and help writers as much as I can. Prior to becoming an agent, I worked heavily on revising manuscripts with authors I truly believed in. A few of my friends nearly rewrote their novel with my advice and ended up signing an agent quite quickly afterward. At some point, I realized that if I were an agent, I wouldn't have to "give up" playing tour guide—I could continue guiding them throughout their career. Interning with The Bent Agency confirmed that desire for me.

How do you feel about writers: I love them, of course! My closest friends are writers or published authors.

How do you feel about editors and publishers: Editors are so much like me—they share the same passion for books. They may seem like the bad guys when they are rejecting a project, but they very much want to find the next amazing project.

How would you describe what you do as an agent to someone (or something) from another planet: I get to spend all day with the written word—whether that means screening new queries or working with clients on revisions or pitching exciting projects to editors. Plus, I spend copious amounts of time reading published works in order to stay up on market trends.

What are your favorite books, movies, and TV shows, and why: Books: *The Season* by Sarah Maclean, *A Match Made in High School* by Kristin Walker, *Hate List* by Jennifer Brown, *Amaranth Enchantment* by Julie Berry, *Wintergirls* by Laurie Halse Anderson, *Hunger Games* by Suzanne Collins…I could go on forever. Movies: I am forever quoting *Empire Records*. There's just something addictive about it. Television: *Veronica Mars* (love her snarky quips!); *House* (I'm sensing a snarky quip trend…); and *The OC* (love the romance and drama!).

Describe the writer/client from hell: Someone who is inflexible with their craft. You simply must be open to revision if you expect to find success in this industry. Work with me (and later, your editor) on polishing your manuscript and meet your deadlines, and we'll be in good shape.

Describe yourself: Driven, enthusiastic, hard-working. My debut novel, *Prada*

and Prejudice, was rejected 26 times, by every publisher in New York and plenty of independent publishers located across the country. I started over from scratch and totally rewrote it, and then we received two offers. If I believe in your project, I'll work just as hard on selling your manuscript as I did on breaking into this industry.

Describe the publisher and/or editor from hell: There are two sorts of editors who can be difficult to work with: the one who is adamant that things be done a certain way—and demands that the revisions be done exactly as they've described—and an editor who waffles, putting the writer through round after round of revisions, sometimes undoing the very things they asked for the first time.

What's the best way for writers to solicit your interest: E-queries! I do not accept snail mail queries at all.

Will e-readers significantly change the business: I answered this question for last year's guide, and I'm already changing my answer! We've seen enormous changes in a single year—and these changes will continue to pick up steam. New e-publishers have gained notice, many well-established authors have left their New York publishers to go solo, and still other successful e-published books and authors have found their way to traditional publishers because they wanted everything that went with the traditional publishing experience. It really will take time to see what the new way of publishing looks like—this industry is historically slow—but there will always be books, always be readers, and always be publishers. We just don't always know just how that will look.

Are you optimistic, pessimistic, neutral, or catatonic about the book biz in the future: Optimistic. I'm a pretty glass-half-full sort of person. This industry will always exist in some form or another. As long as we're flexible and adjust to the changing times, we can find success. It's not like it was ever an easy business to begin with!

Explain what you like and dislike about your job: I have two favorites: Falling in love with a new manuscript and calling an author to tell them I've sold their debut novel. My least favorite parts: Rejecting authors; being one of a half-dozen agents to love a manuscript and not being the one the writer picks for representation; sharing rejections with authors.

Describe a book you might like writing: Since I'm also an author, I already write the books I want to write.

DANA NEWMAN LITERARY, LLC

9720 Wilshire Blvd., 5th Floor, Beverly Hills, CA 90212
about.me/dananewman

Agent's name: Dana Newman
E-mail: dananewmanliterary@gmail.com
Born: June 4, Los Angeles, CA

Education: BA in comparative literature, University of California at Berkeley; JD, University of San Francisco School of Law

Career history: Prior to becoming a literary agent, Dana worked for 14 years as in-house counsel for the Moviola companies in Hollywood, CA, providers of entertainment and communications technologies. Having worked in the entertainment industry during the transition from analog to digital platforms in film editing and audio recording, she's excited about the revolution happening in publishing and enthusiastically embraces new technologies and business models for the creation and distribution of books. Dana is also a transactional and intellectual property attorney, advising author, and creator and entrepreneur on contracts, copyrights, trademarks, and licensing.

Hobbies/Personal interests: Reading (of course), running marathons and half marathons, travel, raising teenage daughters, film, women's issues

Categories/Subjects that you are most enthusiastic about agenting: Nonfiction: narrative and practical nonfiction, memoir, pop culture, lifestyle, health and wellness, business, cultural history, social trends, personal growth; Fiction: literary fiction, upmarket women's fiction (contemporary and historical)

What's the best way for writers to solicit your interest: Please e-mail a query letter to dananewmanliterary@gmail.com that identifies the category, title, and word count; and provides a brief overview of your project, credentials, platform, and previous publishing history, if any. For fiction submissions, please send a query letter and the first five pages of your book in the body of the e-mail (no attachments). If I'm interested in your material, I'll e-mail you a request for a full proposal (for nonfiction) or a synopsis and the first 50 pages (for fiction).

Categories/Subjects writers shouldn't bother pitching to you: Science fiction, fantasy, horror, crime, religion, children's, young adult, poetry, screenplays

If you were not an agent, what might you be doing instead: Writing, or working with writers, editors, and publishers in some other capacity

Do you charge fees separate from your commission or offer nonagenting fee-based services: No

What are some representative titles that you have sold: *The King of Style: Dressing Michael Jackson* by Michael Bush (Insight Editions); *An Atomic Love Story: The Women in Robert Oppenheimer's Life* by Shirley Streshinsky and Patricia Klaus (Turner Publishing); Shirley Streshinsky's backlist titles including *Hers the Kingdom, Gift of the Golden Mountain, A Time Between, The Shores of Paradise,* and *Audubon: Life and Art in the American Wilderness* (Turner Publishing); *How to Read a Client from across the Room: Win More Business with the Proven Character Code System to Decode Verbal and Nonverbal Communication* by Brandy Mychals (McGraw-Hill); *Honey, Do You Need a Ride? Confessions of a Fat Runner* by Jennifer Graham (Breakaway Books); *Combined Destinies: Whites Sharing Grief about Racism* by Ann Todd Jealous and Caroline Haskell (Potomac Books); *On Message: Why Facts Are Overrated, Your Pitch Is Too Complex and Narrative Is the Only Thing That Matters* by Zach Friend (Turner Publishing); *Two Spirits, One Heart: A Mother,*

Her Transgender Son, and Their Journey to Love and Acceptance by Marsha Aizumi (Magnus Books)

How and why did you become an agent: I love reading, and believe in the power of a compelling narrative to influence culture and impact people's lives. My legal background makes me an excellent advocate for authors and helps in navigating the challenges and complexities of the publishing industry in the digital age. I launched my own literary agency in 2010 and have found that it's the perfect fit for my talents and interests.

How do you feel about writers: I have tremendous respect for writers and their ability to creatively express ideas, tell gripping stories, and share inspiring and/or useful information. Reading a well-written book makes life more interesting and is one of its greatest pleasures.

How do you feel about editors and publishers: I admire their dedication to bringing deserving books to the market in a very challenging environment. I have found most editors and publishers to be smart, hard-working, talented people. Publishing a book is a collaborative endeavor, and I enjoy working with editors, publishers, and writers in that process.

How would you describe what you do as an agent to someone (or something) from another planet: My work varies from day to day, which I love. Things I do include assisting writers in polishing their proposals and manuscripts; submitting projects to editors; following up on submissions; negotiating publishing agreements; drafting coauthor agreements; running interference on delivery and production scheduling issues; facilitating cover image discussions; advising on copyright, trademark, and permission issues; working with an author on executing their marketing plan; reading queries, proposals, and manuscripts; and attending writers conferences, where I present workshops on publishing agreements, digital rights, copyright, and trademark issues.

What are your favorite books, movies, and TV shows, and why: Too many to list them all, but some of my favorites are *Bel Canto* by Ann Patchett, *One Hundred Years of Solitude* by Gabriel Garcia Marquez, *Crossing to Safety* by Wallace Stegner, *Rosie* by Anne Lamott, *The Anna Papers* by Ellen Gilchrist, *So Big* by Edna Ferber, anything by Jhumpa Lahiri, Joan Didion, or Jeffrey Eugenides—because they are masterfully crafted stories with distinctive voices, characters, and/or worlds you don't want to leave. I'm partial to movies that have a lot of humor mixed with heartfelt personal or emotional stories (*Jerry Maguire*, *American Beauty*, *Little Miss Sunshine*, *Juno*, *Manhattan*), but I'm also drawn to well-crafted, darker stories that combine history and entertainment, like *The English Patient* and *Atonement*. I'd rather read than watch TV, but I do like character-driven, edgy dramas and comedies like *Homeland*, *Nurse Jackie*, *Girls*, and *The Newsroom*, and I loved *Six Feet Under* when it was on.

Describe the client from hell, even if you don't have any: A writer who has unreasonable expectations about the realities of the book business, won't accept any feedback on their work, is unprofessional, is disrespectful of the author/agent and author/editor relationships, and has no sense of humor

Describe yourself: Endlessly curious, analytical, forthright, a passionate and diligent advocate for people and things I believe in

Describe the publisher and/or editor from hell: Unprofessional, or goes radio silent despite having professed huge enthusiasm for a project; a publisher that doesn't pay its authors according to their contract

What's the best way for writers to solicit your interest: E-mail a well-written, concise query letter with a great hook that demonstrates you've done your research.

Will e-readers significantly change the business: They already have. Sales of e-books are rapidly growing, and the shifting economics of book publishing towards digital production, distribution, and marketing is having an impact on advances, royalties, returns, license terms, books never going out of print, and the reversion of rights.

Are you optimistic, pessimistic, neutral, or catatonic about the book biz in the future: Optimistic. It is easier than ever before for writers to get their work published and distributed worldwide. There will always be a demand for great, well-told stories, and now there are more ways to experience books and for authors to engage with their readers. The need for curation and readers' preference for professionally edited and published content is where those in the publishing industry who adapt to the changing landscape can provide enormous value.

Explain what you like and dislike about your job: I like discovering a voice that really resonates with me, learning something interesting, and seeing a book project come to life. The only thing I really don't like about agenting is all the rejection—both having to decline to represent writers' projects and dealing with the rejections from editors I've submitted to.

Describe a book you might like writing: A narrative nonfiction work that tells a fascinating, little known true story and reads like a novel, a la *Into the Wild*, *Unbroken*, or *The Orchid Thief*.

DANIEL BIAL AGENCY

41 W. 83rd St., Suite 5C, New York, NY 10024
212-721-1786
danielbialagency.com

Agent's name: Daniel Bial
E-mail: dbialagency@msn.com
Education: BA, Trinity College, English
Career history: Editor for 15 years, including 10 years at HarperCollins; founded agency in 1992
Hobbies/Personal interests: Travel, cooking, music, parenting
Categories/Subjects that you are most enthusiastic about agenting: Nonfiction: Biography, business, cooking, current events, history, how-to, humor,

Judaica, language, narrative nonfiction, popular culture, popular reference, popular science, psychology, sports, travel; Fiction: Quality fiction

Categories/Subjects writers shouldn't bother pitching to you: Nonfiction: Academic treatises, crafts, gift books; Fiction: Children's books, genre fiction, poetry, novels by first-time authors with no publishing credits

If you were not an agent, what might you be doing instead: Writer, book doctor, or maybe a freelance celebrity advisor

What's the best way for writers to solicit your interest: E-mail (about one page long with no attachments) or query letter with SASE

What are the most common mistakes writers make when pitching to you: A surprising number of writers devote time in their query letter to telling me about their shortcomings or previous failures. They essentially reject themselves.

Do you charge reading or management fees: No

What categories do you represent, by percentages: Nonfiction: 95 percent, fiction: 5 percent

How would you describe the perfect client: Perfect clients produce trim, tight, ready-to-sell material. They know the business and how to get ahead. They recognize the importance of marketing and know that good intentions don't sell books; hard work does. They take pride in their work and their relationships.

How and why did you become an agent: I love books, good writing, interesting ideas, and being part of the fascinating industry that makes it all happen.

What do you think the future holds for writers, publishers, and agents: Ever since the advent of the computer age, publishers have gotten smarter, and so have most agents and many writers. The old belief that quality sells itself has been proven wrong and replaced with a more practical knowledge of what sells. As a result, publishers are selling more copies, and there are more blockbuster authors than ever before. Publishing has long been threatened by many other entertainment options (movies, games, etc.), and illiteracy remains a problem for the nation as a whole. But despite the occasional doom-and-gloom prediction, the overall business is chugging along quite well.

DANIEL LITERARY GROUP

1701 Kingsbury Dr., Ste 100, Nashville, TN 37215
615-730-8207
www.danielliterarygroup.com

Agent's name: Greg Daniel
E-mail: submissions@danielliterarygroup.com
Born: Lubbock, Texas
Education: BA, Wheaton College; MA, Trinity Divinity School
Career history: I founded Daniel Literary Group in 2007 after more than

10 years in publishing, six of which were at the executive level at Thomas Nelson Publishers, the largest Christian publisher in the world. Most recently I was vice president and associate publisher there.

Hobbies/Personal interests: Cycling, golf, motorcycling, crosswords, taxi driver for my kids

Categories/Subjects that you are most enthusiastic about agenting: Nonfiction only, including such categories as biography/autobiography, business/economics, child guidance/parenting, current affairs, health/medicine, history, how-to, humor/satire, memoirs, nature/environment, popular culture, religious/inspirational, self-help/personal improvement, sports, theater/film, women's issues

Categories/Subjects writers shouldn't bother pitching to you: Fiction, poetry, children's, and screenplays

If you were not an agent, what might you be doing instead: NFL quarterback or Sham Wow spokesman

What's the best way for nonfiction writers to solicit your interest: Do your homework on what I represent and don't represent, and follow my submission guidelines found on my agency website. Sounds basic, but amazingly, 90 percent of the queries I receive ignore this advice. And please don't tell me that your Aunt Ethel or your pet cat read your manuscript and told you it was the most brilliant thing they'd ever read.

Do you charge fees separate from your commission or offer nonagenting fee-based services: No

What are some representative titles that you have sold: *Praying for Strangers* (Berkley/Penguin); *The Mad Bomber of New York* (Union Square); *Close Enough to Hear God Breathe* (Thomas Nelson); *Insurrection* (Howard/Simon & Schuster); *Torn* (Jericho/Hachette); *The Pope Who Quit* (Doubleday Religion); *My Life as a Holy Roller* (WaterBrook/Multnomah Press); *Finding God in the Other* (Jossey-Bass/Wiley); *Wild Things* (Tyndale House); *The Sacredness of Questioning Everything* (Zondervan); *Reimagining Church* (Cook); *Holy Stability* (Paraclete); *Saints in Limbo* (WaterBrook/Multnomah Press)

How and why did you become an agent: I loved being an editor and publisher, but I always envied the diversity of writers that an agent could choose to work with and the ability to concentrate on a smaller group of authors, building their careers and brands. So I finally took the plunge and left life as an editor/publisher to launch my own agency. It's been everything I hoped it would be.

Describe the client from hell, even if you don't have any: One with horns, a tail, and a pitchfork

What do you like best about your clients and the editors and publishers you work with: Book people, whether they're authors or editors, are absolutely the greatest group of people in the world to hang out with. Smart, witty, interesting, and fresh minty breath.

DEFIORE AND COMPANY

47 East 19th Street, Third Floor, New York, NY 10003
www.defioreandco.com

Agent's name: Laurie Abkemeier
E-mail: lma@defioreandco.com
Born: Eureka, California, 1970
Education: Wells College, Aurora, NY; BA in communications, 1992
Career history: My first job was as an editorial assistant at Touchstone/Fireside right out of college. In January 1994, I made a lateral move to Hyperion and worked my way up the ladder from editorial assistant to assistant editor (1994) to editor (1995) to senior editor (1996). I developed a broad list of nonfiction and was responsible for five *New York Times* best sellers, including *Brain Droppings* by George Carlin; *Rock This!* by Chris Rock; *No Shirt, No Shoes, No Problem!* by Jeff Foxworthy; and *First Person Plural: My Life as a Multiple* by Cameron West, PhD. I also acquired and edited the *Business Week* best seller *How to Become CEO* by Jeffrey Fox; *Polish Your Furniture with Panty Hose* by Joey Green; *What No One Tells the Bride* by Marg Stark; *Blue Jelly: Love Lost and the Lessons of Canning* by Debby Bull; and *Living the Simple Life* by Elaine St. James. I left in July 1998 to focus on my growing family but made my way back to publishing in 2003—this time from the agenting side. I've been representing authors on behalf of DeFiore and Company ever since. My list is exclusively nonfiction.

Categories/Subjects that you are most enthusiastic about agenting: Humorous memoir, narrative nonfiction in all subject areas, nature, science, pop culture, history, popular reference, relationships, adventure, food, investigative journalism

Categories/Subjects writers shouldn't bother pitching to you: No fiction, no exceptions. I'm also turned off by anything morose or bleak. But within every category, there's the potential for a book that has my kind of sensibility.

If you were not an agent, what might you be doing instead: A television producer or an entertainment lawyer

Do you charge fees separate from your commission or offer nonagenting fee-based services: No. My editorial services are extensive and included as part of representation.

What are some representative titles that you have sold: *Marley & Me* and *The Longest Trip Home* by John Grogan (William Morrow); *Love in a Time of Homeschooling* by Laura Brodie (Harper); *Meeting Your Half-Orange* by Amy Spencer (Running Press); *How to be a High School Superstar* by Cal Newport (Broadway); *If It Was Easy, They'd Call the Whole Damn Thing a Honeymoon* by Jenna McCarthy (Berkley Books); *Record Collecting for Girls* by Courtney E. Smith (Houghton Mifflin Harcourt/Mariner Books); *The Ugly Christmas Sweater Party Book* by Brian Miller, Adam Paulson, and Kevin Wool (Abrams Image); *It Was the Best of Sentences, It Was the Worst of Sentences* by June Casagrande (Ten Speed Press); *Cheer: Inside the Secret World of College Cheerleaders* by Kate Torgovnick (Touchstone); *Bretz's Flood* by John Soennichsen (Sasquatch Books)

How and why did you become an agent: As an editor for more than six years, I swore I would never be an agent, but motherhood gave me the gift of amnesia. I missed books and wanted to get back into publishing, but an editorial job didn't allow me the flexibility I needed. Becoming an agent seemed like the perfect opportunity to flex my creative muscles and work closely with authors. If authors need one thing in this business, it's a knowledgeable ally and protector. I was fortunate that my former editor-in-chief, Brian DeFiore, was willing to take a chance on me as an agent.

What are your favorite books, movies, and TV shows, and why: My top three movies of all time are *Star Wars* (for its message of mind over matter), *Rear Window* (for its perfect storytelling), and *All the President's Men* (I love investigative journalism). My favorite narrative nonfiction book of all time is *A Civil Action*. That kind of immersion storytelling is rare.

Describe the client from hell, even if you don't have any: Someone who thinks s/he knows more about the publishing process and the industry than I do. Someone who treats me like a mindless henchman. But worst of all, someone who has no interest in rolling up shirtsleeves and promoting his or her own work. These days, being an author means more than putting words on a page.

Describe the publisher and/or editor from hell: Some editors are clueless. They don't understand how a book is created or how the publishing industry operates. They don't bother to keep the author informed. The worst publishers are those who ignore their own marketing instincts and position the book in a way that caters to the category that will get the most copies into the chains. This almost always turns off the book's core audience and usually spells disaster.

What's the best way for writers to solicit your interest: The only way to pitch me is in writing—either by e-mail or snail mail. I cannot properly evaluate a project that is pitched orally.

Will e-readers significantly change the business: The economics are getting harder, but I'm optimistic that the move to digital will attract more people of all ages to books. I also think the digital landscape will make illustrated books more viable. Too many publishers are forced to turn down books because of expensive production costs. Going digital should make a positive difference in this regard.

Agent's name: Brian DeFiore
E-mail: lma@defioreandco.com
Born: August 1956, Brooklyn, New York
Education: BA, SUNY at New Paltz and Queens College
Career history: 1999–Present: president, DeFiore and Co.; 1997–1998: Senior Vice President and publisher, Villard Books, Random House; 1992–1997: Vice President and editor-in-chief, Hyperion; 1988–1992: senior editor/Vice President and editorial director, Dell/Delacorte Press; 1983–1988: editor, St. Martin's Press
Hobbies/Personal interests: Movies, theater, cycling, cooking, being a good dad to my daughters
Categories/Subjects that you are most enthusiastic about agenting: Intelligent

commercial fiction, suspense fiction, narrative nonfiction, psychology/self-help, business, humor, virtually anything that is written beautifully

Categories/Subjects writers shouldn't bother pitching to you: Category romance, poetry, computer books, anything written pedantically

If you were not an agent, what might you be doing instead: Psychotherapy

What's the best way for writers to solicit your interest: A drop-dead brilliant letter (sent by mail or e-mail). Publishing is a medium about the written word; a persuasively written letter indicates the right sort of talent. A sloppy or trite letter indicates the opposite.

Do you charge reading or management fees: No

What categories do you represent, by percentages: Fiction: 35 percent, children's: 10 percent, nonfiction: 55 percent

What are the most common mistakes writers make when pitching to you: Pitching several books at once; telling me how many other agents and/or publishers loved their work, but simply aren't taking new clients (yes, people really do this!)

Describe the client from hell, even if you don't have any: Someone who hears but doesn't listen; someone who thinks an agent's job is solely to bully publishers; someone who has a cynical "I'll write whatever sells" attitude about their work

How would you describe the perfect client: Someone whose work inspires me and who respects and appreciates my role in the process

How and why did you become an agent: After 18 years on the publishing and editorial side of the business, I was ready for a more entrepreneurial challenge. I love the publishing process, but I felt that too much of my time was spent on corporate posturing and not enough on books and authors. Now I can have it both ways.

What can a writer do to increase the odds of you becoming his or her agent: Write brilliantly. There's not much else. Don't send me something until it's absolutely as good as it possibly can be.

How would you describe what you do as an agent to someone (or something) from another planet: I search for talented authors. Using my experience as a publisher, I work with my clients to get their submission material (manuscript or proposal) into the best possible shape to elicit a positive response from publishers. I orchestrate the sale to get the best combination of deal points and publishing house for the project. I negotiate the contract. I sell the subsidiary rights to those projects, often in concert with coagents in Los Angeles and cities around the world. I oversee the publication effort and make sure the publisher is doing what needs to be done. I interpret the publisher's business needs for the author and vice versa. I strategize with my clients to develop their careers.

How do you feel about editors and publishers: I admire the work they do; indeed, I did it myself for several years. I think most editors and publishers have their hearts firmly planted in the right place. I wish that their corporate masters gave them more time and support to do their jobs well. They are under such pressure these last few years that editorial nurturing of authors has evolved into an obsessive quest for "the next big thing." It's always lovely to have "the next big thing," but I've yet to meet the publishing team who always knew what that was 18 months in advance.

I firmly believe that those publishers who focus on editorial quality and integrity over high concept and "platform" are the ones who will win in the end.

What are your favorite books, movies, and TV shows, and why: TV: *Modern Family, The Sopranos, The Daily Show, 30 Rock.* Movies: *The Philadelphia Story, Network, Star Wars.*

What are some representative titles that you have sold: *Following Atticus* (William Morrow); *The Evolution of Bruno Littlemore* (Twelve/Hachette); *When Parents Text* (Workman); *The Pack* (Berkeley); *The Men on My Couch* (Berkeley); *Other People's Love Letters* (Clarkson Potter); *The Monstrumologist* (Simon & Schuster); *Post Secret: Extraordinary Confessions from Ordinary Lives* (Morrow); *Pinch Me* (Touchstone)

DH LITERARY, INC.

PO Box 805, Nyack, NY 10960

Agent's name: David Hendin

Born: December 16, 1945, St. Louis, Missouri

Education: BS in biology, education, University of Missouri, Columbia 1967; MA in journalism, University of Missouri, Columbia, 1970

Career history: Columnist, feature writer, executive (including senior vice president, newspaper syndication, and president, World Almanac Publishing/Pharos Books), United Feature Syndicate, Inc., 1970–1993

What's the best way for writers to solicit your interest: We are not accepting any new clients.

Do you charge reading or management fees: No

What categories do you represent, by percentages: Fiction: 40 percent, nonfiction: 60 percent

How would you describe what you do as an agent to someone (or something) from another planet: I have fun with some talented old friends.

What are some representative titles that you have sold: *Big Nate* books and cartoons by Lincoln Peirce; *Miss Manners Minds Your Business* by Judith and Nicholas Martin (W. W. Norton); *Dead End Jobs* series and *Josie Marcus, Mystery Shopper* series by Elaine Viets (NAL/Signet); *The Time Travelers* by David Toomey (W. W. Norton)

DIANA FINCH LITERARY AGENCY

116 West 23rd St, Suite 500, New York, NY 10011
646-375-2081

How to contact: For queries: No phone calls please. Query by mail with SASE or e-mail address for reply, or by e-mail. Please do not include attachments with e-mail queries. The query should be the text of the e-mail, not a separate attachment. Include the word *query* in the subject heading. E-mail address for queries: queryfinchagency@verizon.net

Agent's name: Diana Finch
E-mail: diana.finch@verizon.net
Born: September 1954
Education: Hanover High School, Hanover, NH, 1972; Harvard, BA cum laude 1976; University of Leeds, Leeds, England, MA, 1977
Career history: I opened my own agency in March 2003, following 18 years at the Ellen Levine Literary Agency, where I handled translation rights for Ellen Levine's clients including Russell Banks, Garrison Keillor, and Michael Ondaatje, while developing my own client list. My first job in publishing was on the other side of the fence, as an editorial assistant and then assistant editor at St. Martin's Press. On the advice of older editors, I decided to try agenting and joined the literary agency of Sanford J. Greenburger Associates, where I agented my first deals. I handle translation rights for a select few literary agents. Among their clients whose work I have sold abroad are Stanford mathematics professor Keith Devlin (*The Millennium Problems*, *The Math Gene*, and *Math Instinct*) and the adventurer and philanthropist Greg Mortenson, author with David Oliver Relin of the best seller *Three Cups of Tea*. My own client list includes other novelists, journalists and foreign correspondents, freelancers and staff writers at *Newsweek*, the *Wall Street Journal*, CNN, and the BBC, authors of popular self-help and reference books, and award-winning children's book authors. I have negotiated assignments for my clients with online and print magazines including *Harper's*, *Salon*, *GQ*, *Outside*, the *New York Times*, and *Vanity Fair*. I am the Chair of the International Committee of the Association of Author Representatives, the membership trade organization for literary agents. The committee meets monthly to focus on issues involved in selling clients' work to foreign publishers. I attend the Frankfurt Book Fair every year, and London Book Fair every few years.
Hobbies/Personal interests: Sports: running, field hockey, soccer; Giants football, Red Sox/Yankees baseball, World Cup soccer; introducing my teenage daughter to the opera
Categories/Subjects that you are most enthusiastic about agenting: Memoir, progressive politics, popular science, economics, literary fiction
Categories/Subjects writers shouldn't bother pitching to you: Romance fiction
If you were not an agent, what might you be doing instead: Certainly a career that involved writing and reading—beyond that, it is hard to say: health, social work, education, environmental issues
What's the best way for fiction writers to solicit your interest: Approach me with a polished proposal and sample chapter, have both a developed platform and a website, be original and don't use a query service.
Do you charge fees separate from your commission or offer nonagenting fee-based services: No

What are some representative titles that you have sold: Azadeh Moaveni, *Time* correspondent, *Honeymoon in Tehran* (Random House) and *Lipstick Jihad* (PublicAffairs); Owen Matthews, *Newsweek* Moscow bureau chief, *Stalin's Children* (Bloomsbury); author and activist Antonia Juhasz, *The Tyranny of Oil* and *The Bush Agenda* (HarperCollins); Robert Marion, MD, *Genetics Rounds* (Kaplan) and the classic *Intern Blues* (HarperCollins); environmental journalist Eric Simons, *Darwin Slept Here* (Overlook); economist Loretta Napoleoni, *Rogue Economics* (Seven Stories Press); novelist and essayist Chris Bauman, *The Ice beneath You, Voodoo Lounge*, and, most recently, *In Hoboken* (Melville House); first novelist Michael FitzGerald, *Radiant Days* (Shoemaker & Hoard); Greg Palast's *Armed Madhouse* and *The Best Democracy Money Can Buy* (Dutton/Plume)

How do you feel about writers: What writers do is very difficult, and it usually does not get easier with practice. Figuring out what to write about and planning a book can be as big an undertaking as actually writing the text of the book.

Describe the client from hell, even if you don't have any: None of my clients fit this description, I'm glad to say.

Describe the publisher and/or editor from hell: I consider it part of my job to keep the publishers and editors with whom I work from descending into this realm.

What do you like best about your clients and the editors and publishers you work with: Their energy and creativity are both inspiring and a pleasure to work with.

You're welcome to share your thoughts and sentiments about the business of writing and publishing: It is not easy and it never gets easier—and it is not always possible to tell what will be the most difficult aspect of writing and publishing a book.

Will our business exist as we know it in 10 years or so: No, of course it will be different and probably more different 10 years from now than it was 10 years ago. The difficult economy will have an impact, and the truly creative will use the Internet and new communication technologies in ways we can't quite predict, and the current edge that celebrities have will I think be diminished as true artists level the playing field.

DON CONGDON ASSOCIATES, INC.

110 William Street, Suite 2202, New York, NY 10038
212-645-1229 | fax: 212-727-2688

Agent's name: Cristina Concepcion
E-mail: dca@doncongdon.com
Career history: Don Congdon Associates, Inc., represents over 100 active authors and eight author's estates, as well as a substantial backlist. The agency is a member of the AAR and has been in business since 1983. Many of its authors have appeared on best-seller lists, including current *New York Times* best seller Kathryn Stockett. They have also won numerous awards: Russell Baker and Edna Buchanan, Pulitzer Prize and George Polk Award winners; Ellen Gilchrist, recipient of the National

Book Award; David Sedaris, James Thurber Prize winner; Richard Matheson, winner of an Edgar and Grand Master of Horror awards; and Ray Bradbury, who has received numerous awards including the National Book Foundation's 2002 medal for Distinguished Contribution to American Letters.

Categories/Subjects that you are most enthusiastic about agenting: Fiction: intelligent and thought-provoking commercial or literary novels with a dramatic story and interesting characters, mysteries, thrillers, historicals with suspense. Nonfiction: classical music, popular music, history, wine, visual and performing arts, sociology, essays and criticism, politics and current affairs, culinary subjects, biography and memoir, science, philosophy, self-help, non-Eastern religion, travel

Categories/Subjects writers shouldn't bother pitching to you: Science fiction, horror, illustrated children's books, poetry, Westerns, books written from the point of view of/or sympathetic to terrorists, spirituality, environmental issues, serial killers, child abuse, Spanish-language books

Do you charge fees separate from your commission or offer nonagenting fee-based services: We only charge fees for expenses such as purchase of books for submission, manuscript copying charges, FedEx, or any extraordinary expense for which the author approves, as per AAR guidelines.

What's the best way for writers to solicit your interest: Via e-mail (for security reasons we will not open attachments—please copy and paste any material to your e-mail) or snail mail (please include an SASE if you wish us to return your material should we decide not to represent it). Query first—we will not read unsolicited manuscripts.

Agent's name: Michael Congdon
E-mail: dca@doncongdon.com
Career history: Don Congdon Associates, Inc., represents over 100 active authors and eight author's estates, as well as a substantial backlist. The agency is a member of the AAR and has been in business since 1983. Many of its authors have appeared on best-seller lists, including current *New York Times* best seller Kathryn Stockett. They have also won numerous awards: Russell Baker and Edna Buchanan, Pulitzer Prize and George Polk Award winners; Ellen Gilchrist, recipient of the National Book Award; David Sedaris, James Thurber Prize winner; Richard Matheson, winner of an Edgar and Grand Master of Horror awards; and Ray Bradbury, who has received numerous awards including the National Book Foundation's 2002 medal for Distinguished Contribution to American Letters.

What topics do you most like to represent: Biography, memoir, history (including military history), politics, current affairs, business, and narrative nonfiction (science, medicine, nature, sports); fiction: commercial, genre (mysteries, thrillers, graphic), and literary

Categories/Subjects writers shouldn't bother pitching to you: Romance, Westerns, speculative science fiction, cozy mysteries, cookbooks, children's, poetry

Do you charge fees separate from your commission or offer nonagenting fee-based services: We only charge fees for expenses such as purchase of books for submission, manuscript copying charges, FedEx, or any extraordinary expense for which the author approves, as per AAR guidelines.

What's the best way for writers to solicit your interest: Via e-mail (for security reasons we will not open attachments—please copy and paste any material to your e-mail) or snail mail (please include an SASE if you wish us to return your material should we decide not to represent it). Query first—we will not read unsolicited manuscripts.

Agent's name: Katie Kotchman
E-mail: dca@doncongdon.com
What would you most like to represent: Literary fiction, mystery/thriller/suspense, up-market women's fiction, young-adult fiction (particularly dystopian suspense/adventure), business, true crime, pop culture, photography, fashion, narrative nonfiction

Categories/Subjects writers shouldn't bother pitching to you: Romance, chick lit, children's illustrated, terrorist plots, spiritual/religious, poetry, cozy mysteries, sci-fi

Do you charge fees separate from your commission or offer nonagenting fee-based services: We only charge fees for expenses such as purchase of books for submission, manuscript copying charges, FedEx, or any extraordinary expense for which the author approves, as per AAR guidelines.

What's the best way for writers to solicit your interest: Via e-mail (for security reasons we will not open attachments—please copy and paste any material to your e-mail) or snail mail (please include an SASE if you wish us to return your material should we decide not to represent it). Query first—we will not read unsolicited manuscripts.

Agent's name: Maura Kye-Casella
E-mail: dca@doncongdon.com
Career history: Don Congdon Associates, Inc., represents over 100 active authors and eight author's estates, as well as a substantial backlist. The agency is a member of the AAR and has been in business since 1983. Many of its authors have appeared on best-seller lists, including current *New York Times* best seller Kathryn Stockett. They have also won numerous awards: Russell Baker and Edna Buchanan, Pulitzer Prize and George Polk Award winners; Ellen Gilchrist, recipient of the National Book Award; David Sedaris, James Thurber Prize winner; Richard Matheson, winner of an Edgar and Grand Master of Horror awards; and Ray Bradbury, who has received numerous awards including the National Book Foundation's 2002 medal for Distinguished Contribution to American Letters.

Categories/Subjects that you are most enthusiastic about agenting: Literary works, young-adult and middle-grade novels, commercial women's fiction, thrillers, ghost stories, multicultural voices, and any well-written novels with quirky characters and/or unique plots and settings. As to nonfiction, she is seeking narrative works (memoirs/adventure/true crime), cookbooks (or food-related projects), parenting, pop culture, and humor.

Do you charge fees separate from your commission or offer nonagenting fee-based services: We only charge fees for expenses such as purchase of books for submission, manuscript copying charges, FedEx, or any extraordinary expense for which the author approves, as per AAR guidelines.

What's the best way for writers to solicit your interest: Via e-mail (for security reasons we will not open attachments—please copy and paste any material to your e-mail) or snail mail (please include an SASE if you wish us to return your material should we decide not to represent it). Query first—we will not read unsolicited manuscripts.

Agent's name: Susan Ramer
E-mail: dca@doncongdon.com
Career history: Don Congdon Associates, Inc., represents over 100 active authors and eight author's estates, as well as a substantial backlist. The agency is a member of the AAR and has been in business since 1983. Many of its authors have appeared on best-seller lists, including current *New York Times* best seller Kathryn Stockett. They have also won numerous awards: Russell Baker and Edna Buchanan, Pulitzer Prize and George Polk Award winners; Ellen Gilchrist, recipient of the National Book Award; David Sedaris, James Thurber Prize winner; Richard Matheson, winner of an Edgar and Grand Master of Horror awards; and Ray Bradbury, who has received numerous awards including the National Book Foundation's 2002 medal for Distinguished Contribution to American Letters.

Categories/Subjects that you are most enthusiastic about agenting: Literary fiction and up-market women's fiction (contemporary and historical) and narrative nonfiction. I am drawn to strong voices and stories that are moving and unpredictable, and I appreciate a sense of humor, especially on the dark side. Nonfiction areas of interest include social history and issues, cultural history and pop culture (including music, film, food, fashion, art), women's and family issues, psychology and mental health, and memoirs with distinctive themes.

Categories/Subjects writers shouldn't bother pitching to you: Genre romance, action/adventure/spy thrillers, crime stories, science fiction, fantasy, military, religion/spirituality, poetry, how-to, cookbooks, illustrated children's books

Do you charge fees separate from your commission or offer nonagenting fee-based services: We only charge fees for expenses such as purchase of books for submission, manuscript copying charges, FedEx, or any extraordinary expense for which the author approves, as per AAR guidelines.

What's the best way for writers to solicit your interest: Via e-mail (for security reasons we will not open attachments—please copy and paste any material to your e-mail) or snail mail (please include an SASE if you wish us to return your material should we decide not to represent it). Query first—we will not read unsolicited manuscripts.

Agent's name: Katie Grimm
E-mail: dca@doncongdon.com
Career history: Don Congdon Associates, Inc., represents over 100 active authors and eight author's estates, as well as a substantial backlist. The agency is a member of the AAR and has been in business since 1983. Many of its authors have appeared

on best-seller lists, including current *New York Times* best seller Kathryn Stockett. They have also won numerous awards: Russell Baker and Edna Buchanan, Pulitzer Prize and George Polk Award winners; Ellen Gilchrist, recipient of the National Book Award; David Sedaris, James Thurber Prize winner; Richard Matheson, winner of an Edgar and Grand Master of Horror awards; and Ray Bradbury, who has received numerous awards including the National Book Foundation's 2002 medal for Distinguished Contribution to American Letters.

Categories/Subjects that you are most enthusiastic about agenting: I am interested in vivid literary fiction, transportive historical fiction, up-market women's fiction, cohesive short-story collections, lurid mysteries and thrillers with exotic settings, high-concept young adult, and middle grade and children's with heart and humor. Most importantly, I am hooked by fiction with emotional resonance and longevity, and in my opinion, this requires an authentic and fresh voice, relatable characters, and a twisting plot that keeps me intrigued. For nonfiction, I am looking for offbeat narrative nonfiction, European history, pressing cultural issues, memoir with distinct voice, religion from a historical or sociological point of view, narrative science and medical, multicultural, illustrated, and counter culture.

Categories/Subjects writers shouldn't bother pitching to you: High fantasy, hard science fiction, thrillers with serial killers or terrorist plots, romance, chick lit, spiritual/inspirational, poetry, Western, political, military, or self-help

Do you charge fees separate from your commission or offer nonagenting fee-based services: We only charge fees for expenses such as purchase of books for submission, manuscript copying charges, FedEx, or any extraordinary expense for which the author approves, as per AAR guidelines.

What's the best way for writers to solicit your interest: Via e-mail (for security reasons we will not open attachments—please copy and paste any material to your e-mail) or snail mail (please include an SASE if you wish us to return your material should we decide not to represent it). Query first—we will not read unsolicited manuscripts.

DOYEN LITERARY SERVICES, INC.

1931 660th St., Newell, IA 50568
712-272-3300
barbaradoyen.com

Agent's name: Barbara Doyen

Career history: Our literary agency was launched on a rural acreage, making it unique for its time. But that was years ago before the world had caught up to us; now many people dream of having successful businesses while living a country lifestyle, and modern technology makes it doable from any location. We began by representing books of all kinds: children's board and picture books, teen and young-adult fiction and nonfiction, and most adult categories. But as the business has grown, we've narrowed our focus to adult trade nonfiction only—the kind of books you find in bookstores for the ordinary reader, plus a few that cross over into the textbook market.

Categories/Subjects that you are most enthusiastic about agenting: All types of trade nonfiction including advice/relationships, business/investing/finance, science, health/diet/fitness, history/politics/current affairs, how-to/DIY, lifestyle, psychology, self-improvement, cookbooks, pop culture, reference, narrative nonfiction, inspirational, biography, memoir, and more. Our service starts with extensive advice about preparing a winning book proposal and continues beyond the publisher's contract—we're there to assist through the whole process to ensure a positive outcome: successful books. We are known for our outstanding nonfiction authors who write knowledgeably and well and who deliver to deadline. We are primarily interested in acquiring excellent writers for all kinds of adult nonfiction books and a few textbooks. Can't write? If you are an expert with a book idea but writing is not your strength, we may be able to help. We frequently pair authors and experts for successful book projects.

Categories/Subjects writers shouldn't bother pitching to you: We are not accepting fiction, poetry, or children's projects; however, we cover most adult nonfiction categories.

What's the best way for nonfiction writers to solicit your interest: In order to consider new clients, we must have a few simple rules: (1) Your first contact to us must be a query letter via e-mail. Please send e-mail through our website, barbaradoyen .com. We no longer accept snail mail queries or submissions. (2) Put the word "Query" in the subject line along with a short title to distinguish your message from spam. (3) Do not include attachments in your query. (4) Contact us about adult nonfiction only. Tip: Include your background and interests when querying us—you just never know what could come of it. We might have a book project for you.

Do you charge fees separate from your commission or offer nonagenting fee-based services: Doyen Literary Services, Inc., operates on a commission basis only; we do not charge fees of any kind.

What are some representative titles that you have sold: *Eating Clean for Dummies* by Jonathan V. Wright, MD, and Linda Larsen; *The Beginner's Guide to Growing Heirloom Vegetables* by Marie Iannotti; *Presidents' Most Wanted* by Nick Ragone

---

DREISBACH LITERARY MANAGEMENT, INC.

PO Box 5379, El Dorado Hills, CA 95762
www.dreisbachliterary.com

Agent's name: Verna Dreisbach
E-mail: verna@dreisbachliterary.com
Born: Native California girl
Education: Sacramento State University, MA and BA in English with a concentration in creative writing and language study; AS, mathematics

Career history: At only 18 years old, I began working as a correctional officer and by 21 years old as a sworn police officer. After 13 years in law enforcement, I stayed home to raise three kids, homeschooling for approximately seven of those years. With an obvious passion for teaching, I returned to school to earn my credentials. During that time, I fell in love with writing and became a literary agent. I started my own nonprofit organization, Capitol City Young Writers (CCYW), for aspiring young writers in junior high and high school. I also teach courses through UC Davis Extension. I have had the great fortune to have a few essays published, but my dream book came along when I was given the opportunity to work with Seal Press on *Why We Ride: Women Writers on the Horses in Their Lives*. I am very grateful for the support of Jane Smiley, who wrote the foreword. And, just when I thought that my first career would have absolutely no relevance to my current career, I joined forces with Lee Lofland (author and former cop) to develop *The Writers Police Academy* for writers who are interested in police procedures and how it can better their writing.

Hobbies/Personal interests: I love animals! I have five dogs, six or more cats (I lose count), one goat, four horses, and two ponies. My husband says that all I need now is a stagecoach. I also love to teach and work with kids, which led me to starting my own nonprofit organization, Capitol City Young Writers. The purpose of CCYW is to educate and inspire youth who share a passion for writing, reading, and publishing.

Categories/Subjects that you are most enthusiastic about agenting: No longer in pursuit of criminals as a police officer, I leave it to writers to bring a life of crime to me in the form of mystery, thriller, and true crime. With two degrees in English, I certainly have an appreciation for literary fiction. I will also look at commercial fiction and young adult. I will consider most nonfiction if there is a great platform and a motivated and passionate author who has a vision—that they, the author, are bigger than their book.

Categories/Subjects writers shouldn't bother pitching to you: Science fiction, fantasy, horror, screenplay, poetry, and picture books

If you were not an agent, what might you be doing instead: With as many animals as I have, I really should have been a veterinarian. The other two career options I dreamt of would have sent me off to a third-world country, one being a doctor with an organization such as Doctors without Borders, the other a photojournalist traveling the world to remote places. Truthfully, I was going to be a Solid Gold dancer, but then the show, ended and I had to find an alternative career choice.

Do you charge fees separate from your commission or offer nonagenting fee-based services: Never

What are some representative titles that you have sold: *The Power of Memoir: How to Write Your Healing Story* by Linda Joy Myers (Jossey-Bass/Wiley); *Walnut Wine and Truffle Groves: Culinary Adventures in the Dordogne* by Kimberley Lovato (Running Press/Perseus); *It Gets Easier! And Other Lies We Tell New Mothers* by Claudine Wolk (Amacom); *Acts of God and Man* by Michael R. Powers (Columbia Business School); *Why We Ride: Women Writers on the Horses in Their Lives* by

Verna Dreisbach (Seal Press/Perseus); *Anomaly* by Christopher Baughman (Behler Publications)

How and why did you become an agent: I became an agent purely by accident. After a first career as a police officer and several years of homeschooling, I returned to college to earn my single-subject English certificate so that I could pursue teaching. A professor recognized my writing ability and suggested I enter the Bazzanella Literary Award contest, which I subsequently won in the category of creative nonfiction. I was surprised not only by the professor's suggestion but by winning as well. I started an internship with a literary agent, reviewing queries and incoming manuscripts. I figured the best way for me to learn about writing and improve my own skills was to see the process up close and personal. I didn't expect that I would fall completely in love with the job. I still have my certification to teach English, but I couldn't see myself removed from the world of publishing and writing. Beginning this career from the mindset of a writer, I believe that I share a passion and understanding with other writers who are trying to navigate their way into the world of publishing.

What are your favorite books, movies, and TV shows, and why: My favorite books tend to be classics. I adore Aristotle and my favorite book is *Candide* by Voltaire. Although, nothing will compare to those childhood favorites that drove me to tears—*Charlotte's Web* and *Where the Red Fern Grows*. I'm not a big fan of TV or the movies, but I'll watch anything starring Sean Connery (love *The Hunt for Red October*) or if it has a sword fight.

What's the best way for writers to solicit your interest: I don't have a preferred method. Referrals are nice, but I also enjoy meeting writers at conferences. I can put a face to a name and the writing, and the process becomes more personal. When I get really busy and my client list is getting full, the cold queries are the first and easiest to say no to. Unfortunate, but true for most agents. I hope it helps some authors to realize that a rejection might not mean they don't have a noteworthy or intriguing project. It could just be a matter of poor timing.

Are you optimistic, pessimistic, neutral, or catatonic about the book biz in the future: The best part of being an agent is when an author tells me that I've made their dreams come true. It can't get any better than that! On the negative side, the amount of time it takes to do the job or when I'm not able to sell a project that I really believe in.

DSM AGENCY

1841 Broadway, Suite #903 New York, NY 10023
212-265-9474 | fax: 212-265-9480
www.dsmagency.com

Agent's name: Delia Berrigan Fakis
E-mail: info@dsmagency.com
Born: Washington, DC, 1981

Education: Georgetown Visitation Preparatory School; BA in English from Drew University; MS in publishing from New York University

Career history: Previously, Delia was the subsidiary rights specialist at the agency. Prior to joining the DSM Agency team in 2005, Delia was an editorial assistant at John Wiley & Sons in Hoboken, NJ, and an editorial assistant and contributing writer at the Connection Newspapers in the Washington, DC, metropolitan area.

Hobbies/Personal interests: Running (especially with her German shorthair pointer), reading, writing, listening to a cappella music, Anglophilia, traveling, ceramics, and attempting to cook and garden

Categories/Subjects that you are most enthusiastic about agenting: The agency specialties are business and self-help books from top professionals in their fields of expertise. We also take on current affairs, narrative, biography and memoir, lifestyle, social sciences, gender, history, health, classical music, sports, women's issues, and literary fiction.

Categories/Subjects writers shouldn't bother pitching to you: No romance, coffee table books, art books, trivia, pop culture, humor, Westerns, occult and supernatural, horror, poetry, textbooks, children's books, picture books, film scripts, articles, cartoons, and professional manuals

Do you charge fees separate from your commission or offer nonagenting fee-based services: No

What's the best way for fiction writers to solicit your interest: The best way for authors to contact us is with a carefully prepared query letter sent via e-mail to query@dsmagency.com. No calls, please.

Agent's name: Doris S. Michaels
Agent assistant: Pauline Hsia
E-mail: info@dsmagency.com
Born: Born in Lodi, CA (May 1955)
Education: BA in English and German literature, University of California at Santa Cruz; MAT. University of California at Berkeley; certificate in computer technology, Columbia University; certificate in book and magazine publishing, 1994 Summer Publishing Institute, New York University. All my life I have loved to read and solidified my passion by majoring in English and German literature at UC Berkeley. It was there that I met my husband (of now over 30 years), Charlie Michaels, and where I learned the business skills to combine my love of reading with practical applications. In the early 80s I began a career in publishing as an acquisitions editor for Prentice Hall. Since I felt left out of the computer revolution, to round out my education I went to Columbia University at nights and on weekends while working full time to earn a certificate in programming and technology. The additional education gave me the qualifications to run the International Information Center for the largest bank in Switzerland (UBS) after my husband was offered the opportunity to start the European Securities area for Goldman Sachs based in Zurich. After four years in Zurich and two years in London, we

returned to the States, and I started my literary agency. Now that the computer world has merged with all other industries, I'm happy to be a part of this new technical world with all the opportunities of e-mail and websites to expand an agency like mine.

Hobbies and personal interests: Music, including listening to classical music and playing the violin; sports, including biking, skiing, and swimming; fluent in German

Categories/Subjects that you are most enthusiastic about agenting: The DSM Agency's specialties are business and self-help books from top professionals in their fields of expertise. We are also looking for books in categories such as current affairs, narrative, biography and memoir, lifestyle, social sciences, gender, history, health, classical music, sports, and women's issues. In the fiction camp, we are currently interested in representing literary fiction that has commercial appeal and strong screen potential.

Categories/Subjects writers shouldn't bother pitching to you: Unfortunately, we are currently not interested in representing science fiction, thrillers, romance, mysteries, coffee table books, art books, trivia, pop culture, humor, Westerns, occult and supernatural, horror, poetry, textbooks, children's books, picture books, film scripts, articles, cartoons, and professional manuals.

If you were not an agent, what might you be doing instead: Perhaps a concert violinist

Do you charge fees separate from your commission or offer nonagenting fee-based services: We do not charge a reading fee. Our commission schedule is standard at 15 percent domestic.

What are some representative titles that you have sold: Please see our website at www.dsmagency.com. Some of the recent titles include *The MELT Method* by Sue Hitzmann (HarperCollins, April 2012); *Thirst* by James Salzman (Overlook Press, October 2012); *The Transformative CEO* by Jeffrey Fox and Robert Reiss (McGraw-Hill, May 2012); *Power Entertaining* by Eddie Osterland (Wiley, September 2012); *Rwanda, Inc.,* by Patricia Crisafulli and Andrea Redmond (Palgrave Macmillan, October 2012); *The Baker's Daughter* by Sarah McCoy (Random House, January 2012); *From Values to Action* by Harry Kraemer (Jossey-Bass, April 2011); *The Time It Snowed in Puerto Rico* by Sarah McCoy (Random House, August 2009); *How to be a Fierce Competitor* by Jeff Fox (Jossey-Bass, March 2010)—11th book; *Influence* by Maddy Dychtwald (Hyperion, May 2010); *Comebacks* by Andrea Redmond and Patricia Crisafulli (Jossey-Bass, May 2010); *Power of Pause* by Nance Guilmartin (Jossey-Bass, January 2010); *The Neatest Little Guide to Stock Market Investing* by Jason Kelly (Plume at Penguin, January 2010)—4th edition; *The House of Dimon* by Patricia Crisafulli (Wiley, March 2009)—*NY Times* best seller; *How NASA Builds Teams* by Charles Pellerin (Wiley, March 2009).

What's the best way for fiction writers to solicit your interest: We prefer pitches as e-mail query letters (with no attachments) sent to our query mailbox at query@dsmagency.com. No phone calls, please.

DUNHAM LITERARY, INC.

156 Fifth Avenue, Suite 625, New York, NY 10010
212-929-0994

Agent's name: Chris Morehouse
E-mail: dunhamlit@yahoo.com
Career history: Attorney admitted to New York State Bar for 25 years; member of the Entertainment, Arts, and Sports Law Section of the New York State Bar Association; member of AAR

Categories/Subjects that you are most enthusiastic about agenting: I like to represent writers of adult nonfiction books in the categories of memoir, health, parenting, relationships, and current affairs. I also represent authors of middle-grade and young-adult fiction and nonfiction. Topics of particular interest to me are sports (especially baseball), psychology, and women's issues (motherhood, work, self-help). I am not interested in the paranormal or religious topics.

What's the best way for fiction writers to solicit your interest: No e-mail queries please! Send Chris Morehouse query letters to 9 Normandy Lane, Manhasset, NY 11030.

How do you feel about writers: Like motherhood, writing is the hardest and loneliest profession, but the rewards are great when you do it well. I love my writers because they handle criticism and rejection with a sense of humor and as a learning experience.

Agent's name: Jennie Dunham
E-mail: dunhamlit@yahoo.com
Career history: Jennie Dunham has been a literary agent in New York City since May 1992. She started her career at John Brockman Associates and then joined Mildred Marmur Associates. She was employed by Russell & Volkening for six years before she left to found Dunham Literary, Inc., in August 2000. She has been a member of AAR (Association of Author Representatives) since 1993. She served on the program committee and was program committee director for several years.

EBELING & ASSOCIATES

303-823-6963
www.ebelingagency.com

Agent's name: Kristina Holmes
Education: BA anthropology, University of Hawaii, Manoa, 2002
Career history: I've been with Ebeling & Associates since 2005, concentrating on practical nonfiction and over the past couple of years, expanding the creative

nonfiction on our list. I'm deeply passionate about the type of books we represent—books that, in some way, educate, enlighten, or inspire readers.

Hobbies/Personal interests: Do I dare say reading?! Beyond my love affair with books, I enjoy physical activities like hiking, biking, surfing, swimming, and going to the gym; nutrition, continuing education, astrology, metaphysics, photography, art, yoga, meditation, friends, and nature.

Categories/Subjects that you are most enthusiastic about agenting: In practical nonfiction, I'm actively looking for titles in health and wellness, mind/body/spirit, spirituality, women's issues, psychology, business, environment/green books, parenting, and pop culture. Practical books must have a distinct premise and be written by authors with established platforms. I am increasingly looking for practical authors who have built a brand, of which the book is just one part. The creative nonfiction I represent varies, but the projects that interest me the most have a very strong and polished voice with a great story behind it.

Categories/Subjects writers shouldn't bother pitching to you: Fiction

If you were not an agent, what might you be doing instead: Traveling

What's the best way for nonfiction writers to solicit your interest: Write a succinct query including a brief statement about your book, what makes it different from what's already been published, why readers will love it, and why you're the person to write it. If you're writing a practical book, please demonstrate your credentials to write your book. I tend to favor queries that are straightforward over ones that attempt to be overly clever.

What are some representative titles that you have sold: *Unjunk Your Junk Food: Healthy Alternatives to Conventional Junk Foods* by Andrea Donsky, Randy Boyer, and Lisa Tsakos (Gallery/Simon & Schuster 2012); *Scammed: How to Save Money and Find Better Service in a World of Schemes, Swindles, and Shady Deals* by Christopher Elliott (Wiley 2011); *Executive Toughness: The Mental Training Program to Increase Your Leadership Performance* by Dr. Jason Selk (McGraw-Hill 2011); *Lead. Serve. Love.* by Gregory Lang (Thomas Nelson 2011); *Kama Pootra: 52 Mind-Blowing Ways to Poop* by Daniel Young (Sourcebooks 2010); *100 Sounds to See* by Marsha Engle and William Huber (Health Communications, Inc. 2010)

How do you feel about writers: I *love* writers. Writers are artists, activists, educators, therapists, and much more. They may bring to light things we know but in a way that most of us can't express. Or perhaps they illuminate aspects of life or of ourselves that we've never considered and need to. In particular, I cherish writers because they make magic happen. They do so by changing the way we think, and as a result, who we are in the world.

Describe the client from hell, even if you don't have any: Unappreciative with a lack of willingness to do their part (write a great manuscript and book proposal, create and implement a successful promotion plan for the book), unable to accept constructive feedback, overly demanding, doesn't follow through with deadlines

Describe the publisher and/or editor from hell: I haven't yet encountered a truly hellish editor, thankfully! Editors work hard and long hours and tend to be very appreciative of the authors we bring their way. A few editors are unprofessional or nonresponsive, but the great majority are amazing people. Thank you, gracious colleagues...

What do you like best about your clients and the editors and publishers you work with: I have the honor of guiding authors in their careers. These are people that I admire and respect deeply and who have made a lasting, professional, and sometimes, personal impact on my life. While I love that our authors are advocating on important issues, at the end of the day I think what I appreciate most about them is that they are genuine, kind people. I enjoy my work so much in no small part because of my clients. In terms of editors and publishers, I think we're in a challenging time right now in publishing, and while I do wonder about the cookie-cutter approach I see some publishers continuing to take, I also see a lot of editors who are dedicated to their craft and want to see this industry succeed. I think most notable is the tremendously long hours that editors work. I'm just amazed.

Describe yourself: On a professional level, I'm extremely determined (debatably to a fault), passionate, and supportive. I represent a younger generation of Americans who have had a lot of freedom to decide what they want in life and less of the societal constrictions that influenced older generations to follow a formulaic approach to life (education, marriage, kids, retirement). This environment has allowed us to consider alternative ways of being and living, which is very necessary for the health of our relationships, environment, economy, and personal satisfaction in life. So, a big thanks to the older generations for helping to shape our history here in the United States. While still so obviously fraught with political and social challenges, we have the opportunity to create our own reality, a freedom that so many others around the world lack. I get a lot of enjoyment out of being a literary agent, but I also look way beyond this to what I'm getting out of and giving to the world. I'm looking forward to being part of the positive growth and evolution occurring globally. Life is a deep mystery and something that I am profoundly grateful to be part of.

Agent's name: Michael Ebeling
Born: June 13, 1963; Escondido, California
Education: BS business, Colorado University; MA holistic health and wellness, Naropa University
Career history: Michael Ebeling brings more than 15 years of publications, consulting, sales, and applied management experience to Ebeling & Associates. Michael's experience with leading authors and publishing companies enables him to effectively advise and support clients in the execution of their goals. Michael spent seven years as the CEO of Alan Cohen Publications (ACP), managing the business and developing Alan's platform and branding from the ground up. During his tenure at ACP, Michael sold several Cohen titles to US publishers and foreign rights to more than 10 countries. In addition to increasing overall sales by 30 percent, Michael managed worldwide book tours and retreats and branded the company message through media such as corporate DVDs, websites, promotional

materials, and press kits. Michael also booked shows for the author on CNN, Fox News with Neil Cavuto, CNBC, and WGN, and had article placements on MSN, CNET, *Psychology Today*, *First for Women*, and *Body and Soul*. Previously, Michael was the marketing director for Art After Five, a publishing house and gift line based in Colorado. During this time, he more than doubled sales and increased the client base by 50 percent. Combining a business degree from the University of Colorado and an MA in health and wellness from the Naropa Institute in Boulder, Colorado, along with his travels to India experiencing and studying the teachings of Indian masters, Michael has a unique background that enables him to merge the worlds of business and spirituality. He enjoys developing long-term relationships built with a deep sense of caring and integrity, and enjoys consulting with authors to create platforms and marketing strategies that drive and sell their books.

Hobbies/Personal interests: Surfing, yoga, Ultimate Frisbee, travel, and reading

Categories/Subjects that you are most enthusiastic about agenting: Prescriptive nonfiction including health, diet, nutrition, sports, self-help/personal growth, mind/body/spirit, humor, business, finance, and career books

Categories/Subjects writers shouldn't bother pitching to you: Fiction

If you were not an agent, what might you be doing instead: I would be a professional traveler.

What's the best way for nonfiction writers to solicit your interest: By adhering to the submission guidelines outlined on our website. We are looking for professional authors with strong platforms that want to get their message out to the world.

Do you charge fees separate from your commission or offer nonagenting fee-based services: Our agency offers consulting services for nonagented clients—usually involves sales/marketing/platform development coaching.

What are some representative titles that you have sold: *Naked: How to Find the Perfect Partner by Revealing Your True Self* by David Wygant (Hay House 2012); *Blissful Bites: Vegan Meals that Nourish Mind, Body, and Planet* by Christy Morgan (BenBella Books 2011); *The Loyalty Cure* by Timothy Keiningham and Lerzan Askoy (BenBella Books 2010); *Counterintuitive: How Neuroscience Is Revolutionizing Management* by Charles Jacobs, PhD (Portfolio/Penguin 2009); *Instant Wealth, Wake Up Rich: Discover the Secrets of the New Entrepreneurial Mind* by Chris Howard (Wiley 2009)

How and why did you become an agent: Because I love the book business and I love to sell. Put those two together and there you are—an agent.

What are your favorite books, movies, and TV shows, and why: TV: *The Daily Show*, *True Blood*, *No Reservations*, *The Sopranos*; Movies: *Ray* and *Avatar*

Describe the client from hell, even if you don't have any: (1) They call all the time. (2) They don't listen to what you tell them. (3) They think they should be on *Oprah*.

You're welcome to share your thoughts and sentiments about the business of writing and publishing: The publishing industry is going to become more and more competitive. It seems that everyone wants to write a book these days and there is only so much shelf space in the bookstores. Writers are going to have a more challenging time finding agents; agents will find it harder to place their clients; and the publishers' margins are shrinking because of this competition.

EDITE KROLL LITERARY AGENCY, INC.

20 Cross Street, Saco, ME 04072
207-283-8797 | fax 207-283-8799

Agent's name: Edite Kroll
E-mail: ekroll@maine.rr.com
Born: Germany
Education: Germany and UK
Career history: Have run my independent literary agency in New York City and Maine for over 25 years. A former editor in London and New York, I represent a small list of adult and children's book writers, as well as artists who write their own books. I have also translated a number of books from German into English.

Hobbies/Personal interests: Learning languages, travel

Categories/Subjects that you are most enthusiastic about agenting: Women writing about their lives in different countries; humor, both narrative and illustrative, for adults and children; fiction for children (middle-grade through young-adult) and limited literary fiction for adults; issue-oriented nonfiction beyond self-help

Categories/Subjects writers shouldn't bother pitching to you: Genre, e.g., romantic fiction, mystery/suspense, cookbooks; no diet books, photographic books, poetry; no single projects—writers only

If you were not an agent, what might you be doing instead: Running a publishing company, restaurant, or bookstore; coaching; translating more books

What's the best way for fiction writers to solicit your interest: A brief letter outlining book and credentials, limited to subjects and areas I am interested in, or an introduction from other clients

Do you charge fees separate from your commission or offer nonagenting fee-based services: I only charge legal fees (previously agreed on) and copying large manuscripts. I offer no nonagented fee-based services.

What are some representative titles that you have sold: *Dreams of Trespass* by Fatema Mernissi, Perseus; *All I Know I Learned from My Cat* by Suzy Becker, Workman; *Work in Progress* by Brett McCarthy, Knopf; *If the Buddha Dated* books by Charlotte Kasl, Penguin; *Benny and Penny* books by Geoffrey Hayes, Raw, Jr.; *Who Wants a Cheap Rhinoceros?* by Shel Silverstein

How and why did you become an agent: After a short stint in marketing (working with a new book division at L'Eggs), publishers only offered me jobs to RUN divisions, and I wanted to work directly with authors and artists. Having started out in subsidiary rights and contracts in the UK (Chatto & Windus), I felt I had a good basic understanding of the business side.

How do you feel about writers: I love their (sometimes hidden) passions and like helping them translate that passion into books.

How would you describe what you do as an agent to someone (or something) from another planet: I am a salesperson, an intermediary between writers and publishers; I represent the writer, not the publisher; and I work on commission only.

What do you like best about your clients and the editors and publishers you work with: Honest dialogue without game playing

Will our business exist as we know it in 10 years or so: Being the eternal optimist, I believe books will continue to exist and be read, though the majority may not continue to be available primarily in printed form.

ELAINE P. ENGLISH, PLLC

4710 41st Street, NW, Suite D, Washington, DC 20016
202-362-5190 | fax: 202-362-5192
www.elaineenglish.com

Agent's name: Elaine P. English
E-mail: Elaine@elaineenglish.com
Born: Asheville, North Carolina
Education: Undergraduate in Latin (magna cum laude) at Randolph Macon Woman's College; MEd (counseling and personnel services) University of Maryland; JD National Law Center at George Washington University
Career history: After pursuing careers in teaching, social services, and personnel management, I completed law school and began working as an attorney for a public interest organization representing reporters and journalists on open government and media issues. I then joined a small firm with a publishing law/agenting practice. After that I had my own firm and managed a small literary agency. For more than 25 years in private practice, I have concentrated on media and publishing issues. About 10 years ago, I decided to expand my practice to include agenting of commercial fiction. Now, on my own, I continue to pursue a practice of both legal and agenting services.
Hobbies/Personal interests: Reading, hiking, nature photography
Categories/Subjects that you are most enthusiastic about agenting: ONLY women's fiction, romance of all subgenres (both contemporary, historical, and paranormal but primarily single titles), and cozy mysteries
Categories/Subjects writers shouldn't bother pitching to you: All nonfiction (including memoirs), children's books, inspirational projects, science fiction and thrillers
If you were not an agent, what might you be doing instead: Simply practicing law
What's the best way for fiction writers to solicit your interest: I accept only e-mail queries sent to queries@elaineenglish.com. I do not accept attachments to e-mails. Generally I will not make a final decision without reading the entire manuscript.
What's the best way for nonfiction writers to solicit your interest: N/A

Do you charge reading or management fees: I charge no reading fees or any upfront costs.

What are the most common mistakes writers make when pitching to you: I hate to see pitches that get bogged down in too much detail, while not giving a complete overview of the project. Also, I find that too many authors rush into submitting their manuscripts before they have actually completed editing, critiquing, and proofreading them.

Describe the client from hell, even if you don't have any: The client who is not open to comments and criticism and who refuses to learn anything about the realities of the publishing business

What's your definition of a great client: A great client is one who sees his/her relationship with an agent as a partnership and is willing to work hard as a professional in this business. Of course, he/she is first and foremost an exceptionally talented writer.

What can a writer do to increase the odds of you becoming his or her agent: Know their target market and have a well-written, solid manuscript with an inventive plot; strong commercial hook; good pacing; strong dialogue; and realistic, strong characters.

How and why did you become an agent: Because I love books, enjoy working with authors, and wanted to contribute, even in a small way, to the creative process by which the reading public is entertained.

What do you see in the near future for book publishing: The book publishing industry is clearly in a period of transition at the moment, and the precise parameters of the future are not clear. I'm confident, though, that books, in some form, will be with us forever.

What are your favorite books, movies, and TV shows, and why: *Jane Eyre* is my all-time favorite book, in part, because it was my introduction into the wonderful world of women's fiction and romance. My taste in TV shows and movies is varied, but I tend to like character-driven series. Frankly, with all the reading I do, there's not much TV time.

In your opinion, what do editors think of you: I hope that they think of me as a fair and reasonable professional who brings them quality projects.

What are some representative titles that you have sold: *The Last Chance* series (most recent *Last Chance Beauty Queen*) by Hope Ramsay (*Forever*/Grand Central); *Getting Played* and *Download Drama* by Celeste Norfleet (Kimani TRU); *The Butterfly House* by Marcia Preston (Mira); and *Tall Dark and Cowboy* by Joanne Kennedy (Sourcebooks)

THE EPSTEIN LITERARY AGENCY

PO Box 356, Avon, MA 02322
www.epsteinliterary.com

Agent's name: Kate Epstein
Born: New York City

Education: BA University of Michigan

Career history: I was an editor at a trade publisher, and I loved it. And then one day I kind of stopped loving it. I still loved books, and I still loved working with authors, but a job that had seemed so varied and interesting was beginning to seem boring. The passion was starting to drip away. Since the money isn't that good, I needed to get that back. One of the best things about making the change to being an agent is that I could follow my heart to be 100 percent the author's advocate. As an editor my sympathies generally lay with the authors, but my paycheck came from elsewhere, so I felt divided ethically. But being your advocate means sometimes telling you that you're wrong.

Hobbies/Personal interests: Raising my two kids. Reading—I've always resisted calling it a "hobby" because I don't consider eating or breathing to be hobbies, and I'm almost that dependent on it. Being very busy I squeeze it in at the oddest times—while doing housework or brushing my teeth. I actually don't know how to go to sleep without reading. Feminism. I also have a vegetable garden and work out every day, but I'm not necessarily proficient at either.

Categories/Subjects that you are most enthusiastic about agenting: 100 percent nonfiction for adults. Particularly interested in (in alpha order) business, crafts, fashion, humor, inspiration, journalism, lifestyles, memoir, nonfiction narrative, parenting, pets, popular culture, reference, relationships, self-help, travel/adventure, women's interests.

Categories/Subjects writers shouldn't bother pitching to you: Fiction, children's, poetry, screenplays

If you were not an agent, what might you be doing instead: The longer I do it, the harder it is to contemplate not agenting, but I loved being an acquisitions editor and could probably love it again. If I didn't work in publishing, I could imagine being a doula.

What's the best way for nonfiction writers to solicit your interest: Make it clear you've read my website. I'm a sucker for compliments, like anyone else—especially if you've read something I agented. I'll also give special consideration if we share an alma mater.

Do you charge fees separate from your commission or offer nonagenting fee-based services: Nope

What are some representative titles that you have sold: *A TV Guide to Life* by Jeff Alexander of *Television Without Pity*, Berkley Books; *Whatever You Do, Don't Run* by Peter Allison, Globe Pequot (North America), Nicholas Brealey (UK, South Africa), Allen & Unwin (Australia), Mouria (Dutch); *Don't Look Behind You* by Peter Allison, Globe Pequot (North America), Allen & Unwin (Australia); *Your 401(canine) Plan* by Mary Jane Checchi, T. F. H. Publications; *The Crochet Dude's Designs for Guys* by Drew Emborsky, The Crochet Dude, Lark Books, of Sterling; *Pets and the Planet* by Carol Frischmann, Howell Book House, a division of John Wiley & Sons, Inc.; *Eagle Walker* by Jeffery Guidry, William Morrow; *The Green Bride Guide* by Kate Harrison, Sourcebooks; *Crossing the Gates of Alaska: One Man and Two Dogs 600 Miles off the Map* by Dave Metz, Citadel; *Knitting the Threads of*

Time by Nora Murphy, New World Library; *Stage Right: Professional Advice to Sell Your Home* by Starr C. Osborne, AMACOM Books; *Nail Your Law Job Interview* by Natalie Prescott and Oleg Cross, Career Press. My website has a complete list.

How and why did you become an agent: I basically became an agent by putting out my shingle. I also took a number of more experienced agents to lunch and picked their brains—a number continue to provide support and advice, and I likewise share my knowledge when it's helpful. Two years in I qualified for membership in the AAR.

How do you feel about writers: Being a solo agent means that writers are my closest colleagues in many ways. I've always loved working with them and have enjoyed nurturing their varied processes—it keeps things interesting. I'm not hugely hip to fame and I think that's why I like being outside the spotlight, and helping my authors to be in the spotlight. I wasn't cool in high school and I didn't want to be. (I wasn't picked on either. I was ignored by most. Good enough.)

What are your favorite books, movies, and TV shows, and why: I'm bad at picking favorite books, and I've become someone that rarely rereads, so in a way my relationship with a book is always temporary. Though when it changes me that may be permanent. I read *Chains* by Laurie Halse Anderson recently and found it a throwback to my teen years, so absorbing that nothing else seemed real. It's very upsetting though, in a way I think far more upsetting to an adult than to a kid. That's the only book I read recently that I'd recommend really widely, though I just enjoyed *Identical Strangers* by Elyse Schein and Paula Bernstein, which deftly wove together two personal narratives and all kinds of interesting information about twins and adoption. Dewey was really quite cute. Favorite TV shows is easy; I like *Battlestar Galactica*, *The Daily Show with Jon Stewart*, and *Saving Grace*. BSG inspires in me a deep love that comes from intriguing plot lines, great characters, and cute boys. As to Jon, he makes the news interesting, which is a feat. I watch while lifting weights the next morning after he broadcasts.

Describe the client from hell, even if you don't have any: Someone who is abusive to me or to editors. Life is too short to work with some people.

What do you like best about your clients and the editors and publishers you work with: I love it when we all believe in a book and its capacity to make people's lives better in some way.

You're welcome to share your thoughts and sentiments about the business of writing and publishing: I think what inspires me most is how intimate the act of reading is, how books enter people's homes and lives. Whatever their subject.

Describe yourself: In some ways I identify with *The Little Engine That Could*. I carry fun and nourishment over the mountain, and I'm very determined.

Will our business exist as we know it in 10 years or so: Yes, I believe it will, though certainly it will change. I'm hopeful about the electronic future. I haven't got a reader yet—I don't commute so it doesn't seem worth it—but I'm hopeful that it will focus readers' attention on the book's text, which after all is its essence. I used to feel books were great decoration—and I still find it odd when I go into a home and see none of them—but I'm finding I have less interest in keeping large numbers of books around than I used to. I think books are to be read and loved, but their physical presence means little to me. And I wouldn't mind getting out of the tree-killing business.

THE ETHAN ELLENBERG LITERARY AGENCY

548 Broadway, New York, NY 10012

Agent's name: Ethan Ellenberg

Career history: Contracts Manager at Berkley, associates Contracts Manager at Bantam 1979–1984

Categories/Subjects that you are most enthusiastic about agenting: All commercial fiction: romance, SF, fantasy, thriller, mystery; all children's fiction: picture books, middle grade, young adult. History, health, science, etc.

Categories/Subjects writers shouldn't bother pitching to you: Poetry

What's the best way for fiction writers to solicit your interest: By mail—see website; synopsis/first three chapters/SASE

What's the best way for nonfiction writers to solicit your interest: By mail—see website; proposal/SASE

Do you charge reading or management fees: No

What are the most common mistakes writers make when pitching to you: Confusing letters; too much personal information

What can a writer do to increase the odds of you becoming his or her agent: Write a great book.

How and why did you become an agent: Love books, felt it was the best job

How would you describe what you do as an agent to someone (or something) from another planet: Represent authors, support them, handle their business

What do you think the future holds for book publishing: The continued impact of Internet will affect us a lot.

What are some representative titles that you have sold: Translation rights to three-time 2009 Hugo Award nominee John Scalzi's *Zoe's Tale* to Heyne in Germany and Eskimo in Russia; two new *Undead* titles and one new paranormal romance anthology to Berkley for Mary Janice Davidson; three new historical romances to NAL for Beatrice Small; five new military science-fiction titles to Avon for Stephen Coonts' coauthor and best seller William Keith; *The Rogue Agent* series of young-adult fantasy to Harper Australia and Orbit US/UK for Karen Miller (w.a. K. E. Mills); two new paranormal romance titles for up-and-coming author Jory Strong to Berkley; six-book deal for best-selling paranormal romance author Christine Warren to St. Martin's; *Last Song*, a new illustrated book by Eric Rohmann to Roaring Brook Press; *Hellcats* by Peter Sasgen to Putnam; *None Left Behind* by Charles Sasser to St. Martin's

FINEPRINT LITERARY MANAGEMENT

57 E. 11th St., Suite 5B, New York, NY 10003
212-777-0047 | fax: 212-228-1660
www.jetreidliterary.com

Agent's name: Janet Reid
Born: Seattle, Washington
Hobbies/Personal interests: Contemporary art, contemporary music, justice, and death penalty issues
Categories/Subjects that you are most enthusiastic about agenting: Narrative nonfiction, particularly history and biography; thrillers; literary fiction
Categories/Subjects writers shouldn't bother pitching to you: Domestic, sexual, pastoral abuse; poetry (although I represent poets for their narrative work); screenplays
If you were not an agent, what might you be doing instead: Stalking Jack Reacher
What's the best way for fiction writers to solicit your interest: Write a compelling query letter on a twenty-dollar bill.
Do you charge fees separate from your commission or offer nonagenting fee-based services: No
What are some representative titles that you have sold: *Crashers* by Dana Haynes; *Even* by Andrew Grant; *Purgatory Chasm* by Steve Ulfelder; *The Pericles Commission* by Gary Corby; *Q* by Evan Mandery; *The Man in the Empty Suit* by Sean Ferrell; *The Avery Cates* series by Jeff Somers; *Without a Paddle* by Warren Richey; *The Killing Court* by Evan Mandery
How do you feel about writers: Their work and their confidence in me allows me to earn a living doing what I love.
How would you describe what you do as an agent to someone (or something) from another planet: I try not to discuss my work when on vacation.
What are your favorite books, movies, and TV shows, and why: *The Wire*. No further explanation needed.
Describe the client from hell, even if you don't have any: Well, I am Satan's literary agent, so I describe him as "mine."
Describe the publisher and/or editor from hell: There are no publishers or editors in hell. They rejected it as "not quite right for them."
What do you like best about your clients and the editors and publishers you work with: Their brilliant writing and creativity. And they are hilarious. I'm so, so fortunate to have them on my list. As for editors, they work magic.
Describe yourself: No. I don't want to scare anyone...yet.
Will our business exist as we know it in 10 years or so: Yes

Agent's name: Amy Tipton
Born: Jan. 27, Arlington, Texas

Education: BA from Naropa University, MA and MFA from New College of California

Career history: I became an agent after working as a literary assistant and office manager at several literary agencies including JCA Literary Agency, Diana Finch Literary Agency, Gina Maccoby Literary Agency, and Liza Dawson Associates. I also worked as a book scout for Aram Fox, Inc., dealing with foreign rights and also worked as a freelance editor to Lauren Weisberger, author of *The Devil Wears Prada*.

Categories/Subjects that you are most enthusiastic about agenting: young adult, commercial women's fiction

Categories/Subjects writers shouldn't bother pitching to you: Science fiction/fantasy

If you were not an agent, what might you be doing instead: Writing or teaching

Do you charge fees separate from your commission or offer nonagenting fee-based services: No

What are some representative titles that you have sold: *Cracked Up to Be* by Courtney Summers (St. Martin's Press); Untitled by Amy Reed (Simon Pulse)

How and why did you become an agent: I just fell into it. I was Peter Rubie's assistant, and he encouraged me to start taking on projects, to see if I could do it.

How do you feel about writers: I love writers. Of course.

What are your favorite books, movies, and TV shows, and why: I probably have too many favorites to name…Books, recently? A lot of young adult: *13 Reasons Why, Such a Pretty Girl, Looking for Alaska, The Fat Girl, Speak, Cracked Up to Be,* etc. All time? *The Abortion: An Historical Romance 1966, Breakfast at Tiffany's, To Kill a Mockingbird, Catcher in the Rye, The Stranger.* Authors I love: Richard Brautigan, Michelle Tea, Eileen Myles, Dorothy Allison, Tawni O'Dell, E. Lockheart, Patrick Carman, Courtney Summers, Daisy Whitney, Lauren Weisberger…As for movies, I love *Breakfast at Tiffany's, Surviving Desire, Secretary, Eternal Sunshine of the Spotless Mind, Down by Law, Ghost World, Serial Mom, Hedwig and the Angry Inch, Muriel's Wedding, Heathers…*I love these books/authors and movies because each one tells a great story.

Describe the client from hell, even if you don't have any: A writer who is (emotionally) high-maintenance is hard to work with; someone who has ego and/or is constantly demanding attention—in the form of e-mail or phone conversations—and second-guessing you as an agent is difficult to work with.

Agent's name: Colleen Lindsay
Born: Burlingame, California; April 13
Education: Life!
Career history: I spent most of my formative years hiding beneath the blankets with a flashlight and a book. My first job in publishing was in Northern California as a mass-merchandise sales rep for Ballantine Books. For five years I served as director of publicity for Del Rey Books, a division of the Random House Publishing Group, where I specialized in the creative publicity and marketing of science fiction, fantasy, pop culture, young-adult fantasy, graphic novels, and third-party licensed media. I've

also worked as a freelance publicist and copywriter for several major trade publishers and as a book reviewer for the *San Francisco Chronicle* under the inimitable Pat Holt. My background in independent book publishing goes even further back to my first job as a bookstore manager in 1984 at the now-defunct San Francisco Bay Area bookstore Central Park Books. I also worked at Printers, Inc., Books in Palo Alto and spent six years as the marketing and events manager at Stacey's Bookstore in San Francisco.

Hobbies/Personal interests: Being faster than a speeding bullet; gratuitous lifting of heavy objects in front of a mirror; nerd-herding; extracting cat claws from sofa; occasionally getting Monopoly and Risk confused, thus resulting in the occasional unfortunate placement of hotels in the Ural Mountains while my army unwittingly invades Park Place (Tragic!); photography; writing; blogging; sleeping whenever possible; and, of course, reading

Categories/Subjects that you are most enthusiastic about agenting: Fiction of all types, both literary and commercial. I love writers who can engage me with amazing characters and a strong voice. Above all, I'm looking for writers who understand the importance of storytelling. I have a particular soft spot for and specialize in genre fiction: science fiction, fantasy, urban fantasy, paranormal romance, slipstream, new weird, horror, steampunk, space opera, military SF, cyberpunk, and surrealism. I love young adult and young-adult fantasy, too. In nonfiction, I'm looking for eloquent narrative nonfiction, works of LGBT interest, and pop culture. I'd also like to see business or career books geared toward young women. And I'm very interested in graphic novels!

Categories/Subjects writers shouldn't bother pitching to you: I don't represent any Christian fiction or nonfiction, inspirational, category romance, children's books, poetry, or short stories.

If you were not an agent, what might you be doing instead: When I was a kid, I wanted to be (in the following order) a small Mexican boy named Pedro (in my head I had a sombrero and a burro), an astronaut, a veterinarian, a writer, and an archaeologist. When I grow up, I still hope to become Indiana Jones. But for now, agenting fits nicely.

What's the best way for fiction writers to solicit your interest: Shout? Wave? Throw an angry Pomeranian at me? Oh, wait, you mean as a writer? The most effective way to make me sit up and take notice is to write a damned good query letter with a strong hook. Let me know that you've actually read my submissions guidelines. This shows me that you're a professional, that you take your own career as seriously as I do.

Do you charge fees separate from your commission or offer nonagenting fee-based services: I'm a freelance copywriter for several large publishers. I specialize in press materials and author Q&As.

What are some representative titles that you have sold: *Better Part of Darkness* by Kelly Gay (Pocket Books), *Total Oblivion, More or Less* by Alan Deniro (Bantam)

How and why did you become an agent: I'd been working in publishing for a number of years in marketing and publicity. While I really enjoyed the work, I also longed to be able to only work on those titles I really felt passionate about. After a layoff in 2007, several of my author and editor friends encouraged me to try to become an agent. The idea appealed to me, but I didn't want to simply hang up my shingle and call myself an agent; too many people try this, and they do a terrible disservice to their clients. I decided the best way to go about it was to do set up some informational interviews with agents to learn more about it. I'd done close to 20 informational interviews by the time I met with Peter Rubie and Stephany Evans at FinePrint. We had a great conversation, talked for a couple of hours, and by the time I got home later than evening, there was a job offer on my voice-mail. It was kismet, I guess.

How do you feel about writers: I love writers. They make what I do possible.

How would you describe what you do as an agent to someone (or something) from another planet: If I met an entity from another planet, I'd be too busy buying him/her a beer and listening to his/her story so I could sell it!

What are your favorite books, movies, and TV shows, and why: TV shows: The new *Battlestar Galactica*: Hands-down the strongest writing, ensemble cast, and cinematography on television. Why this show hasn't won any Emmys for writing is seriously beyond me. Books: Oh, don't ask me that! I've worked in publishing or bookselling for more than 23 years. It would take all day to list all of my favorite books. Here's a random sampling: *Les Miserables* by Victor Hugo, *Always* by Nicola Griffith, *Dark Water's Embrace* by Stephen Leigh, *Perdido Street Station* by China Mieville, *Fall on Your Knees* by Anne Marie McDonald, and *Operation Wandering Soul* by Richard Powers. I love good science fiction, fantasy, mystery, literary fiction, and queer stuff, with the occasional baffling foray into history (Go figure.). Movies: Movies where things explode and pretty people disrobe. *The Lord of the Rings*, *Serenity*, *Wings of Desire*, *Children of Paradise*, Myazaki things.

Describe the client from hell, even if you don't have any: High maintenance. Life is too short for divas, and there are plenty of other writers out there who won't make an agent's or editor's life miserable.

Describe the publisher and/or editor from hell: Editors who are nonresponsive: they sit on manuscripts for months, sometimes years! They don't answer e-mails or return phone calls.

What do you like best about your clients and the editors and publishers you work with: I love pretty much everything about what I do, honestly. I just wish I had more hours in the day to do it.

Describe yourself: Professional nerd. Also, an amateur nerd of epic proportions. It's all good. I've recently overcome my terror of dancing in public. This mustn't be confused with an actual ability to dance, however.

Will our business exist as we know it in 10 years or so: Absolutely! And with the growing acceptance of e-book readers, books will become more accessible than ever before.

Agent's name: Diane Freed
Born: Sandwich, Illinois
Education: BS in journalism, University of Illinois

Career history: I've worked in the field of book publishing my entire career. I began at Prentice Hall as an editor/production coordinator, then on to *U.S.News & World Report* as a book editor and production supervisor. At Time-Life Books I produced direct mail promotional materials, and at Addison-Wesley/Pearson I was a book production supervisor. As owner and manager of my own publishing services company, I worked as a book packager, producing titles for publishers from raw manuscript through electronic files to the printer. I became an agent when I joined the Peter Rubie Literary Agency, which later became FinePrint Literary Management in September 2007. Initially I focused on selling nonfiction, but now I'm representing fiction writers as well and enjoying it tremendously.

In each capacity, I've worked closely with authors in one way or another, so one of my strengths is the ability to collaborate well with them when producing proposals and working on manuscripts. I consider myself a sculptor of sorts: I like putting all the book parts together to make a product that readers can sit with and enjoy, and that they can learn from as well.

Hobbies/Personal interests: Swimming, boating, cooking, travel, movies, theater

Categories/Subjects that you are most enthusiastic about agenting: Nonfiction: Primarily relationship/advice, self-help, spirituality, health/fitness, memoir, current affairs, popular culture, women's issues, environment, humor. Fiction: Commercial and literary fiction, partial to women's fiction. Generally, I can't resist a theme, fiction or nonfiction, in which the characters demonstrate real compassion for others in the lives they lead.

Categories/Subjects writers shouldn't bother pitching to you: Poetry, science fiction

If you were not an agent, what might you be doing instead: I'd be a book editor full time or seriously take up a favorite sport.

What's the best way for fiction writers to solicit your interest: Write an honest, well-written query letter that tells me why your book is important, why it should be published now, and why you are the person to write it.

Do you charge fees separate from your commission or offer nonagenting fee-based services: As an agent, I do not charge fees separate from my commission. However, I do take on occasional, completely separate, editing and proofreading projects.

What are some representative titles that you have sold: *Natural Flexibility* by Charles Kenny (Hatherleigh); *Bufflehead Sisters* by Patricia DeLois (Berkley/Penguin); *Penguins in Amsterdam* by Patricia DeLois (Berkley/Penguin); *The Language of Comforting* by Val Walker (Jeremy Tarcher/Penguin); *Getting Past Your Breakup* by Susan Elliot (Da Capo/Perseus)

How and why did you become an agent: I became an agent because I like discovering new writers and being tuned in to what's on everyone's minds. I took Peter Rubie's course on the role of the literary agent, through New York University, which launched my agenting career.

How do you feel about writers: I can't help but like them a lot, given what I do for a living! Most of all, I admire and respect them incredibly for their patience and perseverance.

How would you describe what you do as an agent to someone (or something) from another planet: I match up aspiring writers with editors at publishing houses that sell the type of books they have written.

What are your favorite books, movies, and TV shows, and why: Tops on my book list would be any and all that had an impact on me when I was growing up, enabled me to see the bigger world, to walk in someone else's shoes: *Black Like Me, All Quiet on the Western Front, To Kill a Mockingbird*, Pearl Buck's stories. Favorite authors today include Lara Vapnyar, Geraldine Brooks, Larry McMurtry, Colm Toibin, Frank McCourt, John Irving, Anne Tyler, Alice Hoffman, Sedaris, Burroughs, and Keillor. Memoir: *Reading* Lolita *in Tehran* by Azar Nafisi, *The Glass Castle* by Jeannette Walls. Movies: *Thelma and Louise, Send Me No Flowers, Matchstick Men, The Sound of Music, Pulp Fiction, West Side Story*. TV: *Boston Legal, The Sopranos, The Office, Charlie Rose Show*. Why? Not sure, but common threads might be that they feature inspirational characters that somehow touch me emotionally, or they just make me laugh. Or best of all, do both.

Describe the client from hell, even if you don't have any: Someone looking for an agent who calls out of the blue or e-mails me a chapter asking if I'll give it a quick critique. Then there is the client who calls at least once a day just to check up on how things are going.

Describe the publisher and/or editor from hell: Someone with poor communication skills and/or who doesn't follow up on things, but fortunately most editors aren't like this.

What do you like best about your clients and the editors and publishers you work with: With clients, I like the collaboration process, discussing how to present the material—both the proposal and the text—in the best way possible so that it will catch an editor's eye. With editors, what I like best is the good feeling we each have upon discovering a new author/book, knowing that we both can appreciate and are excited about promoting what this person has written.

You're welcome to share your thoughts and sentiments about the business of writing and publishing: As an author, you should write from your heart, but be real about what's ahead if you want to be published. It's all about matchmaking from the moment you begin your search for a publisher: Finding the right agent who believes in you and what you've written, who'll then find an editor/publisher who feels the same way, who'll in turn find—match you up with—that bigger audience who'll want to read and buy your book. And, as if you haven't heard this before, the best strategy you can have is to build your platform, especially for nonfiction, as editors always want a strong platform to show that you're getting yourself out there and have real credibility. Blogging regularly shows you have an audience; it's instant, free publicity for the publisher, so consider having your own blog if you don't already.

Describe yourself: (See above.)

Will our business exist as we know it in 10 years or so: I hope so, but I think there will be much more niche stuff given how we can personalize our tastes more now with websites, blogging, and so forth. Perhaps agents will focus on fewer types of books. And I do think that e-books will survive, although I'd predict that they will be more popular as reference books, texts, and the like rather than as mainstream fiction and nonfiction.

Agent's name: Stephany Evans

Born: October 11, 1957; West Chester, Pennsylvania

Education: Elizabethtown College, Elizabethtown, PA

Hobbies/Personal interests: Running, mosaics, gallery hopping, movies, reading, travel

Categories/Subjects that you are most enthusiastic about agenting: Health, wellness, spirituality, food and wine, green/sustainability; narrative nonfiction; literary fiction, mysteries, women's fiction—both literary and commercial (romance, light suspense, paranormal, historical)

Categories/Subjects writers shouldn't bother pitching to you: Poetry, screenplays, children's books, parenting, true crime, fantasy, sci-fi, overtly moralistic tales; no abused women, no abused children

If you were not an agent, what might you be doing instead: Reading, painting, home renovation, operate an art gallery

What's the best way for fiction writers to solicit your interest: Fine wine, flowers…but seriously: write well!

Do you charge fees separate from your commission or offer nonagenting fee-based services: No

What are some representative titles that you have sold: *Solar Power Your Home* and *Alternative Energy* by Rik DeGunther (Wiley/For Dummies); *A Geography of Oysters, Fruitless Fall*, and *American Terroir* by Rowan Jacobsen (Bloomsbury USA); *Do Dead People Watch You Shower?* by Concetta Bertoldi (HarperCollins); *Ina May's Guide to Childbirth* by Ina May Gaskin (BantamDell); *Fully Present: The Art and Science of Mindfulness* by Susan Smalley, PhD, and Diana Winston (Da Capo); *Soul Currency* by Ernest Chu (New World Library); *The Wisdom to Know the Difference* by Eileen Flanagan (Tarcher); *The Extra Mile* by Pam Reed (Rodale); *Something Borrowed* and *Love the One You're With* by Emily Giffin (St. Martin's Press); *The Rose Variations* by Marisha Chamberlain (Soho Press); *Lee* and *Fields of Asphodel* by Tito Perdue (Overlook Press); *SEALed with a Kiss* by Mary Margret Daughtridge (Sourcebooks/Casablanca); *Nice Girls Don't Have Fangs* by Molly Harper (Pocket Books)

How and why did you become an agent: I never had any idea of being an agent. I feel extremely lucky to have met someone who offered me the opportunity, I loved it, and couldn't think of anything I'd like to do more.

How do you feel about writers: Lovely creatures! Many are my best friends.

How would you describe what you do as an agent to someone (or something) from another planet: I so rarely get to talk to such folk at all. We're usually catching up on other subjects.

What are your favorite books, movies, and TV shows, and why: Too many, too many, too many, too many! In books and movies, I tend to gravitate in two directions, either toward something light and funny or something dark and beautiful. In either case, the heart is most important, not the spectacle. TV is where I slum. Aside from PBS's *News Hour* and *Washington Week*, I most often will watch all the reality shows (except the ones where contestants eat gross things). In the little box, spectacle rules.

What do you like best about your clients and the editors and publishers you work with: Their creativity, intelligence, heart, responsiveness, and their willingness to extend themselves, both to further their own careers and to make the world a better, more interesting place

Agent's name: Peter Rubie
Born: Taplow, England, 1950
Education: UK education system, NTCJ (journalism degree equivalent)
Career history: After college I worked in local and regional newspapers before moving to London to work in Fleet Street and then BBC Radio News. In 1981 I moved to the United States and worked a variety of jobs including editor-in-chief of a local Manhattan, NY, newspaper and freelance editor in publishing before becoming the fiction editor at Walker & Co., for six years or so. I left to become a partner in a small two-person literary agency and started my own agency in 2000. In 2007 I merged my company with Imprint to form FinePrint (a company with nine agents as of this writing), of which I am the CEO.
Hobbies/Personal interests: Music, movies, Go, chess, reading, woodworking, computing, parenting, writing
Categories/Subjects that you are most enthusiastic about agenting: Narrative nonfiction, parenting, pop science, history, current events, business; crime fiction, thrillers, off-beat literary, history, young adult and middle grade, literate SF and fantasy, things that excite and interest me
Categories/Subjects writers shouldn't bother pitching to you: Romance, women's fiction, scripts, poetry, poorly written material of any genre
If you were not an agent, what might you be doing instead: Being a professional writer and jazz musician and earning a living as a carpenter (I'd have to be to do the other two things)
What's the best way for fiction writers to solicit your interest: Write really well. Not gimmicky but just with a love of, and grasp of, graceful English. Writing is about THINKING, so I'm looking for that VOICE that will engage me from word one.
Do you charge fees separate from your commission or offer nonagenting fee-based services: No
What are some representative titles that you have sold: *Atherton* series (Little Brown), *Land of Elyon* series (Scholastic), and *Skeleton Creek* (Scholastic)—a cutting-edge multimedia book Internet project—by Patrick Carman; *First Copernican* by Dennis Danielson (Walker); *Enemy of the State* by Michael Scharf and Michael Newton (St. Martin's Press); *On Night's Shore* by Randall Silvis (St. Martin's); *Coyote's Wife* by Aimee and David Thurlo (Tor); *Soul Patch* by Reed Farrell Coleman (Bleak House)

How and why did you become an agent: I decided I spent so much time as an editor arguing on behalf of an author in-house it made sense to actually cross over and become an author's representative. I was one of several people let go by the house I was working for after my boss had the bad taste to accidentally drown, and so it made sense to make the move at that point.

How do you feel about writers: I spend every day talking with writers. The best are smart, funny, imaginative, just whom you would want to spend time with at work or at leisure. I have many friends who are writers, artists, and musicians. The worst are whiny, feel entitled for no good reason, feel aggrieved they're not getting their "due," and are unprofessional in their behavior, acting worse than my six-year-old. Guess who I prefer to be around.

How would you describe what you do as an agent to someone (or something) from another planet: Me, human. Do you know what a book is? It's where human beings do their best thinking and express their best ideas, sometimes in the most beautiful language you can imagine.

What are your favorite books, movies, and TV shows, and why: Too many to mention. All are what I would consider imaginative and well-crafted pieces that throw a light on our world and how we deal with the people in it and our relationships to them.

Describe the client from hell, even if you don't have any: Unprofessional, demanding, doesn't get the industry, and is only concerned with their ill-informed opinion of what life should be, not dealing with what life actually is and making the most of that

Describe the publisher and/or editor from hell: Don't communicate, lie to you, fail to keep promises, fail to follow up and look after your author in-house, are rude and dismissive, too lazy and too ignorant to edit properly

What do you like best about your clients and the editors and publishers you work with: They are smart, funny, imaginative, stimulating people who are a blast to hang out with and work with.

You're welcome to share your thoughts and sentiments about the business of writing and publishing: Publishing at present is struggling to come to terms with the speed that technology is changing the way we do things. The issue is not technology, though, but how technology is changing how things have always been done and what model or models are going to replace the old ways. It's one reason senior publishing executives are leaving their institutions and starting up their own businesses based on their perception of how the industry is moving forward. Writers need to be writing about and coming to terms with these profound changes in the way we view and live our lives for better or worse, but too few are. Save me from another book about a dysfunctional childhood or relationship that is totally engrossed in its own misery and can't or won't relate to the lives of others.

Describe yourself: Still figuring this one out

Will our business exist as we know it in 10 years or so: Yes, but in 25 years—ah, that's a completely different question. People always want to read and always want stories so publishing, and books will still be around and valid. But in what form? Your guess is as good as mine.

Agent's name: Brendan Deneen
Born: Hartford, CT
Education: University of Scranton, University of Glasgow (Scotland)
Career history: Assistant agent at William Morris Agency, story editor at Scott Rudin Productions, director of development at Miramax/Dimension Films, director of production and development at The Weinstein Company, senior vice president at Objective Entertainment, now with FinePrint Literary
Hobbies/Personal interests: Comic-book nerd, film buff
Subject and categories you like to agent: All, but particularly interested in thrillers and young adult right now
Categories/Subjects writers shouldn't bother pitching to you: None. If it's a great idea, I'm interested.
If you were not an agent, what might you be doing instead: Professional breakdancing
What's the best way for fiction writers to solicit your interest: A smart, funny, concise cover letter
Do you charge fees separate from your commission or offer nonagenting fee-based services: I help my clients develop their ideas for the low, low cost of "free."
What are some representative titles that you have sold: *Death's Daughter* by Amber Benson, *Killer's Diary* by Brian Pinkerton, *Drama High* by L. Divine, *The Wildman* by Rick Hautala, *The Hydes* by James A. Moore
How and why did you become an agent: I became an agent because I love the idea of discovering and fostering new talent. I became an agent pretty much by accident.
How do you feel about writers: I love writers, especially ones who understand that this business is all about patience, mixed with a healthy dose of workaholism.
What are your favorite books movies, TV shows, and why: My favorite books include *Grendel* by John Gardner and *Geek Love* by Katherine Dunn. My favorite movies include *Ed Wood* and *Blade Runner*. My favorite TV shows include *Lost* and *The Office*.
Describe the client from hell, even if you don't have any: Someone who thinks constantly badgering me makes me more likely to work hard for them
Describe the publisher and/or editor from hell: Someone who doesn't return calls or e-mails
What do you like best about your clients and the editors and publishers you work with: Patience in my clients and responsiveness from editors/publishers
Will our business exist as we know it in 10 years or so: It may be altered somewhat, but people will always read and watch movies, so I'll still have a job.

Agent's name: Meredith Hays
Born: July 28, 1969, in Lynn, Massachusetts
Education: BA from Skidmore College

Career history: After attending the Radcliffe Publishing Program, I worked at Houghton Mifflin, Co., in Boston in the now defunct trade/reference division, specializing in dictionaries. Moved to NYC and switched gears and worked at agencies, first Writers House, then Linda Chester & Associates, then Judith Ehrlich Literary Management and now FinePrint.

Hobbies/Personal interests: My family (husband, Reed, and son, Henry); animals (especially my cats)

Categories/Subjects that you are most enthusiastic about agenting: Fiction: Exceptionally crafted novels only; must be surprising, refreshing, and deeply satisfying, no matter the subject; Nonfiction: Lifestyle; pop culture; animals/nature; memoir (but no depressing or tragic stories!); crafts

Categories/Subjects writers shouldn't bother pitching to you: Fiction: No romance, Westerns, sci-fi, fantasy, historical fiction, young adult, children's; Nonfiction: Cookbooks, diet, fitness, politics, finance

If you were not an agent, what might you be doing instead: Dog trainer

What's the best way for fiction writers to solicit your interest: A short, well-crafted, spell-checked query letter

Do you charge fees separate from your commission or offer nonagenting fee-based services: No

What are some representative titles that you have sold: *Rollergirl: Totally True Tales from the Track* by Melissa "Melicious" Joulwan (Touchstone); *Lonesome for Bears: A Woman's Journey in the Tracks of the Wilderness* by Linda Jo Hunter (The Lyons Press); *Feltique* by Nikola Davidson (PotterCraft); *The Good Cat Spell Book* by Gillian Kemp (Celestial Arts/Ten Speed Press)

How and why did you become an agent: I went into publishing when I was right out of college and convinced that books were better company than people. When I moved to NYC, the first job I was offered was at an agency, and I liked how hands-on agenting is—how satisfying it is to follow a book from an idea to a manuscript to a finished published book.

How do you feel about writers: I admire their ability to stick with a subject long enough to create a book-length work.

How would you describe what you do as an agent to someone (or something) from another planet: Lots of work, little money

What are your favorite books, movies, and TV shows, and why: Books: *The Giant's House* by Elizabeth McCracken (because it's a lovely, twisted love story); *The Time Traveler's Wife* by Audrey Niffenegger (because it's one of the only truly brave, unique, and memorable stories I've come across); all of Jane Austen (because it's Jane Austen); all of Hemingway (because his dialogue cracks me up); *The End of the Affair* (because it's heart wrenching). Movies: *Rebecca* (because it's pure gothic charm); BBC's *Pride and Prejudice* (because of Colin Firth); *Bridget Jones' Diary* (because it's a guilty pleasure); *The Wedding Singer* (because of the music). TV: *Buffy the Vampire Slayer* (because it's brilliant); original *Mission Impossible* (because it's so stylized).

Describe the client from hell, even if you don't have any: One who is clueless about the industry; oh, and impatient and unkind and contacts me all the time

Describe the publisher and/or editor from hell: One who is mean and not willing to take risks or collaborate

What do you like best about your clients and the editors and publishers you work with: I like to work in tandem with clients and editors to create the best project possible. I'm open to new ideas and suggestions and am all for tweaking a manuscript if it will make it better.

Will our business exist as we know it in 10 years or so: Can't say, because as a new mom, I don't even know what's on my schedule for tomorrow!

Agent's name: June Clark

Education: BA in creative writing/mass media, Queens College, NY; MA in writing and publishing, Emerson College, Boston, MA

Career history: Marketing and promotion in cable TV, brand strategist, professional copywriter, published author, and playwright

Hobbies/Personal interests: Writing, reading, traveling, music, food and wine, pets

Categories/Subjects that you are most enthusiastic about agenting: Accepting limited submissions exclusively in commercial nonfiction areas of film/TV/theater; entertainment biographies; health and beauty; reference and how-to; women's issues; relationships; self-help and pop psychology; food, cocktails, and wine

Categories/Subjects writers shouldn't bother pitching to you: Sci-fi, horror, fantasy; military history; politics; Westerns; poetry; children's books; memoirs; short stories/novellas

If you were not an agent, what might you be doing instead: Writing full time or working in theater

What's the best way for nonfiction writers to solicit your interest: Learn about the types of books I represent and tell me why you think I'm the right agent for your work. Then show a strong platform or experience in the topic being written about and presenting a compelling query about your book.

Do you charge fees separate from your commission or offer nonagenting fee-based services: I provide platform/branding and freelance writing/editing services, but this work is conducted through my other company, Get There Media.

What are some representative titles that you have sold: *Black Comedians on Black Comedy: How African Americans Taught Us How to Laugh* by Darryl Littleton (Applause); *Mean Chicks, Cliques, and Dirty Tricks* by Erika Shearin Karres; *Beatleology: Embracing Your Inner Beatle* by Adam Jaquette and Roger Jaquette (Adams Media); *Simply Elegant Flowers* by Michael George (North Light); *Bad Bosses, Crazy Coworkers, and Other Office Idiots: 201 Smart Solutions to Every Problem at Work* by Vicky Oliver (Sourcebooks); *Forbidden Broadway: Behind the Mylar Curtain* by Gerard Alessandrini (Applause)

How and why did you become an agent: Was helping my agent, Peter Rubie, read query letters and found several projects I liked and was encouraged to pursue them. I continued agenting because it's a sociable job with exposure to interesting ideas and people. And as a writer myself, I can offer a well-rounded perspective to my clients.

How do you feel about writers: Sadly, I feel that being a talented writer is not enough in today's market. It is now necessary to have a great outreach and a reputation in your field or genre in order to get noticed by publishers. That means writers always need to be cultivating an audience for themselves, and that's a tall order for many.

How would you describe what you do as an agent to someone (or something) from another planet: Not much, since they've never asked!

What are your favorite books, movies, and TV shows, and why: In books, I enjoy edgy or witty writers that entertain like Dave Barry, David Sedaris, and Nora Ephron. On TV, I enjoy *The Good Wife*, *Dexter*, *Real Time with Bill Maher*, *30 Rock*, and a few guilty pleasures like *Kitchen Nightmares* and *Fashion Police*. Movies…I rarely, if ever, go to the movies; I prefer live theater.

Describe the client from hell, even if you don't have any: Writers from hell are close minded and resistant to suggestions on how to improve their work. They have difficulty meeting deadlines or effectively communicating with their editors and treat their agent like a secretary.

Describe the publisher and/or editor from hell: Publishers/editors from hell are those who don't return e-mails or phone calls from agents (and their authors), ask to see material but never respond to it, and expect the author to jump through unreasonable hoops or unrealistic delivery of material and then sit on the author's final manuscript for months without reading or honoring their end of the deal.

What do you like best about your clients and the editors and publishers you work with: Open communication, positive attitude, respect for an author's work and editor's time, taking initiative, being proactive in their job or career, and acting professionally

You're welcome to share your thoughts and sentiments about the business of writing and publishing: Publishing is going to have to reinvent itself, especially in our rapidly changing technology age. I think there will be a rise in e-books and print on demand, both of which will make more sense, economically, in the long term. The challenge for all of us, particularly agents, will be in making sure that authors' rights and royalties will be protected. Publishers also need to put more efforts into promotion and place some focus on great concepts and great writing in balance with the whole "platform" issue. They will need to invest time and money in building brand.

Will our business exist as we know it in 10 years or so: I think publishing may go the way of the music business. Writers will become more creative in getting their work seen by the masses and possibly bypass agents and publishers, due to the Internet. I also think readers will become more comfortable with e-books and there may be fewer printed books.

FIREBRAND LITERARY

285 West Broadway, Suite 520, New York, NY 10013
212-334-0025
www.firebrandliterary.com

Agent's name: Danielle Chiotti
Born: September 3, Pittsburgh, PA
Education: University of Pittsburgh, BA, creative writing and communications
Career history: Danielle Chiotti has nearly 10 years' experience with trade fiction and nonfiction publishing. Formerly a senior editor at both Kensington Publishing and Adams Media, she has worked on a wide variety of books ranging from contemporary women's fiction to narrative nonfiction, romance, relationships, humor, and young adult.
Categories/Subjects that you are most enthusiastic about agenting: For fiction: Commercial fiction, multicultural fiction (with a slightly literary edge), romance, paranormal romance, and young-adult fiction for girls. I tend to favor fish-out-of-water stories and stories in which characters get themselves in very sticky situations and must find a way out. I am drawn to gorgeous writing and strong, flawed characters who aren't afraid to take big chances or show a little bit of a dark side. For nonfiction: Narrative nonfiction, memoir, self-help, dating/relationships, humor, current events, women's issues, and cooking (including cookbooks and food narrative). I am looking for compelling projects that present an author's unique voice and point of view or that shed light on a previously unexplored topic.
Categories/Subjects writers shouldn't bother pitching to you: Abuse memoirs, sports, New Age nonfiction, children's books, sci-fi/fantasy, romantic suspense, thrillers, poetry, anything that is described as the "new *Bridget Jones's Diary*"
If you were not an agent, what might you be doing instead: Writing
What's the best way for writers to solicit your interest: For fiction: Have a great first line that provides an immediate insight into your protagonist. For nonfiction: Have a unique/original idea and strong, clear writing. Know your subject area and the audience you're trying to reach, and how you can reach them. Be able to describe your project in one sentence: "It's *The Secret* meets *He's Just Not That into You*." Know your competition!
Do you charge fees separate from your commission or offer nonagenting fee-based services: No
What are some representative titles that you have sold: As I fill out this questionnaire, I am brand-new to agenting, so no sales yet!
How and why did you become an agent: How: I became an agent through serendipitous circumstances, which is the way I got into publishing and the way I've gotten all of my jobs in publishing. Why: I became an agent so I could deal more creatively with a wider variety of authors and genres.
What are your favorite books, movies, and TV shows, and why: Books I

come to again and again for inspiration and comfort: *The Mysteries of Pittsburgh* by Michael Chabon, *The American Woman in the Chinese Hat* by Carole Maso, *Great with Child* by Beth Ann Fennelly, *Charlotte's Web* by E. B. White, *No One Belongs Here More Than You* by Miranda July; books that are plain old fun: *Valley of the Dolls* by Jacqueline Susann, *Bittersweet* by LaVyrle Spencer, anything by Emily Giffin

Describe the client from hell, even if you don't have any: A writer who balks at constructive criticism, who refuses to look outside of themselves and get a sense of the "bigger picture," and who lacks patience with the submission and publishing process

Describe the publisher and/or editor from hell: Lack of communication between editor and author/agent; lack of transparency on the part of the publisher in terms of in-house process, sales figures, publicity/marketing plans for the author

What do you like best about your clients and the editors and publishers you work with: The buzz of excitement when we fall in love with an amazing writer/project, the constant exchange of ideas

---

THE FIRM

9465 Wilshire Blvd., 6th floor, Beverly Hills, CA 90212
310-860-8000 | fax: 310-860-8132

Agent's name: Alan Nevins
Education: Dual major: BS, economics and BA, motion picture/television studies, UCLA
Career history: Created in August 2002, and comprising department head Alan Nevins and a team of literary associates, The Firm's book division rose from the ashes of Renaissance, a successful literary agency of nine years' standing, founded by Alan Nevins and two partners in 1993. Renaissance acquired the Irving Paul Lazar agency in 1993 after the death of famed superagent Irving "Swifty" Lazar. Alan Nevins had been Lazar's final and sole associate prior to forming Renaissance, and the estate approached Nevins about acquiring the Lazar enterprise. This acquisition, and that of the H. N. Swanson Agency, gave the infant Renaissance the enviable legacy of two of Hollywood's most colorful literary agents and solidified its place as a powerhouse literary firm supplying material to the New York publishers as well as the film/television community. When Renaissance dissolved in 2002, Nevins joined music and film mogul the Firm as head of the book division. With longstanding and impressive relationships in Hollywood, London, and New York, the agency currently represents more than 125 writers, boasts an extensive estate list, and partners with more than 30 agencies worldwide for their film and ancillary rights. The Firm book division has major properties in development at the Hollywood studios and with the leading networks, as well as a substantial backlist, and continues to attract some of the world's most sought-after writers for both publishing and film representation.

Awards: Emmy nomination, executive producer, and Christopher Award, executive producer: *Homeless to Harvard: The Liz Murray Story*

Categories/Subjects that you are most enthusiastic about agenting: Commercial fiction, literary fiction, historical fiction, narrative nonfiction, current affairs, lifestyle, women's fiction/chick lit (original voices and storylines), business; children's: unique illustrations and creative storylines that truly stand out; young-adult fiction: focus on strong storytelling, prose, and characters

Categories/Subjects writers shouldn't bother pitching to you: Poetry, short stories

What's the best way for writers to solicit your interest: E-mail query letter and synopsis to query@thefirmbooks.com

What are the most common mistakes writers make when pitching to you: Sending a proposal or manuscript without first contacting us; sending single-spaced or otherwise improperly formatted manuscripts

What are some representative titles that you have sold: *What to Expect When You're Expecting* series (Workman); *A Lotus Grows in the Mud* (Putnam); *Memories Are Made of This* (Harmony); *By Myself and Then Some* by Lauren Bacall (HarperCollins); *Learning to Sing* (Random House); *Lost Laysen* (Scribner); *Tickled Pink* (Time Warner); *Deaf Child Crossing* (Simon & Schuster); *Less Is More* (Portfolio); *The Doors* (Hyperion); Larry Collins and Dominique Lapierre (all titles); *The Black Dahlia Files* (HarperCollins); *Real Life Entertaining* (William Morrow); *Warren Beatty: A Private Man* (Harmony); *Audrey Hepburn: An Elegant Spirit* (Atria); *Hank Zipzer* young-adult series (Penguin); *Baggage Claim* (Simon & Schuster); *Love on the Dotted Line* by David E. Talbert (Simon & Schuster); *Emily's Reasons Why Not* (HarperCollins); *Tonight, Somewhere in New York* (Carroll & Graf); *Sins of the Seventh Sister* (Harmony); Roman Sub Rosa series (St. Martin's); *The Sword of Attila* (St. Martin's); *Tomorrow to Be Brave* (Free Press)

FOLIO LITERARY MANAGEMENT, LLC

630 9th Ave, Suite 1101, New York, New York, NY 10036
212-400-1494 | fax: 212-967-0977
www.foliolit.com

Agent's name: Erin Cartwright Niumata
Born: Scranton, Pennsylvania
Education: BA, University of Delaware
Career history: Erin has been in publishing for over 16 years. She started as an editorial assistant at Simon & Schuster in the Touchstone/Fireside paperback division for several years; moved over to HarperCollins as an editor; and then she went to Avalon Books as the editorial director, working on romance, mysteries, and Westerns. Erin has edited many authors including Leon Uris, Stuart Woods, Phyllis

Richman, Senator Fred Harris, Dean Ornish, Michael Lee West, Debbie Fields, Erica Jong, Brenda Maddox, Lawrence Otis Graham, and Joan Rivers.

Hobbies/Personal interests: Dogs, reading, cycling, running, knitting, sewing

Categories/Subjects you are interested in agenting: Fiction: Commercial women's fiction, historical fiction, psychological thrillers, suspense, humor—I love sassy Southern and/or British heroines; Nonfiction: Cookbooks, biographies, petcare/pets, parenting, self-help, pop culture, humor, women's issues, fashion, decorating

Categories/Subjects writers shouldn't bother pitching to you: Absolutely no romance, Westerns, cozy mysteries, poetry, short-story collections, business, travel memoirs, young adult, or picture books

If you were not an agent, what might you be doing instead: I would be an editor or a teacher.

What's the best way for fiction writers to solicit your interest: I prefer a proposal (nonfiction) or a brief synopsis with the first 50 pages (fiction) with SASE. I receive too many e-mails to handle.

What's the best way for nonfiction writers to solicit your interest: Cover-letter pitch explaining the book and the author's platform along with sample chapters and an outline

Do you charge reading or management fees: No charges; AAR members

What are the most common mistakes writers make when pitching to you: Not following the submission guidelines and sending me something I don't represent; telling me that random people have read the book and think it's fantastic

Describe the client from hell, even if you don't have any: Someone who fights every piece of advice and calls/e-mails incessantly wanting updates or just to "chat"

What's your definition of a great client: Someone who is talented, has a great project, an open-minded attitude, eager to learn, ready to promote the book, and is happy to hear suggestions

How and why did you become an agent: I was an editor for 16 years and decided to try my hand at agenting. So far, so good.

How do you feel about editors and publishers: Editors are overworked, attend entirely too many meetings, have piles of manuscripts that are all urgent, have very little time for anything—which is why agents are crucial for authors.

How do you feel about writers: Most are fantastic.

What are some representative titles that you have sold: *The House on Briar Hill* by Holly Jacobs (Harlequin); *Things That Make Us (Sic)* by Martha Brockenbrough (St. Martin's); *Fabulous Felines* by Sandie Robins (TFH); *Sleeping with Ward Cleaver* by Jenny Gardiner (Dorchester)

Agent's name: Scott Hoffman

Born: Holmdel, New Jersey

Education: BA in government from the College of William and Mary; MBA in finance from New York University's Leonard N. Stern School of Business

Career history: Publishing is a second career for me; before becoming a literary agent I ran a lobbying firm in Washington, DC. After a brief flirtation with finance, I realized my two favorite things in life were books and deals—so I figured out a way to do book deals for a living. In 2006, I was fortunate enough to find Jeff and Paige and start Folio with them.

Hobbies/Personal interests: Chess, poker, opera, bridge, golf, wine

Categories/Subjects that you are most enthusiastic about agenting: Novels that fit perfectly in that sweet spot between really well-written commercial fiction and accessible literary fiction (book-club type books); literary science fiction and fantasy; thrillers of all types; all kinds of narrative nonfiction, journalistic or academic nonfiction; edgy, cool pop-culture nonfiction

Categories/Subjects writers shouldn't bother pitching to you: No kids' books, category romance, Westerns, cozy mysteries, poetry, short stories, stage plays, or screenplays

If you were not an agent, what might you be doing instead: In venture capital or running for office

What's the best way for fiction writers to solicit your interest: Check out our guidelines at www.foliolit.com.

What's the best way for nonfiction writers to solicit your interest: Check out our guidelines at www.foliolit.com.

Do you charge reading or management fees: No charges; AAR members

How do you feel about editors and publishers: I think there are many, many things traditional publishers do very well, and some other things they don't. One of the reasons we started Folio was to help authors market their own works—figure out ways to get individuals into bookstores to pick up their specific title.

How do you feel about writers: It takes a special kind of personality to be able to spend a year in a closet writing a book. I like special personalities.

What do you see in the near future for book publishing: Authors and their agents will begin to take a much more active approach in marketing their titles.

In your opinion, what do editors think of you: That I'm a fair and kind agent with a great eye for talent who's tough enough to always look out for his clients' best interests.

What are some representative titles that you have sold: *Lessons from the CEO's Boss* by Anne Marie Fink (Crown Business); *The Fug Awards* by Heather Cocks and Jessica Morgan (Simon Spotlight Entertainment); *Volk's Game* by Brent Ghelfi (Holt); *The Kommandant's Girl* by Pam Jenoff (Mira); *The Preservationist* by David Maine (St. Martin's Press); *The Superman Wish* by John Hideyo Hamamura (Doubleday)

Agent's name: Celeste Fine
Born: Redlands, California
Education: BA in government, magna cum laude, Harvard University
Career history: After working as an assistant, foreign rights agent, foreign rights manager, and literary agent at Vigliano Associates and Trident Media Group, I joined Folio Literary Management in 2006.
Hobbies/Personal interests: Pool, music, games, tequila

Categories/Subjects that you are most enthusiastic about agenting: Nonfiction: 90 percent of my list is nonfiction—mostly platform-driven projects. Fiction: I do a select list of fiction—mostly projects with memorable characters.

Categories/Subjects writers shouldn't bother pitching to you: Women's fiction, romance, graphic novels

If you were not an agent, what might you be doing instead: Rock star

What's the best way for fiction writers to solicit your interest: E-mail

What's the best way for nonfiction writers to solicit your interest: E-mail

Do you charge reading or management fees: No charges; AAR members

What are the most common mistakes writers make when pitching to you: Not being able to provide a compelling sound bite of the project and not knowing their competition

What's your definition of a great client: A client who is talented, expects to work as hard as I [do] on their project, and understands the business of publishing

What can a writer do to increase the odds of you becoming his or her agent: Be an expert on your subject.

How and why did you become an agent: I fell in love with partnering with authors to make the most of their careers.

How do you feel about writers: A talented writer can change you. That is extraordinary.

What do you see in the near future for book publishing: I imagine there will be a lot of differences. Very exciting.

What are your favorite books, movies, and TV shows, and why: *Tale of Two Cities* and *The Apologist*; *Arrested Development* and *The Closer*; *Confessions of a Dangerous Mind* and *The Departed*.

What are some representative titles that you have sold: *The Alchemy of Aging Well* by Randy Raugh (Rodale); *The LCA's The 30-Day Diabetes Miracle and Cookbook* (Perigee); *The 99¢-Only Store Cookbook* by Christiane Jory (Adams Media); *Eat, Drink, and Be Gorgeous* by Esther Blum (Chronicle); *Unusually Stupid Celebrities* and *Unusually Stupid Politicians* by Kathy and Ross Petras (Villard); *It's Not News, It's Fark* by Drew Curtis (Gotham); *Good Granny, Bad Granny* by Mary McHugh (Chronicle); *Confessions of a Gambler* by Rayda Jacobs (Overlook); *Rightsizing* by Ciji Ware (Springboard Press)

Agent's name: Paige Wheeler
Born: Richmond, Virginia
Education: BA, magna cum laude, Boston University
Career history: After working in bookstores in college, I moved to London and worked for a financial publisher. My first publishing job in the United States was working in editorial for Harlequin/Silhouette. I then worked as an editor for an investment bank before switching over to agenting. My first agenting job was at Artists Agency, where I repped writers for TV, producers, celebrities, as well as book authors. I started my own agency, Creative Media Agency, Inc., and ran that for nine

years before I met Jeff and Scott. Together we decided to form Folio in 2006 to meet the changing needs of authors.

Hobbies/Personal interests: My puppy, reading (!), wine, antiques, interior design/reno

Categories/Subjects that you are most enthusiastic about agenting: Fiction: I'm looking for very well-written commercial and upscale fiction—it should have a fresh and fabulous voice; women's fiction, mysteries, and thrillers (the smarter the better); Nonfiction: Narrative and prescriptive—self-help, how-to, women's issues, business books (all types), pop culture, soft science, politics, travel, design

Categories/Subjects writers shouldn't bother pitching to you: No Westerns, Sci-Fi & Fantasy (SF&F), children's, poetry, plays, screenplays

If you were not an agent, what might you be doing instead: There's another option???

What's the best way for fiction writers to solicit your interest: I prefer an e-mail query with a synopsis, the first few pages embedded (no attachments).

What's the best way for nonfiction writers to solicit your interest: E-mail query with a lot of information about the author and his/her platform. What is unique about this project and why is the author the perfect person to write it?

Do you charge reading or management fees: No charges; AAR members

What are the most common mistakes writers make when pitching to you: Oooh, I love groveling! Seriously, forgetting to include specifics (what the project is about) and not understanding the market for the book.

Describe the client from hell, even if you don't have any: Writers who fail to realize that they are not my only client and aren't appreciative of all the things that I do behind the scenes.

What's your definition of a great client: A fabulous writer who understands the process of publishing, is a go-getter but is also patient and understanding of time constraints and is appreciative of my hard work.

What can a writer do to increase the odds of you becoming his or her agent: If you're an outstanding writer with fresh ideas and an engaging voice, you'll get my attention. For nonfiction, it's about platform, platform, platform—and a unique slant on a concept or idea.

How and why did you become an agent: Again, there's another option????

How would you describe what you do as an agent to someone (or something) from another planet: Um, I don't handle SF&F so I wouldn't be able to communicate with them.

How do you feel about editors and publishers: I think pairing an author with the perfect editor for a project is the difference between merely getting published and building a very successful career. It's our job to find the perfect editor for a particular project.

How do you feel about writers: One of the things I love about this business is that I work with smart and talented people. In general, most writers are super-informed and passionate people who are eager to share their ideas with a larger audience. I like people who possess a viewpoint or don't shy away from an idea and have the information to back it up.

What do you see in the near future for book publishing: Faster adaptation to emerging technologies

In your opinion, what do editors think of you: I'm both intrigued and horrified to find out, but I do hope it's that I'm tenacious, ambitious, and have the drive to succeed.

On a personal level, what do you think people like and dislike about you: Friends and family think that I should probably work less and enjoy life more.

What are some representative titles that you have sold: *Definitely Not Mr. Darcy* by Karen Doornebos (Penguin); *On Strike for Christmas* by Sheila Roberts (Harlequin); *Sit Stay Slay* by Linda O. Johnston (Berkley Prime Crime); *Claimed by the Highlander* by Julianne Maclean (St. Martin's); *Blueberry Years* by Jim Minick (Tom Dunne); *White House Chef* series by Julie Hyzy (Techno/Berkley); *101 Uses for My Ex-Wife's Wedding Dress* by Kevin Cotter (NAL/Penguin); *Slay Bells* by Kate Kingsbury (Berkley)

Agent's name: Rachel Vater
Born: Covington, Kentucky
Education: BA, Northern Kentucky University
Career history: Worked as an editor at Writer's Digest Books before moving to New York City to be an assistant agent at the Donald Maass Literary Agency and then a literary agent with Lowenstein-Yost Associates. She joined Folio in 2007.
Hobbies/Personal interests: Art, piano, theater
Categories/Subjects that you are most enthusiastic about agenting: Fiction: Fantasy, urban fantasy, or anything with a paranormal element, young-adult novels (especially fantasy but also historical or anything dealing with contemporary teen issues), middle-grade novels with a fun, hip voice young teens can relate to; Nonfiction: Pop culture, business, self-help, or humor appealing to professional women

Categories/Subjects writers shouldn't bother pitching to you: No category romance, Westerns, poetry, short stories, screenplays; nothing graphically violent

If you were not an agent, what might you be doing instead: I would be an editor, designer, or musician.

What's the best way for fiction writers to solicit your interest: E-mail or postal mail. Query letter with first few pages. No attachments.

What's the best way for nonfiction writers to solicit your interest: Query via e-mail or postal mail, including credentials, platform, and outline.

Do you charge reading or management fees: No charges; AAR members

What are the most common mistakes writers make when pitching to you: Not knowing what their hook is—what makes the book stand out from the rest out there like it—and failing to emphasize that in the query

Describe the client from hell, even if you don't have any: A writer who won't gracefully accept editorial notes, and if he/she disagrees with any points, argues angrily instead of working with me/the editor to make the manuscript stronger or more clear.

What's your definition of a great client: A writer who mulls over edit notes carefully and implements them well and quickly, keeps a positive attitude, expresses gratitude to his/her agent and editor, is willing to promote his/her books with tireless enthusiasm

What can a writer do to increase the odds of you becoming his or her agent: Know the market. Read a lot in your chosen genre, and know what makes your book/series different and special.

How and why did you become an agent: I was an editor with Writer's Digest Books, where I edited *The Guide to Literary Agents*. I had a chance to meet and interview a lot of agents. It sounded like a dream job to me, and it is.

How do you feel about editors and publishers: It's crucial for agents to know the preferences and quirks of each publishing house and the editors there. Several editors at the same imprint may all have different tastes, so it's important to keep up on who's looking for exactly what.

How do feel about writers: Without them, I wouldn't have a job.

What do you see in the near future for book publishing: The ways in which an author can promote his/her book will keep expanding. New technology makes it easier, faster, and cheaper to find and reach your target readership.

In your opinion, what do editors think of you: I'm a young, ambitious agent building a great list.

What are some representative titles that you have sold: *Wicked Lovely* by Melissa Marr (HarperCollins Children's Books); *Halfway to the Grave* by Jeaniene Frost (Avon/HarperCollins); *Night Life* by Caitlin Kittredge (St. Martin's Press); *I So Don't Do Mysteries* by Barrie Summy (Delacorte Press); *Unpredictable* by Eileen Cook (Berkley)

Agent's name: Jeff Kleinman
Born: Cleveland, Ohio
Education: BA with high distinction, University of Virginia (English/modern studies); MA, University of Chicago (Italian language/literature); JD, Case Western Reserve University
Career history: After graduating from the University of Virginia, I studied Renaissance history in Italy for several years, went to law school, and then joined an art and literary law firm. A few years later, I joined the Graybill and English Literary Agency before becoming one of the founders of Folio in 2006.
Hobbies/Personal interests: Art, history, animals, especially horses (train dressage and event horses)
Categories/Subjects that you are most enthusiastic about agenting: Very well-written, character-driven novels; some suspense, thrillers, historicals; otherwise mainstream commercial and literary fiction; Prescriptive nonfiction: Health, parenting, aging, nature, pets, how-to, etc.; Narrative nonfiction: Especially books with a historical bent, but also art, nature, ecology, politics, military, espionage, cooking, equestrian, pets, memoir, biography

Categories/Subjects writers shouldn't bother pitching to you: No mysteries, romance, Westerns, SF&F, children's or young adult, poetry, plays, screenplays

If you were not an agent, what might you be doing instead: Practicing intellectual property law or training horses, or both

What's the best way for fiction writers to solicit your interest: E-mail only (no attachments, please); include a cover letter and the first few pages of the novel.

What's the best way for nonfiction writers to solicit your interest: E-mail only (no attachments, please). Include a cover letter and perhaps a few pages of a sample chapter, and/or an overview/summary.

Do you charge reading or management fees: No charges; AAR members

What are the most common mistakes writers make when pitching to you: Groveling—just pretend this is a job application and act like a professional; providing too much information—telling too much about the project, rather than being able to succinctly summarize it; sending a poorly formatted, difficult-to-read manuscript

Describe the client from hell, even if you don't have any: Someone who doesn't listen, doesn't incorporate suggestions, and believes that the world "owes" him (or her) a best seller

What's your definition of a great client: Someone who writes beautifully, who has marketing savvy and ability, who is friendly, accessible, easy to work with, fun to talk to, can follow directions and guidance without taking offense

What can a writer do to increase the odds of you becoming his or her agent: For fiction, write a fabulous book with a fresh voice and compelling, unique perspective, and be able to sum up that book in a single, smart, intriguing sentence or two. For nonfiction, ENHANCE YOUR CREDENTIALS. Get published, or have some kind of platform or fresh perspective that really stands out above the crowd. Show me (so I can show a publisher) that you're a good risk for publication.

How and why did you become an agent: My law firm shared offices with an agency, and I did several book contracts. Gradually, I started reading manuscripts, talking to writers, and before long, there I was—a literary agent.

How do you feel about editors and publishers: I think that too often they're overworked and underpaid and often don't have the time to really "connect the dots" in a manuscript or a proposal—so it's crucial that we (the writer and I) connect the dots for them.

How do you feel about writers: It depends on the writer.

What do you see in the near future for book publishing: The future is happening. it's gonna be really cool, too.

In your opinion, what do editors think of you: That I'm honest, ethical, and have a solid list of clients

What are some representative titles that you have sold: *The Memory of Running* by Garth Stein (Harper); *The Widow of the South* and *A Separate Country* by Robert Hicks (Grand Central); *And So It Goes* and *Mockingbird* by Charles Shields (Holt); *The $80 Champion* by Elizabeth Letts (Ballantine); *Unsaid* by Neil Abramson

(Center Street); *Sacco & Vanzetti* and several other titles by Bruce Watson (Viking); *Freezing Point* and *Boiling Point* by Karen Dionne (Berkley); *Learning Bedside Manor* by Nick Trout (Hyperion); *Finn* by Jon Clinch (Random House)

FOUNDRY LITERARY MEDIA

33 West 17th Street, PH, New York, NY 10011
212-929-5064 | fax: 212-929-5471
www.foundrymedia.com

Agent's name: Lisa Grubka
Born: April 19, 1950, Mineola, New York
Education: University of Michigan
Career history: Began career at the publishing house of Farrar, Straus & Giroux, and then spent six years at the William Morris Agency before joining Foundry
Categories/Subjects that you are most enthusiastic about agenting: Fiction: Literary, young adult, and upmarket women's fiction; Nonfiction: Food and wine, memoir, pop-science, narrative
Categories/Subjects writers shouldn't bother pitching to you: Sci-fi, fantasy, romance, crime, mystery, suspense, thrillers
What's the best way for fiction writers to solicit your interest: An engaging and well-written query letter that gives me a sense of the writer's voice, provides me with a thoughtful synopsis, and tells me a bit about the writer
Do you charge fees separate from your commission or offer nonagenting fee-based services: No
What do you like best about your clients and the editors and publishers you work with: I adore my authors—they work hard, are fantastic human beings, and most importantly they love what they do and it shows in their writing.

Agent's name: Mollie Glick
Career history: After graduating from Brown University, Mollie began her publishing career as a literary scout, advising foreign publishers regarding the acquisition of rights to American books. She then worked as an editor at the Crown imprint of Random House, before switching over to "the other side" and becoming an agent at the Jean V. Naggar Literary Agency (JVNLA) in 2003. She joined the Foundry Media team in September 2008. Mollie's list includes literary fiction, narrative nonfiction, and a bit of practical nonfiction. She's particularly interested in fiction that bridges the literary/commercial divide, combining strong writing with a great plot; and nonfiction dealing with popular science, medicine, psychology, cultural history, memoir, and current events. She's very hands-on, working collaboratively with her authors to refine their projects, and then focusing on identifying just the right editors for the submissions.

In addition to her work as a literary agent, Mollie also teaches classes on non-fiction proposal writing at MediaBistro, and a copy of her instructional article on nonfiction proposal writing will be featured in this year's edition of the *Writer's Digest* guide to literary agents.

Hobbies/Personal interests: I'm a bit of a foodie, an amateur film critic, and I love to travel.

Categories/Subjects that you are most enthusiastic about agenting: Literary fiction, narrative nonfiction, memoir, young adult

Categories/Subjects writers shouldn't bother pitching to you: Genre that doesn't cross over; picture books; romance

If you were not an agent, what might you be doing instead: I'd be a food writer, costume designer, or film producer.

What's the best way for fiction writers to solicit your interest: With a killer query letter and great sample chapters

Do you charge fees separate from your commission or offer nonagenting fee-based services: No

What are some representative titles that you have sold: *Drawing in the Dust* by Zoe Klein (Pocket Books); *All about Lulu* by Jonathan Evison (Soft Skull); *Pop Tart* by Kira Coplin and Julianne Kaye (Avon); *Shut Up, I'm Talking: And Other Diplomacy Lessons I Learned in the Israeli Government* by Greg Levey (The Free Press); *Shiny Objects: How We Lost Our Way on the Path to the American Dream and How We Can Find Our Way Back* by Dr. Jim Roberts (HarperOne); *Wounded Warriors* by Mike Sager (Da Capo); *Queen of the Road* by Doreen Orion (Broadway)

How and why did you become an agent: I love the thrill of being the first one to discover a great new writer, and I really enjoy collaborating with my writers.

What are your favorite books, movies, and TV shows, and why: *Lost, Mad Men, Eastbound & Down.* All three shows have strong aesthetic viewpoints, waver between humor and drama, and [have] great character development.

Describe the client from hell, even if you don't have any: A writer who is too insecure or untrusting to collaborate on his/her work

What do you like best about your clients and the editors and publishers you work with: I love clients who take editorial notes and run with them, who strive to understand the business of writing, and who have got original, fresh voices.

Will our business exist as we know it in 10 years or so: Right now, my eyes are on Amazon. Between their Amazon Shorts program, their look-inside-the-book features, and the Kindle, they're reeling out the innovations, and I hope publishers will soon follow their lead.

Agent's name: Chris Park
Education: BA, English, Harvard University
Career history: I spent most of my publishing career on the editorial side—working at Random House and Hachette among other companies—before joining Foundry as an agent in 2007.

Categories/Subjects that you are most enthusiastic about agenting: Memoirs, narrative nonfiction, sports, Christian nonfiction, and women's fiction

Categories/Subjects writers shouldn't bother pitching to you: Genre fiction, New Age

What's the best way for fiction writers to solicit your interest: E-mail query

Do you charge fees separate from your commission or offer nonagenting fee-based services: No!

What are some representative titles that you have sold: *Bible Babel: Making Sense of the Most Talked-about Book of All Time* by Kristin M. Swenson (HarperCollins); *Love, Daddy: A Memoir* by Kambri Crews (Villard/Random House); *High Heat: The Search for the Fastest Pitcher of All Time* by Tim Wendel (DaCapo Press); *How to Be Like God: One Church's Experiment with Living the Old Testament Book of Leviticus* by Daniel M. Harrell (FaithWords)

How and why did you become an agent: I loved my time as an editor but felt that it was increasingly difficult to be the kind of advocate that I wanted to be for my authors. Agenting seemed to feature the perks of being an editor (working closely with authors, editing, advocating) without the unpleasant aspects of working within corporate publishing (having to pledge my firstborn child to get attention for a book).

How would you describe what you do as an agent to someone (or something) from another planet: It's like the movie *Jerry Maguire*, but with less running and more e-mailing.

Agent's name: Stephen Barbara

Born: Born August 1980 in New Haven, Connecticut, to Italian-American family

Education: BA '02 in English literature (with a focus on literary criticism), University of Chicago

Career history: After working briefly on the editorial side at HarperCollins, I spent a year as an assistant at the Fifi Oscard Agency. Then in January of 2006 I became agent and contracts director at the Donald Maass Literary Agency. In early 2009 I brought all of my clients to Foundry, where I'm now a full-time agent.

Hobbies/Personal interests: I follow Italian soccer, enjoy traveling, and am an avid reader of business and narrative nonfiction books.

Categories/Subjects that you are most enthusiastic about agenting: Literary fiction, commercial fiction, young adult, children's, memoir, business, narrative nonfiction

Categories/Subjects writers shouldn't bother pitching to you: Romance novels and screenplays

If you were not an agent, what might you be doing instead: Cry, gnash my teeth, pull my hair out. I love my job!

What's the best way for fiction writers to solicit your interest: Send me a one-page query letter via e-mail with the first five pages pasted into the body of the e-mail. Please mention any writing credits you have and/or endorsements you've received from other writers.

Do you charge fees separate from your commission or offer nonagenting fee-based services: No

What are some representative titles that you have sold: *Before I Fall* and *Delirium* by Lauren Oliver (Harper), *The Big Splash* and *Sidekicks* by Jack Ferraiolo (Harry N. Abrams/Amulet), the *Dead Is* series by Marlene Perez (Graphia), *The Thing about Georgie* and *Umbrella Summer* by Lisa Graff (Harper), *The Secret of Zoom* by Lynne Jonell (Henry Holt), *The November Criminals* by Sam Munson (Knopf), *Mostly Good Girls* by Leila Sales (Simon Pulse), *Splendors and Glooms* by Laura Amy Schlitz (Candlewick Press), *The Catastrophic History of You and Me* by Jess Rothenberg (Dial BfYR). I also represent the boutique literary development company Paper Lantern Lit, the multimedia arts organization The Story Pirates, and the illustrator of *Go the F to Sleep*, Ricardo Cortés.

How and why did you become an agent: Edmund Wilson was probably the writer who most filled me with awe of the New York publishing world when I was growing up, and I knew even in college I wanted to enter into that world and become an editor or agent. But agenting best suited my independent, entrepreneurial instincts.

What are your favorite books, movies, and TV shows, and why: Some of my favorite books include *Feed* by M. T. Anderson, *Liar's Poker* by Michael Lewis, *The Russian Debutante's Handbook* by Gary Shteyngart, *Small Is the New Big* by Seth Godin, and the *Artemis Fowl* series. I'm a big fan of *Burn Notice* and *House*, in terms of TV series. (Hint: I like brash and offbeat heroes and protagonists.)

Describe the client from hell, even if you don't have any: I am happy to report that all my clients are nice, pleasant people in addition to being brilliant writers.

Describe the publisher and/or editor from hell: Many of your problems as an agent go away by signing great writers and pairing them with the most committed and caring editors. But headaches of the job include editors who disappear, editors who package and publish badly or even simply fail to create enthusiasm for their authors' books in-house.

What do you like best about your clients and the editors and publishers you work with: What I like is waking up each day and not knowing what I'll discover next: perhaps a wonderful new writer, perhaps an incredible new work by an existing client. There is the joy of always falling in love with a great new project. Then, too, I like to obsess over the roll-out of a client's book; it's satisfying to see a book released to good reviews and a positive reception with readers.

Will our business exist as we know it in 10 years or so: Certainly not. The current economic recession has highlighted a number of issues the industry must address and respond to: the problem of over-publishing; the coming e-book revolution; the struggles of the chains to maintain profitability; redundant imprints, among others. But at Foundry we're very optimistic about the future. There will always be readers for a great book.

FRANCES COLLIN LITERARY AGENCY

PO Box 33, Wayne, PA 19087-0033
610-254-0555
www.francescollin.com

Agent's name: Sara Yake

Education: MA, English literature, West Chester University

Career history: Bookstore manager for five years, worked in sales for a major publisher for three years, have been with Fran Collin for five years and building my own client list for two years

Categories/Subjects that you are most enthusiastic about agenting: young adult, literary fiction, memoir, narrative nonfiction, travel narrative. I love the West, wilderness, nature, and the great outdoors on a grand scale and am always open to both fiction and nonfiction that can transport me there, especially if it features a strong woman character.

Categories/Subjects writers shouldn't bother pitching to you: Children's picture books, cooking, poetry, crafts, photography

If you were not an agent, what might you be doing instead: Librarian, bookseller, English teacher; definitely something bookish

What's the best way for fiction writers to solicit your interest: Personally, I would rather be wooed than grabbed right off the bat. Often the writers who grab my attention do so for all the wrong reasons, and their queries stick out like sore thumbs, so to speak. A writer woos me by following the generally accepted guidelines for a good, solid, well-written query. Once the query woos me, the writing itself should grab me.

Do you charge fees separate from your commission or offer nonagenting fee-based services: No

How and why did you become an agent: After years spent in other areas of the book business, a series of tiny quirks of fate led me to Fran at just the right time.

How do you feel about writers: I love them!

How would you describe what you do as an agent to someone (or something) from another planet: I try to explain it in the simplest terms and from the ground up. I remember what it's like to know nothing of the strange world of publishing.

What are your favorite books, movies, and TV shows, and why: *Fugitive Pieces* by Anne Michaels; anything by Virginia Woolf; *Zero, Three, Bravo* by Mariana Gosnell; *Cowboys Are My Weakness* by Pam Houston; any of the books by Emily Carr, who was just as good a writer as she was a painter; Philip Pullman's *His Dark Materials* trilogy. TV: *The Vicar of Dibley*, the new *Doctor Who*, *Ace of Cakes*.

What do they all, fiction and nonfiction alike, have in common: GREAT characters!

What do you like best about your clients and the editors and publishers you work with: I'm lucky to be in contact, every day, with people who love books and are dedicated to the art and craft of writing.

You're welcome to share your thoughts and sentiments about the business of

writing and publishing: It's a tough business, and there's no mistaking the fact that it is a business, but there's always room for enthusiasm and passion. It's an honor to be a part of the industry; sounds hokey, but it's true.

FRANCES GOLDIN LITERARY AGENCY, INC.

57 E. 11th St., Suite 5B, New York, NY 10003
212-777-0047 | fax: 212-228-1660
www.goldinlit.com

Agent's name: Sam Stoloff
Born: Nov. 14, 1960, New York City
Education: BA, Columbia University, 1984; MFA, Cornell University, 1988; MA, Cornell University, 1991; PhD, Cornell University (defended dissertation but have not yet received degree, and I may never, just out of laziness)
Career history: I taught college courses in English literature, creative writing, American history, and film studies for a number of years, at Cornell, Ithaca College, and the State University of New York. I've been with the Frances Goldin Agency since 1997. Being an agent is better.
Hobbies/Personal interests: I spend most of my nonworking time these days with my kids, so you could call that my main hobby. I love to cook, and I'm a bit of a foodie and small-time gardener, I sort-of-collect wine, I'm a big fan of the New York Mets, I play tennis, I'm a bit of a political junkie, and I read books (novels, journalism, history) for pleasure when I can. I like a good game of Scrabble or poker. I love movies, but haven't seen many since my first kid was born.
Categories/Subjects that you are most enthusiastic about agenting: Smart journalism, history, books on current events and public affairs, books about food, sports, popular culture, economics, psychology, original graphic works, wonderfully written novels, stories, and memoirs
Categories/Subjects writers shouldn't bother pitching to you: Most genre fiction (unless literary), self-help, diet books, practical nonfiction, pet books, celebrity bios, screenplays
If you were not an agent, what might you be doing instead: I'd probably either be a professor of American studies (literature, history, film), or a writer. Possibly a Washington think-tank type.
What's the best way for fiction writers to solicit your interest: Write a smart, succinct query letter describing the book (only one book, not every available manuscript), and previous publications, if any. I still prefer paper to e-mail, although I can see the writing on the wall.
What's the best way for nonfiction writers to solicit your interest: Write a smart, succinct query letter describing a fabulous project, and previous publications or other credentials, if any.

Do you charge reading or management fees: No

What are the most common mistakes writers make when pitching to you: Failure to actually describe the project; pitching more than one thing at a time; telling me my business (e.g., "Knopf would be the ideal publisher for this book"); assuming an unearned familiarity

Describe the client from hell, even if you don't have any: Thin-skinned, with an aversion to editorial feedback, and an inflated sense of literary importance and wildly unrealistic expectations about what publishing a book means; unable to acknowledge the work of others on their behalf

What's your definition of a great client: Thick-skinned, welcoming of editorial feedback, and with a becoming sense of modesty about themselves; freely expressive of gratitude for the work others do on their behalf. And wonderfully talented, of course.

What can a writer do to increase the odds of you becoming his or her agent: Be professional and courteous.

How and why did you become an agent: Frances Goldin is an old family friend, and I have long admired her integrity, her dedication, her loyalty to her clients, and the quality of the writers she has worked with. It looked pretty good to me!

What do you see in the near future for book publishing: The transition to electronic books will be a gradual one. Reading on paper and on screen will coexist for some time, although I think that when there's a knockout e-book reader with a great screen and a decent price, the migration to e-books will begin in earnest. Book publishers will struggle to adapt, as the means for distributing and consuming words continue to change. Writers will still write, agents will still represent them, but publishers and booksellers face big institutional upheavals.

What are your favorite books, movies, and TV shows, and why: My favorite movie is *Vertigo*. My favorite book is probably *The Great Gatsby* or maybe *House of Mirth*. My favorite TV show is *The Wire*.

What are some representative titles that you have sold: *A Brief History of the Flood* by Jean Harfenist (Knopf); *Jesus Land* by Julia Scheeres (Counterpoint); *Too Late to Die Young* by Harriet McBryde Johnson (Holt); *Blocking the Courthouse Door* by Stephanie Mencimer (Free Press); *Lullabies for Little Criminals* by Heather O'Neill (HarperCollins); *A People's History of Science* by Clifford Conner (Nation Books); *The Daring Book for Girls* by Miriam Peskowitz and Andrea Buchanan (HarperCollins); *Dirty Diplomacy* by Craig Murray (Scribner); *New York at War* by Steven Jaffe (Basic Books).

Agent's name: Matt McGowan
Born: June 19, 1972; Antwerp, Belgium
Education: BA, Colby College
Career history: I started in 1994 as an assistant at St. Martin's Press. After a year I moved on to assist retired Pantheon publisher Fred Jordan revive a small press called Fromm International. Fred was very generous, encouraging me to try just about anything from designing jackets to acquiring books. He was also inspiring in that he

had published these icons like Jack Kerouac and Allen Ginsberg during the heyday of Grove Press/Evergreen Review, where he worked for over 30 years and had these absurd stories about going to a Mets game with Samuel Beckett, drinking in Paris with William Burroughs, and being chased around the Grove offices by Valerie Solanas and her ice pick. I've always looked up to the Grove legacy and Grove founder Barney Rosset and think landing at Frances Goldin, after a short stint at another agency, was really fortunate as Frances has similar convictions about books and writers.

Categories/Subjects that you are most enthusiastic about agenting: Narrative nonfiction; literary, unusual, and/or humorous essays; travel; sports narratives (particularly soccer); smart commercial fiction; distinctive literary fiction; pop culture; music; peculiar histories; quirky and accessible food, business, science, or sociology

Categories/Subjects writers shouldn't bother pitching to you: Romance, religion, diet, reference; I see a lot of "edgy" first novels that romanticize drug use or depravity, which I quickly pass on.

What's the best way for writers to solicit your interest: Query letter or brief e-mail

Do you charge reading or management fees: No

What are the most common mistakes writers make when pitching to you: Making letters too "pitchy." I like a straightforward, informational query letter.

How and why did you become an agent: I read a novel in college which I learned had a really difficult time getting published, and that bred these idealistic notions about publishing and recognizing talented writers and helping them break through. That led to me doing an internship in New York my senior year, and I was actually attracted to the business of it all as much as anything.

What do you think the future holds for writers, publishers, and agents: I doubt books as we think of them today will survive—technology seems to be developing too fast, as well as consumer expectations—but authors and ideas will always be around, and there should always be a market for them.

What are your favorite books, movies, and TV shows, and why: TV: *Entourage, Scrubs, Flip This House,* Anthony Bourdain's show, *No Reservations.* Books: *I Am Not Jackson Pollock* by John Haskell; *Natasha* by David Bezmogzis; *The Miracle of Castel di Sangro* by Joe McGinniss; *Where I Was From* by Joan Didion

On a personal level, what do you think people like and dislike about you: I think my some of my more difficult and literary clients are appreciative that I work hard for them when their work is not clearly commercial. One of them sends me a fruit basket every Christmas, at least. I'm sure there are some things people don't like but let's not go there.

What are some representative titles that you have sold: *The Lifespan of a Fact: An Essay* (FSG); *The Open Curtain: A Novel* (Coffee House); *To Air Is Human: One Man's Quest to Become the World's Greatest Air Guitarist* (Riverhead); *Kicking Out, Kicking On: On the Road with the Fans, Freaks, and Fiends at the World's Biggest Sporting Event, World Cup 2006* (Harcourt); *Neck Deep: Odd Essays* (Graywolf); *The Perfect Baby Handbook: A Guide for the Excessively Motivated New Parent* (HarperCollins); *Bank: A Novel* (Little Brown).

Agent's name: Ellen Geiger

Born: New York, New York

Education: BA, Barnard; MA, University of California

Career history: I started agenting while working as an executive at a PBS station almost 20 years ago and have been at it ever since.

Hobbies/Personal interests: Shockingly enough, I still love to read. I'm also a politics and history fan, and play a mean game of Scrabble.

Categories/Subjects that you are most enthusiastic about agenting: Serious nonfiction of all sorts, history, science, current affairs, business, progressive politics, arts and culture, film, interesting memoirs, cutting-edge issues; In fiction, literary fiction, women's fiction, thrillers, mysteries, historical

Categories/Subjects writers shouldn't bother pitching to you: No New Age or flaky science, romance novels, or science fiction

If you were not an agent, what might you be doing instead: Travel and do more volunteer work; although these days I could work from anywhere if I had my BlackBerry along.

What's the best way for fiction writers to solicit your interest: Be able to write well and have an original idea, which is surprisingly hard to find. Understand the genre you're writing in. Have a track record, ideally, or some writing classes under your belt so you have a good sense of the form. Have done several drafts of your novel: There's nothing that makes my heart sink faster than to read that I'm the first one to read your first draft.

What's the best way for nonfiction writers to solicit your interest: Have a good grasp of your idea and some credentials to back it up. Have researched the market and the competition. Have good writing skills or be willing to team up with a writer to make the book the best it can be.

Do you charge reading or management fees: Absolutely not. No real agent who is a member of the AAR (Association of Author Representatives) does.

What are the most common mistakes writers make when pitching to you: To tell me what a great FILM their book will make; to not be able to summarize the plot briefly or create an interesting hook to get me eager to read more; to submit a query letter filled with typos and grammatical errors

Describe the client from hell, even if you don't have any: Worst is the writer who doesn't trust the agent and second-guesses your decisions, typically someone who solicits advice from everyone in their family including the dog. Another no-no is a bitter, pessimistic person who can't be pleased no matter what happens: If the review of their book is on page 3 of the *NY Times*, they're angry it's not on page 1. Usually I can screen these people out early on, but occasionally I am surprised, as they often masquerade as nice people until publication time.

What's your definition of a great client: Easy. Someone who can write well, and deliver on time! And it's great if that person is also someone who is emotionally mature enough to withstand the natural ups and downs of the publishing process.

What can a writer do to increase the odds of you becoming his or her agent:

A referral is guaranteed to get immediate attention; having a track record and/or good credentials; having a promotional platform for your book or a good plan for one; having studied the craft of writing at reputable schools and workshops; being educated and realistic about the realities of the publishing world.

How and why did you become an agent: It's my calling; I've always worked in arts representation. When I was 25, I owned part of a nightclub, and in a sense, I've been doing that kind of work ever since. I was mentored into the business by a top agent.

How would you describe what you do as an agent to someone (or something) from another planet: In the most general way, do everything possible to get the writer a great deal and help them achieve the best possible publication and promotion of their work. Then make sure they get paid.

How do you feel about editors and publishers: I realize they are under enormous pressure to perform to today's bottom-line oriented standards. Still, I wish they would take more chances and back up their books with real promotion.

How do you feel about writers: By nature, I am predisposed to like creative people and admire those who have the courage of their convictions and believe in their talent.

What do you see in the near future for book publishing: I hope publishers will understand that they must better promote the books they buy. Promotion is the weak link in the chain. We're now in a period of wild experimentation with web-based content, and I think that will shake out in the next few years. And, no matter how sexy they make those e-book readers, people will always prefer holding a real book in their hands.

What are your favorite books, movies, and TV shows, and why: Among our clients, our author Barbara Kingsolver's *Poisonwood Bible* for its sweep, narrative brilliance and social relevance; our author Ann Jones's *Kabul in Winter: Life Without Peace in Afghanistan,* for its brilliant depiction of the forgotten lives of women and men in wartime; our author Dorothy Allison's *Bastard out of Carolina* because it's just one of the best memoirs ever written. *Suite Francaise* for its historical impact and moving origins, *Fieldwork* by Mischa Berlinski for its scope and ideas, Jeffrey Eugenides's *Middlesex* because it's a *tour de force* of writing and history, *Then We Came to the End* for its shrewd, ironic, and ultimately moving insights into contemporary culture. In TV: *Mad Men* for its genius depicting the 1960s era, *The Closer* for Kyra Sedgwick's fab character, *Six Feet Under* and *The Sopranos* for their high-water marks in narrative storytelling. In theater: I love all kinds of theater but recently saw the superb revival of *Sunday in the Park with George* and love it for its tribute to the glory, persistence, and purity of art—surely a theme anyone in our profession can embrace.

In your opinion, what do editors think of you: Smart, fair, dedicated, experienced, a good negotiator, tough on contracts

On a personal level, what do you think people like and dislike about you: Together, organized, friendly, a bit of an egghead, good sense of humor

What are some representative titles that you have sold: Fiction: *Monkeewrench* by PJ Tracy (Putnam); *The Sunday List of Dreams* by Kris Radish (Bantam); *The Penguin Who Knew Too Much* by Donna Andrews (St. Martin's); *The Saddlemaker's*

Wife by Earlene Fowler (Berkley). Nonfiction: *Kabul in Winter: Life Without Peace in Afghanistan* by Ann Jones (Holt/Metropolitan); *The American Plague: The Untold Story of Yellow Fever, the Epidemic That Shaped Our History* by Molly Crosby (Berkley); *If the Creek Don't Rise: My Life out West with the Last Black Widow of the Civil War* by Rita Williams (Harcourt); *How to Read the Bible* by James L. Kugel (Free Press); *Gringos in Paradise* by Barry Golson (Scribner); *Free Exercise, Expensive Gas: A Church–State Road Trip* by Jay Wexler (Beacon)

THE FRIEDRICH AGENCY

136 East 57th Street, 19th floor, New York, NY 10022
www.friedrichagency.com

Agent's name: Paul Cirone
E-mail: pcirone@friedrichagency.com
Born: Brooklyn, NY, June 4th, 1974
Education: Bachelor of Arts from New York University, graduated cum laude
Career history: I began my career at the Aaron Priest Agency, first as an intern, and then apprenticed to Molly Friedrich. Three and half years ago Molly formed her own agency, where I now agent full time.
Hobbies/Personal interests: Besides the obvious answer of reading published books to constantly educate myself on the market, I'm an avid film buff, audiophile, and foodie. I'm also into kickboxing and lifting weights.
Categories/Subjects that you are most enthusiastic about agenting: I gravitate towards literary fiction, first and foremost, but also represent narrative nonfiction and memoir. I'm also open to looking at thrillers, mysteries, commercial fiction, and fantasy/ sci-fi—anything with an original voice, good writing, and compelling story-telling.
Categories/Subjects writers shouldn't bother pitching to you: Romance, business, self-help
If you were not an agent, what might you be doing instead: I'd probably have been the guy who picks music for film soundtracks.
Do you charge fees separate from your commission or offer nonagenting fee-based services: No fees charged. All my reading is done on my time.
What are some representative titles that you have sold: *City of Tranquil Light* by Bo Caldwell (Henry Holt); *American History Revised* by Seymour Morris (Broadway Books); *The Rhinestone Sisterhood* by David Valdez Greenwood (Crown); *Just Don't Fall* by Josh Sundquist (Viking); *So Brave, Young, and Handsome* by Leif Enger (Grove/ Atlantic); *Bury Me Deep* by Megan Abbott (Simon & Schuster); *Service Included* by Phoebe Damrosch (Morrow); *Simon Says* by Kathryn Eastburn (Da Capo); *Queenpin* by Megan Abbott (Simon & Schuster); *Peace Like a River* by Leif Enger
How and why did you become an agent: It evolved from working with and being mentored by Molly Friedrich while at Aaron Priest. It also didn't hurt that

the first book I sold was *Peace Like a River* by Leif Enger. I thought, "This a piece of cake." Then, of course, it wasn't. That kind of writer only comes once in a great while.

How do you feel about writers: I love my writers. I'm pretty blessed.

How do you feel about editors and publishers: It's impossible to generalize. There are editors that I adore, with whom working is a truly collaborative and communicative process, and then there are the ones that fight you tooth and nail just to get a response to an e-mail about print runs!

How would you describe what you do as an agent to someone (or something) from another planet: We're the middleman between the writer and the publisher. We serve as guide, advocate, therapist, financial advisor, defender, man-at-arms, and editor.

What are your favorite books, movies, and TV shows, and why: *The Guernsey Literary and Potato Peel Society* by Mary Ann Schaffer and *Atonement* by Ian McEwan for their blend of history and entertainment; anything by Gabriel García Márquez for his sheer mastery; *Cutting for Stone* by Abraham Verghese for its epic scope and exquisite writing

Describe the writer from hell: A writer with delusions of grandeur!

Describe yourself: I'm a good guy: bright, honest, passionate, hard working, and devoted to good writing!

Describe the publisher and/or editor from hell: The ones that don't collaborate and don't return calls or e-mails

What's the best way for writers to solicit your interest: A query letter via e-mail is preferred.

Will e-readers significantly change the business: Yes, I think e-readers can't be ignored, but I also think books and e-books are going to coexist for a very long time. They won't replace them the way mp3s replaced CDs. The book, after all, is really one of the most perfect inventions.

Are you optimistic, pessimistic, neutral, or catatonic about the book biz in the future: Depending on what I read, my mood fluctuates on the fate of our business. Today I am optimistic that this entry will yield a terrific new writer.

Explain what you like and dislike about your job: I love being the first person to discover a great writer. I hate all the rejections.

Describe a book you might like writing: I'll leave the writing of books to all the real writers out there. Although, maybe when I'm 50 and really lived, I'll have something to say. Who knows?

FULL CIRCLE LITERARY, LLC

7676 Hazard Center Drive, Suite 500, San Diego, CA 92180
www.fullcircleliterary.com

    Agent's name: Lilly Ghahremani
    Born: November 8, Chicago

Education: JD from UCLA School of Law; BA in English from University of Michigan; MBA from San Diego State University

Career history: Following law school, I decided to "use my powers for good." With some editing experience under my belt, I formally began my publishing career with a small firm that specialized in authors' affairs. Although I loved helping authors finalize the paperwork, addressing copyright affairs, and doing some pitching to publishers, I wanted to really dig in and be involved in the creative process more, finding and growing talent and carrying it through to completion, so we launched Full Circle in 2004 to allow us to do just that.

Hobbies/Personal interests: Traveling, reading (of course!), dancing, collecting random pop trivia, yoga

Categories/Subjects that you are most enthusiastic about agenting: Green living, crafting books/do-it-yourself, pop culture, nonfiction how-to books written by an expert with a funny writing voice, and young adult

If you were not an agent, what might you be doing instead: Realistically I'd be doing the lawyer grind. Blech.

What's the best way for fiction writers to solicit your interest: Professionalism is underrated! Authors who do their research and are clear about why they're pitching to me (correctly!) will have my attention.

Do you charge fees separate from your commission or offer nonagenting fee-based services: Absolutely not. Full Circle does not charge any additional fees for its services, nor do we charge a reading fee.

How do you feel about writers: Writers are often the most unappreciated artists out there. Writing a book is no small feat, and writers are some of the most articulate clients you could possibly dream to work with. Plus, they are fellow readers, which automatically brings them close to my heart!

How would you describe what you do as an agent to someone (or something) from another planet: I tell them no, I didn't agent *The Da Vinci Code*!

Describe the writer from hell: The problem writer wouldn't take the time to learn about the industry and what are (or aren't) realistic expectations of an agent or, more importantly, a publisher! On the flipside, a dream author is a self-starter, a self-promoter who realizes they are the foundation of a successful book, and that never changes, even with the biggest publisher or marketing budget.

Describe the publisher and/or editor from hell: Lack of communication. Sending a manuscript and not hearing back is purgatory for agents, whether it's in the submission stage or delivery of a final manuscript.

What do you like best about your clients and the editors and publishers you work with: In general, I try to work with editors I feel a personal connection with—it's important to me that I leave my books in capable, caring hands. I am proud to work with publishers who bring enthusiasm and incredible insight into the projects we share.

What are some representative titles that you have sold: Lilly's recent titles: *The Work-at-Home Success Bible* (Leslie Truex); *Sewing Green* by Betz White

(Stewart, Tabori, & Chang); *Hit Me with Your Best Shot* by Raina Lee (Chronicle Books); *Rockabye Baby* by Penny Warner (Chronicle Books). Stefanie's recent titles: *Preggatinis* by Natalie Boris Nelson; *The Bilingual Edge: Why, When, and How to Teach Your Child a Second Language* by Kendall King and Alison Mackey (HarperCollins); *I Love Dirt!: 52 Activities to Help You and Your Kids Discover the Wonders of Nature* by Jennifer Ward (Shambhala); *Confetti Girl* by Diana Lopez (Little, Brown); *Pele: King of Soccer (Pelé: El rey del fútbol)* by Monica Brown and illustrated by Rudy Guiterrez (Rayo/HarperCollins); *What Can You Do with a Paleta?* by Carmen Tafolla and illustrated by Magaly Morales (Tricycle Press). Jointly agented: *Exclusively Chloe* by Jon Yang.

Agent's name: Stefanie Von Borstel
Born: San Antonio, Texas
Education: BA in English and professional marketing program, University of California, San Diego
Career history: As an undergrad English lit student, I started my first internship in the editorial department of Penguin/PSS, where my first duties included reading submissions and testing copy for *Mad Libs!* I thought, "Wow, what a fun industry; this is for me!" I moved on to the marketing department at Harcourt, where I worked over the course of seven years in various publicity, advertising, and promotions positions. After experiencing both the editorial and marketing/sales side of trade publishing, I decided to combine my experience to help writers navigate the publishing world as an agent.
Hobbies/Personal interests: Cooking and entertaining, flamenco and salsa dancing, tennis, travel, and foreign films
Categories/Subjects that you are most enthusiastic about agenting: Multicultural fiction for adults, teens, and children (especially Latino), nonfiction how-to including parenting, green living, women's interest, and crafts
If you were not an agent, what might you be doing instead: I think I'd like to own a chocolate shop–children's boutique–bookstore—a combination of a few of my favorite things!
What's the best way for fiction writers to solicit your interest: I am always impressed when a writer is familiar with books and authors we've represented.
Do you charge fees separate from your commission or offer nonagenting fee-based services: Absolutely not. Full Circle does not charge any additional fees for its services, nor do we charge a reading fee.
How and why did you become an agent: After working in both the editorial and marketing/sales side of trade publishing, I found that agenting is a great way to be involved in a book from the beginning. So I put my publishing experience to work, and I became an agent to connect books with readers!
How do you feel about writers: I am always amazed at the creative ideas and imagination that seem to fill writers from head to toe. Writing is a true craft!
How would you describe what you do as an agent to someone (or something)

from another planet: Many times people think that since I work with books that I must be a writer OR that I can print their book. I have to explain that while I am fortunate to work with both writers and publishers, I don't write or publish!

Describe the writer from hell: The problem writer wouldn't take the time to learn about the industry and what are (or aren't) realistic expectations of an agent or, more importantly, a publisher! On the flipside, a dream author is a self-starter, a self-promoter who realizes they are the foundation of a successful book, and that never changes, even with the biggest publisher or marketing budget.

Describe the publisher and/or editor from hell: Lack of communication. Sending a manuscript and not hearing back is purgatory for agents, whether it's in the submission stage or delivery of a final manuscript.

What do you like best about your clients and the editors and publishers you work with: I have a passion for the books I represent that I truly share with my authors and the editors I work with. I love the spark of a new idea and seeing it transformed (after lots of work, of course) into a beautiful, printed page!

You're welcome to share your thoughts and sentiments about the business of writing and publishing: Everyone in our industry is in it because they love what they do. I think we're at a time when it's important to support each other and produce the best books that we all can so that readers will continue to read! And more often and at even the earliest age—we all win when there are more lifelong readers!

What are some representative titles that you have sold: Lilly's recent titles: *The Work-at-Home Success Bible* (Leslie Truex); *Sewing Green* by Betz White (Stewart, Tabori, & Chang); *Hit Me with Your Best Shot* by Raina Lee (Chronicle Books); *Rockabye Baby* by Penny Warner (Chronicle Books). Stefanie's recent titles: *Preggatinis* by Natalie Boris Nelson; *The Bilingual Edge: Why, When, and How to Teach Your Child a Second Language* by Kendall King and Alison Mackey (HarperCollins); *I Love Dirt!: 52 Activities to Help You and Your Kids Discover the Wonders of Nature* by Jennifer Ward (Shambhala); *Confetti Girl* by Diana Lopez (Little, Brown); *Pele: King of Soccer (Pelé: El rey del fútbol)* by Monica Brown and illustrated by Rudy Guiterrez (Rayo/HarperCollins); *What Can You Do with a Paleta?* by Carmen Tafolla and illustrated by Magaly Morales (Tricycle Press). Jointly agented: *Exclusively Chloe* by Jon Yang.

HALSTON FREEMAN LITERARY AGENCY, INC.

140 Broadway, 46th Floor, New York, NY 10005

Agents' names: Molly Freeman, Betty Halston

Categories/Subjects that you are most enthusiastic about agenting: 75 percent nonfiction—25 percent fiction. Do not want to see children's books, poetry, textbooks, New Age, erotica, horror.

What's the best way for writers to solicit your interest: Write a compelling query letter. For nonfiction include sample chapters, overview, why you are qualified to write on your subject, biography, and details about any marketing platform you might have. For fiction include synopsis and first three chapters. E-mail or snail mail only. No faxes, phone calls, or attachments. If you e-mail your query, include sample chapters and other requested material in text of the e-mail. Include SASE if you query by snail mail.

Do you charge fees separate from your commission or offer nonagenting fee-based services: We do not charge reading or editorial fees. We charge for photocopying if we accept someone as a client.

What are some representative titles that you have sold: Presently, we have a half-dozen deals pending that are in progress.

What do you like best about your clients and the editors and publishers you work with: We are a hands-on agency specializing in quality nonfiction and fiction. As a new agency, it is imperative that we develop relationships with good writers who are smart, hardworking, and understanding of what's required of them to promote their work.

Describe the writer from hell: A person who won't listen and is, more often than not, late getting requested material submitted

You're welcome to share your thoughts and sentiments about the business of writing and publishing: It is our belief that the publishing industry will be predominantly e-books in 10 years. Technology will improve and become less expensive, making it attractive, especially to younger people, to download books. Brick-and-mortar stores will begin to disappear unless independents and chains can service the e-book market as competitively as online sellers.

HANNIGAN SALKY GETZLER AGENCY

287 Spring Street, New York, NY 10013
www.hsgagency.com

Agent's name: Josh Getzler

Education: BA, University of Pennsylvania, 1990; Radcliffe publishing course, 1990; MBA, Columbia Business School, 1995

Born: May 4, 1968, New York City

Career history: I started in editorial at Harcourt in 1991, and then left to go to business school, expecting to get back into publishing after. Instead, I ended up owning and operating a minor league baseball team for 12 years (Staten Island Yankees), before selling in 2006 and returning to the world of books on the agency side. I worked at Writers House and Russell & Volkening before starting my own agency with partners Jesseca Salky and Carrie Hannigan.

Categories/Subjects that you are most enthusiastic about agenting: Procedural mysteries (particularly, though by no means exclusively, period and foreign), thrillers, literary and commercial fiction, religion (not spiritual guidance—books about religious history or philosophy), sports, music

Categories/Subjects writers shouldn't bother pitching to you: Romance, picture books, religious fiction

If you were not an agent, what might you be doing instead: Sports marketing, working on the business side of a publishing house, editing

What's the best way for fiction writers to solicit your interest: E-mail a clearly and concisely written letter that tells me quickly what kind of book you are pitching. I want to know the genre; I want to know salient details about the story. I don't want to know that you think your book is important and groundbreaking, hilarious and a must-read. I want you to offer it up for evaluation, and I will respect your willingness to put it out there.

Do you charge fees separate from your commission or offer nonagenting fee-based services: No

What are some representative titles that you have sold: *Devil's Trill* by Gerald Elias (St. Martin's Press); *The Crown* by Nancy Bilyeau (Touchstone); *The Chronicles of Egg* by Geoff Rodkey (Putnam)

How and why did you become an agent: When I was selling the baseball team, I was having a conversation with my wife, who told me that it was clear I needed to work in books again. Having 13 years of experience making deals and looking at contracts, I realized I could be suited to agenting. I decided to target existing agencies, rather than start a new one, and got lucky with timing that a position with Simon Lipskar and Dan Lazar at Writers House opened up.

What are your favorite books, movies, and TV shows, and why: Books: *Absalom, Absalom; The Caine Mutiny; The Day of the Jackal; The Tattooed Potato and Other Clues; O, Jerusalem; Sherlock Holmes* (any of them, really). Movies: *Inherit the Wind, Bull Durham, My Cousin Vinny, Murder on the Orient Express, The Great Dictator.* TV shows: *Taxi, Black Adder, Law & Order* (original), *MASH, Prime Suspect.*

Will our business exist as we know it in 10 years or so: Yes, I think so, although there will be a much greater emphasis on electronic rights. We will be even more in the business of representing intellectual property.

HARTLINE LITERARY AGENCY

123 Queenston Dr., Pittsburgh, PA 15235
412-829-2483
www.hartlineliterary.com

Agent's name: Terry Burns
Born: August 21, 1942
Education: BA, West Texas State; advanced studies at Southern Methodist University
Career history: Chamber of commerce executive for 27 years, professional writer

of inspirational fiction 15 years, agent at Hartline for over three years. As a writer I have 24 books in print, and as an agent have a diverse and growing client list.

Hobbies/Personal interests: Camping and RV

Categories/Subjects that you are most enthusiastic about agenting: Historical fiction and romance, mysteries, thriller/suspense, inspirationals, nonfiction, a good well-written book I can see the market for and feel I have the right contacts to address that market.

Categories/Subjects writers shouldn't bother pitching to you: Fantasy and sci-fi, erotica, gay or lesbian, or anything of that nature. [Writers] should know I don't take hard-copy submissions and should check our submission guidelines.

If you were not an agent, what might you be doing instead: Writing more

What's the best way for fiction writers to solicit your interest: Read the submission guidelines and send me just exactly what I want to see in the exact manner I ask to see it.

Do you charge fees separate from your commission or offer nonagenting fee-based services: No; our agency does have a provision to charge for copies and postage if appropriate.

What are some representative titles that you have sold: *Rhapsody in Red* (Moody); *The Birth to Five Book* (Revell); *Beyond the Smoke* (BJU Press); *Tribute* (Kregel); two separate, five-book youth series to Capstone Press; *Rekindle Your Dreams* (Bridge Logos); *Love Rescues*, first book in trilogy (Whitaker House); *By Darkness Hid*, first book in three-book series to Marcher Lord Press and Highland Blessings (Abingdon Press)

How and why did you become an agent: The owner of this agency, Joyce Hart, was my agent for a number of years and still is. She recruited me to work with her. I decided I could do more good by helping a number of people get their work out than doing a book or two a year myself, although I do still write.

How do you feel about writers: Most agents come from a publishing background. I come from a writing background. Whether that is an advantage or a disadvantage, it does give me an unusually good rapport with writers.

How would you describe what you do as an agent to someone (or something) from another planet: To go home, because I don't rep sci-fi

What are your favorite books, movies, and TV shows, and why: I grew up watching *Bonanza* and *Gunsmoke* and Gene and Roy at the movies. I love Westerns. I'd write and rep a bunch of them if there was a market for them right now. As to shows today it takes something pretty interesting to get me away from whatever I'm doing.

Describe the client from hell, even if you don't have any: Let me put it this way: I don't take orders very well.

Describe the publisher and/or editor from hell: The only ones that really bother me are the ones whose idea of a response to a submission is just to never respond. Unfortunately there seem to be more who are doing that.

What do you like best about your clients and the editors and publishers you work with: The love of the words, the desire to get a good story out there that will entertain, that will impact emotions, that will cause someone to stop and think, possibly even bring some change into their lives. I love to work with people on both ends that are trying to make something happen with the written word.

You're welcome to share your thoughts and sentiments about the business of writing and publishing: See above.

Describe yourself: Just a good old boy who likes to try and help people get their words out into the marketplace

Will our business exist as we know it in 10 years or so: Yes. There have been changes over the years, but they have tended to be additional sources of publishing, not replacing previous forms. We will see digital and audio and some of the other changes taking place now continue to grow, but we'll still see publishing as we know it continue to exist.

Agent's name: Tamela Hancock Murray
E-mail: tamelaagents@juno.com
Born: Petersburg, Virginia; September 6
Education: Lynchburg College, honors in journalism
Career history: Tamela has been with Hartline Literary Agency since 2001. She has many happy and successful clients. A professional writer since 1994, she is also an award-winning, best-selling author in her own right.

Hobbies/Personal interests: Reading is Tamela's favorite hobby, a great convenience since her job as an agent requires so much reading! She especially enjoys time spent with her family and friends. Travel fascinates her.

Categories/Subjects that you are most enthusiastic about agenting: Tamela's focus is on inspirational titles. She enjoys fiction and nonfiction. Novelists with stories geared to a mainstream audience stand the best chance of gaining her representation. Writers with an outstanding platform have the best chance of success when submitting nonfiction.

Categories/Subjects writers shouldn't bother pitching to you: Erotica, science fiction, experimental, stream-of-consciousness, horror. I don't mind seeing Christianity explored in a thoughtful manner, but I will not represent any work that is obviously offensive to Christians.

If you were not an agent, what might you be doing instead: Writing for newspapers and magazines

What's the best way for fiction writers to solicit your interest: Client referrals are the number-one way to get my attention. Barring a referral, a top-notch proposal showing me how you will partner with your publisher to make your book a success is the best way to gain my attention. I do review each submission so if you don't hear from me in three months, feel free to resubmit and let me know it's your second try. If you are accepted for representation by another agent before hearing back from me, I would greatly appreciate it if you could let me know so I can disregard your submission and wish you the best.

Do you charge fees separate from your commission or offer nonagenting

fee-based services: I charge no fees. No reading fees, no critique fees, nothing but industry standard commission.

What are some representative titles that you have sold: *A Promise for Spring* by Kim Vogel Sawyer (Barbour Books); *Jewel of His Heart* by Maggie Brendan (Revell); *Mothers of the Bible Speak to Mothers of Today* by Kathi Macias (New Hope Publishers)

How and why did you become an agent: I believe in the books I present to editors, and I love making authors' dreams come true. I became an agent because my agent, Joyce Hart, wanted to expand her business, and she was willing to take a chance on me. I'm so glad she did!

How do you feel about writers: I love writers! Since I'm a writer myself, I understand what they go through to get published and to keep their career momentum going. I understand the frustration of the near miss and the pain of multiple rejections. I also celebrate with them when that all-important contract comes through. Gaining new book contracts never gets old for me. The twentieth book is just as exciting as the first.

How would you describe what you do as an agent to someone (or something) from another planet: I spend a lot of time reading, advising, answering questions, hand-holding, and making friends.

What are your favorite books, movies, and TV shows, and why: My tastes are eclectic. I like to read books on Western mysticism from the Middle Ages. I also enjoy romantic books and suspense. Silent films are a treat. The other night my husband and I stayed up much too late watching *Lorna Doone*. As for TV, *Clean House* is fun to watch. My tastes are often dominated by my mood at the time, whether I want entertainment or wish to be challenged.

Describe the client from hell, even if you don't have any: This writer would refuse to cooperate with editors, send me lots of chain-letter e-mails, and be flighty and unpredictable, with a poor work ethic. Thankfully I have wonderful writers who are just super!

Describe the publisher and/or editor from hell: I really hate having to act as a bill collector. I like when a publisher pays on time. The hellish editor is one who refuses to answer legitimate calls and/or e-mails.

What do you like best about your clients and the editors and publishers you work with: I love how dedicated my clients are to the writing craft and their wonderful attitudes about complying with editors' requests. I love how my editors don't make irrational, unreasonable requests and how they treat my authors with respect. I love publishers who do a top-notch job of marketing.

You're welcome to share your thoughts and sentiments about the business of writing and publishing: A talented, persistent writer willing to be flexible and sensitive to the market has the best chance of success.

Describe yourself: My goal is to be a benefit and a blessing to all who work with me.

Will our business exist as we know it in 10 years or so: Yes, and the quality of our books will only get better. Electronic formats may gain in popularity, but I think we'll always have leather-bound, hardback, and paperback books.

Agent's name: Diana L. Flegal
Born: July 24, Johnstown, Pennsylvania
Education: Certified dental assistant; certified x-ray technologist; 13 credits shy of a degree in anthropology and missions from Maryland Bible College and Seminary
Career history: Served as a third-world health caregiver in Haiti for one year. Chairside dental assistant, 23 years; apologetics teacher at Grace Bible Academy, Sioux Falls, South Dakota; women's Bible study leader; youth leader; Sunday school leader; pastor's wife; editorial assistant to Joyce Hart, CEO and founder of Hartline Literary Agency; literary agent
Hobbies/Personal interests: Crafting, decorating my home, reading, gardening, traveling
Categories/Subjects that you are most enthusiastic about agenting: Inspirational nonfiction, inspirational literary fiction, inspirational gift books, animal books (moving stories about animals and the people that love them)
Categories/Subjects writers shouldn't bother pitching to you: Gay/lesbian, paranormal, New Age, or anything that is not from a Christian worldview. I'll take a look at most anything else if it is well written.
If you were not an agent, what might you be doing instead: Life coaching
What's the best way for fiction writers to solicit your interest: Good story-line with a fast pace. Do not bog me down with minute details of your personal life story. Readers do not want to know these things.
Do you charge fees separate from your commission or offer nonagenting fee-based services: I charge for copies that I must print for submission and the postage for same. That is all. Honest!
What are some representative titles that you have sold: *Fat to Skinny Fast and Easy* by Doug Varrieur (Sterling Publishing Co.); *Be Still and Let Your Nail Polish Dry* by Loree Lough (Summerside Press); *No Strings Attached* by Loree Lough (Whitaker House); *Love Finds You in North Pole Alaska* by Loree Lough (Summerside Press); *Love Finds You in Hershey, Pennsylvania* by Cerella Seachrist (Summerside Press).
How and why did you become an agent: A voracious reader from little on, I have always wanted to be paid to read. As Joyce Hart's first reader, I learned what good writing was, what editors were looking for, and what did not sell. I began to realize that I could be an agent.
How do you feel about writers: I love writers because before I was an agent, I was a reader. I love the printed word, newspapers, magazines, digests, and novels, how tos, etc., so without writers I wouldn't have those precious stolen moments in time when I am swept away to another place and time, country, or planet. My life would not be at all as joyful and varied as it is.
How would you describe what you do as an agent to someone (or something)

from another planet: It is the best reason to relocate to planet Earth. We have free libraries, and you can get your own card. You don't need an extension cord and any battery packs. Just daylight and a comfy chair. It is so worth learning English for!

What are your favorite books, movies, and TV shows, and why: The Bible has the top slot to be sure. As to fiction, I love mysteries best: Elizabeth Peters and her pen name Anne Perry is my absolute favorite author. I have read most everything she has written, and that is a lot of books. Google her sometime. Christy Barritt, Ron and Janet Benrey, too. Maeve Binchy is my favorite secular author, read everything she has written; then nonfiction how-to, John Ortberg, Erwin McManus, T. D. Jakes, Philip Yancey, Max Lucado, John Maxwell, Donald Miller. Writing books: Anne Lamott's *Bird by Bird* is one of the best, then Terry Whalin's *How to Write a Nonfiction Book Proposal*, along with Julia Cameron and William Zinsser. Movies: *The Secret Life of Bees*, *Lord of the Rings*, *K-Pax*. TV shows: *NCIS*, *Bones*, Home & Garden Television.

Describe the client from hell, even if you don't have any: I try to steer clear of them. But I guess they are the ones who write their life's story with every small detail included, expecting it to be a best seller, and it is only interesting to them…

Describe the publisher and/or editor from hell: Don't know too many, but I would say they are the ones who clear their desk and send out the form rejection letters and never give your proposal a glance. Or at the least fail to tell me what exactly they ARE looking for.

What do you like best about your clients and the editors and publishers you work with: The creative comments and critiques that editors give help my writers become better writers. You can tell the ones (editors) who truly love what they do and that they care about representing good writing. They take that extra minute to say a nice thing that keeps you trying all the more to make a match for the writer and the editor. As for my clients, they have become my extended family. We support one another with words and deeds. In my case, we encourage one another to go beyond our limitations to achieve excellence. I care so much for each one and their stories that I [lie] awake at night trying to strategize a plan to enable their success.

You're welcome to share your thoughts and sentiments about the business of writing and publishing: It is a tough business, getting tougher every year, but I believe this means that the really well-turned phrase and good story will shine forth and find its place. And we will be all the better for having known one another and shared the time it takes to read a book together. My life will be enriched as well as the others that just happen to come across that good read, or received a gift or had nothing better to do so out of boredom picked up a book to fill the time. Their lives will be changed, the world will be a better place to live in, and more aliens will desire to visit. They will begin savings accounts and place a poster on the wall of their bedrooms and dream of the day they come to planet Earth and get their very own library card with their name on it.

Describe yourself: I am a lover of books, a dreamer of dreams, an armchair traveler, and a visionary, and a missionary. I'm also a blond by birth.

Will our business exist as we know it in 10 years or so: I plan on being a literary agent until I pass from this life on to the next. It is something that I can do from any-place in the world. I plan to be so successful that I will travel extensively, representing my authors anywhere I go. I appreciate the technology that allows this, and hope I can enjoy the health to follow my dreams of helping dig wells in Africa, build orphanages in third-world countries, and help a school in Tanzania where a friend of mine teaches.

Agent's name: Joyce Hart
Born: August 7, Iowa City, Iowa
Education: Open Bible College, Des Moines, Iowa (now in Eugene, Oregon)
Career history: Started as a secretary to the vice president and editorial staff at Whitaker House, Springdale, Pennsylvania in 1978, until 1989. The last three years I was the vice president of marketing and worked in all aspects of the publishing house.
Hobbies/Personal interests: Reading, traveling, dogs
Categories/Subjects that you are most enthusiastic about agenting: Most adult novels, most genres except fantasy, sci-fi, nonfiction adult books—self-help, spirituality, prayer, family
Categories/Subjects writers shouldn't bother pitching to you: Sci-fi, fantasy, poetry, gay and lesbian, paranormal, memoirs
If you were not an agent, what might you be doing instead: Teaching, working in a bookstore, speaking to women's groups
What's the best way for fiction writers to solicit your interest: A well-written, well-researched proposal. Following our guidelines on our website.
Do you charge fees separate from your commission or offer nonagenting fee-based services: Once in a while we'll charge for postage if it's overnight or very high. Most of the time we don't bother. No fees for nonagenting services. We don't do any editing, etc.
What are some representative titles that you have sold: *An Absence So Great* by Jane Kirkpatrick (WaterBrook Multnomah); three-book series *Lancaster County Secrets*, Suzanne Fisher (Revell); *I Don't Want a Divorce*, David Clark (Revell); *Skipping the Narrows*, Kevin Milne (Center Street); *Blood Ransom*, Lisa Harris (Zondervan); *Scattered Petals*, Amanda Cabot (Revell); *Journey to the Well*, Diana Wallis Taylor (Revell); *Through the Eyes of Love*, Dorothy Clark, Harlequin (Steeple Hill); *Love Finds You in Golden New Mexico*, Lena Nelson Dooley (Summerside Press)

How and why did you become an agent: I became an agent because I quit my corporate job and wanted to stay in this industry. I found my niche. I started Hartline Marketing in 1990 and Hartline Literary in 1992. I was a publisher's rep for 11 or more years and did the literary agency part time. Eventually, the agency became my full-time job.
How do you feel about writers: I like working with authors for the most part. If they are prima donnas, then it's not so much fun. Most are great and my good friends.
How would you describe what you do as an agent to someone (or something) from another planet: I don't know how to answer this one...

What are your favorite books, movies, and TV shows, and why: Books: *The Will of Wisteria* by Denise Hildreth, *Shadows of Lancaster County* by Mindy Sterns Clark, *Healing Stones and Healing Waters* by Nancy Rue and Stephen Arterburn, *A Time to Mend* by Sally John and Gary Smalley. Movies: Two most favorite are *Sound of Music*, because of the music and the story and *Steel Magnolias*—I love the characters and their relationships with one another. TV shows: *Murder, She Wrote*; *Diagnosis Murder*; *Jane Doe*—all mysteries, and I like the characters.

Describe the client from hell, even if you don't have any: One who rewrites and rewrites, not flexible, calls me all hours of the day and night; hard to work with those

Describe the publisher and/or editor from hell: An editor who never responds to e-mails or phone calls. Snobbish editors. Most editors and publishers I work with are good friends.

What do you like best about your clients and the editors and publishers you work with: I like seeing good writing and compelling stories, good nonfiction. I like my clients who are loyal to our agency. Most are willing to work hard and give us a good proposal to present to the editors. Most of the editors are great to work with. I love it when they call me and ask me if I have a client who could write a specific book or on a specific subject. I like to help the author and editor develop a good product.

You're welcome to share your thoughts and sentiments about the business of writing and publishing: I love the publishing world. It is not an easy profession, getting harder all the time. Publishers are asking for "household names" more than ever. Sometimes the "market-driven" part of the business gets discouraging, especially when sales turns down a really good book.

Describe yourself: A pretty ordinary, hard-working woman; the wife of a minister, a mother, and a grandmother; someone who counts her blessings and is grateful for a job that has brought great satisfaction in her life

Will our business exist as we know it in 10 years or so: I think our business will exist in the next 10 years or so. It has changed a lot in the past five years and will continue to change. More and more people are buying online, we're seeing more e-books, but the growth is not huge. However, I think we will always have print books, books that people can hold in their hands.

HEACOCK LITERARY AGENCY, INC.

1020 Hollywood Way, #439, Burbank, CA 91505
www.heacockliteraryagency.com

Agent's name: Catt LeBaigue
E-mail: catt@heacockliteraryagency.com
Born: December 30, California
Education: BA, music, plus a certificate in writing in upper-division and graduate-level courses, California State University, San Bernardino

Career history: Eighteen years in the television and film industry for Columbia, Lorimar, Sony, Fox, Paramount, and Warner Bros. studios. Catt LeBaigue joined the Heacock Literary Agency, working full time as an agent, in 2005. Tom Dark is our newest agent, joining in 2008.

Hobbies/Personal interests: I grew up as an American living abroad in the diplomatic community. A highlight in my life was in 2005, when a full-blooded traditional aboriginal tribe in Australia adopted me, gave me a new name, and invited me to dance in their sacred dances. I raise horses and live close to nature. My interests are meditation, dreams, Jung, reading, travel, drawing, sculpting, and animals.

Categories/Subjects that you are most enthusiastic about agenting: The Heacock Literary Agency was founded in 1978 with a vision to get significant books into the marketplace, books with the potential to empower and fortify consciousness. Books can change the individual from the inside out, and individual consciousness can transform the world. Trade nonfiction: Art, architecture, animal communication, diplomacy, ecology, indigenous cultures, invention, the mind and learning processes, formal science and the connection to inner knowing, social sciences, travel, wilderness awareness, body, mind, and spirit. We seek innovative books that present solutions to problems. Trade fiction: Children's, especially middle grade and young adult. Adult fiction: Literary, no short stories.

Categories/Subjects writers shouldn't bother pitching to you: True crime, abuse accounts, and books that do not contribute to the reader's well-being and peace of mind

If you were not an agent, what might you be doing instead: I see my work as an author's representative, not just as my job, but as the best way that I can contribute to humanity and the health of the planet. If I weren't agenting, I'd be seeking another way that is just as powerful to make a difference.

What's the best way for fiction writers to solicit your interest: E-mail without attachments, unless requested; not accepting postal mail queries

Do you charge reading or management fees: No

What categories do you represent, by percentages: 30 percent adult nonfiction, 40 percent children's, 30 percent fiction

What are the most common mistakes writers make when pitching to you: The writer should take care in composing the inquiry since this is the first impression the agent receives of the writer's ability to convey his or her ideas. Any background information will enhance the writer's chance of attracting interest. Nonfiction books should be presented with a book proposal. Including the word count of the final manuscript is helpful.

Describe the client from hell, even if you don't have any: The client from hell seeks only monetary gain or fame and cannot see beyond themselves.

How would you describe the perfect client: The perfect client delights me with fine writing, is considerate, and expresses appreciation for our efforts.

How and why did you become an agent: Since the founding of the agency by my uncle James B. Heacock and my aunt Rosalie Grace Heacock Thompson, in 1978,

I knew that one day, after a career in Hollywood, I would turn to agenting books. I focused my education with that in mind and followed the publishing business closely through the years, occasionally working for the agency. After spending 18 years in the entertainment industry working in film and television, I felt it was time to switch careers. I joined the agency in 2005, as full-time agent, representing trade fiction and nonfiction. We do not handle screenplays at this time.

What can a writer do to increase the odds of you becoming his or her agent: Timing is the critical element here. If the author is presenting a simply wonderful book about a very crowded subject that already has wonderful books out, the representative cannot spend his or her time trying to place it. The author should be familiar with what is "out there" and concentrate efforts on what needs to be out there.

How would you describe what you do as an agent to someone (or something) from another planet: The literary agent reads and evaluates book proposals and manuscripts, presents those that are accepted to appropriate publishers, negotiates the very best contract possible, and carefully reviews all royalty statements after publication. The literary agent is basically a business manager for the author's writing efforts, serves as a sounding board when the author wants to test new ideas, and distributes the authors' monies promptly.

How do you feel about editors and publishers: Editors and publishers impress me as dedicated, book-loving individuals who behave with integrity and honor.

What do you think the future holds for writers, publishers, and agents: The future is bright for all three. Books continue to be the thought processes of humanity and to make vast contributions to society.

On a personal level, what do you think people like and dislike about you: As Robbie Burns once wrote, "O wad some Power the giftie gie us/To see oursel as ithers see us!"

What are some representative titles that you have sold: The Heacock Literary Agency has sold over 1,100 books to over 100 publishers.

Agent's name: Tom Dark
E-mail: tom@heacockliteraryagency.com
Career history: Tom Dark is a literary agent for Heacock Literary Agency, Inc. Certain of his clients, if they are correct, may point the way toward faster-than-light technology or present classically empirical evidence suggesting that consciousness forms biological matter, not the other way around. If they are wrong, no harm is done. In any case, Dark believes it is time for new ideas: the more basic, more accessible, and less expensive to individual experimentation, the better. Dark has worked as an editor, writer, copywriter, promoter, producer, sound engineer, musician, actor, scriptwriter, political organizer, public speaker, and a host of other occupations largely forgotten except for the philosophical experiment they represented. This experiment began with independent reading during adolescence, when Dark began to wonder what philosophy ever had to do with anything. Forty years into the experiment, the question has become "What makes people keep dismissing philosophy?"

HELEN REES LITERARY AGENCY

14 Beacon St., Suite 710, Boston, MA 02108
617-227-9014
www.reesagency.com

Agent's name: Lorin Rees
E-mail: lorin@reesagency.com
Education: BA, Bard College; MBA, Boston University
Career history: After many years trying to change the world by working in nonprofit organizations and with socially responsible enterprises, I became a literary agent. My journey has exposed me to incredibly diverse and wonderful experiences that inspire me every day. In no particular order, I've worked with underprivileged children, been a park ranger at a national park, advocated for the homeless, consulted small businesses, led the marketing efforts for an innovative food service company, and worked at as line cook. Now, I am dedicated to making an impact through books. I cherish my work and feel extremely fortunate and blessed be a literary agent.

Categories/Subjects that you are most enthusiastic about agenting: Business, history, self-help, literary fiction, popular culture, narrative nonfiction, mystery

Categories/Subjects writers shouldn't bother pitching to you: Romance, fantasy, sci-fi, poetry

If you were not an agent, what might you be doing instead: That's hard to imagine.

What's the best way for fiction writers to solicit your interest: Just present your work. There're no gimmicks or tricks here.

Do you charge fees separate from your commission or offer nonagenting fee-based services: None

What are some representative titles that you have sold: *Words That Work* and *What Americans Really Want…Really* by Frank Luntz (Hyperion); *Blood Makes the Grass Grow Green* and *The Border Crosser* by Johnny Rico (Random House); *Travel Writing* by Pete Ferry (Harcourt); *Primal Health: Stone Age Secrets to Health and Happiness* by Dr. William Meller (Perigee); *It Pays to Be Civil* by Christine Pearson and Christine Porath (Portfolio); *Brandsimple* by Allen Adamson (Palgrave Macmillan); *Who: Solve Your #1 Problem* by Geoff Smart and Randy Street (Random House)

How and why did you become an agent: It was destiny. The clouds parted, the stars aligned, and the moon shone brightly. (I'm not kidding.)

How would you describe what you do as an agent to someone (or something) from another planet: I read a lot.

What are your favorite books, movies, and TV shows, and why: I love too many wonderful books and movies to list.

Describe the client from hell, even if you don't have any: That's a difficult question to answer because I wouldn't work with a client from hell. I not only admire the people I work with, I like them on a personal level and consider many my friends.

Describe the publisher and/or editor from hell: Are you trying to get me in trouble?

What do you like best about your clients and the editors and publishers you work with: There is nothing more satisfying than being part of a successful creative collaboration.

You're welcome to share your thoughts and sentiments about the business of writing and publishing: This is a fair business that requires patience and perseverance. While some terrible books are successful, in the end, truly great books and authors stand the test of time and get, in most cases, the recognition they deserve.

Describe yourself: I'm about 6 feet, 190 lbs, with a shaved head.

Will our business exist as we know it in 10 years or so: Mostly. There will be many differences due to technology and changing demographics, but the elements of publishing will remain the same. Writers will always need a publisher, and publishers will always need writers. And somewhere in the middle there is a literary agent.

Agent's name: Ann Collette

Born: February 11, 1952, Boston, MA

Career history: Worked as a freelance editor and writer for over 15 years before becoming an associate at the Rees Agency almost 10 years ago

Hobbies/Personal interests: Opera, cats, beading, martial arts movies, and ZZ Top

Categories/Subjects that you are most enthusiastic about agenting: Fiction: Mystery, thriller, suspense, literary fiction, women's, horror, vampire; Nonfiction: Military, war, Southeast Asia, historical

Categories/Subjects writers shouldn't bother pitching to you: Children's, young adult, middle grade, sci-fi, fantasy, and anything to do with banking or finances

If you were not an agent, what might you be doing instead: Editing for a big commercial house

What's the best way for fiction writers to solicit your interest: Write a strong, tight, well-focused query letter.

Do you charge fees separate from your commission or offer nonagenting fee-based services: I continue to work as a freelance editor, but I never agent anyone who's paid me to edit their work. These are two distinct careers.

What are some representative titles that you have sold: Steve Sidor: *Skin River, Bone Factory, The Mirror's Edge,* St. Martin's; Vicki Lane: *Signs in the Blood, Art's Blood, Old Wounds, In a Dark Season,* Bantam.

How and why did you become an agent: Helen Rees hired me to evaluate manuscripts for her. She liked my work so much she asked me to become an agent.

How do you feel about writers: I worship the good ones; I try to avoid the pretentious ones.

What are your favorite books, movies, and TV shows, and why: I love Chekhov, the poetry of Raymond Carver, Dennis Lehane, Tom Perrotta, Darrin Strauss, Elizabeth McCracken, Ken Bruen, and Steve McCauley. I love action films, particularly Hong Kong martial arts. I think my favorite film of all time is Sam Peckinpah's

The Wild Bunch. Unfortunately, as I confessed in a previous interview for this guide, I am still enamored of *American Idol.*

Describe the client from hell, even if you don't have any: Somebody who e-mails me a dozen times a day, who doesn't value my time

Describe the publisher and/or editor from hell: One who never gets back in touch with me about a book they initially were eager to see

What do you like best about your clients and the editors and publishers you work with: When we all work together as a team because we have a common goal: publishing the best book possible

You're welcome to share your thoughts and sentiments about the business of writing and publishing: I can't imagine a world without books. But I think publishers need to reevaluate huge advances, especially for celebrity books and the need for fiction writers to have a platform.

Describe yourself: I'm an outgoing, informal woman with a good sense of humor, but I like my solitude.

Will our business exist as we know it in 10 years or so: No; we'll be doing far more e-books.

HELEN ZIMMERMANN LITERARY AGENCY

New Paltz, NY
www.zimmermannliterary.com

Agent's name: Helen Zimmermann
E-mail: submit@zimmagency.com
Born: 1964, Bronxville, New York
Education: BA in English and psychology, State University of New York, Buffalo
Career history: 12 years in book publishing, most of them at Random House, then five years at an independent bookstore. I founded my agency in 2004.
Hobbies/Personal interests: Climbing the 46 high peaks in the Adirondacks (33 down, 13 to go), skiing, being an EMT, oh, and reading!
Categories/Subjects that you are most enthusiastic about agenting: Memoir, relationships, pop culture, women's issues, sports, health and fitness, music, accessible literary fiction
Categories/Subjects writers shouldn't bother pitching to you: Science fiction, horror, tales of male drinking habits, Westerns, poetry, picture books
What's the best way for writers to solicit your interest: By e-mail. Please just send a detailed query letter to start. I will be in touch within three weeks (or sooner) if I want to see more material.
Do you charge reading or management fees: No
What categories do you represent, by percentages: Nonfiction: 85 percent; Fiction: 15 percent

What are the most common mistakes writers make when pitching to you: Sending material that is sloppy or half-baked. If it's obvious you haven't done your homework, I won't be interested.

How and why did you become an agent: Working as the events director for an independent bookstore put me in contact with many aspiring writers. They would always ask, "How do I get published?" My answer was always "You need an agent!" After about the thirtieth inquiry, I decided to become one myself.

How would you describe what you do as an agent to someone (or something) from another planet: If I met someone from another planet, I would ask them if they needed an agent.

How do you feel about editors and publishers: They are smart, hard-working folks in search of projects they deem worthy and that they believe will sell well. Never a good idea to forget that publishing is first and foremost a business.

What are your favorite books, movies, and TV shows, and why: One of my all-time favorite books is *The River Why* by David James Duncan. *Gift from the Sea* kept me on the couch, too.

What are some representative titles that you have sold: *Chosen by a Horse* by Susan Richards (Houghton Mifflin Harcourt); *Seeds: One Man's Quest to Preserve the Trees from Famous Americans' Childhood Homes* by Rick Horan (HarperCollins); *Captain Freedom: A Superhero's Quest to Find the Celebrity He So Richly Deserves* by G. Xavier Robillard (HarperCollins); *The Normal Bar* by Chrisanna Northrup and Pepper Schwartz (Crown/Random House); *Paleoista* by Nell Stephenson (Touchstone/Simon & Schuster); *That Book about Harvard* by Eric Kester (Sourcebooks); *The Wrecking Crew* by Kent Hartman (St. Martin's Press); *Emerald Diamond* by Charley Rosen (HarperCollins)

HIDDEN VALUE GROUP

1240 E. Ontario Ave., Ste. #102-148, Corona, CA 92881
951-549-8891
www.hiddenvaluegroup.com

Agent's name: Jeff Jernigan

Career history: *Christianity Today*, Inc.: marketing manager/publishing; Focus on the Family: director of marketing/publishing; Nest Entertainment: director of marketing/publishing and direct mail; BUY.COM: head of customer relationship manager/online and print; Licensed Professional Coach/LPCC; professionally recognized agent

Hobbies/Personal interests: Rock climbing, reading

Categories/Subjects that you are most enthusiastic about agenting: Family, marriage, parenting, fiction, women's issues, inspirational, self-help, etc.

THE HOLMES AGENCY

1942 Broadway, Suite 314, Boulder CO 80302
720-443-8550
www.holmesliterary.com

Agent's name: Kristina Holmes

E-mail: kristina@holmesliterary.com

Education: University of Hawaii at Manoa: BA anthropology

Categories/Subjects that you are most enthusiastic about agenting: Nonfiction: health/medicine/nutrition, spirituality/personal growth, business, humor, gift, women's issues, nature, environmental issues, science, cooking, relationships, sex, narrative nonfiction

What's the best way for writers to solicit your interest: E-mail query and full proposal to submissions@holmesliterary.com. Further information available on www.holmesliterary.com.

Categories/Subjects writers shouldn't bother pitching to you: Fiction, true crime

Do you charge fees separate from your commission or offer nonagenting fee-based services: I do not charge fees for representation. I also offer publishing consulting services, which are fee-based (for more information, visit www.holmesliterary.com).

What are some representative titles that you have sold: *50 Ways to Say You're Awesome* by Alexandra Franzen (Sourcebooks); *The Cosmic View of Albert Einstein* by Magda Ott and Walt Martin (Sterling Publishing); *Pinfluence: The Complete Guide to Marketing Your Business with Pinterest* by Beth Hayden (John Wiley & Sons); *Stillpower: Excellence with Ease in Sports and Life* by Garret Kramer; (Beyond Words/Atria/Simon & Schuster); *Kissed by a Fox: And Other Stories of Friendship in Nature* by Priscilla Stuckey (Counterpoint Press); *The Mother's Wisdom Deck* by Niki Dewart and Elizabeth Marglin (Sterling Publishing)

How and why did you become an agent: I became an agent in late 2005 with much gusto and naiveté. When the opportunity to become a literary agent appeared, it felt like an inspiring and compelling new career path. So I jumped. I joined a literary agency out of Hawaii, of all places, and gradually learned the business. I love books—and that's fundamental to why I became an agent. However, I've continued as an agent because it's a way I can help others by cocreating and sharing important, beautiful, life-changing books with readers. "Making a difference" is a bit of a cliché at this point, but it is nevertheless at the heart of my work.

How do you feel about writers: I feel about writers as I do people. Some I love...some I like...some strike me odd...and a few are rather difficult.

How do you feel about editors and publishers: Hmm. See above.

How would you describe what you do as an agent to someone (or something) from another planet: I don't feel like I have a "job"; my work is an extension of who I am and what's important to me. While there are clear areas of focus—for example, helping authors develop their book proposal or negotiating a book contract—my work as an agent and consultant varies quite a bit. Of all the things I do, my favorite is probably being a mentor to my authors. I don't pretend I have all the answers—particularly in today's changing marketplace; that would be arrogant—however, I love sharing what I know and using my unique gifts and insights to guide my authors in their careers.

What are your favorite books, movies, and TV shows, and why: I love most everything HBO is producing these days. Some of my favorite series are *Game of Thrones, Boardwalk Empire,* and *True Blood.* I think they're probably running out of ideas for *True Blood,* which is kind of sad. But every show has their day, right? I find HBO's programming to be compelling, sexy, gorgeously filmed, and well casted.

Describe the client from hell, even if you don't have any: I thankfully don't deal with too many writers I would put in the same sentence as the word *hell,* however one thing I do wish is that authors wouldn't cold call me about their projects. I can't tell anything about an author's project and whether it's a match until I've reviewed their query, proposal, and website. The calls I get are usually from well-intentioned, kind authors who want to share their project. That's beautiful; it's just that cold calls aren't productive in my experience. I love speaking to authors after I have reviewed their materials and I am interested in exploring further.

Will e-readers significantly change the business: They already are. And that's okay. Change is good. Books aren't dying…just evolving. That said, I love physical books…

Are you optimistic, pessimistic, neutral, or catatonic about the book biz in the future: I am excited to see what the future holds for book publishing. As we all know, we're in a historic era in publishing where so much is changing. Who knows how it will unfold? I think it's safe to say the future of the book business lies in digital products and on the Internet. Writers developing online audiences are in the strongest position, I feel, because they have a direct line of communication with their audience. They know who their audience is because they talk with them every day. So they can create books that resonate, which is essential. They can e-publish certain books and traditionally publish others. I could go on and on about the opportunities for people with strong online platforms.

Explain what you like and dislike about your job: I love dreaming and brainstorming with my authors, polishing awesome proposals and pitching them to publishers, collaborating with brilliant people, eating chocolate and taking yoga breaks in the middle of my day, coming up with the perfect book title for a project I'm working on, authors who do something special for me out of the blue as a thank-you, the moment I first hold a book I've worked on for years, telling my author they've received an offer on their book, creating change in the hearts and minds of readers through the books I help to publish, researching and talking about online platforms and book promotion, and reading great books. I dislike computer brain, analyzing for most of my waking hours, sitting too much, *either/or* conversations rather than *yes/and* (particularly with regard to the future of the publishing industry), and the number of e-mails in my inbox.

HORNFISCHER LITERARY MANAGEMENT, L.P.

PO Box 50544, Austin, TX 78763

Agent's name: Jim Hornfischer
E-mail: jim@hornfischerlit.com
Born: 1965, Massachusetts
Education: BA, Colgate University; JD, University of Texas at Austin
Career history: President, Hornfischer Literary Management, Austin, 2001–present; agent, Literary Group International, New York, 1993–2001; editorial positions, McGraw-Hill, HarperCollins, New York, 1987–92
Categories/Subjects that you are most enthusiastic about agenting: All types of high-quality narrative nonfiction, including current events, biography, memoir, US and world history, military history, popular science, medicine/health, business, law, and culture
Categories/Subjects writers shouldn't bother pitching to you: Fiction and poetry, and most self-help/inspirational
What's the best way for writers to solicit your interest: A smartly tailored personal letter that suggests professionalism and/or accomplishment, together with 30 to 50 pages of good material that supports your optimism. Please include an overview of the book and its market, author bio (and reviews and other media if available), chapter summaries, and one to three sample chapters.
Do you charge reading or management fees: No reading fees. Commission structure is 15 percent domestic, 25 percent foreign. Sold approximately 16 titles last year. The approximate percentage of all submissions (from queries through manuscripts) that I rejected? The same parade-drenching number as the rest of them.
What are the most common mistakes writers make when pitching to you: Failing to identify the unique space in the universe (or at least in the bookstore) that their proposed book will occupy. Everything follows from that simple act.
How would you describe the perfect client: Thinks big, drinks from glasses that are half full, writes even grocery lists with narrative momentum, keeps an open ear for useful advice and runs with it in brilliant and surprising ways
How and why did you become an agent: Getting a good book published, especially one that might not otherwise have been, can be rewarding in a life-affirming sort of way.
What can a writer do to increase the odds of you becoming his or her agent: Grasp the rudiments of the business (even if as an artist you'd prefer not to bother), temper your ambition with patience and a long view, and refine and improve your craft continuously. It's all in the writing.
How would you describe what you do as an agent to someone (or something) from another planet: My wife always tells me that I shatter dreams for a living, because I send back so many rejections. I prefer to think that, for those writers for whom I do useful work, I help make them. I do a little writing, too: www.jameshornfischer.com.

How do you feel about editors and publishers: Editors: The good ones are the heart and soul of their companies, and management should listen to them more closely. Publishers: I am in awe of the process by which a talented group of people can rally collectively to insert a new voice into the national conversation. It happens all too rarely, but when it does you look back and marvel at the peculiar alchemy of it all.

What are some representative titles that you have sold: *Flags of Our Fathers* by James Bradley with Ron Powers (Bantam); *Traitor to His Class: The Privileged Life and Radical Presidency of Franklin Delano Roosevelt* by H. W. Brands (Doubleday); *The Scent of the Missing: A Handler's Journey Beside a Search-and-Rescue Dog* by Susannah Charleson (Houghton Mifflin); *The Next 100 Years: A Forecast for the 21st Century* by George Friedman (Doubleday); *Ghost: Confessions of a Counterterrorism Agent* by Fred Burton (Random House); *American Pests: The Losing War on Insects, from Colonial Times to DDT* by James E. McWilliams (Columbia); *Rose Bowl Dreams: A Memoir of Faith, Family, and Football* by Adam Jones (Thomas Dunne Books); *How to Break a Terrorist: The US Interrogators Who Used Brains, Not Brutality, to Take Down the Deadliest Man in Iraq* by Matthew Alexander with John Bruning (Free Press); *Mark Twain: A Life* by Ron Powers (Free Press); *Obama: From Promise to Power* by David Mendell (Harper/Amistad); *House to House: A Soldier's Memoir* by David Bellavia with John Bruning (Free Press)

IRENE GOODMAN LITERARY AGENCY

27 West 24th St., Suite 700B, New York, NY 10010
212-604-0330
www.irenegoodman.com

Agent's name: Barbara Poelle
Career history: Barbara Poelle began her publishing career as a freelance copywriter and editor before joining the Goodman Agency in 2007 but feels as if she truly prepared for the industry during her brief stint as a stand-up comic in Los Angeles. She has found success placing thrillers, literary suspense, historical romances, humorous/platform driven nonfiction, and upmarket fiction and is actively seeking her next great client in those genres but is passionate about anything with a unique voice. Barbara has a very hands-on approach with the craft and editorial details of the books she represents and loves working with her clients to take their writing to the next level.

Agent's name: Jon Sternfeld
Categories/Subjects that you are most enthusiastic about agenting: Jon is looking for literary fiction (including well-researched dramas and historical thrillers) and narrative nonfiction that deals with historical, social, or cultural issues a la Erik Larsen or Eric Weiner. He has a particular interest in fiction that has a large, ambitious canvas (exploring a time, place, or culture) or nonfiction that does the same.

Agent's name: Miriam Kriss

Career history: Miriam Kriss joined the Irene Goodman Literary Agency just as she was finishing her master's degree in fine arts at New York University in early 2004 and quickly became one of the hottest young agents in town. Going from Michelangelo to Nora Roberts was not as great a leap as it might seem, as Miriam had been obsessively reading commercial fiction since she found a copy of Judith McNaught's classic *Whitney, My Love* in a rented lakeside cabin when she was 13. A few pages in, not only were some gaps in her Catholic school education filled, but she was hooked. She reads fast: 100 pages an hour, a novel a day, and well, that adds up to a lot of books a year. Miriam likes to say Irene knows the market because she's been doing this for over 25 years and is savvy as all get out, but Miriam herself knows the market because she is the market. And that knowledge has paid off for both her and her clients in a big way. Miriam's focus remains on commercial fiction, and she represents everything from hardcover historical mysteries to all subgenres of romance, from young-adult fiction to kick-ass urban fantasies, and everything in between. If it's fun to read, she probably represents it. She doesn't look for specific stories, focusing instead on finding a voice she can fall in love with and champion. This strategy of taking on only clients she's passionate about has led to six-figure deals for first-time authors and numerous clients appearances on the *USA Today* and *New York Times* best-seller lists. During one memorable week, she had two authors appear on the *Times* list at the same time.

JEANNE FREDERICKS LITERARY AGENCY, INC.

221 Benedict Hill Road, New Canaan, CT 06840
203-972-3011
www.jeannefredericks.com

Agent's name: Jeanne Fredericks
E-mail: jeanne.fredericks@gmail.com
Born: April 19, 1950, Mineola, New York
Education: BA, Mount Holyoke College, 1972, major in English; Radcliffe publishing procedures course, 1972; MBA, New York University Graduate School of Business (now called Stern), major in marketing, 1972

Career history: Established own agency in 1997 after being an agent and acting director of Susan P. Urstadt (1990–1996). Prior to that, I was an editorial director of Ziff-Davis Books (1980–1981), acquiring editor and the first female managing editor of Macmillan's Trade Division (1974–1980), and assistant to the editorial director and foreign/subsidiary rights director of Basic Books (1972–1974). Member of AAR and The Authors Guild.

Hobbies/Personal interests: Crew, swimming, yoga, reading, traveling, casual entertaining, gardening, photography, family activities, volunteering at church

Categories/Subjects that you are most enthusiastic about agenting: Practical, popular reference by authorities, especially in health, science, fitness, gardening, and women's issues; also interested in business, cooking, elite sports, parenting, travel, and antiques/decorative arts

Categories/Subjects writers shouldn't bother pitching to you: Horror, occult fiction, true crime, juvenile, textbooks, poetry, essays, plays, short stories, science fiction, pop culture, guides to computers and software, politics, pornography, overly depressing or violent topics, memoirs that are more suitable for one's family or that are not compelling enough for the trade market, romance, manuals for teachers

If you were not an agent, what might you be doing instead: Reading and traveling more for pleasure, volunteering more, learning to play piano, writing, or perhaps running a publishing company

What's the best way for writers to solicit your interest: Please query with an SASE (or by e-mail without attachments to jeanne.fredericks@gmail.com). No phone calls, faxes, or deliveries that require signatures.

Do you charge reading or management fees: No

Can you provide an approximation by percent of what you tend to represent by category: 1 percent fiction (just from existing nonfiction clients); 0 percent children's; 99 percent nonfiction

What are the most common mistakes writers make when pitching to you: Calling me to describe their proposed books and giving me far too much detail. I'd much rather see that potential clients can write well before I spend valuable phone time with them. Also, claiming to have the only book on a subject when a quick check on the Internet reveals that there are competitive titles.

Describe the client from hell, even if you don't have any: An arrogant, pushy, self-centered, unreliable writer who doesn't understand publishing or respect my time, and who vents anger in an unprofessional way

How would you describe the perfect client: A creative, cooperative, media-savvy professional who is an expert in his or her field and who can offer information and guidance that is new and needed by a sizable audience

How and why did you become an agent: I reentered publishing as an agent because the flexible hours and home-based office were compatible with raising children. I enjoy working with creative authors who need my talents to find the right publishers for their worthy manuscripts and to negotiate fair contracts on their behalf. I'm still thrilled when I open a box of newly published books by one of my authors, knowing that I had a small role in making it happen. I'm also ever hopeful that the books I represent will make a positive difference in the lives of many people.

What can a writer do to increase the odds of you becoming his or her agent: Show me that they have thoroughly researched the competition and can convincingly explain why their proposed books are different, better, and needed by large, defined audiences. Be polite, patient, and willing to work hard to make their proposals ready for submission. Build their media experience and become in demand for regular workshops/presentations.

How would you describe what you do as an agent to someone (or something) from another planet: I select authors, find them the right publishers, negotiate the best deal for them, act as their advocate and diplomat through the publishing process, and handle the money side of the business for them so that they can concentrate on what they do best.

How do you feel about editors and publishers: Having been on the editorial side of publishing for about 10 years, I have great respect for the demands on the time of a busy editor. I therefore try to be targeted and to the point when I telephone or e-mail them and provide them with a one-page pitch letter that gives them the essence of what they need to make a proposal to management. I also make sure that the proposals I represent are focused, complete, and professional to make it easy for an editor to grasp the concept quickly and have a good sense of what the book will be like and why it will sell well. With few exceptions, editors value the creativity and hard work of authors and are intelligent and well meaning. Since they are often overwhelmed with manuscripts, paperwork, and meetings, though, they sometimes neglect some of their authors and need an agent's nudging and reminders. I think that some editors are frustrated by the emphasis on celebrity and platform in the selection process and wish there were more publishers willing to build the careers of authors who have writing talent and authority in their fields of expertise. I share that frustration with them.

What are some representative titles that you have sold: *Your New Green Home* and *Beautiful Solar Homes* by Stephen Snyder and Dave Bonte (Gibbs Smith); *Lilias! Yoga Gets Better with Age* by Lilias Folan (Rodale); *Waking the Warrior Goddess: Dr. Christine Horner's Program to Protect Against and Fight Breast Cancer* by Christine Horner, MD (Basic Health); *The Generosity Plan* by Kathy LeMay (Beyond Words/ Atria); *Canadian Vegetable Gardening* by Doug Green (Cool Springs); *Food Fray: Inside the Controversy over Genetically Modified Food* by Lisa Wessel, PhD (AMACOM); *Stealing with Style* and *The Big Steal* (novels) by Emyl Jenkins (Algonquin); *Raising an Optimistic Child* by Bob Murray, PhD and Alicia Fortinberry (McGraw-Hill); *Palm Springs Gardening* by Maureen Gilmer (Contemporary/McGraw-Hill); *Sentinel of the Seas: Life and Death at the Most Dangerous Lighthouse Ever Built* by Dennis Powers (Kensington); *Melanoma* by Catherine M. Poole and Dupont Guerry, MD (Yale University Press); *Heal Your Heart with EECP* by Debra Braveman, MD (Celestial Arts); *Homescaping* by Anne Halpin (Rodale); *The Monopoly Guide to the Real Estate Marketplace* by Carolyn Janik (Sterling); *Cowboys and Dragons: Shattering Cultural Myths to Advance Chinese–American Business* by Charles Lee, PhD (Dearborn); *The American Quilt* by Robert Shaw (Sterling); *No Limit: From the Cardroom to the Boardroom* by Donald Krause and Jeff Carter (AMACOM); *Rough Weather Seamanship for Sail and Power* by Roger Marshall (International Marine/McGraw-Hill); *Building Within Nature* by Andy and Sally Wasowski (University of Minnesota Press); *The Green Market Baking Book* by Laura Martin (Sterling); *I Ching for Executives* by Donald Krause (AMACOM); *Taking the Sea: Perilous Waters, Sunken Ships, and the True Story of the Wrecker Captains, Tales of the*

Seven Seas by Dennis Powers (Taylor); *The Budget Gardener* by Maureen Gilmer (Cool Springs); *Techniques of Graphite Pencil Drawing* by Katie Lee (Sterling); *Artful Watercolor* by Carolyn Janik and Lou Bonamarte (Sterling)

THE JEFF HERMAN AGENCY

PO Box 1522, Stockbridge, MA 01262
413-298-0077 | fax: 413-298-8188
www.jeffherman.com

Agent's name: Jeff Herman
E-mail: jeff@jeffherman.com
Born: December 7, 1958 in Manhasset, NY
Education: Bachelor's degree in the liberal arts, Syracuse University
Career history: Post-college in the early 1980s, disco died. But that really has nothing to do with my career because I didn't dance and feared crowded noisy rooms. Some people I knew were making a lot of money on Wall Street or in real estate. It seemed like you couldn't lose at either, especially if you were young and hyper. And everybody wore expensive suits and shoes in those days. Facial hair and asymmetrical haircuts were rare. But none of that has anything to do with my career either. I bounced around a variety of jobs in public relations, and hired myself at 26 to be a literary agent, and then stayed that way. Because I didn't have first-hand experience or a mentor, I was able to make a litany of unvolitional mistakes that generated positive results, as mistakes often will. Sometimes I did things the correct way, but that didn't always work out so well. One day I got married and started to have obligations beyond my own immediate needs and had to modify my risks. Skip ahead to 2011, 52 years old. Disco remains dead. I'm still happily married. Crew cuts are cool, even though I don't think so. My business is a good one and I'm happy to go to work most days.

Hobbies/Personal interests: I sing (not well) and speak nonsense to dogs, cats, crows, squirrels, or whatever creatures stand still to listen without trying to have me arrested. I don't know if they say anything in return, but I'm confident that I'm heard even if not understood, which is about the way it usually is with most conversations. This is the closest I can come to what might resemble a hobby.

Categories/Subjects that you are most enthusiastic about agenting: I deal with many areas of nonfiction, especially if it regards a practical, Earth-based topic, or something that makes people's eyes go big for a few moments.

Categories/Subjects writers shouldn't bother pitching to you: I don't comprehend poetry.

If you were not an agent, what might you be doing instead: Something else

Do you charge fees separate from your commission or offer nonagenting fee-based services: Charging fees would be easy and lucrative, but then I would have to keep performing specific tasks of equal value in return or else keep changing my name and address. Either way, it seems easier not to charge fees.

What are some representative titles that you have sold: See www.jeffherman.com.

How and why did you become an agent: Well, like I said above, plus I really like ideas and thinking about things, and structuring deals, and being around positive passion.

How do you feel about writers: I like that they want to express themselves in a way that is perpetual, maybe even eternal. Their words make impressions that bring forth more words, thoughts, and deeds by others. Writers help expand the universe.

How would you describe what you do as an agent to someone (or something) from another planet: I help people make statements that benefit other people, or at least that other people will pay for.

What are your favorite books, movies, and TV shows, and why: I like most zombie movies, because the idea of eating another person's living body without remorse, shame, or indigestion is fascinating. I'm intrigued by the raw undefined force that makes them do that. And I like it when serene suburban neighborhoods suddenly erupt into an orgy of zombies eating their still unzombie neighbors. It seems like it should be something that could actually happen anywhere once in a while. Maybe it does. Maintaining the illusion of sanity and social equilibrium requires too much energy. Horror, especially when real, is the canary.

Describe the writer/client from hell: People who resent others for not being controlled or manipulated; people who lie to themselves

Describe yourself: Just watching and waiting while I work and live, like everyone else. Being creative is more interesting than simply getting stuff done. I like reading because it enables me to talk to myself through other people who aren't there without having to go crazy. It's a kind of internal telepathic conveyance because we can consume information without using our ears or mouths, as is writing.

Describe the publisher and/or editor from hell: When someone is deceptive, intentionally destructive, or deliberately unaccountable for the dissonance they sow.

Describe hell: Whatever is seriously unpleasant can qualify, at least for that moment. On the other hand, it's possible that some people are satisfied with a situation that is seemingly hellish. And then there are those who can bring hell to others through the toxins they deliver, but that can be entirely transient and temporal, like a nasty oil spill. I suppose hopelessness, and absolute apathy and resignation, also qualify. Pushing back, even against seemingly dismal odds, can at least provide a constructive intent and purpose to exist.

What's the best way for writers to solicit your interest: Anyway they dare, but I hope they know I care, even when I seem unaware, because my cupboard of time is so bare I ask them to beware that as I prevail within my little lair, that time can be too rare for me to seem as if I'm always fair. But do not despair—Hares may be fast but often go nowhere.

Will e-readers significantly change the business: Yes. I'm not sure large traditional publishing infrastructures are able to quickly adapt to new economic models that emerging technologies are imposing on the marketplace, and I don't think they internally understand what's happening. Intellectual products are becoming entirely nonphysical, and per-unit pricing and collection methods are unsettled.

Are you optimistic, pessimistic, neutral, or catatonic about the book biz in the future: Optimistic. Especially if some of the large houses and book chains begin to wobble, because good innovations will likely displace them and/or their methodologies.

Explain what you like and dislike about your job: I don't like that I have to do it almost every day, but I like that it gives me something to do almost every day. I wish I had more time to simply be creative and more attentive to certain tasks. I wish I could slow down time and accelerate my productivity. I don't like poor weather, but I don't like it when it's nice out and I'm inside working.

Describe a book you might like writing: That book would challenge the readers to release everything they believe and replace it with the truth. However, I don't have enough content for even the first sentence, so it obviously wouldn't be nearly long enough.

Do you think some/most of these questions are stupid: I don't think they're stupid for the simple reason that they elicit answers, which creates paths to somewhere.

THE JENNIFER DECHIARA LITERARY AGENCY

31 East 32nd Street, Suite 300, New York, NY 10016
212-481-8484, ext. 362 | fax: 212-481-9582
www.jdlit.com

Agent's name: Jennifer DeChiara
E-mail: jenndec@aol.com
Born: New York, New York
Career history: Freelance book editor for Simon & Schuster and Random House; writing consultant for several major New York City corporations; literary agent with Perkins, Rubie Literary Agency and the Peter Rubie Literary Agency; founded the Jennifer DeChiara Literary Agency in 2001
Hobbies/Personal interests: Reading, movies, music, ballet, photography, sports, travel
Categories/Subjects that you are most enthusiastic about agenting: Children's books (picture books, middle-grade, young-adult), literary fiction, commercial fiction, chick lit, celebrity bios, mysteries/thrillers, self-help, parenting, humor, pop culture; in general almost any well-written book, either fiction or nonfiction
Categories/Subjects writers shouldn't bother pitching to you: Romance, erotica/porn, horror, science fiction, poetry
What's the best way for writers to solicit your interest: E-mail queries only, with "Query" in the subject line of the e-mail. No attachments. Go to our website for details: www.jdlit.com.

Do you charge reading or management fees: No

What categories do you represent, by percentages: Children's books: 50 percent, adult fiction: 25 percent, adult nonfiction: 25 percent

What are the most common mistakes writers make when pitching to you: Phoning or faxing queries; calling to check that we received query letter or manuscript; expecting to meet me or showing up uninvited before I've agreed to represent them; interviewing me instead of the other way around; someone who raves about their material when the work has to speak for itself; someone who is more concerned about possible movie deals and marketing angles and the prestige of being an author rather than the actual writing; queries and manuscripts that are poorly written or that have typos; not sending an SASE

Describe the client from hell, even if you don't have any: Someone who calls or e-mails constantly for news; expects a phone call when there's nothing to discuss; expects me to perform according to their timetable; has no knowledge of the publishing business and doesn't think it's their job to learn; doesn't want to work on next book until the first one is sold; can't accept rejection or criticism; needs a lot of hand-holding; has a negative attitude; fails to work as part of a team. Every once in a while a client from hell slips into the agency, but once they show us their horns, we send them back to the inferno.

How would you describe the perfect client: Someone who is passionate about writing; thoroughly professional; appreciative and understanding of my efforts; and who works as part of a team

How would you describe what you do as an agent to someone (or something) from another planet: I help make dreams come true.

What are some representative titles that you have sold: *Naptime for Barney* by Danny Sit (Sterling Publishing); *Heart of a Shepherd* by Rosanne Parry (Random House); *The Chosen One* by Carol Lynch Williams (St. Martin's Press); *A Glimpse Is All I Can Stand* by Carol Lynch Williams (Simon & Schuster); *The Clockmaker's Grimoire* by Matthew Kirby (Scholastic); *The Screwed-Up Life of Charlie the Second* by Drew Ferguson (Kensington Publishing); *Geography Club* by Brent Hartinger (HarperCollins); *The 30-Day Heartbreak Cure* by Catherine Hickland (Simon & Schuster); *His Cold Feet* by Andrea Passman Candell (St. Martin's Press); *The Ten-Minute Sexual Solution* by Dr. Darcy Luadzers, PhD (Hatherleigh Press); *The Write-Brain Workbook* by Bonnie Neubauer (Writer's Digest)

JIM DONOVAN LITERARY

4515 Prentice, Suite 109, Dallas, TX 75206

Agent's name: Jim Donovan
E-mail: jdliterary@sbc.global.net
Born: Brooklyn, New York

Education: BS, University of Texas

Career history: In books since 1981 as a bookstore manager, chain-store buyer, published writer (*The Dallas Cowboys Encyclopedia*, 1996, Carol Publishing; *Custer and the Little Bighorn*, 2001, Voyager Press; *A Terrible Glory*, 2008, Little, Brown), freelance editor, senior editor; Taylor Publishing, five years; literary agent since 1993

Categories/Subjects that you are most enthusiastic about agenting: American history, biography, sports, popular culture, health, business, fiction, popular reference; also, chick lit and parenting (address to Melissa Shultz)

Categories/Subjects writers shouldn't bother pitching to you: Children's, poetry, short stories, romance, religious/spiritual, technical, computer, fantasy/science fiction

What's the best way for writers to solicit your interest: Nonfiction: An intelligent query letter that gets to the point and demonstrates that the writer knows the subject and has something to contribute—and it's not just a magazine article stretched to book length; Fiction: Solid writing and some publishing credentials at shorter length. Snail mail with query and SASE or e-mail: jdlqueries@sbcglobal.net. No attachments please. We will respond to e-mail queries only if we are interested.

Do you charge reading or management fees: No

What are the most common mistakes writers make when pitching to you: The top 10 query letter turnoffs: (1) Don't use a form letter that begins with "To Whom It May Concern" or "Dear Editor." (2) Don't say your writing is better than best-selling writers'. (3) Don't mention your self-published books unless they've sold several thousand copies. (4) Don't refer to your "fiction novel." (5) Don't brag about how great or how funny your book is. (6) Don't quote rave reviews from your relatives, friends, or editors whom you've paid. (7) Don't tell the agent how you're positive your book will make both of you rich. (8) Don't say it's one of five novels you've finished. (9) Don't tell the editor that he'll be interested because it will make a great movie. (10) Don't ask for advice or suggestions (if you don't think it's ready, why should they?).

What can a writer do to increase the odds of you becoming his or her agent: Become published in reputable magazines, reviews, etc., before attempting a book. Most writers simply have no idea how hard it is to garner a contract for an unpublished writer.

How do you feel about editors and publishers: Editors are the miners of the publishing world—they spend days and nights digging through endless layers of worthless material for the occasional golden nugget. Anything the agent or the writer can do to make their job easier is greatly appreciated, so I stress that to potential writers.

What do you think the future holds for writers, publishers, and agents: Most people—and that means most unpublished writers—do not appreciate the importance of good editing and publishing, which is why there will always be a need for editors and publishers—and agents.

What are some representative titles that you have sold: *The Bomber Boys* by Travis Ayres (NAL); *Honor in the Dust* by Gregg Jones (NAL); *Born to Be Hurt* by

Sam Staggs (St. Martin's Press); *The Last Real Season* by Mike Shropshire (Grand Central); *To Hell on a Fast Horse* by Mark Gardner (Morrow); *Resurrection* by Jim Dent (St. Martin's Press)

JODIE RHODES LITERARY AGENCY

8840 Villa La Jolla Drive, Suite 315, La Jolla, CA 92037
www.jodierhodesliterary.com

Agent's name: Jodie Rhodes
Born: Montreal, Canada
Education: BA, Ohio Wesleyan University; pursued MA at Ohio State concurrently with my husband pursuing his PhD at Ohio State but ended up doing his research and writing his papers instead of my own
Career history: A year out of college, I worked as an editor at McGraw-Hill for their school division based in Columbus, Ohio. Left that for a job as a copywriter at a small agency, also in Columbus, Ohio. Then moved to W. B. Doner in Detroit, where I was told no woman could be a copywriter because either directly or indirectly every account was connected to the auto industry and "everyone knew women didn't understand anything about cars," so I became a media buyer. I grew up in Detroit and was eager to leave and see the world, so I took off for San Francisco (what a magical city!) and started my own business there, an upscale employment agency titled simply Rhodes Personnel Agency. At that time, the city was flooded with young women emigrating from Britain. I shall always remember the one who wrote, in the space listing work experience, "general dogsbody." When Hoeffer, Dietrich, and Brown in San Francisco called my agency, looking for a media buyer, I placed myself with them and sold the business. A large regional agency in LA, which handled Mattel Toys among other big accounts, recruited me for twice the money, and I moved down there. Had a brief stint as marketing director for Wham-O Toys. They invented the Hula Hoop. Then joined N.W. Ayer and was promoted to Vice President media director a few years later. Quit to pursue a writing career and sold two novels: one to Bantam and one to Putnam—the latter made the *LA Times* best-seller list its first week in print. Could not sell a third novel and grudgingly went back to advertising but only as a consultant. Here's a story to pop your eyes. The agency I consulted for was supposed to be the new Mary Wells. It had Suzuki when Suzuki was hot. It also had a technology company. I only met the president of it once but was blown away by him. Then I heard the agency dropped the account because they felt this president was too dense to understand their creative strategy. "Are you nuts?" I cried. "This is one of the most brilliant, creative human beings I've ever met." They just sneered at me—after all, I was just a media person. Well, the president's name was Bill Gates and the tech company Microsoft.
Hobbies/Personal interests: A hobby that grew into a vice was option trading.

I was an active trader in the market for many years, concurrent with my positions in advertising. The day I realized I was in trouble was when I had so much money rolling in from option trades that I began regarding my salary as chump change. I now only hold stocks that pay strong dividends. Love bridge and am a life master. Am a passionate but rather inept tennis player. Have always loved horses and riding. Bike regularly. If you'd asked about passions, I would include my deep personal concern with the "throwaway children" in both this country and worldwide. Before I became an agent, I served as a guardian ad litem for the San Diego Juvenile Court Systems and worked (freely, as a volunteer) for Voices for Children. A recent sale, *Chloe Doe* by Suzanne Phillips, is the story of a 17-year-old girl who fled a brutalizing home at age 12 and supported herself by selling her body on the streets of LA since then. I was determined to get this book published and contacted 29 editors simultaneously in the United States and UK. Targeted to the young adult market, it scared many publishers, but I am happy to say we made a big sale and it's created a worldwide buzz.

Categories/Subjects that you are most enthusiastic about agenting: What's really hot today are edgy, literary young-adult/teen novels, and if you're a truly gifted writer who has a strong story idea for one, I'd love to see it. These books are outselling adult fiction three to one. Editors who used to handle only adult trade novels are now acquiring these books. To give you an idea of just how hot they are, editors tend to disappear before major holidays, and it's normally impossible to reach them. But the Friday before Thanksgiving I fell madly in love with a young-adult/teen novel I read nonstop from the moment I opened it to the last page, immediately offered the author representation and was so excited that I spent the weekend writing the pitch letter, mailed it to 14 editors on Monday; on Tuesday 12 of them asked to see the complete manuscript (many e-mailing from their home or their family's home); on Wednesday, editorial director Phoebe Yeh at HarperCollins called me with a preemptive offer of $200,000. Multicultural literature, both fiction and nonfiction, makes my eyes light up. Books that have something important to say and characters with substance. Voice is everything to me in a novel. I'm fascinated by science and have sold many books by a variety of scientists and academics. Mainstream fiction, memoirs, biography, history, literary novels, those rare thrillers and mysteries that are truly original and gripping, world literature, politics, military, international affairs, women's issues, parenting, health, medicine. I am rightly known as an agent who welcomes new writers and the vast majority of books I've sold have been authored by new writers.

Categories/Subjects writers shouldn't bother pitching to you: No romances, religious, spiritual, or inspirational books; no children's books; no erotic works; no science fiction, fantasy, or horror

What might you do if you weren't agenting: Writing. As most writers know, once the writing bug bites you, it's hard to get over. I was fortunate to have sold two novels to major New York houses, but a writer always wants to do more. I am seriously considering writing a nonfiction book titled *Making It*, which should be an interesting insider look at the publishing business from someone who started out as an outsider and had to battle their way inside, just like most of you reading this are doing.

What's the best way for fiction writers to solicit your interest: Be a gifted writer and a fantastic storyteller. Most literary fiction is focused on language and style. There's no compelling story. That's the main reason they get rejected. Sadly, most of the writers who come up with truly interesting plots don't write well enough for their books to sell.

What's the best way for nonfiction writers to solicit your interest: First, have a truly exciting story to tell that either hasn't been written about before or offers exciting new information on the subject. I expect every writer to have thoroughly researched the subject matter and to have a "platform." Publishers want writers with outstanding credentials that will attract reviewers and get media attention. The author should also have a well-planned marketing and promotion strategy of their own which they'll use to generate sales.

Do you charge reading or management fees: I do not charge any fees, upfront or later (not even submission fees).

What categories do you represent, by percentages: 50 percent nonfiction, 35 percent young adult/teen, 15 percent fiction. I might add this is not my choice. I would prefer 70 percent fiction and 30 percent the rest. The magic of fiction is that the author creates life. I love my brilliant scientists, doctors, and academics, but a truly great novel is my passion. Commission structure: 15 percent in all cases except 20 percent for foreign sales or film/TV if it's placed through a subagent. Number of titles sold last year: 45. Rejection rate: 99.5 percent.

What are the most common mistakes writers make when pitching to you: They don't think before they write. They just let it pour out. The result is illogical plots, inconsistent characters, clichéd, superficial writing, and a bored agent. A writer should spend at least two hours of research for every hour of writing. They should know their characters as well as they know their secret thoughts. They should know everything about the situations they put their characters in, including what the streets they walk on look like. Also, you're always off on the wrong foot when you get our name wrong. Form letters addressed to "agent" are sure losers. Query letters with misspelled words and bad grammar are instant rejects. But the most common mistake writers make is telling us how wonderful their book is. Never, ever try to sell us. Experience has taught us that the more modest the writer, the greater the talent, and vice versa. One of the funniest such letters I recently received informed me, "My book is a brilliant, compelling modern-day version of Holden Caulfield's *Catcher in the Wheat.*" Writers are told to keep their query letters short, but one can overdo this as per the following: "Dear Agent, A woman takes her 12 year old daughter out of school and isolates her from the world. The novel is called Elizabeth. Sincerely,…" We do need more information than this. I invite writers to send along the opening 30–50 pages of their book with their query letter. This allows me to get a sense of the writing and the voice and greatly increases the author's chance of interesting me.

Describe the client from hell, even if you don't have any: A client who e-mails or calls you every week after the first round of submissions has been mailed out—who falls apart emotionally when the first rejections come in—who acts as though they're the only client you have—who repeatedly asks what you're going to do after every rejection—who tries to make you feel you and only you are responsible for selling the book—the actual book they wrote has nothing to do with it.

What's your definition of a great client: Intelligent, appreciative, patient, a genuine grown-up who realizes a good agent works as hard as a writer and has enormous demands on their time from many areas

What can a writer do to increase the odds of you becoming his or her agent: NEVER CALL ME ON THE PHONE WHEN I'VE NEVER HEARD OF YOU NOR SEEN ANY OF YOUR WRITING. Be honest, be professional, do your homework before you contact me, research your book, hone your writing craft, don't write for the market (meaning if you're written a book motivated simply by the desire to sell a book, go to some other agent). Write because you had to—because your story, fiction or nonfiction, was that important to you. If you've written a novel and not once during the time you wrote it did you feel excitement, fear, desire, hope, desperation, curiosity, determination—if you never laughed or cried, then you never got inside your book. If you felt nothing, the reader will feel nothing. Give me a bio that will get editors' attention. I cannot begin to tell you how many manuscripts I've requested based solely on the bio info in the query letter. Here's an example: "The first chapter was a finalist in the Harcourt Brace Best New Voices in American Fiction 2007 contest and won the Katie O'Brien Scholarship for Fiction. I was subsequently awarded the Writer-in-Residence at the Footpaths to Creativity Center in the Azores Island. I've worked for 10 years as a wildlife biologist." However, nothing beats an opening description of the book that hooks me.

How and why did you become an agent: One of these days, I may really level and tell you why. Suffice it to say, I knew going in that I had absolutely no chance whatsoever of ever being successful. The odds were just so totally against me. In fact, I never expected a writer to actually contact me since none of the guidebooks responded to the listing I sent in. I had an ulterior motive. Then one day, to my shock, I found a manuscript in my mailbox. *Guide to Literary Agents* had listed me without telling me. I've always been cursed with an overdeveloped sense of responsibility and that lone manuscript forced me to actually try and become a real agent. How I did it was through more work than I ever thought I was capable of. Most everything in my life has come easy to me. When I started my agency in late 1998, I was (and still am) living in La Jolla, California, 3,000 miles from the heart of the publishing business. I didn't have a single writer or know a single editor. I'd never worked as an editor in a New York trade house. I knew nobody and nobody knew me. For the first six months I received nothing but the most ghastly imaginable manuscripts, all of which I rejected. So the first step I took was to write advice columns for writers and convince some regional and national writers' magazines to publish them, in hopes of getting the attention of decent writers. Then I wrote the head of every major New York house (at this time I didn't even have a computer) and said I'd like to interview their editors. I will be grateful all my life to Sally Richardson at St. Martin's and Emily Bestler at Simon & Schuster, who out of the kindness of their hearts, personally called me on the phone and offered me five or six of their editors. After that, everybody was willing to give me interviews. The other thing I did was make what I hoped would be a short-term sacrifice for a long-term benefit. There are about 3,000 people who call themselves agents in this country, and I started out 3,001. Major, talented, polished writers were not querying me. So I took the best of the raw talent and revised, edited, and rewrote their manuscripts into saleable books. There are a multitude of books out there with my writing sprinkled throughout them. Above all, I owe my success to New York editors, and I'm talking major editors for their unbelievable kindness. I had several writers who told me their previous agents never received a single response from editors when they sent submissions. That was the fate I feared. So I introduced myself. I wrote them about myself. They were so gracious! I'll never forget Jane Von Mehren, past Vice President editor-in-chief of Viking Penguin, now at Random House, calling me one day simply to ask how I was doing. Carolyn Marino is a saint. She has cheered me on for years, never letting the fact she has yet to take one of my books deter her from encouraging me to keep sending. The brilliant editor of Ecco Press, Dan Halpren, has taken the time to write notes like, "I'm sorry this one won't work for Ecco, but I remain hopeful." Michael Pietsch, Brian Tart, and Wendy Lamb wrote wonderful recommendation letters to LMP so I could get listed with them (LMP only lists agents who are recommended by major editors), and I'd never even come close to selling them a book. I probably shouldn't start naming editors, because there are so many others who reached out a helping hand. I founded my business on unpublished writers, the majority of whom had been rejected by everyone else for years. Now of course I'm also selling published writers but almost all are writers whose first books I sold and we're now placing their second and third books.

How would you describe what you do as an agent to someone (or something) from another planet: I make people's dreams come true.

How do you feel about editors and publishers: There's a common belief that editors don't really edit these days—they just acquire books. Nothing could be more wrong. Good editors (and most are) do enormous editing. When Robin Desser at Knopf bought *Train to Trieste*, it had gone through five edits—three by me, one by the world-famous author Sandra Cisneros, and one by her personal editor. So what did Robin Desser do? She had the author rewrite the entire book from page one six times! I'd done so much editing on it that I knew the book by heart, but when I read it after Robin's editing, I was blown away. She made it extraordinary. When Phoebe Yeh at HarperCollins bought *The Ghosts of War*, she sent me a copy of her first edit. There wasn't a single page and hardly a single line without her comments and changes. And this was a full manuscript! Since she does this with every book she buys, I can't imagine how she finds time to eat, sleep, or have any personal life (and she's married with children). I hope every writer who reads this begins to see why they keep getting rejected. You can't just write a book and send it out. If it's worth anything at all, you need to rework and hone it time after time until it comes to life and glows. And when it's reached that stage, it will still be only halfway there, but now professionals will take over and bring it to fruition. With rare exceptions, I love editors. They are so bright. Have gained so much knowledge (from their writers, actually), most really deeply care about books and they're all under such pressure all the time—they work enormously long hours and have demands on them writers can't even begin to imagine—yet they will always give new writers a chance. Regarding publishers, it saddens me that making money is so important to them that they'll publish really bad books because there's a celebrity attached or the writer has a *National Observer*–type story. I guess to stay in the business, they have to. But it didn't used to be that way before all the mergers and acquisitions with their companies going public and becoming beholden to Wall Street. I wish they'd reward writers who make money for them by considerably more generous royalties—they know what their break-even point is—after that why not let the author share more fairly in the profits?

How do you feel about writers: My writers are all very special people to me. I consider them my friends. They share their personal life with me and I care about what happens to them. With the enormously gifted fiction writers in particular, I feel a sense of awe at their talent and great thankfulness that they chose me as their agent. As for the brilliant scientists I represent, I am in total awe of their knowledge and expertise. One of the greatest gifts being an agent has brought me is the chance to know such brilliant gifted people.

What do you see in the near future for book publishing: Most of us are very concerned about what's happening to the printed word. Newspapers have lost more than half their circulation. The Internet is the new media, and it becomes more powerful all the time. Kids don't read anymore. We may all end up representing bloggers.

What are your favorite books, movies, and TV shows, and why: I work 15 hours a day, seven days a week, and before I became an agent, I read a minimum of 10 books a week and saw a movie at least once a week. Now I never see movies and never get to read real books. It's horrible, because I need to know what's out there. Thank God for *Publisher's Weekly* and editors who send me their writers' books so I can at least scan them. However, like most people, I am utterly fascinated by the presidential race and tape MSNBC and CNN during the day (do not care for FOX News), then sit up until 1 AM watching. As for dramatic TV, I will watch anything Helen Mirren is in.

In your opinion, what do editors think of you: I'd rather let the editors tell you. From Judith Gurewich at Other Press: "Dear Jodie, Please send us more manuscripts. I can see you understand my love for good writing and heartfelt stories." From Amy Gash at Algonquin: "Jodie, Your books are always so fascinating. I'm interested in this topic and would love to see the proposal. I'm so glad you keep sending projects my way!" From John Aherne at McGraw-Hill: "Hi Jodie, Boy, am I glad I asked to see this. My colleagues and I really liked and responded to this proposal. We all thought it was great! Thanks again for sending this wonderful proposal my way." From Bob Pigeon at Perseus Books: "Dear Jodie, Your query letter has certainly aroused my curiosity and kindled my interest. Please do send this proposal and sample chapter as soon as convenient. Please send it to me via e-mail attachment. Have you sent the proposal to any other imprint in the Perseus Books Group? Looking forward to receiving the material."

On a personal level, what do you think people like and dislike about you: They are enormously grateful that I take chances on them as new and previously rejected writers, that I edit their material, that I continue to market it to multiple publishers after numerous rejections, knowing that I will probably never earn a penny from my work. They like knowing they can trust me and that selling their books is always more important to me than making money. This past year I sold books after 60, 72, 87 rejections and that's just for starters. I sold a book, *3 Minutes on Love*, after representing it and fighting for it for three years and recently sold it after 217 rejections. A debut novel by a Romanian author I took on two years ago, which received 132 rejections, was just preempted by Robin Desser at Knopf, won at auction by Doubleday in the UK with translation rights already sold to Italy, Germany, France, Holland, Greece, Serbia, and Israel. It's currently at auction in Romania. I've had a few books that sell instantly but the majority of books I sell have gone through a minimum of 50 rejections. No wonder I have tendinitis. On the negative side, writers often find it hard to take my blunt criticisms. I don't have time to be polite and beat around the bush. If their writing sucks, I tell them. I also demand they be instantly available when I'm marketing their work and ready to provide editors with any and all material they request.

What are some representative titles that you have sold: *The Goodbye Cousins* by Maggie Martin (Bantam); *Black Boy—White School* by Brian Walker (HarperCollins); *Lies, Damn Lies, and Science* by Sherry Seethaler (Prentice Hall); *Stranded* by Jeanne Dutton (HarperCollins); *The Intelligence Wars* by Steven O'Hern (Prometheus); *How to Survive a Natural Disaster* by Margaret Hawkins (Permanent Press); *Murder at Gravely* by Daniel Craig (Midnight Ink Five Star Mystery); *The Broken Blue Line* by Constance Dial (Permanent Press); *The Make or Break Moment—Physical Science vs. Economists* by Robert and Ed Ayres (Prentice Hall); *The New Biology* by Joseph Panno (Facts on File); *Bacteria—Rulers of the World* by Anne Maczulak (Prentice Hall); *Science through the Ages* by Julie Casper (Facts on File); *Freaked* by Jeanne Dutton (HarperCollins); *The Red Flag in American Bathrooms* by Dr. Wesley Jones (Penguin); *Diagnosis of Love* by Maggie Martin (Bantam); *Murder at Hotel Cinema* by Daniel Craig (Midnight Ink Five Star Mystery); *The Ring* by Kavita Daswani (HarperCollins); *Right Decisions* by Jim Stein (McGraw-Hill); *Choosing the Gender of Your Child* by Daniel Potter and Jennifer Thompson (Prometheus Books); *Messed Up* by Janet Lynch (Holiday House); *A Child's Journey out of Darkness* by Leeann Whiffen (Sourcebooks); *The Ghosts of War* by Ryan Smithson (HarperCollins); *Seducing the Spirits* by Louise Young (The Permanent Press); *A Year with Cats and Dogs* by Margaret Hawkins (Permanent Press); *Internal Affairs* by Connie Dial (Permanent Press); *The Archivist* by M. F. Bloxan (Permanent Press); *Does Israel*

Have a Future by Connie Hilliard (Potomac Books); *Lessons from Baghdad* by Stephen O'Hern (Prometheus Books); *Hoodwinked* by Sherry Seethaler (Prentice Hall's Zoon's Trade Imprint); *America's Covert Military: The Inside Story of Private Contractors* by Shawn Engbrecht (Potomac); *The Truth about Our Energy Crisis* by Jim Mahaffey (Pegasus Books); *The Five-Second Rule* by Anne Maczulak (Perseus/Da Capo); *How Math Can Save Your Life* by James Stein (John Wiley & Sons).

Agent's name: Clark McCutcheon
Career history: Editor for many years at George Braziller in New York, then founded his own publishing company on Long Island, brought out poetry and literary fiction, was affiliated with Billings & Sons, Ltd., and Guilford in London.

JOELLE DELBOURGO ASSOCIATES, INC.

516 Bloomfield Ave., Suite 5, Montclair, NJ 07042
fax: 973-783-6802
www.delbourgo.com

Agent's name: Joelle Delbourgo
E-mail: info@delbourgo.com
Education: BA, magna cum laude, Phi Beta Kappa, Williams College (double major in history and English literature); MA with honors in English literature from Columbia University
Career history: Fall 1999 to present, president and founder of Joelle Delbourgo Associates, Inc. 1996–1999, HarperCollins (1996–1997, vice president, editorial director; 1997–1999, senior vice president, editor-in-chief, and associate publisher); 1980–1996 held various positions from senior editor to vice president, editor-in-chief of hardcover and trade paperback; 1976–1980, various editorial positions at Bantam Books
Hobbies/Personal interests: Cooking, travel
Categories/Subjects that you are most enthusiastic about agenting: Serious nonfiction, including narrative nonfiction, history, psychology, women's issues, medicine and health, business, science, biography, memoir, sports, popular culture, lifestyle, thesis-based books and interdisciplinary approaches to nonfiction subjects; literary fiction; some commercial fiction; some historical fiction; and young-adult books, both fiction and nonfiction. I'm interested in serious thinkers, original ideas, and in a story well told.
Categories/Subjects writers shouldn't bother pitching to you: No category fiction (including romance, Westerns, science fiction, and fantasy); no children's books or technical books
If you were not an agent, what might you be doing instead: I would be a college professor or dean, perhaps, or a writer myself. Anything that involved life as

learning. Publishing has been a continuous graduate school for me and has allowed me to hone my skills and knowledge, while pushing the envelope in those areas I'm curious about. My authors are often pioneers in their fields, and I get a firsthand education working with them. It really works both ways.

Do you charge reading or management fees: We do not charge to read submissions, but by the same token, we are not obligated to analyze your work for you unless you become a client.

What categories do you represent, by percentages: Fiction: 20 percent, nonfiction: 80 percent

What are the most common mistakes writers make when pitching to you: Pretending they know me when they don't; not sending an SASE; writing letters telling me how many other agents have rejected them already, or how little they know about the process. Good-bye!

Describe the client from hell, even if you don't have any: Someone who approaches me by phone, sends materials in minuscule type without an SASE, calls to find out if the package has arrived, won't take no for an answer; clients with a smattering of publishing knowledge that makes them second-guess the agent's every step

What's your definition of a great client: A naturally gifted writer and thinker; the client who has been thinking about the idea or book for a long time and perhaps has tested the idea through research, or presentations such as lectures and workshops; who is passionate, committed, serious, respectful, and works hard over the long term to do right by the book; the client who understands that this is a partnership, between agent and client at first, and then with the editor and publisher; the client who is willing to market a book and is open to being guided in the process. My role is to guide, advise, cheer, facilitate, boost egos, solve problems, and be there when the going gets rough.

What can a writer do to increase the odds of you becoming his or her agent: Write me a fabulous and respectful query and follow the guidelines on my website.

How and why did you become an agent: I had put in 25 years on the corporate side, climbing the ladder from editorial assistant to many years as a top executive. I loved the publishing process, but it also grinds you down. I wanted to get back to what got me into publishing in the first place: working with writers and editors again. I also wanted to work for a company in which I could set the tone, one that is professional and generous and respectful, and the best way to do it seemed to be to create it myself!

How would you describe what you do as an agent to someone (or something) from another planet: I see myself as helping to shape the culture, by choosing to support and develop ideas I find exciting, bodies of information that need to be shared, and literary experiences that will touch readers' hearts and minds. I like being a catalyst in people's lives, occasionally helping them to live their dreams. I am a muse, mother, therapist, advocate, CEO, and friend. Sometimes I wish I had someone like that in my life!

How do you feel about editors and publishers: I'm nuts about them. Occasionally you meet those who aren't smart or good at their job, but most are exceptional. They love what they do and live every day in the hope that they'll discover something that can sell. I love the older, wiser, experienced ones who have perfected their craft, but I'm also very impressed with the taste and talents of the many young editors in the business who have the ear of their management and take their responsibilities very seriously.

How do you feel about writers: I have a great deal of respect for good writers. It is really challenging for any talented person to envision a work and bring it into being. It involves vision, dedication, hard work, and the ability to sustain these qualities on a solitary basis.

What do you see in the near future for book publishing: I get really irritated by all of the gloom and doom about publishing. It's true that the traditional world of book publishing is shrinking, but it's equally true that there are marvelous new opportunities if you keep your eyes open. I'm fascinated with the opportunity that university presses have, for example, to develop what the "big" firms call "mid-list," or by the new trade lists being developed by McGraw-Hill, which was formerly thought of primarily as a business publisher, and Rodale Books, which is rapidly expanding beyond direct mail. More and more, we need to think about new formats, novel ways to market content, and creative new business models. While I am a realist, my philosophy is to think positively and go where the opportunity is. I hate it when people don't agree with me, but, hopefully, I'm right about books more often than I'm wrong; no one "owes" you anything. You want to sell books because they are good and because someone at the publishing house has a vision for how to bring them to market. When it works correctly, it's a beautiful thing.

What are your favorite books, movies, and TV shows, and why: I am a fierce admirer of *Friday Night Lights*, which is one of the smartest series on TV, and AMC's stylish *Mad Men*. I devour anything by Philip Roth, who is probably my favorite American writer but also read lighter fare such as Elinor Lipman's novels. This year's great reads included Anita Shreve's *Testament*, Richard Russo's *Bridge of Sighs*, David Scharch's *Passionate Marriage*, and Daniel Mendelsohn's extraordinary *The Host: A Search for Six of Six Million*. I also read a lot of history, current affairs, and narrative nonfiction.

In your opinion, what do editors think of you: You should ask them! Once an editor, always an editor. Given my editorial background, they recognize me as a member of the tribe, as opposed to an adversary. I believe most respect my judgment, my sense of fairness, and my professional integrity.

On a personal level, what do you think people like and dislike about you: Warm, intense, focused, occasionally intimidating, but most people who are drawn to me like my ability to listen and connect with them.

What are some representative titles that you have sold: *Busted Halo's Freshman Survival Guide* by Nora Bradbury-Haehl with Bill McGarvey (Grand Central), *Talk to Me Like I'm Someone You Love* by Nancy Dreyfus, PhD (Jeremy Tarcher/ Penguin), *Summer Shift* by Lynn Bonasia (Touchstone/Simon & Schuster), *Lessons from the Fat-O-Sphere* by Kate Harding and Marianne Kirby (Perigee/Penguin), *To Kill a Tiger: A Memoir of Korea* by Jid Lee (Overlook Press), *Amen, Amen, Amen* by Abby Sher (Simon & Schuster), *The Sneaky Chef to the Rescue* by Missy Chase Lapine (Running Press/Perseus Publishing), *You Can't Predict a Hero: Leadership in Times of Crisis from Vietnam to Wall Street* by Joseph J. Grano (Jossey-Bass/John Wiley), *The Resilient Stepmother* by Rachelle Katz, EdD (Harlequin Nonfiction), *The Napkin, The Melon, and the Monkey: How to Be Happy at Work and in Life* by Barbara Burke (Hay House), *The Good Girl's Guide to Getting It On* by Joselin Linder and Elena Donavan Mauer (Adam's Media), *Greening Your Small Business* by Jennifer Kaplan (Perigee/Penguin), and *The Gift of Neurodiversity: The Hidden Strengths of Autism, ADHD, Dyslexia, and Other Brain Differences* by Thomas Armstrong (Da Capo/Perseus Publishing)

JOHN HAWKINS AND ASSOCIATES, INC.

71 West 23rd Street, Suite 1600, New York, NY 10019
212-807-7040 | fax: 212-807-9555
www.jhalit.com

Agent's name: William Reiss
Born: 1942, New York, New York
Education: BA, Kenyon College
Career history: Freelance researcher; editorial assistant to Lombard Jones (a graphic designer and editor), encyclopedia editor, Funk & Wagnalls Standard Reference Library
Categories/Subjects that you are most enthusiastic about agenting: Biographies, nonfiction historical narratives, archaeology, science fiction and fantasy, mysteries and suspense, true-crime narratives, natural history, children's fiction, adult fiction (literary and commercial)
Categories/Subjects writers shouldn't bother pitching to you: Romance novels, poetry, plays.
What's the best way for writers to solicit your interest: Telephone or send a letter describing the project, with a few sample pages to provide a sense of writing style
Do you charge reading or management fees: No
What are some representative titles that you have sold: *Shiloh* (S&S/Atheneum Children's Books); *The Madman's Tale* (Ballantine); *White Oleander* (Little, Brown); *Allegiance: Fort Sumter, Charleston, and the Beginning of the Civil War* (Harcourt); *Exit Strategy* (Jove); *Ghosts in the Snow* (Bantam); *Son of a Witch* (Regan Books/HarperCollins)

Agent's name: Anne Hawkins
Education: BA, Bryn Mawr College
Career history: I have been a literary agent for over 12 years. I work with mainstream literary and commercial fiction, including mystery and suspense, and a wide

variety of nonfiction, particularly history, politics, biography, science, natural history, medicine, and women's and family issues. Prior to that, I worked in various businesses and in English education. I also played the bassoon professionally.

Hobbies/Personal interests: I love classical music, ballet, opera, and theater. Cooking is one of my favorite forms of weekend relaxation. I also collect African tribal art.

Categories/Subjects that you are most enthusiastic about agenting: Adult mainstream literary and commercial fiction, including mystery/suspense/thriller, and historicals; a small number of upper-middle-grade and young-adult projects; adult nonfiction projects concerning history, public policy, science, medicine, nature/outdoors, and women's issues

Categories/Subjects writers shouldn't bother pitching to you: Adult fiction: romance, Westerns, horror, science fiction, fantasy; adult nonfiction: advice/relationships, business, self-help, spirituality, most how-to; juvenile: picture books or books for very young readers

If you were not an agent, what might you be doing instead: I might work as a museum curator or in a nursery that specializes in exotic trees and shrubs.

What's the best way for writers to solicit your interest: Write a brief, engaging query letter and include a few sample pages.

Do you charge reading or management fees: No

What categories do you represent, by percentages: Adult fiction: 45 percent, adult nonfiction: 45 percent, upper-middle-grade or young-adult fiction: 10 percent

What are the most common mistakes writers make when pitching to you: Pitching multiple, unrelated projects at the same time is a big mistake, since it's hard enough to find the right agent for even one book. Pitching projects of a type that I don't handle is foolish and a waste of everyone's time. (Readers of this book won't have that problem.)

Describe the client from hell, even if you don't have any: Authors can be a quirky bunch, and "quirky" is fine. But arrogant, unreasonably demanding, inflexible, mean-spirited behavior sours an agent–client relationship every time.

How would you describe the perfect client: Glorious talent aside, the perfect client is distinguished by good sense, good humor, and good manners.

How and why did you become an agent: My brother-in-law, John Hawkins, encouraged me to join the agency.

What can a writer do to increase the odds of you becoming his or her agent: A referral from someone I know (author, other publishing professional, or personal friend) will get my immediate attention. Over 50 percent of my clients have come to me through some kind of referral.

How would you describe what you do as an agent to someone (or something) from another planet: I represent the business interests of authors to publishing houses, provide advocacy, act as a sounding board for editorial issues, and help authors make wise career choices.

How do you feel about editors and publishers: Most people in this industry are smart, interesting, and fun to work with.

On a personal level, what do you think people like and dislike about you: I always try to be forthright and honest. Most people like that, but a few find it daunting.

Agent's name: Warren Frazier
Born: October 1966, New York, New York
Education: BS, New York University
Career history: All with John Hawkins and Associates: began as bookkeeper, promoted to rights director, and currently general manager/literary agent of the agency
Hobbies/Personal interests: Comics, basketball, jigsaw puzzles
Categories/Subjects that you are most enthusiastic about agenting: Multicultural, gay fiction, literary fiction
Categories/Subjects writers shouldn't bother pitching to you: Poetry, children's, military, mafia fiction
If you were not an agent, what might you be doing instead: Running a bed and breakfast
What's the best way for writers to solicit your interest: Query letter, with sample chapters, or e-mail query
Do you charge reading or management fees: No
What categories do you represent, by percentages: Multicultural: 50 percent, fiction—mysteries, literary, science fiction/horror: 30 percent, science/business: 10 percent, other: 10 percent
What are the most common mistakes writers make when pitching to you: Pitching more than one project; misspelling agent's name, information
Describe the client from hell, even if you don't have any: Having unrealistic ideas about publishing industry
How would you describe the perfect client: Good manners, patience, a bit of attitude, and a great sense of humor
How and why did you become an agent: I fell into the business through a client of the agency.
What can a writer do to increase the odds of you becoming his or her agent: [Have] patience and be a great storyteller.
How would you describe what you do as an agent to someone (or something) from another planet: I help place ideas onto various formats, film, books, magazines for mass distribution around the planet.
What are your favorite books, movies, and TV shows, and why: *Mary Tyler Moore Show*, great cast, writing—timeless; *All about Eve*, best movie about art, theater, and people; *The Stand*, probably one of the best epic books about humanity
On a personal level, what do you think people like and dislike about you: I'm brutally honest.
What are some representative titles that you have sold: *Tarnished Beauty* (Atria Books); *White Nights* (St Martin's/Minotaur); *Red Bones* (St. Martin's/Minotaur)

JULIE A. HILL AND ASSOC., LLC

1155 Camino Del Mar #530, Del Mar, CA 92014
www.publishersmarketplace.com/members/hillagent

Agent's name: Julie Hill

E-mail: hillagent@aol.com (no e-submissions please)

Born: Pasadena, California, May 13

Education: BA, University of Arizona; UC Berkeley publishing course.

Career history: Writer then agent…See below.

Hobbies/Personal interests: Gardening, cooking, TRAVEL

Categories/Subjects that you are most enthusiastic about agenting: Psychology; memoir; Jewish memoir, especially anything Holocaust related; self-help and advice are favorites, too, and travel, lots of travel. New spins on New Age, too.

Categories/Subjects writers shouldn't bother pitching to you: Fantasy, horror, children's, business

If you were not an agent, what might you be doing instead: Gardening, traveling, eating!

What's the best way for fiction writers to solicit your interest: Perfect book proposal! Thorough (please, please) market survey and developed platform, including Internet presence

Do you charge fees separate from your commission or offer nonagenting fee-based services: I offer contract consultation at an hourly fee. Often writers sell something themselves and need help with the contract, thus I am here to help! I enjoy contract negotiation.

What are some representative titles that you have sold: A few: *Return to Naples: My Italian Bar Mitzvah and Other Discoveries* by Robert Zweig, PhD (Barricade); *Frommers* and *Dummies* titles for Walt Disney World and Orlando by Laura Lea Miller (four different titles, revised yearly; Barnes and Noble Travel best-seller list); *Café Life: Venice, Café Life: San Francisco,* and *Café Life: Seattle* by Joe Wolff and Roger Paperno, photographer (Interlink Books)—Their *Café Life: Florence* won a Travel Book of the Year Award for 2006; *A Blessing in Disguise* by Andrea Joy Cohen, MD (Berkely/Penguin)—made the *LA Times* (and others) best-seller list

How and why did you become an agent: I was writing for periodicals (and online horoscopes), and I watched my friends who were also writers struggling to find good representation and felt I could help writers get what they deserve. I also wanted to be a career developer and manager, which I do for my authors. Most agents only sell books, which is fine, but there is so much more to making a career out of writing and I want to help my authors prosper.

How do you feel about writers: I love them, of course.

How would you describe what you do as an agent to someone (or something) from another planet: That they don't want it. Space travel has many more benefits, including long-distance travel without airport hassles.

What are your favorite books, movies, and TV shows, and why: *Boston Legal*. So smart, so socially responsible.

Describe the client from hell, even if you don't have any: Cannot/will not take direction; calls to chat; may not know the term *platform*; say they are "going to develop a website."

Describe the publisher and/or editor from hell: Suggests one of your writers formulate a proposal for something they have conceived, and then turns the proposal down. Oh, God, I could go on, but mostly I want to go on the record here as appreciating the good ones, and there are far more good ones that bad. Many are even great.

What do you like best about your clients and the editors and publishers you work with: Smart, smart, smart. Efficient. Don't need a lot of reminding to get the job done.

You're welcome to share your thoughts and sentiments about the business of writing and publishing: Writers' conferences tend to focus on the theme that unknown writers get huge advances, get discovered by Hollywood, and their lives are forever transformed with one book. You may as well bet on Big Brown to win the Triple Crown. Fun to talk about, but unlikely. Someone, somewhere, said, "Publishing isn't a business; it's a casino." More true than not, but one can improve one's odds by doing the work, doing it well, and doing it because "it calls you."

Describe yourself: A pretty nice but short-tempered woman

Will our business exist as we know it in 10 years or so: A great question... Wish I knew...Being an astrologer, I forecast more electronic media, but not as much as the electronic people would have you think. I do feel pubs will do more with agents online; in fact, one of my last deals was done totally by e-mail. The book has been released and is very successful, and I've never heard this editor's voice. I know it seems strange, but we are both happy with the efficiency and happy with having a record of every word that was said, every term ever negotiated, and how it went down. Believe me, this can be very useful going forward, both for me and my author and for the publisher. Further forecast: Despite hundreds of cable channels to keep us entertained, books will thrive because there is nothing more satisfying than a quiet read provided by a great author...nothing.

KELLER MEDIA, INC.

22631 Pacific Coast Highway, Suite 701, Malibu, CA 90265

Agent's name: Wendy Keller
E-mail: Help@KellerMedia.com (NOT for queries! See below!)
Born: Chicago, Illinois, twentieth century
Education: Arizona State University, BA, journalism with minors in history and French
Career history: 1980–1985, print journalist; 1988–1989, agency aide; 1989–present, literary agent/agency owner

Hobbies/Personal interests: Reading very large stacks of books for fun and profit; crew rowing with my team; underwater basket weaving; leaping off tall buildings affirming that I can fly

Categories/Subjects that you are most enthusiastic about agenting: Any nonfiction book intended for adults, including business (sales, management, marketing and finance); spirituality/inspiration (esp. divine feminine/goddess related); women's issues (any from health to family to relationships to other); self-help (parenting, relationships, mental wellness, health, education, etc.); science/physics (esp. quantum physics); history (any—world, American, esp. European); biography (celebrity or known names only); sports; popular psychology; current affairs; chick lit; how-to (do anything); cookbooks (only by authors with their own show on TV or radio, well-known restaurant or big web presence); consumer reference; gift books (illustrated or not)

Categories/Subjects writers shouldn't bother pitching to you: NO to juvenile, fiction, Christian, scripts, erotica, poetry, or true crime. No illustrated books. NO to first-person accounts of overcoming some medical, mental, or addiction trauma. NO to first-person accounts of sexual abuse or crime. NO books written from inside penitentiaries. NO books channeled by dead spirits, dead celebrities, your dog or cat, goldfish, hamster, etc. (YES, we really get those—every month!) That's probably pretty clear. You get the idea, right?

If you were not an agent, what might you be doing instead: Oh, I don't know. I think I'd be running a small, extremely organized, profitable, tidy country somewhere. Or practicing improving my French, Italian, or Spanish language skills. Or finally taking that trip to Morocco…

What's the best way for writers to solicit your interest: www.KellerMedia.com/query

Do you charge reading or management fees: Absolutely not! Agents who do should be immediately burned at the stake! Same with agents who ask for exclusive time periods to consider your work. Heck, if it's good, we will be fighting one another for it. Of course, in a genteel way. Send it to all who ask for it, and then if someone actually offers representation, call the slow ones and give them *X* days to respond. May the best woman win!

What categories do you represent, by percentages: Nonfiction book rights, English language: 70 percent, booking speaking engagements for clients: 10 percent, foreign rights/audio/ancillary: 20 percent

What are the most common mistakes writers make when pitching to you: They send me stuff that is absolutely NOT what I handle (See "Categories/Subjects writers shouldn't bother pitching to you" above), OR they have little to no qualifications for their topic, e.g., male authors who want to write a guide to menopause and aren't even doctors, how-to-be-a-millionaire books by paupers, business books by people who know little more than middle management, science books that have so been done a thousand times before.

Describe the client from hell, even if you don't have any: Clients from hell are those who are so convinced they will make the best-seller list and get a major six-figure advance, but their book is on something like "start your own home-based fertilizer business" or "The 10 Best Potato Salad Recipes in America Today." Geez! Get real! And, of course, unilaterally I get annoyed with people who won't accept editing well, or who lie about their qualifications. Or who tell me it's my job to make them famous. (Note: no!)

How would you describe the perfect client: Read my sold list! www.KellerMedia .com/sold-list. I have so many wonderful clients! Of course, the perfect ones I do not yet represent are people who have their own TV or radio show (or infomercial) broadcasting nationwide and/or a national speaking platform in the USA, or who work for a company—that is or they themselves are a household name. Pulitzer and Nobel Prize winners always welcome!

How and why did you become an agent: I was training to be an Olympic typist, and I crushed my fingers trying to get spare change out of a public payphone.

What can a writer do to increase the odds of you becoming his or her agent: Have a massive, impressive, powerful media or speaking platform already in place, or the finances, drive, team and/or contacts to erect it. Everything else can be arranged.

How would you describe what you do as an agent to someone (or something) from another planet: I make hundreds of phone calls; I fly to New York; I smile at a lot of people, even incoherent cab drivers; I make more phone calls; I cash large checks, skim them for a paltry 15 percent; and I help make smart people really, really happy (and sometimes famous).

How do you feel about editors and publishers: I worship at the feet of publishers and editors. I am grateful for their wisdom and ability to write large checks. I honor their ability to motivate their curmudgeonly publicity departments to work hard for my clients' best interests. In summary, they are the blessed souls paying for my kid's college education.

What do you think the future holds for writers, publishers, and agents: A lot, lot, lot of books, in many forms and formats, now known or which may be developed at some time in the future

On a personal level, what do you think people like and dislike about you: Authors like two things about me: One, I absolutely get the job done, always. I'm extremely focused, efficient, organized, and productive. Two, my mother was a pit bull, my father a Harvard English professor, so I'm a great person to have on your side, unless I skip my distemper shot.

What are some representative titles that you have sold: *Our Own Worst Enemy* (Warner Books); *Inner Wisdom* (Simon & Schuster); *Questions from Earth, Answers from Heaven* (St. Martin's Press); *Who's Afraid to be a Millionaire?* (Wiley); *The Ultimate Smoothie Book* (Warner Books); *Raising a Secure Child* (Viking/Penguin); *101 Ways to Promote Yourself* (HarperCollins); *Hiring Smart* (Crown Books); *The Encouraging Parent* (Random House); *Bringing Home the Business* (Penguin/Perigee); *The Power Path* (New World Library); *Secrets of Successful Negotiation for Women* (Career Press); *Ethics and Etiquette* (Entrepreneur Press); *Heart at Work* (McGraw-Hill); *Seven Secrets* *to Raising a Secure Child* (Penguin); *Never Make Another Cold Call* (Kaplan/Dearborn); *I Closed My Eyes* (Hazelden); *The Acorn Principle* (St. Martin's Press); *Be the Person YOU Want to Be Using NLP* (Random House); *The Jesus Path* (Red Wheel/Weiser)

KEN SHERMAN & ASSOCIATES

9507 Santa Monica Blvd., Suite 211, Beverly Hills, CA 90210

Agent's name: Ken Sherman
Born: Los Angeles, September 19
Education: BS, psychology, Berkeley
Career history: Reader at Columbia Pictures, then training and becoming an agent at the William Morris Agency/Los Angeles for four and a half years, then the Lantz/LA office of NY-based company, then the Paul Koehner Agency, and then my own company starting 1989
Hobbies/Personal interests: Books, film, making art
Categories/Subjects that you are most enthusiastic about agenting: All
If you were not an agent, what might you be doing instead: Drawing
What's the best way for fiction writers to solicit your interest: A good connection through someone I know
Do you charge fees separate from your commission or offer nonagenting fee-based services: No
What are some representative titles that you have sold: A few of my clients are Anne Perry, Tawni O'Dell, the estate of John Updike, Starhawk, the John Hersey estate, Mike Carey (graphic novelist), the Luis Bunuel estate, Louis Begley, etc. Many of my authors are for film and television rights as well as book rights.
How and why did you become an agent: By accident. Books were always a comfort zone and films a passion, so I was always looking and reading, and it seems natural to become involved in writers' professional lives.
How do you feel about writers: I love them and sometimes their work even more.
How would you describe what you do as an agent to someone (or something) from another planet: I don't. They already know.
Describe the client from hell, even if you don't have any: Someone who lacks respect for the agent/author relationship
Describe the publisher and/or editor from hell: The irrational ones who won't let me have my way
What do you like best about your clients and the editors and publishers you work with: Their intelligence and thoughtfulness and ability to tailor each situation as needed
Will our business exist as we know it in 10 years or so: I hope so, but it will morph like the rest of the world.

KIMBERLEY CAMERON & ASSOCIATES

1550 Tiburon Blvd. #704, Tiburon, CA 94920
415-789-9191
www.kimberleycameron.com

Agent's name: Kimberley Cameron
Born: Los Angeles, California
Education: Marlborough School for Girls, Humboldt State University, Mount St. Mary's College
Career history: Former publisher, Knightsbridge Publishing Company. She was a partner with Dorris Halsey at the Reece Halsey Agency from 1993 to 2006.
Hobbies/Personal interests: France, reading for the sheer pleasure of it
Categories/Subjects that you are most enthusiastic about agenting: Writing that touches the heart
Categories/Subjects writers shouldn't bother pitching to you: Children's books, poetry
If you were not an agent, what might you be doing instead: Reading
What's the best way for writers to solicit your interest: Please send all query letters by e-mail to info@kimberleycameron.com. For nonfiction, please attach a complete proposal with sample chapters. For fiction, please attach the first three chapters and a brief synopsis.
Do you charge reading or management fees: No
What categories do you represent, by percentages: Fiction: 50 percent, nonfiction: 50 percent
What are the most common mistakes writers make when pitching to you: We are always impressed by politeness, in a well-written letter or otherwise. Their most common mistake is using too many rhetorical adjectives to describe their own work.
Describe the client from hell, even if you don't have any: One who doesn't know that publishing is a business and should be conducted in a businesslike manner
How would you describe the perfect client: A writer who understands the publishing business and is respectful of an agent's time
How and why did you become an agent: We love books and what they have to teach us. We understand how important and powerful the written word is and appreciate what it takes to be a good writer.
What can a writer do to increase the odds of you becoming his or her agent: Be polite and do your homework—know what we represent and market your work only when it's ready.
How would you describe what you do as an agent to someone (or something) from another planet: READ. Guide writers through the writing and publishing process...
How do you feel about editors and publishers: Editors and publishers are in this business for the love of books—they are all overworked but do the best they can.

What do you think the future holds for writers, publishers, and agents: There will always be readers—what form books will take we cannot imagine. There are searchers for knowledge, spiritual and otherwise that will always be looking for enlightenment.

On a personal level, what do you think people like and dislike about you: They like that I'm serious about helping writers—they might dislike that I must be extremely selective about the material I represent…

What are some representative titles that you have sold: Please visit my website: www.kimberleycameron.com.

KNEERIM, WILLIAMS & BLOOM

475 Park Avenue South, New York, NY 10016
90 Canal Street, Boston, MA 02119
617-303-1650
www.kwblit.com

Agent's name: Hope Denekemp
E-mail: denekamp@kwblit.com
Career history: Hope Denekamp has been with the agency for nearly 20 years and is its financial manager as well as its agency administrator. She manages the day-to-day operations of the agency and also serves as a paralegal on contractual matters. She has been Ike Williams's long-time assistant and enjoys working with the agency's authors and screenwriters. Hope is also a trained chef.

Agent's name: Brettne Bloom
Career history: Brettne Bloom joined Kneerim, Williams & Bloom in 2000 after working at *The Atlantic*. In nonfiction, her interests include memoir, history, current events, biography, travel, adventure, science, popular culture, cooking and food, personal growth, and women's issues. She also represents commercial and literary fiction. Her clients' recent books include the best-selling novel *Commencement* by J. Courtney Sullivan; *The Cradle* by Patrick Somerville, a Barnes & Noble Discover pick and one of Janet Maslin's top 10 books of 2009; *The Kids Are All Right* by Diana Welch and Liz Welch, nominated for an ALA as well as for a Books for a Better Life Award; *Uranium* by Tom Zoellner; *Engaging the Muslim World* by Juan Cole, blogger and expert on Middle Eastern affairs; *The Woman Who Named God* by biblical scholar Charlotte Gordon; and *Rattled!* by Glamour. com parenting blogger Christine Coppa. Brettne is on the board of the Women's Media Group of New York, where she serves as the mentoring coordinator. She grew up in Houston, Texas, and now lives in Manhattan with her husband and two daughters.

Agent's name: Katherine Flynn

Career history: Katherine Flynn joined the agency in 2008. As editorial manager, she evaluates and edits manuscripts and proposals, scouts for new writers, and helps shepherd authors' books through the submission process. After graduating with honors in history from Johns Hopkins University, Katherine worked at the literary agency of Nicholas Ellison/Sanford J. Greenburger Associates, Inc., in New York, where she assisted with authors such as suspense writer Nelson DeMille, women's fiction writer Olivia Goldsmith, and the *Dexter* series author Jeff Lindsay. She then pursued her PhD in history at Brown University, where she is now ABD. Prior to joining Kneerim, Williams & Bloom, Katherine worked at the publishing company of Bedford/St. Martin's. She has also taught English literature and composition to high school students and has worked in a rare book shop.

Agent's name: Jill Kneerim

Career history Jill Kneerim, a founder of Kneerim, Williams & Bloom, represents a wide range of authors, including best-selling novelists Brad Meltzer and Sue Miller; ADD expert Dr. Edward M. Hallowell; scholars Pauline Maier, Stephen Greenblatt, Tanya Luhrmann, and Pulitzer Prize–winner Caroline Elkins; journalists Larry Tye, Bo Burlingham, and David Laskin; biographers Susan Quinn and Gillian Gill; former poet laureate Robert Pinsky; and leading women thinkers such as Jean Kilbourne, Kitty Dukakis, and Dr. Susan Love. Jill is a former editor and publisher who has worked for Simon & Schuster, American Heritage, and Grossman Publishers, a publishing house that she cofounded. She has overseen the creation of countless books and worked with hundreds of authors. She has served on the board of PEN New England and is a member of the advisory board of Grub Street Writing Center. *Boston Magazine* named her one of Boston's 100 most influential women. Jill's interests include a good story on almost any interesting subject; serious fiction; American, African, Asian, and European history; religion; psychology and anthropology; biography and memoir; women's issues; the English language; and good writing.

Agent's name: John Taylor "Ike" Williams

Career history: John Taylor "Ike" Williams, a founder of Kneerim, Williams & Bloom, specializes in biography, history, politics, natural science, and anthropology. He represents Howard Gardner, Joseph J. Ellis, E. O. Wilson, Tim Berners-Lee, Charles Ogletree, Elizabeth Marshall Thomas, James MacGregor Burns, Rev. Peter J. Gomes, Richard Wilbur, Drew Gilpin Faust, and Sara Lawrence-Lightfoot, among others. He was a member of the National Endowment for the Arts (NEA) Literary Panel, chair of the Boston Lawyers Committee for Civil Rights, cochair of the Fine Arts Work Center, and a director of the Boston Book Festival. He also places dramatic rights, such as the feature film *Public Enemies, Vendetta* by Alston Purvis, and a History Channel series based on Howard Zinn's *A People's History of the United States*. As a lawyer, Ike specializes in intellectual property and First Amendment litigation, particularly in publishing, film, television, and new media, and is coauthor of the widely used *Perle & Williams on Publishing Law*. His legal clients include Michael Porter, Muhammad Yunnus, Jeff Kinney, and the estate of John Hersey. Ike is listed in The Best Lawyers in America and the Top 100 Massachusetts Super Lawyers for entertainment, First Amendment, and media law.

THE KNIGHT AGENCY

570 East Avenue, Madison, GA 30650

Agent's name: Pamela Harty
E-mail: submissions@knightagency.net
Born: July; Atlanta, Georgia
Career history: I started at the Knight Agency (TKA) after the birth of my second child. I was eager to work with my sister Deidre Knight after leaving a successful sales career. That was almost nine years ago!
Hobbies/Personal interests: I am a runner and cyclist. I love to paint and, of course…read.
Categories/Subjects that you are most enthusiastic about agenting: I am interested in romance, of course, including historical, suspense, and paranormal, as well as young-adult and women's commercial fiction. I'm also interested in some nonfiction, including health, narrative nonfiction, relationships, and pop culture.
If you were not an agent, what might you be doing instead: Painting and cycling in France

Agent's name: Lucienne Diver
Career history: Lucienne Diver joined TKA in 2008, after spending 15 years at New York City's prestigious Spectrum Literary Agency. With her sharp eye for spotting original new voices, Lucienne is one of the most well-respected agents in the industry. A lifelong book addict, she graduated summa cum laude from the State University of New York at Potsdam with dual majors in English/writing and anthropology. She thus came well equipped for her work as an agent. Over the course of her dynamic career she has sold over 700 titles to every major publisher and has built a client list of more than 40 authors spanning the commercial fiction genres, primarily in the areas of fantasy, science fiction, romance, mystery, suspense, and erotica. Her authors have been honored with the RITA, National Readers' Choice Award, Golden Heart, and Romantic Times Reader's Choice and have appeared on the *New York Times* and *USA Today* best-seller lists. A publishing veteran, Lucienne has superb industry knowledge, numerous editor relationships, and a keen understanding of the foreign rights market. She is a member of the Association of Author Representatives (AAR), Romance Writers of America (RWA), Mystery Writers of America (MWA), and Science Fiction Writers of America (SFWA).

Born: April 27, 1971; Baltimore, Maryland

Education: Graduated summa cum laude from the State University of New York at Potsdam

Career history: I spent 15 years at Spectrum Literary Agency before moving in 2008 to the Knight Agency.

Hobbies/Personal interests: Writing, forensics, theater, beading, scrapbooking, yoga, photography

Categories/Subjects that you are most enthusiastic about agenting: Fantasy, romance, romantica, thrillers, mystery/suspense, young adult

Categories/Subjects writers shouldn't bother pitching to you: Nonfiction, children's books

If you were not an agent, what might you be doing instead: I can't imagine doing anything else.

What's the best way for fiction writers to solicit your interest: Be brilliant. Come up with wonderful ideas in an original voice and keep the pace pounding.

What are some representative titles that you have sold: *The Pawn* (Baker/NAL) by Steven James, *The Girl She Used to Be* (Grand Central) by Dave Cristofano, *Up at the College* (Grand Central) by Michelle Andrea Bowen, *The Sisters Eight* (Houghton Mifflin) by Lauren Baratz-Logsted, *Something Happened* (Simon Pulse) by Greg Logsted

What are your favorite books, movies, and TV shows, and why: I love anything by Joss Whedon. He's got a talent for perfectly melding dark and light, a well-developed sense of the absurd, an amazing flair for dialogue, and wonderful characters. That's what I look for in the books I represent as well.

Will our business exist as we know it in 10 years or so: Absolutely! Books— good stories that challenge our minds and imaginations—are eternal.

Agent's name: Nephele Tempest

Education: The University of Chicago, BA in English language and literature

Hobbies/Personal interests: Reading (naturally), film, theater, music, traveling, photography, and cooking

Categories/Subjects that you are most enthusiastic about agenting: Fiction only; commercial literary, women's fiction, urban fantasy, romantic suspense, historical fiction, science fiction/fantasy, and young adult

Categories/Subjects writers shouldn't bother pitching to you: No mysteries, inspirational, or nonfiction, please

What's the best way for fiction writers to solicit your interest: Please follow our submissions guidelines. Nothing turns me off faster than someone trying to be "clever and original" by ignoring our requests regarding how to submit materials. Beyond that, polish your book to the very best of your abilities, and then give it one more edit before submitting. The extra effort will definitely show.

What are some representative titles that you have sold: *No Regrets* by Shannon K. Butcher (Grand Central Publishing); *Slave to Sensation* by Nalini Singh (Berkley);

Angels' Blood by Nalini Singh (Berkley); *Mayhem in High Heels* by Gemma Halliday (Dorchester); *According to Jane: A Novel about Pride, Prejudice, and the Pursuit of the Perfect Guy* by Marilyn Brant (Kensington); *Burning Alive* by Shannon K. Butcher (NAL); *Major Crush* by Jennifer Echols (Simon Pulse)

What do you like best about your clients and the editors and publishers you work with: I love that I work with a wide range of very different and interesting people, all of whom share my love of books. It makes for a wonderful workday, knowing that at any moment someone might call me with a great new book idea or a recommendation for something fabulous they think I should read. It's a business of kindred spirits.

Agent's name: Melissa Jeginsky
Born: January 11, Pittsburgh, Pennsylvania
Career history: I worked at Harlequin Enterprises for 17 years as an editor before moving to the Knight Agency in September 2008.
Hobbies/Personal interests: I am a rabid crafter: scrapbooking, card making, crocheting, quilting.
Categories/Subjects that you are most enthusiastic about agenting: Romance first and foremost: contemporary, historical, erotica, suspense, inspirational, and category; young adult, both contemporary and historical; women's fiction, from humorous to heart-wrenching
What's the best way for fiction writers to solicit your interest: When a writer has really done their research about our agency and about the marketplace for their work. This shows me they are serious about their craft and that finding an agent and getting published are important to them.

Agent's name: Diedre Knight
Born: July 12
Hobbies/Personal interests: My first true passion is the written word. Beyond reading I have also always been an avid writer, penning my first story when I was seven years old for the *Atlanta Journal-Constitution*. This humble beginning was the start of many great writing adventures, leading me to a love of fan fiction and consequently, my ultimate dream come true, my own publishing contract with Penguin Putnam. I am also passionate about spending time with my family, photography, kayaking, international travel, science-fiction television, the spa, and great music.
Categories/Subjects that you are most enthusiastic about agenting: I am probably most known for my clients within the romance and women's fiction genre (all spectrums), but my tastes are much more broad. I also have a love for great literary fiction, young-adult material, all things paranormal, anything with a Southern flair, and great special-interest nonfiction titles.
Categories/Subjects writers shouldn't bother pitching to you: Our agency is very diverse, and between our five agents, if you have a great story, there is a chance we can find the right agent for your novel. However, despite this diversity, we aren't

interested in children's or picture books, poetry, screenplays, short story collections, biographies, military titles, or anything with gratuitous violence.

If you were not an agent, what might you be doing instead: I am an entrepreneur at heart, so if I hadn't started the Knight Agency, I'm not sure specifically what I would be doing, but I have little doubt I would be running some other business. I'm a natural visionary and a free spirit, so really the possibilities are endless.

What's the best way for fiction writers to solicit your interest: I am easily swayed by enthusiasm and passion. I myself am a very "excitable" person, and so if I can feel your energy in your story I'm instantly hooked.

Do you charge fees separate from your commission or offer nonagenting fee-based services: The Knight Agency doesn't charge any fees for anything related to the publishing process beyond the 15 percent commission we take off of a completed sale.

What do you like best about your clients and the editors and publishers you work with: I think that this industry is one of the greatest businesses out there, hence the reason I have tied myself into it in so many different capacities. It's exciting, dynamic, and it keeps us each on our toes since every day is a new journey. I can think of few other professions where you are blessed enough to meet as many fascinating individuals and cross paths with so many brilliant minds. I'm proud to not only be a associated with the publishing business but a strong contributing force; we are lucky at the end of the day to look at the shelf, see a book, and say, "I did that."

What are some representative titles that you have sold: *Intertwined* (Harlequin) by Gena Showalter, *Rampant* (Harper Teen) by Diana Peterfreund, *Heart Quest* (Berkley) by Robin Owens, *Edge of Hunger* (Harlequin) by Rhyannon Byrd, *Christmas Miracles* (St. Martin's) by Cecil Murphey and Marley Gibson

Agent's name: Elaine Spencer
Born: January 7, Toledo, Ohio
Hobbies/Personal interests: When I'm not reading I love spending time outdoors and in the water, working out, cooking, shopping, traveling, dining out, and cheering on my beloved Georgia Bulldogs.

Categories/Subjects that you are most enthusiastic about agenting: My tastes really run the gamut; I love most anything that has a strong distinctive voice and vivid heartfelt emotional stakes. I am looking for diverse women's fiction and romance, original young-adult and middle-grade stories, edge-of-the-seat suspense, interesting and high-platform nonfiction, and straight commercial and literary fiction.

Categories/Subjects writers shouldn't bother pitching to you: I am wide open to most genres but obviously don't handle those that aren't represented by the agency as a whole. I'm also not the sci-fi gal at the agency, nor am I typically into any boundary-pushing erotica.

If you were not an agent, what might you be doing instead: I would be a personal shopper. I love to shop, whether it's for me or for someone else—tell me what you need and I'm your gal.

What's the best way for fiction writers to solicit your interest: One of the sure-fire ways to impress me is to wow me with your knowledge of the market and your craft right off the bat. I am always inclined to continue reading when I can tell the author is treating their writing life as a career and proceeding as a professional.

What do you like best about your clients and the editors and publishers you work with: I have a very personal and unique relationship with each of my clients. I love that I can relate to each of them on a professional yet individual level. I truly believe that one of the bedrocks of a strong relationship is communication, and I adore the one-on-one tie I have to each of my authors.

What are some representative titles you have sold: *Soul of a Highlander* (Pocket) by Melissa Mayhue, *Stonegate Investigation Agency* (Harlequin) by Candace Havens, *Death by Denim* (Puffin) by Linda Gerber, *Accidentally Demonic* (Berkley) by Dakota Cassidy

---

KRAAS LITERARY AGENCY

13514 Winter Creek Court, Houston, TX 77077
281-870-9770
www.kraasliteraryagency.com

Agent's name: Irene Kraas
E-mail: irenekraas@sbcglobal.net
Born: Are you kidding??? New York, New York
Education: MEd, University of Rochester
Career history: Too long to enumerate: A sample: Beltway bandit (DC consultant); career counselor; agent
Hobbies/Personal interests: Reading, walking, eating, and enjoying life
Categories/Subjects that you are most enthusiastic about agenting: I am looking for psychological thrillers. NO mysteries, please. Think James Patterson, less Patricia Cornwell. In terms of young-adult/juvenile fiction, I am only acquiring those works that show a unique situation (preferably in history) through the eyes of a child or young adult. I am also, especially, looking for innovative middle-grade material. I am still looking for quality adult historical fiction such as *The Courtier's Secret*, *The Red Tent*, and *The Girl with the Pearl Earring*.
Categories/Subjects writers shouldn't bother pitching to you: Please see above.
If you were not an agent, what might you be doing instead: I've done what I've wanted all along and this is the ultimate. However, if I had to choose, I would be a rich publisher and publish all those great books that I've had rejected.
What's the best way for fiction writers to solicit your interest: Please send an e-mail query to me at irenekraas@sbcglobal.net. After that initial correspondence, I will let you know if we wish to see additional material.
What's the best way for nonfiction writers to solicit your interest: Same as above

Do you charge reading or management fees: Under no circumstances do we require an upfront reading fee! We never charge a reading fee. With PDF documents there are no other fees except those described in my contract that pertain to normal commissions.

What are the most common mistakes writers make when pitching to you: Not following my submission guidelines

Describe the client from hell, even if you don't have any: I'll take the fifth, thanks.

How would you describe the perfect client: Great writers who trust me to do the very best for them

How and why did you become an agent: I went from 20 years in business consulting to being the great American writer to agenting. I love using my business acumen in helping first-time authors get a break and helping established authors break out.

What can a writer do to increase the odds of you becoming his or her agent: Be extremely talented—it's a tight market, so understand that it's very competitive and make sure that your manuscript is ready to go when you submit it to me. Also, make sure that what you send me is a genre that I'm actually interested in representing.

How would you describe what you do as an agent to someone (or something) from another planet: I read, read, read. Then I sell, sell, sell.

How do you feel about editors and publishers: Mostly editors are top-notch people interested in good writing. Regarding publishers, well, let's just say that they don't always see the big picture as clearly as we'd like and they don't necessarily have the author's best interests in mind. But, that's why there are agents!

How do you feel about writers: Would I be in this business if I didn't like them? Of course one has to sort between those who have talent and those that don't.

What do see in the near future for book publishing: I think it will remain pretty much as is. People who read still want to hold a book. Of course there will be a few changes regarding electronic editions and print on demand.

What are your favorite books, movies, and TV shows, and why: *24*, *The Sopranos*, you get the idea. I now have to add *Deadwood*. I absolutely love it. I love great ensemble work and high-quality acting and innovative story lines. I don't like comedy.

In your opinion, what do editors think of you: I'm pretty sure they think well of me. After all, you don't stay in this business for 18 years as a very small agency (just me these days), if you don't try to match editors with submissions. When I send something out, they are always ready to read.

On a personal level, what do you think people like and dislike about you: Wow that's a toughie. I assume some like me and some don't. Is there more to be said?

What are some representative titles that you have sold: Authors include Hilari Bell, Janet Lee Carey, Mark Terry, Chelsea Quinn Yarbro, and Richard Uhlig. We have sold far too many books to list here, but please feel free to look at our website (www.kraasliteraryagency.com) or e-mail me.

KT PUBLIC RELATIONS & LITERARY SERVICES

1905 Cricklewood Cove, Fogelsville, PA 18051
610-395-6298
www.ktpublicrelations.com | blog: www.newliteraryagents.blogspot.com

Agent's name: Jon Tienstra
Born: Harvey, Illinois, January 5
Education: BA in English literature; master's in library science
Career history: After graduating college I worked at Alpo Pet Foods as director of product quality control, then for 10 years as director of environmental control. I spent another decade at a competing pet food company because the kids needed shoes. Finally, I was able to leave pet food behind and go back to school, where I took a master's degree in library science. I spent two years at the Rodale Experimental Farm as the organic vegetable gardener before I joined KT Public Relations as an unpaid intern.

Hobbies/Personal interests: I'm an avid reader of most everything. I collect old vegetable gardening books and love car racing of almost all types. You'll find me in the kitchen cooking/creating during off hours. I wish I had more time to paint, but stacks of chapters are always the priority.

Categories/Subjects that you are most enthusiastic about agenting: Fiction: Science fiction/fantasy, mysteries, young adult, literary fiction, police/detective; Nonfiction: Gardening, military

Categories/Subjects writers shouldn't bother pitching to you: Christian, "swords and dragons" fantasy, erotica, children's, poetry, political, inspirational/New Age, short stories, novellas

If you were not an agent, what might you be doing instead: My whole life has led me to this point.

What's the best way for fiction writers to solicit your interest: Do your homework and make your query pitch perfect.

Do you charge fees separate from your commission or offer nonagenting fee-based services: We don't charge any up-front fees. Our commission is the standard 15 percent and, if the book is sold, we subtract postage and copy fees from the advance. We are publicists as well as agents, but we don't publicize our agenting clients' books. We provide publicity/marketing counsel and guidance to our authors as part of our agenting job.

What are some representative titles that you have sold: See Kae's listing.

How and why did you become an agent: All the interesting and fun parts of my life have come together at this focal point.

How do you feel about writers: I really love writers but don't love lazy writers.

How would you describe what you do as an agent to someone (or something) from another planet: I tell them I am on a treasure hunt for an explanation of what it all means.

What are your favorite books, movies, and TV shows, and why: Books: I can't list them all; Movies: *Blade Runner, The Fifth Element, Constantine, Matrix, Apocalypse Now, Das Boot*; TV: HBO and the Speed Channel

Will our business exist as we know it in 10 years or so: Of course not. Change is inevitable. We embrace it as much as possible.

Agent's name: Kae Tienstra
Born: Denver, Colorado on June 3
Education: BA in speech/drama, minor in English
Career history: I stayed at home for 13 years to raise our three children, letting my husband Jon do the hunting and gathering in the corporate world. To save my sanity and bring in a bit of my own money, I began a freelance writing career. I wrote articles for publications like *The Mother Earth News, Organic Gardening,* and our local newspaper and magazines. I also ghostwrote a local history and photography book and penned a one-act play. When Jon quit his job to go back to school, I was hired by Rodale, Inc., as publicity assistant. I moved up quickly to director of publicity for the book division and stayed at Rodale in that capacity for 13 years. I left Rodale to launch my own publicity firm, KT Public Relations, in 1993. (Jon joined the firm a few years after that.) Over the years we've represented large publishers such as Random House, Putnam, HarperCollins, and John Wiley & Sons, as well as smaller publishers and authors. We launched our literary agency in 2006 and changed the name of our company to reflect our two businesses—KT Public Relations and Literary Services.

Hobbies/Personal interests: I'm an avid reader, which is no surprise. Gardening is a passion, especially perennials and herbs. Jon and I spend much of our down time cooking and love to sample great wines. We walk two miles every morning, travel when we can, and try to spend as much time as possible with our grandsons Rob and Max.

Categories/Subjects that you are most enthusiastic about agenting: Fiction: Women's fiction, quirky, contemporary fantasy, mysteries, young adult; Nonfiction: Gardening, health, cookbooks, narrative nonfiction, animals, nature, parenting, psychology, relationships

Categories/Subjects writers shouldn't bother pitching to you: Christian, "swords and dragons" fantasy, erotica, children's, poetry, political, inspirational/New Age

If you were not an agent, what might you be doing instead: I'd be writing my own books.

What's the best way for fiction writers to solicit your interest: In your query letter, by describing in the first sentence the essence of your book. In the next sentence, tell me its genre and word count. Then give me the best written paragraph you can craft about why this book is the cat's pajamas. Then, wind things up by giving me a few sentences about you as a writer. (Don't bother to tell me where you live or who you married.) Then, stop already! If you have done your job, I should want to see some chapters.

Do you charge fees separate from your commission or offer nonagenting

fee-based services: We don't charge any up-front fees. Our commission is the standard 15 percent and, if the book is sold, we subtract postage and copy fees from the advance. We are publicists as well as agents, but we don't publicize our agenting clients' books. We provide publicity/marketing counsel and guidance to our authors as part of our agenting job.

What are some representative titles that you have sold: *Town in a Blueberry Jam* by Alex Haywood (Prime Crime); *The Red Gold Bridge* by Patrice Sarath (Ace); *Gordath Wood* by Patrice Sarath (Ace); *Are You Ready for Lasting Love?* by Paddy S. Welles (Marlowe & Company); *100 Recipes You Can't Eat* by Alexa Lett (Putnam)

How and why did you become an agent: I brought two books to the attention of an agent friend who encouraged me (and Jon) to consider becoming agents ourselves. It seemed the right time to use our knowledge of publishing and publicity to create an agency grounded by this foundation.

How do you feel about writers: I really love writers who know their business. I love writers who are talented but understand that talent will only get them so far. I love writers who study the publishing business, go to writer's conferences, ask questions, and READ, READ, READ. I love writers who read their favorite authors, read out of their comfort zone, and read books, blogs, magazines, websites, and newsletters about book publishing. I love writers who have a sense of humor and who don't take themselves too seriously.

How would you describe what you do as an agent to someone (or something) from another planet: I tell them I am a detective searching for the next great book.

What are your favorite books, movies, and TV shows, and why: Anything by John Steinbeck because of his compassion; *Babbitt* by Sinclair Lewis because of its setting and sense of satire; *The Jump Off Creek* by Molly Gloss because it reminds me what toughness and will can accomplish; *The Naked and the Dead* by Norman Mailer, which I just began reading recently—amazing; *Madame Bovary* by Flaubert—I don't really know why. I don't like Emma Bovary, but this book is perfect. *The Great Gatsby* because no one writes like F. Scott Fitzgerald. Favorite movies: Anything done by Christopher Guest, particularly *Best in Show* because the humor is just my style. Guilty pleasures: Old movies on TBS, especially Fred Astaire when I'm in a bad mood. TV shows: HBO only, especially *Six Feet Under*. (OK, I'll admit to watching *What Not to Wear* on TLC.)

Describe the client from hell, even if you don't have any: Knows nothing about the industry, does not intend to learn, and is sure she/he has the next big book that editors will "buy in a heartbeat." AND this author cannot write her way out of a paper bag.

Describe the publisher and/or editor from hell: My "editor/publisher from hell" does not exist—yet. So far they have all been helpful, kind, and generous to us. It's true! I just remembered one exception, the subsidy publisher who did not come clean about how he works. (But we should have done our homework earlier!)

What do you like best about your clients and the editors and publishers you work with: I like clients who become partners in the process of finding a publisher for their books. These clients don't call, they e-mail. They don't demand, they request. They have good ideas which they share and they also share our enthusiasm for the process. We like the editors and publishers who are open and friendly and who look to us as resources. Some editors tell us where we've gone wrong and we really appreciate it, being new to this side of the business. Other editors give us hints and tips which are so useful.

Will our business exist as we know it in 10 years or so: Everything changes. That's the one true thing. The book business is changing under our feet. In 10 years? Who knows? All we can do is hold on for the ride and try to innovate, not duplicate.

THE LARSEN POMADA LITERARY AGENCY

1029 Jones Street, San Francisco, CA 94109
415-673-0939
www.larsenpomada.com

Agent's name: Elizabeth Pomada
E-mail: larsenpoma@aol.com
Born: June 12; New York, New York
Education: Cornell, '62
Career history: Worked at Holt, Rinehart, and Winston; David McKay; and the Dial Press. Cofounded the agency in 1972. Member: AAR. The agency has sold hundreds of books, mostly by new writers, to more than a hundred publishers.
Hobbies/Personal interests: France, architectural color, reading, travel
Categories/Subjects that you are most enthusiastic about agenting: I like positive narrative nonfiction—something that will make me feel good when I've read it. I like travel narrative that makes me hunt for my passport. And I like fiction of all kinds, from very literary to very commercial, romance, mystery, thriller, etc. Something that will keep me reading past my bedtime.
Categories/Subjects writers shouldn't bother pitching to you: Please do not send poetry, children's books, fantasy, sci-fi, Westerns, misery memoirs, or disease-of-the-month stories. No abuse of any kind.
If you were not an agent, what might you be doing instead: If I weren't agenting, I'd be reading good books. Maybe writing a few.
What's the best way for fiction writers to solicit your interest: The most effective way to grab our attention? Write beautifully. Craft does leap off the page. Follow the submission guidelines on our website.
Do you charge fees separate from your commission or offer nonagenting fee-based services: We do not charge fees separate from our commission or offer nonagenting fee-based services.
How and why did you become an agent: I became an agent when I moved to San Francisco and was told there were no publishing jobs for me in the city. The

employment agent represented writers and artists and she said, pointing to a wall of manuscripts, "Meanwhile, people send me these things, and I don't know what do to with them." I went in every Tuesday afternoon and actually found two books that were salable—so started then.

How do you feel about writers: It depends on when you ask. Most mean well. But too many think the world owes them a living and don't understand that they have to do their homework and be responsible for their success.

How would you describe what you do as an agent to someone (or something) from another planet: We tell them that we're the middlemen, the matchmakers between publishers and authors.

What are your favorite books, movies, and TV shows, and why: Favorite books: *Desiree* by Annemarie Selinko because it's romance that's basically true and historical and *Gone with the Wind* by Margaret Mitchell because in the different readings from when I was a child to now, I've seen different things and learned about life; Favorite movie: *An American in Paris*

Describe the client from hell, even if you don't have any: A noodge who thinks he knows more than I do about the business

Describe the publisher and/or editor from hell: The publisher cheats on royalties and holds back an impossible reserve against returns just so the author won't get any money. The editor simply disappears and doesn't answer phone calls, e-mails, etc. I won't name names, but I could.

What do you like best about your clients and the editors and publishers you work with: I like clients who are genuinely interested in their writing, their careers, the business. It's also special if they are human and interested in me as a human being, too. Friends are nice. I like publishers and editors who are still interested in writers and good writing—even though commerce is important. And all should see publishing/writing as part of life, not the only reason for living.

Will our business exist as we know it in 10 years or so: Our business will exist 10 years or so from now, but not as we know it. Writers will still need to have people on their side, but publishing and selling will change dramatically and machines are sure to take over much of the world—including publishing and bookselling. Do we really have 10 years left?

Agent's name: Laurie McLean
E-mail: queryagentsavant@gmail.com
Education: Bachelor's degree from SUNY Binghamton; master's degree from Syracuse University (Newhouse School of Journalism)
Career history: I was a journalist and then a publicist for a variety of companies and agencies. I was the CEO of an eponymous public relations agency in the Silicon Valley for 20 years. Then I retired and joined Larsen Pomada in 2005.
Hobbies/Personal interests: I enjoy acoustic and ethnic music, cooking, organic gardening, camping, and BOOKS!
Categories/Subjects that you are most enthusiastic about agenting: I handle

adult genre fiction (romance, fantasy, science fiction, mysteries, thrillers, horror, and new Westerns) and middle-grade and young-adult children's books.

Categories/Subjects writers shouldn't bother pitching to you: Don't pitch me memoir, picture books, screenplays, poetry, self-published books, nonfiction, traditional Westerns, erotica, or literary fiction.

If you were not an agent, what might you be doing instead: I would be writing more novels.

Do you charge fees separate from your commission or offer nonagenting fee-based services: I don't charge fees.

What are some representative titles that you have sold: *Xombies* series by Walter Greatshell (Berkley); *Jaz Parks* series by Jennifer Rarding (Orbit); *Hex* series by Linda Wisdom (Sourcebooks); *Iron King* series by Julie Kagawa (Harlequin Teen); *Soul Gatherer* series by Annette McCleave (NAL); *Edge of Night* by Jill Sorenson (Bantam/Dell); *Majix* by Douglas Rees (Harlequin Teen); Uncle Pirate series by Douglas Rees (McElderry); *Deadly Little Secrets* by Jeanne Adams (Kensington); *Geist* by Philippa Ballantine (Berkley)

How and why did you become an agent: I retired from a successful career in high tech PR and wrote a novel. I needed an agent to sell it, and Elizabeth Pomada became my agent. Three books later she still hasn't sold my manuscripts, but I got a great job as a literary agent instead.

How do you feel about writers: Since I also consider myself a writer, I love working with them. They are creative, hard working, and generally idiosyncratic, which I find interesting.

How do you feel about editors and publishers: I love to tangle with them. They are worthy adversaries before the deal and great teammates afterwards.

How would you describe what you do as an agent to someone (or something) from another planet: I sell other people's stories to publishers who turn them into books.

What are your favorite books, movies, and TV shows, and why: Favorite movie: *The Matrix*; favorite book: Tad Williams's Otherland series; favorite TV show: *X-Files*

Describe the writer/client from hell: Arrogant

Describe yourself: Smart with heart

Describe the publisher and/or editor from hell: Overworked to the point of paralysis

What's the best way for writers to solicit your interest: E-mail only to query@ agentsavant.com

Will e-readers significantly change the business: Yes. They already are. And when the current young "gadget" generation begins to make serious money...watch it accelerate.

Are you optimistic, pessimistic, neutral, or catatonic about the book biz in the future: I am optimistic that publishing will change and grow and fragment and reinvent itself. I came from high tech, so I see this as very healthy and positive.

Explain what you like and dislike about your job: I hate the impossibly long hours and hurry-up-then-stop pace. I love the people and the words.

Describe a book you might like writing: "Teen space zombies from a parallel dimension find love and solve the mystery of the Anasazi disappearance while time traveling to the Old West." I think that covers all the genres I rep!

Laurie McLean handles romance, fantasy, science fiction, horror, mystery, suspense, thriller, and "new" Western novels. She also represents children's young-adult and middle-grade fiction. (Young adult is for high school readers and middle grade is for middle school readers.)

At present, my assistant Pam van Hylckama Vlieg and I are only accepting unsolicited queries at queryagentsavant@gmail.com for all kinds of science fiction, fantasy, middle-grade fiction, and young-adult fiction. Otherwise I will take submissions for *everything* I represent from people I meet at conferences or who are referred to me by clients and publishing professionals. I attend more than 20 conferences a year, ranging from free admission for some online cons to $500 or so for the best of the best. Check out the agency's personal appearances page for my schedule.

Alternatives? Our associate agents Kat Salazar and Lindsey Clemons are actively building their lists and are eager to accept queries in the areas they represent. Elizabeth Pomada is also accepting unsolicited queries for romance and mysteries.

I am especially eager to find excellent steampunk, epic fantasy, new weird fantasy, space opera and military science fiction, dark fantasy and urban fantasy. I am also looking for ROMANCE manuscripts in the following subgenres: Regency historicals, Scottish historicals, medieval historicals, paranormal, futuristic, and military (especially yummy special-ops heroes), and steampunk romance. And for the young-adult and middle-grade markets I am searching high and low for young-adult romance, steampunk, paranormal, dark fantasy (no sweet fairy tales), dark reality (dealing with contemporary issues), and anything interesting. Young adult is superhot right now, and I love the teen voice! Plus middle grade is getting as hot as young adult, so I'm looking for boy-based and/or group adventure stories, grounded girl stories, magical realism, dark thrillers, smart/high concept books, fantasy/paranormal, and overall excellent writing.

I DO NOT represent authors of picture books, board books; easy readers; chapter books; memoir; nonfiction; or commercial, literary, or women's fiction. I also do not handle novels about serial killers, cozy mysteries unless the protagonist is unique and compelling (able to anchor a series), Westerns, true-crime dramas, biblical or religious-themed books, role-playing fantasy, superhero fantasy, erotica, erotic romance, inspirational romance, or books with talking animal protagonists.

If you meet these requirements please send the first 10 double-spaced pages and a 1–2 page synopsis in the body of your e-mail (no attachments) to queryagentsavant@gmail.com. (*The submission does not have to be double spaced in the e-mail. The amount of text you send should be the equivalent of 10 double-spaced pages.*) I do not open attachments due to virus concerns, so please include your text in the body of your e-mail message.

If you *mail* me a submission, I will not read it, so please use e-mail only. We live in a digital age. If you can't use e-mail, I am not the right agent for you.

I look forward to reading your work!

Agent's name: Michael Larsen

Born: January 8; New York, New York

Education: CCNY '63

Career history: Worked at William Morrow, Bantam, and Pyramid (now merged with Berkley). Cofounded the agency in 1972. Member: AAR. The agency has sold hundreds of books, mostly by new writers, to more than a hundred publishers. Wrote *How to Write a Book Proposal* and *How to Get a Literary Agent*, both of which are now in their third edition. Coauthored *How to Write with a Collaborator* with Hal Zina Bennett and *Guerilla Marketing for Writers: 100 Weapons for Selling Your Work* with client Jay Conrad Levinson, author of the 25+ [book] Guerilla Marketing series; and Rick Frishman, president of Planned Television Arts.

Hobbies/Personal interests: Going to the movies, listening to jazz (mostly '40s–'60s) and classical music (mostly 1685–1791), seeing plays, visiting France, reading a book without the phone ringing, bringing people together

Categories/Subjects that you are most enthusiastic about agenting: I'm looking for books that will change the world, that will mean something 10 years from now. Books that will add to my knowledge. Nonfiction. Something new and different. Something that will help us face the future.

Categories/Subjects writers shouldn't bother pitching to you: Please do not send books I've already read or sold, diet books, religious tomes, yesterday's news.

If you were not an agent, what might you be doing instead: If I weren't agenting, I'd be publishing, or helping to publish, books that should be published.

What's the best way for fiction writers to solicit your interest: The most effective way to grab our attention? Write beautifully. Craft does leap off the page. Follow the submission guidelines on our website.

Do you charge fees separate from your commission or offer nonagenting fee-based services: We do not charge fees separate from our commission or offer nonagenting fee-based services.

What are some representative titles that you have sold: *The Scalpel and The Soul* by Allan Hamilton (Tarcher); *The Solemn Lantern Maker* by Merlinda Bobis (Delta); *Shadow Isle* by Katharine Kerr (DAW); *Guerrilla Marketing* by Jay Conrad Levinson (Houghton)

How and why did you become an agent: I became an agent when Patty Hearst was captured. I knew there was a book in it and ended up selling it in four phone calls. I figured being an agent was easy! And joined Elizabeth.

How do you feel about writers: It depends on when you ask. Most mean well.

But too many think the world owes them a living and don't understand that they have to do their homework and be responsible for their success.

How would you describe what you do as an agent to someone (or something) from another planet: We tell them that we're the middlemen, the matchmakers between publishers and authors.

What are your favorite books, movies, and TV shows, and why: Favorite book: *The Leopard* by G. Lampedusa: history and life and philosophy all in one. Favorite movie: *Lawrence of Arabia*—best writing, best direction, best acting, best relevance, best music, as true today as it was then.

LAUNCHBOOKS LITERARY AGENCY

566 Sweet Pea Place, Encinitas, CA 92024
760-944-9909
www.launchbooks.com

Agent's name: David Fugate
E-mail: david@launchbooks.com
Born: June 11, 1969, in Richmond, Kentucky. Moved to Springfield, Ohio, when I was two, and then to San Diego, California, when I was eight and have been here ever since.
Education: Bachelor of arts with honors in English/American literature from the University of California, San Diego
Career history: In 1992 I began as an intern at the Margret McBride Literary Agency, while still a student at UC San Diego. Upon graduation I was hired by the McBride Agency to handle submissions and focus on project development. In 1994 I moved to Waterside Productions, Inc., and over the next 11-plus years represented more than 700 book projects that generated over $10,000,000 for authors. In August of 2005, I went out on my own to form LaunchBooks Literary Agency so that I could focus more exclusively on working with authors and projects that I'm truly passionate about.
Hobbies/Personal interests: Reading, a variety of sports (especially basketball, soccer, and skiing), video games, online culture (things like Second Life, blogs, virtual communities, etc.), renewable energy, China, world affairs, new music, and film (especially foreign films, drama, and the few really good sci-fi and comedies that come out each year)
Categories/Subjects that you are most enthusiastic about agenting: Ninety-five percent of the projects I represent are nonfiction, and within that category I have a broad range of interests including history, politics, current affairs, narrative nonfiction, health, business, biography, true crime, memoir, parenting, sports, pop culture, how-to, computers and technology, reference, diet, and humor. In the fiction space I'm interested in humor, science fiction, thrillers, mysteries, and mainstream/topical titles.

Categories/Subjects writers shouldn't bother pitching to you: Religion, spirituality, children's, romance, horror, short stories, poetry

What's the best way for fiction writers to solicit your interest: An e-mail query and a synopsis. However, if an author also wants to attach the first 25–30 pages of their novel as a Word attachment, I'm often happy to read that, as well.

What's the best way for nonfiction writers to solicit your interest: An e-mail query and a proposal

Do you charge reading or management fees: No, I don't charge any upfront or reading fees.

What can a writer do to increase the odds of you becoming his or her agent: It's critical these days that authors have a clear sense of where their book fits into the market and the ability to communicate why their book will sell. It has also become more and more important for an author to have a strong marketing platform. Fortunately, there are now more ways than ever for authors to develop a platform for both themselves and their books, and having one will increase both the odds that I'll offer representation and that a publisher will pick up the book.

What are some representative titles that you have sold: *The Ghost Train* by Jon Jeter (W. W. Norton); *The Making of Second Life* by Wagner James Au (HarperCollins); *Everyday Edisons* by Louis Foreman and Jill Gilbert Welytok (Workman); *Branding Only Works on Cows* by Jonathan Baskin (Grand Central); *The Art of Deception* by Kevin Mitnick and William L. Simon (John Wiley & Sons); *Lifehacker* by Gina Trapani (John Wiley & Sons); *Transcending CSS* by Andy Clarke (Peachpit); *The Zen of CSS* by Molly Holzschlag and Jeff Zeldman (Peachpit); *US Military History for Dummies* by John McManus (John Wiley & Sons)

LES STOBBE LITERARY AGENCY

300 Doubleday Road, Tryon, NC 28782
828-808-7127 | fax: 978-945-0517

Agent's name: Les Stobbe
E-mail: lstobbe@alltel.net
Career history: 1962–1970: *Business* magazine editor; 1970–1978: editorial director, Moody Press; 1978–1982: Vice President and editorial director, Christian Herald Books and Book Club; 1982–1985: editor and director, Here's Life Publishing; 1985–1992: president, Here's Life Publishing; 1993–1996: managing editor, Scripture Press Curriculum; 1996–2001: Vice President of communications, Vision New England; 1993–present: literary agent; 2001–present: editor-in-chief, Jerry B. Jenkins Christian Writers Guild

Hobbies/Personal interests: Boston Red Sox
Categories/Subjects that you are most enthusiastic about agenting: Adult Christian fiction and nonfiction

Categories/Subjects writers shouldn't bother pitching to you: New Age humanistic, children's books, young-adult fiction

If you were not an agent, what might you be doing instead: Writing books

What's the best way for fiction writers to solicit your interest: Get editors at Christian Writers Guild conference to say, "Send me a proposal."

What's the best way for nonfiction writers to solicit your interest: See above.

Do you charge reading or management fees: No

What are the most common mistakes writers make when pitching to you: Sending documents with typos and grammatical mistakes

What's your definition of a great client: One whose proposal is professionally prepared but is willing to improve the pitch

What can a writer do to increase the odds of you becoming his or her agent: Attend a Christian writers conference and talk to editors

How and why did you become an agent: Author friends insisted I represent them

How would you describe what you do as an agent to someone (or something) from another planet: I open doors for clients at publishing houses.

How do you feel about editors and publishers: I was one of them.

How do you feel about writers: I love writers.

What do you see in the near future for book publishing: More consolidations, fewer titles

In your opinion, what do editors think of you: I have a good reputation.

On a personal level, what do you think people like and dislike about you: A caring professional

What are some representative titles that you have sold: *Hearing God's Voice* by Vern Heidebrecht (David C. Cook); *The Evidence* by Austin Boyd (Navpress); *Petticoat Ranch* by Mary Connealy (Barbour Publishing); *The Great American Supper Swap* by Trish Berg (David C. Cook); *Rolling Thunder* by Mark Mynheir (Multnomah-Waterbrook); *Pray Big* by Will Davis Jr. (Baker/Revell); *The 21 Most Effective Prayers of the Bible* by Dave Earley (Barbour Publishing); *From Jihad to Jesus* by Jerry Rassamni (AMG Publishing)

LEVINE GREENBERG LITERARY AGENCY

307 Seventh Avenue, Suite 2407, New York, NY 10001
212-337-0934 | fax: 212-337-0948
www.levinegreenberg.com

Agent's name: Danielle Svetcov

Career history: Danielle Svetcov joined Levine Greenberg in 2001 as a book doctor, and a few years later, began selling books from her "remote" outpost in San Francisco, California.

She looks for titles that make her laugh (e.g., *Skymaul—Happy Crap You Can*

Buy from a Plane) and, if nothing comes along, will write her own laugh track (*The Unconstipated Gourmet—Secrets to a Moveable Feast*). She particularly likes to laugh while she's crying (*Half Baked*), or eating (*Jam It, Pickle It, Cure It*), or parenting (*Balance Is a Crock, Sleep Is for the Weak*), or sweating (*Yoga Bitch*). Also, if you're a mystery writer with snappy elocutionary style, if your book traffics in awkward heroes or charming family dysfunction, please do make contact. Prior to Levine Greenberg, Danielle worked as a freelance writer, an editor, a kitchen slave, and a pastry hawker. She has an MFA in fiction from Warren Wilson College.

Agent's name: Lindsay Edgecombe
E-mail: ledgecombe@levinegreenberg.com
Career history: Lindsay represents a wide range of adult titles, including narrative nonfiction, memoir, lifestyle, and literary and commercial fiction. She is drawn to projects with strong narrators, obscure journeys, and political backbones, but she is an eclectic reader and will take on any project that she's passionate about. Lindsay represents journalists, debut novelists, *New Yorker* cartoonists, Zen abbots, crafty sorts, sommeliers, and Japanophile bloggers, among many others. She loves to uncover new talent and work with her clients to develop great proposals from the spark of an idea. Her authors have contributed to NPR's *This American Life*, written for the *New York Times* and many other publications, and have been on *Oprah* and *The Daily Show*. Writers who make her glad to be able to read include Sarah Vowell, John Updike, Ariel Levy, Anne Fadiman, and above all, E. M. Forster. Lindsay graduated Phi Beta Kappa, summa cum laude from Barnard College, Columbia University, where she edited *The Columbia Review* and worked with students to develop writing in the Writing Fellow program.

Agent's name: Victoria Skurnick
Education: BA, University of Wisconsin
Career history: Began in publishing as copywriter at Avon Books, assistant director of advertising and promotion at Pocket Books, director of advertising and promotion at Holt, Rinehart, and Winston; went on to become senior editor, Pocket Books and St. Martin's Press, and editor-in-chief, Book-of-the-Month Club. Began at Levine Greenberg in 2007.
Hobbies/Personal interests: Writing fiction as half of pseudonymous writing team, Cynthia Victor
Categories/Subjects that you are most enthusiastic about agenting: Fiction of every kind except science fiction, nonfiction including memoir, health, politics, spirituality, all narrative nonfiction
Categories/Subjects writers shouldn't bother pitching to you: Science fiction and children's
If you were not an agent, what might you be doing instead: Writing
What's the best way for fiction writers to solicit your interest: Make the synopsis very short, but include the first chapter or two in the query e-mail.

Do you charge fees separate from your commission or offer nonagenting fee-based services: No

What are some representative titles that you have sold: *Old City Hall* by Robert Rotenberg, FSG; *Bad Things Happen* by Harry Dolan; Amy Einhorn books at Penguin; *Following Polly* by Karen Bergreen, St. Martin's Press; *Chaplin: A Life* by Stephen Weissman; *Exercising Your Spirituality* by Gary Jansen, Warner Faith; *The Unconstipated Gourmet* by Danielle Svetcov, Sourcebooks; *I Met the Walrus* by Jerry Levitan, HarperCollins; *Stay Close* by Libby Cataldi, St. Martin's Press; *Breadline USA* by Sasha Abramsky, Poli Point Press

How and why did you become an agent: I was a writer and editor for many years before I thought about becoming an agent. As the industry changed, the book clubs became less central to the process and I missed the feel of being more hands-on in the process. Being an agent was just about the only part of publishing I had not tried, and it seemed very interesting to me. It turns out to be a perfect fit for my interests and talents and is not corporately run, which fits my temperament.

How do you feel about writers: I am a writer, which makes me sympathetic indeed. They are almost always isolated and need all the help they can get.

What are your favorite books, movies, and TV shows, and why: *Pride and Prejudice*, *The Glass Castle*, *Law & Order*, *Friday Night Lights*. I love narrative, love great characters, and have a tiny penchant for crime—at least on the page.

Describe the client from hell, even if you don't have any: I could give you a name, but it doesn't seem very nice, now does it?

Describe the publisher and/or editor from hell: Giver of false promises

What do you like best about your clients and the editors and publishers you work with: Talent and cooperation

Will our business exist as we know it in 10 years or so: It will be very different indeed. If I could define exactly how, I'd be a very wealthy woman.

Agent's name: Monika Verma
E-mail: mverma@levinegreenberg.com
Career history: Monika Verma is thrilled to be working at Levine Greenberg with Daniel Greenberg and Stephanie Rostan and as an agent. After growing up in Los Angeles, Monika headed east to attend Wellesley College. There she rocked the college radio station, coedited the literary magazine, and studied English. Not getting enough of the cold in Boston, she spent her junior year at Oxford perfecting her punting technique and reveling in her own anglophilia. Monika keeps a special place in her heart for pop culture, humor, narrative nonfiction, fashion, foodie, and music titles. She loves to represent books that makes people's lives just a few degrees sunnier, be those quirky memoirs, satirical humor collections, or old-fashioned cookbooks. On the fiction side, she stays up far too late reading literary mysteries and suspense, especially those from across the pond (some of her favorites are Kate Atkinson and Benjamin Black). She often suspects that she was born in the wrong century and loves books that give her a window into an older way of life. In her

spare time, she enjoys going to concerts, photography, traveling, cheesy Masterpiece Theater adaptations, and searching for the spiciest vegetarian food in New York.

Agent's name: Daniel Greenberg
E-mail: dgreenberg@levinegreenberg.com
Career history: Although Daniel's specialties are popular culture, narrative nonfiction, memoir, and humor, he will take on any project as long as there's a personal connection with the book and he's positively excited about representing the author. No nonfiction topic will ruffle his feathers. As he says, "I can fall in love with a 650-page book on the pencil." Over the years he's worked with, among others, rock critics, novelists, Silicon Valley entrepreneurs, television writers, Onions, conspiracy kooks, performance artists, renowned professors, pug photographers, and *New York Times* reporters. Yet, he often loses sleep worrying that his list is too narrow. His fiction leans towards the literary, and he will generally pass along thrillers, mysteries, romances, Westerns, and the like to his colleagues within the agency. Daniel is a native New Yorker (he went to summer camp with Arielle!), but, he went off to the hinterlands of Madison, Wisconsin, for college. He graduated with honors, a year in Florence under his belt, and a brand-new degree in European history to bring home to his astonished family and friends on the Lower East Side. A brief stint in the Penguin USA subsidiary rights department, coupled with the odd thought that he was Italian, led Daniel off to Italy to work for the Roberto Santachiara Literary Agency in Pavia. In 1994 Daniel returned to New York and joined the agency. In 2002, he became a principal.

Agent's name: James Levine
E-mail: jlevine@levinegreenberg.com
Career history: Founded in 1989 by author and academic entrepreneur James Levine, we have grown into a firm of 12 people with offices in New York and San Francisco. We represent fiction and nonfiction in virtually every category. Most of our titles are published by imprints of the major houses, but we have also worked with almost 50 independent and/or university presses. Our strong foreign rights department works internationally with a respected network of coagents to place our titles with leading foreign publishers, and we are regular participants at the Frankfurt Book Fair and Book Expo America. Our coagents in Hollywood handle movie and television rights with major studios and production companies.

Categories/Subjects that you are most enthusiastic about agenting: Our agents have such wide and varied preferences that our list excludes few genres. As far as fiction is concerned, commercial women's literature, literary fiction, ethnic fiction, young-adult literature, romance, and suspense have been successfully represented by a number of our agents. Additionally, LGLA is no stranger to business, self-help, humor, food, child development, pet, science, narrative nonfiction, and political titles, all of which are of interest to our agents. Our full list can be found at our website.

What's the best way for fiction writers to solicit your interest: The thorough online submission form located at our website (www.levinegreenberg.com), which allows for attaching proposals and sample chapters, is the best way to submit work.

Do you charge reading or management fees: No

What are some representative titles that you have sold: *Predictably Irrational* by Dan Ariely (HarperCollins); *Sex, Drugs, and Cocoa Puffs* by Chuck Klosterman (Scribner); *Love Is a Mix Tape* by Rob Sheffield (Crown); *Fifty Places to Play Golf Before You Die* by Chris Santella; *Green Eggs and Ham Cookbook* by Georgeanne Brennan (Random House); *The Five Dysfunctions of a Team: A Leadership Fable* by Patrick Lencioni (Jossey-Bass); *Queen Bees and Wannabes: Helping Your Daughter Survive Cliques, Gossip, Boyfriends, and Other Realities of Adolescence* by Rosalind Wiseman (Crown); *Why Good Things Happen to Good People: The Exciting New Research that Proves the Link between Doing Good and Living a Longer, Healthier, Happier Life* by Stephen Post, PhD, and Jill Neimark (Broadway); *Extraordinary Knowing: Science, Skepticism, and the Inexplicable Powers of the Human Mind* by Elizabeth Lloyd Mayer, PhD (Bantam); *The Spellman Files* by Lisa Lutz (Simon & Schuster); *The Insufficiency of Maps* by Nora Pierce (Atria); *Getting Warmer* by Carol Snow (Berkley)

Agent's name: Stephanie Kip Rostan

E-mail: srostan@levinegreenberg.com

Career history: A fiction lover who's spent more than one night reading until dawn, Stephanie believes that the compulsion to keep turning pages is as important in a literary coming-of-age story as it is in a serial killer novel. She will take on any kind of fiction that refuses to let her put it down. In the nonfiction arena, she is drawn to books that make our lives better, easier, or more interesting—either through laughter, advice, or the sharing of a true story. Stephanie joined Levine Greenberg after four years as an editor for Bantam Dell and two years as the book producer at iVillage.com. As an editor, she worked on a wide range of fiction and nonfiction, from RITA award-winning romance to literary fiction to true crime to wedding planning. One of her favorite parts of the job was building relationships with authors—another was the free books that fed her out-of-control reading habit. At iVillage, Stephanie spent two years listening to what readers—the over 14 million women who visit the site every month—wanted and why, developing features on book clubs, family and relationships issues, work, home, and diet and fitness. Raised in Andover, Massachusetts, Stephanie is the daughter of a Latin and Greek teacher whose specialty is etymology (ask her dad for a definition, and you'll get a minimum of 36 hours of explanation). This early focus on language led to her obsession with crossword puzzles, a term in Germany as an exchange student, and an English/creative writing major at Princeton. There she became familiar with the slings and arrows of critique groups and revisions, writing under teachers such as Susan Shreve, Stephen Wright, and Joyce Carol Oates. Stephanie now lives with her husband and two children in the New York City area, which makes her green belt in karate a plus—and the fact that she's an incurable Red Sox fan a decided minus.

LINDA KONNER LITERARY AGENCY

10 West 15th Street, Suite 1918, New York, NY 10011
www.lindakonnerliteraryagency.com

Agent's name: Linda Konner
E-mail: ldkonner@cs.com
Born: Brooklyn, New York
Education: BA, Brooklyn College; MA, Fordham University
Career history: Editor, *Seventeen* magazine (1976–1981); managing editor, *Weight Watchers* magazine (1981–1983); editor-in-chief, *Weight Watchers* magazine (1983–1985); entertainment editor, *Redbook* magazine (1985–1986); entertainment editor, *Woman's World* (1986–1993); founding editor, *Richard Simmons Newsletter* (1993–1998); literary agent (1996–present); freelance writer, author of eight books
Categories/Subjects that you are most enthusiastic about agenting: Practical nonfiction (self-help, how-to, popular psychology, health, diet and fitness, relationships, parenting, career, personal finance, business)—all written by or with top experts in their fields, with a national platform
Categories/Subjects writers shouldn't bother pitching to you: Fiction, children's; no nonfiction unless written by/with a top expert
If you were not an agent, what might you be doing instead: Writing (with my honey) the book no one wants to publish: *Apartners: Living Apart and Loving It*
What's the best way for writers to solicit your interest: Send a brief query with a brief bio by mail (with SASE) or e-mail.
Do you charge reading or management fees: No reading fees
What categories do you represent, by percentages: Practical nonfiction: 95 percent; narrative nonfiction, including celebrity autobiographies: 5 percent
What are the most common mistakes writers make when pitching to you: Not being/partnering with a top expert with a good platform
How would you describe the perfect client: Follows through; meets my deadlines; is master of the brief phone call
How and why did you become an agent: Ran out of things to be after having been an author, freelance writer, and magazine editor
What can a writer do to increase the odds of you becoming his or her agent: Have (or write with someone who has) a major platform; have a good sales record with previously published books
Do you have any favorite (current) TV shows, films, or books that you especially like: *Law & Order, What Not to Wear, Ebert & Roeper*

What are some representative titles that you have sold: *The Winner's Brain* by Jeff Brown, PsyD, Mark Fenske, PhD, and Liz Neporent and the editors of Harvard Health Publications (Da Capo/Perseus, spring 2010). *Your Successful Preschooler* by Ann Densmore, EdD, and Margaret Bauman (Jossey-Bass, spring 2010), *A Baby at Last!* by Zev Rosenwaks, MD, Marc Goldstein, MD, with Mark Fuerst (Touchstone Fireside/S&S, summer 2010), *Saying Goodbye* by Barbara Okun, PhD, Joseph Nowinski, PhD, and the editors of Harvard Health Publications (Berkley/Penguin, fall 2010), *Work Smart, Play Hard: How to Make Your First Million by the Time You Turn 30* by Nick Friedman and Omar Soliman with Daylle Deanna Schwartz (Three Rivers Press, spring 2010)

THE LISA EKUS GROUP, LLC

57 North Street, Hatfield, MA 01038
413-247-9325 | fax: 413-247-9873
www.LisaEkus.com

Agent's name: Lisa Ekus-Saffer
E-mail: sia@LisaEkus.com
Categories/Subjects that you are most enthusiastic about agenting: Our primary interest is culinary titles, although we do consider some other nonfiction topics that are complementary, such as books on nutrition, health and wellness, and wine and beverages.

Categories/Subjects writers shouldn't bother pitching to you: Fiction or poetry
What's the best way for writers to solicit your interest: We have proposal guidelines and other information about our agency on our website.

What can a writer do to increase the odds of you becoming his or her agent: The best way for authors to approach us is with a formal query and/or proposal, and we appreciate if people do not call us. We follow up on all formal queries and submissions. We are a full member of the Association of Author Representatives.

What do you think the future holds for book publishing: Despite an increasingly competitive marketplace, we continue to believe in a vibrant cookbook industry full of opportunity.

What are some representative titles that you have sold: Our website offers a comprehensive listing of our authors, book projects, and the many publishers with whom we have worked over the years. The agency celebrated its 28th anniversary this year. We began literary agenting services in 2000 and have negotiated book deals for more than 200 books since then. The business has four primary service areas: public relations, literary agenting, media training, and spokesperson opportunities.

LITERARY SERVICES, INC.

PO Box 888, Barnegat, NJ 08005
609-698-7162
www.LiteraryServicesInc.com

Agent's name: John Willig
E-mail: john@LiteraryServicesInc.com
Born: 1954, New York, NY
Education: Brown University, 1976
Career history: 35 years of publishing experience. I started working as a college sales "traveler" in academic publishing, and over the years became an executive editor for business professional and trade books with Prentice Hall before starting the agency. I was fortunate to grow up surrounded by books and the great Irish love of authors and writing. In my career as an editor and agent, I have negotiated over 700 publishing agreements.

Hobbies/Personal interests: I enjoy a wide range of interests from the arts to athletics…exploring new regions and cities and discovering new "finds" in art, antiques, music, and great food is always of interest! I have been a loyal and long-suffering Jets and Mets fan.

Categories/Subjects that you are most enthusiastic about agenting: We work primarily in nonfiction. Per our website, our core topic areas are in business, investing, careers, self-help, history, science, health, psychology, sports, current events, and global issues. We have started to acquire in crime and mystery fiction, which are some of my favorite personal reading genres.

Categories/Subjects writers shouldn't bother pitching to you: Children's books, science fiction, romance fiction

If you were not an agent, what might you be doing instead: History teacher and baseball or basketball coach. There are days, though, that the allure of the sea and becoming a tuna boat captain sounds just right.

What's the best way for fiction writers to solicit your interest: I'm only interested in crime/mystery fiction at the moment with strong historical story lines.

What's the best way for nonfiction writers to solicit your interest: Per our company website and submission segment, an e-mail answering a few key questions before sending proposals and chapters. I value sample chapters with a well-researched proposal.

Do you charge reading or management fees: No reading fees. In addition to our author representation, we offer content coaching services for authors who are determined (and have decided) to self-publish. This service is based on our extensive editorial, development, and marketing experience working for publishers. It is not intended to be a prerequisite for representation, and it is not a fee we charge to prospective clients. It is intended to help writers venturing into uncharted waters but who have decided that for them the best route is to self-publish or produce their own e-book.

What are the most common mistakes writers make when pitching to you: Exaggerating the market size/potential; spending too much time criticizing the competition/best sellers and not enough on their platform; arrogant tone leading to unreasonable expectations

Describe the client from hell, even if you don't have any: Per the above, I place a high premium on the quality of the author's attitude and learning about what type of person they are and what it will be like to work with them. In my book, character matters.

What's your definition of a great client: Someone with a great learning attitude, a sense of humor, and some humility; organized, responsive, flexible, and collaborative spirit

What can a writer do to increase the odds of you becoming his or her agent: Passion is a given. I worry when there is not enough or too much. I'm more impressed with someone who has done their homework—researching the market, investing time and resources into the writing—and/or has been actively developing their "community" of potential interested buyers of their book through social media, speaking, workshops, etc.

How and why did you become an agent: To work closely with writers in developing their ideas and sharing success (making dreams a reality). I decided to become an agent in the midst of a corporate reorganization (that did not have the best interest of authors on their radar screen).

How would you describe what you do as an agent to someone (or something) from another planet: I work as a writer's advocate and trusted advisor. In doing so, this involves many "hats," such as financial consultant, writing coach, legal counsel, personal advisor/cheerleader, and sometimes therapist.

How do you feel about editors and publishers: Without them I'm on the tuna boat! Having been one, I know how challenging it is to produce successful books, and it is very challenging today. They deserve my respect and admiration—this does not, however, compromise my ability to aggressively represent my clients and their best interests.

What do you see in the near future for book publishing: "Predictions are difficult, especially when they involve the future."—Yogi Berra. And especially when they involve publishing!

What are your favorite books, movies, and TV shows, and why: Books: I love historical/thriller fiction (in the tradition of *The Alienist*, C. Carr). I collect Jazz Age authors Fitzgerald, Hemingway, Wolfe, Stein. Movies: So many!

In your opinion, what do editors think of you: Professional, knowledgeable about publishing; represents high quality authors and projects; can be a good working partner

On a personal level, what do you think people like and dislike about you: I hope as a "good man, father, and friend."

What are some representative titles that you have sold: *Shortcuts to Inner Peace* by Ashley Bush (Berkley); *Good Products, Bad Products* by James Adams (McGraw Hill); *Live Your Dash* by Linda Ellis (Sterling); *Don't Give Up...Don't Ever Give Up* by Justin Spizman (Sourcebooks); *Divine Intuition* by Lynn Robinson (Jossey Bass)

When Giants Fall by Michael Panzner (John Wiley); *The Pursuit of Elegance* by Matt May (Doubleday/Currency); *The 2020 Workplace* by Jeanne Meister (HarperCollins); *Carve Your Own Road* by Jennifer Remling (Career Press); *Love Your Body, Live Your Dreams* by Sarah Maira Dreisbach (Adams Media); *Restoring Who We Are* by Martin Melaver (Chelsea Green Publishers); *The Global Talent Showdown* by Edward Gordon (Berret Koehler); *The Recycling Robot* by Robert Malone (Workman Publishers)

LIZA DAWSON ASSOCIATES

350 7th Avenue, Suite 2003, New York, NY 10001
212-465-9071
www.lizadawsonassociates.com

Agent's name: Liza Dawson
E-mail: queryliza@lizadawsonassociates.com
Education: BA in history, Duke University; graduate of Radcliffe's publishing procedure course.
Career history: Founded Liza Dawson Associates in 1998 after 20 years as executive editor and vice president at William Morrow and Putnam. We are focused on building best sellers in fiction, on finding exceptionally talented children's book authors, and on nurturing and launching serious nonfiction. Our agents include Caitlin Blasdell, Anna Olsanger, Hannah Bowman, Havis Dawson, and Judith Engracia. Chandler Crawford handles our foreign rights.
Hobbies/Personal interests: Local and national politics, archaeology, gardening, and trend watching digital media to discern the future of bookselling
Categories/Subjects that you are most enthusiastic about agenting: Plot-driven literary fiction; upscale historicals and smart mysteries; pacey, well-textured thrillers; multicultural fiction written in a distinctive, memorable voice; history (especially ancient) written by excellent writers; psychology that says something fresh; politics with a point of view; narrative nonfiction, travel, and memoirs written in a lively, moving tone and that take you someplace unexpected
Categories/Subjects writers shouldn't bother pitching to you: Poetry, Westerns, and quirky minimalist fiction
If you were not an agent, what might you be doing instead: Digging for ancient treasure in Italy
What's the best way for writers to solicit your interest: Query via e-mail, Liza@lizadawsonassociates.com
Do you charge reading or management fees: No
What's your definition of a great client: A gifted storyteller who is a funny, focused, fearless workaholic with lots of friends in the media
What are some representative titles that you have sold: *The Guernsey Literary and Potato Peel Society* by Mary Ann Shaffer and Annie Barrows (Dial Press); Robyn

Carr's *Virgin River* series (Mira); *The Executor* by Jesse Kellerman (Putnam); *Fragile Beasts* by Tawni O'Dell (Crown); *Growing Up Bin Laden: Osama's Wife and Son Take Us Inside Their Secret World* by Jean Sasson (St. Martin's); *Darkness Bound* by Stella Cameron (Grand Central); Marie Bostwick's *Cobble Court* series (Kensington); and Annie Barrows's *Ivy and Bean* series (Chronicle)

Agent's name: Havis Dawson
E-mail: queryhavis@lizadawsonassociates.com
Education: BA, Duke University
Career history: Joined Liza Dawson Associates after 20 years of editing business-trade magazines
Hobbies/Personal interests: Smoking cigars and driving cheap, clapped-out sports cars (preferably doing both simultaneously)
Categories/Subjects that you are most enthusiastic about agenting: Military memoirs, southern fiction, fantasy, science fiction, thrillers, business, and practical books, as well as spiritual books
Categories/Subjects writers shouldn't bother pitching to you: Photo books, poetry, sports
If you were not an agent, what might you be doing instead: The pleasantly sinew-taxing chores of gardening: digging holes, chopping tree roots, rolling big stones…
What's the best way for writers to solicit your interest: Query via snail mail or e-mail
Do you charge reading or management fees: No reading fee
What are some representative titles that you have sold: *Flying Through Midnight: A Pilot's Dramatic Story of His Secret Missions over Laos during the Vietnam War* by John T. Halliday (Scribner); *Law of Attraction: The Science of Attracting More of What You Want and Less of What You Don't* by Michael J. Losier (Grand Central)—coagented with L. Dawson

Agent's name: Caitlin Blasdell
E-mail: querycaitlin@lizadawsonassociates.com
Education: BA, Williams College
Career history: Senior editor at Harper and Avon; with the agency since 2002
Hobbies/Personal interests: In the dim past, before being the mother of three small boys, I remember liking cross-country skiing, perennial gardening, baking, and art history.
Categories/Subjects that you are most enthusiastic about agenting: Science fiction, fantasy (for both adults and young adults), parenting, business, thrillers, and women's fiction
Categories/Subjects writers shouldn't bother pitching to you: Horror, especially any books where small children die brutally; Westerns, poetry, cookbooks, business
If you were not an agent, what might you be doing instead: Organizing quality, flexible child care for working mothers

What's the best way for writers to solicit your interest: Query via snail mail or e-mail

Do you charge reading or management fees: No reading fee

What are some representative titles that you have sold: *Saturn's Children* by Charles Stross (Berkeley); *A Writer's Coach: An Editor's Guide to Words That Work* by Jack Hart (Pantheon)

Agent's name: Anna Olswanger

E-mail: queryanna@lizadawsonassociates.com

Education: BA, Phi Beta Kappa, Rhodes College; MA, University of Memphis; certificate in book publishing, NYU

Career history: With the agency since 2005; coordinates the Jewish Children's Book Writers' Conference every fall at the 92nd Street Y; teaches business writing at the Center for Training and Education at Johns Hopkins University and writing for physicians at Stony Brook University Hospital; author of a children's book. She recently launched www.host-a-jewish-book-author.com.

Hobbies/Personal interests: Birds, fine art, Israel

Categories/Subjects that you are most enthusiastic about agenting: Gift books for adults, young-adult fiction and nonfiction, children's illustrated books, and Judaica

Categories/Subjects writers shouldn't bother pitching to you: Horror, occult, military/war, poetry, short-story collections, government/politics, technical, textbooks

If you were not an agent, what might you be doing instead: Building tree houses, traveling, photographing and painting, writing

What's the best way for writers to solicit your interest: Query via snail mail or e-mail

Do you charge reading or management fees: No reading fee

What are some representative titles that you have sold: *The Jewish Woman's Weekly Planner 2010* (Pomegranate); *Ant and Grasshopper* (McElderry/Simon & Schuster); *Sylvie* (Random House Children's Books)

MARKSON THOMA LITERARY AGENCY

44 Greenwich Avenue, New York, NY 10011
212-243-8480 | fax: 212-691-9014
www.marksonthoma.com

Agent's name: Laney Katz Becker

E-mail: info@marksonthoma.com

Born: Toledo, Ohio

Education: BS, School of Communication, Northwestern University

Career history: My background is as a writer. I started as a copywriter at the ad agency J. Walter Thompson. Over the next two decades I also worked as a freelance journalist; my articles appeared in more than 50 magazines, including *Self*, *Health*, *Seventeen*, and *First for Women*. I'm also an author (*Dear Stranger, Dearest Friend*; *Three Times Chai*). Somewhere along the way, I decided that spending seven hours a day in my basement writing books was too solitary for me. I wanted to use my marketing, writing, and reading skills in a new and different way. The agenting world allows me to do just that—and it's never, ever solitary!

Hobbies/Personal interests: Tennis, sewing, reading, writing, theater, spending time with my family, snuggling with my dog

Categories/Subjects that you are most enthusiastic about agenting: Fiction: Anything well suited to book club discussion; anything with a fresh voice; commercial/women's/mainstream/literary; smart, psychological thrillers. Nonfiction: Narratives by experts and/or journalists about fascinating subjects that teach me something new and/or expose me to different ideas, cultures, etc.; stories about people who make a difference in the world.

Categories/Subjects writers shouldn't bother pitching to you: No romance, genre mysteries, children's, fantasy, science fiction, horror, paranormal, young adult, Westerns, poetry

If you were not an agent, what might you be doing instead: Something where I could continue to use my skills as a writer and voracious reader

What's the best way for fiction writers to solicit your interest: I only accept e-mail queries. Authors are encouraged to include the first few pages (or chapter) in the body of the e-mail.

What's the best way for nonfiction writers to solicit your interest: Query via e-mail, only. Convince me there's a need for your book, why you're uniquely qualified to write it, and that you have the platform/ability to attract a readership. Include your proposal as a single Word attachment.

Do you charge reading or management fees: No charges; AAR members

What are the most common mistakes writers make when pitching to you: Long, rambling query letters that leave me bored or confused. Being addressed as "Dear Agent," or "Dear Sir/Madam," or anything else that shows the author is plastering the (agenting) world; being pitched for things I don't represent, which tells me the writers didn't bother to do his/her homework about me.

Describe the client from hell, even if you don't have any: Defensive writers who don't want to revise, don't want to listen, and view agents simply as gatekeepers to editors. I'm also not a fan of writers who fail to say thank you. Writers who, because of my writing background, expect me to do their work for them because, "you know how to do this," are also writers I try to avoid. And finally, writers who immediately send back revisions, rather than taking time to let things sit, reread what they've written, and then—only then—once they're certain their work can't be any better, send it back to me for my review.

What's your definition of a great client: A talented writer who is also a wonderful, thoughtful person; someone who understands that revision is part of the writing process and is willing to go the distance to make their project the very best it can be.

What can a writer do to increase the odds of you becoming his or her agent: If your work is compelling, thought provoking, and well written, you'll get my attention. If your work is fresh, and I don't feel like I've seen the idea/theme a million times before, you'll stand an even better chance of winning me over. If it's nonfiction, someone with a national platform and/or a true expert in his/her field.

How and why did you become an agent: Being an agent allows me to use all the skills I've developed as a writer/reader. Plus, I get to work with lots of interesting people—on all sides of the business.

How would you describe what you do as an agent to someone (or something) from another planet: Read, edit, find talented writers, help authors improve their projects, spend time with editors getting to know their tastes/preferences, sell wonderful manuscripts, help authors understand the publishing process, negotiate contracts, come up with fresh ideas about how to promote authors' works, pitch ideas, and finally…practice conflict resolution and hold an occasional hand or two.

How do you feel about editors and publishers: I think that agents and editors are more alike than different. We've all got piles of manuscripts on our desks, and we're all trying to make the right connections. We love to read and are busy trying to shepherd projects we're passionate about through the process. We're all overworked/underpaid, but we're doing what we do because we love it.

What are your favorite books, movies, and TV shows, and why: Although it's no longer on the air, my favorite TV show of all time is *The West Wing*. My favorite movie is *Apollo 13*. My favorite book? I can't decide on just one.

In your opinion, what do editors think of you: They like the fact that I work so closely with my authors on revisions before I submit anything to them. They also like that I've already done the writing thing and bring those experiences and sensibilities to the table. They tell me they think I've got a good eye and great taste in the projects/authors I represent—and of course, I agree!

On a personal level, what do you think people like and dislike about you: I'm strong, and I don't give up. I've faced many challenges—and keep battling back; I'm a good juggler (of family/friends/work) and a "good picker," as my grandma said, when I introduced her to my future husband.

What are some representative titles that you have sold: *New York Times* and international best-selling author Will Lavender's *Obedience* (Crown/Shaye Areheart) and *Dominance* (Simon & Schuster); *The Crying Tree* by international best-selling author Naseem Rakha (Broadway Books); Barnes & Noble *Discover Great New Writers* pick, *Life's That Way* by actor Jim Beaver (Putnam/Amy Einhorn Books); *Washington Post* best seller, *The Business of Happiness* by Ted Leonsis (Eagle/Regnery); Carol Ross Joynt's memoir *Innocent Spouse*; Barnes & Noble *Discover Great New Writers* selection *Kings of Colorado* by David E. Hilton; *Cemetery Girl* by David Bell

MARTIN LITERARY MANAGEMENT

31 Lake Place North, Danbury, CT 06810
203-797-0993
www.MartinLiteraryManagement.com

Agent's name: Victoria Gould Pryor
E-mail: arcadialit@sbcglobal.net
Education: BA Pembroke College/Brown University (modern literature/history);
MA NYU (modern literature)
Career history: My first job after college was at the John Cushman Agency.
Moved to the Sterling Lord Agency and became hooked on agenting. At the Harold
Matson Agency I began representing authors and then helped found Literistic, Ltd.
Arcadia was begun in 1986.
Hobbies/Personal interests: Science, medicine, classical music and choral sing-
ing, gardening, current/foreign affairs, reading, art, woodworking
Categories/Subjects that you are most enthusiastic about agenting: Nonfiction:
science/medicine, current affairs/popular culture, history, psychology, true crime,
true business, investigative journalism, women's issues, biography, classical music,
memoir, literary fiction
Categories/Subjects writers shouldn't bother pitching to you: Children's/
young adult, science fiction/fantasy, horror, humor, chick lit, technothrillers, picture
books, memoirs about overcoming addiction or abuse
If you were not an agent, what might you be doing instead: I'd be an unhappy
and reasonably solvent doctor or lawyer, a content and struggling woodworker or
landscape architect, or if I had a much better voice, an ecstatic and prosperous
Wagnerian opera singer.
What's the best way for fiction writers to solicit your interest: For fiction: a
concise query letter with brief sample material (the novel's opening paragraphs,
pages, or chapters) and an SASE. In a query letter, I'm more drawn to a novel's
description and themes, as opposed to a detailed plot synopsis. For nonfiction: a
detailed query letter and SASE. It's fine to send a proposal with the letter, but please
take the time to analyze what comparable books are already on the market and how
your proposed book fills a niche. E-mail queries without attachments are fine. If
your subject and query letter are enticing, I'll ask you to send the file—either proposal or manuscript—as an attachment.
**Do you charge fees separate from your commission or offer nonagenting fee-
based services:** No fees or fee-based services
Representative titles: Anjana Appachana: *Listening Now* (Random House);
Philip Dine: *State of the Unions: How Labor Can Revitalize Itself, Seize the National
Debate on Values, and Help Win Elections* (McGraw-Hill); Rob Dunn, PhD: *Every
Living Thing: Man's Obsessive Quest to Catalog Life, from Nanobacteria to New
Monkeys* (Smithsonian Books); *The Wild Life of Our Bodies: Predators, Parasites,*

and *Partners That Shape Who We Are Today* (Harper); Kristin Luker, PhD: *When Sex Goes to School: Warring Views on Sex Since the Sixties* (Norton), *Salsa Dancing into the Social Sciences* (Harvard University Press); Avner Mandelman: *Talking to the Enemy* (Seven Stories Press), *Sleuth Investor* (McGraw-Hill), *The Debba* (Other Press); Diane Powell, MD: *The ESP Enigma: The Scientific Case for Psychic Phenomena* (Walker); Dr. Bernie Siegel: *Love, Medicine and Miracles, Peace, Love and Healing, How to Live Between Office Visits,* and *Prescriptions for Living* (HarperCollins), *Help Me to Heal* (Hay House); Jane Anne Staw: *Unstuck: A Supportive and Practical Guide to Working Through Writer's Block* (St. Martin's); Frank T. Vertosick, Jr., MD: *When the Air Hits Your Brain: Tales of Neurosurgery* (Norton); *Why We Hurt: The Natural History of Pain* and *The Genius Within: Discovering the Intelligence of Every Living Thing* (Harcourt); Jonathan Weiner: *Planet Earth* and *The Next One Hundred Years* (Bantam), *The Beak of the Finch* and *Time, Love, Memory* (Knopf)

How and why did you become an agent: The luck of the draw; I stumbled into the perfect (for me) field, combining a love of reading, people, and business with a smattering of law and social work thrown in on the side.

How do you feel about writers: They're the most fascinating, delightful, talented, hard-working people I know, and life would be very dull without them. Most editors are talented, dedicated, professional, valiant, and extremely overworked. They're often caught in a squeeze between trying to do right by an author and obligations to their employer's bottom line.

How would you describe what you do as an agent to someone (or something) from another planet: An agent is a combination industrial-strength reader, talent scout, business manager/career planner/matchmaker, developmental editor, midwife to creativity, and supporter of professional dreams.

What are your favorite books, movies, and TV shows, and why: Not including my own clients' work, I admire nonfiction that helps us understand and/or changes the way we look at the world past and present (*History of the Jews, Embracing Defeat, And the Band Played On, What's the Matter with Kansas, Temperament*), illuminates areas of science (*Our Kind, How We Die, Love's Executioner, The Man Who Mistook His Wife for a Hat, Anatomy of Love, The Brain That Changes Itself, Emperor of All Maladies*), introduces us to people who lived fascinating lives (*Nora*), and provides quirky and compelling narratives (*Year of Reading Proust, A Heartbreaking Work of Staggering Genius*). Novels by Melville, Faulkner, Greene, Roth, le Carré, and Turow. *The Tin Drum, Love in the Time of Cholera, Ragtime, Life of Pi, Atonement,* etc., and I'm a sucker for literate, character-driven thrillers. TV: Not a lot of time to watch, but I'm a fan of *In Treatment* and any series narrated by Simon Schama. Movies: Another year…

Describe the writer from hell: The writer from hell is not respectful of an agent's or editor's time. He/She is unable to hear or apply whatever information or advice is offered and assumes that business ground rules be set aside for his/her work. Fortunately I don't represent anyone who resembles this.

Describe the publisher and/or editor from hell: Nonresponsive (or very slow to respond); less than flexible and supportive

What do you like best about your clients and the editors and publishers you work with: At its best, my job is about being part of a team of talented, dedicated professionals. It's thrilling to see a book grow from the germ of an idea to a manuscript and then to see the magic that can result when the publisher's expertise and support are added. And it's even more thrilling to help guide an author's career.

Will our business exist as we know it in 10 years or so: The book business will keep chugging along. The trappings will be different, but the core will still be the development and spreading of ideas. Creativity and the imagination will not have changed and will still need nurturing.

THE MAX GARTENBERG LITERARY AGENCY

912 Pennsylvania Avenue, Yardley, PA 19067
215-295-9230
www.maxgartenberg.com

Agent's name: Anne G. Devlin, Dirk Devlin

Career history: The Max Gartenberg Literary Agency has long been recognized as a source for fine fiction and nonfiction. Established in 1954 in New York City, the agency has migrated to the Philadelphia area, growing by two agents in the latest move.

Categories/Subjects that you are most enthusiastic about agenting: Special interests: nonfiction, current events, education, women's issues, celebrity, health, true crime, sports, politics, history, music, biography, environment, narrative nonfiction, thrillers, science fiction, and multicultural nonfiction

Categories/Subjects writers shouldn't bother pitching to you: Poetry, New Age, fantasy

What's the best way for writers to solicit your interest: Writers desirous of having their work handled by this agency should first send a one- or two-page query letter. Simply put, the letter should describe the material being offered as well as relevant background information about the writer and include an SASE for a reply. If the material is of interest, an agent may request a sample or the entire manuscript. Unsolicited material will be returned unread if accompanied by sufficient postage for its return. E-mail queries are also accepted, but hard copies are preferred.

Do you charge reading or management fees: No

What categories do you represent, by percentages: Fiction: 15 percent, nonfiction: 85 percent

What are the most common mistakes writers make when pitching to you: Rather than describing his material and summarizing his qualifications, the writer's query letter asks for information about the agency, information readily available in such directories as *Jeff Herman's Guide* and *Literary Market Place* or on the Web. This tells that the writer is too lazy to do his homework and is probably a poor researcher, to boot.

Describe the client from hell, even if you don't have any: Client who demands unceasing attention and is never satisfied with the deal the agent brings him (he always has friends whose agent got twice as much), who delivers his manuscript late and in such disrepair that it is unacceptable at first glance. And blames the agent for his mess. This is not an imaginary character.

How would you describe the perfect client: A writing professional who can be counted on to produce a well-made, literate, enlightening, and enjoyable book with a minimum of Sturm and Drang. Fortunately, this is not an imaginary character, either.

What can a writer do to increase the odds of you becoming his or her agent: Write a brilliant query letter and, when asked, follow it up with a manuscript or proposal that is even better. Remember that the waiting is the hardest part.

What are some representative titles that you have sold: *Charles Addams: A Cartoonist's Life* (Random House); *Ogallala Blue* (W. W. Norton); *Encyclopedia of Pollution* and *Encyclopedia of Earthquakes and Volcanoes* (Facts On File); *Slaughter on North LaSalle* (Berkley Books); *Jack and Lem* (DaCapo Press); *Passing Gas and Other Towns along the American Highway* (Ten Speed Press); *What Patients Taught Me* and *Country Hospital* (Sasquatch Books); *Winning the Disability Challenge* (New Horizon Press); *Diabetes and You* (Rowman and Littlefield)

MENDEL MEDIA GROUP, LLC

115 West 30th Street, Suite 800, New York, NY 10001
646-239-9896 | fax: 212-695-4717
www.mendelmedia.com

Agent's name: Scott Mendel, managing partner
E-mail: scott@mendelmedia.com
Born: New York
Education: AB, Bowdoin College (Brunswick, Maine); MA, University of Chicago; PhD (ABD), University of Chicago
Career history: With a background in academia, Scott Mendel has worked in publishing since the early 1990s, first as a magazine editor and freelance technical writer and then as an associate and, ultimately, the vice president and director of the late Jane Jordan Browne's Chicago-based literary agency. In November 2002, he opened the Mendel Media Group in New York. Scott holds a bachelor's degree, summa cum laude, from Bowdoin College in Brunswick, Maine. He earned a master's degree in English language and literature from the University of Chicago and is completing his PhD at that institution, with a doctoral dissertation on American Yiddish literature and the meaning of the category "American literature." Scott

has taught literature, English, and Yiddish at a number of institutions, including the Choate-Rosemary Hall Preparatory School in Connecticut, the Hyde Park Cluster of Theological Seminaries in Chicago, Bowdoin College, the University of Chicago, and the University of Illinois at Chicago, where he most recently held an appointment as lecturer in Jewish studies. He wrote the book *A Prosecutor's Guide to Hate Crime*, which was published through a grant from the US Department of Justice and has been in print in new editions for several years. He has been the managing editor of a monthly and quarterly health care magazine, *Positively Aware*, and editor of the Maine literary journal, *The Quill*, which began publishing in 1897. Scott has written a produced play, several works of fiction, and many book columns, news articles, and opinion pieces. He is a member of the Association of Author Representatives, the Author's Guild, the Mystery Writers of America, the Romance Writers of America, the Society of Children's Book Writers and Illustrators, the Modern Language Association, and the American Association of University Professors.

Categories/Subjects that you are most enthusiastic about agenting: History, narrative nonfiction, current affairs, biography, politics, popular culture; smart literary and commercial fiction

If you were not an agent, what might you be doing instead: I was a college instructor for a number of years before becoming an agent. I'd still be doing that.

What's the best way for writers to solicit your interest: Please follow the procedure below. If we want to read more, we'll ask for it by e-mail or phone. If you would like a response, in the event we can't take on your project or don't want to read more, you should include a preaddressed return mailer with sufficient return postage already affixed for the return of your materials—or just include a standard self-addressed stamped envelope, in which case we'll respond with a note but discard the submitted materials. Please do not send inquiries by e-mail or fax. Fiction queries: If you have a novel you would like to submit, please send the first 20 pages and a synopsis by regular post to the address above, along with a detailed letter about your publication history and the history of the project, if it has been submitted previously to publishers or other agents. Nonfiction queries: If you have a completed a nonfiction book proposal and sample chapters, you should mail those by regular post to the address above, along with a detailed letter about your publication history and the history of the project, if it has been submitted previously to publishers or other agents.

Do you charge reading or management fees: No

What categories do you represent, by percentages: My literary agency's clientele includes both fiction writers and nonfiction writers, the latter group comprised mainly of professional journalists and very senior academics writing for the broadest possible trade readership and author–experts writing prescriptive books. On the nonfiction side, I am usually interested in compelling works on history, current events, Jewish topics, personal finance and economics, show business, health, mass culture, sports, politics, science, and biography that I believe will find both a wide readership and critical admiration. I represent a number of people who work in the media, generally in the news business.

What are the most common mistakes writers make when pitching to you: Instead of going to www.mendelmedia.com/FAQ, they call to ask questions about how to send a query. A surprising number of aspiring writers pitch projects that have been unsuccessfully shopped to numerous houses already, so I always ask if a project has already been submitted to and rejected by publishers. Also, we are pitched projects every day by authors who have work we can't help them with: The agency does not represent children's picture books, cozy mystery novels, poetry, drama, screenplays, or any prescriptive nonfiction projects for which the author does not have established professional expertise and/or media credentials.

How would you describe the perfect client: There are as many "dream" clients as there are writers, I think. I like working for clients who are focused on practical career-related matters. Nothing is less impressive to me than a lack of clear focus on goals and expectations, so my dream clients are clear with me and with themselves about what they want to accomplish. I want to be challenged by my clients' work, by their writing, and not by the drama of everyday life.

What are some representative titles that you have sold: First-time novelist Wade Rubenstein, *Gullboy* (Counterpoint Press/Perseus); comedian/screenwriter/novelist Adam Felber, *Schrödinger's Ball* (Villard/Random House); World Trade Center and Jewish Museum Berlin master architect Daniel Libeskind, *Breaking Ground: Adventures in Life and Architecture* (Riverhead/Penguin and numerous publishers around the world); Hoover Institution Senior Fellow and Stanford University professor Larry Diamond, *Squandered Victory: The Story of the Bungled US Attempt to Build Democracy in Iraq* (Times Books/Henry Holt) and *Universal Democracy* (Times Books/Henry Holt); University of Chicago Professor Robert A. Pape, *Dying to Win: The Strategic Logic of Suicide Terrorism* (Random House); Dovid Katz, PhD, *Words on Fire: The Unfinished Story of Yiddish* (Basic Books); Behzad Yaghmaian, PhD, *Embracing the Infidel: Stories of Muslim Migrants on the Journey West* (Delacorte/Bantam Dell); National Public Radio national news anchor Nora Raum, *Surviving Personal Bankruptcy* (Gotham/Penguin); Annie Sprinkle, PhD, *Dr. Sprinkle's Spectacular Sex: Make Over Your Love Life with One of the World's Great Experts on Sex* (Tarcher/Penguin; Goldmann/Random House); Active Parenting founder Michael Popkin, PhD, *Parenting the Spirited Child* (Touchstone Fireside/Simon & Schuster); Anne-Marie Cusac, the George Polk and Project Censored Award-winning longtime investigative journalist at *The Progressive* magazine, *Cruel and Unusual: Punishment in America* (Yale University Press); June Skinner Sawyers, *The Beatles: Alone and Together* (Penguin); Best-selling celebrity biographer Mark Bego, *Piano Man: The Life and Times of Billy Joel* (Chamberlain Bros./Penguin); Lisa Rogak, *The Man behind the DaVinci Code: An Unauthorized Biography of Dan Brown* (Andrews McMeel in the United States, and many other publishers around the world); *Dr. Robert Atkins: The True Story of the Man behind the War on Carbohydrates* (Chamberlain Bros./Penguin; UK, Robson Books; Spanish, Random

House Mondadori Mexico); and *No Happy Endings: The Life of Shel Silverstein* (St. Martin's Press); Dave DeWitt, the best-selling cookbook author, *The Spicy Food Lover's Bible* (Stewart, Tabori & Chang); Ray "Dr. BBQ" Lampe, *Dr. BBQ's Big Time Barbeque: Recipes, Secrets, and Tall Tales of a BBQ Champion* (St. Martin's Press); long-time *Kiplinger's Personal Finance* real-estate writer Elizabeth Razzi, *The Fearless Home Buyer* and *The Fearless Home Seller* (Stewart, Tabori & Chang); novelty and gift book packager Ray Strobel of Strobooks, LLC, *The Panda Principles: A Black Eye Isn't the End of the World* (Andrews McMeel); Paulette Wolf and Jodi Wolf, proprietors of the top-shelf event planning firm Paulette Wolf Events and Entertainment (PWE-E), *Event Planning Made Easy: 7 Simple Steps to Making Your Business or Private Event a Huge Success* (McGraw-Hill); Joanne Jacobs, longtime education writer at the *San Jose Mercury News, Our School* (Palgrave Macmillan)

MEREDITH BERNSTEIN LITERARY AGENCY

2095 Broadway, Suite 505, New York, NY 10023
212-799-1007 | fax: 212-799-1145
www.meredithbernsteinliteraryagency.com

Agent's name: Meredith Bernstein
E-mail: Mgoodbern@aol.com
Born: Hartford, Connecticut
Education: BA, University of Rochester
Career history: Story editor to film producers; literary agent
Hobbies/Personal interests: Reading, of course; travel; film; art; theater; ballet; fashion; contemporary art/craft; jewelry; meeting new people
Categories/Subjects that you are most enthusiastic about agenting: Young adult; almost anything wherein I can learn something new
Categories/Subjects writers shouldn't bother pitching to you: Military history
If you were not an agent, what might you be doing instead: Curating a craft museum; owning a store like Julie on Madison Avenue

MEWS BOOKS, LTD.

20 Bluewater Hill, Westport, CT 06880
203 227-1836 | fax: 203-227-1144

Agent's name: Sidney B. Kramer
E-mail: rnewsbooks@aol.com
Education: New York University, Brooklyn Law School; St. Lawrence University, JD
Career history: One of three founders of Bantam Books: senior vice president

(22 years), founder and managing director of Bantam's London subsidiary, Corgi Books; president, New American Library (formerly Penguin Books); consultant and manager, Cassell and Collier MacMillan, London; president and owner of Remarkable Book Shop, Westport, CT; president of Mews Books, Ltd., literary agents and attorney (NY and CT Bar specializing in literary matters)

Categories/Subjects that you are most enthusiastic about agenting: Children's books, all ages, that are creative, charming, [with] self-sufficient prose suited to a stated age group. Adult books: medical and scientific nonfiction, technical and for the layman; cookery; parenting; reference works; nonfiction all subjects. Fiction: All categories but must be outstanding in their genre for plot and writing.

Categories/Subjects writers shouldn't bother pitching to you: All subjects badly written

What's the best way for writers to solicit your interest: Must have an outline of the work in a page or two in enough detail (but not too much) so that an editor can pick up the story at any point in the manuscript. No cliffhangers like "The readers will be delighted with the new turn of events, everything turns out well." Don't ask us for editorial advice. We want professional work even from first timers. Give your background, accreditation, and market platform in a separate statement. Send all material by snail mail, not e-mail. Do not send manuscript unless requested. SASE. Queries should be less than a page. We want to know if the work has been submitted elsewhere and with what results. We ask for an exclusive while reading so that we don't spin our wheels and duplicate efforts by others (occasional exceptions for established authors). Tell us what else is out there that's comparable. Tell us if you have been published. Pending contracts will be reviewed and negotiated by an attorney.

Do you charge reading or management fees: No reading fees. If we accept your work we do charge for duplication and some direct office overhead incurred in processing, usually less than $100.

What categories do you represent, by percentages: Fiction: 20 percent, children's: 40 percent, nonfiction: 20 percent, other: 20 percent

What are the most common mistakes writers make when pitching to you: Unfocused presentations; misspellings, poor grammar in letter. Presentation should be capable of forwarding to an editor.

Describe the client from hell, even if you don't have any: We have none. A disruptive client is invited elsewhere.

How would you describe the perfect client: All our clients are patient and understanding of the publishing process and understand that editors take their time.

How and why did you become an agent: A perfect fit for a person with my background; a former publisher and an experienced attorney

How do you feel about editors and publishers: Nice people who are overwhelmed by the flood of unpublishable material and the changing marketplace

What are some representative titles that you have sold: Richard Scarry's children's books (some bilingual); *Susan Love's Breast Book*; *Hotter than Hell* and other cookery titles, Jane Butel; *Overcoming Impotence*, Dr. J. Stephen Jones; Tom Wolsky technical media computer books; math series, Debra Ross; *When Bad Grammar Happens to Good People*, Ann Batko; Dr. Gilbert Rose's psychiatry books; Marsha Temlock's *Your Child's Divorce: What to Expect—What You Can Do*; Steve Elman and Alan Tolz's *Burning Up the Air*; Bill Littlefield's *Prospect*, novel and film option

MICHAEL SNELL LITERARY AGENCY

PO Box 1206, Truro, MA 02666
508-349-3718
michaelsnellagency.com

Agent's name: Michael Snell
Born: August 14, 1965, Denver, Colorado
Education: BA, Phi Beta Kappa, DePauw University
Career history: Thirteen years as editor and executive editor for Wadsworth Publishing Company and Addison-Wesley (science, economics, English, computer science, business college textbooks)
Hobbies/Personal interests: Golf, tennis, landscaping, shell fishing
Categories/Subjects that you are most enthusiastic about agenting: Any subject that lends itself to practical self-help and how-to presentation, especially business, management, leadership, entrepreneurship; also health, fitness, psychology, relationships, parenting, pets, women's issues; literary fiction; science fiction; New Age; memoirs; children's books
If you were not an agent, what might you be doing instead: Teaching
What's the best way for writers to solicit your interest: Write an enticing one-page query letter (with SASE), pitching your book/subject and establishing your credentials in the area. We'll tell you what we want to review (proposal, etc.).
Do you charge reading or management fees: No, though we do at times offer collaborative developmental and rewriting services, for which we charge additional commission points. We also represent a number of professional editors, rewriters, ghostwriters, and developmental editors who can help content specialists bring their books to market.
What categories do you represent, by percentages: Adult nonfiction: 95 percent, literary fiction: 5 percent
What are the most common mistakes writers make when pitching to you: A boring or lengthy query that does not get to the point quickly, identifying the subject and the author's credentials in a compelling way. Many new authors oversell their book, when their query letter should achieve one goal: to prompt the agent to ask to see a proposal or material. Also, too many new authors let their egos get in their way, selling too hard with too little humility. Since we only consider new clients on an exclusive basis, authors who have embarked on a fishing expedition, contacting and submitting material to many agents, put us off. Authors forget they're looking

for a marriage partner, not a plumber or electrician. Tiny envelopes with insufficient postage create SASEs that will not accommodate feedback or our brochure on "How to write a book proposal" or our flyer offering a "Model proposal."

Describe the client from hell, even if you don't have any: Editors and agents avoid "high maintenance" authors, those who require constant communication, hand-holding, and reassurance. While agents do form strong bonds with their clients, they run a business that requires efficient, professional, respectful relationships. The worst clients can't see around their own egos: Because they know everything about one thing (their subject), they think they know everything about everything. Poor students make poor clients; bad listeners make bad clients; impatient people who want the publishing process to move quickly make agents' and editors' lives miserable. This is a slow way to make a fast buck: People in a hurry make too many mistakes.

How would you describe the perfect client: The ideal client possesses all the qualities of a good friend and business partner: knowledgeable, patient, humble, respectful, prompt, reliable, professional, perseverant, and funny. Nothing smoothes over the rough patches better than a sense of humor. The agent–author relationship is unique. Because the work involves a certain amount of "art," it engages strong emotions. The best clients don't let their passion for their work undermine a respectful and caring professional relationship with the people who will help them make their dreams come true: their agent and their editor. The quality of the relationship depends on trust: The ideal client trusts her agent's professionalism and listens carefully to guidance and advice. This becomes so crucial to the author–publisher relationship later on: The more an author develops trust with her agent, the better for everyone—not to mention the book's sales—later on.

How and why did you become an agent: Having learned the art of book development as an editor for a book publisher and having helped create dozens of best sellers, I decided I'd rather make 15 percent commission on sales than keep taking home the measly salary publishers pay. I also got weary of the fact that editors were becoming less and less involved in the actual task of development (helping writers turn good ideas into great books). As an agent you can work closely with authors on their manuscripts, when necessary, and you can choose the people and projects that most attract you. I try to honor the same principles I coach my clients to practice: patience, perseverance, and professionalism. To those I'd add passion. I love books, have spent a lifetime overseeing their publication and can think of no greater joy than opening that brand-new baby book and smelling the ink on its pages.

What can a writer do to increase the odds of you becoming his or her agent: Read this listing carefully and approach us with what you've learned about us in mind. When communicating with us, remember Pascal's apology: "I would have made it shorter, if I'd had the time." Time is priceless: don't waste it on long-winded queries and constant phone calls demanding a faster response. By the same token, take your time, pay attention to details when preparing submissions, and slow down. Nothing can kill an emerging relationship faster than hastily assembled material that arrives in our office incomplete and poorly organized. Did I mention patience?

Did I mention approaching us like a good student? You can also request, with SASE, our brochure "How to write a book proposal"; you can read Michael Snell's book *From Book Idea to Best Seller*. And you can ask for information on how to buy a "Model proposal."

How would you describe what you do as an agent to someone (or something) from another planet: We develop book ideas into best sellers.

How do you feel about editors and publishers: We love them. They pay our bills and help pay college tuition for our clients' children.

What do you think the future holds for writers, publishers, and agents: The market for good ideas, valuable information, and graceful communication will keep growing, no matter the form in which it gets packaged. Every 10 years, experts predict the death of the book, and every 10 years the market has expanded.

What are your favorite books, movies, and TV shows, and why: *The Sopranos, Rescue Me, 24, Capote, Crash,* and anything written by David James Duncan or David Foster Wallace

On a personal level, what do you think people like and dislike about you: They like our honesty; they dislike our blunt criticism. They like our humor; they dislike our bad jokes. They like the money we make for them; they dislike the fact that we don't make them more.

What are some representative titles that you have sold: *How Did That Happen?: Holding People Accountable the Positive, Principled Way* by Roger Connors and Tom Smith (Viking/Portfolio); *Recovering the Lost River: Rewilding Salmon, Recivilizing Humans, Removing Dams* by Steve Hawley (Beacon Press); *You, Him, and Her: Coping with Infidelity in Your Marriage* by Dr. Paul Coleman (Adams Media); *Strategic Customer Service* by John Goodman (AMACOM Books); *The Complete Idiot's Guide to the Financial Crisis* by Tom Gorman (Alpha Books); *Gen Y on Board: Managing the New Millennials* by Nicole Lipkin (Career Press); *The Inside Scoop on Business Schools* by David Petersam (Jist Publications); *Introduction to Business Ethics* by Martin Sandby (Prentice-Hall)

Agent's name: Patricia Snell
E-mail: snell.patricia@gmail.com
Born: 1951, Boston, Massachusetts
Education: FIT and Pratt Institute, New York
Career history: Design offices in New York City's garment district and in Manhattan art galleries and museums; 12 years as partner in the Michael Snell Literary Agency
Hobbies/Personal interests: Gardening; landscaping; cooking; tennis; anything involving water (I'm a Pisces): swimming, surfing, fishing, shell fishing; movies, and all areas of design
Categories/Subjects that you are most enthusiastic about agenting: I have broad interests, from the practical to the sublime. Subjects that have the power to solve problems, enhance living, or transform lives gain my attention.

If you were not an agent, what might you be doing instead: Any number of things in design and the visual arts

What's the best way for writers to solicit your interest: Write a brief, one-page query letter. Get to the point right away. Always include sufficient SASE.

Do you charge reading or management fees: No, though we do at times offer collaborative developmental and rewriting services, for which we charge additional commission. But I may negotiate a higher commission on projects on which I agree to collaborate as developmental editor.

What categories do you represent, by percentages: Adult nonfiction: 100 percent, mostly practical how-to and self-help

What are the most common mistakes writers make when pitching to you: Wasting my time with long, boring self-congratulatory letters. Failure to provide the proper return postage. I refuse to waste my time (and money) on those who cannot follow simple, clear directions.

Describe the client from hell, even if you don't have any: Wasting my time, failing to follow directions, being a poor student in the long process of getting published, trying to rush what is an essentially slow process, failing to value my contribution or, worst of all, acting rudely (thankfully a rare occurrence)

MIRIAM ALTSHULER LITERARY AGENCY

53 Old Post Road North, Red Hook, NY 12571
845-758-9408 | fax: 845-758-3118
www.miriamaltshulerliteraryagency.com

Agent name: Miriam Altshuler
E-mail: miriam@maliterary.com
Born: New York, New York
Education: Middlebury College
Career history: Agent for 12 years at Russell & Volkening, Inc.; started my own agency in 1994
Hobbies/Personal interests: Reading, skiing, horseback riding, the outdoors, my children
Categories/Subjects that you are most enthusiastic about agenting: Literary/commercial fiction and nonfiction, narrative nonfiction, memoirs, young-adult novels. See my website: www.miriamaltshulerliteraryagency.com for further guidelines.
Categories/Subjects writers shouldn't bother pitching to you: Genre fiction, how-to, romance. See my website: www.miriamaltshulerliteraryagency.com, for further guidelines.
Do you charge reading or management fees: No reading fees
How and why did you become an agent: I love reading books and love working with people.

NATASHA KERN LITERARY AGENCY

PO Box 1069, White Salmon, WA 98672
www.natashakern.com

Agent's name: Natasha Kern

E-mails: queries@natashakern.com

Education: University of North Carolina, Chapel Hill; Columbia University, New York; New York University

Career history: Publicist and editor for New York publishers and acquisitions editor for New York agents prior to founding her own agency in 1986, Natasha Kern has personally sold over 700 books and has worked on close to 1,000 during her career in publishing.

Hobbies/Personal interests: Gardening, travel, animals and birds, yoga, performing arts, history, geology, and, of course, family and reading

Categories/Subjects that you are most enthusiastic about agenting: Fiction: I am actively looking for big historical novels; inspirational fiction; romantic suspense; romantic comedies; mainstream women's fiction; young-adult fiction. Nonfiction: Narrative nonfiction, health, science, women's issues, parenting, spirituality, self-help, social issues—especially topics that inspire positive thought, action, or change, and books by authorities in their field.

Categories/Subjects writers shouldn't bother pitching to you: Fiction: Horror and fantasy, short stories, children's. Nonfiction: True crime, sports, cookbooks, poetry, gift books, coffee-table books, computers, technical, scholarly or reference books, stage plays, scripts, or screenplays

If you were not an agent, what might you be doing instead: I have been an agent for 20 years because I love doing it. This is a calling for me, and I can't imagine doing anything else. I love my clients. I love books. I like assisting writers to earn a living at what they do best.

What's the best way for writers to solicit your interest: See submission instructions on the website, www.natashakern.com. Send all queries to queries@natashakern.com. We do not accept queries by phone or snail mail. We will contact you within three weeks of receipt of your query if we are interested. Please include your phone number and e-mail address.

Do you charge reading fees or management fees: No

Percentage of representation by category: Fiction: 65 percent, nonfiction: 35 percent

Approximate number of titles sold during the past year: 43 titles

Approximately what percentage of all received submissions do you reject: 99 percent of unsolicited; 85 percent solicited partials, proposals, and manuscripts; and 30 percent of referrals. From 6,000 queries every year, approximately 10 writers are accepted for representation. Write a good query! We are selective, but we do want to find successful writers of the future and have launched the careers of many writers.

What are some of the most common mistakes writers make when pitching to you: Not researching what we represent!; not describing the material or project adequately; not knowing the standards and conventions of the genres we represent; querying by fax, phone, or snail mail; sending unrequested material; exaggerated claims or credentials; comparing themselves favorably to current best-selling authors; lack of professionalism; not knowing the craft of writing; not having an original concept; omitting the ending from a synopsis; not following directions. The majority of queries are rejected because the writer has simply not taken the time to learn, study, and practice to produce something saleable—basically the equivalent of taking a week of music lessons and hoping to play Carnegie Hall.

How would you describe your client from hell: I do not have any clients like this. All of my clients are people I respect and admire as individuals as well as writers. They are committed to their own success and know that I am committed to helping them to achieve it. They understand the complex tasks involved in agenting, including sales, negotiations, editorial, arbitration, foreign and film rights, etc., and we work as a team to ensure the best outcome for their work. Usually problem clients who are difficult to work with are identified before a contract is signed.

How would you describe the perfect client: One who participates in a mutually respectful business relationship, is clear about needs and goals, and communicates about career planning. If we know what you need and want, we can help you to achieve it. A dream client has a gift for language and storytelling, a commitment to a writing career, a desire to learn and grow, and a passion for excellence. This client understands that many people have to work together for a book to succeed and that everything in publishing takes far longer than one imagines. Trust and communication are truly essential. How wonderful that all of my clients are dream clients.

How and why did you become an agent: When I left New York, I knew that I wanted to stay in publishing. However, editorial work was not sufficiently satisfying by itself. I knew I could acquire and develop saleable properties and that my background gave me expertise in sales and running a company. I wanted to work with people long term and not just on a single project or phase of one. Plus, I had an entrepreneurial temperament and experience negotiating big money deals from raising venture capital for high-tech firms. When I developed literary projects for other agents that did not sell, I knew I could sell them myself, so I did. I've never regretted that decision. Agenting combined my love of books, my affinity for deal making, and my preference for trusting my own intuition. I sold 28 books the first year the agency was in business and have sold over 900 personally since then.

What can writers do to increase the odds that they will get you to be their agent: A client who is willing to listen, learn, and work hard to succeed. If there are writing problems I will get this author help to produce a saleable proposal. I have worked with some writers six months or more before their novel or proposal was in top-notch shape to sell it. I am looking for talent and commitment, and if I feel it is a good match, I make a commitment to that writer in return. In nonfiction, the author's passionate belief in the subject as well as expertise and a defined audience are appealing. A strong platform is a must today. In fiction, a wonderful, fresh authorial voice, a page-turning plot that really does keep me up at night, well-structured chapters and imaginative prose, with everything tied to the premise. A writer who can pull me into another point of view and another world I don't want to leave. In fiction, the writing is everything. We are glad to encourage promising writers who still need to master some aspects of craft if they are willing to work with me or an editor.

How would you describe what you do as an agent to someone (or something) from another planet: Unpublished writers often think an agent's job is only sales and negotiations. Of course, every writer wants a sale and to see the book in print. However, an agent's job goes far beyond just deal making because building a career and helping a writer to earn a living from writing requires a long-term strategy and often a complex chess game of moving from one house or genre to another. I am often involved in a book's development from the initial concept through preparation of a proposal, editorial advice, selection of appropriate editors, submissions, negotiations, and contract changes to final signature. Then troubleshooting publication problems begins—from editorial issues to cover problems, title changes, reviewing jacket blurbs, and the myriad things that arise in the course of publication; troubleshooting marketing problems including reviewing publicity planning, press kits and releases, working on cross-promotions and product placement, distribution concerns, suggestions about creating a website, and working with private publicists. Since I represent writers who, for the most part, want a writing career and not just a one-book deal after the first book has been turned in, work begins on a follow-up, fulfilling option clauses (and making sure they do not restrict an author's ability to write whatever she wishes), long-term career planning and strategies, and often multibook deals. Of course, handling an author's financial affairs is paramount, including auditing royalty statements, collecting unpaid monies, providing tax documents like 1099s and foreign tax forms, etc. In addition, I handle legal issues of many kinds from reversion of rights to their allocation; subsidiary sales including foreign rights, film rights, audio, video, and other rights; handling career crises or conflicts with publishers; assisting writers with career transitions or when problems arise like their book being "orphaned"; providing expertise at writers' conferences; educating clients about the publishing industry and its vicissitudes; keeping in touch with editors and their acquisitions interest or concerns about clients; attending industry events like Book Expo; consulting with writing groups—I am currently on the Board of the Faith, Hope, and Love Chapter of the Romance Writers of America (RWA); meeting personally with clients, editors, and others in the industry; traveling to New York and Hollywood several times each year; answering hundreds of e-mails each week; reviewing queries and partials; talking on the phone a lot; reading the work of clients and prospective clients and keeping up with trends; working with office staff and upgrading corporate procedures and technical support; supervising bookkeeper and accountant; articles and interviews for trade publications, etc. It's a long day.

How do you feel about editors and publishers: Editors are indispensable, and every writer should be blessed with a good one. It is one of my primary goals to match each client with the editor who is perfect for him or her. I often succeed, and the result is magical, like all great collaborations: Fred Astaire and Ginger Rogers; Maxwell Perkins and Thomas Wolfe; Gilbert and Sullivan. Writers are more successful in great partnerships. No one can be objective about their own work or realistically expect to recognize all flaws. Most artistic endeavors require a coach—a voice coach, a dance teacher, a master painter. Writing is no exception. There are gifted editors, both private editors and those at publishing houses, who can turn a strong manuscript into a great one, a gifted author into a best-selling one. I want all my clients to have that opportunity. Publishers are going to have some interesting times ahead in the volatile new world of publishing, with challenges at every turn. Developing new talent and valuing the writers who are creating their long-term success would seem to be prerequisites for meeting these challenges. We keep up with changes in the industry like e-books and POD [print on demand] and also work with new emerging presses and imprints as well as major publishers. We can help authors to understand the publisher's point of view (and vice versa) in all situations so a win–win deal will result.

On a personal level, what do you think people like and dislike about you: I think I am liked for my authenticity and honesty, even when I have to tell a writer her material needs more work or a concept isn't saleable. It is entirely possible I may be disliked for my bluntness as well. However, I feel it is a disservice to writers to fail to be clear with them. My passion for the books I represent and the fact that I deeply care about my clients and their success is an asset as well as my industry knowledge and professionalism. My clients appreciate it that I go the extra mile for them to ensure their success. I hate to give up on anything I undertake, so I usually do succeed in achieving my goals and can help my clients to do the same. Even though I have strong opinions, I am also interested in learning new things from the experts—one of the joys of my job.

You're welcome to share your thoughts and sentiments about the business of writing and publishing: Believe in yourself and your own gifts. Keep in mind that the challenge for every writer is twofold—to have something to say and to have the mastery of the craft to say it well. Study and practice plotting, pacing, point of view, etc., so you can express exactly what you want to say. Nothing is more important than being true to your own artistic vision and understanding the requirements of the medium you have chosen to express it, whether you are writing a symphony, a haiku, or a novel. Keep in mind that in imitating other writers you can only be second rate at being them. Expressing your own inner thoughts, feelings, and stories in your own way is the only path to real success. Your world, your history, your experiences, your insights cannot be duplicated by anyone else. Bring us in to share your vision, your imagination. No one can do it better than you can because the truth of your uniqueness is what you are here to offer everyone else. It is what moves us and takes us outside of our own lives when we read what you have written.

What are some representative titles that you have sold: *The Inheritance*, Tamera Alexander (Thomas Nelson); *The Winds of Sonoma*, Niki Arana (Baker); *The Secret Life of God*, David Aaron (Shambhala); *One Bite Stand*, Nina Bangs (Leisure); *Adam's Tongue*, Derek Bickerton (Farrar, Straus); *Up Pops the Devil*, Angela Benson (HarperCollins); *Critical Care*, Candace Calvert (Tyndale House); *Unlawful Contact*, Pamela Clare (Berkley); *Hope Is the Thing with Feathers*, Christopher Cokinos (Tarcher); *Cutting Loose*, Nadine Dajani (Tor); *Body by Night*, Zuri Day (Kensington); *Girlwood*, Claire Dean (Houghton Mifflin); *Ruby's Slippers*, Leanna Ellis (B&H); *Whiskey Gulf*, Clyde Ford (Vanguard); *The Perfect Life*, Robing Lee Hatcher (Thomas Nelson); *The Ecological Garden*, Toby Hemenway (Chelsea Green); *How to Tame a Modern Rogue*, Diana Holquist (Hachette); *The Quiet Game*, Greg Iles (Putnam-Penguin); *Salty Like Blood*, Harry Kraus (Howard S&S); *Scent of Sake*, Joyce Lebra (Morrow); *A Passion Redeemed*, Julie Lessman (Revell); *A Texan's Honor*, Harold Lowry (Leisure); *A Preacher's Passion*, Lutishia Lovely (Dafina); *The Prince of Pleasure*, Connie Mason (Leisure); *A Reason to Believe*, Maureen McCade (Berkley); *Skull Mantra*, Eliot Pattison (St. Martin's); *Bone Rattler*, Eliot Pattison (Counterpoint); *Sucker for Love*, Kimberly Raye (Ballantine); *Gift from the Sea*, Anna Schmidt (Steeple Hill); *The Lady and Libertine*, Bonnie Vanak (Leisure); *The Secret Lives of the Sushi Club*, Christy Yorke (Berkley)

NELSON LITERARY AGENCY, LLC

1732 Wazee Street, Suite 207, Denver, CO 80202
www.nelsonagency.com

Agent's name: Kristin Nelson
E-mail: query@nelsonagency.com
Education: BA University of Missouri—Columbia; MA Purdue University
Career history: The Nelson Agency was established in 2002. Before that, founding literary agent Kristin Nelson worked for Jody Rein Books. She went on her own to represent all types of fiction—including genre fiction like SF&F and romance.

Categories/Subjects that you are most enthusiastic about agenting: The Nelson Literary Agency represents primarily fiction works in the genres of romance (all subgenres except category and inspirational), science fiction, fantasy, young adult, middle-grade, women's fiction, chick lit (including mysteries), commercial, and literary fiction. We also represent some memoir. We are looking for a unique concept and outstanding writing.

Categories/Subjects writers shouldn't bother pitching to you: We don't represent thrillers, nonfiction (except memoir), gift books, cookbooks, picture books, or mysteries (except chick lit).

What's the best way for fiction writers to solicit your interest: We do not accept any queries by snail mail, phone, or in person. We are a paper-free office.

Please visit our website first and then send us an e-mail query letter. If we are interested in your material, we'll e-mail detailed instructions on how to upload your sample pages or proposal to our secure electronic submissions database. We do not accept any queries or materials by snail mail. All materials sent by snail mail will be returned unread.

What's the best way for nonfiction writers to solicit your interest: See above.

Do you charge reading or management fees: No. Any reimbursed expenses are after a work has sold and [are] deducted from a publisher payment.

What are the most common mistakes writers make when pitching to you: Mistakes: (1) Not nailing the pitch blurb in the query letter (or not having a clear story hook); (2) Describing a work as every genre under the sun. What that signals is that you don't have an understanding of your work's place in the market; (3) Antagonistic or whining queries

Describe the client from hell, even if you don't have any: We've been lucky. We truly enjoy all our clients. However, a client from hell would be one who is not Internet or tech savvy (and refuses to work at becoming so).

What's your definition of a great client: Someone who is serious about the business of writing and publishing, who is tech-savvy and is willing to go the distance to promote his or her work. And, he or she writes like a dream and is fast—at least a book a year.

What can a writer do to increase the odds of you becoming his or her agent: Write a terrific novel.

How would you describe what you do as an agent to someone (or something) from another planet: We represent and advocate for authors by placing their materials in front of publishers, negotiating the deal (and watching out for the author's interests), trouble-shooting during the publishing process, and then guiding that author's career.

What are your favorite books, movies, and TV shows, and why: A&E's *Pride and Prejudice*, *Almost Famous*, *Casablanca*, *Clueless*, *Age of Innocence*, *Enchanted April*, *Undercover Brother*, *Star Wars*, *Lord of the Rings*, any Doris Day movie

In your opinion, what do editors think of you: Nice but one tough negotiator

What are some representative titles that you have sold: *Hotel on the Corner of Bitter and Sweet* by Jamie Ford (Ballantine); *Demon's Lexicon* by Sarah Rees Brennan (Simon & Schuster); *Soulless* by Gail Carriger (Orbit); *The Shifter* by Janice Hardy (HarperCollins); *I'd Tell You I Love You But Then I'd Have to Kill You* and *Cross My Heart and Hope to Spy* by Ally Carter (Hyperion Books for Children); *Enchanted, Inc.: Once upon Stilettos* and *Damsel under Stress* by Shanna Swendson (Ballantine); *Code of Love* and *The Winter Prince* by Cheryl Sawyer (New American Library); *Finders Keepers*, *Gabriel's Ghost*, *An Accidental Goddess*, *Games of Command* by Linnea Sinclair (Bantam Spectra); *No Place Safe* by Kim Reid (Kensington); *Prime Time* by Hank Phillippi Ryan (Harlequin); *Magic Lost, Trouble Found* by Lisa Shearin (Ace, Berkley); *Rumble on the Bayou* by Jana Deleon

NORTHERN LIGHTS LITERARY SERVICES, LLC

11248 North Boyer Avenue, Sandpoint, ID 83864
888-558-4354
www.northernlightsls.com

Agent's name: Sammie Justesen

E-mail: sammie@northernlightsls.com

Born: Bedford, Indiana. Let's forget the year!

Education: Purdue University, Indiana University, Harvard (one great year)

Career history: I worked as a registered nurse for over 20 years, but couldn't stay away from writing. I became a clinical editor for Mosby, and then worked as a freelance editor and writer for other medical publishers. I edited fiction for several years until several clients asked me to represent them with publishers. I opened Northern Lights Literary Services in 2004 and began selling books. Though we left the east coast and moved to northern Idaho, the Internet allows us to compete with New York agencies.

Hobbies/Personal interests: Reading (of course), watercolor painting, photography, swimming, and watching wildlife from our office in northern Idaho (moose, bear, elk, turkey, and eagles)

Categories/Subjects that you are most enthusiastic about agenting: We accept fiction and nonfiction in almost any category, as long as it's well written and marketable.

Categories/Subjects writers shouldn't bother pitching to you: We don't accept erotica, fantasy, poetry, horror, or children's and young-adult books.

If you were not an agent, what might you be doing instead: I'd try and make a living with my artwork, which is even harder than succeeding as a writer. I must be a masochist.

What's the best way for fiction writers to solicit your interest: I prefer e-mail queries, well written and to the point. Write your query with a confident voice; don't run yourself down, but don't oversell your book either. Let the writing speak for itself.

Do you charge fees separate from your commission or offer nonagenting fee-based services: No

What are some representative titles that you have sold: *Intuitive Parenting* by Debra Snyder, PhD (Beyond Words); *The Happiness Trap Pocketbook* by Russ Harris, MD (Exisle); *The Confidence Trap* by Russ Harris, MD (Penguin Australia); *The Never Cold Call Again Toolkit* by Frank Rumbauskas, Jr. (Wiley); *Over-the-Counter Natural Cures* by Shane Ellison (Sourcebooks); *Carry a Chicken in Your Lap* by Bruce Johnson and William Ayres (St. Martin's Press); *The Road to Fruition: Recipes from the Smokey Mountains* by Joan Aller (Andrews McMeel); *Kentucky Moon* by Elizabeth Lee (NorlightsPress.com)

How and why did you become an agent: I became an agent because I love discovering new projects and bringing authors and editors together. I crave those moments when I call an author and say, "I have an offer for your book!"

How do you feel about writers: My best friends are writers! I'm a writer! I love writers!

How would you describe what you do as an agent to someone (or something) from another planet: On this planet, millions of beings torture themselves by creating books they hope other humans will read. I try and sell those books to harried editors who hope the public will open their wallets. Beam me up, Scottie!

What are your favorite books, movies, and TV shows, and why: I'm a junkie for self-help books and also love mysteries, memoirs, and biographies. I probably own every how-to-paint watercolor book ever written. I don't watch much television, but I like movies that are cerebral enough to hold my interest. No comic book derivatives, please! My favorite media provides entertainment, teaches me something, and inspires me.

Describe the client from hell, even if you don't have any: Writers from hell go ballistic when I respond to a query with helpful suggestions. Their friends love the book, so it's perfect. Clients from hell expect to hear from me every other day and don't trust me to do my job. Luckily I don't encounter many of these folks. Most writers are great.

Describe the publisher and/or editor from hell: Editors and publishers are wonderful; often overworked and underpaid. I mutter and complain when they hold manuscripts for months without responding, but I understand why that happens.

What do you like best about your clients and the editors and publishers you work with: The camaraderie of working together to create books people fall in love with

Will our business exist as we know it in 10 years or so: The Internet will continue changing the world, but I hope people will never stop reading.

P.S. LITERARY

20033-520 Kerr Street, Oakville, ON, L6K 3C7 Canada
416-907-8325 (Toronto) | 212-655-9276 (New York)
www.psliterary.com
agentcarlywatters.wordpress.com

Agent's name: Carly Watters
E-mail: Queries: query@psliterary.com; general questions: info@psliterary.com
Education: MA from City University London, England—publishing studies; BA honors from Queen's University Kingston, Ontario—English language and literature
Categories/Subjects that you are most enthusiastic about agenting: World literature, multicultural stories, women's fiction, quirky and up-market nonfiction
Categories/Subjects writers shouldn't bother pitching to you: Screenplays, poetry, horror
Do you charge fees separate from your commission or offer nonagenting fee-based services: No

What's the best way for writers to solicit your interest: I only accept pitches via e-mail with a clear subject line and no attachments, following this formula: Paragraph One—Introduction: Include the title and category of your work (i.e., fiction or nonfiction and topic); an estimated word count; and a brief, general introduction. Paragraph Two—Minisynopsis: A concise summary or overview of your work. Paragraph Three—Writer's bio: Tell us a little bit about yourself and your background (awards and affiliations, etc.). Please see our website for more information.

Agent's name: Curtis Russell

Career history: Curtis began his publishing career nearly a decade ago as proprietor of a micro press. In 2005, he crossed to the other side of the desk and founded the P.S. Literary Agency. He has a wide-ranging and diverse client list and is interested in discovering writers with unique ideas, no matter what the category. Curtis is currently acquiring both fiction and nonfiction. In terms of fiction, he is seeking literary, commercial mainstream, women's fiction, romance, young adult/middle grade, and mysteries and thrillers. In terms of nonfiction, he is looking for business, history, politics, current affairs, memoir, health, wellness, pop science, and pop psychology.

Categories/Subjects that writers shouldn't bother pitching to you: Screenplays, poetry

Do you charge fees separate from your commission or offer nonagenting fee-based services: No

What's the best way for writers to solicit your interest: I only accept pitches via e-mail with a clear subject line and no attachments, following this formula: Paragraph One—Introduction: Include the title and category of your work (i.e., fiction or nonfiction and topic); an estimated word count; and a brief, general introduction. Paragraph Two—Minisynopsis: A concise summary or overview of your work. Paragraph Three—Writer's bio: Tell us a little bit about yourself and your background (awards and affiliations, etc.). Please see our website for more information.

PARAVIEW LITERARY AGENCY

40 Florence Circle, Bracey, VA 23919
www.paraview.com/get_a_literary_agent.htm

Agent's name: Lisa Hagan

Born: VA

Education: Virginia Commonwealth University

Career history: I've been an agent since 1993. I love it and can't imagine doing anything else.

Categories/Subjects that you are most enthusiastic about agenting: Spirituality, self-help, memoirs, travel, science, business, and current affairs

If you were not an agent, what might you be doing instead: The only other career that I can see myself in would be teaching; I love to teach, and I enjoy working with everyone, from kids to adults. I am passionate about sharing my love of reading and writing.

What's the best way for writers to solicit your interest: Please send a query submission first via e-mail. Make sure you have a proposal ready to go, and give us your phone number along with e-mail. I have been known to call an author immediately after reading a proposal, if I am really excited. If you send a written query make sure to send a self-addressed stamped envelope if you want a reply.

Do you charge reading or management fees: No

What are the most common mistakes writers make when pitching to you: By not doing their homework: I do not respond to queries that are not in my areas of expertise. I also do not care for a query letter that is not properly addressed; very little irritates me, but that is one thing that really does.

How would you describe the perfect client: I like to connect with my authors on a personal level. This doesn't always happen, but it is nice to be able to call your author your friend as well. It is also nice to have an author who understands what an agent, editor, and pr team do, to know the roles that we all have in making a book a success.

What are some representative titles that you have sold: Please see my website for a complete list. A few of my favorites are *Big Fat Lies Women Tell Themselves* by Amy Ahlers (New World Library); *The Spiritual Girl's Guide to Dating* by Amy Leigh Mercee (Adams Media); *It Doesn't Come with a Title: Uncommon-Practice Leadership* by Nan S. Russell (Career Press); *Keep Out: Top-Secret Places Governments Don't Want You to Know About* by Nick Redfern (New Page Books); *Heal Yourself* by Dr. Lynne Zimmerman (Sunrise River Press); *Choosing Easy World: A Guide to Opting Out of Struggle and Strife and Living in the Amazing Realm Where Everything Is Easy* by Julia Rogers Hamrick (St. Martin's Press); *I See Your Dream Job: A Career Intuitive Shows You How to Discover What You Were Put on Earth to Do* by Sue Frederick; *The Dog Whisperer, The Revised Dog Whisperer,* and *Puppy Whisperer* by Paul Owens with Norma Eckroate—combined over 100,000 copies sold (Adams Media); *The Natural Cat: The Comprehensive Guide to Optimum Care* by Anitra Frazier with Norma Eckroate, 3rd edition—over 500,000 copies sold (Penguin); *Babylon's Ark: The Incredible Wartime Rescue of the Baghdad Zoo* by Lawrence Anthony with Graham Spence—over 75,000 copies sold (Thomas Dunne); *Celebrity Secrets* (Paraview Pocket Books) and *Memoirs of a Monster* by Nick Redfern (New Page Books); *The High-Purpose Company: The Truly Responsible (and Highly Profitable) Firms That Are Changing Business Now* (Collins) and *Cause for Success: 10 Companies That Put Profits Second and Came in First* by Christine Arena (New World Library); *PSIence, Supervolcano: The Catastrophic Event That Changed the Course of Human History, 2013,* and *11:11* by Marie D. Jones (New Page Books); *Zero to Zillionaire* and *The Wealthy Spirit* by Chellie Campbell (Sourcebooks); *The Whole World Was Watching* by Romaine Patterson with Patrick Hinds (Alyson Books); *Talking to Heaven* by James Van Praagh—over 1,2000,000 copies sold (Dutton); *A Knight Without Armor* and *Chasing Down the Dawn* by Jewel Kilcher—combined over 1,000,000 copies sold (HarperCollins); *UFOs, JFK, and Elvis* by Richard Belzer (Ballantine); *The King of Cowboys* by Ty Murray (Atria); *Alien Agenda*—over 50,000 sold—and *Rule by Secrecy* by Jim Marrs—over 200,000 copies sold (HarperCollins); *Crossfire: The Plot That Killed Kennedy* by Jim Marrs—over 200,000 sold (Basic Books); *What Your Doctor May Not Tell You about Menopause* by Dr. John Lee with Virginia Hopkins—over 1,000,000 copies sold (Warner); *The Conscious Universe* (HSF) and *Entangled Minds* by Dean Radin, PhD (Paraview Pocket Books); *Healthy Beauty* by Letha Hadady (Wiley); *Psychic Living* (Paraview Pocket Books); *Secrets of the Signs, Love Secrets of the Signs, Get Psychic* by Stacey Wolf (Warner); *Never Throw Rice at a Pisces* by Stacey Wolf (Thomas Dunne); *The Encyclopedia of Magickal Ingredients* (Paraview Pocket Books); *Power Spells, Easy Enchantments, Zodiac Spells* by Lexa Rosean (St. Martin's); *Bedside Guide to Dreams* by Stase Michaels (Ballantine); *No Soul Left Behind* (Citadel) and *Edgar Cayce: My Life as a Seer* by A. Robert Smith (St. Martin's); *The Coming Global Superstorm* by Art Bell and Whitley Strieber—over 100,000 copies sold (Pocket Books); *Native Heart* and *The Book of Ceremonies* by Gabriel Horn (New World Library). And many more that I am incredibly proud of.

Favorite books to read: I am all over the map; I love history, current affairs, and memoirs, as well as fiction. I will find an author through a friend or a review and then have to read everything that they have written. I can be a bit of a stalker when I find someone whose writing I really resonate with. I love books; I always have several going at once.

Hobbies/Personal interests: I love to be creative, and I have to have a project; whether it is writing, cooking, crafts, gardening, hiking or just being out in nature, I'm doing something interesting and fun.

Additional Services: I assist my authors in crafting the best proposal that we can put together before sending it out to editors. I edit and support them in any way that I can to make it as perfect as possible. I have contacts in every arena if we need to hire a specific professional to make the work top notch.

THE PARK LITERARY GROUP, LLC

270 Lafayette Street, Suite 1504, New York, NY 10012
212-691-3500 | fax: 212-691-3540
www.parkliterary.com

The Park Literary Group was founded in January 2005, when Theresa Park and several colleagues left the venerable literary agency Sanford J. Greenburger Associates. Theresa had been an agent at Greenburger for more than 10 years, but at the age of 37 was eager to try building a new venture. A full-service literary agency, the Park Literary Group represents fiction and nonfiction with a boutique approach: an emphasis on servicing a relatively small number of clients, with the highest professional standards and focused personal attention. With a full-time foreign rights director and excellent relationships with film and television coagents in Los Angeles, the agency brings to bear excellent resources and a wealth of experience in exploiting all rights associated with an author's work.

Agent's name: Theresa Park

Education: BA, University of Santa Cruz; JD, Harvard Law School

Career history: Theresa began her career as a literary agent at Sanford J. Greenburger Associates in 1994. (Prior to that, she was an attorney at Cooley Godward, a Silicon Valley law firm.) She represents a mixture of plot-driven fiction and serious nonfiction. Some of her clients include Nicholas Sparks, Debbie Macomber, Emily Giffin, Laura Zigman, Janice Y. K. Lee, Juliette Fay, Linda Nichols, Robert Whitaker, Lee Silver, B. R. Myers, and Thomas Levenson. She is married to Greg Irikura, a photographer, and has two children.

Categories/Subjects you are most enthusiastic about agenting: Commercial fiction (thrillers, love stories, historical novels, etc.) and serious nonfiction (including narrative history, science, memoir, serious psychology, history, and biography)

Categories/Subjects writers shouldn't bother pitching to you: Cookbooks, diet books, fitness, children's books, humor

If you were not an agent, what might you be doing instead: I can't imagine doing anything else—I really love being an agent and feel privileged to be able to follow my passion.

What's the best way for writers to solicit your interest: A one-page letter, brief synopsis, and one to three chapters, snail-mailed (NOT e-mailed), with an SASE

Do you charge reading or management fees: No—never

What categories do you represent, by percentages: Fiction: 50 percent, nonfiction: 50 percent

What are the most common mistakes writers make when pitching to you: Poor grammar and spelling in written materials; gimmicky attempts to attract attention through means other than a professional query; overly aggressive or unprofessional behavior

How would you describe the perfect client: Professional, disciplined, hardworking, emotionally stable, great people skills and social judgment, down-to-earth, direct

How and why did you become an agent: I love books, I love to work with people, and I love to do deals! Also, given my background as a transactional lawyer, it seemed like the right area of publishing for me. One of the best things about being a lawyer was having clients—I enjoy getting to know people and working closely with them on their manuscripts and proposals; the personal rewards of watching a client's career blossom are the best part of my job.

What can a writer do to increase the odds of you becoming his or her agent: Be professional; send concise, effective query letters.

How would you describe what you do as an agent to someone (or something) from another planet: We are advocates for and advisors to writers—in addition to each acting as a salesperson, negotiator, and long-term strategist.

How do you feel about editors and publishers: Their quality and commitment to authors varies widely—it is impossible to generalize.

What are some representative titles that you have sold: *The Notebook, Message in a Bottle, A Walk to Remember, The Rescue, A Bend in the Road, Nights in Rodanthe, The Guardian, The Wedding, Three Weeks with My Brother, True Believer, At First Sight, Dear John, The Choice* (Warner Books); *Piece of Work* (Warner Books); *Inamorata* (Viking); *Handyman* (Delacorte), *Not a Sparrow Falls, If I Gained the World, At the Scent of Water, In Search of Eden* (Bethany House); *Doomed Queens* (Broadway); *Challenging Nature: The Clash of Science and Spirituality at the New Frontiers of Life* (Ecco); *The Lost Men: The Harrowing Saga of Shackleton's Ross Sea Party* (Viking); *A Reader's Manifesto* (Melville House); *Remember Me: A Lively Tour of the New American Way of Death* (Collins)

Agent's name: Abigail Koons

Education: BA, Boston University

Career history: Eager to work with emerging and established talent, Abigail is currently looking to add to her list of diverse and engaging authors. Her passion for travel makes her a natural fit for adventure and travel narrative nonfiction, and she is also seeking projects about popular science, history, politics, current events, and art. She is also interested in working with commercial fiction. As the foreign rights director, she continues to build on her prior experience with agent Nicholas Ellison, as well as her time with EF Education, a multinational corporation based in Sweden.

Categories/Subjects you are most enthusiastic about agenting: Commercial fiction (thrillers and quirky comedies) and nonfiction (science, political science, art and art history, and business)

Categories/Subjects writers shouldn't bother pitching to you: Young adult, psychology, romance, Westerns

If you were not an agent, what might you be doing instead: In that fantasy world where no one has a full-time job, I would spend my days traveling and reading. This is the next best thing.

What's the best way for writers to solicit your interest: A one-page letter, brief synopsis, and one to three chapters, snail-mailed (NOT e-mailed), with an SASE.

Do you charge reading or management fees: No—never

What categories do you represent, by percentages: Fiction: 50 percent, nonfiction: 50 percent.

What are the most common mistakes writers make when pitching to you: Poor grammar and spelling in written materials; gimmicky attempts to attract attention through means other than a professional query; overly aggressive or unprofessional behavior

How would you describe the perfect client: Professional, disciplined, hardworking, emotionally stable, great people skills and social judgment, down-to-earth, direct

How and why did you become an agent: After dabbling in law and international economics, I decided that my career needed a healthy dose of creativity to balance out the business aspects. Being an agent allows me to utilize my business and organizational skills while working with truly wonderful clients and fascinating projects every day.

What can a writer do to increase the odds of you becoming his or her agent: Be professional; send concise, effective query letters.

How would you describe what you do as an agent to someone (or something) from another planet: We are advocates for and advisors to writers—in addition to each acting as a salesperson, negotiator, and long-term strategist.

How do you feel about editors and publishers: Their quality and commitment to authors varies widely—it is impossible to generalize.

What are some representative titles that you have sold: *Shop Naked: The History of Catalogs* (Princeton Architectural Press)

Agent's name: Amanda Cardinale
Education: BA in European history from Barnard College
Career history: Amanda joined the Park Literary Group in early 2008. She is interested in representing a wide range of fiction and nonfiction from talented new voices. Her fiction interests include commercial, literary, and international fiction. She also seeks provocative nonfiction in the areas of popular culture, entertainment, art, and journalism that focuses on human issues. Drawing on her love of cuisine, Amanda is also interested in food narratives. Prior to joining the Park Literary Group, she worked at International Creative Management and Sterling Lord Literistic.

Categories/Subjects you are most enthusiastic about agenting: Commercial, literary, and international fiction; and nonfiction (popular culture, entertainment, art, and journalism)

Categories/Subjects writers shouldn't bother pitching to you: Young adult, children's, science fiction/fantasy, self-help

Do you charge reading or management fees: No—never

What categories do you represent, by percentages: Fiction: 50 percent, nonfiction: 50 percent.

What are the most common mistakes writers make when pitching to you: Poor grammar and spelling in written materials; gimmicky attempts to attract attention through means other than a professional query; overly aggressive or unprofessional behavior

How would you describe the perfect client: Professional, disciplined, hardworking, emotionally stable, great people skills and social judgment, down-to-earth, direct

What can a writer do to increase the odds of you becoming his or her agent: Be professional; send concise, effective query letters.

How would you describe what you do as an agent to someone (or something) from another planet: We are advocates for and advisors to writers—in addition to each acting as a salesperson, negotiator, and long-term strategist.

How do you feel about editors and publishers: Their quality and commitment to authors varies widely—it is impossible to generalize.

PAUL S. LEVINE LITERARY AGENCY

1054 Superba Avenue, Venice, CA 90291
310-450-6711 | 800-883-0490 | fax: 310-450-0181
www.paulslevinelit.com

Agent's name: Paul S. Levine
E-mail: paul@paulslevinelit.com
Carrier pigeon: Use street address; train pigeon well.
Strippergram: Must be gorgeous and have a great routine
Born: March 16, 1954; New York, NY
Education: B. Comm., Concordia University, Montreal (1977); MBA, York University, Toronto (1978); JD, University of Southern California, Los Angeles (1981)
Career history: Attorney for more than 30 years
Categories/Subjects that you are most enthusiastic about agenting: Commercial fiction and nonfiction for adults, children, and young adults
Categories/Subjects writers shouldn't bother pitching to you: Science fiction, fantasy, and horror
If you were not an agent, what might you be doing instead: Practicing entertainment law; reading good books
What's the best way for writers to solicit your interest: Query letter ONLY by snail mail, e-mail, fax, carrier pigeon, or strippergram
Do you charge reading or management fees: No
What categories do you represent, by percentages: Fiction: 35 percent, children's: 15 percent, nonfiction: 50 percent
What are some of the most common mistakes writers make when pitching you: Telling me that they're writing to me because they're looking for a literary agent. Duh!
Describe the client from hell, even if you don't have any: One who calls, faxes, e-mails, or sends carrier pigeons or strippergrams every day; one who constantly needs reassurance that each rejection letter does not mean that the client's project lacks merit and that the client is an awful person
How would you describe the perfect client: The opposite of the above
How and why did you become an agent: I have loved the book business ever since I started practicing law in 1981. My first client was a major book publisher in Los Angeles.
What, if anything, can writers do to increase the odds that you will become his or her agent: Be referred by an existing client or colleague
How would you describe to someone (or something) from another planet what it is you do as an agent: I represent writers—book authors, screenwriters, and writer-producers.
How do you feel about editors and publishers: I love them.

PEMA BROWN LTD.

11 Tena Place, Valley Cottage, NY 10989
845-268-0026
www.pemabrowneltd.com

> **Agent's name:** Pema Browne
> **E-mail:** ppbltd@optonline.net
> **What are some representative titles that you have sold:** Romance: *The Champion* by Heather Grothaus/Historical/Kensington/Zebra; *Kisses Don't Lie* by Alexa Darin/Contemporary/Kensington/Zebra; *The Highlander's Bride* by Michele Sinclair/Historical/Kensington/Zebra; *Dark Whispers* by Samantha Garver/Historical/Kensington/Zebra Romance. Children's picture books: *The Daring Ms. Quimby* by Suzanne Whitaker (Holiday House); *Sweet Potato Pie* by Kathleen Lindsey/Lee & Low Books; *Say Boo* by Linda Graham Barber/Candlewick Press; *January Rides the Wind* illustrated by Todd Doney/Lothrup/HarperCollins. Nonfiction: *Soul Echoes* by Thelma Freedman, PhD/New Age/Citadel Press; *Identity Theft* by Robert Hammond/Career Press; *Career ReExplosion — Reinvent Yourself in Thirty Days* by Gary J. Grappo/Berkley; *Executive Temping—A Guide for Professionals* by Saralee Woods/John Wiley & Sons

---

PMA LITERARY AND FILM MANAGEMENT, INC.

45 W. 21st St., 4th Floor, New York, NY 10010
212-929-1222 | fax: 212-206-0238
www.pmalitfilm.com

> **Agent's name:** Peter Miller
> **E-mail:** queries@pmalitfilm.com
> **Born:** Atlantic City, New Jersey
> **Education:** BA, Monmouth University
> **Career history:** Known as the "Literary Lion," Peter Miller has been an extraordinarily active literary and film manager for more than 30 years. He is president of PMA Literary and Film Management, Inc., and Millennium Lion, Inc.; he and his company have successfully managed over 1,000 books worldwide as well as dozens of motion picture and television properties. These works include 16 *New York Times* best sellers, and 15 produced films that Miller has managed or executive produced. Three of those films have been nominated for a total of seven Emmy Awards: *Goodbye, Miss Fourth of July* (The Disney Channel, four nominations); *A Gift of Love* (Showtime, two nominations); and *Helter Skelter* (CBS, one nomination). In addition, Miller has a number of film and television projects currently in active development, with some nearing production, in association with Warner

Bros. Features, Sony Pictures Television, Warner Bros. Television, DreamWorks, and many other producers and production companies.

Hobbies/Personal interests: I collect statues and images of lions, which have been celebrated by man since the beginning of time. I also enjoy traveling, films, wine, and adventure.

Categories/Subjects that you are most enthusiastic about agenting: Quality fiction and narrative nonfiction with global marketing and motion picture and television production potential

Categories/Subjects writers shouldn't bother pitching to you: Poetry, pornography, or anything low- or mid-list

If you were not an agent, what might you be doing instead: I would probably be an antique dealer.

What's the best way for fiction writers to solicit your interest: By writing a powerful, succinct, and perfect e-mail or pitch letter

Do you charge fees separate from your commission or offer nonagenting fee-based services: No

What are some representative titles that you have sold: Nonfiction: *The Element* by Sir Ken Robinson and Lou Aronica (Viking); *Strategic Acceleration* by Tony Jeary (Vanguard Press/Perseus Book Group); *Ten Prayers God Always Says Yes To* by Anthony DeStefano (Doubleday Religion); *Nathan Hale* by M. William Phelps (Thomas Dunne Books/St. Martin's Press). Fiction: *The Christmas Cookie Club* by Ann Pearlman (Atria/Simon & Schuster); *The Compass* by Tammy Kling and John Spencer Ellis (Vanguard Press/Perseus Book Group); *No More Good* by Angela Winters (Dafina/Kensington); *A Twisted Ladder* by Rhodi Hawk (Tor); *Perfect Victim* by Jay Bonansinga (Kensington); *Where There's a Witch* (Bewitching Mysteries #5) by Madelyn Alt (Berkley/Penguin).

How and why did you become an agent: When I moved to New York many moons ago, I was producing an off-off-Broadway production. I then met a Broadway producer, and we decided to start a literary agency. I never looked back.

How do you feel about writers: I have the utmost respect for writers, as they are the true geniuses in society.

How would you describe what you do as an agent to someone (or something) from another planet: I would tell them to write something special so I could be the literary manager of the first alien to get published in America.

What are your favorite books, movies, and TV shows, and why: Books: *Being There* by Jerzy Kosinski and *Steppenwolf* by Hermann Hesse; Movies: *Dr. Zhivago*, *The Godfather*, *Austin Powers*, *Juno*, and *The Departed*; TV shows: *Boston Legal*, *Entourage*, and *The Sopranos*

Describe the client from hell, even if you don't have any: One that doesn't know how to communicate but doesn't stop trying to communicate with us

Describe the publisher and/or editor from hell: One that makes an offer during an auction and then disappears

What do you like best about your clients and the editors and publishers you

work with: I like the truly talented authors that we manage who just allow me to do my job and the publishers that do everything they say they're going to do.

You're welcome to share your thoughts and sentiments about the business of writing and publishing: Fortunately, having spent 30 years in the industry, I've learned how to grow with ever-constant sea changes like the one we are presently experiencing in the digital delivery of content.

Describe yourself: I'm a passionate intellectual-property developer who loves to get six-figure advances for his clients. My favorite two words are "bidding war."

Will our business exist as we know it in 10 years or so: Absolutely.

THE QUADRIVIUM GROUP

7512 Dr. Phillips Boulevard, Suite #50-229, Orlando, FL 32819
407-516-1857
www.TheQuadriviumGroup.com

Agent's name: Steve Blount
E-mail: SteveBlount@TheQuadriviumGroup.com
Born: Waycross, GA
Education: BBA, the University of Georgia; MBA, Thunderbird School of Global Management
Career history: After 10 years in banking (profitability analyst, strategic planner, mergers and acquisitions), I made the jump into Christian publishing and retail (LifeWay), starting out on the corporate side doing strategic planning but soon getting into product development, marketing, and sales for the core publishing business. After a successful decade there, I became COO of a faith-based marketing firm that represented major ministry clients such as Billy Graham, Joyce Meyer, Joel Osteen, T. D. Jakes, and more. I've always enjoyed helping those with a compelling message to reach their audiences, whether as their publisher, book marketer, media consultant, or agent.
Categories/Subjects that you are most enthusiastic about agenting: Christian nonfiction, Christian/inspirational fiction, cross-over books
Categories/Subjects writers shouldn't bother pitching to you: Poetry
If you were not an agent, what might you be doing instead: I'd find some other way to help people with compelling life stories or other great messages to reach their audiences.
What can a writer do to increase the odds of you becoming his or her agent: A great proposal, including a powerful hook
Do you charge fees separate from your commission or offer nonagenting fee-based services: Only extraordinary costs with client's permission; no reading fees
How and why did you become an agent: After I left publishing, a number of my authors and publishing colleagues encouraged me to become an agent. There seemed to be a need for someone who understood the inner workings of the business to help

authors with compelling life stories and ideas to navigate through the often difficult publishing process.

QUICKSILVER BOOKS LITERARY AGENTS

508 Central Park Avenue, #5101, Scarsdale, NY 10583
914-722-4664
www.quicksilverbooks.com

Agent's name: Bob Silverstein
E-mail: quickbooks@optonline.net
Born: October 3, 1936; New York, New York
Education: BA, City College of New York
Career history: Bob Silverstein is president of Quicksilver Books (QB), a literary agency and former book packaging and publishing firm established in 1973. QB is responsible for the creation of many national and international best sellers, including novelized versions of such highly acclaimed films as *The Last Tango in Paris, Shampoo,* and *Chariots of Fire.* All of these titles were published in the United States and Canada as Dell/Quicksilver paperbacks. For more than 35 years, Mr. Silverstein has successfully divided his career between books and movies. After graduation from the City College of New York and postgraduate work in comparative literature at the City University of New York (Hunter College), he entered publishing as an associate editor with Gold Medal Books and later became an editor of the Crest and Premier divisions of Fawcett Publications. Between 1962 and 1965, Mr. Silverstein served as managing editor of Dell Books and as senior editor of the newly formed Delacorte Press. In 1965 he joined Anthony Quinn Productions as associate producer and story editor, assisting the actor in preparing his autobiography as well as shaping screenplays for production in the United States and Europe. From 1967 to 1970, Mr. Silverstein was senior unit publicist for United Artists and MGM on major motion pictures filmed on location throughout Europe. In this capacity he worked closely with producers Carlo Ponti, David Wolper, Harry Belafonte, and others. Mr. Silverstein has also coproduced several independent documentary and feature films, as well as a number of television commercials for the Ogilvy & Mather ad agency. In 1971 he returned to publishing as senior projects editor for Bantam Books. Among his acquisitions were such cutting-edge titles as *Gestalt Therapy, Verbatim,* and *In and Out of the Garbage Pail* by Fritz Perls. After several years he left to start his own company, Quicksilver Books, Inc., and since then has collaborated with writers in producing many popular works of fiction and nonfiction, including the previously mentioned movie tie-ins. Other Quicksilver projects, many still in print, include books inspired by new therapies and holistic healing techniques such as gestalt, transactional analysis, rolfing, etc. Among them are *The Body Reveals* (HarperCollins, four editions, 12 printings); *Own Your Own*

Life (McKay/Bantam), *Psychology Today* Book Club (main section); *Chalk Talks on Alcohol* (HarperSanFrancisco, 15 printings); the international best seller *Children Learn What They Live* (Workman); and recent best sellers by Dr. Lois P. Frankel, *Nice Girls Don't Get the Corner Office* and *Nice Girls Don't Get Rich* (Warner Books). As a literary agency (founded in 1987), Quicksilver Books is primarily interested in mainstream adult fiction, with special emphasis on commercial and literary novels. Nonfiction categories include narrative adventure, self-help, psychology, environmental issues, nutrition, health, cooking, healing, alternative therapies, music, New Age, science, medicine, reference, biography, and inspirational memoirs.

Hobbies/Personal interests: Painting, tennis, international travel, spending time with my wife and children

Categories/Subjects that you are most enthusiastic about agenting: Inspirational classics, blockbuster literary novels, best-selling narrative nonfiction, great memoirs and biographies, outstanding cookbooks, meaningful self-help; books that uplift the spirit and that can make a positive difference in people's lives

Categories/Subjects writers shouldn't bother pitching to you: Fantasy, science fiction

If you were not an agent, what might you be doing instead: Painting, traveling, meditating, writing/collaborating on books and movies

What's the best way for writers to solicit your interest: By query letter or e-mail

Do you charge reading or management fees: No

What categories do you represent, by percentages: Fiction (literary fiction, women's novels, suspense thrillers): 15 percent, nonfiction: 85 percent

What are the most common mistakes writers make when pitching to you: They say nothing about themselves. Their letters are full of spelling mistakes. They tell but they don't sell.

Describe the client from hell, even if you don't have any: Full of ego, demanding, unaware of their part in the marketing process

How would you describe the perfect client: Objective, intelligent, sympathetic, humble, emotionally and spiritually attuned

How and why did you become an agent: Initially I was an editor, then a packager/publisher. When the markets changed in the '80s, I went with the flow and became an agent.

What can a writer do to increase the odds of you becoming his or her agent: (1) Have something original to offer; (2) Be aware of market needs and categories; (3) Present it professionally; (4) Have a platform to help market the book.

How would you describe what you do as an agent to someone (or something) from another planet: I consider myself an alchemist/healer-helper to turn lead into gold.

How do you feel about editors and publishers: I come from their ranks. Some stand taller than others. All have a job to do and, for the most part, I respect their efforts. Occasionally, I'm even impressed.

What are your favorite books, movies, and TV shows, and why: I like cooking shows, *This Old House*, *The Sopranos*, *24*, Discovery and History channels, an occasional movie—no sitcoms.

What are some representative titles that you have sold: *Jefferson's Great Gamble* and *Young Patriots* (Sourcebooks); *Look Great Naked* (Penguin); *Sculpting Her Body Perfect* (Human Kinetics); *The Inextinguishable Symphony* (Wiley); *Nice Girls Don't Get the Corner Office* and *Nice Girls Don't Get Rich* (Warner); *The National Public Radio Guide to Building a Classical CD Library* (Workman); *Children Learn What They Live* (Workman); *The Complete Books of Vinyasa Yoga* (Marlowe & Co.); *The Pump Energy Food* (Hyperion); *Real Food Daily Cookbook* (Ten Speed Press); *Help Me to Heal* (Hay House); *The National Public Radio Listener's Encyclopedia of Classical Music* (Workman); *The Complete Book of Ayurvedic Home Remedies* (Harmony); *Dinner at Mr. Jefferson's* (Wiley); *Indian Vegan Cooking* (Perigee); *Macrobiotics for Dummies* (Wiley); *Simply Mexican* (Ten Speed Press)

RAINES & RAINES

103 Kenyon Road, Medusa, NY 12120
518-239-8311 | fax: 518-239-6029

Agents' names: Joan Raines, Keith Korman
What's the best way for writers to solicit your interest: One-page letter
What are some representative titles that you have sold: *Deliverance* by James Dickey; *Forrest Gump* by Winston Groom; *Die Hard* by Roderick Thorp; *Ball Four* by Bouton and Shecter; *The Destruction of the European Jews* by Raul Hilberg; *The Man Who Walked between the Towers* by Mordicai Gerstein (Caldecott winner); *My Dog Skip* by Willie Morris; *Brain Quest* by Chris Welles Feder; *Legacy* by Rich Lowry; *The Contender* by Robert Lipsyte; *Active Faith* by Ralph Reed; *The Glory of Their Times* by Lawrence Ritter; *How to Eat Fried Worms* by Thomas Rockwell; *The Uses of Enchantment* by Bruno Bettelheim; *In My Father's Shadow: A Daughter Remembers Orson Welles* (tentative title) by Chris Welles Feder (Algonquin)

Agent's name: Theron Raines
Education: T. Raines: Columbia, Oxford
What's the best way for writers to solicit your interest: One-page letter
What are some representative titles that you have sold: *Deliverance* by James Dickey; *Forrest Gump* by Winston Groom; *Die Hard* by Roderick Thorp; *Ball Four* by Bouton and Shecter; *The Destruction of the European Jews* by Raul Hilberg; *The Man Who Walked between the Towers* by Mordicai Gerstein (Caldecott winner); *My Dog Skip* by Willie Morris; *Brain Quest* by Chris Welles Feder; *Legacy* by Rich Lowry; *The Contender* by Robert Lipsyte; *Active Faith* by Ralph Reed; *The Glory of Their Times* by Lawrence Ritter; *How to Eat Fried Worms* by Thomas Rockwell;

The Uses of Enchantment by Bruno Bettelheim; *In My Father's Shadow: A Daughter Remembers Orson Welles* (tentative title) by Chris Welles Feder (Algonquin)

RED SOFA LITERARY

2163 Grand Avenue Suite 2, Saint Paul, MN 55105
651-224-6670
www.redsofaliterary.com

Agent's name: Dawn Frederick
E-mail: dawn@redsofaliterary.com
Born: March 2, Atlanta, Georgia
Education: I attended the University of Tennessee, earning a bachelor's degree in human ecology, and master's degree in information sciences from the School of Information Sciences (an ALA-accredited institution).

Career history: I bring experience from the bookstore frontlines, independent publishing, and the library field, over 15 years of experience to be precise. It was pure coincidence (and part fate) my path crossed with Laurie Harper (of Sebastian Literary Agency) in 2002. Over the next five years, I learned the ins and outs of being a literary agent, with marked success. In 2008, I decided to branch out, launching Red Sofa Literary. And yes, I do own a big, red couch.

Hobbies/Personal interests: Where do we start? I am a natural risk taker, and it's very much reflected in my personal life. There are the sports I avidly participate in: roller derby (rolling ref for the Minnesota Rollergirls, known as Mani-Ax), broomball (on three teams now), currently women's lacrosse (taking MN by storm it seems), and bicycling (a much calmer outlet for the energy). Plus, I am a fan of all things quirky, which is a foundation for Red Sofa Literary. So, you should never be surprised if I attend an eclectic event/show/movie, as those are things that always appealing.

Categories/Subjects that you are most enthusiastic about agenting: Biography—historical, media-related, political—NO PERSONAL MEMOIRS; creative nonfiction—it needs to be smart, with noticeable platform, and highly commercial; history; humor; popular culture, especially Americana, and anything quirky; social issues/current affairs—women's studies; sports—less mainstream, more extreme sport, e.g., roller derby; women's narratives—chick lit nonfiction, Latina, African American, and more; young adult—nonfiction. My list is 99 percent nonfiction.

Categories/Subjects writers shouldn't bother pitching to you: I cannot emphasize enough that I will NOT represent any personal memoirs, romances, science fiction, Westerns, parenting, and/or religious books. I sadly get multiple queries in this category daily, and end up rejecting all of them.

If you were not an agent, what might you be doing instead: Going to law school, more than likely

What's the best way for fiction writers to solicit your interest: I love a smart, narrative voice from a writer, and even more so when he/she has done her figurative homework on Red Sofa Literary. That kind of work stands out significantly.

Do you charge fees separate from your commission or offer nonagenting fee-based services: I would only in the event the accepted publisher deal is for an advance of less than $15,000. Red Sofa Literary may charge back a one-time US $100 fee for partial reimbursement for the postage and phone expenses incurred prior to securing the publishing deal. The majority of the time, I never have to worry about this.

What are some representative titles that you have sold: *The Secrets of Skinny Chicks* (McGraw-Hill); *Finding Betty Crocker: The Secret Life of America's First Lady of Food* by Susan Marks (HarperCollins); *Stuck on You: The Indispensable History of Band-Aid Brand Bandages* by Susan Marks (Collector's Press)

What are your favorite books, movies, and TV shows, and why: I have lots of favorite things, however if you cornered me, and I had to list my top 10 TV shows, they would be (in no particular order): *Buffy the Vampire Slayer, Six Feet Under, Sopranos, Alias, 24, Pushing Daisies, Queer as Folk, Sex in the City, L Word,* and *Freaks and Geeks.* Books, that's a hard question; it all depends on my mood and what I'm currently reading. Just know I have lots of favorites, that I'm well-read, and I'm always up for recommendations.

Describe the client from hell, even if you don't have any: Anyone who doesn't promote him-/herself, thereby making it difficult to sell the person's platform, which makes the agent's job more difficult. In addition, too many e-mails/phone calls in a short period of time. I always try to answer them quickly, but if an author has contacted me without giving me time to respond and does this consistently, it tries my patience.

What do you like best about your clients and the editors and publishers you work with: I absolutely love that we all carry a passion for books, good ideas, and our constant desire to find forums to discuss these topics.

REECE HALSEY NEW YORK

450 Seventh Avenue, Suite 2307, New York, NY 10123
www.reecehalseynorth.com

Agent's name: Elizabeth Evans
Born: Milwaukee, Wisconsin
Education: BA Hamilton College, English; MFA in writing, University of San Francisco
Career history: I interned at *Zyzzyva* magazine before beginning my MFA at the University of San Francisco in 2004. While at USF, I joined Reece Halsey North as a reader and editor. I completed my MFA in 2006 and have been an associate agent since that time. In January of 2009 I relocated to New York City to open Reece Halsey New York.

Hobbies/Personal interests: Hobbies: Hiking in the mountains, anything to do with boats. I like fresh air. When the weather keeps me indoors, I'll cozy up with a good book and a cup of tea. Personal interests: Appetizers, bright colors, travels abroad, flowers, aquariums, angel food cake.

Categories/Subjects that you are most enthusiastic about agenting: I represent a wide range of nonfiction and fiction including memoir, pop culture, biography, literary and upmarket commercial fiction, historical fiction, mysteries, and young-adult and middle-grade fiction. I'm especially drawn to voice-driven fiction and narrative nonfiction in unfamiliar or exotic settings. I'm looking for excellent writing that strikes at the heart of the human condition. And I always enjoy a good love story.

Categories/Subjects writers shouldn't bother pitching to you: I do not handle picture books or books for young children, poetry, or screenplays.

If you were not an agent, what might you be doing instead: If not agenting, I would run an organic artisanal cheesery in Wisconsin. Or I'd be a professional organizer.

What's the best way for fiction writers to solicit your interest: I prefer a polite, well-written query letter accompanied by the appropriate submission materials (please see our website). Please do not call the office to pitch your project over the phone. Some ideas might stand out, but great writing is what captures my attention.

Do you charge fees separate from your commission or offer nonagenting fee-based services: No

What are some representative titles that you have sold: *The Dissemblers* (Permanent Press); *The Geography of Love* by Glenda Burgess (Broadway/Doubleday); *Courage to Surrender* by Tommy Hellsten (Ten Speed Press); *A Trace of Smoke* by Rebecca Cantrell (Tor/Forge Books)

How and why did you become an agent: I didn't know about agenting until a writing professor suggested I contact Kimberley Cameron about a reading internship. I knew immediately this was the perfect job for me. Agenting is very business oriented but also appeals to my creative side. I've always enjoyed reading and editing, and I find working with my clients very satisfying. Each day is unique and filled with possibilities.

How do you feel about writers: I have an enormous amount of respect for writers. It takes such determination and discipline to write. And confidence. I admire that. I appreciate the opportunity to read another person's work.

How would you describe what you do as an agent to someone (or something) from another planet: Shhh, don't bother me. I'm reading!

What are your favorite books, movies, and TV shows, and why: *Don't Let's Go to the Dogs Tonight* by Alexandra Fuller, *Housekeeping* by Marilynne Robinson, *Life and Death in Shanghai* by Nien Cheng, *The Power of One* by Bryce Courtenay, *Reading Lolita in Tehran* by Azar Nafisi, *Child of My Heart* by Alice McDermott, *Woman Hollering Creek* by Sandra Cisneros, *The Virgin Suicides* by Jeffrey Eugenides, *Beloved* and *Jazz* by Toni Morrison, *Prep* by Curtis Sittenfeld, *Howards End* by E. M. Forster, anything by Kazuo Ishiguro. All these books give me shivers when I read them. I tend to like films with a sense of whimsy. Favorite movies are *Big Fish*,

The Neverending Story, Moulin Rouge, Rushmore. I don't watch much TV, but I got sucked into *The Tudors* on Showtime. My guilty pleasure is *Gossip Girl*.

Describe the client from hell, even if you don't have any: The writer from hell shows an unhealthy desperation and forgets his/her manners. I enjoy working with writers who are serious and professional and recognize that publishing is a business.

Describe the publisher and/or editor from hell: The publisher/editor from hell? No such thing, they're all angels!

REECE HALSEY NORTH

98 Main Street, #704, Tiburon, CA 94920
415-789-9191
www.reecehalseynorth.com

Agent's name: Amy Burkhardt

Born: New Jersey...I spent half of my childhood there and half outside Boston, Massachusetts.

Education: BA in English, Bates College; candidate for MFA in writing, University of San Francisco

Career history: I worked for three years in various business positions and then moved to San Francisco to begin my MFA in writing. While working on my graduate degree I began interning as a reader at the Reece Halsey North Literary Agency. Since then, I have added responsibilities as an editor and agent.

Hobbies and special interests: Writing; any kind of dance—I have been a dancer since age five; music; art and art history; travel and foreign languages—I speak German and have studied Spanish; hiking/camping, and generally being outside; cooking (but I'm a novice), baking; trying new restaurants; international news and politics; reading, of course!

Categories/Subjects that you are most enthusiastic about agenting: I am open to a wide range of fiction and nonfiction. For fiction, I am drawn to the following categories: literary, upmarket commercial, women's historical, mysteries with a twist. I also enjoy young-adult or character-driven science fiction, but only manuscripts that create an entirely new world for the reader. For nonfiction, I am interested in voice-driven, narrative nonfiction, memoir, travel, lifestyle, and food books. In any genre, I look for accomplished writing, interesting and quirky characters, fresh voices, timely themes, and a good dose of wit. I enjoy stories that teach the reader something new.

Categories/Subjects that writers shouldn't bother pitching to you: Please, no children's, poetry, horror, business books, or screenplays

If you were not an agent, what might you be doing instead: Writing fiction and reading...oh wait, I already do that. Hmmm...traveling the world, learning languages and local dance forms, and writing about it.

What's the best way for fiction writers to solicit your interest: A well-written query letter and a submission that follows our guidelines. For fiction: a one-page synopsis and the first 50 pages of the manuscript. For nonfiction: a proposal and sample chapters. Please no phone pitches…the writing should speak for you.

Do you charge fees separate from your commission or offer nonagenting fee-based services: No

How and why did you become an agent: I began interning at literary agencies to learn about the industry. I have always loved books and knew I wanted to be involved in creating them. As an agent, I have the opportunity to find new authors, to edit and shape their work, and to help them realize their dream of publication. I also have the freedom to choose projects that I am passionate about.

How do you feel about writers: I have the utmost respect and admiration for them, for their powers of creativity, for their dedication, for their perseverance and the face of rejection.

What are your favorite books, movies, and TV shows, and why: I can never pick favorites because it's always changing. Books I like: anything by Edith Wharton and Shakespeare; *To the Lighthouse* by Virginia Woolf; *Atonement* by Ian McEwan; *So Long, See You Tomorrow* by William Maxwell; *The Giver* by Lois Lowry. Movies I like: *Contact, The Thomas Crown Affair, Chocolat*, and *Little Miss Sunshine*. I don't watch much TV, but I loved *Sex and the City, Arrested Development*, and *The Office*.

Describe the client from hell, even if you don't have any: A writer who is unprofessional or rude, who is unwilling to invest real time and effort in editing their manuscript, and who hasn't done their research/has no understanding of the business

Describe the publisher and/or editor from hell: Are we allowed to say bad things about editors?

What do you like best about your clients and the editors and publishers you work with: Everyone loves books, and they are all in it because they are passionate about them.

Will our business exist as we know it in 10 years or so: I wish I knew what it will look like, but I have every confidence it will still exist. People love reading too much for me to imagine a future without books.

REGINA RYAN PUBLISHING ENTERPRISES, INC.

251 Central Park West, New York, NY 10024
212-787-5589
www.reginaryanbooks.com

Agent's name: Regina Ryan
Born: New York, New York
Education: BA Trinity College, Washington DC; graduate work NYU and New School

Career history: Editor: Alfred A. Knopf, Inc.; editor-in-chief, Macmillan Adult Books; founded firm as a book packaging and literary agency in 1977. Now, we are a literary agency only.

Hobbies/Personal interests: Birding, mushroom hunting, wildflowers, cooking, gardening, ballet, modern dance, opera, reading, fine art

Categories/Subjects that you are most enthusiastic about agenting: Books that can change things for the better and/or open our eyes to something new and exciting. Areas of special interest include true adventure, memoir, and well-written narrative nonfiction; also architecture, history, natural history (especially birds and wildflowers), politics, science, the environment, women's issues, parenting, cooking, psychology, health, wellness, diet, fitness, lifestyle, home improvement and design, business, popular reference, leisure activities including sports, travel, gardening.

Categories/Subjects writers shouldn't bother pitching to you: No fiction or children's literature (other than those by clients I already represent); no poetry, movie scripts, or celebrity tell-alls, or anything that involves vampires and/or demons or conspiracy theories

If you were not an agent, what might you be doing instead: I would love to be a park ranger, a botanist, or an ornithologist, but I suspect that in the real world I'd be a lawyer.

What's the best way for nonfiction writers to solicit your interest: I prefer a brief e-mail query or snail mail (with SASE) query describing the project, explaining why it is needed, an evaluation of the competition, and what [the writer's] qualifications are. No telephone queries and no faxes. Please don't send by a method that requires a signature.

Do you charge reading or management fees: No

What are the most common mistakes writers make when pitching to you: They don't get to the point but deliver too much preamble. They don't understand how to analyze the competition by explaining why their books are different and better. They misunderstand the market for their books and often wildly exaggerate the possibilities to the point where it's useless.

Describe the client from hell, even if you don't have any: A client from hell can take several forms. There is the person who doesn't do what is asked of him or her; the person who turns in sloppy work; the person who calls on the phone for no real reason and/or talks endlessly; and finally the person who is never, ever satisfied.

How would you describe the perfect client: A great client is a really good writer who is a smart, hard-working pro who understands the business and who writes and promotes accordingly. My dream client is also polite, respectful, and understands and appreciates what we've accomplished on his or her behalf.

How and why did you become an agent: I had been a book editor in publishing houses for many years before I went on my own, first as an out-of-house editor and then as a packager and agent. It was hard to do both packaging and agenting, so I concentrated for some years on packaging. However, as a packager, most of my ideas came from my own head. I missed the variety of people and ideas that an editor is exposed to daily. Now, as a full-time agent, I delight in the interesting people and ideas that come my way nearly every single day.

What can a writer do to increase the odds of you becoming his or her agent: A great title and a good selling sentence that defines the book really helps. A writer should convince me that first of all, he or she is a really good writer. Then, the writer must show me that the subject is important, that there is a real need for it and a significant market for it. I want to be convinced that the book hasn't been done before and that the author has a good, strong platform.

How would you describe what you do as an agent to someone (or something) from another planet: The first thing I do is to find book projects to represent. This means I either read submissions or approach people who I'd like to see write a book. Once I've committed to a project, I guide the author in shaping a selling proposal using my strong editorial background and my understanding of the marketplace gained over my many years in the business. When the proposal is ready, I bring it to the attention of the editors and publishers I think would be best for it. When a publisher makes an offer, I negotiate terms and review the contract. Then, once it is sold, I exploit whatever other rights are saleable. I hover over the publishing process to help the book and author succeed out in the world in whatever way I can.

How do you feel about editors and publishers: I like editors, and I respect them. They are usually overworked book lovers, just as I am. They work very hard in a very difficult, often frustrating, publishing environment. Publishers—the "suits"— can be the cause of a lot of the above-mentioned frustration—with their sometimes short-sighted view of the possibilities of some of my books, but in general, they, too, work hard and love books and try to do their best.

How do you feel about writers: I like writers. They are usually hard-working, creative, interesting, and smart people. I know because I was married to one for 33 years.

What do you think the future holds for book publishing: I think it's going to get harder and harder to place books with the large publishers, unless nonfiction writers have a golden platform.

What are your favorite books, movies, and TV shows, and why: I read fiction for my pleasure, and recently I have developed a passion for Vladimir Nabokov's *Pale Fire*. Also, Nikolai Bulgakov's *The Master and Margarita*. My favorite movie of late is *Little Miss Sunshine*. I also loved *March of the Penguins* and *The Devil Wears Prada*. On TV I like *Washington Week in Review*, *Book TV*, *Dog Whisperer*, *Top Chef*, *Project Runway*, *Nature*, *Nova*, *Antiques Road Show*, *Mystery*, and good movies on TV. Actually my favorite entertainment is listening to shows on WNYC, our local NPR talk radio station. I always learn something.

In your opinion what do editors think of you: I think they think of me as a pro who understands the business and who represents quality projects.

On a personal level, what do you think people like and dislike about you: I think people think I'm fun, smart, a straight shooter, and a caring and loyal friend.

What are some representative titles that you have sold: *Gilded Mansions: The Stately Homes of America's First Millionaire Society*, Wayne Craven, W. W. Norton;

Chronicle: The 750-Year History of an Eastern European Jewish Family, Michael Karpin, John Wiley; Return to the Middle Kingdom: One Family, Three Revolutionaries, and the Birth of Modern China, Yuan-tsung Chen, Union Square Press; Rain Before Rainbows: How Successful People Failed at First in Their Chosen Fields, Darcy Andries, Sellers Publishing; The Legacy: The Rockefellers and Their Museums, Suzanne Loebl, Smithsonian Press; Escaping Toxic Guilt: Five Proven Steps to Free Yourself from Guilt for Good, Susan Carrell, McGraw-Hill; Mortality Bites: Living with Cancer in Your 20s and 30s, Kairol Rosenthal, John Wiley; Great Smoky National Park and Acadia National Park: FalconGuides primers, Randi Minetor, Globe Pequot Press; 151 Quick Ideas for Great Advertising on a Shoestring, Jean Joachim, Career Press; The Serotonin Power Diet: A Scientifically Proven Weight Loss Program That Uses Your Brain's Ability to Stop Your Overeating by Judith Wurtman, PhD, and Nina Marquis, MD, Rodale; The Bomb in the Basement: How Israel Got Its Nuclear Option and What It Means for the World, Michael Karpin, Simon & Schuster; Anatomy of a Suicidal Mind by Edwin Shneidman, with an introduction by Judy Collins, Oxford University Press; Escape from Saigon, Andrea Warren, a Melanie Kroupa Book, Farrar, Straus & Giroux; What Babies Say Before They Can Talk, Paul Holinger, MD, with Kalia Doner, Fireside Books; The Altruist, Walter Keady, MacAdam/Cage; American Art: History and Culture, Wayne Craven, McGraw-Hill; Beyond the Bake Sale: The Ultimate School Fund Raising Book, Jean Joachim, St. Martin's Press; Lost in the Mirror: Borderline Personality Disorder, Richard Moskovitz, MD, Taylor Publishing; Surviving Hitler: A Teenager in the Nazi Death Camps, Andrea Warren, HarperCollins Junior Books; The Garden Primer, Barbara Damrosch, Workman Publishing; Thomas Eakins by William Innes Homer, Abbeville Press; Organize Your Office! by Ronni Eisenberg and Kate Kelly, Hyperion; Pickups: Classic American Trucks by Harry Moses, photographs by William Bennett Seitz, Random House; Wildflowers in Your Garden, Viki Ferreniea, Random House; Living in Style without Losing Your Mind, Marco Pasanella, Simon & Schuster; The Art of the Table: Table Settings, Table Manners, Table Ware by the Baroness Suzanne von Drachenfels, Simon & Schuster; The Last Childhood: A Family's Memories of Alzheimer's, Carrie Knowles, Three Rivers Press

THE RICHARD PARKS AGENCY

PO Box 693, Salem, NY 12865
518-854-9466
www.richardparksagency.com

Agent's name: Richard Parks
Born: Jacksonville, Florida
Education: BA Duke University, MA University of North Carolina
Career history: I stumbled into the agency business when I took a part-time

summer job at Curtis Brown, Ltd. By the end of the summer, I was hooked. I was at CB for nine years, then left to spend several years working in the movie business, first as an executive at United Artists and then as an independent producer. I produced two movies for HBO but didn't much like it and decided to return to New York and the agency business. I opened my own agency there in 1989. Two years ago, thanks to technology, I shifted my headquarters to the village upstate where I've had a second home for quite some time. I now spend two days a week in New York and five upstate.

Hobbies/Personal interests: Gardening while listening to recorded books

Categories/Subjects that you are most enthusiastic about agenting: Literary and commercial fiction (including mystery, thrillers, and suspense), narrative nonfiction, biography, memoir, history, travel narratives, popular science, parenting, light business, some prescriptive nonfiction

Categories/Subjects writers shouldn't bother pitching to you: Romance fiction, Western fiction; highly technical business or science

If you were not an agent, what might you be doing instead: Teaching

What's the best way for fiction writers to solicit your interest: I read mostly by referral, but a really good query letter will sometimes catch my eye.

Do you charge fees separate from your commission or offer nonagenting fee-based services: I only ask clients to reimburse me for special expenses that I've incurred on their behalf, such as if they ask me to send something to them by FedEx. I do not charge reading fees or any other kinds of fees.

What are some representative titles that you have sold: *Chronic City*, Jonathan Lethem, Doubleday; *The Ballad of West 10th Street*, Marjorie Kernan, HarperPerennial; *A Million Nightingales*, Susan Straight, Pantheon; *The Ghost in Love*, Jonathan Carroll, Sarah Crichton Books/FSG; *The Gerbil Farmer's Daughter, A Memoir*, Holly Robinson, Harmony Books; *7 Steps to Raising a Bilingual Child*, Naomi Steiner, MD, AMACOM; *The Age of Dreaming*, Nina Revoyr, Akashic Books; *South by South Bronx*, Abraham Rodriguez, Akashic Books; *What Ever Happened to Orson Welles?*, Joseph McBride, The University Press of Kentucky; *Deep Focus*, Sean Howe, editor, Soft Skull Press

How and why did you become an agent: See above for how. I became an agent because, once I discovered the business, I loved working with writers. And I've always been an avid reader.

How do you feel about writers: They enhance our lives, giving us insight and knowledge and showing us the world from perspectives other than our own.

How would you describe what you do as an agent to someone (or something) from another planet: I don't have conversations with entities from other planets!

What are your favorite books, movies, and TV shows, and why: There are so many books I love that it's hard to list favorites. I like movies with some substance, not the big action adventure stuff or date comedies. I'm not much of a television watcher at all.

Describe the client from hell, even if you don't have any: Fortunately, I've rarely encountered one.

Describe the publisher and/or editor from hell: Again, perhaps I've been lucky, but I haven't encountered many. Most of the publishers and editors I've dealt with are bright, professional people. I do dislike editors who don't respond to legitimate phone calls, e-mails, or submissions, and I have encountered a few of those.

What do you like best about your clients and the editors and publishers you work with: The fact that they are bright, interesting people who enliven my life

You're welcome to share your thoughts and sentiments about the business of writing and publishing: As we all know, we're going through a difficult time in publishing, along with difficult times in general. But it's not a business that's going to go away. It will evolve and continue to provide readers with entertainment and enlightenment.

Describe yourself: I'm a steady, easy-going person who loves his work and the friends he has made through it.

Will our business exist as we know it in 10 years or so: Some aspects of our business will remain the same, but it's going to change dramatically as electronic publishing continues to grow.

RICK BROADHEAD & ASSOCIATES

47 St. Clair Avenue West, Suite #501, Toronto, ON, Canada M4V 3A5
416-929-0516
www.rbaliterary.com

Don't be scared off by my address! Many of my clients are American experts/authors, and I have made dozens of sales to major American publishers (see below). I welcome queries by e-mail.

Agent's name: Rick Broadhead
E-mail: submissions@rbaliterary.com
Education: BBA, York University; MBA, Schulich School of Business, York University
Career history: I opened my literary agency in 2002 and quickly established myself as one of the leading agencies in the business. In addition to being one of the few literary agents who has a business background and MBA, I have the rare distinction of being a best-selling author. I wrote and cowrote over 30 books prior to establishing my literary agency, and this affords me a unique perspective on the industry that few agents possess and that benefits my clients at every step of the book development and contract negotiation process. I have negotiated millions of dollars in royalties for my authors with such venerable American and Canadian publishing houses as Random House, HarperCollins, Hyperion/Disney, Simon & Schuster, Penguin, St. Martin's Press, Knopf, Rodale, Wiley, Harlequin, Hachette Book Group/Grand Central Publishing, W. W. Norton, Running Press, Chronicle Books, and many others. Books represented by my agency have appeared on best-seller lists,

been shortlisted for literary awards, translated into multiple languages, and through my agency's partnerships in Hollywood, been optioned for film and television development. One of my first book sales was quickly optioned by Paramount/CBS for development as a television sitcom. My marketing and business expertise were acknowledged by my alma mater, York University, which awarded me its prestigious marketing medal for demonstrated excellence in marketing. My vast knowledge of the publishing industry, both as an author and an agent, and my strong relationships with editors have allowed me to consistently negotiate excellent deals for my clients. I'm a meticulous negotiator, and I have secured many six-figure deals for my clients.

Categories/Subjects that you are most enthusiastic about agenting: The agency's clients include accomplished journalists, historians, physicians, television personalities, bloggers and creators of popular websites, successful business executives, and experts in their respective fields. They include science journalist and *New York Times* best-selling author Sam Kean, author of *The Disappearing Spoon: And Other True Tales of Madness, Love, and the History of the World from the Periodic Table of the Elements*; Yale University physician and US Surgeon General nominee Dr. David Katz; hormone expert Dr. Natasha Turner, author of the best-selling book, *The Hormone Diet*; survival skills expert and Discovery Channel host Les Stroud (*Survivorman*); former *New York Times* reporter Jerry Eskenazi (who has written over 8,000 stories for the *New York Times*); ice road trucker Alex Debogorski, costar of History television's hit show, *Ice Road Truckers*; intelligence expert and national security historian Matthew Aid; Princeton scholar and Yemen expert Gregory Johnsen; former CNN Senior Political Analyst Bill Schneider; sports journalist and *ESPN: The Magazine* contributor Gare Joyce; *Wall Street Journal* best-selling author and marketing guru Ryan Allis; award-winning military historian Tim Cook; ornithologist/biologist Dr. Glen Chilton, author of *The Curse of the Labrador Duck*; musician Steven Page, former lead singer of the Barenaked Ladies; comic-book blogger Brian Cronin; and golf blogger Neil Sagebiel, author of *The Longest Shot: Jack Fleck, Ben Hogan, and Pro Golf's Greatest Upset*. I love history, politics, sports, natural history (birding/nature/environment), current affairs, biography, science and pop science, pop culture, self-help, health, medicine, military history, national security/intelligence, business, and humor. I especially love working with journalists, and I have found many of my best clients after seeing their work in magazines or newspapers. I've also sold many books based on popular websites and from authors who have wowed me with a great book pitch.

Categories/Subjects writers shouldn't bother pitching to you: Fiction/novels/novellas, children's books, poetry, screenplays

What's the best way for nonfiction writers to solicit your interest: A short query letter is best. Describe the book project and your credentials/expertise/platform. You can contact me via e-mail or send a letter by mail.

Do you charge fees separate from your commission or offer nonagenting fee-based services: I do not charge fees or offer fee-based services. Like most literary agents, I am paid on a commission basis.

What are the most common mistakes writers make when pitching to you: Overly long query letters; sending me a proposal that has clearly not been vetted for grammar and spelling mistakes; not having confidence in your work; pasting chapters into the body of an e-mail; sending attachments without asking first; copying the same query letter to multiple literary agents simultaneously; not personalizing a query letter; sending a manuscript or multiple chapters (electronically or in hard copy) before an agent has requested it; pitching multiple book projects simultaneously. Make sure you have a solid proposal ready *before* you contact a literary agent. It's quite demotivating when an author pitches an idea, gets me excited, and then tells me the proposal is still in progress and weeks away from completion.

What's your definition of a great client: The best clients, not surprisingly, are those who make my job easier. They're professional, patient, prepared, flexible, open to my input, prompt to respond to my questions and needs, and their proposals are outstanding. Incessant phone calls and e-mails make my job very difficult since they take time away from selling.

What can a writer do to increase the odds of you becoming his or her agent: First of all, you should know what types of books I'm most interested in, as I'm most likely to be receptive to a pitch if the book fits my interests and the subject categories I'm looking for. Check my website at www.rbaliterary.com to see the types of books I have sold. Second, your proposal needs to be polished. There are three major criteria I look for when evaluating book proposals (and query letters): (1) a talented writer; (2) a great concept (ideally, a book that is different from other books currently on the market); (3) an author with a platform, credentials, and the relevant expertise. Books rarely sell themselves these days, so publishers look for authors who have a "platform." If you're a leading expert in your field or you have experience writing for major newspapers or magazines, or if you've been on television or radio, or if you've done something really different or compelling, I'm more likely to have success selling you to a major publisher. Similarly, if you have a popular blog or website or you have a large audience of potential book buyers or you're affiliated with a major organization or university/college, publishers are more likely to be interested in you. Remember that a literary agent has to sell your project to an editor, and then the editor has to sell your project internally to his/her colleagues (including the marketing, publicity, and sales staff), and then the publisher has to sell your book to the book buyers at the chains and bookstores and persuade them to buy lots of copies. At each stage in the process, it needs to be clear what's going to make your book sell. You're most likely to get my attention if you write a succinct pitch letter and then follow up (if requested) with a polished proposal that persuasively demonstrates your expertise and platform, the market potential of your book, and why your book is different. In short—get me excited! In the marketing section of your proposal, do not put together a full-blown marketing plan that includes a laundry list of general ideas for book signings, press releases, a website, etc. This is one of the biggest mistakes authors make when crafting a book proposal. Publishers are most interested in the *existing* connections and relationships you have—people you know, publications you have written for, and/or any success you've already had. For example, if you have an existing website that has a sizeable audience, that's an important selling point for your book (rather than your plan to build a website when your book comes out). Similarly, if you've written for any well-known magazines or newspapers, or if you've appeared on radio or television, that experience is more meaningful to a publisher than a list of media outlets you're going to pitch when your book is released. Endorsements from best-selling authors and/or experts are also extremely valuable and can be helpful when I'm pitching your book proposal to a publisher.

How and why did you become an agent: I'm an entrepreneur at heart, and I love the business side of publishing—finding great authors, pitching book ideas, negotiating deals, and being a part of an exciting and dynamic industry. I became a best-selling author early in my career, and eight years later, after several successive best sellers, I decided to put my business savvy and passion for publishing to work for other authors. I love what I do, and I love getting excited about a new book project that I can pitch to the publishers and editors I work with. There's something special about holding a book in your hand and realizing you played a part in its creation.

How would you describe what you do as an agent to someone (or something) from another planet: I help make dreams come true! A lot of writers question the value of an agent, but my involvement will always result in a better deal for the author, whether it's in the advance/royalties, the selection of the publisher/editor, or better contract terms.

What are some representative titles that you have sold: *The Pirates of Somalia: Inside Their Hidden World* by Jay Bahadur (Pantheon/Random House); *King of the Road: True Tales from a Legendary Ice Road Trucker* by Alex Debogorski (Wiley); *The Curse of the Labrador Duck: My Obsessive Quest to the Edge of Extinction* by ornithologist Dr. Glen Chilton (Simon & Schuster); *Wikibrands: Reinventing Your Company in a Customer-Driven Marketplace* by business strategists Sean Moffitt and Mike Dover (McGraw-Hill); *Northern Armageddon: The Battle of the Plains of Abraham* by military historian Peter MacLeod (Knopf/Random House); *Survive!—Essential Skills and Tactics to Get You out of Anywhere—Alive* by survival-skills expert Les Stroud, host of *Survivorman* on the Discovery Channel (HarperCollins); *See Mix Drink: A Refreshingly Simple Guide to Crafting the World's Most Popular Cocktails* by Brian Murphy (Little, Brown); *The Secret Sentry: The Top-Secret History of the National Security Agency* by intelligence historian Matthew Aid (Bloomsbury Press); *The Flavor Point Diet* by David Katz, MD (Rodale); *Do Chocolate Lovers Have Sweeter Babies?— Exploring the Surprising Science of Pregnancy* by former Random House editor Jena Pincott (Bantam Dell/Random House); *Which Comes First, Cardio or Weights?— Fitness Myths, Training Truths, and Other Surprising Discoveries from the Science of Exercise* by *Popular Mechanics* contributing editor Alex Hutchinson (HarperCollins); *Portrait of Camelot: A Thousand Days in the Kennedy White House* by Richard Reeves and Harvey Sawler (Abrams); *The Longest Shot: Jack Fleck, Ben Hogan, and Pro Golf's Greatest Upset* by golf blogger Neil Sagebiel (Thomas Dunne Books/St. Martin's Press); *Insultingly Stupid Movie Physics: Hollywood's Best Mistakes, Goofs, and Flat-Out*

Destructions of the Basic Laws of the Universe by engineer and science teacher Tom Rogers (Sourcebooks); *The Quantum Ten: A Story of Passion, Tragedy, Ambition and Science* by science journalist Sheilla Jones (Oxford University Press); *101 Foods That Could Save Your Life* by registered dietician David Grotto (Bantam Dell/Random House); *Bad Bridesmaid: Bachelorette Brawls and Taffeta Tantrums—What We Go through for Her Big Day* by journalist Siri Agrell (Henry Holt); *10 Years Thinner: The Ultimate Lifestyle Program for Winding Back Your Physiological Clock—and Your Bathroom Scale* by Christine Lydon, MD (Da Capo Press/Perseus Books Group); *The Menopause Makeover* by Staness Jonekos (Harlequin)

RITA ROSENKRANZ LITERARY AGENCY

440 West End Avenue, Suite 15D, New York, NY 10024-5358
212-873-6333
www.ritarosenkranzliteraryagency.com

Agent's name: Rita Rosenkranz
E-mail: rrosenkranz@mindspring.com
Career history: Editor at various major New York publishing houses before becoming an agent in 1990; member of AAR, Authors Guild, International Women's Writing Guild (IWWG)
Categories/Subjects that you are most enthusiastic about agenting: Animals; anthropology/archaeology; art/architecture/design; biography/autobiography; business/economics; child guidance/parenting; computers/electronic; cooking/foods/nutrition; crafts/hobbies; current affairs; ethnic/cultural interests; gay/lesbian issues; government/politics/law; health/medicine; history; how-to; humor/satire; interior design/decorating; language/literature/criticism; military/war; money/finance; music/dance; nature/environment; New Age/metaphysics; photography; popular culture; psychology; religious/inspirational; science/technology; self-help/personal improvement; sports; theater/film; women's issues/studies. This agency focuses on adult nonfiction, stresses strong editorial development and refinement before submitting to publishers, and brainstorms ideas with authors. Actively seeking authors who are well paired with their subject, either for professional or personal reasons.
Categories/Subjects writers shouldn't bother pitching to you: Fiction, children's books, and poetry
What's the best way for writers to solicit your interest: Send query letter only (no proposal) via regular mail or e-mail. Submit proposal package with SASE only on request. No fax queries. Considers simultaneous queries. Responds in two weeks to queries. *Tips:* Identify the current competition for your project to make sure the project is valid. A strong cover letter is very important.
What categories do you represent, by percentages: Nonfiction: 100 percent
What are some representative titles that you have sold: *Get Known Before the*

Book Deal: Use Your Personal Strengths to Grow an Author Platform by Christina Katz (Writer's Digest Books); *29 Gifts* by Cami Walker (DaCapo Press); *See Me after Class: Experienced Teachers Share the Lessons They Learned the Hard Way* (Kaplan); *Twenty Strengths Adoptive Parents Need to Succeed* by Sherrie Eldridge (Bantam Dell); *Lifelines: The Black Book of Proverbs* by Askhari Johnson Hodari and Yvonne McCalla Sobers (Broadway Books); *Encyclopedia of Jewish Food* by Gil Marks (Wiley)

RIVERSIDE LITERARY AGENCY

41 Simon Keets Road, Leyden, MA 01337
413-772-0067 | fax: 413-772-0969
www.riversideliteraryagency.com

Agent's name: Susan Lee Cohen
E-mail: rivlit@sover.net
Born: New York, New York
Career history: I have been a literary agent for almost 30 years. I began my publishing career at Viking Penguin and subsequently worked as a literary agent at Richard Curtis Associates and Sterling Lord Literistic before founding Riverside Literary Agency in 1990.

Categories/Subjects writers shouldn't bother pitching to you: Genre fiction (romance, science fiction/fantasy, Westerns), children's books, poetry

Do you charge fees separate from your commission or offer nonagenting fee-based services: No

What are some representative titles that you have sold: *The Myth of Sanity* (Viking), *The Sociopath Next Door* (Broadway), and *The Paranoia Switch* (Farrar Straus & Giroux) by Martha Stout; *Reviving Ophelia* (Putnam/Ballantine); *The Shelter of Each Other* (Putnam/Ballantine); *Another Country* (Putnam/Ballantine); *The Middle of Everywhere* (Harcourt); *Letters to a Young Therapist* (Basic Books); *Writing to Change the World* (Riverhead) and *Seeking Peace* (Riverhead) by Mary Pipher; *Pawprints of Katrina* by Cathy Scott (Wiley); *Right, Wrong, and Risky* by Mark Davidson (Norton); *The Secret Magdalene* by Ki Longfellow (Crown); *Please Kill Me* by Legs McNeil and Gillian McCain (Grove/Atlantic); *Stop Running from Love* by Dusty Miller (New Harbinger); *Buddha Is as Buddha Does* (HarperOne), *The Big Questions* (Rodale), *Awakening to the Sacred* (Doubleday), *Awakening the Buddhist Heart, Letting Go of the Person You Used to Be* (Doubleday), and *The Mind Is Mightier than the Sword* (Doubleday) by Lama Surya Das

RLR ASSOCIATES, LTD.

7 West 51st Street, New York, NY 10019
212-541-8641 | fax: 212-541-6052
www.rlrassociates.net

Agent's name: Scott Gould
E-mail: sgould@rlrassociates.net
Born: Baltimore, Maryland
Education: New York University
Career history: I began my career in the editorial department at *Playboy* magazine, and later, handling rights at another agency before building my client list at RLR.

Categories/Subjects that you are most enthusiastic about agenting: I represent and am always on the lookout for literary and commercial fiction (including genre fiction) and all kinds of well-written, narrative nonfiction, from history to pop science to humor.

Categories/Subjects writers shouldn't bother pitching to you: I don't represent poetry or screenplays.

What's the best way for fiction writers to solicit your interest: The best way to stand out is to e-mail (or snail mail) a query letter that tells me everything about the project and you in an interesting and professional way, along with a few pages or more of the manuscript. Creativity counts, but in the end the book stands for itself, so don't kill yourself over a query letter.

Do you charge fees separate from your commission or offer nonagenting fee-based services: We follow the AAR guidelines and do not charge any reading or other fees.

What are some representative titles that you have sold: *Cash from Chaos: Creating and Building a Successful Gen X/Y Brand* by Eric Boyd and Sean Murphy (Prentice Hall/Pearson); *The Greatest Yankees Myths* by Peter Handrinos (Triumph Books); *Nathanael Greene: A Biography of the American Revolution* by Gerald Carbone (Palgrave Macmillan)

How and why did you become an agent: I became an agent because I love seeking out talent and making good books happen.

What are your favorite books, movies, and TV shows, and why: Books: *Confederacy of Dunces, Jesus' Son, Lolita, Andy Kaufman Revealed!, Fear and Loathing in Las Vegas.* Movies and TV: *The Big Lebowski, The Wire, The Sopranos.*

You're welcome to share your thoughts and sentiments about the business of writing and publishing: This really is a business of relationships, which is generally a good thing because book people tend to be interesting people.

ROBIN STRAUS LITERARY AGENCY

7 West 51st Street, New York, NY 10019
212-541-8641 | fax: 212-541-6052
www.robinstrausagency.com

Agent's name: Robin Straus
E-mail: info@robinstrausagency.com
Education: Wellesley BA, NYU School of Business MBA
Career history: Started at publishing houses, doing editorial work at Little, Brown and subsidiary rights at Doubleday and Random House; Vice President Wallace & Sheil Agency for four years, and started Robin Straus Agency, Inc. in 1983

Categories/Subjects that you are most enthusiastic about agenting: High-quality literary fiction and nonfiction. Subject is of less importance than fine writing and research.

Categories/Subjects writers shouldn't bother pitching to you: Genre fiction such as science fiction, horror, romance, Westerns; poetry; no screenplays or plays

If you were not an agent, what might you be doing instead: Traveling the world; raising horses and dogs; going to medical school

What's the best way for writers to solicit your interest: A great query letter and sample material that speaks for itself. Caution: We are a very small agency and unable to take on more than a few clients per year, so we would have to be completely smitten.

Do you charge reading or management fees: No

What categories do you represent, by percentages: Nonfiction: 60 percent (history, social science, psychology, women's interest, education, travel, biography, art history, and many other fields); fiction: 40 percent

What are the most common mistakes writers make when pitching to you: Bad grammar in letters, clichés, overstating claims for book being revolutionary; asking us to download queries and manuscripts

Describe the client from hell, even if you don't have any: Being awakened every morning by a client's phone call

How would you describe the perfect client: A captivating writer who can make any subject interesting; receptive to suggestions on how to improve work; appreciative that the publishing process is a collaborative effort; imaginative about ways to market self and books

How and why did you become an agent: I started out my career working on manuscripts, but discovered I also liked the business end of publishing and moved into rights. Agenting seemed the best way to combine editorial and selling activities and be a strong advocate for authors.

What can a writer do to increase the odds of you becoming his or her agent: Convince me with your arguments. Dazzle me with your prose. Make me fall in love with your characters.

How would you describe what you do as an agent to someone (or something)

from another planet: When I want to represent an author, I work with him/her to help shape proposals and manuscripts to entice editors to make an offer. I submit material to publishers, negotiate contracts, vet royalty statements, sell translation, serial, film, and audio rights on behalf of client. I generally act as the business manager for the author and intercede whenever necessary throughout the entire publishing process. I view my relationship with my clients as a continuum that extends over many books.

How do you feel about editors and publishers: They do less editing than they used to, probably because they are under more pressure.

What do you think the future holds for writers, publishers, and agents: Even with all the competition for our time, books will always have an important place and publishers will continue to exist and figure out ways to stay central. With the rise of the Internet and other electronic media, there is a huge need for content, and authors increasingly will find other venues and audiences for their work beyond paper over board volumes. The challenge will be in finding fair ways to compensate the writers while simultaneously protecting their work.

What are some representative titles that you have sold: Fiction such as *The No. 1 Ladies Detective Agency* and other series (Pantheon/Anchor), *The Ivy Chronicles* (Viking), *Coma* (Riverhead), *The Year of the French* (NY Review), *Budapest Noir* (HarperCollins), *The Go-Between* (Houghton Harcourt), *Becoming Jane Eyre* (Penguin), *The Rose Labyrinth* (Atria). Nonfiction such as *Ideas* (HarperCollins), *Outfoxing Fear* (Norton), *Character Matters* (Touchstone), *A Writer at War* (Pantheon), *Mismatch* (Scribner), *Higher Education?* (Times), *The German Genius* (HarperCollins), *Fishface* (Phaidon), *The Healthiest You/Program* (Atria), *Polar Obsession* (National Geographic), *Simple Skin Beauty* (Atria), Jimmy Connors's memoir (Harper), *Trotsky* (Yale), *Who Do You Think You Are* (Touchstone), *The Time of Their Lives* (St. Martin's), *Couples in Art* (Prestel), *The Fall of Berlin* (Viking)

SANDRA DIJKSTRA LITERARY AGENCY

1155 Camino del Mar, PMB 515, Del Mar, CA 92014
858-755-3115
www.dijkstraagency.com

Agent's name: Sandra Dijkstra
Born: New York, New York
Education: BA in English, Adelphi; MA in comparative literature, UC Berkeley; PhD in French literature, UC San Diego
Career history: University professor, literary agent
Hobbies/Personal interests: Reading, films
Categories/Subjects that you are most enthusiastic about agenting: Specialize in literary and commercial fiction and nonfiction, especially biography, business,

current affairs, health, history, psychology, popular culture, science, self-help, narrative nonfiction

Categories/Subjects writers shouldn't bother pitching to you: Westerns, science fiction, romance, poetry collections, screenplays

If you were not an agent, what might you be doing instead: I would be an editor and/or college professor.

What's the best way for fiction writers to solicit your interest: Please send a query letter by regular mail (e-mail submissions are NOT accepted) with 50 sample pages of your manuscript (double-spaced, single-sided), and a one- to two-page synopsis. Please refer to our website, www.dijkstraagency.com, for our most updated submission guidelines.

What's the best way for nonfiction writers to solicit your interest: Send one to two sample chapters, profile of competition, intended audience and market, author bio, and brief chapter outline.

Do you charge reading or management fees: No

What are the most common mistakes writers make when pitching to you: Incessant phone calls to check on the status of their submissions or demanding reading notes on an unsolicited submission. Writers should also be careful not to overhype their projects and to remember to let us know about your platform or previous writing credentials.

Describe the client from hell, even if you don't have any: The client from hell is never satisfied and has expectations that exceed all possibilities of realization.

What's your definition of a great client: Dream clients ask the right questions, offer useful support material, and trust their agents. They do not e-mail and/or call daily. These clients keep us apprised of progress and are professionals who understand that we are their partners and advocates. They help us to represent their best interests, trust us, and work like hell to make [their] book happen after writing the best book possible.

What can a writer do to increase the odds of you becoming his or her agent: They should try to find a publisher, bookseller, librarian, or established author to recommend them to us. They should also try to publish their work in magazines, newspapers, or online—leading us to chase them!

How and why did you become an agent: I became an agent to publish books that help writers realize their dreams and make a difference in the world.

How would you describe what you do as an agent to someone (or something) from another planet: I read manuscripts and hope to fall in love. Then, when I do, I talk on the phone with editors and prepare them to fall in love. When I discover talent, I support it with all my heart, brain, and soul.

How do you feel about editors and publishers: Editors are overworked and underpaid. They are (most of them) dedicated and passionate about authors and books. In a perfect world, publishers would have more support, more money, and more time! Publishers would be "making public the book," in the fullest sense, which they try to do, often.

How do you feel about writers: Writers are our inspiration! Their work drives our work. There's nothing better than nurturing and campaigning for their books in the world.

What do you see in the near future for book publishing: Lots of joy when the publishing process works as it should. Lots of sorrow when it doesn't.

What are your favorite books, movies, and TV shows, and why: Bill Maher, Jon Stewart, Keith Olbermann

In your opinion, what do editors think of you: That I'm pushy—on the front and back end of the publishing process, which is my job

What are some representative titles that you have sold: Nonfiction: *Devil's Highway* by Luis Urrea (Back Bay Books); *Religious Literacy* by Stephen Prothero (Harper San Francisco); *Winter World* by Bernd Heinrich (Harper Perennial); *God on Trial* by Peter Irons (Viking); *The Little Book That Beat the Market* by Joel Greenblatt (Wiley). Fiction: *Saving Fish from Drowning* by Amy Tan (Ballantine Books); *Snow Flower and the Secret Fan* by Lisa See (Random House); *Empress Orchid* by Anchee Min (Houghton Mifflin); *Lethally Blond* by Kate White (Warner); *Sweet Revenge* by Diane Mott Davidson (William Morrow)

SANFORD J. GREENBURGER ASSOCIATES

55 Fifth Ave., New York, NY 10003
212-206-5675
www.sjga.com

Agent's name: Matthew Bialer
Born: December 20, 1962
Education: BA, Vassar College
Career history: Spent 14 years in the book department at the William Morris Agency; have been in the business since 1985
Hobbies/Personal interests: Painting, photography, outdoors, music (rock, jazz, classical)
Categories/Subjects that you are most enthusiastic about agenting: Thrillers, urban fantasy, epic fantasy, cross-over science fiction, some romance, pop music books, narrative nonfiction, literary fiction, women's fiction, sports
Categories/Subjects writers shouldn't bother pitching to you: Self-help, diet books
If you were not an agent, what might you be doing instead: Paint (watercolor) and take black-and-white street photographs
What's the best way for fiction writers to solicit your interest: Be aware of what I represent (at least some of it) and see if what you wrote jibes with my taste.
What's the best way for nonfiction writers to solicit your interest: Letter
Do you charge reading or management fees: No

What are the most common mistakes writers make when pitching to you: They just shotgun it out there without any thought as to who the agent is and what they do.

Describe the client from hell, even if you don't have any: That's a tough one. Generally speaking, it is a client who does not listen, who does not get how things are properly done in the business.

What's your definition of a great client: Listens. Trusts. And has a good rapport. A great relationship with the client is me not telling the writer what to do by an ongoing dialogue. I like clients who can teach me a thing or two.

What can a writer do to increase the odds of you becoming his or her agent: Do the homework on what is out there and successful that is like your project. And be realistic about it. And find out about the agent to whom you are pitching.

How and why did you become an agent: I love books and publishing. I like creativity. I like to help make a project come to fruition. I became one because I started at an agency and just never looked back.

How would you describe what you do as an agent to someone (or something) from another planet: I manage book careers. I help a writer sell his or her book to a publisher. I am a matchmaker between project and editor/publisher and then I help manage the publishing of the book in both the United States and throughout the world.

How do you feel about editors and publishers: In a perfect world, I love them both, but of course I have my preferences. Some editors and publishers are more effective than others or better at a certain kind of book.

How do you feel about writers: Love them

What do you see in the near future for book publishing: Still trying to find itself in a world full of competing media whether a million TV channels, computers, iPods, etc.

What are your favorite books, movies, and TV shows, and why: Books: Cormac McCarthy, Tolkien, Stephen King, Hemingway, Dennis Lehane, Tad Williams, Pynchon, Phil Dick. TV: *Heroes, Without a Trace*. Movies: Too many to name.

In your opinion, what do editors think of you: I think I am well respected and am well known in the industry.

On a personal level, what do you think people like and dislike about you: They love me!

What are some representative titles that you have sold: *Otherland and Shadowmarch* series by Tad Williams; *The Name of the Wind* by Patrick Rothfuss; *The Ice-Man: Confessions of a Mafia Contract Killer* by Philip Carlo; *The People* series by Michael Gear and Kathleen O'Neal Gear; *Truancy: Some Kids Were Rebellious* by Isamu Fukui; *Zanesville* by Kris Saknussemm; *The Bone Thief* by Thomas O'Callaghan

SARAH JANE FREYMANN LITERARY AGENCY

59 West 71st Street, #9b, New York, NY 10023
212-751-8892
www.sarahjanefreymann.com

Agent's name: Katharine Sands

Career history: A literary agent with the Sarah Jane Freymann Literary Agency, Katharine has worked with a varied list of authors who publish a diverse array of books. Highlights include *XTC: SongStories*; *Chasing Zebras: THE Unofficial Guide to House, MD*; *Make Up, Don't Break Up* with Oprah guest Dr. Bonnie Eaker Weil; Playwright Robert Patrick's novel, *Temple Slave*; *The Complete Book on International Adoption: A Step-by-Step Guide to Finding Your Child*; *Hands Off My Belly: The Pregnant Woman's Survival Guide to Myths, Mothers, and Moods*; *Under the Hula Moon*; *The New Laws of Attraction*; *Whipped: A Professional Dominatrix's Secrets for Wrapping Men Around Your Little Finger*; *The Gay Vacation Guide*; *City Tripping: A Guide for Foodies, Fashionistas, and the Generally Style-Obsessed*; *Writers on Directors*; Ford model Helen Lee's *The Tao of Beauty*; *Elvis and You: Your Guide to the Pleasures of Being an Elvis Fan*; *New York: Songs of the City*; *Taxpertise: Dirty Little Secrets the IRS Doesn't Want You to Know*; *The SAT Word Slam*; *Divorce After 50*; *The Complete Book of Bone Health*; *The Safe and Sane Guide to Teenage Plastic Surgery*; to name a few. She is the agent provocateur of *Making the Perfect Pitch: How to Catch a Literary Agent's Eye*, a collection of pitching wisdom from leading literary agents. Actively building her client list, she likes books that have a clear benefit for readers' lives in categories of food, travel, lifestyle, home arts, beauty, wisdom, relationships, parenting, and fresh looks, which might be at issues, life challenges, or popular culture. When reading fiction she wants to be compelled and propelled by urgent storytelling, and hooked by characters. For memoir and femoir, she likes to be transported to a world rarely or newly observed.

Agent's name: Sarah Jane Freymann

Born: London

Education: Although I spent most of my childhood in New York City, I went to a French school—the Lycée Français de New York. I also studied ballet with Balanchine and grew up in a home where the environment was intensely 19th-century European.

Career history: My first job was with the United Nations. I also worked as a model…in real estate…and as an editor in a publishing company.

Hobbies/Personal interests: I am interested in journeys and adventures of every kind—both inner and outer. My personal interests and hobbies keep changing. Right now, I am into teaching…yoga…and, as soon as my shoulder heals, kayaking.

Categories/Subjects that you are most enthusiastic about agenting: Nonfiction: Spirituality, psychology, self-help; women's issues, health/medicine (conventional and alternative); cookbooks; narrative nonfiction; natural science, nature; memoirs;

cutting-edge journalism; multicultural issues; parenting; lifestyle; history. Fiction: Sophisticated mainstream and literary fiction with a distinctive voice: historical and biblical fiction; edgy young-adult fiction.

Categories/Subjects writers shouldn't bother pitching to you: Westerns, screenplays, and almost anything channeled

If you were not an agent, what might you be doing instead: Working with Doctors Without Borders; with children and adolescents; competitive ballroom dancing; singing opera (if I could); cultivating a quiet haven by the sea

What's the best way for fiction writers to solicit your interest: Via a well-written and interesting query letter (include e-mail address) or via an e-mail query (with no attachments). Please send queries to submissions@sarahjanefreymann.com.

What's the best way for nonfiction writers to solicit your interest: Via a well-written and interesting query letter (include e-mail address) or via an e-mail query (with no attachments). Please send queries to submissions@sarahjanefreymann.com.

Do you charge reading or management fees: There are no reading or upfront fees.

What are the most common mistakes writers make when pitching to you: Calling and attempting to describe projects over the phone; characterizing a project as "The best…Startling…Never before in publishing history…" and so on…

Describe the client from hell, even if you don't have any: I honestly wouldn't know because I've always made sure never to take on such a client, but it would be someone who isn't honest with us about themselves or the work, or who has seen it in the past or is reviewing it now. Or someone who is a generally difficult, mean-spirited human being.

What's your definition of a great client: Someone who is not only a natural storyteller and writes beautifully, with passion and intelligence, but who is also a nice human—in other words, a *mensch*. Someone with a sense of humor, who has the patience, the willingness, and the humility to rewrite their material when necessary. And someone who appreciates the hard work and the passion that their agent brings to the job. I am fortunate to have several such clients.

What can a writer do to increase the odds of you becoming his or her agent: Submit a strong, clear, well-written query that sells both the book and its author, with the promise of substance rather than hype.

How and why did you become an agent: I became an agent by rushing in where angels feared to tread, and if I knew then what I know now…I'd do the same thing all over again.

How would you describe what you do as an agent to someone (or something) from another planet: That I am a treasure hunter in search of new universes and galaxies, and of new ways of looking at our old, familiar universe; that I assist writers in getting published by helping them edit and shape their proposals, and then by being a deal-maker, a matchmaker, and a negotiator once the work is ready to be launched.

How do you feel about editors and publishers: I love editors. They are intelligent, idealistic, well informed, incredibly hardworking, and absolutely devoted to their books and to their authors.

How do you feel about writers: I have great respect for writers. They have the capacity to reveal the truth and create new visions for the world.

What do you see in the near future for book publishing: Like all arts and industries, publishing is going through a sometimes painful transition. In large measure, due to the Internet, the publishing universe (like the rest of the world) is becoming increasingly global. This is a challenge—but a challenge we should accept and even welcome.

In your opinion, what do editors think of you: I would imagine editors think I'm a straight shooter and a tough negotiator—but someone who is always fair, invariably gracious, and has terrific projects.

On a personal level, what do you think people think of you: People say that I am charming, generous, elegant, warm, intuitive, kind, and passionate about life. By the same token, I have strong opinions and at times, according to my daughter, I can be self-righteous.

What are some representative titles that you have sold: *Souls of the Air: Invoking the Essence of Birds* by Sy Montgomery (Simon & Schuster); *The Perfect One-Dish: Simple Meals for Family and Friends* by Pam Anderson (Houghton Mifflin); *Mediterranean Hot and Spicy* by Aglaia Kremezi (Random House/Broadway); *Birth Day: A Pediatrician Explores the Science, the History, and the Wonder of Childbirth* by Dr. Mark Sloan (Random House/Ballantine); *100 Places Every Woman Should Go* by Stephanie Elizando Griest (Traveler's Tales) and *Mexican Enough* (Simon & Schuster/Atria); *Stylish Sheds and Elegant Hideaways* by Debra Prinzing and William Wright (Clarkson Potter); *Tossed and Found: Customization, Reclamation, and Personification for Your Home* by John and Linda Meyers (Stewart, Tabori & Chang); *I Want to Be Left Behind: Rapture Here on Earth* by Brenda Peterson (a Merloyd Lawrence book); *That Bird Has My Wings: The Autobiography of an Innocent Man on Death Row* with an Introduction by Pema Chodrun (Harper One); *Taxpertise* by Bonnie Lee (agent Katharine Sands) (Entrepreneur Press); *How to Make Love to a Plastic Cup: and Other Things I Learned While Trying to Knock Up My Wife* by Greg Wolfe (HarperCollins); *The Fatigue Prescription* by Linda Hawes Clever, MD (Viva/Cleis Press); *Wisdom 2.0: Ancient Secrets for the Creative and Constantly Connected* by Soren Gordhamer (HarperOne); *Emptying the Nest: Launching Your Reluctant Young Adult* by Dr. Brad Sachs (Palgrave Macmillan)

Agent's name: Steve Schwartz
E-mail: steve@sarahjanefreymann.com
Categories/Subjects that you are most enthusiastic about agenting: Nonfiction: Business, sports, humor, men's issues, politics, new technology. Fiction: Mystery/crime, thrillers, fantasy, historical sagas, adventure, sports—popular fiction in almost any genre as long as it grabs me from the first paragraph and doesn't let go.

Categories/Subjects writers shouldn't bother pitching to you: Westerns, screenplays, and almost anything channeled

SCHIAVONE LITERARY AGENCY, INC.

3671 Hudson Manor Terrace, #11H, Bronx, NY 10463-1139
Corporate Offices, 236 Trails End, West Palm Beach, FL 33413-2135
561-966-9294 | 718-548-5332

Agent's name: Jennifer DuVall

E-mail: jendu77@aol.com

Born: New York, New York

Education: BS, MA, New York University; EdD Nova University; professional diploma, Columbia University; advanced studies: University of Rome, Italy

Career history: Director of reading, Monroe County (FL) Public Schools; professor emeritus of developmental skills at the City University of New York; literary agent

Categories/Subjects that you are most enthusiastic about agenting: Celebrity biography, autobiography and memoirs, general fiction, mystery, romance, fantasy/ science fiction, business/investing/finance, history, religious, mind/body/spirit, health, travel, lifestyle, children's (no picture books), African American, Latino, ethnic, science

Categories/Subjects writers shouldn't bother pitching to you: Poetry, short stories, anthologies, or children's picture books. No scripts or screenplays. We handle film rights, options, and screenplays only for books we have agented.

If you were not an agent, what might you be doing instead: Teaching graduate courses on the psychology of reading, writing nonfiction

What's the best way for writers to solicit your interest: Query letters only, one-page preferred (no phone or fax). For fastest response (usually same or next day), e-mail queries are acceptable and encouraged. For queries by post, include SASE. No response without SASE. Do not send large envelopes with proposals, synopsis, sample chapters, etc., unless specifically requested. Queries must be sent to the main office in West Palm Beach, except for those directed to Jennifer DuVall at the New York City branch office or those addressed to Kevin McAdams in Manhattan.

Do you charge reading or management fees: No reading fee

What categories do you represent, by percentages: Nonfiction: 51 percent, fiction: 41 percent, children's: 5 percent, textbooks: 3 percent

What are the most common mistakes writers make when pitching to you: Make initial contact via phone/fax; failure to query first before sending proposals, synopsis, etc.

How would you describe the perfect client: A published author who remains loyal to the author/agent partnership

How and why did you become an agent: I have enjoyed a lifetime love of books and reading. I served as a reading specialist in schools and colleges and authored five trade books and three textbooks. I enjoy representing creative people and successfully working with them as partners in achieving and augmenting their career goals.

What can a writer do to increase the odds of you becoming his or her agent: If a request is made for additional material, the author should prepare an outstanding, professionally written proposal along with sample chapters. For fiction, a brief well-stated synopsis accompanied by compelling initial chapters can make the difference in an offer of representation.

How would you describe what you do as an agent to someone (or something) from another planet: Sell creative work of authors/clients to major publishing houses; negotiate contracts; handle business details—enabling authors to concentrate on the craft of writing

How do you feel about editors and publishers: I have been fortunate in working with the best editors in the industry. Generally, they are conscientious, indefatigable, and sincere in bringing an author's work to press. Agenting would be impossible without them. Publishers are the backbone of the industry. I am grateful for the serious consideration they give to my highly selective submissions.

What do you think the future holds for writers, publishers, and agents: The future holds unlimited opportunities for all, especially the reading public.

On a personal level, what do you think people like and dislike about you: My clients tell me that they appreciate the unlimited contact they have with me. I am always available to discuss their needs and concerns as writers. The editors I work with have always appreciated the time, care, and consideration I put into my submissions to them. While dislikes may exist, they haven't been expressed to me.

What are some representative titles that you have sold: *A Brother's Journey* (Warner); *A Teenager's Journey* (Warner); *Inside: Life behind Bars in America* (St. Martin's); *Bedlam South* (State Street Press/Borders)

THE SCOTT MEREDITH LITERARY AGENCY

200 West 57th Street, Suite 904, New York, NY 10019
646-274-1970
www.scottmeredith.com

Agent's name: Arthur Klebanoff
E-mail: info@scottmeredith.com
Education: Yale, BA; Harvard Law School, LLB
Career history: Cofounder, Morton Janklow Associates; head of publishing for International Management Group; purchased Scott Meredith Literary Agency in 1993; founder, RosettaBooks, an e-book publisher
Categories/Subjects that you are most enthusiastic about agenting: Category leaders in nonfiction
Categories/Subjects writers shouldn't bother pitching to you: First fiction
Do you charge fees separate from your commission or offer nonagenting fee-based services: No

What are some representative titles that you have sold: *The Conscience of a Liberal* by Paul Krugman (Norton); *The New American Story* by Bill Bradley (Random House); *10* by Sheila Lukins (Workman); *Field Guide to North America* by Roger Tory Peterson (Houghton Mifflin); *Mayo Clinic Book of Alternative Medicine* (Time Inc. Home Entertainment); *Janson's History of Art* (Prentice Hall)

Arthur Klebanoff, owner and president of the Scott Meredith Literary Agency, has been a leading literary agent and influential presence in the publishing industry for over 35 years, representing books with more than $1 billion in retail sales. He is the founder (2001) and CEO of Rosetta Books, LLC, the leading independent electronic publisher specializing in introducing to the e-book space authors whose print titles are a vibrant element of the ongoing cultural dialogue, from the contemporary such as Stephen Covey's *The Seven Habits of Highly Effective People* and the *Rainbow Magic* series, to such sought-after classics as *Brave New World*, *Slaughterhouse-Five*, *A Passage to India*, *Shoeless Joe*, Winston Churchill's *The Gathering Storm*, and many others. As cofounder and partner in the literary agency Morton L. Janklow Associates, Inc., he worked over a 10-year period on more than 30 seven-figure book deals, most involving commercial fiction. Arthur previously led the publishing division of International Management Group. He has represented a broad range of authors and publishing programs, including Michael Bloomberg, Danielle Steel, Bill Bradley, Nobel Laureate Paul Krugman, Barbara Taylor Bradford, Judith Krantz, Richard Nixon, masterful Civil War artist Mort Kunstler, Daniel Patrick Moynihan (for whom he worked in the White House between college and law school), and the Mayo Clinic. He orchestrated the precedent-setting sales of Linda Goodman's *Love Signs* and has overseen the management of her record-setting backlist; there are more than 60 million copies of her books in print worldwide. Arthur is a graduate of Harvard Law School (Law Review, 1972) and Yale University (where he won the Alpheus Henry Snow Prize for "inspiring in his classmates an admiration and love for the best traditions of high scholarship"). He is an advisor to the Roger Tory Peterson Institute for Natural History, a nature-in-education organization. Arthur is also author of the book *The Agent: Personalities, Politics and Publishing* (2002).

SCOTT TREIMEL NY

434 Lafayette Street, New York, NY 10003
212-505-8353
www.scotttreimelny.com

Agent's name: Scott Treimel
Born: San Diego, California
Education: BA Antioch College, American history
Career history: Curtis Brown, Ltd. (trained by Marilyn Marlow); Scholastic;

United Features Syndicate; HarperCollins Children's Books; founding director of Warner Bros. Worldwide Publishing

Hobbies/Personal interests: Theater, dogs, politics, entertaining, history, architecture, good deeds

Categories/Subjects that you are most enthusiastic about agenting: All categories of children's books, from board books through teen novels. No adult projects; no toy-only projects, no screenplays.

Categories/Subjects writers shouldn't bother pitching to you: Religious/ evangelical

If you were not an agent, what might you be doing instead: Theatrical producer or beach bum

What's the best way for fiction writers to solicit your interest: Via website only

What's the best way for nonfiction writers to solicit your interest: Via website only

Do you charge reading or management fees: No

What are the most common mistakes writers make when pitching to you: (1) Explaining the market; (2) overselling; not allowing their work to speak for itself; (3) infusing a pitch with gimmicks

Describe the client from hell, even if you don't have any: One with unreasonable expectations, who is impatient with matters I can't control and will not listen to advice, from me or an editor; one who sends revised manuscripts in rapid succession and confuses our submissions to editors; one who writes "Have you heard from…" e-mails suggesting that we do not *religiously* inform clients of all goings-on as they happen

What's your definition of a great client: Consistent, productive, passionate about craft, able to work well with the variety of personalities that contribute to making and marketing books and a client who actively promotes his or her books

What can a writer do to increase the odds of you becoming his or her agent: It is 99.9 percent about the content of the work. Therefore, to increase the odds, be original and write brilliantly. One key problem we see with new writers is derivative storylines and too-familiar characters. I advocate imaginative boldness. That'll do it.

How and why did you become an agent: I worked on both sides, buying and selling intellectual property, and then I wanted to be closer to the key ingredient to the whole process: the creator. I am not beholden to corporate oversight and am able to advocate for the people who make the first and greatest contribution— the creators.

How do you feel about editors and publishers: We have many talented editors. I worry their publishers put so much pressure on them that they are unable to take chances, try new things. I like independent vision, which the present committee-style publishing discourages. It is also true that editors are editing less these days, and publishers have off-loaded services they once provided.

What do you see in the near future for book publishing: (1) More focus on fewer titles; and (2) the increasing development of electronic distribution of literary work

What are your favorite books, movies, and TV shows, and why: I like cartoons, not the animated movies that wink at the adults in the audience, but cartoons on television. The old-style *Looney Tunes* and *Tom and Jerry* gag fests have been replaced with well-plotted storytelling—often solidly structured. I also dig the high visual style and experimenting. I watch *South Park* and *Sponge Bob*, but also *Camp Lazlo*, *Foster's Home for Imaginary Friends*, *The Grim Adventures of Bill and Mandy*, *Pokemon*, *Dexter's Laboratory*, *Robot Chicken*, *The Powerpuff Girls*, *Squidbillies*. Writers for children can do well to tune in and discover the level of social sophistication and cultural references cartoon characters resource. My greatest dislike is a sentimentalized recollection of childhood. Cartoons source a more authentic point of view. Going way, way back, I love Monty Python. Favorite book: *Middlemarch*, of course!

In your opinion, what do editors think of you: They think I am honest, direct, reasonable but not a softie. I believe they also think I have good taste and interesting projects.

On a personal level, what do you think people like and dislike about you: Straightforward, energetic, earnest, funny

What are some representative titles that you have sold: *Orphans* by Gail Giles (Candlewick); *Boogie Monster* by Kevan Atteberry (Compendium); *The Hunchback Assignments* (series) by Arthur Slade (HarperCollins Canada and Random House/Wendy Lamb Books); *Monkey Ho Ho* by J. C. Phillips (Viking); *Lucky Me* by Richard Scrimger (HarperCanada); *Zomboy* by Richard Scrimger (HarperCanada); *Boy and Bot* by Ame Dyckman (Knopf); *Lovabye, Dragon!* by Barbara Joosse (Candlewick); *Tea Party Rules* by Ame Dyckman (Viking); *Frankenstein* by Rick Walton (Feiwel and Friends); *Hooray Parade* by Barbara Joosse (Viking); *Frankie Goes to School*, illustrations by Keven Atteberry; *Cakes and Miracles* by Barbara Golden (Marshall Cavendish)

SCOVIL CHICHAK GALEN LITERARY AGENCY, INC.

276 Fifth Avenue, Suite 708, New York, NY 10001
212-679-8686 | fax: 646-349-1868
www.scglit.com

Agent's name: Anna Ghosh
E-mail: annaghosh@scglit.com
Born: Bristol, United Kingdom
Education: New School for Social Research, New York; Hampshire College, Massachusetts; Woodstock International School, India
Career history: Agent at SCG since 1995
Categories/Subjects that you are most enthusiastic about agenting: Literary nonfiction, current affairs, investigative journalism, history, science, social and cultural issues, travel, and adventure

What's the best way for writers to solicit your interest: Send a well-written and thoughtful query letter.

Do you charge reading or management fees: No

What categories do you represent, by percentages: Nonfiction: 70 percent, fiction: 30 percent

What are some representative titles that you have sold: *Last True Story I'll Ever Tell: An Accidental Soldier's Account of the War in Iraq* (Riverhead); *Ambitious Brew: The Story of American Beer* (Harcourt); *Living Cosmos* (Random House); *Churchill's Choice: Empire, War, and the Great Bengal Famine* (Basic); *Reading Claudius* (Dial Press); *All Is Change: The Two-Thousand Year Journey of Buddhism to the West* (Little Brown); *Is Gluten Making Me Ill?* (Rodale); *Art of War for Women* (Doubleday)

THE SEYMOUR AGENCY

475 Miner Street Road, Canton, NY 13617
315-386-1831
www.theseymouragency.com

Agent's name: Mary Sue Seymour

E-mail: marysue@twcny.rr.com

Born: September 21, New York

Education: BS from State University of New York plus 30 graduate hours mostly in education; New York State teacher's certificate

Career history: Began agency in 1992

Hobbies/Personal interests: Hiking in the Adirondacks, walking my golden retriever, watching *American Idol* and *Walker, Texas Ranger*, going to church, reading my Bible, baking apple pies and homemade cinnamon rolls, traveling to writers conferences, and presenting workshops

Categories/Subjects that you are most enthusiastic about agenting: Christian books of any type, especially historical Christian romance, category romance, and any type of secular romance

Categories/Subjects writers shouldn't bother pitching to you: Fantasy romance, sci-fi romance, erotica, short stories, poetry, general novels

If you were not an agent, what might you be doing instead: Teaching art

What's the best way for fiction writers to solicit your interest: A great query letter describing the project to a T—show me you can write.

Do you charge fees separate from your commission or offer nonagenting fee-based services: No

How and why did you become an agent: I was writing while teaching school. I had three agents—a couple of them were pretty bad, and I wondered if I could be a successful agent. The first book I sent out sold a four-book deal to Bantam, so I believe it was meant to be. I quit teaching.

How do you feel about writers: I sympathize with them. There is a lot of room for error when you write a book, yet writers have to have them perfect, and editors are so selective these days. Also the economy isn't that good, and editors are buying more conservatively. It's a tough life, and I have nothing but the greatest respect for authors. The key to being a happy author is to have other things you do simultaneously that you're good at. Then you will always have success in your life.

What are your favorite books, movies, and TV shows, and why: I absolutely love *Walker, Texas Ranger* on the Hallmark Channel, and I watch it whenever I can. It's so funny in some ways, and of course the good guys always win. There are certain Christian undertones in the show that I like as well.

Describe the client from hell, even if you don't have any: I have never had one.

Describe the publisher and/or editor from hell: I have never dealt with one. Editors are always professional or they wouldn't be editors.

What do you like best about your clients and the editors and publishers you work with: They're nice, real people just like I try to be.

Describe yourself: I love to travel to conferences and meet writers; I do about one conference a month. Conferences I plan to attend this year include a Christian conference in Asheville, NC; RWA National in Washington DC; WOW in Las Vegas; Put Your Heart in a Book in New Jersey; Central Florida Writer's Conference; Space Coast Writer's Conference in Cocoa Beach, FL.

Will our business exist as we know it in 10 years or so: The advent of DVDs [is] taking over writing a little bit. I am anxious to see where the book industry will be in 10 years.

SHEREE BYKOFSKY ASSOCIATES, INC.

PO Box 706, Brigantine, NJ 08203
shereebee.com

Agent's name: Sheree Bykofsky

E-mail: shereebee@aol.com

Born: September 1956, Queens, New York

Education: BA, State University of New York, Binghamton; MA, in English and comparative literature, Columbia University

Career history: Executive editor/book producer, the Stonesong Press (1984–1996); freelance editor/writer (1984); general manager/managing editor, Chiron Press (1979–1984); author and coauthor of a dozen books, including three poker books with coauthor Lou Krieger

Hobbies/Personal interests: Poker, Scrabble

Categories/Subjects that you are most enthusiastic about agenting: Popular reference, adult nonfiction (hardcovers and trade paperbacks), quality literary and commercial fiction (highly selective)

Categories/Subjects writers shouldn't bother pitching to you: Children's, young adult, genre romance, science fiction, horror, Westerns, occult and supernatural, fantasy

What's the best way for fiction writers to solicit your interest: Send an e-query letter, pasted into the body of your e-mail, to submitbee@aol.com. No attachments will be opened.

What's the best way for nonfiction writers to solicit your interest: See above.

Do you charge reading or management fees: No

What are the most common mistakes writers make when pitching to you: Excessive hubris; not explaining what the book is about; comparing book to best sellers rather than showing how it is unique; paranoia (we're not going to steal your idea); sloppy grammar, punctuation, and spelling

What's your definition of a great client: One who is not only a talented writer but also professional in every sense

What can a writer do to increase the odds of you becoming his or her agent: I love a query letter that is as well written as the proposed book or a polished, perfect, professional proposal.

What are some representative titles that you have sold: *Boyfriend University* (Wiley); *1001 Ways to Live Green* (Berkley); *Conspiracy Nation* (Chicago Review); *Junk Jewelry* (Clarkson Potter); *The Thrill of the Chaste* (Thomas Nelson); *When the Ghost Screams* (Andrews McMeel); *Death Waits for You* (Pocket)

SIMENAUER AND GREENE LITERARY AGENCY, LLC

PO Box 770968, Naples, FL 34107-0968
239-597-9877
www.sgliterary.com

Agent's name: Jacqueline Simenauer
E-mail: jsliteraryagent@gmail.com
Born: New York, New York
Education: Fordham University
Career history: After working as an articles editor for a national publication, I decided to start my own literary agency, and as a result of this, I coauthored a number of books with my clients. Some of the six books that I was involved with include the best-selling *Beyond the Male Myth*, which was featured on *Oprah*; *Husbands and Wives, Singles: The New Americans*, which gained the attention of the White House; and *Not Tonight, Dear*. They went on to sell over 200,000 copies. My work has also been featured in most of the nation's magazines and newspapers including *Time*, *Readers Digest*, *Ladies Home Journal*, *The New York Times*, and *The Washington Post*. In addition, I have appeared in 100 radio/TV showings, including *Good Morning America* and the *Today Show*.
Hobbies/Personal interests: I have always worked so hard that I never found

time to even think about a hobby. However, I do love classical concerts. I am a member of a wine society; I love the Broadway theater and great fiction.

Categories/Subjects that you are most enthusiastic about agenting: I like a wide range of strong commercial nonfiction books that include medical, health, nutrition, popular psychology, how-to/self-help, parenting, women's issues, spirituality, men's issues, relationships, social sciences, beauty, controversial subjects.

Categories/Subjects writers shouldn't bother pitching to you: This agency doesn't handle crafts, poetry, and children's books.

If you were not an agent, what might you be doing instead: You would probably find me cruising around the world.

What's the best way for nonfiction writers to solicit your interest: Please write a really good query letter. This is so important. If you can't get your idea across effectively, then you've lost the agent.

Do you charge fees separate from your commission or offer nonagenting fee-based services: We do not charge a reading fee. The agency can draw on professionals to do book doctoring when requested, and the fee for that is currently $2.50 per page. In rare instances, we also offer ghostwriting services (utilizing published writers on a contract basis). This represents a small part of our business—probably in the range of 5 percent or less.

What are some representative titles that you have sold: *The Insulin Resistance Diet* by Dr. Cheryle Hart and Mary Kay Grossman, RD (McGraw-Hill); *The Thyroid Guide* by Dr. Beth Ann Ditkoff and Dr. Paul Lo Gerfo (Harper); *Overcoming Anxiety without Tranquilizers* by Dr. Edward H. Drummond (Dutton); *The Feel Good Diet* by Dr. Cheryle Hart and Mary K. Grossman, RD (McGraw-Hill); *The Endometriosis Sourcebook* by Mary Lou Wallweg (Contemporary); *Decoding the Secret Language of Your Body* by Dr. Martin Rush (Fireside/Simon & Schuster); *Fasting and Eating for Health* by Dr. Joel Fuhrman (St. Martin's Press); *What to Do after You Say I Do* by Dr. Marcus J. Goldman and Lori Goldman (Prima); *Why Did It Happen?* by Janice Cohn, DSW (Morrow); *The Mind Factor* by Dr. Jean Rosenbaum (Prentice Hall); *Bride's Guide to Emotional Survival* by Rita Bigel-Casher, PhD (Prima); *Money Secrets the Pros Don't Want You to Know* by Stephanie Gallagher (AMACOM); *What Is Fear?* by Dr. Jean Rosenbaum (Prentice Hall); *Husbands and Wives* by Dr. Anthony Pietropinto; *The Healing Mind* by Eileen F. Oster (Prima); *Singles: The New Americans* (Simon & Schuster); *How to Avoid Divorce* by Dr. Jean Rosenbaum (Harper); *Biotypes* (Times Books); *The Joy of Fatherhood* by Dr. Marcus Goldman (Prima); *The Yankee Encyclopedia* by Mark Gallagher (Sagamore); *Every Woman's Guide to Investing* by Francie Prince and Douglas Pi (Prima); *Brave New You* by Mary Valentis, PhD (New Harbinger Publications); *Beyond the Male Myth* by Dr. Anthony Pietropinto; *The Real Truth about Mutual Funds* by Herbert Rongold (American Management); *The Single Woman's Travel Guide* by Doris Walfield (Citadel Press); *Conquering Loneliness* by Dr. Jean Rosenbaum; *The Clinic* by Dr. Anthony Pietropinto; *Reengineering Yourself* by Dr. Daniel L. Araoz and Dr. William S. Sutton (Adams Media); *The Dream Girl* by Dr. Anthony Pietropinto (Adams

Media); *Kleptomania* by Dr. Marcus Goldman (New Horizon); *Is Your Volkswagen a Sex Symbol?* by Dr. Jean Rosenbaum; *How I Sold a Million Copies of My Software* by Herbert R. Kraft (Adams Media); *Single's Guide to Cruise Vacations* (Prima)

How and why did you become an agent: I seemed to have always been involved with the publishing world, in one way or another. I had worked for a national publication as an articles editor, I was a freelance writer and coauthor. Agenting seemed the likely next step so I opened an agency. At first I was the only one. Then I was joined by my colleague Carole Greene, who has now become my partner.

How do you feel about writers: I think my background as a freelance writer and coauthor makes me even more sympathetic to struggling writers. I understand what it feels like to see your name on a book jacket and appear on a major TV show, and if I can help you achieve your dream, then it becomes mine as well. But understand that it takes a great deal of perseverance to go from an idea to a proposal strong enough to get the attention of the publishing world.

Agent's name: Carole J. Greene
Born: Anderson, IN, October 14, making me a Libra; yep, I'm balanced.
Education: Two degrees from Ball State University, Muncie Indiana: BA and MA in English
Career history: After a decade as a high school and college educator focusing primarily on composition and creative writing, I became a full-time independent journalist. I wrote more than 1,000 articles for national and regional magazines on a wide range of topics including medical, business, finance, lifestyle, home improvement, community development, real estate, and golf. I also wrote a humor column for a monthly newspaper. I created award-winning marketing materials—advertising copy, brochures, newsletters, video scripts—for private clients. I then turned my attention to book projects, as a ghostwriter, coauthor, and author of numerous books, and editor of a couple dozen more (so far), both for private clients and publishers. Since 1985, I've belonged to the same writers group (all members have been published), where each week we lovingly critique one another's works in progress. After teaching, freelancing, ghosting, editing, and critiquing, the next logical step was agenting. Ta-da!
Hobbies/Personal interests: In addition to traveling the world with my hubby, I enjoy theater, movies, fine dining, music, golf, bridge, and reading. Lots of reading. Mostly before publication.
Categories/Subjects that you are most enthusiastic about agenting: I find my tastes are quite eclectic: almost anything that is well written and has a chance of being salable. Fiction attracts me more than nonfiction. Query me about an intriguing story beautifully told that demonstrates expert use of the English language. But if it needs a little polish to make it shine, I have a red pen, and I'm not afraid to use it!
Categories/Subjects writers shouldn't bother pitching to you: Arts and crafts, poetry, children's books, horror, or fantasy
If you were not an agent, what might you be doing instead: When I'm not working with/for my clients, I am writing SOMETHING—from pro bono

materials for groups I support to grocery lists. I'm still tinkering with a novel I began several years ago…Who knows?, maybe this is the year I'll finish it. Probably not.

What's the best way for fiction writers to solicit your interest: The most effective way is to write a query letter that demonstrates their grasp of language skills and their commitment to delivering their message in an interesting, professional manner. Just owning a computer and a word processing program is not enough to make you a writer, so forget the stylized graphics for your cover and concentrate on making that query letter so enticing that I salivate to see more of your material.

Do you charge fees separate from your commission or offer nonagenting fee-based services: NO

How do you feel about writers: I am totally supportive of the creative life. If you love to mess around with words and have a story to tell that would benefit others, I'll be the wind beneath your wings. The best writers through the ages have made the world a better place. If you aspire to that lofty goal, I would love to help you get your message out.

Describe the client from hell, even if you don't have any: I wouldn't describe any writer, editor, or publisher as "from hell" as long as they put forth sincere effort to produce a book that people will be glad they read. That applies to agents too, so don't bug me if you're my client. I'm putting forth sincere effort even if you don't hear from me for weeks!

You're welcome to share your thoughts and sentiments about the business of writing and publishing: One of my writing group friends once said, "Writing is the hardest work I ever loved." It IS difficult, much harder than nonwriters comprehend. Getting your FIRST book published can be daunting; however, every successful author has that FIRST book. Don't ever let fear of rejection stand in your way of attaining the goal of publishing your work. Changes in the publishing industry occur so fast that the wisest sage would be unable to foresee the future. Will we continue to read books? Absolutely; it's in our DNA. The method of delivery will continue to evolve, with e-books and Kindle right now and, who knows, maybe a microchip inserted directly into our bodies that will autodownload books as they're being published. It's an exciting industry and I'm thrilled to fulfill my role in it—until someone has to pry that red pen out of my cold, still fingers.

STEELE-PERKINS LITERARY AGENCY

26 Island Lane, Canandaigua, NY 14424
585-396-9290

Agent's name: Pattie Steele-Perkins
E-mail: pattiesp@aol.com
Career history: Prior to becoming an agent Pattie Steele-Perkins was creative director for a television production company. Prior to that, she was a producer/director.

Categories/Subjects that you are most enthusiastic about agenting: Romance and women's fiction

Categories/Subjects writers shouldn't bother pitching to you: Nonfiction

What's the best way for writers to solicit your interest: A brief e-mail query that includes a synopsis

Do you charge reading or management fees: No

What categories do you represent, by percentages: Romance and women's fiction: 100 percent

What are the most common mistakes writers make when pitching to you: They don't research what I handle, or they do research and pitch the story as if it were romance, even though it isn't.

Describe the client from hell, even if you don't have any: Clients that use foul language rather than just "stet" on copy edits; clients that rant and rave online about their editor or publishing house

How would you describe the perfect client: Someone who loves to write and has stories to tell

How do you feel about editors and publishers: They are the smartest people I have ever met and they love books.

THE STEINBERG AGENCY, INC.

47 East 19th Street, 3rd Floor, New York, NY 10003
212-213-9120
www.steinbergagency.com

Agent's name: Peter Steinberg

Born: April 23, Queens, NY

Education: BFA in film production at New York University's film school

Career history: After graduating from film school, I was temping at HarperCollins (to pay the bills) while focusing my energy on writing screenplays, and realized—much to my own surprise—that I really enjoyed the world of publishing. At that time, there was an assistant opening at a prestigious (although I didn't know it at the time) boutique literary agency called Donadio & Ashworth (now called Donadio & Olson) and I got the job, fell in love with being a literary agent, and I've been an agent ever since. And in the fall of 2007, I opened my own shop, which has been extraordinarily fulfilling.

Hobbies/Personal interests: Spending time with my wife and kids

Categories/Subjects that you are most enthusiastic about agenting: A broad range of novels and short story collections and the occasional young-adult title. Nonfiction interests include memoir, humor, biography, history, pop culture, fitness, and narrative nonfiction.

Categories/Subjects writers shouldn't bother pitching to you: Screenplays, poetry, romance

If you were not an agent, what might you be doing instead: In the movie business in some creative capacity

What's the best way for fiction writers to solicit your interest: Great writing in combination with a referral

Do you charge fees separate from your commission or offer nonagenting fee-based services: Absolutely none

What are some representative titles that you have sold: *Angels of Destruction*, Keith Donohue, Shaye Areheart Books (Crown); *Gossip of the Starlings*, Nina de Gramont (Algonquin); *Are You Ready!*, Bob Harper (Broadway Books); *Eden's Outcasts*, John Matteson (W. W. Norton); *The Expeditions*, Karl Iagnemma (The Dial Press); *I'm a Lebowski, You're a Lebowski* by Lebowskifest (Bloomsbury); *Towelhead*, Alicia Erian (Simon & Schuster); *Jars of Glass*, Brad Barkley and Hepler Hepler (Dutton Children); *The Post-War Dream*, Mitch Cullin, Nan A. Talese Books (Doubleday); *The Heaven of Mercury*, Brad Watson (W. W. Norton); *The 351 Books of Irma Arcuri*, David Bajo, Viking; *Comeback Season*, Cathy Day (Free Press); *The Affected Provincial's Companion*, Lord Whimsy (Bloomsbury); *Don't Make Me Stop Now*, Michael Parker (Algonquin); *Identical Strangers*, Paula Bernstein and Elyse Schein (Random House)

How and why did you become an agent: See "Career history."

How do you feel about writers: I love interacting with writers on a daily basis. It's why I do what I do.

How would you describe what you do as an agent to someone (or something) from another planet: I would tell them I have a love/hate relationship with e-mail.

STIMOLA LITERARY STUDIO, INC.

308 Livingston Court, Edgewater, NJ 07020
201-945-9353
www.stimolaliterarystudio.com

Agent's name: Rosemary Stimola
E-mail: info@stimolaliterarystudio.com
Born: November 6, 1952; Queens, New York
Education: BA in elementary education/theoretical linguistics, Queens College; MA in applied linguistics, NYU; PhD in linguistic/educational psychology, NYU
Career history: Professor of language and literature, children's bookseller, freelance editor, education consultant, literary agent
Hobbies/Personal interests: Beach combing, Latin dance, cockapoos
Categories/Subjects you are most enthusiastic about agenting: Preschool through young-adult fiction/nonfiction; concept cookbooks
Categories/Subjects writers shouldn't bother pitching to you: Adult fiction
If you were not an agent, what might you be doing instead: Working in publishing, editorial, or marketing

What's the best way for writers to solicit your interest: Referral through editors, clients, or agent colleagues always helps. See SUBMISSION GUIDELINES on website. Prefer e-mail queries, but no attachments please!

Do you charge reading or management fees: No

How do you feel about writers: I am in awe of good writers and admire those less talented for their efforts.

Describe the client from hell, even if you don't have any: Desperate for money, has unrealistic expectations and a major ego, resistant to editor guidance and revision

How would you describe the publisher or editor from hell: Does not answer calls or respond to e-mails; late with paperwork; does not deliver what is promised in time or production

How and why did you become an agent: It was an evolving state, allowing me to put the literary aesthetics I developed as an educator and the publishing knowledge I acquired as a bookseller to use in one role.

How would you describe what you do as an agent to someone (or something) from another planet: In the space between authors and publishing personnel, I serve as an advocate, facilitator, champion, and troubleshooter, all in the service of making the best possible book, one that I can then bring to foreign and film markets.

What do you like best about your clients and the editors and publishers you work with: We are all lovers of story, dazzled by well-crafted written words and their ability to touch head and heart.

Will our business exist as we know it 10 years from now: Our business will certainly exist, but with world and technological changes, we must change as well. I couldn't say what the face of publishing will look like in the future, but I would stake my life on its being an important force.

What are your favorite books, movies, and TV shows, and why: *Harold and the Purple Crayon* (the perfect children's book); *Now, Voyager* (Bette Davis at her best!); *The Shawshank Redemption* (love this tale of friendship and triumph of spirit); *To Kill a Mockingbird* (read at 12 years of age, a life-changing book for me); *Fried Green Tomatoes* (words and characters pull at my heart strings); *Starman* (attracted to the human element in this sci-fi tale); *Sophie's Choice* (a perfect novel); *Cider House Rules* (characters to die for)

What are some representative titles that you have sold: The *Hunger Games Trilogy* by Suzanne Collins (Scholastic); *Bridge of Time* by Lewis Buzbee (Feiwel and Friends); *Getting over Garrett Delaney* by Abby McDonald (Candlewick Press); *The Jenna Fox Chronicles* by Mary E. Pearson (Holt); *Inside Out and Back Again* by Thanhha Lai (Harper Collins); *Amy and Roger's Epic Journey* by Morgan Matson (Simon & Schuster); *Barbie, for Better or Worse* by Tanya Lee Stone (Viking); *Another Brother* by Matthew Cordell (Feiwel and Friends); *The Flying Beaver Brothers* by Maxwell Eaton III (Knopf)

STROTHMAN AGENCY, LLC

6 Beacon Street, Suite 810, Boston, MA 02108
www.strothmanagency.com

Agent's name: Dan O'Connell
E-mail: info@strothmanagency.com
Career history: Dan O'Connell has devised and executed marketing and publicity campaigns for small presses, mid-sized publishers, and trade houses. As assistant publicity director at Houghton Mifflin's Trade and Reference Division, he worked with a range of distinguished authors including PEN Faulkner Award winner John Edgar Wideman (*Hoop Roots*), Harvard psychologist Daniel Schacter (*Seven Sins of Memory*), NBA finalist and science writer Steve Olson (*Mapping Human History, Count Down*), National Book Award winner James Carroll (*Secret Father*), and award-winning psychologist Pumla Gobodo-Madikizela of the University of Cape Town (*A Human Being Died That Night*). O'Connell devised brand-building campaigns for two of Houghton's most significant lines—*The American Heritage* line of dictionaries and *The Peterson Field Guides*. As assistant marketing director at Beacon Press, O'Connell managed publicity campaigns for two national best sellers, Cornel West's *Race Matters* and Marian Wright Edelman's *The Measure of Our Success*. Before joining Beacon, O'Connell was marketing manager at Alyson Publications, the leading publisher of books for gay and lesbian readers. He began working in book publishing at The Brookings Institution in Washington, DC, where he handled subsidiary rights, among other marketing duties.

Categories/Subjects that you are most enthusiastic about agenting: We specialize in narrative nonfiction, memoir, history, science and nature, arts and culture, literary travel, current affairs, and some business. We have a highly selective practice in fiction and young-adult literature.

Categories/Subjects writers shouldn't bother pitching to you: We do not handle romance, science fiction, picture books, gift books, poetry, or self-help.

What's the best way for writers to solicit your interest: Fiction: Send a synopsis and two or three chapters of your work with a self-addressed stamped envelope. Nonfiction: We specialize in nonfiction. Send a query letter outlining your qualifications and experience, along with a synopsis of your work and a self-addressed stamped envelope. We are now accepting submissions via e-mail. Please see our website for more information and the submission e-mail address.

Do you charge fees separate from your commission or offer nonagenting fee-based services: We do not charge any upfront fees.

What are some representative titles that you have sold: A book of advice on "etiquette, ethics, and everything in between" by Robin Abrahams (Times Books); *The Sound of Freedom: Marian Anderson, the Lincoln Memorial, and the Democratic Imagination* by Ray Arsenault (Bloomsbury Press); *The Weeping Time: Anatomy of a Slave Auction* by Anne Bailey (HarperCollins); *Choke: What the Secrets of the*

Brain Reveal about Success and Failure at Work and at Play by Sian Beilock (Simon & Schuster); *A Slave No More* by David W. Blight (Harcourt); *The Problem of Slavery in the Age of Emancipation* by David Brion Davis (Knopf); *Columbus and the Quest for Jerusalem* by Carol Delaney (Free Press); *The Race Card* by Richard T. Ford (Farrar, Straus & Giroux); *A Patent Lie* and *Errors and Omissions* by Paul Goldstein (Doubleday); *Addled: A Novel* by JoeAnn Hart (Little, Brown); *New Boy* by Julian Houston (Houghton Mifflin); *Kaufman Field Guide* series and *Flights against the Sunset* by Kenn Kaufman (Houghton Mifflin); *High Crimes: The Fate of Everest in an Age of Greed* by Michael Kodas (Hyperion); *Education's End: Why Our Colleges and Universities Have Given Up on the Meaning of Life* by Anthony T. Kronman (Yale); *Freedom for the Thought That We Hate: Biography of the First Amendment* by Anthony Lewis (Basic Books); *Stranger from Abroad: Hannah Arendt, Martin Heidegger, and the Experience of Germans and Jews in the 20th Century* by Daniel Maier-Katkin (Norton); *Snow Falling in Spring: Coming of Age in China During the Cultural Revolution* by Moying Li (Farrar, Straus & Giroux); *Attack on the Liberty* by James Scott (Simon & Schuster); *Poisoned Profits: The Toxic Assault on Our Children* by Philip and Alice Shabecoff (Random House); *Sun and Shade: Three American Families Journey from Black to White* by Daniel Sharfstein (Penguin Press); *The Book of Getting Even* and *Tales out of School* by Benjamin Taylor (Steerforth Press); *Backcast: Fly Fishing, Fatherhood, and a River Journey through the Heart of Alaska* by Lou Ureneck (St. Martin's); *Shell Game: Rogues, Smugglers, and the Hunt for Nature's Bounty* by Craig Welch (HarperCollins); *Skipjack: Tracking the Last Sailing Oystermen* by Chris White (St. Martin's Press); *Riddled with Life: Friendly Worms, Ladybug Sex, and the Parasites That Make Us Who We Are* by Marlene Zuk (Harcourt)

Agent's name: Wendy Strothman
E-mail: info@strothmanagency.com
Career history: Wendy Strothman, who led the turnarounds of two venerable Boston publishers, Beacon Press and Houghton Mifflin's Trade and Reference Division, has 30 years of publishing experience. As executive vice president and head of Houghton Mifflin's Trade and Reference Division from 1996 through July 2002, she turned an unprofitable division into one of the most profitable in the industry. Strothman's efforts to publish books at the highest standards led the company to receive more literary awards than at any time in its history: two Pulitzer Prizes, one National Book Award, three Caldecott Medals, and two Newbery Medals, among many other honors. At Houghton Mifflin, Strothman also acquired and edited books by key authors, including James Carroll (*An American Requiem*, winner of the National Book Award; *Constantine's Sword*, *New York Times* best seller), Philip Roth (four novels, including *American Pastoral*, winner of the Pulitzer Prize, and *The Human Stain*, *New York Times* best seller), John Kenneth Galbraith, Arthur M. Schlesinger Jr. (*A Life in the Twentieth Century*), and Paul Theroux. She vigorously pursued the defense in the lawsuit brought by the Margaret Mitchell estate

to block publication of Alice Randall's *The Wind Done Gone*, a parody of *Gone with the Wind*. From 1983 to 1995, Strothman headed Beacon Press, a Boston publisher founded in 1854. She led Beacon to new prominence, publishing two *New York Times* best sellers (*The Measure of Our Success* by Marian Wright Edelman and *Race Matters* by Cornel West) and one National Book Award winner, Mary Oliver's *New and Selected Poems*. Strothman began her career in 1973 at the University of Chicago Press, where she launched the *Critical Edition of the Works of Giuseppe Verdi*. Strothman was the senior fellow and the secretary of the Brown University Corporation; at Brown she has funded the annual Wendy J. Strothman Faculty Research Award in the Humanities to facilitate research planned for publication. She has served on the board of governors of Yale University Press and the board of trustees of the Cantata Singers in Boston, and now serves as a trustee of Deerfield Academy and on the board of 826 Boston, an affiliate of 826 Valencia. She has served as an expert witness on publishing matters and provides business consulting services to small nonprofit publishers. In addition, she has led workshops in publishing for the American Academy of Arts and Sciences, the Nieman Foundation at Harvard University, and other institutions. Known as an advocate for authors and freedom of expression and as a friend to independent booksellers, Ms. Strothman has received numerous awards, including the Publisher of the Year Award from the New England Booksellers Association, the Person of the Year Award for "permanent and significant contributions to the book industry" from the Literary Market Place, the 1994 PEN New England "Friend to Writers" Award, and a doctor of humane letters from Meadville Lombard Theological School in Chicago and a doctor of human letters from Brown. She is a frequent speaker at industry, library, and university events.

Categories/Subjects that you are most enthusiastic about agenting: We specialize in narrative nonfiction, memoir, history, science and nature, arts and culture, literary travel, current affairs, and some business. We have a highly selective practice in fiction and young-adult literature.

Categories/Subjects writers shouldn't bother pitching to you: We do not handle romance, science fiction, picture books, gift books, poetry, or self-help.

What's the best way for fiction writers to solicit your interest: Fiction: Send a synopsis and two or three chapters of your work with a self-addressed stamped envelope. Nonfiction: We specialize in nonfiction. Send a query letter outlining your qualifications and experience, along with a synopsis of your work and a self-addressed stamped envelope. We are now accepting submissions via e-mail. Please see our website for more information and the submission e-mail address.

Do you charge fees separate from your commission or offer nonagenting fee-based services: We do not charge any upfront fees.

Agent's name: Lauren MacLeod
Career history: Lauren MacLeod joined the Strothman Agency after graduating cum laude from Emerson College with a BFA in writing, literature, and publishing.

Lauren is drawn to highly polished literary fiction. Her specialties include young-adult and middle-grade fiction and nonfiction of all types.

Categories/Subjects that you are most enthusiastic about agenting: We specialize in narrative nonfiction, memoir, history, science and nature, arts and culture, literary travel, current affairs, and some business. We have a highly selective practice in fiction and young-adult literature.

Categories/Subjects writers shouldn't bother pitching to you: We do not handle romance, science fiction, picture books, gift books, poetry, or self-help.

What's the best way for fiction writers to solicit your interest: Fiction: Send a synopsis and two or three chapters of your work with a self-addressed stamped envelope. Nonfiction: We specialize in nonfiction. Send a query letter outlining your qualifications and experience, along with a synopsis of your work and a self-addressed stamped envelope. We are now accepting submissions via e-mail. Please see our website for more information and the submission e-mail address.

Do you charge fees separate from your commission or offer nonagenting fee-based services: We do not charge any upfront fees.

THE TALBOT FORTUNE AGENCY

980 Broadway, Suite 664, Thornwood, NY 10594
www.talbotfortuneagency.com

Agent's name: Gail Fortune
E-mail: queries@talbotfortuneagency.com
Education: BS, Northwestern University (Medill School of Journalism)
Career history: Gail Fortune is a literary agent and former book editor with 18 years of publishing experience. Prior to becoming an agent she spent 16 years at Putnam Berkley (now part of Penguin Group (USA)), where she rose from assistant to the editor-in-chief to executive editor. Her authors won six RITAs and were nominated for Edgar and Anthony awards. She published two *Publishers Weekly* books of the year. She edited many other national best sellers in romance, mystery, and narrative nonfiction.

Categories/Subjects that you are most enthusiastic about agenting: I am most enthusiastic about representing narrative nonfiction, commercial women's fiction, historical fiction, and romance novels. Narrative nonfiction can cover almost any subject, but history, food, travel, and Christian spirituality are particular interests of mine. Newspaper and magazine experience is helpful; many books are generated from concepts first tried out in articles. In fiction, I am looking for a voice that grabs me and a narrative that keeps me turning the pages. I like original voices.

Categories/Subjects writers shouldn't bother pitching to you: I do not represent children's books, science fiction, fantasy, Westerns, poetry, prescriptive nonfiction, or screenplays.

What's the best way for fiction writers to solicit your interest: Query via e-mail only. Please see SUBMISSION GUIDELINES page [of company website].

What's the best way for nonfiction writers to solicit your interest: Query via e-mail only. Please see SUBMISSION GUIDELINES page.

Do you charge reading or management fees: We do not charge any reading fees.

What are the most common mistakes writers make when pitching to you: Not following the submission guidelines; pitching multiple projects in one query letter; sending queries that ramble; using pressure tactics; knocking published authors; not trusting us or the business in general; thinking someone's going to steal their idea; relaying incomplete representation, submission, or publishing histories; not being truthful or straightforward

Describe the client from hell, even if you don't have any: The client from hell doesn't respect our time. They fail to recognize the publisher's justly proprietary attitude towards marketing, book design, and other facets of publication. They won't take suggestions for change, no matter how minor or well reasoned. They complain about writing and treat being published as a right instead of the opportunity and privilege it is.

What's your definition of a great client: The perfect client respects our personal and professional lives. They trust us. They are open to input from their editor. They love to read, and they love to write. They are enthusiastic about their ideas and about what they do.

What can a writer do to increase the odds of you becoming his or her agent: Please respect our time. Make sure your query is clear and succinct, and includes all of your contact information. Make sure your proposal (for nonfiction) or manuscript (for fiction) is complete and ready to go if we're interested. In general, approach publishing as a business and try to be as professional as possible right from the start. Of course, having a great project that's well researched and well executed goes a long way toward the above.

How and why did you become an agent: Becoming an agent was a natural progression from being editors. The work is similar, but we're able to spend less time in meetings and more time working with authors. We can also handle a more eclectic range of material, and we get to work with editors throughout the industry who share our passions and enthusiasms.

How do you feel about editors and publishers: Editors are without a doubt the hardest working and most idealistic people in book publishing. Publishers represent the best opportunity for gifted writers to get wide distribution, readership, and money in what is an often difficult business.

What are some representative titles that you have sold: *The Great Swim* by Gavin Mortimer (Walker Books); *Texas Princess* by Jodi Thomas (Berkley); *Twisted Creek* by Jodi Thomas (Berkley); *Married in Black* by Christina Cordaire (Madison Park Press); *A Notorious Woman* by Amanda McCabe (Mills & Boon/ Harlequin Historicals)

Agent's name: John Talbot

E-mail: queries@talbotfortuneagency.com

Education: BA, DePauw University

Career history: John Talbot is a literary agent and former book editor with 24 years of publishing experience. Prior to becoming an agent he spent seven years with Putnam Berkley (now part of Penguin USA), where he rose to the rank of senior editor and worked with such major best-selling authors as Tom Clancy, W. E. B. Griffin, and Jack Higgins, as well as rising literary stars such as Tom Perrotta. He published national best sellers in hardcover, trade paperback, and mass-market paperback, along with five *New York Times* notable books. He began his editorial career at Simon & Schuster.

Categories/Subjects that you are most enthusiastic about agenting: I am most enthusiastic about representing narrative nonfiction of all types, thrillers, commercial women's fiction, and literary fiction. Narrative nonfiction can cover almost any subject, but history, current events, participatory journalism, sports, pop culture, business, and Christian spirituality are particular interests of mine. Newspaper and magazine experience is helpful; many books are generated from concepts first tried out in articles. A marketing platform, i.e., a website or blog with a fan base in the tens of thousands or a list of corporate clients and customers, and a track record of speaking engagements and media appearances can be the deciding factor in getting a nonfiction sale. In fiction, I'm keenly interested in well-crafted thrillers with new or unusual hooks, and good genre fiction in growth categories. I am also looking for the fresh and occasionally edgy voice, no matter the subject or genre. Writers with minority backgrounds and unusual experiences and perspectives interest me, as do writers of what Sue Miller calls domestic realism. Previous publication in literary journals and magazines is a plus.

Categories/Subjects writers shouldn't bother pitching to you: I do not represent children's books, science fiction, fantasy, Westerns, poetry, or screenplays.

What's the best way for writers to solicit your interest: Query via e-mail only. Please see SUBMISSIONS GUIDELINES page.

Do you charge reading or management fees: We do not charge reading fees.

What categories do you represent, by percentages: 50 percent fiction, 50 percent nonfiction

What are the most common mistakes writers make when pitching to you: Not following the submission guidelines; pitching multiple projects in one query letter; sending queries that ramble; using pressure tactics; knocking published authors; not trusting us or the business in general; thinking someone's going to steal their idea; relaying incomplete representation, submission, or publishing histories; not being truthful or straightforward

Describe the client from hell, even if you don't have any: The client from hell doesn't respect our time. They fail to recognize the publisher's justly proprietary attitude towards marketing, book design, and other facets of publication. They won't take suggestions for change, no matter how minor or well reasoned. They complain about writing and treat being published as a right instead of the opportunity and privilege it is.

How would you describe the perfect client: The perfect client respects our personal and professional lives. They trust us. They are open to input from their editor. They love to read, and they love to write. They are enthusiastic about their ideas and about what they do.

How and why did you become an agent: Becoming an agent was a natural progression from being editors. The work is similar but we're able to spend less time in meetings and more time working with authors. We can also handle a more eclectic range of material, and we get to work with editors throughout the industry who share our passions and enthusiasms.

What can a writer do to increase the odds of you becoming his or her agent: Please respect our time. Make sure your query is clear and succinct, and includes all of your contact information. Make sure your proposal (for nonfiction) or manuscript (for fiction) is complete and ready to go if we're interested. In general, approach publishing as a business and try to be as professional as possible right from the start. Of course, having a great project that's well researched and well executed goes a long way toward the above.

How do you feel about editors and publishers: Editors are without a doubt the hardest working and most idealistic people in book publishing. Publishers represent the best opportunity for gifted writers to get wide distribution, readership, and money in what is often a difficult business.

What are some representative titles that you have sold: Fiction: *Tom Clancy's Endwar* (Berkley); *24 Declassified: Vanishing Point* (HarperEntertainment); *Becoming Finola* (Pocket Books); *Under Darkness* (Signet Eclipse); *The Brothers Bishop* (Kensington); *If Wishing Made It So* (Signet Eclipse); *CSI: Nevada Rose* (Pocket Books); *Forgive the Moon* (NAL Accent); *French Pressed: A Coffeehouse Mystery* (Berkley Prime Crime). Nonfiction: *All Hands Down: The True Story of the Soviet Attack on the USS Scorpion* (Simon & Schuster); *Sundays in America: A Yearlong Road Trip in Search of Christian Faith* (Beacon); *While Europe Slept: How Radical Islam Is Destroying the West from Within* (Doubleday); *Last Flag Down: A Civil War Saga of Honor, Piracy, and Redemption on the High Seas* (Crown)

TALCOTT NOTCH LITERARY

2 Broad Street, Second Floor, Suite 10, Milford, CT 06460
203-876-4959 | fax: 203-876-9517
www.talcottnotch.net

Agent's name: Gina Panettieri
Born: June 8, 1960, Peekskill, New York

Education: Long Island University Southampton, University of Virginia (double major writing/pre-med)

Career history: I came into agenting through one of the less common routes, by way of writing. I began as a freelance writer while still in college, writing anything from confession stories for *Modern Romance* to consumer protection and health articles. Later, I ran an ever-expanding critique group out of my home and became very involved with writer support groups and organizations and was represented myself by two well-known agents who taught me a great deal both about writing and about the business. But it was after assisting a number of writers in negotiating their own contracts that I became an agent myself and found my true calling. Within the last few years, I've begun writing again in addition to agenting and am the author of *The Single Mother's Guide to Raising Remarkable Boys* (Adams Media 2008) and *Honey, We're Spoiling the Kids* (Adams Media 2009). Since most agents who write themselves either write about publishing, or write novels, I suppose in becoming a parenting author I'm still sticking to the less common career routes!

Hobbies/Personal interests: I enjoy gardening (mind you, I didn't say I was particularly good at it, but the survival rate is improving), old movies (think *Royal Wedding* or *Arsenic and Old Lace*, NOT *Ferris Bueller's Day Off*), collecting cobalt glass and miniatures (houses, furniture, animals. I'm looking for a miniature cow if anyone knows a breeder). I love decorating for the holidays (Halloween is particularly fun). Researching for my own books keeps me reading a lot of psych, education, and child-development journals, which I actually enjoy. Finally, my own kids are a constant source of amusement and a limitless source of material for my books, to their great embarrassment.

Categories/Subjects that you are most enthusiastic about agenting: I primarily handle nonfiction, and my tastes are quite eclectic. I do a great deal of parenting, relationship, self-help, health, business/career, cooking, "green" works, memoir, and current events, as well as children's nonfiction. I'm not limited to those areas, though, and writers shouldn't hesitate to query me on nearly any nonfiction project. In fiction, I work mostly with mystery/suspense/thrillers and women's fiction, but I'll also do a bit of young adult and middle-grade and some fantasy, action-adventure, and science fiction.

Categories/Subjects writers shouldn't bother pitching to you: Picture and board books, early readers, poetry, short stories

If you were not an agent, what might you be doing instead: Probably writing full time and continuing to be very involved in writing organizations

What's the best way for nonfiction writers to solicit your interest: Show you understand the market for your work, what's already been written on the subject, and how your own work fills an existing need. Don't just use links to websites in lieu of writing a real query.

Do you charge fees separate from your commission or offer nonagenting fee-based services: No, never

What are some representative titles that you have sold: *Fall* by Ron Franscell, winner of the 2007 Ippy for True Crime and the 2007 *Foreword Magazine* Book of the Year Award in True Crime (New Horizon, released in paper as *The Darkest Night* by St. Martin's Press); *The Connected Child* by Dr. Karyn Purvis, Dr. David Cross, and Wendy Lyons Sunshine (McGraw-Hill); *Breaking the Cosleeping Habit* by Dr. Valerie Levine (Adams Media); *The Essential Supervisor's Handbook* by Brette and Terrence Sember (Career Press)

How and why did you become an agent: (The second half of this question was answered in an earlier question.) I love being an agent because it allows me to read so many fascinating works. I feel like I'm constantly learning. Agenting's an unending education. It's also terribly exciting to find something truly wonderful, important, and meaningful, and be instrumental in bringing it to the world.

How do you feel about writers: I certainly respect what they do, and because I write myself, I can relate to many of their issues. I think that helps me present constructive criticism in ways that are more easily accepted and also gives me a deeper perspective into the craft of writing. I also love their creative energy and the generosity of spirit of many writers. This is one industry where so many successful practitioners eagerly help new hopefuls.

How would you describe what you do as an agent to someone (or something) from another planet: I find new works that will help to enlighten people and enrich lives, and that entertain, comfort, or possibly provoke the readers. Books make life vastly more interesting. I help bring those books to the people.

What are your favorite books, movies, and TV shows, and why: I find reality programs like *The Deadliest Catch* and *Ice Road Truckers* to be interesting (for a while) because they make you aware of a different way of life and also because they feature people who have not yet spurned the idea of a real challenge, hard work, testing their own limits, understanding self-sacrifice. Perhaps for the same reason, I love old movies and shorts, since they're often time capsules of earlier ways of life. I listen to old radio shows on CD (the most fascinating are the World War II–era broadcasts), as well. In diving into what life was in America 60 years or 70 or even 80 years ago, again, you're learning, but this time about ourselves, and where we came from. It gives a new perspective on the present, on social roles, on the evolution of culture, on what's gone right and wrong. With books, my tastes are eclectic and voracious, but again, I want to learn.

Describe the client from hell, even if you don't have any: Someone who has completely unrealistic expectations, such as instant success, or that worrying about such trivial issues as spelling and grammar is "what the editor is for"; or someone who is unreasonably demanding of my time, since that would mean they're not respecting the time I must give to others

Describe the publisher and/or editor from hell: Someone who pulls out all the stops to acquire a project and then loses steam afterward and doesn't continue to shepherd the project zealously. In those cases, everybody loses.

What do you like best about your clients and the editors and publishers you work with: The exchange of ideas and energy

You're welcome to share your thoughts and sentiments about the business of writing and publishing: This is an exciting, but challenging, time to work in publishing. The industry continues to meet new demands and pressures. From finding ways to "go green" in what's traditionally been a huge carbon-footprint business, to exploring new ways to promote and publicize works, to looking ahead to predict the needs of consumers in a changing economy, publishing is stimulating, stressful, joyous, frustrating, rewarding, and exhausting. Never a dull moment.

Describe yourself: Mom/agent/activist/tree-hugger/writer/helpmate/friend

Will our business exist as we know it in 10 years or so: Yes, it will. It will continue to change to meet new demands and embrace new technology, but those things will occur in tandem and as a complement to the business as we know it today.

TED WEINSTEIN LITERARY MANAGEMENT

307 Seventh Avenue, Suite 2407, New York, NY 10001
www.twliterary.com

Agent's name: Ted Weinstein

Education: Bachelor's degree in philosophy from Yale College, master's degree in public and private management from Yale School of Management

Career history: Ted Weinstein has broad experience on both the business and editorial sides of publishing. Before founding the agency, he held senior publishing positions in licensing, marketing, publicity, and business development. Also a widely published author, Ted has been the music critic for NPR's "All Things Considered" and a commentator for the *San Francisco Chronicle* and many other publications.

Categories/Subjects that you are most enthusiastic about agenting: Wide range of intelligent nonfiction, especially narrative nonfiction, popular science, biography and history, current affairs and politics, business, health and medicine, food and cooking, pop culture, and quirky reference books

Categories/Subjects writers shouldn't bother pitching to you: Fiction, stage plays, screenplays, poetry, or books for children or young adults

What categories do you represent, by percentages: Nonfiction: 100 percent.

What are the most common mistakes writers make when pitching to you: Submitting a proposal for a type of work I do not represent; sending a proposal that isn't polished, professional, and typo free; telephoning the agency to query; sending a mass e-mail, cc-ing me and every other agent in the business

Describe the client from hell, even if you don't have any: Someone who doesn't act like a professional—missing deadlines, personalizing business issues. Publishing is a business and success is always more likely to come to those who are disciplined and hard working and who treat the people they work with respectfully.

How would you describe the perfect client: Talented, professional, hard working—someone who treats his or her writing like a career (even if it isn't their only career)

How and why did you become an agent: Before becoming an agent, I spent many years in different areas of publishing—editorial, marketing, business development, licensing—and agenting is an endlessly fun, fascinating, and rewarding combination of all these areas.

What can a writer do to increase the odds of you becoming his or her agent: We accept e-mail submissions only. Treat your writing as a long-term career, not just a one-book opportunity. Constantly improve your writing by getting feedback from writing groups, editors, and other thoughtful coaches. Increase your public profile by publishing your words and ideas via newspapers, magazines, and radio.

How would you describe what you do as an agent to someone (or something) from another planet: I'm a combination of editor, cheerleader, advocate, negotiator, marketing consultant, lawyer, accountant, career coach, and therapist, in varying proportions depending on what each client needs from me to help them succeed.

How do you feel about editors and publishers: They are smart businesspeople, without whom talented authors are unlikely to reach the audience they deserve, and they are some of the smartest readers anywhere. My clients and I carefully review every comment we receive from editors. No two editors will have the same reaction to any proposal, but the insights from each one are enormously valuable in helping my clients improve their work.

What do you think the future holds for writers, publishers, and agents: Authors increasingly need to think of themselves as CEOs of their own multimedia empires, promoting and publicizing themselves and their talents in every possible venue and looking to enhance and exploit the value of their insights and writing in every possible medium.

On a personal level, what do you think people like and dislike about you: Professionalism-with-a-sense-of-humor, wide-ranging insights and creativity, forthrightness and integrity

What are some representative titles that you have sold: Marina Gorbis' *SocialStructing: The End of the Organization and the Birth of the Amplified Individual* (Simon & Schuster/Free Press); Austin Kleon's *How to Steal Like an Artist: 10 Things Nobody Told Me about the Creative Life* (Workman); Andrew J. Polsky, PhD, *Victory in the Balance: Why Presidents Fail at War* (Oxford); *The Willpower Instinct* by Kelly McGonigal, PhD (Penguin/Avery); *Inside Steve's Brain: The Leadership Secrets of Steve Jobs* by Leander Kahney (Penguin/Portfolio); *The Body Toxic* by Nena Baker (Farrar Straus & Giroux); *The Unfinished Game: Pascal, Fermat, and the Birth of Probability Theory* by Keith Devlin (Perseus/Basic); *Blank Spots on the Map: State Secrets, Hidden Landscapes, and the Pentagon's Black World* by Trevor Paglen (Penguin/Dutton); *The Autobiographer's Handbook: The 826 Valencia Guide to Writing a Memoir* (Holt); *The New New Deal* (Penguin/Portfolio); *American Nightingale: The Story of Frances Stanger, Forgotten Heroine of Normandy* by Bob Welch (Simon & Schuster/Atria); *Ancient Wisdom, Modern Kitchen: Recipes from the East for Health, Healing, and Long Life* (Perseus/Da Capo); *One-Letter Words: A Dictionary* by Craig Conley (HarperCollins); *Momma Zen: Walking the Crooked*

Path of Motherhood by Karen Miller (Shambhala); *The Probiotics Revolution* by Sarah Wernick and Gary B. Huffnagle (Random House/Bantam)

TESSLER LITERARY AGENCY, LLC

27 West 20th Street, Suite 1003, New York, NY 10011
www.tessleragency.com

Agent's name: Michelle Tessler

Education: Master's degree in English literature and member of the Association of Author Representatives

Career history: Before forming her own agency, Michelle Tessler worked as an agent at Carlisle & Company, now part of InkWell Management. She also worked at the William Morris Agency and the Elaine Markson Literary Agency. In addition to her agenting experience, Michelle worked as an executive of business development and marketing in the Internet industry. In 1994, just as the Internet was becoming a mainstream medium, she was hired by best-selling author James Gleick to help launch The Pipeline. She then went on to serve as vice president of New Media at Jupiter Communications, and later at ScreamingMedia, before returning to traditional publishing. Her experience marketing content, products, and services to appeal to both general and niche audiences is of great benefit to her authors as they look for creative and effective ways to get the word out on their books and grow their readerships.

Categories/Subjects that you are most enthusiastic about agenting: The Tessler Literary Agency is a full-service boutique agency. We represent writers of quality nonfiction and literary and commercial fiction. Our nonfiction list includes popular science, reportage, memoir, history, biography, psychology, business, and travel. Committed to developing careers and building the readerships of the authors we represent, our agency offers personalized attention at every stage of the publishing process. Sharp editorial focus is given to clients before their work is submitted, and marketing support is provided along the way, as publishers begin to position the book in the marketplace through catalog copy, jacket designs, and marketing, promotion, and launch strategies. We handle all domestic, foreign, and subsidiary rights for our clients, working with a network of dedicated coagents who specialize in film and translation rights.

What's the best way for fiction writers to solicit your interest: Please submit initial queries via the webform at www.tessleragency.com.

What's the best way for nonfiction writers to solicit your interest: See above.

What are some representative titles that you have sold: *Flower Confidential* by Amy Stewart—a *New York Times* best seller (Algonquin); *Body Clutter* by Marla Cilley (aka The Flylady) and Leanne Ely (aka The Dinner Diva), a *New York Times* best seller (Touchstone); *Presidential Doodles* from the creators of *Cabinet* magazine

(Basic); *A Sense of the World* and *The Extraordinary Journeys of James Holman* by Jason Roberts—finalist for the National Book Critics' Circle Award (HarperCollins); *Sixpence House: Lost in a Town of Books* by Paul Collins—a *Booksense* best seller (Bloomsbury); *How to Be Lost* by Amanda Eyre Ward (Macadam Cage/Ballantine); *Saving Dinner* by Leanne Ely (Ballantine); *The Mommy Brain: How Motherhood Makes You Smarter* by Katherine Ellison (Basic); *Our Inner Ape: The Past and Future of Human Nature* by Frans De Waal—a *New York Times* notable book (Riverhead); *Mediated* by Thomas De Zengotita (Bloomsbury); *Defining the Wind: The Beaufort Scale and How a 19th-Century Admiral Turned Science into Poetry* by Scott Huler (Crown); *Sink Reflections* by Marla Cilley (aka The Flylady) (Bantam); *Suburban Safari: A Year on the Lawn* by Hannah Holmes (Bloomsbury); *Forgive Me* by Amanda Eyre Ward (Random House); *In the Furnace of the Nation-Empires* by Michael Knox Beran (Free Press); *A Mid-Sized and Immodest Mammal: A Natural History of Myself* by Hannah Holmes (Random House); *The Fruit Hunters: Inside the Fruit Underworld* by Adam Gollner (Scribners); *The Miracle: The Epic Story of Asia's Quest for Wealth* by Michael Schuman (HarperBusiness); *A Nuclear Family Vacation: Travels in the World of Atomic Weaponry* by Sharon Weinberger and Nathan Hodge (Bloomsbury); *Vatican II: A People's History* by Colleen McDannell (Basic); *Bottomfeeder: An Ethical Eater's Adventures in a World of Vanishing Seafood* by Taras Grescoe (Bloomsbury); *The Day We Lost the H-Bomb: The True Story of a Missing Bomb and the Race to Find It* by Barbara Moran (Presidio)

THOUGHT LEADERS INTL./INTELLECTUAL PROPERTY MANAGEMENT

109 Barbaree Way, Tiburon, CA 94920
415-789-9040
www.thoughtleadersintl.com

Agent's name: Leanne Sindell
E-mail: lsindell@thoughtleadersintl.com
Born: Near Seattle, WA
Education: Bible college in Sweden, England, and Seattle, WA; liberal arts studies in Kuopio, Finland, Stockholm University, Sorbonne University, and American University in Paris; degree in fashion design and illustration from Studio Bercot, Paris; securities and commodities/futures licensed from 1984–2005

Career history: Financial sales in the securities and managed futures industry for 20 plus years; took a three-year hiatus to study fashion design in Paris and designed in NYC for a year; commercial illustrator and artist. In 2007, I started my own literary agency.

Personal interests/hobbies: Painting, reading, cooking, films, travel, learning languages, classical/jazz/world music

Categories/Subjects that you are most enthusiastic about agenting: Business books, memoir

Categories/Subjects writers shouldn't bother pitching to you: Fiction, poetry, diet books, health/fitness, New Age/spiritual

Do you charge fees separate from your commission or offer nonagenting fee-based services: No

What representative titles you have sold to publishers: *The Econosphere* by Craig Thomas (FT Press); *The Genius Machine, The 11 Steps That Turn Raw Ideas into Brilliance* by Gerald Sindell (New World Library); *The Art of Managing Professional Services* by Maureen Broderick (Wharton School Publishing); *The Yahoo! Style Guide: The Ultimate Sourcebook for Writing, Editing, and Creating Content for the Digital World* by Cris Barr and the senior editors at Yahoo! (St. Martin's Press); *Genereux ou egoiste? Etes-vous de ceux qui prennent ou de ceux qui donnent?* by Cris Evatt and Bruce Feld (Payot et Rivages)

How and why did you become an agent: I decided to use my love of books and ideas and combine it with my knowledge of business and sales skills.

How do you feel about writers: I love writers and have a great respect for them.

Describe yourself: Curious, ethical, funny, serious, open-minded, artistic, fair, impatient, opinionated, and empathetic

What's the best way for writers to solicit your interest: E-mail query letter is the best way to start a conversation.

Will e-readers significantly change the business: I think they already have and continue to do so. I imagine there will be many new forms of a book in the future.

Are you optimistic, pessimistic, neutral, or catatonic about the book biz in the future: Mostly optimistic

---

TRACY BROWN LITERARY AGENCY

PO Box 772, Nyack, NY 10960
914-400-4147

Agent name: Tracy Brown
E-mail: tracy@brownlit.com
Born: Omaha, Nebraska
Education: Williams College; Columbia University
Career history: I worked my way up (and down) the book publishing editorial ladder for 25 years before becoming an agent in 2004. I came into the business at the age of 28 as an assistant in the publicity department at E. P. Dutton and then moved to junior editorial positions at Holt and Penguin. In 1988 I was offered the job of editorial director of Quality Paperback Book Club. Returning briefly to trade publishing in 1992, I initiated a new trade paperback list at Little, Brown called Back Bay and served as its first editorial director. In 1993 I returned to the book clubs when I

was offered the position of editor-in-chief of Book-of-the-Month Club, a position I held until 1996 when I returned to the trade as an acquiring editor at Holt and then at Ballantine. In 2004 I decided to become an agent. My first three years were spent in association with Wendy Sherman Associates. I opened my own agency in 2007.

Hobbies/Personal interests: Travel, cooking, farmer's markets, Bob Dylan's music

Categories/Subjects that you are most enthusiastic about agenting: 80 percent nonfiction: Current affairs, memoir, psychology, travel, nature, health; 20 percent literary fiction

Categories/Subjects writers shouldn't bother pitching to you: Science fiction, romance, young adult

If you were not an agent, what might you be doing instead: That's a scary thought.

What's the best way for fiction writers to solicit your interest: Write a succinct and informative query letter that clearly states who you are and what you want to write about.

Do you charge fees separate from your commission or offer nonagenting fee-based services: No fees

What are some representative titles that you have sold: *Mating in Captivity: Unlocking Erotic Intelligence* by Esther Perel (HarperCollins); *Perfect Girls, Starving Daughters* by Courtney E. Martin (Free Press); *The Man in the White Sharkskin Suit* by Lucette Lagnado (Ecco); *Why We're Losing the War on Cancer* by Clifton Leaf (Knopf); *Full Frontal Feminism* by Jessica Valenti (Seal Press); *Super in the City: A Novel* by Daphne Uviller (Bantam).

How and why did you become an agent: I'm amazed that I survived in corporate publishing for 25 consecutive years. Then there came a time when I wanted more freedom to select the authors I want to work with. The transition from editor to agent was relatively easy for me; acquiring books and selling them involve essentially the same skills.

How do you feel about writers: Their words have impacted my life more than any other art form.

How would you describe what you do as an agent to someone (or something) from another planet: Don't even try to make sense of the book business. Nobody knows why some books sell and others don't. This irrationality can be frustrating at times but is also a large part of why so many of us are attracted to the challenge of bringing worthy books to the public's attention.

Describe the client from hell, even if you don't have any: A client needs to trust that an agent knows how to do his/her job. Trying to micromanage the process is going to make everyone miserable.

Describe the publisher and/or editor from hell: I've known a few (luckily very few) editors and publishers who seem to feel that the agent is nothing but a trouble-maker who must be thwarted at every turn.

What do you like best about your clients and the editors and publishers you work with: I enjoy these relationships most when the topic of conversation is not always about work.

Describe yourself: I receive a lot of queries addressed to "Ms." Tracy Brown. I'm used to this and don't mind, but it's probably best for potential clients to know that I'm one of the rare males with the name Tracy.

Will our business exist as we know it in 10 years or so: Definitely not as we know it today. But there will always be people who want to tell stories and other people will want to hear them. So most likely there will be a need for somebody to facilitate the process. I'm not worried—yet.

TRIADAUS LITERARY AGENCY

PO Box 561, Sewickley, PA 15143
412-401-3376
www.triadaus.com

Agent's name: Uwe Stender
Born: Germany
Education: PhD, German literature
Career history: Literary agent (since 2004), university lecturer (writing, German), teacher
Hobbies: Soccer (runner-up national high school coach of the year 2007), playing squash, reading
Categories/Subjects that you are most enthusiastic about agenting: I am open to pretty much anything.
If you were not an agent, what might you be doing instead: I might be in the music industry as a producer.
What's the best way for fiction writers to solicit your interest: Send me a well-written and error-free e-mail query.
Do you charge fees separate from your commission or offer nonagenting fee-based services: No
What are some representative titles that you have sold: *86'd* by Dan Fante (Harper Perennial); *Covert* by Bob Delaney with Dave Scheiber (Union Square Press/Sterling); *The Equation* by Omar Tyree (Wiley); *Lost's Buried Treasures* by David Lavery and Lynnette Porter (Sourcebooks); *What's Possible* by Daryn Kagan (Meredith)
How and why did you become an agent: I have always been interested in literature (PhD and taught at universities), and after years of researching the field from a publishing perspective, I decided to become an agent (with a lot of guidance and mentoring from several well-connected publishing insiders). I love the thrill of discovering a GREAT book.
How do you feel about writers: Without them, I would not be doing my dream job.
How would you describe what you do as an agent to someone (or something) from another planet: It's like discovering new planets every day!
What are your favorite books, movies, and TV shows, and why: Love things

that move me on an emotional level. All of the following do: (1) Books: *The Little Prince*, St. Exupery; *The Tin Drum*, Grass; *Huckleberry Finn*, Mark Twain (2) Films: *Cinema Paradiso*; *Goodbye, Lenin*; *It's a Wonderful Life* (3) TV shows: *Bonanza*, *Life on Mars* (British Version), *Seinfeld*

What do you like best about your clients and the editors and publishers you work with: These folks are hard-working, smart, and committed to making dreams come true.

VAN HAITSMA LITERARY

204 N. El Camino Real, Suite E-431, Encinitas, CA 92024
www.vanHaitsmaLiterary.com

Agent's name: Sally van Haitsma

Categories/Subjects writers shouldn't bother pitching to you: Horror, fantasy, romance, historical, chick-lit, sci-fi, screenplays, and poetry

If you were not an agent, what might you be doing instead: Make documentaries, garden, read, travel, bake pies, and lounge on the beach slathered in sunscreen

What's the best way for fiction writers to solicit your interest: Query letter, four pages of sample writing, plus a one-page synopsis

What's the best way for nonfiction writers to solicit your interest: Query letter listing credentials, education, and experience plus any marketing ability, social media, etc. If applicable, a formal book proposal, less than 50 pages.

Do you charge reading or management fees: No

What are the most common mistakes writers make when pitching to you: Unprofessional presentation, spelling errors, lack of knowledge about the publishing industry; lack of information about themselves; lack of brevity; submitting more than one project at a time; thinking of writing books as a get-rich-quick scheme rather than focusing on their craft

Describe the client from hell, even if you don't have any: Not listening to our advice, not trusting our judgment; telling us what to do and how to do it; not telling the truth

What's your definition of a great client: Appreciative, loyal, trusting, trustworthy, knowing that we care deeply about their work; sense of humor and resilience

What can a writer do to increase the odds of you becoming his or her agent: Write a query that will knock our socks off. Be referred by editors, clients, other professionals, or simply be a brilliant writer.

How and why did you become an agent: I was seduced by the ghost of Thomas Hardy.

How would you describe what you do as an agent to someone (or something) from another planet: We sell manuscripts from writers unknown and known to publishers, who magically turn them into books.

How do you feel about editors and publishers: Thank God for all of them

How do you feel about writers: It depends if they can write.

What do you see in the near future for book publishing: Much like smart phones revolutionized simple voice communication into a multimedia experience, e-books will enhance the reading experience in ways we can't even imagine yet. Tangible books, however, will continue to be popular and cherished.

What are your favorite books, movies, and TV shows, and why: Books: *Return of the Native, The Road, The Glass Castle, Jane Eyre, The Devil in the White City.* TV shows: *Homeland, Enlightened, Fringe, Walking Dead, Boardwalk Empire, True Blood, The Mentalist.* Movies: *Chopping Block* movies; *The House of Sand and Fog; La Strada; The Waterfront; Fannie and Alexander; Hannah and Her Sisters; GATTACA; In Thin Air; Das Boot; Chinatown; Aguirre, The Wrath of God; The Piano; The Best Years of Our Lives; Fargo*

In your opinion, what do editors think of you: They respect and like us. We are consummate professionals, aggressive when we need to be but always polite and pleasant. They recognize integrity, and they are aware of our good reputation.

On a personal level, what do you think people like and dislike about you: Everyone loves us, why wouldn't they? Our friends think we have a very glamorous job. We don't tell them the truth.

What are some representative titles that you have sold: *Wesley the Owl* by Stacey O'Brien (Free Press/Simon & Schuster); *America Libre* by Raul Ramos y Sanchez (Grand Central); *The Leisure Seeker* by Michael Zadoorian (Morrow/ Harper); *Hick* by Andrea Portes (Unbridled Books); *Film School* by Steve Boman (BenBella Books); *Death in a Wine Dark Sea* by Lisa King (The Permanent Press); *NATO 2.0* by Sarwar Kashmeri (Potomac Books); *Does This Mean You'll See Me Naked?* by Robert Webster (Sourcebooks)

VERITAS LITERARY AGENCY

601 Van Ness Avenue, Opera Plaza Suite E, San Francisco, CA 94102
415-647-6964 | fax: 415-647-6965
www.veritasliterary.com

Agent's name: Katherine Boyle
Born: June 16 (Bloomsday!) 1969, Stanford, California
Education: BA, English and psychology, Stanford University
Career history: After graduation I worked at a variety of Bay Area independent presses and agencies while pursuing a publishing certificate at Berkeley. Veritas was established in 1995, and thereafter I joined the AAR and the Authors Guild.
Hobbies/Personal interests: Music and visual art addiction, foreign films, running, hiking, chapbook making, pet adoration, eating
Categories/Subjects that you are most enthusiastic about agenting: Literary fiction, multicultural fiction, historical fiction, new fabulist and literary speculative

fiction, southern fiction, literary thrillers and mysteries, narrative nonfiction, reportage, memoir, popular science, popular culture, natural history, current events and politics, women's issues, art- and music-related biography

Categories/Subjects writers shouldn't bother pitching to you: New Age, romance, military history, Westerns

If you were not an agent, what might you be doing instead: It's a toss-up between whale scientist or London stage actress.

What's the best way for fiction writers to solicit your interest: Well-written, concise queries

Do you charge fees separate from your commission or offer nonagenting fee-based services: No

What are some representative titles that you have sold: *Hedwig and Berti* by Frieda Arkin (St. Martin's); *Sickened* by Julie Gregory (Bantam); *If I Am Missing or Dead* by Janine Latus (Simon & Schuster/Random House UK); *Free Burning* by Bayo Ojikutu (Crown); *I Was a Teenage Gumby* by Jean Gonick (Hyperion); *Sometimes the Soul* by Gioia Timpanelli (W. W. Norton/Vintage); *Deliberate Acts of Kindness* by Meredith Gould (Doubleday); *The Nature of Music* by Maureen McCarthy Draper (Riverhead/Putnam); *American Sideshow* by Marc Hartzman (Tarcher/Penguin); *65 Successful Harvard Business School Application Essays* by The Harbus (St. Martin's); *The Essential Nostradamus* by Richard Smoley (Tarcher/Penguin); *The Twins of Tribeca* by Rachel Pine (Miramax); *The Creative Writing MFA Handbook* by Tom Kealey (Continuum)

How and why did you become an agent: I've always loved books and great writing, but I'm too fond of social interaction to thrive as a librarian. I couldn't ask for a better career to satisfy the introverted/extroverted poles of a Gemini personality.

How do you feel about writers: I adore them. It's a tough job, and they're certainly doing more than their share to keep the culture on life support, generally earning a fraction of what video game designers make.

How would you describe what you do as an agent to someone (or something) from another planet: Storytelling is an ancient and universal art. Since dreams probably come from these other planes, it shouldn't be too hard to explain the field to an interested entity. All beings likely share the intuition that there's more wisdom embedded in a story than we'll ever know.

What are your favorite books, movies, and TV shows, and why: Books: *Housekeeping, The Sea, The Restraint of Beasts,* and anything by Alice Munro, William Maxwell, and Italo Calvino. All of these authors can shift a reader's level of perception almost instantaneously. Movies: *I'm Not Scared, Dreams, The 400 Blows, Nights of Cabiria,* and *The After Life:* all strange, beautiful, life affirming. TV: *Flight of the Conchords* and *Prime Suspect,* because hilarity and Helen Mirren are also important.

Describe the client from hell, even if you don't have any: Someone who calls to pitch a "great idea" on the phone before they've even written a word.

Describe the publisher and/or editor from hell: Luckily I've been spared that circle so far.

What do you like best about your clients and the editors and publishers you work with: I couldn't ask for a better cadre of kindred spirits. There's no greater rush than celebrating a book's success with a brilliant author and a wonderfully committed editor. Of course they're all individuals, but on the whole it's so reassuring to be surrounded by so many sane, thoughtful, intellectually curious, passionate, witty, and good-natured people. I just wish that they weren't spread so far apart—we could throw some great parties.

Describe yourself: "Trying to define yourself is like trying to bite your own teeth."—Alan Watts

Will our business exist as we know it in 10 years or so: While the tectonic plates are certainly shifting, books will always be beloved and necessary in this world. To sustain authors, however, it may be increasingly important to pursue alternate subrights arenas—pitching a historical-fiction series to a video game producer, for example. A protean instinct will serve both authors and agents well, but the importance of craft, originality, and excellence will never disappear.

Agent's name: Megan O'Patry
Born: San Diego, California; 1984
Education: BA in pre- and early-modern literature, UC Santa Cruz; MFA in creative writing, San Francisco State University
Career history: A long time ago when the earth was green and there were more kinds of animals than you've ever seen…
Hobbies/Personal interests: Playwriting, black and white movies, teaching infants to swim
Categories/Subjects that you are most enthusiastic about agenting: Literary fiction, narrative nonfiction, mainstream fiction, young adult, to name a few
Categories/Subjects writers shouldn't bother pitching to you: Self-help, guidebooks
If you were not an agent, what might you be doing instead: Working in Elmore Leonard's coffee shop
What's the best way for fiction writers to solicit your interest: A well-written query. Don't sell try to sell me a used car. I don't need a car, I live in the city. Please don't drop me into the middle of your story with aggressive adverbs; be honest and to the point. Always spellcheck.
Do you charge fees separate from your commission or offer nonagenting fee-based services: No
How and why did you become an agent: It was a stage of evolution, more or less. I followed Katherine Boyle home one day and lived under the dining room table for a while, next to a slush pile. The rest, as they say, is in development.
How do you feel about writers: Writers are like M&Ms. They come in a variety of colors, and you stuff them in your mouth, hoping for a hallucinatory effect. And sometimes you wake up on the side of the road in your underwear. I love writers!
How would you describe what you do as an agent to someone (or something)

from another planet: I'm very tight lipped. I communicate with bumper stickers. I pass on and receive a lot of intergalactic wisdom this way, such as "Go North for the cold beer."

What are your favorite books, movies, and TV shows, and why: *A Hero of Our Time, The House of Leaves, Lolita, The West Wing, Deadwood, Weeds, The Last Unicorn, The Seven Faces of Dr. Lao,* because of the writing, my friends, the writing!

Describe the client from hell, even if you don't have any: Someone who is unrealistic in their expectations, resistant to constructive criticism, and unacquainted with courtesies like *please* and *thank you*

What do you like best about your clients and the editors and publishers you work with: They love what they do, and they come into any project with an open mind. We extend them the same necessity. At the end of the day, we may want different things but by the end of the week, we're all lined up.

Will our business exist as we know it in 10 years or so: I have a bumper sticker somewhere that addresses this very issue...

VICTORIA SANDERS & ASSOCIATES, LLC

241 Avenue of the Americas, Suite 11H, New York, NY 10014
www.victoriasanders.com

Agent's name: Victoria Sanders
Born: Los Angeles, California
Education: BFA, Tisch School of the Arts at New York University; and JD from Benjamin N. Cardozo School of Law
Career history: WNET/Channel 13, Simon & Schuster, Carol Mann Agency, Charlotte Sheedy Agency
Hobbies/Personal interests: Architecture, reading, art, film
Categories/Subjects that you are most enthusiastic about agenting: All things that are great reads and teach me something in some way
Categories/Subjects writers shouldn't bother pitching to you: Sadly, I am the wrong person for science and math, my own failing.
If you were not an agent, what might you be doing instead: Furniture design
What's the best way for fiction writers to solicit your interest: A terrific query letter
Do you charge fees separate from your commission or offer nonagenting fee-based services: No
What are some representative titles that you have sold: *Fractured* by Karin Slaughter (Bantam); *Undone* by Karin Slaughter (Bantam); *Can't Stop, Won't Stop: A History of the Hip-Hop Generation* by Jeff Chang (winner of the American Book Award, St. Martin's Press); *Who We Be: The Colorization of America* by Jeff Chang (St. Martin's Press); *100 Young Americans* by Michael Franzini (Collins Design/HarperCollins); *So Happy Together* by Maryann McFadden (Hyperion); *Hold Love Strong* by Matthew

Goodman (Touchstone/Fireside); *What Doesn't Kill You* by Virginia DeBerry and Donna Grant (Touchstone/Fireside); *Flow* by Elissa Stein and Susan Kim (St. Martin's Press); *Sisters and Husbands* by Connie Briscoe (Grand Central); *Never Make the Same Mistake Twice: Straight Talk on Love and Life from a Real Housewife* by NeNe Leakes and Denene Millner (Touchstone/Fireside); *The Invisible Mountain* by Carolina De Robertis (Knopf); *The Journey Home* by Sejal Ravani (Putnam); *The Opposite of Me* by Sarah Pekkanen (Atria); *Damaged* by Kia Dupree (Grand Central)

How and why did you become an agent: Simply, books. They have always been critically important to me. I grew up with my nose stuck in one, and I learned very early on that most authors are underappreciated.

How would you describe what you do as an agent to someone (or something) from another planet: I am a writer's advocate.

What are your favorite books, movies, and TV shows, and why: *Ugly Betty, Entourage, CBS Sunday Morning* (it's all about Nancy Giles), *Good Morning, America* (Robin and Diane!)

Describe the client from hell, even if you don't have any: All clients are nervous, and that's normal. However, someone who, once signed, needs to go off and finish the project but likes to give daily updates or even weekly—that's too much, unless we're working closely together editorially, and it's crunch time.

Describe the publisher and/or editor from hell: Someone who is nonresponsive. Just rip the Band-Aid and tell me the truth. Don't ignore calls or e-mails.

What do you like best about your clients and the editors and publishers you work with: I love it when we all get jazzed on the work.

You're welcome to share your thoughts and sentiments about the business of writing and publishing: Everything is cyclical. Good books will still be published, and those who work hard and are passionate will survive.

WALES LITERARY AGENCY, INC.

PO Box 9426, 415 1st Avenue North, Seattle, WA 98109-0426
206-284-7114
www.waleslit.com

Agent's name: Elizabeth Wales
E-mail: waleslit@waleslit.com
Born: March 30, 1952
Education: BA, Smith College; graduate work in English and American literature, Columbia University
Career history: Worked in the trade sales departments at Oxford University Press and Viking Penguin; worked in city government and served a term on the Seattle school board; also worked as a bookseller and publisher's representative
Categories/Subjects that you are most enthusiastic about agenting: A range

of narrative nonfiction and quality commercial fiction; especially interested in non-fiction projects that could have a progressive cultural or political impact; in fiction, looking for talented mainstream storytellers, both new and established; some well-crafted psychological thrillers and young adult; especially interested in writers from the Northwest, Alaska, West Coast, and Pacific Rim countries

Categories/Subjects writers shouldn't bother pitching to you: Children's books, how-to, self-help, and almost all genre projects (romance, true crime, horror, action/adventure, most science fiction/fantasy, techno thrillers)

Do you charge fees separate from your commission or offer nonagenting fee-based services: No reading fees

What are some representative titles that you have sold: *It Gets Better: Coming Out, Overcoming Bullying, and Creating a Life Worth Living,* edited by Dan Savage and Terry Miller (Dutton/Penguin, 2011); *Heat* by Bill Streever (Little, Brown, 2012); *Unterzakhn: A Graphic Novel and Story of the Lower East Side* by Leela Corman (Schocken/Pantheon, 2012)

How and why did you become an agent: For the adventure and the challenge; also, I am a generalist—interested in variety.

WENDY SCHMALZ AGENCY

Box 831, Hudson, NY 12534
518-672-7697 | fax: 518-672-7662

Agent's name: Wendy Schmalz
E-mail: wendy@schmalzagency.com
Born: Willow Grove, Pennsylvania
Education: BA, Barnard College
Career history: I started right out of college in the film department of Curtis Brown, Ltd. After a year, I went to Harold Ober Associates, where I continued to handle film rights but also built my own list and represented the estates of F. Scott Fitzgerald and Langston Hughes. I opened my own agency in 2002.

Hobbies/Personal interests: Woodworking, history

Categories/Subjects that you are most enthusiastic about agenting: I represent adult and children's fiction and nonfiction.

Categories/Subjects writers shouldn't bother pitching to you: I don't represent genre fiction such as sci-fi, romance, or fantasy. I'm not looking for books for very young children and I'm not interested in taking on any new picture-book writers. I don't handle self-help or Christian books.

If you were not an agent, what might you be doing instead: Forensic pathology

What's the best way for fiction writers to solicit your interest: When I get a submission letter, I want to know the writer wants me specifically to represent him or her—that she isn't just fishing for an agent. I want the sense that they know what

I represent and want me to represent them because they think I'd be right for the kind of writing they do.

What's the best way for nonfiction writers to solicit your interest: Same as above

Do you charge reading or management fees: No

What are the most common mistakes writers make when pitching to you: It's a mistake to be overly confident, but it's also bad to be insecure. I don't like it when someone says his book is so great that it will sell millions of copies and be a major motion picture, nor do I like sniveling letters that beg me to read the work.

How and why did you become an agent: When I was a teenager, I read Tennessee Williams's autobiography. He went on and on and how great his agent was. Before that, I didn't know what an agent was, but it sounded like a cool way to make a living.

What are some representative titles that you have sold: *She Loves You, She Loves You Not* (Little Brown) and *By the Time You Read This, I'll Be Dead* (Hyperion) by National Book Award finalist Julie Anne Peters; *Girl, Stolen* (Holt) by April Henry; *The False Friend* (Doubleday) and *Bee Season* (Doubleday) by Myla Goldberg; *Now Is the Time for Running* (Little Brown) by Michael Williams; *The Flatiron* by Alice Alexiou (St. Martin's)

What's the best way for writers to solicit your interest: I accept e-mail queries only. Please include a synopsis in the body of the e-mail. Do not attach the manuscript. Because of the number of queries I receive, I only respond to those whose manuscripts I want to read.

WENDY SHERMAN ASSOCIATES, INC.

450 Seventh Avenue, Suite 2307, New York, NY 10123
212-279-9027 | fax: 212-279-8863

Agent's name: Wendy Sherman

Born: New York, New York

Education: University of Hartford, bachelors in special education; BA 1998, Sarah Lawrence College

Career history: Opened this agency in 1999, was previously with the Aaron Priest Agency; vice president, executive director at Henry Holt; vice president, associate publisher at Owl Books; vice president, sales and subsidiary rights (1998–1999); also worked at Simon & Schuster and McMillan

Hobbies/Personal interests: Reading, traveling

Categories/Subjects that you are most enthusiastic about agenting: Quality fiction, women's fiction, suspense, narrative nonfiction, psychology/self-help

Categories/Subjects writers shouldn't bother pitching to you: Science fiction, fantasy, horror, mysteries, and children's books

If you were not an agent, what might you be doing instead: I could be back in corporate publishing but choose not to pursue that career path.

What's the best way for fiction writers to solicit your interest: Query letter via regular mail to the agency, with a first chapter

What's the best way for nonfiction writers to solicit your interest: Query letter via regular mail describing their book and credentials

Do you charge reading or management fees: No

What are the most common mistakes writers make when pitching to you: The most common mistakes are not targeting the right agent and being unclear about your book in your query letter. Writers should do their research and find an agent who is a good fit for their material.

Describe the client from hell, even if you don't have any: The client from hell is unreasonably demanding and doesn't trust our judgment and experience.

What's your definition of a great client: The perfect collaboration between agent and author is one of mutual goals and respect.

What can a writer do to increase the odds of you becoming his or her agent: Have a fully polished book or proposal that's timely and well done

How and why did you become an agent: After leaving Henry Holt, I had the opportunity to work for the Aaron Priest Agency. I had thought about agenting for some time, and it seemed like the perfect way to make the change from working for a publisher to becoming an agent.

How would you describe what you do as an agent to someone (or something) from another planet: We bring writers to the attention of the best possible/most enthusiastic editor and publisher. We then do our best to ensure the book is published with the utmost enthusiasm.

How do you feel about editors and publishers: More than ever, editors have a very tough job. They not only have to find manuscripts they want to publish, but then they have to convince in-house colleagues in editorial, marketing, and sales to support the acquisitions.

How do you feel about writers: We love writers; they are why we became agents. The best writers bring an immense amount of talent to the table and take direction well.

What are your favorite books, movies, and TV shows, and why: *Watership Down* by Richard Adams; *A Tree Grows in Brooklyn* by Betty Smith; *The Glass Castle* by Jeannette Walls; all of Jane Austen and George Eliot; *Middlesex* by Jeffrey Eugenides. And so many more.

What are some representative titles that you have sold: Fiction: *Love in 90 Days* by Dr. Diana Kirschner (Center Street); *Kockroach* by Tyler Knox (William Morrow); *Marked Man* by William Lashner (William Morrow); *Souvenir* by Therese Fowler (Random House); *The Cloud Atlas* by Liam Callanan (Delacorte); *The Judas Field* by Howard Bahr (Henry Holt); *The Vanishing Point* by Mary Sharratt (Houghton Mifflin); *The Ice Chorus* by Sarah Stonich (Little, Brown); *Crawling at Night* by Nani Power (Atlantic Monthly Press). Nonfiction: *My First Five Husbands* by Rue McClanahan (Broadway); *Confessions of a Prep School Mommy Handler* by Wade Rouse (Harmony); *Why Men Fall Out of Love* by Michael French

(Ballantine); *Cash In on Your Passion* by Jonathan Fields (Broadway); *Real Love* by Greg Baer (Gotham); *Feed the Hungry* by Nani Power (Free Press)

Agent's name: Michelle Brower
Born: Berlin, New Jersey
Education: The College of NJ, BA; and New York University, MA
Hobbies/Personal interests: Crafting, cooking, film, animals
Categories/Subjects that you are most enthusiastic about agenting: Pop culture, music, humor, crafting, commercial fiction, thriller, literary fiction, narrative nonfiction, young adult, and graphic novels; books with elements of horror, fantasy, or science fiction that are for a mainstream audience

Categories/Subjects writers shouldn't bother pitching to you: Cozies, children's picture books, category romance

If you were not an agent, what might you be doing instead: I would probably be working in editorial.

What's the best way for fiction writers to solicit your interest: Query and first chapter, by e-mail or regular mail

What's the best way for nonfiction writers to solicit your interest: Query letter via regular mail describing their book and credentials

Do you charge reading or management fees: No

What are the most common mistakes writers make when pitching to you: The most common mistakes are not targeting the right agent and being unclear about your book in your query letter. Writers should do their research and find an agent who is a good fit for their material.

Describe the client from hell, even if you don't have any: The client from hell is unreasonably demanding and doesn't trust our judgment and experience.

What's your definition of a great client: The perfect collaboration between agent and author is one of mutual goals and respect.

What can a writer do to increase the odds of you becoming his or her agent: Have a fully polished book or proposal that's timely and well done.

How and why did you become an agent: I started with Wendy Sherman Associates in 2004 after receiving my master's degree in literature, and I love working with clients to develop their ideas, shape their proposals, and take their fiction to the next level.

How would you describe what you do as an agent to someone (or something) from another planet: We bring writers to the attention of the best possible/most enthusiastic editor and publisher. We then do our best to ensure the book is published with the utmost enthusiasm.

How do you feel about editors and publishers: More than ever, editors have a very tough job. They not only have to find manuscripts they want to publish, but then they have to convince in-house colleagues in editorial, marketing, and sales to support the acquisitions.

How do you feel about writers: We love writers; they are why we became agents. The best writers bring an immense amount of talent to the table and take direction well.

WORDWISE MEDIA SERVICES

4083 Avenue L-8, Suite 255, Lancaster, CA 93536
866-739-0440 | fax: 866-501-4280
www.wordwisemedia.com
info@wordwisemedia.com

Agent's name: Steven Hutson

Categories/Subjects that you are most enthusiastic about agenting: We represent a wide range of fiction and nonfiction books for adults and children. Spiritual themes a specialty.

What's the best way for writers to solicit your interest: Download the query form at our website, and follow the instructions.

Born: 1962 in Los Angeles

Education: Los Angeles City College, major in business administration

Career history: From a very early age I always wanted to be a writer. Instead I took the easy (but boring) road, following a career in office jobs and retail stores. But I continued writing on the side, hoping to make it big someday. I attended writers' conferences and sat at the feet of a couple of mentors, and finally had my first book published in 2006. At that point I set up a manuscript editing service for aspiring authors. And life was good. A couple of years later I was asked to take over the management of a local writers' conference, which has grown every year since. The literary agency is the next logical step on that path.

Hobbies/Personal interests: I've always enjoyed swimming; it's the only sport that I have ever done well. Cooking and gardening keep my hands busy.

Categories/Subjects writers shouldn't bother pitching to you: Please no screenplays, poetry, erotica, picture books, or chainsaw murders. You've been forewarned, and we won't respond to submissions for such.

If you were not an agent, what might you be doing instead: I would probably continue in my writing in some fashion. Apart from that you might find me working in a cubicle as an accountant.

Do you charge fees separate from your commission or offer nonagenting fee-based services: No fees for representation clients, ever. I might bill you for reimbursement on extraordinary expenses I incur on your behalf, such as postage on a huge manuscript. We still offer editing services, but we will not represent editing clients for at least a year after the most recent editing project.

What are some representative titles that you have sold: *Unexpected Love* by Julie Zine Coleman, Thomas Nelson, 2013; *Noir(ish)* by Evan Guilford-Blake, Dutton, 2012; *Faith Like Steel* by Dave Beckwith, Group Publishing, 2013; *Sand in*

the Gears by Andrew Smith, Potomac, 2012; *Wind over Marshdale* by Tracy Krauss, Astraea Press, 2012; *Dark Biology* by Bonnie J. Doran, Pelican, 2012

How and why did you become an agent: In the summer of 2010, my editing service received an e-mail from a potential client who asked me to recruit writers for a series of books and pitch the ideas to publishers. Happily, I already knew most of the people I needed to make this happen, and many responded favorably. With this newfound confidence, I felt emboldened to set up shop as a literary agency at the beginning of 2011.

How do you feel about writers: As a writer myself, I know how vulnerable it feels to show my work to someone and think, "Please be kind. Please like me." For this reason, even when I turn down a potential client, I try to offer some type of useful feedback. Perhaps they can leverage it into a new-and-improved manuscript in the future.

How do you feel about editors and publishers: Now that I'm working as an agent, I can (at least partly) understand the difficulty of their job. I can't help everyone, and I often have to deliver bad news.

How would you describe what you do as an agent to someone (or something) from another planet: At the beginning of each day, I have the opportunity to help make someone's dreams come true. Nothing more exciting than that.

What are your favorite books, movies, and TV shows, and why: Book: *Phantom Tollbooth* by Norton Juster. It's the ultimate existential experience for a child, even if he has to read it three times to understand it. Movie: *Footloose* with Kevin Bacon. The guy who chases a dream against all odds, sometimes wins. TV show: *The West Wing* on NBC. It has taught me much about how to write nonfiction and persuade someone of my point of view.

Describe the client from hell, even if you don't have any: Won't follow instructions, return e-mails or phone calls, or take my advice

Describe the publisher and/or editor from hell: Won't respond to my e-mails or phone calls. As a writer I've learned to take rejection gracefully, but the worst part is the waiting.

Will e-readers significantly change the business: I don't know. I don't have one, and I'm not in a big hurry to get one. I like dead trees.

Are you optimistic, pessimistic, neutral, or catatonic about the book biz in the future: I'm irrationally optimistic. There will always be a market for books, in one form or another. Whether for education or for pleasure, people will always seek them out.

Explain what you like and dislike about your job: I love it when a client thanks me again and again for helping her succeed. I hate it when she argues over every edit I suggest.

Describe a book you might like writing: All through school, I hated history class; it's the only subject I ever flunked. But today I love researching history and showing people why they should care.

LITERARY AGENTS

WRITERS HOUSE

21 West 26th Street, New York, NY 10010
3368 Governor Dr., #224F, San Diego, CA 92122
www.writershouse.com

Agent's name: Kenneth Wright
Education: BA, University of Colorado, Boulder; MA, Boston College
Career history: Editor through publisher positions at Oxford University Press, Simon & Schuster, HarperCollins, Henry Holt, and Scholastic
Categories/Subjects that you are most enthusiastic about agenting: Adult fiction and nonfiction, children's middle-grade and young-adult fiction and nonfiction
Categories/Subjects writers shouldn't bother pitching to you: Fantasy, romance, genre, picture books
What's the best way for fiction writers to solicit your interest: Make me laugh. Keep it short. Know your readers.
Do you charge fees separate from your commission or offer nonagenting fee-based services: No. Honest.
What are some representative titles that you have sold: David Macaulay (Roaring Brook/MacMillan); *The Lost Girls* by Amanda Pressner, Jennifer Baggett, and Holly Corbett (HarperCollins); *Why Santa Teleports* by Greg Mone (Bloomsbury)

Agent's name: Steven Malk
Born: Johannesburg, South Africa
Education: BA, political science and BA, history, University of California San Diego
Career history: Opened a West Coast office for Writers House in 1998; worked for the Sandra Dijkstra Literary Agency prior to that
Categories/Subjects that you are most enthusiastic about agenting: Books for children, middle-grade readers, and young adults
Categories/Subjects writers shouldn't bother pitching to you: Books that aren't intended for children, middle-grade readers, or young adults
If you were not an agent, what might you be doing instead: Playing center field for the San Diego Padres (not really, but it's a nice thought)
What's the best way for fiction writers to solicit your interest: Write a carefully thought-out, focused query that demonstrates a strong command of your work and also explains why you're querying me, specifically.
Do you charge fees separate from your commission or offer nonagenting fee-based services: No
What are some representative titles that you have sold: *The True Meaning of Smekday* by Adam Rex (Hyperion); *Clementine* by Sara Pennypacker, illustrated by Marla Frazee (Hyperion); *King Dork* by Frank Portman (Delacorte Press); *Your Own, Sylvia: A Verse Portrait of Sylvia Plath* by Stephanie Hemphill (Knopf); *John, Paul, George,*

and Ben by Lane Smith (Hyperion); *Repossessed* by A. M. Jenkins (HarperCollins); *Collect Raindrops: The Seasons Gathered* by Nikki McClure (Abrams); *Knucklehead: Tall Tales and Almost-True Stories of Growing Up Scieszka* by Jon Scieszka (Viking); *The Secret Order of the Gumm Street Girls* by Elise Primavera (HarperCollins); *We Are the Ship: The Story of Negro League Baseball* by Kadir Nelson (Hyperion)

How and why did you become an agent: It allowed me to be involved in both the creative and business sides of the industry and to work closely with and on behalf of authors I greatly admire. It was also the perfect outgrowth of bookselling for me, as I was able to apply everything I'd learned as a third-generation bookseller to my work as an agent.

What are your favorite books, movies, and TV shows, and why: Books (not including books that I've represented, obviously): anything by Barbara Cooney or Roald Dahl; also *The Westing Game* by Ellen Raskin, *I'll Fix Anthony* by Judith Viorst, *The Carrot Seed* by Ruth Krauss, *Dear Genius: The Letters of Ursula Nordstrom* by Leonard Marcus, and many, many more. Movies: *Hoosiers, Rushmore, Ghost World, Election, The Straight Story*

Agent's name: Dan Lazar

Born: Jerusalem, Israel

Career history: I started as an intern and worked my way up to senior agent.

Categories/Subjects that you are most enthusiastic about agenting: Literary and commercial fiction, women's fiction, historical fiction, thrillers, mysteries, gay and lesbian, young adult, middle grade, graphic novels or memoirs, Judaica, memoir, narrative nonfiction, pop-culture, humor

Categories/Subjects writers shouldn't bother pitching to you: Romance, picture books, cookbooks

What's the best way for fiction writers to solicit your interest: A great query letter and the first five pages of their manuscript

Do you charge fees separate from your commission or offer nonagenting fee-based services: No fees

What are some representative titles that you have sold: *Island of Lost Girls* by Jennifer McMahon (Harper); *Final Theory* by Mark Alpert (Touchstone); *Eve* by Elissa Aliott (Bantam); *Savvy* by Ingrid Law (Dial/Walden); *The Last Invisible Boy* (Ginee Seo/Atheneum); *Haiku Mama* (Quirk Books)

How and why did you become an agent: I loved books and reading. I applied for an internship at both publishers and agencies—Writers House hired me for the summer and happily so! I've been here ever since.

How would you describe what you do as an agent to someone (or something) from another planet: You don't go to court without a lawyer or buy a house without a real estate agent. Same for publishing—we're the author's champion and partner. Ideally (and more and more realistically), we're the one constant in the author's career, since editors move jobs, and publishers are changing constantly.

What are your favorite books, movies, and TV shows, and why: Favorite movies: *The Incredibles, Monsters, Inc.*; favorite TV shows: *The Daily Show, Will & Grace, Dirty Sexy Money, Frasier, Freaks and Geeks*

What do you like best about your clients and the editors and publishers you work with: I love their books, and I admire their persistence and passion. Different tastes are what make this business tough and rewarding all at once, but we're all in it ultimately for the same reason.

Will our business exist as we know it in 10 years or so: The business as we know it changes every day! But it's not going anywhere.

ADVICE FOR WRITERS

Dear Reader,

The purpose of the Essay Section is to provide knowledge, and maybe even some wisdom. To most effectively utilize all the raw data in this book, I highly recommend that you fortify yourself with proven road maps. Eventually, your own experiences will serve as your best teacher. Until then, you will need to draw from what others might share.

Whenever I teach about how to get published, I ask my students to listen to everything I say and then forget it. Why? Because within anarchy can be found holiness. Information can be either empowering or entrapping. The human mind will "see," "feel," and "hear" whatever the environment "tells" it. It is difficult to re-direct the way an individual or an entire society perceives its reality. It has been said that the best way to hide something as outlandish as extraterrestrials would be to simply put them in the middle of Times Square, because the vast majority of people would "refuse" to perceive what "cannot" be there. Some people might report that they saw something quite odd, but most of them would probably be talked out of it by the non-silent majority that relies upon reason and good sense. In the end, some unsubstantiated and inconsistent rumors might filter into the supermarket tabloids about an ET invasion in Times Square. Once that happens, nobody who ever wants to be taken seriously again will admit to seeing anything out of the ordinary, and would likely convince themselves that it was all perfectly explainable. Of course, Times Square is a strange place anyway.

The greatest measure of everlasting success tends to belong to those who create something new and enduring. It could be an intangible idea that somehow alters the course of history. Or it could be a physical thing or process that makes humanity more capable of manipulating time and space (like the wheel, which was presumably invented by Mrs. Wheel). People who innovate are in a way the ultimate liberators and rule breakers. It's their frustration, hunger, and lack of passive complacency that moves them to focus their energies for the purpose of changing what is. By nature, they are expansive. It's safe to assume that such individuals face tremendous opposition from the status quo. The vast majority of people are understandably threatened when confronted by the requirement to change, even when it is best for them to do so. All of us are capable of thinking beyond what already exists, and that approach to life will tend to be an asset when seeking to become a published writer. However, the risk of failure and rejection is always real, and can stand tall as the personal executioner of our dreams. To be eligible for success, a writer must be willing to endure all the pain that there might be.

Our nation's Puritan founders were fond of saying: *God is no respecter of persons.* That sentiment fit their belief system that human choices were mere manifestations of a preordained universe. If you accept that as your truth, then it will be pointless to resist what your heart and soul ask of you. If you don't accept such a paradigm, then there is no excuse for you not to pursue what you see as your truthful path. There is also a middle ground, which is to accept that reality is indeed predetermined, and yet live as if it is entirely your own free will that will bring you to tomorrow.

Writing, and the effort to become published, may at times resemble a dead end surrounded by the walls of a brutal confinement. But even then there is a path, and where there is a path there is a way. I hope that these essays will serve to strengthen you.

Jeff Herman

THE BATTLE OF THE "UNS"
(UNAGENTED/UNSOLICITED SUBMISSIONS)

JEFF HERMAN

Most major publishing houses claim to have policies that prevent them from even considering unagented/unsolicited submissions. "Unagented" means that a literary agent did not make the submission. "Unsolicited" means that no one at the publisher asked for the submission.

It's possible that you, or people you know, have already run into this frustrating roadblock. You may also be familiar with the rumor that it's more difficult to get an agent than it is to get a publisher—or that no agent will even consider your work until you have a publisher. On the surface, these negatives make it seem that you would have a better shot at becoming a starting pitcher for the Yankees or living out whatever your favorite improbable fantasy might be.

But, as you will soon learn, these so-called policies and practices are often more false than true, especially if you develop creative ways to circumvent them.

I have dubbed the previous obstacle course the Battle of the "UNs."

If you're presently unagented/unsolicited, you're one of the UNs.

Welcome! You're in good company.

Nobody is born published. There is no published author who wasn't at one time an UN. Thousands of new books are published each year, and thousands of people are needed to write them. You can be one of them.

In this chapter I'll show you how to win the Battle of the UNs. But first let me clarify an important distinction. When I use the word "win" here, I don't mean to say that you'll necessarily get your work published. What I mean is: You'll gain reasonable access to the powers that be for your work, and you'll learn how to increase the odds—dramatically—that your work will in fact be acquired.

Please be realistic. For every published writer, there are, at minimum, several thousand waiting in line to get published. "Many are called, but few are chosen."

It's completely within your power to maximize your chances of getting published. It's also within your power to minimize those chances. There are reasons why some highly talented people habitually underachieve, and those reasons can often be found within them. If you fail, fail, and fail, you should look within yourself for possible answers. What can you do to turn it around? If you find some answers, then you haven't failed at all, and the lessons you allow yourself to learn will lay the groundwork for success in this and in other endeavors.

Having an agent greatly increases the likelihood that you will be published. For one thing, on the procedural level, established agents can usually obtain relatively rapid (and serious) consideration for their clients. One basic reason for this is that editors view agents as a valuable screening mechanism—that is, when a project crosses the editor's desk under an agent's letterhead, the editor knows it's undergone vetting from someone in the industry who is familiar with the applicable standards of quality and market considerations.

I usually recommend that unpublished writers first make every attempt to get an agent before they start going directly to the publishers.

It's significantly easier to get an agent than it is to get a publisher—not the other way around. Most agents I know are always on the lookout for fresh talent. Finding and nurturing tomorrow's stars are two of our functions.

However, one of my reasons for writing and researching this book is to reveal to you that as a potential author, not having an agent does not necessarily disqualify you from the game automatically. Before I show you ways to win the Battle of the UNs, I'd like you to have a fuller understanding of the system.

YOU ARE THE EDITOR

Imagine that you're an acquisitions editor at one of America's largest publishing firms in New York City. You have a master's degree from an Ivy League college and you, at least, think you're smarter than most other people. Yet you're earning a lot less money than most of the people who graduated with you. Your classmates have become lawyers, accountants, bankers, and so forth, and they all seem to own large, well-appointed apartments or homes—whereas you, if you fall out of bed, might land in the bathtub of your minuscule New York flat.

On the other hand, you love your job. For you, working in publishing is a dream come true. As in other industries and professions, much of your satisfaction comes from advancement—getting ahead.

To move up the career ladder, you'll have to acquire at least a few successful titles each year. To find these few good titles, you'll be competing with many editors from other publishers and perhaps even with fellow editors within your own firm. As in any other business, the people who make the most money for the company will get the choice promotions and the highest salaries. Those who perform less impressively will tend to be passed over. (Of course, being a good editor and playing politics well are also important.)

There are two tried-and-true sources for the titles that publishers acquire: literary agents and direct solicitations.

LITERARY AGENTS

As an editor on the move, you'll cultivate relationships with many established literary agents. You'll want them to know what you like and what you don't like. And, by showing these agents you're disposed to acquiring new titles to build your position in the company, you'll encourage them to send you projects they think are right for you.

When you receive material from agents, you usually give it relatively fast consideration—especially if it's been submitted simultaneously to editors at other houses, which is usually the case.

When something comes in from an agent, you know it's been screened and maybe even perfected. Established agents rarely waste your time with shoddy or inappropriate material. They couldn't make a living that way because they'd quickly lose credibility with editors.

DIRECT SOLICITATIONS

If you're an ambitious editor, you won't just sit back passively and wait to see what the agents might bless you with. When you're resourceful, the opportunities are endless. Perhaps you'll contact your old American history professor and ask her to do a book showcasing her unique perspectives on the Civil War.

Or maybe you'll contact that young, fresh fiction writer whose short story you just read in a leading literary journal. You might even try reaching that veteran United States senator who just got censured for sleeping with his young aides.

One place you'll tend not to use is the "slush pile." This is the room (more like a warehouse) where all the unagented/unsolicited submissions end up.

Looking through the slush pile isn't a smart use of your limited time and energy. The chances that anything decent will be found there are much less than 1 percent. You have less-than-fond memories of your first year in the publishing business, when, as an editorial assistant (which was basically an underpaid secretarial job), one of your tasks was to shovel through the slush. Once in a great while, something promising could be found; but most of the stuff wasn't even close. At first, you were surprised by how unprofessional many of the submissions were. Many weren't addressed to anyone in particular; some looked as if they had been run over by Mack trucks; others were so poorly printed they were too painful for tired eyes to decipher—the list of failings is long.

No, the slush pile is the last place—or perhaps no place—to find titles for your list.

Now you can stop being an editor and go back to being whoever you really are. I wanted to show you why the system has evolved the way it has. Yes, though it's rational, it's cold and unfair, but these qualities aren't unique to publishing.

You're probably still wondering when I'm going to get to that promised modus operandi for winning the Battle of the UNs. Okay, we're there.

OUT OF THE SLUSH

The following steps are intended to keep you out of the infamous slush pile. Falling into the slush is like ending up in jail for contempt of court; it's like being an untouchable in India; it's like being Frank Burns on *M*A*S*H*. My point is that nobody likes the Slushables. They're everyone's scapegoat and nobody's ally.

Once your work is assigned to the slush pile, it's highly unlikely that it will receive effective access. Without access, there can be no acquisition. Without acquisition, there's no book.

Let's pretend that getting published is a board game. However, in this game you can control the dice. Here are several ways to play.

GET THE NAMES!

If you submit to nobody, it will go to nobody. Sending it to "The Editors," "Gentlemen," or the CEO of a $100-million publishing house equals sending it to no one.

Use the directory in this book to get the names of the suitable contacts.

In addition to using this directory, there are two other proven ways to discover who the right editors may be:

1. Visit bookstores and seek out recent books that are in your category. Check the acknowledgments section of each one. Many authors like to thank their editors here (and their agents). If the editor is acknowledged, you now have the name of someone who edits books like yours. (Remember to call to confirm that the editor still works at that publishing house.)

2. Simply call the publisher and ask for the editorial department. More often than not, a young junior editor will answer the phone with something like, "Editorial." Like people who answer phones everywhere, these people may sound as if they are asleep, or they may sound harried, or even as if they're making the most important declaration of their lives. Luckily for you, publishers plant few real secretaries or receptionists in their editorial departments, since it's constantly reconfirmed that rookie editors will do all that stuff for everyone else—and for a lot less money! Hence, real editors (although low in rank) can immediately be accessed.

Returning to the true point of this—once someone answers the phone, simply ask, "Who edits your business books?" (Or whatever your category is.)

You can also ask who edited a specific and recent book that's similar to yours. Such easy but vital questions will bring forth quick and valuable answers. Ask enough times and you can build a list of contacts that competes with this book.

DON'T SEND MANUSCRIPTS UNLESS INVITED TO DO SO!

Now that you're armed with these editors' names, don't abuse protocol (editors yell at me when you do—especially when they know where you've gotten their names). Initiate contact by sending a letter describing your work and encouraging the editor to request it.

This letter, commonly referred to as a query letter, is in reality a sales pitch or door-opener. (Please see the following chapter in this book about query letters for a full overview of this important procedure.) In brief, the letter should be short (less than 1½ pages), easy to read and to the point, personalized, and well printed on good professional stationery. Say what you have, why it's hot, why you're a good prospect, and what's available for review upon request.

In addition to the letter, it's okay to include a résumé/bio that highlights any writing credits or relevant professional credentials; a brief summary (two to three pages) if the book is nonfiction, or a brief synopsis if it's fiction; a photo, if you have a flattering one; and promotional materials. Be careful: At this stage your aim is merely to whet the editor's appetite; you don't want to cause information overload. Less is more.

Also include a self-addressed stamped envelope (SASE). This is an important courtesy; without it, you increase your chances of getting no response. Editors receive dozens of these letters every week. Having to address envelopes for all of them would be very time-consuming. And at 45 cents a pop, it's not worth doing.

The SASE is generally intended to facilitate a response in the event of a negative decision. If the editor is intrigued by your letter, he may overlook the missing SASE and request to see your work—but don't count on it.

You may be wondering: If I have the editor's name, why not just send her my entire manuscript? Because you're flirting with the slush pile if you do. Even though you have the editor's previously secret name, you're still an UN, and UNs aren't treated kindly. An editor is inundated with reams of submissions, and her problem is finding good stuff to publish. If you send an unsolicited manuscript, you'll just be perceived as part of that problem. She'll assume you're just another slushy UN who needs to be sorted out of the way so she can go on looking for good stuff.

A bad day for an editor is receiving a few trees' worth of UN manuscripts; it deepens her occupational neurosis.

On the other hand, a professional letter is quite manageable. It is, at least, likely to be read. It may be screened initially by the editor's assistant, but will probably be passed upstairs if it shows promise.

If the editor is at all intrigued by your letter, she will request to see more material, and you will have earned the rank of being solicited.

Even if your work is not ultimately acquired by this editor, you will have at least challenged and defeated the UNs' obstacle course by achieving quality consideration. Remember: Many people get published each year without the benefits of being agented or initially solicited.

It's okay, even smart, to query several editors simultaneously. This makes sense because some editors may take a very long time to respond or, indeed, may never respond. Querying editors one at a time might take years.

If more than one editor subsequently requests and begins considering your work, let each one know that it's not an exclusive. If an editor requests an exclusive, that's fine—but give him a time limit (four weeks is fair).

Don't sell your work to a publisher before consulting everyone who's considering it and seeing if they're interested. If you do sell it, be sure to give immediate written and oral notification to everyone who's considering it that it's no longer available.

The query-letter stage isn't considered a submission. You only need to have follow-up communications with editors who have gone beyond the query stage, meaning those who have requested and received your work for acquisition consideration. If you don't hear back from an editor within six weeks of sending her your letter, it's safe to assume she's not interested in your work.

If you send multiple queries, don't send them to more than one editor at the same house at the same time. If you don't hear back from a particular editor within six weeks of your submission, it's probably safe to query another editor at that house. One editor's reject is another's paradise; that's how both good and bad books get published.

We've just covered a lot of important procedural ground, so don't be embarrassed if you think you've forgotten all of it. This book won't self-destruct (and now, presumably, you won't either).

COLD CALLS BREED COLD HEARTS

One more thing: It's best not to cold-call these editors. Don't call them to try to sell them your work. Don't call them to follow up on query letters or submissions. Don't call them to try to change their minds.

Why? Do you like it when someone calls you in the middle of your favorite video to sell you land in the Nevada desert, near a popular nuclear test site?

Few people like uninvited and unscheduled sales calls. In some businesses, such as public relations, calling contacts is a necessary part of the process—but not in publishing. Furthermore, this business is based on hard copy. You may be the greatest oral storyteller since Uncle Remus, but if you can't write it effectively and engagingly, nobody will care. You'll end up soliciting their hostility. Of course, once they are interested in you on the basis of your hard copy, your oral and physical attributes may be of great importance to them.

On the other hand, some people are so skilled on the telephone that it's a lost opportunity for them not to make maximum use of it as a selling method. If you're one of these extremely rare and talented people, you should absolutely make use of whatever tools have proved to work best for you.

Everything I've said is my opinion. This is a subjective industry, so it's likely—no, it's for certain—that others will tell you differently. It's to your advantage to educate yourself to the fullest extent possible (read books, attend workshops, and so forth)—and in the end, to use your own best instincts about how to proceed.

I'm confident that my suggestions are safe and sound, but I don't consider them to be the beginning and the end. The more you know, the simpler things become; the less you know, the more complex and confusing they are.

BREAKING THE RULES

Taken as a whole, this book provides a structure that can be considered a set of guidelines, if not hard-and-fast rules. Some people owe their success to breaking the rules and swimming upstream—and I can certainly respect that. Often such people don't even know they're breaking the rules; they're just naturally following their own unique orbits (and you'll find a few illustrations of this very phenomenon elsewhere in these essays). Trying to regulate such people can often be their downfall.

On one hand, most of us tend to run afoul when we stray from established norms of doing business; on the other hand, a few of us can't succeed any other way (Einstein could have written an essay about that).

If you're one of those few, hats off to you! Perhaps we'll all learn something from your example.

Keep reading!

THE LITERARY AGENCY FROM A TO Z

HOW LITERARY AGENTS WORK

JEFF HERMAN

Literary agents are like stockbrokers and real estate agents. They bring buyers and sellers together, help formulate successful deals, and receive a piece of the action (against the seller's end) for facilitating the partnership.

Specifically, literary agents look for talented writers, unearth marketable nonfiction book concepts, and discover superior fiction manuscripts to represent. Simultaneously, agents cultivate their relationships with publishers.

When an agent detects material she thinks she can sell to a publisher, she signs the writer as a client, perhaps works on the material with the writer to maximize its chances of selling, and then submits it to one or more appropriate editorial contacts.

HOW AGENTS WORK FOR THEIR CLIENTS

A dynamic agent achieves the maximum exposure possible for the writer's material, which greatly enhances the odds that the material will be published.

Having an agent gives the writer's material the type of access to the powers that be that it might otherwise never obtain. Publishers assume that material submitted by an agent has been screened and is much more likely to fit their needs than the random material swimming in the slush pile.

If and when a publisher makes an offer to publish the material, the agent acts on the author's behalf and negotiates the advance (the money paid up front), royalties, control of subsidiary rights, and many other important and marginal contract clauses that may prove to be important down the line. The agent acts as the writer's advocate with the publisher for as long as the book remains in print or licensing opportunities exist.

The agent knows the most effective methods for negotiating the best advance and other contract terms and is likely to have more leverage with the publisher than an unagented writer does.

There's more to a book contract than the advance-and-royalty schedule. There are several key clauses that you, the writer, may know little or nothing about, but would accept with a cursory perusal in order to expedite the deal. Striving to close any kind of agreement can be intimidating if you don't know much about the territory; ignorance is a great disadvantage during a negotiation. An agent understands every detail of the contract and knows where and how it should be modified or expanded in your favor.

Where appropriate, an agent acts to sell subsidiary rights after the book is sold to a publisher. These rights can include serial rights, foreign rights, dramatic and movie rights, audio and video rights, and a range of syndication and licensing possibilities.

THE AGENT'S PERSPECTIVE

No agent sells every project she represents. Even though authors are signed on the basis of their work's marketability, agents know from experience that some projects with excellent potential are not necessarily quick-and-easy big-money sales. And, yes, each and every agent has at least on occasion been as bewildered as the author when a particularly promising package receives no takers. Some projects, especially fiction, may be marketed for a long time before a publisher is found (if ever).

THE AUTHOR'S EXPECTATIONS

What's most important is that you, the author, feel sure the agent continues to believe in the project and is actively trying to sell it.

For his work, the agent receives a commission (usually 15 percent) against the writer's advance and all subsequent income relevant to the sold project.

Although this is an appreciable chunk of your work's income, the agent's involvement should end up netting you much more than you would have earned otherwise. The agent's power to round up several interested publishers to consider your work opens up the possibility that more than one house will make an offer for it, which means you'll be more likely to get a higher advance and also have more leverage regarding the various other contractual clauses.

The writer-agent relationship can become a rewarding business partnership. An agent can advise you objectively on the direction your writing career should take. Also, through her contacts, an agent may be able to get you book-writing assignments you would never have been offered on your own.

WHO'S THE BEST AGENT FOR YOU

There are many ways to get an agent. The best way to gain access to potential agents is by networking with fellow writers. Maybe some of your colleagues can introduce you to their agents or at least allow you to drop their names when contacting their agents. Most agents will be receptive to a writer who has been referred by a current and valued client.

This book features a directory of literary agencies, including their addresses, the

ADVICE FOR WRITERS

names of specific agents, and their specialty areas, along with some personal remarks and examples of recent titles sold to publishers.

QUERY FIRST

The universally accepted way to establish initial contact with an agent is to send a query letter. Agents tend to be less interested in—if not completely put off by—oral presentations. Be sure the letter is personalized: Nobody likes generic, photocopied letters that look like they're being sent to everyone.

Think of the query as a sales pitch. Describe the nature of your project and offer to send additional material—and enclose a self-addressed stamped envelope (SASE). Include all relevant information about yourself—along with a résumé if it's applicable. When querying about a nonfiction project, many agents won't mind receiving a complete proposal. But you might prefer to wait and see how the agent responds to the concept before sending the full proposal.

For queries about fiction projects, most agents prefer to receive story-concept sheets, plot synopses, or both; if they like what they see, they'll request sample chapters or ask you to send the complete manuscript. Most agents won't consider manuscripts for incomplete works of fiction, essentially because few publishers are willing to do so.

If you enclose an SASE, most agents will respond to you, one way or another, within a reasonable period of time. If the agent asks to see your material, submit it promptly with a polite note stating that you'd like a response within four weeks on a nonfiction proposal, or eight weeks on fiction material. If you haven't heard from the agent by that time, write or call to find out the status of your submission.

CIRCULATE WITH THE FLOW

You're entitled to circulate your material to more than one agent at a time, but you're obligated to let each agent know that such is the case. If and when you do sign with an agent, immediately notify other agents still considering your work that it's no longer available.

At least 200 literary agents are active in America, and their individual perceptions of what is and isn't marketable will vary widely—which is why a few or many rejections should never deter writers who believe in themselves.

BUYER AND SELLER REVERSAL

When an agent eventually seeks to represent your work, it's time for her to begin selling herself to you. When you're seeking employment, you don't necessarily have to accept the first job offer you receive; likewise, you do not have to sign immediately with the first agent who wants you.

Do some checking before agreeing to work with a particular agent. If possible, meet the agent in person. A lot can be learned from in-person meetings that can't be gathered from telephone conversations. See what positive or negative information you can find out about the agent through your writers' network. Ask the agent for a client list and permission to call certain clients. Find out the agent's specialties.

Ask for a copy of the agent's standard contract. Most agents today will want to codify your relationship with a written agreement; this should protect both parties equally. Make sure you're comfortable with everything in the agreement before signing it. Again, talking with fellow writers and reading books on the subject are excellent ways to deepen your understanding of industry practices.

When choosing an agent, follow your best instincts. Don't settle for anyone you don't perceive to be on the level, or who doesn't seem to be genuinely enthusiastic about you and your work.

SELF-REPRESENTATION: A FOOL FOR A CLIENT?

Agents aren't for everyone. In some instances, you may be better off on your own. Perhaps you actually do have sufficient editorial contacts and industry savvy to cut good deals by yourself. If so, what incentive do you have to share your income with an agent?

Of course, having an agent might provide you the intangible benefits of added prestige, save you the hassles of making submissions and negotiating deals, or act as a buffer through whom you can negotiate indirectly for tactical reasons.

You might also consider representing yourself if your books are so specialized that only a few publishers are potential candidates for them. Your contacts at such houses might be much stronger than any agent's could be.

ATTORNEYS: LITERARY AND OTHERWISE

Some entertainment/publishing attorneys can do everything an agent does, though there's no reason to believe they can necessarily do more. A major difference between the two is that the lawyer may charge you a set hourly fee or retainer, or any negotiated combination thereof, instead of an agency-type commission. In rare instances, writer-publisher disputes might need to be settled in a court of law, and a lawyer familiar with the industry then becomes a necessity.

BOTTOM-LINE CALCULATIONS

The pluses and minuses of having an agent should be calculated like any other business service you might retain—it should benefit you more than it costs you. Generally speaking, the only real cost of using an agent is the commission. Of course, using the wrong agent may end up causing you more deficits than benefits, but even then you may at least learn a valuable lesson for next time.

Your challenge is to seek and retain an agent who's right for you. You're 100 percent responsible for getting yourself represented and at least 50 percent responsible for making the relationship work for both of you.

AN ALTERNATIVE INTRODUCTION TO LITERARY AGENTS

JEFF HERMAN

The title of this essay may be puzzling. I hope so, because it's meant to be. Let me explain. I wrote the essay preceding this one, also about agents, 20+ years ago and have not changed it since. *Writer's Digest* magazine paid me $200 in 1987 to write that essay, and I have recycled it in this book through all 22 of its previous editions. My rationale was/is: *If it ain't broke, don't fix it.*

So is that essay broken? No, it's okay. Except it was written by a 20-something guy. Two decades since, that guy has morphed into me. What agents are and what we do has not changed too much over time, but I have. That's simply not the essay I would write today for numerous reasons. The number-one reason is that I am struggling every day to forget what I know, or at least pretend that I don't know it. What am I talking about?

At 27 I had a few years under my belt as a diversified publicist. I understood how to use the media to promote products, people, and ideas. I had learned how to buy and wear a suit; how to keep my hair and face neat; how to function in an office; how to interact with other humans for the purpose of getting tasks done; how to work for jerks; and how to talk on a phone. I of course learned other things as well, but I have to stop the list somewhere.

A constellation of choices and circumstances brought me to the book business. Sensing that I had little to lose and an adventure to gain, I rented some office space and appointed myself a literary agent. It was the second half of the 1980s, disco was dead, and New York was still recovering from the humiliations of the '70s. I only had nominal experience and knowledge about the occupation that I had hired myself for, and I made the mistakes to prove it. Fortunately, the errors were to my own detriment and no one else's. But it was exciting. I was creating something and having fresh experiences along the way. I liked observing people's personalities and egos, and learning about their histories and the directions they chose. I was surprised to see how some of the most successful people were so clearly scared and self-doubting. And I was annoyed by the way some very gifted people could be so self-destructive and unwilling to own any accountability for their actions. I was especially intrigued by the way some people were able to make things happen for themselves and those who were with them. Native intelligence and formal education did not seem to matter as much as I expected. In the unstructured free-for-all entrepreneurial ways that are the emblem of our nation, those who may have spent their student careers in Special Ed classes could emerge from secret telephone booths as Masters of the Universe. People could be very interesting.

The passage of time and raw experience taught me what I know about the book business, and about people. Sometime in the mid-1990s I fell into a routine. My workload and commitments mushroomed. I would make decisions on the basis of other people's advice or the bottom-line calculations. The more visceral messages from my heart and gut lost their traditional primacy in the constitution of my life. I continued to succeed on the basis of hard work and intellect, and by riding the momentum that my earlier years established. But it was not so much of an adventure as it was a job. And that was changing me.

The changes were subtle. Looking back, I recall that I felt the urge to watch more TV; to eat more; to go out less; to be more fixed in my routines. I was inclined to think more and feel less. My time and energy belonged to the mounting tasks that my success generated. I was employed by what had to get done. I had essentially abdicated being the Master of my Domain. Of course, once I had a family to support, it could no longer be just about me. I didn't need much, but a family does. Like many people before me and since, I transitioned from being an explorer into being an expert. Explorers keep moving, looking, touching, consuming and discovering. Experts stand still and cultivate their crops. Each harvest is likely to follow the same template as the ones before, though the goal is to expand the bounty by making better use of the available resources. No accident that the root word for *husband* means "farmer." A responsible farmer does not leave his land; he roots himself into the soil with every seed he sows, and conjures the earth's power to make food out of dirt, water, and light.

Without experts, we'd all be nomads like our prehistoric ancestors. No steady homes; no security; no nuclear families; no settlements; no growers of wheat and barley, and no commerce between them. To this day, we would be herds of two-legged entities chasing after herds of the four-legged kind. But without the explorers our cars would have square tires. Without the explorers we might have nothing. In fact, we might be nothing. The experts probably held their ground as the fury of serial floods, droughts, and ice ages swatted them into oblivion. To the contrary, the explorers instinctively shrugged off what was left behind, and discovered the future; our future. And that's still what they do every day. It is good for a society to have different kinds of people. Perhaps it's equally as good for each of us to embrace vast differences within our own beings, no matter how conflicted that may seem. Self-directed rejection and repression leads to decades of quiet desperation. Your bills may get paid, but you will owe yourself a fortune.

I digress. If you're still with me, let's talk about literary agents.

Actually, everything I said over 20 years ago is still valid. Just read the essay that precedes this one. I did make a few revisions to reflect contemporary conditions.

WRITE THE PERFECT QUERY LETTER

DEBORAH LEVINE HERMAN
JEFF HERMAN

The query is a short letter of introduction to publishers or agents, encouraging them to request to see your fiction manuscript or nonfiction book proposal. It is a vital tool, often neglected by writers. If done correctly, it can help you to avoid endless frustration and wasted effort. The query is the first hurdle of your individual marketing strategy. If you can leap over it successfully, you're well on your way to a sale.

The query letter is your calling card. For every book that makes it to the shelves, thousands of worthy manuscripts, proposals, and ideas are knocked out of the running by poor presentation or inadequate marketing strategies. Don't forget that the book you want to sell is a product that must be packaged correctly to stand above the competition.

A query letter asks the prospective publisher or agent if she would like to see more about the proposed idea. If your book is fiction, you should indicate that a manuscript or sample chapters are available on request. If nonfiction, you should offer to send a proposal and, if you have them, sample chapters.

The query is your first contact with the prospective buyer of your book. To ensure that it's not your last, avoid common mistakes. The letter should be concise and well written. You shouldn't try to impress the reader with your mastery of all words over three syllables. Instead, concentrate on a clear and to-the-point presentation with no fluff.

Think of the letter as an advertisement. You want to make a sale of a product, and you have very limited space and time in which to reach this goal.

The letter should be only one page long, if possible. It will form the basis of a query package that will include supporting materials. Don't waste words in the letter describing material that can be included separately. Your goal is to pique the interest of an editor who has very little time and probably very little patience. You want to entice her to keep reading and ask you for more.

The query package can include a short résumé, media clippings, or other favorable documents. Do not get carried away, or your package will quickly come to resemble junk mail. Include a self-addressed stamped envelope (SASE) with enough postage to return your entire package. This will be particularly appreciated by smaller publishing houses and independent agents.

For fiction writers, a short (one- to five-page), double-spaced synopsis of the manuscript will be helpful and appropriate.

Do not waste money and defeat the purpose of the query by sending an unsolicited manuscript. Agents and editors may be turned off by receiving manuscripts of 1,000-plus pages that were uninvited and that are not even remotely relevant to what they do.

The query follows a simple format (which can be reworked according to your individual preferences):

1. lead;

2. supporting material/persuasion;

3. biography; and

4. conclusion/pitch.

YOUR LEAD IS YOUR HOOK

The lead can either catch the editor's attention or turn him off completely. Some writers think getting someone's attention in a short space means having to do something dramatic. Editors appreciate cleverness, but too much contrived writing can work against you. Opt instead for clear conveyance of thoroughly developed ideas and get right to the point.

Of course, you don't want to be boring and stuffy in the interest of factual presentation. You'll need to determine what is most important about the book you're trying to sell, and write your letter accordingly.

You can begin with a lead similar to what you'd use to grab the reader in an article or a book chapter. You can use an anecdote, a statement of facts, a question, a comparison, or whatever you believe will be most powerful.

You may want to rely on the journalistic technique of the inverted pyramid. This means that you begin with the strongest material and save the details for later in the letter. Don't start slowly and expect to pick up momentum as you proceed. It will be too late.

Do not begin a query letter like this: "I have sent this idea to 20 agents/publishers, none of whom think it will work. I just know you'll be different, enlightened, and insightful, and will give it full consideration." There is no room for negatives in a sales pitch. Focus only on positives—unless you can turn negatives to your advantage.

Some writers make the mistake of writing about the book's potential in the first paragraph without ever stating its actual idea or theme. Remember, your letter may never be read beyond the lead, so make that first paragraph your hook.

Avoid bad jokes, clichés, unsubstantiated claims, and dictionary definitions. Don't be condescending; editors have egos, too, and have power over your destiny as a writer.

SUPPORTING MATERIAL: BE PERSUASIVE

If you are selling a nonfiction book, you may want to include a brief summary of hard evidence, gleaned from research, that will support the merit of your idea. This is where you convince the editor that your book should exist. This is more important for nonfiction than it is for fiction, where the style and storytelling ability are paramount. Nonfiction writers must focus on selling their topic and their credentials.

You should include a few lines showing the editor what the publishing house will gain from the project. Publishers are not charitable institutions; they want to know how they can get the greatest return on their investment. If you have brilliant marketing ideas or know of a well-defined market for your book where sales will be guaranteed, include this rather than other descriptive material.

In rereading your letter, make sure you have shown that you understand your own idea thoroughly. If it appears half-baked, the editors won't want to invest time fleshing out your thoughts. Exude confidence so that the editor will have faith in your ability to carry out the job.

In nonfiction queries, you can include a separate table of contents and brief chapter abstracts. Otherwise, it can wait for the book proposal.

YOUR BIOGRAPHY: NO PLACE FOR MODESTY

In the biographical portion of your letter, toot your own horn, but in a carefully calculated, persuasive fashion. Your story of winning the third-grade writing competition (it was then that you knew you wanted to be a world-famous writer!) should be saved for the documentary done on your life after you reach your goal.

In the query, all you want to include are the most important and relevant credentials that will support the sale of your book. You can include, as a separate part of the package, a résumé or biography that will elaborate further.

The separate résumé should list all relevant and recent experiences that support your ability to write the book. Unless you're fairly young, your listing of academic accomplishments should start after high school. Don't overlook hobbies or non-job-related activities if they correspond to your book story or topic. Those experiences are often more valuable than academic achievements.

Other information to include: any impressive print clippings about you; a list of your broadcast interviews and speaking appearances; and copies of articles and reviews about any books you may have written. This information can never hurt your chances and could make the difference in your favor.

There is no room for humility or modesty in the query letter and résumé. When corporations sell toothpaste, they list the product's best attributes and create excitement about the product. If you can't find some way to make yourself exciting as an author, you'd better rethink your career.

HERE'S THE PITCH

At the close of your letter, ask for the sale. This requires a positive and confident conclusion with such phrases as "I look forward to your speedy response." Such phrases as "I hope" and "I think you will like my book" sound too insecure. This is the part of the letter where you go for the kill.

Be sure to thank the reader for his or her attention in your final sentence.

FINISHING TOUCHES

When you're finished, reread and edit your query letter. Cut out any extraneous information that dilutes the strength of your arguments. Make the letter as polished as possible so that the editor will be impressed with you, as well as with your idea. Don't ruin your chances by appearing careless; make certain your letter is not peppered with typos and misspellings. If you don't show pride in your work, you'll create a self-fulfilling prophecy; the editor will take you no more seriously than you take yourself.

Aesthetics are important. If you were pitching a business deal to a corporation, you would want to present yourself in conservative dress, with an air of professionalism. In the writing business, you may never have face-to-face contact with the people who will determine your future. Therefore, your query package is your representative.

If editors receive a query letter on yellowed paper that looks as if it's been lying around for 20 years, they will wonder if the person sending the letter is a has-been or a never-was.

You should invest in a state-of-the-art letterhead—with a logo!—to create an impression of pride, confidence, and professionalism. White, cream, and ivory paper are all acceptable, but you should use only black ink for printing the letter. Anything else looks amateurish.

Don't sabotage yourself by letting your need for instant approval get the best of you. Don't call editors. You have invited them to respond, so be patient. Then prepare yourself for possible rejection. It often takes many nos to get a yes.

One more note: This is a tough business for anyone—and it's especially so for greenhorns. Hang in there.

QUERY TIPS

If you have spent any time at all in this business, the term *query letter* is probably as familiar to you as the back of your hand. Yet no matter how many courses you've attended and books you've read about this important part of the process, you may still feel inadequate when you try to write one that sizzles. If it's any consolation, you're far from being alone in your uncertainties. The purpose of the query letter is to formally introduce your work and yourself to potential agents and editors. The immediate goal is to motivate them to promptly request a look at your work, or at least a portion of it.

In effect, the letter serves as the writer's first hurdle. It's a relatively painless way for agents and editors to screen out unwanted submissions without the added burden of having to manhandle a deluge of unwanted manuscripts. They are more relaxed if their in-boxes are filled with 50 unanswered queries, as opposed to 50 uninvited 1,000-page manuscripts. The query is a very effective way to control the quality and quantity of the manuscripts that get into the office. And that's why you have to write good ones.

The term *query letter* is part of the lexicon and jargon of the publishing business. This term isn't used in any other industry. I assume it has ancient origins. I can conjure up the image of an English gentleman with a fluffy quill pen composing a most civilized letter to a prospective publisher for the purpose of asking for his work to be read and, perchance, published. Our environments may change, but the nature of our ambitions remains the same.

Let's get contemporary. Whenever you hear the term *query letter*, you should say to yourself "pitch" or "sales" letter. Because that's what it is. You need the letter to sell.

QUERY LETTER TIPS

+ *Don't be long-winded.* Agents/editors receive lots of these things, and they want to mow through them as swiftly as possible. Ideally, the letter should be a single page with short paragraphs. (I must admit I've seen good ones that are longer than a page.) If you lose your reader, you've lost your opportunity.

+ *Get to the point; don't pontificate.* Too many letters go off on irrelevant detours, which makes it difficult for the agent/editor to determine what's actually for sale—other than the writer's soapbox.

+ *Make your letter attractive.* When making a first impression, the subliminal impact of aesthetics cannot be overestimated. Use high-quality stationery and typeface. The essence of your words is paramount, but cheap paper and poor print quality will only diminish your impact.

+ *Don't say anything negative about yourself or your attempts to get published.* Everyone appreciates victims when it's time to make charitable donations, but not when it's time to make a profit. It's better if you can make editors/agents think that you have to fight them off.

WHY NOT SIMPLY SUBMIT MY MANUSCRIPT?

Q: Why can't I bypass the query hurdle by simply submitting my manuscript?
You may—and no one can litigate against you. But if you submit an unsolicited manuscript to a publisher, it's more likely to end up in the so-called slush pile and may never get a fair reading. If it's sent to an agent, nothing negative may come of it. However, most agents prefer to receive a query first.

Sending unsolicited nonfiction book proposals is in the gray zone. Proposals are much more manageable than entire manuscripts, so editors/agents may not particularly mind.

But you may want to avoid the expense of sending unwanted proposals. After all, the query is also an opportunity for you to screen out those who clearly have no interest in your subject.

Also, you shouldn't be overly loose with your ideas and concepts.

These pointers, in combination with the other good information in this book and all the other available resources, should at least give you a solid background for creating a query letter that sizzles.

THE KNOCKOUT NONFICTION BOOK PROPOSAL

JEFF HERMAN

The quality of your nonfiction book proposal will invariably make the difference between success and failure. Before agents and publishers will accept a work of fiction (especially from a newer writer), they require a complete manuscript. But nonfiction projects are different: A proposal alone can do the trick. This is what makes nonfiction writing a much less speculative and often more lucrative endeavor (relatively speaking) than fiction writing.

You may devote five years of long evenings to writing a 1,000-page fiction manuscript, only to receive a thick pile of computer-generated rejections. Clearly, writing nonfiction doesn't entail the same risks.

On the other hand, writing fiction is often an emotionally driven endeavor in which rewards are gained though the act of writing and are not necessarily based on rational, practical considerations. Interestingly, many successful nonfiction writers fantasize about being fiction writers.

As you'll learn, the proposal's structure, contents, and size can vary substantially, and it's up to you to decide the best format for your purposes. Still, the guidelines given here serve as excellent general parameters.

An excellent model proposal is featured later in this chapter.

APPEARANCE COUNTS

+ Your proposal should be printed in black ink on clean, letter-sized (8½" x 11"), white paper.

+ Letter-quality printing is by far the best. Make sure the ribbon or toner or ink cartridge is fresh and that all photocopies are dark and clear enough to be read easily. Publishing is an image-driven business, and you will be judged, perhaps unconsciously, on the physical and aesthetic merits of your submission.

+ Always double-space, or you can virtually guarantee reader antagonism— eyestrain makes people cranky.

- Make sure your proposal appears fresh and new and hasn't been dog-eared, marked-up, and abused by previous readers. No editor will be favorably disposed if she thinks that everyone else on the block has already sent you packing. You want editors to think you have lots of other places to go; not nowhere else.

Contrary to common practice in other industries, editors prefer not to receive bound proposals. If an editor likes your proposal, she will want to photocopy it for her colleagues, and your binding will only be in the way. If you want to keep the material together and neat, use a binder clip; if it's a lengthy proposal, clip each section together separately. Don't e-mail or send CDs unless the agent or editor consents to receiving that way.

THE TITLE PAGE

The title page should be the easiest part, but it can also be the most important, since, like your face when you meet someone, it's what is seen first.

Try to think of a title that's attractive and effectively communicates your book's concept. A descriptive subtitle, following a catchy title, can help to achieve both goals.

It's very important that your title and subtitle relate to the book's subject, or an editor might make an inaccurate judgment about your book's focus and automatically dismiss it.

For instance, if you're proposing a book about gardening, don't title it *The Greening of America*.

Examples of titles that have worked very well are:

How to Win Friends and Influence People by Dale Carnegie
Think and Grow Rich by Napoleon Hill
Baby and Child Care by Dr. Benjamin Spock
How to Swim with the Sharks Without Being Eaten Alive by Harvey Mackay

And, yes, there are notable exceptions: An improbable title that went on to become a perennial success is *What Color Is Your Parachute?* by Richard Bolles. Sure, you may gain freedom and confidence from such exceptional instances. By all means let your imagination graze during the brainstorming stage.

However, don't bet on the success of an arbitrarily conceived title that has nothing at all to do with the book's essential concept or reader appeal.

A title should be stimulating and, when appropriate, upbeat and optimistic. If your subject is an important historic or current event, the title should be dramatic. If a biography, the title should capture something personal (or even controversial) about the subject. Many good books have been handicapped by poorly conceived titles, and many poor books have been catapulted to success by good titles. A good title is good advertising. Procter & Gamble, for instance, spends thousands of worker-hours creating seductive names for its endless array of soap-based products.

The title you choose is referred to as the "working title."

Most likely, the book will have a different title when published. There are two reasons for this:

1. A more appropriate or arresting title (or both) may evolve with time; and

2. The publisher has final contractual discretion over the title (as well as over a lot of other things).

The title page should contain only the title; your name, address, and telephone number—and the name, address, and phone number of your agent, if you have one. The title page should be neatly and attractively spaced. Eye-catching and tasteful computer graphics and display-type fonts can contribute to the overall aesthetic appeal.

OVERVIEW

The overview portion of the proposal is a terse statement (one to three pages) of your overall concept and mission. It sets the stage for what's to follow. Short, concise paragraphs are usually best.

BIOGRAPHICAL SECTION

This is where you sell yourself. This section tells who you are and why you're the ideal person to write this book. You should highlight all your relevant experience, including media and public-speaking appearances, and list previous books, articles, or both, published by or about you. Self-flattery is appropriate—so long as you're telling the truth. Many writers prefer to slip into the third person here, to avoid the appearance of egomania.

MARKETING SECTION

This is where you justify the book's existence from a commercial perspective. Who will buy it? For instance, if you're proposing a book on sales, state the number of people who earn their living through sales; point out that thousands of large and small companies are sales-dependent and spend large sums on sales training, and that all sales professionals are perpetually hungry for fresh, innovative sales books.

Don't just say something like "My book is for adult women and there are more than 50 million adult women in America." You have to be much more demographically sophisticated than that.

AUTHOR PLATFORM

The platform has become a crucial piece of the proposal in recent years. It's expected that as a minimum the author is sufficiently savvy about social media to have a large digital network of like-minded "friends" who can be tapped to purchase the book. It's all about the number of relevant people ("communities") you can access, and the expectation they will either buy your book or at least tell others about it ("viral marketing").

COMPETITION SECTION

To the uninitiated, this section may appear to be a set-up to self-destruction. However, if handled strategically, and assuming you have a fresh concept, this section wins you points rather than undermines your case.

The competition section is where you describe major published titles with concepts comparable to yours. If you're familiar with your subject, you'll probably know those titles by heart; you may have even read most or all of them. If you're not certain, check *Books in Print*—available in virtually every library—which catalogues all titles in print in every category under the sun.

Don't list everything published on your subject—that could require a book in itself. Just describe the leading half-dozen titles or so (backlist classics, as well as recent books) and *explain why yours will be different*.

Getting back to the sales-book example, there is no shortage of good sales books. There's a reason for that—a big market exists for sales books. You can turn that to your advantage by emphasizing the public's substantial, insatiable demand for sales books. Your book will feed that demand with its unique and innovative sales-success program. Salespeople and companies dependent on sales are always looking for new ways to enhance sales skills (it's okay to reiterate key points).

PROMOTION SECTION

Here you suggest possible ways to promote and market the book. Sometimes this section is unnecessary. It depends on your subject and on what, if any, realistic promotional prospects exist.

If you're proposing a specialized academic book such as *The Mating Habits of Octopi*, the market is a relatively limited one, and elaborate promotions would be wasteful.

But if you're proposing a popularly oriented relationship book along the lines of

The Endless Orgasm in One Easy Lesson, the promotional possibilities are also endless. They would include most major electronic broadcast and print media outlets, advertising, maybe even some weird contests.

You want to guide the publisher toward seeing realistic ways to publicize the book.

CHAPTER OUTLINE

This is the meat of the proposal. Here's where you finally tell what's going to be in the book. Each chapter should be tentatively titled and clearly abstracted.

Some successful proposals have fewer than 100 words per abstracted chapter; others have several hundred words per chapter. Sometimes the length varies from chapter to chapter. There are no hard-and-fast rules here; it's the dealer's choice.

Sometimes less is more; at other times a too-brief outline inadequately represents the project.

At their best, the chapter abstracts read like mini-chapters—as opposed to stating "I will do...and I will show..." Visualize the trailer for a forthcoming movie; that's the tantalizing effect you want to create.

Also, it's a good idea to preface the outline with a table of contents. This way, the editor can see your entire road map at the outset.

SAMPLE CHAPTERS

Sample chapters are optional. A strong, well-developed proposal will often be enough. However, especially if you're a first-time writer, one or more sample chapters will give you an opportunity to show your stuff and will help dissolve an editor's concerns about your ability to actually write the book, thereby increasing the odds that you'll receive an offer—and you'll probably increase the size of the advance, too.

Nonfiction writers are often wary of investing time to write sample chapters since they view the proposal as a way of avoiding speculative writing. But this can be a shortsighted view; a single sample chapter can make the difference between selling and not selling a marginal proposal. Occasionally, a publisher will request that one or two sample chapters be written before he makes a decision about a particular project. If the publisher seems to have a real interest, writing the sample material is definitely worth the author's time, and the full package can then be shown to additional prospects, too.

Many editors say that they look for reasons to reject books and that being on the fence is a valid reason for rejecting a project. To be sure, there are cases where sample chapters have tilted a proposal on the verge of rejection right back onto the playing field!

Keep in mind that the publisher is speculating that you can and will write the book upon contract. A sample chapter will go far to reduce the publisher's concerns about your ability to deliver a quality work beyond the proposal stage.

WHAT ELSE?

There are a variety of materials you may wish to attach to the proposal to further bolster your cause. These include:

- Laudatory letters and comments about you

- Laudatory publicity about you

- A headshot (but not if you look like the Fly, unless you're proposing a humor book or a nature book)

- Copies of published articles you've written

- Videos of TV or speaking appearances

- Any and all information that builds you up in a relevant way, but be organized about it—don't create a disheveled, unruly package.

LENGTH

The average proposal is probably between 15 to 30 double-spaced pages and the typical sample chapter an additional 10 to 20 double-spaced pages. But sometimes proposals reach 100 pages, and other times they're 5 pages in total. Extensive proposals are not a handicap.

Whatever it takes!

MODEL SUCCESSFUL NONFICTION BOOK PROPOSAL

What follows is a genuine proposal that won a healthy book contract. It's excerpted from *Write the Perfect Book Proposal* by Jeff Herman and Deborah Adams (John Wiley & Sons) and includes an extensive critique of its strongest and weakest points. All in all, it's an excellent proposal and serves as a strong model.

The book is titled *Heart and Soul: A Psychological and Spiritual Guide to Preventing and Healing Heart Disease* and is written by Bruno Cortis, MD. This project was sold to the Villard Books division of Random House.

Every editor who saw this proposal offered sincere praise. Ironically, several of these editors regretted not being able to seek the book's acquisition. From the outset I was aware this might happen. The past few years have given us numerous unconventional health and healing books—many of which are excellent. Most publishers I approached felt that their health/spirituality quota was already full and that they would wind up competing with themselves if they acquired any more such titles.

Experienced agents and writers are familiar with the market-glut problem. In many popular categories it's almost endemic. If you're prepared for this reality from the outset, there are ways to pave your own road and bypass the competition. Dedicated agents, editors, and writers want to see important books published, regardless of what the publishers' lists dictate.

Furthermore, it is not necessary for every publisher to want your book (though that is the proven way to maximize the advance).

In the end, you need only the right publisher and a reasonable deal.

Let's look first at the title page from the book proposal.

HEART AND SOUL

(This is a good title. It conjures up dramatic images similar to a soulful blues melody. And it has everything to do with what this proposal is about. The subtitle is scientific and provides a clear direction for the patients.)

**Psychological and Spiritual Guide to
Preventing and Healing Heart Disease
by
Bruno Cortis, MD
Book Proposal**

The Jeff Herman Agency

(The title page is sufficient overall. But it would have been better if the software had been available to create a more striking cover sheet. To a large degree, everything does initially get judged by its cover.)

OVERVIEW

(One minor improvement here would have been to shift the word "Overview" to the center of the page—or otherwise styling the typeface for such headings and subheadings throughout the proposal to make them stand out from the body text.)

Heart disease is the number-one killer of Americans over the age of 40. The very words can sound like a death sentence. Our heart, the most intimate part of our body, is under siege. Until now, most experts have advised victims of the disease, as well as those who would avoid it, to change avoidable risk factors, like smoking, and begin a Spartan regimen of diet and exercise. But new research shows that risk factors and lifestyle are only part of the answer. In fact, it is becoming clear that for many patients, emotional, psychological, and even spiritual factors are at least as important, both in preventing disease and in healing an already damaged heart.

(This is a powerful lead paragraph. The author knows a lot of books are out there about heart disease. The first paragraph of the overview immediately distinguishes this book proposal and draws attention to "new research." Anything that is potentially cutting edge is going to catch the eye of a prospective publisher.)

Like *Love, Medicine, and Miracles* by Bernie Siegel, which showed cancer patients how to take charge of their own disease and life, *Heart and Soul* will show potential and actual heart patients how to use inner resources to form a healthy relationship with their heart, actually healing circulatory disorders and preventing further damage.

(The preceding paragraph contains the central thesis for the project, and it is profoundly important. In retrospect, this could have worked exceedingly well as the first paragraph of the proposal, thereby immediately setting the stage. This is a clever comparison to a highly successful book. It indicates an untapped market that has already proved itself in a similar arena. Instead of merely making unsubstantiated claims based on the success of Dr. Siegel's work, the author shows what this book will do to merit the same type of attention.)

The author, Bruno Cortis, MD, is a renowned cardiologist whose experience with hundreds of "exceptional heart patients" has taught him that there is much more to medicine than operations and pills.

(It is good to bring the author's credentials into the overview at this juncture. A comparison has been made with a highly successful and marketable doctor/author—which will immediately raise questions as to whether this author has similar potential. The author anticipates this line of editorial reasoning and here makes some strong statements.)

Dr. Cortis identifies three types of heart patients:

+ Passive Patients, who are unwilling or unable to take responsibility for their condition. Instead, these patients blame outside forces, withdraw from social contacts, and bewail their fate. They may become deeply depressed and tend to die very soon.

+ Obedient Consumers, who are the "A" students of modern medicine. Following doctors' orders to the letter, these patients behave exactly as they are supposed to, placing their fates in the hands of the experts. These patients tend to die exactly when medicine predicts they will.

+ Exceptional Heart Patients, who regard a diagnosis of heart disease as a challenge. Although they may have realistic fears for the future, these patients take full responsibility for their situation and actively contribute to their own recovery. While they may or may not follow doctors' orders, these patients tend to choose the therapy or combination of therapies that is best for them. They often live far beyond medical predictions.

(This is an exceptional overview—especially where it defines the three patient types.)

It is Dr. Cortis's aim in this book to show readers how to become exceptional heart patients, empowering them to take responsibility for their own health and well-being.

(The remaining paragraphs of this overview section show a highly focused and well-thought-out plan for the book. The writing collaborator on this project had to condense and assimilate boxes and boxes of material to produce this concise and to-the-point overview that leaves no questions unanswered. Although it took a great deal of effort for the writer to write such a good proposal, there is no struggle for the editor to understand exactly what is being proposed and what the book is going to be about.)

Although Dr. Cortis acknowledges the importance of exercise, stress management, and proper nutrition—the standard staples of cardiac treatment—he stresses that there is an even deeper level of human experience that is necessary in order to produce wellness. Unlike other books on heart disease, Heart and Soul does not prescribe the same strict diet and exercise program for everyone. Instead it takes a flexible approach, urging readers to create their own unique health plan by employing psychological and spiritual practices in combination with a variety of more traditional diet and exercise regimens.

While seemingly revolutionary, Dr. Cortis's message is simple: You can do much more for the health of your heart than you think you can. This is true whether you have no symptoms or risk factors whatsoever, if you have some symptoms or risk factors, or if you actually already have heart disease.

MARKET ANALYSIS

Heart and Soul could not be more timely. Of the 1.5 million heart attacks suffered by Americans each year, nearly half occur between the ages of 40 and 65. Three-fifths of these heart attacks are fatal. While these precise statistics may not be familiar to the millions of baby boomers now entering middle age, the national obsession with oat bran, low-fat foods, and exercising for health shows that the members of the boomer generation are becoming increasingly aware of their own mortality.

(The writer would be well advised to ease off the use of the term baby boomer. It is so often used in book proposals that many editors are undoubtedly sick of it. It might have been better merely to describe the exceptional number of people in this pertinent age bracket—without attempting to sound trendy. Good use of facts, trends, and the public's receptivity to what some would characterize as an unorthodox treatment approach.)

This awareness of growing older, coupled with a widespread loss of faith in doctors and fear of overtechnologized medicine, combine to produce a market that is ready for a book emphasizing the spiritual component in healing, especially in reference to heart disease.

Most existing books on the market approach the subject from the physician's point of view, urging readers to follow doctor's orders to attain a healthy heart. There is very little emphasis in these books on the patient's own responsibility for wellness or the inner changes that must be made for the prescribed regimens to work. Among the best known recent books are:

(Not a big deal in this instance—but ordinarily it would be better to have identified this portion of the proposal as the competition section, set it off under a separate heading.)

Healing Your Heart, by Herman Hellerstein, MD, and Paul Perry (Simon & Schuster, 1990). Although this book, like most of the others, advocates proper nutrition, exercise, cessation of smoking, and stress reduction as the road to a healthy heart, it fails to provide the motivation necessary to attain such changes in the reader's lifestyle. Without changes in thinking and behavior, readers of this and similar books will find it difficult, if not impossible, to follow the strict diet and exercise program recommended.

In *Heart Talk: Preventing and Coping with Silent and Painful Heart Disease* (Harcourt Brace Jovanovich, 1987), Dr. Peter F. Cohn and Dr. Joan K. Cohn address the dangers of "silent" (symptomless) heart disease. While informative, the book emphasizes only one manifestation of heart disease and does not empower readers with the motivational tools needed to combat that disease.

(This section is termed the market analysis, which in this proposal actually departs from the approach of the typical marketing section of most proposals. Instead of telling the publisher how to sell the book, the writing collaborator [see the About the Authors section further on] shows special insight into the target audience. The key is that this analysis is not merely a statement of the obvious. This type of in-depth analysis of the potential reader can be very persuasive.)

The Trusting Heart, by Redford Williams, MD (Times Books, 1989), demonstrates how hostility and anger can lead to heart disease, while trust and forgiveness can contribute to wellness. While these are important points, the holistic treatment of heart disease must encompass other approaches as well. The author also fails to provide sufficient motivation for behavioral changes in the readers.

(The author does a good job of demonstrating the invaluable uniqueness of this particular project—especially important when compared with the strong list of competitors.)

The best book on preventing and curing heart disease is Dr. Dean Ornish's

Program for Reversing Heart Disease (Random House, 1990). This highly successful book prescribes a very strict diet and exercise program for actually reversing certain types of coronary artery disease. This still-controversial approach is by far the best on the market; unfortunately, the material is presented in a dense, academic style not easily accessible to the lay reader. It also focuses on Dr. Ornish's program as the "only way to manage heart disease," excluding other, more synergistic methods.

(The writer collaborator directly analyzed the competition, highlighting the most relevant books on the market without listing each one directly. Although you do not want to present the editor with any unnecessary surprises, if there are too many similar books out in your particular subject area, you might want to use this approach. The writer confronts the heaviest competition directly by finding specific distinguishing factors that support the strength of his proposed project.)

APPROACH

Heart and Soul will be a 60,000- to 70,000-word book targeted to health-conscious members of the baby boom generation. Unlike other books on heart disease, it will focus on the "facts of the connection between the mind and the body as it relates to heart disease, showing readers how to use that connection to heal the heart." The book will be written in an informal but authoritative style, in Dr. Cortis's voice. It will begin with a discussion of heart disease and show how traditional medicine fails to prevent or cure it. Subsequent chapters will deal with the mind-body connection, and the role in healing of social support systems, self-esteem, and faith. In order to help readers reduce stress in their lives, Dr. Cortis shows how they can create their own "daily practice" that combines exercise, relaxation, meditation, and use of positive imagery. Throughout the book, he will present anecdotes that demonstrate how other Exceptional Heart Patients have overcome their disease and gone on to lead healthy and productive lives.

In addition to a thorough discussion of the causes and outcomes of coronary artery disease, the book will include tests and checklists that readers may use to gauge their progress, and exercises, ranging from the cerebral to the physical, that strengthen and help heal the heart. At the end of each chapter readers will be introduced to an essential "Heartskill" that will enable them to put the advice of the chapter into immediate practice.

Through example and encouragement *Heart and Soul* will offer readers a variety of strategies for coping with heart disease, to be taken at once or used in combination. Above all an accessible, practical book, *Heart and Soul* will present readers with a workable program for controlling their own heart disease and forming a healthy relationship with their hearts.

(This is a good summary statement of the book.)

ABOUT THE AUTHORS

Bruno Cortis, MD, is an internationally trained cardiologist with more than 30 years' experience in research and practice. A pioneer of cardiovascular applications of lasers and angioscopy, a Diplomate of the American Board of Cardiology, contributor of more than 70 published professional papers, Dr. Cortis has long advocated the need for new dimensions of awareness in health and the healing arts. As a practicing physician and researcher, his open acknowledgment of individual spirituality as the core of health puts him on the cutting edge of those in traditional medicine who are beginning to create the medical arts practices of the future.

(This is a very good description of the author. The writing collaborator establishes Dr. Cortis as both an expert in his field and a compelling personality. All of this material is relevant to the ultimate success of the book.)

Dr. Cortis has been a speaker at conferences in South America, Japan, and Australia, as well as in Europe and the United States. His firm, Mind Your Health, is dedicated to the prevention of heart attack through the development of human potential. Dr. Cortis is the cofounder of the Exceptional Heart Patients program. The successful changes he has made in his own medical practice prove he is a man not only of vision and deeds, but an author whose beliefs spring from the truths of daily living.

(A formal vita follows in this proposal. It is best to lead off with a journalistic-style biography and follow up with a complete and formal résumé—assuming, as in this case, the author's professional credentials are inseparable from the book.)

Kathryn Lance is the author of more than 30 books of nonfiction and fiction (see attached publications list for details). Her first book, *Running for Health and Beauty* (1976), the first mass-market book on running for women, sold half a million copies. *The Setpoint Diet* (1985), ghosted for Dr. Gilbert A. Leveille, reached the *New York Times* best seller list for several weeks. Ms. Lance has written widely on fitness, health, diet, and medicine.

(Though she wasn't mentioned on the title page, Lance is the collaborator. This brief bio and the following résumé reveal a writer with virtually impeccable experience. Her participation served to ensure the editors that they could count on the delivery of a high-quality manuscript. Her bio sketch is also strong in its simplicity. Her writing credits are voluminous, but she does not use up space here with a comprehensive listing. Instead she showcases only credits that are relevant to the success of this particular project. Comprehensive author résumés were also attached as addenda to the proposal package.)

ADVICE FOR WRITERS

HEART AND SOUL
by
Bruno Cortis, MD
Chapter Outline

(Creating a separate page [or pages] for the entire table of contents is a useful and easy technique to enable the editor to gain a holistic vision for the book before delving into the chapter abstracts. In retrospect, we should have had one here.)

(The following is an exceptional outline because it goes well beyond the lazy and stingy telegraph approach that many writers use, often to their own detriment. [Telegrams once were a popular means of communication that required the sender to pay by the word.] Here each abstract reads like a miniature sample chapter unto itself. It proves that the writers have a genuine command of their subject, a well-organized agenda, and superior skills for writing about it. Together they are a darn good team. Whatever legitimate reasons a publisher may have had for rejecting this proposal, it had nothing to do with its manifest editorial and conceptual merits. Some writers are reluctant to go this editorial distance on spec. However, if you believe in your project's viability and you want to maximize acquisition interest and the ultimate advance, you'll give the proposal everything you've got.)

Contents

Introduction: Beating the Odds: Exceptional Heart Patients

Chapter 1
YOU AND YOUR HEART
Traditional medicine doesn't and can't "cure" heart disease. The recurrence rate of arterial blockage after angioplasty is 25–35 percent, while a bypass operation only bypasses the problem, but does not cure it. The author proposes a new way of looking at heart disease, one in which patients become responsible for the care and well-being of their hearts, in partnership with their physicians. Following a brief, understandable discussion of the physiology of heart disease and heart attack, further topics covered in this chapter include:

(This is a good technique for a chapter abstract. The writer organizes the structure as a listing of chapter topics and elaborates with a sample of the substance and writing approach that will be incorporated into the book. The editor cannot, of course, be expected to be an expert on the subject, but after reading this abstract will come away with a good sense of the quality of the chapter and the depth of its coverage.)

Heart disease as a message from your body. Many of us go through life neglecting our bodies' signals, ignoring symptoms until a crisis occurs. But the body talks to us and it is up to us to listen and try to understand the message. The heart bears the load of all our physical activity as well as our mental activity. Stress can affect the heart as well as any other body system. This section explores the warning signs of heart disease as "messages" we may receive from our hearts, what these messages may mean, and what we can do in response to these messages.

Why medical tests and treatments are not enough. You, the patient, are ultimately responsible for your own health. Placing all faith in a doctor is a way of abdicating that responsibility. The physician is not a healer; rather, he or she sets the stage for the patient's body to heal itself. Disease is actually a manifestation of an imbalance within the body. Medical procedures can help temporarily, but the real solution lies in the patient's becoming aware of his own responsibility for health. This may involve changing diet, stopping smoking, learning to control the inner life.

(Although the abstracts are directed to the editor who reviews the proposal, the writer incorporates the voice to be used in the book by speaking directly to the reader. This is an effective way to incorporate her writing style into the chapter-by-chapter outline.)

Getting the best (while avoiding the worst) of modern medicine. In the author's view, the most important aspect of medicine is not the medication but the patient/physician relationship. Unfortunately, this relationship is often cold, superficial, professional. The patient goes into the medical pipeline, endures a number of tests, then comes out the other end with a diagnosis, which is like a flag he has to carry for life. This view of disease ignores the patient as the main component of the healing process. Readers are advised to work with their doctors to learn their own blood pressure, blood sugar, cholesterol level, and what these numbers mean. They are further advised how to enlist a team of support people to increase their own knowledge of the disease and learn to discover the self-healing mechanisms within.

How to assess your doctor. Ten questions a patient needs to ask in order to assure the best patient-doctor relationship.

Taking charge of your own medical care. Rather than being passive patients, readers are urged to directly confront their illness and the reasons for it, asking themselves: How can I find a cause at the deepest level? What have I learned from this disease? What is good about it? What have I learned about myself? Exceptional heart patients don't allow themselves to be overwhelmed by the disease; rather, they realize that it is most likely a temporary problem, most of the time self-limited, and that they have a power within to overcome it.

Seven keys to a healthy heart. Whether presently healthy or already ill of heart disease, there is a great deal readers can do to improve and maintain the health of their hearts. The most important component of such a plan is to have a commitment to a healthy heart. The author offers the following seven keys to a healthy heart: respect your body; take time to relax every day; accept, respect, and appreciate yourself; share your deepest feelings; establish life goals; nourish your spiritual self; love yourself and others unconditionally. Each of these aspects of heart care will be examined in detail in later chapters.

Heartskill #1: Learning to take your own pulse. The pulse is a wave of blood sent through the arteries each time the heart contracts; pulse rate therefore provides important information about cardiac function. The easiest place to measure the pulse is the wrist: place your index and middle finger over the underside of the opposite wrist. Press gently and firmly until you locate your pulse. Don't use your thumb to feel the pulse, because the thumb has a pulse of its own. Count the number of pulse beats in fifteen seconds, then multiply that by four for your heart rate.

This exercise will include charts so that readers can track and learn their own normal pulse range for resting and exercising, and be alerted to irregularities and changes that may require medical attention.

(The inclusion of this technique shows how specific and practical information will be included in the book—important for a nonfiction book proposal. Editors look for what are called the program aspects of a book, because they can be used in promotional settings—and may also be the basis for serial-rights sales to magazines.)

Chapter 2
YOUR MIND AND YOUR HEART

This chapter begins to explore the connection between mind and body as it relates to heart disease. Early in the chapter readers will meet three Exceptional Heart Patients who overcame crushing diagnoses. These include Van, who overcame a heart attack (at age 48), two open-heart surgeries, and "terminal" lung cancer. Through visualization techniques given him by the author, Van has fully recovered and is living a healthy and satisfying life. Goran, who had a family history of cardiomyopathy, drew on the support and love of his family to survive a heart transplant and has since gone on to win several championships in an Olympics contest for transplant patients. Elaine, who overcame both childhood cancer and severe heart disease, is, at the age of 24, happily married and a mother. The techniques used by these Exceptional Heart Patients will be discussed in the context of the mind-body connection.

(The authors do not save the good stuff for the book. If you have interesting case studies or anecdotes, include them here: The more stimulating material you can include, the more you can intrigue your editor. In general, this chapter-by-chapter synopsis is exceptionally detailed in a simplified fashion, which is important for this type of book.)

How your doctor views heart disease: Risk factors v. symptoms. Traditional medicine views the risk factors for heart disease (smoking, high blood cholesterol, high blood pressure, diabetes, obesity, sedentary lifestyle, family history of heart disease, use of oral contraceptives) as indicators of the likelihood of developing illness. In contrast, the author presents these risk factors as *symptoms* of an underlying disease, and discusses ways to change them. Smoking, for example, is not the root of the problem, which is, rather, fear, tension, and stress. Smoking is just an outlet that the patient uses to get rid of these basic elements, which he or she believes are uncontrollable. Likewise high cholesterol, which is viewed by the medical establishment as largely caused by poor diet, is also affected by stress. (In a study of rabbits on a high-cholesterol diet, narrowing of arteries was less in rabbits that were petted, even if the diet remained unhealthful.) Other elements besides the traditional "risk factors," such as hostility, have been shown to lead to high rates of heart disease.

A mind/body model of heart disease. It is not uncommon to hear stories like this: They were a very happy couple, married 52 years. Then, suddenly, the wife developed breast cancer and died. The husband, who had no previous symptoms of heart disease, had a heart attack and died two months later. All too often there is a very close relationship between a traumatic event and serious illness. Likewise, patients may often become depressed and literally will themselves to die. The other side of the coin is the innumerable patients who use a variety of techniques to enlist the mind-body connection in helping to overcome and even cure serious illnesses, including heart disease.

Rethinking your negative beliefs about heart disease. The first step in using the mind to help to heal the body is to rethink negative beliefs about heart disease. Modern studies have shown that stress plays a most important role in the creation of heart disease, influencing all of the "risk factors." Heart disease is actually a disease of self, caused by self, and is made worse by the belief that we are its "victims." Another negative and incorrect belief is that the possibilities for recovery are limited. The author asserts that these beliefs are untrue, and that for patients willing to learn from the experience, heart disease can be a path to recovery, self-improvement, and growth.

The healing personality: tapping into your body's healing powers. Although the notion of a "healing personality" may sound contradictory, the power of healing is awareness, which can be achieved by anyone. The author describes his own discovery of spirituality in medicine and the realization that ultimately the origin of disease is in the mind. This is why treating disease with medicine and surgery alone does not heal: because these methods ignore the natural healing powers of the body/mind. How does one develop a "healing personality"? The starting point is awareness of the spiritual power within. As the author states, in order to become healthy, one must become spiritual.

Writing your own script for a healthy heart. Before writing any script, one must set the stage, and in this case readers are urged to see a cardiologist or physician and have a thorough checkup. This checkup will evaluate the presence or absence of the "risk factors" and assess the health of other body organs as well. Once the scene is set, it is time to add in the other elements of a healthy heart, all of which will be explored in detail in the coming chapters.

Making a contract with your heart. We see obstacles only when we lose sight of our goals. How to make (either mentally or on paper) a contract with one's heart that promises to take care of the heart. Each individual reader's contract will be somewhat different; for example, someone who is overweight might include in the contract the desire that in six months she would weigh so much. The point is to set realistic, achievable goals. Guidelines are provided for breaking larger goals down into small, easily achievable steps. Creating goals for the future makes them a part of the present in the sense that it is today that we start pursuing them.

What to say when you talk to yourself. In the view of the author, the greatest source of stress in life is negative conversations we have with ourselves. These "conversations," which go on all the time without our even being aware of them, often include such negative suggestions as "When are you going to learn?" "Oh, no, you stupid idiot, you did it again!" When we put ourselves down, we reinforce feelings of unworthiness and inadequacy, which leads to stress and illness. Guidelines are given for replacing such negative self-conversation with more positive self-talk, including messages of love and healing.

Heartskill #2: *Sending healing energy to your heart.* In this exercise, readers learn a simple meditation technique that will help them get in touch with their natural healing powers and begin to heal their hearts.

Chapter 3
THE FRIENDSHIP FACTOR:
PLUGGING INTO YOUR SOCIAL SUPPORT SYSTEM

Heart disease is not an isolated event, and the heart patient is not an isolated human being. Among the less medically obvious "risk factors" involved in coronary disease are social isolation. In this chapter the author discusses the importance of maintaining and strengthening all the social support aspects of the patient's life, including family, friendship, community, and sex. He shows how intimacy and connection can be used not just for comfort but also as actual healing tools.

Sexual intimacy: the healing touch. Following a heart attack, many patients may lose confidence due to a fear of loss of attractiveness or fear of death. Citing recent studies, the author points out that there is a difference between making sex and making love. The desire for sex is a human need and is not limited to healthy people. Anybody who has had a heart problem still has sexual needs and ignoring them may be an additional cause of stress. Guidelines for when and how to resume sexual activity are offered. Other topics covered in this chapter include:

> *Keeping your loved ones healthy, and letting them keep you healthy*
> *How you may be unwittingly pushing others out of your life*
> *The art of nondefensive, nonreactive communication*
> *Accepting your loved ones' feelings and your own*
> *How to enlist the support of family and friends*
> *Joining or starting your own support group*

> Heartskill #3: *Mapping your social support system*

Chapter 4
OPENING YOUR HEART:
LEARNING TO MAKE FRIENDS WITH YOURSELF

In addition to enlisting the support of others, for complete healing it is necessary for the patient to literally become a friend to himself or herself. This may entail changing old ways of thinking and responding, as well as developing new, healthier ways of relating to time and other external stresses. In this chapter the author explores ways of changing Type A behavior, as well as proven techniques for dealing with life's daily hassles and upsets. An important section of the chapter shows readers how to love and cherish the "inner child," that part of the personality that needs to be loved, to be acknowledged, and to have fun. Equally important is the guilt that each of us carries within, and that can lead not only to unhealthy behaviors but also to actual stress. The author gives exercises for learning to discover and absolve the hidden guilts that keep each of us from realizing our true healthy potential. Topics covered in this chapter include:

> *A positive approach to negative emotions*
> *Checking yourself out on Type A behavior: a self-test*
> *Being assertive without being angry*
> *Keeping your balance in the face of daily hassles and major setbacks*

ADVICE FOR WRITERS

Making a friend of time
Identifying and healing your old childhood hurts
Letting go of hurts, regrets, resentments, and guilt
Forgiving yourself and making a new start
The trusting heart

Heartskill #4: *Forgiveness exercise*

Chapter 5
IDENTIFYING AND ELIMINATING STRESS IN YOUR LIFE

The science of psychoneuroimmunology is beginning to prove that the mind and body are not only connected, but also inseparable. It has been demonstrated that changes in life often precede disease. Lab studies have shown that the amount of stress experienced by experimental animals can induce rapid growth of a tumor that would ordinarily be rejected. For heart patients, the fact of disease itself can become another inner stress factor that may worsen the disease and the quality of life. One out of five healthy persons is a "heart reactor," who has strong responses under stress that induce such unhealthful physiological changes as narrowing of the coronary arteries, hypertrophy of the heart muscle, and high blood pressure. In this chapter the author shows readers how to change stress-producing negative beliefs into constructive, rational beliefs that reduce stress. Included are guidelines to the five keys for controlling stress: diet, rest, exercise, attitude, and self-discipline.

Why you feel so stressed out
Where does emotional stress come from and how does it affect your heart?
Your stress signal checklist
Staying in control
Calculating your heart-stress level at home and on the job
Stress management

Heartskill #5: *Mapping your stress hotspots*

Chapter 6
YOUR FAITH AND YOUR HEART

As the author points out, there are few studies in the field of spirituality and medicine, because physicians, like most scientists, shy away from what is called "soft data." Soft data are anything outside the realm of physics, mathematics, etc.: the "exact sciences." As a physician, the author has grown ever more convinced of the body's natural healing power, which is evoked through mind and spirit. No matter how "spirit" is defined, whether in traditional religious terms or as a component of mind or personality, the truth is that in order to become healthy, it is necessary to become spiritual.

In a ten-month study of 393 coronary patients at San Francisco General Hospital, it was proven that the group who received outside prayer in addition to standard medical treatment did far better than those who received medical treatment alone. Those in the experimental group suffered fewer problems with congestive heart failure, pneumonia, cardiac arrests, and had a significantly lower mortality rate. This chapter explores the possible reasons for this startling result and illuminates the connection between spirit and health.

The difference between spirituality and religion. A discussion of the differences between traditional views of spirituality and the new holistic approach that sees mind, body, and spirit as intimately connected and interdependent.

Faith and heart disease. The healing personality is that of a person who takes care of his own body. He may also use such other "paramedical" means to get well as physical exercise, a proper diet, prayer, meditation, positive affirmations, and visualization techniques. The author surveys these techniques that have been used for centuries to contribute to the healing of a wide variety of diseases. Other topics exploring the connection between faith and a healthy heart include:

> *Tapping into your personal mythology*
> *Forgiving yourself for heart disease*
> *Keeping a psychological-spiritual journal*

> Heartskill #6: *Consulting your inner adviser*

Chapter 7
PUTTING IT ALL TOGETHER:
HOW TO DEVELOP YOUR OWN DAILY
PRACTICE FOR A HEALTHY HEART

Daily Practice as defined by the author is a personalized program in which readers will choose from among the techniques offered in the book to create their own unique combination of mental and physical healing exercises. Each component of the daily practice is fully explained. The techniques range from the familiar—healthful diet and exercise—to the more spiritual, including prayer, meditation, and visualization. Included are examples of use of each of these techniques as practiced by Exceptional Heart Patients.

> *The benefits of daily practice*
> *Meditation: how to do it your way*
> *Stretching, yoga, and sensory awareness*

Hearing with the mind's ear, seeing with the mind's eye
The psychological benefits of exercise
Healthy eating as a meditative practice
The healing powers of silent prayer
Creating your own visualization exercises
Creating your own guided-imagery tapes
Using other types of positive imagery

Heartskill #7: *Picking a practice that makes sense to you*

Chapter 8
LEARNING TO SMELL THE FLOWERS

In our society, pleasure is often regarded as a selfish pursuit. We tend to feel that it is not as important as work. And yet the key element in health is not blood pressure, or cholesterol, or blood sugar; instead it is peace of mind and the ability to enjoy life. Indeed, this ability has been proven to prevent illness. In this chapter the author focuses on the ability to live in the moment, savoring all that life has to offer, from the simple physical pleasures of massage to the more profound pleasures of the spirit. Topics covered in this chapter include a discussion of Type B behavior, which can be learned. The secrets of this type of behavior include self-assurance, self-motivation, and the ability to relax in the face of pressures. The author shows how even the most confirmed Type A heart patient can, through self-knowledge, change outer-directed goals for inner ones, thus achieving the emotional and physical benefits of a Type B lifestyle. Other topics discussed in this chapter include:

Getting the most out of the present moment
Taking an inventory of life's pleasures
Counting down to relaxation
Hot baths, hot showers, hot tubs, and saunas
Touching; feeding the skin's hunger for human touch
Pets, plants, and gardens as healing helpers

Heartskill #8: *Building islands of peace into your life*

Chapter 9
CREATING YOUR FUTURE

The heart may be viewed in many different ways: as a mechanical pump, as the center of circulation, as the source of life. The author suggests viewing the heart above all as a spiritual organ, the center of love, and learning to figuratively fill it with love and peace. A positive result of heart disease is the sudden knowledge that one is not immortal, and the opportunity to plan for a more worthwhile, fulfilling life in the future. In this final chapter, Dr. Cortis offers guidelines for setting and achieving goals for health—of mind, body, and spirit. For each reader the goals, and the means to achieve them, will be different. But as the author points out, this is a journey that everyone must take, patients as well as doctors, readers as well as the author. No matter how different the paths we choose, we must realize that truly "our hearts are the same."

> *The Art of Happiness*
> *Choosing your own path to contentment*
> *Goals chosen by other exceptional heart patients*
> *Developing specific action steps*
> *Reinforcing and rethinking your life goals*
> *Finding your own meaning in life and death*

> Heartskill #9: *Helping others to heal their hearts*

Recommended Reading

Appendix I:
FOR FRIENDS AND FAMILY:
HOW TO SUPPORT AN EXCEPTIONAL HEART PATIENT

Appendix II:
ON FINDING OR STARTING A SELF-HELP GROUP

Appendix III:
ABOUT THE EXCEPTIONAL HEART PATIENT PROJECT

Authors' Notes

Acknowledgments

Index

(Appendices are always a valuable bonus.)

(It is great to be able to include an actual endorsement in your proposal package. Quite often, writers state those from whom they intend to request endorsements—but do not actually have them lined up. Perhaps unnecessary to say, but valuable to reiterate, is that editors and agents are not overly impressed by such assertions. They do, however, nod with respect to those authors who demonstrate that they can deliver on their claims. The inclusion of at least one such blurb creates tremendous credibility.)

Gerald G. Jampolsky, MD
Practice Limited to Psychiatry
Adults and Children

April 1, 1998

Mr. Jeff Herman

The Jeff Herman Agency, Inc.
140 Charles Street, Suite 15A
New York, NY 10014

Dear Jeff:
You may use the following quote for Bruno's book:

"Dr. Bruno Cortis writes from the heart—for the heart. This is a much-needed and very important book."

Gerald Jampolsky, MD,
Coauthor of *Love Is the Answer*

With love and peace,
Jerry
Gerald Jampolsky, MD

(The author, Dr. Cortis, is very well connected in his field. He solicited promises from several prominent persons to provide cover endorsements like this one. Having these promises to provide such blurbs at the time I marketed the proposal further enhanced the agency's sales position.)

PROFOUND QUESTIONS AND HUMBLE ANSWERS

JEFF HERMAN

In the course of my ongoing participation in publishing workshops, seminar presentations, and panels at writers' conferences, certain questions arise time and again. Many of these requests for information go straight to the heart of the world of book publishing.

The following questions are asked from the gut and replied to in kind. In order to be of value to the author who wishes to benefit from an insider view, I answer these serious queries in unvarnished terms, dispensing with the usual sugarcoating in order to emphasize the message of openness and candor.

Q: I have been at this for a long time, and can't get published. How come?
Well, your stuff may not be good. That's the easy answer, which probably applies to most of what gets written and, frankly, to some of what actually gets published. After all, books get published for many reasons, including the possibility that they are of high quality. But lack of quality is not, never has been, and never will be the only factor as to why books do or don't get published. That said, it's good to make your product the best it can be.

It's safe to say that everyone who works in publishing will agree that countless works of excellence don't make it to publication. That's unfortunate. But is it unfair? Who's to say?

Many works get published because the writer managed to get them to the right people at the right time. How and why did that happen?

Other fine works fail to "connect," in spite of the diligent efforts made by the writer to sell them. Why? I don't know. Why are some people very pretty, while others are very ugly? I don't know. Some consequences can be logically traced backwards to a cause or causes, or a lack of necessary acts.

But sometimes there is no apparent pathology behind what does and doesn't happen. And that's when we must simply surrender. There's an ancient Jewish saying, "Man plans, God laughs." Some things are left to our discretion and control, whereas other things obviously are not. It's possible that that may be why you did not sell your manuscript. But I don't know.

Q: Why are memoirs and autobiographies hard to sell?
Because the vast majority of us lead lives of quiet desperation that would bore even a 300-year-old turtle. None of us ever truly listen to each other. That's why a lot of us pay strangers $90 or more an hour to listen to us. Or at least we think they're listening.

So why should someone actually pay you to read about your life? If you can effectively answer that question, you may be qualified to write a book about YOU.

Now, there are ways to maneuver around this conundrum. For instance, you can place your life within the context of fascinating events. People do connect to events and situations that mirror their own lives and feelings right back at them.

You can think ahead by doing something notable or outrageous for the sole purpose of having a platform for writing about yourself. A lot of us do ridiculous things anyway, so why not do them in a planned, conscious way? It's said that we all write our own script in life. So, if you are the designer of your own life, who do you have to blame for leading a boring life? Think about your life as a feature film, and start living it within that context. Preempt the cutting room floor whenever possible. Become someone that other people will pay to watch, read about, and listen to.

Even if you don't get anything sold, you may still end up with more friends.

Q: Why do editors, agents, and some writers seem so snobby?
Because maybe they are. Why should you care? Because you want validation and snobs counter that. A long time ago, when I was young and a bit more stupid, I told a snobby editor to come clean my bathroom for me. He didn't. Neither did I; I hired a housekeeper. To this day I enjoy foiling people who think they are better then the rest. Sometimes, I think I'm better than the rest. But my better angels take care of that by hiding my car in a parking lot, or causing me to wash my mouth with shampoo. My list of due personal humiliations is infinite, and appreciated.

Snobbery is a burden, and a punishment unto itself. Let the snobs have their burden, and keep writing.

Q: Is it more difficult to get an agent than it is to get a publisher?
I believe it's substantially easier to get an agent than it is to get a publisher.

The primary reason for this is that no agent expects to sell 100 percent of the projects she chooses to represent. Not because any of these projects lack merit (though some of them may), but because only so many titles are published per year—and many excellent ones just won't make the cut. This is especially true for fiction by unknown or unpublished writers, or for nonfiction in saturated categories. As a result, many titles will be agented but never published.

Naturally, a successful agent prefers to represent projects that she feels are hot and that publishers will trample each other to acquire. But few, if any, agents have the luxury of representing such sure-bet projects exclusively. In fact, the majority of their projects may be less than "acquisition-guaranteed," even though they are of acquisition quality.

The agent assumes that many of these projects will eventually be sold profitably, but probably doesn't expect all of them to be. Every experienced agent knows that some of the best cash cows were not easily sold.

Make no mistake—it's not easy to get a reputable agent. Most agents reject 98 percent of the opportunities that cross their desks. They accept for representation only material they believe can be sold to a publisher. That is, after all, the only way for them to earn income and maintain credibility with publishers. If an agent consistently represents what a publisher considers garbage, that will become her professional signature—and her undoing as an agent.

But don't despair. This is a subjective business, composed of autonomous human beings. One agent's reject can be another's gold mine. That's why even a large accumulation of rejections should never deter you as a writer.

Some people get married young, and some get married later!

Q: Is there anything I can do to increase my odds of getting an agent?
Yes.

First consider the odds quoted in the previous answer. The typical agent is rejecting 98 percent of everything he sees. That means he's hungry for the hard-to-find 2 percent that keeps him in business.

If you're not part of that 2 percent, he'll probably have no use for you or your project. Your challenge is to convince him that you're part of that select 2 percent.

Q: What do agents and editors want? What do they look for in a writer? What can I do to become that kind of writer?
Let's back up a step or two and figure out why agents want to represent certain projects and why editors want to buy them. This industry preference has little to do with quality of writing as such.

Many highly talented writers never get published. Many mediocre writers do get published—and a number of them make a lot of money at it. There are reasons for this. The mediocre writers are doing things that more than compensate for their less-than-splendid writing. And the exceptional writers who underachieve in the publishing arena are (regardless of their talents) most likely doing things that undermine them.

In other words, being a good writer is just part of a complex equation. Despite all the criticism the educational system in the United States has received, America is exceedingly literate and has a motherlode of college graduates and postgraduates. Good, knowledgeable writers are a dime a dozen in this country.

Profitable writers, however, are a rare species. And agents and editors obviously value them the most. Once more: Being an excellent writer and a financially successful writer don't necessarily coincide. Ideally, of course, you want to be both.

To maximize your success as a writer, you must do more than hone your ability to write; you must also learn the qualifiers and the disqualifiers for success. Obviously, you wish to employ the former and avoid the latter. Publishing is a business, and agents tend to be the most acutely business-oriented of all the players. That's why they took the risk of going into business for themselves (most agents are self-employed).

If you wish, wear your artist's hat while you write. But you'd better acquire a business hat and wear it when it's time to sell. This subtle ability to change hats separates the minority of writers who get rich from the majority who do not.

In my opinion, rich writers didn't get rich from their writing (no matter how good it is); they got rich by being good at business.

Many good but not-so-wealthy writers blame various internal or external factors for their self-perceived stagnation. My answer to them is: Don't blame anyone, especially yourself. To lay blame is an abdication of power. In effect, when you blame, you become a car with an empty gas tank, left to the elements. The remedy is to fill the tank yourself.

Learn to view mistakes, whether they be yours or those of the people you relied upon, as inconvenient potholes—learning to move around them will make you an even better driver. Remember the old credo: Only a poor workman blames his tools.

Observe all you can about those who are successful—not just in writing, but in all fields—and make their skills your skills. This is not to insist that making money is or should be your first priority. Your priorities, whatever they are, belong to you. But money is a widely acknowledged and sought-after emblem of success.

If an emphasis on personal gain turns you off, you may, of course, pursue other goals. Many successful people in business find the motivation to achieve their goals by focusing on altruistic concepts—such as creating maximum value for as many people as possible. Like magic, money often follows value even if it wasn't specifically sought. If you're unfortunate enough to make money you don't want, there's no need to despair: There are many worthy parties (including charities) that will gladly relieve you of this burden.

Here are specific ways to maximize your ability to get the agent you want:

+ *Don't start off by asking what the agent can do for you.* You're a noncitizen until the agent has reason to believe that you may belong to that exclusive 2 percent club the agent wants to represent. It's a mistake to expect the agent to do anything to sell herself to you during that initial contact. You must first persuade her that you're someone who's going to make good money for her business. Once you've accomplished that, and the agent offers you representation, you're entitled to have the agent sell herself to you.

+ *Act like a business.* As you're urged elsewhere in this book, get yourself a professional letterhead and state-of-the-art office equipment. While rarely fatal, cheap paper and poor-looking type will do nothing to help you—and in this business you need all the help you can give yourself.

Virtually anyone—especially someone intellectually arrogant—is apt to be strongly affected on a subliminal level by a product's packaging. People pay for the sizzle, not the steak. There is a reason why American companies spend billions packaging, naming, and advertising such seemingly simple products as soap. We would all save money if every bar of soap were put into a plain paper box and just labeled "Soap." In fact, the no-frills section does sell soap that way—for a lot less. But few people choose to buy it that way. Understand this human principle, without judging it, and use it when packaging yourself.

♦ *Learn industry protocol.* I never insist that people follow all the rules. As Thomas Jefferson wisely suggested, a revolution every so often can be a good thing. But you should at least know the rules before you break them—or before you do anything.

For instance: Most agents say they don't like cold calls. I can't say I blame them. If my rejection rate is 98 percent, I'm not going to be enthusiastic about having my ear talked off by someone who is more than likely part of that 98 percent. Just like you, agents want to use their time as productively as possible. Too often, cold calls are verbal junk mail. This is especially true if you are a writer selling fiction; your hard copy is the foot you want to get through the door.

Speaking for myself, most cold calls have a neutral effect on me (a few turn me off, and a few rouse my enthusiasm). I try to be courteous, because that's how I would want to be treated. I will allow the caller to say whatever he wants for about one minute before I take over to find out what, if anything, the person has in the way of hard copy. If he has some, I invite him to send it with an SASE. If he doesn't have any, I advise him to write some and then send it. Usually, I don't remember much about what he said on the phone; I may not even remember that he called. But that doesn't matter; it's the hard copy that concerns me at first. This is the way it works with most agents. We produce books, not talk.

An agent's time is an agent's money (and therefore his clients' money). So don't expect any quality access until the agent has reason to believe you're a potential 2 percenter. If you're the CEO of General Motors, for instance, and you want to write a book, then all you need to do is call the agent(s) of your choice and identify yourself; red carpets will quickly appear. But the vast majority of writers have to learn and follow the more formalized procedures.

♦ *As explained elsewhere in this book, view the query letter as a sales brochure.* The best ones are rarely more than 1½–2 pages long and state their case as briefly and efficiently as possible.

Here are the most common query mistakes:

1. Long, unfocused paragraphs.

2. Pontificating about irrelevancies (at least, matters that are irrelevant from the agent's perspective).

3. Complaining about your tribulations as a writer. We all know it's a tough business, but nobody likes losers—least of all, shrewd agents. Always be a winner when you're selling yourself, and you'll be more likely to win.

Most agents are hungry for that golden 2 percent, and they dedicate a great deal of time shoveling through mounds of material looking for it. You must be the first to believe that you are a 2 percenter, and then you must portray yourself that way to others. Reality begins in your own head and is manifested primarily through your own actions—or lack thereof.

Every agent and editor has the power to reject your writing. But only you have the power to be—or not to be—a writer.

Q: Should I query only one agent at a time?
Some of my colleagues disagree with me here, but I recommend querying 5 to 10 agents simultaneously, unless you already have your foot in the door with one. I suggest this because some agents will respond within 10 days, while others may take much longer or never respond at all. Going agent by agent can eat up several months of valuable time before a relationship is consummated. And then your work still has to be sold to a publisher.

To speed up this process, it's smart to solicit several agents at a time, though you should be completely up front about it. If you go the multiple-submissions route, be sure to mention in your query letters to each agent that you are indeed making multiple submissions (though you needn't supply your agent list).

When an agent responds affirmatively to your query by requesting your proposal or manuscript, it's fine then to give the agent an exclusive reading. However, you should impose a reasonable time frame—for instance, two weeks for a nonfiction proposal and four weeks for a large manuscript. If it's a nonexclusive reading, make sure each agent knows that's what you want. And don't sign with an agent before talking to all the agents who are reading your work. (You have no obligation to communicate further with agents who do not respond affirmatively to your initial query.)

Most agents make multiple submissions to publishers, so they should be sensitive and respectful when writers have reason to use the same strategy agents have used with success.

Q: How do I know if my agent is working effectively for me? When might it be time to change agents?

As I remarked earlier, agents don't necessarily sell everything they represent, no matter how persistent and assertive they may be. In other words, the fact that your work is unsold doesn't automatically mean that your agent isn't doing his job. To the contrary, he may be doing the best job possible, and it may be incumbent upon you to be grateful for these speculative and uncompensated efforts.

Let's say 90 days pass and your work remains unsold. What you need to assess next is whether your agent is making active and proper attempts to sell your work.

Are you receiving copies of publisher rejection letters regarding your work? Generally, when an editor rejects projects submitted by an agent, the work will be returned within a few weeks, along with some brief comments explaining why the project was declined. (In case you're wondering, the agent doesn't have to include an SASE; the editors want agent submissions.) Copies of these rejection letters should be sent to you on a regular basis as the agent receives them. While no one expects you to enjoy these letters, they at least document that your agent is circulating your work.

If you have received many such rejection letters within these 90 days, it's hard to claim that your agent isn't trying. If you've received few or none, you might well call the agent for a status report. You should inquire as to where and when your work has been submitted, and what, if anything, the results of those submissions have been. In the end, you will have to use your own best judgment as to whether your agent is performing capably or giving you the run-around.

If it ever becomes obvious that your agent is no longer seriously trying to sell your work (or perhaps never was), you should initiate a frank discussion with the agent about what comes next. If the agent did go to bat for you, you should consider the strong possibility that your work is presently unmarketable and act to preserve the agent relationship for your next project. Remember, if your work remains unsold, your agent has lost valuable time and has made no money.

If the evidence clearly shows that your agent has been nonperforming from day one, then your work has not been tested. You should consider withdrawing it and seek new representation.

Agent-hopping by authors is not rampant, but it's not uncommon either. Often the agent is just as eager as you—or more so—for the break-up to happen. One veteran colleague once told me that when he notices he hates to receive a certain client's phone calls, then it's time to find a graceful way to end the relationship.

The wisdom of agent-jumping must be assessed on a case-by-case basis. The evidence shows that many writers have prospered after switching, while others have entered limbo or even fallen far off their previous pace.

Before you decide to switch agents, you should focus on why you are unhappy with your current situation. It may be that if you appeal to your agent to discuss your specific frustrations—preferably in person, or at least by phone—many or all of them can be resolved, and your relationship will be given a fresh and prosperous start.

Agents are not mind readers. You only have one agent, but your agent has many clients. It is therefore mostly your responsibility as a writer client to communicate your concerns and expectations effectively to your agent. Your relationship may require only occasional adjustments, as opposed to a complete break-up.

Q: Who do agents really work for?
Themselves! Always have and always will.

True, agents serve their clients, but their own needs and interests always come first. Of course, this is the way it is in any business relationship (and in too many personal ones). You should never expect your lawyer, accountant, or stockbroker (and so on), to throw themselves into traffic to shield you from getting hit.

As long as the interests of the agent and the writer are in harmony, everything should work out well. However, on occasion the writer may have expectations that could be detrimental to the agent's own agenda (not to mention state of mind). Writers must never lose sight of the truth that publishers are the agent's most important customers. Only a foolish agent would intentionally do serious damage to her relationships with individual editors and publishing houses. It should be further noted that there is, therefore, a fine line that an agent will not cross when advocating for her clients.

Q: What do agents find unattractive about some clients?
Agents are individuals, so each will have his own intense dislikes. But, generally speaking, a certain range of qualities can hamper any and all aspects of an agent's professional association with a client—qualities that often have similarly negative effects in realms other than publishing. Here's a litany of displeasing client types and their characteristics.

+ The Pest. Nobody likes a nag, whether at home or at the office. A squeaky wheel may sometimes get the grease—not that anyone likes the effect—but more often this person gets the shaft.

+ The Complainer. Some people can never be satisfied, only dissatisfied. It seems to be their mission in life to pass along their displeasure to others. These folks are never any fun—unless you're an ironic observer.

+ The BS Artist. Even if they believe their own distortions, the bottom-line is that all their promises and boasts are as containable as bovine gas eruptions.

+ The Screw-Up. These clients miss trains, planes, and deadlines. Their blunders can create major hassles for those who count on them.

+ The Sun God. Some people believe they are more equal than others and will behave accordingly. It's a real pleasure to see Sun Gods humbled.

+ The Liar. Need I say more?

Sometimes these wicked traits combine, overlap, and reinforce themselves in one individual to create what an agent may rate as a veritable client from hell. Enough said on this subject for now, except that I would be remiss if I did not insist that no trade or professional class is immune to this nefarious syndrome—not even literary agents.

Q: How does someone become an agent?
For better or worse, anyone in America can declare himself an agent—at any time. But what people say and what they do are different things. Legitimate literary agents earn most or all of their income from commissions. The less-than-legitimate agencies most often depend on reading and management fees for their cash, with few, if any, actual book sales to their credit.

Most agents earn their stripes by working as editors for publishers. But that is by no means the only route, nor is it necessarily the most effective training ground. Good agents have emerged from a variety of environments and offer a broad range of exceptional credentials. What's most important is the mix of skills they bring to their agent careers, such as:

1. Strong relationship skills—the ability to connect with people and earn their confidence.

2. Sales and marketing skills—the ability to get people to buy from them.

3. Persuasion and negotiating skills—the ability to get good results in their dealings.

4. An understanding of the book market and of what publishers are buying.

5. An ability to manage many clients and projects at the same time.

Q: Who owns book publishing?
Many decades ago, book-publishing entities were customarily founded by individuals who had a passion for books. Though they obviously had to have business skills to make their houses survive and thrive, money was not necessarily their primary drive (at least, not in the beginning), or they would have chosen more lucrative endeavors.

The vestiges of these pioneers can be found in the family names still extant in the corporate designations of most of today's publishing giants. But apart from the human-sounding names, these are very different companies today. Much of the industry is owned by multinational, multibillion-dollar conglomerates that have priorities other than the mere publication of books. The revenues from book operations are barely noticeable when compared with such mass-market endeavors as movies, TV/cable, music, magazines, sports teams, and character licensing. Stock prices must rise, and shareholders must be optimally satisfied for these firms to feel in any way stable.

Q: How does this type of ownership affect editors and the editorial-acquisition process?
This rampant corporate ownership translates into an environment in which book editors are pressured to make profitable choices if their careers are to prosper. At first look, that doesn't sound radical or wrongheaded, but a downside has indeed developed—editors are discouraged from taking risks for literary or artistic rationales that are ahead of the market curve or even with an eye toward longer-term development and growth of a particular writer's readership.

The bottom line must be immediately appeased by every acquisition, or the non-performing editor's career will crumble. The editor who acquires blockbusters that the culturally elite disdain is an editor who is a success. An editor with books that lose money and are universally praised by critics is an editor who has failed.

Of course, the previous comparison is extreme. Most editors are not single-minded money-grubbers and do their best to acquire meaningful books that also make commercial sense. Where the cut becomes most noticeable is for the thousands of talented fiction writers who will never write big money-makers. While slots still exist for them, large publishers are increasingly reluctant to subsidize and nurture these marginally profitable writers' careers. Commercially speaking, there are better ways to invest the firm's resources.

Q: What, if any, are a writer's alternatives?
Yes, the big kids are dominant on their own turf and intend to extend their claim to as much of book country as they can. But this isn't the end of the story. The heroes are the thousands of privately owned "Mom and Pop" presses from Maine to Alaska who only need to answer to themselves. Every year, small presses, new and old, make an important contribution to literate culture with books that large publishers won't touch. It's not uncommon for some of these books to become best sellers. University presses also pump out important (and salesworthy) books that would not have been published in a rigidly commercial environment.

Q: Is there anything positive to say about the current situation?
I don't mean to imply that the corporate ownership of the bulk of the book industry is absolutely bad. Indeed, it has brought many benefits. Publishers are learning to take better advantage of state-of-the-art marketing techniques and technologies and have more capital with which to do it. The parent entertainment and communications firms enable the mainstream commercial publishers to cash in on popular frenzies, as with dinosaur mania, the latest and most salacious scandals, fresh interest in the environment or fitness, or celebrity and other pop-culture tie-ins, such as Gump and Madonna books.

The emergence of superstores enables more books to be sold. The stores create very appealing environments that draw much more traffic than conventional old-style bookstores. Many people who hang out at the superstores were never before motivated to go book shopping. But once they're in one of these well-stocked stores—whether at the bookshelves, ensconced in a reading seat, or perched by a steaming mug at an in-store cafe—they're likely to start spending.

The unfortunate part is that many small independent bookshops cannot compete with these new venues. However, many others are finding clever ways to hang on, by accenting special reader-interest areas or offering their own individual style of hospitality.

Q: How profitable is publishing?
One way to measure an industry's profitability is to look at the fortunes of those who work in it. By such a measure, the book business isn't very profitable, especially when compared to its twentieth-century sisters in entertainment and information industries: movies, television, music, advertising, and computers. Most book editors require a two-income family if they wish to raise children comfortably in New York or buy a nice home. The vast majority of published authors rely upon their day jobs or spouse's earnings. A handful of authors make annual incomes in the six and seven figures, but it's often the movie tie-ins that get them there and in turn push even more book sales.

A fraction of book editors will climb the ranks to the point at which they can command six-figure incomes, but most never attain this plateau. Almost all of those writers just starting in the business earn barely above the poverty level for their initial publishing endeavors—if that.

A well-established literary agent can make a lot of money. The trick is to build a number of backlist books that cumulatively pay off healthy commissions twice a year, while constantly panning for the elusive big-advance books that promise short-term (and perhaps long-term) windfalls.

In many ways, the agents are the players best positioned to make the most money. As sole proprietors, they're not constrained by committees and can move like lightning. When everything aligns just right, the agent holds all the cards by controlling access to the author (product) and the publisher (producer).

The publishing companies themselves appear at least adequately profitable, averaging about 5 to 10 percent return on revenues (according to their public balance sheets). The larger companies show revenues of between $1 billion and $2 billion, sometimes nudging higher.

These are not sums to sneeze at. But most of those sales derive from high-priced non-bookstore products like textbooks and professional books. Large and midsize publishers alike are dependent upon their cash-cow backlist books for much of their retail sales. These books entail virtually no risk or investment, since the customers are essentially locked in for indefinite periods, and the publisher has long ago recouped the initial investment. Many backlist books are legacies from editors and business dynamics that current employees may know nothing about.

The real risk for the current regime is their front-list, which is the current season's crop. Large houses invest tens of millions of dollars to acquire, manufacture, market, and distribute anywhere from 50 to a few hundred "new" books. A small number of big-ticket individual titles will by themselves represent millions of dollars at risk. Most titles will represent less than $50,000 in risk on a pro-rata basis.

In practice, most of these front-list titles will fail. The publisher will not recoup its investment and the title will not graduate to the exalted backlist status. But like the fate of those innumerable turtle eggs left in the sand, it's expected that enough spawn will survive to generate an overall profit and significant backlist annuities well into the future.

In the fairness of a broader picture, it is known that most motion pictures and television shows fail, as do most new consumer products (such as soap or soft drinks) that have engendered enormous research-and-development costs. It's the ones that hit—and hit big—that make the odds worth enduring for any industry.

Q: What about attending writers' conferences?
Over the past 15 years I must have attended more than 100 writers' conferences in my role as an agent. I've gone to small towns, big cities, and luxury resorts. In all of them, I have discovered one common denominator: Writers' conferences are for writers what fertilizer is for crops.

It's invaluable for a writer to enter into communion with others of a like mind, at least once a year. The various classes about the usual subjects and the abundant networking opportunities are worthwhile bonuses. But the real benefit is what is received "between the lines." When does someone who writes actually become a writer? What is the initiation process? Most people who write can easily fall into an isolation zone. Family members and friends may at best be indifferent about the person's passion for writing. At worst, they may belittle it as a wasteful self-indulgence that will never mean anything. Of course, once the writer starts accumulating impressive bylines or has a book published, or best of all starts making a lot of money from writing, people may show more respect. But at any given moment most writers have not yet penetrated the ceiling that takes them into the world of actual publication, and those are the writers who need the most support and comfort. Writers' conferences are that special place where struggling writers can connect with fellow travelers, and meet those who have been "there" and suffered the same way before they arrived at greener pastures. A good conference experience will empower writers to be firmer in their identity and more determined to achieve their goals.

There are hundreds of writers' conferences each year and they are well spread out. Chances are there is at least one being given during the next 12 months within 150 miles from where you live. They are usually scheduled on weekends and sponsored by nonprofit community-based writers' clubs. The tuition is often quite modest and only intended to recoup expenses. Ask your librarian or check the Internet for information about writers' clubs and conferences near you.

Q: Is there "ageism" in book publishing?
I have only been asked about racism in publishing once or twice. Each time I answered that I have neither witnessed it nor practiced it, but that does not mean that racism does not exist beyond my limited view. But there is a related question that I hear more frequently, which is: *Do book editors discriminate against elderly*

writers? That question makes me uncomfortable because I have mixed feelings about how to answer it.

I can absolutely say that there is no organized program of discrimination against writers of a certain age. That said, there is the evidence of what does and does not get published, and the more subtle evidence of what agents and editors say to each other off the record. Now here I am going out on a limb, and I have not scientifically researched the facts. Nevertheless, I am suggesting that when it comes to fiction, that young unpublished writers have an edge over elderly unpublished writers. I do not believe that the same can be said for nonfiction. Why is this? Introducing new writers to the reading public is a tricky and risky business. The primary target market for new fiction tends to consist of younger readers who have not yet formed strong ties to existing authors. Because of their relative youth, they will be most attracted to themes and styles that they can personally relate to. We also see this emphasis on youth with new films, television shows, and consumer products. It follows that writers who look like and talk like the readers who are being targeted, will be the writers who are offered contracts. If you accept that this is the case, then yes, elderly writers are discriminated against, and to say otherwise is to be disingenuous or blindfolded.

Assuming the above situation is a fact, is it a valid or immoral condition? Frankly, I don't know how to assess the morality of it for one big reason: The marketplace has its own morality. Look, the new fiction writer is as much a part of the product as anything that goes between the pages. Is it reasonable to expect that younger readers will gravitate to new fiction written by people who remind them of their parents or grandparents? Now I'll step aside and let other people pick up the debate, assuming anyone has even read this deeply into the essay section of this book.

However, writers who are of a certain age should avoid making certain mistakes. For instance, when I read a query letter or author bio section, there usually is no reason why I need to be told how old the writer is, unless his or her age is somehow relevant to the material. Once writers start broadcasting how old they are, certain impressions will be formed in the eye of the reader, which can range from the positive to the negative. Why? Because that's what humans do, we form impressions, which get recalled by the information we are given. If your age is a variable of no consequence in the context of what you have written, then just keep it to yourself.

Q: Should I e-mail my query letters to agents?
I think you should consider both e-mail and snail mail. Material that gets electronically delivered is easier to review and process then the submissions that get sent via hard copy. But like a lot of what I say, this is merely my impression. I have not scientifically evaluated what delivery methods are likely to achieve enhanced access, and I would also assume that a lot of it depends upon the preferences of the individual agent. As a marketer, I believe that receiving items that boast physicality can make a bolder impression than an e-mail.

Q: What about agency fees?

Not that stupid question again. It keeps popping up wherever I meet writers. Clearly intelligent people describe the ridiculous abuses they get drawn into by people who claimed to be agents. If you pay a fee, especially to someone who has no documented track record of actually selling books to publishers, then you are making it possible for publishing scams to sustain and surpass the $50 million annual level that the FBI estimated several years ago.

THE AUTHOR-AGENCY CONTRACT

JEFF HERMAN

The author-agent relationship is first and foremost a business partnership. Like any business relationship, it is best to carefully and lucidly document what each party's respective responsibilities and due benefits are. Memories are short, but the written word is forever, assuming you don't lose the paperwork. If there is ever a disagreement or simple confusion about what's what, all you need to do is refer to the contract. A good contract that anticipates all reasonably plausible circumstances is the ultimate arbitrator, and will cost you no additional fees or aggravation.

Below is my agency's standard client contract. I consider it to be fair and liberal, and have had very few complaints about it over the years. To my knowledge, most agencies use contracts that are similar in content.

The key aspects to look for in the agency contract are as follows.

1. COMMISSIONS

Most agencies will charge a 15 percent commission against all advances and royalties they generate for the client. International and dramatization deals often require the agent to retain a coagent, who has the necessary relationships in each respective country where a foreign rights deal might be made, or who has the requisite expertise to deal with the Hollywood jungle. When a coagent is used, the two agents will evenly split the total commission, but this will require the overall commission to be increased to as much as 30 percent.

2. SCOPE OF REPRESENTATION

The contract should be clear about what properties are being represented at the current time, and perhaps into the future. The most liberal arrangement from the author's perspective will be to limit the scope only to the project "in hand." It's best for the author to keep his options open regarding future books. Exceptions to this may be next works that are clearly derived from the first work, or an ongoing series.

3. DURATION OF CONTRACT

This is an area of variance for agency contracts. Some clearly state a six-month or longer term; others are completely open-ended. I prefer the latter. I believe that the agent or writer should be at liberty to end the whole thing whenever they feel compelled to do so. Obviously, the author will still be charged any due commissions that were earned prior to the termination, including any deals that result from the agent's pitches, even if consummated post-breakup.

4. FEES AND/OR REIMBURSABLE EXPENSES

As has been stated elsewhere in this book, a legitimate agent will only make money from the client if a book deal is entered into, thereby paying the agency its due commission. If the agency contract is structured in a way that enables the agency to show a profit even if the work is not sold to a publisher, then the author needs to be concerned. The ways this might show up include large upfront "management fees" or "retainers for expenses." If a so-called agency were to collect $500 five times a week, and never did anything to actually sell any of these works, it would be a very profitable scam, which is much more common than it ought to be. It is perfectly legitimate for an agency to track certain out-of-pocket expenses such as photocopying and shipping, and request reimbursement from the client at some point at cost.

5. REVIEWING AND NEGOTIATING THE AGENCY CONTRACT

It's the author's responsibility to understand and be comfortable with the contract before signing it. The author should not feel awkward about asking the agent to clarify items in the contract, and it is acceptable for the author to request that some reasonable revisions get made. Some authors prefer to have all their contracts vetted by their attorney. This is okay as long as the attorney understands the customs and protocols of the book publishing business. Otherwise, the attorney may go after certain provisions that are generally left alone, and end up wrecking the relationship before it can get off the ground. Assuming that the attorney does have some legitimate points for discussion, then the author should be willing to deal directly with the agency about them, and not turn the attorney loose on the agent.

SAMPLE LETTER OF AGREEMENT

This Letter of Agreement (Agreement) between The Jeff Herman Agency, LLC (Agency), and WILLIAM SHAKESPEARE (Author), issued on JANUARY 2, 1625, will put into effect the following terms and conditions when signed by all parties to it.

REPRESENTATION

- The Agency is exclusively authorized to seek a publisher for the Author's work, referred to as the "Project," on a per-Project basis. The terms and conditions of this Agreement will pertain to all current and future Projects the Author explicitly authorizes the Agency to represent through written expression. Separate Agreements will not be required for future Projects, unless the terms and conditions differ from this Agreement and/or the Author requests a separate Agreement in each instance. The Agency cannot legally bind the Author to any Publisher contracts.

COMMISSION

+ If the Agency sells the Project to a publisher, the Agency will be the Agent-of-Record for the Project's income-producing duration with the publisher, and will irrevocably receive and keep 15 percent of the Author's advance and royalty income relevant to sold Project received from the publisher. Unless otherwise stated, the Agency commission will also pertain to the Project's subsidiary rights, which commonly means dramatic, foreign, audio, video, merchandising, and electronic adaptations of the primary Project. If the Agency uses a subagent to sell foreign or film rights, and the subagent is due a commission, the Agency commission for such will be 10 percent and the subagent's commission will not be more than 10 percent. The Agency will not be required to return any legitimately received commissions in the event the Author-Publisher contract is terminated due to the Author's breach of contract, nor will the Agency bear any responsibility for errors and breaches committed by the Author. There will be an "Agency Clause" included in the body of the Author-Publisher contract memorializing the Agency's standing as a "third-party beneficiary," and providing for the Agency to receive due commission payments directly from the publisher and for the Author to receive due payments minus the commission directly from the publisher, the exact wording for which shall be subject to Author approval. These terms will be binding on the Author's estate in the event of his/her demise. If the Author's Project is placed with a publisher by the Agency, the Agency's status herein will extend to any subsequent contracts between Author and Publisher that pertain to a subsequent edition or revision of the Project, or are clearly derivative of the Project.

EXPENSES

+ The Agency will be entitled to receive reimbursement from the Author for the following out-of-pocket expenses (at actual cost): Manuscript/proposal copying; necessary overnight deliveries; postage for submission of materials to publishers; foreign shipping and communications. An itemized accounting and records of such items will be maintained by the Agency and shown to the Author. No expense events in excess of $75.00 will be incurred without the Author's prior knowledge and consent.

PROJECT STATUS

- The Agency will forward to the Author copies of correspondence and documents received from Publishers in reference to the Author's Project(s).

REVISIONS

- This Agreement can be amended through written expression signed by all parties to the Agreement.

TERMINATION

- Any party to this Agreement can terminate it at any time following its execution by notifying the other parties in writing to that effect. However, the Agency shall remain entitled to all due commissions which may result from successful Agency efforts implemented prior to the termination, and the Agency's existing standing as a third-party beneficiary in any existing Author-Publisher contract cannot be revoked without the Agency's expressed written consent. Termination of the Agency's representation of one or more Author Projects will not imply termination of this entire Agreement, unless such is specifically stated in writing.

Signatures below by the parties named in this Agreement will indicate that all parties concur with the terms and conditions of this Agreement, and will honor their respective responsibilities in good faith.

THE JEFF HERMAN AGENCY, LLC, JEFFREY H. HERMAN, PRESIDENT

_____

Author's name: WILLIAM SHAKESPEARE

Signature:_____

Specific Project(s) represented at this time ("working" or tentative title): *101 Ways to Please a Wench*

SECRETS OF GHOSTWRITING AND COLLABORATION SUCCESS

TONI ROBINO

Thousands of people in the world have valuable information to share or incredible stories to tell. But only a few of them have the ability or the time to write their own books. That's where you—the professional writer—come into the picture. If you're a strong, clear writer, have the ability to organize thoughts and ideas into a logical order, and can put your ego in the back seat, you may have what it takes to be a successful ghostwriter or collaborator.

The life of a professional writer has its share of pains, but it also has an ample amount of perks. To begin with, it provides a means of escape from the Monday through Friday, 9-to-5 grind. The pay is good, and as you improve your skills and broaden your network, it gets better. In addition to being paid to learn and write about interesting people, philosophies, and methods, being a professional writer puts you in touch with a wide array of fascinating people.

I've had the chance to interview some of the planet's most brilliant people and to explore the work of trendsetters and pioneers in the fields of business, psychology, health, fitness, relationship building, astrology, and metaphysics. I have been flown to Paris to meet with leaders in the field of innovation, wined and dined at some of New York's most exclusive restaurants, and collected agates on the Oregon coast, all in the name of "work." If this sounds appealing, keep reading.

WHAT'S THE DIFFERENCE BETWEEN GHOSTWRITING AND COLLABORATING?

One of the most common questions I'm asked is "What's the difference between a ghostwriter and a collaborator?" The answer can vary from project to project. But, typically, a ghostwriter gathers the author's original materials and research and turns them into a book, based on the author's specifications (if the book will be self-published) or the publisher's specifications (if the book has been sold through the proposal process). Theoretically, although ghostwriters do conduct interviews and undertake additional research, they do not contribute their own thoughts or ideas to the content of the book.

In reality, the boundaries of the ghostwriter are not always so clear. As a ghostwriter, I have created 80 percent of the exercises in a number of self-help books, provided many original ideas for content, and "given away" plenty of great title ideas. I don't regret these choices because they felt right and, in the cases mentioned, I was being fairly paid for my ideas, as well as for my services. My being generous with my contributions also made my clients happy and helped to build the foundation of my business. But don't take this too far. For one thing, it's not always a wise choice—particularly if you're giving away original ideas that are perfect for your own book. For another thing, the author you're working with may not appreciate this type of input from you. Do not overstep your boundaries as a ghostwriter by adding your own thoughts to a book, unless the author specifically asks you to do this.

In my more naïve days, and following two glasses of Chardonnay, I made the mistake of sharing my unsolicited input with the author of a health book that I was ghostwriting. In the midst of my enthusiasm, I started brainstorming ideas that she might use to illustrate some of the book's major points. Suddenly, she sprung out of her chair, pointed at me, and declared, "Let's get something straight. This is MY book!" Ouch! I was offering ideas without being asked, but on the other hand, I was only suggesting. Even so, take the word of an initiate and tread softly on your client's turf.

Nowadays, if an author wants me to contribute my own ideas and create original material to support the book, I work with that person as a collaborator and generally receive a coauthor credit, either on the cover or on the title page. Getting credit isn't the most important thing when you're starting out, but if you want to publish your own books in the future, stringing together a list of credits can give you a considerable advantage.

If a book cover says "by John Doe and Jane Smith," they were probably equal collaborators. That can mean:

+ they're both experts and one or both of them wrote the book,

+ they're both experts and they hired a ghostwriter to write the book, or

+ the first author is the expert and the second is a professional writer.

If a book cover says "by John Doe with Jane Smith," Jane probably wrote the book. It could also mean that Jane was a contributor to the book.

Whether you will be serving as a ghostwriter or a collaborator should be clarified up front. Which way to go depends on the project and the people involved. Some of my clients want me to be a "ghost" because they want exclusive cover credit, or they want people to think they wrote their own book. (If this bothers you, now would be a good time to bail out.) Other clients say, "I'm not a writer. This is my material, but I don't want to pretend I wrote this book," or "You deserve credit for what you're doing." On the flip side of the coin, you may be willing to write some books that you don't want your name on. Let's hope this is not because you haven't done a good job!

Perhaps you're trying to establish yourself in a particular field of writing and may not want to be linked with projects outside of your target area. That's a judgment call, and you're the best one to make it.

BEING "INVISIBLE" HAS ITS ADVANTAGES

Years ago, after signing my first contract to ghostwrite a book about personal development, I called a friend to share the great news. But instead of being happy for me, she said, "That's not fair. Why should you write a book and not get any credit for it? You teach that stuff in your seminars. Why don't you write the book yourself?" She was also upset that I wouldn't divulge the name of the "mystery author."

She had no way of knowing how challenging it can be to publish your first book flying solo. The author whom I was writing for was well known and regularly spoke to huge crowds of people all around the world. He had created the perfect platform for this book and was in the prime position to make it a success. He had been previously published and his depth of knowledge in this topic was far greater than my own.

For me, it was a chance to learn more about one of my favorite topics from one of the best sources available. It was also a chance to slip into the publishing world through the back door. I dashed in and never looked back. Once I completed that book, the author referred me to a friend who hired me to write a book about her spiritual journey. She, in turn, introduced me to a professional speaker who wanted to self-publish a book on personal coaching, but could never find the time to write it. And so it goes. If you do a good job, one book can easily lead to the next.

Besides that, being invisible has its advantages. I can zip into the grocery store in purple sweatpants, hair in a ponytail on top of my head, and not a stitch of makeup, and nobody notices or cares! I can kiss my husband in public without camera flashes going off around us, and nobody shows up at my door uninvited, except my mother-in-law.

WHEN CREDIT IS DUE

After you've ghostwritten your first book or two, you'll have more confidence in yourself and your abilities. You will probably start fantasizing (if you haven't already) about seeing your name on the cover, instead of tucked into the acknowledgments section—if that! My name didn't even appear in the first few books that I wrote. Beginning with the fourth book, I asked for a credit in the acknowledgments. Since then, I've been thanked for being a wordsmith, editorial adviser, writing coach, editor, and a "great friend." At least, that was a step in the right direction. However, as much as I relish my anonymity, I also look forward to the day when I'm writing more of my own books than other people's! For that reason, most of the professional writing that I do now is as a collaborator/coauthor.

TEN STEPS TO SUCCEEDING AS A PROFESSIONAL WRITER

There are a number of things to consider before quitting your job and striking out as a professional writer. Writing is a constant process and no matter how good a writer may be, that individual can always get better. Another point to consider is that being a great writer doesn't ensure your success. Writing is a business, and the more you learn about running a business, the better off you'll be. If you're stagnating in a job you abhor, reframe your situation so that you see it as an opportunity to continue earning an income while you make the transition to your writing career. Meanwhile, focus on polishing your writing and interpersonal skills and learn as much about operating a business as you can. The more you learn now, the fewer mistakes you'll make later.

1. ASSESS YOUR WRITING SKILLS

Now is the time to be as objective about your writing as possible. Regardless of where you believe you could or should be along your writing path, what counts at the moment is where you are right now. What writing experience do you have? Have you taken any writing courses? Does your writing flow from one thought logically to the next, or does it need to be better organized? Is your writing smooth and conversational, or does it sound stiff or overly academic? What sorts of positive and negative comments have you received about your writing? Have you had anything published? If not, get going!

If you're too close to your writing to be objective, hire an editor, book doctor, or writing coach to give you some forthright feedback. This assessment will help you to learn where you excel and where you should focus your efforts for improvements. The good news is that there's a market for writers at all points on the professional spectrum. You may not be ready to take on your first book, but you could be qualified to ghostwrite an article, collaborate on a chapter, or polish someone else's work. Begin at your current skill level and commit to a path of improvement. By doing this, you will increase your abilities and your income.

2. MAKE YOUR FIRST LIST

Everyone knows at least a few experts. Whether the experts in your life are doctors, professors, psychologists, interior decorators, photographers, archaeologists, or magicians, chances are that some of them have a goal to write a book. Unless these people are good writers and have a lot of free time, which very few experts have, their book will remain on their "wish list" until someone like you shows up to help them. So begin to make a "potential author" list by answering the following questions. For each question, list as many names as you can think of.

Do you know people who are pioneers or experts in their field?
Do you know people who are famous, either in general or in their area of expertise?
Who are the experts, celebrities, or trendsetters whom your friends or associates know?

Once you've made your list, number the names, starting with number one for the person you would most like to work with. Resist the urge to contact these people until you have professionally prepared for your meeting, by learning more about them and taking Steps 3 and 4.

3. PREPARE A PROFESSIONAL PACKAGE

Put together a promotional package for yourself, or hire a professional to help you do it. This package should include your résumé or bio, the services you offer, and a variety of writing samples, showing different styles and topics. You might also insert a page of testimonials from people you have helped with your writing skills or from teachers and coaches who can attest to your abilities. If you've been published, include clean copies of a few of your best clips. If you haven't, enclose a few essays that demonstrate your ability to write clearly and deliver a message effectively.

When you send out your promotional package, enclose a personal pitch letter. Basically, you are telling people what you believe they have to offer the world through their experience or expertise. You're also telling them why you are the perfect person to write the article, manuscript, or book proposal.

4. SET YOUR RATES

Some writers enclose a rate sheet in their promotional package, but I don't recommend it. I do recommend that you make a rate sheet for your own reference. This will be your guide when you are deciding what to charge your clients. Since every project is a little different, don't commit to a price until you estimate how much time and money it will take for you to do the job well.

Calculate how fast you can write final copy, by keeping track of the actual hours spent writing, editing, and proofreading an article or sample chapter. When the piece is completed to your satisfaction, follow this formula:

Total number of words in final copy
Divided by
Total number of hours to complete final copy
Equals:
Your average speed per hour

The idea isn't to race. This exercise is designed to give you a reality check. If you don't know your average speed for producing final copy, you won't be able to create realistic deadline schedules and you'll have no idea how much you're earning for a day of work.

While you may be able to speed through a first draft, the chapter isn't finished until you've edited, polished, and proofread it.

In addition to estimating your actual writing time, build in time for research, interviews, and meetings with the author. You should also estimate the amount of postage, phone charges, faxes, audio tapes, transcription services, and anything else that will be money out of your pocket. Once you've done your homework, you can present the client with a Letter of Agreement (see Step 7) that includes what you will charge and what they will get for your fee.

Writers' rates vary wildly. I was paid $10,000 for the first few books that I ghost-wrote, and this is still a great starter rate for a nonfiction book ranging from 70,000 to about 85,000 words. You may not be able to charge this much the first time or two, but with each publication that you add to your list, you can inch up your price. When you reach the point where you are earning $15,000 or more on a book, you will be in the company of some of the most successful ghostwriters. The average fee to write a book proposal can range from $1,000 up to $8,000 or more. When you turn writing into a full-time adventure and write several proposals and books each year, while perhaps editing others, you'll be well on your way to ongoing financial and publishing success!

Many times, if you are working as a "writer for hire," you are paid a flat fee and do not receive royalties from book sales. If you are ghostwriting the book, you may be able to negotiate for royalties. (Royalties for ghostwriting can range from 10 percent of the author's royalties to 50 percent.) If you're a collaborator, in most cases you're entitled to a percentage of the book sales. However, many contracts state that the writer does not begin to receive royalties until the publisher has recouped the initial advance for the book. In some cases, the writer's royalties do not begin until the author has recouped the amount invested in the writer. The bottom line is that most ghostwriters don't receive a dime in royalties until thousands of books have been sold. I suggest that you charge what you're worth up front and think of royalties as icing on the cake.

5. POLISH YOUR INTERPERSONAL SKILLS

Unfortunately, some of the best writers are not comfortable talking to people or selling themselves to potential clients. If you see this as a possible pitfall in building your business, make it a priority to develop your interpersonal skills. Plenty of books, tapes, and seminars address personal development, communication skills, networking, and conflict resolution. Devote yourself to learning how to be more comfortable and effective in your interactions with others.

Practice listening closely to what your client is saying, without interrupting. Growing up in an Italian family with everyone talking at once, I had no problem paying attention to what my clients were saying. (If you can listen to three people at once, you can easily hear one at a time!) However, mastering the discipline to keep my mouth shut until it was my turn to talk was another matter entirely. While inter-jecting and simultaneous talking is considered par for the course in some settings, many people are offended by interruptions and consider them rude. If you have an exciting idea or pertinent question on the tip of your tongue, jot it down, and wait until your clients complete their thoughts, before chiming in.

Learn how to communicate with your clients in a way that is open and caring. For example, rather than telling an author that the file of notes she sent you was so disorganized that dealing with it was like "stumbling blindfolded through a maze," tell her you appreciate her ability to think of so many things at once. Then tell her what you want her to do. "Please put all of your notes under specific category headings, so I can keep all of your great ideas organized." The rule is to think before you speak. There are usually better ways to communicate a thought than the first words that pop into your head or out of your mouth!

Another skill that is essential for a ghostwriter and important for a collaborator is learning how to keep your ego in check. It's not uncommon for a writer to start feeling attached to a project and have a desire for greater freedom or control of the content or writing style. Remind yourself that this book is not yours. Your day will come, and working as a professional writer is paving the way for that to happen.

One of the surest ways to nip your ghostwriting career in the bud is to break the code of confidentiality that you have with the author of the book. Degrees of "invisibility" differ by project, but if the author doesn't want anyone to know you are writing the book, zip your lips. Other than perhaps your spouse, there is no one, and I mean no one, that you should tell. You can say you're writing a book, and you can divulge the general topic, but that has to be the end of the conversation. To this day, my best friends have no idea who I've ghostwritten books for—except in the cases where the authors have publicly acknowledged me for my participation.

Finally, one of the most beneficial interpersonal skills that a writer or anyone else can possess is a sense of humor. Things are bound to go wrong somewhere along the way, and being able to laugh together with your client will ease tension and stress and make the project a whole lot more fun. It's also valuable to learn to laugh at yourself. My father always said, "If you can look at yourself in the mirror at the end of the day and laugh, you'll make it in life." Oftentimes, when I write a book I create a blooper file, just for my own entertainment. This file contains all of the funny, startling, and obscene typos that I find when I proofread my work.

Keep in mind that there are scores of great writers in the world. Why would an author choose to work with someone who's cranky, arrogant, or self-absorbed if it's possible to work with someone equally talented who is also pleasant, down to earth, and fun?

6. KNOW WHEN TO RUN!

Some day, in the not too distant future, you will have a chance to write a book that you know in your gut is not a good match. This might be because it's a topic that bores your pants off, the point of view is in direct opposition to your own beliefs, or the material is leagues away from your scope of knowledge, experience, or ability for comprehension. In spite of all this, you may be tempted to leap into this "opportunity." Maybe your rent is due, the phone company is threatening to disconnect you, or maybe you just can't wait any longer to write your first book. Before you rationalize this decision or override your instincts, take a step back and think about it for at least two days before you commit. For instance, I should have failed algebra class, but my professor gifted me with the lowest passing grade. Even so, when I was offered a chance to ghostwrite *Understanding the Intrigue of Calculus*, I was tempted to do it. Fortunately, two bounced check notices (caused by my math errors) snapped me back to reality, and I graciously declined the offer.

Aside from making a good match with a topic, it is imperative that you feel good about the book's author. It usually takes about nine months to write a book and doing it with someone else can be compared to having a baby together—minus the sex. If you like each other, it can be a wonderful journey filled with creative energy. If you don't like each other, it can be a recurring nightmare that doesn't go away when you wake up.

Years ago, I took on the daunting task of "saving a book." The complete manuscript was due in three months and the author's writing team had mysteriously jumped ship. When I spoke with author for the first time, she was both friendly and enthusiastic, but she also seemed a little desperate. I ignored my instincts, and two days later I was sitting in her apartment discussing the book. Several things happened that day, and each one of them should have set off warning flares in my mind. To begin with, the author's materials were in complete disarray. (No problem, I told myself. I'm a great organizer.) Second, in between telling me how important it is to speak to our mates with respect, she was berating her husband for his lack of photocopying abilities and sundry other things that he couldn't do right to save his life. (She's just stressed out, I justified.) And third, as I leafed through the disheveled stacks of unnumbered pages, I came across a few very cryptic and angry-sounding notes from the writing team that had bailed out. (I reassured myself that even if others had failed, I would not.)

These rationalizations would soon come back to bite me. And not just once. As it turned out, nine writers had attempted to complete this manuscript before I was contacted. Four writers quit, one writer had a nervous breakdown, three of them disappeared into thin air, and another had his phone disconnected. Ironically, the week the book was released, I had the pleasure of meeting one of the writers who had wisely run for her life. We traded our "Crazy-Author Horror Stories" over steaming plates of fried rice and laughed until tears streamed down our cheeks. At that point it was funny, but not a moment before! If you connect with an author who enters the scene waving red flags, run for your life!

7. CLOSE THE DEAL

Verbal agreements are not enough. If you're working with a publishing house, the author or the author's agent will usually have a contract for you to sign. Make sure you understand this agreement before you sign it. Don't be afraid to ask questions. These contracts are written in "legalese" and can be daunting the first time you encounter one. If you're working with an author who plans to self-publish, create a "letter of agreement" that specifies exactly what services you are providing, the fees involved, the date of delivery, and any other considerations that should be put into writing. This document should be signed by both you and the author; it will help to prevent assumptions or other misunderstandings concerning your business agreement.

8. CAPTURE THE AUTHOR'S VOICE

Whether you're working as a ghostwriter or a collaborator, one of your jobs is to capture the voice of the author. Simply put, you want to write in a way that makes it sound like the author is talking. It shouldn't sound like another author whose style you admire, and it most certainly should not sound like you!

Practice reading a few paragraphs from a favorite book, and then write a few of your own, mimicking the author's voice. Do this with a wide variety of authors, and over time, you will develop an "ear" for others' voices.

One of the best ways to write in the author's voice is to conduct taped interviews with the author and have them transcribed onto computer disk. You can cut and paste the pertinent information into each chapter, in the author's own words, and then smooth it out and expand it as needed.

9. CREATE AND KEEP DEADLINES

There are nearly as many methods of meeting deadlines as there are writers. I tend to take a very methodical approach, dividing up the work into equal parts, circling my "days off," and carefully penciling each chapter deadline on my desk calendar. (I can't help it, I was born this way.) Other writers would go mad with this approach. One of the best writers I know creates 10 percent of the book the week she signs the contract and the other 90 percent the month before the manuscript is due. I couldn't even conceive of this approach and would never have believed it could be done if I hadn't witnessed it personally. The secret is to find out what works best for you. But don't kid yourself. Very few writers can write a great book in less than six months. At least until you settle into your own rhythm, pace yourself. Set reasonable deadlines and find a way to stay accountable to those dates.

Staying accountable to my own deadline schedule was initially much harder than I thought it would be. (There are so many tempting diversions in life!) Frequently, when I was supposed to be writing, I was toying with an art project, combing the forest floor in search of gourmet mushrooms, or just staring out the window. My sense of urgency wasn't ignited until my cash flow began to dwindle. That was when I discovered my motivation. Food, shelter, electricity. It may sound like common sense, but for me it was an "aha" moment. I do have some built-in motivation, but it's keeping my cash flow going that moves me from the sunroom to my office each day.

Linking productivity with payments works well. Ask for one-third of your fee up front. This assures you that the author is serious and provides income so you can focus on the book. Schedule your second payment of one-third to coincide with turning in 50 percent of the manuscript. The final one-third is slated for the date you deliver the final manuscript to the author. If you feel you need more deadlines, divide your fee into four or more payments, each contingent on completing a certain amount of work.

10. ASK FOR REFERRALS

I don't have a business card that says "writer." I don't advertise my writing or editing services, and networking requires an hour's drive from the sanctuary of my forest home into the nearest city, which translates into: I rarely do it. By all sensible accounts, I shouldn't be making it as a ghostwriter. And yet I am, and have been for more than a decade. The secret to my success is word-of-mouth marketing. My clients are happy with my work and me, so they hire me again. They also tell their friends and associates about me, and the wheel continues to spin, seemingly of its own volition.

I know there are many more approaches to marketing, but I've learned that personal referrals usually provide clients whom I want to work with. It's possible for a satisfied client to refer you to an author whom you'd rather eat glass than work with, but most of the time, personal referrals increase your chances of connecting with authors and projects that are interesting and appealing.

When you've completed your work and satisfied your client, ask for referrals. If you've delivered the goods, they'll be happy to brag about you to their friends and associates who "just can't seem to find the right writer."

MAINTAIN YOUR BRIDGES

After the manuscript is complete, the author will be busy with promotional plans and getting back to regular business. You will be focusing on your next project. It's easy to get caught up in the day-to-day happenings and neglect to maintain the bridges that you've already built.

Make it a point to connect with satisfied clients from time to time. Hearing from you will help them think of you for future projects and will increase the likelihood that they'll remember to refer you to someone else. Every couple of months, send a card, a funny e-mail, or an upbeat fax. I phone previous clients only on occasion, and when I do, I call them at their office and keep it short. You want to be the person they look forward to hearing from, not the one who won't go away!

COLLABORATION AGREEMENT

This Collaboration Agreement ("Agreement") entered into on [Date], by and between ("Author") and ("Writer"), will put the following terms and conditions into effect when signed by both parties.

1. The Author and Writer agree to work together in writing a book about ("Concept").

2. The Writer in consultation with the Author will write a nonfiction book proposal ("Proposal") for the purpose of soliciting and obtaining a book publishing contract. The Proposal will consist of the customary elements as per industry standards and as explained in the book, *Write the Perfect Book Proposal* (John Wiley & Sons), and will include one sample chapter. The Author will make available to the Writer necessary access to herself and other relevant sources and materials for the purpose of generating the Proposal. The Proposal will not be deemed as complete and ready for showing to prospective publishers until the Author accepts it as such.

3. The Writer promises to complete a first draft of the proposal and chapter by [Date], assuming the Writer receives necessary cooperation from the Author and other necessary sources.

4. If a publisher's contract is entered into, both parties will be signatories to it and equally subject to it, unless otherwise stated. The Writer will proceed to write the manuscript to the publisher's satisfaction as per the terms and conditions of the publisher's contract, in collaboration with the Author.

5. The Writer will not submit the manuscript or any portion of it without the Author's consent. Only the Author will be permitted to accept or reject editorial suggestions made by the publisher, though the Writer will be consulted.

6. The Author will be the book's sole spokesperson, and the Author's name will appear before and in bigger print than the Writer's name in all instances. The word "With" will precede the Writer's name.

7. The Author and Writer will jointly own the book's copyright. The Author will retain sole ownership of original material used in the book to which she already possesses ownership, and no assignments of such ownership are included or implied beyond said usage in the book.

8. The Author agrees to indemnify the Writer against any damages the Writer suffers due to the publication of any material in the book provided by the

Author. The Author will bear sole responsibility for confirming the veracity and legally unencumbered nature of all material and information that is provided by the Author, including the acquisition of necessary permissions, and will be held solely responsible for paying the costs and possible damages from any libel suits resulting from the book's publication.

9. If the Proposal is used to generate a deal from a publisher, but the Writer no longer wishes to write the manuscript, or the Author does not want the Writer to do so, the Writer will be entitled to a one-time "kill-fee" in the amount of $, to be paid within 30 days of the Author's receipt of first-proceeds from the publisher, in consideration of the Writer's generating the Proposal that generated the book contract. Upon termination, the Writer will automatically relinquish any rights whatsoever to any other payments or any ownership of the material in the proposal, and agrees not to ever use the material or other proprietary information in any fashion whatsoever, and will promptly return to the Author any notes, documents, photos, or audios relevant to the book.

10. If the Writer fails to generate a Proposal that is acceptable to the Author, then this Agreement will terminate and the Author will be prevented from using any of the written expression generated by the Writer for any purposes whatsoever, and the Writer will promptly return all materials in his possession provided by the Author and will be proscribed from using any information or material provided by the Author for any purposes whatsoever.

11. If no publishing offers are received by [date], 2013, this Agreement will automatically terminate, unless renewed through written expression attached hereto. The Writer will be proscribed from using the proposal or anything in it provided by the Author without the Author's expressed consent, and will promptly return all items as stated above. If the Author uses the Proposal to secure a publishing deal at a later point, then the Writer will be entitled to the "Kill fee" stated above. Otherwise, the Writer will not be due any compensation apart from due reimbursements.

12. If after entering into a publisher's contract, the publisher refuses to accept the manuscript for editorial purposes and demands reimbursement of some or all of advance payments made to the Author and Publisher as per the terms of the publisher's contract, then both Author and Writer will be separately responsible for returning their portions to the publisher. Any such publisher rejection and termination will also cause this Agreement to automatically terminate as per the terms and conditions stated in Paragraph 11, unless both parties choose to extend it through written expression attached hereto.

13. This Agreement will remain binding upon both parties' estates.

14. Neither party can assign or transfer their obligations herein without the written consent of the other party attached hereto.

15. This Agreement can be amended upon the expressed written consent of both parties attached hereto.

16. All advance and/or royalty revenues derived from the book's publication shall be divided as follows between the parties: Fifty-fifty, 50 percent-50 percent.

17. All revenues derived from any movie/TV/dramatization licenses or options based upon the book will be divided as follows: 80 percent to the Author, 20 percent to the Writer.

18. The Writer will not receive any revenues received by the Author from the following activities: Appearances, speaking, endorsements, interviews.

19. Expenses relevant to writing the Proposal and the manuscript shall be divided as follows: 50 percent Author, 50 percent Writer. The accounts shall be balanced from first-proceeds received from a Publisher. Otherwise, the party who is due reimbursement will be promptly reimbursed by the other party. Neither party will spend more than $50 without the expressed e-mail consent of the other following an expressed e-mail description of what the spending is for. All expenses must be documented in order to be reimbursed.

(Signatures follow)

WHEN THE DEAL IS DONE

HOW TO THRIVE AFTER SIGNING
A PUBLISHING CONTRACT

JEFF HERMAN

ongratulations! You've sold your book to an established publishing house. You've gained entry to the elite club of published authors. You'll discover that your personal credibility is enhanced whenever this achievement is made known to others. It may also prove a powerful marketing vehicle for your business or professional practice.

Smell the roses while you can. Then wake up and smell the coffee. If your experience is like that of numerous other writers, once your book is actually published, there's a better-than-even chance you'll feel a bit of chagrin. Some of these doubts are apt to be outward expressions of your own inner uncertainties. Others are not self-inflicted misgivings—they are most assuredly ticked off by outside circumstances.

Among the most common author complaints are: (1) Neither you nor anyone you know can find the book anywhere. (2) The publisher doesn't appear to be doing anything to market the book. (3) You detest the title and the jacket. (4) No one at the publishing house is listening to you. In fact, you may feel that you don't even exist for them.

As a literary agent, I live through these frustrations with my clients every day, and I try to explain to them at the outset what the realities of the business are. But I never advocate abdication or pessimism. There are ways for every author to substantially remedy these endemic problems. In many cases this means first taking a deep breath, relaxing, and reaching down deep inside yourself to sort out the true source of your emotions. When this has been accomplished, it's time to breathe out, move out, and take charge.

What follows are practical means by which each of these four most common failures can be preempted. I'm not suggesting that you can compensate entirely for what may be a publisher's defaults; it's a tall order to remake a clinker after the fact. However, with lots of smarts and a little luck you can accomplish a great deal.

A PHILOSOPHY TO WRITE BY

Let me introduce a bit of philosophy that applies to the writer's life, as well as it does to the lives of those who are not published. Many of you may be familiar with the themes popularized by psychotherapists, self-awareness gurus, and business motivators that assert the following: To be a victim is to be powerless—which means you don't have the ability to improve your situation. With that in mind, avoid becoming merely an author who only complains and who remains forever bitter.

No matter how seriously you believe your publisher is screwing up, don't fall into the victim trap. Instead, find positive ways to affect what is or is not happening for you.

Your publisher is like an indispensable employee whom you are not at liberty to fire. You don't have to work with this publisher the next time, but this time it's the only one you've got.

There are a handful of perennially best-selling writers, such as John Grisham, Anne Rice, and Mary Higgins Clark, whose book sales cover a large part of their publisher's expense sheet. These writers have perhaps earned the luxury of being very difficult, if they so choose (most of them are reportedly quite the opposite).

But the other 99.98 percent of writers are not so fortunately invested with the power to arbitrate. No matter how justified your stance and methods may be, if you become an author with whom everyone at the publishing house dreads to speak, you've lost the game.

The editors, publicists, and marketing personnel still have their jobs, and they see no reason to have you in their face. In other words: Always seek what's legitimately yours, but always try to do it in a way that might work for you, as opposed to making yourself *persona non grata* till the end of time.

ATTACKING PROBLEM NO. 1: NEITHER YOU NOR ANYONE YOU KNOW CAN FIND THE BOOK ANYWHERE

This can be the most painful failure. After all, what was the point of writing the book and going through the whole process of getting it published if it's virtually invisible?

Trade book distribution is a mysterious process, even for people in the business. Most bookstore sales are dominated by the large national and regional chains. Publishers always have the chain stores in mind when they determine what to publish. Thankfully, there are also a few thousand independently owned shops throughout the country.

Thousands of new titles are published each year, and these books are added to the seemingly infinite number already in print. Considering the limitations of the existing retail channels, it should be no surprise that only a small fraction of all these books achieves a significant and enduring bookstore presence.

Each bookstore will dedicate most of its visual space to displaying healthy quantities of the titles it feels are safe sells: books by celebrities and well-established authors, or books that are being given extra-large printings and marketing budgets by their publishers, thereby promising to create demand.

The rest of the store will generally provide a liberal mix of titles, organized by subject or category. This is where the backlist titles reside and the lower-profile newer releases try to stake their claims. For instance, the business section will probably offer two dozen or so sales books. Most of the displayed titles will be by the biggest names in the genre, and their month-to-month sales probably remain strong, even if the book was first published several years ago.

In other words, probably hundreds of other sales books were written in recent years that, as far as retail distribution is concerned, barely made it out of the womb. You see, the stores aren't out there to do you any favors. They are going to stock whatever titles they feel they can sell the most of. There are too many titles chasing too little space.

It's the job of the publisher's sales representative to lobby the chain and store buyers individually about the merits of her publisher's respective list. But here, too, the numbers can be numbing. The large houses publish many books each season, and it's not possible for the rep to do justice to each of them. Priority will be given to the relatively few titles that get the exceptional advances.

Because most advances are modest, and since the average book costs about $20,000 to produce, some publishers can afford to simply sow a large field of books and observe passively as some of them sprout. The many that don't bloom are soon forgotten, as a new harvest dominates the bureaucracy's energy. Every season, many very fine books are terminated by the publishing reaper. The wisdom and magic these books may have offered are thus sealed away, disclosed only to the few.

I have just covered a complicated process in a brief fashion. Nonetheless, the overall consequences for your book are in essence the same. Here, now, are a few things you may attempt in order to override such a stacked situation. However, these methods will not appeal to the shy or passive:

- Make direct contact with the publisher's sales representatives. Do to them what they do to the store buyers—sell 'em! Get them to like you and your book. Take the reps near you to lunch and ballgames. If you travel, do the same for local reps wherever you go.

- Make direct contact with the buyers at the national chains. If you're good enough to actually get this kind of access, you don't need to be told what to do next.

- Organize a national marketing program aimed at local bookstores throughout the country.

There's no law that says only your publisher has the right to market your book to the stores. (Of course, except in special cases, all orders must go through your publisher.) For the usual reasons, your publisher's first reaction may be "What the hell are you doing?" But that's okay; make the publisher happy by showing her that your efforts work. It would be wise, however, to let the publisher in on your scheme up front.

If your publisher objects—which she may—you might choose to interpret those remarks simply as the admonitions they are, and then proceed to make money for all. This last observation leads to ways you can address the next question.

ATTACKING PROBLEM NO. 2: THE PUBLISHER DOESN'T APPEAR TO BE DOING ANYTHING TO MARKET THE BOOK

If it looks as if your publisher is doing nothing to promote your book, then it's probably true. Your mistake is being surprised and unprepared.

The vast majority of published titles receive little or no marketing attention from the publisher beyond catalog listings. The titles that get big advances are likely to get some support, since the publisher would like to justify the advance by creating a good seller.

Compared to those in other Fortune 500 industries, publishers' in-house marketing departments tend to be woefully understaffed, undertrained, and underpaid. Companies like Procter & Gamble will tap the finest business schools, pay competitive salaries, and strive to nurture marketing superstars. Book publishers don't do this.

As a result, adult trade book publishing has never been especially profitable, and countless sales probably go unmade. The sales volumes and profits for large, diversified publishers are mostly due to the lucrative—and captive—textbook trade. Adult trade sales aren't the reason that companies like Random House can generate more than $1 billion in annual revenues.

HERE'S WHAT YOU CAN DO

Hire your own public relations firm to promote you and your book. Your publisher is likely to be grateful and cooperative. But you must communicate carefully with your publishing house.

Once your manuscript is completed, you should request a group meeting with your editor and people from the marketing, sales, and publicity departments. You should focus on what their marketing agenda will be. If you've decided to retain your own PR firm, this is the time to impress the people at your publishing house with your commitment and pressure them to help pay for it. At the very least, the publisher should provide plenty of free books.

Beware of this common problem: Even if you do a national TV show, your book may not be abundantly available in bookstores that day—at least, not everywhere. An obvious answer is setting up 800 numbers to fill orders, and it baffles me that publishers don't make wider use of them. There are many people watching *Oprah* who won't ever make it to the bookstore, but who would be willing to order then and there with a credit card. Infomercials have proved this.

Not all talk or interview shows will cooperate, but whenever possible you should try to have your publisher's 800 number (or yours) displayed as a purchasing method, in addition to the neighborhood bookstore. If you use your own number, make sure you can handle a potential flood.

If retaining a PR firm isn't realistic for you, then do your own media promotions. There are many good books in print about how to do your own PR. (A selection of relevant titles may be found in this volume's "Suggested Resources" section.)

ATTACKING PROBLEM NO. 3: YOU DETEST THE TITLE AND JACKET

Almost always, your publisher will have final contractual discretion over title, jacket design, and jacket copy. But that doesn't mean you can't be actively involved. In my opinion, you had better be. Once your final manuscript is submitted, make it clear to your editor that you expect to see all prospective covers and titles. But simply trying to veto what the publisher comes up with won't be enough. You should try to counter the negatives with positive alternatives. You might even want to go as far as having your own prospective covers professionally created. If the publisher were to actually choose your version, the house might reimburse you.

At any rate, don't wait until it's after the fact to decide you don't like your cover, title, and so forth. It's like voting: Participate or shut up.

ATTACKING PROBLEM NO. 4: NO ONE AT THE PUBLISHING HOUSE SEEMS TO BE LISTENING TO YOU

This happens a lot—though I bet it happens to certain people in everything they do. The primary reasons for this situation are either (1) that the people you're trying to access are incompetent; (2) that you're not a priority for them; or (3) that they simply hate talking to you.

Here are a few things you might try to do about it:

+ If the contact person is incompetent, what can that person really accomplish for you anyway? It's probably best to find a way to work around this person, even if he begins to return your calls before you place them.

+ The people you want access to may be just too busy to give you time. Screaming may be a temporary remedy, but eventually, they'll go deaf again. Obviously, their time is being spent somewhere. Thinking logically, how can you make it worthwhile for these people to spend more time on you? If being a pain in the neck is your best card, then perhaps you should play it. But there's no leverage like being valuable. In fact, it's likely that the somewhere else they're spending their time is with a very valuable author.

+ Maybe someone just hates talking to you. That may be this person's problem. But, as many wise men and women have taught, allies are better than adversaries. And to convert an adversary is invaluable. Do it.

CONCLUSION

This essay may come across as cynical. But I want you to be realistic and be prepared. Many publishing success stories are out there, and many of them happened because the authors made them happen.

For every manuscript that is published, probably a few thousand were rejected. To be published is a great accomplishment—and a great asset. If well tended, it can pay tremendous dividends.

Regardless of your publisher's commitment at the outset, if you can somehow generate sales momentum, the publisher will most likely join your march to success and allocate a substantial investment to ensure it. In turn, the publisher may even assume all the credit. But so what? It's to your benefit.

FICTION DICTIONARY

JAMIE M. FORBES

In book publishing, people describe works of fiction as they relate to categories, genres, and other market concepts, which, coming from the mouths of renowned industry figures, can make it sound as if there's a real system to what is actually a set of arbitrary terminology. Categories are customarily viewed as reflecting broad sectors of readership interest. Genres are either subcategories (classifications within categories) or types of stories that can pop up within more than one category—though genre and category are sometimes used interchangeably.

For instance, suspense fiction (as a broad category) includes the jeopardy story genre (typified by a particular premise that can just as easily turn up in a super-natural horror story). Or, again within the suspense fiction category, there's the police procedural (a subcategory of detective fiction, which is itself a subcategory of suspense that is often spoken of as a separate category). The police procedural can be discussed as a distinct genre with its own special attributes; and there are partic-ular procedural genre types, such as those set in the small towns of the American plains or in a gritty urban environment. As a genre-story type, tales of small-town American life also surface in the context of categories as disparate as literary fiction, horror stories, Westerns, and contemporary and historical romance.

As we can see, all of this yackety-yak is an attempt to impose a sense of order onto what is certainly a muddy creative playing field.

The following listing of commonly used fiction descriptions gives an indication of the varieties of writing found within each category. This is not meant to be a strict taxonomy. Nor is it exhaustive. The definitions associated with each category or genre are fluid and personalized in usage and can seem to vary with each author interview or critical treatise, with each spate of advertising copy or press release, or they can shift during the course of a single editorial conference. One writer's "mystery" may be a particular editor's "suspense," which is then marketed to the public as a "thriller."

Then, too, individual authors do come up with grand, original ideas that demand publication and thereby create new categories or decline to submit to any such des-ignation. But that's another story—maybe yours.

ACTION-ADVENTURE

The action-oriented adventure novel is best typified in terms of premise and scenario trajectory. These stories often involve the orchestration of a journey that is essentially exploratory, revelatory, and (para)military. There is a quest element—a search for a treasure in whatever guise—in addition to a sense of pursuit that crosses over into thrillerdom. From one perspective, the action-adventure tale, in story concept if not explicit content, traces its descent from epic-heroic tradition.

In modern action-adventure we are in the territory of freebooters, commandos, and mercenaries—as well as suburbanites whose yen for experience of the good life, and whose very unawareness in the outback, takes them down dangerous trails. Some stories are stocked with an array of international terrorists, arms-smugglers, drug-dealers, and techno-pirates. Favorite settings include jungles, deserts, swamps, and mountains—any sort of badlands (don't rule out an urban environment) that can echo the perils that resound through the story's human dimension.

There can be two or more cadres with competing aims going for the supreme prize—and be sure to watch out for lots of betrayal and conflict among friends, as well as the hitherto unsuspected schemer among the amiably bonded crew.

Action-adventures were once thought of as exclusively men's stories. No more. Writers invented new ways to do it, and the field is now open.

COMMERCIAL FICTION

Commercial fiction is defined by sales figures—either projected (prior to publication, even before acquisition) or backhandedly through actual performance. Commercial properties are front-list titles, featured prominently in a publisher's catalog and given good doses of publicity and promotion.

An agent or editor says a manuscript is commercial, and the question in response is apt to be: How so? Many books in different genres achieve best seller potential after an author has established a broad-based readership and is provided marketing support from all resources the publisher commands.

Commercial fiction is not strictly defined by content or style; it is perhaps comparative, rather than absolute. Commercial fiction is often glitzier, more stylishly of the mode in premise and setting; its characters strike the readers as more assuredly glamorous (regardless of how highbrow or lowlife).

A commercial work offers the publisher a special marketing angle, which changes from book to book or season to season—this year's kinky kick is next year's ho-hum. For a new writer in particular, to think commercially is to think ahead of the pack and not jump on the tail-end of a bandwagon that's already passed. If your premise has already played as a television miniseries, you're way too late.

Commercial works sometimes show elements of different categories, such as detective fiction or thrillers, and may cut across or combine genres to reach out toward a vast readership. Cross-genre books may thus have enticing hooks for the reading public at large; at the same time, when they defy category conventions they may not satisfy genre aficionados. If commercial fiction is appointed by vote of sales, most popular mysteries are commercial works, as are sophisticated best-selling sex-and-shopping oh-so-shocking wish-it-were-me escapades.

CRIME FICTION

Related to detective fiction and suspense novels, in subject matter and ambiance, are stories centered on criminal enterprise. Crime fiction includes lighthearted capers that are vehicles in story form for the portrayal of amusingly devious aspirations at the core of the human norm. Crime stories can also be dark, black, noir, showing the primeval essence of tooth-and-nail that brews in more than a few souls.

Some of the players in crime stories may well be cops of one sort or another (and they are often as corrupt as the other characters), but detection per se is not necessarily the story's strong suit. It is just as likely that in the hands of one of the genre's masters, the reader's lot will be cast (emotionally, at least) in support of the outlaw characters' designs.

DETECTIVE FICTION

Varieties of detective fiction include police procedurals (with the focus on formal investigatory teamwork); hard-boiled, poached, or soft-boiled (not quite so tough as hard-boiled); and the cozy (a.k.a. tea-cozy mysteries, manners mysteries, manor house mysteries).

Detectives are typically private or public pros; related professionals whose public image, at least, involves digging under the surface (reporters, journalists, computer hackers, art experts, psychotherapists, and university academics, including archaeologists); or they may be rank amateurs who are interested or threatened via an initial plot turn that provides them with an opportunity (or the necessity) to assume an investigatory role.

The key here is that the detective story involves an ongoing process of discovery that forms the plot. Active pursuit of interlocking clues and other leads is essential—though sometimes an initial happenstance disclosure will do in order to kick off an otherwise tightly woven story.

The manifold denominations of modern detective fiction (also called mysteries, or stories or novels of detection) are widely considered to stem from the detective tales composed by the nineteenth-century American writer Edgar Allan Poe. Though mysterious tracks of atmosphere and imagery can be traced in the writings of French symbolists (Charles Baudelaire was a big fan of Poe), the first flowering of the form was in Britain, including such luminaries as Arthur Conan Doyle, Agatha Christie, and Dorothy L. Sayers. Indeed, in one common usage, a traditional mystery (or cozy) is a story in the mode initially established by British authors.

The other major tradition is the American-grown hard-boiled detective story, with roots in the tabloid culture of America's industrial growth and the associated institutions of yellow journalism, inspirational profiles of the gangster-tycoon lifestyle, and social-action exposés.

The field continues to expand with infusions of such elements as existentialist character conceits, the lucidity and lushness of magic-realists, and the ever-shifting sociopolitical insights that accrue from the growing global cultural exchange.

Occasionally, detective fiction involves circumstances in which, strictly speaking, no crime has been committed. The plot revolves around parsing out events or situations that may be construed as strange, immoral, or unethical (and are certainly mysterious), but which are by no means considered illegal in all jurisdictions.

FANTASY FICTION

The category of fantasy fiction covers many of the story elements encountered in fables, folktales, and legends; the best of these works obtain the sweep of the epic and are touched by the power of myth. Some successful fantasy series are set within recognizable museum-quality frames, such as those of ancient Egypt or the Celtic world. Another strain of fantasy fiction takes place in almost-but-not-quite archaeologically verifiable regions of the past or future, with barbarians, nomads, and jewel-like cities scattered across stretches of continent-sized domains of the author's imagination.

Fair game in this realm are romance, magic, and talking animals. Stories are for the most part adventurous, filled with passion, honor, vengeance—and action. A self-explanatory subgenre of fantasy fiction is termed sword-and-sorcery.

HORROR

Horror has been described as the simultaneous sense of fascination and terror, a basic attribute that can cover significant literary scope. Some successful horror writers are admired more for their portrayal of atmosphere than for attention to plot or character development. Other writers do well with the carefully paced zinger—that is, the threat-and-delivery of gore; in the hands of skilled practitioners, sometimes not much more is needed to produce truly terrifying effects.

The horror genre has undergone changes—there is, overall, less reliance on the religiously oriented supernatural, more utilization of medical and psychological concepts, more sociopolitical and cultural overtones, and a general recognition on the part of publishers that many horror aficionados seek more than slash-and-gore. Not that the readers aren't bloodthirsty—it is just that in order to satisfy the cravings of a discerning audience, a writer must create an augmented reading experience.

The horror itself can be supernatural in nature, psychological, paranormal, or techno (sometimes given a medical-biological slant that verges on sci-fi), or can embody personified occult/cultic entities. In addition to tales of vampires, were-creatures, demons, and ghosts, horror has featured such characters as the elemental slasher/stalker (conceived with or without mythic content), a variety of psychologically tormented souls, and just plain folks given over to splatter-house pastimes. Whatever the source of the horror, the tale is inherently more gripping and more profound when the horrific beast, force, or human foe has a mission, is a character with its own meaningful designs and insights—when something besides single-minded bloodlust is at play.

At times, the horror premise is analogous to a story of detection (especially in the initial setup); often the horror plot assumes the outlines of the thriller (particularly where there is a complex chase near the end); and sometimes the horror-story scenario ascribes to action-adventure elements. However, rather than delineating a detailed process of discovery (as in a typical mystery) or a protracted hunt throughout (as in the thriller), the horror plot typically sets up a final fight to the finish (until the sequel) that, for all its pyrotechnics and chills, turns on something other than brute force.

LITERARY FICTION

The term *literary* describes works that feature the writer's art expressed at its most refined levels; *literary fiction* describes works of literature in such forms as the novel, novella, novelette, short story, and short-shorts (also known as flash fiction). In addition to these fictional formats, literary works include poetry, essays, letters, dramatic works, and superior writing in all nonfiction varieties, covering such areas as travel, food, history, current affairs, and all sorts of narrative nonfiction, as well as reference works.

Literary fiction can adhere to the confines of any and all genres and categories, or suit no such designation. A work of fiction that is depicted as literary can (and should) offer the reader a multidimensional experience. *Literary* can designate word selection and imagery that is careful or inspired or that affects an articulated slovenliness. A literary character may be one who is examined in depth or is sparsely sketched to trenchant effect. Literature can postulate philosophical or cultural insights and portray fresh ideas in action. Literary works can feature exquisitely detailed texture or complete lack of sensory ambiance.

Structurally, literary fiction favors story and plot elements that are individualistic or astonishingly new, rather than tried-and-true. In some cases the plot as such does not appear important, but beware of quick judgment in this regard: Plotting may be subtle, as in picking at underlying psychology or revelation of character. And the plot movement may take place in the reader's head, as the progressive emotional or intellectual response to the story, rather than demonstrated in external events portrayed on paper.

To say that a work is literary can imply seriousness. Nonetheless, many serious works are not particularly sober, and literary reading should be a dynamic experience—pleasurably challenging, insightful, riveting, fun. A work that is stodgy and boring may not be literary at all, for it has not achieved the all-important aim of being fine reading.

Obviously, a book that is lacking with respect to engaging characters, consciousness of pace, and story development, but that features fancy wordplay and three-page sentences, is hardly exemplary of literary mastery. Though such a work may serve as a guidepost of advanced writing techniques for a specialized professional audience, it is perhaps a more limited artifice than is a slice-and-dice strip-and-whip piece that successfully depicts human passion and offers a well-honed story.

Commercial literature, like commercial fiction in general, is essentially a back-definition; *commercial literature* indicates works of outstanding quality written by authors who sell well, as opposed to just plain *literature*, which includes writers and works whose readership appeal has not yet expanded beyond a small core. Noncommercial literary works are staples of the academic press and specialized houses, as well as of selected imprints of major trade publishers.

When a literary author attracts a large readership or manages to switch from the list of a tiny publisher to a mammoth house, the publisher might decide a particular project is ripe for a shot at the big time and slate the writer for substantial attention, accompanied by a grand advance. If you look closely, you'll note that literary authors who enter the commercial ranks are usually not just good writers: Commercial literary works tap into the cultural pulse, which surges through the editorial avenues into marketing, promotion, and sales support.

In day-to-day commercial publishing discourse, to call a piece of work literary simply means it is well written. As a category designation, literary fiction implies that a particular book does not truly abide by provisos of other market sectors— though if the work under discussion does flash some category hooks, it might be referred to in such catch-terms as a *literary thriller* or *literary suspense*.

MAINSTREAM FICTION

A mainstream work is one that can be expected to be at least reasonably popular to a fairly wide readership. In a whim of industry parlance, to various people in publishing the label *mainstream* signifies a work that is not particularly noteworthy on any count—it's a work of fiction that's not literary, according to circumscribed tastes, and not something easily categorized with a targeted, predictable base of readership. They may not be particularly profitable either, especially if the publishing house is bent on creating best sellers. A mainstream work may therefore be seen as a risky proposition, rather than a relatively safe bet.

Let this be a cautionary note: In some publishing minds, a plain-and-simple mainstream book signifies midlist, which equals no sale. In a lot of publishing houses, midlist fiction, even if it's published, gets lost; many commercial trade houses won't publish titles they see as midlist (see Midlist Fiction).

A mainstream work may be a good read—but if that's all you can say about it, that's a mark against its prospects in the competitive arena. When a story is just a good story, the publisher doesn't have much of a sales slant to work with; in publishing terms that makes for a dismal enough prognosis for an editor or agent to pass.

If a manuscript has to sell on storytelling merits or general interest alone, it most likely won't sell to a major publisher at all. If mainstream fiction is what you've got, you, the writer, are advised to return to the workshop and turn the opus into a polished piece with a stunning attitude that can be regarded as commercial, or redesign the story line into a category format such as mystery, suspense, or thriller. A mainstream mystery or mainstream thriller may contain characters that aren't too wacko and milieus that aren't overly esoteric. Such works are eminently marketable, but you might suppress the mainstream designation in your query and just call your work by its category or genre moniker.

If you've got the gifts and perseverance to complete a solid story, and you find yourself about to say it's a mainstream book and no more, you'll be farther along faster if you work to avoid the midlist designation. Think commercially and write intrepidly.

Please note: Many editors and agents use the term *mainstream fiction* more or less synonymously with *commercial fiction* (see Commercial Fiction).

MIDLIST FICTION

Midlist books are essentially those that do not turn a more-than-marginal profit. That they show a profit at all might testify to how low the author's advance was (usually set so the publisher can show a profit based on projected sales). Midlist books may be category titles, literary works, or mainstream books that someone, somewhere believed had commercial potential (yet to be achieved).

The midlist is where no one wants to be: You get little if any promotion, few reviews, and no respect. Why publish this kind of book at all? Few publishers do. A midlist book was most likely not intended as such; the status is unacceptable unless the writer is being prepped for something bigger and is expected to break through soon. When a writer or series stays midlist too long, they're gone—the publishers move on to a more profitable use of their resources.

If the publishers don't want you, and the readers can't find you, you're better off going somewhere else, too. (See Commercial Fiction or any of the other category designations.)

MYSTERY

Many people use the term *mystery* to refer to the detective story (see Detective Fiction). When folks speak of traditional mysteries, they often mean a story in the British cozy mold, which can be characterized—but not strictly defined—by an amateur sleuth (often female) as protagonist, a solve-the-puzzle story line, minimal body count (with all violence performed offstage), and a restrained approach to language and tone. Sometimes, however, a reference to traditional mysteries implies not only cozies, but also includes stories of the American hard-boiled school, which are typified by a private eye (or a rogue cop), up-front violence as well as sex, and vernacular diction.

On the other hand, mysteries are seen by some to include all suspense fiction categories, thereby encompassing police procedurals, crime capers, thrillers, and even going so far afield as horror and some fantasy fiction.

In the interests of clarity, if not precision, here we'll say simply that a mystery is a story in which something of utmost importance to the tale is unknown or covert at the outset and must be uncovered, solved, or revealed along the way. (See Crime Fiction, Detective Fiction, Fantasy Fiction, Horror, Suspense Fiction, and Thriller.)

ROMANCE FICTION

The power of love has always been a central theme in literature, as it has in all arts, in all life. For all its importance to the love story genre, the term *romance* does not pertain strictly to the love element. The field can trace its roots through European medieval romances that depicted knights-errant and women in distress, which were as much tales of spiritual quest, politics, and action as love stories. The Romantic movement of the nineteenth century was at its heart emblematic of the heightened energy lent to all elements of a story, from human passion, to setting, to material objects, to psychological ramifications of simple acts.

Thanks to the writers and readers of modern romances, they've come a long way from the days of unadulterated heart-stopping bodice-rippers with pampered, egocentric heroines who long for salvation through a man. Today's romance most often depicts an independent, full-blooded female figure in full partnership with her intended mate.

Modern romance fiction is most assuredly in essence a love story, fueled by the dynamics of human relationships. From this core, writers explore motifs of career and family, topical social concerns, detective work, psychological suspense, espionage, and horror, as well as historical period pieces (including European medieval, Regency, and romances set in the American West) and futuristic tales. Romance scenarios with same-sex lovers are highlighted throughout the ranks of vanguard and literary houses, though this theme is not a priority market at most trade publishers or romance-specialist presses.

Among commercial lead titles tapped for best seller potential are those books that accentuate the appeal of romance within the larger tapestry of a fully orchestrated work. (See also Women's Fiction.)

SCIENCE FICTION

Take humankind's age-old longings for knowledge and enlightenment and add a huge helping of emergent technology, with the twist that science represents a metaphysical quest—there you have the setup for science fiction. Though the basic science fiction plot may resemble that of action-adventure tales, thrillers, or horror stories, the attraction for the reader is likely to be the intellectual or philosophical questions posed, in tandem with the space-age glitter within which it's set. In terms of character interaction, the storyline should be strong enough to stand alone when stripped of its technological trimmings.

In the future fiction genre, the elements of science fiction are all in place, but the science tends to be soft-pedaled, and the story as a whole is character-based. In a further variation, the post-apocalyptic vision presents the aftermath of a cataclysm (either engendered by technology or natural in origin) that sets the survivors loose on a new course that demonstrates the often-disturbing vicissitudes of social and scientific evolution. Such scenarios are generally set in the not-too-distant future, are usually Earth-based, or are barely interstellar, with recognizable (but perhaps advanced) technology as the norm.

Purity of genre is at times fruitless to maintain or define. Is Mary Shelley's *Frankenstein* a science fiction tale or a horror story, or is it primarily a literary work? Is Jules Verne's *20,000 Leagues under the Sea* science fiction or a techno-thriller—or a futuristic action-adventure?

Stories of extraterrestrial exploration, intergalactic warfare, and other exobiological encounters are almost certain to be placed within the science fiction category, until the day when such endeavors are considered elements of realism.

SUSPENSE FICTION

Suspense fiction embraces many literary idioms, with a wide range of genres and subdivisions categorized under the general rubric of suspense. Indeed, in broad terms, all novels contain suspense—that is, if the writer means for the reader to keep reading and reading, and reading on… way into the evening and beyond.

Suspense fiction has no precise formula that specifies certain character types tied to a particular plot template. It is perhaps most applicable for a writer to think of suspense as a story concept that stems from a basic premise of situational uncertainty. That is: Something horrible is going to happen! Let's read! Within suspense there is considerable latitude regarding conventions of style, voice, and structure. From new suspense writers, editors look for originality and invention and new literary terrain, rather than a copycat version of last season's breakout work.

However, that said, writers should note that editors and readers are looking for works in which virtually every word, every scene, every blip of dialog serves to heighten suspense. This means that all imagery—from the weather to social setting, to the food ingested by the characters—is chosen by the writer to induce a sense of unease. Each scene (save maybe the last one) is constructed to raise questions or leave something unresolved. Every sentence or paragraph contains a possible pitfall. A given conversational exchange demonstrates edgy elementals of interpersonal tension. Everything looks rosy in one scene? Gotcha! It's a setup to reveal later what hell lurks underneath. Tell me some good news? Characters often do just that, as a prelude to showing just how wrong things can get.

The jeopardy story (or, as is often the case, a woman-in-jeopardy story) reflects a premise, rather than being a genre per se. A tale of jeopardy—a character under continuous, increasing threat and (often) eventual entrapment—can incorporate what is otherwise a psychological suspense novel, a medical thriller, an investigatory trajectory, or slasher-stalker spree.

Additional subdivisions here include romantic suspense, in which a love relationship plays an essential or dominant role (see Romance Fiction); erotic suspense, which is not necessarily identical to neurotic suspense; and psychological suspense (see immediately following).

SUSPENSE/PSYCHOLOGICAL

When drifts of character, family history, or other psychodynamics are central to a suspense story's progress and resolution, the tale may aptly be typified as psychological. Sometimes superficial shticks or gimmicks suffice (such as when a person of a certain gender turns out to be cross-dressed—surprise!), but such spins work best when the suspense is tied to crucial issues the writer evokes in the characters' and readers' heads and then orchestrates skillfully throughout the storyline.

There are, obviously, cross-over elements at play here, and whether a particular work is presented as suspense, psychological suspense, or erotic suspense can be more of an advertising-copywriting decision than a determination on the part of editor or author.

THRILLER

The thriller category is exemplified more by plot structure than by attributes of character, content, or story milieu. A thriller embodies what is essentially an extended game of pursuit—a hunt, a chase, a flight worked fugue-like through endless variations.

At one point in the history of narrative art, thrillers were almost invariably spy stories, with international casts and locales, often set in a theater of war (hot or cold). With shifts in political agendas and technical achievement in the real world, the thriller formula has likewise evolved. Today's thriller may well involve espionage, which can be industrial or political, domestic or international. There are also thrillers that favor settings in the realms of medicine, the law, the natural environs, the human soul, and the laboratory; this trend has given rise to the respective genres of legal thriller, medical thriller, environmental thriller, thrillers with spiritual and mystical themes, and the techno-thriller—assuredly there are more to come.

The thriller story line can encompass elements of detection or romance and certainly should be full of suspense, but these genre-specific sequences are customarily expositional devices or may be one of many ambient factors employed to accentuate tension within the central thriller plot. When you see a dust jacket blurb that depicts a book as a mystery thriller, it likely connotes a work with a thriller plot trajectory that uses an investigatory or detective-work premise to prepare for the chase.

WESTERN FICTION

The tradition of Western fiction is characterized as much by its vision of the individualist ethic as it is by its conventional settings in the frontier milieu of the American West during the period from the 1860s to the 1890s, sometimes extending into the early 1900s. Though the image of the lone, free-spirited cowpoke with an internalized code of justice has been passed down along the pulp-paper trail, it has long been appreciated by historians that the life of the average itinerant ranch-hand of the day was anything but glamorous, anything but independent.

Whatever the historical record, editors by and large believe readers don't want to hear about the lackluster aspects of saddle tramps and dust-busting ruffians. Nevertheless, there have been inroads by books that display the historically accurate notions that a good chunk of the Western scene was inhabited by women and men of African American heritage, by those with Latino cultural affinities, by Asian expatriates, and by European immigrants for whom English was a second language, as well as by a diversity of native peoples.

Apart from the traditional genre Western, authors are equipped for a resurgence in a variety of novels with Western settings, most notably in the fields of mystery, crime, action-adventure, suspense, and future fiction. Among the newer Western novels are those replete with offbeat, unheroic, and downright antiheroic protagonists; and the standardized big-sky landscape has been superseded by backdrops that go against the grain.

Family sagas have long included at least a generation or two who drift, fight, and homestead through the Western Frontier. In addition, a popular genre of historical romance is set in the American West (see Romance Fiction).

Many contemporary commercial novels are set in the Western United States, often featuring plush resorts, urban and suburban terrain, as well as the remaining wide country. The wide variety of project ideas generated by writers, as well as the reader response to several successful ongoing mystery series with Western elements, indicates a lively interest out there.

WOMEN'S FICTION

When book publishers speak of women's fiction, they're not referring to a particular genre or story concept (even if they think they are). This category—if it is one—is basically a nod to the prevalence of fiction readers who are women. Women's fiction is a marketing concept. As an informal designation, women's fiction as a matter of course can be expected to feature strong female characters and, frequently, stories offered from a woman's perspective.

As for the writers of books in this category—many (if not most) are women, but certainly not all of them are; the same observation applies to readers. Men can and do read these works, too—and many professional male writers calculate potential readership demographics (including gender) as they work out details of story and plot.

In essence, what we've got is storytelling that can appeal to a broad range of readers, but may be promoted principally to the women's market. It makes it easier to focus the promotion and to pass along tips to the publisher's sales representatives.

Many women writers consider their work in abstract compositional terms, regardless of whom it is marketed to. Other women writers may be publicized as cultural pundits, perhaps as feminists, though they don't necessarily see their message as solely women-oriented. Are they women writers or simply writers? So long as sales go well, they may not even care.

Some women writers adopt the genderless pose of the literary renegade as they claw their way through dangerous domains of unseemly characterization, engage in breakthrough storytelling techniques, and explore emergent modes of love. (After all, how can a force of nature be characterized by sex?) Any and all of these female wordsmiths may find themselves publicized as women authors.

Romantic fiction constitutes one large sector of the women's market, for many of the conventions of romance tap into culturally significant areas of the love relationship of proven interest to women book buyers.

Descriptive genre phrases pop in and out of usage; some of them trip glibly from the tongue and are gone forevermore, while others represent established literary norms that endure: kitchen fiction, mom novels, family sagas, domestic dramas, historical romances, chick lit, lipstick fiction, erotica, and thrillers. When these popular titles are written, promoted, or both, in ways intended to pique the interest of women readers, whatever else they may be, they're automatically women's fiction.

SELF-PUBLISHING

JEFF HERMAN

Many books in print have sold hundreds of thousands of copies but will never appear on any lists, nor will they ever be seen in a bookstore, nor will the authors ever care. Why? Because these authors are self-publishers and make as much as a 90 percent profit margin on each copy they sell.

Their initial one-time start-up cost to get each of their titles produced may have been $15,000, but after that, each 5,000-copy print run of a hardcover edition costs about $1.25 per unit. The authors sell them for $25 each. When they do a high-volume corporate sale, they're happy to discount the books 20 percent or more off the $25 list price.

Now, we said that no bookstores are in the picture. Then how and where are the authors selling their books? The answer to this question is also the answer to whether it makes sense for you to self-publish. Here's what these authors do:

1. A well-linked website and Internet campaign designed to sell and up-sell.

2. A well-oiled corporate network, which translates into frequent high-volume orders by companies that distribute the book in-house as an educational tool or distribute them at large as a sales vehicle (customized printings are no problem).

3. Frequent public speaking events where backroom sales happen.

4. Frequent and self-generated publicity that's designed to promote the books and leads people to the website, a toll-free number, or both.

Obviously, most of us don't have this kind of in-house infrastructure, which brings us back to the most important question: How will you sell copies of your self-published book? If you don't have a realistic answer in place, then self-publishing may not be a viable option after all, or at least your initial expectations have to be reoriented.

Why can self-publishers make so much money? Because they get to keep it. Here's how a conventional book publisher's deal gets divided up:

*   Start with a trade paperback listed at $20.

* $10 goes to the retailer.

- $1.50 goes to the author.

- The first $15,000 goes to set the book up.

- $1.00 goes to printing each copy.

- $? Corporate overhead. (If the publisher overpaid on the advance, then this number goes higher.)

- $?? Publisher's profit. (This is a real wild card. If a publisher is an inefficient operation, then any profit may be out of reach. If too few books sell, there are only losses, no matter how lean and mean the publisher may be.)

A secondary source of no-overhead revenues for both publishers and self-publishers is ancillary rights, which include exports, translations, and audio editions.

What's clear is that the published author makes a tiny fraction of the per-unit sale versus what the self-publisher makes. But the publisher also absorbs all the risks. And then there's the distribution factor…

WHAT'S DISTRIBUTION?

AND WHY DO SELF-PUBLISHERS HAVE A TOUGH TIME WITH IT?

Because everyone else does, too. Distribution is the process that gets books onto shelves, theoretically. Strong distribution does not ensure that bookstores will elect to stock the title. Too many books are published, compared to the quantity and quality of shelf space to accommodate them. You can have a big-name publisher and an invisible book. Distribution only generates the potential for the book to be available in stores, and nonexistent distribution deletes that potential.

All established book publishers have proven distribution channels in place, consisting of warehouses, fulfillment and billing operations, and traveling or regional salespeople who pitch the stores.

Smaller-sized presses may not be able to afford all of that, so they'll pay a 15 percent commission to a large house to handle it for them, or they will retain an independent distributor that does nothing but distribute for small presses.

Brick-and-mortar bookstores are not eager to open accounts with self-publishers. It's too much of a hassle. Same goes for independent distributors.

Several brilliant self-publishing consultants have devised ways to bypass these distribution obstacles. Look for their books in the "Suggested Resources" section of this book.

Vanity publishing is for morons. I don't mean to be insulting. It's just that you end up spending so much more than necessary, all for the illusion that you've been published in the conventional sense. In truth, all you'll get out of the deal are boxes of expensive books that were probably not edited or well produced.

Hiring qualified editors, consultants, and so on, to help you make the best self-published book possible does not fall under the vanity label.

CAN SELF-PUBLISHERS SELL THEIR BOOKS TO CONVENTIONAL PUBLISHERS? SHOULD THEY WANT TO?

THE ANSWERS TO THE ABOVE QUESTIONS ARE "YES" AND "MAYBE."

For the sake of clarity, a "conventional" publisher is a house that publishes books that are written by other people, as opposed to having been written by the same people who own or run the house. From here on, I'll refrain from having to use the word *conventional*.

A self-published book may have sold as many as one million copies (a few actually have), but publishers may still deem the book as virtually unpublished. Why? Because publishers essentially focus on retail sales, and within retail sales, most of their focus is on bookstores. Few publishers have the capacity or mandate to sell books in other ways. Large non-store sales frequently happen, but generally because the buyers have come to the publisher to purchase or co-market the title in question, not because the publisher has been especially aggressive or innovative about generating such deals.

It follows that if a self-published book hasn't penetrated bookstore shelves in any meaningful way, then it can still be seen as virgin meat by publishers, even if sales have been tremendous beyond the stores. As publishers see it, the bookstore represents an entirely new population of potential consumers who have not yet been tapped by whatever other sales activities the author has in place. Consumers who purchase books in stores are different from consumers who purchase books in other ways.

Also, just because a book is very successful outside the stores, does not necessarily mean that it will achieve the same or any success in the stores. The reverse is also true. Why? The answer should be obvious in a general sense: Consumers who buy books through infomercials, websites, SPAMs, direct mail, and at public events, may never go to bookstores. Conversely, consumers who go to bookstores may not be nearly as reachable through these other channels.

At a minimum, publishers evaluate self-published books as if they are untested raw manuscripts, and all consideration will be based upon the publisher's sense of the work's salability in bookstores. At a maximum, the publisher will take into consideration the self-published book's sales history and the author's ability to manifest those results. If it's believed that the author can duplicate her proven capacity to sell books once the product makes it into the stores, then that will add leverage to the kind of deal the author can make with a publisher.

Even if a self-published book did not sell very many copies, a publisher may still be very happy to pick it up if they can see that it has unfulfilled potential once it has distribution behind it. Publishers do not have any expectations that self-publishers can or should be able to succeed by themselves. But once again, even a successful self-publisher may not be able to interest a publisher, if the publisher does not think that the success can be transferred to bookstores.

Why would a successful self-publisher even want to give up his rights to a publisher? After all, the per-copy profit margin greatly surpasses the per-copy royalty. However, there are several good reasons why going over to the "other side" can be a shrewd move. Basically, the self-publisher would want to achieve the best of both worlds. She would want to be able to buy copies of the book from her publisher at a very high discount, so that she can still sell the copies through non-bookstore channels at an excellent margin. At the same time, the publisher would be selling the book in her behalf through bookstores, something she was unable to do by herself, thereby generating new revenues that would not have been earned otherwise.

If one of the self-published author's goals is to use the book as a medium for selling additional goods and services, then maximizing distribution may actually be more crucial than the per-copy profits, and bookstores are a wonderful way to "meet" quality consumers.

What all of this reveals is that self-publishers have to develop a flexible form of logic when it comes to understanding who buys books, and who conventional publishers know how to sell books to. Pretty much everyone buys certain kinds of food and clothing in predictable ways. But until you immerse yourself into the "laws" of the book market, you may be confused at what first appears to be the relative randomness of what books people buy, and how and where they get bought. If you are able to accept the apparent nonsense of it all, and open your mind to seeing through the dissonance into the way the book universe functions, then 2 + 2 will again equal 4, and you will also end up being a bit smarter than you were before.

THE AMAZON FACTOR

Over the last couple of years, many self-publishers have discovered clever ways for their books to reach the top 100 ranking on Amazon; a few have even managed to hit the #1 spot. The same is also true for some conventionally published authors.

Several highly paid consultants have made it their specialty to teach authors how to manipulate Amazon sales. It basically comes down to getting as many people as possible to buy the book from Amazon on a given day, which artificially spikes its ranking. Due to the growing prevalence of this strategy, it's not uncommon for an obscure book to abruptly become an Amazon Best Seller for a single day, and then revert to its natural stratospheric ranking.

The Amazon sales probably have nil impact on brick-and-mortar sales, and the marketing costs to drive the sales probably eat whatever extra revenues are generated. So why do it? There are many valid reasons, such as: (1) Even fleeting visibility generated by a high ranking might attract lasting momentum and attention. (2) It's valuable and feels good to say and document that you were an Amazon Best Seller. (3) It might achieve specific professional benefits that go beyond simply selling a book.

THE GOOGLE FACTOR

Not only can none of us ever hide, but we can also make sure people find what we want them to.

Google has become the dominant search engine, to the extent that people now routinely say, "Google me/yourself/it/them." That could change, by the way. A few decades ago we used to say, "Make me a Xerox." I can't recall the last time I've seen a Xerox machine in person. Whatever the brand, search engines are obviously here to stay, and will become progressively more precise and invasive.

Like the Amazon Factor, many consultants have emerged who charge top dollar to help people achieve top Google rankings. You can also just pay Google a lot of money for high visibility. One common formula is to pay every time you get a "hit." However, this has been a big mistake for some entrepreneurs who ended up owing a lot of money for a huge surge of hits that failed to generate any actual sales. Everything has a learning curve, and we all try not to be the ones who get smashed into the curve while taking calculated risks. The bottom line is that search engines, and the Internet in general, are still relatively new frontiers for creative "small fries," which includes self-publishers, to score outsized results.

THE DIGITAL PUBLISHING FACTOR

The above information was written over the past few years but still remains accurate. What's changing is the immensity of opportunities to become a highly successful self-publisher with nominal financial investment. You don't need to understand how the technology works in order to exploit it, anymore than you need to understand how your phone works. You simply need to understand the intended functions, and then perhaps go beyond that by envisioning additional uses that haven't been contemplated, yet. Geeks-for-hire can always be found for not much money to conjure the programs.

The fast-growing ubiquity of hand-held reading devices has finally brought the future to digital publishing. For a decade, the so called e-book was mostly an over-hyped abstraction, because there wasn't a decent mass-market way to access them. Imagine the usefulness of TV programs if sets couldn't be purchased for less than $10,000, and were still blurry. E-books can now be easily purchased and read without needing to ever exist in physical form, and without ever needing to exist in bookstores or any other physical locations. All that's needed are ways to reach and persuade targeted consumers all over the world to purchase your digital product. The logistical means for accomplishing this are available to all. Obviously, it's up to each of us to build what people will buy, and to effectively let them know that they want to buy it. What constitutes good products, good service, and good marketing is timeless.

Bottom-line: for a few-hundred dollars you can retain an online service to convert whatever you write into a state-of-the art digital "book." What happens after that is anyone's guess, but be aware that 90 percent of self-published digital books sell less than 10 copies a year. That's a lot of publishing against nil commerce.

MYFACE, SPACEBOOK, TEXASSING, TWITTERING, BOREAGING, ANTI-SOCIAL MEDIA

I mean no disrespect. Like it or not, none of us who want to be current can afford to ignore social media, especially Facebook. If you want to communicate with as many people as possible without having to repeat yourself countless times, then you have to know where the most people can be found at any particular time. There are brilliant ways, most of them undiscovered, for how to exploit social media into massive digital selling machines Where there are people there are wallets; where there are wallets there is plastic; where there's plastic there's impulse opportunism. Follow the crumbs to find the loaves.

SELF-PUBLISHING OPTIONS FOR ASPIRING AUTHORS

JASON R. RICH

If you're an up-and-coming or aspiring author, but just can't seem to get your foot in the door at a major publishing house or capture the attention of a reputable literary agent to represent you, you're certainly not alone. Not only has the book publishing business become much more competitive in recent years, but bookstores are dramatically cutting back on the newly published book titles they order, which means publishing houses have to be even more selective about the authors they opt to work with and the book titles they publish.

Even if you can't get your book published and distributed right away through a major publisher, there has never been a better time in the entire history of publishing to self-publish your work. Thanks to print-on-demand technology, you can publish your book in hardcover or softcover format, and have it sold though Amazon.com, BN.com, and other online-based booksellers, for a relatively small investment.

There are several ways to self-publish your work and have it printed in traditional book form. The least expensive and easiest option is to work with an established print-on-demand publisher that offers a fee-based turnkey solution for publishing a manuscript and having it distributed online.

However, when you self-publish your work, you will be taking on the role of author, publisher, editor, marketing person, sales executive, and promotional coordinator, not to mention cover designer and fact-checker. Even if you're a highly skilled writer, for your self-published book to be successful and potentially be taken seriously by a major publisher or a literary agent in the future, it's essential that you not just write an amazing manuscript that will appeal to the book's target audience; you also need to have that book professionally edited, and pay a graphic designer to create a professional-looking book cover and page layout design for you.

Plus, if you plan to include photos or any type of graphics within your self-published book, they too need to look highly professional. Your goal as a self-published author should be to create a published book that is as good, if not better, from a content and appearance standpoint, than any book you'd see on the shelf of your favorite bookstore.

While many of the print-on-demand turnkey solutions offer a la carte manuscript editing, critiquing, page design, and cover design services, your best bet is to hire experienced freelance professionals to work with you in order to achieve your desired results. Then, use the services of a print-on-demand publishing company to publish and distribute your book, and arrange to have it sold through the major online booksellers.

The trick to creating a popular self-published book, however, involves much more than writing an amazing manuscript and having it printed. You also need to truly understand who the target audience is for your book, cater to that reader, and have the know-how and wherewithal to self-promote and advertise your book to that niche audience in order to generate sales.

Simply having a self-published book available on Amazon.com and BN.com, for example, is only the first step. As a self-published author, it's also your responsibility to promote your book and sell it. This is a lot easier if you already have a following, or a way to easily and inexpensively promote and advertise your work to your intended audience.

You'll quickly discover that it's not financially viable as a self-published author to invest a fortune in paid advertising for your book. Thus, you'll need to devise no-cost or low-cost ways to generate book sales, through personal appearances, public relations efforts, getting book reviews published in the media, getting yourself interviewed by the media, or through the use of online social networking sites like Facebook and Twitter.

Also, be sure to seek out well-known bloggers with established and dedicated followers and ask them to write reviews of your book within their blogs, and perhaps to include an interview with you as the author as well.

Plus, as you create your book listings for the major online booksellers like Amazon.com or BN.com, fully utilize keywords and well-written book descriptions to ensure that people who search for a book that relates to your topic will easily find your book. Utilizing keywords and well-written descriptions is also useful if you opt to launch your own website or blog as a promotional tool, or utilizing inexpensive keyword-based advertising via Google AdWords (www.google.com/adwords), Microsoft Advertising on Yahoo! and Bing (www.advertising.microsoft.com/home), or Facebook (www.facebook.com/advertising), that is highly targeted, in order to generate interest in your book.

Before you invest any money in self-publishing your book, however, develop a detailed business plan and budget, keeping in mind that beyond hiring an editor, cover designer, and print-on-demand publisher, you will also need to invest time and money into advertising and promoting your book in order to generate sales. Yet, you still need to generate a profit from the sale of your books, keeping in mind that between the print-on-demand publisher and the online bookseller, your costs will be up to 60 or even 70 percent of the book's cover price.

As a self-published author, it's important to have realistic expectations. In reality, it is almost certain that your self-published book will not get mainstream bookstore distribution, no matter how good the book is. Also, unless you have a proven way to inexpensively and consistently generate sales, don't expect to sell more than a few hundred, or if you work really hard, a few thousand printed copies of your self-published book.

In other words, for the majority of authors who pursue the self-publishing route, this is not a get-rich-quick business model. Instead, being a published author can be used as a way to boost your professional reputation and position yourself as an expert in your field, which can lead to higher earnings or career advancement.

Self-publishing a book can also lead to higher paying freelance writing or consulting jobs. Depending on its topic, your book can be used as a sales or promotional tool for your company, or as a way to generate leads for a service-driven business. The possibilities are limited only by your creativity, determination, and how hard you're willing to work to promote and sell your book once you get it published.

Once you decide to pursue self-publishing and opt to publish your manuscript as a traditional hardcover or softcover book, there are many companies that can serve as your print-on-demand publisher, including Trafford (www.trafford.com), Amazon CreateSpace (www.createspace.com), Lulu (www.lulu.com), and iUniverse (www.iUniverse.com).

Each of these companies offer slightly different services at different price points, so it's important to analyze your needs, define your objectives, and then choose a print-on-demand publisher that offers the best solution or publishing package for you, at an affordable rate.

You should also understand that if your ultimate goal is to have your book picked up by a major publisher, this is still possible. The majority of major publishers don't consider self-published books to have been previously published, since they don't get traditional bookstore distribution. However, if through your own sales efforts for the self-published edition of your book you can prove to a publisher there is a demand for your work, this will certainly help you get noticed.

THE E-BOOK ALTERNATIVE

Within the past two or three years, literally tens of millions of people have purchased e-book readers, including the various models of the Amazon Kindle, the Barnes & Noble Nook, and Apple's iPad. As a result, the e-book business has become extremely viable and is very inexpensive and easy for a self-published author to break into.

Once your manuscript is created as a Microsoft Word document, for example, you can hire a company for just a few hundred dollars to custom format your edited manuscript into an e-book format that is Kindle, Nook, and/or iPad compatible. These same companies can also be hired to get your e-book listed and sold directly on Amazon.com, BN.com, and Apple's iBookstore, typically within a week or so.

While readers will be able to find your e-book using a keyword search and then purchase and download it to be read on their e-book reader, it remains your responsibility as a self-published e-book author to promote and advertise your book in order to generate sales.

Self-publishing an e-book is faster and cheaper than using a print-on-demand publisher to create a softcover or hardcover edition of your book. In fact, Amazon offers its Kindle Direct Publishing Program, which allows you to format a Word document into Kindle e-book format yourself, and get the e-book listed and sold on Amazon.com. To learn more about this service, visit Kindle Direct Publishing (kdp .amazon.com/self-publishing/signin).

The alternative is to hire an e-book publishing turnkey solution, such as BookBaby (www.bookbaby.com), that will provide all of the fee-based services you need to publish and distribute your pre-edited e-book through all of the major online-based booksellers, and make it available in all popular e-book reader formats.

If you already have your e-book preformatted in an acceptable e-pub format, the cost to get started distributing your book through BookBaby, which gets it listed on Amazon.com, BN.com, iBookstore.com, and other online booksellers, is just $99.00 (as of this writing).

Remember, simply writing the manuscript for an e-book is just the first step. To give your book credibility and position yourself as a professional writer/author, you will definitely want to hire an editor or proofreader to review your manuscript, and hire a professional graphic designer to create a visually appealing e-book cover graphic.

Of course, if you discover or can create a demand for your work, you can always use a print-on-demand publisher to create a hardcover or softcover edition of your book, and also publish it in all popular e-book formats.

Self-publishing offers a wonderful way for you to establish yourself as a writer and author, while maintaining 100 percent control over your book project from start to finish. As a self-published author, you retain the copyright related to your work. Be sure, however, to research your various options, develop your business plan, and pursue the best opportunities based on the realistic goals you have for your book.

Jason R. Rich (www.JasonRich.com, Twitter: @JasonRich7) is the best-selling author of more than 48 books, 3 of which have been self-published by print-on-demand publishers, and also made available in e-book form. He is also the author of *Self-Publishing for Dummies* (Wiley), and a frequent contributor to numerous national magazines, major daily newspapers, and popular websites.

THE WRITER'S JOURNEY
THE PATH OF THE SPIRITUAL MESSENGER

DEBORAH LEVINE HERMAN

If you have decided to pursue writing as a career instead of as a longing or a dream, you might find yourself focusing on the goal instead of the process. When you have a great book idea, you may envision yourself on a book-signing tour or as a guest on a talk show before you've written a single word.

It's human nature to look into your own future, but too much projection can get in the way of what the writing experience is all about. The process of writing is like a wondrous journey that can help you cross a bridge to the treasures hidden within your own soul. It is a way for you to link with God and the collective storehouse of all wisdom and truth, as it has existed since the beginning of time.

Many methods of writing bring their own rewards. Some people can produce exceptional prose by using their intellect and their mastery of the writing craft. They use research and analytical skills to help them produce works of great importance and merit.

Then there are those who have learned to tap into the wellspring from which all genius flows. They are the inspired ones who write with the intensity of an impassioned lover. They are the spiritual writers who write because they have to. They may not want to, they may not know how to, but something inside them is begging to be let out. It gnaws away at them until they find a way to set it free. Although they may not realize it, spiritual writers are engaged in a larger spiritual journey toward ultimate self-mastery and unification with God.

Spiritual writers often feel as if they're taking dictation. Spiritual writing has an otherworldly feeling and can teach writers things they would otherwise not have known. It is not uncommon to read something after a session in "the zone," and question if indeed you had written it.

Writing opens you up to new perspectives, much like self-induced psychotherapy. Although journals are the most direct route for self-evaluation, fiction and nonfiction also serve as vehicles for a writer's growth. Writing helps the mind expand to the limits of the imagination.

Anyone can become a spiritual writer, and there are many benefits to doing so, not the least of which is the development of your soul. On a more practical level, it is much less difficult to write with flow and fervor than it is to be bound by the limitations of logic and analysis. If you tap into the universal source, there is no end to your potential creativity.

The greatest barrier to becoming a spiritual writer is the human ego. We treat our words as if they were our children—only we tend to be neurotic parents. Children are not owned by parents, but rather must be loved, guided, and nurtured until they can carry on, on their own.

The same is true for our words. If we try to own and control them like property, they will be limited by our vision for them. We will overprotect them and will not be able to see when we may be taking them in the wrong direction for their ultimate well-being. Another ego problem that creates a barrier to creativity is our need for constant approval and our tendency toward perfectionism. We may feel the tug toward free expression, but will erect blockades to ensure appropriate style and structure. We write with a "schoolmarm" hanging over our shoulders, waiting to tell us what we are doing wrong.

Style and structure are important to ultimate presentation, but that is what editing is for. Ideas and concepts need to flow like water in a running stream. The best way to become a spiritual writer is to relax and have fun. If you are relaxed and pray for guidance, you'll be open to intuition and higher truth. However, writers tend to take themselves too seriously, which causes anxiety, which exacerbates fear, which causes insecurity, which diminishes our self-confidence and leads ultimately to mounds of crumpled papers and lost inspiration. You are worthy. Do not let insecurity prevent you from getting started and following through.

If you have faith in a Supreme Being, the best way to begin a spiritual writing session is with the following writer's prayer:

Almighty God (Jesus, Allah, Great Spirit, etc.), Creator of the Universe, help me to become a vehicle for your wisdom so that what I write is of the highest purpose and will serve the greatest good. I humbly place my (pen/keyboard/Dictaphone) in your hands so that you may guide me.

Prayer helps to connect you to the universal source. It empties the mind of trash, noise, and potential writer's blocks. If you are not comfortable with formal prayer, a few minutes of meditation will serve the same purpose. Spiritual writing as a process does not necessarily lead to a sale. The fact is that some people have more commercial potential than others. Knowledge of the business of writing will help you make a career of it. If you combine this with the spiritual process, it can also bring you gratification and inner peace. If you trust the process of writing and make room for the journey, you will grow and achieve far beyond your expectations.

Keep in mind that you are not merely a conduit. You are to be commended and should take pride in the fact that you allow yourself to be used as a vessel for the Divine. You are the one who is taking the difficult steps in a world full of obstacles and challenges. You are the one who is sometimes so pushed to the edge that you have no idea how you go on. But you do. You maintain your faith and you know that there is a reason for everything. You may not have a clue what it is… but you have an innate sense that all of your experiences are part of some bigger plan. At minimum they create good material for your book.

In order to be a messenger of the Divine you have to be a vessel willing to get out of the way. You need to be courageous and steadfast in your beliefs because God's truth is your truth. When you find that your inner truth does not match that of other people, you need to be strong enough to stay true to yourself. Your soul, that inner spark that connects you to all creation, is your only reliable guide. You will receive pressure from everywhere. But your relationship with your creator is as personal as your DNA. You will be a house divided if you accept things other people tell you to please them while sensing that it does not resonate with your spirit.

When you do find your inner truth your next challenge is to make sure that you do not become the person that tries to tell everyone else what to believe. When a spiritual writer touches that moment of epiphany it is easy to become God-intoxicated. There is no greater bliss than to be transformed by a connection to the source of all creation. It is not something that can be described. It is individual. This is why it is important for a spiritual writer to protect this experience for another seeker. The role of a spiritual messenger who manifests his or her mission through the written word, is to guide a person to the threshold of awakening. Bring them to the gate but allow God to take them the rest of the way. Your job is to make the introduction. From there the relationship is no longer your responsibility. Your task is to shine the light brightly for some other seeker to find it.

It is difficult to believe so strongly in something while feeling unable to find anyone to listen to you. If you try too hard you might find that there are others who will drain your energy and life force, while giving nothing in return. They may ridicule you and cause you to step away from your path. You do not have to change the world by yourself. You need to do your part. Whether it is visible or as simple as helping someone know you care, you are participating in elevating the world for the better. Some people like it exactly as it is. There are those who thrive on chaos and the diseases of the soul. Your job as a spiritual writer is to protect your spirit as you would your own child. Do not give away your energy; make it available for those who truly want it and will appreciate it. When you write, expect nothing in return. While following the protocols of the business world, do not set your goal too high as needing to transform people's souls. If you do, you will elevate your responsibility beyond the capability of simple humans. If you do the groundwork, God will do the rest.

The world of the spiritual writer can be a very lonely place. It is easier to love God, creation, and humanity than it is to feel worthy of receiving the love in return. Those of us who devote our energy to wanting to make a difference through our writing forget that God has given us this gift as a reward for our goodness, faith, and love. It is a two-way street. What we give we can also receive. It maintains the balance. It replenishes our energy so we can continue to grow and fulfill our individual destiny. We are all loved unconditionally. God knows everything we have ever thought, done, or even thought about doing. We judge ourselves far more harshly than God ever would. We come into this world to learn and to fix our "miss" takes. We only learn through object lessons. We have free will. Sometimes we have to burn our hands on the stove several times before we learn that it is too hot to handle. I personally have lived my life with the two-by-four-on-the-head method. While not recommended, it is the only way I have been able to learn some of my more difficult lessons. I have often considered wearing a helmet.

When we connect with our inner truth we can become intoxicated with our own greatness. It is a very heady thing to write, especially if we are able to see our name in print. If we have people listening to what we have to say, we can believe that we are the message and forget that we are merely the messenger. Spiritual writers need to start every day praying for humility. If we don't, and there is danger that we are going to put ourselves before the purity of Divine truth, we will not be able to be the pure vessel that we had hoped to become. The universe has methods of protecting itself. We will experience humiliation to knock us down a few pegs to give us the opportunity to get over ourselves. I have experienced many instances of humorous humiliation such as feeling amazed with myself, only to literally splat on my face by tripping over air. No injury, except to my inflated pride. God has a sense of humor.

On a more serious note, spiritual messengers who are taken in by their own egos are vulnerable to negativity. The information they convey becomes deceiving and can help take people off their paths. This is why spiritual writers should always begin each session with a prayer to be a vessel for the highest of the high and for the greater good. While readers have the choice to discern the wheat from the chaff, in this time of rapid spiritual growth, it is important to help seekers stay as close to their paths as possible. There is no time for major detours. We all have a lot of work to do.

We are all here to improve the lives of each other. We are blessed with living in an information age where we can communicate quickly and clearly with one another. However, technology also serves to make us separate. We all cling to our ideas without respecting the paths of one another. We are all headed to the same place, the center of the maze, where there is nothing and everything all at once. We are all headed for the place of pure love that binds all of us to one another. We don't want to get caught up with trivial arguments about who is right and who is wrong. Our goal right now needs to be how to foster everyone's path to his or her own higher truth. We share what we have so others can find it, without wasting time arguing the point to win them to our side. Too many battles have been fought over who is the most right. We all come from the same source.

When it comes down to it, spiritual writers are the prophets of today. You are here to give God direct access to our world in ways that we as human beings can understand. We need to listen to the essence of the message rather than focusing on who is the greater prophet. In the business of writing, there is no sin in profit. But in the mission of writing, one must not forget that we all answer to the same boss and serve the same master.

You are also a messenger. When you agree to be a spiritual writer, you are also agreeing to bring light into the world. This is no small commitment. Remember to keep your ego out of it. While it is important to learn to promote and support your work, you must not forget that you are the messenger and not the message. If you keep this at the center of your heart and remember that you serve the greater good, you are a true spiritual writer who is honoring the call. May God bless you and guide you always.

HOW TO MAXIMIZE YOUR BLOGGING EFFORTS

ARIELLE FORD

I am often asked how people can increase their platform when seeking a publisher for their books. Any aspiring writer would benefit from starting a blog before writing a book or book proposal and before creating an overall promotion plan for their online marketing. This gives you access to a built-in audience and helps you develop material you know will be of interest to your audience. Blogging is not difficult. Intuitively I understood the importance of blogging for increasing traffic to my site, growing my e-mail list, search engine optimization, earning expert status, and the list goes on. On a practical level I initially saw blogging as one more platform on which I needed to create value-added content. Don't get me wrong, I love providing support to people on the topics I feel very passionate about, but I was not sure I could stay on top of it or how to integrate social networking into my marketing plan. I was happy to learn that I was wrong on both points and if I can find a process that works for me and if I can make heads or tails of it all, so can you! I would like to share my strategies and some of the results I have seen so far.

CREATING YOUR BLOGGING STRATEGY

Stay on topic: Brand expansion through blogging requires that you, well, blog about your brand! Remain consistent with your messaging, your tone, and your reason for sharing with your audience. If you feel strongly about a topic or event outside of your industry, always tie it back with appropriate relevance and provide insight related to how it may impact your reader. Use self-promotion blogs sparingly, as your visitors will get bored and annoyed by this and they will not return.

Plan ahead: Although it may seem difficult at first to brainstorm multiple blog topics in advance, it is important to plan out what and when you will blog so that you stay on track and hold yourself accountable. Look at some of the comments people have been making on your social networking sites for inspiration. Of course there will be times that a particular current event may spur your interest for blogging and that's great. On your editorial calendar,

ADVICE FOR WRITERS

remember to always plan a blog before a book signing, speaking engagement, or teleclass to create a buzz. Also post a blog within 48 hours after an event so that you can share a great audience question and provide your answer for those who did not attend.

Create a community: Whenever appropriate, elicit comments to your blog post. If your blog is a "How to" or "10 Steps…" ask your readers what has worked best for them. By doing this you create a discussion and community from which you and others can learn. Who knows, you may even come up with another blog idea, or even your next book!

Blog page effectiveness: Make it easy for any visitor to connect with you once they are on your blogging page. If you are program-savvy do it yourself or have someone else add a Twitter, Facebook, or LinkedIn button to your blog page. Also, your subscriber form should be very visible on this page because once the visitor likes what you have to share and how you share it, they will want to learn more from you.

Creating social media infrastructure: If you are taking the time and mental energy to create great content on your blogs, it would be a shame if no one knew about it or read it. I use my Facebook personal profile, Fan Page, and Twitter accounts to announce a new post and drive traffic to the blog.

Craft interesting status updates (at least five per blog post) and use a shortened url account such as Bit.ly to track how many people are going to your blog (Click Through Rates).

Have your blogs automatically posted to your Facebook account through the networked blog feature and the auto blog import via the Notes feature.

Use a scheduling account such as SocialOomph to preplan the posting of your updates for time efficiency and Retweet effectiveness (Hint: there are certain times of the day and week that are the best for getting great Click Through Rates and Retweets, as I mentioned in a blog post on *The Huffington Post*).

My results: Within only six weeks of consistent blogging, I saw my Click Through Rates grow from 150 to as high as 863. My Facebook fans increased by 60 percent and my e-newsletter consistently obtained new subscribers. I have also seen colleagues earn solid teleclass and webinar participation as a result of regularly posting value-added content. Strong results will not happen overnight. You will gain traction if you continue to be present and add value to your community before they will become loyal fans and engaged consumers. There is no need to start from scratch trying to figure this all out on your own. Find a blogging buddy who can help with brainstorming, accountability, and collaboration or seek out the support of a professional.

Arielle Ford is a leading pioneer and personality in the personal growth and contemporary spirituality movement. For the past 25 years she has been living, teaching, and promoting consciousness through all forms of media. Her stellar career includes years as a prominent book publicist, author, literary agent, TV lifestyle reporter, television producer, Sirius radio host, publishing consultant, relationship expert, speaker, columnist, and blogger for the Huffington Post. www.arielleford.com

Arielle was instrumental in launching the careers of many *New York Times* best-selling self-help authors including Deepak Chopra, Jack Canfield, Mark Victor Hansen, Neale Donald Walsch, and Debbie Ford. She was the publicist for dozens of other top selling authors such as Wayne Dyer, Gary Zukav, Dean Ornish, Joan Borysenko, Louise Hay, Jorge Cruise, and don Miguel Ruiz.

She is a gifted writer and the author of seven books including *The Soulmate Secret*, now in 21 languages.

Arielle is the creator of the at-home publishing study course Everything You Should Know about Publishing, Publicity, and Building a Platform (everythingyoushouldknow.com) and the annual www.21stcenturybookmarketing.com event, which is the premiere book-marketing event for authors.

ADVICE FOR WRITERS

REJECTED...AGAIN

THE PROCESS AND THE ART OF PERSEVERANCE

JEFF HERMAN

Trying to sell your writing is in many ways similar to perpetually applying for employment, and it's likely you will run into many walls. That can hurt. But even the Great Wall of China has a beginning and an end—for it's simply an external barrier erected for strategic purposes. In my experience, the most insurmountable walls are the ones in our heads. Anything that is artificially crafted can and will be overcome by people who are resourceful and determined enough to do it.

Naturally, the reality of rejection cannot be completely circumvented. It is, however, constructive to envision each wall as a friendly challenge to your resourcefulness, determination, and strength. There are many people who got through the old Berlin Wall because for them it was a challenge and a symbol—a place to begin, not stop.

The world of publishing is a potentially hostile environment, especially for the writer. Our deepest aspirations can be put to rest without our having achieved peace or satisfaction. But it is within each of us to learn about this special soil and blossom to our fullest. No rejection is fatal until the writer walks away from the battle, leaving the written work behind, undefended and unwanted.

WHY MOST REJECTION LETTERS ARE SO EMPTY

What may be most frustrating are the generic word-processed letters that say something like: "not right for us." Did the sender read any of your work? Did that person have any personal opinions about it? Could she not have spared a few moments to share her thoughts?

As an agent, it's part of my job to reject the vast majority of the submissions I receive. And with each rejection, I know I'm not making someone happy. On the other hand, I don't see spreading happiness as my exclusionary purpose. Like other agents and editors, I make liberal use of the generic rejection letter.

Here's why: Too much to do, too little time. There just isn't sufficient time to write customized, personal rejection letters. To be blunt about it, the rejection process isn't a profit center; it does consume valuable time that otherwise could be used to make profits. The exceptions to this rule are the excessive-fee-charging operations that make a handsome profit with each rejection.

In most instances, the rejection process is "giveaway" time for agents and editors since it takes us away from our essential responsibilities. Even if no personal comments are provided with the rejections, it can require many hours a week to process an ongoing stream of rejections. An understaffed literary agency or publishing house may feel that it's sufficiently generous simply to assign a paid employee the job of returning material as opposed to throwing it away. (And some publishers and literary agencies do in practice simply toss the greater portion of their unsolicited correspondence.) Agents and editors aren't *Dear Abby*, though many of us wish we had the time to be.

Therefore, your generic rejection means no more and no less than that particular agent/editor doesn't want to represent/publish you and (due to the volume of office correspondence and other pressing duties) is relaying this information to you in an automated, impersonal way. The contents of the letter alone will virtually never reveal any deeper meanings or secrets. To expect or demand more than this might be perceived as unfair by the agent/editor.

KNOW WHEN TO HOLD, KNOW WHEN TO FOLD

It's your job to persevere. It's your mission to proceed undaunted. Regardless of how many books about publishing you've read, or how many writers' conferences you've attended, it's up to no one but you to figure out how and when to change your strategy if you want to win at the book-publishing game.

If your initial query results are blanket rejects, then it may be time to back off, reflect, and revamp your query presentation or overall approach. If there are still no takers, you may be well advised to reconceive your project in light of its less-than-glorious track record. Indeed, there might even come a time for you to use your experience and newfound knowledge of what does and doesn't grab attention from editors and agents—and move on to that bolder, more innovative idea you've been nurturing in the back of your brain.

AN AUTHENTIC SUCCESS STORY

Several years ago, two very successful, though unpublished, gentlemen came to see me with a nonfiction book project. My hunch was that it would make a lot of money. The writers were professional speakers and highly skilled salespeople, so I arranged for them to meet personally with several publishers, but to no avail.

All told, we got more than 20 rejections—the dominant reason being that editors thought the concept and material weak. Not ones to give up, and with a strong belief in their work and confidence in their ability to promote, the authors were ultimately able to sell the book for a nominal advance to a small Florida publishing house—and it was out there at last, published and in the marketplace.

As of this writing, *Chicken Soup for the Soul*, by Jack Canfield and Mark Victor

Hansen, has sold millions of copies and has been a *New York Times* best seller for several years straight. Furthermore, this initial success has generated many best-selling sequels.

We all make mistakes, and the book rascals in New York are definitely no exception. Most important, Canfield and Hansen didn't take no for an answer. They instinctively understood that all those rejections were simply an uncomfortable part of a process that would eventually get them where they wanted to be. And that's the way it happened.

A RELENTLESS APPROACH TO SELLING YOUR BOOK

I once heard a very telling story about Jack Kerouac, one from which we can all learn something. Kerouac was a notorious literary figure who reached his professional peak in the 1950s. He's one of the icons of the Beat Generation and is perhaps best remembered for his irreverent and manic travel-memoir-as-novel *On the Road*.

SALES TALES FROM THE BEAT GENERATION

The story begins when Kerouac was a young and struggling writer, ambitiously seeking to win his day in the sun. He was a charismatic man and had acquired many influential friends. One day Kerouac approached a friend who had access to a powerful publishing executive. Kerouac asked the friend to hand-deliver his new manuscript to the executive, with the advice that it be given prompt and careful consideration.

When the friend handed the manuscript to the executive, the executive took one glance and began to laugh. The executive explained that two other people had hand-delivered the very same manuscript to him within the last few weeks.

What this reveals is that Kerouac was a master operator. Not only did he manage to get his work into the right face, but also he reinforced his odds by doing it redundantly. Some might say he was a manipulator, but his works were successfully published, and he did attain a measure of fame in his own day, which even now retains its luster.

...AND FROM THE BEATEN

I will now share a very different and more recent story. It starts in the 1940s, when a best-selling and Pulitzer Prize–winning young-adult book was published. Titled *The Yearling*, this work was made into an excellent movie starring Gregory Peck. The book continues to be a good backlist seller.

In the 1990s, a writer in Florida, where *The Yearling*'s story takes place, performed an experiment. He converted the book into a raw double-spaced manuscript and changed the title and author's name—but the book's contents were not touched. He then submitted the entire manuscript to about 20 publishers on an unagented/

unsolicited basis. I don't believe the submissions were addressed to any specific editors by name.

Eventually, this writer received many form rejections, including one from the book's actual publisher. Several publishers never even responded. A small house in Florida did offer to publish the book.

What is glaringly revealed by this story? That even a Pulitzer Prize–winning novel will never see the light of day if the writer doesn't use his brain when it's time to sell the work.

HOW TO BEAT YOURSELF & HOW NOT TO

People who are overly aggressive do get a bad rap. As an agent and as a person, I don't like being hounded by salespeople—whether they're hustling manuscripts or insurance policies. But there are effective ways to be heard and seen without being resented. Virtually anyone can scream loud enough to hurt people's ears. Only an artist understands the true magic of how to sell without abusing those who might buy. And we all have the gift to become artists in our own ways.

Here's an example of what not to do:

It's late in the day and snowing. I'm at my desk, feeling a lot of work-related tension. I answer the phone. It's a first-time fiction writer. He's unflinchingly determined to speak endlessly about his work, which I have not yet read.

I interrupt his meaningless flow to explain courteously that while I will read his work, it's not a good time for me to talk to him. But he will not let me go; he's relentless, which forces me to be rude and cold as I say "Bye" and hang up.

I then resent the thoughtless intrusion upon my space and time. And I may feel bad about being inhospitable to a stranger, whatever the provocation.

Clearly, the previous scenario does not demonstrate a good way to initiate a deal. I'm already prejudiced against this writer before reading his work.

Here's a more effective scenario.

Same conditions as above. I answer the telephone. The caller acknowledges that I must be busy and asks for only 30 seconds of my time. I grant them. He then begins to compliment me; he's heard I'm one of the best, and so forth. I'm starting to like this conversation; I stop counting the seconds.

Now he explains that he has an excellent manuscript that he is willing to give me the opportunity to read and would be happy to send it right over. He then thanks me for my time and says good-bye.

I hang up, feeling fine about the man; I'll give his manuscript some extra consideration.

In conclusion, relentless assertiveness is better than relentless passivity. But you want your style to be like Julie Andrews's singing voice in *The Sound of Music*, as opposed to a 100-decibel boom box on a stone floor.

TRIBULATIONS OF THE UNKNOWN WRITER (AND POSSIBLE REMEDIES)

JEFF HERMAN

Many nations have memorials that pay homage to the remains of their soldiers who died in battle and cannot be identified. In a way, it seems that the legions of unpublished writers are the *Unknown Writers*. As has been expressed elsewhere in this book, it cannot be assumed that the unknown writer and her unknown work are of any lesser quality than those works that achieve public exposure and consumption, any more than those soldiers who died were less adept than those who got to go home. To the contrary, perhaps they were more adept, or at least more daring, and therefore paid the ultimate price.

No warrior aspires to become an unknown soldier, let alone a dead soldier. Every soldier prefers to believe that her remains would be known; would perhaps even explain what happened towards the end, and would be presented to her loved ones for final and proper farewells. It is much the same for the writer. No writer worth her ink wants to believe that her legacy of expression will be forever unknown. Even if her other accomplishments in life are magnificent, it is still those words on the pages that she wants revealed, preferably while she's still around to experience and enjoy it.

Obviously, in life and beyond, there are many unknown writers. That's just the way it is.

It may just be that the fear of living and dying as an unknown writer is the extra push you need to bring your work to the first step on the road to publication—getting your work noticed by a publishing professional, be it agent or editor. If you are still reading this essay, then it is absolutely true that you are willing to try harder to reach that goal. In recognition and respect for your aspirations and determination, I will provide additional insights and strategies to help you help yourself avoid the fate of the unknown writer.

But let's make sure that your goals, at least in the early stages of your publishing life, are reasonably measured. It is suitable to imagine yourself one day at the top of the publishing food chain. Why not? Genuine humans have to be there at any given moment, so why not you? However, it is improbable that you will arrive there in one step. Your odds will be enhanced through your dedication to learning, calculating, and paying the necessary dues. For the purposes of the lesson at hand, I will encourage you to focus on the more humble goal of simply transitioning to the realm of being a published writer. For sure, there is more to do after that, but we will leave those lessons for other places in this book, and for other books.

WAYS TO BE SEEN IN A CROWD

Established literary agencies, including yours truly's, are inundated with unsolicited query letters (both hard-copy and digital), proposals, pieces of manuscripts, and entire manuscripts. This stream of relentless *intake* easily runs from 50 to 150 uninvited submissions per week, depending on how visible the agency in question is to the world of writers at large. These numbers do not account for the many works that the agency has requested or was expecting from existing clients. Frankly, many successful agents are simply not hungry for more than what they already have, and make efforts to be as invisible and unavailable as possible.

The above scenario only tells of the agencies. It's likely that the publishers, both big and small, are receiving the same in even greater volumes, which is of dubious value since many publishers will simply not consider anything that is unsolicited or unrepresented, period.

How can your work go from being an unseen face in the crowd to a jack-in-the-box whose presence cannot be denied? Here are some suggested steps.

1. Don't merely do what everyone else is already doing. That doesn't mean that you should entirely refrain from doing what's conventional or recommended. After all, the beaten track is beaten for a reason: It has worked before and it will work again. But be open to the possibility of pursuing specific detours along the way. Look upon these excursions as a form of calculated wild-catting. If nothing happens, or if you end up puncturing the equivalent of someone's septic tank, then just take it as a lesson learned.

2. Make yourself be seen. A pile of No. 10 envelopes is simply that, and none of the component envelopes that form the pile are seen. Someone once sent me a letter shaped like a circle. It could not be grouped with that day's quota of query letters; it demanded to be seen and touched and dealt with, immediately. Another time I received a box designed as a treasure chest, which contained an unsolicited proposal. I did not appreciate receiving a bag of white powder with a certain proposal. The powder was flushed down the toilet and the manuscript returned without being read.

3. Be generous. Most submissions are actually a demand for time, attention, and energy. During a long day in the middle of a stressful week in the throes of a month in hell, none of those submissions will be seen as good faith opportunities from honorable people. To the contrary, they will feel like innumerable nuisances springing forth from the armpits of manic brain-eating zombies, with drool and odor. I can recall opening a package to find a handwritten card from a stranger telling me how much he appreciated my

ADVICE FOR WRITERS

wonderful contributions to the business and how much I have helped him and others, etc., etc. I always remember those kinds of things; wouldn't you?

4. Don't be a nag, be a gift. Everyone likes gifts, and nobody likes nags. So why do so many aspiring writers (and others) act out like nags? It's counterintuitive. Of course, nature teaches us from the moment we are born that the noisy baby gets the tit. Passivity invites neglect. Noise attracts attention. What an interesting conundrum. Nagging is bad. Passivity leads to death. Noise can't be ignored. Well, all of that is equally valid, and none of it disqualifies the original point that you are a gift, so act like one.

5. Keep knocking, even after the door is opened. That does not make sense, and it might not be appreciated. But if someone were to keep knocking on my door even after I opened it, I would simply have to ask that person why he or she is doing that, and therein is the beginning of a conversation. Of course, it may all go downhill from there, but then it may not. What happens next depends on the nature of the conversation that has just been launched, regardless of its weird genesis.

6. Don't ask for anything, but offer whatever you can. If that is the energy projected throughout your communications, you will attract due wealth. However, the word *due* is rather crucial in this context. A well-intentioned worm may end up on the end of a fish hook, and a nasty frog may be well fed all summer. Too often people stop at just being nice, and then they become prey. Is it fair that they are eaten for doing nothing at all? Actually, that's exactly what they asked for, to end up nourishing the needs of others. We must all serve a purpose, and we must all consume to survive. If you don't wish to be consumed, then don't present yourself for that. The universe is a layered place of lessons and challenges, and being a writer is just one of many ways to play the game. Don't just give yourself away, any more than you would throw yourself away. If you value the gems you wish to share, you will discern with whom to grant them, and simply refuse to participate with others.

7. Know your gifts and appreciate them. I can tell right away when I am reading a query letter from a writer who believes in herself and the quality of her product, and I can see those who are not so sure that they should even be trying. Sometimes the writer is apologetic, or even goes as far as asking me if they should be trying. Ironically, the writer's quality as a writer cannot be predicted by their native sense of self-worth. In fact, great literature has emerged from the hearts of those who are seemingly committed to a life of losing. But there is a logical explanation for that: To each writer is assigned a muse. Some writers may hate themselves while loving their muse, and it shows.

WHEN NOTHING HAPPENS TO GOOD (OR BAD) WRITERS

AKA IGNORED WRITER SYNDROME (IWS)

JEFF HERMAN

I will not be ignored!" screams Alex Forrest, the book editor played by Glenn Close, to her philandering lover played by Michael Douglas in the classic film, *Fatal Attraction*.

What perfect karma, a book editor being ignored, even though her job was not relevant to the conflict. Too bad about the rabbit, though.

It's an inalienable truth that any writer who aggressively pitches his or her work will encounter abundant rejections along the way. You know that. But what you may not have been prepared for was the big-loud-deafening nothing at all. You followed the given protocols; have been gracious, humble, and appreciative; and have done nothing egregious. And you would never boil a rabbit. So what's your reward? Absolutely nothing; you have been ignored.

A document stating that your work has been rejected, even if clearly generic, may be a much more welcome outcome than the silence of an empty universe. At least that formal rejection letter reflects that you are part of a genuine process. True, you have been turned away at the gate, but it still seems that you belong to a fraternity of sorts. It's like you're an understudy, or simply wait-listed. Your existence is acknowledged even if unwelcome, whereas to be ignored is proof of nothing. Nature abhors a vacuum, and any writer with nerve endings will understand why soon enough, if not already.

I write this essay because of the frequent feedback I receive from readers complaining about the non-responsiveness of editors and agents. I have carefully considered this phenomenon and how it must negatively affect the morale and stamina of those who are endeavoring in good faith to be published. I have decided that to be ignored deserves its own category in the travails of writing, and that it inflicts even more pain and frustration than the proverbial rejection. I shall designate it with a logical term: Ignored.

Why are so many writers ignored by editors and agents? I will respond to that with questions of my own. Why are so many children ignored? Why are so many of the poor and needy ignored? Why are so many social problems ignored? I could ask this question in countless ways, and the primary universal answer would essentially remain the same: It's far easier to do nothing.

ADVICE FOR WRITERS

Let's get back to our specific context. Agents and editors have demanding, often tedious, workloads that overwhelm the typical 40-hour work week (they tend to put in way more hours than that, even though they can rarely bill by the hour or receive extra pay). They are rewarded for generating tangible results, which is most often measured in the form of monetary revenues. Taking the time to respond to writers, even in a purely perfunctory manner, might be the courteous thing to do, but neither their businesses nor their bosses will reward their kindness. You may feel such inaction is a misguided and shortsighted "policy," and you might be right, but it doesn't change the facts as they are.

Does being ignored mean that you have actually been read and rejected? This question can't be answered, because you're being ignored. It's possible that someone did read your work and rejected it, and then threw it out even if an SASE was attached. Why would someone do that? Because it's much easier to and they can't justify the time it would take to answer as many as 100 submissions per week. It's also possible that your submission has not been read and may never be read, because nobody is available to screen the "incoming" in any organized fashion. It's not out of the question that submissions will accumulate in numerous piles and boxes for several years before they are simply discarded, never to be opened. Does this strike you as harsh or ridiculous? Whatever; it is the way it is.

What is certain is that if your work is read and accepted, you will hear about it.

In closing, my message to you is that you not allow being ignored to diminish your dreams and goals. It's simply a part of the process and part of the emotional overhead you might encounter on your road to success. It's also a crucial reason why you should not put all of your manuscripts in one basket. To do so may be tantamount to placing your entire career into a bottomless pit. Making multiple submissions is reasonable and wise if you consider the possible consequences of granting an exclusive without any deadline or two-way communications. Please refer to the other essays and words of advice in this book to keep yourself from becoming a victim of Ignored Writer Syndrome (IWS).

POST-PUBLICATION DEPRESSION SYNDROME (PPDS)

JEFF HERMAN

If you're struggling to get published, then this essay isn't for you, yet. If you're currently under contract, now is a good time to read this. If you have already been published and experienced what the above title indicates, then hopefully this essay will help you heal and realize you are far from alone.

You don't need to be reminded how much passion, fortitude, and raw energy goes into crafting your work, followed by the grueling process of getting it published. What you're probably not prepared for is the possibility of post-publication blues.

No one directly discusses or recognizes this genuine condition because newly published authors are expected to be overjoyed and grateful for the achievement of being published. After all, each published author is amongst the fortunate "one-out-of-a-thousand" struggling writers who make it to the Big Show. In reality, people who reach the pinnacle of success in any field of endeavor will often feel an emotional letdown in the wake of their accomplishment. The feelings can be comparable to a state of mourning, as the thrill of chasing the goal instantly evaporates and is replaced by nothing. Writers are especially prone to wallowing alone, as theirs is a solitary process by design, and only other writers who have been through the same cavern can be truly empathetic.

Emotional letdowns happen when results don't fulfill expectations. Everything preceding the point of publication involves drama, excitement, and anticipation. Butterflies flutter in the belly and endorphins soar through the brain. One day the writer's goal will be manifested in the body of a published book, and the self-constructed dreams will be displaced by a reality that seems to lack sizzle. What follows might feel sad and unnourishing. No matter how much is achieved, something crucial might feel left behind.

Achieving awesome goals is a reward unto itself, but it may not be enough to satisfy what's needed. The writer's imagination may have drawn fantastic pictures of glamorous celebrity parties, profound talk-show appearances, instantaneous fame, and goblets of money. But just as the explosive passions and idealized assumptions of first love might experience an anticlimactic consummation, finally receiving the bound book in hand might prove to be surprisingly uneventful.

Sometimes the publication is everything the writer hoped for, which of course is a wonderful outcome. But for many it feels like nothing much happened at all. The media aren't calling; few people show up for signings/readings; and perhaps most upsetting of all, friends and relatives report that the book can't be found. Meanwhile, no one from the publisher is calling anymore and they act like their job is done. In truth, most of the publishing team is probably absorbed with publishing the endless flow of new books, whereas what's already been published is quickly relegated to "yesterday's list." A chirpy in-house publicist may be available, but he/she may not appear to be doing or accomplishing much while adeptly saying imprecise things in a glib, patronizing manner.

There's abundant information available about how to be a proactive author and successfully compensate for the universal marketing deficits endemic to the book publishing business. But that's not the purpose of this essay. For sure, it's constructive to take practical steps for mitigating disappointments and solving existential problems, but such activities may also distract the troubled writer from the tender places crying somewhere inside. These feelings must be recognized and soothed separate from business-oriented solutions. It's good to sell as many copies as possible, but unwise to turn away from needs radiating beneath the skin.

Seeking or initiating communities of "published writers in pain" should be what the doctor ordered. If done right, such personal connections will help level the loneliness and despair that defines post-publication depression. However, the community must consciously dedicate itself to a positive process. Nothing useful will be accomplished by reinforcing anger, resentment, or sense of victimhood. Even worse is unsupportive competitiveness or negativity that pushes people down. And as can happen in any inbred community, distortions, misinformation, and poor advice might circulate with a bogus badge of credibility.

Life is rarely a clear trail. If it looks to be, then unexpected destinations are likely to prevail. Writers will eat dirt and wear thorns in exchange for self-compassion and self-discovery. Pain isn't punishment but a consequence that expands the writer's integrity, authenticity, and relevance. Post-publication depression is an item on a menu in a script written by the writer for the writer. Never fear the pain, just be prepared to live through it and learn it, and to help others do the same.

WRITING & PUBLISHING IN 2013 & BEYOND

JEFF HERMAN

Writing is innately immune from transformation because the need to communicate, learn, and be entertained is organically human, and not provoked or hindered by technology. Computers can process many kinds of information faster and more reliably than the human brain, but they are unable to purely create, imagine, dream, emote, or be a fulfilling social companion for most of us. As long as people have hearts and minds, there will be writers, readers, and other kinds of humans.

Electromagnetic energy isn't a human creation, but humans are rapidly mastering the ability to manipulate it. Digital information can be produced in infinite quantities and immediately distributed to all people with current hardware and digital connections. You or I could instantaneously distribute, or advertise, our "unpublished" manuscript(s) to every existing e-mail address on Earth. There are services that can penetrate state-of-the-art spam catchers or stealthily hack away at any website without constraint. You know this because you get unwanted e-mail, and perhaps your account has been "possessed" by parties unknown who used your base to unilaterally "communicate" with everyone you've ever e-mailed with.

There's no reason to believe that digital security will ever outpace digital porosity. Anything that flows through the digital stream becomes as public as the molecules in the air we breathe. We can and do make laws declaring some data to be proprietary, but laws are only for those who either choose to obey them or lack the skills to do otherwise.

Literary agents and publishers receive countless unsolicited digital manuscripts that are simultaneously distributed to ALL of us. The digital age has enabled the pace and volume of random submissions to surge like never before. Cheap copy machines, printers, and PCs were huge production and distribution accelerators, but barely a warm-up for what's happening now. The ability to massively distribute content makes the avoidance of massive dismissal the real challenge.

Once upon a time manuscripts and documents required steady hands, smooth stones, or nonperishable animal skins. In-person encounters were the primary method for expressing and delivering information. The staggered introductions of paper, ink, printing presses, postal systems, telegraphs and codes, telephones, motorized transportation, and radio transmissions carried Western societies ever deeper into the Modern Age. Communications became progressively less personal, less intimate, and more officious. Family and communal relationships became much less binding. It became much easier for different peoples to discover each other, which triggered new economic opportunities and the blending of diverse cultures. But it also manifested unprecedented opportunities for stronger societies to exploit weaker ones, and that tendency hasn't dissipated.

As we become even more digitally connected and reliant, we risk becoming increasingly lonely and socially alienated. Online "relationships" are just that, and can't substitute for the real thing. Much of the developed world's social chaos and self-destructive behavior is attributable to the breakdown of the undeniable human need to be genuinely intimate and communal. We won't succeed at digitally faking out what DNA demands.

Unfortunately, technology hasn't been an equal-opportunity benefit, and won't be as long as current dynamics prevail. The gulf between rich and poor is unnecessarily growing, not contracting. The vast majority of people in undeveloped countries, and large pockets of people in developed countries, are left behind. Social elites (which presumably include the writer and readers of this essay) are emotionally insulated from the way disadvantaged people live, and are intellectually deceived about the underlying currents. Elites are conditioned to believe that poor people are envious, covetous, perhaps less worthy, and eager to steal what they want in ruthless ways. This provokes fear, defensiveness, isolation, and an unnecessary sense of scarcity. Instead of generosity, we end up with a sense of cold competiveness, besiegement, and antipathy towards others.

The media sometimes make a dramatic show of the world's abundant misery and injustice, which elicits rivers of donations and genuine compassion, though many donors ensure that their names are visibly attached to their deeds. However, there's an absence of discussion about the underlying causes of the world's miseries. The victims are implicitly blamed for not being able to cultivate functional societies, or for being unable to thrive within wealthy countries. It's rarely stated that poverty could be universally phased out everywhere if power, wealth, and opportunities were equitably and justly distributed. The dying majority would be remade into valuable contributors to themselves and the world at large. But elites are locked into not seeing how their societies are systematically exploiting the mineral resources and cheap labor impoverished countries richly possess.

Americans refer to its domestic restless hordes as ignorant rednecks or urban hooligans, and refer to third-world malcontents as incorrigibly hateful of what America "stands for." The word *terrorist* is a catch-all for anyone who aggressively seeks to turn the status quo upside-down. There are many psychopathic bad seeds sowing destruction in the name of justice, but many other so-called terrorists are using the only leverage available to confront truly unjust circumstances. In turn, defenders of the status quo often use ruthless tactics in the name of law and order.

Misguided violence erupts by design when deliberate fallacies about racial, cultural, and religious conflicts are deployed to confuse and exploit valid grievances. People are easily distracted from recognizing the real reasons for their own and other people's pain. As a result, kindred interests are frequently divided against each other through the infusion of calculated lies, and fail to take a united stand against the real reasons for their shared plight.

Violence, regardless of its alleged cause or purpose, becomes the apparent problem and everything shifts to both promoting and confronting it at the expense of constructive solutions. Those who possess the cherished throne of power will assume a self-righteous posture, and claim to be defending a just system against agents of chaos. It's easier to erase those who oppose you for religious, racial, or political reasons, and not because they simply want you to reslice the proverbial pie.

None of the above necessarily represents this writer's point of view, but all of it is germane to this essay and a plausible portrayal of current/future events. Chaos is a consequence of injustice. Power and wealth need to be evenly disbursed if only for the simple reason that nature abhors disequilibrium, and will invariably seek balance. People can try to obstruct natural laws, but the costs will multiply until the structure either corrects or eliminates itself. Man plans, nature laughs.

Research is underway to combine human attributes and biology with human-made technology. It will be convenient to run a vacuum cleaner or lawn mower with our thoughts instead of our muscles. It will be thrilling to immediately know French by the painless insertion of a "stick" into the tiny piercings (ports) leading into our brains. Eventually, humans could become so physically and mentally enmeshed with high-tech components, that infants will receive "postpartum construction" in addition to any vestigial forms of upbringing that might still exist. The dreaded day may arrive when factions of our species are in conflict with the existence of souls. But as long as there are writers who see and express the truth, there will be hope for positive choices and outcomes.

At their best, writers deliver reality and universal values. Sometimes they may only impress a few, or their words may be dormant for generations before suddenly blooming when needed. Movements and revolutions are shaped, and humans are formed, by what's written. The past is documented and understood on the basis of what's written, which provides a context for future choices. History becomes a guessing game once we go beyond the written record. Memories and oral accounts rarely match the range of feelings and impressions written in real-time.

A steamy romance novel, a practical how-to book, or profound treatise, are all equal because each is written to benefit those who need or want them. With obvious exceptions, no writer should judge the merits of what they or others are called to write. The most seemingly basic forms of entertainment or mundane self-help/how-to guides can make very significant differences in people's lives, and the future won't take that away.

Traditional commercial publishing models may not survive into the near future. Today's dominant publishing institutions are burdened with obsolete infrastructures unsuitable for the digital age. They will either fail or be radically restructured. Jobs will be lost but new ones created. Large sums of money will be lost but large capital investments will flow. The dominant brick-and-mortar book chains may lose their purpose for existing, but the mom-and-pop stores and independent presses will be poised to successfully adapt and survive, and will continue generating decent revenues for many years by doing things the old-fashioned way for Baby Boomers and volitional luddites.

Book publishers aren't bringing the digital future; they're being dragged into it kicking and screaming. They are being forced to comply with technology and marketplace preferences. Yes, writers who are published by the large houses will be collateral passengers on the roller coaster, as will their agents. But writers have always been the most versatile tool in the shed, and only need the air to breathe and some bread to eat to keep writing.

FIND YOUR PASSION
AND PISS IT AWAY

JEFF HERMAN

Headlines mean a lot; sometimes everything. Either they attract immediate attention or they fail. Of course, a high level of preexisting interest in the subject matter can compensate for a feeble headline. An easy example would be any tag line referencing notorious "Tot Mom" Casey Anthony during the summer of '11.

The first rule when trying to get attention is to get attention. Guess what? Getting attention is easy. Just watch a bored kid or ornery dog. But getting positive or appropriate attention is challenging. Return to the above headline. It's magnetically provocative because it's countercultural to the point of deviant. It's not what Tony Robbins would say, or at least not without a smile; though he's always smiling.

The second rule is to understand that further rules won't matter until you accomplish the first rule. Assuming you will, proceed to the third rule.

The third rule is to understand that no rules apply to you unless you choose to follow them, regardless of who makes them. Rules have power if they can be enforced, and many nonsensical rules prevail because defiance is costly. Tax evasion is an example. Many rules are perpetual for the simple reason that enough people mindlessly follow them. Society intrinsically attempts to impose conformity. However, at least 10 percent of any given community will be inherently unable to comply with rules, and many of them are antisocial criminals. Other serial nonconformists will be condemned to a life of quiet desperation. But a crucial remnant will succeed at creating original realities and innovative possibilities that will potentially deliver progress, destruction, or a combination of both.

The fourth rule is to manage the consequences of the attention you will hopefully attract. For instance, using the above headline requires me to quickly explain the method to my apparent madness, and attempt to bring readers to my real purpose. However, I'm not trying to sell anything and may never know if anyone even reads this essay, whereas you will be pitching for, and will be mindful of, specific results. Obviously, you want to begin your sales letters and documents in ways that will maximize attention. But if you take risks by opening your material in absurd ways, then you had better have an immediate conversion process built into the text, or the initial attention you capture may devolve into the equivalent of an errant missile to nowhere, or an unintended destination.

The fifth rule is to remember that beauty without attention equals beauty without attention; whereas mediocrity with attention can be rewarding. If Sophia Loren had agoraphobia and never left her house, countless generations of men (OK, not all men and some women) wouldn't have been able to include her in their fantasies. It's plausible that women even more beautiful and talented than Ms. Loren were simply unable to tolerate or negotiate what it takes to get attention, and will therefore be forever unknown. Conversely, Mae West wasn't a classic beauty, but yet was one of the most famous and sexualized women in the world for decades.

The sixth rule is to devise as many other rules as you wish, and then you may destroy or morph them, because that's the process that helps keep us vibrant and connected to the lives we live.

THE INDEPENDENT EDITORS

Over the past few years, independent editors (aka "Book Doctors") have become much more numerous and are more frequently an important part of the publishing process. This relatively new and potentially indispensable utility player has earned a section all its own.

Simply stated, an independent editor is someone who is retained by a writer at a negotiated fee, for the purpose of helping to make the writer's proposal, pitch letter, marketing materials, story summary, chapters, entire manuscript, or any combination thereof, as professionally perfect as possible. These services are not to be confused with ghostwriting, collaborating, or coauthoring, as it is not the editor's function to actually write anything, but to merely help the writer reach her best potential, though some freelance editors might also provide collaboration services.

In-house editors may recognize an unpublished writer's rich potential, but lack the time or incentive to help chisel the raw product into a publishable form, and therefore reject it. In some cases the editor will conditionally reject it with the generous suggestion that if the writer can somehow make it better, he's welcome to resubmit it, which in turn opens the door for an independent editor. It's not uncommon for agents to do the same. Some writers decide to preempt or reduce the chance of rejection by retaining editorial support prior to pitching anything to anyone.

A significant trend, which has hopefully peaked, is the endemic downsizing that has plagued corporate publishing for more than a dozen years. Many excellent veteran editors were granted the proverbial "golden parachute" for the purpose of eliminating overhead. For obvious reasons, this brain drain hasn't been good for in-house quality, but that's for another essay. This displaced talent pool includes more than a few who have edited the most important and successful books that have been published over the past generation. These same editors are now available to help eligible writers reach their full potentials, for fees that are modest when compared to unrelated professional services.

The community of downsized and retired editors lends itself to mutual support and combined marketing efforts. For instance, those who are best suited for memoirs can make referrals to those who specialize in romance. It can be inefficient and lonely to be an isolated freelancer, so forming loosely organized groups came naturally to those who had spent years in offices working with others. The initial groups didn't want to become too crowded or structured, so several new groups have been spawned to absorb the increasing supply of independent editors.

Presented here is verbatim information presented by each of the groups and their respective members. While I endorse the concept of using an independent editor when appropriate, and have confidence in the veracity and quality of everyone listed here, I do not specifically endorse any of them. In future editions, I hope to expand this section by including qualified independent editors who are not affiliated with a group. If you are one of them, feel free to contact me.

Jeff Herman

SCAMS AND BOOK DOCTORS

IN THAT ORDER

JEFF HERMAN

Publishing scams have become an epidemic. I read somewhere that writers are getting ripped off for more than $50 million a year, and some scam artists have even gone to jail.

Let's start by looking at ethics. I don't like ethics. They're like organized religion—prone to promoting arrogance, subjective judgment, and hypocrisy. I do like honesty. Honesty's best defense is the fast and consistent enforcement of consequences against those people who harm others.

The best defense is not to be a victim in the first place. Without becoming a paranoid lunatic, you must accept that bad deeds are hovering around waiting to happen. Sometimes, you may be tempted into being a perpetrator. That's why houses have glass windows and why the universe can't stay angry, or else we'd all have to go to hell. It's more likely, however, that you'll be a victim, not a doer, on any given day; though it's hoped you'll be neither. Both extremes may be mostly, or completely, within your power to be or not to be. For instance, I'll never understand why women jog by themselves in Central Park when it's dark out. And I'll never understand why writers send fat checks to virtual strangers.

To what extent should society protect its citizens from making stupid choices? I've seen smart men and women date and marry morons, with predictably disastrous results. I've done enough stupid things in my life to qualify for the Infra-Mensa society many times over. How about you? Should someone have stopped us? And if we were stopped, might we not have been even more stupid the next time?

Basically, I'm praising stupidity as a natural right and gift. It's unnatural to overly protect people from themselves. We all see what happens to individuals who are excessively parented or to entire communities that are enabled to subsist in perpetual poverty and social decay.

So what about writers who get scammed? Well, they should stop doing it.

- They should stop sending money to get people to "read" their work, since there are several hundred real agents who will do that for free.

- They should stop smoking and stop eating other fat mammals.

- They should stop giving money to unproven strangers who promise to get them published, since there are several hundred real agents who will do that on a contingency.

- + They should wear seatbelts, especially when in New York taxis.

- + They should stop giving money to unproven strangers who promise to "fix" the work, especially since there are at least dozens of real book editors who can genuinely fix your work.

- + They should stop maintaining balances on their credit cards.

- + They should always ask for evidence of ability whenever asked for money.

If we, as writers, walk the previous line, then parasitic acts could not exist and thrive. We would not need more laws, more people working for government, or any ethics. Such things only exist in the absence of honesty and in the dissonance that follows.

As a service, I have attached information about specific "Book Doctor" organizations and individuals that I'm familiar with and trust. These are people who either have deep experience working as real editors at real publishers, have "doctored" many manuscripts to the point of publication, or both. Retaining their skills will often make the difference between getting a deal or being a "close call."

I endorse none of these people or the expectations they might create. I simply want you to have a safe place to turn if you need help and are ready to receive.

The following is an actual pitch letter from a fee-charging agency, with only the names and other identifying information changed. Such correspondence is typical of the alluring invitations writers often receive in response to their agent submissions.

If a writer chooses to explore this route, I strongly advise following these preliminary steps:

1. Ask for references. You're being asked to shell out hundreds of dollars to a virtual stranger. Get to know those who would eat your money.

2. Ask for a list of titles sold. Find out whether the so-called agency actually has an agenting track record. Or is this particular operation just a high-priced reading service with an agency façade?

3. Better yet, call or write to non–fee-charging agents and ask them to recommend book doctors, collaborative writers, or editorial freelancers whom they use to shape and develop their own clients' works, or see the "Book Doctor" section in this book. This may be a better place to spend your money.

BEWARE OF SHARKS!

The following correspondence is genuine, though all names and titles have been altered. My purpose for exposing these ever-so-slightly personalized form letters isn't to condemn or ridicule anyone. I simply wish to show how some subsidy publishers hook their clients.

SHARK HOUSE PUBLISHERS

Mr. Bourne Bate
Brooklyn Bridge
East River, NY 00000
Dear Mr. Bate:

Your manuscript *A Fish's Life* is written from an unusual perspective and an urgent one. In these trying economic times that have created despair and anguish, one must give thought to opportunities, and this upbeat and enthusiastic book makes us realize that those opportunities are out there! My capsule critique: Meticulous aim! With a surgeon's precision we're taught how to work through everything from raising money to targeting areas. There is a sharp eye here for all of the nuances, studded with pointers and reasoning, making it a crucial blueprint.

What can I say about a book like this? It stopped me in my tracks. I guess all I can do is thank you for letting me have the opportunity to read it.

The editors who read this had a spontaneous tendency to feel that it was imbued with some very, very good electricity and would be something very special for our list and saw such potential with it that it was given top priority and pushed ahead of every other book in house. The further problem is that publishing being an extremely rugged business, editorial decisions have to be based on hard facts, which sometimes hurt publishers as much as authors. Unfortunately, we just bought several new nonfiction pieces… yet I hate to let this one get away. Publishing economics shouldn't have anything to do with a decision, but unfortunately, it does and I was overruled at the editorial meeting.

Still I want you to know that this is a particularly viable book and one that I really would love to have for our list. Furthermore, this might be picked up for magazine serialization or by book clubs because it is so different. Our book *Enraptured* was serialized six times in *International Inquirer* and sold to Andorra. *The Devil Decided* sold well over 150,000 copies, and we have a movie option on it. *Far Away*, serialized in *Places* magazine and *Cure Yourself*, was taken by a major book club.

I really want this book for our list because it will fit into all the areas that we're active in. Therefore, I'm going to make a proposition for you to involve yourself with us. What would you think of the idea of doing this on a cooperative basis? Like many New York publishers these days, we find that sometimes investors are interested in the acquisition of literary properties through a technique that might be advantageous under our tax laws. There is no reason that the partial investor cannot be the writer, if that person so chooses. Tax advantages may accrue.

I'd be a liar if I promised you a best seller, but I can guarantee that nobody works as hard promoting a book as we do: We nag paperback, book clubs, magazines, and foreign publishers with our zeal and enthusiasm. We do our PR work and take it seriously because this is where we're going to make the money in the long run. One of our authors hired a top publicist on his own for $50,000. He came limping back to us, saying they didn't do the job that we did, and which we don't charge for. This made our office feel very proud of all our efforts.

I feel that your book deserves our efforts because it is something very special. Think about what I've written to you, and I will hold the manuscript until I hear from you. I truly hope that we can get together because I really love this book and believe it is something we can generate some good action for vis-à-vis book clubs, foreign rights, etc., because it is outstanding and has tremendous potential.

Sincerely,

Eda U. Live

Eda U. Live
Executive Editor

The writer of *A Fish's Life* wrote back to Shark House (all names have been changed) and informed the vanity press that he did not want to pay any money to the publisher to have his book published.

The vanity house responded with the following letter.

(This publisher has probably learned from experience that some exhausted writers will return to them with open wallets after fruitless pursuit of a conventional commercial publishing arrangement.)

SHARK HOUSE PUBLISHERS

Mr. Bourne Bate
Brooklyn Bridge
East River, NY 00000
Dear Mr. Bate:

I have your letter in front of me and I want you to know that I think very highly of the book. Before I go any further, I want to tell you that it is a topnotch book and it hits the reader.

In order for us to do a proper job with a book, there is a great deal of PR work involved and this is very costly. To hire an outside agent to do a crackerjack job would cost you upward of $50,000. Yet here we do not charge for it because it is part of our promotion to propel a book into the marketplace, and it is imperative that this be done. The author has to be booked on radio and TV, stores have to be notified, rights here and abroad have to be worked on, reviewers contacted, autograph parties arranged, and myriad details taken care of.

In view of this, why did I ask you to help with the project? I think the above is self-explanatory, especially when we are in the midst of a revolution between books and television. Publishers are gamblers vying for the same audience. Just because a publisher loves a book is no guarantee that the public is going to love it. In times when bookstores are more selective in the number of books they order, the best of us tremble at the thought of the money that we must put out in order to make a good book a reality.

Be that as it may, I have just come from another editorial meeting where I tried to reopen the case for us, but unfortunately, the earlier decision stands.

As a result, I have no choice but to return the manuscript with this letter. I would also like to tell you that you must do what the successful writers do. Keep sending it out. Someone will like it and someone will buy it.

I wish you every success. Live long and prosper.

Sincerely,
Eda U. Live

Eda U. Live
Executive Editor

NINE SIGNS OF A SCAM BOOK DOCTOR

JERRY GROSS

Working with an expert, ethical book doctor can often make the difference between being published or remaining unpublished. Conversely, working with an unqualified, unethical book doctor can often be hazardous—even fatal—to your career.

You've worked hard to save the money to hire a book doctor. Make sure that the book doctor you hire will turn out to be a good investment. Here are nine signs that someone who claims to be a professional book doctor may be trying to scam you.

1. **A scam book doctor states that you can't get published unless you hire a book doctor.**

   You may hear that editors and publishers demand that a manuscript be professionally edited before they will consider it for publication, or that agents won't take on a client unless the writer first works with a book doctor to polish the manuscript.

   Not true. Agents and editors still take on manuscripts that need a lot of work, but, to be candid, they don't do it too often because they are usually overworked and overwhelmed by the volume of material submitted to them. That's why working with a good book doctor can at least improve your odds of being accepted by an agent and an editor.

2. **A scam book doctor guarantees, or at least implies, that his editing will get you accepted by an agent.**

   Not true! No reputable book doctor can make this statement because no book doctor can persuade an agent to represent a project that the agent does not like, believe in, or see as commercially viable. Beauty is in the eye of the beholder, and editors and agents often see a manuscript's potential through very different eyes.

3. **A scam book doctor guarantees, or strongly implies, that once she's edited your manuscript, an agent will definitely be able to sell it.**

   Not true. The vagaries, shifts of taste, and trends in the publishing marketplace are such that agents themselves cannot be sure which manuscripts will be salable.

4. **A scam book doctor admits (or you discover) that he has a "financial arrangement" with the person or company who referred you to him.**

In plain English, this means that he kicks back part of his fee for the referral.

This is inarguably unethical. There should be no financial relationship between the book doctor and the referring party. If one exists, it can adversely affect the honesty and integrity of his evaluation of your manuscript, or both.

5. **A scam book doctor does not guarantee that she will edit your manuscript personally.**

Since you are hiring the editor for her specific expertise, insist that she guarantee in writing that she will edit the manuscript herself. If she won't do this, look elsewhere for an editor.

6. **A scam book doctor tells you that he can't take on your project, but will subcontract it.**

However, he won't tell you who will edit it, and he won't provide you with that editor's background, samples of that editor's work, or any references. And he does not give you the right to accept or refuse the editor he suggests.

If you do decide to work with another editor because the one you wanted is overbooked or otherwise unavailable, then you have every right to know as much about the person recommended by him as you know about the editor making the recommendation. You also have every right to decide whether you want to work with the editor whom he recommends.

7. **A scam book doctor won't provide references from authors or agents she's worked with.**

Obviously, the editor won't provide you with names of dissatisfied clients, but you can learn a lot by gauging the enthusiasm (or lack of it) with which the client discusses working with the book doctor. Ask questions: "Was she easy and friendly to work with?"; "Was she receptive to ideas?"; "Was she available to discuss her approach to line editing, critique of the manuscript, or both?"; "Did you feel that you got good value for your money?"

8. **A scam book doctor won't provide samples of his editing or critiques.**

Engaging in a book doctor without seeing how he line edits or addresses problems in a manuscript is akin to buying oceanfront property in Arizona from a real estate salesman on the phone or on the Web. Talk is cheap, but good editing is expensive. Make sure you are buying the expertise you need; demand to see samples of the editor's work. If he balks, hang up the phone!

9. A scam book doctor sends you an incomplete Letter of Agreement that does not specify all the costs you will incur, what she will do for each of her fees, a schedule of payment, and a due date for delivery of the edited or critiqued manuscript.

Every one of your contractual obligations to each other should be spelled out clearly in the Letter of Agreement before you sign it. If changes are agreed upon during the course of the author-editor relationship, these changes should either be incorporated into a new Letter of Agreement that both parties sign or be expressed in rider clauses added to the Agreement that are initialed by both editor and author. There should be no hidden or "surprise" costs at the time of the final payment to the book doctor.

A final caution: Be convinced that you are hiring the right book doctor before signing the Letter of Agreement. Not only your money, but also your career is at stake!

Jerry Gross has been a fiction and nonfiction editor for many years, the last 19 as a freelance editor/book doctor. He is editor of the standard work on trade-book editing *Editors on Editing: What Writers Need to Know About What Editors Do*. He also creates and presents workshops and panels on editing and writing at writers' conferences. He can be reached at 63 Grand Street, Croton-on-Hudson, NY 10520-2518 and at jgross@bookdocs.com.

THE INDEPENDENT EDITORS

AN EDITOR OF ONE'S OWN

BY THE EDITORS OF WORDS INTO PRINT (WWW.WORDSINTOPRINT.ORG)

Are book doctors really worth it? What do they do that agents and in-house editors might not? With all the help a writer can get on the journey from manuscript to published book, why hire an editor of one's own?

Literary and publishing staff used to be the first industry insiders to read a proposal or manuscript. Today, however, the focus on business interests is so demanding and the volume of submissions so great—agents alone take in hundreds of query letter a month—that a writer's work has to be white-hot before receiving serious consideration. In light of these developments, a writer may turn to an independent editor as the first expert reader. In addition, as the ways of producing a book continue to evolve, an independent editor can be your guide in choosing among the different venues—from traditional publishing to self-publishing to e-books.

WHAT ELSE DO INDEPENDENT EDITORS DO, AND HOW MUCH DO THEY CHARGE?

Services. Not every writer and project will call for the services of an independent editor. However, if you are looking for the kind of personalized and extensive professional guidance beyond that gained from workshops, fellow writers, online sources, magazines, and books, hiring an editor may well be worth the investment. An editor of your own can provide a professional assessment of whether or not your project is ready to submit, and to whom you should submit it; expert assistance to make your manuscript or book proposal as good as it should be; help with preparing a convincing submissions package; and an advocate's voice and influence to guide you in your efforts toward publication.

Another key role an independent editor plays is to protect writers from querying their prospects before their material is irresistible. Premature submissions cause writers needless disappointment and frustration. Your editor can zero in on the thematic core, central idea, or storyline that needs to be conveyed in a way that is most likely to attract an agent and a publisher. In short, an editor of your own can identify the most appealing, salable aspects of you and your work.

Rates. "Good editing is expensive," our venerable colleague Jerry Gross prudently notes. What kind of editing is good editing and how expensive is it? The Internet and other sources quote a wide range of rates from a variety of editors. The numbers are not necessarily accurate or reliable. We've seen hourly rates ranging from about $25 to well above $200. Several factors account for this spread: the type of editing, the editor's level of experience, and the publishing venue. For example, rates for copyediting are lower than those for substantive editing. Moreover, standards in book publishing are particularly rigorous because books are long, expensive to produce, made to last, and vulnerable to the long-term impact of reviewer criticism.

Process. Book editors are specialists. Every book project arrives on the desk of an independent editor at a certain level of readiness, and the first task is to determine what the project needs. A deep book edit is typically a painstaking, time-consuming process that may move at the pace of only 3 or 4 manuscript pages per hour—or, when less intensive, 8 to 12 pages per hour. Occasionally a manuscript received by an independent is fully developed, needs only a light copyedit, and may well be ready to submit as is. In other cases, the editorial process may require one or more rounds of revisions. If you are hiring an editor to critique your work, you should be aware that reading the material takes considerably more time than writing the critique. Sometimes a flat fee, rather than an hourly rate, may be appropriate to the project. Sometimes an editor will offer a brief initial consultation at no charge. A reputable independent book editor will be able recommend a course of action that may or may not include one or more types of editorial services, and give you a reliable estimate of the time and fees involved.

BUT WON'T THE IN-HOUSE EDITOR FIX MY BOOK?

Sometimes. Maybe. To an extent. Independents and in-house editors are, in many ways, different creatures. For starters, in-house editors spend much of the day preparing for and going to meetings. Marketing meetings. Sales meetings. Editorial meetings. Production meetings. The mandate for most of these in-house editors is to acquire new book projects and to shepherd those that are already in the pipeline. With so many extended activities cutting into the business hours, the time for actually working on a manuscript can be short.

Many in-house editors have incoming manuscripts screened by an already overworked assistant. (The days of staff readers are long gone.) The only quiet time the editor has for reading might be evenings and weekends. We have known editors to take a week off from work just to edit a book and be accessible to their authors. These days, too, the acquiring editor may not do any substantive work on a book project under contract, leaving that task to a junior editor. There is also a distinct possibility the acquiring editor may leave the job before that book is published, and this can occur with the next editor, too, and the next, threatening the continuity of the project. All of which doesn't mean that there aren't a lot of hard-working people at the publishing house; it means that editors have more to do than ever before and must devote at least as much time to crunching numbers as to focusing on the writer and the book.

Independent editors, on the other hand, spend most of their business days working exclusively with authors and their texts. They typically handle only a few manuscripts at a time and are free from marketing and production obligations. An independent editor's primary interest is in helping you to get your book polished and published. An editor of your own will see your project through—and often your next book, too.

WHAT DO AGENTS SAY ABOUT INDEPENDENT EDITORS?

"As the book market gets tougher for selling both fiction and nonfiction it is imperative that all submissions be polished, edited, almost ready for the printer. Like many other agents I do as much as possible to provide editorial input for the author but there are time constraints. So independent editors provide a very valuable service these days in getting the manuscript or proposal in the best shape possible to increase the chances of impressing an editor and getting a sale with the best possible terms." —Bill Contardi

"Agents work diligently for our clients, but there are situations in which outside help is necessary. Perhaps a manuscript has been worked on so intensively that objectivity is lacking, or perhaps the particular skill required to do a job properly is not one of an agent's strong suits. Maybe more time is required than an agent can offer. Fortunately, agents and authors are able to tap into the talent and experience of an outside editor. The outside editors I've worked with offer invaluable support during the editing process itself and for the duration of a project. Their involvement can make the difference between an author getting a publishing contract or having to put a project aside, or the difference between a less-or more-desirable contract." —Victoria Pryor

"The right editor or book doctor can make all the difference in whether a manuscript gets sold. A debut novelist, for example, may have a manuscript that is almost there, but not quite. With the input of a good editor, the novel can reach its full potential and be an attractive prospect to a potential publisher. Similarly, someone writing a memoir may have had a fascinating life but may not really have the God-given writing talent that will turn that life into a compelling and readable book. An editor can take that person's rough-hewn words and thoughts and turn them into a memoir that really sings on the printed page." —Eric Myers

"Occasionally a novel will land on my desk that I feel has talent or a good concept behind it but for whatever reason (the writing, the pacing) needs an inordinate amount of work. Instead of just rejecting it flat-out I may then refer the author to a freelance editor, someone who has the time and expertise to help the author further shape and perfect their work." —Nina Collins

"I have had several occasions to use the help of freelance editors, and think they provide incalculable good service to the profession. In these competitive times, a manuscript has to be as polished and clean as possible to garner a good sale to a publisher. If it needs work, it simply provides an editor with a reason to turn it down. My job is to not give them any excuses. I do not have either the time or the ability to do the editorial work that may be required to make the manuscript salable. Paying a freelance professional to help shape a book into its most commercially viable form ultimately more than pays for itself." —Deborah Schneider

SO, HOW CAN I FIND THE RIGHT EDITOR?

You've searched online. You've looked in annual directories such as this one. You've asked around. A personal recommendation from a published writer-friend who has used an independent editor may or may not do the trick. Every author has different needs, every author-editor dynamic a different chemistry.

Although sometimes an author and editor "click" very quickly, many editors offer free consultations, and it's fine to contact more than one editor at this stage. A gratis consult may involve an editor's short take, by phone or in writing, on sample material the editor asked you to send. But how to distinguish among the many independent editors?

Some editorial groups are huge, and they are open to all who designate themselves as editors; it might take some additional research to identify the members who are most reputable and best suited to your work. The smaller groups consist of editors who have been nominated, vetted, and elected, which ensures the high quality of the individual professionals. They meet with regularity, share referrals, and discuss industry developments. Your consultation, references offered, and the terms of any subsequent agreement can tell the rest.

Another way to find the right editor is to prepare your manuscript to its best advantage—structurally, stylistically, and mechanically. Jeff Herman's annual guide, for example, is filled with directions on manuscript preparation, and it is a good idea to follow them. Asking the opinion of one or more impartial readers—that is, not limiting your initial reviewers to friends and relatives—is a great strategy as well. If you have the benefit of a disinterested reader, you may be able to make some significant changes before sending an excerpt to an independent editor. One more element to consider: editors often will take your own personality and initial written inquiry into account as carefully as they do your writing. Seasoned independents do not take on every project that appears on the desk; they can pick and choose—and, working solo, they must.

TALES FROM THE TRENCHES

We hope we've given you a sense of what an editor of your own can do for you and where we fit into the publishing picture. But next to firsthand experience, perhaps nothing communicates quite as sharply as an anecdote. Here are a few of ours:

"An in-house editor called me with an unusual problem. He had signed up an acclaimed author for a new book project. She had written a number of stories—nonfiction narratives about her life in an exotic land. The problem was this: some of the stories had already been published in book form in England, and that collection had its own integrity in terms of theme and chronology; now she had written another set of stories, plus a diary of her travels. How could the published stories and the new ones be made into one book?

"I decided to disregard the structure of the published book altogether. As I reexamined each story according to theme, emotional quality, geographical location, and people involved, I kept looking for ways in which they might relate to each other. Eventually, I sensed a new and logical way in which to arrange them. I touched not one word of the author's prose. I did the same thing I always try to do when editing—imagine myself inside the skin of the writer. A prominent trade book review had this to say about the result: 'One story flows into the next...'" —Alice Rosengard

"A writer had hired me to help with his first book after his agent had sold it to a publisher because he wanted to expedite the revisions and final approval of his manuscript. As a result of our work together, the book came out sooner than anticipated; it also won an award and the author was interviewed on a major TV news program. The same author hired me a year later for his second book, purchased by a larger publisher, and this book, too, entailed some significant developmental editing. At that point we learned the in-house editor had left the publisher and a new one had come aboard. This editor not only objected strongly to one whole section of the book, she also gave the author a choice: revise the section in one week or put the project on hold for at least six more months.

"From halfway across the world, the writer called me on a Friday to explain his publishing crisis, which was also coinciding with a personal crisis, and asked if we could collaborate closely on the fifty pages in question over the weekend. I agreed, cancelled my weekend plans, and we camped out at each end of the telephone and e-mail boxes almost nonstop for three days. He resubmitted the book on Tuesday, the book received all requisite signatures in-house, and a month later it went into production. This hands-on and sometimes unpredictable kind of collaboration with writers helps illustrate the special nature of independent editing." —Katharine Turok

"In August of 2005, a young woman who had just been fired from her very first job contacted me. She wanted my help writing a book about her experience. I asked if she'd written much before and I suppressed my groan when she said she hadn't, but what she lacked in credentials she made up for in energy and enthusiasm. She told me she had graduated at the top of her Ivy League college class and done everything right—good grades, great internships—to land a plum job at a consulting firm, but when she got there she quickly discovered that she didn't know how to have a job—she lacked the tools to deal with sexist bosses; she hadn't mastered PowerPoint; she believed her female coworkers would be supportive, not catty. She was determined to share what she'd learned to help other young women.

"As we worked together on her proposal, we not only structured her book but found ways to use her youth and inexperience in her favor—especially in terms of marketing. She built up her platform by writing for neighborhood papers, national newspapers, and eventually high-profile websites. All the pieces added up, the timing was right and she landed a great agent who secured a two-book deal." —Alice Peck

"My work on a book about a near-extinct species of birds was greatly enhanced when the author gave me a tour of a California estuary. Guided by his passion and on-site expertise, I was able to spot exquisite birds, hear bird-watching lingo, and see his high-end scope in action. Now I understood the thrill of what he was writing about, and was better able to help him communicate it.

"One of my most challenging assignments was to add action scenes to a memoir by an Olympic fencing champion. Here was a subject I knew nothing about. I tried to bone up in advance through reading, but my author had a better idea. Working his way across my living room floor, he sparred with an invisible opponent, demonstrating what he wished to describe in his book. I wrote down what I saw.

"As an independent editor, I have the time and freedom to work 'outside the book,' to literally enter the worlds my authors are writing about." —Ruth Greenstein

YOUR BOOK MAY BE BETTER THAN YOU (AND THEY) THINK

BY THE EDITORS OF THE CREATIVE LITERARY ALLIANCE (WWW.CREATIVELITERARYALLIANCE.COM)

As independent editors, we are often approached by writers who are "stuck." They may have spent a great deal of time crafting their manuscript or book proposal, only to find their energy and confidence waning. Some have received repeated rejections from literary agents or publishers. Others may be grappling with confusing feedback from writing workshops, or well-meaning but indiscriminate praise from family members or friends. Suddenly—or gradually—these authors have come to feel that it just may not be worth the effort.

They may even be wondering, "Is my book really that bad?"

Perhaps it's not.

We've all heard stories about best-selling authors who were rejected by virtually every publisher before finally selling their work. Luckily for these writers, they didn't give up in despair. But you can bet they asked themselves whether their work was any good, and if anyone would find it worth publishing.

The truth is, agents and in-house editors are so overworked that few of them have time to tell a writer precisely why they are passing on his work, and what he needs to do to fix it. In fact, many of them don't read far enough into a manuscript or proposal to know for sure whether it has any value. They know that they'll have to reject a large portion of submissions, and so any of a number of fixable issues may trigger their rejection—freeing them to move on to the next in the pile.

This is where a good independent editor can help. She will look at your manuscript or proposal the way industry professionals would view it, if they had the time. She can show you exactly where the weak points are, help you formulate a plan to address them, and guide you along the way. She can help you answer such common questions as:

Why have I received so many rejection letters?

You may get dozens of rejections without knowing why, and what you can do about it. If there are personalized comments in those rejection letters, an independent editor might discern some common thread in them that would help you understand why. In addition, your editor will know the sort of material agents and publishers are looking for, and can help you bring out the elements of your work that are most likely to sell. She can also guide you in defining your market. It may be that with some shift of language or perspective, your book would appeal to a broader or very different group of people than you originally had in mind.

My family and friends love my book, so why can't I get an agent?

Thank goodness for supportive family and friends—where would we all be without them? Yet the fact is that because they are so close to you, they can't possibly be objective about your work. Even a relative who is a published, successful author may not be the best person to critique your book. Enjoy the compliments, but put your trust in an independent editor who understands the publishing business *and* has your best interests at heart.

How do I make sense of all the conflicting feedback I've received in writing workshops?

Unfortunately, workshops are not always helpful. The group members are not publishing professionals; they may be too kind, failing to point out your book's flaws, or too critical, because they are competitive or simply not knowledgeable. Plenty of good manuscripts have permanently ended up in bottom drawers because their authors received discouraging workshop feedback. An independent editor, on the other hand, can be like a breath of fresh air. He knows publishing from the inside out, and has no agenda but helping you to make your book the best it can be.

I'm really nervous about sending my manuscript out. It's my baby. What if an agent or house editor "rips it to shreds"?

If you're sitting on a manuscript because you are afraid to let it out into the world, to possibly be exposed to harsh scrutiny, relax. An independent editor can be an excellent first reader. She will emphasize your manuscript's strong points, while gently showing you how it can be improved. She wants you to succeed, and understands the complicated emotions authors may feel. She has had years of experience in communicating with writers in ways that they can understand and use.

What kind of publishing is best for my work?

Are you aiming for traditional (commercial) publication, self-publishing, or an e-book? Would you be happy with a limited edition, privately printed for friends, family, or clients? Do you see your book as part of an overall media strategy, in conjunction with a website or online marketplace? Perhaps you want publication to help further your career, or even as a stepping stone to a new career. An independent editor can help you define your publication goals.

I've gone over my work countless times and I've done as much as I can on my own. But how do I really know if it's ready for submission?

Working together, you and your independent editor will review your manuscript or proposal, looking for anything that might need improvement. If your work is fiction or a memoir, your editor will be looking at such aspects as character development, point of view, plot, structure, tone, dialogue, theme, pacing, and originality. If you're writing a nonfiction book or proposal, your editor will evaluate your basic concept and idea development, your planned approach and writing style, your platform, and the market for your book.

It's very possible that with the proper guidance and some reworking, you will find your manuscript or proposal is not just better than you thought, but a work you can be proud of—and one that will catch the attention of agents and publishers.

The Creative Literary Alliance, www.creativeliteraryalliance.com, is a group of expert independent editors and publishing consultants who work with authors, literary agents, and publishers.

THE LISTINGS

WORDS INTO PRINT

www.wordsintoprint.org

Words into Print is one of New York's top networks of independent book editors, writers, and publishing consultants. Founded in 1998, WiP is a professional alliance whose members provide editorial services to publishers, literary agents, and book packagers, as well as to individual writers. Members of WiP have extensive industry experience, averaging 20 years as executives and editors with leading trade book publishers. As active independent professionals, members meet individually and as a group with agents and other publishing colleagues; participate in conventions, conferences, panels, and workshops; and maintain affiliations with organizations that include PEN, AWP, the Author's Guild, the Women's National Book Association, the Modern Language Association, and the Academy of American Poets.

The consultants at Words into Print are committed to helping established and new writers develop, revise, and polish their work. They also guide clients through the publishing process by helping them find the most promising route to publication. WiP's editors and writers provide:

- Detailed analyses and critiques of proposals and manuscripts

- Editing, cowriting, and ghostwriting

- Expert advice, ideas, and techniques for making a writer's project the best it can be

- Assistance in developing query letters and synopses for literary agents and publishers

- Referrals to literary agents, publishers, book packagers, and other publishing services

- Guidance in developing publicity and marketing strategies

- Project management—from conception through production

- Inside information writers need to make their way successfully through the publishing world

Words into Print's editors offer top-tier assistance at competitive rates. Brief profiles appear below. For more information, please visit www.wordsintoprint.org.

Marlene Adelstein
E-mail: madelstein@aol.com

Thorough, constructive critiques, editing, advice on material's commercial potential, and agent referrals when appropriate. Over 20 years' experience in publishing and feature film development. Specializes in commercial and literary fiction: mysteries, thrillers; women's fiction, romance, historical; young adult; memoir; nonfiction proposals; screenplays.

Martin Beiser
E-mail: Martin.Beiser@gmail.com

Has spent three decades in the book and magazine publishing world. At Free Press, he edited numerous best-selling and award-winning books. He was managing editor at GQ magazine for 12 years. Offers thorough critiques, line editing, and developmental editing. Specializing in narrative nonfiction, history, current affairs, politics, sports, business, biography, memoir, travel/adventure, magazine journalism, nonfiction proposals, the extended essay.

Linda Carbone
E-mail: lindacarbone@optonline.net

Twenty-five years of experience editing all types of nonfiction, particularly memoir, health, and psychology, but including parenting, self-help, and social science. Former senior developmental editor with Basic Books. Has worked with Paul Bloom, Stephen Carter, Lama Surya Das, Seth Godin, and Alice Miller. Offers detailed critique, rewriting/book doctoring, and developmental, substantive, and line editing of manuscripts and proposals. Can assist with finding an agent when appropriate.

Ruth Greenstein
E-mail: rg@greenlinepublishing.com

Over 20 years' experience with literary fiction, biography/memoir, social issues, cultural criticism, arts, travel, nature, popular science, health, psychology, religion/spirituality, poetry, photography, media companions, reference. Cofounder of WiP; formerly with Harcourt and Ecco. Has worked with Anita Shreve, Erica Jong, John Ashbery, Gary Paulsen, Alice Walker, Sallie Bingham, and Dennis Lehane. Offers a full range of editorial services, as well as synopsis writing, submissions guidance, and Web presence development.

Melanie Kroupa
E-mail: mkroupa@verizon.net

Thirty-five years of editing literature for children and young adults, including one winner and three finalists of the National Book Award, as well as Newbery and Caldecott Honor Books. Most recently at Farrar, Straus & Giroux / Melanie Kroupa Books. Manuscript and proposal evaluation, developmental, substantive, and line editing of picture books, fiction, nonfiction, and memoir. Authors include Phillip Hoose, Debby Dahl Edwardson, Martha Brooks, Cari Best, Ibtisam Barakat, Terry Farish.

Alice Peck
E-mail: alicepeck@alicepeck.com

Edits, evaluates, and rewrites memoir, narrative, spirituality, and fiction (especially first novels); writes and edits proposals. Acquired books and developed them into scripts for film and television (David Brown to MTV) before shifting her focus to editing in 1998. Authors include Alison L. Heller, Chase N. Peterson, Don Handfield, Dr. Jeffrey B. Rubin, Hannah Seligson, Jeri Parker, Joanie Schirm, Kim Powers, Kristen Wolf, Lama Surya Das, Laurence Klavan, Susan McBride, and Tim Cockey.

Alice Rosengard
E-mail: arosengard1@yahoo.com

Developmental and detailed editing, manuscript, and proposal evaluation. Concentrations: literary and mainstream fiction, history, memoir, biography, science, international affairs, cookbooks. Over 35 years of experience guiding new and established writers published by HarperCollins, Palgrave Macmillan, Doubleday, Basic Books, St. Martin's, and Bantam, among others. Authors worked with include Stephen Mitchell, Martha Rose Shulman, Larry Sloman, Bette Bao Lord, John Ehle, Avner Mandelman, Sue L. Hall, MD, Jay R. Tunney, and George C. Daughan.

Katharine Turok
E-mail: kturok@gmail.com

Manuscript evaluation; developmental, substantive, and line editing; rewriting; condensing. Literary and mainstream fiction, autobiography/memoir, biography, contemporary issues, film, history, nature, poetry, psychology, popular reference, theater, travel, visual arts, women's issues, translations. Over 20 years' international experience acquiring and editing works from new and established writers and published by major houses including Bloomsbury, Dutton, Folger Shakespeare Library, Scribner, and independent presses.

Michael Wilde
E-mail: michaelwildeeditorial@earthlink.net

Provides first-time and experienced authors with all manner of editorial services and help with writing. More than 20 years' experience working with leading authors and publishers in subjects ranging from scholarly and professional books to popular culture, literary and mainstream fiction, children's books, and young adult novels. Can assist in finding an agent when appropriate.

INDEPENDENT EDITORS GROUP

www.bookdocs.com

The Independent Editors Group is a professional affiliation of highly select, diverse, experienced freelance editors/book doctors who work with writers, editors, and agents in trade book publishing. They are: Sally Arteseros, Maureen Baron, Harriet Bell, Susan Dalsimer, Paul De Angelis, Michael Denneny, Joyce Engelson, Jerry Gross, Susan Leon, Richard Marek, James O'Shea Wade, Betty Sargent, and Genevieve Young.

Years of distinguished tenure at major publishing houses made them eminently qualified to provide the following editorial services on fiction and nonfiction manuscripts.

+ In-depth evaluations and detailed critiques

+ Problem-solving

+ Plot restructure

+ Developmental and line editing

+ Reorganization, revision, and rewriting

+ Book proposals and development

+ Ghostwriting and collaboration

If any editor is unavailable, referrals will be made to other appropriate IEG members. Inquiries are welcomed; please do not send manuscripts. Fees, references, and résumés are available from editors on request.

Whenever you have a project calling for freelance editorial expertise, get in touch with the best editors in trade book publishing today to solve your manuscript problems.

Sally Arteseros
E-mail: sarteseros@cs.com

Edits all kinds of fiction; literary, commercial, women's, historical, contemporary, inspirational. A specialist in short stories. And in nonfiction: biography, autobiography, memoir, psychology, anthropology, business, regional books, and academic books. Editor at Doubleday for more than 25 years.

Maureen Baron
150 West 87th Street, #6C
New York, NY 10024
212-787-6260

Former vice president/editor-in-chief of NAL/Signet Books continues to work with established and developing writers in all areas of mainstream fiction and non-fiction. Specialties: medical novels and thrillers; women's issues; health matters; African American fiction; biography; memoirs. Knows the market and has good contacts. Book club consultant.

Harriet Bell
315 E. 68th Street
New York, NY 10065
E-mail: harrietbell@verizon.net
www.bellbookandhandle.com
www.bookdocs.com

More than 25 years as editor and publisher at leading trade houses. Areas of interest and expertise: Nonfiction including business, cooking, crafts, diet, fitness, health and lifestyle, how-to, gastronomy, illustrated books, memoir, nonfiction narrative, popular psychology, reference, and wine.

Susan Dalsimer
Editorial Consultant
320 West 86th Street
New York, NY 10024-3139
212-496-9164 | fax: 212-501-0439
E-mail: SDalsimer124@aol.com

Edits fiction and nonfiction. In fiction edits literary and commercial fiction as well as young-adult fiction. In nonfiction interests include the areas of memoir, spirituality, psychology, self-help, biography, theater, film, and television. Authors worked with include Paul Auster, Fredric Dannen, Thomas Farber, Annette Insdorf, Iris Krasnow, Padma Lakshmi, D.J. Levien, Anthony Minghella, John Pierson, Martin Scorsese, and Veronica Webb.

Paul De Angelis Book Development
273 Town Street
West Cornwall CT 06796
860-672-6882
E-mail: pdeangelis@bookdocs.com
www.bookdocs.com

Manuscript evaluations, rewriting or ghostwriting, and editing. Thirty years' experience in key positions at St. Martin's Press, E. P. Dutton, and Kodansha America. Special expertise in history, current affairs, music, biography, literature, translations, popular science. Authors worked with: Delany sisters, Mike Royko, Peter Guralnick, Barbara Pym, Alexander Dubcek.

Michael Denneny
459 Columbus Ave., Box 204
New York, NY 10024
212-362-3241
E-mail: mldenneny@aol.com

Thirty-four years' editorial experience at the University of Chicago Press, the Macmillan Company, St. Martin's Press, and Crown Publishing. Works on both fiction and nonfiction manuscripts for publishers, literary agents, and authors, doing editorial evaluations, structural work on manuscripts, and complete line editing, as well as helping with the preparation of book proposals. Published, among others, Ntozake Shange, Buckminster Fuller, G. Gordon Liddy, Linda Barnes, Joan Hess, and Steven Saylor. Has won the Lambda Literary Award for Editing (1993), the Literary Market Place Editor of the Year Award (1994), and the Publishing Triangle Editor's Award (2002).

Jerry Gross
63 Grand Street
Croton-on-Hudson, NY 10520-2518
E-mail: GrosAssoc@aol.com

More than 40 years of specific, problem-solving critiques. My reports offer specific suggestions for solutions to these problems. I do restructuring and line editing in all areas of quality fiction and nonfiction, adult and young adult, upmarket women's and men's fiction, historical novels, thrillers, crime novels, espionage novels, memoirs, social history, politics, mass culture: films and the stage, popular health and medicine, etc. My aim is to help the author write to the best of his or her ability, and to make the manuscript as effective and salable as possible.

Susan Leon
21 Howell Avenue
Larchmont, NY 10538
914-833-1429

Editor specializing in preparation of book proposals and collaborations, including two *New York Times* best sellers. Fiction: All areas—commercial, literary, historical, and women's topics. Nonfiction: History, biography, memoir, autobiography, women's issues, family, lifestyle, design, travel, food. Also, law, education, information, and reference guides.

Richard Marek

240 Hillspoint Road
Westport, CT 06880
203-341-8607

Former president and publisher of E. P. Dutton specializes in editing and ghost-writing. Edited Robert Ludlum's first nine books, James Baldwin's last five, and Thomas Harris's *Silence of the Lambs*. As ghostwriter, collaborated on six books, among them a novel that sold 225,000 copies in hardcover and more than 2 million in paperback.

Betty Kelly Sargent

212-486-1531 | fax: 212-759-3933
E-mail: bsargent@earthlink.net

Betty Kelly Sargent is a veteran book and magazine editor with over 30 years of experience in the publishing business. Most recently she was editor-in-chief of William Morrow and before that books and fiction editor at *Cosmopolitan Magazine*. She has been an executive editor at large at HarperCollins and executive editor of Delacorte Press, and started out as a senior editor at Dell Books. Now a writer and freelance editor, she is coauthor of *Beautiful Bones Without Hormones* with Leon Root, MD, *What Every Daughter Wants Her Mother to Know* and *What Every Daughter Wants Her Father to Know* with Betsy Perry. She specializes in women's fiction as well as memoir, diet, health, lifestyle, self-help, and general nonfiction.

James O'Shea Wade

1565 Baptist Church Road
Yorktown Heights, NY 10598
914-962-4619

With 30 years' experience as editor-in-chief and executive editor for major publishers, including Crown/Random House, Macmillan, Dell, and Rawson-Wade, I edit and ghostwrite in all nonfiction areas and specialize in business, science, history, biography, and military. Also edit all types of fiction, prepare book proposals, and evaluate manuscripts.

Genevieve Young

30 Park Avenue
New York, NY 10016
fax: 212-683-9780

Detailed analysis of manuscripts, including structure, development, and line editing. Areas of special interest include biography, autobiography, medicine, animals, modern Chinese history, and all works with a storyline, whether fiction or nonfiction.

THE CONSULTING EDITORS ALLIANCE

The Consulting Editors Alliance is a group of highly skilled independent book editors, each with a minimum of 15 years' New York publishing experience.

We offer a broad range of services, in both fiction and nonfiction areas. These services include development of book proposals, in-depth evaluation of manuscripts, project development, line editing and rewriting, "book doctoring," and collaboration and ghostwriting.

We work with writers both published and unpublished, literary agents, packagers, and editors at major publishers and at small presses across the country.

Arnold Dolin
212-874-3419 | fax: 212-580-2312
E-mail: abdolin@consulting-editors.com

Specialties: Contemporary issues/politics, popular psychology, business, memoir/biography, literary fiction, gay fiction, theater, films, music. Arnold Dolin has held various editorial and executive positions during his nearly five decades in publishing. Most recently he was senior vice-president and associate publisher at Dutton Plume. He has edited a wide range of fiction and nonfiction, including *The Cause Is Mankind* by Hubert Humphrey, *On Escalation* by Herman Kahn, *Martha Graham: A Biography* by Don McDonagh, *With Child* by Phyllis Chesler, *Parachutes and Kisses* by Erica Jong, several books by Leonard Maltin, *Cures and Stonewall* by Martin Duberman, *Inside Intel* by Tim Jackson, *Defending the Spirit* by Randall Robinson, and *RFK* by C. David Heymann. His services are available as an editor and a consultant.

Moira Duggan
914-234-7937 | fax: 914-234-7937-*51
E-mail: mduggan@consulting-editors.com

Specialties: Self-help, health, sports (especially equestrian), travel, nature, architecture, illustrated books, biography. Moira Duggan offers critique and solutions in all phases of adult nonfiction book development: concept, presentation, writing style, factual soundness. Whether as an editor, collaborator, or ghost, she aims for excellence of content and peak marketability in every project. Before turning freelance, she was managing editor at The Ridge Press, which conceived and produced quality illustrated books. She has written eight nonfiction titles, including *Family Connections: Parenting Your Grown Children* (coauthor), *The Golden Guide to Horses*, and *New York*. Her editorial philosophy: Respect and guide the writer; be committed, tactful, and reliable; deliver on time.

Sandi Gelles-Cole

914-679-7630

E-mail: sgelles-cole@consulting-editors.com

Specialties: Commercial fiction and nonfiction. Other: First novels; "wellness" issues for women; general fiction or nonfiction on behalf of nonwriter experts or celebrities. Sandi Gelles-Cole founded Gelles-Cole Literary Enterprises in 1983, after 11 years as an acquisitions editor for major New York publishers. Strong points include: developing concept and integrating for fiction and nonfiction, concretizing concept and integrating it throughout the work; for fiction: structuring plot, developing subplot, deepening characterization, collaboration, rewriting, preparing proposals. Some authors Sandi Gelles-Cole has worked with: Danielle Steel, Alan Dershowitz, Victoria Gotti, Christiane Northrup, Rita (Mrs. Patrick) Ewing, and Chris Gilson, whose first novel, *Crazy for Cornelia*, was sold in an overnight preemptive sale as a major hardcover and became a *Los Angeles Times* best seller.

David Groff

212-645-8910

E-mail: dgroff@consulting-editors.com

Specialties: Fiction, biography/memoir, science, current affairs. David Groff is a poet, writer, and independent editor focusing on narrative. For the last eleven years, he has worked with literary and popular novelists, memoirists, journalists, and scientists whose books have been published by Atria, Bantam, HarperCollins, Hyperion, Little Brown, Miramax, Putnam, St. Martin's, Wiley, and other publishers. For 12 years he was an editor at Crown, publishing books by humorist Dave Barry, novelists Colin Harrison and Paul Monette, and journalists Patrice Gaines, Michael D'Antonio, and Frank Browning. He coauthored *The Crisis of Desire: AIDS and the Fate of Gay Brotherhood* by Robin Hardy, and *An American Family*, with Jon and Michael Galluccio. David's book *Theory of Devolution* was published in 2002 as part of the National Poetry Series.

Hilary Hinzmann

212-942-0771

E-mail: hhinzmann@consulting-editors.com

Specialties: History, science, technology, business, sports, music, political/social issues, biography/memoir, and fiction. Formerly an editor at W.W. Norton, Hilary Hinzmann has edited *New York Times Book Review* Notable Books of the Year in both fiction and nonfiction. Books he has worked on include *Winfield: A Player's Life* by Dave Winfield and Tom Parker (a *New York Times* best seller), *Marsalis on Music* by Wynton Marsalis, *Virgil Thomson: Composer on the Aisle* by Anthony Tommasini, *The Perez Family* by Christine Bell, the Kevin Kerney mystery series by Michael McGarrity, and *The Symbolic Species: The Coevolution of Language and the Brain* by Terrence W. Deacon. He is now assisting fiction and nonfiction writers with development of their work, editing manuscripts for publishers, ghostwriting, and cowriting.

THE INDEPENDENT EDITORS

Judith Kern

212-249-5871 | fax: 212-249-4954

E-mail: kernjt@aol.com

Specialties: Self-help, spirituality, lifestyle, food, health, and diet. Other: Mysteries, women's fiction. Judith Kern was an in-house editor for more than 25 years, most recently a senior editor at Doubleday, before becoming an independent editor and writer. She has worked with well-known fiction writers including Charlotte Vale Allen, Jon Hassler, Bette Pesetsky, and Patricia Volk, and Edgar award-winning mystery writers Mary Willis Walker and John Morgan Wilson. Her best-selling and award-winning cookbook authors include Alfred Portale, Pino Luongo, Michael Lomonaco, and Madeleine Kamman. She has collaborated with Jennifer Workman on *Stop Your Cravings* (The Free Press); with Joe Caruso on *The Power of Losing Control* (Gotham); and with Dr. Jane Greer on *The Afterlife Connection* (St. Martin's Press). She also worked with Alan Morinis on *Climbing Jacob's Ladder* (Broadway); Dr. Arlene Churn on *The End Is Just the Beginning* (Doubleday/Harlem Moon); and Ivan Richmond on *Growing Up Zen in America* (Atria). She is a member of the Author's Guild, The James Beard Society, and the International Association of Culinary Professionals.

Danelle McCafferty

212-877-9416 | fax: 212-877-9486

E-mail: dmccafferty@consulting-editors.com

Specialties: Thrillers, mysteries, women's contemporary and historical fiction, romances, and inspirational novels. Other: Self-help, religion/spirituality, theater, and true crime. A former senior editor at Bantam Books, Danelle McCafferty started her own editorial services business in 1990. She works on all stages of a manuscript, from outline and plot development to line editing and/or rewriting. Over the past 25 years, she has edited best-selling novels by Tom Robbins, Dana Fuller Ross, Peter Clement, Frank Perretti, Nora Roberts, Patricia Matthews, and Janelle Taylor, among others. Nonfiction authors include Bill Ury (negotiating), Ed Jablonski (theater), and Eileen MacNamara (true crime). As editorial director for a packager, she oversaw six highly successful mystery series. The author of two nonfiction books and numerous articles, she is a member of the American Society of Journalists and Authors and the Editorial Freelancers Association.

Nancy Nicholas

E-mail: nnicholas@consulting-editors.com

Specialties: Fiction, including first novels, historical fiction, and mysteries; biographies and autobiographies, history, theater, hobbies, and gay issues. Nancy Nicholas has worked at three book publishers and three magazines in a variety of roles. In 18 years at Knopf, she worked on literary and popular fiction, serious nonfiction, and translations. At Simon & Schuster, she edited fiction and nonfiction by a number of celebrities, including Joan Collins, Marlene Dietrich's daughter

Maria Riva, Jerry Falwell, Jesse Jackson, Shirley Conran, and Shelley Winters. At Doubleday, she worked on the revised Amy Vanderbilt etiquette book. She was also a senior editor at *Vogue*, *Mirabella*, and *Connoisseur* magazines. Since becoming a freelancer, Nicholas has handled projects for many publishers, from editing Nick Malgieri's baking books and Michael Lee West's "Crazy Lady" Southern fiction to riding herd on the project that became Bill Gates's *The Road Ahead* and writing *Cooking for Madam* with Marta Sgubin, Jacqueline Kennedy Onassis's cook.

Joan B. Sanger

voice/fax: 212-501-9352
E-mail: jsanger@consulting-editors.com

Specialties: Mainstream commercial fiction, primarily legal and medical thrillers, mysteries, contemporary women's fiction. Other: Structuring nonfiction proposals, biography, and autobiography. Joan Sanger has been an independent editorial consultant for over 10 years, primarily developing and editing commercial fiction. Her referrals come from agents, publishers, and private clients. Her authors, who are published by Berkeley, Warner Books, HarperCollins, and Simon & Schuster, include Gary Birken, MD, an author of medical thrillers who is working on his fourth novel, James Grippando, and Bonnie Comfort. Prior to setting up her consultancy she was a senior editor for 15 years at Simon & Schuster, founder, vice-president and editor-in-chief of the hardcover division of New American Library, and vice-president and senior editor at G.P. Putnam. Among her best-selling authors are Irving Wallace, Kitty Kelley, Anne Tolstoi Wallach, Henry Fonda, and Arthur Ashe. She has been a member of the Women's Media Group for 20 years.

Carol Southern

E-mail: csouthern@consulting-editors.com

Specialties: Personal growth, relationships, spiritual/inspirational, health/beauty, women's issues, biography, memoir, lifestyle. Carol Southern is a consultant, editor, book doctor, and ghostwriter. Prior to starting her own business in 1998, she held editorial and executive positions at Crown and Random House, where she was publisher of her own imprint, Carol Southern Books. She has edited many successful authors, including Donald Kauffman, *Color*; Ron Chin, *Feng Shui Revealed*; Sonia Choquette, *The Psychic Pathway*; biographer Carol Brightman; and Pulitzer Prize winners Naifeh and Smith (*Jackson Pollock*), as well as best-selling lifestyle authors Martha Stewart, Lee Bailey, and Chris Madden.

Karl Weber

voice/fax: 914-238-6929
E-mail: kweber@consulting-editors.com

Specialties: Business, including management, personal finance, and business narratives; also current affairs, politics, popular reference, and religious/spiritual. Karl Weber is a writer, book developer, and editor specializing in nonfiction, with a focus on business-related topics. In 15 years as an editor and publisher with McGraw-Hill, the American Management Association, John Wiley & Sons, and Times Business/Random House, Weber edited many best sellers in fields such as management, investing, careers, business narratives, and memoirs. He helped to create Wiley's acclaimed *Portable MBA* book series, and, when *Worth* magazine in 1997 selected the 15 best investment books of the past 150 years, two were titles edited by Weber. He also edited three best-selling books by former President Jimmy Carter, *Living Faith*, *Sources of Strength*, and *An Hour Before Daylight*.

THE EDITORS CIRCLE

www.theeditorscircle.com

We are a group of independent book editors with more than 100 years of collective experience on staff with major New York book publishers. We have come together to offer our skills and experience to writers who need help bringing their book projects from ideas or finished manuscripts to well-published books.

As publishing consultants (or "book doctors"), we offer a variety of editorial services that include defining and positioning manuscripts in the marketplace; evaluating and critiquing complete or partial manuscripts and book proposals; editing, ghostwriting, or collaborating on manuscripts and proposals; offering referrals to agents and publishers; helping authors develop platforms and query letters; and consulting on publicity and marketing.

So if you need help refining your book idea, editing or restructuring your manuscript, or defining and positioning your project in the marketplace, the book publishing professionals of The Editors Circle can offer you the editorial services you seek, a successful track record of projects placed and published, and the behind-the-scenes, hands-on experience that can help you take your idea or manuscript wherever you want it to go.

The editorial professionals of The Editors Circle include:

Bonny V. Fetterman

Editing and consulting: Academic and popular nonfiction, with special expertise in Judaica and books of Jewish interest (Jewish history, literature, religion, culture, and Bible); general nonfiction (history, biography, memoirs); works of scholarship (social sciences). Currently based: Jamaica, New York. Previous on-staff experience: senior editor of Schocken Books (15 years). Currently literary editor of *Reform Judaism* magazine.

Rob Kaplan

Editing, ghostwriting, and collaborating on nonfiction books and book proposals, including business, self-help, popular psychology, parenting, history, and other subjects. Currently based: Cortlandt Manor, New York. Previous on-staff experience: AMACOM Books (American Management Association), Macmillan, Prentice Hall, HarperCollins.

Beth Lieberman

Editing, collaborating, and proposal preparation: Parenting, psychology/motivational, women's issues, Los Angeles–interest, memoir, Judaica, commercial women's fiction, general fiction. Currently based: Los Angeles, California. Previous on-staff experience: New American Library (NAL), Warner Books, Kensington Publishing, Dove Books, and Audio, NewStar Press.

John Paine

Commercial and literary fiction, including thrillers, women's suspense, historical, African American, and mystery. Trade nonfiction, including adventure, memoirs, true crime, history, and sports. Currently based: Montclair, New Jersey. Previous on-staff experience: Dutton, New American Library, Prentice Hall.

Susan A. Schwartz

Ghostwriting: fitness, memoirs, other nonfiction subjects. Nonfiction editing: Popular health, parenting, business, relationships, memoirs; popular reference books (all subjects); book proposals, assessments, and evaluations; corporate marketing publications (histories, biographies, conference materials); website content. Fiction editing: Women's fiction; medical, legal, and political thrillers; general categories. Currently based: New York, New York. Previous on-staff experience: Random House, Doubleday, Facts on File, NTC/Contemporary Books.

THE CREATIVE LITERARY ALLIANCE

The Creative Literary Alliance is a group of independent New York City publishing professionals, offering clients worldwide a broad range of writing and editorial services. Each CLA professional at least 20 years' experience in the field, working with authors, literary agents, and every major publisher. They are specialists in both fiction and nonfiction, and are accessible via telephone, e-mail, and/or in person.

Members of the Creative Literary Alliance can help writers with:

+ A detailed evaluation and critique of a manuscript or proposal

+ Idea development

+ Substantive editing, rewriting, and polishing of any written material

- Book collaboration, coauthoring, and ghostwriting

- Assistance with query letters and book synopses

- Coaching throughout the writing process

- Project management, from conception through production

- Getting manuscript produced and distributed as an e-book and/or self-published as a print on demand (POD) book.

- Advice on platform development and marketing strategies

- Referrals to literary agents, publishers, and other literary services

- Advice on all aspects of the publishing process

Penelope Franklin

E-mail: Penelope@creativeliteraryalliance.com

Specialties—Nonfiction: art, biography/memoir, women's issues, health, history, social sciences, food, narrative nonfiction, natural history, self-help, paranormal, humor, travel.

Penelope Franklin is a writer, editor, and ghostwriter with over 30 years of publishing experience. She works closely with first-time authors as well as established ones, helping each to discover and develop a unique voice. She has worked with the publishers Reader's Digest Books, Ballantine, Harper's, Oxford University, Columbia University, *American Heritage* magazine, and *Current Biography* magazine. A veteran of United Nations publishing, she has helped writers worldwide who use English as a second language.

Penne, a member of the Association of Personal Historians, is particularly drawn to biographies, memoirs, and family histories. She is a pioneer in the pet history genre and has written, designed, and published limited-edition volumes for many pet lovers (www.PetPersonalHistories.com).

Janet Spencer King

E-mail: janet@creativeliteraryalliance.com

Specialties—Nonfiction: adventure, biographies, health, diet/fitness/nutrition, medical, memoirs, self-help/popular psychology, women's issues. Fiction: popular mainstream, women's literature.

Janet Spencer King has been an editor and writer for more than 25 years. She was for a time a literary agent, working closely with first-time and experienced nonfiction and fiction authors to prepare their proposals as well as editing their manuscripts to become fully ready for publication. In addition Janet has authored or coauthored four books published by leading publishing houses. Janet was also active in the magazine field, as editor-in-chief of three national magazines and as a writer of many magazine articles on subject ranging from family dynamics to health/medical/nutrition topics. In keeping with the changing publishing world Janet has developed expertise on guiding authors through self-publishing to produce their book as an e-book and/or through print on demand (POD).

Diane O'Connell
E-mail: diane@creativeliteraryalliance.com
Specialties—Fiction: commercial/mainstream, thrillers, mysteries, suspense, supernatural, young adult. Nonfiction: business, biography/memoirs, health/fitness/nutrition, lifestyle, self-help/popular psychology, spirituality.

An award-winning writer and editor with 25 years' experience, Diane O'Connell was an editor at Random House, and is the author or coauthor of five books published by leading publishing houses, including *Divorced Dads: Shattering the Myths* (Tarcher/Putnam), which was the subject of a *20/20* report. Diane is an expert at working with first-time authors, guiding them in every step of the writing and publishing process. She is equally at home with helping authors get traditionally published, as well as guiding them through the self-publishing and e-book maze. Diane is available to work with fiction and nonfiction authors at every stage of the writing and publishing process. She particularly welcomes first-time authors to contact her.

Olga Vezeris
E-mail: olga@creativeliteraryalliance.com
Specialties—Fiction: commercial/mainstream for historical, sagas, thriller/mystery/suspense, women's market. Nonfiction: art/architecture, business, crafts/hobbies, food/entertaining, gift books, health/fitness/nutrition, illustrated books, lifestyle/decorating, narrative nonfiction, self-help/popular psychology, spirituality/New Age, travel, true crime. She edits manuscripts and works with authors to develop book proposals and projects for traditional and self-publication as well as special markets and custom publishing.

Olga Vezeris has some of the most extensive experience in the publishing industry, having had senior editorial and subsidiary rights positions in companies including Simon & Schuster, Grand Central Publishing (and Time Life), Workman, HarperCollins Audio, and the Book of the Month Club group, where she has acquired, edited, or licensed many commercial fiction and nonfiction titles. Olga has lectured at the New York University publishing programs.

RESOURCES FOR WRITERS

WEBSITES FOR AUTHORS

One of the most valuable aspects of the World Wide Web for writers is that it provides the opportunity to explore the world of publishing. This annotated list of websites offers descriptions of some of the most useful sites for writers.

Now more than ever there's an infinite amount of resources available for writers on the Internet in anything from membership/subscription sites to personal websites of authors who also list agents of the same genre.

The trend of blogging has spread among publishers—it is now common for trade and university publishers to keep a blog, or even separate blogs for different imprints. Publishing bloggers keep things mixed up with guest pieces by house authors, book reviews, interviews, links, industry news, current events, videos, and more. Publishers use blogs to keep the public aware of new releases, establish goodwill between press, authors, and customers, and as an outlet for interesting topical content related to their books.

Not only publishers keep blogs, though. The blogging trend has spread across the whole spectrum of the book world. Many literary agents keep blogs that give writers invaluable advice, critique mistakes, and lend crucial insights into their individual preferences and personalities. Writers keep blogs chronicling their own publishing experiences and hurdles. And others, from critics to businessmen, printers, and engineers, lend their own unique and valuable opinions about the publishing world.

We are aware that blogs sprout up quickly, and while a fairly large list has been gathered, it is far from comprehensive. Follow links, sample, and explore and you will learn much about what people are thinking and how to approach them.

Below is a sampling of what's available on the Web, grouped according to the following categories:

- Anthology Resources

- Blogging Resources

  - Literary/Industry Blogs

  - Literary Agent Blogs

  - Publisher Blogs

  - University Press Blogs

- Children's Literature Resources

- Funding Resources

- Horror Resources

- Mystery Resources

- Poetry Resources

- Romance Resources

- Science Fiction Resources

- Screenwriting Resources

- Western Resources

- General Resource Sites

ANTHOLOGY RESOURCES

ANTHOLOGIESONLINE

www.AnthologiesOnline.com

Writers will find more than great articles and frequent postings of calls for manuscripts. From *Chicken Soup* to horror, anthology publishers post their calls for writers. Subscribers have advance notice of calls for manuscripts and may apply for a free promotional page.

The site has a comprehensive, up-to-date list of paying markets for writers of science fiction, fantasy, horror, and slipstream. One page lists all markets; other pages break out markets by pro, semi-pro, anthologies, and contests, as well as by print and electronic formats. Listings include summaries of guidelines and indications of markets' "aliveness," plus website URLs.

LITERARY/INDUSTRY BLOGS

BLOG OF A BOOKSLUT

www.bookslut.com/blog

Bookslut, the alias of eminent litblogger Jessa Crispin, features prolific magazine and book reviews, columns, interviews, essays, news, unusual links, history, book society, and much more.

BOOKDWARF

www.bookdwarf.com

The blog of Megan Sullivan, one of the frontlist buyers at the Harvard Book Store. She writes on books, reading reports, publishing news, film adaptations, humor, and opinion.

BOOKENDS, LLC

bookendslitagency.blogspot.com

Bookends is a literary agency focusing on fiction and nonfiction books for adult audiences. Their blog features publishing advice, views from the agent's perspective, industry opinions, book reviews, and inspiration.

BOOKNINJA

www.bookninja.com

Founded by Canadian editor and publisher George Murray, Bookninja is the premier Canadian literary site and is frequented by thousands of people from around the globe. It posts unusual publishing-related stories, hearsay, industry news, humor, and technology.

BOOKSQUARE

www.booksquare.com

The primary blog of Kassia Krozser. Honest, entertaining, and often hilarious writing on the publishing industry, technology, the Internet, markets, and writers.

CONFESSIONS OF AN IDIOSYNCRATIC MIND

www.sarahweinman.com

Confessions of an Idiosyncratic Mind is the blog of Sarah Weinman, the *Baltimore Sun*'s crime fiction columnist and writer of "Dark Passages," a monthly mystery and suspense column for the *Los Angeles Times Book Review*. It provides commentary on crime and mystery fiction, industry links, and genre news.

CONVERSATIONAL READING

www.conversationalreading.com

The blog of Scott Esposito, member of the National Book Critics Circle, reviewer and essayist, has been singled out by the *New York Times*, *The Village Voice*, and *Variety*, among others. It features literary news, interviews, reviews, rants, opinions, links, and more.

DEAR AUTHOR...

www.dearauthor.com

Six devoted readers serve up fiction book reviews (primarily romance and fantasy with some nonfiction and manga thrown in) and provide honest commentary on the romance genre and publishing industry.

THE ELEGANT VARIATION

www.marksarvas.blogs.com

According to Fowler's, "The Elegant Variation" is a term for the inept writer's pained efforts at freshness or vividness of expression. The acclaimed blog itself is the work of Mark Sarvas, writer, book reviewer, screenwriter, and newspaper editor. The posts feature quotes, marginalia, book reviews, contests, interviews, publishing news, book giveaways, and videos.

GALLEYCAT

www.mediabistro.com/galleycat

Galleycat is an all-purpose literary weblog that features updates in the writing world, announcements, profiles, essays, interviews, events, industry and bookseller news, and multimedia.

GOLDEN RULE JONES

www.goldenrulejones.com

This blog was started to cover literary events in Chicago, specifically fiction, poetry, and literary nonfiction.

LAILA LALAMI

www.lailalalami.com/blog

The blog of Laila Lalami, Moroccan-born writer, novelist, Fulbright fellow, and professor. It features journal entries, news, commentary, links, photographs, and opinions.

LITBLOG CO-OP

www.lbc.typepad.com

The Litblog Co-Op is made up of a coalition of bloggers for the purpose of drawing attention to the best of contemporary fiction, authors, and presses. A variety of participating bloggers post their opinions about fiction, publishing news, reviews, and podcasts.

THE LITERARY SALOON

www.complete-review.com/saloon

The Literary Saloon offers opinionated commentary on literary matters, news, links, and tirades. Updated daily, it offers plenty on commentary and updates on the industry, both at home and internationally.

MAUD NEWTON

www.maudnewton.com

Brooklyn editor and writer Maud Newton's entertaining blog has been widely praised by publications as various as the *New York Times Book Review*, *Forbes*, *New*

York Magazine, the *Washington Post*, and *Entertainment Weekly*. It features literary links, politics, humor, rants, recipes, essays, complaints, gossip, and more.

PUBLISHING FRONTIER

www.pubfrontier.com/about

Started by Peter Brantley, the director of the Digital Library Federation, Publishing Frontier aims to conduct provocative public discussion of the publishing revolution and how it affects readers, society, economics, and fundamental values such as privacy. Posts follow on technology, popular culture, book printing, publishing practice, business, science, gadgets, and more.

PUBLISHING INSIDER

www.publishinginsider.typepad.com/publishinginsider

Written by Carl Lennertz of HarperCollins Publishers, Publishing Insider reflects a fascination with how and why books sell. Movies, music, and museums are also explored as he studies how word of mouth operates in larger society. Posts on style, songs, best sellers, reissues, and marketing.

THREE PERCENT

www.rochester.edu/College/translation/threepercent

Three Percent has the goal of becoming a destination for readers, editors, and translators interested in finding out about modern and contemporary international literature. The title is taken from the fact that only 3 percent of books published in the United States are works in translation (and for poetry and fiction the number is closer to 0.7 percent). The site is a part of the University of Rochester's translation program. It posts on translation exercises, international book series, reviews, magazines, international events, and publishing.

WOULDN'T YOU LIKE TO KNOW?

www.isabelswift.blogspot.com

The blog of Isabel Swift, a member of Harlequin's New Business Development team, it offers posts about publishing, editing, business, relationships, romance, and storytelling in the 21st century.

LITERARY AGENT BLOGS

AGENT IN THE MIDDLE

agentinthemiddle.blogspot.com

The blog of NY-based literary agent Lori Perkins, AITM focuses on horror, social science fiction, dark fantasy, erotica, and pop culture. She posts on conventions, titles-I'd-like-to-see, erotica, romance, advice for writers, and agenting stories.

AGENTSPEAK

raleva31.livejournal.com

The blog of literary agent Rachel Vater, with Folio Literary Management. She posts on inspirational author tales, announcements, queries, blogs, websites, publicity, deals, and rejections.

BG LITERARY

bgliterary.livejournal.com

Children's book agent Barry Goldblatt writes about books he loves, books he's sold, events in children's publishing, and details in the life of an agent.

DHS LITERARY SHOW + TELL

dhsliterary.blogspot.com

The blog of DHS Literary (short for David Hale Smith Literary) releases information on new releases, deals, best-of lists, and industry buzz.

DYSTEL AND GODERICH LITERARY MANAGEMENT

www.dystel.com

The excellent Dystel and Goderich blog has posts on advances, insider publishing information, opinions, the business of writing, conferences, pitching, do's and don'ts, publicity, and essays.

ET IN ARCAEDIA, EGO

arcaedia.wordpress.com

The blog of Jennifer Jackson, agent at the Donald Maass Literary Agency. Jennifer writes "letters from the query wars," chronicling the war-torn battlefield of query submission and rejection, observations, links, lists, and small essays on writer-agent relations.

THE EVIL EDITOR

www.evileditor.blogspot.com

The Evil Editor's blog features writing exercises, cartoons, fill-in-the-captions, feedback, horror, science fiction, obituaries, and plots.

FULLCIRCLELIT

fullcirclelit.blogspot.com

The blog of Full Circle Literary is chock-full of literary links and excerpts culled from all corners of the Web.

THE KNIGHT AGENCY

knightagency.net/blog

The blog of the Knight Agency features member blogs, book reviews, news, recent deals, and manuscript submission.

LIT SOUP

litsoup.blogspot.com

The blog of Jenny Rappaport, literary agent at the L. Perkins Agency. Posts on upcoming events, query rejections, interns, cat tales, advice for writers, and titles.

THE REJECTER

rejecter.blogspot.com

This is the anonymous blog of an assistant at a literary agency. S/he writes: "On average I reject 95 percent of the letters immediately and put the other 5 percent on the 'maybe' pile. Here, I'll talk about my work." He posts on vanity presses, Amazon, podcasts, fiction, blogs, platforms, writer advice, and genres.

MISS SNARK

missssnark.blogspot.com

Although discontinued in May 2007 after receiving over 2.5 million hits, the archives of Miss Snark, the Literary Agent, are definitely worth perusing, especially for the writer who wants an extremely candid view of how poor submissions are received. Writers ask questions about the various details of the submission process, courting an agent, how queries should be structured, etc., and Miss Snark provides her very meticulous, professional, and uncensored opinions on what writers can do better.

NATHAN BRANSFORD

nathanbransford.blogspot.com

Nathan's excellent and regularly updated blog sports lengthy posts that give writing tips, critiques, and his opinions on publishing. His blog also has a thriving message board community, regularly garnering 75–100+ comments on each post. Read for advice on queries, submitting, and what goes on in the mind of an agent.

PUB RANTS

pubrants.blogspot.com

The blog of Denver-based literary agent Kristin, PubRants features advice for writers, opinions on details of query structuring, beginning-writer mistakes, videos, journal entries, and music updates.

PUBLISHER BLOGS

THE ABBEVILLE MANUAL OF STYLE

www.abbeville.com/blog

The blog of Abbeville Press, producer of fine art and illustrated books. Their posts feature interviews, photography, news, reviews, contests, videos, and opinions.

ADDENDA & ERRATA

addenda-errata.ivpress.com

Addenda and Errata is a blog from the editors of InterVarsity Press and brings readers up to date on issues, trends, and news related to evangelical publishing program of IVP Academic.

AMISTAD CONFIDENTIAL

www.amistadconfidential.blogspot.com

Amistad Confidential publishes books by and for the people of the African Diaspora. Posts on writers, upcoming books, African and African American issues in publishing, and more.

ANDREWS MCMEEL PUBLISHING, LLC NEWS

andrewsmcmeelpublishing.blogspot.com

The Andrews McMeel blog has book reviews, print and YouTube interviews, publishing news, author press, and links.

BANTAM DELL NEWS

www.randomhouse.com/bantamdell/news

The Bantam Dell blog features free excerpts, links to audio readings, author awards, sweepstakes info, podcasts, and event announcements.

THE BEST WORDS IN THE BEST ORDER

www.fsgpoetry.com

The venerable publishing house Farrar, Straus, & Giroux has an excellent poetry blog that features giveaways, audio poetry readings, posts by FSG poets, reviews, and poetry links.

CHELSEA GREEN

www.chelseagreen.com

The front page of Chelsea Green's website doubles as a blog with posts on environmental news, new books, international events, podcasts, video interviews, YouTube, environmental events, profiles, green tips, and recipes.

CHRONICLE BOOKS BLOG

www.chroniclebooks.com/blog

The Chronicle Books blog's mission is to let visitors know "what we're reading, what we're publishing, what makes us laugh, and what excites us." It features giveaways, book release info, event announcements, design ideas, photographs, tips, and television reviews.

DAVID R. GODINE, PUBLISHER

www.drgodine.blogspot.com

The blog of David R. Godine, Publisher, and Black Sparrow Books features upcoming titles, book reviews, articles, literary links, translations, blogs, bookstores, announcements, eulogies, and interviews.

FLOG!

www.fantagraphics.com/index.php?option=com_myblog

FLOG!, the blog of Fantagraphics, publisher of comic and art books, features doodles, art scans, convention coverage, cartoons, podcasts, interviews, sales, author and artist spotlights, and signings.

GIBBS SMITH BOOKS BLOG

gibbs-smithbooks.blogspot.com

Lifestyle and design publisher Gibbs Smith's blog has posts on new releases, author events, pictures, YouTube videos, kitchen tips, design tips, and interviews.

HARLEQUIN AMERICAN ROMANCE AUTHORS

harauthors.blogspot.com

The blog of authors who write Harlequin American Romance, the HAR blog features journal-style entries by authors on writing strategies and experiences, new releases, recipes, families, and pets.

HARLEQUIN HISTORICAL AUTHORS BLOG

harlequinhistoricalauthors.blogspot.com

Harlequin Historical authors discuss new releases, book excerpts, writing, and offers and promotions.

HARLEQUIN'S PARANORMAL ROMANCE BLOG

paranormalromanceblog.com

This blog features frequent posts by Harlequin Paranormal Romance authors, talking about their books, writing experiences, inspirations, and personal stories. There are also interviews and convention updates.

HIPPOCRENE BOOKS LANGUAGE AND TRAVEL BLOG

hippocrenebooks.blogspot.com

This very interesting blog features free samples of language learning programs, travel writing, vocabulary, and language.

INTRIGUE AUTHORS BLOG

intrigue-authors.blogspot.com

Harlequin Intrigue authors write about romance, writing, sexy books, journal-style experiences, and new releases.

LONELY PLANET TRAVEL BLOG

www.lonelyplanet.com/blogs/travel_blog

Lonely Planet's 326 authors and 400 travel-loving staff use their blog network to bring the best in travel blogging—buzzword events, breaking news, tough travel, odd corners, and the world's craziest kitsch.

NOLO BLOGS

www.nolo.com/blogs.cfm

The hub of Nolo legal publishing, it features numerous blogs on legal economics, divorce, estate planning, real estate, fundraising, patents, LLCs, law reform, and bankruptcy.

THE OLIVE READER

olivereader.com

The Olive Reader is the weblog of the Harper Perennial imprint of HarperCollins. It features posts on movies, a literary quote generator, info on books, the book world, event coverage and announcements, up-and-coming writers, amusing anecdotes, tattoos, pictures, and T-shirts.

ORBIT BOOKS

www.orbitbooks.net

Orbit is a UK-based leading publisher of science fiction and fantasy, recently established in the United States as an imprint of the Hachette Book Group USA. Their blog features items on Orbit books, info on author appearances, interviews, links, sci-fi—related news, and movies.

O'REILLY RADAR

radar.oreilly.com

The O'Reilly Radar features tech reviews and laments, guest bloggers, Internet, social networks, updates on the press, new books, statistical charts, and computer networks.

PANTHEON GRAPHIC NOVELS NEWS

graphic-novels.knopfdoubleday.com

The blog of Random House's graphic novel imprint, Pantheon Graphic Novels, has updates on author appearances, comic book news, animated movies, reviews, event announcements, awards, and upcoming publications.

PENGUIN BLOG (USA)

www.us.penguingroup.com/static/html/blogs

Reveals what life is like for Penguin editors, articles by Penguin authors and guest bloggers, podcasts, Penguin imprint news, and upcoming books.

ROWMAN AND LITTLEFIELD PUBLISHERS BLOG

rowmanblog.typepad.com

The Rowman and Littlefield blog features lengthy, high-quality articles and opinion by R&L authors, current events, political science, economics, literary updates, and education.

SIMON & SCHUSTER CANADA

simonschusterca.tumblr.com

This eclectic blog features YouTube posts, new books, scandals, appearances, recipes, photographs, author appearances, contests, book expos, and technology.

SOURCEBOOKS NEXT

www.sourcebooks.com/blog

Sourcebooks Next explores how the digital world is transforming the publishing industry and provides the latest Sourcebooks news on its books, authors, and other activities.

THE TYNDALE BLOG

www.tyndale.com/blog

The Tyndale Blog offers a closer look at Tyndale's products and its authors, including upcoming media interviews, information about publishing trends, and Tyndale corporate initiatives.

THE WINGED ELEPHANT

theoverlookpress.blogspot.com

The book blog and book vlog of The Overlook Press, the Winged Elephant has posts on book reviews, new releases, literary essays, author profiles, and announcements.

ZONDERVAN BLOG

zondervan.typepad.com/zondervan

Zondervan's mission is to express the current evangelical POV as manifested in author commentary, book excerpts, interviews, trends analysis, stimulating links, news from behind the scenes, and user comments.

UNIVERSITY PRESS BLOGS

BEACON BROADSIDE

www.beaconbroadside.com

Beacon Press's blog features political writing, articles by Beacon authors, book updates, political links, opinion essays, interviews, and news.

BOOKMARK

www.uapress.blogspot.com

Bookmark, the blog of the University of Arkansas Press, has reviews, announcements, links to UA author press, event info, and new books.

BROOKINGS PRESS BLOG

brookingspress.typepad.com

The blog of the Brookings Institution has new and featured books, excerpts from Brookings Press authors, essays, links, and politics.

THE CHICAGO BLOG

pressblog.uchicago.edu

The blog of the University of Chicago Press includes posts on author essays, interviews, excerpts, documentaries, book reviews, recent releases, current events, opinion, magazines, and links.

COLUMBIA UNIVERSITY PRESS BLOG

www.cupblog.org

The Columbia University Press Blog features posts on CUP titles, current events, reviews, politics, interesting books, posts by CUP authors, radio, and press.

DUKE UNIVERSITY PRESS

www.dukeupress.typepad.com

News from Duke University Press includes posts on current events, recent releases, videos, guest posts, reviews, and contests.

HARVARD UNIVERSITY PRESS PUBLICITY

www.harvardpress.typepad.com

HUP's blog features posts on book news and reviews, event notifications, current events, author interviews, and links.

ILLINOIS PRESS BOOK BLOG

www.press.uillinois.edu/wordpress

As the tagline puts it, the UIP blog brings "author appreciation, broadcast bulletins, event ephemera, and recent reviews from the University of Illinois Press." Publishing news and links, trivia, amusements, and reviews.

INDIANA UNIVERSITY PRESS BLOG

iupress.typepad.com/blog

The Indiana University Press blog features book reviews, feeds, history, Indiana-related material, choice links, catalogs, and Twitter updates.

LSU PRESS

blog.lsupress.org

The Louisiana State University Press blog features interviews, release info, literature news, amusing videos, author events, essays, and photography.

MITPRESSLOG

mitpress.mit.edu/blog

MIT Press features posts on technology, video games, international relations, academic news, environment, music, video, award news, the Internet, blog watches, author links, architecture, math, philosophy, and more.

NEWS FROM THE UNIVERSITY OF GEORGIA PRESS

ugapress.blogspot.com

The University of Georgia Press blog features book news, reviews, awards, press news, and info on UGA Press authors.

OUPBLOG

blog.oup.com

The blog of Oxford University Press USA features links, publishing updates, pop-culture articles, curious facts, words of the week, short biography, and much more eclectic material.

SAGE HOUSE NEWS

cornellpress.wordpress.com

Sage House News, the blog of the Cornell University Press, features author interviews, recent releases, links to articles, a Publicity Roundup, current events, blog reviews, podcasts, author news, and science.

THERE'S A HOLE IN THE BUCKET

holeinthebucket.wordpress.com

The blog for the University of Alberta Press features posts by the editors, new books, reviews, event reports, awards, announcements, many photographs, info for authors, and links.

UNIVERSITY OF CALIFORNIA PRESS BLOG

www.ucpress.edu/blog

The University of California Press Weblog features posts on book reviews, science, author posts, excerpts, press news, photographs, interviews, wine, podcasts, poetry, websites, awards, and current events.

UNIVERSITY OF HAWAI'I PRESS LOG

uhpress.wordpress.com

One the most respected publishers of Asian and Pacific studies in the world, the UHP blog includes posts on awards, recent releases, reviews, articles on Asian and Pacific history and current events, and Hawai'ian book event announcements.

UNIVERSITY OF NEBRASKA PRESS BLOG

www.nebraskapress.typepad.com

This blog has info on new releases, Tuesday trivia, history, UNP author guest blogs, reviews, interviews, and event announcements.

UNIVERSITY OF PENNSYLVANIA PRESS LOG

pennpress.typepad.com/pennpresslog

The UPenn Press blog features posts on new and forthcoming titles, excerpts, previews, interviews, links, current events, publishing updates, and commentary.

UNC PRESS BLOG

uncpressblog.com

The University of North Carolina Press blog has reviews, new releases, a Today in History feature, roadtrip journals, audio links, history, blogosphere updates, awards, and event reports.

YALE PRESS LOG

yalepress.wordpress.com

The Yale Press blog features recent releases, Yale Press author opinion, photo contests, podcasts, video, awards, eulogies, and summer reading lists.

CHILDREN'S LITERATURE RESOURCES

THE CHILDREN'S BOOK COUNCIL

www.cbcbooks.org

"CBC Online is the website of the Children's Book Council—encouraging reading since 1945." It provides a listing of articles geared toward publishers, teachers, librarians, booksellers, parents, authors, and illustrators—all those who are interested in the children's book field.

CHILDREN'S BOOK INSIDER

www.write4kids.com

"Whether you're published, a beginner, or just someone who's always dreamt of writing for kids," here you'll find a free library of how-to information, opportunities to chat with other children's writers and illustrators, links to research databases, articles, tips for beginners, secrets for success as a children's writer, message boards, a children's writing survey, the chance to ask questions of known authors, and the opportunity to register in the website's guestbook to receive free e-mail updates filled with news and tips. The site also features a listing of favorite books, Newbery Medal winners, Caldecott Award winners, current best sellers, and a link to its own children's bookshop.

THE SOCIETY OF CHILDREN'S BOOK WRITERS AND ILLUSTRATORS

www.scbwi.org

This website "has a dual purpose: It exists as a service to our members, as well as offering information about the children's publishing industry and our organization to nonmembers." It features a listing of events, awards and grants, publications, information for members, information on how to become a member, and a site map.

VERLA KAY'S WEBSITE FOR CHILDREN'S WRITERS

www.verlakay.com

This site is packed with information to assist writers of children's stories. Whether you are a beginner or a multipublished writer, there is something here for you. A chat room with nightly chats with other children's writers, online workshops and transcripts of past workshops, a Getting Started page, and a Published Writers page are just some of the features of this award-winning website.

FUNDING RESOURCES

ART DEADLINES LIST

artdeadlineslist.com

Art Deadlines List is a "monthly newsletter providing information about juried exhibitions and competitions, call for entries/proposals/papers, poetry and other writing contests, jobs, internships, scholarships, residencies, fellowships, casting calls, auditions, tryouts, grants, festivals, funding, financial aid, and other opportunities for artists, art educators, and art students of all ages. Some events take place on the Internet."

THE FOUNDATION CENTER

foundationcenter.org

The Foundation Center website is dedicated to assisting writers in finding grants. It offers "over 200 cooperating sites available in cities throughout the United States. Of particular note is its large online library, with a wonderful interactive orientation to grant seeking. You'll even find application forms for several funding sources here."

FUNDS FOR WRITERS

www.fundsforwriters.com

Funds for Writers specializes in leading writers to grants, awards, contests, fellowships, markets, and jobs. The two websites and three newsletters provide a weekly abundance of sources for writers to reference and put checks in the bank. The other sites teach you how to write. Funds for Writers tells you where to make a living doing it.

MICHIGAN STATE GRANT INDEX FOR WRITERS

staff.lib.msu.edu/harris23/grants/3writing.htm

This index includes a list of websites containing information on poetry grants, award programs, science writing, screenwriting, contests, scholarships, fellowships, reference, and student writing. The website is divided into categories for easy browsing.

NATIONAL FOUNDATION FOR THE ARTS

www.nea.gov/grants/apply/Lit.html

The National Foundation for the Arts believes that through literature, a nation expresses its hopes and fears and tells its stories to its citizens and to the world. Their website includes information on grants for arts projects, literature fellowships, radio and television programs, and more.

NATIONAL WRITERS UNION

www.nwu.org

The union for freelance writers working in US markets offers grievance resolution, industry campaigns, contract advice, health and dental plans, member education, job banks, networking, social events, and much more.

SOUTHERN ARTS FEDERATION

www.southarts.org

The Southern Arts Federation, a nonprofit regional arts organization founded in 1975, creates partnerships and collaborations; assists in the development of artists, arts professionals, and arts organizations; presents, promotes, and produces Southern arts and cultural programming; and advocates for the arts and arts education.

WESTERN STATES ARTS FEDERATION

www.westaf.org

The WSAF is a "nonprofit arts service organization dedicated to the creative advancement and preservation of the arts. Focused on serving the state arts agencies, arts organizations, and artists of the West, WSAF fulfills its mission by engaging in innovative approaches to the provision of programs and services and focuses its efforts on strengthening the financial, organizational, and policy infrastructure of the arts in the West."

HORROR RESOURCES

DARK ECHO HORROR

www.darkecho.com/darkecho/index.html

Dark Echo Horror features interviews, reviews, a writers' workshop, dark links, and a newsletter. Articles relate to topics such as the perception and psychology of the horror writer, the "best" horror, and reviews of dark erotica. The site also offers information and links to fantasy writing.

HORROR WRITERS ASSOCIATION

www.horror.org

The Horror Writers Association (HWA) was formed to "bring writers and others with a professional interest in horror together, and to foster a greater appreciation of dark fiction in general." Bestower of the Bram Stoker Awards, HWA offers a newsletter, late-breaking market news, informational e-mail bulletins, writers' groups, agents, FAQ, and links.

MASTERS OF TERROR

www.horrorworld.org

Masters of Terror offers information about horror fiction, book reviews, new authors, horror movies, author message boards, HorrorNet chat room, and a reference guide and critique of horror fiction that features some 500 authors and 2,500 novels. The site also includes exclusive author interviews, book and chapbook reviews, and horror news.

MYSTERY RESOURCES

CLUELASS HOME PAGE

www.cluelass.com

The ClueLass Home Page offers awards for mystery fiction and nonfiction, information about conferences and conventions, and mystery groups for writers and fans. It includes information about markets, other contests, reference material, and online support, as well as listings of mystery magazines and newsletters, an international directory of mystery booksellers and publishers, and factual links about crime, forensics, and investigation.

MYSTERY WRITERS OF AMERICA

www.mysterywriters.org

Mystery Writers of America "helps to negotiate contracts, watches development in legislation and tax law, sponsors symposia and mystery conferences, and publishes books." The site includes mystery links, awards, a calendar of events, writers' discussions, and a new online mystery every day. It was established to promote and protect "the interests and welfare of mystery writers and to increase the esteem and the literary recognition given to the genre."

SHORT MYSTERY FICTION SOCIETY

www.shortmystery.net

The Short Mystery Fiction Society "seeks to actively recognize writers and readers who promote and support the creative art form of short mysteries in the press, in other mystery organizations, and through awards." The site offers a newsletter and other resources.

SISTERS IN CRIME

www.sistersincrime.org

Sisters in Crime is a website that vows to "combat discrimination against women in the mystery field, educate publishers and the general public as to inequities in the treatment of female authors, raise awareness of their contribution to the field, and promote the professional advancement of women who write mysteries." The site includes information about local chapters of Sisters in Crime and offers mystery links and online bookstores.

POETRY RESOURCES

ACADEMY OF AMERICAN POETS

www.poets.org/index.cfm

The Academy of American Poets website offers news regarding contest opportunities and winners, an online poetry classroom, the first-ever poetry book club, events calendars, and a search feature to find a specific poet or poem. Users can also listen to an author read a poem in RealAudio. The "My Notebook" feature allows visitors to keep a file of favorite poems or readings from the site. There are also discussion group and literary links sections.

ELECTRONIC POETRY CENTER

wings.buffalo.edu/epc

There are perhaps more poetry websites online than for any other literary genre, so picking one representative site is really quite pointless. But we do recommend the Electronic Poetry Center at the University of New York at Buffalo, which is the heart of the contemporary poetry community online, having been around since the early days of gopher space—practically the Dark Ages in computer time. Of particular note are the active and well-respected poetics mailing list, the large collection of audio files, and an extensive listing of small press poetry publishers.

THE INTERNATIONAL LIBRARY OF POETRY

www.poetry.com

The International Library of Poetry website offers information about its writing competitions, which focus on "awarding large prizes to poets who have never before won any type of writing competition." The site also includes Internet links, a list of past winners, anthologies of winning poems, and chat rooms.

POETRY SOCIETY OF AMERICA

www.poetrysociety.org

The Poetry Society of America website includes information about the newest developments in the Poetry in Motion project, which posts poetry to seven million subway and bus riders in New York City, Chicago, Baltimore, Portland, and Boston. It also includes news about poetry awards, seminars, the tributes in libraries program, the poetry in public program, and poetry festivals.

POETS & WRITERS

www.pw.org

Poets & Writers is an online resource for creative writers that includes publishing advice, message forums, contests, a directory of writers, literary links, information on grants and awards, news from the writing world, trivia, and workshops.

ROMANCE RESOURCES

ROMANCE WRITERS OF AMERICA

www.rwa.org

Romance Writers of America (RWA) is a national nonprofit genre writers' association—the largest of its kind in the world. It provides networking and support to individuals seriously pursuing a career in romance fiction.

SCIENCE FICTION RESOURCES

CRITTERS WRITER'S WORKSHOP

www.critters.org

Critters is a free online workshop/critique group for writers of science fiction, fantasy, and horror. Writers interested in having their work dissected send short stories or chapters to the submission queue, whereupon members read it and deliver a critique in a week. Critters has several thousand members and has handled thousands of manuscripts. There is also a system in place for evaluating full novels.

ONLINE WRITING WORKSHOP FOR SCIENCE FICTION, FANTASY, AND HORROR

sff.onlinewritingworkshop.com

At this writing workshop members submit, review, rate, and improve their manuscripts. There are dozens of reviews and submissions each day and links to other workshop resources, such as critique guides. It is free the first month and afterwards membership costs $49.

SCIENCE FICTION AND FANTASY WRITERS OF AMERICA

www.sfwa.org

The official website of the Science Fiction and Fantasy Writers of America offers information about the organization, its members, affiliated publications, an art gallery, and various awards.

SFNOVELIST

www.sfnovelist.com/index.htm

SFNovelist is "an online writing group dedicated to novelists who write 'hard science' SF." It is a highly structured and organized system of the exchange of science fiction manuscripts for consideration by other writers. Its goals are to "become in the marketplace a premier source of novelists who write believable/hard science" SF; garner the attention of SF publishers, SFWA, and other writers' organizations for SF novelists; and develop a cadre of strong novelists, most of whom become published. Behind every great writer is usually a group of fellow writers who are equally serious about their writing, establish a presence at major SF writer conferences and conventions, and provide services and information to members that will help them in their search for self-improvement and in getting published. This includes contacts with other known writers and publishers and sources of distribution and marketing.

SCREENWRITING RESOURCES

HOLLYWOOD SCRIPTWRITER

www.hollywoodscriptwriter.com

Hollywood Scriptwriter is an international newsletter that offers articles on craft and business "to give screenwriters the information they need to work at their careers." The site includes low-budget and indie markets available for finished screenplays, as well as a listing of agencies that are currently accepting submissions from readers of Hollywood Scriptwriter. According to Hollywood Scriptwriter, "people like Harold

Ramis, Francis Ford Coppola, and Larry Gelbart have generously given of their time, knowledge, and experiences to share with HS's readers."

SCREENWRITER'S RESOURCE CENTER

www.screenwriting.com

The Screenwriter's Resource Center aims to "provide links to products and services for screenwriters, compiled by the staff at the National Creative Registry." It includes links to many screenwriting sites and offers advice and copyright words of warning for writers posting original work on the Internet.

SCREENWRITER'S UTOPIA

www.screenwritersutopia.com

Screenwriter's Utopia includes "helpful hints for getting screenplays produced, script development services, and contest information." The site includes a screenwriters' work station, tool kit, agent listings, and creative screenwriting magazines. Interviews with the screenwriters of *Sleepless in Seattle*, *Blade*, and *The Crow: City of Angels* are featured, and other interviews are archived. The site also includes chat rooms, message boards, a writer's directory, and a free newsletter.

WESTERN RESOURCES

WESTERN WRITERS OF AMERICA, INC.

www.westernwriters.org

"WWA was founded in 1953 to promote the literature of the American West and bestow Spur Awards for distinguished writing in the Western field." The site offers information about Old West topics, a listing of past Spur Award winners, and opportunities to learn about WWA and the Spur Award, to apply for membership in WWA, to subscribe to *Roundup Magazine*, or to contact Western authors whose work interests you.

GENERAL RESOURCE SITES

1001 WAYS TO MARKET YOUR BOOKS

www.bookmarket.com/1001bio.html

1001 Ways to Market Your Books is a site that offers a book marketing newsletter, consulting services, and book marketing updates. Other topics include success letters, author bios, sample chapters, and tables of contents.

3AM MAGAZINE

www.3ammagazine.com

3am is a webzine dedicated to countercultural, radical, and the cutting edge of fiction, poetry, and nonfiction. It features author profiles, interviews, links, and samples of poetry and fiction.

ABSOLUTE WRITE

www.absolutewrite.com

Absolute Write is the "one-stop Web home for professional writers." It offers specific resources for freelance writing, screenwriting, playwriting, writing novels, nonfiction, comic book writing, greeting cards, poetry, songwriting, and more. The site also features interviews, articles, announcements, and a newsletter.

AGENT QUERY

www.agentquery.com

Agent Query is meant to be the one-stop writer's resource on the Web about literary agents and publishing. It aims to help writers navigate through the arcane world of book publishing and offers a free searchable database of over 900 agents and profile information.

AMERICAN BOOKSELLERS ASSOCIATION

www.bookweb.org

The American Booksellers Association is a trade association representing independent bookstores nationwide. The site links members to recent articles about the industry and features Idea Exchange discussion forums.

AMERICAN DIALECT SOCIETY

www.americandialect.org

The American Dialect Society website offers discussion lists, a newsletter, and a contacts list. Writers will find the "Dialect in Literature Bibliography" useful, as well as digital dictionaries and style and grammar guides.

AMERICAN JOURNALISM REVIEW

www.ajr.org

This redeveloped site includes more editorial content, updated links to news industry sites, an improved job search function called "The Employment Section," and other interactive features.

AMERICAN SOCIETY OF JOURNALISTS AND AUTHORS

www.asja.org

The American Society of Journalists and Authors is "the nation's leading organization of independent nonfiction writers." It offers its members professional development aids, such as confidential market information, an exclusive referral service, seminars and workshops, and networking opportunities. The site offers all visitors a newsletter, legal updates from the publishing world, and professional links.

THE ASSOCIATION OF WRITERS & WRITING PROGRAMS

www.awpwriter.org

The Association of Writers & Writing Programs website offers information about the AWP annual conference, a list of writers' conferences, a list of AWP member schools, articles and information on writing and writing programs, and a sample of articles and news from the AWP magazine *The Writer's Chronicle*. Members of AWP enjoy an online conferencing system, career advice, career placement service, a subscription to *The Writer's Chronicle*, and notice of contests and awards.

AUTHOR NETWORK

author-network.com

Author Network is a flourishing international community for writers. The site includes articles, monthly columns, a newsletter, message board, discussion group, critique service, and thousands of links to other writing sites. The writer in residence, Paul Saevig, provides a regular supply of instructional essays that may help new writers or even established authors. Other material and articles are provided by regular contributors, who are generally published authors themselves. Author Network promotes individual writers and other sites of interest to writers, as well as competitions, conferences, and courses.

AUTHOR'S GUILD, THE

www.authorsguild.org

For more than 80 years the Guild has been the authoritative voice of American writers… its strength is the foundation of the US literary community. This site features contract advice, a legal search, information on electronic rights and how to join the organization, a bulletin index, publishers' row, a listing of board members, and current articles regarding the publishing field. There is also a link for Back-in-print.com, an online bookstore featuring out-of-print editions made available by their authors.

AUTHORLINK

www.authorlink.com

This information service for editors, literary agents, and writers boasts more than 165,000 loyal readers per year. Features include a "Manuscript Showcase" that contains 500-plus ready-to-publish, evaluated manuscripts.

BLACK WRITERS REUNION & CONFERENCE

www.blackwriters.org

The Black Writers Alliance is the "first literary arts organization to utilize the power of the online medium to educate, inform, support and empower aspiring and published black writers. The Black Writers Alliance (BWA) is dedicated to providing information, news, resources, and support to black writers, while promoting the Internet as a tool for research and fellowship among the cultural writing community." The site offers users access to its media kit, a forum, a directory of speakers, a photo album, mailing lists, and chat rooms. The Black Writers Alliance is the first online community that has hosted an annual conference for its members.

BOOKLIST

www.booklistonline.com

Booklist is a "digital counterpart of the American Library Association's *Booklist* magazine." In the site is a current selection of reviews, feature articles, and a searchable cumulative index. Review topics include books for youth, adult books, media, and reference materials. The site also includes press releases, the Best Books list, and subscription information.

BOOKTALK

www.booktalk.com

Want to find out how to click with the people who talk books? Booktalk is a site where writers and readers learn more about the publishing industry. Besides an extensive literary agent list, there are articles about how to get published, writing tips from authors, and a bulletin board. The host for many author home pages, Booktalk allows readers to interact with best-selling authors, learn about new releases, read book excerpts, and see what's upcoming. A slushpile section lists conferences and publishing links.

BOOKWIRE

www.bookwire.com

Partners with *Publishers Weekly, Literary Market Place,* and the *Library Journal,* among others, BookWire is a site that offers book industry news, reviews, original fiction, author interviews, and guides to literary events. The site features publicity and marketing opportunities for publishers, authors, booksellers, and publicists, and it includes a list of the latest BookWire press releases.

THE BURRY MAN WRITERS CENTER

www.burryman.com

With members and visitors in 104 countries, the Burry Man truly is "a worldwide community of writers." Working professionals and beginning writers find exclusive articles on the craft and business of writing, an extensive list of freelance job resources, a vast section focusing on Scotland, and links to more than 3,000 primary sources of information, giving writers the chance to speak to one another and use the Internet to hone their skills.

THE ECLECTIC WRITER

www.eclectics.com/writing/writing.html

This site is an information source for those interested in crime, romance, horror, children's, technical, screen, science fiction, fantasy, mystery, and poetry writing. It features articles, a fiction writer's character chart, resources by genre, reference materials, research, general writing resources, online magazines and journals, writing scams, awards, and a writing-related fun page.

THE EDITORIAL EYE

www.eeicom.com

The Editorial Eye website consists of a sampler of articles originally printed in the newsletter by the same name. The articles discuss techniques for writing, editing, design, and typography, as well as information on industry trends and employment. *The Eye* has been providing information to publication professionals for 18 years.

GRANTA

www.granta.com

The *Granta* website offers information about the most current issue of this highly regarded literary journal. The introduction is an explanation and background info about the topic around which the issue is based. The contents of the issue are listed, and visitors to the site may read a sample from the issue, as well as obtain subscription and ordering information. It also offers similar information about back issues and a readers' survey.

HELIUM

www.helium.com

Helium is a community of writers who share expert information on virtually any topic. Helium welcomes essays and articles on subjects as diverse as cooking, traveling, and computers, rated and classified by the user community itself. Helium also features a Marketplace for Freelance Writers section where publishers advertise assignments and writers can submit their material.

HOLLYLISLE.COM

hollylisle.com

HollyLisle.com offers a community of supportive writers helping each other reach their writing goals. Led by full-time novelist Holly Lisle, the community includes crit circles, discussion and research boards, workshops, free real-time writing classes with professional writers and people who can offer their expertise in areas of interest to writers, writing articles, free writing e-books, and the award-winning free e-zine *Vision: A Resource for Writers*, plus chapters, cover art, works in progress, and surprises for readers.

LITERARY MARKET PLACE

www.literarymarketplace.com

The Literary Market Place website offers information about publishers, which are categorized by US book publishers, Canadian book publishers, and small presses, as well as literary agents, including illustration and lecture agents. The site also offers trade services and resources.

THE MARKET LIST

marketlist.com

The Market List was started in 1994 as an e-zine on AOL and Compuserve. The first comprehensive writers market guidelines online.

MIDWEST BOOK REVIEW

www.midwestbookreview.com

Responsible for *Bookwatch*, a weekly television program that reviews books, videos, music, CD-ROMs, and computer software, as well as five monthly newsletters for community and academic library systems and much more, the Midwest Book Review was founded in 1980. This site features its reviews.

THE NATIONAL WRITERS UNION

www.nwu.org

The National Writers Union is the trade union for freelance writers of all genres. The website provides links to various services of the union, including grievance resolution, insurance, job information, and databases.

PARA PUBLISHING

www.parapublishing.com

The Para Publishing Book Publishing Resources page offers "the industry's largest resources/publications guide," a customized book writing/publishing/promoting information kit, as well as current and back issues of its newsletter. The site also includes research links, a listing of suppliers, and mailing lists.

RESOURCES FOR WRITERS

PEN AMERICAN CENTER

www.pen.org

PEN is an international "membership organization of prominent literary writers and editors. As a major voice of the literary community, the organization seeks to defend the freedom of expression wherever it may be threatened, and to promote and encourage the recognition and reading of contemporary literature." The site links to information about several PEN-sponsored initiatives, including literary awards.

PUBLISHERS LUNCH

publisherslunch.com

Publishers Lunch is the publishing industry's "daily essential read," read by more than 30,000 publishing people every day. It gathers together stories from all over the Web and print media of interest to the professional trade book community, along with original reporting, perspective, and wisecracking.

PUBLISHERS MARKETPLACE

publishersmarketplace.com

Publishers Marketplace shares a brand with and is run by the same people as Publishers Lunch, but is a different service. For a registration fee, Publishers Marketplace provides real-time information on book deals, profiles of agents and publishers, a publishing industry Job Board, Publishers Lunch Deluxe, and reviews.

PUBLISHERS WEEKLY ONLINE

publishersweekly.com

Publishers Weekly Online offers news about the writing industry, as well as special features about reading and writing in general and genre writing. The site also includes news on children's books, bookselling, interviews, international book industry news, and industry updates.

R. R. BOWKER

www.bowker.com

R. R. Bowker is a site that offers a listing of books in print on the Web, books out of print, an online directory of the book publishing industry, a data collection center for R. R. Bowker publications, and a directory of vendors to the publishing community.

SHARPWRITER.COM

www.sharpwriter.com

SharpWriter.Com is a practical resources page for writers of all types—a "writer's handy virtual desktop." Reference materials include style sheets, dictionaries, quotations, and job information. The Office Peacemaker offers to resolve grammar disputes in the workplace.

UNITED STATES COPYRIGHT OFFICE

www.copyright.gov

The United States Copyright Office site allows the user to find valuable information about copyright procedures and other basics. In addition, the user can download publications and forms, then link to information about international copyright laws.

WOODEN HORSE PUBLISHING

www.woodenhorsepub.com

Wooden Horse Publishing is a complete news and resource site for article writers. Visitors get news about markets, including planned, new, and folding magazines; editor assignments; and editorial changes. The site features a searchable market database of over 3,000 US and Canadian consumer and trade magazines. Entries include full contact information, writer's guidelines, and—only at Wooden Horse— reader demographics and editorial calendars. Newsletter describes new markets and industry trends.

WRITE FROM HOME

www.writefromhome.com

Whether you're a freelance writer, author, or writing from home but employed by a publication, this site strives to offer work-at-home writers tips, information, and resources to help you balance your writing career and children under one roof. You'll also find lots of writing and marketing resources to help you achieve the success you desire. It features a chat room, e-mail discussion list, and a monthly e-zine, featuring articles, markets, guidelines, tips, and more.

WRITER'S CENTER, THE

www.writer.org

The Writer's Center is a Maryland-based nonprofit that "encourages the creation and distribution of contemporary literature." The website provides information on the organization's 200-plus yearly workshops and links to its publication *Poet Lore and Writer's Carousel*.

WRITERS FREE REFERENCE

writers-free-reference.com

Writers Free Reference is a unique resource site with many eclectic features and links. Its most outstanding asset is a continuously updated list of literary agents and their e-mail addresses.

WRITERS GUILD OF AMERICA

www.wga.org

The WGA West site provides information about the Guild and its services, such as script registration. Other links to writing resources are provided as well.

WRITER'S MANUAL

www.writersmanual.com

Writer's Manual is an online writer-related information warehouse. It receives information from writers, publishers, and agents worldwide, which includes links, announcements, articles, book reviews, press releases, and more. The site features free writer-related articles, links and resources, recommended books, and a vast job board that lists jobs for traditional and online publishing markets, syndication markets, publishers, grants/fellowships, and contests. The site hosts contests on a monthly basis, including the Writer Critique Contest, in which a published author edits and critiques the writing of one winner.

WRITERS NET

www.writers.net

Writers Net is a site that "helps build relationships between writers, publishers, editors, and literary agents." It consists of two main sections, "The Internet Directory of Published Writers," which includes a list of published works and a biographical statement for each writer, and "The Internet Directory of Literary Agents," which lists areas of specialization and a description of the agency. Both are searchable and include contact information. It is a free service that hopes to "become an important, comprehensive matchmaking resource for writers, editors, publishers, and literary agents on the Internet."

WRITERS ON THE NET

www.writers.com

"Writers on the Net is a group of published writers and experienced writing teachers building an online community and resource for writers and aspiring writers." A subscription to the mailing list provides a description and schedule of classes offered by the site and a monthly newsletter.

WRITERS WRITE

www.writerswrite.com

This "mega-site" provides myriad resources, including a searchable database of online and print publications in need of submissions. The Writers Write chat room is open 24 hours a day for live discussion.

WRITERS-EDITORS NETWORK

writers-editors.com

The Writers-Editors Network has been "linking professional writers with those who need content and editorial services since 1982." The site features agent listings, articles on marketing tools, and a database of over 10,000 e-mail addresses of editors and book publishers. The site also links to fabulous how-to e-books of dream jobs for writers.

WRITERSPACE

www.writerspace.com

"Writerspace specializes in the design and hosting of websites for authors. We also provide Web services for those who may already have websites but wish to include more interactivity in the way of bulletin boards, chat rooms, contests, and e-mail newsletters." The site features an author spotlight, contests, workshops, mailing lists, bulletin boards, chat rooms, romance links, a guestbook, information on adding your link, Web design, Web hosting, its clients, and rates.

WRITERSWEEKLY.COM

www.writersweekly.com

This is the home of the most current paying markets to be found online. Writers Weekly publishes a free weekly e-zine featuring new paying markets and freelance job listings. Serving more readers than any other freelance writing e-zine, it is dedicated to teaching writers how to make more money writing.

WRITING CORNER

www.writingcorner.com

Writing Corner is dedicated to the reader and writer alike, providing a one-stop place for author sites, chats, and giveaways, along with articles on all aspects of writing. The weekly "JumpStart" newsletter is designed to motivate writers at every level, while the "Author's Corner" newsletter keeps readers apprised of author events. The site features market information, resource listings, book reviews, and vast archives of writing information for fiction, nonfiction, and corporate writers.

WRITING.ORG

www.writing.org

Writing.org is a very simple but very useful website. It includes links to articles and interviews with agents, tips on finding an agent, tips on avoiding scam artists, and other "no-nonsense" tips on being an aspiring writer. This site's creator is a published author, former editor, former agent, and has been helping writers online for almost ten years.

YOUCANWRITE

www.youcanwrite.com

YouCanWrite is one of *Writer's Digest's* 101 Best Sites for Writers and is the brainchild of two long-time publishing professionals who know the business from the inside out. Aspiring nonfiction writers can get the real story on what agents and editors look for in a salable manuscript. The site offers a wealth of free information, and its Insider Guides are practical, fun to read e-books that cover all the bases—from agents to books proposals to contracts.

SUGGESTED RESOURCES

SUGGESTED RESOURCES

SELF-PUBLISHING RESOURCES

Aiming at Amazon: The New Business of Self-Publishing, or, How to Publish Books for Profit with Print on Demand
by Lightning Source
and *Book Marketing on Amazon.com*
by Aaron Shepard (Shepard Publications, 2007)
www.shepardpub.com

Business and Legal Forms for Authors and Self-Publishers
by Tad Crawford (Allworth Press, 2005)
10 East 23rd Street, Suite 210, New York, NY 10010
212-777-8395

The Business of Writing for Children: An Award-Winning Author's Tips on Writing Children's Books and Publishing Them
by Aaron Shepard (Shepard Publications, 2000)
www.shepardpub.com

The Complete Guide to Self-Publishing: Everything You Need to Know to Write, Publish, Promote and Sell Your Own Book
by Tom Ross, Marilyn J. Ross (Writer's Digest Books, 2002)
4700 E. Galbraith Road, Cincinnati, OH 45236
512-531-2690

The Complete Guide to Successful Publishing
by Avery Cardoza (Cardoza Pub, 2003)
132 Hastings Street, Brooklyn, NY 11235
800-577-WINS, 718-743-5229; fax: 718-743-8284
e-mail: cardozapub@aol.com

Dan Poynter's Book Publishing Encyclopedia
by Dan Poynter (Para Publishing, 2006)
PO Box 8206-240, Santa Barbara, CA 93118-8206
805-968-7277; fax: 805-968-1379; cellular: 805-680-2298
e-mail: DanPoynter@aol.com, 75031.3534@compuserve.com

The Fine Print of Self-Publishing: The Contracts and Services of 45 Self-Publishing Companies Analyzed, Ranked, and Exposed
by Mark Levine (Bascom Hill Publishing Group, 2008)
212 3rd Ave. North, Suite 570, Minneapolis, MN 55401

How to Self-Publish & Market Your Own Book: A Simple Guide for Aspiring Writers
by Mark E. Smith, Sara Freeman Smith (U R Gems Group, 2006)
PO Box 440341, Houston, TX 77244-0341
281-596-8330

How to Self-Publish Your Book with Little or No Money!: A Complete Guide to Self-Publishing at a Profit!
by Bettie E. Tucker, Wayne Brumagin (Rainbow's End Company, 2000)
354 Golden Grove Road, Baden, PA 15005
724-266-2346; fax: 724-266-2346

Indie Publishing: How to Design and Publish Your Own Book
by Ellen Lupton (Princeton Architectural Press, 2008)
37 E. 7th Street, New York, NY 10003
212-995-9620; e-mail: editorial@papress.com

Make Money Self-Publishing: Learn How from Fourteen Successful Small Publishers
by Suzanne P. Thomas (Gemstone House Publishing, 2000)
PO Box 19948, Boulder, CO 80308
800-324-6415

Perfect Pages: How to Avoid High-Priced Page Layout Programs or Book Design Fees and Produce Fine Books in MS Word for Desktop Publishing and Print-on-Demand
by Aaron Shepard (Shepard Publications, 2006)
www.shepardpub.com

Print-on-Demand Book Publishing: A New Approach to Printing and Marketing Books for Publishers and Self-Publishing Authors
by Morris Rosenthal (Foner Books, 2008)
www.fonerbooks.com

Self-Publishing for Dummies
by Jason R. Rich (Wiley)
111 River Street, Hoboken, NJ 07030-5774
201-748-6000

The Self-Publishing Manual: How to Write, Print & Sell Your Own Book
by Dan Poynter (Para Publishing, 2007)
PO Box 8206-240, Santa Barbara, CA 93118-8206
805-968-7277; fax: 805-968-1379; cellular: 805-680-2298
e-mail: DanPoynter@aol.com, 75031.3534@compuserve.com

*Sell Your Book on Amazon: Book Marketing Coach Reveals Top-Secret "How-To" Tips
Guaranteed to Increase Sales for Print-on-Demand and Self-Publishing Writers*
by Brent Sampson and Dan Poynter (Outskirts Press, 2007)
10940 S. Parker Rd., PO Box 515, Parker, CO 80134

*Top Self-Publishing Firms: How Writers Get Published, Sell More Books, and Rise to
the Top*
by Stacie Vander Pol (CreateSpace, 2008)
100 Enterprise Way, Suite A200, Scotts Valley, CA 95066
e-mail: info@createspace.com

The Well-Fed Self-Publisher: How to Turn One Book into a Full-Time Living
by Peter Bowerman (Fanove Publishing, 2006)
3713 Stonewall Circle, Atlanta, GA
770-438-7200

INDUSTRY RESOURCES

*30 Steps to Becoming a Writer and Getting Published: The Complete Starter Kit for
Aspiring Writers*
by Scott Edelstein (Writer's Digest Books, 1993)
4700 E. Galbraith Road, Cincinnati, OH 45236
512-531-2690

1,818 Ways to Write Better & Get Published
by Scott Edelstein (Writer's Digest Books, 1997)
4700 E. Galbraith Road, Cincinnati, OH 45236
512-531-2690

Children's Writer's & Illustrator's Market
by Alice Pope (Writer's Digest Books, 2009)
4700 E. Galbraith Road, Cincinnati, OH 45236
512-531-2690

Guide to Literary Agents
by Chuck Sambuchino (Writer's Digest Books, 2009)
4700 E. Galbraith Road, Cincinnati, OH 45236
512-531-2690

Novel & Short-Story Writer's Market
by Rachel McDonald (Writer's Digest Books, 2009)
4700 E. Galbraith Road, Cincinnati, OH 45236
512-531-2690

Poet's Market
by Nancy Breen, Editor (Writer's Digest Books, 2009)
4700 E. Galbraith Road, Cincinnati, OH 45236
512-531-2690

Screenwriter's and Playwright's Market
by Chuck Sambuchino (Writer's Digest Books, 2009)
4700 E. Galbraith Road, Cincinnati, OH 45236
512-531-2690

Writer's Market
by Robert Brewer (Writer's Digest Books, 2009)
4700 E. Galbraith Road, Cincinnati, OH 45236
512-531-2690

Advice to Writers: A Compendium of Quotes, Anecdotes, and Writerly Wisdom from a Dazzling Array of Literary Lights
by John Winoker, Compiler (Vintage Books, 2000)
299 Park Avenue, New York, NY 10171
212-751-2600

Alchemy with Words: The Complete Guide to Writing Fantasy, vol. 1
by Darin Park and Tom Dullemond (Dragon Moon Press, 2008)

The American Directory of Writer's Guidelines: More Than 1,700 Magazine Editors and Book Publishers Explain What They Are Looking for from Freelancers
by Steven Blake Mettee, Michelle Doland, and Doris Hall (Quill Driver Books, 2006)
1831 Industrial Way, #101, Sanger, CA 93657
fax: 559-876-2170; e-mail: sbm12@csufresno.edu

The Art of the Book Proposal
by Eric Maisel, PhD (Tarcher, 2004)
375 Hudson Street, New York, NY 10014-3657

The Autobiographer's Handbook: The 826 National Guide to Writing Your Memoir
by Jennifer Traig (Holt Paperbacks, 2008)
175 Fifth Avenue, New York, NY 10010
646-307-5151

Book Business: Publishing: Past, Present, and Future
by Jason Epstein (W.W. Norton & Company, 2002)
500 Fifth Avenue, New York, NY 10110
212-354-5500; fax: 212-869-0856

Book Proposals That Sell: 21 Secrets to Speed Your Success
by W. Terry Whalin (WriteNow Publications, 2005)
The Stables, Priory Hill, Dartford, Kent, DA1 2ER UK

Business and Legal Forms for Authors and Self-Publishers
by Tad Crawford (Allworth Press, 2005)
10 East 23rd Street, New York, NY 10010
fax: 212-777-8261; e-mail: groberts@allworth.com

*The Business of Writing for Children: An Award-Winning Author's Tips on Writing
Children's Books and Publishing Them*
by Aaron Shepard (Shepard Publications, 2000)

The Career Novelist: A Literary Agent Offers Strategies for Success
by Donald Maass (Heinemann, 1996)
22 Salmon Street, Port Melbourne, Victoria 3207, Australia
e-mail: customer@hi.com.au

The Case of Peter Rabbit: Changing Conditions of Literature for Children
by Margaret MacKey (Garland Publishing, 1999)
29 W. 35th Street, New York, NY 10001-2299
212-216-7800; fax: 212-564-7854; e-mail: info@taylorandfrancis.com

Christian Writer's Market Guide: The Essential Reference Tool for the Christian Writer
by Sally Stuart (WaterBrook Press, 2009)
12265 Oracle Blvd., Suite 200
Colorado Springs, CO 80921
719-590-4999

The Complete Guide to Book Marketing
by David Cole (Allworth Press, 2004)
10 East 23rd Street, New York, NY 10010
212-777-8395

The Complete Guide to Book Publicity
by Jodee Blanco (Allworth Press, 2004)
10 East 23rd Street, Suite 210, New York, NY 10010
212-777-8395

The Complete Guide to Writer's Groups, Conferences, and Workshops
by Eileen Malone (John Wiley & Sons, 1996)
605 Third Avenue, New York, NY 10158-0012
212-850-6000; fax: 212-850-6088; e-mail: info@wiley.com

The Complete Guide to Writing and Selling the Christian Novel
by Barbara Kipfer (Writer's Digest Books, 1998)
4700 E. Galbraith Road, Cincinnati, OH 45236
512-531-2690

A Complete Guide to Writing for Publication
by Susan Titus Osborn, Editor (ACW Press, 2001)
5501 N. 7th Ave., # 502, Phoenix, AZ 85013
877-868-9673; e-mail: editor@acwpress.com

The Complete Idiot's Guide to Getting Published, 4th Edition
by Sheree Bykofsky, Jennifer Basye Sander (Alpha Books, 2006)
201 West 103rd Street, Indianapolis, IN 46290
317-581-3500

The Complete Idiot's Guide to Getting Your Romance Published
by Julie Beard (Alpha Books, 2000)
357 Hudson Street, New York, NY 10014
212-366-2000

The Complete Idiot's Guide to Publishing Children's Books, 3rd Edition
by Harold D. Underdown et al. (Alpha Books, 2008)
357 Hudson Street, New York, NY 10014
212-366-2000

The Complete Idiot's Guide to Writing Christian Fiction
by Ron Benrey (Alpha Books, 2007)
357 Hudson Street, New York, NY 10014
212-366-2000

The Copyright Permission and Libel Handbook: A Step-by-Step Guide for Writers, Editors, and Publishers
by Lloyd J. Jassin, Steve C. Schecter (John Wiley & Sons, 1998)
605 Third Avenue, New York, NY 10158-0012
212-850-6000; fax: 212-850-6088; e-mail: info@wiley.com

The Craft and Business of Writing: Essential Tools for Writing Success
by Robert Brewer and the Editors of Writer's Digest Books (Writer's Digest Books, 2008)
4700 E. Galbraith Road, Cincinnati, OH 45236
512-531-2690

Directory of Poetry Publishers
by Len Fulton (Dustbooks, 2007)
PO Box 100, Paradise, CA 95967
530-877-6110, 800-477-6110

Directory of Small Press/Magazine Editors & Publishers
by Len Fulton, Editor (Dustbooks, 2008)
PO Box 100, Paradise, CA 95967
530-877-6110, 800-477-6110; fax: 530-877-0222

Editors on Editing: What Writers Need to Know about What Editors Do
by Gerald Gross, Editor (Grove Press, 1994)
841 Broadway, New York, NY 10003
212-614-7850

The Fast Track Course on How to Write a Nonfiction Book Proposal
by Stephen Blake Mettee (Quill Driver Books, 2008)
1254 Commerce Ave, Sanger, CA 93657
559-876-2170; fax: 559-876-2180

The First Five Pages: A Writer's Guide to Staying Out of the Rejection Pile
by Noah T. Lukeman (Fireside, 2005)
1230 Avenue of the Americas, New York, NY 10020
212-698-7000

Formatting & Submitting Your Manuscript (Writer's Market Library series)
by Jack Neff (Writer's Digest Books, 2004)
4700 E. Galbraith Road, Cincinnati, OH 45236
512-531-2690

Get Known Before the Book Deal: Use Your Personal Strengths to Grow an Author Platform
by Christina Katz (Writer's Digest Books, 2008)
4700 E. Galbraith Road, Cincinnati, OH 45236
512-531-2690

Get Your First Book Published: And Make It a Success
by Jason Shinder, Jeff Herman, Amy Holman (Career Press, 2001)
3 Tice Road, PO Box 687, Franklin Lakes, NJ 07417
201-848-0310

Getting It Published: A Guide for Scholars and Anyone Else Serious about Serious Books
by William Germano (University of Chicago Press, 2008)
1427 East 60th Street, Chicago, IL 60637
773-702-7700; fax: 773-702-9756

Guerilla Marketing for Writers: 100 Weapons to Help You Sell Your Work
by Jay Conrad Levinson, Rick Frishman, and Michael Larsen (Writer's Digest Books, 2000)
4700 E. Galbraith Road, Cincinnati, OH 45236
512-531-2690

Hooked: Write Fiction That Grabs Readers at Page One & Never Lets Them Go
by Les Edgerton (Writer's Digest Books, 2007)
4700 E. Galbraith Road, Cincinnati, OH 45236
512-531-2690

How to Be Your Own Literary Agent: The Business of Getting a Book Published
by Richard Curtis (Houghton Mifflin Company, 2003)
222 Berkeley Street, Boston, MA 02116-3764
617-351-5000

How to Do Biography: A Primer
by Nigel Hamilton (Harvard University Press, 2008)
79 Garden Street, Cambridge, Massachusetts 02138
800-405-1619

How to Write a Book Proposal
by Michael Larsen (Writer's Digest Books, 2004)
4700 E. Galbraith Road, Cincinnati, OH 45236
512-531-2690

How to Write a Damn Good Mystery: A Practical Step-by-Step Guide from Inspiration to Finished Manuscript
by James N. Frey (St. Martin's Press, 2004)
175 Fifth Avenue, New York, NY 10010
212-674-5151

How to Write a Damn Good Novel
by James N. Frey (St. Martin's Press, 1987)
175 Fifth Avenue, New York, NY 10010
212-674-5151

How to Write a Damn Good Novel II: Advanced Techniques for Dramatic Storytelling
by James N. Frey (St. Martin's Press, 1994)
175 Fifth Avenue, New York, NY 10010
212-674-5151

How to Write Irresistible Query Letters
by Lisa Collier Cool (Writer's Digest Books, 2002)
4700 E. Galbraith Road, Cincinnati, OH 45236
512-531-2690

How to Write Killer Fiction
by Carolyn Wheat (Perseverance Press, 2003)
PO Box 2790, McKinleyville, CA 95519
707-839-3495

Immediate Fiction: A Complete Writing Course
by Jerry Cleaver (St. Martin's Press, 2005)
175 Fifth Avenue, New York, NY 10010

Inside Book Publishing
by Giles Clark (Routledge, 2008)
270 Madison Avenue, New York, NY 10016
212-216-7800 fax: 212-563-2269

The Joy of Publishing: Fascinating Facts, Anecdotes, Curiosities, and Historic Origins about Books and Authors
by Nat G. Bodian (Open Horizons, 1996)
PO Box 205, Fairfield, IA 52556

*Jump Start Your Book Sales: A Money-Making Guide for Authors, Independent
Publishers and Small Presses*
by Marilyn Ross, Tom Ross (Writer's Digest Books, 1999)
4700 E. Galbraith Road, Cincinnati, OH 45236
512-531-2690

*Keep It Real: Everything You Need to Know About Researching and
Writing Creative Nonfiction*
by Lee Gutkind (W. W. Norton, 2009)
500 Fifth Avenue, New York, NY 10110
212-354-5500 fax: 212-869-0856

Kirsch's Guide to the Book Contract: For Authors, Publishers, Editors and Agents
by Jonathan Kirsch (Acrobat Books, 1998)
PO Box 870, Venice, CA 90294
fax: 310-823-8447

Kirsch's Handbook of Publishing Law: For Authors, Publishers, Editors and Agents
by Jonathan Kirsch (Acrobat Books, 1994)
PO Box 870, Venice, CA 90294
fax: 310-823-8447

Literary Agents: A Writer's Introduction
by John F. Baker (IDG Books Worldwide, Inc., 1999)
919 E. Hillsdale Boulevard, Suite 400, Foster City, CA 94404-2112
800-762-2974

*Literary Marketplace: The Directory of the American Book Publishing Industry with
Industry Yellow Pages*
by Karen Hallard, Mary-Anne Lutter, and Vivian Sposobiec (Information Today)
630 Central Avenue, New Providence, NJ 07974
888-269-5372; e-mail: info@bowker.com

Make a Real Living as a Freelance Writer: How to Win Top Writing Assignments
by Jenna Glatzer (Nomad Press, 2004)

Making the Perfect Pitch: How to Catch a Literary Agent's Eye
by Katherine Sands (Watson-Guptill, 2004)
770 Broadway, New York, NY 10003
e-mail: info@watsonguptill.com

Negotiating a Book Contract: A Guide for Authors, Agents and Lawyers
by Mark L. Levine (Moyer Bell Ltd., 1988)
Kymbolde Way, Wakefield, RI 02879
401-789-0074, 888-789-1945; fax: 401-789-3793
e-mail: sales@moyerbell.com

Nonfiction Book Proposals Anybody Can Write: How to Get a Contract and Advance Before Writing Your Book
by Elizabeth Lyon (Blue Heron Pub, 2000)
1234 SW Stark Street, Suite 1, Portland, OR 97205
fax: 503-223-9474; e-mail: bhp@teleport.com

The Plot Thickens: 8 Ways to Bring Fiction to Life
by Noah Lukeman (St. Martin's Press, 2003)
175 Fifth Avenue, New York, NY 10010
212-674-5151

Plug Your Book! Online Book Marketing for Authors, Book Publicity through Social Networking
by Steve Weber (Weber Books)
www.weberbooks.com

The Portable Writers' Conference: Your Guide to Getting and Staying Published
by Stephen Blake Mettee, Editor (Word Dancer Press, 2007)
1831 Industrial Way, #101, Sanger, CA 93657
559-876-2170; e-mail: sbm12@csufresno.edu

Publicize Your Book: An Insider's Guide to Getting Your Book the Attention It Deserves
by Jacqueline Deval (Perigee Trade, 2008)
375 Hudson Street, New York, NY 10014
212-366-2000

Secrets of a Freelance Writer: How to Make $85,000 a Year
by Robert W. Bly (Henry Holt, 1997)
115 West 18th Street, New York, NY 10011
212-886-9200; fax: 212-633-0748; e-mail: publicity@hholt.com

Self-Editing for Fiction Writers
by Renni Browne, Dave King (HarperCollins, 2004)
10 East 53rd Street, New York, NY 10022-5299
212-207-7000

The Shortest Distance Between You and a Published Book
by Susan Page (Broadway Books, 1997)
841 Broadway, New York, NY 10003
212-614-7850

A Simple Guide to Marketing Your Book: What an Author and Publisher Can Do to Sell More Books
by Mark Ortman (Wise Owl Books, 2001)
24425 Fieldmont Place, West Hills, CA 91307
818-716-9076; e-mail: apweis@pacbell.net

Telling Lies for Fun & Profit
by Lawrence Block, Sue Grafton (Introduction); (William Morrow & Company, 1994)
1350 Avenue of the Americas, New York, NY 10019
212-261-6500

This Business of Books: A Complete Overview of the Industry from Concept Through Sales
by Claudia Suzanne, Carol Amato, and Thelma Sansoucie, Editors (Wambtac, 2004)
17300 17th Street, #J276, Tustin, CA 92780
800-641-3936; fax: 714-954-0793; e-mail: bookdoc@wambtac

The Well-Fed Writer: Financial Self-Sufficiency as a Freelance Writer in Six Months or Less
by Peter Bowerman (Fanove Publishing, 2000)
3713 Stonewall Circle, Atlanta, GA 30339
770-438-7200

Write the Perfect Book Proposal: 10 Proposals That Sold and Why
by Jeff Herman, Deborah M. Adams (John Wiley & Sons, 2001)
605 Third Avenue, New York, NY 10158-0012
212-850-6000; fax: 212-850-6088; e-mail: info@wiley.com

Writer Tells All: Insider Secrets to Getting Your Book Published
by Robert Masello (Holt Paperbacks, 2001)
115 West 18th Street, New York, NY 10010
212-886-9200

Writer's & Illustrator's Guide to Children's Book Publishers and Agents
by Ellen R. Shapiro (Prima Publishing, 2003)
3000 Lava Ridge Court, Roseville, CA 95661

The Writer's Legal Companion: The Complete Handbook for the Working Writer
by Brad Bunnin, Peter Beren (Perseus Press, 1998)
11 Cambridge Center, Cambridge, MA 02142
e-mail: info@perseuspublishing.com

The Writer's Legal Guide (2nd ed.)
by Tad Crawford, Tony Lyons (Allworth Press, 2002)
10 East 23rd Street, Suite 210, New York, NY 10010
212-777-8395

The Writer's Little Instruction Book: 385 Secrets for Writing Well and Getting Published
by Paul Raymond Martin, Polly Keener (Writer's World Press, 2005)
35 N. Chillecothe Road, Suite D, Aurora, OH 44202
330-562-6667; fax: 330-562-1216; e-mail: Writersworld@juno.com

The Writer's Market Companion
by Joe Feiertag, Mary Carmen Cupito (Writer's Digest Books, 2004)
1507 Dana Avenue, Cincinnati, OH 45207
513-531-2222; fax: 531-531-4744

Writing the Breakout Novel
by Donald Maass (Writer's Digest Books, 2002)
4700 E. Galbraith Road, Cincinnati, Ohio 45236
513-531-2690

Writing the Breakout Novel Workbook
by Donald Maass (Writer's Digest Books, 2004)
4700 E. Galbraith Road, Cincinnati, Ohio 45236
513-531-2690

Writing Down the Bones: Freeing the Writer Within
by Natalie Goldberg (Shambhala Publications, 2005)
PO Box 308, Boston, MA 02117
617-424-0030; fax: 617-236-1563

Writing Fiction: The Practical Guide from New York's Acclaimed Creative Writing School
by Gotham Writers' Workshop (Bloomsbury USA, 2003)
175 5th Ave., 8th floor, New York, NY 10010
212-780-0115

Writing Life Stories: How to Make Memories into Memoirs, Ideas into Essays, and Life into Literature
by Bill Roorbach (Writer's Digest Books, 2008)
4700 E. Galbraith Road, Cincinnati, Ohio 45236
513-531-2690

Writing Successful Self-Help and How-To Books
by Jean Marie Stine (John Wiley & Sons, 1997)
605 Third Avenue, New York, NY 10158-0012
212-850-6000; fax: 212-850-6088; e-mail: info@wiley.com

Writing the Nonfiction Book
by Eva Shaw, PhD (Rodgers & Nelsen Publishing Company, 1999)
PO Box 700, Loveland, CO 80537
970-593-9557

You Can Make It Big Writing Books: A Top Agent Shows How to Develop a Million-Dollar Bestseller
by Jeff Herman, Deborah Levine Herman, Julia DeVillers (Prima Publishing, 1999)
3000 Lava Ridge Court, Roseville, CA 95661

Your Novel Proposal: From Creation to Contract: The Complete Guide to Writing Query Letters, Synopses and Proposals for Agents and Editors
by Blythe Camenson (Writer's Digest Books, 1999)
4700 E. Galbraith Road, Cincinnati, OH 45236
512-531-2690

E-PUBLISHING RESOURCES

Electronic Publishing: Avoiding the Output Blues
by Taz Tally (Prentice Hall, 2001)

Electronic Publishing: The Definitive Guide
by Karen S. Wiesner (Avid Press, 2003)
5470 Red Fox Drive, Brighton, MI 48114
810-801-1177; e-mail: cgs@avidpress.com

ePublishing for Dummies
by Victoria Rosenborg (Hungry Minds, Inc., 2000)
909 Third Avenue, New York, NY 10022

From Entrepreneur to Infopreneur: Make Money with Books, E-Books, and Information Products
by Stephanie Chandler (Wiley, 2006)
111 River Street, Hoboken, NJ 07030-5774
201-748-6000

How to Publish and Promote Online
by M. J. Rose, Angela Adair-Hoy (Griffin Trade Paperback, 2001)
175 Fifth Avenue, New York, NY 10010
212-647-5151

How to Write a "How-to" Book (Or e-book): Make Money Writing About Your Favorite Hobby, Interest, or Activity
by Shaun Fawcett (Final Draft!, 2006)
803-746-4675

How to Write and Publish Your Own e-book in as Little as 7 Days
by Jim Edwards and Joe Vitale (Morgan James Publishing, 2007)
1225 Franklin Avenue, Suite 325, Garden City, NY, 11530
516-620-2528

Self-Publishing EBooks and PODS: One Step at a Time
by Timothy Sean Sykes (The Forager, 2006)

Write Your eBook or Other Short Book—Fast!
by Judy Cullins, Dan Poynter, and Marshall Masters (Your Own World Books, 2005)
PO Box 67061, Scotts Valley, CA 95067
775-546-1472

Writing.Com: Creative Internet Strategies to Advance Your Writing Career
by Moira Anderson Allen (Allworth Press, 2003)
10 East 23rd Street, Suite 210, New York, NY 10010
212-777-8395

SUGGESTED RESOURCES

GLOSSARY

GLOSSARY

A

abstract A brief sequential profile of chapters in a nonfiction book proposal (also called a synopsis); a point-by-point summary of an article or essay. In academic and technical journals, abstracts often appear with (and may serve to preface) the articles themselves.

adaptation A rewrite or reworking of a piece for another medium, such as the adaptation of a novel for the screen. (*See also* **screenplay**.)

advance Money paid (usually in installments) to an author by a publisher prior to publication. The advance is paid against royalties: If an author is given a $5,000 advance, for instance, the author will collect royalties only after the royalty moneys due exceed $5,000. A good contract protects the advance if it should exceed the royalties ultimately due from sales.

advance orders Orders received before a book's official publication date, and sometimes before actual completion of the book's production and manufacture.

agent The person who acts on behalf of the author to handle the sale of the author's literary properties. Good literary agents are as valuable to publishers as they are to writers; they select and present manuscripts appropriate for particular houses or of interest to particular acquisitions editors. Agents are paid on a percentage basis from the moneys due their author clients.

American Booksellers Association (ABA) The major trade organization for retail booksellers, chain and independent. The annual ABA convention and trade show offers a chance for publishers and distributors to display their wares to the industry at large and provides an incomparable networking forum for booksellers, editors, agents, publicists, and authors.

American Society of Journalists and Authors (ASJA) A membership organization for professional writers. ASJA provides a forum for information exchange among writers and others in the publishing community, as well as networking opportunities. (*See also* **Dial-a-Writer**.)

anthology A collection of stories, poems, essays, and/or selections from larger works (and so forth), usually carrying a unifying theme or concept; these selections may be written by different authors or by a single author. Anthologies are compiled as opposed to written; their editors (as opposed to authors) are responsible for securing the needed reprint rights for the material used, as well as supplying (or providing authors for) pertinent introductory or supplementary material and/or commentary.

attitude   A contemporary colloquialism used to describe a characteristic temperament common among individuals who consider themselves superior. Attitude is rarely an esteemed attribute, whether in publishing or elsewhere.

auction   Manuscripts a literary agent believes to be hot properties (such as possible best sellers with strong subsidiary rights potential) will be offered for confidential bidding from multiple publishing houses. Likewise, the reprint, film, and other rights to a successful book may be auctioned off by the original publisher's subsidiary rights department or by the author's agent.

audio books   Works produced for distribution on audio media, typically audiotape cassette or audio compact disc (CD). Audio books are usually spoken-word adaptations of works originally created and produced in print; these works sometimes feature the author's own voice; many are given dramatic readings by one or more actors, at times embellished with sound effects.

author tour   A series of travel and promotional appearances by an author on behalf of the author's book.

authorized biography   A history of a person's life written with the authorization, cooperation, and, at times, participation of the subject or the subject's heirs.

author's copies/author's discount   Author's copies are the free copies of their books the authors receive from the publisher; the exact number is stipulated in the contract, but it is usually at least 10 hardcovers. The author will be able to purchase additional copies of the book (usually at 40 percent discount from the retail price) and resell them at readings, lectures, and other public engagements. In cases where large quantities of books are bought, author discounts can go as high as 70 percent.

autobiography   A history of a person's life written by that same person, or, as is typical, composed conjointly with a collaborative writer ("as told to" or "with"; *see also* **coauthor**; **collaboration**) or ghostwriter. Autobiographies by definition entail the authorization, cooperation, participation, and ultimate approval of the subject.

B

backlist   The backlist comprises books published prior to the current season and still in print. Traditionally, at some publishing houses, such backlist titles represent the publisher's cash flow mainstays. Some backlist books continue to sell briskly; some remain best sellers over several successive seasons; others sell slowly but surely through the years. Although many backlist titles may be difficult to find in bookstores that stock primarily current lists, they can be ordered either through a local bookseller or directly from the publisher.

backmatter Elements of a book that follow the text proper. Backmatter may include the appendix, notes, glossary, bibliography and other references, lists of resources, index, author biography, offerings of the author's and/or publisher's additional books and other related merchandise, and colophon.

best seller Based on sales or orders by bookstores, wholesalers, and distributors, best sellers are those titles that move the largest quantities. List of best-selling books can be local (as in metropolitan newspapers), regional (typically in geographically keyed trade or consumer periodicals), or national (as in *USA Today*, *Publishers Weekly*, or the *New York Times*), as well as international. Fiction and nonfiction are usually listed separately, as are hardcover and paperback classifications. Depending on the list's purview, additional industry-sector designations are used (such as how-to/self-improvement, religion and spirituality, business and finance); in addition, best seller lists can be keyed to particular genre or specialty fields (such as best seller lists for mysteries, science fiction, or romance novels, and for historical works, biography, or popular science titles)—and virtually any other marketing category at the discretion of whoever issues the best seller list (for instance, African American interests, lesbian and gay topics, youth market).

bibliography A list of books, articles, and other sources that have been used in the writing of the text in which the bibliography appears. Complex works may break the bibliography down into discrete subject areas or source categories, such as General History, Military History, War in the Twentieth Century, or Unionism and Pacifism.

binding The materials that hold a book together (including the cover). Bindings are generally denoted as hardcover (featuring heavy cardboard covered with durable cloth and/or paper, and occasionally other materials) or paperback (using a pliable, resilient grade of paper, sometimes infused or laminated with other substances such as plastic). In the days when cloth was used lavishly, hardcover volumes were conventionally known as clothbound; and in the very old days, hardcover bindings sometimes featured tooled leather, silk, precious stones, and gold and silver leaf ornamentation.

biography A history of a person's life. (*See also* **authorized biography; autobiography; unauthorized biography.**)

blues (or bluelines) Photographic proofs of the printing plates for a book. Blues are reviewed as a means to inspect the set type, layout, and design of the book's pages before it goes to press.

blurb A piece of written copy or extracted quotation used for publicity and promotional purposes, as on a flyer, in a catalog, or in an advertisement (*See also* **cover blurbs**).

book club A book club is a book-marketing operation that ships selected titles to subscribing members on a regular basis, sometimes at greatly reduced prices. Sales of a work to book clubs are negotiated through the publisher's subsidiary rights department (in the case of a best seller or other work that has gained acclaim, these rights can be auctioned off). Terms vary, but the split of royalties between author and publisher is often 50 percent/50 percent. Book club sales are seen as blessed events by author, agent, and publisher alike.

book contract   A legally binding document between author and publisher that sets the terms for the advance, royalties, subsidiary rights, advertising, promotion, publicity—plus a host of other contingencies and responsibilities. Writers should therefore be thoroughly familiar with the concepts and terminology of the standard book-publishing contract.

book distribution   The method of getting books from the publisher's warehouse into the reader's hands. Distribution is traditionally through bookstores but can include such means as telemarketing and mail-order sales, as well as sales through a variety of special-interest outlets such as health-food or New Age venues, sports and fitness emporiums, or sex shops. Publishers use their own sales forces as well as independent salespeople, wholesalers, and distributors. Many large and some small publishers distribute for other publishers, which can be a good source of income. A publisher's distribution network is extremely important, because it not only makes possible the vast sales of a best seller but also affects the visibility of the publisher's entire list of books.

book jacket   (*See* **dust jacket**.)

book producer or **book packager**   An individual or company that can assume many of the roles in the publishing process. A book packager or producer may conceive the idea for a book (most often nonfiction) or series, bring together the professionals (including the writer) needed to produce the book(s), sell the individual manuscript or series project to a publisher, take the project through to manufactured product—or perform any selection of those functions, as commissioned by the publisher or other client (such as a corporation producing a corporate history as a premium or giveaway for employees and customers). The book producer may negotiate separate contracts with the publisher and with the writers, editors, and illustrators who contribute to the book.

book review   A critical appraisal of a book (often reflecting a reviewer's personal opinion or recommendation) that evaluates such aspects as organization and writing style, possible market appeal, and cultural, political, or literary significance. Before the public reads book reviews in the local and national print media, important reviews have been published in such respected book-trade journals as *Publishers Weekly*, *Kirkus Reviews*, *Library Journal*, and *Booklist*. A gushing review from one of these journals will encourage booksellers to order the book; copies of these raves will be used for promotion and publicity purposes by the publisher and will encourage other book reviewers nationwide to review the book.

Books in Print Listings, published by R. R. Bowker, of books currently in print; these yearly volumes (along with periodic supplements such as *Forthcoming Books in Print*) provide ordering information, including titles, authors, ISBNs, prices, whether the book is available in hardcover or paperback, and publisher names. Intended for use by the book trade, *Books in Print* is also of great value to writers who are researching and market-researching their projects. Listings are provided alphabetically by author, title, and subject area.

bound galleys Copies of uncorrected typesetter's page proofs or printouts of electronically produced mechanicals that are bound together as advance copies of the book (compare **galleys**). Bound galleys are sent to trade journals (*see* **book review**) as well as to a limited number of reviewers who work under long lead times.

bulk sales The sale at a set discount of many copies of a single title (the greater the number of books, the larger the discount).

byline The name of the author of a given piece, indicating credit for having written a book or article. Ghostwriters, by definition, do not receive bylines.

C

casing Alternate term for binding (*see* **binding**).

category fiction Also known as genre fiction. Category fiction falls into an established (or newly originated) marketing category (which can then be subdivided for more precise target marketing). Fiction categories include action-adventure (with such further designations as military, paramilitary, law enforcement, romantic, and martial arts); crime novels (with points of view that range from deadpan cool to visionary, including humorous capers as well as gritty urban sagas); mysteries or detective fiction (hard-boiled, soft-boiled, procedurals, cozies); romances (including historicals as well as contemporaries); horror (supernatural, psychological, or technological); thrillers (tales of espionage, crisis, and the chase); Westerns; science fiction; and fantasy. (*See also* **fantasy, horror, romance fiction, science fiction, suspense fiction,** and **thriller**.)

CD or **computer CD** High-capacity compact discs for use by readers via computer technology. CD-ROM is a particular variety; the term is somewhere between an acronym and an abbreviation. (CD-ROMs are compact computer discs with read-only memory, meaning the reader is not able to modify or duplicate the contents.) Many CDs are issued with a variety of audiovisual as well as textual components. When produced by publishers, these are sometimes characterized as books in electronic format. (*See also* **multimedia**.)

children's books Books for children. As defined by the book-publishing industry, children are generally readers aged 17 and younger; many houses adhere to a fine but firm editorial distinction between titles intended for younger readers (under 12) and young adults (generally aged 12 to 17). Children's books (also called juveniles) are produced according to a number of categories (often typified by age ranges), each with particular requisites regarding such elements as readability ratings, length, and inclusion of graphic elements. Picture books are often for very young readers, with such designations as toddlers (who do not themselves read) and preschoolers (who may have some reading ability). Other classifications include easy storybooks (for younger school children), middle-grade books (for elementary to junior high school students), and young adult (sometimes abbreviated YA, for readers through age 17).

coauthor One who shares authorship of a work. Coauthors all have bylines. Coauthors share royalties based on their contributions to the book. (Compare **ghostwriter**.)

collaboration Writers can collaborate with professionals in any number of fields. Often a writer can collaborate in order to produce books outside the writer's own areas of formally credentialed expertise (for example, a writer with an interest in exercise and nutrition may collaborate with a sports doctor on a health book). Though the writer may be billed as a coauthor (*see* **coauthor**), the writer does not necessarily receive a byline (in which case the writer is a ghostwriter). Royalties are shared, based on respective contributions to the book (including expertise or promotional abilities as well as the actual writing).

colophon Strictly speaking, a colophon is a publisher's logo; in bookmaking, the term may also refer to a listing of the materials used, as well as credits for the design, composition, and production of the book. Such colophons are sometimes included in the backmatter or as part of the copyright page.

commercial fiction Fiction written to appeal to as broad-based a readership as possible.

concept A general statement of the idea behind a book.

cool A modern colloquial expression that indicates satisfaction or approval, or may signify the maintenance of calm within a whirlwind. A fat contract for a new author is definitely cool.

cooperative advertising (co-op) An agreement between a publisher and a bookstore. The publisher's book is featured in an ad for the bookstore (sometimes in conjunction with an author appearance or other special book promotion); the publisher contributes to the cost of the ad, which is billed at a lower (retail advertising) rate.

copublishing Joint publishing of a book, usually by a publisher and another corporate entity such as a foundation, a museum, or a smaller publisher. An author can copublish with the publisher by sharing the costs and decision making and, ultimately, the profits.

copyeditor An editor, responsible for the final polishing of a manuscript, who reads primarily in terms of appropriate word usage and grammatical expression, with an eye toward clarity and coherence of the material as presented, factual errors and inconsistencies, spelling, and punctuation. (*See also* **editor**.)

copyright The legal proprietary right to reproduce, have reproduced, publish, and sell copies of literary, musical, and other artistic works. The rights to literary properties reside in the author from the time the work is produced—regardless of whether a formal copyright registration is obtained. However, for legal recourse in the event of plagiarism or other infringement, the work must be registered with the US Copyright Office, and all copies of the work must bear the copyright notice. (*See also* **work-for-hire**.)

cover blurbs Favorable quotes from other writers, celebrities, or experts in a book's subject area, which appear on the dust jacket and are used to enhance the book's point-of-purchase appeal to the potential book-buying public.

crash Coarse gauze fabric used in bookbinding to strengthen the spine and joints of a book.

curriculum vitae (abbreviated CV) Latin expression meaning "course of life"—in other words, the résumé.

D

deadline In book publishing, this not-so-subtle synonym is used for the author's due date for delivery of the completed manuscript to the publisher. The deadline can be as much as a full year before official publication date, unless the book is being produced quickly to coincide with or follow up a particular event.

delivery Submission of the completed manuscript to the editor or publisher.

Dial-a-Writer Members of the American Society of Journalists and Authors may be listed with the organization's project-referral service, Dial-a-Writer, which can provide accomplished writers in most specialty fields and subjects.

direct marketing Advertising that involves a "direct response" (which is an equivalent term) from a consumer—for instance, an order form or coupon in a book-review section or in the back of a book or mailings (direct-mail advertising) to a group presumed to hold a special interest in a particular book.

display titles Books that are produced to be eye-catching to the casual shopper in a bookstore setting. Often rich with flamboyant cover art, these publications are intended to pique bookbuyer excitement about the store's stock in general. Many display titles are stacked on their own freestanding racks; sometimes broad tables are laden with these items. A book shelved with its front cover showing on racks along with diverse other titles is technically a display title. Promotional or premium titles are likely to be display items, as are mass-market paperbacks and hardbacks with enormous best seller potential. (Check your local bookstore and find a copy of this edition of this *Guide*—if not already racked in "display" manner, please adjust the bookshelf so that the front cover is displayed poster-like to catch the browser's eye—that's what we do routinely.)

distributor An agent or business that buys books from a publisher to resell, at a higher cost, to wholesalers, retailers, or individuals. Distribution houses are often excellent marketing enterprises, with their own roster of sales representatives, publicity and promotion personnel, and house catalogs. Skillful use of distribution networks can give a small publisher considerable national visibility.

dramatic rights Legal permission to adapt a work for the stage. These rights initially belong to the author but can be sold or assigned to another party by the author.

dust jacket (also **dustcover** or **book jacket**) The wrapper that covers the binding of hardcover books, designed especially for the book by either the publisher's art department or a freelance artist. Dust jackets were originally conceived to protect the book during shipping, but now their function is primarily promotional—to entice the browser to actually reach out and pick up the volume (and maybe even open it up for a taste before buying) by means of attractive graphics and sizzling promotional copy.

dust-jacket copy Descriptions of books printed on the dust-jacket flaps. Dust-jacket copy may be written by the book's editor but is often either recast or written by in-house copywriters or freelance specialists. Editors send advance copies (*see also* **bound galleys**) to other writers, experts, and celebrities to solicit quotable praise that will also appear on the jacket. (*See also* **cover blurb**.)

E

e-book Refers to any book that exists in digital form, regardless of whether or not it also exists in a traditional physical form.

editor Editorial responsibilities and titles vary from house to house (often being less strictly defined in smaller houses). In general, the duties of the editor-in-chief or executive editor are primarily administrative: managing personnel, scheduling, budgeting, and defining the editorial personality of the firm or imprint. Senior editors and acquisitions editors acquire manuscripts (and authors), conceive project ideas and find writers to carry them out, and may oversee the writing and rewriting of manuscripts. Managing editors have editorial and production responsibilities, coordinating and scheduling the book through the various phases of production. Associate and assistant editors edit;

they are involved in much of the rewriting and reshaping of the manuscript and may also have acquisitions duties. Copyeditors read the manuscript and style its punctuation, grammar, spelling, headings and subheadings, and so forth. Editorial assistants, laden with extensive clerical duties and general office work, perform some editorial duties as well—often as springboards to senior editorial positions.

Editorial Freelancers Association (EFA) This organization of independent professionals offers a referral service, through both its annotated membership directory and its job phone line, as a means for authors and publishers to connect with writers, collaborators, researchers, and a wide range of editorial experts covering virtually all general and specialist fields.

el-hi Books for elementary and/or high schools.

endnotes Explanatory notes and/or source citations that appear either at the end of individual chapters or at the end of a book's text; used primarily in scholarly or academically oriented works.

epilogue The final segment of a book, which comes "after the end." In both fiction and nonfiction, an epilogue offers commentary or further information but does not bear directly on the book's central design.

F

fantasy Fantasy is fiction that features elements of magic, wizardry, supernatural feats, and entities that suspend conventions of realism in the literary arts. Fantasy can resemble prose versions of epics and rhymes or it may be informed by mythic cycles or folkloric material derived from cultures worldwide. Fantasy fiction may be guided primarily by the author's own distinctive imagery and personalized archetypes. Fantasies that involve heroic-erotic roundelays of the death-dance are often referred to as the sword-and-sorcery subgenre.

film rights Like dramatic rights, these belong to the author, who may sell or option them to someone in the film industry—a producer or director, for example (or sometimes a specialist broker of such properties)—who will then try to gather the other professionals and secure the financial backing needed to convert the book into a film. (*See also* **screenplay**.)

footbands (*See* **headbands**.)

footnotes Explanatory notes and/or source citations that appear at the bottom of a page. Footnotes are rare in general-interest books, the preferred style being either to work such information into the text or to list informational sources in the bibliography.

foreign agents Persons who work with their US counterparts to acquire rights for books from the United States for publication abroad. They can also represent US publishers directly.

foreign market Any foreign entity—a publisher, broadcast medium, etc.—in a position to buy rights. Authors share royalties with whoever negotiates the deal or keep 100 percent if they do their own negotiating.

foreign rights Translation or reprint rights that can be sold abroad. Foreign rights belong to the author but can be sold either country-by-country or en masse as world rights. Often the US publisher will own world rights, and the author will be entitled to anywhere from 50 percent to 85 percent of these revenues.

foreword An introductory piece written by the author or by an expert in the given field (*see* **introduction**). A foreword by a celebrity or well-respected authority is a strong selling point for a prospective author or, after publication, for the book itself.

Frankfurt Book Fair The largest international publishing exhibition—with five hundred years of tradition behind it. The fair takes place every October in Frankfurt, Germany. Thousands of publishers, agents, and writers from all over the world negotiate, network, and buy and sell rights.

Freedom of Information Act Ensures the protection of the public's right to access public records—except in cases violating the right to privacy, national security, or certain other instances. A related law, the Government in the Sunshine Act, stipulates that certain government agencies announce and open their meetings to the public.

freight passthrough The bookseller's freight cost (the cost of getting the book from the publisher to the bookseller). It is added to the basic invoice price charged the bookseller by the publisher.

frontlist New titles published in a given season by a publisher. Frontlist titles customarily receive priority exposure in the front of the sales catalog—as opposed to backlist titles (usually found at the back of the catalog), which are previously published titles still in print.

frontmatter The frontmatter of a book includes the elements that precede the text of the work, such as the title page, copyright page, dedication, epigraph, table of contents, foreword, preface, acknowledgments, and introduction.

fulfillment house A firm commissioned to fulfill orders for a publisher—services may include warehousing, shipping, receiving returns, and mail-order and direct-marketing functions. Although more common for magazine publishers, fulfillment houses also serve book publishers.

G

galleys Printer's proofs (or copies of proofs) on sheets of paper, or printouts of the electronically produced setup of the book's interior—the author's last chance to check for typos and make (usually minimal) revisions or additions to the copy (*see* **bound galleys**).

genre fiction (*See* **category fiction.**)

ghostwriter (or **ghost**) A writer without a byline, often without the remuneration and recognition that credited authors receive. Ghostwriters often get flat fees for their work, but even without royalties, experienced ghosts can receive quite respectable sums.

glossary An alphabetical listing of special terms as they are used in a particular subject area, often with more in-depth explanations than would customarily be provided by dictionary definitions.

H

hardcover Books bound in a format that uses thick, sturdy, relatively stiff binding boards and a cover composed (usually) of a cloth spine and finished binding paper. Hardcover books are conventionally wrapped in a dust jacket. (*See also* **binding; dust jacket.**)

headbands Thin strips of cloth (often colored or patterned) that adorn the top of a book's spine where the signatures are held together. The headbands conceal the glue or other binding materials and are said to offer some protection against accumulation of dust (when properly attached). Such bands, placed at the bottom of the spine, are known as footbands.

hook A term denoting the distinctive concept or theme of a work that sets it apart as being fresh, new, or different from others in its field. A hook can be an author's special point of view, often encapsulated in a catchy or provocative phrase intended to attract or pique the interest of a reader, editor, or agent. One specialized function of a hook is to articulate what might otherwise be seen as dry albeit significant subject matter (academic or scientific topics; number-crunching drudgery such as home bookkeeping) into an exciting, commercially attractive package.

horror The horror classification denotes works that traffic in the bizarre, awful, and scary in order to entertain as well as explicate the darkness at the heart of the reader's soul. Horror subgenres may be typified according to the appearance of were-creatures, vampires, human-induced monsters, or naturally occurring life forms and spirit entities—or absence thereof. Horror fiction traditionally makes imaginative literary use of paranormal phenomena, occult elements, and psychological motifs. (*See* **category fiction; suspense fiction.**)

how-to books An immensely popular category of books ranging from purely instructional (arts and crafts, for example) to motivational (popular psychology, self-awareness, self-improvement, inspirational) to get-rich-quick (such as in real estate or personal investment).

hypertext Works in hypertext are meant to be more than words and other images. These productions (ingrained magnetically on computer diskette or CD) are conceived to take advantage of readers' and writers' propensities to seek out twists in narrative trajectories and to bushwhack from the main path of multifaceted reference topics. Hypertext books incorporate documents, graphics, sounds, and even blank slates upon which readers may compose their own variations on the authored components. The computer's capacities to afford such diversions can bring reader and hypertext literature so close as to gain entry to each other's mind-sets—which is what good books have always done.

I

imprint A separate line of product within a publishing house. Imprints run the gamut of complexity, from those composed of one or two series to those offering full-fledged and diversified lists. Imprints also enjoy different gradations of autonomy from the parent company. An imprint may have its own editorial department (perhaps consisting of only one editor), or house acquisitions editors may assign particular titles for release on appropriate specialized imprints. An imprint may publish a certain kind of book (juvenile or paperback or travel books) or have its own personality (such as a literary or contemporary tone). An individual imprint's categories often overlap with other imprints or with the publisher's core list, but some imprints maintain a small-house feel within an otherwise enormous conglomerate. The imprint can offer the distinct advantages of a personalized editorial approach, while availing itself of the larger company's production, publicity, marketing, sales, and advertising resources.

index An alphabetical directory at the end of a book that references names and subjects discussed in the book and the pages where such mentions can be found.

instant book A book produced quickly to appear in bookstores as soon as possible after (for instance) a newsworthy event to which it is relevant.

international copyright Rights secured for countries that are members of the International Copyright Convention (*see* **International Copyright Convention**) and that respect the authority of the international copyright symbol, ©.

International Copyright Convention Countries that are signatories to the various international copyright treaties. Some treaties are contingent upon certain conditions being met at the time of publication, so an author should, before publication, inquire into a particular country's laws.

introduction Preliminary remarks pertaining to a piece. Like a foreword, an introduction can be written by the author or an appropriate authority on the subject. If a book has both a foreword and an introduction, the foreword will be written by someone other than the author; the introduction will be more closely tied to the text and will be written by the book's author. (*See also* **foreword**.)

ISBN (International Standard Book Number) A 10-digit number that is linked to and identifies the title and publisher of a book. It is used for ordering and cataloging books and appears on all dust jackets, on the back cover of the book, and on the copyright page.

ISSN (International Standard Serial Number) An eight-digit cataloging and ordering number that identifies all US and foreign periodicals.

J

juveniles (*See* **children's books**.)

K

kill fee A fee paid by a magazine when it cancels a commissioned article. The fee is only a certain percentage of the agreed-on payment for the assignment (no more than 50 percent). Not all publishers pay kill fees; a writer should make sure to formalize such an arrangement in advance. Kill fees are sometimes involved in work-for-hire projects in book publishing.

L

lead The crucial first few sentences, phrases, or words of anything—be it a query letter, book proposal, novel, news release, advertisement, or sales tip sheet. A successful lead immediately hooks the reader, consumer, editor, or agent.

lead title A frontlist book featured by the publisher during a given season—one the publisher believes should do extremely well commercially. Lead titles are usually those given the publisher's maximum promotional push.

letterhead Business stationery and envelopes imprinted with the company's (or, in such a case, the writer's) name, address, and logo—a convenience as well as an impressive asset for a freelance writer.

letterpress A form of printing in which set type is inked, then impressed directly onto the printing surface. Now used primarily for limited-run books-as-fine-art projects. (*See also* **offset**.)

libel Defamation of an individual or individuals in a published work, with malice afore-thought. In litigation, the falsity of the libelous statements or representations, as well as the intention of malice, has to be proved for there to be libel; in addition, financial damages to the parties so libeled must be incurred as a result of the material in question for there to be an assessment of the amount of damages to be awarded to a claimant. This is contrasted to slander, which is defamation through the spoken word.

Library of Congress (LOC) The largest library in the world is in Washington, DC. As part of its many services, the LOC will supply a writer with up-to-date sources and bib-liographies in all fields, from arts and humanities to science and technology. For details, write to the Library of Congress, Central Services Division, Washington, DC 20540.

Library of Congress Catalog Card Number An identifying number issued by the Library of Congress to books it has accepted for its collection. The publication of those books, which are submitted by the publisher, is announced by the Library of Congress to libraries, which use Library of Congress numbers for their own ordering and cataloging purposes.

Literary Market Place (LMP) An annual directory of the publishing industry that contains a comprehensive list of publishers, alphabetically and by category, with their addresses, phone numbers, some personnel, and the types of books they publish. Also included are various publishing-allied listings, such as literary agencies, writer's confer-ences and competitions, and editorial and distribution services. *LMP* is published by Information Today and is available in most public libraries.

literature Written works of fiction and nonfiction in which compositional excellence and advancement in the art of writing are higher priorities than are considerations of profit or commercial appeal.

logo A company or product identifier—for example, a representation of a company's initials or a drawing that is the exclusive property of that company. In publishing usage, a virtual equivalent to the trademark.

M

mainstream fiction Nongenre fiction, excluding literary or avant-garde fiction, that appeals to a general readership.

marketing plan The entire strategy for selling a book: its publicity, promotion, sales, and advertising.

mass-market paperback Less-expensive smaller-format paperbacks that are sold from racks (in such venues as supermarkets, variety stores, drugstores, and specialty shops) as well as in bookstores. Also referred to as rack (or rack-sized) editions.

mechanicals Typeset copy and art mounted on boards to be photocopied and printed. Also referred to as pasteups.

middle grade Just like the name implies; 4th to 8th grade.

midlist books Generally mainstream fiction and nonfiction books that traditionally formed the bulk of a publisher's list (nowadays often by default rather than intent). Midlist books are expected to be commercially viable but not explosive best sellers— nor are they viewed as distinguished, critically respected books that can be scheduled for small print runs and aimed at select readerships. Agents may view such projects as a poor return for the effort, since they generally garner a low-end advance; editors and publishers (especially the sales force) may decry midlist works as being hard to market; prospective readers often find midlist books hard to buy in bookstores (they have short shelf lives). Hint for writers: Don't present your work as a midlist item.

multimedia Presentations of sound and light, words in magnetically graven image— and any known combination thereof as well as nuances yet to come. Though computer CD is the dominant wrapper for these works, technological innovation is the hallmark of the electronic-publishing arena, and new formats will expand the creative and market potential. Multimedia books are publishing events; their advent suggests alternative avenues for authors as well as adaptational tie-ins with the world of print. Meanwhile, please stay tuned for virtual reality, artificial intelligence, and electronic end-user distribution of product.

multiple contract A book contract that includes a provisional agreement for a future book or books. (*See also* **option clause/right of first refusal.**)

mystery stories or **mysteries** (*See* **suspense fiction.**)

N

net receipts The amount of money a publisher actually receives for sales of a book: the retail price minus the bookseller's discount and/or other discount. The number of returned copies is factored in, bringing down even further the net amount received per book. Royalties are sometimes figured on these lower amounts rather than on the retail price of the book.

New Age An eclectic category that encompasses health, medicine, philosophy, religion, and the occult—presented from an alternative or multicultural perspective. Although the term has achieved currency relatively recently, some publishers have been producing serious books in these categories for decades.

novella A work of fiction falling in length between a short story and a novel.

O

offset (offset lithography) A printing process that involves the transfer of wet ink from a (usually photosensitized) printing plate onto an intermediate surface (such as a rubber-coated cylinder) and then onto the paper. For commercial purposes, this method has replaced letterpress, whereby books were printed via direct impression of inked type on paper.

option clause/right of first refusal In a book contract, a clause that stipulates that the publisher will have the exclusive right to consider and make an offer for the author's next book. However, the publisher is under no obligation to publish the book, and in most variations of the clause the author may, under certain circumstances, opt for publication elsewhere. (*See also* **multiple contract.**)

outline Used for both a book proposal and the actual writing and structuring of a book, an outline is a hierarchical listing of topics that provides the writer (and the proposal reader) with an overview of the ideas in a book in the order in which they are to be presented.

out-of-print books Books no longer available from the publisher; rights usually revert to the author.

P

package The package is the actual book; the physical product.

packager (*See* **book producer.**)

page proof The final typeset copy of the book, in page-layout form, before printing.

paperback Books bound with a flexible, stress-resistant, paper covering material. (*See also* **binding.**)

paperback originals Books published, generally, in paperback editions only; sometimes the term refers to those books published simultaneously in hardcover and paperback. These books are often mass-market genre fiction (romances, Westerns, Gothics, mysteries, horror, and so forth) as well as contemporary literary fiction, cookbooks, humor, career books, self-improvement, and how-to books—the categories continue to expand.

pasteups (*See* **mechanicals.**)

permissions The right to quote or reprint published material, obtained by the author from the copyright holder.

picture book A copiously illustrated book, often with very simple, limited text, intended for preschoolers and very young children.

plagiarism The false presentation of someone else's writing as one's own. In the case of copyrighted work, plagiarism is illegal.

platform Refers to the author's professional connections and popularity, measured by Internet and media presence, and the extent to which such can be leveraged to sell books.

preface An element of a book's frontmatter. In the preface, the author may discuss the purpose behind the format of the book, the type of research upon which it is based, its genesis, or underlying philosophy.

premium Books sold at a reduced price as part of a special promotion. Premiums can thus be sold to a bookseller, who in turn sells them to the bookbuyer (as with a line of modestly priced art books). Alternately, such books may be produced as part of a broader marketing package. For instance, an organization may acquire a number of books (such as its own corporate history or biography of its founder) for use in personnel training and as giveaways to clients; or a nutrition/recipe book may be displayed along with a company's diet foods in non-bookstore outlets. (*See also* **special sales**.)

press agent (*See* **publicist**.)

press kit A promotional package that includes a press release, tip sheet, author biography and photograph, reviews, and other pertinent information. The press kit can be put together by the publisher's publicity department or an independent publicist and sent with a review copy of the book to potential reviewers and to media professionals responsible for booking author appearances.

price There are several prices pertaining to a single book: The invoice price is the amount the publisher charges the bookseller; the retail, cover, or list price is what the consumer pays.

printer's error (PE) A typographical error made by the printer or typesetting facility, not by the publisher's staff. PEs are corrected at the printer's expense.

printing plate A surface that bears a reproduction of the set type and artwork of a book, from which the pages are printed.

producer (*See* **book producer**.)

proposal A detailed presentation of the book's concept, used to gain the interest and services of an agent and to sell the project to a publisher.

public domain Material that is uncopyrighted, whose copyright has expired, or that is uncopyrightable. The last includes government publications, jokes, titles—and, it should be remembered, ideas.

publication date (or pub date) A book's official date of publication, customarily set by the publisher to fall six weeks after completed bound books are delivered to the warehouse. The publication date is used to focus the promotional activities on behalf of the title—so that books will have had time to be ordered, shipped, and be available in the stores to coincide with the appearance of advertising and publicity.

publicist (press agent) The publicity professional who handles the press releases for new books and arranges the author's publicity tours and other promotional venues (such as interviews, speaking engagements, and book signings).

publisher's catalog A seasonal sales catalog that lists and describes a publisher's new books; it is sent to all potential buyers, including individuals who request one. Catalogs range from the basic to the glitzy and often include information on the author, on print quantity, and on the amount of money slated to be spent on publicity and promotion.

publisher's discount The percentage by which a publisher discounts the retail price of a book to a bookseller, often based in part on the number of copies purchased.

Publishers' Trade List Annual A collection of current and backlist catalogs arranged alphabetically by publisher, available in many libraries.

Publishers Weekly (PW) The publishing industry's chief trade journal. *PW* carries announcements of upcoming books, respected book reviews, interviews with authors and publishing-industry professionals, special reports on various book categories, and trade news (such as mergers, rights sales, and personnel changes).

Q

quality In publishing parlance, the word "quality" in reference to a book category (such as quality fiction) or format (quality paperback) is a term of art—individual works or lines so described are presented as outstanding products.

query letter A brief written presentation to an agent or editor designed to pitch both the writer and the book idea.

R

remainders Unsold book stock. Remainders can include titles that have not sold as well as anticipated, in addition to unsold copies of later printings of best sellers. These volumes are often remaindered—that is, remaining stock is purchased from the publisher at a huge discount and resold to the public.

reprint A subsequent edition of material that is already in print, especially publication in a different format—the paperback reprint of a hardcover, for example.

résumé A summary of an individual's career experience and education. When a résumé is sent to prospective agents or publishers, it should contain the author's vital publishing credits, specialty credentials, and pertinent personal experience. Also referred to as the curriculum vitae or, more simply, vita.

returns Unsold books returned to a publisher by a bookstore, for which the store may receive full or partial credit (depending on the publisher's policy, the age of the book, and so on).

reversion-of-rights clause In the book contract, a clause that states that if the book goes out of print or the publisher fails to reprint the book within a stipulated length of time, all rights revert to the author.

review copy A free copy of a (usually) new book sent to electronic and print media that review books for their audiences.

romance fiction or romance novels Modern or period love stories, always with happy endings, which range from the tepid to the torrid. Except for certain erotic specialty lines, romances do not feature graphic sex. Often mistakenly pigeonholed by those who do not read them, romances and romance writers have been influential in the movement away from passive and coddled female fictional characters to the strong, active modern woman in a tale that reflects areas of topical social concern.

royalty The percentage of the retail cost of a book that is paid to the author for each copy sold after the author's advance has been recouped. Some publishers structure royalties as a percentage payment against net receipts.

S

sales conference A meeting of a publisher's editorial and sales departments and senior promotion and publicity staff members. A sales conference covers the upcoming season's new books, and marketing strategies are discussed. Sometimes sales conferences are the basis upon which proposed titles are bought or not.

sales representative (sales rep) A member of the publisher's sales force or an independent contractor who, armed with a book catalog and order forms, visits bookstores in a certain territory to sell books to retailers.

SASE (self-addressed stamped envelope) It is customary for an author to enclose SASEs with query letters, with proposals, and with manuscript submissions. Many editors and agents do not reply if a writer has neglected to enclose an SASE with correspondence or submitted materials.

satisfactory clause In book contracts, a publisher will reserve the right to refuse publication of a manuscript that is not deemed satisfactory. Because the author may be forced to pay back the publisher's advance if the complete work is found to be unsatisfactory, the specific criteria for publisher satisfaction should be set forth in the contract to protect the author.

science fiction Science fiction includes the hardcore, imaginatively embellished technological/scientific novel as well as fiction that is even slightly futuristic (often with an after-the-holocaust milieu—nuclear, environmental, extraterrestrial, genocidal). An element much valued by editors who acquire for the literary expression of this cross-media genre is the ability of the author to introduce elements that transcend and extend conventional insight.

science fiction/fantasy A category fiction designation that actually collapses two genres into one (for bookseller-marketing reference, of course—though it drives some devotees of these separate fields of writing nuts). In addition, many editors and publishers specialize in both these genres and thus categorize their interests with catchphrases such as sci-fi/fantasy.

screenplay A film script—either original or one based on material published previously in another form, such as a television docudrama based on a nonfiction book or a movie thriller based on a suspense novel. (Compare with **teleplay**.)

self-publishing A publishing project wherein an author pays for the costs of manufacturing and selling his or her own book and retains all money from the book's sale. This is a risky venture but one that can be immensely profitable (especially when combined with an author's speaking engagements or imaginative marketing techniques); in addition, if successful, self-publication can lead to distribution or publication by a commercial publisher. (Compare with **subsidy publishing**.)

self-syndication Management by writers or journalists of functions that are otherwise performed by syndicates specializing in such services. In self-syndication, it is the writer who manages copyrights, negotiates fees, and handles sales, billing, and other tasks involved in circulating journalistic pieces through newspapers, magazines, or other periodicals that pick up the author's column or run a series of articles.

serial rights Reprint rights sold to periodicals. First serial rights include the right to publish the material before anyone else (generally before the book is released, or coinciding with the book's official publication)—either for the United States, a specific country, or for a wider territory. Second serial rights cover material already published, either in a book or another periodical.

serialization The reprinting of a book or part of a book in a newspaper or magazine. Serialization before (or perhaps simultaneously with) the publication of the book is called *first serial*. The first reprint after publication (either as a book or by another periodical) is called *second serial*.

series Books published as a group either because of their related subject matter (such as a biographical series on modern artists or on World War II aircraft) and/or single authorship (a set of works by Djuna Barnes, a group of books about science and society, or a series of titles geared to a particular diet-and-fitness program). Special series lines can offer a ready-made niche for an industrious author or compiler/editor who is up to date on a publisher's program and has a brace of pertinent qualifications and/or contacts. In contemporary fiction, some genre works are published in series form (such as family sagas, detective series, fantasy cycles).

shelf life The amount of time an unsold book remains on the bookstore shelf before the store manager pulls it to make room for newer incoming stock with greater (or at least untested) sales potential.

short story A brief piece of fiction that is more pointed and more economically detailed as to character, situation, and plot than a novel. Published collections of short stories—whether by one or several authors—often revolve around a single theme, express related outlooks, or comprise variations within a genre.

signature A group of book pages that have been printed together on one large sheet of paper that is then folded and cut in preparation for being bound, along with the book's other signatures, into the final volume.

simultaneous publication The issuing at the same time of more than one edition of a work, such as in hardcover and trade paperback. Simultaneous releases can be expanded to include (though rarely) deluxe gift editions of a book as well as mass-market paper versions. Audio versions of books are most often timed to coincide with the release of the first print edition.

simultaneous (or multiple) submissions The submission of the same material to more than one publisher at the same time. Although simultaneous submission is a common practice, publishers should always be made aware that it is being done. Multiple submissions by an author to several agents is, on the other hand, a practice that is sometimes not regarded with great favor by the agent.

slush pile The morass of unsolicited manuscripts at a publishing house or literary agency, which may fester indefinitely awaiting (perhaps perfunctory) review. Some publishers or agencies do not maintain slush piles per se—unsolicited manuscripts are slated for instant or eventual return without review (if an SASE is included) or may otherwise be literally or figuratively pitched to the wind. Querying a targeted publisher or agent before submitting a manuscript is an excellent way of avoiding, or at least minimizing the possibility of, such an ignoble fate.

software Programs that run on a computer. Word-processing software includes programs that enable writers to compose, edit, store, and print material. Professional-quality software packages incorporate such amenities as databases that can feed the results of research electronically into the final manuscript, alphabetization and indexing functions, and capabilities for constructing tables and charts and adding graphics to the body of the manuscript. Software should be appropriate to both the demands of the work at hand and the requirements of the publisher (which may contract for a manuscript suitable for on-disk editing and electronic design, composition, and typesetting).

special sales Sales of a book to appropriate retailers other than bookstores (for example, wine guides to liquor stores). This classification also includes books sold as premiums (for example, to a convention group or a corporation) or for other promotional purposes. Depending on volume, per-unit costs can be very low, and the book can be custom-designed. (*See also* **premium**.)

spine That portion of the book's casing (or binding) that backs the bound page signatures and is visible when the volume is aligned on a bookshelf among other volumes.

stamping In book publishing, the stamp is the impression of ornamental type and images (such as a logo or monogram) on the book's binding. The stamping process involves using a die with a raised or intaglioed surface to apply ink stamping or metallic-leaf stamping.

subsidiary rights The reprint, serial, movie and television, and audiotape and videotape rights deriving from a book. The division of profits between publisher and author from the sales of these rights is determined through negotiation. In more elaborately commercial projects, further details such as syndication of related articles and licensing of characters may ultimately be involved.

subsidy publishing A mode of publication wherein the author pays a publishing company to produce his or her work, which may thus appear superficially to have been published conventionally. Subsidy publishing (alias vanity publishing) is generally more expensive than self-publishing, because a successful subsidy house makes a profit on all its contracted functions, charging fees well beyond the publisher's basic costs for production and services.

suspense fiction   Fiction within a number of genre categories that emphasize suspense as well as the usual (and sometimes unusual) literary techniques to keep the reader engaged. Suspense fiction encompasses novels of crime and detection (regularly referred to as mysteries). These include English-style cozies, American-style hard-boiled detective stories, dispassionate law-enforcement procedurals, crime stories, action-adventure, espionage novels, technothrillers, tales of psychological suspense, and horror. A celebrated aspect of suspense fiction's popular appeal—one that surely accounts for much of this broad category's sustained market vigor—is the interactive element: The reader may choose to challenge the tale itself by attempting to outwit the author and solve a crime before detectives do, figure out how best to defeat an all-powerful foe before the hero does, or parse out the elements of a conspiracy before the writer reveals the whole story.

syndicated column   Material published simultaneously in a number of newspapers or magazines. The author shares the income from syndication with the syndicate that negotiates the sale. (*See also* **self-syndication**.)

syndication rights   (*See also* **self-syndication; subsidiary rights**.)

synopsis   A summary in paragraph form, rather than in outline format. The synopsis is an important part of a book proposal. For fiction, the synopsis portrays the high points of story line and plot, succinctly and dramatically. In a nonfiction book proposal, the synopsis describes the thrust and content of the successive chapters (and/or parts) of the manuscript.

T

table of contents   A listing of a book's chapters and other sections (such as the front matter, appendix, index, and bibliography) or of a magazine's articles and columns, in the order in which they appear; in published versions, the table of contents indicates the respective beginning page numbers.

tabloid   A smaller-than-standard-size newspaper (daily, weekly, or monthly). Traditionally, certain tabloids are distinguished by sensationalism of approach and content rather than by straightforward reportage of newsworthy events. In common parlance, "tabloid" is used to describe works in various media (including books) that cater to immoderate tastes (for example, tabloid exposé, tabloid television; the tabloidization of popular culture).

teleplay   A screenplay geared toward television production. Similar in overall concept to screenplays for the cinema, teleplays are nonetheless inherently concerned with such TV-loaded provisions as the physical dimensions of the smaller screen, and formal elements of pacing and structure keyed to stipulated program length and the placement of commercial advertising. Attention to these myriad television-specific demands is fundamental to the viability of a project.

terms The financial conditions agreed to in a book contract.

theme A general term for the underlying concept of a book. (*See also* **hook**.)

thriller A thriller is a novel of suspense with a plot structure that reinforces the elements of gamesmanship and the chase, with a sense of the hunt being paramount. Thrillers can be spy novels, tales of geopolitical crisis, legal thrillers, medical thrillers, technothrillers, domestic thrillers. The common thread is a growing sense of threat and the excitement of pursuit.

tip sheet An information sheet on a single book that presents general publication information (publication date, editor, ISBN, etc.), a brief synopsis of the book, information on relevant other books (sometimes competing titles), and other pertinent marketing data such as author profile and advance blurbs. The tip sheet is given to the sales and publicity departments; a version of the tip sheet is also included in press kits.

title page The page at the front of a book that lists the title, subtitle, author (and other contributors, such as translator or illustrator), as well as the publishing house and sometimes its logo.

trade books Books distributed through the book trade—meaning bookstores and major book clubs—as opposed to, for example, mass-market paperbacks, which are often sold at magazine racks, newsstands, and supermarkets as well.

trade discount The discount from the cover or list price that a publisher gives the bookseller. It is usually proportional to the number of books ordered (the larger the order, the greater the discount), and typically varies between 40 percent and 50 percent.

trade list A catalog of all of a publisher's books in print, with ISBNs and order information. The trade list sometimes includes descriptions of the current season's new books.

trade (quality) paperbacks Reprints or original titles published in paperback format, larger in dimension than mass-market paperbacks, and distributed through regular retail book channels. Trade paperbacks tend to be in the neighborhood of twice the price of an equivalent mass-market paperback version and about half to two-thirds the price of hardcover editions.

trade publishers Publishers of books for a general readership—that is, nonprofessional, nonacademic books that are distributed primarily through bookstores.

translation rights Rights sold either to a foreign agent or directly to a foreign publisher, either by the author's agent or by the original publisher.

treatment In screenwriting, a full narrative description of the story, including sample dialogue.

U

unauthorized biography A history of a person's life written without the consent or collaboration of the subject or the subject's survivors.

university press A publishing house affiliated with a sponsoring university. The university press is generally nonprofit and subsidized by the respective university. Generally, university presses publish noncommercial scholarly nonfiction books written by academics, and their lists may include literary fiction, criticism, and poetry. Some university presses also specialize in titles of regional interest, and many acquire projects intended for commercial book-trade distribution.

unsolicited manuscript A manuscript sent to an editor or agent without being requested by the editor/agent.

V

vanity press A publisher that publishes books only at an author's expense—and will generally agree to publish virtually anything that is submitted and paid for. (*See also* **subsidy publishing.**)

vita Latin word for "life." A shortened equivalent term for curriculum vitae (*See also* **résumé**).

W

word count The number of words in a given document. When noted on a manuscript, the word count is usually rounded off to the nearest 100 words.

work-for-hire Writing done for an employer, or writing commissioned by a publisher or book packager who retains ownership of, and all rights pertaining to, the written material.

Y

young-adult books Books for readers generally between the ages of 12 and 17. Young-adult fiction often deals with issues of concern to contemporary teens.

young readers or younger readers Publishing terminology for the range of publications that addresses the earliest readers. Sometimes a particular house's young-readers program typifies books for those who do not yet read, which means these books have to hook the caregivers and parents who actually buy them. In certain quirky turns of everyday publishing parlance, young readers can mean anyone from embryos through young adults (and "young" means you when you want it to). This part may be confusing (as is often the case with publishing usage): Sometimes younger adult means only that the readership is allegedly hip, including those who would eschew kids' books as being inherently lame and those who are excruciatingly tapped into the current cultural pulse, regardless of cerebral or life-span quotient.

Z

zombie (or zombi) In idiomatic usage, a zombie is a person whose conduct approximates that of an automaton. Harking back to the term's origins as a figure of speech for the resurrected dead or a reanimated cadaver, such folks are not customarily expected to exhibit an especially snazzy personality or be aware of too many things going on around them; hence some people in book-publishing circles may be characterized as zombies.

INDEX

INDEX

INDEX

AGENTS AND AGENCIES

INDEX

PUBLISHERS AND
IMPRINTS BY SUBJECT

PUBLISHERS AND IMPRINTS BY SUBJECT

ADULT NONFICTION

PUBLISHERS AND IMPRINTS BY SUBJECT

BOOKS FOR CHILDREN/TEENS

COOKING

CRAFTS

MIND/BODY/SPIRIT

RELIGION

ROMANCE

ABOUT THE AUTHOR

Jeff Herman is the founder of the Jeff Herman Agency in Stockbridge, Massachusetts, where he can often be found with his wife and partner, Deborah Herman, and their canine partners, Gracie the Whippet and Fee-Bee the Hybrid. There, they all toil and grind away at their various tasks with high hopes, passion, and gratitude. Over the years they have agented many hundreds of published books, and have helped many thousands of writers become published. Their book, *Write the Perfect Book Proposal*, is an excellent resource. The Hermans enjoy teaching what they've learned, and love learning from and with those they teach. Visit them at www.jeffherman .com. Write to them at jeff@jeffherman.com and Deborah@jeffherman.com.

ABOUT THE WRITER
ENTREPRENEUR NETWORK

The Writer Entrepreneur Network, theWENet.ning.com, helps writers form powerful partnerships for mutual success. This network is a sister site to the Writers Agents and Editors Network. It moves beyond craft, connections, and content about the industry to the nuts and bolts of becoming a professional writer. The industry is changing rapidly. This network brings its members real time updates and information to keep everyone ahead of the curve. It also has products, services, and tools to assist in the tasks of self-promotion and monetization of a writing career.

Writers write because they often feel compelled to do so. However, most writers dream of the day when they can kiss their day jobs goodbye. Not everyone can fund vacation homes, luxury, and philanthropy through writing. However, all writers would like to receive benefit, recognition, and prosperity from their labor. The Jeff Herman Agency stands for quality. Jeff and Deborah Herman have been providing writer education for over 20 years. This endeavor anticipates the growing need for Writer Entrepreneurship. The industry is changing, and the savvy writer can change with it.